LANDMARK COLLECTOR'S LIBRARY

A Georgian Gent & Co.
The Life and Times of Charles Roe

Dorothy Bentley Smith

Published by

Landmark Publishing Ltd
Ashbourne Hall, Cokayne Ave, Ashbourne, Derbyshire DE6 1EJ England
Tel: (01335) 347349 Fax: (01335) 347303
e-mail: landmark@clara.net
website: www.landmarkpublishing.co.uk

ISBN 1 84306 175 9

© **Dorothy Bentley Smith 2005**

Print: Cromwell Press Ltd, Trowbridge

Design: Mark Titterton

Cover: James Allsopp

Front cover & page 3: Portrait of Charles Roe painted
by Joseph Wright of Derby 1769, reproduced with the kind permission of
"The Churches Conservation Trust".

Back cover: The map of Anglesey is one of a series which
appeared in a French publication entitled *'L'Angleterre ou Description Hist et
Topographique du Royaume Uni de la Gran Bretagne'* by G.B. Deeping (6 vols.).
The French geographer was Michel Perrot and engraver M. Migneret.

The golden fleece and cavern represent Parys Mountain,
and the broken classical column, early Roman occupation. It is a very rare map;
others of similar design are known in the trade as the "gravestone series"
inspired by the shape of the ornamental cartouche.
Reproduced by courtesy of John Booth
from *'Antique Maps of Wales'* (1977)

LANDMARK COLLECTOR'S LIBRARY

A Georgian Gent & Co.
The Life and Times of Charles Roe

Dorothy Bentley Smith

Landmark Publishing

CONTENTS

ACKNOWLEDGEMENTS

A book of this size would not have been possible without the help, assistance and genuine interest of so many people. Unfortunately, as is often the case, it is impossible to mention all by name, otherwise a further three or four chapters would be necessary; therefore it is incumbent upon me to be succinct for the sake of brevity.

Many individuals are appropriately mentioned by name in the references and photographic attributions; to all go my sincere thanks. To those who should be mentioned individually for putting up with my sheer doggedness on occasion, I can only apologise and thank them sincerely for all their efforts. Into this category fall all the staff of Record Offices and Libraries listed in the abbreviations. However, there are those who deserve special mention.

Firstly Clare Mortin (now retired) and her staff of Macclesfield Public Library, in particular the former local history librarian, Barbara West, who made every effort to satisfy my unceasing requests. Secondly F.I. Dunn and his excellent staff at the Cheshire County Record Office, and likewise Glenys Matheson and her staff of the John Rylands Library, Manchester where I have spent many happy hours.

Further afield I have been greatly assisted by Tomos Roberts, former librarian of the University of Wales, Bangor, and the Leeds District Archivist, W.J. Connor. The staff of the Cumbria Record Office, Kendal, have also given considerable support, for which I am very grateful. My sincere thanks go to the factor, David B. Boyd, Islay Estates Company, for taking time out from his busy schedule to provide valuable information, and for the enthusiasm shown by members of the Derbyshire Caving Club, together with that of the former Bishop of London's personal assistant.

I was privileged to attend the Northern Ceramic Summer School at Keele University for seven years under the course director, Terry Lockett. Those courses were invaluable to me, not only for inspiring 17th to 19th century research, but for the wealth of knowledge imparted by individuals who have since become good friends. One in particular, Patrick Latham, has been an excellent mentor for 18th century research; to him and his wife Gerda, who have accommodated me on several occasions on my treks to London, a very special thank you.

I also owe a great deal to a member on the Hodgson family tree, David Bates, who has saved me hours of research and confusion by compiling the Hodgson family information, extracting additional details of the Irish mining and discovering papers presented to The Royal Society by A. Mills. To him and wife Sylvia, who have entertained me admirably from time to time, I can only say "Thank goodness you were part of the team". My thanks also go to Tim and Julie Brinton for all their assistance with regard to Christ Church, and to the Legal and Engineers Departments of Macclesfield Borough Council for their considerable help in locating deeds and plans relevant to my research.

Lastly I must express my deepest gratitude to my late husband, James, and immediate family. Following three years of research I had begun to write when James suffered a massive stoke and heart attack which left him with brain damage, yet he tried hard to assist. The following eight years would have been difficult without my children, Victoria, Nicholas, Alexandra and subsequent son-in-law Paul, who, despite all the demands of University educations to higher degrees, never failed to help, when called upon. Before his illness my husband had assiduously extracted considerable information from the River Weaver books; it had been his desire to edit and advise on text but this became impossible, so I am very much indebted to Eileen Talbot who enthusiastically stepped into the breach.

This book is testimony to my love and respect for James, not only as a professional, but as a humanist, humanitarian, husband and father; I therefore dedicate it to him with all my heart.

WHY?

One of the smallest questions in the English language yet often requiring one of the longest answers. A business succeeds when all the odds are stacked against it; another fails when everything seems to be in its favour. Why?

The answer lies in something which economic historians find difficult to equate – personality. Throughout history individuals have worked and given beyond what was required of them for an employer they have admired and respected. And whilst financial reward has played a key role, beyond a certain point it has never been the only consideration. Of course, there are those who will work hard for whoever they find in charge, and conversely there are those who will not. But the vast majority will look for personalities with whom they can relate, whether at work or at play. It is as relevant today in the age of computers as it was when prehistoric man chiselled upon a stone.

The interweaving of personalities is what makes history so fascinating, but today's would-be historians will never interpret the past with any degree of competence if they do not understand today's people. Accoutrements might change with time yet the genes are the same, they just present themselves in slightly differing forms.

These convictions, deduced over many years from my experiences as a Civil Servant; a creator of a personnel department for a division of the Rank Organisation with responsibility for over 1500 staff members, and finally as a successful guest house proprietress, were well and truly tested when I became involved with local history.

My home town of Macclesfield, famed for its silk industry throughout the world during the 19th and first half of the 20th century, was an obvious target for research. The impetus for its success had, of course, begun much earlier, the question was "Why?" In searching for the answer I soon appreciated the importance of using primary sources wherever possible and applying my 'formulae' to my discoveries. The resultant revelations were surprising, not only with regard to local history but to British history of the 18th century. Also revealed was the extent of one of the most important British industries of the period – the smelting of copper and its associate trades – and, of course, the characters, without whom this book would not have been worth writing.

In the course of my research there have been occasions when, on a visit to a Record Office, library or other establishment, someone has asked me "What are you researching?" My answer "Brass and copper", had invariably drawn the same response – "Why?" Perhaps it seemed strange that a woman should be interested in such a subject, but after giving them a brief synopsis of my findings, hence the desire to write the story, each would leave me purporting to have a genuine interest in my project and an intention to "watch out for the book" when published.

Here is the book: I hope they will not be disappointed.

PROLOGUE

In the mid-18th century Charles Roe set the town of Macclesfield in Cheshire on the road to success with its silk industry, which eventually became second to none in the world. Having succeeded with one business he diversified into another, vital for the British economy at that time - copper smelting. One could not imagine two more diametrically opposite concerns, and both requiring the greatest expertise in their own spheres, yet he took up the challenge and succeeded against all the odds, not only in providing the first large silk spinning mill for Macclesfield, but also in becoming one of the greatest copper and brass producers of the period.

The lives of both Charles Roe (1715-1781) and his son William (1746-1827) cover virtually the whole of that elusive period in English History called 'Georgian' (1714-1830), therefore "A Georgian Gent. & Co." seemed an appropriate title, particularly as the story encompasses, not only their lives and considerable business interests, but also the company they kept.

They crossed the paths of many famous men, including those of Handel, Josiah Wedgwood and Dr. Johnson, which made the task more interesting, for the period presented in my school-days had seemed the most boring and least absorbing in British history. It comprised reams of economics, politics, a social history of downtrodden poor, gin drinking and depravations, the perfect combination to leave a student with a desire to close the books and never open them again.

After many years I was reintroduced to the Georgian Period through a love of antiques. Surely the people who produced such beautiful, exquisite objects with great attention to detail, and the people who bought and appreciated them, deserved a second look? What came to light was an incredible period of English history full of fascinating people. Far from the handful of wealthy aristocrats and hundreds of poor, it became dominated by an enormously wealthy middle class, as varied and eclectic as today. The myths and legends were about to be exploded, and now I could turn my attention to Charles Roe.

I cannot better the comments of those who have written before me:

"Often the best book to write is the one you have long sought and never found. This is one such".
Irene H. Franck and David M. Brownstone. *The Silk Road: A History*.

"I have made many good friends in unexpected places, friends who I can justly claim have been introduced to me by Bess herself"
David N. Durrant. *Bess of Hardwick*. (reprint 1988) I must substitute Charles for Bess.

"One of the benefits of writing a work such as this is the interest in new subjects which is required."
Eric Delieb and Michael Roberts (1971). *The Great Silver Manufactory*.

"Before you write a book you should have read at least 10,000". Chinese proverb.

Whilst bearing in mind the latter, although I have not complied, I plead mitigation on the grounds that the sheer volume of documentation which has passed before my eyes could not have been more edifying. There I do not rest my case, on the contrary it now begins.

I make no apology for the amount of information contained within these pages; this is a history book and every facet is vital in understanding what has gone before. Every day we are bombarded with data from the media and our own experiences; our minds learn to sift out what is significant or interesting and reject the rest, that is until a circumstance arises whereby memory recalls a snippet of information, and suddenly an inconsequentiality takes on new appeal.

At first an individual can often make little impression, yet, as the name begins to appear in different contexts, so one's curiosity grows. The name becomes a real person from whom and about whom we can learn many things, whatever our motivation in doing so. In life we become acquainted with a variety of people, the vast majority of whom we shall never meet, but, inexplicably, the feeling is one of a mutual relationship. The historian operates in exactly the same way when delving into the past; the difference is that he or she never considers the available original information out of date; it is sifted, recorded, accepted or rejected according to the subject under review, and appears as fresh and often as vibrant as any news today. And whilst it can be argued that portraits were, in general, doctored for appeal, how often have we met someone for the first time, having seen a photograph or image on television, and been surprised at the lack of resemblance?

The people who weave in and out of the following pages must be treated in similar fashion: if they are important enough they will reappear at various intervals and their names will recall their characters with ease; if not then it matters not, they are simply insignificant to the reader. That they have been included by name is vital; for example, the headmaster of a school is not always the same man, and it could be significant to know which particular headmaster was responsible for a certain action. Also a name might be of relevance to one reader, although not to another.

I have taken the liberty of abbreviating dates and numbers as much as possible, and to present them in an easily recognised form. Their inclusion is vital and adds fascination to a book which, out of necessity, has to present some economics of the period. Figures represent people's lives; they can be taken off the pages and transformed into portraits of everyday living, far from the boring concepts they at first inspire.

I have also simplified the problem of dating prior to 1752, when the calendar was adjusted and eleven days removed so that the day after the 2nd September became the 14th instead of the 3rd. The old year had begun on Lady Day, 25th March, but the adjusted calendar produced a year commencing 1st January. A date such as 1st February 1750 would have been shown as 1st February 1749/50, but I have preferred to use the modern approach and qualify it as the year 1750 only.

To encourage others to delve into the annals of the 18th century I have chosen to use the language of the period as much as possible, considering modern phrases such as cash flow or managing director as anachronistic. Other words such as vacation, tenement, coastwise, which many tend to think of as part of modern American vocabulary, were actually part of 18th century English and frequently used. The fact that Roe & Co. refer to themselves in the plural - "We, the House of Roe & Co."- has been the consideration for likewise adopting the plural form. Occasionally choices have had to be made when using company jargon, but again I have adhered, as much as possible, to the nuances of the period.

The 18th century was an extraordinary time when everyone seemed to be play acting; innovativeness was the order of the day as each sought to perform his or her chosen role upon the stage. The jostling for the limelight was intense, as opportunity after opportunity presented itself. But who would be remembered for their performances, and how many deserved the credits given, or criticisms levelled? And how many more have been left waiting in the wings ready to take their bow? Enter centre stage Roe and company, your adjudication is about to begin.

PART I

1

THE ROE FAMILY

The best laid schemes o' mice an' men,
Gang aft a-gley

On the eleventh day of January in the year 1669 Rev. William Roe prepared his will. He had lived a long life during which many changes had taken place, traumatic changes causing great difficulties, but ones which he and his wife Robina had successfully overcome.

William had been presented to the living of the church of Wem in 1615 by Alathea, Countess of Arundel. Alathea was the grand-daughter of Bess of Hardwick. Her father, Gilbert Talbot (son of the Earl of Shrewsbury), had married her mother, Mary (daughter of Bess), at the Church of St. Peter and St. Paul in Sheffield. The Parish Church of Wem was also dedicated to St. Peter and St. Paul. Although Bess and her four husbands and families had faithfully embraced the Church of England, only her daughter, Mary, had adhered to the Roman Catholic faith. Could this have been due in part to the influence and presence of Mary, Queen of Scots, held captive so long within their family? Whatever the reason, Mary Talbot ensured that her children were also brought up according to the Roman Catholic tradition, and consequently Alathea had married Thomas Howard, the Roman Catholic Earl of Arundel. Rev. William had made a good marriage and must have been well-known either to the Arundels or their close acquaintances, and one wonders whether or not it was partly by his influence that on Christmas Day 1615 (the year of his presentation) the Earl of Arundel forsook the Church of Rome for the Church of England, to the "great grief of his mother", although at the time it was presumed by many to have been a matter of convenience.

What is certain is the fact that from this time onwards Rev. William's faith and loyalty to the principles of the Church of England were to remain unshaken, and many generations of the Roe family were to follow his example. Unaware that dark thunder clouds were gathering on the distant horizon, he and Robina moved into the Parsonage House close by the church and settled down to serve God and the people of Wem.

Wem was a very small hamlet, by modern standards, but significant enough in the 17th century. There were many fine half-timbered residences with wattle work and rubble filling, having roofs of thatch or shingles.

The villagers had the usual diverse occupations of "tanner, joyner, miller, potter and shoemaker" amongst others, and here, as in other parts of England, were to be found the all important woollen workers. For the few large landowners there was plenty of hunting, hawking and fishing – rights which were purchased with the ownership or leasing of land, and could be subleased to someone else. These rights were jealously guarded, and Heaven help anyone who transgressed because the most severe penalties could be inflicted, and on occasion were. On the other hand, many Lords of the Manor were often engaged elsewhere, and with such a small population, enormous expanses of unpolluted countryside and rich woodlands, many a true and worthy soul must have succumbed to the temptation of helping himself.

Being close to Shrewsbury certainly had its advantages. Built by the Romans, Watling Street had been used by generations of travellers and pilgrims alike. They passed through the towns of Shrewsbury, Chester and Bangor en route to Holyhead for the crossing to Ireland. Wem was also in close proximity to another Roman Road (now the A49T) going northwards to Whitchurch, where it joined the route to Nantwich. This made easy the carriage of salt from Cheshire and later aided the proliferation of the Puritan cause. Many petty chapmen, together with wealthy and important merchants and citizens, used these roads going to and from the Great Fairs. Judging from the several references to alewomen in the records, it would seem that the ales of Wem were just as popular then as they are today, and much appreciated by the weary voyagers who came within the compass of their production. Bearing this in mind Rev. William began to lay the foundations for his 'dynasty' and also to help his fellow creatures in a very practical way.

In the first instance, having chosen his bride, he would approach Robina's father with a view to proposing a marriage settlement. Marriage settlements were very much a reciprocal arrangement, and the future son-in-law would often have to match his future father-in-law's offer, pound for pound in value. The father, anxious that his daughter should not be left destitute if her husband died, made it obligatory for the money 'given' by him to be invested, in order to provide a pension plan, should such an event occur. He was also anxious that his family should not lose the benefits of his contribution, and so it was compulsory for this capital investment to be used only for the children of the marriage in question, and under no circumstances be put to the use of, or benefit, any other children from a subsequent marriage. Should it so happen that the couple were childless, and the husband survived the wife, the onus would be upon the husband to pay his wife's share of the settlement to his father-in-law's heirs (usually nephews, or if nieces, to be kept in trust and settled at the time of their marriages etc.) thus returning the money back to the family from whence it came. From at least the Elizabethan period, the marriage settlement was one of the most important legal arrangements and the relevant document was signed in the presence of a lawyer and usually witnessed by a representative on behalf of each family. (Ironically today it is the divorce settlement which has taken the place of the marriage settlement).

Before signing the document, Rev. William would have carefully checked the contents, making sure no extra clauses or further conditions had been included, other than those agreed upon. Sometimes an unscrupulous potential father-in-law would try a little blackmail at the last minute. After all the anxieties, negotiations and ultimate triumphs, it seemed incumbent upon the bridegroom to dig deep into his money bag and make purchase of a marriage licence in order to secure his prize. This marriage licence was a form of affidavit to the Bishop declaring that neither party had already negotiated a marriage contract with anyone else, and that there was no 'Let' or ' Impediment' or any other reason why they might not 'Lawfully marry together'. The marriage could then take place almost immediately without the necessity of waiting for the marriage banns to be read. Just how much was business and how much was pleasure may never be known, but it did unite couples of compatible status, if nothing else. From 18th century letters there is evidence that some of these marriages were very happy, in fact the young couples had actually fallen in love first, and then hoped that 'Dearest Papa' would not make things too difficult at the 'negotiating table'.

His marriage having taken place, Rev. William endeavoured to find a suitable investment for the Roe money, but finding nothing locally, had to look further afield. His first action would be to contact a well-known local lawyer or barrister and advise him of the amount of money he had available for investment.

The lawyer or barrister was the vital business link in both the 17th and 18th centuries. He acted as estate agent, stock broker, banker and financier apart from performing his normal legal duties, and in doing so had the opportunity more than anyone else, to make the right investments at the right time. By the beginning of the 18th century there were already many wealthy barristers; they tended to invest in land and securities. No doubt the lawyer or barrister contacted by Rev. William, would have been approached already by one or two of his landowning clients, with a view to borrowing money. A loan was usually negotiated if there was land or property available as security. When money changed hands, new property deeds were signed. The lender's name, together with a mention of the loan, was included on them, as though he temporarily owned a share of that property. The lender was entitled to receive interest on his loan, usually at the rate of 4% per annum, payable twice yearly; popular dates were Lady Day (25th March) and the Feast of St. Michael the Archangel (29th September). In the due course of time, if the borrower was unable to make payment of the interest due, the lender was entitled to go to court and claim part of the property in lieu of his capital and interest. This action was known as a 'seizure' and often occurred.

At this period in English history many huge estates which had been developed in the Elizabethan period, were being divided. There was a shortage of cash amongst the landed aristocracy, either through marriage settlements, overspending on estates or luxuries, not to mention pleasures, and slowly but surely they began to mortgage parts of their land and properties.

Such a landowner was Sir John Corbett who owned many tenements and parcels of land in Hadley, a hamlet within fifteen miles distance of Wem and close by the township of Wellington. These lands and tenements were subleased to several individuals, and gradually over a period of time, possibly because Sir John and his heirs needed more and more money, Rev. William took possession of portions of the Hadley estate. This meant that he also took over the leases of the tenants, which proved to be a valuable source of income. The Roman Catholic monks, in their day, had shown great enterprise by producing meads and wines for the local populace, now it was the turn of the Church of England, in the form of Rev. William Roe, investing in the beer brewing industry of Hadley. His investments included the Hadley Mill, leased to the Wright family; a tenement in possession of a widow, Margaret Golbourne and a John Whitfield; houses and buildings including corn and malt mills, together with water rights, fishing, land, meadows and lanes, formidable acquisitions for a parson of the Church of England, and yet this would be far from an isolated instance.

For many parsons like the Roes, it was an ideal way of demonstrating their paternal instincts. They could look after their tenants, make sure there were no evictions, lend or give money to those in need and keep the community together in a Christian manner. Sadly, as always, the seeds of greed and envy were growing, and some unscrupulous individuals, in order to obtain for themselves good livings within the Church, began to falsify documents and letters of recommendation. Some even went so far as to bribe a patron of a living, to 'put in a good word' for them with a friend who had connections in another Diocese, and where they were unknown to the Bishop. As yet this practice had not really taken hold, but when it did, it was to cause great problems and embarrassment for the Church of England, particularly as the 18th century progressed.

During the summer of 1617 Robina found that she was pregnant. Childbirth was awesome, fraught with great dangers for both mother and child. There were the 'old wives' tales' to contend with, and superstition and witchcraft. (After the severity of the Lancashire Witches trials in Lancaster during August 1612, when several 'so-called' witches were hanged, a shiver was felt throughout the nation. James I encouraged the seeking out and persecution of these alleged miscreants, and the effect of this continued well beyond his reign.) It was usual for the mother-to-be to return to her parents' home in order to prepare herself for the birth of her first child, for there experience and help were available. Robina need not have worried for early in the following year, she was delivered safely of a baby boy. As soon as the child drew his first breath his destiny was ordained, at least as far as his parents were concerned. He would follow in his father's footsteps and become a parson of the Church of England;

...is to take place – his baptism. Quite
...he parish register by the parsons (or
... their family Bible. The acceptance
...f God, signified by baptism, was the
..., this usually took place as soon as

...unlike today where Orson Cart and
...e child is given all the names of his
...he first born was usually named after
...o, until more names were required.
...so on through the family, thus baby
...rch in Wem, on 15th February 1618.
...he year of the execution of Sir Walter

After the death of Elizabeth I in March
...m Scotland. In that country James had
been strictly brought up, ...yterian nobles. How would he try to
manipulate the Church of England? Its ministers could only wait and see.

All had been well for a while, but after two years on English soil, the Gunpowder Plot had taken place, which had instilled in James such terror that he had reacted by encouraging the passing of further severe laws against the Roman Catholics.

By the year 1611, a new translation of the Bible had been completed and received James's approval. He took great pleasure in his right as King of England to appoint the Bishops of the Church, a practice not to be tolerated in the Church of Scotland. He was also an ardent believer in the Divine Right of Kings, but unfortunately went too far in publishing his theories, implying that the King could do as he wished.

Possibly as a direct result of James's severe and restricted upbringing, he had responded by adopting an extravagant life style. Vast quantities of money were squandered on his amusements, particularly his passion for hunting. Due to rising prices in the 16th century the income from Crown land had decreased considerably and James would not curtail his spending, so the inevitable happened – desperate for money he would have to approach the city merchants for a loan. It had been done before by monarchs in need, and therefore why should they refuse him? James however had misread the mood of the city and it would not be long before the whole country heard the news that the Lord Mayor of London had been forced to take a stand against him.

The Lord Mayor had been summoned and commanded to obtain a loan of £20,000 for the King, (at least £2 million today) from the city merchants; this was refused. James, in his anger threatened to remove the courts of law, his own Court and even Parliament itself to either Winchester or Oxford. The Lord Mayor, with a slight contemptuous bow, told the King he could do as he wished commenting "but she [the city of London] humbly desires that whenever Your Majesty shall remove your Courts, you would please to leave the Thames behind you". A polite yet poignant reminder of the commercial importance of the great river without which neither the King nor city could thrive. Having antagonized the city it was next the turn of the Church. Despite his hatred of Roman Catholics and his intense dislike of High Church ritual, James somehow managed to increase the bitterness of the Puritan elements within the Church of England who, finding that they had no alternative, chose to break away and became known as Independents.

The reign of James I was reaching its end when a son and daughter of Rev. William were baptised Thomas and Dorothy on 25th May 1624, in their father's church at Wem. Thomas must have died early, because on 3rd April 1628, a second Thomas was baptised in the same church. This was in keeping with yet another tradition, that of naming a new born child after a deceased brother or sister. (At the time of preparing his will in 1669, Rev. William had at least one more surviving daughter, named Elizabeth, who had grown up and married a Robert Ferrington).

James I's death occurred in 1625. It came too late to stop the war with Spain, encouraged by his favourite the Duke of Buckingham.

On the face of it James's reign would seem to have been an almost complete disaster, resulting in a depletion of resources and capital; yet so often the old adage "It is an ill wind that blows no one any good", can be applied to the most critical of circumstances.

One of the most important events of James I's reign was the sending to India of Sir Thomas Roe in order to establish the East India Company. It is entirely possible that Rev. William was related to his contemporary, Sir Thomas (born circa 1581, died 6th November 1644). Sir Thomas's grandfather, another Sir Thomas, had been Lord Mayor of London in 1568 and his son, Robert, baptized Thomas after his famous grandfather. It would never occur to Robert that his son would become even more famous than his namesake, when some years later he was sent by James I to the Court of the Great Mogul. It is interesting to note that the Christian names which occur in Rev. William's branch of the Roe family i.e. Thomas, Robert and William were also established in Sir Thomas's family, and during the 17th and 18th centuries other members of the Roe family, whether in Devon, Shropshire, Derbyshire or elsewhere had strong connections with the Church of England; many of their number being parsons.

The East India Company would bring wealth, luxuries and commodities to the subjects of James I and help to make England a great nation. The Dutch East India Company had certainly achieved this for the Netherlands, and the Eastern trade of the Italian States, initiated by Marco Polo, had brought tremendous riches and prosperity to the Adriatic coast, particularly Venice, for almost 350 years. The same year, in which Rev. William had been presented to the living of Wem (1615), Thomas Roe had set sail on the 3rd February, "with a fleet of six good ships". He was given letters of credence and a royal missive to the Great Mogul together with detailed instructions for his guidance. He was also told to impress upon the Mogul the greatness of James I and the naval strength of his kingdom. After months of arduous and complicated negotiations, Thomas Roe returned triumphant to a delighted King, having achieved the first 'foothold' in the continent of India on behalf of the British East India Company.

* * * * * * *

When Charles I ascended the throne he was faced with an unenviable task. He inherited his father's debts, a war with Spain and a disenchanted nation. However he tried he could not possibly hope to succeed.

The year 1628 was to prove an eventful one. Apart from young Thomas's baptism, word came of the assassination of the Duke of Buckingham. A less noted fact was the entry into Parliament of the son of a prosperous squire from East Anglia, by the name of Oliver Cromwell. Had Rev. William been aware of it, he could hardly have envisaged the dramatic sequence of events which this particular personality was to set in motion. His mind was busy with his own problems. His family was growing more numerous, and with an adequate financial situation it was time for him to look around for some security of tenure. The parsonage house was only for his benefit whilst he remained parson of Wem. Possibly his subconscious warned him that an uneasy situation was developing, the vibrations from the capital were not good, and there were those around in Shropshire who were promoting the Puritan way of life.

One such person was Richard Baxter, born at High Ercall not far from Wem. He complained of the lack of observance of the Lord's Day, and was irritated by the distractions which the Sabbath brought, particularly by the players of pipe and tabor (a small drum popular from the Middle Ages, struck with one hand, while the other held the pipe.). Even the morris dancers did not escape his displeasure, for they often entered the church complete with "livery, scarfs and antic dresses with the morris bells jingling at their legs; and as soon as common prayer was read, did hasten out presently to their play again.".

Meanwhile in the city, King Charles was making great endeavours to co-operate with Parliament. By 1628 he held an original loan which then stood at £222,897 and two shilings, with two further advances of £120,000 and £25,000 (by today's values totalling at least £40 million). As was usual the loan was made with the security of property and therefore it was necessary for Charles to execute a large deed during that year, conveying over 1,000 manors in various parts of the England to certain trustees. It would be impossible for him to repay these enormous sums of money and so in due course legal 'seizure' of the manors was inevitable. The trustees would sell them as necessary for the recovery of the City's money. The widespread distribution of property amongst the middle classes further helped the dissemination of wealth, which was to provide a good foundation for the 18th century.

By Indenture of 10th September 1628 Rev. William Roe came into possession of the 'Manor of Arleston'. All properties were leased for three lives, which in this case would be his own, his wife's and his son's (William Jnr.). The lease was given by Francis Forester, whose family had held the position of hereditary custodians of the portion of Wrekin Forest known as Wellington Hay, since the 12th century (and still do so today). Local tradition insists that the property, originally built by Francis Forester, had been the hunting lodge of James I, and the circumstances tend to support this. Whether or not it had been given to James, leased by him or put at his disposal, is at present unknown; however it was available for lease in 1628 and coincides with the mortgaging of the royal estates. James had been fanatical about his hunting, and even in 1638 Charles I was very concerned about poachers in the area. He sent a letter to certain magistrates, referring to offenders who kept greyhounds and who were devious enough to hunt, course and destroy hares, pheasants, partridges etc. when others were attending "divine service" on "Saboth dayes" and also at other "unfitt and inconvenient tymes".

Today, Arleston Manor still stands, a house much loved and cared for by its present owner. It is a fine black and white timbered building, having been built in two distinct halves. The original hunting lodge carries the date 1614 on the front gable and contains a remarkable plaster ceiling in the drawing room. The entire surface of this ceiling is covered in geometric devices which are representative of the Forester Family, including the Forester's Head with plumed hat.

The second part of the house, built in the same style as the original, bears the date of 1630 on its front gable. It is interesting that this extension was either built for Rev. William or by him with permission. It is smaller than the original building. There is a big chimney stack with a beautiful cluster of shafts at the top, and the sides are adorned with a chevron ornament which continues in the projecting cornice. This chimney stack is representative of the tax subsequently paid on three hearths (6/-) by William Jnr.; Arleston was listed on the tax roll under Bradford Hundred, South.

For the moment Rev. William remained parson of Wem and continued to occupy the parsonage house. During 1629, whilst the extension of the hunting lodge was being built, the overseers of the poor organised a petition to the Dowager Countess of Arundel, Ann Howard, to which Rev. William added his signature. They informed her that many poor cottagers had lived for a very long time upon her land and had been given work in her woods, but the last winter had been hard. Work had temporarily been found for them in her "Pool", but now the employment was coming to an end. The parish and manor had grown poor and not able to relieve them, and they hoped she would give them some allowance for which they would ever "pray for her health in this world, and in the world to come eternal glory". It was always a sensible idea to remind the wealthy landowner of his or her responsibilities from time to time, whether or not the parish could afford to give payment to the poor. No doubt this time it was genuine and perhaps some of the cottagers were set to work on the enlarging of Rev. William's house at Arleston.

The wealthy landowners did have responsibilities and some of them accepted these, realising their role in society; they were in effect Chief Executives of their own large companies. As ever the hand of the Church guided in all matters as much as possible. It was the strong link between the people and those in authority. Many gentry realized that it was foolish to antagonize their estate workers. Some were genuinely great benefactors but, as always, there were those few who could not care less, and the responsibility and burden of management fell heavily upon someone else's shoulders; in some instances with devastating effects. They received petitions from groups of people and individuals on all sorts of matters, and often were called upon to act as arbitrators in local disputes. If a particular landowner was in the army or had connections

An early 17th century Protestant Minister.

with a high ranking naval official, then it was usual for the sons of his estate workers to ask for recommendations in the army or navy.

Many local families who were tenants of the Lords of the Manor would follow their landlord's loyalties, and all too soon the choice would be either 'King or Parliament'. Charles I made the same foolish mistake as his father in allowing himself to come under the influence of the Duke of Buckingham, and succeeded in declaring war on France. The King took his first irrevocable step towards his execution when he decided to rule alone. He concluded the war with France in 1629 and with Spain in 1630, hoping to gain support from his people, together with extra finances – wars were expensive operations. For eleven long years, commencing in 1629, Parliament was to remain banished.

In the midst of all this young William Roe entered university. The Church of England was there to educate and it was a role which it took seriously. No one more than Rev. William realized how important education was, and his ambitions were beginning to take shape. He resigned his living in Wem during the year 1634. He must have been well-known and respected within the vicinity of Wellington, and one suspects that he received great encouragement from the Forester family and their associates, because having left Wem quickly and quietly, he became involved with a school at Arleston. When Rev. Samuel Garbet M.A. wrote his *'History of Wem'* between 1740 and 1753 – although not published until 1818 – he noted that "He (Rev. William) had many children by his wife Robina and dying at the parsonage house in Wem 12th November 1637 was buried in the church . . . without any monument or inscription as a memorial to him". For some reason Garbet had presumed him dead, but this fine character of a man was not to be got rid of so easily, and God allowed him a further thirty two years in which to do His work.

* * * * * * *

During the Civil Wars and after, many documents were destroyed and some official records discontinued for a period; therefore it is not possible to be specific about certain events, they can only be deduced from circumstantial evidence.

By 1637 or 1638 William Jnr. would have obtained his B.A., which took three years to complete; it is possible that he also obtained his M.A. which was usually a matter of course and non-residential, by which time the Civil War had started in 1642. With all the growing uncertainties, the circumstances made it impossible for William Jnr. to be presented to a living, or officially recognized as a parson of the Church of England. His father would never renounce his allegiance to that church and neither would he.

On 10th November 1637 "Mr. William Roe, Schoolmaster . . . exhibited his licence to teach boys under the seal of this Court" (Wellington). This date conveniently relates to within two days of Garbet's 'death' of William Snr. at Wem. This was also the year in which Francis Forester died.

It is known that William Jnr. became a noted schoolmaster, married an Elizabeth and that his first son, Robert, was born at Arleston. It seems logical to conclude, therefore, that father and son started a school in the extension at Arleston Manor. What better way to keep the principles of the Church of England alive during difficult times?

Some legal arrangement must have been proposed by the Forester family by which Rev. William was allowed to lease a large area of land which encompassed Arleston village, and to purchase for himself rights, which officially declared him to be Lord of the Manor of Arleston.

By 1640 the King had come to his senses and recalled Parliament, but it was only the calm before the storm. Parliament was full of angry men and within two years the unthinkable happened, the Civil War was underway. Families divided in their loyalties, many wives having to support their husband's families against their father's. Village turned against village and it was difficult at times to know who was friend and who was enemy.

At first there was Royalist activity around Wem, but suddenly with the arrival of Sir William Brereton, the great Cromwellian General, both willing and unwilling townspeople were set to work to fortify the town. Great consternation must have been felt in Arleston Manor. The Parliamentarians were determined to hold Wem, as one of their despatches read "the place is necessary to the recovery of a rich and considerable county". Small wonder the poor had been gathering there for a number of years; prosperity always attracts the needy, beggars, thieves and the like.

The siege of Wem was about to begin, for the town was strategically important because of its position between Shrewsbury and Chester. The Cavalier and Roundhead reports were to differ considerably as to the exact details of operations, but the main sequence of events cannot be challenged. Twice the Royalists attacked and twice they were rebuffed. According to the Parliamentarian report many Royalists lost their lives and carts loaded with bodies were carried away or lay "miserably torne with the shott and lying in the fields". As the Puritan reinforcements had not arrived to defend Wem, it is said that the old women were dressed in red cloaks and took up conspicuous positions to deceive the Royalists. These women are immortalized in a rhyme:

> "The Women of Wem and a few musketeers,
> Beat the Lord Capel and all his cavaliers".

Lord Capel withdrew, and joining the forces returning from Nantwich, beat a hasty retreat to Shrewsbury. The Royalists held Chester and Shrewsbury, but Nantwich and Wem were strong Parliamentarian garrisons from which the Roundheads did very well in harassing and capturing convoys of ammunitions and prisoners. The following year, one of the finest Royalist commanders, Prince Rupert, came to survey the garrison at Wem, but decided it was not worth the effort to attack.

Prince Rupert was the nephew of Charles I, son of his sister Elizabeth, who, on marrying Frederick V elector palatine, had become Queen of Bohemia. She was a great admirer and friend of Sir Thomas Roe, and until his death in 1644 he was Elizabeth's counsellor and adviser. When Prince Rupert first visited England from 1636 to 1637, Sir Thomas wrote to the Prince's mother "I have observed him . . . full of spirit and action, full of observation and judgement". This handsome, brilliant young man seemed to excel in everything. He had a talent for languages, a reputation for being 'a master at all weapon' and (after the Restoration) was considered to be one of the best tennis players in England. Before those halcyon days returned, however, Prince Rupert, zealous as ever, was to bring so much blood and destruction into the cities of England, that Sir Thomas advised his mother to persuade him to return to his father's Court; but his successes were far too important for King Charles to remove him at this particular juncture.

Rupert joined the Cornish forces in an assault on the city of Bristol and forced Fiennes to capitulate, but despite many such triumphs, the Puritan army slowly but surely gained the advantage.

At this period life in Wem was extremely difficult. On one occasion the town was desperately short of food and being on the point of starvation, many deserted. Rev. William must have thanked his Maker daily for the deliverance of his family from such a predicament. No doubt he would have to supply succeeding armies with corn from his barns; beef, bacon, butter and cheese from the store in his house; and hens (for eggs); and poultry (for eating) from his farm yard.

About this time William Jnr. married Elizabeth and they appear to have remained with his family at Arleston Manor. They must have wondered what the future held for them. Elizabeth bore William at least four children: Robert born circa 1646, the year in which the Roundheads from the garrisons of Wem and Oswestry took Shrewsbury by a surprise attack; Richard born circa 1648, who died at the age of twenty one years; Thomas born circa 1651 and a daughter, Jane, who married into the Cotton family in due course. Rev. William was ever mindful of his grandchildren's future. He still held his tenements and lands in Hadley from which he received the rents, but now being closer to these sources of income, he could keep a watchful eye on them.

As the Civil War progressed, Oliver Cromwell became the dominant Puritan personality and established himself as England's supreme general. In 1648 Parliament at last managed to take hold of the King. There was great speculation and argument as to what would happen next. Much to the horror and consternation of many families, both Puritan and Royalist and, of course, the Church, the King was tried for treason and sentenced to death. Never before in England had a monarch been put on trial. Even some of the enemies of Charles must have hesitated to condone such an act, but Parliament was adamant, and on 30th January 1649 he was executed as a traitor to the Commonwealth of England. Having accomplished what seemed like the impossible, Parliament, now unsure of itself, struggled on in great disorder for four years, until Cromwell, exasperated at its ineptitude, marched to the House of Commons with a detachment of troops. He literally threw out the Speaker, together with the mace and sceptre, and dissolved Parliament. He assumed the title Lord Protector and ruled Britain with a firm hand for five years until his death in 1658.

These years must have been difficult ones for the Roe family. Parliamentarian county committees had been established, similar to the county councils of today. They collected rents and fines and assigned leases etc. and in effect carried out a compulsory purchase scheme. Any Royalist who had been actively engaged against them had his lands sequestrated, and in due course parts or parcels of these lands were sold to Puritans. This was to cause great problems at the Restoration. (Tragically in the case of the Earl of Derby, he not only suffered temporary forfeiture of his lands, subject to a heavy fine, but also the loss of his life by execution). Many others were taxed heavily, and if this tax (or fine) was not paid, part of their land could be confiscated in lieu of payment. Tenants who were Royalists with former Royalist landlords, suddenly found themselves under Puritan dominance.

There is no doubt that the Roes would be fined, and it is doubtful whether or not they would be allowed to teach; but even if they were not allowed to teach other people's children, they determinedly taught their own. Everyone knew that Cromwell could not live for ever and that his son, Richard, was just a shadow of his father. The only question was, how long must they endure the austerity of Cromwellian rule? The clergymen were all ejected from their livings if they did not renounce the Thirty Nine Articles, one of which was allegiance to the Monarch as head of the Church of England; no doubt some acceded to the Puritan demands, as typified by the song "The Vicar of Bray".

In the meantime Prince Rupert, who had left England on 5th July 1646, was building up a reputation as a swashbuckling buccaneer, sometimes in the employ of the French government, sometimes attending to the interests of his cousin, Prince Charles, or sometimes attacking the English (Lord Protector's) ships. However impetuous these actions seemed, when he did return to England, he was to take an important part in revitalising the nations industries.

* * * * * * *

No one today can appreciate the sheer joy and elation which the Restoration of the Monarchy created on 29th May 1660. At the end of the 17th century, church bellringers were still receiving payment for the ringing of bells on Restoration or Oak Apple Day; it was compulsory for a period. In the early years of the 18th century many inventories included pictures of Charles II which were being willed to a further generation within the family. The mood of the people was obvious; never again would they allow such an appalling situation to manifest itself. With the Civil War well and truly behind them, they set about building for the future with renewed energy and enthusiasm.

At last grandfather Roe could organise his resources with some confidence, and in his few remaining years, after Robina had died, he and his son William (now in his late forties) shared everything, in the hope that they could provide adequately for the next generation. Granddaughters, Elizabeth and Dorothy, would have to be provided with sufficient marriage settlements to be able to make good marriages; grandsons, Robert and Thomas, (also Richard until he died in 1670) were to receive the best education. Even so they laboured under great difficulties for five or six years. Robert lacked his brother Thomas's scholastic abilities, but at the age of eighteen years he was accepted at Queen's College, Oxford. He entered as a "serv" (servant). At Cambridge these humble students were called sizars, but in both universities their status was the same, they performed certain duties in part payment for their education and maintenance which often included running errands, helping tutors or on occasion scrubbing floors. Socially this was no detriment to them, and some of the greatest characters in Church history began their student days in this way.

The Roes obviously had little spare money, and as soon as Robert had obtained his B.A. in 1667, his brother Thomas replaced him at the university, being recorded as "pleb" (plebian). This meant that he was accepted as an ordinary student and could concentrate on his studies, instead of working to reduce his fees. The Roe finances were at last improving.

Thomas did very well for himself. He entered the university aged sixteen years, obtained his B.A. in 1671, his M.A. in 1674 and his Bachelor of Divinity at Pembroke College. When he died unmarried in 1703, he had been rector of Marston Mortaine in Bedfordshire for five years.

After the Restoration, the Church of England was again reorganised, and a new word was about to become commonplace in the English language, that of Dissenters. The ministers of the church were given the option to conform once more and accept the Thirty Nine Articles. If they chose not to do so, then they had to resign. Many obstinately refused, but continued preaching in the area around the church which they had been forced to vacate. They were obviously well supported by the Puritan members of their former congregations. Finally in 1665 an Act of Parliament was passed prohibiting any minister from living within five miles of any place where he had preached. The Dissenting ministers and their small congregations formed yet another breakaway group, to the further detriment of the Established Church.

* * * * * * *

Sir Thomas Roe's endeavours early in the century were now reaching fruition, and England had established trading links not only in India, but also in China, Turkey, Africa and with many small islands in the Indian ocean where ships often had to put in for emergency supplies or repairs. Bumbay (Bombay) belonged to Portugal, but when Charles II married the King of Portugal's sister, it was given to him. He made very little profit from it and so he gave it to the East India Company, who fortified it and kept a garrison of soldiers there.

During the next century this trade with the Far East established in England an enormously wealthy merchant class; nor were the affluent aristocrats to be left behind, in fact quite often they were there leading the way. Many vigorously developed the resources on their estates as in the instance of coal, iron, lead and copper mines, and clay for the potteries, giving much encouragement to the advancement of science which went hand in hand with mineralogy. They also invested in ships plying to and from the East, and used their power and influence through their seats in the House of Lords to ensure their schemes were successful.

Prince Rupert had returned to England in November 1661, and in the following February his mother had died. She was buried in Westminster Abbey having left him her jewels, which further antagonised the already strained relationship between himself and his elder brother, the elector. He was welcomed enthusiastically by Charles II, his cousin, who was having problems with the Dutch. The 'Hollanders' had a long established trade with the Far East and jealously guarded their monopolies. There was much pirating of ships and Prince Rupert was the ideal person to be involved in such activities. In 1663 the Prince became one of the patentees of the Royal African Company, which built forts along the coast of Africa to safeguard the developing trade. This trade brought to England gold, drugs, elephants' teeth, wax and commodities; it also encouraged what seemed like a sensible idea at the time – the slave trade.

* * * * * * *

When Sir Thomas Roe first visited Africa for provisions, the conditions under which the inhabitants lived were appalling. Their old people they left "in some open place in the dark night" for the wild beasts to devour them. They had habits of sheep-skins, thonged together, which covered their bodies to the middle; for jewellery they wore about their necks "Bullocks, or Sheeps-guts full of excrement" and when they were hungry they shook out some of the "filthy pudding out of the guts". One of these "poor wretches" was brought back to England by the Commander of an English ship and kept for six months in the house of Sir Thomas Smith, Governor of the East India Company. There he was given a good diet, good clothes, good lodgings and an ornamental breast and neck piece made of brass "his beloved Metal". When he had learnt a little English, however, he cried to go home and his wish was granted. "He had no sooner set footing on his own shore, but presently he threw away his clothes, his linnen, with all other covering, and got his sheeps skins upon his back, guts about his neck, and such a perfum'd Cap . . . upon his head" (These caps were made with cow dung "mingled with a little stinking grease").

Kettle-brass and iron hoops from empty casks were traded for cattle and sheep, and an Italian traveller wrote:

"Here ye must know, that this people of all metals seem to love Brass, I think . . . for the rankness of its smell; with which they make great Rings to wear about their Wrists; yea, so taken are they with this base metal, that if a man lay down before them a piece of Gold worth two pounds sterling, and a piece of brass worth two pence, they will leave the Gold and take the brass".

The African tribes had been fighting amongst themselves for long enough, and the Dutch and Portugese had turned it to their advantage. Instead of the prisoners being put to death, they could be used in the mines and plantations of South America. The more belligerent African tribes now saw an opportunity to obtain the 'luxuries' they desired, and waged war unnecessarily upon the more peace-loving tribes. In return for Indian cottons, Venetian beads and brass ornaments they captured and ironically fed well, and kept in perfect condition, prisoners ready for the foreign ships.

There must have been great debates in England amongst the merchants who saw an ideal opportunity for themselves. The plantations in America and the West Indies were developing and suitable local labour could not be found. The African, being so used to living in tropical conditions, seemed ideal, but the voice of the Church was strong and had to be heard. Missionaries were sent out by the score. They travelled with the Africans to the plantations and the people in England thought all was well. As far as they were concerned, the superior peace loving tribes had been saved from the cruel and torturous conditions in South America. They were being taken to plantations where there was plenty to eat, where they were given at least one new full suit of clothes each year. Each man had a shirt or smock made from approximately three yards of 'coarse' cotton, and breeches and white knitted stockings. Just as many of the landed gentry in England took pride in the appearance of their estate workers, often providing uniforms for messengers and others, so many of the plantation owners took pride in the efficiency and appearance of their plantation workers. Once again, however, greed and avarice were to rear their ugly heads, and certain English men would act no better than their Dutch and Portugese counterparts. For many years to come the ordinary English citizen, whether weaving striped cotton for the shirts of negro slaves, or growing beans for their food, or making coppers for the sugar plantations, would not even give them a second thought.

* * * * * * *

The slave trade was certainly of no concern to the Roe family of Arleston in Shropshire, nor were they at all affected by the London plague; or the great fire which broke out in Pudding Lane on 2nd September 1666, during Robert's term at Oxford. Their only concern would be the carrying of the plague into their area of Shropshire by travellers from the City; or that Robert might be infected by students and others, returning to the university after visiting friends and relatives in London.

Once more fears and superstitions were aroused. In many towns and hamlets throughout the country, strict watches were kept by appointed individuals who had to report to those in authority when strangers appeared in their streets or highways; then appropriate steps were taken to have them 'removed'. The bubonic plague filled people with terror, and rightly so, it was rumoured that because of it, half the population of London had died. In the 14th century it had appeared in the form of the Black Death, but in the year 1665 it was the pulmonary plague. The first symptoms were swellings on the body followed by a red rash and great difficulty in breathing, hence the name.

Sadly for one Derbyshire village called Eyam, the precautions were of no avail. The disease was transmitted by fleas lodged in a bale of cloth, ordered from London by a tailor. Today this village is still a living testament of man's love for his neighbour. During the year in which the plague raged (1665/66), out of a population of 350 only 80 survived. Many heeded the words of the parson, Rev. Mompesson, when he asked them not to panic or run away because of the danger of spreading the plague throughout the North of England. In due course of time this village, set in one of the richest lead mining areas of the country would become well-known to Rev. Robert's eldest son.

* * * * * * *

When Robert's grandfather died, after completing his will on 11th January 1669, he left his half share of the livestock, and all other chattels relating to the Arleston Estate, to his son William Jnr. (Robert's father), excepting two beds complete with bedding, which were given, one to each grandson (Robert and his brother Thomas). There was still one life left on the lease for the Manor, which was valued at £20 in the inventory, and as it appertained to William Jnr. he decided to remain there until his death in 1680, having outlived his father by only ten years. The two daughters and grandchildren were all provided for by yearly payments, to be made out of the various rents received from the Hadley investments. Son, Thomas, was not included and presumably had died. For the eldest grandson, Robert, Rev. Roe left "all those corn mills and Malt mills at Hadley aforesaid with all houses buildings and Pooles Dams . . . To have and to hold for . . . his heires males forever", together with a gift of four silver spoons.

At last Robert was in a position to negotiate a marriage settlement and find himself a wife. He was a man of "large stature, but mean capacity"; yet despite the fact that he had acquired a reputation for being rather dull and not a good conversationalist, he did succeed in marrying Elizabeth (a daughter of Thomas Steadman). The 'Stedman' family, who had lived at the "White House", Aston Munslow for over 400 years, are credited with being entrusted with the Holy Grail by the Glastonbury Monks at the time of the Reformation. The blackened olive wood cup, said to have been used by Christ at the Last Supper and brought to Glastonbury by Joseph of Arimathea, had remained with the family for almost 300 years when, because of female descent in the 18th century, it passed to the Powells of Nantoes. With or without the influence of his wife's family, Robert had also been successful in obtaining the position of headmaster at Diddlebury School, Munslow, (which was situated approximately fifteen miles south of Shrewsbury) from 20th September 1670. At this period the grammar schools were so small that quite often the headmasters were the only teachers in them. Occasionally there was a second master, but always both the positions could only be filled by parsons. Shortly after taking up this appointment, Robert's first born child, a son, Thomas, (named after his wife's father) was baptised at Munslow on 8th November 1670. Thomas was quickly followed by William (1672) and Elizabeth (1674).

Now an excellent opportunity presented itself. The Free Grammar School in Wem had been founded in 1650, during the Commonwealth Period, by a gentleman called Thomas Adams. Adams had been brought up in Wem and eventually went to Cambridge, destined for the Church. Here, once more, it seemed likely that the influence of Rev. William prevailed – at least for a little while. Adams eventually decided to settle in London where he became a wealthy and successful draper, and also Lord Mayor in 1646. Unfortunately, being a staunch Royalist, he found himself imprisoned in the Tower for a period, but after the Restoration he was made a baronet, Father of the City, President of St. Thomas's hospital and even founded the Chair of Arabic at Cambridge University. He gave money and lands as an investment for the Grammar School, which at first was situated in a large room over the market house, but then was moved to the Church until the new school was built in 1670. In 1676 the post of headmaster became vacant. There were many Royalist families in the area who would remember Rev. William being parson of the Parish Church. Probably because of this and other connections, Robert was successful in gaining the headship of the school and almost immediately moved from Munslow to take up the position. He was just in time to meet the Bishop on his Visitation round in 1676.

Each Bishop, in each Diocese of the Church of England, visited every parish within his Diocese, usually once every three years. He was accompanied by a clerk, and they collected the transcripts (i.e. the Bishop's copies of all the births, marriages and deaths entered in the registers by the parsons or clerks), for the previous three years. They also collected all tithes due to the Bishop, either in money or in kind, and any other payments. They ensured that grammar school masters were qualified and kept schools in good order. They also set up a small 'court' where complaints could be heard, and the Bishop would advise or take action accordingly. The Bishop's Visit was a significant occasion, when he was entertained by the local 'dignitaries'. If the Visit took place in a town which was important enough to have a corporation, then the Mayor, Aldermen and Burgesses, together with the Bishop, enjoyed a Civic Reception with plenty of food and wine, much to the detriment of the Mayor's funds. The Mayor was always very careful to enter the expenditure in his accounts, which were presented after the end of his year in office. They were duly audited and,with appropriate admonitions where necessary, entered in the Corporation Minute Book; some of these make delightful reading to 21st century eyes, whilst others seem just as appropriate now as then.

On the occasion of the Bishop's next Visit to Wem in 1679 Robert was again entered in the book as schoolmaster, but this time instead of making a personal appearance, he "Exhibited Licence through William Smith".

Between these two Visitations a terrible tragedy had occurred. On Saturday 3rd March 1677, at about seven to eight o'clock in the morning, a young girl of 14 years of age went upstairs to bring down fuel which was stored beneath a bed. Her sister was washing linen at the well, and the girl hoped to have a good fire for her sister's return, but in her hurry, she placed her candle too close to a twig, which ignited, setting the thatch ablaze. Agitated by a strong wind, nothing could save the house. Burning thatch and shingles were blown in all directions, and as the season had been dry, house after house caught alight with great rapidity until there was a raging inferno. It was of no avail to try to use the old fire hook, with auxiliary pole, for detaching the burning roofs or pulling down walls. Within the space of an hour every building in town seemed to be alight. There was panic everywhere. People tried to save what they could from their homes, but the poor shoemaker, having retrieved a parcel of shoes from his shop, disappeared under the falling mass of the market house. Another man, trying to save some cattle, also vanished into the flames. Gone were over one hundred houses, barns and other buildings, almost the whole of the church and the steeples, but incredibly the school was virtually the only building left standing.

Robert's house was razed to the ground and he must have lost a great deal. The children would have been terrified; Thomas was six years of age, William four and Elizabeth only two. Baby Robert, baptised just one month earlier on the 2nd February, does not seem to have survived.

Garbet wrote "In the streets they were scorched with excessive heat, in the fields they were ready to perish with cold". Many people were forced to leave for other towns and villages; some never to return.

Robert and his family moved into the upper storey of the school and made it their home. The library was converted into his bed-chamber and the other room reorganised as a kitchen, where he had a chimney built at his own expense. He did his best, under the circumstances, and had part of the schoolhouse rebuilt in brick. Poor Robert must have been very much affected by the tragedy. He was later criticized because he was unable to keep up the reputation of the school. "His heavy genius, and the loss of his scholars exposing him to affronts, he thought fit to relinquish a post which he could not keep with honour".

On 15th April 1678, the year after the great fire, Robert purchased from Mr. Richard Roderick several parcels of land in Wem, which were subsequently conveyed to his father as security for his brother, Thomas. These lands were purchased by loans, using the Hadley properties as security, and both the names of Robert and his father appeared on the Bonds (the Bonds were the IOUs in the form of a certificate legally prepared by a solicitor).

The church was still in ruins after the fire, and it was brought to the attention of the Bishop by Mr. R. Jebb, churchwarden, that John Smyth, sadler of Wem, had taken lead from a window and from the font, and employed it "to his own estate". The bells had actually melted down with the tremendous heat caused by the blaze, but the tower survived, and helped by one or two phases of restoration work still stands today. The chancel was not rebuilt by Daniel Wycherley, Lord of the Manor, until 1680, so after Jonathan's birth, father Robert and the family had to travel to St. Mary's, Shrewsbury for his baptism on 31st May 1679.

When William Jnr. died early in 1680, his wife would no longer be entitled to live at Arleston Manor, but she was entitled to receive the benefit of her marriage settlement; in fact, a wife was entitled to claim up to one third of her late husband's estate. Although the corn and malt mills and other properties in Hadley had been willed to Robert and his heirs by his grandfather, his mother received the income from these tenements until her death.

It is interesting to note that there seems to have been no attempt made to replace either of the two lives terminated on the lease. Usually, when a life was lost on a property lease, it was possible to negotiate a new one in its place, at a price, of course. Perhaps the Roes had tried to negotiate but had been refused. Shortly after the death of William Jnr. coal mines were being worked on the Arleston Estate. There are account books in existence from 7th January 1685 relating to a mining lease granted by the Forester family. Possibly the Foresters had endeavoured to work the mines for themselves, when the Roe lease expired, but found that the most economic proposition was to sublease to someone else. It is more than likely that William Jnr., having learnt well from his father, had already been enjoying the benefit of these coal seams, which would certainly account for his rapid increase in prosperity during his last ten years at Arleston. Apart from one servant, who had been with them for some years, the family could now afford more, and when William Jnr. prepared his will, being a generous and kindly man he gave each of his servants a gift which seemed to represent two weeks' wages. The retainer was given the option of a yearly pension of £4, or her full wages due + 25% (in all a lump sum of £20) which she could then invest at an interest rate of at least 4% per annum (i.e. 16/- which was probably equal to about three weeks' wages). By this period there were many goods available for the servants to buy.

Once more there were plenty of petty chapmen travelling the roads and selling their wares to a variety of people. Some came on pack horses, many walked. Ordinary villagers and townspeople were now beginning to take a pride in their homes, whether they were tiny cottages or townhouses. Striped brown and white calico was sold to hang for both window and bed curtains, and came in lengths of 10 yards for seven shillings to nine shillings the piece. Indian cottons were popular, some chequered and flowered which were suitable for bed linen. 'Long cloth', a cheaper Indian variety sold for $1/2$d. or $1/4$d. a yard, with a coarse one for eight pence or nine pence a yard. The gentry preferred 'bridges holland' for sheets, which was 45 inches wide, and a fine 'gulix holland' for sheets, shirts and shifts. Tablecloths and napkins were sold in suites, the tabling being three times as wide as the napkinning and there were two lengths of napkin breadth to every length of tabling. It was also possible to buy sewing needles, linen thread, scissors and a variety of little printed story books and maps etc. It encouraged a desire to learn to read, and promoted the expansion of etiquette and good manners which were to become so pronounced in the 18th century.

Robert remained at the Adams Grammar School in Wem until 1682; the church being almost completed, he was able to have a daughter, Dorothy, baptised there on 8th June 1681. Where his mother resided is not known. He then purchased the Hadley Manor for his family from Sir John Corbet (presumably by loans), which complemented the other holdings of land in

Hadley; and from 1682 onwards he had his own private grammar school in the manor house. His mother, Elizabeth, now resided in Hadley, possibly with the family, and when she died Robert obtained the Administration of her estate during March 1691. Before she died, however, Elizabeth had the pleasure of seeing Robert's last three children baptised in the church of All Saints, Wellington; she had done her duty well and borne him nine children.

Brother Thomas, had the security of a large area of land in Hadley known as Grice's Tenement, and also the lands in Wem – until the interest on the loans no longer could be paid.

The Roe finances were once more diminishing. Robert's eldest son, Thomas, aged fifteen years, had entered All Souls' College, Oxford on 11th November 1685, recorded as 'pleb'. He obtained his B.A. in 1689 and his M.A. from St. Mary's Hall in 1692. By the time brother William entered Trinity College, Cambridge on 20th June 1699, he was in the same position in which his father had found himself on entering Oxford some years previously. The life of a sizar was very hard and he was only fifteen years old, but by the time he had reached twenty five years of age, he was a son to be proud of. He had obtained his B.A. after three years and his M.A; he was ordained Ordinary Deacon in London and priest, and he was presented to two very good livings in Shropshire not far from Arleston. Firstly he took Frodesley and then held it together with Pitchford, which was close by. On 30th November 1708 he married Isabella, the daughter of the parson of Bishop Stortford, and was able to come to his father's rescue in 1710 before the Hadley Estate was seized.

On the 12th June 1700 all the lands in Hadley, left by grandfather, Rev. William Roe, to both Robert and his brother, Thomas, had been seized. The loans had been made, or taken over, by two London barristers, one of the Middle Temple and the other of the Inner Temple, and now they had demanded their rights. There was probably a little money surplus from the seizure of these lands. If the value of the lands or property sold, was in excess of the loan plus interest owed, then the balance would be paid to the borrower. Rev. Robert had just sufficient resources to manage his two eldest daughters' marriage settlements, but even the Hadley Manor was now in danger of seizure. In almost one hundred years things had never been so bad, not even during the Civil Wars.

William's great grandfather would have been proud of him, for he did not allow the seizure to take place. Gathering together as much money as he could (again one suspects by loans) he purchased the Hadley Manor from his father, Robert, in 1710. Robert lived out the rest of his days there, and managed a further marriage settlement for his daughter, Jane. He still had plenty of furniture, tables, chairs, stools, a couple of chests; two feather beds complete with bedding; pewter and brass wares and a silver cup and spoons. There were plenty of kitchen items, and in the parlour a pendulum clock and case. When Robert died in 1717 all these items he left to his youngest daughter, Alice "for her care of me, as for her mother", and Alice, then twenty eight years of age, was made sole executrix. Each of the three married daughters received 5 shillings, William received one shilling and his brother, John, who was a widower, received a pair of shoes. But what of Thomas, the eldest son, who should have inherited the Hadley Estate? He received his shilling and his father's gold signet ring.

Thomas's eighth and last child, a son called Charles, was just two years of age. Even if the child survived to reach adulthood, he seemed to have very little chance of success in early 18th century England. Although things were bad, they were still not at their worst; in only six years time Rev. Thomas would have died, closely followed by his wife. Before these events took place, however, Thomas had forsaken his native Shropshire, home of the Roe family for so long, and ventured forth into unknown territory.

2

BEER, BUTTONS AND BOLES

I will lift up my eyes unto the hills,
From whence cometh my help

The Mayor, Aldermen and Burgesses of Macclesfield were attending a Corporation meeting in the old medieval Guildhall, close by the Parochial Chapel of All Hallows. It had been brought to their attention that the Minister of the church, Mr. Hulme, considered "that the burthen" of the place was so great, he could not possibly perform his duties without an assistant. Having discussed the matter, it was duly noted in the Corporation Minute Book, on that day, 6th October 1690, that an allowance of £20 per annum would be given for a Curate in addition to surplice fees, and that "Mr. Hulme shall have allowance as to King's Preacher and Curate and Parsonage House – will amount to £60 per annum." Samuel Hulme had previously been Clerk of Knutsford in Cheshire, having replaced Rev. Kettlesbie Turner, who had been buried there on 17th August 1686. Knutsford was only a chapelry of Rostherne, and after two years Hulme sought to better himself by moving to the Macclesfield Chapel. Although the Macclesfield chapelry was subordinate to Prestbury Parish Church, Hulme probably considered that a Corporation might conceivably be more generous than a patron of a living, and within the year had tested out his theory. Exactly when he engaged his 'assistant' is not known. It would seem that he deferred the appointment for a while to enable him to accrue a little money. Some eighteen months later repairs were carried out to the parsonage house, and a new kitchen and staircase were built at the expense of the Corporation. At some time shortly after this date, Rev. Thomas Roe, having obtained his M.A. from St. Mary's Hall, was offered, and accepted the appointment as Curate of the Parochial Chapel.

The mystery is why Thomas came to Macclesfield and did not obtain a living within the Diocese of Lichfield, where the Roe family was well represented. Lichfield was an enormous Diocese covering the whole of Derbyshire, Staffordshire, the northern part of Shropshire and elsewhere, consequently presenting many opportunities. There was already a Roe family in the Macclesfield area, but with whom Thomas seems to have had no obvious connections. At this period of English history very little was coincidence, so someone, somewhere, had ensured that he was available for the position. On leaving Oxford University, Thomas had probably returned to the Hadley School until a post presented itself; whatever experience he gained in that quarter seemed to have made him determined to avoid the tradition of school teaching, to which three generations of his family had doggedly adhered. On arriving in Macclesfield, Thomas must have thrown himself enthusiastically into his work because, on 14th September 1694, the Corporation Minute Book records a pay increase "Ordered that Mr. Rowe" (there was often a variation of spelling at this period) "the Curate of Macclesfield shall have £30 per Annum salary over and besides the surplice fees from Michaelmas next so long as he shall continue Curate there to be paid out of the Revenues of the said Town until further notice." The Corporation was being generous, indicating that the small township was quite prosperous, and during the next four years of Thomas's stay within the Borough it was to become even more so. Thomas would soon be made aware of the history of the chapel and also of the Hundred of Macclesfield.

* * * * * * *

At the time of the Domesday survey Cheshire was divided into seven hundreds, one of which was Macclesfield, situated on its extreme eastern boundary. It was sparsely populated with very little cultivated land, but its predominant feature was a magnificent forest, which spread in a south-easterly direction like a huge green cloak folding its way in and out of the valleys towards the Derbyshire hills. Here deer, wild boar, pheasants and other game could be hunted at leisure. Out of this mass of trees and foliage flowed a river, which gently meandered along the floor of a shallow valley, from a southerly direction. On reaching the northern extremity of this small valley, the river curved sharply westwards to continue its journey across the north eastern region of the county. The Domesday Record states "There is a mill to supply the hall", so at this early date the valley and its river had already been adopted. There seems to have been only a handful of people living within the area, but because the Norman Earls of Chester had such an interest in the forest, the first signs of development began to appear. Seven large areas of land were enclosed by either fences or walls and were called the Heys.

In the year 1237 the Hundred, Forest and Manor of Macclesfield were appropriated by the Crown, and by the year 1261 there was such a thriving small community along the fringes of the western bank of the river, that the 'town' of Macclesfield was granted its first Charter by Edward, Earl of Chester, for which it duly made payment. Thus Macclesfield became a free Borough with permission to create a Merchant Guild and enjoy many privileges, including the right of the Burgesses to give, sell or mortgage their burgages and to choose a leader for themselves, who in due course was given the office of Mayor.

As unusual set of circumstances pertained during the years 1270 to 1347, which gave rise to 'the liberty of Macclesfield Hundred'. This was the period when the manor was separated from the affairs of the county of Cheshire and given in dower to two queens of England. The first was Eleanor, consort of Edward I, to whom is accredited the founding of the Parochial Chapel. The chapel, probably begun in 1278, was dedicated by the Bishop of St. Asaph to All Hallows or All Saints; it can be no coincidence that Eleanor and Edward had been married on All Saints Day, 1st November 1254. To this day the choristers are entitled to wear red cassocks as a symbol of the royal foundation.

Towards the end of the 14th century, John of Macclesfield, an official at the Court of Richard II, built for himself a crenallated residence or castle, which was situated halfway down the steep hill, leading from the southern end of the hamlet up to the tiny market place; there stood the market cross, close by the Guildhall and Parochial Chapel. His land was surrounded by a substantial stone wall, and covered an acre of ground which sloped down to the river, where the small brooks and tributaries, draining from the western regions of the hamlet, gathered together to enter its course. This boggy area, overlooked by both the castle and the Parochial Chapel, had acquired the name of Waters.

Leading from the market cross northwards out of the hamlet, and dropping steeply down the far side of the hill, was a way known as Jordangate, which still exists to this day.

To the south-west of the hamlet lay an area designated the 'Lord's Park', and because of Macclesfield's royal connections, this area became the royal demesne. From the time of Edward I's visits, it was stocked with cattle and horses. The manorial accounts for the year 1296/7 give evidence of a stud being in existence in Macclesfield Park comprising seven mares, but with a borrowed stallion; however, there is a record of the purchase of a bay stallion in 1301 "for the stud". Although the stud was removed to Denbigh in 1360, this small beginning established in the Macclesfield area a tradition for the breeding and selling of horses, which was to be of great significance during the later part of the 17th and 18th centuries.

(It is interesting to note that horses were bred for working, albeit for hunting or military use, and it was not until the 18th century that horse racing became established. Initially this caused considerable resistance, so in the year 1740 an Act of Parliament (Geo II 13 Cap XIX) was passed "to prevent excessive Increase of Horse Races" because "the Breed of strong and useful Horses hath been much prejudiced". By this Act a person was only allowed to own one horse for racing purposes; however, the passion for horse racing was here to stay despite a further attempt in 1745 when an Act (Geo II 18 Cap XXXIV) to prevent gambling, in particular cards, dice and roulette, had included at the end "and to restrain and prevent the excessive Increase of Horse Races . . .".)

Over the centuries, as more and more timber was taken from the forest for the making of stockades, bridges, houses, carts and furniture amongst other things, the forest began to diminish considerably, and by the 18th century fir timber was being imported from America for the building of Macclesfield houses.

The only other area of immediate importance to the hamlet was the Common or waste lands situated on the eastern banks of the river, where the local populace enjoyed unrestricted rights to pasture sheep, horses and cattle; rights which remained unimpeded until the 17th century. This land rose steeply, almost immediately from the banks of the river, and apart from a level area of ground halfway up the hill, continued its steep ascent to the summit. From the elevated position of this level ground, a splendid view of the valley was obtained, displaying the layout of the hamlet below, which after the 14th century was highlighted by John de Macclesfield's castellated mansion on the opposite brow, together with a clear view of the Parochial Chapel, now complete with a "very high spire steeple" silhouetted against the skyline. Barely discernible were the Macclesfield mills situated alongside the river, which were the subject of a dispute early in the 17th century.

In March 1691 Macclesfield Corporation decided to erect its own malt mill, which was built on Dog Lane, one of the earliest of the 'town's' streets, and it seems probable that this had replaced an earlier timber framed mill. The eastern end of Dog Lane was entered from the Market Place, directly opposite the Parochial Chapel, and ran in a westerly direction; the mill was situated on the southern side about two-thirds of the way along. (Today this is the site of the Grosvenor Centre and Indoor Market; Castle Street running immediately along the southern side of the complex, which is of recent creation, experiences at its western extremity the full force of any wind sweeping across the Cheshire plain and rising towards the Kerridge Hills and Derbyshire). This would have been an ideal position for the original mill.

Two water mills, which belonged to the Crown, were actually in the adjoining parish of Sutton, and were part of what had been the original manor of Macclesfield. At some time in the medieval period Sutton Manor had been created and the house renamed Sutton Hall, which is still standing.

By the early 17th century the Macclesfield mills were in the possession of three Johns with the surnames of Faulkner, Newton and Barlowe, for which they paid a fee farm rent to His Majesty. The inhabitants, not only of Macclesfield, but also of the surrounding hamlets of Sutton, Wincle, Hurdsfield, Broken Cross and elsewhere in the 'Burrough, Manor and Forrest', brought their ground or spent corn, grain and pulse, to the mills. The fact that these grains were already ground or spent indicates that the several customers had hand mills or querns, a simple device consisting of two circular stones. The upper stone had a hole in the centre through which the grain was poured, and another hole near the edge, through which a stick was pushed to act as a handle. Sometimes this upper stone was two-handled (known as a saddle quern), but whichever device was used, the method was the same, the upper stone was revolved or moved backwards and forwards against the lower one, thus crushing the grain trapped in between. This initial operation was presumably followed by a primitive refining with a sieve, to collect the better quality parts of the mass for immediate use according to their intended purpose e.g. wheat for bread or malt for beer brewing. The coarser parts would be put in separate sacks and brought to the Macclesfield mills for further crushing, after which the spent grains would be used as cattle food.

On 4th December 1629 (the year in which Rev. William Roe was busy extending his hunting lodge at Arleston) a certain gentleman by the name of James Pickford, together with two other defendants, were summoned to appear in the Court of the Exchequer in Chester. Pickford was accused of having erected water course mills, handmills or querns and horsemills, "in or near the said town of Macclesfield" to the damage of the Macclesfield mills. James Pickford, Mayor of Macclesfield during 1626/27, had family connections in Derby through his sister's marriage, and the principal trade of Derby was malting from which Staffordshire, Lancashire and the greater part of Cheshire were supplied. A considerable portion was also taken to London "by which many good estates have been raised". (A comment written by a historian, Mr. Woolley in the year 1712 and publlished in a *History of Derby* 1826)

James Pickford did confess to erecting one handmill or quern in Wildboarclough, but pointed out that it was situated four miles from Macclesfield. He agreed that he had brought the malt from Derby, but stood by his right to do so. The case was delayed for discussion, and after much debate it was decided that he and the other defendants should be dismissed, unless someone could show further cause for prosecution within two days – which apparently no one could. Some eleven years later, on the 12th February during the 16th year of the reign of Charles I (1640) James Pickford had an Exemplification of Exchequer Proceedings prepared – in simple terms he obtained a copy of the Court proceedings – presumably because he was becoming affluent and someone was beginning to cause problems again.

Only six weeks earlier Pickford had leased land in Macclesfield from the Earl of Derby, but as the land was barren at that time, he was spending a large amount of money on improving it. It would seem that this piece of land was complementary to his residence, because already by this date he appears to have been living in what remained of John de Macclesfield's castle.

The castle had come into possession of the Earls of Derby in the late 16th century and must have fallen into disrepair, with the land also neglected. On 14th January 1632 the then Earl of Derby had sold the lease of the property to a Richard Blacklach, a woollen merchant and chapman, the latter involving him in the small linen and silk industry, including the making of buttons and buttonholes, which had already found roots in and around the areas of Leek, Congleton, Macclesfield, and as far north as Stockport, along the eastern border of Cheshire. When Blacklach died in 1635, James Pickford the Elder, Alderman and once more Mayor, leased the property shortly afterwards. In 1641, during his third term of office as Mayor, there followed the leasing of further property.

The Civil War was, of course, just beginning, and Macclesfield, as elsewhere, would not escape its repercussions. Sir William Brereton, Commander of the Parliamentary forces, lived at Handforth, only a few miles distance from Macclesfield, and after his successful siege of Nantwich in 1643, Crewe Hall and other Royalist Houses in south Cheshire quickly fell to the Parliamentary army. All too soon it was the turn of Macclesfield, and the army, under the direction of Colonel Mainwaring, took the township. Colonel Legh of Adlington Hall, being an ardent Royalist, was quick to respond, but Mainwaring had the assistance of the Manchester forces, and after a gallant defence of the Hall itself, Macclesfield and district fell to the overwhelming might of the Parliamentarians, with Colonel Legh eventually taken prisoner at Nantwich.

About the time of Robert Roe's birth in 1646, when the Roundheads took Shrewsbury by a surprise attack, Pickford the Elder made out his Will, leaving to his son, James the Younger, Alderman and Mayor (1645/46), all his goods and chattels in the Macclesfield house, but James the Elder lived longer than he expected and completed a further term of office as Mayor in 1652/53, followed once more by his son in 1655/56. Perhaps candidates were hard to find under the restraining influence of the Puritan way of life, however, there was certainly no lack of enthusiasm on the part of the Pickford family. It was this son, who in due course bitterly complained that when Cromwell was Lord Protector, he had been taken to Court and had spent a great deal of money proving that the original barren parcel of land had been legally leased from an ancestor of the Earl of Derby, for the benefit of his family.

With the Restoration the time had come to settle old scores, and not only did the Pickfords again have to face legal action with regard to their land acquisitions, but also the old allegation of the handmill at Wildboarclough. The case, however, was an excuse to sort out exactly who was legally entitled to which parcels of land in Macclesfield Forest, as the pre-Parliamentarian owners, the King and Earl of Derby, had both been beheaded, and various areas of their land sequestrated. Boundaries were difficult to establish, and with both successors anxious to reclaim their fathers' possessions everyone was reliant on the people who lived in the forest to recall where those boundaries had been.

The outcome of the subsequent Pickford trial is not known, but was apparently to the advantage of both the Earl and Pickfords, for John, son of James the Younger, having embraced the legal profession had gained one of the most prestigious positions in the Hundred which carried great influence. Charles, then eighth Earl of Derby, having succeeded to the title after his father's execution, appointed John Clerk of the Forest and Hundred of Macclesfield "to take into his charge and custody all Court Rolls Court Books Records . . . belonging to the Court for terme of his natural life. . ." Needless to say, under the auspices of such a title, both John and his father took great steps in establishing themselves as an important family, not only within the Borough but elsewhere.

It was during the Mayoralty of James Pickford the Younger, on 8th December 1655 that the first mention of the button industry was made in the Corporation Minute Book:

> "Forasmuch as by the industry & care of many of the Burgesses & freemen of this Borough & Corporation in the trade & manufacture of the skillful & well making of Buttons here & the Blessing of God there upon the inhabitants thereof – places adjacent are much bettered in their livelihood & estates than heretofore . . ."

During the aftermath of the Civil War it had been difficult to assemble many of the Common Burgesses for the Corporation Meetings, despite fines levied for absenteeism. In fact, between the years 1651 and 1654 no meetings whatsoever had taken place. Once Oliver Cromwell had established himself as Lord Protector, slowly but surely things began to return to normal, which included the Mayor, Aldermen and Burgesses of Macclesfield.

At the December Meeting of the Corporation in 1655 it had been noted that many "foreigners & strangers" had been making buttons and bringing them into Macclesfield on market days to sell at a cheaper rate than the ones produced and sold by the freemen of the Borough. This situation had to be remedied and consequently fines were to be imposed from the following 1st January. It was during this year that James Pickford purchased from the Mayor of Macclesfield, his predecessor, what appears to have been quite a large area of waste land for the substantial sum of £6. By the early 1660s the Pickfords, in relation to their trades, had developed their land well; they were now in possession of several properties and further plots of land, mostly purchased from the Mayor, Aldermen and Burgesses of Macclesfield.

In addition to tanning and malting businesses, the Pickfords were also involved in the local textile trade, having built a dyehouse at the end of a stonewall leading from one of the old castle walls. This was conveniently situated close by the brook flowing across the Waters to join the river originally known as Jordan, subsequently named 'the Water of E", but which by this period had been given the universal name of Bollin.

Whether or not the establishment of either the silk, linen or cotton trades had also been brought by the Pickfords from Derby, may never be known. It is interesting to note, however, that in the year 1634, a property known by the name of Newhouse had been erected close by the southern side of the Parochial Chapel. By 24th June 1640 a citizen and haberdasher of London, by the name of John Gatley, was mentioned in an assignment of the lease. A haberdasher was a shopkeeper who supplied "the taylor" (tailor) with buckram, wadding, hair-cloths, buttons, mohair, silk, thread, stay-tape, binding and all sorts of trimmings except gold and silver lace, which was supplied by the laceman. The property seems to have been held under the Legh family of The Ridge, who had connections with the Leghs of both Lyme and Adlington Halls.

By the time James Pickford the Younger died in 1665 he had certainly done a great deal in promoting the early industries of the area, and by entering into a financial arrangement with the Corporation he ensured that each week twelve loaves of bread were given to twelve poor residents of Macclesfield.

Four years later, on 15th June 1669 Jonathan Pickford married a Mistress Alice Lees, and until his death in 1689 seems to have kept two residences; one in Macclesfield and the other, presumably because of the marriage settlement, at Altehill, Ashton-under-Lyne. It was at Altehill where the children were christened and where the Pickfords established themselves as cotton manufacturers, eventually owning an extensive business during the 18th century with cotton mills established in Royton, Oldham and elsewhere in Lancashire. However, they still retained their interests in Macclesfield; in fact they eventually acquired at least one third of the land development in the town. Nor were the Pickford interests in Macclesfield purely commercial, it would seem.

In the year 1650, during the Civil War, a certain George Fox, lodging in the town of Derby, attended a meeting. Finding the army present, but being very concerned about the state of religion in England, he addressed the gathering. Some thought him drunk so he was escorted by soldiers to the gaol for an overnight stay. However, in due course, having been examined by the magistrate, Fox warned the company present to "tremble at the voice of God". From that moment, having been ridiculed and called a Quaker by the judge, a new sect came into being. George Fox subsequently became a very wealthy man and married the widow of a Judge Fell of Swartmoor Hall, situated about one half mile from the port of Ulverston. Quakerism had arrived early in the Lake District where the Church of England had a firm hold, and many irritations it would cause. It also arrived early in Macclesfield.

Circumstantial evidence seems to indicate that the Pickfords were responsible. Jonathan whose sister, Ellen, had married William Fletcher of Derby, also had a brother who took the name Jedediah, at the time of his 'conversion'. Many Biblical names such as Micah, Obadiah and Nehemiah were adopted by the Quakers, and Jedediah followed the Quaker call to the port of Bristol, which was fast becoming their stronghold, and where they worked hard developing the African trade and the trade with America.

In June 1691 William Opie and Jedediah Pickford, Merchants of Bristol, leased a one sixteenth part of the freight on board the ship "Joseph", for a voyage from Bristol to Virginia or Maryland and back, paying £12 for every four hogsheads of tobacco laden plus a 2/- duty on each hogshead. (A hogshead holds fifty four gallons and a barrel, thirty six. When empty they were ideal for use as packing cases in respect of all sorts of goods).

Shortly after Thomas Roe's arrival in Macclesfield, Jedediah had died without leaving issue. The Trustees of his brother Jonathan's children, sent the young James of Altehill to Bristol, to be apprenticed to a Michael Pope for seven years from 4th October 1695. They paid Mr. Pope £200 for the privilege (at least £20,000 today) with the intention of James becoming a free Burgess of the City of Bristol when the apprenticeship was completed. After two years James would stay no longer. A refund of £60 was made by Michael Pope, together with a written relinquishment of the covenant made by James; and when the young man returned to Ashton-under-Lyne he became a staunch member of the congregation attending the Parish Church there.

* * * * * * *

Thomas Roe must have been very impressed with the 'modern' Macclesfield which he discovered on his perambulations through the Borough. The "Great streets" of the small market town were paved or part paved and were kept clean and tidy by scavengers engaged by the Corporation. Modernisation of some of the Elizabethan properties on Chestergate was taking place, where old frontages were being extended by the addition of verandas, supporting extra rooms on upper floors. The fashion had possibly spread from Chester which was considered to be a unique city in England, because of the fact that a person could walk from one end of the city to the other without ever getting wet. One or two of the older cottages on Back Street (today King Edward Street) had been replaced by good sized brick dwelling houses and the residents enjoyed the pleasure of their gardens and orchards, interspersed with stables where often a cow was kept.

Thomas would be interested in the newly built malt mill belonging to the Corporation on Dog Lane and compare it with his father's mills in Hadley. Just beyond the malt mill at the far end of Dog Lane was a tithe barn, and, on making enquiries, Thomas would be told that this barn had been constructed by, and belonged to the Pickford family, although the present Mr. Pickford was living at Altehill. The highway which swept round from Chestergate to link up eventually with Mill Street, by which the barn stood, had simply been given the name Barn Street, being largely unadopted apart from one or two houses and cottages.

The Corporation seemed full of industrious active men and during the year 1693 they were particularly busy. After the erection of the malt mill had come the laying down of a bowling green during the previous summer of 1692. It was situated just a little way up the hill on the other side of the River Bollin. Now the water supply needed their attention. There did exist an excellent source of water in the centre of the town, due to the 'initiative' of the Corporation, but as more inhabitants wanted to avail themselves of the service, it was putting undue strain on the system, so something had to be done. Negotiations were under way with a certain gentleman by the name of Mr. George Sorocold, who was held in high esteem in various parts of the country as a hydraulics engineer. The outcome produced a cistern, constructed for the use of the waterworks at the Cross, on the principle laid down by Mr. Sorocold, the cost of which was £50.

Originally two aldermen had seen an ideal opportunity to make a handsome profit. The hamlet was supplied with wells, the most important of which was situated almost in the backside of the Pickford property on Mill Street, and close by the Gatehouse of the old castle; consequently the small surrounding area had become known as Wellmouth. The well which supplied the cottages at the lower end of Mill Street would eventually be given the name of Pickford's well, when James Pickford, late apprentice of Bristol, took it upon himself to lease a large area of land in that vicinity from Earl Barrymore. A third well, just a short distance from the last mentioned, supplied the area of Parsonage Green with its handful of cottages and, of course, the parsonage house itself; whilst high up on Macclesfield Common, above the area of level ground, there was an excellent supply of water at a place called the Stone-pit Well.

The natural drainage of the area, beneath the gritstone ridge, collected together a good clean water supply ideal for drinking purposes, and it was from this source that Aldermen Lunt and Booth piped the water in lead pipes all the way down into the valley, across the River Bollin and up to the Cross in the Market Place, no mean achievement. However, someone must have suddenly realized the implication of their actions – monopolies of this nature could not be tolerated – the outcome was seen to be executed with the greatest respect and decorum. Lunt was reimbursed for his expenses of laying out the aqueduct (a sum of £35 8s.) and was given the privilege of having Lunt Hill named after him, at the southwestern end of the Common. Booth was presented with a piece of plate to the value of £5 "as an acknowledgement of his services to the said borough concerning the waterworks", and the Mayor, Aldermen and Burgesses conveniently commandeered the whole operation in the year 1681.

There had been some activity on Macclesfield Common for many years due to the working of coal seams, and it would be part of Rev. Thomas's duty to administer to the miners in the event of any accidents, and in the case of fatal ones to comfort and help any widow or children who might be left destitute. The Church and Corporation worked very well together in looking after the needs of the poor, in fact mining on the Common was only permitted by the Corporation on the understanding that coal getters and coal carriers paid a stipulated sum to an officer, which was held, together with any other monies acquired, for the relief of the poor, and distribution from this fund was made at certain times as and when appropriate. All had worked well until recently, when the Earl of Macclesfield had taken over the lease for the encroachments on the Common from the Crown, and now it was expected that the Corporation should pay 50 shillings per annum in respect of such encroachments. The Corporation found itself involved in instigating proceedings to claim exemption; it would be emphatically pointed out that any profit made from the Common was for the benefit of the poor and any demands made by the lease would be to the detriment of the fund and also the poor.

Appropriately, the old way across the Common was named Black Road; it linked the very steep ascent at the northern end (which continued over the hills in the direction of Buxton in Derbyshire) to the roadway leading upwards towards the stone quarry at the southern end, the lower part of which was now known as Lunt Hill. The most direct route to the Common from the centre of town was across the Eyes, but as this area was privately owned by the Pickford family, and now subleased to several tenants, no right of way was possible. Another steep descent proceeded immediately down the hillside, close by the southeastern extremity of the Chapel (famous today as "The Hundred and Eight Steps"), but only led to the Waters.

The King's Oven or Bakery stood close by the Guildhall, and this would be where the sacks of flour were brought and stored for the baking of bread and where some of the inhabitants brought their own loaves and pastries for baking.

All sorts of recipes were available, published in small booklets which were sold by chapmen at the fairs or during their meanderings around the countryside.

French bread was becoming very popular: Pain ala Mountrau was made with milk and water plus the addition of a little salt, and had fennel seeds beaten and scattered in the dough. It was highly recommended for dipping in wine, preferably 'Mascadel' (Muscadel) or Canary. Pain D'Gentilly was made in the same way as Pain ala Mountrau except a little sweet butter was added. A further variety, having the exotic name of Pain Benit O Brioche required, not only the addition of a pound of fresh butter, but also "a new fresh curd cheese" to be added two hours after the butter. The latter when baked had to be placed on a wicker hurdle to keep it from breaking. (Today brioche rolls are still very much enjoyed). The 'varnish' was made with the yolk of fresh beaten eggs, but sometimes a more economic idea was to use honey, in which instance the oven had to be "slackened". There was even a recipe which included two French curd cheeses and a dozen fresh eggs.

> "NOTE: That all Stale Bread set a new into the Oven, will much
> recover it, and if it be eaten immediately, little different
> from what is now made."

According to custom, the inhabitants of Macclesfield were still obliged to use the King's Oven, or as it was now known, the Town Bakehouse, for their own baking, and a reasonable toll was levied. A great favourite was gingerbread which had the advantage of keeping longer than ordinary bread. For the baking of white bread or gingerbread one penny was charged for every twenty pennyworth. For every measure of corn made into brown bread or every score of mince pies or tarts, a charge of four pence was made, and for every four pies or custards only one penny. The giblet pies were the most expensive costing one penny each to bake.

To Thomas's eyes Monday must have presented some incredible scenes, in sharp contrast to the quiet observance of the previous Lord's Day. In order to make his way to and from the Parochial Chapel he would have to push through crowds of chattering people, and weave his way around tables set out on the pavements covered with a variety of goods for sale; because Monday was market day. There were stalls selling pewter wares and pottery and glass. The baker had been busy from early morning preparing extra bread and plenty of gingerbread for the gingerbread stall. The fishmen and butchers always sold plenty, and the hatters and glovers were well represented. There were even paper men present, sellers of ropes and cords, tallow chandlers and sellers of "burnt fearn ashes". The whole lively scene must have been greatly enriched by the delicious aromas filling the market place from the direction of the bakery.

The local inhabitants who also kept shops, displayed their goods, not only through their small thick glass paned windows, but also upon their pavements outside. Some years previously, Jonathan Pickford had obtained permission from the Corporation to hang shades or boards from the side of his house in Mill Street, "for keeping dry of such persons as shall have standing under them." The lessee of his house and shop now not only had the advantage of keeping her prospective customers dry, but also her goods.

If market days seemed busy then the great fairs were even more so, and the small tolls gathered on market days were substantially augmented by the great tolls of the fair days. The fairs were held twice yearly, one upon the Feast of St. Barnabas in June and the other on All Saints day.

Stallage was a toll which was charged on everything possible, and no one could be exempted by pretending that it only related to the erection of stalls; only freemen were not charged. Even bands of strolling players or troupes of actors were charged stallage for the time they spent in the town. Puppet shows were very popular together with lotteries and raffles, all suitably tolled. The medical profession was represented by a "Quack Doctor" who put in an appearance at both the markets and fairs, being charged $1^1/_2$d on market days and 2d at the fair.

The sale of livestock, mostly sheep, oxen and cattle, took place all the year round, but the greatest attractions were the horse fairs when people travelled from Yorkshire, Derbyshire, North Staffordshire and all parts of Cheshire to purchase fine horses. Perhaps the success of the Macclesfield chapmen came from the fact that they owned more packhorses between them than almost anywhere else in England.

The strength of Macclesfield was, and still is, its position in relation to the rest of the country. It is ideally situated for routes east to west i.e. from the Peak District of Derbyshire across the Cheshire Plain to Chester and North Wales; north to Stockport and Manchester thence to Carlisle or York, and south via Leek, Ashbourne and Derby en route for London. The Corporation, ever mindful of the many visiting traders and chapmen, particularly in the summertime from Scotland travelling south, was concerned to keep the common highway within the Borough in a good state of repair, and at the July Meeting of 1693 they legislated to levy a tax on the inhabitants for that purpose.

This fine body of men was becoming very powerful. It had confidence to take on anything or anybody, having sufficient resources to defend any law suit which was necessary for its attainments. With the departure of the Aldermen Pickford, the Corporation was endeavouring to monopolise the beer brewing industry by forcing everyone to use the new malt mill. The other lucrative concern over which it tried to exercise control was the button industry, and during the last Corporation Meeting of the year in December 1693, the following legislation was adopted – whereas previously buttons could be taken back if not sold, and credit given, from now onwards they had to be sold absolutely. Only freemen who had been apprenticed to the trade for five years or more would be allowed to practise the button trade. The poor were to be engaged in the making of the buttons, but it was emphatically stated that the materials had not to be given out elsewhere. If the buttons produced were not of a sufficiently high standard then the person concerned would be punished.

Proposals for the employment of the poor and "the prevention of idleness and begging" had been published in a general letter dated 27th October 1681. This gave an account of a book written by a Mr. Thomas Firman, a gentleman in the Parish of St. Botolph, Aldersgate in London, who had adopted the idea from the Dutch with great effect, and had set up his own model workhouse. In Holland a woman was paid 5/- per week to teach twenty or thirty poor boys and girls to spin, some on single and some on double wheels. Some of the children earned 6d per day and they also were allowed time for "the learning of reading and other necessaries". This was obviously the sort of arrangement that the Macclesfield Corporation had in mind.

Having provided for the children, Mr. Firman's next care was for "grown Persons" whom he supplied with materials in their own houses and he found that he could trust them. He also gave full instructions in his book for spinning on double wheels, the sorting of his yarns and also for the "keeping of books" showing clearly the prices paid for flax, hemp, spinning and weaving and how to keep an account of the expenses and profit. This suggestion would soon be taken up by others in the textile trade; it was a novel idea that by giving credit and delivering goods he would enable more people to work. Meanwhile in Macclesfield the important button industry was progressing well alongside the linen and silk industries.

Perhaps Thomas was interested enough to ask some of his congregation where the idea of the button making came from, and why it had established itself in Macclesfield. At the beginning of the century the Dutch had supplied the English with buttons in large quantities. During their wars with the French, the Dutch East India ships on the last stage of their journey home, being laden with rich cargoes did not dare to run the gauntlet through the Channel, but chose the safer route around the English coast, by way of Scotland. These East Indiamen put in at many British ports and traded goods, and it is understood that a group of Dutch immigrants, or 'Hollanders' as they were known throughout the 17th century, settled in Chester. The name Holland is said to have been assumed by at least one Dutch immigrant family, although the name was already established in the Macclesfield area from at least the 14th century, having been adopted by a family from Upholland in Lancashire. As early as 1634 a Philipp Holland was leasing a house and tenement in the Parish of Hurdsfield (now part of the town of Macclesfield) close by the river Bollin, from the Earl of Derby. This Philipp Holland was a parson, later to become a Dissenting minister, but other members of the family were in the area, and just like the Rev. William in Hadley, parsons of the Church of England were investing very early in British industry.

* * * * * * *

Macclesfield had close connections with Chester because, by an ancient charter, freemen and burgesses of Macclesfield did not have to pay tolls there. However, in the year 1678 some Macclesfield merchants had been distrained upon and their goods retained in custody, and it was significant enough for "a law suit at the expense of the Corporation to be put in force." Records also exist of horses being purchased by Macclesfield chapmen at Chester horse sales.

Wool and wool dyeing had always been important in the area but now the linen and linen thread had also become an integral part of Macclesfield commerce. On a Macclesfield property deed dated 15th March 1663 there is a mention of a James Stopford of Dublin, who was a member of a local family. Large quantities of linen, presumably including linen yarn, were being imported through the port of Chester from Dublin and would be brought across Cheshire by packhorse. The Irish linen was of superior quality; local flax was only suitable for cord, rope and canvas, but in addition, it would be extremely useful for making sacks and outer wrappings necessary for the transportation of raw materials. A later House of Commons report, however, reveals that until the second quarter of the 18th century the preference was for yarn imported from Hamburg, because it made a whiter thread. John Marriott, a thread maker of Manchester, who had strong connections with Macclesfield merchants, was using 'German and Holland' linen thread in 1737.

The old Roman road to Carlisle (today the A6) was a very busy road and a vital link between Scotland and London. When, in 1672, a Phillipp Swettenham, heir apparent to a considerable estate near Macclesfield, married Elizabeth, the eldest daughter of Edward Wilson of Dallam Tower near Kendal, Westmorland, it forged links between the two areas with families and retainers passing to and fro, and it seems to have encouraged the settlement in the Macclesfield area of some of the Lakeland families. (By the middle of the 18th century, Kendal had a well established waste silk industry which operated in exactly the same way as the Macclesfield one i.e.waste silk was supplied from London, boiled in soap, a process called "scowering", after which it was combed and spun by women, then doubled to make it more substantial; dressed, and sent back to London again).

It was stated in the late 17th century that "Our Prodigality in (the) wearing of Silk" created by the Turkish and East India Traders, was increasing to such an extent "that in time (it) may spoil the Silk Work of all Europe."

Only small amounts of raw silk were actually arriving in England at this time. Most imported silk was wrought, but some raw silk was brought on East India ships from Turkey by the Levant Company. It was not the best quality, but ideal for use in the button trade. There was great danger in the Turkish trade from Barbary pirates, and many English sailors were captured and sold as slaves. Some were lucky; if an English ship was in a port where English slaves were kept, the crew of the vessel would make a collection on board and buy the men back again. Wrought silks including stockings were bought in Naples and Sicily, which at this time were subject to the Crown of Spain. English ships had a considerable trade with Naples, supplying that great port with herrings from North Yarmouth in Nova Scotia and fish from Newfoundland.

Leghorn was an important port under the government of the Duke of Florence and some silk could also be purchased there. The silk industry in Northern Italy was well established by the late 17th century, but the processes were jealously guarded. It was said that in the middle of the 6th century, two Persian monks had smuggled some silk worms' eggs out of China to Constantinople, where they had been successful in hatching and rearing the worms; from there the industry spread into Europe, eventually reaching Northern Italy, in particular the areas around the cities of Venice, Milan, Florence and Lucca, bringing with it great wealth. Italian banks were established, which in due course were copied by the Dutch, resulting in the foundation of the great Bank of Amsterdam.

The East Indiamen operating through the port of London brought the raw silk together with other cargoes, including tea and blue and white Nankeen chinaware from China, and pepper and spices from the islands in the Indian Ocean.

Macclesfield had long established trading connections with London. In the year 1675 a Francis Dashwood, Esq., of the City of London and his son, had a considerable trade in the town and were admitted as burgesses on the payment of £40 (at least £4,000 today); previously they had been charges stallaged (a corporation fee) for their transactions. Francis Dashwood was a Turkey Merchant, which meant that he obtained a good deal of mohair and some silk from Turkey in exchange for wool. He was also a member of the Saddlers' Guild, presumably because there was no Turkey Merchants' Guild, although there was a Mercers' Guild. Quite often traders became members of whatever guild they could manage by this period, unlike the medieval period when a man belonged to the guild relating to his particular trade. Perhaps the answer lies in the fact that merchants were diversifying by the late 17th and 18th centuries and no one trade stood alone but was interdependent with others. Saddlers, for example, not only supplied saddles but everything else relating to "Horse-Furniture". They used "leather, awl, waxed thread" and bought a variety of goods from other tradesmen such as wood from a "Tree-maker"; buckles, studs, brasses etc. from a founder; linen from a linen-draper; buckram, silk and thread from a haberdasher and, therefore, through Francis Dashwood's dealings in Macclesfield, he could have reaped quite a considerable business amongst his fellow guild members.

By 1678 the Dashwoods were amongst the leading silk importers of England, and the following year they were responsible for a third of the raw silk imported through the East India Company.

Francis Dashwood, founder of the Dashwood fortunes lived in Dashwood House, Bishopsgate, London and had Alderman's Walk named after him. On his death in 1683, he left a bequest of £100 (today at least £10,000) to the poor of Macclesfield, reflecting his gratitude for the privilege of being accepted as a Freeman of the Borough. His son became Sir Francis and lived at Wanstead, until he bought West Wycombe in 1698 from his brother-in-law; and it was the grandson, the 2nd Baronet who became famous, or infamous, as the founder of the Hell Fire Club at West Wycombe. Some of the profits from the Macclesfield button industry appear to have contributed towards the financing of some unusual activities.

Just a few years before Thomas Roe's arrival in the town, in the year 1686, James Nixon, a chapman, had also made payment of £40 on behalf of John Whiteman, 'Silkman of the City of London', who was accordingly admitted as a freeman.

On his visits around the Borough and in the Forest of Macclesfield, Thomas would see the making of buttons in the houses of the few selected families who, to use a delightful expression of the period, would have been shown the 'art and mystery' of the making of buttons. Initially a buttonmaker, who was a man, made the moulds out of wood. The wood preferred appears to have been holly tree wood. The English holly tree (*Ilex aquifolium*) can grow to a height of almost 50ft. The timber is fine-grained, heavy and compact and is particularly valued by both the turner and instrument maker. Holly tree wood is white and must be dried either in the open air or in kilns before use, in order to reduce shrinkage, swelling and weight. It must also be protected from decay, insects and fungi, which in the 17th and 18th centuries would be done with a coating of oils or common salt dissolved in water.

The Free Grammar School owned a large area of land at this period, on the eastern bank of the River Bollin, which stretched from the water's edge, up the hill towards the Round Fountain. During the reign of Queen Anne it was known as the Hollyfields, but the name was subsequently corrupted to Hallefields, a name which remains today. This suggests a source for some of the wood, not only for button making but for the later establishment of chair making, the latter being carried out by an early 18th century Quaker with the delightful name of Micajah Wortsley, who had leased a plot of land close by from John Pickford. The Hollyfields were leased out by the Free Grammar School as part of their income.

Having prepared the button moulds, these were then padded with scraps of material and covered or embroidered with linen thread, silk, mohair, goat or horsehair, or a combination of all or any of these materials. This intricate part of the work was done by women. Whether or not the horsehair was a by-product of the famous Macclesfield horse fairs, or whether it again came from Chester, where occasional consignments of horsehair (presumably from Flanders) and goat hair were received, is difficult to say. Human hair for wigs was usually also part of the lading. It is interesting to discover that the main production of buttons about this period and early into the 18th century does seem to be from either goat or horsehair. On occasion white ox hair was used because it could be dyed easily. Two items of buttons being exported through the port of London in the early part of 1683 are recorded as "Buttons Hair Gross 154, Buttons Tin Gross 31".

As the mohair and silk came from the London merchants to be twisted, doubled and dyed, initially it would be the waste or scraps from this trade which would be put to good use in button making, until it developed into a lucrative business in its own right.

During Thomas Roe's curacy at the Parochial Chapel he saw two silk weavers buried; one by the name of Francis Dale in 1696, and the following year a William Allen, who left a considerable estate at Leek in Staffordshire. There were very few silk weavers in the North West at this period; one is recorded in Chester and another in Manchester. The passing of the Macclesfield weavers seemed to mark the end of an era. In 1698 legislation was brought in to protect further the woollen industry, with magistrates, judges, professors and students forced to wear woollen gowns; this was in addition to burials in wool, encouraged from 1667 onwards. It was proving very difficult to get hold of raw silk, as the Chinese insisted that the East India Company purchase their wrought silks only. The Chinese silk was, of course, the finest quality and ideal for weaving, but with the 'wrought silk only' policy the English weavers were finding it difficult to survive in their trade. On the other hand, the button industry, relying only partially on silk, had no such problems. An *"Intreaty for Help on Behalf of Eight silk weavers"* was published in 1699. They referred to the policy,

"That no Foreign-made Buttons should be imported into England with which our Dutch Friends before had plentiful served us . . . And though their numbers at Macclesfield & Sherbourn & the adjacent country are great yet I am confident . . . in one parish in London not many years since weavers & throwsters exceeded them . . . But the Buttonmakers may thank God that they do not have an East India Company to cope with."

Apart from its thriving little industries, Macclesfield was very fortunate in having a Free Grammar School founded by Sir John Percival and housed in the newly built Savage Chapel of 1504, just to the south of the main chapel. After its refounding on 25th April 1552 it was situated behind the Parochial Chapel, a little to the northeast, where it would remain until 1748. The Rev. Hulme and Thomas were not involved in the day to day running of the school, the headmaster was Rev. Timothy Dobson M.A., former head of Stockport Grammar School. The dozen or so boys would attend all services at the Parochial Chapel and would be, no doubt, members of the choir. One wonders what thoughts passed through Thomas's mind as he acknowledged their presence; perhaps he spared a thought or two for his father, Rev. Robert growing weary after all those years of responsibilities and teaching, but because of his financial embarrassment as yet unable to retire, still having young William to support through university.

* * * * * * *

Three significant events took place during the following year of 1694, the first of which was to have such far reaching effects, that it has to be one of the most important in modern English history; the founding of the Bank of England, encouraged by William and Mary.

After the death of Charles II, his brother James had succeeded, who by his first wife had two daughters, Mary and Anne. James was left a widower, but on remarrying had been persuaded to the Roman Catholic faith by his new wife, Mary of Modena. On the birth of their son, James (father of Bonnie Prince Charlie) the country had once more been thrown into confusion, but fortunately nothing catastrophic had ensued, as at the time of the Civil War. Mary, sister of James II and Charles II had married William of Orange, and it was their son, William who married his cousin Mary, daughter of James II by his first wife. This young William and Mary were invited to take the throne of England by a group of English 'gentlemen', amongst whom the 4th Earl of Devonshire (a direct descendant of Bess of Hardwick) played an important part. The Glorious Revolution, as it was called, succeeded in

1688, and James with his wife and son found themselves exiled in France.

William and Mary brought to England a sense of security, a great encouragement of trade and the means by which this could be carried into effect. Their idea was for a central Bank of England which they hoped would become as important and influential as the great Bank of Amsterdam. Their desire was realised finally in the year 1694 and history was to prove that their aspirations were greatly exceeded.

Sadly this was also the year of Mary's death and William remained to rule alone; and the 4th Earl of Devonshire was given his Dukedom "for services rendered".

The founding of the Bank of England might not have been significant to Thomas Roe, but certainly the Queen's death would be, and the third event was definitely only of significance to him personally – he received the increase of his stipend as curate of the Macclesfield chapel. At least he was one small step nearer to providing for a wife, but he knew that for any possibility of advancement he would have to be recommended to a living, if and when the opportunity arose. The Rev. Hulme was well aware of his junior's situation and would look for an opportunity to help in the best way he could. In the meantime the Parish work kept them busy; Prestbury was a very large parish and they would assist the parson, often by travelling long distances around the parish and visiting many of the villages and hamlets which fell within their sphere. The countryside must have reminded Thomas very much of his native Shropshire, the rich greens of the pastures, the luxurious hills and valleys with their sparkling streams and rivers providing excellent water for industry, and the sheep with the same thick, soft, creamy fleeces unlike their scraggier cousins further north.

* * * * * * *

Later when Thomas came to review the short period of his life spent in Macclesfield, perhaps he would recall only two discordant incidents which are worth the mention.

The first was a local speculation which caused some excitement during the early part of the year 1696. The Corporation had given permission on the 8th January for Nicholas Thornley to build a brickworks on the Common. Macclesfield was busy 'modernising' and bricks were needed for houses to replace the wattle and daub structures of earlier periods. However, the incident concerning the waterworks and Booth and Lunt was still remembered, and perhaps either one of these two gentlemen acted surreptitiously in inciting several persons to spoil and destroy "a considerable quantity of bricks upon the Common for the use of Nicholas Thornley and other Burgesses." The situation was quickly remedied by the prosecution of the ringleader.

The second incident took place in the spring of 1696, when news reached Macclesfield of a dispute near the village of Alderley, on the Edge itself. It seemed that for the past three years or so, a group of men working as a partnership, had been spending a great deal of time and money searching for copper in that vicinity. Lots of myths and legends had grown up about the Edge; stories of King Arthur and his knights sleeping in the caves, sightings of witches' covens, sufficient perhaps to keep the more timorous souls away, especially after dark, but certainly not disconcerting to the stout-hearted miners who were determined to make a fortune for themselves.

Initially the search for copper had been inspired by Prince Rupert, who after the Restoration had returned to England at the invitation of his cousin Charles II, and was granted an annuity of £4,000 per annum. Eventually, he attained the position of First Lord of the Admiralty (9th July 1673 to 14th May 1679) but was involved in a variety of schemes to promote business, which included becoming one of the patentees of the Royal African Company. He loved scientific experiments and invented a method of making gunpowder ten times the ordinary strength, and of manufacturing hailshot. In order to carry out his experiments Prince Rupert built a laboratory and a forge. It was becoming imperative for England to develop her metallurgic industries, particularly the brass and copper, for which we were paying high prices abroad. The copper was brought mostly from Sweden, with a little from Japan, but earlier in the century some had been brought from Africa, only to be found inferior in quality. The Civil War had put an end to the small developing industry and now Prince Rupert saw the necessity for England to be as self sufficient as possible. During 1665 there had been a petition to Parliament pointing out that much of our calamine production (this was the zinc ore used at that period for brass making) was being exported to Sweden in return for brass. In 1668 Prince Rupert was chosen as governor of "The Governors, Assistants and Societies of the Mines Royal, the Mineral and Battery Works". He was given eight deputy governors and thirteen assistants with which to work his miracle. He was credited with the invention of 'Princes-metal', a mixture of copper and zinc, the zinc being greater in proportion than that found in brass, although this has subsequently been disputed. However, there is an interesting note in the Patent Office records for Patent No. 162, dated 8th January 1671; Lord Anthony Ashley, to whom this patent had been granted, was requested not to divulge the fact that Patent No. 161 of the same date, had been granted to Prince Rupert. Unfortunately, with Rupert's death in 1682 the metallurgic industry lost its momentum.

Up to this time only the Company (The Mines Royal) was permitted to carry out the mining of the precious metals gold and silver, and as these were usually intermixed with other metals, the situation was very confusing, because officially copper, tin, lead and iron were also included. No one would have dared to upset the existing 'arrangements' concerning the tin mines of Cornwall or the lead mines in the King's Field in Derbyshire, where mining had continued uninterrupted, to a greater or lesser degree, for centuries. These mines were leased under an arrangement with the Crown, and then subleased by the miners.

It is possibly because of this anomaly, and also the restricting influence on the search for copper, that in 1689 the Mines Royal Act was passed, declaring that in future no mine of copper, tin, lead or iron should be considered royal. (This was, of course, the year following the Revolution – perhaps indicating that William and Mary were more enlightened about the subject than their predecessors had been.) The flood gates were now open to all who wanted to take advantage. One such person in the Macclesfield area was Thomas Legh of The Ridge, close by the Derbyshire hills, whose family had originally owned the Newhouse near the Parochial Chapel.

Thomas Legh had married a Mary Ashenhurst of the village of Beard in Derbyshire during the year 1663, and various lands in the areas of the Ridge, Sutton and Wincle became part of the marriage settlement. By the year 1670 Thomas Legh found himself in debt and was forced to apply for an Act of Parliament to allow him to sell five messuages in Wincle in order to cover the debts. The Act (Charles II 22.) was necessary to release the properties from the marriage settlement, otherwise legally they were not his to sell. Having extricated himself from a difficult financial situation, it would seem that his business interests greatly improved over the next two decades or so, because by the 1690s Legh had sufficient capital to form a partnership with two associates, and begin the mining of Alderley Edge. He also had sufficient credit to purchase Wincle Grange in 1694 from Lawrence Baskervyle, fishmonger of London, who had previously invested in the property when Edward Hollinshed, merchant taylor of London (related to a family in Gawsworth near Macclesfield) had been declared bankrupt. Fishmongers were very wealthy people and theirs was one of the most important Guilds in the City; in fact, one of their members, Sir William Scawen M.P., London merchant, was one of the first directors of the Bank of England in 1694 and held the position of Governor from 1697 to 1699. Obviously Thomas Legh had important connections in the City and these would be needed if he was successful in locating copper ore.

Living so close to the lead mines of Derbyshire, Thomas Legh seems to have assumed, or conveniently presumed, that the laws relating to lead mining might be contrived in some way to relate also to copper mining.

Derbyshire lead mining was literally a law unto itself. Exactly ten years after founding the Parochial Chapel in Macclesfield Edward I, held an Inquisition at Ashbourne in 1288 which ensured that the lead mining laws were set down at the request of the miners. These were to remain virtually unaltered for six centuries and any disputes were settled by a jury of twenty four miners at the great Barmote courts of either the High Peak or the Wapentake of Wirksworth. Always the Barmasters have been the officials with jurisdiction over lead mining in Derbyshire. In the 18th century they seem to have had some legal training and they certainly had considerable authority. "Should it happen that any Miner be killed Slain dampe'd or murder'd upon the Mine or within the Grove neither Officer Coroner nor any other Officer ought to meddle therein but only the Barmaster or his Deputy".

Anyone had the right to go and search for lead ore within the King's Field without hindrance from the landowner. When a new vein of lead ore was discovered an application was made to the Barmaster to register the name of the vein in his book, and at the same time two dishes of ore were presented to him in order to 'free' the mine. The Barmaster then allowed the miners two meers of ground, which measured 32 yards each in the High Peak, although this measurement varied slightly in other areas. Having worked through these, the third meer belonged to the Lord of the mine. In 1690 the 4th Earl of Devonshire, living at Chatsworth House, leased the mineral duties in the High Peak from the Duchy of Lancaster and consequently became entitled to the Lord's meers. This third meer was usually bought by the miners after the Barmaster and the members of the Barmote Court had visited and valued it. The miners could then continue working through the third meer, and thereafter claim Taker meers as they worked on, but if no work was done in a particular mine for a period of three weeks, then the Barmaster was entitled to claim the mine and assign it to others.

The land on Alderley Edge was waste or common land, but Sir Thomas Stanley of The Old Hall, Alderley was apparently Lord of the Soil or Lord of the Manor of Alderley. By this period, this branch of the family had no close connection with the Earls of Derby, in fact, Sir Thomas Stanley is accredited with supporting Oliver Cromwell during the Civil War, and consequently the family seem to have had strong Protestant tendencies. Thomas Legh and partners must have considered that they had the right to enter upon the land and search for copper, although it must be remembered that lead is also present in the Alderley mines, and this could have been the pretext used for carrying out a search under the same conditions as in the High Peak. One suspects that Legh had already been involved in some sort of mining in the High Peak area because he was an arbitrator in a dispute between a Mrs. Ratcliffe and a Mr. Torr about "ore gotten at a certain new vein in the new Rake" in Bradwell Liberty on 21st April 1692. The story of the Alderley Mine, as later revealed at the Cheshire Quarter Sessions commencing 14th July 1696, was somewhat strange in the telling.

The case commenced with an Anthony Goodman declaring that he had been steward and agent for over a year to a Mr. Thomas Crosse, merchant, Mr. John Appleby and Mr. Daniel Kingston "who were entitled to certain Copper Mines and a Smelting Milne in Over Alderley under a Lease for a great many yeares yett to come from Sir Thomas Stanley Bart." Mr. Goodman had been present in a dwelling house in Alderley on the previous Friday afternoon when he overheard Hough, Horderne and William Sellars in a lower room, discussing the mines and mill. He deduced that Thomas Legh of The Ridge (referred to as Mr. Legh) had persuaded Horderne to some mischief at the mine, telling him that he could only be bound to good behaviour. Three neighbours of Alderley next gave evidence as witnesses, declaring that on the previous Friday evening, as they were smoking their pipes of tobacco in the High Lane, they saw and overheard Horderne and Sellars planning to "break down the locks and go into the mines or bee killed". The very next day, on the Saturday morning at an early hour, the two schemers accompanied by several others went to the mines with picks. Mr. Goodman, agent to Mr. Crosse, had been forewarned and several of his workmen were guarding locked doors on the site, sufficient to deter Horderne and his mob who subsequently went away.

The next person to give evidence was John Hough of Over Alderley, husbandman, who said that he had been at the mines the previous evening from about ten o'clock; at about two o'clock in the morning there arrived six or seven persons, including Hugh Horderne, who broke open the locks and doors stating that they had orders to do so. On gaining entry they put up new doors and remained in possession. Some time later, on Tuesday 12th May, Thomas Legh's workmen were busy getting ore in the mine when John Hough arrived with supporters from Alderley and declared "he would have them out or tear them in pieces". Using ropes Hough and his men tried to carry out their threat, but one quick actioned workman cut himself free, whereupon Hough brought a pair of horse chains from his father's house. In no time at all the horse chains were thrust around the 'intruders' and then fastened to a rope, and the rope to a windlass; in the same manner as ore was drawn out of a mine, so were Horderne and company. The witness to the last scene of violent action "sayth that the said Mr. Legh and his partners had been in peaceable possession of the mines for the space of three years and a quarter".

Exactly what position Sir Thomas Stanley took in all this is a mystery. He must have known that the search for ore was under way by Legh and partners, but ignorance of the legal situation perhaps made him reluctant to intervene. It is possible that copper had not been found in the first instance for quite some time, and that he was awaiting the discovery before taking action. On the other hand, perhaps Legh and company, being unsuccessful, had withdrawn for a period and this had given Sir Thomas the opportunity to lease the mine to Thomas Crosse and partners, which would provide some income whilst the search for ore continued.

The legal situation does seem to have been very uncertain, the judgement being that the persons implicated on both sides were bound to be of good behaviour. After the Court hearings at Nantwich both Thomas Legh and Thomas Crosse seem to have withdrawn from their mining speculations, because some two years later a petition was presented to Parliament on which appeared the names of Messrs. Appleby, Kingston and Hath, London merchants, mining at Alderley Edge. Mr. Hath had obviously replaced Thomas Crosse in that particular partnership. Thomas Legh turned his attention to politics; he is recorded as M.P. for Newton near Warrington from 1698 until his burial in Macclesfield on 23rd March 1703.

The structure of these business transactions reveals a significant factor; that of a tiny population scattered across the country, with people travelling great distances to keep up communications, and seemingly totally undeterred by any adversities which they encountered on their journeys. It is also important to appreciate the enormous influence which the City of London exerted on the rest of the country at this period, it was like a giant octopus drawing into itself everything it could find, and as the population within the city increased, it was necessary to reach further and further along the communications network for sufficient food to supply its swelling numbers. It is also important to appreciate that many families 'in the country' had second homes in London. Merchants sent their sons to establish business connections and as there was constant 'to-ing and fro-ing', it was a matter of convenience and economy to have properties in both places. Many of the aristocracy were M.P.s and kept second homes in and around London, which again created considerable movement as retainers and family journeyed between the two residences. England was full of activity, the Industrial Revolution was already under way. As already seen in Macclesfield, from late in the 17th century there was evidence of organised economic activity concerned with the manufacture and processing of raw materials. It is a sad reflection on human nature, however, that success and affluence for some, no matter to what purpose or benevolence they put their extra hard gained finances, automatically creates a destructive and selfish malevolence in others.

Thomas Roe must have sensed a restlessness emerging in the small town of Macclesfield. A good strong personality was needed, someone of sufficient stature to command respect from all sections of the community, and until that person presented himself, a struggle for power would develop over the next few years, as different personalities were drawn into the borough in the hope of making their fortunes.

* * * * * * *

Thomas, now in his mid-twenties, showed no concern for local politics, he could only hope and pray that he would find the answer to his problems, and he did not have long to wait.

When Rev. Hulme had taken up his previous duties as Clerk of Nether Knutsford, he had replaced Rev. Kettlesbie Turner, who had been Minister there for sixteen years. Turner was not an old man when he died, being only in his mid-forties. Details of his early life are not known but he had matriculated at Jesus College, Oxford and obtained his B.A. there in 1664. He and his wife, Mary, baptised a daughter, Mary, at Nether Knutsford on 1st November 1670, shortly after he had taken up duties in the area. They subsequently had three sons who all died in early infancy, and a daughter who seems to have survived. One week after the birth of the third son, Mrs. Turner died and was buried on 1st July 1679, whilst the child only survived till October. Daughter, Mary, was nine years of age. She would be expected to help as much as possible with the household duties and the care of the three younger children, Thomas, five years of age, Sarah, only two and baby Kettlesbie until he died. The following year Turner married Ann Burghall (by Licence) on the 15th September at Marton by Congleton, just a few miles to the south of Macclesfield.

The Burghalls were an interesting family, well established in the Nantwich area, in fact, Ann seems to have been the niece of Rev. Burghall, Puritan vicar of Acton-by-Nantwich at the time of the Civil War. He wrote a diary about the events of that period in Cheshire, (now considered a plagiarism) the manuscript of which is housed in the British Museum. In the year following Turner's second marriage, young Thomas died and was buried during the month of August, but Ann Turner was already pregnant and when the baby son was born, he was given the name of Thomas in memory of his half brother. Another son, Josiah, was born, only to be buried in June 1686, shortly followed by his father during August.

Poor Mary, only sixteen years of age, had learnt to grow up quickly and face the realities of life. Her experiences deputising as a young mother stood her in good stead and she became an excellent cook. She was to be loved by many who came to know her, being a good Christian, full of kindness and always willing to help others. Mary presumably stayed with her stepmother and at some time came to Macclesfield. One suspects that Rev. Hulme kept a watchful eye on the little family. They were great friends of the Barbor family, as was Thomas Roe. Josiah Barbor was a burgess of Macclesfield and quite a wealthy man. Other members of the family lived around the Glossop and Castleton areas of Derbyshire.

Hulme was obviously well-known around the Knutsford area, where the Birtles family of the Hill-within-Birtles lived. The Birtles family had become involved in the button trade and Thomas Birtles had good business and family connections in the town of Leek in Staffordshire. He had married into the important Bagshawe family of the Castleton area in Derbyshire, and when he and his wife, Elizabeth, presented their first-born son, Thomas, for baptism on 31st (sic) June 1679 it was Rev. Kettlesbie Turner who had performed the ceremony.

It must have been a delight to all concerned when Thomas Roe married Mary Turner in October 1698. The Marriage Licence dated the 6th October was witnessed by Josiah Barbor and his wife, Margaret, and it was no surprise that Thomas and Mary immediately set off for Castleton, where Thomas had been offered a reasonable living, thanks to the endeavours of his friends. The title to the Rectory and Parsonage of Castleton at this time belonged to a gentleman by the name of Thomas Charlesworth, of another important Peak District family, who were to become well-known to the Roes.

Mary was exactly one week older than her husband. They were an ideal match, and at twenty eight years of age, with very little to offer in the way of a marriage settlement, both must have decided that the chances of marriage were very remote indeed, until they had been introduced. Both had a strong Church of England background and despite Mary's stepmother's Puritanical family, she and Thomas possessed a portrait of King Charles, declaring themselves to be fervent Royalists. Packing what few possessions they had acquired, they doubtless travelled with packhorses by way of Chapel-en-le-Frith, on the journey into Derbyshire.

They would pass through the small coal-mining village of Rainow along a route which provided a superb view of the Cheshire Plain stretching out westwards towards the distant horizon, with the Mersey Estuary visible on a clear day. As winter was fast approaching the air would be growing cooler, and with the first flurries of snow, this route would soon become hazardous, though not impassable to the stout breed of horses, so familiar on these hills. The winding track passed through yet another coal mining village by the name of Kettleshulme, to the Derbyshire border and the hamlet of Whaley Bridge. After arriving in Chapel-en-le-Frith the final most difficult stage of the journey would begin.

The countryside had now taken on a bleaker appearance, with plateau shaped hills filling the near horizon and large outcrops of limestone imposing themselves on the landscape as they approached the village of Castleton. This was an entirely different world from the one they had just left behind. Gone were the buttons, the linen thread and the silk; this was leadmining country, hard and rugged. Derbyshire people were good honest folk who were used to battling against nature and seemed to enjoy all the challenges she threw in their way. Life in many ways was less sophisticated, but God was needed here in the Peaks the same as on the Cheshire Plain, and Mary would support her husband in every way she could.

The cottages and houses of Castleton were made of stone, built to endure the constant changes of weather experienced in the High Peak. The parsonage house was an old building; in fact Thomas and Mary would be the last parson and wife of St. Edmund's to reside there. It stood close by the River Noor (Noe), which flowed, cold and clear, from out of the Peak Cavern. About the time of their arrival, Castleton received one of its many visitors to see the 'Wonders of the Peak'. This particular lady, by the name of Celia Fiennes, was the daughter of the Cromwellian General Fiennes, who during the Civil War had been attacked by Prince Rupert and the Cornish forces, whilst trying to hold the city of Bristol, but finally had been forced to capitulate. Miss Fiennes wrote:

> "The 6th Wonder is at Castleton . . . this is what they call the Devilles Arse a Peake, the hill on one and jutting out in two parts and joyns in one at the top . . . you enter a great Cave which is very large, and severall poor little houses in it built of stone . . . now, none but very poor people live there which makes some small advantage by begging and by lighting the strangers into the Cave."

She continued by describing the rocks dripping water and hanging down in many places and was surprised at the loftiness of the Cavern in parts. The company reached the river, which was about 12 yards wide, through which it was possible to wade, although the water reached above waist high.

The other 'Wonder' described by Celia Fiennes was Mamtour (Mam Tor) a very high hill, situated close by both Winnats Pass and Odin, the latter being one of the oldest lead mines in England. Mam Tor or the Shivering Mountain continuously crumbles on one side, particularly after frost or heavy rain, and sheds grit stone, shale or sand at an amazing rate, and the constant sound of falling rocks, emulating gun shots, can be heard at a great distance down the valley. Celia Fiennes wrote "on that broken side the sand keeps trickling down allwayes especially when there is least wind, of which I believe this Country scarce ever is without". She also observed "you scarce see a tree and no hedges at all over the Country, only dry stone walls that incloses ground no other fence".

She surprisingly omitted a description of the Peak Castle perched high up on the very edge of the rocky escarpment, above and to the east of the Cavern or Peak Hole. It had been built by William Peveril, natural son of William the Conqueror, but had eventually come into the possession of Edward III, who gave it to his son, John of Gaunt, Duke of Lancaster, and it had remained part of the Duchy of Lancaster ever since. There it was fixed, like some sort of rocky gargoyle, a weather-worn ruin but a significant one, overlooking the peaceful village comprising hall, cottages and church of St. Edmund, huddled around the market place below.

When Celia Fiennes departed, she made her way south towards Ashbourne, where she saw some of the copper mines, "here they dig them like a well but secure the side with wood and turffe bound with the wood like laths or frames across and longwayes, to secure it". This description may refer to Ecton Hill, just over the border in Staffordshire, although generally, it has been understood that very little mining, if any, was taking place at Ecton during this period. Having reached Uttoxeter, she mentions several mills "which are used for their prepareing the metal they take out of the mines. I had a piece of Copper given to me by one of the Managers of them." Celia Fiennes, no doubt, tucked her piece of 'treasure' inside her saddlebag as a souvenir of her travels in the Peak District.

Thomas Roe's interest was in the lead mines of the Castleton area, which would provide a valuable supplement to his stipend. Signs of lead mining and smelting were in evidence in many places, and as Thomas travelled around on his horse, he would notice these activities. In the very early years of lead mining (there is a reference to the Odin lead mine in the 13th century) the melt was smelted in a very primitive way on these summits. The boles or wind hearths were heated by fires of wood and always faced westwards to gain the full effect of the prevailing winds. They were constructed from large rough stones and were built to form a cavity of approximately 2 ft square and 14 ft long. The ore was allowed to run out into rough moulds, but it was far from pure. When cool the blocks of lead were removed from the moulds, ready for transportation. Two blocks together made a pig and eight pigs a fodder.

The 17th century was drawing to a close. It had been a traumatic one for English History and who could foretell what the 18th would bring, although many soothsayers tried.

Ancient mining tools, found at Hill Top Mine, Great Hucklow, Derbyshire, from *The Reliquary* Vol. IV 1863-4

PART 2

3
THE EARLY YEARS

Give us this day our daily bread.

The High Peak of Derbyshire, E. Bowen 1758.

The 18th century had arrived and with it a son for Thomas and Mary Roe. Given his father's name, he was baptised by Thomas at St. Edmund's Church, Castleton, on 7th March 1700. Word would quickly be sent to Hadley in Shropshire, where Rev. Robert Roe was in financial difficulties and, therefore, unfortunately unable to provide for his grandson, as his grandfather had provided for him. Nevertheless the assumption would be that this welcomed addition to the family meant yet another generation of Roes would continue their great tradition of providing ministers for the Church of England.

Daughter Frances, born on 9th and baptised on 30th December 1701, was probably named after one of Mary's grandmothers, although it is possible that Mary had an elder sister with the same name, born before her parents had moved to Knutsford.

During March 1702 came the news of the death of the King, William III; he had been thrown from his horse the previous month whilst riding from Kensington Palace to Hampton Court. Anne, sister of his deceased wife, Mary, now accepted the responsibilities of the Crown, but in France, the Old Pretender, as he became known, son of James II and half brother to Anne, was awaiting his opportunity to lay claim to the English Throne. In Macclesfield the Roes' good friend, Josiah Barbor, Alderman, had been elected mayor for the year 1702/3, but sadly he died during the following year and by his will, made on 18th August (proved 29th September 1704) he gave "unto Mary wife of Thomas Roe of Castleton in the County of Derby Clerke tenne pounds" (over £1,000 today). It was very unusual at this period to leave money to others except family and servants, and the gift would be much appreciated. Josiah's house was a large one, which suggests the possibility of Thomas having lodged with the family during the time he had lived in Macclesfield.

Meanwhile Thomas's second son, William, had been born on 10th and baptised 26th August 1703. Mary was busy, now thirty three years of age she still had plenty of childbearing years ahead of her. On the 26th November, when William was only three months old, a terrible storm raged throughout England. It caused tremendous devastation, particularly around the coasts, and an estimated one thousand sailors died with the loss of hundreds of boats and ships. Great havoc was caused by the destruction, not only of houses, barns and other buildings, but of hundreds of windmills which were either blown down or caught fire due to the gale force winds rotating the sails at a high velocity. Another fatality was the Eddystone lighthouse. It was a beautiful wooden structure, built between 1696 and 1699, on rocks in the English Channel, fourteen miles off Plymouth. Its designer, Henry Winstanley, was actually present in the lighthouse when the disastrous storm began. He, and his creation, did not stand a chance, and when the waves had subsided and the storm cleared, there was not a single trace of either of them. The Roes survived, and St. Edmund's Parish Register records the births and baptisms of three more sons:

Robert, born 3rd September, baptised 26th September 1705.
John, born 24th September, baptised 16th October, died 16th November 1707.
James, born 18th June, baptised 5th July, 1711.

Daughter, Mary, named after her mother was almost a Christmas baby, born on 23rd December 1712, and there must have been some concern regarding her baptism on the following 9th January. Winter babies had great difficulty in surviving, it was far better to be born in the spring.

Thomas, being a true cleric, had entered all his children's names in Latin in the Register, and when the final and eighth child was born, his name was subsequently recorded as Carolus born 7th May and baptised 2nd June 1715, but no one could have guessed what the future held for young Charles, least of all his parents. By the time of James's birth, Rev. Thomas seems to have exhausted the list of male Christian names within the family and resorted to the choice of royal names for his two youngest sons, demonstrating once more his allegiance to the Crown.

Thomas's income had improved considerably since his arrival in Castleton. The lands belonging to the Parsonage, which were given to the vicar for his use, were known as the glebe lands. In Castleton these were more than adequate for his own use and some parts were subleased. In fact, one of the main lessees was Richard Bagshawe, High Sheriff of Derbyshire 1700/1 and brother-in-law of Thomas Birtles, button merchant of Birtles Hall near Macclesfield, who had now taken over the title of the parsonage from 10th September 1708 and had also leased the 'tythes' (tithes) from the Bishop of Chester. (There exists a lease dated 6th July 1716, relating to the tithes, but this appears to be a renewal lease. Thomas Charlesworth, held the lease at the time of Rev. Thomas's induction, however, shortly afterwards, this must have been transferred to Richard Bagshawe, indicated by his involvement in a legal dispute during 1704).

Although the Bishop of Chester was entitled to two-thirds of some of the tithes and the vicar the remaining third, the actual ecclesiastical jurisdiction remained in the hands of the Bishop of Lichfield. It is possible that the connection with the Bishop of Chester came from the fact that both the port of Chester and the lands of Castleton were part of the Duchy of Lancaster, and that one of the earlier Bishops had been allowed privileges within the Duchy which had continued to his successors. Obviously it would have been very inconvenient for the Bishop to claim his tithes in kind, Castleton being quite some distance from Chester, so in this instance he preferred to lease them to someone locally, and in doing so obtained a regular annual income instead.

The tithe system seemed very complicated, but it was worked out to the simplest and most beneficial form for all concerned.

Within the town or liberty of Castleton every eleventh stack of corn was given as tithe. For every five lambs, one lamb was given, but if under five one halfpenny for each lamb (etc.) this was the 'Wooll and Lamb' tithe but it also included calves. The third tithe was for the ore, from which every tenth dish was given, and out of these dishes of ore paid as tithe, a charge of one penny was made by the miners for washing and cleansing every ten dishes of ore. These three tithes were the ones which were shared between Richard Bagshawe (Thomas Charlesworth originally) and Thomas in proportions of two-thirds and one third respectively, and they, between themselves, came to a convenient arrangement. If Rev. Thomas did not wish to keep the lambs, but have them sold, then Richard Bagshawe sold them together with his own and paid Thomas accordingly e.g. entry in Bagshawe's Account Book – "1708/9 to Rectory rec'd for tyth Lambs & Wooll sold £8-18-6d". The lead ore they could not possibly smelt themselves, so an arrangement was made by which Thomas would receive an appropriate value in cash when the lead ore was sold to the smelters.

Richard Bagshawe had a considerable interest in the Odin mine from the year 1704. Apparently little work appears to have taken place since a dispute during the year of 1673, but Bagshawe and partners carried out several trials during 1704, which proved successful. Had the Bishop of Chester known what profits were about to be made, he would never have leased out his tithes.

A tithe of lead ore seemed a contradiction in terms, because a tithe was a duty payable on items which grew and therefore replaced themselves. Initially, miners were under the misapprehension that lead ore grew and renewed itself in the vein, but even after appreciating the truth, they acknowledged a duty of tithe payable to the Church in addition to other duties payable to the king or his lessees – at least, until the Parliamentarian period. Obviously many Royalist families in the High Peak and elsewhere in Derbyshire seized the opportunity to rid themselves of the levy and at the same time deprive the Puritan ministers of part of their income, and all miners were incited to rebel. During the year 1652, when Parliament was in utter chaos and about to be 'evicted' by Cromwell, a bill was presented by the parsons of Derbyshire demanding their right to tithe ore, and Parliament supported them. In reality, however, the system fell apart. In some parishes the miners accepted the judgment, but in others parsons had to be grateful for whatever they were given, and some never again received tithe ore. It has been stated in several sources that tithes upon ore were only paid in Eyam and Wirksworth, including Cromford and Middleton, after the dispute. As the Odin mine appeared to have been unworked for just over thirty years until 1704, Richard Bagshawe and Thomas Roe, by a Suit in Chancery dated 19th January 1704, were awarded the right of receiving payment of lead tithe within the liberty of Castleton.

Apart from the three main tithes, there were small dues which the Rev. Thomas received wholly himself; these related to pigs, swarms (of bees) and eggs. He also received the dues arising from "Weddings Churchings & Burialls":

Weddings – fee 1/- where Banns published (6d. to Vicar, 6d. to Clerk).
Weddings by Licence – double fees.
Churchings (of women after childbirth) – 6d. to Vicar.
Burials – fee 1/- (9d. to Vicar, 3d. to Clerk).

The vicar was also entitled to Easter dues. The Parish clerk had little or no wage but he was entitled to a piece of meadow land and received £1 each year for looking after the clock and for ringing curfew.

Obviously if there was going to be any appreciable increase of income for Thomas it would emanate from the lead tithe. Richard Bagshawe's reckoning book states, that for the period from October 1704 to early March 1705 a total of 4,713 dishes of ore were "gott" at the Odin mine. This was an excellent start for the mine, in some instances it took months, and sometimes years, and a great deal of finance to bring a mine into production. The first payment of tithe ore would be 471 dishes of which Thomas was entitled to one third i.e. 157 dishes. A dish of ore held in weight between 60lbs. and 75lbs. of lead ore, depending on the quality, and nine dishes made up a load, therefore Thomas's dishes approximately made up a litttle more than 17 loads. It is difficult to estimate how much this represented in cash, but accepting the fact that, apart from the occasional erratic increases and decreases in commodities etc. which occurred from time to time, prices in general remained the same throughout the 18th century (unlike today's inflation rates), it is possible to make a comparison. In the parish of Wirksworth in 1775 the vicar received 200 loads of lead ore which realised £315 and the following year 279 loads for which he was paid £430. At this time smelted lead was selling for approximately £9 per ton, but the price varied, of course, depending on the quality. It is known that in the year 1720 it was at its lowest price of £3 per ton, just one third of the aforementioned. The vicar of Wirksworth was receiving almost £1 11 6d. a load for his ore, so at the very least Thomas would receive one third of this figure i.e. 10/6d. for each load. His first payment should therefore have been at least £9.3.9d. (almost £1000 today). Figures of production (to the nearest load) are extant for Odin for the period 1709 to 1715. There is very little variation for any of the seven years, when Thomas received an average tithe of 115 loads, realising at least £60 per annum.

It is interesting to note that separate Lead Account Books of the East India Company begin in the year 1705, and there is no doubt that during the next few years, large quantities of Derbyshire lead found their way to India and the Far East, and not only lead. Samuel Bagshawe of Ford Hall had a son, Samuel Jnr. born 1713, who was to become a J.P. for the county of Derby; M.P. for Tallagh, County Waterford in Ireland and Colonel of the 93rd. Regiment of Foot. He was to have a distinguished career as a soldier and become second in command in India for the East India Company, serving there for quite some time. He eventually died in the year 1762, having lost a leg at the siege of L'Orient in France and an eye in India.

The vein at Odin proved to be extremely rich and by late in the year 1706 the workings had reached more than 500 yds. deep under the shales of Mam Tor. In April of that year forty one men and eight women were employed at the mine. In mines generally in England women worked mostly on the surface standing, or as at Ecton Mine in Staffordshire sitting back to back, and using flat hammers known as buckers to beat and crush the ore into smaller pieces, which was then sorted. Later in the century children were used to sort the ore; this was done usually by girls, whilst the boys helped to wheel out the waggons laden with ore sometimes accompanied by women.

The money received from the lead tithe was needed by Thomas for the education of his children. Young Thomas, being the eldest, would have to attend a good school. In the 17th century there had been a school in Castleton, but now it seemed that it no longer existed. Thomas had replaced a vicar by the name of Samuel Cryer, who had conscientiously carried out his duties at St. Edmund's for fifty three years from 1644 until his death in 1697, in spite of the Civil War. The last mentioned schoolmaster was a Stephen Hall who appeared on a deed referring to a transfer of land on 30th December 1687, so apparently it had not been part of the vicar's duties to teach in the school. Because of a growing concern about the numbers of Roman Catholics in England (brought about by the question of succession on the death of Queen Anne), during the years 1705 and 1706 Papal Returns had to be completed by the parsons of all English parishes, and sent to the appropriate archbishops. Thomas endorsed his 1705 Return "Nil", dated 14th November. The 1706 Return was more searching and asked what advowsons or rights of presentation or donation of churches, benefices or schools were in the hands of Papists or reputed Papists. Thomas completed this on the 2nd October 1706 as follows:

"There is no Papist nor reputed Papist that I know of dwelling within my parish, nor is the advowson of my church in the disposition of any such.
We have no school.

Thomas Roe vicar."

In the Bishop's Visitation Book of 1714, Thomas Roe is entered as 'Vicar' but the space against 'LUD' (schoolmaster) is left blank. One can only assume that there was no school in Castleton for the children to attend, during the early years of Thomas's ministry.

Unfortunately school records at this period are very sparse indeed, even grammar school records. There were three grammar schools which Thomas must have considered for his sons i.e. Retford, Derby and (closer to home) Tideswell, all with excellent reputations. No Roes are recorded at Retford for the period 1700 to 1730, but there is a mention of a Thomas Roe at the Derby School in 1704, however, this seems a little too early for young Thomas of Castleton. Schools usually had three or four forms. In the first, boys learnt to read; in the second there was writing and arithmetic and this was usually where the free school ended. At the third form the grammar school commenced, for which fees had to be paid. Here began the learning of 'higher parts' of arithmetic, and if the boys were intending to go to sea or enter commerce they also learnt book-keeping and navigation. If intended for the Church, they learnt Latin grammar in the fourth form and started the first book *Corderius Colloquies*. After this they read Nepos, Caesar, Ovid and Virgil and sometimes also learnt Greek and began the Greek testament. After leaving the grammar school the boys would have to attend either Oxford or Cambridge University to enable them to obtain their B.A.s for entry into the Church of England and other careers.

By the time Charles was born in 1715, Thomas, now fifteen years of age would be approaching his entry into university but some great upset occurred. Young Thomas never entered university; his father banished him from their lives and none of the other Roe children ever gave the name of Thomas to any of their children, despite the fact it was also their father's name. Mary, being Mary, somehow kept in touch, probably secretly and quietly. Thomas was her son and Mary could not forget it. Perhaps as Charles grew up he dare not ask what had happened to his brother, and had to surmise as everyone else did.

* * * * * * *

The River Trent, winding its way across the centre of England, was a very busy and exciting river. It carried great cargoes, including lead from Derbyshire, to the great port of Hull. Derby was a storehouse for lead, where it was brought on horses from Wirksworth and other areas with smelting mills. From Derby it was carried in carts and waggons to Wilne Ferry, a distance of five miles, for embarkation by craft. On its course, the river, navigable from Burton-on-Trent, passed through Newark and the port of Gainsborough, eventually meandering to the estuary and the port of Hull. Hull and Gainsborough had a considerable trade with London and many young boys must have been tempted to work the vessels and eventually join the ships to that great city.

There was a Thomas Roe who settled in Paull, a tiny fishing village just to the east of the great port of Hull, and he seems to be a likely contender for the part of the missing son. He was very remote and many miles away from any of the other Roe families of either Yorkshire or Derbyshire, and he was a sailor. It is recorded in the Paull Church Register that Thomas Roe, Sailor married Frances Gaul on 10th January 1722 and baptised a son in December of the same year.

The Royal Navy had very few ships in commission in the early years of the 18th century, but by 1727 there was a Thomas Roe (spelt Row) serving on board *H.M.S. Pearle*, attached to the Woolwich Quarters. She began rigging on 12th May 1727, the date from which the wages were paid, and commenced victualling on the 16th. Her complement was one hundred and ninety men and her Captain was Commander William Knight. For the next four years she carried out duties between England and the West Indies, making calls at "Barbados, Domineco, Monserat" etc. and Thomas was finally discharged from this particular period of duty on 24th March 1731. The naval ships were there to guard our merchantmen with their rich cargoes, returning from either China, India, the West Indies or America. Apart from the periods when we had been at war with the Dutch or the French, the great danger was from pirates, and they could be of any nationality; in fact, not long after Rev. Thomas had arrived in Castleton, during the year 1700, a collection had been made and recorded in the Parish Register "for the redemption of poore English captives in slavery at Machanes under the Emperor of Fez and Moroccoe" the amount collected was £1.4.8d.

Thomas and Mary had a very good friend, Robert Charlesworth, who was a man of some standing and greatly respected in the Castleton area; he was also a partner in the Odin mine. His son, Thomas, settled in Hull and became a merchant there, probably attending to the onward despatch of the lead, amongst other things, to London, and maybe through this connection Mary received news of her eldest son from time to time.

The situation suggests that young Thomas had been attending a school some distance from Castleton and completely outside his father's supervision. This would have been a great expense for Rev. Thomas and the indications are that second son, William, attended the local Tideswell Grammar School (for which virtually no records exist). Rev. Samuel Cryer's daughter, Dorothy, had married Jacob Creswick, vicar of Tideswell, and the Creswicks and Roes became firm friends. When Rev. Creswick died, Dorothy returned to live in Castleton close by the Roes.

* * * * * * *

Queen Anne had died in 1714 and the choice of monarch fell upon her second cousin, who was German and also the nephew of Prince Rupert. He was not very happy or comfortable in England, much preferring his native Hanover, but he was a Protestant, and was subsequently crowned George I. Thus began the Georgian Period and baby Charles, born 1715, unlike his brothers and sisters, was well and truly Georgian. During the winter of 1715/16 there were several disturbances in Scotland and some parts of the North, as James Edward, the Pretender, son of James II, made his presence felt in a bid to claim the English throne. The government, with the aid of Dutch soldiers, managed to quell the small rebellion, which forced James Edward to leave Scotland in the February of 1716, never to return.

One year later, during February 1717, a strange phenomenon occurred. Young Robert Roe, only twelve years of age, died and was buried on the 26th January and within one week of his death a brilliant star was seen in the sky, shining "at all hours of day and night". It was reported from all parts of England. A young man by the name of Thomas Secker, who owned shares in some Derbyshire lead mines, and was later ordained by the Bishop of Durham, wrote a letter from London to his sister in Chesterfield . . . "did you see the strange Light in the skies last Tuesday night if you had as much of it as we I doubt not but you have Monsters and Prodigies enough to fill a sheet with. Here it has been improved into Armies fighting, Heads appearing and what not. One good woman in Moorfields sat preaching and preparing us all for the Day of Judgment. Another who had a great turn to Politicks than to Religion explained it against the King for not reprieving the two Lords, till another informed us it was actually done and so spoiled the Scheme. But the last Conjecture I heard was that it was Lord Darentwaters Soul marching in State out of Purgatory. Since then I have met with some People who were doubtless either Presbyterians or Atheists that imagined the whole Business was only a Quantity of Matter, of which by reason of the bad Weather the Air must be prodigiously full, set on Fire by the increasing Heat of the Sun, as is very usual in cold countries." (The age of enlightenment was just beginning).

A Mr. Whillock, who lived in the High Peak, kept a notebook in which he entered many interesting items. He also reported the star, as seen by himself and several others. The winter was fine and moderate and by the 20th April it was so very warm, that all the cattle were turned out to grass and the sowing was done early. May was very stormy and a terrible tragedy took place on the fourteenth when the wife of George Tunnicliffe of the village of Mappleton, just north of Ashbourne "died in her own house, great with child, being struck by a thunder bolt." This was also the year in which grandfather Robert died in Hadley, and Uncle William decided not to sell the Hadley Estate, which he had purchased seven years previously from his father, but to keep it as part of the inheritance for his eldest son.

In between the tragedies, myths and legends, there were the fun days, particularly in summer when Peak District families travelled to Ashbourne or Grindon (just over the border in Staffordshire) for the fairs. Close by Castleton, the village of Eyam with its lovely old church, was still recovering from the terrible visitation of the plague, but life went on, with the traditional sheep roasting taking place at the end of the summer, to which other villages were invited. There was also the comic excitement of the bull baiting, which was growing in popularity. The poor old bull, on his way to the market to be killed, would be tied by means of a strong rope, to an iron ring which was well and truly fixed in the roadway, close by the centre of the village (with a public house nearby). The spectacle of a tiny bull terrier charging the bull and pitting its strength against the enormous creature, brought roars of laughter from the crowd. If the bull's horns were too sharp, a pad of leather was fitted over them, and as a ping-pong ball rebounds from a bat, so the little dog rebounded from off the bull's head. As the small sturdy creature somersaulted through the air after impact, the people in the crowd jostled for position in order to catch the dog and set him down, ready for his next charge. The little dog, refusing to be disconcerted, would once more gather speed, hoping that he could sink his teeth into the rolls of flab, invitingly hanging down in layers from the beast's enormous neck, before the head caught him another stunning blow. If the terrier succeeded, to the slight irritation of the bull, a wooden wedge would have to be manoeuvred into the dog's mouth in order to 'unhook' him from his antagonist.

In Castleton itself, there has long been a tradition in connection with the Garland Festival, which takes place each year on Restoration or Oak Apple Day, the 29th May (when oak leaves were originally worn to commemorate King Charles II's escape after the Battle of Worcester by hiding in an oak tree). It is not certain when this ceremony of hanging the Ringers' garland of flowers on one of the pinnacles of the church tower actually started, but taking into consideration Thomas and Mary's royalist sympathies, and the fact that Thomas was accustomed to the ringers of the Parochial Chapel in Macclesfield performing with great enthusiasm on Oak Apple Day, it would be surprising if the ceremony had not been encouraged by them. Throughout the Georgian (and Victorian) period, the ceremony was organised by the church bellringers, who toured the village with the garland, performing morris dances and making a collection for themselves, before congregating in the churchyard to witness the actual placing of the huge, colourful garland, high up on the church tower, where it remained until it withered away. Morris dancing had experienced a strong revival since the sombre Puritan days and was reminiscent of the village of Wem in Shropshire.

The whole essence of life was to be as self-sufficient as possible and as young Charles Roe grew up, it was a lesson which he never forgot. The most important over-riding factor was to be able to feed oneself and family, and the whole of life revolved around this basic necessity. Almost every article or booklet which was written about any subject whatsoever, usually came under the general title of 'Husbandry', because everything in one way or another related to the land. Even articles about trade appeared in publications entitled *'Husbandry and Trade'*.

Everyday life was one great economy and consequently nothing was wasted. Oxen were the most useful animals, they could pull very heavy loads and were steadier than horses, and when killed they provided plenty of meat for the butchers. On 22nd March 1718, Mr. Whillock sent one of his oxen to be killed at Leek market; included in the payment he received was an amount for the hide and one for the pounds of tallow taken from around the kidneys, which were used by the tallow chandlers for making candles.

There were two methods of making candles, but first the wicks had to be prepared from cotton spun "for the purpose" and cut into correct lengths. One method was to use lead or tin moulds and attach a wick to the centre of each, pour in the melted tallow and leave to solidify. The other method was to secure five or six wicks to a short stick and dip them in melted tallow which was kept liquid "by standing in a vat of boiling water". The wicks were dipped over and over again, then allowed to drip and solidify, until the candles were of the required thickness. Apart from normal domestic use, candles were required in great numbers for the lead mines; it would have been impossible to work without them. Fortunately they could be used virtually without fear of explosions, but sadly the same thing could not be said of coal mines where many serious accidents occurred caused by pockets of gas, particularly as the mines became deeper. One method used to keep fresh air circulating in mines was to sink shafts at certain intervals along the surface to penetrate through the ceiling of the main tunnel, fires were then lit on the surface at every top of a shaft, thus drawing air along the part of the main tunnel between the bottom of the shafts close by, and up the shaft where the fire was suspended at the mouth. Eventually chimneys were erected over the mouths of the shafts and the fires were lit, suspended inside the chimneys, which was a far more efficient method. Sometimes huge bellows were used to try to pump air into the shafts or clay pipes were laid, but again without very good results. As is the way with all hazardous occupations, the lead miners in general were found to be very superstitious and it is said that one of the customs of Castleton was to take a child down the mine, with a candle strapped to his head, to assure the miners of success.

So this was the world into which Charles was born. A rural England where people worked hard and played hard, and in spite of the bull baiting and cock fighting, a people who respected their animals and appreciated the role they played in the teamwork required to harness nature. A world in which his father did his utmost to combat the fears and superstitions, particularly of the poorer people, by the influence of the Church, in an area which had been described in 1675 as having long held the reputation as "a stage or two beyond Christendom". And a world in which the family played the most important part, with the uniting of families by marriage, acting as a strengthening link to an already well established connection within a profession, trade, vocation or neighbourhood.

The Roe family, as was the case with many Church of England parsons and their families, held an important respected position within the community. By many it was looked upon and accepted as a privileged position, and whether or not the clergy were rich or poor, it gave their offspring a deep sense of belonging in the community and a confidence with which to obtain distinct positions; in fact, as the 18th century progressed, many clergymen's sons, although not necessarily following in their father's footsteps, were to become famous or important people.

There was plenty of good food available. At the time of Thomas and Mary's marriage in 1698 a collection of recipes had been published within a periodical and some were quite delicious e.g.:

To Stew Beef Steaks

"Take three pound of any good Beef, beat it well with a Rowling-pin, and put into a Tin-Stew-Pan, (of which those that have double bottoms are durable,) with half a pint of Ale, and half a pint of Claret, with a shred Onion, and set it at two hands distance over a gentle Fire, and when it is half ready, which may be in half an hour, put in a blade or two of Mace, a bunch of sweet Hearbs, an Anchovie, and when ready,which may be in half an hour or more, take the Liquor out, and put into it a little fresh Butter, Nutmeg, and the juyce of a Lemmon squeezed on it, and serve it up".

A Frigacy of Rabbets or Chickens.

"Take two Rabbets, quarter them, break all their Bones, clap them into a large Frying-Pan with a Cover, into which put a pint of White Wine, a pint of fair Water, half a pound of Bacon thin sliced, two Anchovies, a small bunch of sweet-Herbs to the value of a farthing, chopt small, two pennyworth of Capers, let all these simmer or gently Fry an hour, then take half a Porringer of the Broth, beat it up with the yolks of six boyled Eggs, put all in a Dish, and squeeze on the juyce of a Lemmon".

Fish recipes were also popular. Cheshire was renowned for the stocks of fish in its lakes and meers, which were easily supplied to the surrounding counties. Oysters were very popular in the North, being brought up from London in barrels of water.

To Stew Salmon

"Take a Jowl of Salmon, wash it very clean in an Earthen Pan, put it into a Kettle fit for it, with a Pint of White Wine Vinegar, half a Pint of fair Water, some Lemmon Peel, a bunch of sweet Herbs, a pennyworth of large Mace, three Wallnut-Tree-leaves (which may always be had at seed shops) a quart of Oysters with their own Liquor, a Pint of Shrimps, and simmer all these for about an hour till they are (done) enough, and then serve it up with the Liquor in a Dish".

Other recipes included roasting a fillet of veal, making potted beef or "to preserve a Breast of Veal in Pickle for three months in the Summer-time". Several instructions were given for preserving food with salt. Lumps of butter were to be potted up and kept 'sunk' in brine and would last six months. A leg of mutton buried in a heap of hard dry Portsea-salt was found to have kept for three months.

(NOTE). "I am credibly informed that Eggs have been packt up in a barrel of Salt, that the same have kept good to Jamaica . . . whereas others packt in Meal or Flour quickly became musty".

For those women of a hamlet or village who could not read, there would always be some good housewife who would show them how to cook the recipes. Perhaps this is where vicars' wives earned their reputation for making jams, preserving fruits and producing lots of good country baking which they often generously distributed to the poorer families within the parish. Not everyone had a room which was specifically a kitchen, but as more houses were built, kitchens were being added. Mary Roe's kitchen was well stocked with the following items:

"24 pewter dishes, 44 plaits.
4 pewter Rings, 3 Salvers and a pewter Cup.
2 Morter and pestills.
Callender, Caster and Cheestoster.
Jack and 2 Spitts, a pair of Racks.
A tin Driping pan, 2 Iron Driping pans.
brass Chaising Dish, 2 old brass pans.
A water pan, 2 Sauce pans.
A Caldron, a Skellett, a Iron pott.
A frying pan, a Laidle and 2 flesh forks."

There was also available a good selection of seeds, herbs and plants. In a letter dated 16th April 1698 sent from a London stockist to a shopkeeper in the High Peak area, an enormous variety of items had been supplied from which the following are but a few examples:

Seeds for "Cucumber, Mellon, Onion, Carrot, Leek, Parsnep, Turnep, Parsley, Rosemary, Cabbage lettuce and Lap lettuce, small Indian Cresses, Selleree, Dutch Asparagrass, Best Collyflower, Windsor Beans, White Kidney Beans and Liver collourd Kidney Beans" etc.

Flower seeds included "African Marygold, Wallflower, Double Hollyhock, Polyanthus, Stock Julyflower, London Pride" etc.

Apart from the seeds, small plants were also sent e.g."200 asparagrass plants" and "100 Artichoke plants" there was also listed a pair of garden shears for which a charge of 3/6d. was made, making them approximately the same price as today – valued at about £18.

Mary would have the assistance of her eldest daughter, Frances, whom she would teach to read and write and cook and sew, but poor Frances died on 14th June 1719; she was only seventeen years of age. When one child fell ill and died there must have been a few anxious weeks of wondering whether or not another child would follow. From the eight original children born to the Roes, now, with Thomas gone, there were only four. On the 2nd June of the following year (1720) William fulfilled his father's ambition and matriculated at Brasenose College, Oxford aged sixteen years. Brasenose College was originally founded in 1512 by William Smyth, Bishop of Lincoln and Richard Sutton, Knight of Prestbury Parish, Cheshire. These "Founders endowed the said college with Goods Profits & Emoluments . . . or one Principal & twelve Fellows; six of whom were to be elected from Persons born in the County Palatine of Lancaster and the other six from Persons born in the County Palatine of Chester, but with Preference always to be given to any Candidate born in the respective Parishes of the said Founders, namely Prescot in the County of Lancaster & Prestbury in the County of Chester". . . Once more the Macclesfield connection was working for Thomas.

Charles, now five years of age, was left with his brother, James, of nine years and his sister, Mary, of seven years and consequently a special bond developed between the trio. James was proving to be a very clever boy; soon it would be his turn to go to school. Young Mary took on the role of 'little mother' now that Frances had died, and Charles, from the expertise shown later in his life, seems to have found his way around Castleton and become fascinated with anything connected with lead mining. One can imagine him following other village children, who had a reputation of being fleet of foot and very agile, over the rocks and in and out of the caverns. His curiosity to see where his father's lead tithe came from, would make him conversant with the Odin mine. Later events were to prove it was a love and fascination which became part of his life and which would never leave him, although at this early age he knew that he would be expected to enter the Church, and in all fairness to Charles, it seemed to be his desire to do so.

Charles would soon learn that not only did his father receive payment for tithe ore from Odin, but he had used some of the money for investing in

The Cavern at Castleton in which many lead miners lived in the 18th century.

another lead mining venture close by the village of Eyam. This would have been very exciting for the young boy, who must have been taken along to see the work in progress. One can imagine all his questions; and those his father could not answer would be dealt with by his father's partners who were actually working the mine.

A very practical arrangement existed regarding the partnership formed to carry out mining; some of the partners were the miners or managers themselves, whilst others were 'gentlemen' who had money to invest, as in Thomas's case. The partners, who were also actually involved in the work, received a wage which was calculated at a certain rate per day. It is possible, of course, that some poorer workmen were employed who had no money to invest, and there were also to be taken into account wages for the women and children, who sorted and crushed the ore. After the deduction of all wages and other expenses, the partners divided the remainder of the profit between them according to their shares, and payment was made at regular intervals each year, which seemed to correspond more or less to quarter days. The size of shares varied a good deal, but it did make calculations or 'reckonings' easier (remembering that under the old English monetary system 12 pence = one shilling and there were 240 pence in one pound) when shares were in multiples of dozens; the most common being $\frac{1}{24}$, $\frac{1}{48}$, $\frac{1}{96}$, or $\frac{1}{192}$. Quite often shares were willed to several children and if a man held a $\frac{1}{48}$ share which was divided between four, then each would receive a $\frac{1}{192}$ share, (therefore it can be appreciated that there were not necessarily 192 people investing in one mine). This worked very well when the mine was making a profit, but what happened when a loss was incurred? Instead of receiving a payment, the partners received a demand (in effect an invoice) for their share of the loss arising; and should a 'one-off' item or expense occur i.e. the hiring of a Newcomen engine to pump water from a mine for a specific period, when an emergency arose, then the amount due was divided between the partners and 'invoiced' immediately, in the hope that everyone would pay up quickly to enable the situation to be rectified.

The accounting system suggests that had the Odin mine made a loss, Thomas would still have received his entitlement of tithe ore from any ore taken from the mine; the expenses being no concern of his. This situation is probably what caused the agitations of the Derbyshire miners in the first instance when they originally protested against the payment of tithe ore. The same provision would be made for the payment of the wages i.e. the wages would have been paid before the loss was calculated. This meant, in effect, a working partner would be paying back part or the whole of his wage to cover his share of the loss, whereas his partner who was an investor only, by making his payment of the loss was helping to supplement the wages bill. The system seemed quite fair and very few queries arose. Where there were disputes, as more and more mining took place, they tended to be in the actual working of the mines themselves. A situation could arise where two different partnerships were working two separate mines, and suddenly the mines intersected. On these rare occasions the Barmote Court found itself very busy. In some cases, the miners realising that a considerable amount of time and money could be spent on legal wrangles, all joined together in a new partnership and continued working on as a joint venture.

Fortunately, Thomas's involvement in the lead mining industry was in the early days of its 'renaissance' when problems of this nature had not often arisen. As everything was proceeding well at Odin, it was time for investment elsewhere in the area and attention was concentrated on the Hucklow Edge near Eyam. Having accrued a little money, he entered a partnership in which Richard Bagshawe was involved and purchased for himself a $\frac{1}{48}$ share.

Travelling in a southeasterly direction from Castleton, through the village of Bradwell, a visitor would approach a high gritstone ridge, which followed a line running from west to east, just north of the village of Eyam. This was the Hucklow Edge, and at its western end were the villages of Little and Great Hucklow. From some time late in the 17th century mining had been in progress, with shafts driven between 600 to 800 ft through gritstone and shale, until the miners had reached the mineralised limestone which contained the lead. It had been a large investment, initially, but the miners had done very well in determining the course of the Hucklow Edge vein, which was proving very rich, until their progress had been beset by problems. As the shafts went deeper and deeper, water began to seep into the mine. There was an old mine by the name of Have-At-All, which had been driven into the Hucklow Edge vein as a drainage system, but had been only partially successful. The Hucklow Edge vein dipped under Hucklow Edge, having been worked westwards from Gt Hucklow. Systematically one sough after another (going eastwards) was driven to intersect the vein, with a shaft sunk from the hill top once the sough had found it. This was a risky exercise, particularly as the vein split at least twice. However, it was rich and therefore worthy of speculation. Over several decades, exploration advanced eastwards. The splitting of the vein caused problems identifying which belonged to whom (and the risks of being dispossessed) as well as the greater capital outlay of ever-deepening shafts. However for speculators like the Roes, it was an interesting exercise worthy of the risk.

Work commenced on the Have-At-All sough during the year 1711, just about the time when Charles's brother James was born. Permission was obtained the following year from the landowner of Foolow Pasture to continue the sough through his land and the mine proved successful. Two years later, however, Richard Bagshawe, sensing that the rich Hucklow vein was there for the taking, grew impatient and yet another partnership was formed to work another sough. Again Rev. Thomas was an investor purchasing a further $^1/_{48}$ share and during 1714 the sough masters were granted meers on the eastern range of what they thought was the Hucklow Edge vein. Hopes were high as the miners once more battled their way through the rock to form the sough which they called Brookhead, and by the time Charles was five years old the work was well in progress. In this particular partnership, Thomas was joined by Rev. William Street, curate of Edale, who had now become a good friend to the Roe family.

Edale was a small village or hamlet just to the north of Castleton, and the chapel had been built in the year 1633, consecrated the following year and was responsible to the Mother church of St. Edmund's, Castleton. The curate was provided and maintained at "ye Charge of ye inhabitants thereof who allow him about Seventeen pounds Ten shillings per annum". This was hardly a wage, but Street supplemented his income by teaching, as many curates and parsons did, and he would be the one who prepared young James for grammar school. He also managed to save a little money for his investment of a $^1/_{96}$ share in the Brookhead sough on which everyone was building their hopes.

The miners had been favoured with some mild winters during the past few years, in fact, during the previous winter of 1719 "much buying of Oxen" had taken place in the High Peak for the London market. Mr. Whillock recorded in his notebook "They took them to kill in London by March before they were half fat". Thomas Secker, still writing to his sister in Chesterfield, but on this occasion from Calais, commented in his letter "I find myself able to talk French amongst them better than I expected but here every Body talks English."

* * * * * * *

The year 1720 was an eventful year in England and has been remembered to this day, because many people lost 'considerable fortunes' by investing in a company formed as part of a scheme for funding war (a sort of mini-Civil Service department) and it received loans from the Bank of England and the (New) East India Company. By 1711 large arrears had accrued in respect of navy victualling and transport and army debentures. A separate fund was established in order to make regular payments of interest due on the loans, and it was incorporated, becoming known as the South Sea Company. This company was given trading rights, and intended to try to capture part of the South Seas trade from Spain, with whom we were at war. It sounded like a marvellous idea and many people rushed to invest, so that by

1715 the capital of the company had reached ten million pounds. The Bank of England was trying to sail a steady course, in spite of its large investment in the company, but complications set in. The trading of the company was utterly futile and it finally involved itself in payments of bribes to public men amounting to one and a quarter million pounds, in order to keep them quiet regarding a fraud which had been perpetrated. On 18th August 1720 the general public was suddenly made aware of what was happening, and a panic started which resulted in a total collapse of the company and many people with it. It is often forgotten that some of the early investors in the scheme did very well out of it; one such example was King's College, Cambridge which bought £1950 of South Sea stock between 1716 and 1719 and fortunately sold whilst the share prices were rapidly rising. During 1720, in the month of June alone, the shares more than doubled in value before the extent of the fraud was revealed. Fortunately none of the Roe family had invested in the speculation and neither had Thomas Secker, although his family in Chesterfield were informed of his many friends and acquaintances in the City who had been 'ruined' by it all.

Mary Roe's dear friend and neighbour, Dorothy Creswick, died during the early winter of 1720/21 and Thomas Roe was Executor for which he received £5. One of the witnesses was another good friend, Robert Charlesworth. Dorothy's son, Samuel, had already been provided for so that her daughter was given the benefit of her house, garden and orchard, together with "Profits arising from the tythe of Alton and Thornhill". The faithful housekeeper (as was usual at this period) was given the contents of her own room, which included the bed with its bedding, sheets and hangings "as it now stands and which she usually lies in. With one pair of sheets more". A brass sauce pan and kettle, two tables, two pewter dishes, two plates, two chairs, two stools and the old brass candlestick. She also received two suits of clothing together with four "petty coats", three shifts and three flaxen aprons. The remainder of the estate, which presumably meant the other items left in the house and any other small amounts of cash or income (although the latter seems unlikely as they had not been specified) were willed to Mary Roe, representing once more a significant gesture by someone who appreciated Mary's kindness and friendship.

Young James was ready for grammar school and Thomas must have learnt of the excellent school in Stockport which was within easy reach of home should an emergency arise. The old Roman road could be joined at Chapel, which then passed through Stockport on its way to Manchester. Enquiries would have been made and the following details obtained. The patrons of the school were the Goldsmiths Guild of London, who confirmed the appointments of the masters, and on 1st December 1703 they had confirmed the appointment of a Rev. Joseph Dale, who was the son of a minister of Denton, near Manchester, and related to the Dale family of Leek in Staffordshire. Dale was a brilliant teacher. His salary, as headmaster of Stockport Grammar School, had been increased to £10 per annum from 1711, with a further small increase some five years later. In 1717 he had been given both the curacy of Chorlton Chapel at a rate of £10 per annum and Birch Chapel at £3 10s. per annum; in the not too distant future he would also obtain the curacy of the Chapelry of Denton (1723), at £20 per annum. Not an exceptional income by any means and yet by the time this man died in 1759 he left a considerable fortune; one item alone was a sum of £8,000 which he had invested through his son, Edward, and from which he was receiving interest.

Though Thomas and Mary would not live to appreciate it, the fact that they chose Stockport Grammar School for their son, James, was the most significant thing they ever did, and would prove to have the most important bearing on the future of their family.

William Street had proved himself to be a good teacher, and possibly with the encouragement of Thomas, Richard Bagshawe during 1721 conveyed a dwelling house to the use of a school for Castleton, which was "now in possession tenure or occupation of William Streete, Clerk Edale whom Richard Bagshawe had appointed to be schoolmaster there". The consequence of this would be that young Mary and Charles were able to join other children from the village and surrounding areas for lessons, provided locally in the new schoolhouse.

On 21st December 1721, although Thomas was only fifty one years of age, he felt it necessary to write out his will. He did not have a formal one prepared, but had his own witnessed by three local inhabitants. By 25th May 1723 he had died and was buried at St. Edmund's Church. A visitor to the church in the late Victorian period saw the gravestone within the Communion rails, but today there is no trace. After the payment of funeral debts he left everything, including the share of the mines, to his wife, to be disposed of for the bringing up of the children; and if she should die before the children had grown up, then he appointed his son, William, and his dear friends Rev. William Street of Edale and Robert Charlesworth of Castleton, as trustees for the children "Requesting that they will take care of the bringing them up & placing them to such honest Callings as they in their Judgments shall think meet". There was no mention of son, Thomas. Mary had the will proved at Lichfield with an affidavit from William Street, confirming that it was the last Will and Testament of Mr. Thomas Roe Clerk so far as he knew and believed. The largest single item in the Inventory was "Debts due on Specialities £300" out of a total of £454 13 4d. There was plenty of furniture, which included "a Clock & Chimes & Weather Glass", "a Writing-Desk Looking-Glass Several Maps", "2 presses" and "a Chest of Drawers".

Mary had a big decision to make. Now fifty three years of age, she was not a young woman and had daughter, Mary, aged ten years and Charles, aged only eight years to consider. Her main priority was to keep the family together; William, fortunately, was in his final year at Oxford. There is no doubt that Mary would make the journey to Stockport as quickly as she could, to seek the help and advice of Joseph Dale, and he, being true to his nature, set the 'wheels' of the Church in motion, so that practical help could be given as soon as possible. Mary saw no alternative but to move herself and the two younger children to Stockport to be near James. She disposed of some of the larger items of furniture, together with saddles and saddle bags, brewing equipment, and the livestock of which they had a horse, cow, sow and pig. She kept sufficient beds and bedding for four persons, together with various chairs and tables and the clock, several family portraits and the portrait of King Charles. As soon as a suitable dwelling house was found to rent, their belongings were loaded into a wagon and Mary left the home she had known for the past twenty five years. She must have felt apprehensive about the move to Stockport, because she was either given, or bought for herself, a gun. As Charles left his beloved Derbyshire, he must have wondered what would happen next. In all probability Street and Charlesworth were there to see them on their journey and to reassure Mary that they would look after the Roe interests in the local lead mining industry. Charles would miss his visits to the mines but he knew that he would return. He loved and understood the miners, and had learnt to speak their language; the knowledge he had gained during his few short years would stand him in good stead for the future.

* * * * * * *

Perhaps Charles and sister Mary were a little excited about taking up residence in Stockport, which was close by Manchester. Manchester seemed to be the most important town in England after London. It had once been famous for its woollen industry which had now been superseded by cotton and linen. It appeared to have connections 'everywhere' through the ports of Hull, Chester and Liverpool, and, during the summertime, the Scottish chapmen journeyed south through Carlisle and the Lake District, passing through Manchester and Stockport on their way to London. Over a period of time several of them had taken shops and settled in the Manchester area. There was a great deal of coming and going to London, which meant that everyone was kept up-to-date with news from the Capital.

Stockport was a busy little town and well patronised by the Legh family of Lyme Hall near Disley. Peter Legh the Elder was a very kind man, who looked after his large estates (some of which were situated in South Lancashire) and employees to the best of his ability. He engaged the services of John Ward, who was a very important lawyer, probably a barrister-at-law, of the Inner Temple and who lived at Capesthorne Hall near Macclesfield. On 16th January 1704 John Ward had written to Peter Legh "I have seen great Variety of yer Oar at ye Mine Adventure. And my Lord Barnard who has great mine in Durham will furnish me with instructions for you". This was to be the beginning of an extremely important and lucrative coal mining industry in South Lancashire which was to serve the Leghs well for many years to come. They eventually developed pits at Haydock near Liverpool, Lowton near Warrington, and, nearer to home, at Norbury close by Poynton, just to the north of Macclesfield. It was also one of the inspirations for a gentleman by the name of Thomas Patten to invest in the building of copper works on the edge of the River Mersey at Bank Quay, Warrington, in the year 1717. He was already a merchant dealing in sugar and tobacco and possessed the best wharf site in the town. A great deal of money was needed to bring a copper smelter into production, and there was no doubt that sugar and tobacco from the West Indian and American trades through the port of Liverpool were providing considerable fortunes for many. From 1st. January 1719 Thomas Patten Jnr. had joined his father in partnership with a William Wood, and it was this son who further developed the considerable trade they had in Manchester. He was a great stalwart of the Church of England, involving himself in all sorts of schemes, usually in the capacity of trustee, for the benefit of the poor, particularly in Manchester itself; and because of his attainments, he found himself 'courted' by both Peter Legh of Lyme and the Bishop of Chester.

Thomas Patten learnt very early that it is easier to take copper ore to coal, than vice versa, because three tons of good coal were needed to smelt one ton of copper, and so he contracted to purchase his coal from Peter Legh of Lyme. Because of the constant supervision needed on the Legh Estates, the Estates manager, his deputy and other workmen in the employ of Peter Legh were frequently seen in Stockport on their way to, and returning from, Warrington and Liverpool. Many purchases, both personal and on behalf of the Legh family, were made in the town, and as Peter Legh also had property in Macclesfield, close by the Market Place, a further vital link in the communications network was maintained between the two places.

* * * * * * *

William Roe obtained his B.A. on 21st January. 1724, but before the end of the year tragedy struck once more when his mother, Mary, died and was buried at St. Mary's, the Parish Church of Stockport, on 28th November 1724. In her will, Mary more or less reiterated what Thomas had requested in his, but she was more specific and added one further notable bequest. After payment of the funeral expenses and debts, the whole of her estate had to be kept together, including the profits from the mines, until Charles (or if he died, the youngest remaining child) had reached the age of twenty four years.The trustees were once more Rev. William Street and Robert Charlesworth who were given power, if necessary, to dispose of any of the estate "for the education & placing to honest Callings my three younger Sons & Daughter". After the children had received their education then the estate could be distributed viz:

Daughter, Mary, was to be given two hundred pounds and one half of the share in the "Groove call'd Brookhead". She was also to receive all the linen and wearing apparel.

The remainder of the estate, goods and money had to be equally divided between William, James and Charles but the shares in the Derbyshire mines had to be shared between her four sons, Thomas, William, James and Charles. Mary obviously knew of Thomas's whereabouts and the distribution seems to suggest that he was already married.

William took on the responsibilities of the little family, and it was to this older brother that James, Mary and Charles now looked for help and guidance.

4
THE RETURN

Train up a child in the way he should go: and
when he is old, he will not depart from it.

By strange coincidence, it always seemed to be the sons named William who took on the burdens of care and duty during periods of crisis in the Roe family.

William, some time during the year of his mother's death (1724), was given a curacy of the Parochial Chapel in Macclesfield, but this post did not come under the auspices of the Macclesfield Corporation, as his father's position had done, it seems to have been created at the discretion of the Churchwardens, unless they were responsible for making him additional payments. This unusual arrangement must have arisen from the fact that, on the accession of George I, due to a series of litigations, the Borough was without a Charter for about nine years from 1716 to 1724. In the wardens' accounts for the years 1726 to 1729 appear payments of £5 per annum, with an occasional payment, "Paid Mr. Roe for wine for a Privat communion 6d". It is also possible, as in the case of Rev. Joseph Dale of Stockport, that William held more than one curacy in the area.

There is little doubt that Charles and Mary lived with William, possibly remaining for a short while in the rented house at Stockport. The main concern of the trustees and Rev. Dale, was that there should be sufficient money to complete the education of James, who was living up to his reputation of being an excellent scholar. William's small stipend was hardly sufficient to support the family, but surely there would be adequate income from the lead mining shares to provide James with a good education; in the meantime William could teach Charles and Mary. Young Charles seems to have loved William and looked upon him as a father figure. Perhaps Charles's relationship with his father had been rather a distant one. He certainly acquired his mother's trait for endeavouring to help others, together with a personality which endeared itself to a few exceptional people who thought as he did. When Charles Roe made a friend it was for life. The indications are that, as he grew up, he became a strong well built man of large stature, acquiring at least this one characteristic from his grandfather, Rev. Robert of Hadley. He had a very strong conscience, which was almost his downfall on occasion, and, like all tolerant people, when he was pushed beyond the limits of his generosity and patience, his sudden rush of anger knew no bounds. But this was for the future; the present, creating many difficulties and problems, was helping to build and strengthen his character.

In the first instance, Robert Charlesworth, Rev. William Street and William Roe must have decided that the most logical course of action was to allow James income from as many lead mining shares as possible, and only retain the investment in one mine in respect of William himself, and Charles.

Matters were not proceeding very well in Derbyshire. Unfortunately the Brookhead sough was being driven at too high a contour to be effective for hand pump arrangements. By the year 1722 it had been decided to start another sough to locate and unwater the Hucklow

Edge Vein, and it would seem that Thomas had already invested in this shortly before his death. The sough, named Stoke, was driven westwardly from the Derwent valley through gritstone and shale, but the costs of this work were mounting rapidly. Another attempt to locate the Hucklow Edge Vein was made from January 1724, when Magclough sough was started; however, during the next decade a sum of £4,859 was expended without results. This was the mine in which William and Charles held a $^1/_{48}$ share. They are entered on a list of "Partners at Eyam Groves" (unfortunately undated but definitely before 1730). Included also on this list is a Mr. Wroe with the following shares:

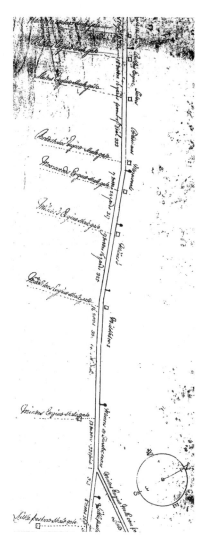

Part of an 18th c. plan of lead mines at Eyam Edge. Also shows vein splitting – see p. 58.

Brookhead $^1/_{48}$	Miners $^1/_{48}$
Middleton $^1/_{96}$	Founders & Barkers $^1/_{48}$
Milnes Engine $^1/_{96}$	Moorwood Engine $^1/_{92}$

There is no doubt that these shares were held for James, who entered St. John's College, Cambridge as a sizar, on 26th July 1729. Fortunately his income was supplemented by a 'Bell' scholarship. The Great Bell, hung in Tudor times, had required a young scholar to mount the stairs of the tower and ring the morning peal at 4 a.m., no doubt with a good deal of weariness. He returned at nightfall to signal the locking of the college gates and additionally to call everyone to chapel for the delivery of a sermon. Queen Elizabeth I's favourite, Robert Devereux, Earl of Essex, had subsequently donated a bell which was placed "in one of the Inner Turrets as you enter into St. John's College" i.e. the south-west turret. At different times the bell had been recast, however, by the time young James ascended the turret, the morning peal had moved to the more civilised hour of 6a.m., but the 'job' was not without its dangers. On certain occasions more strokes were required, and one exhausted pupil in the early 17th century had been lifted high by the bell rope then thrown down onto his head. He remained unconscious for most of the day and everyone feared for his life; but he survived to tell the tale. Young James too survived and graduated B.A. in 1732.

Apart from the shares reserved for James Roe, one half of the share in the Brookhead sough should have been held in trust for his sister, Mary, as requested in his mother's will; no doubt with the intention of being used as part of her marriage settlement in due course. This group of soughs in which James held his shares, appear to have been worked simultaneously from about the year 1715. They were situated to the northwest of Eyam and proceeded from the southern side of the Hucklow Edge Vein, in a northerly direction, to intersect the vein itself. Whether or not Rev. Thomas had invested in these from their beginnings is not known, but the probability is more than likely. They certainly seem to have been productive. Where records exist from the 1730s onwards, they indicate that mining produced a good yield.

* * * * * * *

Not too long after the Roes' departure from Castleton, Daniel Defoe arrived in the area as part of his tour through England and Wales (1724-28). His description of the High Peak as a "howling wilderness" has been reiterated as an exemplification of hostile desolation by many writers, but also he used the word "wondrous", indicating that the area excited him in some way, and for which, obviously, he felt a strange appeal. He wrote an excellent description of his visit to Brassington Moor, near Wirksworth, during which he met a lead miner and his family. He and his companions were directed to a high mountain where, it was said, a giant was buried (superstitions still prevailed). "Here we missed the imaginary wonder, and found a real one", he wrote. They discovered:

> "a large hollow cave, which the poor people by two curtains hang'd cross, had parted into three rooms. On one side was the chimney and the man, or perhaps his father, being miners, had found a means to work a shaft or tunnel through the rock to carry the smoke out at the top . . . Everything was clean and neat tho' mean and ordinary. There were shelves with some earthenware, and some pewter and brass. There was . . . a whole flitch or side of bacon hanging up in the chimney and by it a good piece of another. There was a sow and pigs running about at the door, and a little lean cow feeding upon a green place just before the door."

Defoe learnt that the woman's husband with good luck could earn "about five pence a day, but that he worked by the dish", the ore being measured in a wooden bowl known as a dish. The woman worked "the oar" for which, if she worked hard, she could earn three pence a day. She had five small children who "look'd plump and fat, ruddy and wholesome: and the woman was tall, well shap'd clean." Defoe and his companions proceeded to a valley where there were several grooves "so they call the mouth of the shaft or pit by which they go down into a lead mine . . . we were agreeably surprized with seeing a hand, and then an arm, and quickly after a head, thrust up out of the very groove we were looking at". The miner demonstrated to them that "by setting his feet upon pieces of wood fixt cross the angles of the groove like a ladder" he could come up or go down easily, with his elbows resting on the wooden pieces as well as his feet. The man was clothed completely in leather, wearing a cap without a brim, and he had some tools in a little basket which he drew up with him. He was "lean as a skeleton, pale as a dead corps, his hair and beard a deep black, his flesh lank". Besides the tools in the basket, the miner lifted out of the mine about three quarters of one hundred weight of ore. On enquiring, Defoe learnt that the mine was 60 fathoms deep, with two miners working at 11 fathoms and a further three miners working 15 fathoms deeper. The miner, on being given "two small pieces of better mettle, called shillings" by Defoe and company, made off towards the alehouse to purchase some "good pale Derby". Defoe was so struck by the contentment and happiness of the lead mining people that he felt compelled to present the story in the greatest detail, using it as a parable "to show the discontented part of the rich world how to value their happiness."

This was certainly a sentiment with which the Roes would have concurred, and as poor William struggled onwards with regard to Charles and Mary, at least he knew that he was fulfilling his mother's and father's wishes in respect of James. There was certainly no spare money with which to educate Charles, so Stockport Grammar School was out of the question. One has to assume that, because of William's connection with Macclesfield, Charles probably attended the Macclesfield Free Grammar School for the first two forms, for which no fees were payable. Therefore, he would have learnt to read in the first, and completed writing and arithmetic in the second form. In later years he was always very self conscious about his inadequate education, and when occasions arose on which he had to put pen to paper, his abrupt style was an embarrassment to him, and he would conclude with phrases such as "Excuse my being in a hurry".

* * * * * * *

During the year 1727 George I died and was succeeded by his son, George II, who inherited a land which was poised on the edge of a fascinating period of its history and one of incredible potential. It was as though all the restless power and spirit of the 17th century had gathered itself together and at last found its true direction; it would burst forth like a flower from its bud, creating admiration, appreciation and inspiration in all who came into contact with it. Simultaneously it would envelop the great city of London, the smallest hamlets, the larger villages and towns of which Macclesfield was no exception.

On 13th February 1729 William married Anna Barbor in the Parochial Chapel, Macclesfield. The details of the marriage settlement will probably remain a mystery, but it seems possible that Anne was related to his father's old friend, Josiah, and could have come from the family at Glossop. She was to become a good 'mother' to the Roe children. On the move to Macclesfield, the house in Stockport would have been subleased. After only fourteen months of marriage, William died suddenly and was buried in the graveyard of the Parochial Chapel on 23rd April 1730, but whatever he left in the way of assets is unknown. Charles and Mary must have felt dreadfully shocked and insecure. Again this final trauma seems to have had a deep lasting effect on Charles, making him determined to find security and stability whenever possible. When the time came that he had sufficient money to do so, he invested in property. This was his security, reflected in the fact that whatever properties he acquired, he never sold but kept them for the rest of his life.

Charles was almost fifteen years of age when brother William died, and something had to be done, for there was his new 'mother' Anne to support and his sister, Mary. James was managing to work his own way through university on his small income, but Charles now had to face the reality that a university education was impossible for him, and he would be denied the vocation of a Church of England parson. In later years, a close associate and friend related that whilst in his youth, Charles had made himself a promise; if he was fortunate enough for God to bestow success upon him in the financial world, then he would build a church as an acknowledgement. Living in Macclesfield was certainly not an advantage, as Charles would have insufficient money to enter into an apprenticeship in the town. Circumstantial evidence suggests that Rev. Dale came to the rescue.

* * * * * * *

The town of Macclesfield was experiencing a period of retrogression. About the time that the Pickford family had taken up their main residence at Alte Hill, Ashton-under-Lyne, towards the end of the 17th century, their place had been taken by a family with the unusual name of Hollinpriest. This was probably no coincidence, because the Hollinpriests seem to have been involved in the cotton and linen thread trade, and by this period the Pickfords also were heavily involved in cotton. There were three Hollinpriest brothers, Edward, Samuel and Robert who had moved to the area from south Manchester. Edward lived in the township of Hurdsfield and was an attorney. This did not necessarily mean that he had received legal training, as in the case of a solicitor, but it did indicate that he was a resident of some standing and respectability who could be trusted to act or represent someone else in a legal situation, having been appointed by them to do so. He had died, however, on 21st January 1703.

The other two brothers, Samuel and Robert, had several children baptized in the Parochial Chapel during the decade commencing 1713, and they lived in two of the largest houses in the small town. One of them lived in the old Pickford residence on the site of what remained of the medieval castellated mansion leased from the Earl of Derby. The other brother lived in a huge house on the corner of Dog Lane and Mill Street, which was, in effect, a small manufactory or workhouse; the word manufactory came more into general use during the second half of the 18th century. This was the period in between the cottage industry and the mills, when an employer had a large residence, part of which was used for his trade, and where he employed possibly half-a-dozen people 'at home'. This particular Hollinpriest had a house with a frontage of 17 yards, which was built in brick and covered with slate. There were nine bays consisting of nine lower rooms and nine upper rooms, a cellar, one backside, three gardens, a barn and two stables. Running the full length of the property i.e. 50 yards, there was a twisting yard of 5 yards wide. All this information was according to a survey of rented properties, carried out in 1709 on behalf of the Earl of Derby.

The twisting yard would be where the linen or cotton thread, mohair or silk was actually twisted. Usually it was done by two boys, one standing at one end of the yard, with bobbins of thread attached to a belt around his waist, and the other running the full length of the yard, drawing with him from the bobbins held by the first boy, however many threads were considered desirable, and at the same time twisting them into a stronger fibre. The process could also be carried out with the use of a strange looking machine resembling a penny-farthing bicycle, but having the small wheel over the top of the large one.

A drawing of what I refer to as a 'penny-farthing machine' showing a small boy and a woman twisting the long strands of silk in a twisting yard.

Courtesy of Macclesfield Museums Trust.

There is no mention of the Hollinpriests in Macclesfield after the mid 1720s; they seem to have mysteriously disappeared. Perhaps they emigrated either to the West Indies or America, or simply moved over the border into Derbyshire. Wherever bound, their exodus did leave the remaining families in the town competing for power, particularly the Dissenters and Quakers, after the renewal of the Borough Charter in 1724. Meanwhile the surrounding hamlets of Leek, Congleton, Gawsworth and Poynton were rapidly advancing and threatening to leave Macclesfield behind.

* * * * * * *

The town of Leek in Staffordshire, 12 miles south of Macclesfield, was a very busy little place. Much land in the area was owned by the Earl of Macclesfield, and as there were no Guilds or Corporation to restrict individuals, free enterprize was the order of the day. This situation was also developing in Birmingham, where many craftsmen had settled, including Huguenots, but Leek had a greater advantage being situated on an important road to Ashbourne and Derby, thence to London. During the year of 1685 a collection had been made in St. Edward's, the Parish Church of Leek, on behalf of French refugees. It was said that some came from Coventry to settle in the town, where they introduced ribbon and ferret weaving (narrow bindings) as they did also in Derby. Already, as in Macclesfield, the silk, mohair, horsehair and linen buttons were being made in a variety of patterns, and by 1730 there were three prominent families who appear to have been involved in the lucrative business.

One was the Birtles family, of whom Thomas had settled at Birtles Hall, near Macclesfield, where his family had been for generations.

Another was the Lankford family (sometimes spelt Langford or Laneford), who seem to have come from the Nottingham area, and one of their number was about to play an important role in the affairs of Macclesfield.

The third was, of course, the Dales, of whom Joseph was headmaster of the Stockport Grammar School. All of these families were staunch members of the Church of England and all held properties within the parish of Leek.

It can only be surmised that because of Dale's connections in Leek, he obtained a position for Charles in the mohair and silk trade with a certain gentleman, from the Lankford family, named Samuel.

Samuel Lankford had a strong personality and was sometimes a little unscrupulous in getting what he wanted. His intentions seemed to be honourable, but on occasion, events were to cast a slight shadow of doubt in that direction. However, he appears to have come from a wealthy family and was an excellent businessman from whom Charles, no doubt, learnt the first rudiments of economics and good business practice.

Situated near the Derbyshire border was the Staffordshire village of Sheen, where the vicar at that period was Rev. Ralph Sleigh. The Sleigh family of Derbyshire was an important one which had been in the area for generations. (One of them, Samuel, had been Sheriff of Derbyshire in 1648 and again in 1666). Ralph and his wife, Elizabeth, had several children, one of whom, Thomas, married a Catherine Buckley at Rocester in Staffordshire, on 12th May 1702. Within the year (13th April 1703) they had a daughter, Elizabeth baptized in the village of Alstonfield, but Thomas died and it was his widow, Catherine, who married Samuel Lankford at Ilam, on 31st January 1722. Apart from Rocester, to the south west, all these villages are very close together, a little to the north of the town of Ashbourne, and situated in the area where Daniel Defoe visited the lead mines during 1725.

On 1st November 1723 Samuel Lankford entered into partnership with seven other investors, two of whom, Thomas and John, were members of the Sleigh family and possible in-laws. Their speculation was in a lease for part of Ecton Hill from the Duke of Devonshire in order to subcontract work to teams of miners in the search for copper ores. Initially they appear to have met with some success, but eventually abandoned the enterprise because of lack of funds.

* * * * * * *

It is interesting to note how property and money could transfer from one family to another, within two or three generations, because of marriage settlements and premature deaths. The wife of the Rev. Ralph Sleigh, Elizabeth, was the daughter and heiress of Richard Gratton of the village of Brassington, in Derbyshire. In 1620 a Richard Gratton, amongst others, "had compounded with the king's commissioners for confirmation of his customary estate." There is also a Richard Gratton recorded in the horse sale book of Brassington, at the Easter Fair of 1659, as being a witness to a sale. Young Thomas Sleigh inherited from his grandfather, Richard Gratton, through his mother, Elizabeth, part of the Brassington Estate. On the death of Thomas this inheritance would be held in trust for his daughter Elizabeth's children; but, although Elizabeth subsequently married and was widowed, she had no children. On her mother's remarriage to Samuel Lankford another daughter was born, who surprisingly was again named Elizabeth. Catherine died in October 1727 and Samuel Lankford, presumably with the two young girls, appears to have moved to Marbrook (Meerbrook) close by Leek, where he purchased a large estate called the New Grange, near Blackshaw Moor. A future transaction indicates that Samuel Lankford must have held part of the Brassington Estate on behalf of his step daughter, probably in the capacity of trustee within the framework of the marriage settlement, and this was to be of importance to the Roe family at a later date.

Meerbrook was a small village where, it was recorded by J. Cox:

> "they have an Act of burning Fern green, which they do commonly on the side of an Hill lying to a fresh Gale of Wind for which they alledge it as a Reason that the Ashes might not fly away, as they certainly would if it was burnt dry; but the true reason is (says Dr. Plot) that there is an Oiliness in green Fern which remains in the Ashes, when it is far burnt which makes them fit for the Use they put them to, which is to wash their Buckings with, because Wood-Ashes are not commonly to be had in this County where Coal is the general Fuel for their Fires."

These burnt fern ashes were, the ones sold on market days at the Macclesfield market, and the "Buckings" referred to were simply their dirty linen or washing: in fact, a buckbasket was a basket in which the dirty clothes were carried to the wash.

The New Grange estate seems to have been the centre of Samuel Lankford's business operations; it was conveniently situated for travelling across the hills between Cheshire, Derbyshire and Staffordshire. This area known generically by the strange name of Flash, though not geographically, is a name taken from a village hidden amongst the hills, close by the route from Leek to Buxton. The chapmen of the district, who dealt in the button and haberdashery trade, became known as 'Flashmen'. This would be the area primarily in which Charles worked, and where he would have the opportunity to travel to Castleton, keeping in touch with both the lead mining and the old friends of the Roe family.

The main centre of distribution for the button trade was, from north to south, Stockport, Macclesfield, Congleton and Leek. It is known from a later deed that Thomas Birtles, button merchant, acquired what became his business premises on Chestergate in Macclesfield. He

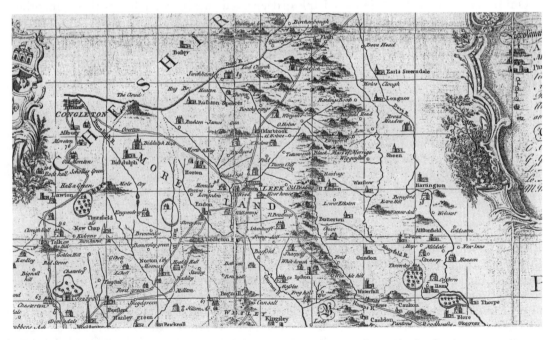

Staffordshire Moorland. The route from Leek to Flash, running north-east is clearly shown passing Meerbrook village where Charles Roe married his first wife, Elizabeth. The map by Joseph Browne was produced in 1682.

appears to have operated a sort of warehouse arrangement, having other buildings and a barn close by. There it would seem that linen or silk thread was kept for sale to Manchester merchants, and as he was a button merchant, presumably he had the buttons collected and brought to his premises also, for onward despatch. The buttons in Macclesfield itself, were now being made by old men and women and young children (many probably orphans) in one or two of the 'modern' workhouses situated close by Thomas Birtles's offices.

Dyeing was still a very important industry in the town, and the biggest dyehouse which was, no doubt, the one originally erected by the Pickford family, at the end of a wall leading from the castle wall on Waters, had now acquired the grandiose title of the Copperas House Works. It was here in this "Building commonly used in or about the making of Copperas" that the "Brasses Boyling pans Cisterns Coolers Weights Scales Implements" were kept, indicating that apart from the actual production of copperas, which would be supplied to the other dyehouses in the area, dyeing itself was taking place.

By definition, according to Dr. Samuel Johnson's *Dictionary*, copperas was:

"A name given to three sorts of vitriol; the green, the bluish green and the white, which are produced in the mines of Germany, Hungary & other countries. But what is commonly sold here for copperas is an artificial vitriol, made of a kind of stones found on the seashore in Essex, Hampshire & so westward ordinarily called gold stones from their colour. They abound with iron, and are exposed to the weather in beds above ground and receive the rains and dew, which in time breaks and dissolves the stones: the liquor which runs off is pumped into boilers, in which is first put old iron, which, in boiling, dissolves. When the boiling is finished, the liquor is drawn off into coolers, where it shoots into crystals of a fine green colour. This factitious [artificial] copperas, in many respects, perfectly agrees with the native green vitriol of Germany and is used in dying hats and cloths black, and in making ink."

Today copperas, or ferrous sulphate heptahydrate, is produced on a large scale by exposing heaps of iron pyrites (commonly known as fool's gold) to the action of air and moisture. The liquor drained off contains ferrous sulphate and sulphuric acid. The sulphuric acid is also converted into copperas, or ferrous sulphate, by adding scrap iron and is still used in dyeing, the manufacture of ink and also the dressing of crops. Apart from actually being used as a dye, copperas is used as a mordant. Without mordants many dyes would 'bleed' badly or fade when rinsed. Copperas has been used as a mordant for wool and cotton from the earliest times, but has a hardening effect on fibres and tends to darken or 'sadden' colours, so it has to be used with care. With certain plants it produces beautiful greens or greys. Copperas can never be used for silk because it is too harsh, therefore, one can only presume that very little silk was being dyed (if any) in Macclesfield at this time, and that the main production was for the cotton and woollen industries.

* * * * * * *

As the interest in mineralogy increased with the progress in mining, so did the experiments of the alchemists and apothecaries. They established themselves in their respective communities as an elite profession in the same way as the lawyers or solicitors, although barrister remained supreme. They were the forerunners of today's doctors and chemists, and their surplus cash was invested in a variety of ways e.g. properties for leasing, shares in mines and other small industries etc. One such apothecary, by the name of Francis Nicholson, lived in Macclesfield.

The Nicholsons were descended from a Cumberland family and had settled in the Stockport area during the 17th century, acquiring vast parcels of land and consequently were very well-known. Francis's father had moved to Macclesfield and had baptised his son after his brother, Rev. Francis of Stockport. They were also acquainted with the Leghs of Lyme Hall, particularly Peter Legh the Elder, and when the time came for young Francis to open his own 'chemist shop', he appears to have leased a property in Macclesfield belonging to Peter Legh, which was situated at the northern end of Mill Street, close by the Market Place. The indications are that Francis grew into a very self-opinionated young man and was part of a family who were always quarrelling amongst themselves. His father, Ralph, had held the position of Common Clerk of the Macclesfield Borough, but on 28th July 1714 it was recorded in the Corporation Minute Book that for the three years 1709-11 he had made "divers faults of enrolling admissions of the Burgesses", so a fine of £3 was imposed, but as Ralph had died, a payment of £3 was deemed to be due to him, thus cancelling the fine.

By the late 1720s Francis had pushed himself forward in Macclesfield society, being conscious of the fact that to be considered of any importance at all he would have to become an Alderman. Initially he certainly seems to have impressed the overseer of the Steward of Lyme Hall: an entry in the account books dated 4th February 1729 reads, "Paid to Doctor Nicholson his bill in full of all a/cs to 5th February, 1728-9 as per receipt £2 12 5d." However, by 26th November of the same year a further entry reads "Mr. Nicholson Apothecary in Macclesfield" paid 5/- for "his Visit to old Jno. Richardson & George Platt". One wonders what happened to John Richardson and George Platt because by January the following year the accounts record a payment to plain Francis Nicholson.

The account books kept by both the Steward of Lyme, Mr. Peter Orford and his overseer make interesting reading. Macclesfield was the place where soap, stockings and silk thread were purchased, the latter used extensively by tailors. The soap is later referred to as castle soap and then castile soap and was also purchased in Stockport and Ashton-under-Lyne. It was bought, together with candles, from William Warsop "soap boyler" of Macclesfield, until at least 1730. He subsequently became Mayor of Macclesfield for the year 1733/4. From 15th March 1734, another soap maker in Macclesfield lived at the lower end of Mill Street opposite Pickford's well. The premises were a group of cottages, close by the dyehouses on the Pickford land, and situated just to the south of the castle site. It is tempting to think that this castle soap was an early instance of the use of a brand name.

The Lyme accounts for the early 1730s also record purchases of mohair and horse "hare" buttons, a few dozen bought from Francis Nicholson in his capacity as a retailer. Possibly Charles Roe was the middleman or salesman connected with these transactions. The Nicholsons must have known the Roes at this early period, not only because of the Stockport connection but also because William had been Curate of the Parochial Chapel until his death in 1730.

The Roe family also had a connection with William Roe's successor, Rev. John Robinson. Although John Robinson's father is recorded as a husbandman of Cheshire, his son was baptised in the village of Lyddington, nine miles to the southwest of Stamford in Lincolnshire, which was a very important town lying on the Great North Road (today the A1) from London to York. John Jnr. had been admitted to St. John's College, Cambridge as a sizar during 1726, when he was 24

A label adapted from an 18th century soap and toiletry manufacturer's trade card.

years of age. This was, of course, the college which young James Roe had also entered as a sizar during 1729, when he was 18 years of age. As only a handful of students were admitted to each University College at this period, the two students must have known each other, even if only for a few brief months, until John Robinson obtained his B.A. during 1729/30; being of a personal nature, it was a significant connection which was so important to the structure of Georgian Society. When James returned home during vacation periods, he and Robinson would be able to discuss theology and other matters, as both received tuition from the same masters who seemed to have a more liberal and 'down to earth' approach with regard to the position of the Church of England.

James graduated B.A. in 1732 and apparently returned to live with the family in Macclesfield until a position became available. He did not have long to wait; by 31st July 1733 he became incumbent of Disley near Stockport, suggesting a recommendation from Joseph Dale, because the patron of the living was none other than Peter Legh the Elder of Lyme Hall.

The following year an event took place which gave everyone cause to celebrate, Dorothy, the daughter of Joseph Dale, became the second wife of Samuel Lankford of Meerbrook. They were married in the church of St. Edward's, Leek on 14th May 1734. The marriage settlement must have been quite an involved affair and of some great value, particularly with the inclusion of the Meerbrook and Brassington estates. It is understood locally in Brassington Village that an old stone building, still standing close by the ancient manor house, was known to have been used in connection with the silk industry. Whether or not this was developed by Samuel Lankford is at present unknown, but he was certainly a very active and ambitious man, who would appreciate the reciprocal vitality which was present in the disposition of his young associate, Charles Roe. After the wedding, he seems to have remained in residence at the New Grange estate with his wife, Dorothy. The large house was well situated, having a background of superb scenery. It was overlooked by a huge ridge, known as 'The Roaches', straggling the heather covered hills. During late summer and autumn the dense masses of the evergreen Eurasian shrub spread their small bell-shaped flowers into a glorious carpet of deep purple, which contrasted beautifully with the magnificent bleak rocky outcrop, the latter hiding from view both the way to Buxton and the village of Flash.

Charles Roe was, by then, 19 years of age, and with neither father nor family able to support him in local politics, he knew that it would be a tough struggle to achieve anything at all. He had, however, a great attribute in his favour, he would never allow himself to do anything dishonest or illegal. There would be times in the years ahead when he would choose to overlook such transgressions in others, but only on a temporary basis, whilst he concentrated all his energies on attaining his goal before they did, thus ultimately 'scuttling' their operations. Charles knew, as did Francis Nicholson the apothecary, that he would have to become a burgess of Macclesfield if he wanted to realise his ambitions and also to have a say in the progress of the Borough, but the first step on the rung of the ladder was to own a burgage. The inscription on his monument tells us that "with a slender Portion on his entrance into Business, (he) carried on the Button and Twist manufacture in this Town, with the most active Industry, Ingenuity and Integrity", and whilst he worked hard and saved the money with which to buy his precious property, he would be perfectly well aware of the intrigues and disruptions which were taking place elsewhere in the Borough.

The person who seemed to be at the centre of the disturbances was a character by the name of Peter Davenport. The Davenport family had long been established at Bramall Hall and he was possibly the great grandson of a Peter Davenport, heir of Bramall, and his wife Anne, a member of the Legh family of Adlington Hall, who had produced a large family in the middle of the 17th century.

* * * * * * *

Peter Davenport is first recorded in Windsor, where on 1st September 1707 he became Lieutenant to Major Sol. Rapin in Lord Mohun's Regiment of Foot. By 1709 he was transferred to Lt. General Cadogan's Regiment of Horse, the 5th Dragoon Guards, where he was a Quartermaster responsible for accommodation, food and equipment. Three years later he gained a small promotion to Cornet, the lowest rank of commissioned cavalry officer in the British Army. Some years later, when William Bagshawe of Ford, near Chapel-en-le Frith, wrote to his nephew, he commented "I have also been informed that ye Adjutant's Comissary & other Collatoral Officers . . . seldom or never receive any further preferrment. Comissary Davenport of Macclesfield is an Instance of this, who was in the Post, I believe, in Queen Anne's Reign . . ."

Because of the War of the Spanish Succession, during Queen Anne's reign about fifty regiments had been raised for service in Spain and Portugal, but by the end of 1712 many were reduced and the officers placed on half pay. The fighting ultimately ended in 1714 with the signing of the Treaty of Utrecht, and the remaining regiments were put on a peace footing. Peter Davenport's final appointment seems to have been as Lieutenant in Colonel James Dormer's newly raised Regiment of Dragoons on 22nd July 1715, which would see action during the Jacobite disturbances of the following winter.

By 1723 Commissary Davenport was once more ensconced in the Macclesfield area, having married "Phebe" Smale in the fashionable Parish Church of Prestbury, on the 25th August. Although having buried at least two wives, it does not seem to have discouraged Phoebe's willingness to accept his name. She came from a family which was to grow in importance as the silk industry developed, and there is a suggestion from a later property deed that the Smales owned a twisting croft on Back Street in Macclesfield, which was almost opposite the handsome house which Peter Davenport would 'purchase' for himself some years later. It is more than likely that Peter Davenport was already a tenant in the house, giving the impression of affluence, acquiring the services of a servant, Mottershead, who later became his retainer, and presenting himself as a dashing 'young' officer in the Dragoons. A marriage settlement would, of course, be arranged and there is no doubt that Davenport would find his wife's portion very useful. As a Quartermaster in the Regiment of Foot he would have received 4s 8d. per day; in the Dragoons 5s 6d. per day, but on promotion to Cornet the increase would be to only 8s 0d. per day. This was hardly sufficient to support his intended life style, and throughout the 1730s he made purchases of secondhand clothes from the Steward of Peter Legh of Lyme. It can only be assumed that the Steward, Peter Steele, had received some sort of legal training for he recorded several amounts of one guinea for preparing leases. He also appears to have sold odd items of clothing to others; perhaps they were his own, or maybe he sold them on behalf of a relative of someone then deceased; however, amongst other things Peter Davenport acquired in February 1734 an old pair of shoes for one shilling and in October 1738 "a silk Camelot Coat Buttons & Breeches" etc. for a guinea, and his final purchase in May 1741 was for a "Drab fustian coat (excepting the buttons)" £1 5 0d., but by this period his position in society was very different indeed.

On 8th November 1728 Davenport had baptised a daughter, Elizabeth, in the Parochial Chapel, Macclesfield: her mother was not Phoebe, but Lucy Francis, daughter of John Legh of Adlington Hall and sister to Elizabeth and Charles Legh; Phoebe had died and Davenport had married yet again. Lucy's father is known to have been extremely upset about the whole affair, yet despite this her brother, Charles, seems to have gone some way towards accepting Commissary Davenport into the family. It would be impossible to speculate upon the sort of arrangements which were made regarding the jointure, if any at all under the circumstances. Charles Legh was by nature a most generous and affable man, who initially seems to have come very much under the influence of his older brother-in-law, because on 20th December 1733 the following entry was made in the Macclesfield Corporation Minute Book:

"Whereas Peter Davenport Esq. & Charles Leigh Esq two of His Majesty's J.P.s for County of Chester have lately taken upon themselves the authority of acting as J.P.s within the said Borough & consined two inhabitants Daniel Robson & John Whittaker to the prison of the Castle of Chester for demeases committed within the Borough. . ."

A suit was to follow against the "said interfering Justices" and an order was made to empower John Stafford and John Hawkins "to solicit all such suits for and upon the behalf of this said Corporation."

Charles Legh learnt his lesson, he would never again intrude upon the Macclesfield establishment but rather win his way into it and make substantial contributions towards the development of the Borough in due course. This ultimate act of arrogance by Peter Davenport seems to have been, on the one hand, a trial of strength with a newly established authority in the town, and on the other, a form of revenge for an incident which had taken place some months earlier.

General James Cholmondeley, whose family seat was near Nantwich, owned a vast area of park land in Macclesfield which was leased to several tenants. This land was part of the marriage settlement when he had married Penelope, daughter of Earl Barrymore. Apart from one or two cottages here and there, and the area which was leased and developed by the Pickford family and their lessees, the remainder was used for the growing of crops and the grazing of cattle and so forth, with some parcels converted into arable crofts, not twisting crofts. General James was the son of George, 2nd Earl of Cholmondeley, who died on the 7th May 1733 having led a distinguished military career. The Earl was succeeded by his eldest son, another George, who was then 30 years of age, and the brother of General James. As the Cholmondeleys had such extensive holdings within the Borough they, of course, took an interest in its affairs. James and his wife were to die without issue, so that the estates eventually passed via his brother to the Earls of Cholmondeley.

A surviving document relates that an election was to take place in Macclesfield for officials in the Court of the Manor and Forest and that General Cholmondeley was on his way to the town accompanied by Mr. Crew from the neighbouring town of Congleton; both were prospective candidates. As they proceeded, mounted, along the road from the south towards Macclesfield, a crowd of well-wishers, including the Mayor and Aldermen, met and escorted them all the way to the Market Place. Despite the fact that they had considerable support from the local gentry, which included Sir William Meredith of Henbury Hall and Peter Legh the Elder of Lyme, Peter Davenport, totally undeterred, considered that he was the better candidate. He had literally rallied his troops and was therefore supported by some of his military friends. Assisted by such a force, his retainer, Mottershead, had the audacity to strike Peter Legh, knock the hat off Sir William Meredith's head and use abusive language. "The Gentlemen thus affronted lookt upon this proceeding to be intended for a provocation to raise a Mob & Quarrells & therefore took no notice of it for fear any disorders might arise about it but went away". It was intended, and reported in the town, that the candidates would return to give entertainment to their friends and supporters; elections were always a marvellous opportunity for exuberance. Commissary Davenport, however, on the testimony of witnesses allowed a further rumour to circulate "that Mr. Crew had given up the Election & wo(ul)d stand no longer & thereupon he set the Bells aringing".

Word was sent to General Cholmondeley and Mr. Crew, exhorting them to return as soon as possible on another day before the election. On the next occasion of their visit, Peter Davenport was also joined by a member of the Lunt family (of the waterworks dispute in the 1690s). A great throng gathered shouting support for Cholmondeley and Crew "thereupon C(ommissary) D(avenport) struck a person twice with his Caine & after him Mottershead his Retainer Box'd him" . . . A fracas then developed, during which one of Davenport's friends charged out of his house with a "Drawn Hanger" (a short sword) threatening to cut off someone's head. After an exchange of blows, peace reigned for awhile during which Peter Davenport and his friends retired to the Angel Inn, close by in the Market Place.

The opposition supporters were already there making merry and drinking in a crowd gathered around the Market Cross. Davenport sent out a barrel of ale for his supporters, but before much ale was consumed "The Populace pulled the Bung out of it & turned the Liquor into the Channel". During the pandemonium which ensued several windows in the Angel were smashed by hurtling bricks, and finally, with a great deal of difficulty, the Mayor accompanied by Justices read the Riot Act, which had been brought into law as recently as the year 1714.

Meanwhile Messrs. Cholmondley and Crew were taking a 'quiet' drink with friends in another inn, totally unaware of what was happening. They later joined a gathering in the Grammar School where a new governor was being elected, after which they were entertained by the production of a play. The whole proceedings took four hours, and as the company dispersed, much to their consternation they found Commissary Davenport and a great many of his party armed with clubs, sticks and bricks, waiting for them on the street leading up to the school. Even the ladies were not spared, and as they waited terrified indoors, two of their coaches were damaged on arrival by having bricks thrown at the coachmen and horses. Peter Davenport subsequently insinuated that Messrs. Cholmondeley and Crew had brought a mob with them from Congleton for the intention of causing a riot. At least one influential inhabitant of the Borough felt moved to take action, and discreetly compiled a letter, the contents of which were brought to the attention of the Earl of Derby, who was responsible for the functioning of the Court of the Manor and Forest as hereditary steward. The letter contained in the greatest detail the events which had taken place.

James, 10th Earl of Derby, was not slow in taking action. It is fortunate for Macclesfield that he did not die until 1736, when the direct line became extinct and the Earldom passed to a distant cousin, Edward, because he would be fully conversant with the position of the great families in the area and would know whose opinions to rely upon. There was always the problem that his residences, situated at Knowsley and Ormskirk, were at a great distance from the town. Even his deputy, William Taylor, who had been appointed Clerk of the Court in 1715, also lived in Ormskirk, and it was appreciated that someone nearer to the area was needed in order to keep control. It was, therefore, decided to appoint a deputy Clerk as a subordinate to William Taylor, and the choice could not have been a better one. This was the man needed by the Borough to re-establish stability, someone of great stature and ability, capable of the designated task; and with his appointment Macclesfield entered a new era. His name was John Stafford.

* * * * * * *

Throughout English history the Staffords were one of those unfortunate families who had suffered many trials and tribulations, culminating in their forced surrendering of the Barony of Stafford by Roger, the last male heir, to King Charles I by an enrolled deed dated 7th December 1639. One of the junior branches of this great family had been settled in Eyam, Derbyshire, for many generations, but with the birth of five daughters in the middle of the 17th century, Humphrey Stafford's line had ended. Another minor branch was established at Bottoms (previously Botham) Hall, Mellor near Stockport, and John Stafford's coat of arms, still displayed in the entrance hall of his former dwelling house on Jordangate in Macclesfield, confirms that he was descended from the Staffords of both Eyam and Botham Hall.

The Staffords of the 17th century have long perplexed genealogists, because there appears to be a missing branch of the family. John Stafford had in his possession a portrait of "Stafford of Botham, Derby, dressed in silken hose with a white lawn collar, and his auburn hair uncovered". The painting is of the School of Vandyck, the Flemish painter favoured by Charles I. This suggests a close family relationship and was possibly John Stafford's grandfather or great grandfather. A tombstone, which formerly existed in the graveyard of Manchester Cathedral, was inscribed with the Coat of Arms of the Staffords of Botham, together with a record of the deaths of several members of a family which included the parents, John and Sarah, all dated during the second decade of the 18th century. John Stafford would later choose the name Sarah for his eldest daughter. It would seem that he and his sister, Frances were orphans, brought up by guardians within the Stafford family.

There was a connection with a Mr. Anthony Stafford of Strands, near Mellor, and as there were two Anthony Staffords living close together at this period, Mr. Stafford of Strands is always given his full designation. Baptised at Mellor on 29th December 1681, the son of John Stafford of Shaw (pronounced Shay), a farmhouse between Mellor and New Mills, Anthony Stafford appears in the Entrants Register of Gray's Inn on 5th June 1700. There is no record of him being called to the Bar, but the records of Gray's Inn are incomplete at that period; it seems more probable that he practised as an attorney rather than a barrister. He is mentioned in the Lyme Accounts, and John Ward of Capesthorne Hall refers to him as early as 13th November 1707 in a letter written to Peter Legh the Elder of Lyme Hall "Mr. Stafford has been with me with some allegations or reasons in writing for his Bill". Later in his life, John Stafford was certainly in possession of vast areas of land around the area of Mellor, which are referred to as "late in possession of Mr. Stafford" (Anthony); these included Strands, Thorset Hamlet and Middlecale.

The John Stafford buried at Manchester Cathedral on 3rd January 1712, was the son of a John Stafford of London who is known to have died during the year 1743. The circumstances suggest that young John and his sister were brought up in London by this possible grandfather, and because of the association of Anthony Stafford with John Ward of the Inner Temple, young John was accepted into Clifford's Inn, one of the preparatory schools for the Inner Temple.

The Inns of Court have always commanded respect, generating a somewhat mystical aura, perpetuated from their earliest inauguration by the Knights Templar, as a city within a city. In the year 1128, the Knights Templar (founded in 1118 to guard the roads to the Holy City of Jerusalem) came to England and settled in Holborn on a site, which is today, nearby Chancery Lane. They grew wealthy, and on this Temple estate built a monastery, church, barrack and council chambers, together with residences. However, in the year 1312 the Order was accused of corruption and evil practices, and although the charges never seem to have been substantiated, it was dissolved by the Pope. The whole of the estate passed into private hands, from whom it was leased by the Knights of St. John. After years of chaos, when unqualified persons had been practising as lawyers, it was Edward I who stepped in to bring order out of confusion by commanding that only those appointed by the Chief Justice of the Common Pleas could plead in court. Thus it became necessary to study law at a recognised school in order to become a barrister, and out of these medieval law schools, the Inns of Court grew. By 1326, the Knights of St. John were subleasing houses to professors of common law.

The Middle Temple is first mentioned in a bequest of 1404, and the Inner Temple is referred to as a "college" in a letter dated 1440. Lincoln's Inn records begin during 1422 but seem to have been pre-dated by Gray's Inn. Although the actual dates of establishment are uncertain, these four great Inns of Court have been in existence for over 500 years, and throughout their history, to qualify as a lawyer has always cost a considerable sum of money. It has also been accepted that only the sons of noble families entered these Inns of Court.

Although today the Inns of Chancery have ceased to function and many buildings have been demolished, at the beginning of the 18th century they still existed, and the Inner Temple regarded Clifford's, Clement's and Lyon's Inns as its preparatory schools. The Stafford family, therefore, must have had a considerable amount of money invested in the education of both Anthony and John. The suggestion made by some genealogists, that the family was impoverished, can now, perhaps, be regarded in a different vein. Certainly the impact of John

Stafford's presence in Macclesfield was enormous and possibly indicates the influence of John Ward and Peter Legh the Elder of Lyme in suggesting his name to the Earl of Derby.

John Stafford seems to have been born in the early years of the century and, although his early life is a mystery, he must have qualified as a lawyer judging from the cases with which he became involved. Sadly, the records of the Inner Temple suffered considerable damage during the Second World War, but certain aspects of his career seem to suggest that he was called to the Bar and was, therefore, a barrister-at-law of the Inner Temple.

Like Peter Davenport and Charles Legh, John Stafford is recorded in Macclesfield for the first time, at that fateful meeting of the Corporation on 20th December 1733, although his signature appears as a witness on a deed dated 20th March 1733, with regard to a sale of several acres of land in Townscliffe near Mellor. The outcome of the law suit, instigated by the Macclesfield Corporation against Peter Davenport and Charles Legh, is not known, but from that time onwards Peter Davenport abandoned his political ambitions in the borough. There seems no doubt that Messrs. Stafford and Hawkins (the retiring mayor) won the day, and John Stafford was appointed Deputy Town Clerk to the Corporation from 25th March 1734, so that he now held two entirely separate legal positions at the same time.

Within the year, on 21st November 1734 he married Lucy Tatton of Stockport, by licence, at the beautiful church of Taxal, not too far distant from Mellor. This was an important marriage, Lucy being the sister of William Tatton of Wythenshawe. Her brother's second marriage to Hester Egerton assured the inheritance of the Egerton Estates to their son, William Tatton Egerton, who was, of course, Lucy and John Stafford's nephew; and it was this nephew who started the rebuilding of the mansion, bequeathing a considerable part of the magnificent hall of Tatton Park near Knutsford, as we see it today. An intriguing letter survives, dated 1724, which was written by William Tatton from Wythenshawe to Peter Legh the Elder of Lyme, and seems to indicate that at that time Lucy's brother was in financial difficulties and was hoping for some assistance, being related to Peter Legh by marriage:

> "there is an absolute necessity of a speedy redemption of this Estate, or it must unavoidably sink under its heavy Burden. I purpass to waite on you at Lime in a little time, where I hope to meet with some further encouragement to the satisfation of Yr. Most Obediant Kinsman & Obliged Humble Servant, William Tatton."

No doubt he received his "encouragement", the Tatton Estates survived; Peter Legh could be a very accommodating man.

The baptism of the Stafford first born, a son, named William after his grandfather, at present cannot be traced, but the subsequent baptisms of the three daughters are recorded at the Parochial Chapel in Macclesfield.

John Stafford was quickly accepted as the bastion of Macclesfield Society, and with its latest 'recruit' the Corporation took on a new lease of life. He was elected mayor for the year 1736-37, and on 19th August 1736, an amount of £20 was paid out of public funds, to enable Mr. Thomas Heywood and Mr. Francis Nicholson (apothecary) to bring from London, one or more fire engines for the public service of the inhabitants of the Borough. The well in Wallgate, used by innkeepers, was considered to be a nuisance and was immediately "stopt up". This could have been a legitimate excuse for increasing the revenue received from water rates, by encouraging an expansion of the water supply into further parts of the town. In December of the same year, it was agreed that the position of Town Clerk, which was held for life, should be remunerated with a payment of £15 per annum.

By June 1738 the Visitation of Samuel, Bishop of Chester, was planned and he was to be entertained at the mayor's house. As the mayor for that year was none other than Francis Nicholson, he seems once more to have elevated himself beyond his station, but his delusions of grandeur were brought to an abrupt halt when, at a public meeting on the 3rd November, it was ordered:

"That for the future no Mayer of this Borough shall lend or hire the Upper Room of the Guildhall of this Borough upon any public or private occassion to any person or persons whatsoever under penalty of £5."

During this time, Davenport, although warranting no further comments in the Corporation Minute Book, had been far from idle. Having buried Lucy, and accepted condolences with the comment "God will I hope inable me to get Thorough it, as I have formerly don on the Like Occasfsions", he had married Mary Duckinfield in 1736, a year after the burial of her husband, William. The Duckinfields of Duckinfield were well acquainted with Davenport for he had leased the collection of heriots due on Death or Alienation of any tenant within the Liberty of the High Peak, and therefore had reason to call on the grieving widow. Heriots were forms of medieval death duties and fines. He also purchased a field adjoining his house on Back Street on 1st May 1736 from Sir Charles. But significantly Mary was one of the daughters of Thomas Patten, copper smelter of Warrington, and already Davenport was planning his next enterprise.

The old medieval guildhall of Macclesfield replaced by the present Town Hall in the 1820s. This print hung on the wall of the Police Department, at one time situated in the cellars of the present Town Hall. Reproduced by courtesy of A. Rowbotham.

5

THE MACCLESFIELD COPPER MINE

Much Ado About Nothing.

About the year 1735, someone climbed the steep track known as Lunt Hill, leading across the southern end of Macclesfield Common, to take a closer look at an area, just to the west of the region, where small coal mining and stone quarrying activities were taking place. A little above this area of level ground, was situated the Stone-Pit Well with its magnificent view of the valley below. Fed by a series of springs and a stream from Rulow's Hollow, it had remained the supplier of excellent water down into the town, since the dispute in 1681 when the Mayor, Aldermen and Burgesses had taken over the 'waterworks'.

Another stream, known as the Black Brook, bubbled and gurgled its way, unimpeded, down the hillside, passing close by the Stone-Pit Well. The lower catchment area for all these brooklets covered at least an estimated 200 acres, and after a storm or heavy showers of rain, the volume of water pouring down the hillside was a force to be reckoned with, causing flooding on occasion, particularly on the lower reaches of the Common. The eventual destination of the Black Brook was the River Bollin, which flowed rapidly through the valley below.

During long periods of drought, the streams became almost trickles, and it was this inconsistency in the supply of water in similar areas, that had been turned to advantage by the Romans, during their prolonged occupation of our islands centuries earlier. It has been said that the Romans brought to Britain their recipes for cheese making, which certainly benefited the county of Cheshire, as did their exploitation of the salt mines (although the latter has been disputed); but they also brought their ability to seek out mines of metal, and after hundreds of years those methods were still in use. They observed rivers and streams and looked for discoloration along the banks, due to the presence of mineral ores. Sudden torrents arising out of hills and mountains after heavy rainfall were particularly sought, and the proximity of copper ores was often detected by the harsh disagreeable taste of the water. Another method was to immerse a piece of bright iron in the stream for two or three days, and if the copper was present, the iron took on the copper colour. A candle or piece of tallow could also be submerged, in which instance the indication would be a tinge of green colour.

The interested party on Macclesfield Common was also searching for the presence of minerals, and some trace of what appeared to be copper ore must have been found, for within a few months part of the Common was staked out.

Any invasion of the Common, for whatever purpose, would be keenly observed by anyone and everyone, and because of the close proximity to the coal seams, perhaps the initial reaction was to presume that the designated area was for the intention of 'coal-getting'. In the first instance the somewhat clandestine operation must have aroused curiosity and a considerable amount of speculation because of the method used, and would soon be brought to the attention of the Mayor, Aldermen and Burgesses.

The earliest evidence of this mining is a memorandum dated "Febry 14th 1736", part of which reads:

"It is hereby agreed between Sam(ue)l Finney and John Tamblyn that the said Saml Finney shall discharge exonerate and free the s(ai)d John Tamblyn from all and every part Share or dole in the Copper Mine on Macclesfield Common . . ."

The original partnership agreement could not have been in existence very long, as the evidence on site reveals today, but this interesting episode of Macclesfield history was to be the 'acorn' from which an enormous 'oak tree' would grow. Some weeks later, on 21st May 1736, an Indenture was drawn up (the copy of which has survived) between the Right Honourable William, Lord Harrington, Baron of Harrington, on the one part and a partnership between Samuel Finney of Fulshaw near Wilmslow, Cheshire and Peter Davenport of Macclesfield on the other. As one suspects, nothing was ever straightforward when Peter Davenport was involved, and in due course, the whole procedure would take on the semblance of a comic opera. But, before recounting this event, it is necessary to understand something of the history of copper, and to establish what had taken place to inspire the interest in the site on Macclesfield Common; and also to discover who the original speculators were.

* * * * * * *

Although copper ranks very low in the order of abundance in the earth's crust, it was one of the first metals to be used by man some 10,000 years ago, after the period known as the Stone Age. It was used in the making of weapons, tools, utensils and ornaments, the latter often embellished with pieces of the ore itself, polished and shaped like precious stones, many in the form known as cabochon. The malleability of the metal and its natural outcrops made it a useful accessory for the cave dwellers, and thus the extraction, smelting and working of copper is amongst the oldest achievements of the human race. Within the last 30 years, the earliest complete smelting installations in the world have been discovered in the Timna Valley, Wadi Arabah in Israel, close by the Gulf of Akabar. They date back to at least the fourth millennium B.C. and are referred to in the Bible.

This art of copper production spread from the Eastern Mediterranean to Northern Europe towards the end of the Middle Ages. Copper artefacts have been found in many different areas, particularly Sumeria (modern Iran and Iraq), Israel and Egypt. In fact, the symbol used for copper +, known as the ankh, was originally created by the Egyptians to denote both copper and eternal life. The Greeks referred to it as "chalkos" from which many associated names have been derived, including the copper ore, chalcopyrite, which is a yellow ore. The mines of Cyprus were well-known to the Romans, which gave them the opportunity to compete with the Greeks in providing another group of associated words derived from Latin, of which cuprous and cupric are examples.

The malleability of copper has already been mentioned, and in common with other metals it has some excellent properties which include electrical and thermal conductivity, intermediate strength, absence of magnetism and a resistance to corrosion and fatigue. It also has good forgeability, which means that it is ideal for coinage, coppersmithing and drawing (important for wire making). Apart from, perhaps, the iron based alloys, copper alloys provide a degree of versatility and useful properties that cannot be approached by any other metal. The alloy of copper, revered by the Africans for its brightness and rankness of smell, was brass. It looked well and was considerably stronger than any other alloy, even after years of wear. It was particularly prized for escutcheons, handles, locks and other forms of furniture hardware and ornamental castings. Because of its copper content, it was also suitable for drawing into wire, and this had made it invaluable for use in the woollen industry from at least the medieval period. One of the woollen processes was carding which involved the use of wool cards. A wool card was actually a piece of wood with a handle on one-side and wire teeth set into leather on the other. Two cards were used together, one in either hand, and a piece of wool, having been placed between them, was combed from one to the other with great dexterity, until the wool was a mass of interlaced fibres, which could then be spun by the use of spinning wheels. Later this also appertained to the cotton and waste silk industries where fibres also had to be spun. The wire teeth in the cards were made from either iron or brass, but obviously the brass ones were preferred because of their greater durability and non-corrosive nature.

Until the reign of Elizabeth I no brass had been made in England. Her father, Henry VIII, had paid dearly for the brass required for ordnance and the woollen industry, which had to be imported from the Continent. He understood the importance of being self-sufficient, but it was left to his daughter, Elizabeth, to try to encourage the development of the industry.

During the summer of 1564, representatives from the firm of Haug & Company of Augsburg came to England bringing several mining experts with them, as a consequence of an indenture signed three years earlier which had resulted in the formation of a company to work the English mines.

In May 1565 copper ore containing silver was discovered in Cumberland, and permission obtained to bring three or four hundred foreign workmen to settle in the area and to work the mines. A period of prosperity began and the German miners brought with them a variety of tools including crucibles, assay cupels, weights, compasses etc. and even established their own brewery. This was the first time that foreign workers, on such a large scale, had actually come to England to invest in industry, without being victims of persecution. However, before long, there was such ill feeling and resentment among the local villagers, that Queen Elizabeth personally intervened by writing to the J.P.s of both Cumberland and Westmorland, urging them to placate the local populace. Their efforts, in time, were successful, as was the whole project. Smelting mills were erected and the Mines Royal Company was finally incorporated during 1568.

Whilst the main objectives had been achieved i.e. the locating and extraction of copper ore and the successful smelting of it, the industry was somewhat limited without the production of brass. At this time brass was produced by combining copper with the zinc ore, calamine. To produce good brass was a difficult process, requiring great expertise, and to this end a sister company was formed with the title, "Society of Mineral and Battery Works". The search for calamine commenced, and after several unsuccessful trials, the company was on the point of importing the mineral, when deposits were discovered on the western end of the Mendips in Somerset.

A site could now be selected on which to commence brass production, but even this proved difficult, so finally temporary smelting operations were started in Bristol Castle, which culminated in the erection of wireworks near Tintern Abbey on the river Wye. Eventually more German workmen were brought from the Tyrol to set up a workshop in which they made all sorts of wrought goods, and trade was built up with London and Keswick, but by the year 1579 Haug & Company, who felt that they were not reaping the rewards of their investments, withdrew.

The industry managed to survive for a further period by developing mines in Cornwall, Devon and Cardiganshire and one of the German personnel from Keswick, Ulrich Frosse, was made manager of a newly erected smelter at Neath in South Wales. Because of problems with mining, the industry barely survived the period up to the Civil War in the 17th century; that it did so at all was mostly due to the descendants of the German miners. The resurgence, of course, took place under the guidance of Prince Rupert, after the Restoration, but still there was insufficient impetus to keep the progression motivated, until it was suddenly realised that the demand for copper was growing with the development of the plantations in the West Indies.

The island of Barbados had become Britain's first West Indian possession in 1625, and almost immediately had been cleared for sugar cane. By the end of the 17th century it was the richest island and was the most densely populated. Jamaica, originally discovered and claimed on behalf of the King and Queen of Spain by Christopher Columbus, had a chequered history. It was finally attacked and claimed for Britain by Admiral Penn, the father of the Quaker, William Penn, together with General Venables, as a compensatory move to allay the wrath of Oliver Cromwell, Lord Protector, for their miserable failure in attacking the larger island of Hispaniola. This was in 1655, but, for many years afterwards, despite the fact that peace between England and Spain was made in 1660, the island was the subject of several attacks, and the unofficial war in the Caribbean continued, involving also the Dutch and the French. The island soon became home to hundreds of pirates and the city of Port Royal was built on its south east coast, which became the richest seaport in the Caribbean. It was known as the 'wickedst city in the world' and when it was hit by an enormous earthquake in the year 1692, it was considered to be 'the judgement of God'. Jamaica recovered only slowly, but during the early 18th century it too was beginning to develop as a profitable sugar island.

It cannot be coincidence that the Quaker Community of Bristol, closely followed by Thomas Patten of Warrington, all of whom were deeply involved in the sugar and tobacco trades, suddenly turned their attentions to copper.

Apart from land and property acquisitions, which were obviously limited, the security of one's money presented quite a problem at this period. The Bank of England was hardly 'off the ground' and there were no branch banks in England available for investors. Some Government stocks could be purchased, but with the erratic investments in the South Sea Company and the eventual victims falling 'fast and furious', anyone with a considerable amount of hard earned cash would look to expand their businesses further by diversification.

A considerable amount of capital was needed to bring a copper smeltworks into production. Initially, potters could manage with small ovens in which to bake their wares, and the boles on the Derbyshire hillsides were not excessive for the primitive smelting of lead ores, but it was impossible for a copper smelter to begin in such a small way. The considerable heat required for copper smelting could only be produced in a larger furnace, which had to be correctly lined to ensure the heat was retained, and also built in such a way as to prevent contamination of the metal. The constant renewal of oven bottoms, the repairing of the lining fabric, which were absolute essentials, and also the fact that the industry had to be highly organised with constant supplies of copper and coal, added further to the cost. Also the site for the intended smelters had to be carefully chosen to ensure as little pollution as possible to the neighbourhood, keeping in mind the direction of the prevailing winds. The purchase or leasing of such land could be an expense, particularly if penalty clauses or certain conditions were included. The pigs of copper would, of course, be transported and sold to individuals and companies for the manufacture of articles, but a copper smelter would not wish to limit his production only to the metal stage, if he was already involved in a business where copper articles were of use, or where they could be sold alongside his other products. This further extension to his smelting business involved the beating or rolling of the metal, for which a considerable amount of waterpower was needed to work the machinery. A large water wheel was imperative, in order to set in motion the pairs of rollers through which the copper passed, or to motivate the large hammers which were used in the beating and pounding of the copper.

Apart from their surfeit of cash, perhaps the incentive for the Bristol merchants and Thomas Patten was their involvement in the sugar trade, and their observations of the Dutch influence in that area.

From the middle of the 16th until the beginning of the 18th century, the vast majority of people owned pewter wares which they willed to their beneficiaries, and over 80% of these items were utilitarian table wares such as plates, dishes, chargers and saucers. The remainder included many candlesticks, drinking pots and cups.

Pewterers tended to work as individuals in London and the provincial towns, and usually employed two or three apprentices. The composition of pewter was not standardised but varied from place to place. Pewter is an alloy of tin to which additions are made in order to prevent cracking when heated, and fracturing with daily usage. The combination of lead, copper and tin was originally found to be ideal; the copper added strength and the lead workability. Analysis has shown that plates contained a higher proportion of tin than most other objects, giving them more durability, whereas flagons and measures, which were always cast, had a higher proportion of lead in their composition. Given all the variations, however, the copper content was very rarely higher than 1.5%, and the lead 3.5%.

Many pewter wares, except flatwares which were beaten, were made in moulds and these moulds were usually brazen. Brass ware at this period came under the general heading of brazen wares, and as the 17th century progressed, more and more copper, brass and bronze objects were purchased. The largest proportion of these items were cooking pots and cauldrons, with the remaining quarter comprising skillets, mortars, skimmers and ladles, chafing dishes, basins, ewers and candlesticks. By the end of the century an enormous variety of copper and brass objects were coming into use, including buttons, pins and needles, tobacco boxes and objets d'art etc. Whether or not the majority of these were made in England is in doubt; many of the pieces still in existence have the characteristic shapes of Dutch manufacture. Imports through the Port of London for the month of May 1680 have revealed cargoes of such battery, predominantly from Rotterdam, but also from Hamburg.

As previously mentioned, apart from the spasmodic periods of mining in England, the copper metal itself, essential for the production of pewter, together with the brass required for ordnance and wire etc. were actually coming from Sweden, with occasional cargoes of chests of Japanese copper brought home on East Indiamen towards the end of the century; and the Swedes, desperate for calamine, were exchanging part of their brass production for quantities of the English zinc ore.

The great brass-producing countries of Sweden, Germany and Holland, united by their Germanic origins, were renowned for their traditions in metallurgy. Their cultures were built upon myths and legends, depicting the earth as a great furnace, and their gods as giants who forged all manner of things with their anvils and hammers. This was their strength, their superiority, and the story of the god, Thor, who was depicted as an excellent blacksmith, had been handed down from generation to generation.

This great tradition also produced objects for industrial development, which included the making of huge receptacles called coppers. A copper was "a vessel of copper; commonly used for a boiler larger than a movable pot". The vessels were used in the textile industry for washing, boiling and dyeing and must have also been used in the sugar refining industry, although it has been stated that the latter were made from iron. In the early days of the sugar industry this was probably true; iron forges had been in existence in England for many centuries, but once copper became more readily available, its advantages for the sugar industry far outweighed those of iron. Another important indicator is the fact that the port of Venice had once been the centre for sugar refining in Europe, but with typical Dutch ingenuity, the centre of mercantile power had been transferred away from the Adriatic to Amsterdam, and now it was the port of Antwerp, just over the Dutch border, which controlled the Continental sugar production.

Although copper was known to give off poisonous oxides when it came into contact with acids or their salts, and therefore all copper food vessels were lined with tin, the boiling of the juice from the crushed sugar cane was carried out with the addition of milk of lime (calcium hydroxide), which removed the impurities and was ladled off. Milk of lime was alkaline and consequently there was no danger of poisoning. Coppers would heat up more quickly than iron pans, and because of the long boiling time required for the syrup to become more and more concentrated, there was less danger of contamination; iron is a more volatile metal, and likely to produce iron oxide (rust) under such conditions. After three boilings the raw sugar was transported to England for refining. The plantation owners in the West Indies were probably offered coppers for sale by the Dutch, which would be extremely expensive, and the Bristol merchants, particularly the Quakers, dedicated to their policy of being as self-sufficient as possible, would seize the opportunity, not only to satisfy their own requirements, but to provide merchandise for what was becoming a growing market for copper and brass goods.

The Dutch, who had been highly successful in the East Indies, had never really gained a hold in the trade of China. In the year 1638 they had obtained the sole right to trade with Japan, and it was from that country that chests of copper were imported.

Alongside the development of the West Indies and the Eastern seaboard of America, came the growing trade with West Africa. The Dutch had already well developed this trade in order to purchase 'negro' labour for the gold mines in Brazil. In some areas a form of currency was used comprising cowrie shells and manillas. The Dutch imported the cowrie shells into Amsterdam from the Maldive Islands, and manufactured the manillas, which were a form of brass bracelet.

The growing market for goods from England demanded cottons, beads, clay pipes, brass in the form of rods, brass manillas and bowls of all shapes and sizes. Some of these bowls acquired a ritual use as containers for fetishes. The English cottons were often rejected, but the imported Indian cottons were highly prized, as were the beads. Venice was the supplier of beads, and as the English merchants, including the Turkey merchants, sent their ships into the Mediterranean Sea to deliver herrings to Naples and wool to the Turks, they would bring back the Venetian beads together with Turkish mohair and silk, and Italian silk from Leghorn. Thousands of pounds worth of beads would eventually find their way to the West African coast; it was to become a very lucrative business.

By the beginning of the 18th century a complicated interweaving of trade was already established between the maritime nations of Europe, their infant colonies and the Continents of Asia, India, Africa and the Americas. Each was an integral part of another, but the competition created, by what appeared to be insatiable markets, was intense.

The African trade was becoming an important facet in the requirements of our plantations in the West Indies and America, as more and more strong negroes were required. Even today sugar cane cannot be cut successfully with machinery, it has to be done by hand. Indian cottons and Venetian beads for this trade had to be imported, and so it would seem brass and copper goods also.

On 23rd July 1691 the Government once more endeavoured to stimulate the waning copper industry by approving the formation of the Governor & Company of Copper Mines in England. The Mines Royal Company was still in existence, although somewhat ineffectual, particularly after the passing of the Mines Royal Act in 1689 which had taken away the restriction on the search for copper ore. Again prospecting for copper was under way, only this time there were individuals with sufficient resources and inducement to retain the momentum once the initial inspiration had faded away.

In 1692 Dockwra's Copper Company was established near Esher in Surrey, with smelting and brass production, including a wire manufactory for the important pin making trade, and another important company was founded in 1702 in Bristol, known as the Bristol Wire Company. The erection of these and other smelters produced a rush of speculators all intent on supplying copper ore to the works, from which they could make their fortunes.

Up to this time, traditionally Cheshire had not been a copper mining county; it had always held a reputation for its cheese and salt, but within the next few years that was to change.

* * * * * * *

After the dispute at the Alderley Edge copper mine during 1696, between Thomas Legh and Thomas Crosse, mining had been continued for a short period by the London merchants, Appleby, Kingston and Hath, but little is known of their activities. Initially the mining would have taken the form of opencast, but having located a vein of ore, the miners would work along the vein and follow it into the ground.

As the name indicates, the Edge is the brink of an uplifted block of sandstones, mudstones and marl, which was formed some 180 million years ago, in the Triassic period of prehistory. In effect, though not geologically, it is the last rocky 'outpost' of the Peak District, projecting just a little way into the Cheshire Plain. On a clear day, an uninterrupted view of the Mersey Estuary can be seen, with the lush green pastures of Cheshire, representing some of the finest agricultural land in the world, spreading westwards as far as the eye can see.

At various stages throughout its history, this small area has been wooded, and then left barren for a while during periods of increased activity, and consequently much surface erosion has taken place from time to time. It has previously been suggested that, due to volcanic activity far below the earth's surface, the deposits of copper ore, which are predominantly green malachite and the bright blue mineral azurite, infiltrated into the area through fissures and faults after the formation of the rock. Subsequent weathering and penetration of rainwater over a considerable period of time caused the infiltration of the sandstones by copper ores, creating a speckled effect. Recently, however, further theories have been put forward and the subject is still open to debate.

Perhaps the first indication of the presence of copper was due to the malachite, because in certain areas above the veins, the vivid rich colour of the green vegetation is instantly noticeable and must have attracted the original speculators to the site. This early mining, with the use of picks and hammers, appears to have taken place on the Eastern side of the Edge, where part open cast workings have been discovered at Engine Vein and in the northern area of the old Alderley quarry. The mines adjacent at Stormy Point, which are mostly situated just over the parish border in Over Alderley, could also have been worked at this early period.

According to a *"General View of the Agriculture in Cheshire"* written by Henry Holland and published in London during 1808, a gentleman by the name of Mr. Abbadine of Shropshire, who creates the impression of having been a somewhat elusive character, had been mining the Edge about one hundred years earlier i.e. circa 1708. From information now emerging, this date appears to be too early and more than likely occurred during the first half of the 1730s.

Already Bristol was developing into a Quaker stronghold, and Abraham Darby, later to become famous as an ironmaster, had moved there during 1699. The Quakers grew to dominate the copper and brass industries of the Bristol area, and remembering that Sir Thomas Stanley of the Old Hall, Alderley, had been a strong Puritan, it is entirely possible that Mr. Abbadine was searching for copper ore with the intention of supplying the Bristol works, rather than the Church of England copper smelter, Thomas Patten of Warrington.

Other fragments of associated evidence exist, but must not be taken as conclusive. The names of Hibberdine and Mottershead are entered as joint occupiers of a property on Chestergate in Macclesfield in the year 1743, for Land Tax purposes. Hibberdine is an unusual name, but Abbadine seems non-existent; so was this the same person, or a member of the same family?

There was a small family of Hibberdines living in London, early in the 18th century, who were possibly Dissenters. The Mottersheads were also known to have been Puritan sympathisers, with a member of the family collecting rents in the Macclesfield area, during and after the Civil War, on behalf of Sir William Brereton, Commander of the Parliamentary forces. The Mottersheads, unlike the Hibberdines, were a numerous family, with several of them living in and around the Alderley area. Thomas was a recurring Christian name amongst their members, and one of them had made a large fortune in London, during the

Commonwealth period, as a dungster, presumably responsible for the disposal of human and animal excrement by its conversion into manure. He had used part of this money as an investment by purchasing several properties in Chester, some situated on Foregate Street and Fleshmongers Lane. He bought them on 6th June 1662 from Peter Warburton of Arley, whose descendants have provided the beautiful gardens of Arley Hall in Cheshire for our pleasure and enjoyment today. Perhaps Thomas Mottershead had organised the supply of cartloads of manure for the original gardens. Manure was an important commodity which was sometimes mentioned on property deeds relating to land, particularly where it was leased. A clause was included to ensure that any manure kept on the land at the time of vacation, was to be left for the use of the next occupier.

The Mottershead, who was jointly occupying the Chestergate property with Mr. Hibberdine, was more than likely related to Peter Davenport's retainer, who had interests in one or two other properties close by.

The only other documented mine in Cheshire to be worked for copper ore up to this time was located at Bickerton near Chester, and the spasmodic periods of mining there followed the same pattern as Alderley. There is a reference to the Chester copper mines as early as the 1670s, and one suspects that Alderley had also been surveyed about that time. By 1690 the Bickerton mine was being worked by a handful of men on behalf of the owner, Sir Philip Egerton. Almost two years after the Alderley dispute, in 1697, Sir Philip was contacted by Sir Humphrey Mackworth of Gnoll near Neath in South Wales suggesting that he should send his copper ore to a public copperworks which Sir Humphrey proposed to build. Here, once more, was a strong Puritan family becoming involved in the industry. Sir Humphrey's grandfather, Colonel Mackworth, had presided over the fateful trial of the Earl of Derby at Chester, on the 29th September 1651. Sir Humphrey himself put money into a mine in Merioneth during 1697, followed by a copper mine in Pembrokeshire and tin mines in Cornwall, but all without success. He did, however, establish "The Governor and Company of the Mine Adventurers of England" known briefly as "The Mine Adventurers of England" in 1699. The Governor was the Duke of Leeds and Sir Humphrey was the Deputy. The Company seemed a great success, having been funded by a form of lottery, but by 1707 they were accused of scandalous frauds and a Commons Committee found Mackworth both responsible and guilty. He was a very powerful man and survived by sheer personality; within a short time he was drawing up proposals for another company and writing political pamphlets. This was, of course, the period in which the South Sea Bubble was growing and many financial intrigues were afoot. One cannot help wondering if the choice of company name was a deliberate ploy to cause confusion with the Governor and Company of the Copper Mines in England, encouraging people to invest in what they thought was a Government scheme, when actually it was the brainchild of Sir Humphrey.

The Mackworths had originated from the village of Mackworth in Derbyshire, and on their family tree were members of the Church, including a Dean of Lincoln. By a strange turn of fate Sir Humphrey's son, Herbert felt that he was also destined for the Church, but his father refused to allow such a thing. It might be politic for the family to attend the Church of England once more, but actually to contribute towards its survival by allowing his son to devote his time and energies to it, was an entirely different matter. Years later this was to have a significant effect on relations between the Mackworth Company and an important copper company based in Macclesfield.

The owner of the Bickerton mine, Sir Philip Egerton, died in 1698 and was succeeded by his son, John. Several attempts to work the mine took place during the first two decades of the century, and although the quality of the copper ore raised was exceptional, its occurrence in the veins was patchy, so that little quantity was actually mined. After a few unproductive years, a letter was written on 10th April 1735 by a William Church of London, on behalf of a Shropshire gentleman, enquiring about the possibility of re-working the mine. He personally carried out an inspection, agreed a royalty of $^1/_6$ of the ore raised and obtained a lease; work recommenced once more, but after raising 44 tons of capital ore (good quality) no further mining seems to have taken place for the remainder of the 18th century.

Although the people and events may or may not be closely connected, one important fact emerges, that since the days when Elizabeth I had brought German miners from the Tyrol to find her copper ores, and had been successful for a time working the mines of Keswick in the Lake District, apart from Ecton Hill in Staffordshire, copper had been mined as a secondary ore in the tin and lead mines and in the Royal mines where gold and silver were found, but now the race was on to find mines predominantly of copper. Whoever monopolised these mines would also monopolise the copper smelting industry of England and Wales. The Quakers knew this and were well aware of the consequences. One Quaker family in particular would become notorious for their machinations as the 18th century progressed, for they ruthlessly dedicated themselves to a complete take-over of everything in which they became involved. The patriarch of this family was Nehemiah Champion, merchant of the City of Bristol, who had a close association with Abraham Darby.

Abraham Darby's family were farmers and nailmakers in the Midlands, but about the year 1702 he became concerned with brass production. The process of converting copper into brass was still not understood properly in England, and it is said that Darby went to Holland and hired some Dutch workmen, who helped him set up the brass works at Baptist Mills. After six years Darby became interested in cast iron and built a foundry in Cheese Lane, Bristol, but a year later, in 1709, his enthusiasm took him to Coalbrookdale, where he established a blast furnace for which he used coke. Darby's friend, Nehemiah Champion, seems to have replaced him at Baptist Mills, which subsequently became known as the Bristol Brass Company, and Nehemiah continued the experiments of brass making until finally he took out a patent No. 454 on 20th April 1723, part of which reads:

> "A Method of converting Copper into Brass by a New Way of Preparing the Copper to receive a much greater Proporcon of Calamy & make a much greater increase of Brass from Coppe . . . in much less time & less Expence than has been done by any Method before . . . (also) a new Way of Nealing the Plates & Kettles with Pitt Cole . . ."

The staunch Church of England family involved in Bristol copper and brass were the Costers, who were rivals to the Bristol Copper Company. Thomas Coster, the eldest of three brothers, was elected M.P. for Bristol in 1734. By coincidence Rev. Thomas Secker, whose letters to his family in Chesterfield have provided so much delightful information regarding the South Sea Bubble, the mysterious light in the sky and his trip to France some years earlier, was now Bishop of Bristol. On 14th June 1735 he wrote to his brother:

> "I shall be glad to put my Share of the Leadmines intirely into the Hands of the good Friend you intimate. But to tell you a Truth which perhaps you will wonder at, though I have had good Preferment a great while and have now I believe £1100 and neither I nor my wife are negligent yet partly with the Expence of coming into Preferments and partly with living and giving away suitably to them, I am not one shilling richer that when I lived with you . . ."

Another of the Coster brothers, John, who had formed a syndicate to work some Cornish mines, was said to be supplying many Bristol concerns with copper until his death in 1731. This change of circumstance possibly disrupted the availability of the copper ore and encouraged individuals such as Samuel Finney of Fulshaw near Wilmslow, Cheshire to try to fill the gap.

The Finneys were an important family whose name was originally Finnie or Fiennes, again suggesting a strong Puritan connection, as in the case of Celia Fiennes and her father, the Cromwellian General. Samuel I, born circa 1630, had been a merchant in Barbados and made a fortune out of sugar and cotton. He married Mary, the daughter of a planter Mr. Evans, whose family at that time were quite famous, one of them being Lt. Governor of Pennsylvania. He returned to England and to Cheshire, where he bought the Alcock Green Estate which had formerly belonged to the Davenports of Chorley. His next purchase was the Old Hall at Fulshaw near Wilmslow, which he demolished in order to provide a suitable location for his 'perfect' family home. This was completed by 1684, having taken two years and a good deal of planning, which included a model of the proposed house carved in wood. Together with his son, John, he accompanied William Penn, the Quaker, to Pennsylvania and helped to organise the colony.

John returned to England during 1711 and about this time his father died, but the name of Samuel had been given to John's eldest son, who was subsequently known as Samuel II. This Samuel grew into a totally irresponsible young man. His secret marriage in 1718 to Esther, the daughter of Ralph Davenport of Chorley, incurred his father's "extreme displeasure"; but by 1721 his father-in-law had provided a business for him as a linen merchant in Warrington, the town in which Thomas Patten was now carrying on the successful business of copper smelting. Within the year, Samuel ll was in partnership with members of his wife's family in Manchester and held interests in the Davenport mining concerns in Cornwall. During the early 1730s he gave up the Manchester connections and returned to Fulshaw Hall, where he carried out extensive repairs and additions, but his extravagant life style would ultimately cause problems.

From Finney's extant accounts and papers he appears to have owned a ship, the captain of which sailed under his instructions. Cotton and linen goods were taken down the coast, probably to Bristol for onward despatch to the West Indies and America in larger sea-going vessels. Several household items and provisions were also loaded, destined for Cornwall, after the discharge of which, copper ore was taken on board for the return voyage to Bristol. One presumes that the return cargo from Bristol would be predominantly sugar, raw cotton and tobacco brought in from the Colonies. No journey was ever wasted, and after the specified lading had been placed on board, ships' captains would often pick up whatever goods they could, to try to ensure that as far as possible they sailed with their holds full.

Samuel II continued his investments in the mines of Cornwall, and for the eight years 1730-38, he held shares in tin, lead and copper mines in the Parish of St. Columb Major and Budock. During February 1731 he had purchased a $1/16$ part of a lease for fifty guineas in the 'Whale' Swallow lead mine in Truro from a Mr. Thomas Dewstoe, and on 13th July 1731 he had paid ten guineas for a $1/16$ share of the Wheal Trugo copper mine in the parish of St. Columb Major, which he still held in 1738. His investments in Truro were further extended during 1734 with the involvement in a tin mine called 'Whale' Roseland, and finally in the October of that year he "allowed Captain Tamblyn £22 2 10d. for sundry wares sold him in July last & likewise £3 2 2d. for cost of Whalan Chance".

Captain Tamblyn could have been an officer in the army, because both the Finneys and Davenports had military connections, but he was more than likely a Captain in one of the larger Cornish mines. Captain was a title given to the man who directed the work above and below ground. He was an experienced miner who had under him "Bottoms-Captains", who worked below ground and "Grass Captains", who worked above the ground. (A Grass Captain in a copper mine was called the Dresser and he was responsible for keeping a day book and delivering materials, such as gunpowder, shovels, candles etc. to the men). It was presumably this Captain Tamblyn who had entered into a partnership agreement with Samuel Finney to sink a mine on Macclesfield Common. For reasons best known to himself, Captain Tamblyn quickly withdrew before a mining lease could be completed, but Finney confident of success looked around for another partner, ironically finding Peter Davenport (a possible relative by marriage). Who talked whom into what, must have been quite amusing. Finney, anxious that no more time should be wasted and no more partners lost, this time approached Baron Harrington for a formal lease.

At the time of Thomas Roe's curacy at the Parochial Chapel, the Earl of Macclesfield had taken over the lease for encroachments on the Common, but in the year 1712 this had been re-assigned to William Stanhope, diplomatist and statesman, who had been created Baron Harrington on 6th January 1730.

There still seemed to be some confusion regarding legislation relating to copper mines, but as copper was usually located in mines in a three lode situation i.e. lead, zinc and copper, or as in Cornwall, tin and copper, the mining of it in Cornwall was usually covered by the tin mining or Stannary Laws, whereas in Derbyshire (where the three lode occasionally pertained), the lead mining laws, upheld by the Barmoot Court, sufficed. The lease was obviously drawn up to cover for the discovery of any or all of the three associated ores, tin, copper or lead, and one would have expected the lead mining laws of Derbyshire to be applied on Macclesfield Common; it is interesting to note that Samuel Finney, being conversant with the mining techniques of Cornwall, must have suggested the alternative. The lease stipulates that Samuel Finney together with Peter Davenport "shall and will work these Mines . . . according to the rules . . . Escribed by the Stannary Law or Customs in the County of Cornwall." Under this Law, as the mine was to be sunk on Common ground, Samuel Finney was compelled to give three months notice in a Stannary Court so that the Lord of the soil (i.e. Baron Harrington in this instance) could object. How Finney managed this in Cheshire is not known, but as Baron Harrington seemed in favour of the idea, perhaps this formality was ignored, although the statutory three months notice seems to have been complied with. Captain Tamblyn had withdrawn from the partnership on 14th February, and it was just over three months to the dating of the lease on the 21st May.

The next preliminary event was the selection of the site upon which the mining would be allowed to take place, under the terms of the lease. The piece or portion of land to be "enjoyed" by the owner of the mine was approximately one acre, and as a Cheshire acre was considerably larger than a normal acre, being 10,240 square yards, (a statute acre is 4,840 square yards) perhaps Samuel Finney realized that he was literally able to gain ground by adopting the Cornish mining laws rather than those of Derbyshire. The bounds or outer limits of this area could take the form of either a square or triangle, depending on whether three or four "Corners" were formed. A "Corner" was a hole cut in the turf with the soil turned back on top of the turf, in the form of a mole hill. On completion of the three or four "Corners", straight lines were drawn from one to another, creating an outer limit. It was then possible to sink shafts anywhere within the area.

From the site evidence today, the piece of ground chosen by Finney was triangular shaped, and he succeeded in claiming a Cheshire acre. The lease was to run for 21 years, and the partnership allowed to build "any Engine or Engines, Burninghouse or houses Stamp or Stamps" etc. and, of course, were entitled to water rights. Lord Harrington was to be given $1/6$th share of the ore when it had been dressed and was fit for sale. For this purpose two buddles were dug out almost immediately alongside the Black Brook, so that sufficient water could be diverted into them for the washing of the ore. The buddles, which were circular, appear to have been the same shape as the ones on Ecton Hill in Staffordshire. Once the ore had been taken out of the ground, the first job, usually done by two men, was to break it into small pieces with hammers; then it was sorted, usually by small girls. At Ecton there were three grades, best, second and worst. Keeping the heaps separate, the ore was once more crushed with flat hammers, this time by women. They sat back to back on a bench to enable them to buck or beat the ore into a fine sand. In Cornwall they were known as bal maidens. The ore could now be transferred to the buddles for washing. This operation had to be superintended carefully, otherwise some of the best ore particles could be washed away.

By this method, if the copper ore was a good grade, it was sifted initially with a griddle or iron wire sieve of one inch mesh or less, and put for sale without dressing. The remainder of the ore, which had passed through the griddle or sieve, was then crushed into pieces the size of peas and washed repeatedly with the aid of other sieves, each successive sieve becoming progressively finer. The ore remaining in each of these sieves was then graded for sale.

* * * * * * *

Very little ore could have been raised on Macclesfield Common, although at least six shafts have been discovered on the site. However, Samuel Finney had commenced his operations in great style, and had built and furnished a house, close by the mine, for the convenience of the miners. He had also purchased the necessary timber from a near neighbour of his, called John Leigh. His expenses must have been mounting because one of the shafts, which has been surveyed, is beautifully constructed. It is approximately 75 ft deep, circular in execution, with a diameter of 7 ft 6 in. The top 15 ft, which represents the depth of the clay soil, is neatly lined with bricks; the remainder is hewn out of rock strata with bedrock at the bottom.

After the initial burst of activity, at this point in the operations Samuel Finney disappeared, without having paid John Leigh for the timber. Leigh endeavoured for some time to contact him, as apparently did other creditors, and finally on learning that Peter Davenport was Samuel Finney's partner, he took out a lawsuit against Peter Davenport.

Peter Davenport was forced into action. He did not engage John Stafford to take on his case (presumably because of the Corporation law suit), instead he approached Edward Chetham, Recorder of Macclesfield, who, himself, was the subject of a strange set of circumstances. The draft of Davenport's legal answer is both amusing and revealing. He denied that he had been in partnership with Samuel Finney before 1st June 1737, but confirmed that from that date the partners in the Macclesfield copper mine were as follows:

"Peter Davenport	$2^{1}/_{2}$	shares representing	$^{5}/_{16}$ths.
Robert Heys (now deceased)	1	shares representing	$^{2}/_{16}$ths.
Samuel Finney (A.W.L.)*	$3^{1}/_{2}$	shares representing	$^{7}/_{16}$ths.
Daniel Finney	1	shares representing	$^{2}/_{16}$ths."

* Presumably this meant 'Absent Without Leave'.

It took almost nine foolscap sheets of paper, containing a carefully worded explanation, to produce the following details. Peter Davenport had discussed the idea of a partnership with Samuel Finney some time during May 1736. Lord Harrington was contacted by the four intended partners in respect of a lease being drawn up, but at that time and for some considerable time afterwards, Davenport had "continued in London". As the existing document is only a copy of the original lease, and bears no signatures, confirmation of the actual partners cannot be ascertained, but the copy definitely refers to only Samuel Finney and Peter Davenport.

Samuel Finney must have taken Davenport's word and commenced operations. Davenport stated that he was surprised to receive a letter from one of the other partners, Mr. Heys, in which he was informed that Samuel Finney had built and furnished a house upon the Common for the miners "having not then agreed upon a Partnership with him".

At the commencement of the partnership on lst June 1737, Samuel Finney delivered to the other partners a statement of expenses which had been allowed, with the money advanced to partnership stock. Davenport confirmed that Finney was a near neighbour of John Leigh's, and having dealt with him previously, he might have bought some timber and other goods from him during 1736, but Davenport did not know.

Davenport expressly denied that on 17th September 1736 he and Samuel Finney had paid John Leigh £10 as part of his demand, nor did he know "that Samuel Finney alone paid the £10". On the advice of Samuel Finney, John Leigh had drawn up a bill for £17, in the names of Samuel Finney and Peter Davenport, representing the remainder of the money due. As Leigh owed money to one of his creditors, Edward Cherry, he asked that the order "with words and figures" be made "payable to one Edward Cherry". Davenport denied all knowledge of Edward Cherry and stated that the bill must have remained unpaid because "Finney was not able or not willing to pay it". Davenport suggested that Finney had accepted the bill on his own private account and not as a partner, and that the bill had not been included in his expenses claim to the partnership. Davenport concluded this part of his denial by stating that he did believe the bill was "settled in Macclesfield".

Samuel Finney had kept out of the way of his creditors for some time, but having made some arrangements with them, he was again seen in public until February 1738, when he finally "went beyond the seas".

Peter Davenport claimed that he had been at his own dwelling house in Macclesfield for several months, only five miles from John Leigh, and that neither he nor the other two partners, Robert Heys and Daniel Finney, had received any demands for a period of up to six months after Samuel Finney had absconded. The bill presented was now in the amount of £19 15 7^{1}/$_{2}$d. (presumably because interest had been added).

During the month of August 1736, it was understood that Samuel Finney had assigned his share of the partnership to James Marsden and Joshua Marriott, merchants of Manchester, by way of mortgage for securing certain sums of money, and "within a few days they asked for possession of Samuel Finney's shares towards satisfaction of their debts."

Nothing further is known of the mining venture. During 1738, Samuel Finney appeared in the developing city of Philadelphia in Pennsylvania. He never returned to England, and was lost to his family for long periods. He lived for a time in Port Lewis on the River Delaware and Annapolis in Maryland, but was last heard of, again in Philadelphia, in the year 1764.

Peter Davenport turned his attentions to his military connections in Chester. His former brother-in-law, Charles Legh, who had married Hester, daughter and co-heiress of Robert Lee, of Wincham near Chester, had begun to take an active part in County affairs, becoming a Colonel of Militia, and this family connection certainly helped to further Peter Davenport's career. He managed to obtain the position of Receiver General for the County, which was in effect Collector of Taxes, and through this newly acquired authority once more interfered whenever possible in the affairs of Macclesfield.

Edward Chetham, barrister-at-law and Recorder of Macclesfield from 1740 to 1750, who had prepared Peter Davenport's answer to the suit, was a member of the famous Chetham family of Manchester, whose ancestor had built the Library close by St. Mary's Church, (now Manchester Cathedral), and founded the Chetham Society. Edward Chetham's presence in Macclesfield is a mystery except for the fact that he was distantly related to the Stafford family. The last Stafford heir of Botham Hall in Mellor, was Thomas, who had a son, Tristram, and the two of them are known to have sold the Estate to the Chetham family in 1704, because it was heavily mortgaged. The probable truth is that the Chethams had loaned money to the Staffords, and had claimed the estate by right of seizure. Perhaps some pressure was put on John Stafford, and as an obligatory gesture he was instrumental in obtaining for Edward Chetham the position of Recorder. After leaving Macclesfield, Edward Chetham took a post in Castleton near Rochdale, Lancashire and using his legal position, fraudulently acquired the Chetham estates from his young nephew who was in the army. Chetham had actually torn the leaf out of the Salford Register on which the baptism of his nephew was recorded, to insinuate that the boy was illegitimate. The fraud was eventually proved and Edward Chetham "at last blew his brains out in a room at Castleton in 1789."

Of the remaining personalities involved in the Macclesfield copper mine, James Marsden and Joshua Marriott, merchants of Manchester, who had acquired Samuel Finney's share, were an important link in the chain of events which was about to take place.

At this period there is virtually no evidence of Charles Roe's activities, they can only be deduced from what is known of the economic background, the circumstances which pertained in the area and the facts which emerge from 1739 onwards.

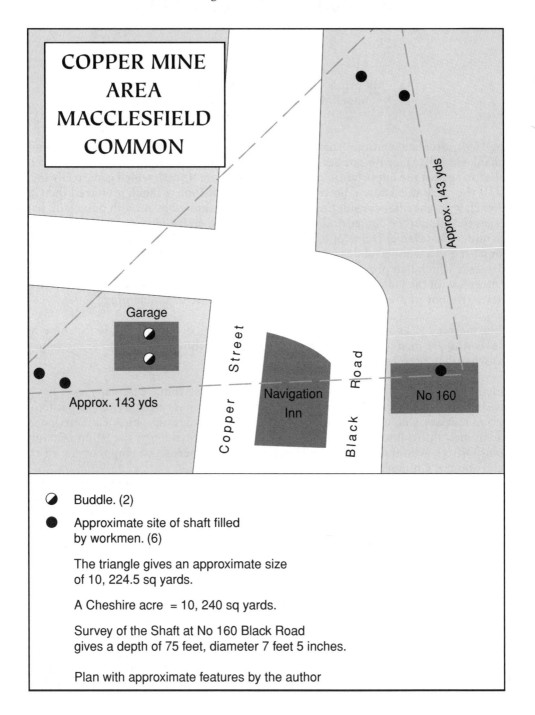

COPPER MINE AREA MACCLESFIELD COMMON

Approx. 143 yds

Garage

Copper Street

Navigation Inn

Black Road

No 160

Approx. 143 yds

◐ Buddle. (2)

● Approximate site of shaft filled by workmen. (6)

The triangle gives an approximate size of 10, 224.5 sq yards.

A Cheshire acre = 10, 240 sq yards.

Survey of the Shaft at No 160 Black Road gives a depth of 75 feet, diameter 7 feet 5 inches.

Plan with approximate features by the author

6
ADMITTED GRATIS

My prime of life in wand'ring spent and care,
Impell'd with steps unceasing, to pursue
Some fleeting good....

During 1699, after lamentations from silk weavers, when they had declared "the Buttonmakers may thank God that they do not have an East India Company to cope with", they did obtain prohibition against the importation of wrought silks from 'India', which generically included China. If the truth was known, however, the English customers much preferred the Chinese and French wrought silks, considering them far more fashionable. As with porcelain, patterns were sent to China to be copied and were either woven, embroidered or painted on the silk. By the mid-1720s Daniel Defoe observed "that the silk manufacture of England is increased and improved to a wonderful degree." We were now producing broad-silks, velvets, brocades and damasks which had previously been imported from Italy and France. Unfortunately for the mercers, with the ladies' preference for French silks, Defoe eagerly pointed out they had no alternative but to pretend that English silks were French, commenting:

> "the mercer . . . knows that there are master-weavers in Spitalfields, with whom he deals who are men of exquisite art . . . (and) that nothing comes from France equal to what they perform here."

Had the silk weavers known what problems the East India Company was having in purchasing raw silks, particularly from China, they might have been more sympathetic; it is surprising that any Chinese raw silk was being taken on board the ships. Chinese merchants were extremely difficult to deal with, being officially superintended by the Hoppo, an Imperial Customs Officer, who represented the Emperor. Both Emperor and Hoppo were, of course, Manchu and not Chinese.

Crew members were allowed their own purchases which were limited according to rank. Many of these were sold on arrival home and a handsome profit made, though often denied by the gainer. Amongst the private trade, silk handkerchiefs were very popular; a handkerchief piece contained twenty handkerchiefs, each measuring one yard square. Very few ships were making the long voyage to China and the Far East each year; returning the following year, but nevertheless their imports were significant. Two ships dispatched from Canton during the winter of 1729-30 had private cargoes on board which included:

> 'Mr. William Fazakerley Handkerchiefs 758 pieces each 20 handkerchiefs. Captain Elliston Handkerchiefs 50 pieces' (presumably each 20 handkerchiefs).

Until the year 1731 it had been the practice to pack all raw and wrought silks in chests, but from that year a new method was adopted; the raw silk from Nankeen was kept in the package in which it was contained, then covered with a good wax cloth, over which a matt cloth was secured. The bale was then "rattan'd" i.e. further secured with canes in a sort of wickerwork arrangement, thus reducing its size and enabling more goods to be taken on board than when the silk was stowed in chests. (The silks imported from other countries apart from China had always been in bales).

The first direct purchase of tea from China, an amount of 2lbs 2ozs. bought by the East India Company Directors, had been made in 1664. It was a small beginning, but by 1718 tea was starting to displace woven silks, probably encouraged by the prohibition policy.

Large quantities of sago were also brought back. The sago was shovelled directly into the hold and those pieces of Chinese porcelain which were hollow wares, such as bowls, dishes, spittoons etc, were actually packed in, and filled with, the sago to reduce breakages.

Copper importations continued; in 1700 the copper and tea purchases were approximately equal in weight. By 1702 larger quantities of copper were demanded, and in 1703 both "Japan" (Japanese copper in the form of cakes, not pigs) and China copper were bought at Macao; however, the charge for the Japanese copper was almost 30% more than the Chinese, which resulted in the purchasing of Chinese copper only for the next few years. This copper came from the province of Yunnan, which is situated on the borders of Burma, Laos and Vietnam. The region is very mountainous but rich in minerals, and at the same time as the copper purchases were made, the valuable metal tungsten was obtained, but in smaller quantities, which was (and still is) found in the same region. From this time onwards, of course, the search for English copper was progressing.

Copper, exported out of the Port of London to India at the beginning of the century, took the form of plates from Sweden and was required by the East India Company for use in the forts developing to protect trade. Goods taken to China were mostly woollens and lead, but the great demand was for silver; however, the greatest difficulty was in providing any English products which the Chinese would buy, whilst at the same time supplying the large quantities of silver demanded.

Some raw silk was purchased in Bengal, India, but this was becoming increasingly expensive. By the 1730s hardly any raw silk could be obtained from China, and none at all arrived during the year 1736. This was an important year because there ascended the throne of China a talented young man by the name of Kienlung. During his long reign, which would last until 1795, he encouraged overseas trade, although in his early years his orders were often conveniently manipulated. In 1750 the English Parliament would reduce the duty on Chinese raw silk to that of Italian, by which time, however, a resurgence of the importation of Chinese raw silk was already taking place.

The year 1736 was also important in England, for at last the medieval shackles were shaken loose and we stepped into the modern world with the Repeal of the Witchcraft Act.

Unfortunately at this time, the button trade, concentrated around the area comprising Stockport, Macclesfield, Congleton and Leek, was suffering a decline, and a group of merchants took action. Amongst them was Samuel Lankford of Leek, who personally attended a House of Commons Committee meeting where he, together with several others, put forward their grievances.

It is amusing to see the tactics employed by the merchants outside London, who were determined to ensure that they received trade protection through legislation in order to prevent the trade of the capital completely monopolising the whole country. The fact that the East Indiamen could only be unloaded in the Port of London was in itself very restrictive, particularly to the Northern Counties, so time after time, as the 18th century progressed, more and more "thousands of poor" were added to petitions; but where were they in reality?

An official census never took place during the 18th century, and people really had no idea of crowd capacities. The population of Macclesfield in 1720 has always been quoted as approximately 4,400, based on a figure of 925 families collated by Bishop Francis Gastrell, Bishop of Chester, but on evidence now emerging from property deeds, this figure seems to be the approximate number of people rather than families. Certainly the population could not have been in excess of 1,500 in 1720, and by 1737 had probably reached about 2,000. A list of poor exists for the town dated 1722, on which 150 names appear, some of whom would only have been temporarily considered as poor e.g. a man sustaining injuries which would keep him from his work for a while.

The petitioners contended that 30,000 people were employed in the button trade of the counties of Chester, Stafford and Derby, but of late many were suffering great difficulties because of its decline. This large figure would not only include the entire estimated population within the Flash area, which covered the borders of Cheshire, Staffordshire and Derbyshire, but also London importers and their families and servants, chapmen who came from other areas, together with their families at home, and probably the crews of the ships sailing to Turkey, Italy and China to bring back raw materials. How often today are figures contrived to prove all sorts of conclusions?

An Act of 1722 was referred to, by which the prohibition of wearing buttons and buttonholes made of cloth, serge and other stuffs encouraged the consumption of raw silk and mohair yarn, which had given great stimulation to the trade. Merchants stated that once again raw silk was being imported from Italy together with Turkish silk, and that one or two consignments were arriving on East Indiamen, (probably from Bengal).

* * * * * * *

By 1736 Charles Roe was 21 years old and had certainly fostered connections in the townships of both Stockport and Leek. Whilst in his teens he must have travelled to London and Chester in order to buy the essential raw materials for the Macclesfield area, leaving home shortly after dawn to make full use of daylight hours.

The journey to Chester would take Charles close by the Birtles estate en route for Monk's Heath, an important crossroads approximately four miles distant from the market cross of Macclesfield. Within a further five miles, the road came close to the birthplace of Mary, Charles's deceased mother. As mentioned, her father had been curate of Nether Knutsford, a chapelry of the parish of Rostherne, but now Knutsford was growing in importance to such an extent, that from 1741 it would become a parish in its own right. The town, situated on a main highway from the south, via Warrington to Liverpool, was already a post town, which gave it an 'elite' position and brought in extra revenue. John Ward, barrister-at-law of Capesthorne Hall, in a letter dated 30th April 1706, writing from the Inner Temple to a friend, had concluded:

"P.S. Macc(lesfield), friend, have been a little out of ye way about ye post & you turn Manchester post to Knutsford road, there's an end of all hopes of making Macclesfield a post town."

After leaving Knutsford the level route continued onwards across the Cheshire Plain to Northwich, a town with growing potential. Its location, just below the confluence of the rivers Weaver and Daven (Dane) had made its selection a necessity for the construction of quays and wharfs as part of the River Weaver Navigation Scheme. The Weaver ended its journey by flowing into the estuary of the Mersey, giving convenient access to the small but rapidly improving port of Liverpool, at the mouth of the great river.

As recently as the year 1720, the Weaver was navigable for six miles above Frodsham Bridge, but only at high tide. In that year a group of "gentlemen" had formed a syndicate to fund and obtain an Act of Parliament in order to extend the navigability of the river from Frodsham Bridge, beyond Northwich to Winsford Bridge, a distance of some 20 miles. Charles would observe these advancing improvements with interest, but during the early years of his life it would not be necessary for him to travel to Liverpool, a situation which he would later well regret. He might have made the journey out of curiosity and interest, but as always, taking goods for sale and not returning empty handed. The highlight of this journey would be a visit to the smelt works of Thomas Patten in Warrington, which were becoming quite a tourist attraction, and no doubt making contact with some of the personnel in the employ of Peter Legh the Elder of Lyme, which enabled him to assess the activities taking place in the coalfields of South Lancashire. At this time, however, his principal involvement does seem to have been with the city of Chester.

A convenient stop for refreshment was in Northwich, from where one of the most delightful parts of the journey was about to take place; it was the section through the Delamere Forest.There several hamlets lay nestled between the trees, and large numbers of red fallow deer darted across the path of unsuspecting visitors. It was a comparatively short ride out of the forest to the East Gate, an arched stone gateway, one of the four entrances into the city.

For many centuries Chester had been an important port, having under its jurisdiction the outports of Lancaster, Liverpool and several smaller harbours, but by the beginning of the 17th century, the silting up of the Dee Estuary had reached an advanced stage, causing sea-going vessels to anchor by the town of Neston, a distance of ten miles. This gave rise to the small but convenient quay of Parkgate being constructed on the shore below the town, with goods transported overland to and from Chester city. Two Acts of Parliament, passed in the reign of William and Mary, enabled a channel to be cleared to the port, and an Act of 1732 further encouraged the progress. The formation of the River Dee Company was 'in the offing', but although the situation would temporarily improve, many were to lose substantial amounts of money by this undertaking, whilst others, realistically judging the situation, began to send sons and relatives to the port of Liverpool in order to establish roots for the future.

Not only did the Chester families grasp these early opportunities, which is possibly why there was no obvious resentment when Liverpool swiftly and steadily expanded during the 18th century, but they unwittingly encouraged a corresponding reaction in the port of Lancaster. The merchants from this northerly port, subordinate to the comptroller of Chester, saw an opportunity to gain the upper hand and further enlarge their family fortunes. A great struggle for power was about to take place as the small handful of established Liverpool merchants and their families were courted by some, and ruthlessly manipulated by others (in particular a faction of merchants from north Lancashire), until ultimately one person would effectually gain control; a situation which Liverpool seems subjected to about once every two hundred years, as past and recent events have shown.

Unfortunately the constriction of the Dee Estuary was not the only problem; the river during the winter season was unpredictable, as any heavy rain or snowfall in the Welsh mountains precipitated the flow of a large volume of water down into the lower reaches of the river, which on occasion was both frightening and devastating. Within living memory the inhabitants would recall many being drowned and a newly built quay, together with warehouses full of goods, being swept away.

The impressive walled city of Chester, complete with its castle and Rows, was a hive of activity. Its travellers and merchants brought news from a vast area including North Wales, the Isle of Anglesey, Ireland and the Severn Estuary. The houses, for the most part built of timber, were very large and spacious, having galleries, piazzas or covered walks adjacent. The ancient castle, constructed on the southern side of the city and still in use as a garrison, was kept in good repair, containing storehouses and magazines (hence the Commissary Davenport connections). If any disturbances arose along the northwest coast or in Ireland, the garrison was of great importance for military preparations.

In general the citizens of Chester were extremely wealthy merchants and shopkeepers, creating an intercourse of trade over a large area far beyond the hinterland of the port. Each year the great fairs of the city were patronised by groups of tradesmen from Bristol and

Dublin, encouraged by the importation from Ireland of the large quantities of linen. At these fairs, of course, horses were also bought and sold. Much lead and coal were brought down the River Dee by ponts in the summertime, and Charles would make himself conversant with the news from the mining areas in the Welsh mountains. On occasion, some of the Derbyshire miners held interests in or worked the lead mines of Wales, often returning to their home county in due course.

No journey was ever wasted and Charles would carry with him items for sale in Chester. Silk thread was in great demand; until the invention of nylon it was the toughest fibre, its versatility due to the combination of high strength with high elasticity. Not only was it used by tailors for sewing clothes but also by cordwainers (makers of leather goods) for stitching seams, including those of shoes. Chester was receiving cow hides from Dublin and had a large glove industry using imported kidskins, lambskins and, no doubt, Macclesfield silk thread. The thread would also be required by the Chester silk weavers, two of whom gained prominence in the Assembly, one becoming an almsman in 1737 and the other an alderman in 1738. Silk thread used for weaving materials and stockings was also employed in the making of fishing nets.

As a replacement for his sales goods, Charles would purchase and arrange for the transportation to Macclesfield of horse or goat hair and linen thread, and would probably carry back with him any household goods or items requested by family and friends. Furs were becoming very popular with the importation of beaver, musquash and ermine from Canada. Wines from overseas and English cider were also available.

Which ever maiden journey Charles undertook, he would accompany the more experienced merchants so that he could be correctly introduced into the closely developed commercial circles; or he would carry letters of recommendation from V.I.P.s such as John Stafford, Peter Legh of Lyme or senior merchants who were well-known and trusted by the people concerned.

The first important connection was the Church, and whenever anyone travelled to a new area it was imperative for them to attend the services of the local church. If they were Dissenters then they would find the nearest Dissenting chapel, whilst Quakers and other religious minorities would likewise seek out their own groups. Churches and chapels held extra services on market and fair days where merchants and customers alike attended, creating strong commercial links within their own religions. St. Oswald's (now Chester Cathedral) must have been the inspiration, not only of the spirit, but also for the completion of many good business transactions. Here Charles would attend services, quickly identifying the Clerk of the Pentice (Town Clerk), the Mayor, Aldermen and other important officials and families within the City, presenting himself to them with his credentials, or being presented by a close associate.

As no branch banks existed, the greater percentage of business was carried out on trust supplemented by credit notes, for it was very difficult personally to carry large sums of money. In an area where constant business transactions took place, Charles would make arrangements with a person of repute i.e. a lawyer or substantial business man, so that he could loan cash or have either his own or someone else's promissory notes discounted, or where he could deposit cash in advance and know that it would be safely kept for him. No doubt there would be occasions when Charles would be asked to carry out business transactions on behalf of an associate in Macclesfield, and would be recompensed accordingly.

It was possibly because of the necessity for discounting bills, and other monetary and business arrangements with members of the Chester Assembly, that Charles made a very important contact in the city. The Brocks were one of Chester's most significant families. By trade they were pewterers and braziers, owning lands near Gresford in Denbighshire and property in Chester, comprising a house and business premises on Fleshmongers Lane (today part of the site of the multi-storey car park on Pepper Street) and a public house by the name of *Blew anchor* on Watergate Street, where Charles was possibly accommodated during his visits. Needless to say Thomas Brock (the elder), with his son and grandson of the same name, and his nephew, Richard (son of his deceased brother, Richard) were great stalwarts of the Church of England. The name suggests Dutch origins, and in a Huguenot return of 1593 there is an entry No. 118 for Peter Brocke and wife, a Dutchman born in Solingen under the Duke of Cleveland, a member of the Dutch Church, by trade a cutler. Today Solingen is part of Germany and still famous for its cutlery.

Thomas Brock the elder had become a freeman of Chester on 14th October 1697 and was admitted to the Company of Smiths, Cutlers and Plumbers on 12th September 1699; he subsequently became Sheriff of Chester for the year 1715/16 and Mayor for 1729/30. He gained a reputation for his superb brass candelabra, two of which dated 1726 were originally in the church at Malpas in Cheshire, but which now hang at Aston Hall, Birmingham. Thomas, who would live to a great age, was joined in the business by his son, but the grandson, educated to be a solicitor, was to have a very impressive career, and it was this grandson with whom Charles became intimately acquainted, although he apparently had business dealings with other members of the family.

* * * * * * *

Apart from the influential Chester connections, it was also necessary to make contact with merchants in the City of London to enable purchases of mohair and raw silk to be made.

The journey to London was, of course, considerably longer. On occasion John Stafford was known to travel back to Macclesfield by boat rather than overland. The River Thames was navigable to Lechlade only 12 miles from Cirencester, from whence the old Roman road of Ermine Street took travellers the distance of 15 miles into the port of Gloucester on the Severn Estuary. From there sea-going vessels made regular sailings to Chester and Liverpool, and Stafford would use the opportunity to carry out business transactions in Liverpool on behalf of Peter Legh or the Earl of Derby, before continuing his boat journey to Northwich from where he would make the comparatively easy ride home to Macclesfield. On occasion, presumably, the journey would be undertaken in reverse. But for Charles a better alternative would be to travel to Shrewsbury along one of the packhorse routes, boat down the Severn to Gloucester, and then trek the 27 miles to Lechlade for the final boat journey down the Thames to London.

Assuming Charles went overland, he would take the route out of Macclesfield later to be favoured by coaches, along the Leek road via the hamlet of Bosley. He would, no doubt, make contact with Samuel Lankford at Meerbrook, and pay his compliments to the Misses Lankford before riding through Leek. Samuel and Dorothy were now the proud parents of a son, baptised Henry after his paternal grandfather, on the 8th April 1735 at St. Edward's in Leek but henceforth known as Harry. It seems more than probable that Charles would be accompanied by two or three packhorse teams as they commenced the next stage of their journey to Ashbourne.

Ashbourne was an excellent market town, full of good stone buildings, boasting a splendid Elizabethan grammar school and one of the finest parish churches in England. Many of the beautiful churches in this part of Derbyshire had been enhanced and furnished from the profits of the lead mines. Already Samuel Johnson had made the acquaintance of his future life-long friend Dr. Taylor, and Ashbourne, where he resided from time to time in the Taylor household close by the parish church, was to become his haven during some of the difficult and depressing periods of his life.

From Ashbourne there followed an easy ride to Derby, a distance of some 12 miles, passing through the village of Mackworth, home of Sir Humphrey Mackworth's forefathers on the outskirts of the town. The church of All Saints (now Derby Cathedral) contained the tomb of Bess of Hardwicke, ancestor of the Duke of Devonshire. Close by were the almshouses generously provided by Bess, which overlooked one of Derby's most famous tourist attractions, the first silk throwing mill in England.

The silk works were built on an island in the River Derwent, part of St. Michael's parish. The best view of them could be obtained by standing on St. Mary's Bridge and observing them from their northern and eastern sides across the river. The most impressive building was the largest one referred to as 'The Silk Mill'; built in Italian style it was operated by an enormous waterwheel. This was the inspiration for Charles's premier business venture, and he would certainly take part in a tour of the works, a replication of which had already been built in Stockport. The story of the Derby silk mill had become almost as famous as the one about Dick Whittington and his cat.

* * * * * * *

The first description of a silk throwing mill in Derby was written by Mr. Woolley in 1712. He referred to St. Michael's parish as "small" and "the poorest in town". Its lanes led to St. Michael's Mills, which were malt and flour mills belonging to the Corporation, but close by was a silk throwing mill built by Mr Cocket. Near to these mills was one of George Sorocold's ingenious water supply inventions (the engineer whose water cistern had been adopted by the Macclesfield Corporation); it took the form of a water engine, which, from the operation of only one wheel, threw up water to a cistern adjoining St. Michael's Church. From there the water was conducted in pipes which supplied not only "all parts of the town" at a cheap rate, but, at the same time, turned the malt mill and bored elm trees for pipes – the whole operation managed by one man.

The name of the pioneer silk industrialist was actually Thomas Cotchet not Cocket, a local lawyer, who must have had family connections in the textile trade. In the year 1702 he had built the original building which became known as the "Old Shop". It was 62 ft in length, 28 ft 5 inches wide and 35 ft high, contained three stories, and was sited on one of the islands in the River Derwent which at that point was closest to the shore. The west front of the building was brick, having six handsome windows in each of the first two stories; the third storey, used as a lumber room, had six dormant (dormer) windows set in the roof. The shop contained eight double Dutch mills (machines) set up in two groups of four, one set on the ground floor and the other set on the first floor; each mill or machine had 148 spindles. All these machines were turned simultaneously by one water wheel $13^1/_2$ ft in diameter which held 24 ladle boards. The wheel, said to have been devised by George Sorocold, was placed with its shafts and heads below the level of the lower floor and operated on the same principle as a water corn mill. The eastern side of the building was a studded wall covered with plaster work, and the two rows of windows continued around the whole length of the building. The light entering the shop was sufficient for 24 doublers to work at each row of six windows. Although the water wheel was a great labour saving device in the throwing of silk, no automatic machinery was available for carrying out the doubling process which still had to be done on hand machines.

Whereas some employees had previously worked in their employer's home, or the employer had collected finished goods from employees working at home, and had set up a sort of warehouse (factory) within his own dwelling house, or had engaged apprentices in a workshop next to the house in which he lived, now businesses progressed one stage further with the development of wind or water driven machinery. The first small shops, which later expanded and acquired the name manufactories, were accompanied by a dwelling house in which the owner usually lived, and which later could be subleased to a manager when the owner had made sufficient money to move out to a new estate.

Accordingly a brick dwelling house, with sashed windows, was built near to the Old Shop comprising a kitchen, parlour, dining room and three bed chambers, complete with a garret at the top. Adjacent to this house (and again this became common practice) a 'compting' house was erected where the book-keeper worked and where business dealings took place and company records were kept. On another island belonging to the works an ornamental garden was created which measured 124 ft in length and 27 ft in width; at the southern end a handsome summerhouse was built. Early industrial development was very much part of a scheme to appreciate and adorn the landscape and create aesthetically pleasing views. A "handsome gravel walk", leading to the dwelling house, allowed sight of the weir which turned water to the wheel displaying a beautiful cascade set against the background of the delightful island garden beyond.

There are several versions of the next part of the story but they all agree on the principal sequence of events. One writer includes the additional information that John Lombe, whose family lived in Norwich, was apprenticed to Thomas Cotchet, and this is entirely possible. The machinery for the mills was inspired by the Dutch connections encouraged during the reign of William and Mary, and Norwich had long held trading links with Holland. John Lombe's father was a worsted weaver, and his eldest brother, Thomas, born in 1685 during his father's first marriage, had been sent to London to be apprenticed to a mercer. In due course he was admitted to the Mercers' Company and became a freeman of the City and an alderman of Bassishaw ward. Thomas was said to have imported silk through English agents, Glover and Unwin in Leghorn, Northern Italy. At this point in the story there is a suggestion that Mr. Cotchet's machinery was not as efficient at throwing the filatures of silk as desired by the silk weavers, many of whom were concentrated in certain areas of London. Before Mr. Cotchet's enterprise silk thread was bought "ready worked" from Italy, which presumably meant thrown, twisted and wound onto bobbins ready for the weavers to use. This was very expensive to buy, retaining the superiority of silk production for the Italians.

The logical answer was for someone to go to Italy and carry out, what today is termed 'industrial espionage'. Thomas Lombe, unlike Mr. Cotchet, was financially secure and, seizing on a great opportunity to promote both himself and his business, must have been persuaded by his half brother, John, to become involved in the silk throwing industry. It is possible that Mr. Cotchet had borrowed money from Thomas Lombe in the usual way of a mortgage on part of the premises, so that consequently the Lombe name would have been included on the deeds of the silk mills, although the island was under lease from the Derby Corporation for £8 per annum. However it was done, Thomas provided the finances for John to travel to Italy about the year 1715 (the year of Charles Roe's birth), in order to assimilate the technical details of the Italian throwing machinery. Thomas Lombe was later to inform Members of Parliament that the Italians had "the most severe laws" in order to "preserve the mystery among themselves for a great number of years", and that anyone attempting to discover the secrets of their silk industry would have to forfeit both their goods and life.

Although his destination is not stated, John Lombe appears to have infiltrated the silk industry of the State of Piedmont, because the machines or mills of which he supposedly made copies were described as Piedmontese. For centuries Piedmont had been ruled by the House of Savoy and was traditionally French speaking, but in 1563 its duke favoured the Italian territories and moved the capital from Chambery, in the Province of Savoy, to Turin in the State of Piedmont and subsequently the language became Italian.

From the 16th century Spain had dominated Northern Italy, but under the Treaty of Utrecht in 1713 Austria gained Milan, Naples and Sardinia, whilst Piedmont was given Sicily, triggering a disturbed period for the next few years, particularly in the regions where the Italian silk trade was important. The Duke of Savoy was probably preoccupied with the encroachment of the Austrian Empire towards his borders, which would create emphasis more on external than internal security, and presented John Lombe with the ideal opportunity during 1715 to enter the State and copy the machinery. He was also successful in persuading two of the Italian workmen to accompany him back to Derby during the following year.

The story of John Lombe's adventures in Italy was, without a doubt, romanticised and elaborated and Charles Roe would certainly have heard the exciting details and the melodramatic ending.

John Lombe, in order to gain access to the machinery, is said to have masqueraded as an Italian workman and obtained the help of a Roman Catholic priest. The further assistance of Messrs. Glover and Unwin in Leghorn, was forthcoming, although they were based in the State of Tuscany, which at that period was still ruled by the Medici Family until their line died out in 1737.

On his return, John Lombe initially installed hand machines in buildings near to the Derby town hall, where he was able to train workers whilst the construction of the new machinery and buildings was underway on the island in the Derwent.

On 9th September 1718 brother Thomas obtained a patent for the sole use of the machines, which was granted for 14 years. The machines were of three designs; the winding engine, known to the Italians as 'il inganatore'; the spinning machines which became known to the English workmen as the 'filatoes'; the twisting mills also Anglicised to 'tortoes'.

Thomas Lombe now came into possession of Thomas Cotchet's original buildings; perhaps he claimed them by 'seizure' because of Cotchet's inability to pay the interest due on the loan, or perhaps an arrangement was made between them. The designs and ideas of the Italian workmen must have been taken into consideration because, not only did the machines conform to Italian construction, but also the buildings in which they were to be accommodated.

Cotchet's island, 540 ft long and $52\frac{1}{2}$ ft wide, at this stage was only occupied by his original buildings in the north eastern corner. Now the whole island was to be utilised, and building commenced in typical Venetian style with the sinking of piles which were doubly planked in order to provide firm foundations. A courtyard was laid out around which buildings were constructed, the largest of these soon became known and famous throughout England as 'The Silk Mill'. At the same time as the Lombes progressed, Thomas Patten of Warrington was building his copper smelter; the Champions of Bristol together with Abraham Darby were carrying out experiments in metallurgy; Newcomen was producing his new steam engine and Sorocold, long involved in the competent supplying of water for various systems, had turned his attention to the building of docks, particularly Rotherhithe in London and the first dock for Liverpool; the Industrial Revolution was well under way.

The Silk Mill had stonework built to a height of 4 ft immediately laid on top of the piles, and onto this were constructed 13 handsome stone arches on either side of the building. Five stories rose above these arches, having walls of stone measuring 18 ins thick for the first two stories and 14 ins thick for the upper three. A flattish roof was added, well protected with lead of 10lbs to the foot and hidden from view by a series of battlements. When completed the Silk Mill was 110 ft long, 39 ft wide and $55\frac{1}{2}$ ft high with the east and west fronts having 70 windows each, set in rows of 14. Each window was sashed and measured 6 ft high and 3 ft 2 ins wide, allowing as much light as possible to enter the building.

The machinery was now installed with George Sorocold as the engineer in charge. Into the three upper stories were placed the winding engines, 26 on each floor, each having swifts, spindles and spinning bobbins, with some kept in reserve. Into the two lower stories were placed the filatoes or spinning mills and the tortoes or twisting mills. These were fascinating machines, and any sightseers being taken round the Silk Mill must have been very impressed with what they saw. Each filato resembled a wooden cage of tubular form, having a diameter of just over $12\frac{1}{2}$ ft and a height of 19 ft 8 inches, and stood on the ground floor, but rose upwards through a hole cut out of the ceiling and continued to the ceiling of the first floor. Altogether there were eight of these mills, each of them containing 6 rounds and 575 spindles; these spindles were used for both the filatoes and the tortoes. There were four tortoes of exactly the same height as the filatoes but almost half a foot wider, which took up the remaining spaces in the two lower stories. Each torto contained 4 rounds of spindles, 384 to each mill,

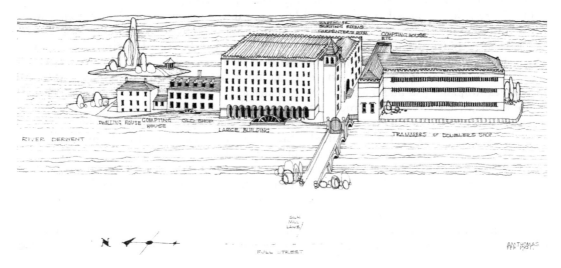

An impression of the Silk Works at Derby on the River Derwent from a description by William Wilson. courtesy of Alan M. Thomas.

with several hundred bobbins and several hundred star wheels of different sizes for altering the throw of the silk threads as required.

All these mills had upright shafts in their centres and connected with shafts suspended over the top of the machinery, which in turn were linked to a main shaft, $10^{1}/_{2}$ ft long and 21 ins in diameter, the latter passing through "a navel-hole in the middle of the building" to the water-wheel on the western side. The whole ensemble was worked by means of this large undershot water-wheel which had a diameter of 23 ft and 42 ladle boards on its rims and cantells, making it almost twice the size of Mr. Cotchet's original one.

The Italian Mill adjoined the Old Shop and was impressively situated on the opposite side of the courtyard from the entrance to the silk works. Visitors, having viewed the buildings from St. Mary's bridge, would cross the River Derwent and make their way round to Silk Mill Lane in order to gain entry to the 'inner precinct'. Many had never seen anything like this before in England, but Charles would have witnessed the building of the Stockport silk mill when he was just 17 years of age, and would be eager to make comparisons.

The approach to the island was well orchestrated; a fine bridge of three arches, built in brick and plaster to imitate stonework, crossed from the lane to the larger island, and had, on the second pier, "two handsome stone pillars, 14 feet high, 3 feet square to which are hung a pair of neat iron gates, 19 feet high and 10 feet wide, weighing 18 hundredweights". The bridge was 55 ft in length with a width of 12 ft, providing an excellent view of the courtyard and Italian silk mill through the wrought iron gates. Having crossed the bridge and entered the courtyard, the buildings on the right hand side could then be observed.

The first building was the Trammers' or Doublers' shop of two stories, with cellars and a brewhouse underneath. It was almost 45 ft wide, 21 ft deep and reached a height of $39^{1}/_{2}$ ft. On the ground floor were three windows and a door facing the yard, with two windows on each of the other sides. All windows were sashed, measuring 7 ft 2 ins high and 3 ft 3 ins wide. Close by was the compting house commissioned by the Lombes, behind which a building stretched for 139 ft. It was only 18 ft wide comprising three stories built to a height of $41^{1}/_{2}$ ft but contained only three rooms, one to each floor. Each room was sufficiently illuminated by 51 windows on either side, to accommodate in all 306 doublers, one to each window. Besides the employees the rooms also contained doublers' wheels, spindles and parts, jacks with glass eyes, boxes for doublers' work and "any other necessaries".

On the remaining side of the courtyard lay the warehouses, carpenter's room and other offices in a building of three stories, being slightly higher that the Doublers' Shop on the opposite side, but only 30 ft in length and 26½ ft in width. This building was not well endowed with windows, having them only on the sides facing east and the courtyard, thus taking into account the adverse effect of daylight on stored fibres, which can cause discolouration, and also making security a little easier.

An Italian style staircase contained within a tower, rose to an impressive height of 64 ft, giving access to all floors of the Italian Works. This was well supplied with windows, no doubt serving a dual purpose, not only did they allow plenty of light to fall upon the stairs but also provided a panoramic view of the courtyard below and, one would suppose, a prospect of the islands together with a considerable area of Derby. At the apex of the tower was constructed a small canopy like roof under which hung a bell just 1 ft in length; a necessity for calling workers to the mills on time.

The Lombes had made great endeavours to succeed in the business, but on 16th November 1722 John Lombe was dead. It was judged that he had been poisoned by an Italian woman, who had been sent by the ruler of Piedmont to carry out his revenge. Whether or not there

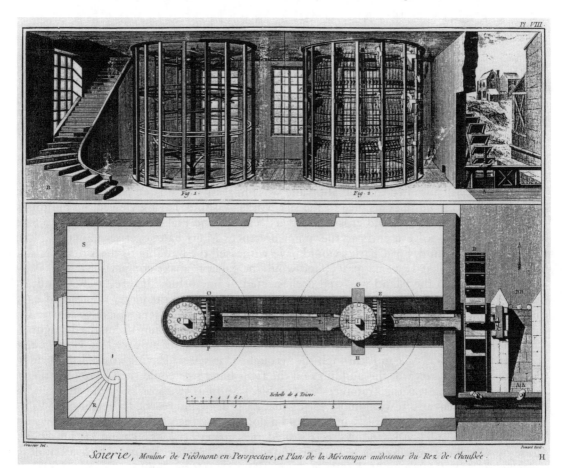

Soierie, Moulins de Piémont en Perspective, et Plan de la Mécanique audessous du Rez de Chaussée.

The silk machines operating in Piedmont as copied by John Lombe and patented by Thomas Lombe for the Derby silk mill.

was any truth in the story will probably always remain a mystery, but the Duke of Piedmont or, as he became known, King of Sardinia, did command that no raw silk was to be exported to England. This seems to have had some effect for a while, because without the Chinese and Italian raw silk, which was of the highest quality and suitable for weaving, there remained only occasional consignments of silk from Bengal and the poorer quality silk from Turkey, adding further difficulties to the progress of silk weaving in England.

In 1727, the year of George II's accession, Thomas Lombe was fortunate to have been elected sheriff of his London borough and as a consequence received a knighthood. The patent obtained by Sir Thomas expired in 1732; he petitioned for its renewal but without success. The government, anxious to prevent monopolies and wishing to encourage other individuals to become involved in the silk industry, offered Sir Thomas the substantial sum of £14,000 together with a pension if he would allow his machinery to be copied by others. The outcome seemed inevitable, Sir Thomas acquiesced and placed a model of his loom (or mill) in the Patents Office at the Tower of London. He died on 3rd January 1739 at his house in Old Jewry in the City of London and was, by modern standards, a millionaire many times over. The silk works were sold during that year by Lady Lombe to the Wilson family of Leeds.

* * * * * * *

As stated by the button makers in their petition to Parliament in 1737, silk was once again arriving from Italy, and with the Emperor Kienlung on the throne of China, the future development of the English silk industry looked full of promise.

Until Charles Roe had visited London for the first time, he would not have been able to comprehend fully the many aspects of the silk industry. Each subsequent visit would bring a greater understanding of the importation difficulties, the processes necessary for the preparation of silk to enable the English silk weavers to produce silks of the highest quality, and the establishment of contacts with a variety of merchants within the City (usually accomplished through attendances in coffee houses, where daily newspapers were provided for customers to read, whilst politics, religious matters, gossip and business dealings were all discussed, argued about and enlarged upon).

The journey to London from Derby continued along the old Roman road which had brought travellers from Carlisle via Manchester and Buxton. It proceeded south through the villages of Loughborough and Leicester to Market Harborough from where two alternative routes were possible to St. Albans. The Carlisle road passed through Bedford and Luton to join Watling Street (A5), whilst the second route made its way to Northampton and joined Watling Street further north to continue through Dunstable. From St. Albans, Watling Street was a very busy road, taking travellers on the final stage of their journey to Charing Cross in London.

By 1737 a form of waggon known as the "Gee-ho" began to supplant pack horses. It was intended for transporting goods and had a team of eight horses with an extra pair at the rear in case of emergencies, the latter inevitably required for hauling the waggon out of bogs and quagmires particularly during periods of bad weather. The old Roman roads had served well for centuries but were now desperately in need of repair. A new era in road transport was beginning and if businesses were to succeed, better and quicker communications were necessary.

Pack horses were still ideal for the transportation of Macclesfield buttons to the Capital; however, if the silk trade was to develop to any substantial degree then the use of waggons would be inevitable. As more and more valuable goods, wealthy merchants and visitors moved along the roads the hazard of highwaymen increased, in fact highway robbery was becoming quite a thriving business. Everyone in England would remember the case of Jonathan Wilde whose execution at Tyburn on Monday, 24th May 1725 had been given national publicity. Although Charles was only ten years old at the time, the story had caused such a stir that the vast majority of the British public would remember and talk about it for some years to come, and as Charles approached the outskirts of London with his merchandise, the details of the story must have crossed his mind.

Jonathan Wilde appears to have had some sort of legal training and presumably started his career with the best of intentions. Initially he seems to have been approached by a client who had lost a bundle of goods worth a considerable amount of money, from a coach travelling in London. An advertisement was duly placed in *The Daily Courant* on Saturday, 28th March 1719, stating that the bundle contained a parcel of muslin, a parcel of printed calico, 2 cambricks, 10 silk handkerchiefs and a remnant of flowered muslin – the reward was 4 guineas, a substantial amount. One would suppose that the price of the advertisement would also have to be taken into account plus Jonathan Wilde's fee. From that time onwards many similar advertisements appeared in the newspapers, always requesting that the goods be delivered to Jonathan Wilde, whereupon a reward would be given and no questions asked. The items now began to include not only lost but stolen goods:

"Taken out of Winchcomb Waggon on Monday night 90 pounds of Thrown Liege Silk – Reward 20gns." (even by today's standards a considerable reward, more than £2,000).

The Daily Courant, Saturday 9th May 1719.

By 13th June of that year, Jonathan Wilde was describing himself as "The British Thief Taker at the Old Bailey" and had received a warrant from the Lord Chief Justice to apprehend two highwaymen in Oxfordshire.

Business continued to do well; almost two years later the same newspaper ran an advertisement on 13th February 1721, and although the reward was 10 gns., the value of items stolen was surprising and included a silver tobacco box and stopper, 2 silver heads of canes and one gold, a pair of silver spurs, 2 pairs of silver buckles, 2 silver snuff boxes, 5 silver tea spoons, a pair of silver tongs, 2 dozen pewter plates, a warming pan, a set of mocha stone buttons, a parcel of India waistcoats and breeches, caps, handkerchiefs and neckcloths and other sundry parcels of linen. One conclusion which can be drawn is that Liege silk was very highly prized.

Just how far Jonathan Wilde had master minded this apparently legitimate business is difficult to say, but at last someone realised the significance of the undertaking and legislation was brought in. It is reminiscent of the Mafia problems in America when Al Capone was finally brought to trial for tax evasion, because on Saturday, 22nd May 1725 it was reported that Jonathan Wilde had finally been brought to trial for not prosecuting "Persons who had committed Thefts which had been made a Felony by a late Statute". He admitted his guilt and pleaded for transportation, but the Death warrant "came to Newgate". The newspaper, which had quite happily accommodated his advertisements, now included a large etching of Jonathan going to the place of execution, together with a full report of the proceedings. Journalism and sensationalism were here to stay.

Depending on the season and weather conditions Charles would have spent three or four days on the road travelling from Macclesfield to London and staying at hostelries overnight, or with relatives of friends and associates if appropriate. Inn food was traditionally very good. Menus included "Toasted Cheshire cheese", considered to be a delicious dish, with salmon dressed in oil and vinegar for supper. Cheshire cheese was also served with fine wheaten bread and butter, and yet another popular dish was roast meat with salad. The favourite beverage was ale, brewed on the premises usually by the landlady. Brewhouses were an integral part of the English way of life, as indicated by the inclusion of one in the buildings of the Derby Silk Mill, and as industrial development progressed, any large sized business was not complete without one – it was the forerunner of today's factory canteen.

Having obtained reasonable accommodation for himself, Charles's next regard would be for his horse. The welfare of horses was a great concern, judging from the number of letters on the subject kept amongst family papers. In the same way that people recommended recipes to each other for curing ailments, they also recommended cures for horse illnesses. A good horse doctor was 'worth his weight in gold' and if a master was staying in his London house when one of his horses fell ill, it was not uncommon for him to send a message to his country horse doctor requesting him to send down a prescription for his groom, or even to ask the doctor to attend personally. On occasion the reverse applied, it was the London doctor who advised the country groom, as evidenced by the following letter:

> "Sir, by the Discription the Groom gives me of the mare I am afraid she is in great Danger if shes inclined to the Yellows the best Way's to take Two large handfulls of sharp pointed Dockshoots cut into slices a handfull of Chamomile Flowers half an ounce of Turmerick bruis'd half an Ounce of Castile Soap. Let these be boild in Two Quarts of Water to Three Pints and let her take Two or three hornfulls of it Three times a day squesing a little Saffron into it, Let her (have) nothing but scalded Bran or dry Bran for her Diet and Hay but no Oats.
>
> As for the Coach Horse if he has had any hurt or Strain in his Loins, I dont know any better Advice than to let him have as much rest as possible till he recovers that Weakness they may bath it with Spirit of Wine and Vinegar ownce a day."

Having arrived in London, Charles would make his way to Cheapside to find his cousin, Christopher. The small Roe family of Macclesfield, now comprising only James, Mary and Charles, together with 'mother' Ann, had always maintained contact with their relatives in Shropshire. Uncle William, rector of Frodesley and Pitchford, who had rescued the Hadley Estate in 1710, was father to a numerous family and his two eldest sons, William and Samuel, had entered the Church. The third son, Christopher, who was 18 months older than his cousin, Charles, had settled in Cheapside in the City with his first wife, Susanna. In the 17th century many houses in Cheapside had been replaced by business premises, including a row of goldsmiths' shops, and it was fast becoming the centre of London's wealth. As part of the marriage settlement Christopher invested money in the purchase of four freehold properties in the area, part of which would presumably be subleased. At this time he was possibly a mercer, a dealer in silks and velvets. Until the 15th century mercers were dealers in small wares, but with the advent of the silk industry into England the word took on a new connotation. There is no doubt that the two cousins worked together, and through this association Charles would make some valuable contacts within the City. The fact that there is also a later association with a linen merchant close by in Cornhill, seems to suggest that some of the Irish linen and thread entering through the Port of Chester, was finding its way to London via Macclesfield.

* * * * * * *

The London with which Charles first became familiar was to alter considerably during his lifetime. Until the middle of the century, Old London Bridge was to remain the only bridge in existence, and it was very old, necessitating considerable expenditure on repair work. Many wealthy citizens inhabited the bridge, portraying a city in miniature stretching across the water. Spaces had been preserved between the buildings wherever possible to enable pedestrians to keep out of the way of "carts, cars and droves of cattle" which otherwise would have proved dangerous. The bridge, constantly in use, was the only way out of London to the southeast. Its southern side still occasionally displayed grim reminders of the punishments meted out to traitors and other convicted persons, by the continuing habit of impaling heads on the turrets of the gate.

Westminster Abbey was also in a dilapidated condition and from the end of the 17th century Parliament had granted an annual sum towards its restoration. This had sufficed for a while but of late was proving insufficient, forcing a further petition for aid during 1738, which was only obtained with some difficulty. Westminster Hall was used not only as a banqueting hall and court room but also as a market.

George II and Queen Caroline resided at Kensington Palace where the Queen took a great interest in the gardens. During 1730 William Kent had altered and decorated Kensington Palace, and it was said that the Queen engaged him to help her put into effect the new plans for the gardens. Caroline took 100 acres from Hyde Park and allowed the flower beds of William of Orange to be re-arranged. During the years 1730-33 a lake called the Serpentine was formed on the course of the old Westbourne River, and on completion the Queen opened Kensington Gardens to the public on Saturdays, with the proviso that those attending were to wear "full dress".

It is possible that Charles viewed these gardens, although he personally did not seem to have much regard for formal gardening. Some years later when he acquired his grand "messuage fit for a gentleman" in Macclesfield, together with its seven Cheshire acres of land (about 15 statute acres), he did have a small garden adjacent to the house, but being a practical man, the remaining acreage comprised a croft, orchard and meadows representing one of Charles's main principles of life, self-sufficiency wherever possible.

Buckingham House (later to become Buckingham Palace) would certainly have attracted his attention. It was built on a piece of land purchased by James I in 1609 in an attempt to create an English silk industry. Five acres had been planted with mulberry trees (later incorrectly presumed to have been of the wrong variety), but with the subsequent failure of the project, the whole area became a public park known as Mulberry Gardens. It was during 1703 that the Duke of Buckingham had built his house in this park, which in due course was purchased and totally rebuilt by George III.

Another attempt to rear silk worms in England had been made at the beginning of the 18th century when John Apletre (often referred to as "Appletree") took out Patent No. 420, but again the project failed. Charles Roe might have been tempted to try his hand at rearing silk worms, however horticulture was not one of his strong points. It would soon become apparent that ground surfaces were the means by which he would try to interpret what lay beneath; his fascination was with mineralogy rather than aesthetically pleasing landscapes. Nor would he have much concern for the Vauxhall pleasure gardens, in existence since 1661 and situated on the south bank of the river in the borough of Lambeth. (The gardens of Ranelagh in Chelsea were shortly to open to the public during the year 1742). There concerts and balls were held and exhibitions of 'up and coming' young artists such as Hogarth and Hayman. Games were very popular, in particular cards and bowls, and there existed little alcoves where tea was exquisitely sipped whilst listening to the latest in popular music, with Handel a firm favourite.

Charles, a hard worker and dedicated to business, would find his interests in the City where the Merchant Guilds still had a firm hold on commerce, although they were losing power in many provincial areas. No evidence exists of Merchant or Craft guilds before the 12th century; the ones which did exist were a form of protection against vandalism and robbery. When Merchant and Craft guilds were established it was on a religious basis, each one choosing a patron saint for its protection. Guilds were recognised by the confering of a royal charter establishing their corporations, but sometimes this took years, even centuries of struggle to achieve. Early monarchs resisted their formation; however guilds commanded wealth, and a sovereign at war, out of necessity, needed to ensure that City backing was available, so inevitably the more powerful guilds were successful in achieving their ambitions. There had always been great jealousy between the guilds, which in the medieval period had sometimes created open warfare on the London streets, but by the 18th century, after the traumas of the Civil War and the Great Fire (the latter having destroyed many of the medieval halls) they were able to function once more in a decisive manner.

There is no evidence of Charles, or any other member of the Roe family, ever having been a member of a guild. This is not surprising in Charles's case because there was never any money available for an apprenticeship, so the next best thing was to cultivate a friendship with a member of a guild and work through him.

The enormous area of London destroyed by the Great Fire had created an opportunity to lay out the most beautiful city. The part of London untouched by the flames was the district around Smithfield and St. Bartholomew Fair, which had become the slum area of the Capital by the 18th century. This was where Hogarth lived and where he delighted in depicting all its depravities in some of his etchings and paintings. He lived amongst thieves, pick pockets and gin drinkers, whilst he became a member of the Hell Fire Club at West Wycombe. St. Bartholomew's hospital had been rebuilt during 1730 by James Gibbs, architect of St. Martin-in-the-Fields and during 1736 Hogarth had been commissioned to paint the pictures on the grand staircase. Smithfield was an important cattle market; during the year 1731 it had been recorded that 8,304 head of cattle had been sold there.

Until the Great Fire the Lord Mayors of London had lived in their own houses during their year of office, but afterwards a house in New Court, Bow Lane was made available until it was decided to build the Mansion House. The building commenced in 1739, but it would not be completed until 1753, and Charles, together with cousin Christopher, would be able to watch its progress with interest from accommodation close by.

* * * * * * *

The year 1739 was a very important one for Charles, now 24 years of age, because by Indentures of Lease and Release dated 15th and 16th of October he was able to purchase a burgage property in Macclesfield and lease the plot of land on which it stood. The purchase price is not recorded in the existing deeds, and where Charles previously invested his money is intriguing. Although, by his mother's will, her estate was out of trusteeship on his 24th birthday, yet there could have been very little left to dispose of. Much of his capital would be 'tied-up' on a short term basis in the purchasing of raw materials for the business of button merchant and in the stock of buttons, but as in the case of the button merchant, Thomas Birtles, the scope of the business covered a far wider area. A large part of the business would be to ensure that the supplies of linen thread and silk thread, together with the various sorts of hair, were suitably prepared. Only a small part of these threads would actually be used for buttons, especially after the building of the Stockport silk mill when much greater quantities of twisted and thrown silk thread would be available in the area. A considerable part of the Stockport production must have been transported down to London for the weaving of materials, particularly around the Cheapside and Spitalfield areas. The demand for fine thrown silk thread by the London weavers was increasing, and in the not too distant future cousin Christopher would set up as a silk throwster in Spitalfields.

The obvious explanation for the source of Charles's purchase money for his property would be that his savings were out on loan at interest. The main possibilities seem to be either in London, Macclesfield and district or both, and if in Macclesfield the transactions would have taken place through John Stafford, as it was from this quarter that he received his first vital assistance. The burgage plot of land on which the property stood was situated on the western side of Jordangate Street almost opposite Cockshoot Lane (today the lower part of Hibel Road) and was part of the estate purchased by John Stafford from a Cheshire solicitor, Samuel Harriman. John Stafford's house stood (and still stands, though part of it much altered) at the top of the hill, also on the western side of Jordangate, and was complemented by another impressive house standing directly opposite on the eastern side, bearing the date 1728. This latter house remains virtually unaltered and is known as Jordangate House, formerly Pear Tree house, and is believed to have been built by either of two brothers,

Thomas or John Glover.

The Glovers were an important silk family and Thomas appears to have been a mercer from Prescot in Lancashire with connections in Stockport and Manchester, who had probably become involved in the Macclesfield trade because of his association with William Taylor of Prescot, Deputy to the Earl of Derby. There was also a William Taylor, chapman of Macclesfield but whether or not this was the same man, or a relative, is not known, however he did lease a large dwelling house or burgage on part of John Stafford's land. William Taylor must have had some close business connections with Charles Roe and some influence with John Stafford because, at his nomination, John Stafford sold Charles Roe the house and William Taylor the plot of land. This meant that Charles would pay a ground rent to William Taylor for the land, which at the rear of the house was divided into three twisting crofts. The frontage of the property on Jordangate Street was quite wide by modern standards, at least 19 yards with an average length backwards of 27 yards. Charles held this property for the rest of his life and William Taylor held the land until it subsequently passed to his only daughter, Mary.

At this early period in the 18th century a thriving little industry had developed in this small area of Jordangate, with at least three twisting crofts known also to exist behind the dwellings on the eastern side of the street, below the Glover property. This small community seemed to be on very good terms one with another, and all seemingly linked by the Earl of Derby connection and their strong affiliations with the Church of England.

Meanwhile the Quakers, mostly settled on the Pickford land in the southern part of the town, were busily engaged in their various occupations, some of which included the button trade. A group of Dissenters, which at this period included the Brocklehurst family (set to become one of the giants amongst the silk families of the 19th century), were also busily engaged in the coarse button trade, which they still operated on a cottage basis i.e. outworkers covering and embroidering the buttons at home. The Dissenters were mostly to be found in the northern part of the town, close by the Dissenting Chapel on Back Street, or in the Hurdsfield area on land, the possession of which had been under dispute at the time of the Civil War because it was the inheritance of the Earl of Derby.

Unfortunately 17th century prejudices had not been curbed, and each community worked as independently as possible, seeing the others as great rivals. It was the perfect atmosphere for the stimulation of trade, commerce and invention, which were beginning to gain momentum by the 1740s.

With the acquisition of his property, Charles now took on an unofficial status in the town's affairs. He and brother James were on very good terms with John Stafford; however, within the Corporation discrimination remained and it took a further three years before an entry was made in the Corporation Minute Book on 8th October 1742, stating that Charles Roe, Gent. had been admitted a freeman of the Borough of Macclesfield "Gratis". The fact that he did not have to pay for the privilege, as the majority did, indicates how hard he must have worked to gain the respect of fellow members, although at the same time it must be noted that Samuel Lankford, Gent. whilst still residing near Leek, had probably brought some influence to bear on the decision, because two years earlier on 3rd October 1740 he had also been admitted a freeman of the Borough "Gratis".

The suffix "Gent." simply meant the second male in seniority in the family. Whereas 'Esquire' had originally denoted a Knight, and 'Gentlemen' his sons, by the early Georgian period etiquette had transformed their meanings to 'Esquire' indicating the head of the family and 'Gentleman' the next in seniority. The remaining sons were referred to as 'Yeomen', which did not necessarily mean that they were freeholders who cultivated their own land, but that they were younger sons.

Whether or not the eldest brother, Thomas, was still alive seemed a matter for conjecture. To all intents and purposes, so far as the Roe family members were concerned, whilst Rev. James was living Charles would always be addressed as 'Gent.'

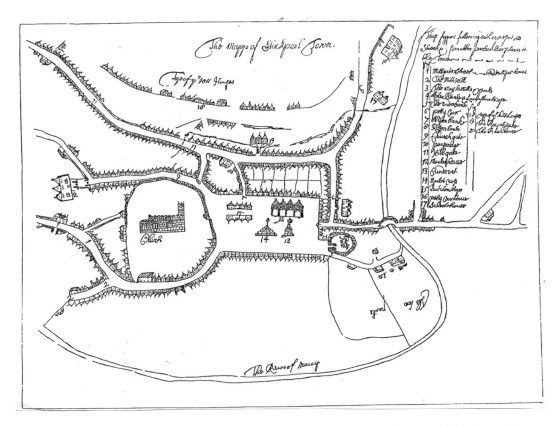

17th century Map of Stockport with the 'Schoolhouse' numbered 17. Courtesy of Stockport Library.

7
SILKS AND TARTANS

Ne'er the twain shall meet.

On the expiration of Sir Thomas Lombe's patent in 1732, the first group of individuals who had shown any initiative with regard to silk throwing on a large scale had been six men with connections in or around the Stockport area.

They were an interesting group, and would need to be so when one considers that Sir Thomas, on making application to Parliament for prolonging the patent beyond the 14 years limit (which incidentally caused great interest because it was the first instance of such an action), pointed out that a considerable amount of capital had been absorbed by the venture, and that the period of protection afforded by the patent had expired before the true potential and benefit of the silk machinery had become of use to him. Perhaps being more conversant with the situation in Derby and the silk trade in general than the vast majority of the citizens of London, the Stockport partnership regarded Sir Thomas Lombe's claims with some irony and decided that they stood a good chance of success, having found an ideal site.

The course of the River Mersey described a large loop as it flowed around the town of Stockport, changing direction from a northerly to a westerly route. The exaggerated curve of the bend provided a natural contour for the area of the parkland, which actually comprised two parks. One was known simply as the 'Park' and the other as the 'Furthermost Park', and it was in the latter area that the Park silk mill was to be constructed.

The group was led by Thomas Eyre, Esq., of Stockport, a principal merchant of the Manchester area. When the Trustees for the employment of the Poor of Manchester had invested a large sum of money by loaning out an amount of £474 9s. at interest, they had shown confidence in three merchants viz. Thomas Patten of Warrington, copper smelter, Thomas Eyre, who appears to have been related to the important Eyre family of the High Peak in Derbyshire involved in lead mining, and John Dickenson, an associate with interests in the cotton and linen trade, whose business was so successful that he was able to purchase for his own use, or to build, one of the largest town houses in Manchester (now part of the site of the Arndale Centre).

As the 18th century progressed, the pattern establishing itself in any large scale business was to include a lawyer or solicitor in the partnership, and in the case of the proposed Stockport silk mill this position was taken by Alexander Elcocke, Gent., of Stockport who described himself as Attorney-at-law. By coincidence, during the 17th century, both the Eyre and Elcocke families had branches established in the vicinity of Nantwich, a town important for its salt trade. Mary, the wife of Alexander Elcocke, appears to have been married previously to the son of another partner, Thomas Hadfield of Heaton Norris, a chapman. Mary must have been widowed young without children, but despite her remarriage Thomas Hadfield always regarded her as his daughter-in-law.

Thomas Hadfield was already an old man when he became involved in the silk mill venture, but he had made a good living resulting in the possession of lands and property across the

River Mersey from the town of Stockport, in the district of Heaton Norris. He also had a warehouse which was subleased for a period to George Nicholson, another chapman and member of the partnership.

George Nicholson was the brother of none other than Francis Nicholson, apothecary of Macclesfield; however their relationship was not a very harmonious one, as future events would prove.

The fifth partner, Jonathan Gurnell, was a merchant in the City of London. This also became common business practice for companies outside London; a partner well established in the capital was essential to oversee and supervise business transactions, which helped create a more efficient and lucrative concern. Quite often it was a relative of a local family, who had been despatched there at an earlier date to deal with family business. By trade, Jonathan Gurnell was predominantly a mohair merchant, sending great quantities of the yarn to his warehouse in Stockport, beginning in the year 1730. He estimated that he sold 145 sacks of mohair in the town in each of the first 3 years, amounting to £7,786 each year (a considerable trade - in total almost £2½ million today). He appeared before the House of Commons Committee in 1737 alongside Samuel Lankford, with regard to the petition of the Button-makers, but no reference was made of his connection with the Stockport partnership. Perhaps discretion was the better part of valour.

The sixth and last partner was Talbot Warren, a man of middle age who had served in the army. He was a member of the Warren family of Poynton, landed gentry who owned considerable estates including several closes in the town of Stockport, part of which extended along the banks of the River Mersey. At the age of 48 years he had married Frances, the daughter of William Davenport of Bramhall (a relative of Commissary Davenport of Macclesfield). His important connection was his elder brother, Edward, High Sheriff of Cheshire for the year 1731, and successor to the Warren estates, which included two mills and the two parks on the banks of the Mersey.

On or about the 24th June 1732 (previously quoted as 1st June), Edward Warren leased to the partnership an area of the parkland of Stockport just to the east of Lancashire Bridge, which included the water corn mill and was adjacent to the other mill known as the "Logwood Mill". The latter could possibly have been a dye mill, because logwood is used with the mordant alum to produce the colours of dark grey, violet grey, purple and black, all popular Georgian colours and obtained successfully in the dyeing of silk. It was also used with urine, copperas and foxglove leaves to dye wool and felt black.

Henry Heginbotham, a Victorian historian, when writing his book *Stockport, Ancient and Modern* published in 1892, had obviously seen either a copy of, or the original deeds, which unfortunately are now missing. However, later deeds have survived which partly recite back to the original Indentures, confirming some of the details. The following extract is quoted from Heginbotham, who was referring to the partnership:

> "they propose to carry on a design imitable of Sir Thomas Lombe's engines, and to fix and work the same, with power to make a sluice to divert part of the water from the mill sluice to turn a wheel, but not to damage the supply to the water wheel of the Logwood Mill." The lease was subject to these conditions: The payment of a halfpenny a yard annually as chief rent, with five per cent. upon the profits. The fish in the river was to be preserved, and continue to be the property of the lord of the manor, fishing both in the river and the sluice being strictly protected. An offer was then made to John Guardivaglio, the other Italian who accompanied Lombe from Piedmont, to construct these works, which he accepted, and induced some of the workpeople to accompany him from Derby. The mills were completed and commenced working with such success that on May 1st, 1740, the Logwood Mill was taken and added thereto."

From existing deeds a yearly rent of £12 5 9d. was payable and there is a reference to an Indenture dated 1st May 1740. As the Logwood Mill is included with the premises on a later deed, it can be accepted that its addition was made by this Indenture. It is possible that although expansion was necessary, the intrinsic reason for the addition of the mill was to obtain a better supply of water for the functioning of the large water wheel.

The year 1740 saw Stockport growing in importance, due in no small part to the expansion of its silk mill; however, the reference to John Guardivaglio by Heginbotham is confusing.

Of the two Italians who had accompanied John Lombe on his return journey from Piedmont to Derby, only details relating to one are known, at present the other must remain anonymous. The available information relates to a young man called Ignatius (not John) Guardavaglio, a surname which was to cause problems for several parish clerks, but one which, in spite of the numerous variations of spelling, was quite distinctive and could easily be recognised. He seems to have settled well in Derby, possibly brought about by the fact that a famous family called Bassano had lived there for many years. They were always referred to as Italians, although it was an ancestor of theirs who had settled in England at the time of Henry VIII and had become one of the King's court musicians. The musical and artistic traditions had remained within the family and they were much loved and respected by the people of Derby.

On the supposition that Ignatius had arrived during the year 1716, it was eight years before he married Hannah Endsor, on 27th September 1724 at St. Peter's Church, situated on the opposite side of the town from the Silk Mill in St. Michael's parish. It would have taken a considerable amount of hard work and savings for Ignatius to have been able to enter into a marriage settlement. After the marriage the couple probably took up residence in St. Alkmund's parish, which was next to St. Michael's and adjacent to the Silk Mill, because on 31st January 1727 the parish register records the baptism of their son, John and the fact that his father was "a native of ye Kingdom of Sicily". As already mentioned, the Ruler of Piedmont had been given Sicily under the Treaty of Utrecht in 1713, which suggests that Guardavaglio had either travelled or been sent to Piedmont, to work in the silk mills of that state because of the assimilation. Perhaps he was not happy there and was grateful for the opportunity provided by the intercession of John Lombe, albeit dangerous, which had brought about his exodus to England.

The family unity lasted for only a brief period; Hannah was buried at St. Alkmund's on 8th July 1729, recorded as the wife of "Nath", she had probably died in childbirth. Ignatius had obviously anglicised his name to Nathaniel. He must have felt the necessity for providing his young son with a mother, as so often happened in the Georgian period when young men were left as widowers with small children, because six months later, on 13th January 1730, he married Sarah Gaunt in the same church, and there also took place the baptism of his second son, Nathaniel, on 25th April, 1732. (Apart from Sarah's burial, recorded many years later, on 10th November 1761, widow of Nathaniel, there appears to be no further entries in any of the Derby registers for this family).

The suggestion that a Guardavaglio helped with the construction of the Stockport silk mill is supported by circumstantial evidence, however, young John was only 13 years old in 1740 and would not have had enough experience to take charge of such an undertaking. It now seems likely that Ignatius took his son, John, to Stockport and left his wife, Sarah in Derby – a possible sign of discontentment with his second marriage. Although another alternative could be that Sarah went with him to Stockport for a while, but eventually returned home. There is no record of what happened to baby Nathaniel, nor do any further baptisms appear to have taken place for the couple.

In the records of St. Mary's Church, Stockport, on 3rd February 1753, there is a burial relating to Joseph Guardivaglio of Stockport, described as a labourer. Was this the man who has been recorded as assisting in the building of the Stockport silk mill? Until quite late in the 18th century, builders were not defined as such, but were usually referred to as joyners (joiners), bricklayers, plaisterers (plasterers), or labourers. As this is the only occasion on which the Christian name Joseph appears in the family, could it possibly have been miscopied for a badly written Ignatius? Or was Ignatius accompanied to England by another family member named Joseph? The only positive conclusion is that the Guardivaglio family was largely responsible for the introduction and establishment of a superior silk throwing industry in England.

One suspects that by 1740, young John, English by birth and not Italian, was an apprentice in the Stockport silk mill. It is difficult to calculate how long it took to build the mill after the leasing of the original plot of land in June, 1732. The shares were divided into twelfths, reminiscent of the lead mines of Derbyshire, making easy reckoning; but hardly had the partnership begun when Talbot Warren died on 21st December 1734, followed 16 months later by Thomas Eyre on 15th April 1735. Although Talbot Warren was middle aged, Thomas Eyre was a comparatively young man, and must have died fairly quickly, because he had only prepared his will four days earlier on the 11th April. This sequence of events must have curtailed the building of the mill to some degree. There is no specific mention of the silk mill in Thomas Eyre's will, only that his Executors, William Wright of Offerton, his good friend Jonathan Gurnell of the City of London and John Dickenson of Manchester had to sell and dispose of all his real and personal estate and allow his wife £600 in satisfaction of her dower, with the residue divided amongst the children.

There is an interesting stipulation included in the will which dictates that his servant Gervase Cartwright was to serve and assist the Executors, and for as long as he did so, was to receive £40 per annum. A letter, written by John Stafford from his house in Macclesfield to Peter Legh the elder of Lyme, dated 21 February 1736, contains this intriguing final paragraph:

> "I stay'd at Stockport in my way to Haydock severall hours, where Mr. Worthington met us, & by the assistance of Mr. George Nicholson I hope ye affr is put into so true a light that Mr. Eyre's Exts. (Executors) will safely settle it, but as nobody on their part was there except Mr. Cartwright (agent of ye late Mr. Eyre) we c'd only go threw it as it appeared & he promised to lay ye papers before ye Exts. the next opportunity & ye affr sho'd then be ended."

Whatever "ye papers" referred to, seems to have been a straightforward once and for all matter. The direct involvement of Peter Legh in the affairs of the silk mill does not seem feasible, as the land belonged to the Warren family. Perhaps it related to something in which Thomas Eyre was personally involved and for which he had accrued a debt. One possible explanation is that he had approached Peter Legh of Lyme with a view to purchasing timber for building the mill, water wheel and machinery. This would be similar to the actions of Samuel Finney of Fulshaw, in connection with the Macclesfield copper mine, who at that very same period was making purchases of materials, including timber, for the construction of the buildings on Macclesfield Common on behalf of the company, with the intention of receiving reimbursement from the other partners in due course (except for the fact that Finney had not paid for them in the first instance). Although possibly a comparable situation, Thomas Eyre could be exonerated for non-payment of debt or part debt having 'expired'.

Whoever took over the available shares in the silk mill is at present unknown, but the mill was apparently completed by 1740 and operating with such success that the addition of the Logwood Mill was deemed necessary. Henceforth the whole manufactory became known as the Park silk mills.

As this was only the second silk mill to be built in England, using machinery relating to Sir Thomas Lombe's patent, one would suppose that the building and installation of such machinery, and the actual development of the mill as a whole, would closely follow the methods used in Derby, with small adaptations made where necessary; from a later 19th century plan this appears to have been the case.

* * * * * * *

In the first instance it would be vital to bring together and train a small work force, in exactly the same way in which John Lombe's initial project had begun in the Derby town hall; and for this purpose a group of smaller buildings would be built in preparation for the subsequent erection of the large silk mill, designated to contain the Lombe machinery. This would take time and is possibly why there is no specific mention of any buildings relating to the silk mill in Thomas Eyre's will dated 11th April 1735.

The original Stockport silk mill was built on the same plan as that of Derby i.e. having a gateway which led into the courtyard on the opposite side to the five storey building which contained the filatoes and tortoes, operated by means of a large water wheel. From the measurements of the Derby mill this building, which housed the tortoes and filatoes, provided for a space of approximately 5 ft minimum around each machine, on the assumption that they were arranged in pairs and evenly placed throughout the first two floors of the five storey building. The corresponding five storey building in Stockport was of the same width, just over 39 ft, but was 13 ft shorter, which suggests that instead of accommodating twelve machines as in Derby, the Stockport mill held ten. One can only presume that the three upper floors, as in the Derby counterpart, contained the winding machines. The general layout of all the buildings was similar in both cases, including the brewhouse, stables, mechanics' (carpenters') shop, warehouses and, of course, the compting house next to a dwelling house.

Anyone and everyone from around the region would be full of curiosity to see how the new mills were progressing. The Derby mills, in operation for nearly 20 years, were, of course, offered for sale during 1739 due to the death of Sir Thomas Lombe, placing the initiative with the partnership at Stockport, which had already gained an advantage by the incorporation of some of the Derby workers, including the Guardavaglios, into its manufactory.

Rev. Joseph Dale, headmaster of Stockport Grammar School, who by this time had added yet another curacy of £40 per annum to his income, (having accepted the one at St. Mary's Church in Stockport from the year 1733), would be able to recount first hand the developments taking place in the silk works to his son-in-law, Samuel Lankford of Leek. The progress would also be transmitted to Francis Nicholson by his 'enviable' brother, George. To be able to take part in such a scheme must have raised the social standing of those concerned.

Charles Roe was never one to ignore competition. He was meticulous in everything he did and seems to have assumed an air of confidence during his early years of struggle, which gave him the will to succeed in whatever he became involved. He must have been aware that the Park silk mills were not only proving to be an excellent investment for those concerned, but also providing employment for many people. And, so far as one can tell , not only Charles, but Samuel Lankford, was conscious of the necessity for providing employment for the underprivileged. With these motivating influences prevalent in his mind, Charles conceived an ambitious scheme for Macclesfield and took, what must have been, a great and very bold step. So certain was he of Samuel Lankford's confidence in his ability to succeed, that he asked for the hand in marriage of Lankford's second daughter, Elizabeth. This was an interesting choice; not Elizabeth the eldest (step) daughter (who had actually married Edward Cheney at Mackworth in 1741), but Elizabeth, the only daughter of Lankford's marriage to Catherine Sleigh, who was a few years younger than the 28 year old Charles.

The negotiated marriage settlement was very large and essential for the plans envisaged by both father and future son-in-law. Lankford's share was "to the value of £1800", but how this was composed is difficult to say. However, his apparent fortune seems to have been derived in part from the fact that he was once more involved in mining speculations at Ecton Hill in Staffordshire. He was one of a quartet who had negotiated a new lease with the 3rd Duke of Devonshire to run from 12th December 1739 to Michaelmas (29th September 1760). Another of the partners was Alexander Taylor, landlord of Buxton Hall and baths. Although original accounts are no longer extant, it has been possible to estimate their considerable success from the surviving duty payments made to the Duke as lessor. Even these are at present incomplete but sufficient to deduce that by 1743 the profits were considerable.

For his part Charles included his Jordangate property and may have borrowed some money in order to meet this fortune with a comparable amount of his own. Nevertheless this was no mean achievement for an orphan who, from the age of 15 years, had borne the responsibility of a sister and sister-in-law without any visible means of support, except what he could make for himself. Obviously there had been great moral support through their connections, yet Charles had not buried nor wasted his talents but had taken full advantage of every opportunity presented to him. At the same time it must be pointed out that he seems to have inherited the Roe tradition of public spiritedness and that whatever success was forthcoming, he did not regard as purely for his own or family's social benefit but as an advantage gained from a genuine desire to help others, which then became the instrument and means by which he could fulfil his commitments.

Looking at the subsequent sequence of events, it is reasonable to suppose that initially Charles did not reveal the full extent of his ambitions to Samuel Lankford, otherwise he would probably have received a much smaller portion for his wife, either because Lankford would have considered the scheme far too ambitious for one person, or else because Lankford would more than likely have demanded a partnership, restricting Charles and denying him the sole right to make decisions. So far as Samuel Lankford was concerned the money would be invested in property and an expansion of the 'button' business.

As Thomas Birtles's business premises in Chestergate were used as a sort of distribution centre, to a certain extent he would be able to monopolise the established trade and presumably charge as he pleased for his services; Charles must have decided to break away from the system and become independent. This would mean that some sort of warehousing, including a compting house, was essential. By 1743, not only was Charles involved in the button trade but he was dealing in a more general way with silk merchandise, as witnessed by information contained in a letter written to Peter Legh the elder by his brother, Rev. James on 8th February 1743:

> "My best Complimts attend Mrs. Legh. I rec'd her Silk, my Bror. tells me the Hanks will be work'd into any form, & w'd be glad if she w'd send him a pattern of Silk, such as she w'd have it, as to the other, the mice he's afraid have quite spoil'd it."

This information can be interpreted in many ways. Had the hanks of thrown silk come from Spitalfields or Stockport? As James had received the hanks, the argument seems to favour Stockport. Presumably Mrs. Legh had originally bought some wrought silk, possibly French, and required more of the same pattern. Charles had requested a piece from which the pattern could be copied in order to purchase a greater quantity in London, or to have it woven by Spitalfield weavers or made locally (although at this period the latter does not seem feasible). Mice had ruined the piece to be used for this purpose, but in the meantime Mrs. Legh had bought some thrown silk from the Park silk mills and had sent it to Macclesfield, care of James, because he was more likely to be at home than Charles, who was often travelling on business. Charles, now in possession of the hanks from which the new piece was to be woven, discovered that the pattern piece was ruined, hence the request in his brother's letter. Although this nicely fits the facts, the only undisputed suggestion is that whatever connections the Park silk mills had with the London weavers, Mrs. Legh had chosen Charles to execute the order for her, which in itself was complimentary (at least before the vermin had been at work).

Mrs. Legh's action also suggests that despite the close proximity of the excellent thrown silk available from the Park silk mills, Messrs. Roe and Lankford preferred to use silk thrown locally in the twisting crofts for the employment of the elderly and the young engaged in the embroidery of buttons in the Macclesfield workhouses, which helped to alleviate the conditions of the poor in Macclesfield. Had Charles been purchasing thrown silk from Stockport, he would surely have chosen some for Mrs. Legh. For the moment it would have to be business as usual until his marriage had taken place, but in the meanwhile family and parochial matters took over.

* * * * * * *

Parsons and curates of livings kept in frequent touch with their patrons, and James Roe was no exception. When they did not meet in church or private chapel, or socially at balls or dinner parties which were growing in popularity, the clergyman kept his benefactor informed by letter of anything of interest which was happening within the area; always anxious to pay compliments, be of service in a variety of ways not only religious, act as a messenger or put forward pleas on behalf of others. These letters were often entertaining, informative and full of interest.

Although James Roe was curate of Disley, he still preferred to live with his family in Macclesfield, but he always maintained a steady stream of correspondence with his patron, Peter Legh the elder of Lyme. His letter of 8th February 1743, referred to above, was a very chatty letter in response to one received from Peter Legh, which reflected the latter's somewhat despondent mood. Roe's little philosophies of life were already taking shape "no state of Life, however gay prosperous or happy it may ap'ear in the Eyes of the World, is totally free f(ro)m Cares & Uneasinefs." His first piece of family news was obviously a surprise and not a pleasant one by any means, insinuated by his comment "I shall be apt to blame myself for not having endeavour'd to prevent it." The event to which he referred was the unexpected marriage between Anne Roe, widow of his deceased brother, William, and Francis Nicholson, apothecary.

Francis Nicholson had first married Ellen Endon of Macclesfield in 1730 and their ten years of marriage had produced four daughters and three sons, but the second son, Ralph, had died and, consequently, on the birth of their third son, the name Ralph was also adopted. Here once again was a widower with small children. His wife, buried on 3rd February 1741, had been preceded by their youngest child, Alice, buried the previous December and only two months old. Exactly one year after his first wife's burial Francis Nicholson married Anne Roe in the Parochial Chapel of Macclesfield.

Someone must have provided for Anne's share of the marriage settlement, but who? Francis Nicholson having realised his civic ambitions of Alderman and Mayor, was by no means impoverished, and someone must have provided Anne with a fairly substantial sum, because her dower from William's marriage could not have been of any great value, and was possibly one of the contributory factors for her 12 years of widowhood. The Derbyshire lead mining shares had provided nothing from Magclough sough for years, in fact Charles would have been asked to make significant payments towards the cost of maintaining the mine, and must also have paid them on Anne's behalf in respect of William's half share of the $1/48$ inherited from their father; it is therefore reasonable to suppose that he also assisted in some way with Anne's marriage settlement.

There is no doubt that Charles made regular visits to the mine from which he gained valuable knowledge. Hopes had been raised in January 1735 when the first measure of ore had been taken, obtained from sumps sunk into the vein below sough level. By this time the sough was about 6,000 ft in length driven through gritstone and shales. It had almost reached the Brookhead sough and was driven with the same intention i.e. to locate and unwater the Hucklow Edge vein. As the Brookhead sough had originally been driven at too high a contour, it was now rendered obsolete by the advancement of Magclough, but to no avail. Although James had now lost his half of the Brookhead share left by his father, he still retained his other shares, and from limited details available two of the mines in particular were producing quite substantial yields:

Miners Engine from 24/4/1733 to 28/6/1736 Loads 10,761 (price not known).

Moorwoods Engine from 1/2/1734 to 31/3/1739 Loads 4,533 = £4986 10s.

It is extremely difficult to estimate the value of this income to James and, whilst expenses might have been due in respect of his shares in other mines, by making the simplest and briefest of calculations he was probably receiving something in the region of between £5,000 and £7,000 per annum by today's values. Not a fortune by any means, yet certainly worth having. Unfortunately sister Mary had also lost the half share of her father's interests in the Brookhead sough, which would have been deemed part of her marriage settlement, so in due course, should the need arise, alternative arrangements would have to be made.

Whatever the pecuniary agreement between Anne Roe and Francis Nicholson, they did ask James to live with them:

"They have persuaded me to one thing contrary to my own Inclinations w[hi]ch is to live w[i]th them- I thought ye Family w[oul]d be large enough, but was urg'd in such a maner yt [that] without Ingratitude I c[oul]d not resist."

A letter written in September of the same year did confirm James's residence in an amusing way and indirectly reflected his lack of confidence in Francis Nicholson's professional abilities . . . "Tho' I live in some sort in an Apothecary's Shop, yet let me advise You not to dabble too much in Physick."

Charles presumably lived in his property on Jordangate, with his sister Mary keeping house for him, although it is possible that the Jordangate property was already leased to a tenant when Charles bought it (and this he would have to respect), in which case it seems entirely possible that the large family referred to by James also included Charles and Mary.

* * * * * * *

Macclesfield Town was becoming well-known throughout the country. The peregrinations of its chapmen would take them to many parts, where they would be closely observed by the local inhabitants. The quality of their hats and wigs, the number of horses they owned, the excellence of their clothes and merchandise: all would be assessed and judged. The impression imparted seems to have been one of a certain amount of affluence, suggesting that the town was an important centre, easily accessible and socially desirable. Its proximity to Buxton also helped. More and more people were becoming aware of the remedial effects of spring waters, and Buxton was beginning to develop into an important spa and social centre where merchants and their ladies, from as far afield as Liverpool and the Midlands, began to meet friends at least once a year. Bristol and Bath were also developing simultaneously and seaside resorts were keeping pace. As early as July 1736 an advertisement had appeared in *The Kentish Post* encouraging bathing in sea water:

"This is to inform all Persons that Thomas Barber, Carpenter, at Margate in the Isle of Thanett, hath lately made a very convenient Bath, into which the Sea Water runs through a Canal about 15 Foot long. You defcend into the Bath from a private Room adjoining to it . . ."

The foundations of the great British holiday resorts were already being laid.

Health and leisure activities were actively being encouraged as large numbers of citizens no longer had to economise to survive, but were finding themselves with money surplus to requirements which gave them the opportunity to purchase the smaller luxuries of life.

As is the paradoxical way with most things, the towns and places which were beginning to thrive and attract the wealthier, more cultured and better behaved visitors, also found themselves playing host to a sophisticated band of confidence tricksters, thieves and pickpockets, amongst whom some members of the clergy were no exception, much to the dismay of James Roe.

In Macclesfield the year 1743 proved quite eventful in this respect. Towards the middle of the year, Peter Legh the elder was growing very ill and as his legitimate heir was his nephew, Peter Legh the younger, Rev. James naturally kept in close touch with his future patron. He had previously reported the arrival in town of a Parson Parr who had decided to take up residence, but when news arrived that he was under suspension "for Bastardy & his Living under Sequestration", the parson immediately packed and left. James Roe generously giving him the benefit of the doubt, wrote "& in the Hurry forgot to pay for his Board".

The other parson, by the name of White, who had arrived in town, was more divisive. He allowed the rumour to circulate that he was on intimate terms with Peter Legh the younger, and had actually been entertained at the latter's home. As a consequence many Macclesfield families had made him welcome, until it was discovered that his business was "an Intrigue" with a certain married lady. She had retired from Chester with her husband, a former attorney of the city, and now resided with Nathaniel Barton who kept an inn. Poor James declared, "I begin to be afham'd of the Cloth myself," having previously remarked that "a Parson & a Villain are look'd upon here as Synonimous Terms."

The year 1743 also brought Peter Davenport into prominence once more, and James, unable to contain himself, was moved to write "He seems Determin'd to be a Plague to the Town, till [th]ey are so happy as to get him six feet under Ground". After rejection by the Borough, when Davenport had used his Chester and family connections to obtain the important position of Receiver General for Cheshire, his responsibilities now included the collection of Land Tax throughout the whole county. The 1743 Land Tax was proposed by Act of Parliament 1742 16 Geo.2. Cap 1, which stated:

"An Act for granting Aid to His Majesty by a Land Tax to be raifed in Great Britain for the Service of the Year One thousand seven hundred and forty three"
– the rate was to be four shillings in the pound (20%).

Incidentally two more Acts passed that year are of interest: An earlier act 15 Geo.2. Cap 35 reflects the shortage of copper by restraining the exportation of copper bars which had already been imported into this country. This was more likely to affect the English colonies in America and the West Indies. The act also incorporated legislation for the encouragement of making sail cloth in Great Britain and silk manufactures.

A later act 16 Geo.2. Cap 29 allowed for carts to be drawn by four horses instead of two, which had considerable repercussions even to this very day. The act covered for all sorts of vehicles, brewers' drays, carts belonging to scavengers who transported dirt and soil from the streets, also cars and carriages which were the forerunners of modern taxis. Most of these conveyances had wheels shod with iron, which caused great damage to pavements, not to mention pedestrians, as "great Inconveniences" arose from the "irregular Behaviour of Carmen, Draymen" etc. who could now in effect 'exceed the speed limit' with their increased horse power, causing considerable havoc, particularly in the streets of London and other 'large' cities. This act was to cause such devastating effects that by 1745 the clause would be repealed under 18 Geo.2. Cap 33. and carts etc. allowed to be drawn by three horses only. Because of the many accidents which occurred in the interim, further legislation demanded that any owner of such vehicles who resided within the stipulated limits (the Cities of London and Westminster, the suburbs and Borough of Southwark), would have to "enter his Name and Place of abode with the Commissioners for licensing Hackney carriages" and place on some conspicuous part of his vehicle the name of the owner and the number, to enable prosecutions to be brought if necessary. The charge was to be one shilling.

It is fortunate that a copy of the 1743 Land Tax Return for Macclesfield was kept in John Stafford's office and has survived the rigours of time. With the greatest confidence can the details entered on those pieces of paper be relied upon, because without any shadow of doubt, Peter Davenport ensured that every single penny of the tax was collected from every single inhabitant of Macclesfield who was liable to pay, and he possibly tried to force the issue with a few who were not. Whatever 'traumas' this operation produced, John Stafford would do his utmost to ensure that the collection proceeded in the strictest legitimate manner.

For his services, Peter Davenport was knighted as a Crown Servant, Collector of Land Tax, on 8th June 1744. With the bestowal of this Knighthood, he considered that he had been given carte blanche to oversee the authority used by the Macclesfield Corporation, and many legal wrangles ensued. To add further to the problems, the mayor, poor Thomas Hooley, who bore the brunt of Peter Davenport's rancour, died in the month of September, but not before he had been served with a writ to appear in the Court at Chester. Davenport had insisted that tollage must be paid by a travelling Jew, and now the mayor and corporation were to be sued by the gentleman concerned, which was by no means the first instance of such an action. The new mayor, William Clayton, bookseller, button merchant, mercer and previously half share owner of the Copperas House dyeworks, was a much tougher character, and once he took office there seemed to be more solidarity within the Corporation in the stand against "the Great Major Davenport". But it must not be thought that Thomas Hooley had quietly acquiesced, quite the reverse. During a public meeting at the cross outside the Angel Inn in the town square, Davenport and he had been involved in a heated argument, during which the mayor had refused to be intimidated by his military antagonist, and had remained the victor.

Nor had Peter Davenport's activities been confined to the Borough; he was still collecting heriots in the High Peak, as evidenced by a bond executed in his favour in connection with the will of William Leese, surgeon of 'Chappell in le Frith' dated 14th July 1740. His visits to the area had gained him the acquaintance of the Bagshawes. They had quickly learnt their lesson some three years earlier when, in the autumn of 1737, William Bagshawe of Ford Hall near Chappell had contacted Commissary Davenport with a view to obtaining the release of his nephew, who was on active service in Gibraltar and who was apparently either very badly injured or ill. Davenport had promised to pay Mr. Bagshawe a visit when in Castleton, but not having heard anything from the Commissary, William Bagshawe had directly approached the Duke of Devonshire, and asked him to intercede on his nephew's behalf. Unexpectedly a letter arrived from Davenport, addressed from Castleton, excusing himself for not having visited Ford Hall. It was obvious that he had on earlier occasions over-emphasised his military connections, and that William Bagshawe had readily believed his fabrications. Davenport assured Mr. Bagshawe that his nephew would be home in the spring, if he lived that long. As his original contact had let him down rather badly, he had been forced to approach "a very particular friend", Captain Crosby of Chester, who had lately been made Major to a Regiment at Gibraltar. It was the Major's intention to deal with the matter immediately on his arrival there after Christmas, but Davenport craftily concluded that his original contact had suggested to the Major that he would receive 20 guineas (£21) for his trouble.

Apart from the money, William Bagshawe panicked; he had no intention of allowing Commissary Davenport's schemings to jeopardise his plans, and thought it better that Captain Crosby "could be stopt from making any instances for his return".

* * * * * * *

At this period Charles Roe's name is markedly absent from the Corporation records, apart from his admission as freeman. He does not seem to have involved himself in local politics or intrigues. Even his marriage to Elizabeth Lankford was far from a grandiose affair. It did not take place at the fashionable East Cheshire churches of either Prestbury or Wybunbury, nor even at St. Edward's Leek or the Macclesfield Parochial Chapel, despite the fact the latter had been greatly enlarged during 1740, which had necessitated the removal of the old north wall together with the wooden spire. The addition of high pews, galleries and an extension in the classical style would have made it an ideal venue for a wealthy merchant's wedding. Instead they chose the small ancient chapel of Meerbrook, built in 1538, during the reign of Henry VIII; possibly an indication of Elizabeth's character, unpretentious and rather shy. Today very little remains of the original chapel; the present delightful and beautiful church was almost totally rebuilt during 1873. The chapel was, of course, very close to Samuel Lankford's estate, and after the ceremony, which had to take place between the hours of 8 a.m. and 12 o'clock noon, one would suppose that the wedding breakfast would have been lavishly provided by him.

The marriage was performed on 26th May 1743, granted by Licence dated the 23rd, and witnessed by Charles's friend and colleague, William Hyde. Willam Hyde at that time was living in the parish of Leek, but his family were from the area of Denton and Stockport. He would later return to Stockport, where the family owned several properties including a dyehouse and warehouse. At his death in 1780, described as a 'Silk Throwster', he bequeathed all his messuages, dwelling houses, silk mills, lands and premises, situated in Heavily and Shaw Heath (today part of the town of Stockport) to his wife, Sarah.

In the vast majority of cases a Georgian honeymoon did not entail a holiday trip or, to use a Georgian word which would grow in popularity, vacation; after the breakfast feast the husband and wife usually returned to their prepared marital abode and settled into the new routine of everyday life. Dr. Johnson, in his inimitable way, defined a honeymoon as "The first month after marriage when there is nothing but tenderness and pleasure."

Where Charles and Elizabeth lived, after their marriage, cannot be stated with certainty, but it had to be in Macclesfield. There is a sedan chair (previously on display in the West Park Museum) which traditionally was left by Charles Roe's wife to the poor of the town. The story relating to this has never varied since the mid-Victorian period, and recounts how Mrs. Roe, from her window, saw the older people of the Poorhouse struggling up the hill to attend services at the Parochial Chapel. If Charles and Elizabeth lived in the Jordangate property, which was sited at the top of the hill almost opposite Cockshoot Lane, then the story has a ring of truth to it. The most direct routes to the Chapel, by way of either Goose Lane or The 108 Steps, were very, very steep, and older inhabitants would find it easier to take the longer more gradual climb up Cockshoot Lane, for the Poorhouse was situated down the hill on the eastern bank of the River Bollin (in the area referred to as the Waters Brook). As the Poorhouse was quite small until 1757, the gift of a sedan chair, for use by a very small number of elderly residents, then becomes less of an absurdity to modern minds.

Another more sensible connotation of the phrase "for the benefit of the Poor" would have been that the sedan chair was to be sold and the money realised given to the Poorhouse. Which does not discredit the story of Elizabeth observing the poor people toiling up the hill.

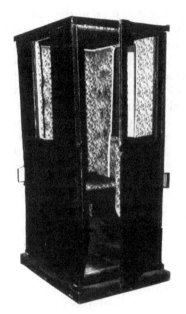

Until a few years ago, for as long as anyone could remember, the sedan chair had been kept in the Parish Church of St. Michael and All Angels, formerly the Parochial Chapel, and seems to support the idea that it could have been hired by members of the congregation returning home after church services, and the money placed in the Poor box. From time to time this money would then have been used "for the benefit of the Poor". Whatever the truth, to the people of Macclesfield the sedan chair is regarded as a very important and significant part of their history. It symbolises the name of a great benefactor who laid the foundations for an outstanding industry which made the name Macclesfield so synonymous with silk, particularly during the 19th century, that even today Macclesfield is known as Silk Town.

* * * * * * *

As soon as the marriage had taken place, Charles set the wheels in motion for his ambitious scheme, which was to build a silk mill in the town, using the principles of the Thomas Lombe machinery. Having already familiarised himself with both the Derby and Stockport silk mills, he knew that the first essential was water power.

The Roe Sedan chair Courtesy of Macclesfield Museums Trust.

Charles must have looked hard and long for the ideal site and now he faced a dilemma. All the lands alongside the Bollin and its tributaries were either owned or under lease, and the largest investor within the Macclesfield boundary was the Pickford family. Fortunately Joseph Pickford, now resident in Ashton-under-Lyne, was a member of the Church of England, but any leases entered into by his ancestors with the Quaker families would be jealously guarded by them. Charles had no alternative but to look to an associate and a member of his own faith, in order to persuade someone to sublease either the whole or part of the property which would be most advantageous to him.

The person whose co-operation Charles sought and received was John Pickering. A survey carried out on behalf of the Earl of Derby in 1709 records John Pickering as lessee of two cottages in Wellmouth, close to the castle properties and the town well. On 5th May 1728, described as a twister, Pickering leased from James Pickford, the father of Joseph, of Altehill, Ashton-under-Lyne:

"All that old piece of building . . . near to Pickford Bridge called the Dyehouse containing Three Bays of buildings . . . with liberty to alter and convert the said buildings into a shade (shed) or Twisting House," The rent was £1 17 6d. per annum for 21 years commencing on the following 25th March. At the end of the term, the buildings on the land were to be left "in good and Substantial Tenantable repair".

Throughout the 18th century the brook which flowed across Parsonage Green was an open watercourse. At the far side of the Green, as an extension to Mill Street, was Pickford bridge, which allowed for the passage of people and carts from the town square, down the steep narrow winding way of Mill Street, onto the flat green meadow land of the Green, then southwards to the Leek road. From this point, the brook (today known as Dams brook) continued to flow parallel to the River Bollin through the Brook meadow, at a distance of some 150 yards. It then meandered in a north-easterly direction to join the River Bollin across the area known for many years as Waters Green. Another rivulet (which now flows underground from the direction of Church Street) gurgled its way down from the north-western corner of the Green after supplying the obsolete town's well ("Stop'd up" by the Corporation in 1736). In the medieval period the interjection of the streams created an island, which was transformed into a boggy area in later centuries because of soil erosion. This was subsequently drained by someone creating a proper channel to the Bollin.

The likely candidate for this scheme was the ancestor James Pickford, who had leased a barren area of land from the Earl of Derby and spent a great deal of money on improving it, and, under threat of sequestration by Oliver Cromwell, followed eventually by the re-instated Earl of Derby, had attended Court to prove it was legally his. This area of land adjoined the castle property and spread downhill towards the River Bollin, and it was here that the Pickford family had built one of their dyehouses, presumably making use of the water from the smaller brook, or that superfluous from Wellmouth.

The other dyehouse was, of course, near to Pickford Bridge and in both areas there existed long sheds on posts, listed in a survey of the Commonwealth period. These were essential for hanging up to dry the hanks of various fibres after dyeing. Wet or damp fibres must have plenty of fresh air in which to dry, otherwise mildew is a hazard, and by suspending the hanks across lines hung from post to post, they would also be protected from vermin, another vulnerability indicated by James Roe's letter.

On 4th September 1732, for some reason John Pickering had to sign a further lease in respect of the building near Pickford Bridge, which had now been converted into a twisting house. The reason could have been due to the change of usage. James Pickford had died, and this new lease was executed by his son, Joseph, but the rent remained at £1 17 6d. per annum. This time permission was given for a cart to go "up the backside belonging to the dwelling house wherein Mary Barbour Widow now dwells" which was situated at the northern end of the bridge. Three years later, on 31st December 1735, John Pickering married Ellen Henshaw in the village of Goostrey (today close by the Radio Telescope at Jodrell Bank). They were both residents of Macclesfield and John Pickering was entered in the Register as a "Button-maker", which suggests that he actually made button moulds, although the 17th century meaning was probably more literal than that used in the 18th century, when 'Button-maker' seems to refer to an employer whose employees, however few, made the complete buttons for him to sell to the mercers. As he had created the twisting house, John Pickering must have had at least two or three employees engaged in twisting thread on the premises. Whether or not the embroidery of the buttons also took place there, is not known.

*(The deeds originally seen by W. H. Chaloner M.A. Ph.D. of Manchester University, when writing his article entitled, "Charles Roe of Macclesfield (1715-81), An Eighteenth Century Industrialist, Part 1", which was publilshed in the *Transactions of the Lancashire & Cheshire Antiquarian Society* 1950-51, Volume 62, have now disappeared. Whilst part of the information given can be confirmed, the remainder must be accepted. However, it is the omissions from these deeds which have created some ambiguity and have concealed the truth until now. I have been fortunate in tracing many Pickford family papers, including property deeds, which were responsibly deposited by a firm of London Solicitors some years ago in the offices of The Royal Commission on Historical Manuscripts, Chancery Lane, London, and it is thanks to the endeavours of both parties, that a significant portion of Macclesfield history has been preserved and is now safely housed in the Leeds Archives. For further information please refer to the references. The new sources of information have been used in conjunction with the old).

*Professor Chaloner stated "From the lease it appears that at some date between 13 July 1743 and 15 February 1744 Roe had" (with the consent of the then lessee, John Pickering, twister of Macclesfield, and the owner of the land, Joseph Pickford, of Althill, Lancs.) "taken down all the buildings" on a piece of land in Macclesfield "near to Pickford Bridge 26 yards long and 11 yards in breadth". On this cleared space he had "at a very great expense erected a large pile of buildings intended for a silk mill for throwing of raw silk by means of a wheel to be turned by water". Roe also secured water rights in "the brook, stream or water-course running by the side of the said building" together with certain rights over a "sough or tunnel" (essential to the working of the water mill) which ran through property occupied by other tenants of Pickford. To the lease is attached a note "For Mr. Roe" dated December 14, 1744 from John Ward of Capesthorne Hall, near Macclesfield, and the Inner Temple, "the great conveyancer" which ends: "I wish you success in your mills"."

It is true that Charles would have to obtain consent from both the owner and the lessee of the land and buildings, in order to take down any buildings which at that time were still standing, and it would be a great expense for him to erect new ones, but the important words are "intended for a silk mill" . . . in all other instances of intended buildings appearing on property deeds, the subsequent deed has always contained the phrase "which was then built". Professor Chaloner makes no mention of this. One also must assume that the phrase within parentheses viz: "essential to the working of the water mill" was a deduction on the part of Professor Chaloner. The sough or tunnel referred to, must have been the one at the far end of the lesser brook, built by the Pickford family to drain the land and direct the stream into the River Bollin. Under no circumstances would Charles have been given rights over a sough or tunnel with the likelihood of impeding the water supply to other Pickford tenants. If, however, he intended in some way to increase the water supply for powering a water wheel, then it was necessary for him to be able to enlarge the sough in order to take away the extra volume of water after it had turned the wheel.

The transfer of the lease from John Pickering to Charles Roe was apparently made for the payment of a guinea and a yearly rent of £1 18 6d, and was for the term of three lives, i.e. that of Charles Roe, his wife and Joseph Pickord. If one of them died within the year, then a replacement life could be made. The original lease was for the building only, and the fact that the dyehouse had been converted into the twisting house, seems to indicate that it was the same building being leased, which technically included the ground it occupied. The site of the building, 26 yards long by 11 yards wide, was not a very large area, but sufficient for Charles to erect on the vacated space a group of smaller buildings in which to bring together and train his small workforce in preparation for the building of the larger mill to contain the Lombe machinery. It is significant that about this time the three twisting crofts behind Charles Roe's house on Jordangate were converted into a garden or orchard, perhaps another indication that Charles and Elizabeth were residing in the house, and that the small twisting business had been transferred to Parsonage Green.

Now there was a legal change of circumstances; up to this point in time the building had always belonged to the Pickford family, but the new buildings belonged to Charles Roe. The land had been, and still remained, the inheritance of the Pickfords and therefore the payment of £1 18 6d. to be made each year on the 25th March (Lady Day) was, in effect, a ground rent. Unfortunately, this is the reason why no counterparts of the deeds relating to the subsequent buildings, completed by either Charles or any other person, are retained with the Pickford papers, simply because the new buildings no longer belonged to them.

It is interesting to see that the lease was prepared by John Ward of Capesthorne Hall and not John Stafford – the old establishment being preferred, which could have been at the insistence of Joseph Pickford. John Ward was a delightful character who loved to amplify his name by the addition of "the great conveyancer" suggesting a life time of dealing with many transfers of property.

Silk is silk, and always has been, but cotton at various times has had a more universal meaning. In the 16th century, Lancashire cottons would appear to have been wool. By the 17th century cotton wool was being used, together with silk, to produce a cloth called "satten cotton or bumbazie". The great parish of Manchester became famous for its cotton and linen smallwares, and the weaving of linen was very much on the increase. By the 18th century fustians and cotton-linen both used flax for warp and cotton for weft, and Manchester retained its superiority in all branches of the trade including dyeing, bleaching and providing markets.

The connection between certain Manchester merchants and Macclesfield was well-established by the 18th century, and therefore it must be accepted that Charles was not only dealing in silk with Spitalfields and Cheapside in London, but must also have been sending some silk thread to Manchester, besides linen thread and possibly spun cotton, which was easy to prepare and needed no special treatment. The mohair seems to have been mostly consumed by the button trade in the Flash area; in fact, Samuel Lankford was listed as a mohair merchant of Leek in 1736. With the international situation being so unpredictable and causing great concern over the reliability of supplies of raw materials, any one merchant would be foolish to put "all his eggs in one basket" – Charles Roe would definitely think so.

One particular Manchester merchant, Samuel Touchet, in partnership with Joseph Hague, built up what today would represent a multi-million pound business, in the cotton trade. Touchet was on the committee of the Africa Company, and because of his enormous export business was able to provide currency exchanges for other merchants trading abroad and for the public in general. One of his customers was Colonel Samuel Bagshawe of Castleton, M.P. for Tallagh, county Waterford in Ireland, who found it necessary from time to time to exchange English money for Irish, and vice versa. Relying on the enormity of the business, Touchet foolishly did not diversify, and by 1761 found himself well and truly bankrupted despite a last minute dash to London by his brother, who succeeded in raising a subscription of £100,000 in two days. (Someone must have had confidence in him, even today £10 million pounds in 48 hours would be difficult to find).

For the remaining years of the 1740s no further information has been supplied by Professor Chaloner from the Royal Depot Mills deeds, but fortunately other Pickford deeds are extant, and one in particular is of vital importance. However, before Charles could proceed any further with his intended silk mill, a traumatic event intervened.

* * * * * * *

During 1744 the British Government learnt of plans for a Jacobite invasion of England and the British fleet, under the command of Admiral Norris, was put on full alert; but it was not until the late autumn of the following year that Charles Edward Stewart, son of the Old Pretender, now exiled in Italy, made his daring attempt to claim the English throne for his father. He quietly sailed out of Nantes in the *Doutelle (Du Teillay)*, accompanied by the ship, *Elizabeth,* a well-armed privateer, which carried arms and ammunition for the Prince's forces. After a six hour battle, due to the interception of a British warship, the *Elizabeth* managed to regain the French coast, badly damaged, but the *Doutelle* made her way to Scotland where it was possible for the Prince to land with seven of his companions. Many of his father's old supporters soon rallied to the cause, bringing sons and other family members with them, and by the 12th November the Young Pretender found himself before the gates of Carlisle, at the head of a substantial army. In just over six weeks he had captured Edinburgh, beaten the English army at Prestonpans and marched to the English border. From the moment that Bonnie Prince Charlie set foot on English soil, many of the people with whom he became personally involved, have been found to have had significant connections with Macclesfield. This, in a way, is not surprising, when one considers that the route chosen was, in effect, the English silk trail from Scotland to London, which was traversed, mainly during the summer months, by chapmen, many of whom were acquainted with the town.

The first appearance of the Prince on the 12th November caused consternation and confusion amongst the remaining inhabitants of Carlisle; several of their number, together with a large group of militia, had already disappeared. He gave them until the following day to surrender peaceably, thus avoiding repercussions, and made his departure. Immediately an irregular meeting took place in the town hall, when the Mayor, Aldermen and Burgesses voted on the issue. The town clerk, John Pearson, whose step father was a captain in the English army, did not want to surrender, but the remaining populace was dwindling rapidly and the Corporation was forced to seek terms with the rebels when they returned the next day. The Corporation Minute Book ominously recorded the votes. The Mayor, anxious to capitulate, led the rest, but Pearson abstained.

As soon as Carlisle had succumbed to the presence of the Jacobite rebel army, shock waves were generated throughout the Lake District and people took action. Many of the old Westmorland and Cumberland families were great Hanoverian royalists, including their tenants and servants, so quickly and stealthily a plan of action was put into effect. As many head of cattle as could be herded together in the time available were taken to a remote valley, and the army was denied essential supplies.

Bonnie Prince Charlie marched south as quickly as he could. It was difficult to calculate how large the army was, rumours and propaganda enlarged it to about 10,000, whereas in truth it was probably somewhere between 5,000 to 6,000, predominantly male but with a few females and children. The young boys had been trained to dart quickly in between the legs of the English horses so as to inflict injury to the animals with knives, once battle commenced. It was no secret that the rebels were marching for Manchester, where many Scottish tradesmen had settled and where a warm welcome was expected. As they proceeded en route to the city via Preston, warnings were sent ahead. Someone wrote to John Stafford, and from his subsequent reply, which was in the way of a report with enclosures, the person concerned would seem to be Edward, Earl of Derby.

The direct line of descent in respect of the Earls of Derby had become extinct in 1736 with the death of James, when he had been succeeded by a distant cousin, Edward. By a quirk of fate, due to the marriage of Lady Amelia-Sophia, daughter of the 7th Earl of Derby, to the Duke of Athol, Edward was distantly related to Lord George Murray, the then Duke of Athol, who became, in reality, commander-in-chief of the Prince's army having the greatest military ability and knowledge. The Earl of Derby would, therefore, be anxious to allay any suspicions of any collaboration with the rebels. John Stafford's letter included the following:

> "Dear Sir,
> I thank you for yr. kind advice, but it came too late, for in a few hours after I received the Letter, we were alarmed with the approach of the Rebells . . . We had heard of their coming into Manchester, and of the great rejoycings there, and that they raised recruits very fast, from whence we concluded they would have made some stay in the Town."

At each sojourn the Prince was provided with the best amenities available, and Manchester was no exception. However, for the time being it was not the prospect of any military action which was causing him concern, but the enormous problem of accommodation and food for such a large army.

The house chosen to be his abode was the town house of John Dickenson, associate of, and executor for, Thomas Eyre of Stockport (the Eyre family are known to have been Roman Catholic). Dickenson, like John Pearson before him, must have found himself in an extremely difficult position. Dictated by the mood of the town, he had no alternative but to welcome the Prince into his home, however, the family knew where their loyalties lay and any action would have to be taken with the greatest caution. But it is possible that a Protestant tutor of the young Pretender's brother, Henry, known as "Mr. Dicconson", (a variant of the name Dickenson, and one which appears on some documents relating to the Dickensons of Manchester) could have been related to the family; he had died in Italy during October 1743.

The Dickensons were (and remain) a very important and ancient family of the Lake District, particularly of the iron mining region around Lamplugh, a tiny village a few miles to the east of Whitehaven. Alternatively, one wonders if the scouts of Bonnie Prince Charlie had received advance knowledge of the importance and wealth of John Dickenson on their journey south, or whether it was just coincidence that his town house was chosen as accommodation for their Prince. During that year John Dickenson had purchased the Birch Hall Estate (Rusholme) as his main family residence, including Birch Chapel, the curate of which was Rev. Joseph Dale, Headmaster of Stockport Grammar School. At the time of the Prince's entry into Manchester, John Dickenson was still resident in the town. His splendid town house stood at the top of Market Street Lane which was principally occupied by many black and white timber buildings, but was beginning to show signs of modernisation as a number of wealthier merchants were in the process of constructing fine stone mansions, financed from the proceeds of the Manchester trade.

Two neighbours and associates of John Dickenson were Joshua Marriott and James Marsden, linen thread merchants and partners who had taken shares in the Macclesfield copper mine some years earlier, but apparently to no avail. (Joshua Marriott, also a fustian manufacturer, was an associate of Thomas Birtles whose business address was Chestergate, Macclesfield). They both owned large stone built residences; James Marsden's house occupied a site on Market Street Lane near to the Dickenson property, and Joshua Marriott's was just around the corner in Brown Street. Their importance can be assessed by the fact that a 'Plan of the Towns of Manchester and Salford', produced by Caffon and Berry circa 1750, includes a series of important buildings displayed as side borders and at the top of the centre panel; from the eleven insets depicting merchants' houses, four of them relate to Touchet, Dickenson, Marriott and Marsden.

John Dickenson was very well-known to John Stafford, having been for some time Lord of the Manor of Taxal, on the Cheshire and Derbyshire border. Two years earlier a dispute had arisen between Dickenson and Edward, Earl of Derby, concerning a parcel of tenanted waste land in Kettleshulme, near Macclesfield, containing 14 statute acres (not Cheshire) 2 roods and 30 perches, which was set between lands owned by both parties. They had agreed to go to arbitration to settle the matter and judgement was given by Charles Legh of Adlington Hall and Edward Downs of Worth, the latter another associate and great friend of John Stafford, who had connections in Macclesfield. The decision was to divide the land equally within a specified period of time, and the demarcation was a stone wall erected at the expense of John Dickenson, but with part reimbursement from the Earl. This was amicably accepted by both parties.

Dickenson, 46 years of age in 1745, had three sons and four daughters. The eldest son, John, was 19 years old when Charles Edward Stuart imposed himself upon them, but the family afterwards reported that the Prince was a man of great charm and good manners. The bed upon which he slept during his three nights stay was removed to Birch Hall when the family took up permanent residence there, and for many years afterwards was a showpiece for visitors, together with a silk handkerchief which the Prince inadvertently left behind in his hurry to depart for Macclesfield.

In the early hours of Sunday, 1st December, the army set forth quickly and quietly, hoping to provide an element of surprise. John Stafford later speculated that their spies had been advised of a party of some 20 Dragoons of the King's forces who had entered Macclesfield on the previous evening, but it now seems likely that the Prince was acting upon a valuable piece of information which he had received. He was desperate for professional assistance, and throughout the journey spies were sent ahead to enquire from would-be sympathisers of some standing, where the people most likely to help on the next stage of their route were located. Someone in the Dickenson household, most probably John Dickenson himself who had relations in Macclesfield, saw a marvellous opportunity to act. Whilst appearing to assist the rebel army, which ensured no reprisals, the effect would be the opposite. The name of Sir Peter Davenport, Commissary in the English Army, experienced in providing food and equipment for large numbers of forces, was put forward as a suggested contact. Davenport was not above being bribed, but he would certainly be able to turn the situation to his advantage and to the disadvantage of the rebels, through his family and military connections, without allowing himself to become involved in a situation where he could be tried for treason. Here was an excellent opportunity for someone to take retaliation on Davenport by placing him in a compromising situation. His unpopularity was widespread but, although modern historians have accused him of being a Jacobite - that he certainly was not.

The Prince and his forces crossed the River Mersey in two divisions. The bridges, destroyed in advance by resistance groups, forced the divisions to ford the river; the first at Stockport, led by the Prince, and the second at Cheadle. The Cheadle group continued through the villages of Wilmslow and Chorley, climbed Alderley Edge and made a rendezvous with the first group who had traversed the low ground between Woodford and Prestbury. At about 10 o'clock that Sunday morning, news came into Macclesfield from "the country people that the Rebells were within a quarter of a mile of the Town". Consternation knew no bounds.

A young officer, Commander of the small group of Dragoons, was taking breakfast with the Mayor's wife. His reassuring words "Never fear, Ma'am – we'll protect you" had scarce left his lips when the alarm was given. "Down went his dish", and in the fastest time possible, he, his group of Dragoons, and the Mayoress, 'Madame Frances', disappeared out of the town. Despite the fact that the service at the Parochial Chapel was only half way through, the congregation rushed out of doors to join the other townsfolk on the streets, adding further to the confusion and panic.

John Stafford, in his letter, confessed his initial fright, having found himself at the top of the house peeping out of the garret window. However, overcome by shame, on seeing his wife and her two sisters below at the gates, he joined them and watched "the whole army pass by my own door, except a regiment of Horse commanded by Lord Elcho, and some forces which came in late."

The quartermasters rode to the cross, followed on foot by John Stafford, who was now rapidly gaining confidence:

> "They enquir'd for Sir P. Davenport's house – whether he was in town or not, and being answ'd not, they gave him a Curse, and asked when he left it, and soon afterwards rode to his house, and after viewing it inside and out, marked the door with the word 'Prince'."

On enquiring the size of the army and receiving the answer, 10,000, John Stafford returned home dismayed. Almost immediately a Regiment of Horse arrived, commanded by the Duke of Perth, containing within its ranks a poor wretched individual guarded by four fearsome looking soldiers with drawn swords. Fright had mesmerised the prisoner to such a degree, that for some time friends and neighbours were unable to recognise him. It was, in fact, Samson Salt who had been sent to Stockport a few days earlier to gain information of the advancing army, but when he had not returned, the Establishment including John Stafford, had erroneously presumed that the Jacobites intended to remain in Manchester for several days. Samson Salt, by trade a Macclesfield grocer, had endeavoured to sell his business on Mill Street by placing an advertisement in *The Manchester Magazine* on Tuesday, 21st August 1742, which included an incentive of 12 months credit provided proper security could be given. It was also from him that two locks had been purchased some years earlier (1738) for the Parochial Chapel, indicating that a variety of goods could be bought from the shop. (Shopkeepers stored whatever they could sell, as witnessed by Francis Nicholson's stock of buttons in his Apothecary's shop). On realising that Samson Salt was a townsman of

Macclesfield, the guards began to ridicule him and make fun of his distress in front of the onlookers. The spectacle of his discomfort was fortunately short lived, as the sound of approaching bagpipes heralded the arrival of the remaining regiments, both Horse and Foot, who were attired in Highland dress. As they approached John Stafford's house, each one marching with a Colonel at its head, news of Bonnie Prince Charlie's arrival reached the crowd. John Stafford reported:

> "You may safely imagine we were all very attentive to see him, and it happen'd that a halt was made just opposite my door for a minute or two, which gave us the opportunity of having a very full view of him. He was in Highland Dress with a blue waistcote trim'd with silver, and had a blue Highland cap on, and was surrounded by about 40 who appeared as his Guard. He is a very handsome person of a man, rather tall, exactly proportioned, and walks very well . . . He walked on foot from Manchester, as he had done, 'tis said, all the way from Carlisle; and I believe they made their best appearance into the Town, expecting to have been received as at Manchester; but there was a profound silence, and nothing to be seen in the countenances of the Inhabitants but horror and amazement. Endeavours were used to have given 'em a peal of the Bells, for fear of insults. But 4 Ringers were all that could be got, and they rung the Bells backwards, not with design, but through confusion."

Whether or not Charles Edward Stuart was quartered in Peter Davenport's house, is debatable, but from that time on it was referred to as Holyrood House. Another version suggests that the Prince stayed in the inn almost opposite John Stafford's house, but lower down Jordangate. The hostelry subsequently became known as the 'Palace Inn', and as the house of John Dickenson acquired the name 'Palace House', there appears to have been some connection.

The Mayor was asked to declare the Prince's father King, and John Stafford was summoned with instructions to wear his gown. He sent word that he would attend but that his gown "was out of the way". After the Mayor had made the proclamation, repeated by the Town Clerk and two or three of the Aldermen, the Jacobites gave themselves a cheer but received little response from the assembled populace.

John Stafford and his family were fortunate to have a young Lowlander, though in Highland dress, quarter himself with them. His appearance was unpromising but proved to be deceptive, concealing a character of good education and breeding. The women folk soon felt at ease and from him they learnt much about the army, as he identified the Chiefs and Clans marching by. Over dinner in the evening the young man remarked what a glorious town Manchester was, but seemed unable to understand the lack of enthusiasm encountered elsewhere since their arrival in England. Many thought that if they could cross the border into Wales, the anticipated fervour would greatly enhance their cause, but having obtained information regarding the movements of the Duke of Cumberland and his army, the Prince's secretary later revealed that "there was a council of war held at Macclesfield in which it was unanimously agreed to make some forward marches so as to get between the Duke's army and London and then march on as fast as they could to the capital."

John Stafford, unaware of the strategical debates which were taking place, was unobtrusively gathering information. The army had gone to great lengths to conceal its numbers. Where a house received orders to billet 40 to 50 troops, only half arrived, but in other instances residents had double the expected number. Everyone had been given orders to illuminate their houses at dusk, upon pain of execution. About 9 o'clock in the evening, a very ordinary looking man arrived at John Stafford's door with a billet which read "Mr. Stafford – 408"; having received an earlier one for 10 men and 5 horses, resulting in the arrival of the young officer, his servants and 5 horses, John Stafford's premature relief was shattered. After a short while the soldier assured his 'host' that the note was meant to indicate 40 men and 8 officers, but a further period of time elapsed during which no more individuals arrived, so the man declared that he believed no one else would come that evening. The Stafford family spent a miserable night, unable to relax with their latest 'guest' within the household. Although he professed to be a doctor, he was judged by everyone to be a highwayman. In spite of the presence of townsmen, who had volunteered to serve as guards for the night, several "odd things" went missing and the locks in John Stafford's bureau and his wife's closet, which were in the room where the soldier had slept, were found to have been tampered with.

The next morning, Monday, 2nd December, John Stafford rose early and went across the way to investigate the situation in the house of one of his neighbours who had been given a company of 50 common men for the evening. "The house floor was covered with straw and men, women and children lay promiscously together like a kennel of hounds and some of 'em stark naked". From all accounts the army intended to remain in the town that day, so John Stafford obtained a pass to take his wife and sisters, together with several other females, to his friend's house at Shrigley. He left his clerk and servants to secure his property and, complete with entourage, walked on foot "thro' the bye-roads" up to the house of Edward Downs (one of the adjudicators in the Dickenson – Earl of Derby dispute at Kettleshulme). The Scottish soldiers had already paid Mr. Downs a visit, and from their knowledge of the fire arms which he kept, it was apparent someone had readily supplied information. John Stafford, concluding his letter, wrote . . . "those villans could not come to the knowledge of these things but through greater villans."

The following day the rebel army was on the march again. Lord George Murray took an advance column to Congleton from whence he drove the Duke of Kingston and a small contingent of English Horse along the Newcastle road, which succeeded in persuading the Duke of Cumberland that this was their designated route. In the meantime the remaining forces made their way to Leek in Staffordshire where the brother of Samuel Lankford found himself entertaining the Duke of Perth for the evening.

The Jacobites made rapid progress to Derby arriving there the next day, Wednesday, 4th December, looking dirty and fatigued. They made their entry as formidable as possible, bearing eight standards, white with red crosses, accompanied by the determined playing of bagpipes. Bonnie Prince Charlie was accommodated in the town house of the Earl of Exeter (demolished in 1854) which was situated in Full Street, and the remainder of the troops were dispersed as usual, throughout the town. The sheer endurance required by the ill-equipped troops to carry themselves from Leek to Derby within the day, had taken its toll. Exhaustion can play tricks with the mind; quarrelling broke out amongst the officers which ensured a further day's stay in Derby, allowing the Duke of Cumberland to realise his mistake and regain ground towards the rebels. By Thursday, 6th December, Charles Edward Stuart, angry, disillusioned and having to accept the reasons for the disconsolation of his troops, resentfully agreed to retreat.

One of the stories concerning the occupation of Derby, to be recounted at a later date, was that of the Wright family. Mr. John Wright, Attorney of Derby, later to become Town Clerk, was such an honest man that he had earned the nickname "Equity Wright". His son, Joseph, born at 28, Irongate, close by the church of All Saints on 3rd September 1734, was destined to become an eminent painter, subsequently known as Wright of Derby, which distinguished him from another painter of the same name. On hearing of the approach of the Jacobite army, Wright took his wife, two daughters and son, Joe, to Repton, thinking it inconceivable that any of the soldiers would cross the River Trent, as there was no bridge in the area to aid the crossing. The two eldest sons were already attending Repton Grammar School, under the tuition of the Rev. Mr. Ashley, but much to the surprise of all concerned, 3 officers and 40 men quartered themselves in the house. During their stay the soldiers saw a small gun and enquired of its maker, when they were told that young master Joseph had made it "they wished they could see the little gentleman . . . they were sure he must be an ingenious boy." It was during this stay at Repton that young Joseph, 11 years of age, became fascinated with a "Christmas-piece" belonging to one of the boys, of which he made an excellent drawing. This was the start of Joseph's artistic career, which did not meet with his father's approval, but on the return to Derby, totally undaunted, Joseph spent many hours in the attic of the house secretly copying several of the interesting public-house signs displayed in the town.

In the scramble to return to Scotland, the retreating army broke up into several disorganised groups and one contingent, numbering about 1,500, made its way back through Macclesfield, although the Prince and his party, on leaving Leek, headed in the direction of the Roaches and stayed near the village of Flash in a cottage which became known as the 'Royal Cottage'.

John Stafford learnt that shortly after his departure for Shrigley, 20 common men, 3 officers and 6 horses had taken lodgings in his premises, but thanks to the restraining influence of his 'custodians', only a looking glass was broken. As he joyfully hurried homewards on the Tuesday morning, having been advised of their departure, about a mile from Macclesfield he was met by several people with some alarming news; the town was under threat of being burnt to the ground. Undeterred John Stafford rushed onwards to learn that one of the Scottish soldiers, attacked in a hosier's shop in the Market Place, had been cut on the head and stabbed in the thigh with his own sword by a young local man who, on entering the shop, had been standing behind him. The young man made a hasty exit and could not be found, but such was the outcry that the 30 or 40 soldiers remaining in the town had threatened to burn the place down. They offered a reward of £50 to anyone apprehending the assailant, but he was gone, so a mercer and an innkeeper, who had houses adjacent to the hosier's shop, were taken as hostages instead.

Seeing the last of the intruders depart, John Stafford made his way back to Shrigley and returned with the family the next day. The local inhabitants had hardly time to recover from their ordeals when news of the Jacobite retreat from Derby, together with the fact that many were returning by way of Macclesfield, instilled a greater shock than had their original arrival on the outskirts of the town. The thought of the rebels' revenge was uppermost in everyone's mind, particularly after the wounding of one of their compatriots. The Mayor and many inhabitants locked up their houses and fled, causing outrage amongst the returning dejected troops. Once more John Stafford's family were evacuated to Shrigley, and by Saturday evening, the 7th December, the town was again occupied. Orders were issued to the High Constable, John Brocklehurst, that if anyone withheld provisions or accommodation, military executions would be carried out. On receiving this account from his clerk, John Stafford immediately walked back from Shrigley the next morning to take charge of the situation. He was well aware of his responsibilities as Deputy Clerk of the Manor and Forest of Macclesfield, even if the Civic dignitaries chose to think otherwise of theirs. John Stafford was personally in some danger, having sent a messenger to Leek carrying a letter in which he wrote disparagingly of the Jacobites. Had this letter fallen into enemy hands, he feared dreadful reprisals.

The young officer of former acquaintance paid a visit to the Stafford household, although not staying on this occasion, and spoke of an expected French landing of some 15,000 men in the South of England, but sounded unconvincing. That night John Stafford again made the tedious journey to Shrigley to be with his family. The next morning the rebels were gone, but not before they had discovered that a subscription had been raised in the town from loyal subjects, in support of the Government. The Mayoress refused to impart any further information to them, despite their numerous menaces, but her husband's clerk, appreciating the seriousness of the situation hurried away and procured the list of subscribers. A further message from John Stafford's clerk produced an instruction for him to pay the sum due on his master's behalf, to the rebel army, in order that he would not suffer retribution if John Stafford refused to pay. This done, he was correctly given a receipt for the payment, which

John Stafford eventually sent with his report. From behind the locked doors, the rebels took their revenge by pilfering money, bedding and clothes, inflicting suffering on both the poor and better off alike.

Samson Salt, taken by the Jacobite army on their march south to Leek, managed to escape and contacted the King's forces at Stone in Staffordshire, but being mistaken for a Jacobite spy was kept confined for two or three days, half delirious, and finally turned out of the camp, from where he quickly hastened home. His arrival coincided with news of the Jacobites' return, whereupon the poor man "sunk down and died instantly".

The second and final report from John Stafford was included at the end of a business letter. Apart from the Macclesfield news, he had also gathered information from outlying areas:

> "As they went from hence to Stockport, stragling partys of 'em pilfered and plundered all the way. Mr. Legh of Adlington and his tenants suffered prodigiously . . . he lost 6 horses and 2 of his servts . . . great quantities of Hay and corn beside many other valuable things. They had taken only 2 Horses of Mr. Legh of Lyme: what other damage they had done I can't tell, but I fear some of the tenants are almost ruined."

Peter Legh the elder had died the previous year and it was his nephew, Peter the younger M.P., who now occupied Lyme Hall. John Ward, the faithful counsellor had written (letter undated):

> "I am concerned I canot attend yo'r Uncle (with whom I have so long a friendship) to the grave. I durst not venture to Winwick at this season having been so long confined to ye house by a cold . . ."

After the Jacobite retreat he again wrote to the nephew on 21st December 1745 from Capesthorne:

> "I am glad to hear by Mr. Roe [this would be James] that you escaped . . . better than some of yo'r neighbours. My poor tenants in Capesthorne (lost) 17 horses out of 18 . . . some will be ruined having no horses nor money to buy."

He continued by explaining that teams of horses had been taken to draw "ye Chevalier's Carriages" and were eventually left near Preston, together with carts from Peter Legh's coal pits. It had been a great expense for someone to retrieve them, but the carts were now returned and the person responsible was demanding 10 shillings for each, towards damages.

John Stafford advised that the rebels had behaved very badly on their return through Stockport, and Alexander Elcocke, Attorney-at-law and partner in the Park Silk Mills, had been dragged around the town with a halter round his neck, together with two or three more citizens, but fortunately they were afterwards released, apparently suffering only humiliation.

In the penultimate paragraph of his letter, John Stafford, not wishing to appear pompous, but obviously very proud of the succeeding event, mentioned the advent of the Duke of Cumberland to the town . . . "it was a particular felicity to me that my house happen'd to be the most convenient in the Town for his Quarters." That visit of William Augustus, second son of King George II and Queen Caroline, gave the name Cumberland House to John Stafford's residence, which it has retained to this day, (and which now comprises a doctors' surgery with many original features still preserved, and a dental practice). By contrast, Holyrood House, the home of Sir Peter Davenport, was demolished many years ago and is now the site of an approach road containing traffic lights, at the entrance to a large roundabout.

A soldier in the Duke's army recorded many details of their journey through England in pursuit of the retreating rebels; he commented that Macclesfield was "a good handsome large town having many good houses" and noted also that "Congleton, as well as this Town are chiefly employed in making Mohair Buttons (etc) for Manchester." The Duke of Cumberland with the King's forces left Macclesfield on Tuesday, 11th December 1745 and headed North. After crossing the River Bollin our correspondent described their journey through part of the large forest of Macclesfield and saw on every side "Pitts where they dig Turf in squares like Bricks, and in these Pitts nothing is more common than to see Fir Trees lie here buried from ten to twenty Foot deep which the Men who work here dig up for various Uses but chiefly for Splinters which are very resinous and when lighted serve the Poor for Candles".

Through every place they passed the behaviour of the rebels on their hasty retreat north was communicated to the army:

> "wherever they rested they had let fall their Odour all over the Towns and at People's Doors (and) so caused the Towns to stink intolerably, many of them also fouled their Beds and commonly the Rooms."

They stole clothes and horses, and whilst one rebel lifted a townsman off his feet, another grabbed his shoes.

The inhabitants of Stockport turned out to watch the Duke's army pass by, but as the bridge over the Mersey had been blown up to delay Prince Charles's original march south, His Majesty's forces and their wives had to wade through "up to their Middles".

Manchester was judged to be the most beautiful town seen in England, yet resembling Holland for its industry. The children, all employed, were able to earn their bread, and the manufacture of "Cottons, Buttons, Fillettings, Checks and all Kind of . . . Small Wares", produced vast quantities of goods for export, particularly to the West Indies.

The army followed the Jacobites back to Scotland where they won a decisive victory at the Battle of Culloden on 16th April 1746. On arrival in Carlisle the Duke of Cumberland's authoritative attitude towards the people had caused great concern, for without hesitation he took into custody the Mayor, Joseph Backhouse, the Town Clerk, John Pearson and eight other individuals who were accused of having surrendered the city. They were immediately sent off to London where they were detained without trial for some time. John Pearson was released, obviously grateful he had abstained from the crucial vote, but the Mayor, thanks to his misplaced bravado in leading the faction wishing to capitulate, paid for his action with imprisonment.

* * * * * * *

During the interim between Charles Roe's initial development of the land near Pickford Bridge and the departure of His Majesty's forces from the town, what other events had occupied his mind?

Primarily Charles's scheme must have advanced rapidly during the summer of 1743, after his marriage. He ensured that Elizabeth's name was included on the lease so that in the event of his death she would have security of tenure, and would be able to lease out the buildings, providing her with a means of support, until the claim for her third part of the estate could be established. That first winter of their marriage brought a very heavy snowfall, which is unusual for the town. Heavy snowfalls mean that Macclesfield is occasionally cut off from the outside world for short periods, but this is due to conditions on the surrounding hills, as very little snow collects in the town itself. The winter of 1743 produced an uncommon item of expenditure in the Church warden's accounts in respect of the Parochial Chapel viz:

"Paid for cleaning the roof after the Great Snow 1-0d. (one shilling)."

It could have been difficult to continue building in such conditions, and any further progress was possibly delayed. It was in the spring that Elizabeth conceived, and their first child, a daughter, was born just after Christmas on the 27th December. By tradition the first child was usually born in the home of the wife's parents, so Charles would take Elizabeth to the Meerbrook Estate, where her step-mother, Dorothy, daughter of Rev. Joseph Dale of Stockport, was able to offer help and advice. This also seems to have been a severe winter, unless Elizabeth had a difficult birth, because it was not until the following 18th April that Catherine, named after her maternal grandmother, was baptised at the Parochial Chapel in Macclesfield (now to be referred to as St. Michael's Church after the rebuilding and extensions of 1740). It was not normal to delay a baptism for such a long period; generally this took place within two weeks of birth, at the most one month, because of the high infant mortality rate, and this does seem to suggest that they were away from the town, and that their return was delayed for some reason.

Later that year, great consternation must have been felt in Charles Roe's household on learning that the Scottish forces were making their way towards Macclesfield during the early part of December. Catherine was not quite one year old and Elizabeth was five months pregnant with their second child. Charles's first priority would have been to ensure their safety and consequently would take them to Meerbrook, where they would most likely join the Lankford household and perhaps retire to the Brassington Estate for the duration of the Jacobite infiltration into the area. Charles's dilemma must have been great: concern for his house and goods, not to mention his newly built business premises on Parsonage Green yet, at the same time, anxiety for the safety of his family. But whether or not circumstances forced him to keep faith with his neighbours and remain in the town during the crisis, may never be known. Every penny he had was tied up in his grand scheme, and fear of theft and destruction must have encouraged him to keep a vigilant watch on his possessions. After all, premises of any large size were at a premium and necessary for the accommodation of Jacobite soldiers. After the Scottish army's crushing defeat in April 1746, life could once more return to normal and plans be made for the future.

8
AN EVENTFUL YEAR

The busy candidates for power and fame,
Have hopes, and fears, and wishes, just the same;

During the year 1595, in the reign of Elizabeth I, the burgesses of Macclesfield had obtained a new charter to consolidate their position as a Corporation. This established a form of local government which continued, virtually unaltered, until the year 1834. The Corporation comprised:

A Mayor – elected yearly by the Capital Burgesses, on the Friday after Michaelmas.
2 Aldermen.
24 men (of better and honest sort) to be called Capital Burgesses.
A High Steward.
One or more men 'learned-in-law' to be his deputies.
A Sergeant at Mace.

The original number of burgesses was 120, all owning burgages or house plots in the town, but as the 18th century progressed this number reached 280, probably caused by subdivision of plots, or, as in the case of Charles Roe, one person continuing to own the land but selling the property standing on it to someone else.

Charles was elected Mayor for the year 1747-48, commencing in the autumn term. He had been proudly recorded as Alderman in St. Michael's register against his children's baptismal entries. Catherine now had two brothers: William, born on 10th April and baptised on 2nd May 1746, and Charles (Jnr.) born on 3rd and baptised on 24th July 1747. Charles, breaking with tradition, named William, not after one of the child's grandfathers, but after his deceased elder brother, whom he had loved and regarded as a father figure during the most vulnerable period of his life. Sadly young Charles did not survive, dying at an early age.

Another death, that of William Hawkins, burgess, meant that John Stafford was elected Town Clerk to replace him, commencing 23rd April 1748. This position, usually for life, was held in conjunction with his prime office, which by then was Clerk to the Court of the Manor and Forest of Macclesfield. John Stafford was becoming a very busy man, due in no small part to the death of John Ward, barrister-at-law of Capesthorne, in the same year; it was the end of an era. This kindly man, on his wife's death in 1744, had written:

"It pleased God ye 20th last month to take my dear Wife If we had both lived to August we should have been married 50 years After so long an Union I find it hard to part but we must submit to ye wise Disposer of all things She is released from an infirm state of health & if anybody was well prepared for another world she was I pray God fit us all for our great Change."

John Stafford's growing reputation ensured that several of the Ward clientele placed their confidence and cases in his hands. One such important client was Peter Legh the younger of Lyme, but he was not the same affable character as his uncle had been. He was more remote, emotionless and matter-of-fact, yet to his credit he was aware of this and on occasion tried to make amends.

John Stafford would greatly appreciate the extra remuneration required to maintain his position in society, particularly as his wife, Lucy, was a member of the Tatton family, who were always in the height of fashion. Son William destined to be a solicitor, had to be provided with a good education, and should the need arise, his three daughters, Sarah, Lucy and Penelope Margaret, would have to be furnished with respectable marriage portions, if they were to marry well. There is evidence to suggest that John Stafford had become the guardian of a young girl, Elizabeth Blagg, whose family had lived in Macclesfield for at least two centuries, and of which she was the only remaining member.

Elizabeth's uncle, Edward, had invested in a large estate called 'The Fence' or 'Lowerfence' in Hurdsfield (now part of the site of the King's School for Girls on Fence Avenue) upon his marriage to Elizabeth Janney, using her marriage portion of £1,500. The estate was originally purchased on 3rd August 1728, but the couple died without issue and so it devolved upon Elizabeth's father, William, heir-at-law. This would create an interesting situation whereby William would have to return to his brother's wife's family the appropriate sum in compensation for her marriage settlement, but he in turn, in negotiating his own marriage settlement, would hope to be recompensed by a comparable figure from his future father-in-law. This sort of situation was more than likely responsible for the instances in which a widower married his deceased wife's sister (although it was considered illegal in the eyes of the Church) because it would conveniently maintain the status quo so far as the marriage settlement was concerned, thus avoiding any financial embarrassment and awkward situations where money was invested in business assets.

On 30th July 1738, William Blagg married Anna Norton and lived in Fence House, where their only surviving child, Elizabeth, was born. Anna was a good Christian who stood up for her beliefs. On one occasion, one of the younger workmen on the estate, David Pickford, had received his weekly wage on the Saturday evening as usual with the rest of the workers, when he was harassed by them in an attempt to force him to accompany them to the alehouse. They had probably learnt that he had attended a small gathering of the so-called Methodists at Shrigley Fold, Higher Hurdsfield. No one knew very much about the Methodists except, like the Dissenters before them, they were mainly part of the Church of England congregation that wished to rid themselves of the hierarchy within the Church. They wanted to create a more down-to-earth religion, feeling that it would reach the lower social levels of society in a more positive way than the rituals and practices still upheld by the Church of England. The inspiration for their movement had come from a young minister called John Wesley, who had no intention of leaving the Church, but who was hoping in some way to bring about a reformation by his actions.

Wesley had made an unsuccessful tour of America during 1737, followed by a tour of Germany in 1738, but despite his travels at home, had made very little impact on English Society at this time. The Methodists in their desire for sobriety had created an impression of 'kill-joys' which was not very appealing to the public in general, attracting ridicule and bigotry, and this was the situation in which David Pickford had found himself. Having refused to join his workmates for a jug of ale, the overlooker ordered him to fetch his tools and go home, threatening to "turn him away". Unsure of whether or not he would be allowed back onto the estate to work, he hurried home upset, having the welfare of his wife and four young children to consider. That night he dreamed that he had to tell Mrs. Blagg, which gave him the courage to go and see her. Anna was determined that David would not be dismissed and shortly afterwards the overlooker was discharged and David "put in his place".

At the time of Elizabeth's baptism on 12th October 1740, her father, William, was recorded as

Alderman in St. Michael's register, but he did not live long; it is possible that his position of Alderman had been taken by Charles Roe. Unfortunately the Corporation records leave much to be desired until the acceptance of John Stafford as Town Clerk, when his ability to create order, and the thoroughness with which he discharged his duties, brought a professional attitude to the administration of the Borough including a more meticulous method of recording information.

William Blagg's will, dated 15th February 1742, was witnessed by Rev. James Roe, Charles Roe and John Stafford. The original will and codicil are missing but there remains an unusual affidavit signed and sworn by Joseph Hobson, a button merchant and Quaker. It refers to the codicil made almost three weeks later on the 5th March, by which Hobson was nominated and appointed executor. This seems strange when one considers that William Blagg was a loyal member of the Church of England and already had three reliable witnesses. By the affidavit dated 15th September 1743, Joseph Hobson emphatically refused "to take upon him the Execution thereof". From a land transaction 20 years later, there is an indication that Hobson had lent money to William Blagg and was therefore concerned about the repayment of it. John Stafford would be anxious for Hobson not to try to force a sale of part of the premises so that the estate could be run to the best possible advantage for Elizabeth, only four years of age. The interest payable on any loans would be calculated and paid when it became due. Quakers, like the Jews, were hard-working business enthusiasts, and many of them by this time had accrued vast sums of money, in spite of fines they had suffered earlier for their beliefs. They were always anxious to invest money and had no scruples about lending it to persons outside their groups; in fact, if the interest was not paid in due course, they had a valid reason for land seizure, which further consolidated their position. For whatever reason, something or someone had persuaded Joseph Hobson to 'leave well alone' and relinquish his Executorship, allowing John Stafford to take full responsibility for the child and her inheritance. Elizabeth appears to have been brought up in the Stafford household and the Fence estate leased to tenants.

An important part of the Blagg estate was income from coal mines in the Rainow area known as 'upper and lower Clift near Clift (Cliff) Lane'. William Blagg had specifically requested that the mines should not be let to others, but continue to be worked by his trustees for the benefit of his daughter, until she reached 21 years of age.

About this time, no doubt at the insistence of Lucy, his wife, John Stafford modernised his house and had a Venetian window installed in his drawing room.

Fortunately the Glover residence across the way from Cumberland House, in which a large group of Jacobites had slept on the straw strewn floor, was left untouched. Samuel Glover's money was needed for a very important project in which he had become involved, so the facade, reminiscent of the Blenheim style, remained, and still remains unaltered.

Thomas Birtles, no doubt following the Stafford lead, also modernised. He had the outside of his premises on Chestergate rebuilt, retaining many internal features, including a fine Jacobean 'barley-sugar twist' staircase, but converting the former properties into one large house with the addition of a Venetian window in the drawing room at the rear. This is probably why he borrowed £300 from his uncle, Richard Bagshawe of Castleton, by bond dated 14th October 1748. He was already heavily in debt, having travelled to Ford Hall in June of that year in order to accompany his cousin to a solicitor's office and present the property deeds relating to the Birtles Estate, for inspection. The land was reckoned to cover 100 Cheshire acres (210 statute acres), and against this Thomas Birtles had already borrowed £1,500. Charles Roe's new enterprise must have had a formidable effect on Thomas Birtles's business profits, and must have caused some antagonism, resulting in the removal of Samuel Lankford from the Meerbrook Estate to Macclesfield; Leek was a stronghold for the Birtles family. An additional reason could have been the death of Lankford's second wife and a desire to be closer to his son-in-law's venture.

Lankford's eldest son, Harry, now 13 years old, would presumably attend Stockport

Grammar School, where his grandfather was headmaster. The other two children, Mary aged seven years and Samuel only three would remain with their father. Samuel Lankford was already in Macclesfield by 1747, described as a 'Buttonmaker' when his name appeared on a deed as trustee of Francis Stavely Coutsbury, Derbyshire in connection with a lead mine called Whale Sough. On the same day that John Stafford was appointed Town Clerk, Samuel Lankford became a Capital Burgess and leased Rainow Hall for himself and his family. This involved a steep climb eastwards from the town through Hurdsfield, passing the small warehouse and twisting shop of the Brocklehurst family on the righthand side, then traversing a winding track rising sharply to the village of Rainow, nestling snugly behind Kerridge Hill. With him moved his centre of operations for his button trade.

A happy event took place at St. Michael's church on 16th August 1748 when Charles Roe's sister, Mary, married Rowland Atkinson, second master of the Macclesfield Free Grammar School. Charles must have been particularly pleased because Mary was nearly 35 years of age, making her the senior of her husband by almost 10 years.

* * * * * * *

The Atkinsons were an old Lakeland family from the district of Troutbeck, near Windermere. Both Rowland's grandfather and father were doctors, and his father had married Agnes Cookson, who came from an important family in the North East, involved in the business of lead and iron, both mining and smelting. Rowland was the youngest of four brothers and three sisters. The eldest, John, had followed in the footsteps of his father and grandfather, providing yet another M.D. for Troutbeck Bridge. Christopher, born in 1713, just 15 months younger than John, was a vicar, having obtained his M.A. from Queens College, Oxford. The third brother, Thomas, was involved in ironworks at Cockermouth and near Whitehaven, encouraged by his mother's family's connections in the trade. The union between Mary and Rowland was to have an important effect on Charles's future.

The Free Grammar School records, like the Corporation records, are scant before this period, but it is possible to piece together the sequence of events which provided Rowland Atkinson with his appointment in Macclesfield.

In 1672 the marriage linking the Swettenham family of Swettenham near Macclesfield, and the Wilsons of Dallam Tower near Milnthorpe, Co. Westmorland has, of course, been mentioned. The Swettenhams were closely related to the local Comberbach and Glegg families who had strong military and legal connections (hence their affiliations with Masonic lodges). John Baskervyle, friend and associate of John Stafford, who would later change his name to Glegg to inherit a family estate, was a governor of the Macclesfield Grammar School. Another colleague, Joseph Comberbach, prepared and witnessed the Articles of Agreement dated 28th May 1748 for the new grammar school premises. The final link was between the Wilsons of Dallam Tower and the Flemings of Rydal Hall, Coniston.

Sir William Fleming, 1st Baronet, at the age of 67 years had successfully married a young lady, Dorothy Rolandson, aged 22 years. By the time Sir William died in 1736, aged 80 years, his marriage had produced three daughters, who subsequently married well. The eldest, Dorothy, married Edward Wilson of Dallam Tower in 1746, and the youngest, Catherine, would marry Sir Peter Byrne in 1755, who in order to inherit the Tabley Estate near Knutsford in Cheshire, adopted the family name, Leycester. These marriages demonstrate that the close family ties had been maintained from one generation to the next; the Tabley Estate lies approximately eight miles to the north of Swettenham village.

The Rydal Hall estate was entailed, which meant that it passed to Sir William's brother, Sir George, Bishop of Carlisle. Upon his death in 1747, once again the estate passed to another male heir, his nephew, Sir William.

It was whilst the estate was in the hands of Sir George, Bishop of Carlisle, that Rowland

Atkinson's brother, Christopher, was recommended and obtained the post of Usher (Second Master) at the Macclesfield Grammar School.

The Atkinson, an important and highly respected family, had second cousins who were solicitors in Kendal and numbered amongst their friends a Sheriff of Cumberland.

Christopher Atkinson, on leaving Queens College, Oxford, had accepted the curacy of Troutbeck from 13th January 1735. During the following year his father died and was buried there. Shortly afterwards he had married Jane Johnson of Old Hall near Kendal, and as a consequence their first child, a boy, born 6th March 1739 was given the unlikely name of Johnson Atkinson. Not to be outdone the eldest brother, John, M.D. of Troutbeck Bridge, six months later baptised his first child, also a boy, Cookson Atkinson, the surname of his mother's family. These two unusual names would subsequently appear on many occasions in the records of a future Macclesfield company.

Christopher remained at Troutbeck for 10 years during which time his family grew; he would eventually have 12 children. He knew the Bishop of Carlisle very well and would have communicated to him his anxiety to obtain a good living. The Flemings, as most families of that period, were in constant touch with their close relatives, arranging visits, exchanging letters, helping with petitions and requests on behalf of estate workers and associates in the professions. The Swettenham family near Macclesfield, and the Wilson and Fleming families of the Lake District, being so intimately connected, would discuss a whole variety of matters amongst themselves, putting forward recommendations to each other, including a good deal of gossip, which not only sustained the bond between them but stimulated connections over a much wider area, incorporating their friends, associates and servants. Obviously the Bishop of Carlisle had let it be known amongst his nieces and their families that he had a very good curate who deserved a better living, and, should such a situation arise, he would be obliged by their assistance.

In the middle of the year 1745, before the arrival of Charles Edward Stuart, Macclesfield Grammar School required a headmaster. The Governors met on 2nd July and appointed Rev. Edward Ford M.A. who had to give bonds in the sum of £5,000. They were determined to improve the standard of the school by ensuring that a person of high calibre was appointed, particularly after their problems of the last few years when certain masters had not fulfilled their promise. The Second Master, Rev. John Ashworth, was a very old man and by receiving a substantial payment of £240 needed very little persuading to take 'early' retirement. This gave the Governors the opportunity to appoint a new Usher at the same time as the Headmaster, so Rev. Christopher Atkinson B.A. arrived in Macclesfield to take up his appointment. Surprisingly he was also compelled to present bonds of £5,000 and to resign his 'spiritual preferment' i.e. the curacy of Troutbeck, within six months. This astronomical sum must have equalled the value of all school assets, and in the unlikely event of anything going wrong, as in the case of a fraud being perpetrated, the Governors would have some guarantee of recompense. Christopher would not be able to substantiate the total amount himself and would need others to act as sureties.

The Governors called a meeting on 2nd September at which it was recorded in the Minute Book that Mr. Ford had resigned and a payment had been made to him of £10 10s. out of School Revenues "in consequence of Expenses he hath been put to in his application." It is more than likely that he could not fulfil the requirement of the bond, and must have been surprised at its enormity. Immediately Christopher Atkinson was elected Headmaster "unanimously" at a salary of £60 per annum with the perquisite of the school house rent free, whilst brother Rowland was accepted as Second Master, salary £40 per annum, but the stipulation of a bond was waived. Had Christopher made such an outstanding impression on the School Governors, or was it the involvement of the Bishop of Carlisle which had been the deciding factor? Perhaps, in fairness, it was both.

After the Estate had devolved upon the Bishop's nephew Sir William in 1747, John Atkinson, the eldest brother, became doctor to the next generation of Flemings now resident at Rydal Hall. The family were again referred to as 'le Fleming', Sir William having reinstated the 'le' as part of the family name at his son's baptism. It had originally been deleted by an ancestor, but the Georgian trend for individualism and novelty had promoted its acceptance as fashionable once more. The le Flemings had a long tradition of being M.P.s and J.P.s, and in this respect Sir William was beginning to work closely with John Pearson, Town Clerk of Carlisle, who was instructing him on the procedures of the Quarter Sessions and other legal matters.

Charles Roe, now kinsman to this very important family, found himself introduced into a much wider social circle. However, Mary's marriage must have presented him with some problems in respect of the settlement. Rev. James would not be able to contribute in any way, so Charles, as usual, would have to take the responsibility. Apart from Charles's concern with education, which was of mutual interest to both himself and the Atkinsons, his connections with lead mining also formed a significant bond. He appears to have offered to Rowland, as part of the marriage settlement, a share of the Roe interests in the Derbyshire lead mines, thus compensating for Mary's loss of the half share in the Brookhead Sough. This would have been discussed with Rev. James, and to this end the investments were reorganised.

* * * * * * *

During 1746 Magclough sough had finally reached the Great-brook-head vein and all the partners of the two mines, being sensible and not wishing to become involved in lengthy and expensive litigations, combined operations. This was the mine in which William and Charles had held an interest inherited from their father. A 'Reckoning at Gt. Brookhead' for the period '8/12/46 - 2/5/47' shows 'Mr. Wroe' holding a $1/96$ share. The meeting took place in Sheffield viz:

> "Sheffield 20th Nov. 1746,
> It is agreed that all the Veins & Mineral Interests of Mag-clough & Great-brook-head be consolidated & made one united Mineral Interest that the Tools & Engines at each Mine be valued . . . and the partnership that hath the lefser Quantity of Tools . . . pay a sum of Money to the other partnership to bring them to an Equality" . . .

One of the leading shareholders in both mines was still Richard Bagshawe, Esq., which considerably helped the consolidation. The Roe share for the whole mine was $1/48$ which was now converted into a $1/96$ share in the new partnership, Consolidated Tytles. The adjustment made between the shares of the old and new enterprise meant that "Mr. Roe" received £25 for a $1/6$ part.

In 1747 reorganisation of the soughs along Eyam Edge relating to the Old Great Vein, or Great-brook-head, took place with the closure of Magclough. A note headed "The Rev'd Mr. Roe Extrs – 1747" could either refer to father, Thomas, or brother, William, but it is of no consequence which, because as only James and Charles were involved, they seem to have decided to share all the lead mining investments. The shares listed on the note are:

Stoke	$1/192$
Consolidated Tytles	$1/96$
Ladywash	–

The Stoke sough, originally begun in 1720-22, like Magclough had been intended to underwater the Hucklow vein; there is no evidence of investment in it by Rev. Thomas Roe. In 1734 it was said to have lowered the water in the Eyam Edge mines, but by 1738 the costs had risen to between £11-12,000. Due to a dispute the sough was then dammed up until

1747 when it was re-opened in order to supersede Magclough. The intention was to drive the branch northwesterly in order to reach the Ladywash possessions; Rev. James and Charles bought a $^1/_{192}$ share in this undertaking.

Rev. James still held from his original shares:

Miners	$^1/_{48}$
Milnes & Middleton	$^1/_{96}$ (now combined)
Moorwood	$^1/_{192}$

All these soughs had directly developed from exploration eastwards on the Hucklow Edge vein. As these were producing a good steady income, it was decided to hold the shares jointly. There had been a dispute relating to this group of mines, which because of its complicated nature had not been settled by the Barmote Court but was tried at "the Court of King's Bench by a Derbyshire Jury" in the Easter term of 1745, and as a result, a consolidation had taken place. During the next five years (1748-1753), the Moorwood Engine would be worked in conjunction with Bradshaw's Engine sough and the Roes would acquire a $^1/_{192}$ share in Old and New Bradshaw's, indicating that as the Moorwood sough was driven towards Bradshaw's Engine, a new working from Bradshaw's was also driven towards Moorwood, until the two intersected.

James appreciated that he had received the benefit of the majority of the shares during his years of education, but the time had now arrived for Charles and Mary also to benefit. By her mother's will Mary was to receive an additional £200, which normally would have been invested in safe securities such as Government Bonds. If the £200 had been invested on Mary's behalf by the Trustees, then it would have been mentioned in either the will of Rev. William Street or of Robert Charlesworth of Castleton. The latter will contains details of money outstanding to a Sheffield family for whom Charlesworth was Trustee, but there is no mention of any Roe investments. Perhaps it had been used by the Roe family in their struggle to survive, and brother William would have taken responsibility for that. Charles must have accepted that only he could provide the £200 with the addition of interest due, towards Mary's marriage portion, though how he achieved this is not known. In no way was Rowland Atkinson allowed a share in the silk venture, this was tied up with the marriage settlement of Charles and Elizabeth Lankford and any benefit arising therefrom, was reserved for the children of their marriage.

* * * * * * *

Secretly, Charles must have been profoundly grateful for the absence of one particular controversial character during his year as Mayor. Sir Peter Davenport, conspicuous by his disappearance at the time of the Jacobite approach, had passed out of Macclesfield's history. The circumstances of his death are not known, except that he was buried in the Parochial Chapel on 27th January 1747. His daughter Elizabeth at 18 years of age was still a minor, and as such was deemed incapable of managing her father's estate. She nominated her uncle, Charles Legh of Adlington, together with George Legh of Tatton and Francis Jodrell of Twemlow to be her administrators. There were probably some outstanding debts to be settled as it was considered necessary to sell the property on Back Street and the adjacent land. The Macclesfield Free Grammar School, close by St. Michael's, had become inadequate for the ambitious schemes envisaged by the Governors; it was a very old building. Holyrood House, with its outbuildings including stables and sufficient land, seemed an ideal alternative. The purchase was made by John Stafford, acting as trustee for the Governors. Articles of Agreement, drawn up between himself and the three administrators on 28th May 1748, agreed a purchase price of £550, payable in two equal instalments of £275 on the following

29th September and 25th December. Even at this early date fixtures and fittings were considered part of the sale:

> "It is agreed between the partys that all Chimney Pieces Wainscote & Locks on the Doors and Lead Cisterns and such other things that are fixed and usually go along with the house sold" . . . were to be included.

Permission was given to start alterations before the first payment was made, in particular the stable furniture could be sold and alterations made to the outbuildings. The Articles of Agreement were witnessed by both Christopher and Rowland Atkinson on 24th June 1748. They benefited greatly by being able to take up residence in Holyrood House, which became the home of the Headmaster.

The old school building and plot of land known as School Bank were sold to Nathaniel Bradock in 1748 for £120, and he is said to have converted the premises into a button manufactory.

* * * * * * *

Just after the completion of Charles's year in office as Mayor, George Nicholson, brother of Francis and a partner of the Park Silk Mills, wrote a rather scathing letter to John Stafford, at least by Georgian standards. Given the height of indignation, the majority of letters were written in a well-mannered and polite fashion, it was the basis of Georgian society. Everything, as much as possible, was found to be "agreable". Business letters were always concluded with respects to the family of the recipient, concerns for health matters, and final courtesies such as "Your most obliged Friend & Humble Servant"; "Your very Humble Servant"; "I am Dear Father, Your most Dutiful & Affectionate Son", and so forth. The tone of George Nicholson's letter, dated 14th November 1748, was an indication of some financial instability. He referred to "this Mad Affair" in which his brother, Francis and John Stafford seemed so indifferent "as if it was of no manner of consequence to me to have my Right invaded & my Property detained from me by force of Arms". He asserted that he had endeavoured "to Avoid & Stem the Torrent of Distruction that seems to threaten the Family through the obstinacy of the One & the Sapine negligence of the Other Executor". Strong words: the former a reference to his brother, Francis and the latter, John Stafford. He was referring to the execution of his mother's will.

Alice Nicholson, a resident of Macclesfield, had been buried at St. Mary's Stockport on 18th January 1747. Her will, prepared some years earlier, on 28th November 1741, appointed her son, George and John Stafford as Executors. George was bequeathed £80 and her silver cup. Francis had already received his £80 in advance as a loan, on which he paid his mother £4 per annum interest, but he was to receive two silver spoons. Brother, Ralph and sister, Alice, whose husband was a goldsmith, were also left £80 and two silver spoons each. The "China, linnen & wearing apparell" amongst other items were to be divided amongst the grandchildren and Alice was to be given her mother's spinning wheel.

The only person who could have been causing problems for George Nicholson in his capacity as Executor, was his sister's husband, Josiah Stringer, goldsmith. Francis, already given the benefit of his money, would also have access to his mother's chattels. George had been visited by the bailiffs, "they have allready got my Coat by Law [would] You have me give them my Cloak also . . . He was obviously short of cash either due to his own extravagances or a depletion in the profits of the Park Silk Mills. He had borrowed £170 from his mother, on 2nd February 1734, no doubt needed for investment in the Silk Mill, but this had been repaid. Nothing more is known of George Nicholson until his death in 1755.

By 1743 the Stockport Silk Mill had been proving very profitable, as witnessed by the will of Alexander Elcock, Attorney, prepared on the 22nd December 1743 in which he stated:

"AND WHEREAS I am pofsefsed of & Intitled unto One undivided Twelfth part or Share of & in the Silk Mills called the Park Mills in Stockport . . . which s'd Twelfth share (altho' I reckon it valluable) may by Misfortunes in trade and inevitable accidents be reduced however till that happen . . . the Annuall profitts . . . will bring in a comfortable Subsiftence to and for my Dear & Loving Wife & family . . ."

As a subsequence of his calculation Elcock designated £50 per annum to his wife; the residue to be used for the children's education and divided equally amongst them. There were two sons and three daughters to be considered, so he must have presumed a profit of at least £100 to £150 per annum. This provides some idea of the potential of the Silk Mill at this time. The expenses would be heavy, including the wages of the workforce, which would have been little less than the Derby Mill, but if a $^1/_{12}$ share was taken as £125 per annum on average, then the total profit for the year would be somewhere in the region of £1,500. It must be remembered that the silk business provided only part of each partner's income; of the details known, all held properties and lands from which they received rents, some were merchants in their own right, whilst Alexander Elcock had his own law practice in and around the town of Stockport.

So far as the estate was concerned, Alexander's wife was to be allowed the use and benefit of the properties, but on her death it was to pass to the eldest son. Elcock died on 2nd August 1748 and with his departure from the Park Mills partnership, the driving force seemed to disappear. If his investments had brought him any sort of satisfaction, he had been called upon to pay for it in other ways. First the humiliation of being dragged around the streets of Stockport by the Jacobite rebels, and then the tragedy of his eldest son, John, to whom he intended leaving his law books and estate. The anguish which he suffered in adding a codicil to his will on 7th February 1746, is demonstrated by three alterations in the opening phrases which were left to read:

"Whereas I the Testator Alex'r Elcock having found by sad experience since publishing of my s'd will . . . that my Eldest son John grows more and more unadvisable & lefs capable of Governing himself when in Liquor to which he is but too much addicted . . ."

The codicil revoked John's inheritance which was left instead to the second son, Thomas.

* * * * * * *

April 1748 saw the end of a long and complicated war which had started in 1740 over the question of the Austrian Succession. Britain had been at war with Spain since 1739, but only indirectly with France as an ally of Austria since 1741, until France finally declared war on England in 1744. This, of course, had temporarily given the English silk industry a chance to dominate with the reduction of French imports, which were so popular. War, however, was fought very much on a local basis at this period, with people passing freely to and fro across Europe, avoiding the battle grounds. Even without the help of smuggling, many French goods would still be arriving in our ports by devious means; if a profit could be made, there were always those who would find a way to make it, just as today.

The Bank of England had received a renewal of its Charter in 1742, and although the war was a strain on national finances, the Bank coped well. With the restoration of international peace in 1748 came a period of great stability, producing a good working relationship between the Treasury and the Bank, and an involvement in experimental banking both in England and Scotland, which provided a solid platform for British industries at an important stage of their development.

Charles had judged well the time to expand his silk interests, but since 1746 had been experiencing difficulties with regard to the main part of his plan, the building of the large silk mill intended to house replicas of the Lombe machinery. His business of button merchant had continued, probably in co-operation with John Pickering, who seems likely to have overseen the making of the moulds, or been responsible for the button production on a subcontract basis i.e. working as a small manufactory within a larger manufactory, which became very much a pattern of the Georgian industrial scene as the century progressed. This kept the book-keeping simple as each party worked as a separate entity, charging goods from one to another on a credit note system. The embroidery of the buttons, and also buttonholes, would still be carried out by workers at home, who in the main were married women with small children and babies to look after. It would also be continued in the Corporation Poorhouse by the young orphans and older residents. Another probability was that Charles was supplying the raw materials to other workhouses or small button manufactories in the town, and ensuring the collection of the finished articles, to be sold onwards on a co-operative basis.

One of the first buildings, therefore, to have been erected on the Parsonage Green site would have been a small workshop for the joiners, who would not only produce button moulds but also any machinery required. Next would be a building containing large rooms for the twisters and doublers; the twisters were mostly men or boys and the doublers women and older girls. Charles was now fully occupied in organising and expanding his business in the one location, on a scale hitherto unknown in Macclesfield. The women with young children and babies staying home, would require the help of an older daughter to assist with the numerous household chores. Their small garden plots still had to be looked after and any animals attended to. Supplies of milk and water were essential and the laborious duties of washing, baking, collecting fuel, feeding hens and helping with the pigs in the middingsteads all took time. Predominantly it would be the husbands, sons and other daughters who would go out to work, experiencing for the first time the excitement of working together in large buildings erected especially for the purpose. One can imagine the dilemmas which occurred, with mothers insisting that their husbands kept a strict eye upon the children, particularly the girls, in order that no untoward behaviour took place. The majority of the employees would be from the congregation of St. Michael's, and James concerned himself with the welfare of these silk-worker in the same way as his father and elder brother had administered to the miners on the Common.

Another two buildings of great importance and absolute necessity were the compting house and warehouse. A good clerk and also a book-keeper were needed and had to be of exemplary character, because not only was absolute trust essential in the handling of cash and other matters, but it was imperative that customers' accounts be kept correctly. One young man who would certainly fulfil these requirements was the son of Rev. John Robinson, Prime Curate of St. Michael's; he would eventually become a partner in the concern and a button merchant at a later date.

Charles's connections in London developed rapidly as he undertook more journeys to ensure a steady supply of silk for his workers. (The mohair was more than likely being supplied by Samuel Lankford.) Raw silk arrived at the Port of London in two different forms. Firstly hanks, which had been wound directly from the fine silk thread shrouding the silkworm (species *Bombyx mori*) by a process known as reeling, and secondly, bales of waste silk. The Chinese and Italian silk was of a far superior quality to that of Turkey or India, the latter (as mentioned) was used 'mostly in the Button, and Twist, and Stocking Way', but 'White China Silk' was considered 'absolutely necessary for fine Gauze Silk Stockings'.

* * * * * * *

An old engraving showing the Emperor Justinian receiving from the monks the first silkworm eggs to reach the western world.

A sixteenth-century engraving showing peasants feeding silkworms on mulberry foliage.

Courtesy of the European Council for the Promotion of Silk

The initial process of silk production took place in the country of origin where the silkworms were reared. China can claim to be the first country to produce silk, accredited to the Empress Hsi Ling Shi about the year 2640 B.C. The Chinese love to give credence to their legends by allocating dates, and the development of sericulture is always attributed to this Empress. The monopoly was remarkably preserved in China for about 3000 years, from where it spread into Korea, a country over which China had long claimed suzerainty. Of the incredible silk stories concerning its diffusion throughout the East, the one relating to a Japanese mission in the 3rd century, sent to capture silkworm eggs and workers, seems to be the most acceptable, but there is also the story of a Chinese princess travelling to India for her marriage to a prince and hiding a batch of eggs in her headdress. Two Persian monks, previously mentioned, claimed responsibility for its advent into the West via Constantinople, from where it was transported into Spain, Sicily and Italy by the involvement of the Arabs.

In the first instance eggs would be allowed to complete their life cycle, emerging as moths from the pupae in due course. After mating female moths lay their eggs on the leaves of mulberry trees, which must be of a suitable variety. Within a week ant like creatures hatch out, their sole concern in life to eat and eat both day and night, until five weeks later, having shed several skins, each one has grown from 1 to 70 or 80 millimetres long. About this time each resultant caterpillar or silkworm begins to change its behavioural pattern as it feels the urge to create a cocoon. It emits a pair of endless filaments from two apertures, one on each side of its head; these threads are bound together as one by a gummy substance secreted by the worm called sericin. This resultant thread or filature is manoeuvred into figures of eight, as the caterpillar moves its head from side to side, in the process of wrapping itself up inside its cosy, sticky cocoon. The sericin hardens allowing the caterpillar to change into a chrysalis, from which the moth eventually emerges by dissolving the sericin with a brown solution and forcing its way through.

For the production of silk, it is essential that during the cocoon stage, the chrysalis is killed and the filature unwound from around its body, but obviously some silkworms must be allowed to complete the metamorphosis in order to produce eggs for the following year's crop. This is done by keeping eggs of both sexes, which are easily distinguishable, in a cool atmosphere, it arrests their urge to spin cocoons, and enables the silk-workers to store them until the following spring when, with a little encouraging warmth, they return to their predestined occupation.

At the appropriate time the silk cocoons are gathered for the first process to be carried out, that of reeling. A 16th century engraving portrays one method used by showing cocoons placed in shallow trays over the tops of stoves or ovens; heat applied in this way not only killed the chrysalis but softened the gum. Another method was to place several cocoons in a container of boiling water for some time, and then allow it to cool a little. Once the end of a filature was loose, the unravelling could begin by passing the thread through a small wire loop positioned over the top of the stove. One filature was so incredibly fine that it was necessary to wind several together to make the strands more manageable. It was found convenient to pass the filatures of 6 or 7 cocoons through the same loop for reeling, because as the gum solidified once more, it bound them together as one substantial thread, which could then be tied to a large wooden frame. As several wire loops were in position, held in line above the trays, it created a process of multiplicity, enabling many strands to be attached to the revolving wooden frame which was turned by a handle, thus allowing hanks to be formed at various intervals along its length.

As much silk as possible was removed from the cocoons by this method, but the shells, with their residue of silk and sericin still adhering, were packed together as solidly as possible and exported in large sticky, dirty bales. This was the waste silk, which at first glance would be considered totally unusable. Amazingly it was from this waste that the finest silk was produced. It required more attention, but the trouble was well worthwhile.

Originally Charles would be purchasing raw silk in the form of hanks only, for his twisters in the twisting crofts, and also when they were first transferred to Parsonage Green. The job

The process of reeling silk from cocoons in Piedmont.

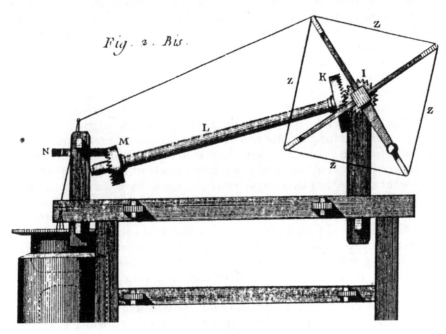

The reeling machine in detail showing the conversion of the silk
threads from the cocoons to hanks.

Details from Diderot's *Encyclopedie.*

of the twisters and throwsters was to twist and double the filature into more substantial yarns, depending on the requirements of the weavers, because different fabrics demanded different thicknesses of thread. Once Charles had brought together the throwsters under one roof, it would then be possible to use double Dutch mills operated by a small water wheel, identical to the process carried out in Mr. Cotchet's original mill in Derby. He had already obtained water rights in the Dams Brook which flowed by the side of the building, and the facility of this water also made it possible for him to handle waste silk, although the transportation of this from London would not be as convenient as the hanks.

In order to handle waste silk it was necessary to have large copper containers in which to boil up the masses of sticky, dirty cocoons. To purchase these containers would be expensive, and whether or not Thomas Patten Jnr. of Warrington would be able to supply either copper sheets, which could be shaped and set into position over the stoves, or the large copper containers at this time is debatable. The most likely source for the receptacles would be Bristol.

The waste silk had to be boiled up with plenty of soap, which was already being produced adjacent to the site, at the bottom of Mill Street, in the cottages which extended eastwards to St. James Square. When the waste silk had been thoroughly cleaned and rinsed, it was imperative that it should be dried as quickly as possible in a building where plenty of warm air could circulate.

The next stage required that the silk, now soft and lustrous, be combed. Charles would have to purchase expensive brass wire for his combs, iron had been used in the past, but brass was far superior. The brass wire was being produced at Thomas Patten's wire mill at Alton, near Cheadle, Staffordshire and Charles would definitely have made the journey to purchase the valuable commodity himself, and take stock of the works.

After the silk had been combed, it was spun, in exactly the same way as cotton or wool, but the ensuing process of doubling was unique to silk production. All the silk, whether from the original hanks still containing sericin or the spun silk without sericin, had to be created into more substantial threads for the weavers, and a careful count taken of the numbers of threads twisted together; these could then be doubled and twisted again, and this action called 'throwing' was repeated many times if required. It was also necessary to establish a method of regulating the number of twists in each inch so that identical yarn could be reproduced if and when requested.

One final process was necessary for the waste silk only; because of the nature of its creation, it was inevitable that whiskers and bits of fluff remained attached to the fibres and it was desirable for the weavers to have these removed. This process was called singeing, necessitating the finished yarn to be passed quickly through a flame. Large candles would be used, again conveniently supplied by the soapmaker, who was also the tallow chandler, close by. The Park Silk Mills of Stockport contained a singeing house for this purpose, and Charles would also need to include one on his site.

From later developments, it appears that at this stage the silk was left in hanks or skeins and used primarily for the button trade, although some of the better quality might have been acceptable to the London weavers and weavers within the region, including the stocking weavers of Macclesfield. Some weavers preferred to weave silk containing sericin, it made the task easier, but in this condition the silk could not be dyed. Large quantities of material were very difficult to dye evenly and to dry, so often garments were made up first by the tailor or dressmaker, then washed thoroughly in soapy water to remove any trace of sericin, and afterwards dyed. This had the additional advantage of ensuring that the silk sewing thread, used in the preparation of the garments, was dyed the same colour as the material, the garments could then be trimmed with all manner of ribbons, laces, buttons and buttonholes. A new fashion was growing amongst the ladies whereby trimmings, in particular elaborate collars, lace frills and fringes etc. were actually pinned onto plain dresses. This meant that the same dress could be worn on several occasions, but made to look different by changing the accessories.

If the silk was to be dyed before weaving, it had to be tied in convenient batches of five or six hanks. Silk expands considerably when wet and must be given plenty of room, it also tangles easily, which meant that each hank would have to be loosely tied in four or five places, before placing in batches. The waste silk could immediately be mordanted and then put in the dye bath, but any hanks containing sericin would have to be washed thoroughly first, to remove all trace of the gummy substance. After boiling in good soapy water for at least an hour, the hanks were rinsed, and immediately mordanted and dyed; it was unnecessary to dry them after rinsing if the intention was to dye them.

Charles would not concern himself with the dyeing process, he was fortunate that within 150 yards distance, on the banks of the River Bollin, next to Watercoates Bridge and situated on Pickford land, was the dyehouse of John Turner the younger. The indications are that John Turner was encouraged to build his dyehouse during 1743, about the same time as Charles started his project. Apart from the fact that the Copperas House Works would have had to adapt its dyeing methods for silk, it was more inconveniently placed for receiving the wet hanks.

Dyers also required large coppers in which to mordant and dye yarns, as witnessed by the inventory of the Copperas House Works, and John Turner would be no exception. Silk is particularly sensitive to alkalis and requires neutral or acid dyebaths. Mr. Turner would be able to use copper sulphate solution as a mordant, but with the addition of cream of tartar to prevent loss of lustre. The copper sulphate came from low grade copper pyrites, and cream of tartar was easily produced from the fermentation of wine. Dyes were readily available; silk responds excellently to natural dyes and a good colour range would be obtained from madder (scarlet), indigo (blue), sloes (deep pink) and blackberry tops (mid green).

During the first three years of Charles Roe's development of his Parsonage Green site, it can be confidently assessed that the "pile of buildings" referred to in the deeds included a joiners' shop, stables, a building comprising at least two large rooms for the throwsters (i.e. twisters and doublers), a warehouse, a compting house, a drying shed, a boiling house for waste silk, with stone floors inset with channels to take away the soapy water, a singeing house.

There would be no necessity to build a brewhouse on the premises because barrels of ale could easily be supplied from the brewhouses close by, and one in particular, kept by the Huxley family seemed best to qualify. Thomas Huxley had leased the burgage of the Pickford family on Jordangate Street, situated on the corner close by the market cross, from 29th December 1726, together with several parcels of land and use of the middingstead on Dog Lane. The property became an inn known as the "Queen's Head", and Thomas's son, Samuel, in due course took over the premises; he was also a button merchant and a member of St. Michael's congregation. As mentioned, adjacent to the site was the soap maker/tallow chandler with the dyehouse close by. Coal was easily obtained from the Common, just up the hill to the east of the old copper mine, and would have to be stored near to the boiling pans and drying shed.

The materials for Charles Roe's actual buildings were also readily available in the vicinity, mostly from the Common. Bricks came from the brickworks near to the clay pits, stones from the nearby quarry and an abundance of wood, which was probably supplied by either the Fauconberg family from their Sutton estate, or from the wood in Wildboarclough. Apart from the button moulds, wood from holly trees could also be used for stools and other items of furniture.

Charles had expended a considerable sum of money, time and effort in co-ordinating the different sectors of his industry, but his main concern would be the functioning of the water wheel. Perhaps he had hoped to persuade other tenants of the Pickford family, particularly on the River Bollin, to allow him to negotiate further water rights once his mills were under construction, but this did not occur. Instead he was left with a small section of the Lesser Brook which was a fairly insignificant stream of water. It drained from the western end of the parkland down into the region called the Dams, where it was joined by two smaller brooks before flowing across Parsonage Green, under Pickford Bridge and past his silk mills. There was no possible means of providing a head of water for an overshot wheel, and only after heavy rain or winter snows would there be anything like the force required to keep an undershot wheel turning continuously. A long dry summer would prove disastrous so far as the supply of water was concerned, because of inadequate facilities for the construction of a reservoir. One presumes that in such conditions the throwsters would have to return to the old traditional way of throwing until the double Dutch looms were operative once more. It has been previously suggested that James Brindley, to become famous for his canal engineering, had possibly helped; however this now seems most unlikely.

James Brindley, born in 1716 in the village of Tunstead, near Buxton, had been apprenticed at the age of 17 years to Abraham Bennett, wheelwright of Sutton near Macclesfield. Brindley supposedly worked on silk mills in Macclesfield; if this was the case then the work would have been mostly undertaken for Quaker families, many of whom had settled on the Pickford land. Before Charles built his mills, only Thomas Vardon had a small shed close by the river Bollin in which were one or two mills. There were, of course, the corn mills, which were notorious for catching fire due to worn mill stones causing sparks in an atmosphere full of dust, and Smiles's suggestion that Brindley worked on mills which had caught fire, could have related to any of these. On the death of Abraham Bennett, James Brindley completed his master's work but had returned to Leek by 1742 from where he subsequently gained great experience repairing and renovating old machinery, and became involved with canals. His diaries (or notebooks) give no suggestion that he undertook work for Charles Roe.

* * * * * * *

On 30th September 1748 Rev. James and Rowland Atkinson, both conveniently described as "Gents.", were admitted as freemen of the Borough at a meeting of the Mayor, Aldermen and Burgesses in the Guildhall . Charles Roe's year in office was almost at an end; it had proved to be an eventful one in many ways and not least of all because at last the great project was underway, the construction of the Silk Mill to house the Lombe-style machinery.

Charles had appreciated that if he was to develop his silk production further and supply the London weavers with finest quality silks, he had no option but to experiment with the Lombe machinery, which would ultimately necessitate the construction of a large water wheel to provide sufficient power for the number of large machines. It is understood that he engaged a mechanic to assemble one of the Italian machines, possibly in the belief that it would inspire someone to transfer their lease to him. The fact that Sir Thomas Lombe, patron of the Derby Silk Mill, had been a 'multi-millionaire' by today's standards, and that six wealthy partners had proved necessary in contributing towards the Stockport scheme, must have forced Charles to appreciate that however brilliant, self-sufficient and dedicated he was, beyond a certain point he could not continue alone. About this time he took into partnership his father-in-law, Samuel Lankford, who probably withdrew from the Ecton mining partnership in order to invest in the enterprise. There is no mention of the copper concern in Lankford's will prepared 1758, nor any indication of the fortune he would have made had his investment continued. The extant Ecton figures suggest that whilst profits were ample up to 1750, the mine may not have reach its considerable potential until 1752, in which case Lankford had withdrawn two years too soon.

It also seems likely that at the same time as Lankford, Charles Roe also admitted into the silk mill partnership Rev. John Robinson, curate of St. Michael's, who resided in a house with yards appurtenant, adjacent to the Parsonage Green mills. This house and yards seem to have been considered as part of the Roe complex, therefore Rev. Robinson would have been a tenant. It is known that the Parsonage House was in a dilapidated condition, and together with its gardens and stables was leased out by a subsequent curate; this situation must already have been applicable during John Robinson's curacy. The extra money provided by the two partners would be usefully employed in developing the new machinery, but it also provided Samuel Lankford with an opportunity to interfere if he so desired.

At this juncture negotiations must have taken place between Charles Roe and three of his neighbours in Jordangate Street. Who took the first initiative is not known, but the events which did take place have had to be reconstructed by a process of elimination.

Originally on 29th December 1726 Thomas Huxley, landlord of the Queens Head, had leased several parcels of land from John Pickford of Ashton-under-Lyne, some of which had formerly been in possession of a W. Crooke, and are not readily identifiable; however, as most of the Pickford family holdings are known, the only plot which seems to correspond with Mr. Crooke's former lease was situated down stream from Charles Roe's mills on the Lesser Brook. The area was "formerly part and parcel of . . . two Meadows . . . called Birtles Eyes and the Palace Yard." The latter forming part of the meadow lands originally belonging to the Castle site owned by the Earls of Derby, and presumably the barren and waste land drained and developed by James Pickford the younger in the 17th century.

Thomas Huxley had a son, Samuel, button merchant and Mayor of Macclesfield for the year 1746/47, the year before Charles Roe. Samuel, together with two of his friends and associates, Samuel Glover and William Greaves, who were also merchants, came into possession of the plot of land in the Waters, one can only assume by virtue of Samuel Huxley's father. William Greaves, Mayor during 1740/41, was no doubt related to a wealthy butcher, George Greaves of Mill Street, who for several years had been sub-lessee of other meadow land under lease to the Pickford family by General Cholmondley and situated in the Dams area.

The outcome was a partnership between Charles Roe and his two partners together with the merchant trio. This was very similar to the Stockport partnership where six partners operated the Silk Mill as a separate business apart from their main occupations.

Charles was obviously the person to be in charge of the actual building of the Silk Mill, meanwhile Samuel Huxley and associates negotiated water rights with Joseph Pickford to enable them to provide the extra water power required to drive a large water wheel. Charles already had rights over a sough or tunnel which was adjacent to the site in the Waters, and on 24th October 1748 a lease was drawn up between Joseph Pickford of Altehill, Ashton-under-Lyne, and the three merchants, Glover, Huxley and Greaves whereby they had liberty "to erect upon or cross the said Brook, Stream or Watercourse" a wear for "the raising and impounding" of the water. This refers to the River Bollin and not to the Lesser Brook. They were also allowed to "make any Tunnel Sough Drain or other device" through the adjacent fields thereby "conveying or drawing any part of the water through the fields". This sluice at some point would have had to incorporate a sluicegate in order to control the amount of water flowing from the River Bollin into the Lesser Brook; the position for this seems likely to have been near the Bollin. At the same time the trio acquired rights over "that other brook in a certain field now in possession of John Bayley lying next and adjacent to before lands", this refers to the part of the Lesser Brook which flowed between Charles Roe's land and the lands now in possession of Glover, Huxley and Greaves. The stipulation was "for the use of the said Silk Mill"; the rent £2 per annum for 21 years next ensuing.

There were already five small cottages at the southern end of the intended Silk Mill site, and from an Enclosure Plan of 1796 and a drawing of Waters Green in 1810, it is possible to discover how the site was developed. The five cottages stood in a row running approximately from north to south. Adjacent to the northern end, the partnership built a fine Georgian house (today the site of the Queens Hotel), complemented by three poplar trees planted in the narrow front garden which overlooked the Green. The two cottages immediately next door to the house had their roofs removed and an extra storey added so that they acquired the same height as the house. At the northern end of the house was added a smaller building of two stories, which must have been the compting house. From the compting house a wall was built extending to the north-eastern corner of the site, but it did allow access through large gates to the Silk Mill. Along the northern boundary at some time a row of nine cottages was built, although this was more than likely included at a later date when other alterations took place. The southern boundary coincided with what is today a culvert which runs underground diagonally across the former bus station complex. The western boundary was the Lesser Brook, its course adapted by the widening and deepening of its channel so that it gained the form of an elongated reservoir.

The designated area for the Italian style Silk Mill was towards the northern end of the plot and was laid out in a direction from southwest to northeast. Its western side, which was 52 ft long, was constructed alongside the elongated reservoir. Its southern side was 112 ft long, but the northern side was a few feet longer which meant that at the eastern end, which was also the entrance, half of the building had the benefit of the extra few feet. This part, which obviously projected out further, lay next to the compting house, but to allow access to the southern side of the mill, space had to be allowed behind the compting house thus restricting the length of the mill's southern half by a few feet.

Charles in his own inimitable way, altered the layout of the Lombe machinery from that seen in the Derby and Stockport mills, making more economic use of the space available. Without taking into account the extra few feet of space at the eastern end of the building, Charles had at his disposal a rectangle of 52 ft wide and 112 ft long into which he installed 14 Italian machines, two more than Derby and four more than Stockport. The looms were placed in the space of the two lower floors, and the only possible way in which they could have been accommodated, ensuring a minimum space around each machine of approximately 5 ft as had been found necessary in both the Derby and Stockport mills, was to place them in three rows lengthways, in the formation of five, four and five. If the looms in the outer rows of five were each placed 5 ft away from the walls, this created a space lengthways of 10 ft between the looms, but sideways of 17 ft. Each loom in the middle row of four, when positioned exactly in the middle of the space created by the two looms to its right and the two looms to its left, was found to be the necessary 5 ft away from each of these four surrounding looms.

The Macclesfield Silk Mill was only four stories high instead of five as at Derby and Stockport, but the overall floor space in the two upper stories of the Roe mill was very little different in area from the three upper stories of the other two mills, they being only 39 ft wide as compared to the width of 52 ft in the Roe mill. The three upper stories in the Derby mill were, of course, used to house the winding machinery which completed the final process of winding the hanks of silk onto wooden bobbins, ready for use by weavers. Presumably the two upper stories of the Macclesfield mill were used for the same purpose. Careful consideration would have to be given, however, to the light entering the building. As the Italian looms in the lower stories alternated in position, the light from the windows would not have been impeded to any of these machines, but the light penetrating the upper stories might have caused problems. From the 1810 drawing only 13 windows appear across the length of the northern side of the building in each of the four stories, whereas the Derby mill, which was a few feet shorter, contained 14 windows in each of its five stories. It is always difficult to make a judgment from drawings which appear to be free hand and not to scale, but if a comparison has to be made, it would seem that the Roe windows were slightly larger than their counterparts at Derby.

The reproduction of the silk mill on Charles Roe's monument in Christ Church, Macclesfield, depicts the mill as originally built; it also appears on the drawing of Waters

Green in 1810, making a comparison possible. The most obvious difference is that the original mill had another building close by, on the north-eastern corner of the site; this also had a height of four stories and contained six windows in each of the upper three, with five windows and a door on the ground floor level. If the scene portrays the front of the mill, then this building would face the perimeter wall. The side of this building contained only two windows in each of the four levels which, if used as an indication of its width, suggests a depth of approximately half that of the main building i.e. 26 ft. This building was probably demolished at the same time as the removal of the large water wheel, considered redundant with the advent of steam power during the last quarter of the 18th century. The extra space gained would allow for the building of the row of nine cottages together with certain other smaller premises as shown by the 1810 drawing. A Victorian Indenture mentions stables together with the cottages, but the stables would already have been part of the premises from the beginning.

The large water wheel fixed on the northern side of the Macclesfield mill presumably operated the machinery on the same principle as the one in Derby. It was certainly more impressive to view, although it must be remembered that because of the depth of the River Derwent both of the Derby water wheels were placed with their shafts and heads below the level of the first floor, and therefore considered as low-breast wheels, a position impossible to achieve on the Lesser Brook. The water wheel depicted on the Roe monument reaches almost to the level of the second floor or the approximate height of the Italian machines, which was just less than 20 ft, and appears to be about two thirds above ground level. This suggests a height of about 18 ft making the diameter around 27 ft. It can also be confirmed by the fact that the wheel at maximum covered the width of three full windows, representing almost a quarter of the length of the rectangle (112 ft) i.e. $\frac{1}{4}$ of say 108 feet = 27 feet. This seems an impossible size for the period so, allowing for artistic licence, in all probability it was most likely nearer 24 ft in diameter, a size which Roe & Co. would use in North Wales some years later. Unfortunately no other measurements exist to provide precise calculations, but even allowing for errors, the Macclesfield Silk Mill water wheel appears slightly larger than the Derby one of 23 feet diameter, and adds weight to the argument that the Macclesfield mill housed more machines and required more power. As the Macclesfield wheel was further out of the water, its circumference would need to be greater to accommodate more ladle boards on its rims and cantells in order to take full advantage of the flow of the water, which in turn would provide a greater force to effect the rotation of the huge wheel.

Both representations of the mill clearly show a chimney at the front end, just over the apex of the roof, closely followed by a miniature bell tower in imitation of an Italian campanile. The Italian version was actually a bell tower standing separate from other buildings; the Derby tower was more authentic, but even there it was attached to the Silk Mill, allowing access to all floors by means of its staircase. The Macclesfield bell would have been included for its utilitarian 'appeal', to ensure that the workers did not arrive late, and from the illustration available it originally supported a weather vane. In the area immediately south of the Silk Mill, between the long reservoir and the Georgian house, was laid out a fine garden with a row of trees neatly planted alongside the buildings, presumably in the spaces between the windows. The garden was divided into four parts with walk ways in between, and a pentagon-shaped reservoir, no doubt disguised as an ornamental pool, was created in the south-west corner of the plot, close by the long reservoir.

The water course must have continued from the northern end of the long reservoir, along the north side of the mill to drive the water wheel, then turned south underground to pass through the sough or culvert over which Charles Roe held water rights, before entering the River Bollin. During recent rebuilding on the site the remains of a culvert were discovered in the cellars beneath the cottages adjacent to the southern wall of the Queens Hotel. A considerable amount of flooding has occurred in the cellars of the hotel over many years, and even within living memory the landlord has been known to have dived under 3 or 4 ft of water to rescue barrels of beer.

Today the north-eastern corner of the site is occupied by the showrooms of Cookson's garage, a family business which has been established on part of these premises since 1911; in the cellars there remains a large section of stone wall indicative of a very old building which occupied the corner site before the brick buildings of the Victorian Era. There is also an underground well, now covered over, situated in the vicinity of where the original watercourse of the Lesser Brook flowed along the northern side of the mill.

Apart from visual evidence for the site of the buildings, the most conclusive appears on a Land Tax return. From 1784 onwards all the Land Tax returns for the remaining years of the Georgian Period exist, but before that year it has only been possible to trace two. The first one already mentioned was for the year 1743, over which Peter Davenport had authority and responsibility for the collection. The second one, previously undated, relates to either 1756 or 57; listed under "Houses & Buildings" are the following entries:

Parsonage Green.		
Messrs Lankford & Roe	Silk Mills & Do (i.e. etc.)	£25.0. 0
The Revd. Mr. Robinson	House & Yards	
Waters.		
Messrs Glover	Shade (shed)	£16.0. 0
"	4 dwellings	8.0. 0
"	4 "	5.0. 0
Mr. Wm. Greaves		6.0. 0
Messrs Glover & Company for Silk Mill (work)Shop & Warehouses)		46.0. 0
Mess'er Roe's Cpany)		

It is interesting to see the arrangement adopted from these entries, bearing in mind the complications that might arise should any individual or group decide to withdraw, and also the fact that the Lankford & Roe mills on Parsonage Green were an investment from the marriage settlement. By far the largest group in the whole of Macclesfield was the Silk Mill complex valued at £46 in Waters, and shared by both companies.

Subsequent Indentures dated 3rd and 4th February 1767, upon the marriage of Joseph Pickford, reveal the following description of his Macclesfield holdings incorporated in his marriage settlement. The properties included were, in effect owned by him at that period, and signify the value of his land and confirm that he was entitled to the (ground) rents from such properties:

"30 Mefses [Messuages] 5 Barns 1 Silk Mill, 5 Acres of Land 5 Acres of Meadow 8 Acres of Pasture 50 Acres of Moor" . . .

Obviously there was only one building on the Pickford land which purported to be a silk mill so far as Mr. Pickford's solicitor was concerned, the others were considered to be either messuages or barns. In fact one could say that there was only one building in the whole of Macclesfield which was regarded as a silk mill, certainly Dr. Johnson thought so seven years later. It is worth quoting two entries from his journal, because he had visited Derby on the previous day:

"19th July 1774,
We went then to the Silkmill at Derby where I remarked a particular manner of propagating motion from a horizontal to a vertical wheel."

"20th July 1774.
At night we came to Macclesfield, a very large town in Cheshire, little known. It has a silk mill. It has a handsome church, which however is but a chapel for the town – belongs to some parish of another name as Stourbridge lately did to Old Swinford. Macclesfield has a town hall, and is, I suppose a corporate town."

Although the Macclesfield Silk Mill was completed during 1748/49 there was still much to be done before anyone could claim success.

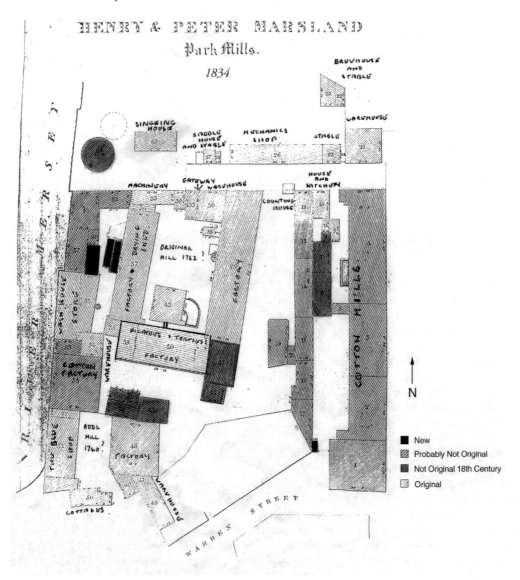

Henry & Peter Marsland – Park Mills 1834. This plan shows all the buildings on site in 1834. I have shaded in the buildings added to the original mill of 1740, when the wheel was removed and steam power introduced, so that the adapted plan shows the original layout of the Stockport Silk Mill. Names have been added to the numbered buildings according to an additional list in the folios.

Details courtesy of Stockport Library.

Marsland's Park Mills, Stockport - The terrible fire 17th March 1851 as depicted in *The Illustrated London News* causing the death of 22 men. By this time it had been converted from silk to cotton and the fire seems to have started in the large warehouse by the River Mersey.

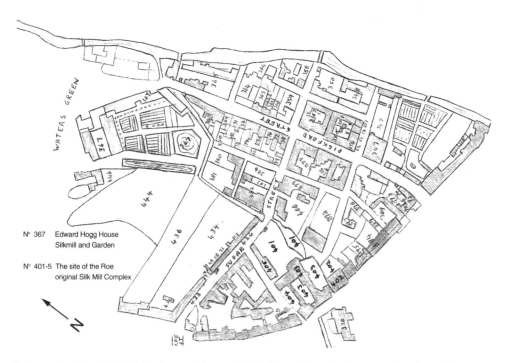

Nº 367   Edward Hogg House
          Silkmill and Garden

Nº 401-5 The site of the Roe
          original Silk Mill Complex

Details from the Macclesfield Enclosure Map c. 1804: Note that the intended Pickford Street actually became Sunderland Street and Sugar Street became Pickford Street. The silk mill no. 367, owned by Edward Hogg was the one originally owned by Glover & Co. and partly shared with Roe & Co. courtesy of Cheshire and Chester Archives and Local Studies. Reference LBM 2039 c.1795 (part).

9
FROM SILK TO COPPER

Then first she calls the useful many forth;
Plain plodding industry, and sober worth:

By the year 1750, despite all concerted efforts, the Macclesfield Silk Mill was not operating at full capacity due to an insufficient water supply. Maximum power would be achieved only when weather permitted, despite the additional water diverted from the River Bollin; so something had to be done.

Just to the south of Parsonage Green, across the boundary in the parish of Sutton, stood the water corn mills of the Earl of Fauconberg, called Sutton Mills. At some distant time in the past, water "flowing from a certain water course" passed in a northerly direction through "the Wilderness and Garden at Sutton Hall", home of the Fauconberg family, supplying themselves, their farms and tenants, then turned to run into "the Pool belonging to the said Corn Mills for the purpose of altering and securing a Head and Fall of Water for the turning of any Mills or Manufactories". After leaving the Pool the stream joined the Moss Stream flowing towards Macclesfield from Danes Moss, which passed through Moss End Farm, shortly before entering the Bollin. In order to establish the corn mills, ancestors of the Fauconbergs had constructed a weir less then 100 yards from the point at which it entered the Bollin and diverted some of the water. (The Bollin itself flows westwards until it receives the waters of Moss Stream, after which it also changes direction to take a northerly course).

The construction of the weir, together with a paddle device, built up a head of water which, after being redirected into the artificial watercourse, continued to flow along the western bank of the Bollin so that the two ran parallel for a distance of approximately half a mile, through a meadow area subsequently named Mill Green; it was in this area that the corn mills had been constructed. The artificial watercourse entered the River Bollin as it turned sharply eastwards to traverse a small wasteland along the southern boundary of Parsonage Green, before entering Pickford Eyes.

The Fauconbergs, whose family name was Bellasyse, had always sustained their Roman Catholic beliefs, that is until the 18th century. The junior branch of the family at Sutton Hall had maintained a chapel there, and during the traumas of the previous century this had been the sanctum in which the small Roman Catholic community of the Macclesfield area had been able to congregate. In 1700 the Fauconberg title and estates had devolved upon Thomas Bellasyse of Sutton Hall as a result of his uncle's death at Bolton in Lancashire. His own death, on 26th November 1718, ensured the transfer of title and properties to his son, Thomas, who became the third Viscount Fauconberg; however it was this son who apostatised and embraced the Church of England in 1734.

The nearest regular place of worship for the Fauconbergs, when at Sutton Hall, was St. Michael's, which meant that they would be very well acquainted with Rev. John Robinson. The chapel within the Hall apparently continued in use for Church of England services, but for any service to take place in the chapel, arrangements would have to be made with the vicar of Prestbury Church so that either himself or one of his curates within the parish could attend, or a clergyman of their own choosing who was well-known or recommended to them. The Fauconbergs would pay the fee for whichever clergyman officiated, no doubt taking place on Sunday afternoons when the family were gathered together after dinner. The Devonshire family at Chatsworth House in Derbyshire often engaged the services of a local parson on Sunday afternoons, as did many other families in similar positions.

Circumstances seem to indicate a more than casual acquaintance between the Roe family and the Fauconbergs, due in no small part to Rev. James, whose reputation as a minister was growing. He had probably been recommended by Robinson for duties in the chapel allowing him to supplement his income. In 1750 James was 39 years of age and still unmarried, so he had to give consideration to any marriage settlement in which he might become involved. His presence in Sutton is confirmed by the fact that on 2nd January 1753 he would marry, Elizabeth Harper, daughter of the rector of Malpas, Cheshire, in the chapel at Sutton Hall, which must have been quite a privilege. One of his sermons, preached in Congleton at a later date and subsequently published after his death, gives a clear indication of his sentiments and influences. He pointed out that a mistake made by many men was to consider themselves good Christians by simply being members of a "particular church or party". He continued:

> "This is one of thefe dangerous principles which the church of Rome hath admitted; taking upon it to give all thofe, who are members thereof, the name and title of Good Catholicks and feverly to cenfure, nay to pronounce eternal Damnation on all thofe who are out of it; whom they ftyle Hereticks. And, it grieves me to fay, we have reafon to complain of fome, who pretend to be members of our own Church for copying too clofely after this unchristian pattern."

Because of Rev. James's involvement at Sutton, any social gatherings would include brother, Charles, now one of the leading townsmen of Macclesfield, and Samuel Lankford of Rainow Hall, who had married for the third time on 17th July 1749. His wife, Rebecca, was a member of the Hulley family, of which two brothers had married two sisters from the Hooley family, causing great confusion. Both families were responsible for providing several aldermen and mayors for Macclesfield during the first half of the 18th century. Rebecca's uncle, Thomas Hooley, was the mayor who had died just before the end of his term in office, but not before Peter Davenport had sent him a writ to appear in court at Chester as the representative of Macclesfield Corporation on the charge of not fining a travelling Jew.

The impression created by Samuel Lankford was that of a man dedicated to the task in hand, which in his case was the promotion in society of Samuel Lankford. His entry into the Silk Mill business added further conviction to the already powerful personality that he was destined to become Macclesfield's premier townsman. A lesser man, having Samuel Lankford as his father-in-law, would have had problems, but Charles seems to have handled the situation very well, co-operating sufficiently so as not to cause offence, but not becoming involved in anything which was against his principles. Being the youngest son, he had learnt to defer to the initial judgement of older men, until his wisdom taught him otherwise. Even in the choice of names for his sons, Charles had shown himself to be of strong character. Despite the enormous sum of money placed at his disposal by Samuel Lankford under the terms of the marriage settlement, he had chosen to disregard the name of Samuel for his two eldest sons, naming them after his elder deceased brother and himself; only on the birth of his third son was the name Samuel adopted.

On 25th March 1750 a deed was drawn up between Thomas, Earl of Fauconberg, and Charles Roe, together with Samuel Lankford. According to Professor Chaloner the lease was for 21 years at a yearly rent of £2 2s. which included the Sutton Mills together with "full power to direct and convey waste and useless water to the silk mills in Macclesfield". This

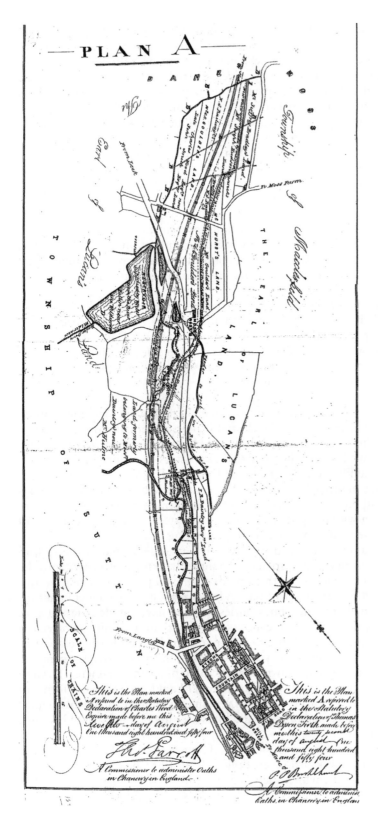

Plan of 1854: The watercourse to Sutton Mills showing the various stages of development from the Middle Ages to the 19th century reproduced by kind permission of the owner.

rent seems very reasonable if the corn mills were also included, but it is more than likely that the deed was only for the water rights after the water had passed through the mills. The fact that Messrs. Glover, Huxley and Greaves were not included on this original deed but only on a later renewal, seems strange. Perhaps Samuel Lankford and Charles saw an opportunity to charge the partnership a rent for the extra water supply, thus making a profit on it, or perhaps it was considered less complicated to allow Charles and Samuel Lankford to deal with the Earl of Fauconberg, knowing him on a personal basis. As Glover, Huxley and Greaves were already responsible for the sough from the Bollin, which included keeping it in good order and cleaning it out from time to time, they were probably quite happy to allow Charles and Samuel Lankford the responsibility for the other. Whichever reason prevailed, the outcome was the same, and another instance of Charles Roe's ingenuity, to overcome yet another obstacle, was put into action.

A large reservoir existed, adjoining the corn mills to the west of Mill Green, the flow of water from which would be controlled by a sluicegate. This artificial watercourse, instead of entering the River Bollin, was altered to continue flowing more or less parallel to the river, even after the Bollin turned eastwards across the wasteland and into Pickford Eyes. Today traces of this old watercourse remain under Mill Lane, the road which leads southwards out of the town towards Leek. The water flowed up the middle of the present road through a tunnel until it reached Parsonage Green, where it turned eastwards mirroring the course of the Bollin. The old sough or tunnel can be traced crossing Brook Street but then disappears. The reason seems to be that Charles, wanting to use the extra water supply to good effect, dropped the tunnel into the sough constructed by Glover, Huxley and Greaves which was already conveying water from behind the weir on the River Bollin; this, of course, necessitated an enlargement to the sough, which was mentioned by Professor Chaloner. Matters improved for a while, but were still not as desirable as the partnership would have wished.

Within six weeks of the signing of the deed, Charles's wife, Elizabeth, died. Their fourth child, Samuel, born on 11th November 1749 and baptised only two days later, seems to have given his mother a difficult birth from which Elizabeth never really recovered. Her burial, entered in St. Michael's register on 1st May 1750, recorded Charles once more as Alderman. It must have been a very demanding time for him, but his sister, Mary, and sister-in-law, Ann Nicholson were there to support the family.

* * * * * * *

Since her marriage, Mary had been very busy. On 9th May 1749 her husband, Rowland Atkinson had been appointed Headmaster of the Free Grammar School on the resignation of his brother, Christopher, who had accepted the living of Thorp Arch in Yorkshire, where he would remain for the rest of his life. Mary and Rowland now had the benefit of the Headmaster's House, the former residence of Sir Peter Davenport, where their first child, Frances, was born but died young. At the time of Elizabeth's death Mary was expecting her second child, who unfortunately also would not survive childhood.

Sister-in-law, Ann Nicholson and husband Francis only had one child, a daughter, Margaret, baptised on 28th March 1744. Francis Nicholson's eldest child, Ralph, by his first wife, was now 16 years of age and the decision had been taken for him to enter the Church of England as his uncle, Rev. Francis of Stockport, had done. Plenty of help and guidance were assured from the minsters Rowland Atkinson, James Roe and John Robinson, and no doubt Rev. Joseph Dale also on his visits from Stockport to see the family.

Another family with whom the Roes were becoming intimately connected, was the Leghs of Adlington Hall. Charles Legh had inherited the estate upon the death of his father in 1739, and become patron of the Parish Church of Prestbury, which encompassed the chapel of St. Michael's in Macclesfield. During the 1740s, together with his wife, Hester, he had started to modernise their Elizabethan house in the fashion of the day.

Nothing could have been a greater contrast to the brown and cream Tudor houses, built with clay, plaster and oak beams, using techniques known as lath and plaster or wattle and daub, than the Italian classical architecture, popularly called Palladian style. Named after Andrea Palladio, a famous Italian architect of the 16th century, its use of bricks and stones, mimicking parts of the ancient buildings of Greece and Rome, incorporating pediments supported by columns, was still being received with great enthusiasm. Whilst many completely rebuilt in the new classical style, many also adapted their existing houses, preferring to ignore the incongruity created on occasion by their efforts. Today, however, the existence of original Tudor features, enveloped by the balanced and mathematical proportions of the Georgian Era, adds quaintness and charm to what some people might consider to be an architectural 'hotchpotch'. The Leghs, initiating their 'modernisation programme', began by changing one or two internal features in their Tudor Hall.

The Great Hall of Adlington, originally completed in the year 1505, had been considerably embellished over the years. Its most remarkable feature was, and still is, an organ tentatively attributed to Bernard Smith c. 1670, incorporating the console of a pre-Cromwellian instrument. The organ is raised from the floor by being set on a gallery above the large entrance door into the Hall, and is built between two oak trees which have their roots in the ground. Having been carved at some time with an adze, each of these oaks has been formed into an ornate octagonal column. The murals on either side of the organ were completed about 1705 and represent music, portrayed by St. Cecilia playing her harp on the righthand panel, complimented by a female lutenist on the left, both accompanied by angels performing on various instruments. Apart from the south wall which contains the windows, the two remaining walls, panelling excepted, are covered with superb murals which appear to predate the 17th century. On entering the Great Hall through the doorway below the organ, one is faced with an elaborate canopy at the far end of the room, larger than the mural it overshadows. This canopy, divided into 60 panels by moulded oaken ribs, contains a fine set of armorial shields representing the chief Cheshire families, said to have been completed in 1581.

It was upon the organ in this splendid Hall that Handel had played during his visit of 1741. Handel, born in Halle, Germany first visited England during 1710; after returning home the following year, he finally settled in England in 1712, taking on British nationality by becoming naturalised. He enjoyed periods of great popularity, but there were times also when he was out of favour.

Charles Legh's eldest sister, Elizabeth, was a fine player of the harpsichord and for many years had lived in Hanover Square, London. She died unmarried at the age of 40 years in 1734, having been part of London society at a time when Handel and his music were very much in demand. Both she and her brother, Charles, were musical and also staunch admirers of Handel, knowing him personally. He was also known to the Wesley brothers, John and Charles, and had set some of Charles Wesley's words to music, which made fine hymns; that their sentiments were in accord is hardly surprising, because Handel had been brought up in a Lutheran household.

Even if only casually, Handel was also known to John Stafford. The organist to the Society of the Inner Temple from 1734 was John Stanley, blinded by an accident when only two years old. Stanley had graduated from Oxford at the age of 16 years, which is the youngest recorded age for an Oxford musical graduate, and it was said that on many occasions 40 or 50 organists, Handel included, assembled in the Inner Temple to hear the last voluntary.

Unfortunately in 1740 Handel had been accused of pirating works from other composers and, whatever the truth, he suffered considerably. The Duke of Devonshire, in his capacity as Lord Lieutenant of Ireland, had come to his rescue in the autumn of 1741 by inviting the composer to Dublin for a series of concerts, and it was at this time, in connection with his Irish journey, that he had first visited Adlington Hall. Local tradition maintains that Handel

Hadley Manor purchased in 1682 by Rev. Robert Roe in which he created a school. Courtesy of Neil Clarke.

Old Water Tower – a famous landmark, and part of the Hadley Estate.

Photograph of the historical plaque on the old Water Tower .

A Victorian watercolour of the Macclesfield Chapel c. 1413-1739 now the Parish Church in the Market Place, founded by Eleanor of Castile in 1278.

The tomb effigy of Queen Eleanor in Westminster Abbey, reproduced by courtesy of The Dean and Chapter of Westminster'.

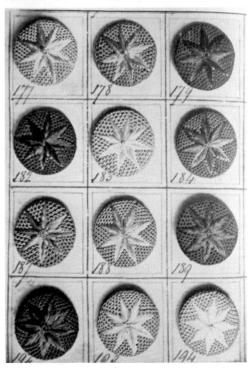

18th century Macclesfield silk buttons. Courtesy of the Macclesfield Museums Trust.

This 17th century painting depicts Sir Francis Dashwood busy with his accounts. Through the open window can be seen his ships sailing down the River Thames laden with wool for Turkey; the sheep represents his flocks on the Sussex Downs. print by the Courtauld Institute of Art, reproduced by courtesy of the present Sir Francis Dashwood. Dutch School.

Left: Castleton –
A view of Peveril
Castle from
St. Edmund's
churchyard.

The steep descent down The Winnats to Castleton, Derbyshire.

Odin Mine – the 19th century ore crushing circle on the opposite side of the road from the lead mine; this replaced an earlier one.

St. Edmund's, Castleton on Oak Apple Day 1987. The tower is bedecked with leaves and the Ringers' garland of flowers.

The Norman font in St. Edmund's church at which Charles Roe was baptised.

The River 'Noor' (Noe) flowing from the Cavern.

Edwardian Edale.

Early 20th century Middleton Dale.

John Lombe as seen on a building overlooking the Market entrance in the centre of Derby. Note the snake under his right foot, symbolic of his poisoning.

A model of the Lombe silk throwing machine, part of the Silk Heritage exhibition in Macclesfield. It has been constructed from the Italian design used in the Derby Silk Mill and is one-third of the original in size.

The reconstructed Derby Silk Mill by the River Derwent in Derby, now a museum.

John Stafford.

Stafford Coat of Arms, Cumberland
House, Macclesfield.

Penelope Margaret Stafford – courtesy of the
Derby Museum Service.

Lucy Stafford - courtesy of Sotheby's Auctioneers.
This is now on loan to The National Trust.

All three portraits were painted by Joseph Wright of Derby in Liverpool in 1769. Unfortunately the copy of John Stafford is the only one available; every endeavour has been made to trace the owner of the original portrait but without success.

Cumberland House – the home of John Stafford, Jordangate, Macclesfield. The left half of the facade is original. The right half was reconstructed at the beginning of the 19th century to accommodate a separate solicitor's office.

Prince Charles Edward Stuart in his early thirties by Jean-Louis Tocqué. Reproduced by courtesy of the Duke of Atholl from his collection at Blair Castle, Blair Atholl, Perthshire.

Jordangate House formerly known as Pear Tree House. It was built in 1728 as the home of the Glover family and It stands opposite Cumberland House.

Charles Roe's original mill on Parsonage (Park) Green. The larger building on the left was constructed c.1810 and became known as the Royal Depot Mill. The smaller Roe mill has erroneously been referred to as 'The Button Mill'.

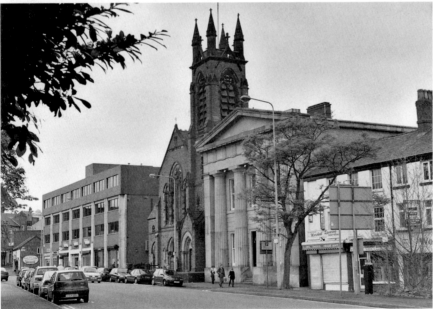

The area of Park Green today which was originally occupied by Charles Roe's silk mill complex. The building on the left occupies the site of the Royal Depot Mill and the original Roe mill; the church is on the site of the Pickford Hall and barn, subsequently leased by Charles Roe for the expansion of his premises. The classical styled former bank and neighbouring shop are where the winding rooms stood.

Left: The Macclesfield Silk Mill depicted on the Roe monument in Christ Church.

Above: 'Waters Green c. 1810 – on the right is the large silk mill shared by Glover & Co. and 'Mess'er Roe's Company'. By this period it had been converted to steam power.

Left: Waters Green today. The Queen's Hotel now occupies the group of buildings in the centre of the 1810 scene. The original silk mill was replaced by another mill in the 19th century which now towers over the hotel and is converted into showrooms.

Adlington Hall – the Georgian facade completed by 1750.

Portrait of Charles Legh of Adlington Hall. Courtesy of the late Charles Legh.

The Old Hall Hotel, Buxton leased to Brian Hodgson Snr. by William, 3rd Duke of Devonshire c. 1750.

An early 19th century print of St. Martin's-in-the-Fields, London where Charles Roe married Mary Stockdale in April 1752.

Charles Roe House, Chestergate, home of the Roe family from 1753 onwards including the original offices of Roe & Co.

The Venetian window at the rear of Charles Roe House which overlooked the garden mentioned by his niece Hester in her diary.

The Quay at Lancaster c. 1790.

Coniston Copper Mine now a Heritage Site.

Alderley Edge showing the Derbyshire Caving Club at work; Wood Mine, late 1980s.

Dolcoath Mine, Cornwall showing bal maidens at work. Engraving by J. Thomas from a drawing by T. Allen. It was printed in *Cornwall Illustrated*, 1831.

The Grey House, Ashbourne, home of Brian Hodgson Snr. from c. 1767 till his death in 1784. Courtesy of Lindsey Porter.

Winter in the hills around Macclesfield Forest. The packhorses carrying copper ore from Ecton would occasionally face such conditions on their journeys via Axe Edge. There they would join the Buxton Road at the Cheshire border en route for the Roe & Co. smelters on Macclesfield Common.

added the final details to his oratorio *Messiah* during this short visit; the work was actually performed by rehearsal in Chester before the composer sailed from Parkgate to Dublin, however the organist was not of sufficient experience and proved detrimental to the proceedings. Fortunately the rehearsal in Dublin on 8th April 1742, and the first official public performance on the 13th, produced such a profound impression that the work was repeated on 3rd June.

Handel must have been extremely flattered by Elizabeth Legh's devotion to his works. Although dying intestate she had prepared a draft will in which she had directed "that all my music books that are composed by Mr. Handel may be put in some library or public room at Cambridge, there to be seen or copied but will have all fastened by a chain to ye wainscote or wall, that so none of them can be carried away or stole". The draft will also revealed that Elizabeth had cultivated a horror of being buried alive, hence the instructions that after her death, she was not to be buried with "undue haste". Nor did this satisfy her paranoia, the possibility of a postmortem had not escaped her attention either – "when I die I do positively charge not to be opened or cut up by surgeons or any person whatsoever."

It was shortly after Handel's visit that the Leghs began their refurbishment of Adlington. The Elizabethan fireplace in the Great Hall was replaced by a larger one of new classical design, and at the same time the lower parts of the walls were panelled. Extensions were then carried out to create a complete Georgian facade with a central portico at ground level along the south front, at either end of which were to be two projecting bays incorporating a new west wing and the old Elizabethan east wing. By 1749 Charles Legh had built the west wing, containing a staircase, dining-room and drawing-room, and added several rooms in the north-west corner. His next step was to create a ballroom which occupied the full length of the first floor, and which must have been completed in time for Handel's visit of 1751.

Handel's fortunes had oscillated considerably in the intervening years since his first visit to Adlington, but the popularity of his oratorio, *Messiah,* had grown steadily and become known as his masterpiece. To this day it has remained a great favourite and is performed throughout the country, but nowhere more so than in Macclesfield which, over the years, has gained a reputation for producing excellent choirs. The seeds of the town's musical involvement were sown way back in the 18th century, particularly by Charles Legh. His musical inspirations (and aspirations) were taken up by families such as the Roes and the Atkinsons, and there seems no doubt that Charles Legh would have organised a ball for his guest of honour, to celebrate the completion of his new ballroom, to which many local families would have been invited. Something certainly stimulated a musical awareness in the lives of Charles Roe and Rowland Atkinson, both of whom later encouraged appreciation of music amongst their children, and Charles Roe's dedication to Handel's music seems to suggest that he had met the renowned composer.

During his visit of 1751, Handel once again played the organ in the Great Hall and also composed a Hunting Song to which Charles Legh wrote the words. This manuscript is still carefully retained at Adlington, complete with addendum in Handel's neat handwriting which reads "Presented by him in this his own handwriting to Charles Legh Esqr in the year 1751".

Charles Legh at this time was very much preoccupied with County affairs, which strengthened his connections in Chester. He was a Colonel of the Militia and finally elected High Sheriff of Cheshire for the year 1747. The Legh family had suffered a great deal during the Civil War because of their Royalist loyalties, but this was never recognised at Court. Totally undaunted, they had carried on their traditional role in the County, together with genuine concern and interest in local affairs until the unfortunate incident with the Mayor, Aldermen and Burgesses of Macclesfield in December of 1733, when Charles Legh had been somewhat misled by Peter Davenport. There seems no doubt that his father, John Legh, one of the two M.P.s for Bodmin, whose wife was the granddaughter of the first Earl of Radnor, would have had no hesitation in condemning the over zealous action, and in directing his son in the execution of his duties; he was there to serve and not to effect an aggrandisement of his position. Some influence had certainly been brought to bear on Charles Legh, whether or not his father's reprimand may not be known, but nothing would have changed the manner or attitude of his brother-in-law, Peter Davenport, listed as a Gentleman of the Grand Jury at Chester Assizes in 1746.

By 1747 the situation had resolved itself; to paraphrase James Roe's comments, many people would be greatly relieved that Sir Peter was 'six feet under', but as is the paradoxical way with most things, in some quarters he would be missed. People who are often annoying, overbearing and the creators of great irritations, for some inexplicable reason often leave a void when they are gone. In retrospect one cannot say that they are regarded with affection, but rather with a strange sort of admiration for their sheer vitality and persistence, which ensures that others actively uphold their principles instead of passively allowing them to fade away.

* * * * * * *

During the early 1750s Charles Roe was beginning to widen the scope of his activities. Although there was concern regarding his investment in the Macclesfield Silk Mill, he seems to have realised that delegation was necessary in respect of the ordinary everyday running of the business, in order to allow him time to develop his talents as a merchant. Certainly his connections in Derbyshire intensified, which suggests that he was involved in the sale of lead. His knowledge of the actual mining of lead was excellent, but he needed to be fully conversant with the industry in every respect, including the smelting and sales procedures, if he was to become a merchant of any worth.

The Brassington estate was very useful, allowing him to stay at the house whilst developing further this part of his business. It was situated only three miles from Wirksworth, one of the most important lead mining centres of the period, close to the Derwent valley. An article concerning the area had been published in *The Universal Magazine* for October, 1748; it described the River Derwent as rising in the Peak and seeming to divide the Shire in two. The eastern and southern parts were well cultivated "fruitful in all kinds of grain especially in barley" and contained many Gentlemen's houses (referred to as seats) and parks. The western bank of the Derwent consisted of black hills and high mountains, some of which were inaccessible and barren. Except for a few fields of oats, and grass in the vales where great flocks of sheep and cattle fed, the surface was bare and dismal, yet the mountains were rich in mines of lead, antimony, iron, coal, alum, green and white vitriol, a coarse sort of crystal, marble, alabaster, azure, spar, mill stones, scythe stones and grindstones. The principal towns were listed as Derby, Ashbourne, Wirksworth, Alfreton, Winster, Bakewell, Chesterfield, Tideswell, Chapel-in-Frith, and Dronfield.

At this time Matlock, known as Matlock Bridge, hardly existed, and was just a handful of cottages close by the bridge; this situation would change over the next few years as the Georgian concern for health rapidly grew with the development of the old Roman bath closely following the one at Buxton.

The smelting mills were concentrated along the banks of the River Derwent in the Matlock area, stretching southwards to Cromford and Wirksworth; the region was known as the Low Peak and Wirksworth Wapentake. The market town of Wirksworth was also mentioned in the article:

> "it lying commodious for the fmelters, whose furnaces are at Creich (Crich), a small village near this town, on the other side of the Derwent . . .
> The ore is melted down with great fires; and running through canals, framed on purpofe, it is made into great maffes, which the smelters call Sows. And it deferves the obfervation of the curious, that the fmelters, who refine and run the lead, chufe (chose) the time of the W(est). wind as the moft proper for their purpofe; becaufe it has been found the moft conftant and lafting of all winds in thofe parts."

Charles was also very much involved in London at this time and he probably made the journey from Wilne Ferry (where the Derwent enters the River Trent) five miles south of Derby, along its tortuous route north, through the towns of Nottingham, Newark, Gainsborough and the important centre of Stockwith. Here the lead from the High Peak of Derbyshire arrived for onward transportation to the port of Hull; this included lead from the mines of the Eyam area in which the Roes had investments.

One of the smelting centres for the High Peak was around Calver, therefore it was easier to transport the pigs overland to Chesterfield from Rowsley, a distance of eight miles, and onwards from Chesterfield to Bawtry via Blyth, a further 20 miles. At Bawtry they were loaded onto small boats to negotiate the River Idle, and taken the 10 miles to Stockwith where they joined consignments of lead from the Low Peak. The journey was completed on the River Trent to the Humber Estuary and the port of Hull. It was the practice to weigh lead at the wharf of embarkation by "sworn Porters" making it unnecessary "to have it landed at Hull to be weigh'd over again – it pays a duty upon exportation of one shilling per Hundred", instead it could "be delivered without handling, out of the Keels Directly into the Ships that go either to foreign parts or Coastways".

A large percentage of the coastal trade in lead was to London, where it was essential for London based merchants to deal with the onward selling to the East India Company, the Royal Africa Company, the Navy Board or agents in the rapidly developing American colonies and the West Indies. It was important for Charles to establish good contacts in the City for his adventure into the metal trade; he was already well established in the textile and button business but the metal industry was just beginning to expand and opportunities had to be taken. Already a group of Quakers, trading as The London Lead Company, had organised themselves in the Winster area, just to the north of Brassington.

It had been in the year 1720 that two members of this Quaker company had transferred their attentions from lead mines in Flint to Derbyshire. They had negotiated leases and taken over earlier workings to rework the Mill Close mine. Over the years these workings progressed steadily and were all situated in an area to the north-east of Winster, on the northern side of the Millclose Brook, which flowed eastwards to join the River Derwent. Originally The London Lead Company had experienced transportation problems, which had forced them to sell ore to the local smelters or remove part of it to their mills in Flint. Eventually they leased Bowers Smelt Mill at Ashover, and between 1735 and 1737 removed the existing furnaces and replaced them with new ones to their own design. Shortly afterwards the Company had introduced a low arch reverberatory furnace, completing their self-sufficiency in the area. It was always important, when working mines, to plan for several years ahead, and to try to calculate if and when flooding problems might arise as the mines became deeper. As a consequence soughs were begun well in advance which hopefully, whilst providing ore as work progressed, would ultimately act as a drainage channel for water seeping into the main mine in a particular area. To this end a new sough called Yatestoop or Cowley at the Yatestoop mine was commenced by the Quakers in the year 1751.

Once again Charles would not miss the opportunity to make himself fully conversant with all the activities which were taking place in the area, and to establish contact with an important family called Tissington. The family operated under the title 'Anthony Tissington & Co.' but in their activities outside Derbyshire they were also referred to as 'The Derbyshire Company'.

Anthony Tissington, known to be of Swanwick or Matlock, presumably holding property in both areas, was Deputy Barmaster at Matlock (recorded at Allen Hill sough in 1738) and a mineralogical writer.

George Tissington of Matlock Bridge was Barmaster of Matlock and the brother of Anthony. George was also mineral agent at Winster, and is recorded as owning over eight acres of land in the Manor. In the early 1740s he endeavoured to obtain a lease on behalf of the Tissington company to work what would prove to be, a very rich copper mine at Middleton Tyas in

Yorkshire (today near to Scotch Corner on the A1) and a further important stimulus for the metallurgic industry in the North of England.

* * * * * * *

The first intimation of copper mining at Middleton Tyas is an agreement of 1738, relating to the land of Leonard Hartley, although a little spasmodic mining is understood to have taken place a few years earlier. Two other local landowners also seized the initiative and decided to exploit their ground. One was Lady D'Arcy, who was to have a running feud with Hartley, and the other was Richard Shuttleworth, lord of the manor, who owned extensive estates in Lancashire and sat as Tory M.P. for the county. It was Shuttleworth who engaged George Tissington to explore his lands for copper. Apparently Tissington was successful; he also offered to make a trial in the lands of another adjoining landowner, Mr. Wilkinson, but his offer was rejected. On 15th October 1746, however, he was partner to an agreement regarding the sale of copper and ore. This agreement was between himself and a partnership of John Rotton Gent. of Duffield, to the north of Derby and John Gilbert-Cooper, of Locko near Spondon, to the east of Derby.

The Rotton family was obviously of some standing, anyone becoming involved in the copper industry had to have a considerable amount of capital available for investment, but little is known of them. On the other hand much is known of John Gilbert-Cooper who was another intriguing Georgian character.

Originally there had been two manors in Brassington, and during the year 1630 King Charles I had granted the Duchy Manor of Brassington to Charles Harbord, Esq., who within two or three years had divided the land into four parts and sold it to others. Because of complications in borrowing money for these land purchases, moieties were seized at Court, and one fourth part was conveyed to a William Savile of Bakewell. William Savile was a man of considerable means: a receipt dated 10th May, 1639 confirms that for the sum of £950 he had also made purchase from the Duke of Kent of one third of a large estate including the other Manor of Brassington. William Savile was the great grandfather of John Gilbert-Cooper, and the latter had eventually inherited these family estates but had sold them as recently as 1749. It was obviously from this connection with the Brassington area that George Tissington had become well acquainted with John Gilbert-Cooper.

The Gilbert family had inherited Thurgarton Priory in Nottinghamshire in 1736, but in doing so were compelled to use the surname and arms of the Cooper family, to which they conformed by Act of Parliament. Their Denby estate, nine miles from Derby, was rich with seams of high quality coal and it was here that young John, only 16 years of age in 1739, had proceeded to develop an important family business. He was signatory to a lease for Ecton copper mine during that year, and his partnership with Rotton produced an important smelter on the Denby estate, interests in mining, and a connection with the Derby Copper Works.

The Derby Copper works, established in 1737 on the eastern part of a large island called 'Holms', were situated approximately one mile south of the island containing the Silk Mill. A Swedish visitor, Angerstein, during his visit of 1753-55 was to comment "Close to the Whitewares factory is a slitting and rolling mill, which belongs to Mr. Evins and Mr. Storr, iron manager at Derby . . . At this rolling-mill they also sometimes roll copper plates, which are manufactured at a copper-mill 9 miles from this." The latter is obviously a reference to Denby, and at a later date John Rotton would become personally involved with this mill. It is of interest to note the reference to the Whitewares (manu)factory situated on Cockpit Hill, which would eventually close down in March 1779, allowing the already established manufactory on Nottingham Road, close by St. Mary's Bridge and the Silk Mill, to become famous and renowned throughout the world for its production of Derby porcelains.

Incredibly John Gilbert-Cooper's copper interests seem to have been more of a hobby than necessity, and to a large extent he was probably quite happy to allow John Rotton to take full control of the business, whilst he indulged himself in his passion for writing. He had been educated at Westminster School, entering Trinity College, Cambridge in 1743; however, after only two years and a marriage to the granddaughter of Sir Nathan Wright, recorder of Leicester, intentions of obtaining a degree had been abandoned. In 1746 he had sold Locko Park and most of the Denby estate for £13,000 and had taken up residence at Thurgarton, but had retained under lease 6 acres of land at Denby, presumably relating to his smelter site. After this, his time seems to have been divided between London and Thurgarton, and by the early 1750s he was publishing poetry, miscellaneous tracts and books, promulgating his philosophical ideas about harmony within nature and the soul. Meanwhile George Tissington was furthering his interests at Middleton Tyas.

* * * * * * *

The glebe land for the benefit of the parson of the Parish Church of Middleton Tyas was situated within the area where copper ore was likely to be found. The land adjacent to the church brought into consideration a mining law which had to be observed: no mining could take place beneath the church itself; however it did not deter anyone from mining in the vicinity and creating spoil heaps on the 'doorstep'. A future parson would disapprove of this state of affairs and use his ingenuity to insist that any spoil from new workings had to be used to create a terrace across the field to the church, and planted with an avenue of trees.

George Tissington, who must have been attending the church when in the area, would have become well-known to the parson, Rev. Dr. John Mawer, and would certainly have let it be known that he held the important position of Barmaster at Matlock and an agent of good repute in Winster; he obtained a lease for the glebe mineral rights from Rev. Mawer during 1750. The living was a good one, but was to be considerably augmented by the royalties which Rev. Mawer would receive until his death in 1763. The total sum of his receipts is calculated to be in the region of £4,000. His epitaph in the Parish Church leaves no doubt that he was an extraordinary character. "He was able to speak & write twenty two languages, and particularly excelled in the Eastern Tongues". Known to Frederick, Prince of Wales, he had put forward his wish to promote the Christian religion in the Abyssinian Empire, but the untimely death of the Prince on 20th March 1751, had forestalled his ambitions.

Fortunately analysis of the ore obtained at Middleton Tyas proved that it contained an extremely high copper content said to be the richest in Europe. The initial figure was an astonishing 45% (later 66%) equalled only by very rare consignments of ore imported from a mine near New York. The mines of Cornwall averaged approximately 9% and in other areas, designated as yielding only a poor copper content, the average was 4%-5% (today with modern mining techniques yields as low as 0.5% are considered economically viable).

The high copper content considerably simplified what was normally an extremely complicated and difficult smelting process, and as a result the partnership in which Lady D'Arcy was involved, which had been so successful in raising ore, had decided by 1744 that it was worth its while to build a smelt mill. Fortunately the low sulphur content of the ore also made it unnecessary to carry out the initial calcining process. In other areas where ores contained a high percentage of sulphur it was desirable to burn them in order to reduce impurities, particularly the sulphur, before removing them for smelting. This process required large mounds of ore to be placed on open ground and set alight; the ore smouldered for weeks, often months, giving off sulphurous fumes which, to use a Georgian expression, was 'an unwholesome business'.

The refining process at Middleton Tyas, using coal deposits within the area, considerably alleviated the difficulties of carriage relating to large quantities of copper ore over long distances, and as part compensation for smelting charges savings would be made on transportation costs. The pigs of copper still contained small quantities of impurities which would require a minimal amount of refining at the destination centre. It is not clear whether or not George Tissington built his own smelter, but the suggestion given by correspondence relating to Leonard Hartley, is that Tissington's was a very crude affair, producing unrefined ore "once through the fire" only. This would rid the ore of a considerable amount of impurities and was sufficient for Tissington's customers, John Rotton and John Gilbert-Cooper, who would have no desire to spend extra cash on purchasing coal when they had abundant supplies of their own on the Denby estate. At Middleton Tyas, to smelt and refine copper ore probably required a ratio of two tons of coal to one ton of copper; in other areas the ratio would be higher. Because of this initial smelting the Denby partnership would only require approximately one ton of coal to refine one ton of copper.

The copper pigs would be placed in large casks and transported from Tissington's smelter in waggons down the old Roman Road of Dere Street (A1), then via York to the Humber Estuary, and would presumably make the reverse journey to that of lead i.e. down the River Trent. This is suggested by a letter from a relative of John Rotton's regarding the purchase of copper ore and addressed from Eaton (now known as Long Eaton), which was the nearest point on the Trent to the Denby smelter, where once again an old Roman road conveniently connected the two places.

* * * * * * *

At this time, through his various contacts, Charles Roe's attention must have been directed more and more towards the concerted efforts of those searching for copper ore; here was the potential to develop a very important industry. By the year 1752 he had not only established a considerable business network in the Northwest, Derbyshire and the City of London, but his interests in the capital had diffused beyond the City itself. He had become acquainted with Joseph Stockdale of Castle Street close by the "Royal Mewse" in the Parish of "St. Martin's-in-the-Fields". (Today known as St. Martin-in-the-Fields with Trafalgar Square occupying the site of the 18th century Royal Mews and Charing Cross Road roughly follows the layout of its predecessor, Castle Street). How this contact was established is not known, but the facts which are, offer a variety of what appear to be coincidences.

Charles was conversant with the King's Theatre in the Haymarket, which was only five minutes walk from Joseph Stockdale's house. It was at this theatre during the 1740s that Handel established himself and performed many operas. He used the theatre as his centre of operations, often conducting and playing upon the organ. Theatre organs at this period were difficult and expensive to install, and with the likelihood of fire, as witnessed by the great rapidity with which theatres burnt down due to the use of candlelight, it was considered impracticable to lay out a great deal of money for the assembly of such instruments. Handel often complained about the organ, insisting that if he could be allowed to build one for the theatre, he would know exactly how it should be done. Apart from the 40 operas performed by Handel at the King's Theatre, he also committed himself, though not entirely successfully, to a series of Lenten performances at Covent Garden, again not too far distant from Castle Street and St. Martin's-in-the-Fields.

Although his antecedents are unknown, Joseph Stockdale was apparently a merchant whose two dearest friends were Daniel Golden, a linen draper, Parish of St. Clement Danes and John Davis, an ironmonger and brazier, Parish of St. Andrew, Holborn. (Also close by was Cousin Christopher Roe's younger brother, John, born October 1724, who had become an iron and tin plate worker in the Parish of St. John's Clerkenwell; all, therefore, living within one square mile).

Recorded at the Bank of England is the firm of Scawen and Stockdale, which opened an account in 1694, the year in which the Bank was first established. Bills were discounted for the partnership during 1708, but unfortunately it was not customary to record addresses on account pages. It is possible that they were associated with Sir William Scawen, a London merchant and M.P. who was a director of the Bank from 1694-1722, serving as Deputy Governor from 1695-1697 and as Governor 1697-1699. This Stockdale would, of course, be the generation before Joseph, yet whilst at present no relationship can be proved, both were obviously men of means.

A family of Stockdales was established in the Lake District during the 17th century, some of whom became Dissenters but feeling unsettled, travelled south to London; amongst them was the parson, Richard Hogarth, whose son, William, would later seek revenge by 'poking fun' at the Establishment through his creation of ribald caricatures and paintings. The Hogarths had settled in the Clerkenwell Smithfield area, the poorer part of London left untouched by the Great Fire, and it was in areas such as this that Rev. John Wesley, 47 years of age in 1750, had been making a great impact.

The Church of England had not been complacent in understanding its own deficiencies; as early as 1737 Thomas Secker, formerly Bishop of Bristol but then of Oxford, had reported a new instruction to the Church, that by the 34th Canon:

"No Bishop shall henceforth admit any Person into sacred Order which is not of his own Diocese, except he be either of one of the Universities of this Realm, or except he shall bring Letters dismissory from the Bishop of whose Diocese he is."

However, the Church still had an enormous task ahead, and not until the end of the 18th century, when a brilliant and enlightened Bishop of London would sweep away many prejudices, misunderstandings and ignorance, revitalising the thinking within the Establishment, would that task begin in earnest.

John Wesley's father, Samuel, formerly a Dissenting minister, had subsequently conformed to the Church of England and brought up his large family in the Epworth Rectory in Lincolnshire. On leaving his childhood behind it is said that John Wesley was eventually persuaded to a simple faith by a Moravian Peter Bohler, having attended a meeting of Moravians on 14th May 1738 in Aldersgate Street, London, under the auspices of the Church of England. During this meeting Luther's preface to the Letter of Paul to the Romans had been read, which had greatly affected Wesley, who from that time onwards imbibed the doctrines of Martin Luther, the German monk who had challenged the practices of the Roman Catholic Church early in the 16th century.

Wesley travelled extensively, but many parsons would not allow him to preach within their churches, fearing the effect of his words. Initially he had felt ill at ease preaching out of doors, but soon adapted to the innovation, considering it pertinent to the needs of the tin miners in Cornwall, the potters of Staffordshire, the coal miners of the Northeast and the textile workers of Manchester and elsewhere. His influence in London had grown considerably, particularly among the more Protestant members of the community. He appealed to the Huguenot silk workers of Spitalfields and the Dissenting families who had gathered in the capital from outside, and even within the Royal Parish of St. Martin's-in-the-Fields his ideas and doctrines were welcomed enthusiastically.

At the beginning of the 18th century it had been decided to replace the Old Church of St. Martin with a new one. The foundation stone, laid in the year 1721, marked the commencement of the work. The following year the Governor of Carolina had sent a quantity of cedar wood to be used for the interior. During digging of the foundations, bones of an individual purporting to be eight ft tall were found, fuelling the idea that he had been a giant appearing at one of the Charing Cross fairs. Samuel Pepys's diary contains an entry for August 1664, mentioning that he had been to Charing Cross and walked, complete with hat on, under the arms of a great Dutch giant.

The beautiful church was finally completed and consecrated by the Bishop of London, Dr. Edmund Gibson on 20th October 1726. It was considered to be, and still is, the finest Parish Church of the Grecian style of architecture in the country. Its interior was "of such noble proportions" that it was decided not to spoil the effect with the reinstatement of ornaments and monuments from the old church, nor were any new ones to be added, or objects fixed to the walls. Many of the original monuments were set up in the vaults and crypt of the new church, and even the Earl of Bridgewater, whose family monument had been set in the south side of the original chancel, had to comply with the orders of the 'Rebuilding Commissioners'.

The church could now seat 1,500 persons, but subsequent alterations would reduced the capacity by about 300. The total bill relating to the building was £33,661 16 7d. and the following expenditure also incurred:

Decorating and altering Communion Plate	£1,109 2 10d.
Fees to Bishop for Consecration	£ 21 14 0d.
The copper ware and bell cost	£ 51 12 9d.

These individual items represent vast sums of money. The Royal family attended services in the new church which necessitated additions of screens leading to the royal pews, and a fireplace for the King.

It was in this magnificent church that Charles Roe married Mary, second daughter of Joseph Stockdale, on 25th April 1752. The parish clerk made the mistake of entering Charles's surname as 'Bee' in the register, although the marriage licence correctly records Roe. Here is an amusing coincidence, the predominant part of the Roe family coat of arms is a beehive. The marriage licence dated 12th March, suggests that Charles had hurried home before the wedding took place to inform the family of his intentions, and to make preparations for the home coming of his London bride. It is also possible that Mary travelled to Macclesfield with him in order to meet her future step children, William, Catherine and Samuel, and was accompanied by at least one or two other members of the Stockdale family.

Joseph Stockdale and his wife, Martha, had a numerous family of seven daughters and three sons, but only five survived to adulthood. They had all been baptised in the new church, and Mary's baptismal date of 27th April 1729, meant that she was just 23 years old at the time of her marriage, making her almost 14 years younger than Charles.

There was a significant community of Methodists in the Parish of St. Martin's-in-the-Fields, and the Stockdales were amongst them. Subsequently, upon the rebuilding of the old church, the Methodists, who were using the adjacent Long Acre chapel, were given the option of purchasing the building together with three houses in Chapel Court, and the pulpit. Here was a sign that even the Church of England was endeavouring to be more 'accommodating' with regard to the wishes of some of the members of its congregation.

It was later reported that Charles Roe "when in London often heard the Methodists", and that Mary:

> "had been brought up amongst the people in derision called Methodists; and though when married, she gave way so far to a tender husband, as not to attend the means of grace among the people she loved. She was a pattern of meekness, and all her manners were so strict and upright that many thought her righteous overmuch."

This marriage seems to have had little effect on Catherine and William, now seven and six years of age respectively, but Samuel who had barely known his real mother, was only two and a half years old when Mary took over the household; his subsequent development very much reflects Mary's influence, to the extent that he would have no problem considering himself part of Charles and Mary's progeny. Catherine would always retain her passion for the luxuries of life, an attitude inherited from the Lankford family, which was in no way ever considered a detriment to their Christian attributes. William would become 'his father's son', indefatigable, hard working, with an overwhelming sense of duty, so traditional of the Roe family. There would never be any antagonism shown by Catherine and William towards their future half-brothers and sisters, their Georgian values and good manners would never have allowed it.

Complete with a marriage settlement, which included a payment of £500 from Joseph Stockdale, Charles was about to begin another phase of his life. The fact that his first wife, Elizabeth, had died before him, meant that he was freed from any obligations to the Lankford family, but would have to ensure that in due course his first three children would receive the benefit of their mother's investments in property and the silk business.

At this point in time Charles Roe's interests were so diversified that he does not appear to have made a specific investment on behalf of his second wife, and Joseph Stockdale does not seem to have insisted upon it, excepting that Charles had in mind the purchase of a more substantial residence.

By July of the same year, Thomas Birtles was heavily in debt. Two years earlier he had borrowed money from Joshua Marriott (amongst others), linen merchant of Manchester and partner in the Macclesfield copper mine, which he was now compelled to redeem. Further loans were either obtained from, or were deliberately taken over by Francis Nicholson, apothecary, John Stafford, lawyer and a third party, John Baskervyle, also a lawyer and associate of John Stafford. Within two weeks, which seems an incredibly short time, the trio had taken legal action by a Chirograph 2b Geo.2 dated 15th August, whereby Thomas Birtles and his wife, Ellen, were forced to sell the Macclesfield estate. As a consequence, an advertisement was placed in the Chester newspaper, Adams' *Weekly Courant,* during the weeks of September and October, and finally for week ending 7th November, declaring that a sale of the premises would take place in Macclesfield at the Angel on Tuesday, 14th November 1752. In the meantime the property could be viewed and details obtained from John Stafford.

Once again John Stafford seems to have become involved in the proceedings, although whether or not he actively sought to acquire the property for Charles Roe, or whether what occurred was pure coincidence, is difficult to deduce.

The advertisement was headed "To be SOLD, Together or in Parcels" and proceeded:

> "A Capital Meffuage (fit for a Gentleman's Family . . . with convenient Out-Offices and Buildings, a Garden and five Clofes (lying directly behind the House) containing together 7 Cheshire Acres of Land and upwards – And two small Dwelling houses and a Barn (near to the Capital Meffuage)."

Also included were three farms or estates in Hurdsfield, Rainow and Bollington, all leased out and having considerable quantities of timber, coal mines and stone quarries "all which, by the Custom of the Manor the Copyholder is entitled to".

The Chirograph actually contained greater detail of the Macclesfield property, listing "Three Messuages one shippon Two Barns Two Stables three gardens Four acres of Land Three acres of meadow three acres of pasture Common of pasture for all manner of Cattle and Common of Turberry . . ."

The Capital Messuage was the house situated on Chestergate, and the one which Charles desired. Given the probable situation regarding the button trade, Charles could in no way directly approach Thomas Birtles in order to purchase; he also appears to have been 'playing for time' in order to obtain the required sum, and John Stafford assisted in the transactions.

On 4th February 1753, Charles and Mary's first child was born, a daughter baptised Martha after her grandmother Stockdale. By 23rd May 1753, Charles had made a part payment towards the premises and as a consequence held a $1/10$th part of the estate. It must have been difficult for all concerned to find the cash so desperately needed by Thomas Birtles, but at the same time it must have also been difficult for Charles to assure everyone who had put forward loans, that he would redeem them as quickly as possible, in the hope that none of them would force the house and premises to be sold separately. Even John Stafford's brother-in-law, William Tatton, made a loan, together with James Roe. The total sum of all the loans was £1,370 and James Roe and Rowland Atkinson acted as Trustees and Guarantors on behalf of Charles.

About this time, Charles, now 38 years of age, took up residence in the Chestergate House (today known as Charles Roe House). There is no evidence to suggest that he also purchased the estates in Hurdsfield, Rainow and Bollington, only the substantial area of land extending westwards and southwards from his residence, comprising almost 15 acres or 7 Cheshire acres. His boundary to the south met the area of parkland then in possession of General Cholmondeley, (the result of Cholmondeley's marriage to Earl Barrymore's daughter). This boundary almost reached the Lesser Brook or Dams Brook as it came to be known, which gurgled its way downhill in a southerly direction, descending sharply into the region called the Dams, where it was joined by the two smaller brooks, one of which had travelled from the area which is now South Park, and the other which had trickled its way down the steep slope from the north-western corner of the parkland.

The Pickford family, after purchasing the land know as the Eyes from the Earl of Derby in the 17th century, had consolidated their holdings by leasing several closes of land, originally from Earl Barrymore, through which the Lesser Brook flowed. Some of these appear on an Indenture dated 10th September 1729. Two of the closes, the Highmost Brooke Meadow and the Little High Field, were immediately adjacent to Charles Roe's southern boundary, followed by the Lower Dams, from where the Lesser Brook flowed across Parsonage Green, under Pickford Bridge and into Pickford Eyes passing Charles Roe's mills. Charles approached Joseph Pickford of Altehill with a view to leasing, what was to him, this very important area of land. By this period, the Pickford family was well established in the Lancashire cotton trade and had no further commercial ambitions in Macclesfield, apart from land leases, and so Charles was successful.

He also negotiated a lease renewal to add the life of this son, William, to the original one for the Silk Mill in place of his wife Elizabeth's, after her death on 28th April 1750. On 26th December 1753 the land holding was again enlarged, and this further lease with Joseph Pickford recites all leases to that date and confirms Professor Chaloner's quotations from the original mill lease from 25th March 1744; it also verifies that the sough or tunnel, to accommodate the stream flowing alongside, led from the eastern side of the building. The plot of land, now incorporated with that of the mill, was the adjacent parcel to the south, with the mill stream flowing between the two (today site of the United Reformed Church). On it stood an old house, originally known as Pickford Hall, together with its tan yard. And according to Professor Chaloner another Indenture dated 5th April 1754 obtained from Joseph Pickford the leasing of yet another close of land on the southern side of what had been the tan yard (today site of Barclay's Bank on Park Green) which included "all that barn or parcel of building called Pickford Barn . . . near to a place called Pickford Bridge." On these premises soon afterwards Roe constructed "a reservoir, dam or head of water . . . for the better supplying (of) the silk mills". Evidently there were still problems with an insufficient water supply. Part of Pickford Barn was also converted into a "winding-room" for the partnership. The lease was for 21 years at a rent of £16 10s. per annum. All the Pickford leases were restricted to 21 years under the terms of Joseph Pickford's marriage settlement.

Charles was now almost totally self-sufficient. The stream provided water for his livestock kept on the meadow land. He also established an orchard, and a croft which would provide vegetables together with a garden, albeit small, which could be viewed from the Venetian window in the Drawing Room. His acquisition of further water rights over the Lesser Brook meant that he had control over the watercourse commencing on the southwestern boundary of his land, continuing down through the fields to Parsonage Green, under Pickford Bridge, between his "pile of buildings", until it became that part of the stream over which Glover, Huxley and Greaves held rights.

At the same time Charles turned his attention to the smaller brooklet which flowed out of the parkland (South Park) and gradually descended towards the Dams. Just above the point at which a sharp incline occurred, enabling it to rapidly enter the Lesser Brook in the Lower Dams region, Charles constructed a reservoir which must have incorporated a sluicegate in order to control the outflow. (Today the site of this former reservoir is represented by the gardens, yards and pathway behind the houses on the western side of Nelson Street). The water being fed to the Macclesfield Silk Mill could, therefore, be controlled from three directions i.e. the water from the corn mills in Sutton, the River Bollin and the Lower Dams; included in the system were two reservoirs which were able to provide water during the summer months as necessary.

The addition of the Pickford barn to the mill complex on Parsonage Green is interesting, particularly as part of it was converted into a winding room. This is a possible indication that problems of lighting were being experienced in the two upper floors of the large Silk Mill. The winding room also indicates that yarn was being wound onto bobbins for use by weavers. At last silk of a sufficiently high quality was being provided, predominantly for the silk weavers of the Spitalfields area in London, but also for silk weavers elsewhere.

By 29th June 1754 Charles found it necessary to obtain a loan of £2,000 through his contacts in London, in order to rid himself of the loans nearer home. He presumably did not disclose the source of his apparent affluence, in order to promote confidence and respect should any future business transactions arise. He obtained a loan of £1,000 from Robert Mandeville who, having served his apprenticeship, had been made free in 1750 and become a linen draper in Cornhill, close by the Bank of England. From 1754 Mandeville was on the livery of the Drapers' Company and must have been very well acquainted with Charles to have placed such a substantial sum at his disposal. The second loan of £1,000 was made by Samuel

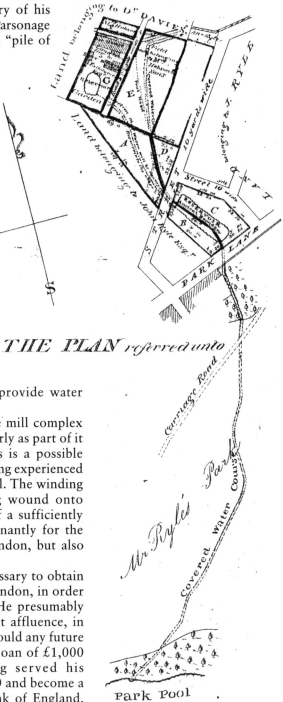

THE PLAN referred unto

Park Stream. A plan of 1806 courtesy of CCALS Ref. D 1128/5 (part).

Holland, a druggist of London, who was probably related to Robert Mandeville. Charles, although executing a Bond for £2,000 on 29th June, did not redeem the other loans on his property until Indentures dated 17th and 18th September were prepared. The interest due on the Bond was to be calculated at 4% per annum, payable in two equal instalments each year on 29th June and 29th December.

Having settled his financial situation and gained the occupation of a considerable area of land on his southern boundary, Charles created a garden at the rear of his house out of part of his 'Barn-field'. This necessitated an adjustment to his eastern boundary. However, whilst his house and garden occupied the large corner site juxtaposed with both Chestergate and Barn Street, the strip of land with buildings, running immediately south of his residence along the western side of Barn Street (and therefore along Charles Roe's eastern boundary), was owned by a Thomas Sheldon. This created a problem, because part of the boundary line between the Roe garden and the gardens at the rear of two of the neighbouring properties, was irregular. Agreement was reached whereby each exchanged a strip of land and Charles accepted responsibility for the erection and maintenance of the 'Palisadoes' on either side of the pathway thus created. This allowed access from the Roe house, through the garden to a minor roadway. The agreement was signed on 23rd December 1755 with Charles decribed as 'Silk Merchant' and Thomas Sheldon as 'Jersey Comer'.

* * * * * * *

During this period in time the Macclesfield Silk Mill must have been very successful due, not only to the endeavours of the partners, but also to the decline of the Park Silk Mills, as yet another member of the original partnership had died during 1753. This time it was Thomas Hadfield who, by his will dated 28th February 1752 (which was possibly 1753, because 1752 was the year in which the calendar had been adjusted) stipulated that his Executors must "sell and dispose of All my Share Interest and Benefit in the Park silk mills in Stockport," and also requested that he was to be buried "without the Ceremony of the Bearers" and "that such of my particular friends and acquaintances as shall attend my Funeral shall have hatbands and Gloves"; these items would be bought for the mourners and charged as funeral expenses by the executors upon the estate of the deceased.

Amongst the several bequests contained in the will there is mention of a warehouse, stables and outbuildings under lease to George Nicholson, adjacent to the garden or orchard at the rear of Thomas Hadfield's dwelling house in Heaton Norris.

By the time George Nicholson prepared his will, on 27th November 1755, no mention was made of the Park Silk Mills. At some time during the two years following the death of Thomas Hadfield, the mills had come into possession of a Richard Blackburn and would remain in his occupation until the early 1780s. The situation must have been identical to the one in which the Stockport business had gained an advantage over the Derby Silk Mill at the time of Sir Thomas Lombe's death, but this time the advantage was with Macclesfield and one which it would retain for nearly 200 years.

One indication of the decline of the Stockport silk trade was the fact that John Guardivaglio had moved to Macclesfield with his family and baptised a daughter, Sarah, on 2nd March 1755 at St. Michael's. He was to remain in the town with his wife, Mary, and children until at least 1760, no doubt providing considerable expertise for the Silk Mill. Although the name of the mechanic who originally built a Lombe machine for Charles Roe is unknown, it does seem appropriate to speculate that it was one of the Guardivaglios from Stockport.

The year 1753/54 had been an important one for Samuel Lankford; he had achieved his ambition of becoming mayor of Macclesfield. One can only presume that he used his position to further his connections with General James Cholmondeley, because during the following year he took an extraordinary course of action.

The King's court house, situated in the town of Macclesfield, had also made the custom of maintaining the King's prison or gaol a necessity close by. The gaol house, together with lands appurtenant, which were adjacent to St. Michael's church, had been leased from the Crown by Earl Rivers subject to the payment of a yearly rental of one shilling.

It was Richard Savage, Earl Rivers, who had been involved in a great scandal culminating in the *Earl of Macclesfield's Case* presented to the House of Lords in 1697-98, by which Lord Macclesfield had obtained a divorce from his wife, Ann, Countess of Macclesfield, on the grounds of her adultery with the Earl. The result of the Countess's illicit union with Earl Rivers was a son baptised Richard, who was subsequently brought up by a shoemaker and his wife. Earl Rivers died in 1712, but on his death bed had expressed a desire to leave young Richard an inheritance; however a visit from Lady Macclesfield had assured him that the child was dead and the young boy put forward as Richard, none other than the shoemaker's son. This boy grew up claiming that his mother, Lady Macclesfield, had robbed him of his inheritance. He became a great friend of Dr. Johnson's who, although always complaining of Richard's boorish behaviour, defended his friend's allegations and derided Lady Macclesfield. Dr. Johnson's great friend and companion, Boswell, finally carried out his own investigations but was unable to discover any evidence to support Richard's story; on the other hand neither could he disprove it. With the death of Richard Savage, Earl Rivers, the Savage family line ended after 300 years. His daughter, Elizabeth, had married James Barry, Earl of Barrymore, and the marriage of their daughter, Penelope, had placed the Savage estates at the disposal of her husband, General James Cholmondeley; but in spite of Penelope's death in 1742, the General had retained the parkland of Macclesfield together with certain rights over the Savage Chapel adjoining St. Michael's church, the adjacent plot of land and the gaol house.

The gaol, together with the office of Bailiff, was leased to a keeper, who in turn had subleased to Moses Berry, officiating at the time of Samuel Lankford's mayoralty. At the "latter End of May or beginning of June 1755" Samuel Lankford, having taken over the original lease from the keeper, turned out Moses Berry and put Edmund Brough in his place. Berry delivered his prisoners, one of whom was awaiting execution, into Mr. Brough's custody. Brough continued to attend Court and carry out his duties for some time, for which he received fees, but it was subsequently drawn to the attention of William Taylor, Clerk and John Stafford, Deputy Clerk of the King's Court that Brough had allowed the prisoners "to go at large & had refused to receive into the sd Gaol some other prisoners who for want of Bail had been brought to the sd Gaol". On being questioned about his actions, Brough had insisted that he was acting upon the instructions of his landlord, Mr. Lankford, who was determined "it should be a Gaol no longer". Samuel Lankford insisted that he was acting under the orders of General Cholmondeley, whereupon petitions were prepared to the General, stipulating that the jurisdiction of the Court extended over a quarter of the County of Cheshire, including two of the largest market towns, and that the withdrawal of the use of the prison was a considerable inconvenience. This dispute was to continue for four years, during which time William Taylor and John Stafford would finally prepare their case.

What could have been the reason for this extraordinary turn of events? Perhaps a clue lies with an entry in a Town Hall directory some years later, which records James Pickering and James Cholmondeley as Button manufacturers on Park (Parsonage) Green in 1773. It is obvious that General Cholmondeley would not be personally involved in the practical making of buttons, but in his list of rentals for 1775 appears an entry "Pickering John two New buildings on Park Green 8/-". Perhaps the person responsible for the compilation of the directory mistakenly assumed James Cholmondeley was a partner with John Pickering in the button business, because he owned both the land and buildings. This Pickering was more than likely the son of the man originally involved in the silk venture with Charles Roe. On the other hand it is possible that the General had invested some money in the button business, but this seems extremely improbable. This tenuous connection, however, does lead one to presume that Samuel Lankford had initially suggested to General Cholmondeley the idea that the gaol house would make an ideal button manufactory from which they could both greatly benefit. Lankford probably also emphasised the fact that he would be able to employ many more old men, women and poor children, which would considerably alleviate the hardships suffered by many.

This argument is further supported by the fact that the Quaker, Joseph Hobson, who had taken his turn as an Overseer of the Poor, began to make overtures concerning the enlargement of the existing Poorhouse close by the River Bollin. Charles Roe, Overseer during the years 1743/44 and 1748/49, found himself serving on the Vestry Committee of St. Michael's when, at a meeting attended by Samuel Glover, James Hulley, Maltster, "the said Mr. Hobson" and two others, the following entry was made:

"10th February 1757.
Present Poorhoufe shall with all convenient speed be enlarged for the use of the Poor of the Burrough of Macclesfield according to a plan & Estimate heretofore drawn up by Mr. Hobson & signed by several principal inhabitants & lay payers".

James Hobson had evidently been busy preparing his petition realising that Samuel Lankford was intent on monopolising that part of the button trade as it related to the poor of the town, and in no way was Hobson prepared to allow this to happen. He was insisting that arrangements for the poor should be kept with the rightful authorities and not exploited by a particular individual outside their control. Charles appears to have agreed with Hobson's stance; he never involved himself with the saga of the gaol house. In fact, from the time of Samuel Lankford's take over of the lease, Charles had already begun to distance himself from his father-in-law's schemes. On 13th September 1756, he had added his signature to an Indenture relating to the leasing of a copper mine from Sir William Fleming at Coniston in the Lake District. And despite Samuel Lankford's original involvement with Ecton copper mine, he would never become a partner in any of Charles Roe's copper mining interests.

10
CHARLES ROE & CO.

The Copper sparkling next in ruddy streaks,
And in the gloom betrays its glowing cheeks.

A letter dated 9th December 1754 contains the statement "Miss Kitty Fleming has called in near £4,000, which will make money very scarce in these parts where it is mostly let out". Catherine, or Miss Kitty as she was known, was the third daughter of Sir William, 1st Baronet of Rydal Hall who had died in 1736. Her elder sister, Barbara, had married Edward Parker of Broosholm during 1754 and anxiety regarding Barbara's marriage settlement, and possibly her own because of her intended marriage to Sir Peter Byrne-Leycester of Tabley Hall near Knutsford, must have forced her into taking action in order to recover some of the money due from the estate as provision for their dowers.

Sir William, through the customary services of his lawyer, would have loaned out money to many business and professional people within the area of Coniston and, as indicated by the aforementioned letter, Kitty's action of 'calling in' such a vast sum would have had an incisive effect on the economy of the region; however, the reality was that a considerable period of time would elapse before her action reached fruition.

Kitty's uncle, Sir William 3rd Baronet now heir of Rydal, seemed to be labouring under great difficulties, no doubt brought about by the demands made on the estate in respect of the various marriage settlements relating to the numerous Fleming daughters.

Although the routine book-keeping and everyday running of Rydal was in the hands of the steward, John Moore, who also held the position of Captain of the Westmorland Militia, Sir William personally endeavoured to promote further business schemes, which included the leasing of mineral rights, in the hope of providing more income for the beleaguered estate. The Coniston mines, said to have been worked originally by the Germans as a consequence of their activities in Keswick during the reign of Queen Elizabeth I, had been unproductive for many years, but on 29th June 1748 Sir William had granted a lease for 51 years to John Gorsuch, Gent., of London a possible relative of Thomas Gorsuch, goldsmith of London who, during the previous year, had negotiated a lease for a mine at Tilberthwaite from Sir John Pennington. The Coniston lease referred to gold, silver, copper, lead, tin, iron etc. excepting coal, slate and stone. The Gorsuchs were presumably only interested in precious metals and as very little attention appears to have been paid to the mines, one must deduce that their trials were unsuccessful.

The following year Sir William surprisingly asked a Quaker by the name of John Lawson to send someone to inspect Coniston mine. Lawson accordingly paid an individual by the name of Joseph Vipone 16s. 0d., which included an amount of 4s. 0d. for horse hire for four days. Whether or not as a direct result of this survey, within a short period of time the mine was being worked by a partnership referred to as "Kendal gentilmen".

On 6th July 1754 an interesting letter was addressed to Sir William from the village of Dent in north-west Yorkshire, close by the border with Westmorland (today, due to boundary changes, Dent is in Cumbria). The writer, James Stephens, claimed to be "Now Steward for the Warrington Copper Company" which was, of course, Thomas Patten's company. He referred to himself also as "the man that came to Rydal with adam fleming" about the weighing of the first parcel of ore at Coniston "in those gentilmen's time". Adam Fleming was, at that time, rent collector for Coniston Manor, and Stephens, presumably an independent merchant intent on buying copper or other ore which he could sell on. Perhaps his services to Thomas Patten were such that he was hired on a permanent basis. He was enquiring on behalf of "some gentilmen" who were interested in leasing the mine. This could have been a reference to anyone, including himself or Tissington & Co. who were also mining in the North Riding at this period, but it would certainly not relate to Charles Roe. James Stephens had taken some trouble to discover that, if the mines were not worked for six calendar months, then the lease was void and "there never has Ben (been) four mainers (miners) at work at one time Since Christmas Last". His penultimate request was a desire that Sir William would not disclose his name to the "Kendal gentilmen" should they still hold the lease for the mine, otherwise "they will not throw up there Lease if . . . they think I know of Som ore Lyin there that I never informed them [of]".

He also mentioned that a search for ore was taking place in Dent, and a brief postscript conveyed greetings from George Mason and his wife, a member of a family which would become famous for its pottery and porcelain, in particular ironstone china, which is still in production today.

Evidence on site at Coniston mine confirms that work had been in progress and had reached at least as deep as the old hand chiselled level known as Cobbler's, which had been taken down to the Bonsor Vein. The fact that the ore was becoming more difficult to extract seems to have dissuaded the group from making further progress and suggests that they had had very little experience of mining, and thus the clause concerning the termination of the lease by the lessor, Sir William, was brought into effect. The mineral rights were once more available for leasing.

For some time the Warrington company had been experiencing an ever-growing demand for copper goods from the port of Liverpool, as the African trade rapidly developed. The number of ships sailing from the port to West Africa in 1737 had been 33, but by 1753 had more than doubled to 72. Thomas Patten, through an association with one of his partners in the wire mill at Alton in Staffordshire, had taken premises in the Greenfield Valley in Flintshire during the early 1740s, where a powerful source of water provided the necessary power for the establishment of rolling mills for his copper. On 12th July 1755, together with brother Robert and two Warrington merchants, Thomas formed a partnership to make plate and roll copper at the Greenfield mills "fit to work into vessels for sale in Foreign markets by the coppersmiths". This, of course, would necessitate a greater supply of copper ore for the smelters at Warrington, and one must presume that two very reliable merchants offered to acquire the requisite ore, if at all possible. One was Charles Roe and the other was Legh Dickenson, son of John, merchant of Manchester, who had played host to Bonnie Prince Charlie. As regards Legh Dickenson, it must be admitted that it seems more probable he had moved to Cornwall to join other members of the family who had been established in Falmouth for several years and who had possibly been involved with the purchase of copper ore. Records show that Patten & Co. had been acquiring reasonable consignments of Cornish copper ore from at least 1729.

Legh Dickenson was still in the Manchester area on 5th March 1754 when his distinctive signature was added to a property deed as a witness to a sale of land in Macclesfield Park. His brother, John, had married into the Chetham family who were already related to another important Macclesfield family, surname Hawkins.

On 26th May 1757 Legh Dickenson signed the register of St. Euny, (or Uny) Parish church of Redruth in Cornwall, when he married a widow, Patience Michell, by licence. Patience, baptised 23rd April 1728, was the daughter of William Churchill who had originated from Devon. There were several branches of the Churchill family in the West Country, one of which became famous when John Churchill, appointed by King William to the position of Commander-in-chief of the allied forces against France in the War of the Spanish Succession, effected four of the greatest victories in English military history. Although at present no close connection can be traced, by strange coincidence Henrietta, eldest daughter of John Churchill, lst Duke of Marlborough, had married Francis Godolphin in March 1699, and the Godolphin estate was but a short distance from what has become one of the most famous and remarkable mines in Cornwall, Dolcoath in Camborne. This mine was worked continuously longer than any other, and was the deepest in Cornwall. Like the Odin mine of Castleton in Derbyshire it had been worked for centuries; both claiming to be the oldest mine in England.

The Godolphins were also concerned with mining, particularly tin; in fact the grandfather, after whom Francis had been named, had been so successful in his management of the stannaries during the reign of Elizabeth I, that he had been sent to North Wales by her successor, James I, to oversee and certify trials of ore, and also particularly in Cardiganshire.

In spite of the oft repeated intelligence that the Romans came to Britain for metals, they appear to have paid very little attention to the south-west area of England. The limited remains of their occupation in the region represent only a small association with tin mining. The Roman copper mining was apparently concentrated in North Wales where the ore could be easily extracted; as in the rest of England, the true beginnings of the copper industry in Cornwall can be traced to the 16th century.

The first intimation of copper was c. 1580, when the Mines Royal Company leased its mining rights in Cornwall for £1,000, representing a five year rental. The lease was taken by Daniel Hochstetter (in charge of the Keswick venture) and Thomas Smythe, Collector of Customs for the Port of London, and a shareholder of the Mines Royal. Hochstetter died in 1581 but Smythe continued, considering it well within his means. At a later date Smythe also leased the mining rights of Wales from the Mines Royal.

A small smelting works was set up in Neath, South Wales, with the help of Germans; and Ulrich Frosse, before taking up the management of the works, was initially in charge of mining operations in Cornwall, where he resided for a time. At this early period unsuccessful attempts were made to smelt in Cornwall, but Neath superseded, that is until the winter of 1585-86 when Frosse complained that the works were at a standstill due to lack of ore. Thomas Smythe ultimately lost money, and the mines of Keswick and Cornwall became unprosperous. At present very little is known of the smelting taking place in Neath, but somehow the works appear to have survived, probably due to the importation of copper ore, particularly from Sweden.

After the Mines Royal Acts of 1689 and 1693 releasing the mines from Crown monopoly, the encouragement given in the search for copper ore was noticeable amongst the personnel already concerned with workings in lead mines. One such person was John Coster, son of a Forest of Dean ironmaster, who had been involved with lead smelting for many years in Bristol. During the 1680s he had moved to Redbrook on the River Wye near Monmouth, and had set up a copper smelter which was supplied with small cargoes of Cornish ore shipped to Chepstow. He died in 1718.

During her travels of 1685 to c. 1712 Celia Fiennes gave various descriptions of the Cornish mines and also made a particular point of mentioning "I saw not a windmill all over Cornwall or Devonshire tho' they have wind and hills enough, and it may be its too bleake for them". She noted that the "tinn mines" produced not only tin but also stone and a sort of spar, similar to that mined in the lead mines of Derbyshire, and "stones as cleer as Christal which is called Cornish Diamonds". She visited "Mr. Bescawens Trygoltny a Relation of mine". This refers to Mr. Boscawen's house Tregothnan, from which she described the view; "eastward and the south was the Great Ocean which runs into Falmouth thats the best harbour for shipps in that road; the north to the hills full of Copper mines". The next day she made her way to Land's End by Redruth "mostly over heath and downs which was very bleake and full of mines; here I came by the Copper mines, which have the same order in the digging and draining tho' here it seemes dryer and I believe not quite soe annoy'd with water; the oar is something as the tinn only this looks blackish or rather a purple colour and the glistering part is yellow as the other is white; they do not melt it here but ship it off to Bristol by the North Sea . . . at St. Ives they do melt a little but nothing that is considerable".

About the year 1700 attempts had again been made to smelt copper ore locally, by means of a smelter built near St. Austell which was shortly afterwards followed by another, the latter having been built by a partnership of John Pollard of Redruth and Thomas Worth of St. Ives, but both failed due to the expense of obtaining coal.

Following the death of John Coster Snr. who had become known as the 'father of Cornish mining', his son, John Jnr. considered it necessary in 1719 to form what today would be termed a syndicate, in order to ensure that finances were available for the development of Cornish mines. The Costers were yet another staunch Church of England family; to a degree they were rivals of the Bristol Brass Company which came under the control of Abraham Darby and the Champions respectively. Yet despite the immense Quaker involvement in the Bristol area, and the rivalries, John Jnr. took control of operations for the 'consortium' which included several partners from various Bristol copper works, one of which was the Quaker company of the Champions. Cornish copper mining began to expand rapidly, involving not only John Coster Jnr. but also his two brothers, Thomas and Robert. Documentation relating to the year 1727 proves that John was supplying at least three Bristol concerns with copper, which continued until his death in 1731.

This apparently successful period of early copper mining concentrated attention on the area, although in some quarters the difficulty of obtaining copper ore, as opposed to tin, was probably not fully appreciated until investments had been made.

Tin was seldom rich enough to work beyond a depth of 50 fathoms and the copper was found in no great abundance until a depth of 100 fathoms or more, consequently copper mining necessitated a greater skill in "hydraulicks and mechanicks" and proved to be considerably more expensive to mine than tin, requiring substantial supplies of coal, candles, timber, leather, ropes, gunpowder and various other materials, not to mention an increased wages bill in respect of the extra labourers employed.

This, however, had not deterred William Churchill who, having lived in Penzance, Helston (where his daughter, Patience was baptised) and Redruth, was mining Dolcoath for copper ore when he signed the accounts "Errors excepted" on 5th March 1733, and would continue to do so until his death early in 1765. It is entirely possible that he had commenced mining two or three years earlier, because the set of accounts relating to this period begins in 1731 and is evidence that the mine, (part of the North Downs Adventure for accounting purposes) was producing copper at that time. Other records show that previous owners had made a substantial profit, reputed to be more than a million pounds in the decade 1718 to 1728. William Churchill would consequently become a very wealthy man, and High Sheriff of Cornwall in 1765, the year of his death. His residence is believed to have been on Fore Street in Redruth, today the site of a shopping arcade. He invested his profits in several properties and other mining ventures which, by 1737, together with John Enys, Esq., included interests in the following mines:

Pendarvis Wheale	Owla
Wheale Widen	Wheale Moore
Wheale Veriah	Wheale Rose.

Apart from Wheal Rose, which adjoined the Great North Downs mine and was known to be yielding rich copper ore about the year 1739, very little is known of the others mentioned above, except that ore was being purchased from Wheal Owla and Veriah in 1729, and by 1734 all the mines except Wheal Moore were in production.

* * * * * * *

By 1740 William Churchill, described as "an Inn keeper" in Redruth, had obtained lease of the Redruth market. In 1747 he possibly witnessed John Wesley's first visit to the town where, on 4th July, Wesley preached in the street. Redruth at this time comprised one main street only, and was referred to in legal documents as "the town or village". Wesley was to make several visits to the area over the next few years, but was not always well received; however, a Methodist Society was formed early which met in a house close by the town.

The parson of the Parish of Redruth was Rev. John Collins who had been a fellow student of Wesley's at Oxford, and who was later to save Wesley from a mob in the Parish of Wendron. In spite of his concern for his friend's welfare, Collins did not condone the effect John Wesley's actions were having on certain members of the community, and on 16th September 1749 wrote to the Bishop of Exeter concerning the curate, Rev. Thomas Vivian "had it not been for Mr. Vivian whom I take to be a false-hearted brother, the sect had never increased as it did, in this Parish". The curate was a member of a family whose name would become synonymous with copper smelting, particularly during the early years of the 19th century, when Vivian & Co. would come to monopolise the smelting industry of the Neath Valley in South Wales.

The Churchill family were now ardent members of the Parish Church of St. Euny, situated about a quarter of a mile from the market town of Redruth "at the very western extremity of the parish", and it was here, on 25th June 1753, that Patience married into the eminent local family of Michell. Her husband, Francis, was an apothecary who, no doubt, carried out the very important task of assaying her father's mineral ores, but by 17th February 1755 he had died and was buried in the graveyard of St. Euny's. Patience was left to enjoy their several properties and profits and, together with other executors, to manage the estate until their small son, Francis William, came of age to claim his inheritance. Sadly young Francis died shortly after his father, leaving the estate unadministered, but the inheritance due to the child would now automatically pass to Francis's nephew who was already a beneficiary under the will. As this nephew was also a minor, in due course execution of the estate was taken by someone else on his behalf. Patience would be entitled to her third share in compensation of her dower, and this would be included in negotiating her marriage settlement with Legh Dickenson.

It was an important marriage for Patience, and the fact that Legh Dickenson was accepted into the community as a gentlemen of some consequence, seems to indicate that something was known of his background. There was already a Dickenson family established in Falmouth from the 1720s who were more than likely cousins, involved in supplying goods for Legh's father in Manchester in the same way that the Finney and Davenport families were operating. In all probability Legh Dickenson's removal to Cornwall took place about the middle of 1756, at the time when Charles Roe was considering the idea of leasing the Coniston copper mine; his position in Cornwall was, however, vastly different from the one which Charles envisaged for himself. Legh does not appear to have become involved personally in mining, as no evidence exists to suggest that he was ever a shareholder in any of the Cornish mines. He was there as an agent to purchase copper ore on behalf of a particular company which, one has to assume, at that time was the Warrington company of Thomas Patten Jnr. and his partners, because of his father's close connections with Thomas Patten Snr. There was also the connection with Charles Roe, not only because of the linen and silk thread trade but from the fact that Rev. Joseph Dale, headmaster of Stockport Grammar School, was also curate of Birch Chapel at Rusholme of which the Dickenson family were patrons.

* * * * * * *

Tin in Cornwall had been produced 'time out of mind' and there were already established ways of operating. If found on common land (as mentioned in Chapter 5), the Stannary Laws were applied, but elsewhere the grant for tin was the same as for copper and not bounded by these Laws. The dues or dish payable to the lord of the soil (i.e. the individual who had leased rights from the Crown) was usually $\frac{1}{6}$ $\frac{1}{7}$ $\frac{1}{8}$ $\frac{1}{9}$ or even $\frac{1}{12}$. The dues for copper ore only, were payable in money, but for tin, payment was made in stone or mineral ore. Purchases of Cornish ore took place by ticketing, a system begun in 1725. It was presumably devised to avoid monopolies taking place, but just as at auction sales today, agreements could be reached between bidders in advance of sales. Accounts, said to have been faithfully transcribed from Copper Ore buyers books, provide the following details in respect of Cornish copper ore sales for the period 1726 to 1755 i.e. from the year in which ticketing was fully operative until the year before Legh Dickenson's arrival in Redruth:

1726-35 64,800 tons @ £7 15 10 = £473,500 Av.p.a. 6,480 tons £47,350.
1736-45 75,520 tons @ £7 8 6 = £560,106 Av.p.a. 7,552 tons £56,010.
1746-55 98,790 tons @ £7 9 0 = £731,457 Av.p.a. 9,879 tons £73,145.

In order to allow some sort of perspective to be formed, by using the multiplication figure of at least 100 to give an approximate comparative figure today, it can be seen that almost £180 million of copper ore had been sold in the 30 year period.

By 1755 a handful of copper companies had agents in the area bidding for ore viz. (Bristol) Brass-Wire Co., the English Copper Co., Wayne & Co., Chambers & Co. and "a gentleman from Wales" who more than likely represented the Mackworth Co. now in the hands of Sir Herbert of the Gnoll Estate near Neath in South Wales; his father, Sir Hubert, had died in 1727.

The procedure of ticketing was unique to Cornwall. Existing records indicate that it took place once a fortnight, alternating between Tabb's Hotel, Redruth and the Royal Hotel, Truro, though in the early days it probably took place only in Redruth and less frequently.

Before the day of ticketing, it was necessary for the interested parties to determine the quality of the ore on offer by assay, allowing them to make a realistic bid should their companies decide to purchase. As soon as sufficient quantities of ore were dressed and ready for sale at an individual mine, agents were invited to attend on an appointed day to obtain their samples.

The dressed ore was divided into parcels of different weights e.g. 2 parcels x 100 tons, 1 x 42 tons, 1 x 7 tons, and the day before sampling one parcel of convenient size, depending on the number of agents attending, would be mixed again and again. If the weight was less than 10 tons it was usually divided into three "Doles" or piles. Upon the arrival of the samplers, each dole was divided into quarters by means of a shovel and samples obtained from different parts of the ore, so that 2 or 3 cwts. were then carried to a clean floor. Here it was well mixed on the boards, divided again into four, and two of the adverse quarters returned to the original dole. The remaining two quarters were mixed once more, broken up into pieces sufficiently small enough to pass through a coarse sieve, then thoroughly and finally mixed three or four times. After this each sampler in turn helped himself to 1 or 2 lbs. of the ore which he placed in a bag and took away for assaying.

The sampling day took place two weeks before the day appointed for ticketing, to enable the agents to receive instructions from their respective companies.

Whether or not each company had its own assay house is difficult to ascertain, or whether there was a co-operative arrangement whereby each agent could commission his own assayer to carry out the tests using the same premises and equipment as the others, has apparently not been recorded at that time. In the early years perhaps the latter was the norm, but as more companies became involved in purchasing ore from Cornwall, it became a greater convenience for each to establish its own assay office. There is a suggestion at a later date that Legh Dickenson was possibly engaged in the dual role of agent and assayer, in which instance he would have initially required a good deal of instruction and practice to be able to do so.

A common wind or reverberatory furnace was used, with a hole in the side. A brick clay door had to be constructed to fit exactly the hole, but with a small aperture in the centre through which the assay could be inspected. When the test was underway, the aperture needed to be 'stopped up' with a piece of clay. As iron has a higher melting point than copper, iron tools were always preferred to others by men working with the furnaces, and iron was also used for the bars or grate of the furnace which was laid down over the ash pit.

The first essential was to heat up the furnace by filling it with coal, sometimes referred to as sea coal, and allowing it to reduce to charcoal. Sea coal was something of a misnomer and possibly derived from the fact that Londoners received their coal by ship from North-umberland, although another suggestion comes from the centuries old tradition of women combing beaches and filling baskets with pieces of coal washed down from the cliffs. Whilst the furnace was prepared, the sample ore was powdered and sieved through a hair sieve and placed on a piece of paper in a heap of about a half inch thick. From this was taken a troy ounce, which was actually one and a quarter ounces. Next a large crucible was placed almost at the top of the furnace and raw coal added around it to keep down the flames. After placing the powdered ore in the crucible, some of the bricks were gently placed in position to raise the heat of the fire. As soon as the ore became dusky red in colour, the stirring began to prevent it "running into lumps". The iron rod used for stirring was two and a half feet in length, "as thick as the end of a little finger" with one end flattened to 'suit' the bottom of the crucible. It was not necessary to stir continuously, only briskly from time to time to prevent the powder forming lumps. In between times the rod had to be removed from the crucible but was left in the furnace with the upper end protruding through the hole. This process, called calcining, took about 45 minutes during which large quantities of "sulphureous and arsenical fumes" were emitted. Having rid the ore of most of its impurities by burning off, the next stage could then begin.

The crucible was removed and the powdered ore weighed so that one ounce could be mixed with one and a quarter ounces of black flux (glass), a thimble full of powdered culm (coal slack) and covered with a half ounce of sea salt. The furnace was filled with fresh charks (charcoal), the crucible re-instated and surrounded by charcoal up to the brim. A cover was placed on the crucible which had to be of the same material. The crucibles of Redruth were to acquire a worldwide reputation, exceeding those of Germany when, in 1760, John Juleff would establish a crucible works at Pednandrea and one in Redruth itself. The crucibles were made of clay mixed with granite to withstand the intense heat. This clay known as Grouan was also used for bricks from which fireplaces and furnaces were built.

The hole or mouth in the side of the furnace was now completely bricked up resulting in a rapid rise in temperature which caused the contents of the crucible to melt and boil. The boiling could clearly be heard for some time, but on cessation it was necessary to remove some of the bricks and inspect. If further bubbling took place, the fire had to be tended, the bricks reinserted and further time allowed until the contents of the crucible flowed like oil. Only when this condition pertained could the crucible and its contents be removed from the furnace and allowed to cool. When cold the crucible had to be broken in order to separate the metal, now a solidified residue at the bottom, from the scoria (the scum from off the top of the boiling metal which had now also solidified). If the scoria was glassy, clear and black without containing grains of copper, then the process had been successfully completed. This process should only have taken 15 to 20 minutes to complete. The quantity of copper extracted from the ore could then be measured and judgement made as to the quality.

Apart from this method of calcining the ore, there was an alternative way by the regule (or regulas) method, but it did take longer. Briefly the copper ore sample was pulverised, sifted and mixed with an equal quantity of powdered black glass, a quarter or fifth part of 'nitre' and the same amount of borax. After mixing together they were placed in the crucible and covered with a quarter inch of 'common salt'. The furnace was bricked up to obtain maximum heat until the mixture melted and flowed freely. The crucible was removed, allowed to cool then broken to separate the regule from the scoria. The regule thus obtained was placed into another crucible and the process repeated.

On the day of ticketing a dinner "almost equal to a city feast" was provided at the expense of the mines, each mine contributing in proportion to the amount of ore it had for sale. This enabled the mine owners, their agents and the company agents to assemble together. As soon as the dinner was finished and tables cleared, the tickets containing the offers from the different companies were produced, registered by the agents of both buyers and sellers and the originals given to the mining proprietors. The highest bid for a particular parcel or lot of ore was accepted. This part of the procedure took very little time at all, and within half an hour "ten thousand pounds worth of Ores may be sold".

Most of the copper ores mined in Cornwall have been found in slate and provide a fascinating group, representing almost every colour in the spectrum. Those mined in the 18th century were given the following descriptions:

Grey copper ore (chalcocite), found to be the richest sort, very similar to lead. In Dolcoath mine this was found in an iridescent form.

Black copper ore (bornite – first discovered by a Count Bournon), bluish black in colour, also very rich.

(Both chalcocite and bornite are sulphides, which means they contain the element sulphur, necessitating an initial roasting to rid the ore of the impurity.)

Red copper ore (cuprite), the most valuable, usually worth double or treble the price of the others i.e. £14 to £20 per ton, but was difficult to smelt because of the iron content.

Yellow copper ore (chalcopyrite – similar in composition to bornite), found in four different states. The first was shallow amongst the black ore but could easily be scraped into a rich yellow dust. The second was a rich gold flaky ore, worth £12 to £15 per ton. The third, a brass colour, worth only £7 to £10 a ton, found in large quantities in some areas and therefore worth the effort of mining although it was at least 50 fathoms deep. The deepest ore was a pale yellow colour, greatly inferior to the others and worth only £4 to £6 per ton.

The most beautiful and elegant sort, as regards colour, was called 'Peacock' which produced an iridescent effect, but when exposed to the atmosphere for a long period the colour faded away. Beneath the surface it was said to be yellow. This presumably relates to a formation found in Cornwall whereby bornite, called peacock ore by the miners, forms striations or bands within the chalcopyrite.

Of the precious stones, malachite, with its rich greens, has been found in Cornwall, and azurite with its beautiful deep blue colour, has been found at Redruth, but neither match the description of any of the ores mined in the 18th century. At that period, chemistry was already an important subject, and alkaline salts were known to produce a blue colour with copper, which changed to green when acid was added.

* * * * * * *

Apart from one brief recorded journey north, Legh Dickenson was to remain in Cornwall for the rest of his life. It seemed as though he and his brother, John, now a merchant of London, felt the embarrassment of the episode concerning 'the Young Pretender' and had no desire to remain in the Manchester area where the family was well-known.

On the other hand Charles Roe seemed determined to stay in Macclesfield, the town he had adopted as home. The Land Tax return for 1756-57 contains an entry on page 5 confirming his occupation of the Chestergate house, giving a yearly value of £27, together with the land of 7 acres and 2 roods £30, and an outbuilding listed on the adjoining Barn Street £2. This latter property was in effect the registered office of his very own company – "Chas Roe & Co." – created for his own mercantile business, to be kept separate from the silk partnership.

When comparing properties in Macclesfield he was now the equal of John Stafford, whose Jordangate house was valued at £25 and land of 8 acres and 2 roods £29 10s. The two of them occupied by far the two largest houses in town.

The most astonishing difference between the 1743 Land Tax return and that of the mid-1750s is the increase in population. Some entries, of course, only relate to land, but an approximate residential figure gives 400 entries for 1743, and 680 entries for 1756-57, however, at least a hundred of the latter relate to two or more dwellings indicating that some of the larger residences were now subdivided. These figures suggest an increase in excess of 1,000 people in little more than a decade, bringing the Macclesfield town population to within 3,500.

The obvious explanation has to be the building of the Silk Mill complex by Charles Roe and his partners. Macclesfield was experiencing a great influx of people anxious to be part of, and to have a share in, what promised to be a valuable industry. It seems logical to suppose that many had followed the example of John Guardavaglio and moved from Stockport, bringing with them skills and knowledge vital to the early success of the business.

With the advent of the silk workers extra housing was essential and about one third of the increase was accommodated on Jordangate Street, the Land Tax return showing that the residences had doubled in number. Some burgesses would take the opportunity to sub-lease parts of their large houses opposite the old guildhall, but the steep slope in the middle of Jordangate, which accommodated John Stafford's house on the western side and the Glover residence on the east, remained unaltered. Charles Roe's old property was divided into three dwellings and sub-leased and many small residences appeared. The street must have partly extended along what is today Beech Lane, which was very convenient for the workers who would be able to walk down Cockshoot Lane and along Waters Green to the mill, a matter of only five minutes.

Another area of rapid development was Barn Street, the greater part of which ran parallel to Charles Roe's land, but not quite adjacent. Along both sides small dwellings mushroomed, and at the lower end where it curved to join Mill Street, an area called Newgate (at present the site of the car park on the northern side of the Silk Heritage Centre) now supported several houses, gardens and barns, including two workhouses (workshops).

There was hardly any increase in the tenancies on the Pickford land as regards residential dwellings, it was mostly occupied by industrial development, but the last significant area of new dwellings was in the land known as Watercoates on the opposite bank of the River Bollin. It was in fact part of Macclesfield Common, sandwiched between the Halleyfields (Hollyfields) belonging to the Grammar School and the lands of Sutton owned by the Fauconbergs. The locality of Watercoates was a strip of land bordering the Bollin and following the contour of the river as it changed direction from a northerly to an easterly course. As there was apparently no alternative, the encroachment of 40 or so cottages on the very border of the Common must have been conveniently overlooked by the Corporation, particularly as the Silk Mill partners were all dominant figures within its assembly.

This was an ideal situation for the location of almost 200 persons, they were only two or three minutes walk from the mills on Parsonage Green, five minutes from the large silk mill, with the River Bollin providing an important source of clean water. The vast majority of Georgian housewives took a pride in their homes and families, and several sources provide adequate information to indicate plenty of scrubbing, cleaning, care and attention to both houses and gardens. How could members of a population who were rapidly acquiring skills and artistry of the highest standards, a desire for the meticulous, an appreciation of symmetry and beauty which encompassed the smallest button, household objects or the largest garden, be so ignorant and neglectful of the dwellings in which they lived, as has previously been suggested?

Needless to say there was always the problem of sanitation, but at that time it was not quite so critical as it would become in the last decade of the century when the rapid increase in population outstripped resources. The larger houses had, what were politely called, garderobes. Literally translated it means wardrobe, but it was becoming fashionable to use French words which created slight connotations in translation, although in this particular instance it must be admitted that the word had been popular since 1066, the Normans having installed garderobes complete with cess pools in their castles. In the more affluent households the garderobes would be created down one particular corner of the building so that each floor had one, whereas in others it would be on the ground floor at the rear of the house. A garderobe was simply a room with a hole in the floor over which was placed a wooden seat, with the receptacle below strewn with straw, which was swept out usually about once a week. The contents were collected on a regular basis by the scavengers. In Macclesfield the scavengers were employed by the Corporation and collected the excrement usually once a week in carts, after which it would be taken to the fields to be used as manure.

The smaller houses and cottages, which were originally arranged in squares, usually had a middingstead within their confines in which was placed a small building to be used as a toilet. Once again the floor would be strewn with straw and cleaned out as necessary. These privies were included on house deeds as witnessed by one dated 24th December 1778 relating to Pott Croft (now the site of the loading bay at the rear of the Marks and Spencer's store on Mill Street) which stated: "Liberty & privelege of going to & returing from & using the Common Privy House or House of Ease in Pott Croft aforesaid from time to time as need or occasion shall require".

It must be reiterated that nothing was ever wasted, and even urine had its value. It had to be at least two weeks old, termed 'stale', and because of its ammonia content and its cheapness was ideal as a mordant for the dyehouses. As previously stated however, silk is sensitive to alkalis and therefore the stale urine would only be used for wool, cotton or linen and was probably in great demand at the Copperas House works. From later evidence the dyehouse of John Turner Jnr. situated on the opposite bank of the River Bollin from Watercoates and which in due course passed to Thomas Ryle, dyer, must have been used for dyeing materials other than silk, because it is recorded that Thomas Ryle was receiving consignments of copperas. On the other hand this could be an indication of resourcefulness; when the silk industry was in one of its temporary declines the dyer turned once more to other materials to keep himself occupied.

The principal mordant for silk is alum; it can be used for linen after the initial softening procedure involving soft water, a rich lather (obtained from pure soap) and the addition of an alkali. In the 18th century alum was also important in leather tanning, the manufacture of parchment and the hardening of candles.

Dr. Johnson's *Universal Concise Dictionary*, 1755 edition, describes alum as principally produced in England, Italy and Flanders. In England roche alum was made from a bluish stone frequently found in the hills of Yorkshire and Lancashire. It was used in dyeing and colouring for binding "the colour upon the stuffs". Until the middle of the 19th century the most important region for alum was north-east Yorkshire, around the North York Moors. It had been worked from the late 16th century, which coincided with the advent of the silk industry in England, encouraged by Elizabeth I. However, the Lancashire hills referred to by Dr. Johnson were actually situated in the Lake District and records exist of several alum or potash pits on the eastern shore of Lake Coniston, and at the south-western edge of Lake Windermere, just to the north of Backbarrow; it would be from this region, close by the Coniston mine, that alum was transported to Macclesfield.

There was for a period a copperas works in the vicinity of Whitehaven, in the area where Thomas Atkinson, brother of Rowland, had his ironworks, and this again was the most likely source of Macclesfield's supply of copperas. Although at present no further details are known, Charles Roe, more than anyone else in Macclesfield, had the connections and opportunities to purchase these requisite commodities for the local industries.

It now becomes apparent that Charles was a merchant in every sense of the word, buying whatever he could, wherever he could, and selling on to make a profit. Goods would be stored, if appropriate, in the upper rooms of his Chestergate House. The roof, now vastly restored, takes the form of an inverted W and allows for a considerable area of storage space, ideal for materials and buttons, away from the problems of vermin and damp on the stones of the ground floor level. This is further confirmed by the remains of a pulley-block over the central top floor window facing Chestergate, which would formerly have operated with a hoist-rope to lift goods from the street level to the upper floors.

After his second marriage to Mary Stockdale of London, his business interests became progressively more involved with minerals, possibly dictated by his father-in-law's business connections, and to this end he not only looked for areas in which to purchase the necessary ores, but took the bold step of actually finding them for himself. His experience gained in the lead mines of Derbyshire was about to be put to the test.

* * * * * * *

During the summer of 1756 Sir William Fleming had become ill and as a consequence travelled down from Rydal Hall to Buxton in the hope of obtaining a cure from the waters of the old Roman baths.

Buxton's renown for its natural thermal springs had been regained during the late 16th century when the Earl of Shrewsbury, fourth husband of Bess of Hardwick, was given the unenviable custodianship of Mary, Queen of Scots, who was forever complaining of her rheumatism. The Earl built a house for his royal 'guest' close by St. Anne's Well, which in time passed to the Dukes of Devonshire as a consequence of their descent from Bess. A fire in 1670 caused alterations and extensions to be carried out on the premises, then known as the Hall or Buxton Hall. It was described by Celia Fiennes some 20 years later as being "the largest house in the place tho' not very good". This description confirms that the property was by then subleased and converted to an inn. By the 1750s three baths were enclosed within its walls resulting in a waiting list of six weeks for accommodation. Buxton was the place to be. Many prominent personalities began to flock to the small town, and the Duke of Devonshire suddenly found himself with a potentially valuable source of income.

If the waters had any beneficial effect at all for Sir William it could only have been of short duration, for he died the following year. However, the trip to Buxton must have presented Charles Roe with an ideal opportunity to approach the baronet with a proposal for leasing the Coniston mine. Charles would have learnt of the availability of the lease from Dr. Atkinson, physician to the Fleming family and brother to Rowland, his sister's husband. Dr. Atkinson was more than likely already overseeing the transportation of raw materials from the Lake District to Macclesfield, and judging from later events his son, Cookson, 17 years of age, must have been assisting operations and at the same time gaining experience by working in the ironworks of uncle Thomas.

The Coniston lease, dated 13th September 1756, but effective from 29th September 1756, was between Sir William Fleming, and the partnership of Charles, described as "Merchant" and his brother-in-law, Rowland Atkinson, Gent. As Rowland had very little money for investment in a project of such magnitude, once again his share must have been part compensation for his wife Mary's marriage settlement.

The lease refers to all mines and veins of lead or copper ore within the "Manor of

Cunningstone, in the County of Lancaster", permission being given for the two lessees or their assigns (deputies etc.) to dig or sink mines, to make soughs or drains, erect engines or buildings for which purpose they were allowed any stones, clay, timber or wood upon the ground of the Manor. Permission was also given for servants, chapmen, workmen, horses, carts and carriages to go through or over the land. Water could be obtained from "a convenient place", and smelting on site was allowed, as consent had been given for "making Merchantable lead or copper ore". This phrase is significant, at this time Charles had no smelter for refining ore and therefore must have been intent on selling it. If he found lead, this could easily be smelted as in Derbyshire and transported as pigs, but copper ore was a different matter and Charles would have no alternative but to sell it to the nearest and most accessible copper smelter, who was Thomas Patten of Warrington. It seems feasible, therefore, that before committing himself to the undertaking, Charles would have come to some sort of arrangement with Thomas Patten.

Any ores raised during the first six months of the lease were to be duty free, but after that period a $1/12$ share of lead or copper ore was due to Sir William after it had been dressed, cleaned and made 'merchantable'. The usual stipulation of ensuring no neglect of the mines, was included, and this time the workings could only remain "unwrought for the space of three months together in any one year", not the six months as contained in previous deeds. The mines also had to be made available for inspection by Sir William or anyone designated by him in order to ensure proper working was taking place.

The deed was "Duly Stampt" in the presence of Joseph Comberbach (admitted as a freeman of Macclesfield ex gratia at the same time as Rev. James Roe and Rowland Atkinson on 13th September 1748 and destined to become Town Clerk of Macclesfield in 1759. Surprisingly John Stafford had already resigned his position of Town Clerk in 1754). The other person present was Joseph Stockdale, Charles Roe's father-in-law, who must have been visiting Macclesfield at that time.

The transaction having been completed, Roe & Co. were now in a position to begin their task of mining, but exactly when operations commenced is not known. However, during the following month of October 1756, Anthony Tissington & Co. began work on the westerly edge of the sett on ground which eventually became known as Paddies End, leaving Roe & Co. to rework the old mine of Bonsor Vein situated $3/4$ mile to the east.

Whether or not at the onset Charles intended combined operations with another partnership is a matter for speculation. It seems more probable that after all the interest shown in North Yorkshire, he was approached by Tissington & Co. for he did allow them to buy $13/24$ of the mine shares, thus placing at his disposal the extra capital necessary for his first venture into a very vulnerable business. It was exactly the same sort of arrangement as had been concluded with the silk business; two separate partnerships working independently, yet co-operating as necessary within the framework of, what could loosely be termed, a consortium of the two groups.

During the 17th century iron ore had been mined in the vicinity on Coniston Fell, which resulted in Sir Daniel Fleming sending two workmen on 14th January 1675 to view the area for his "intended forge". The forge was subsequently built and Sir Daniel purchased the land appurtenant called the Holme for £15 from John Dixon of Dixon-ground in Coniston on the 12th September 1676, thus avoiding payment of an annual (ground) rent. During 1692 a smithy had been built at the mines, but from 1693 onwards the ironworks were leased to a tenant.

Extensive accounts exist for the working and repairing of the iron forge and buildings, which comprised a dwellinghouse for the hammerman and two coal-houses together with a garden. With the death of Sir Daniel during 1701, the 18th century accounts become much less detailed, but an unsigned copy agreement indicates that from 1735 Sir William allowed a Quaker partnership, the Backbarrow Company, to lease the ironworks for 21 years at £30 per year.

About this period many problems seem to have arisen as a result of one or two factions within the community, so much so that Sir William's presence was requested at Troutbeck Bridge in April 1750 together with others, including Dr. Atkinson and one of the Dixon family (the latter appearing to have Quaker connections), with the plea that "The Design of this meeting is to establish Peace and good Neighbourhood in Troutbeck & to which good End you may be a most material Instrument, and I hope every one will lend their best afsiftance to so good a work". Perhaps the Quakers felt that they were being deprived of their rights because they were a dissenting minority within an otherwise strong Church of England community.

In 1755, Sir William, endeavouring to be unprejudicial, appointed James Dixon of Orrest in Applethwaite "to the Office of my Bailiff untill I shall Appoint another".

During 1757 the lease of the iron forge and buildings in respect of the Backbarrow partnership was due to expire and Robert Barker, agent for Anthony Tissington & Co. being unable to find reasonable accommodation for his workmen, obtained a lease of the forge houses from the spring of that year "at the same rent as they had been let for before".

The first week in July 1758 marked the arrival of Mr. Hale, in his capacity as book-keeper, "to act for near one half of the mine", which was the remaining $^{11}/_{24}$ owned by Roe & Co. Presumably work had already begun in the Old Mine but not as yet on any large scale, because Josiah Wagstaff, a member of a lead mining family from Darley Dale near Matlock and Winster in Derbyshire, was already on site and would be working as ground agent ensuring that mining was being carried out in a correct manner. Charles had chosen his employees carefully, under no circumstances would he have allowed amateurs to take control of a business into which he was about to invest a considerable sum of money. Perhaps he had in mind Dr. Leigh's comments when writing his *Natural History of Lancashire, Cheshire and the High Peak,* published in 1700, "were the Mines rightly manag'd, we should not have any neceffity to import our Copper from Sweden".

Together with Charles, John Hale (often referred to in error as Hall) and Josiah Wagstaff were connected with the group of lead mines near Eyam called Consolidated Titles, and in particular the one known as Miners Engine. These mines were, of course, originally owned by Richard Bagshawe Snr. of the Oakes-in-Norton (today part of Sheffield), the great friend of Charles Roe's deceased father, Thomas. At his death in 1750 Richard's younger sons, William and John appear to have inherited the Miners Engine shares. Their elder brother, Richard Jnr., involved in Consolidated Titles for some time, presumably inherited from his father additional shares in the other mines. John Hale had been engaged as book-keeper by the Bagshawe family from at least 1741, at which time he must have been quite a young man. It was an important position and one of great trust, as it was incumbent upon him to handle sums of money on behalf of the family. Josiah Wagstaff, being one of the partners in the concern, would know John Hale very well, and after the dispute and consolidation with the Stoke sough partnership in 1748, and the death of Richard Snr. in 1750, perhaps after five years or so with the new establishment, they were happy to accommodate Charles Roe's request for their engagement at Coniston.

(There had also occurred an upset with the overseer, William Hill, subsequently discharged from his duties, and when the partners of Consolidated Titles had met to appoint a new one in 1755, Anthony Tissington's name was included on the list, acting on behalf of a Mrs. Galliard).

Evidence on site and the accounts for copper ore weighed at Coniston suggest that with the arrival of Mr. Hale work began in earnest at the Bonsor vein. Until his arrival just three lots of ore had actually been weighed viz:

6th Feb.	1758	10 tons.
27th May	1758	10 tons.
5th July	1758	14 tons 8 cwts. (hundredweights).

These amounts could, of course, relate partly or wholly to Tissington & Co. but as they were to relinquish their share of the mining in a little over a year's time, this suggests that they were unsuccessful. Ironically the Paddy End Vein would prove to be richer than any of the others, but not until the 1850s. With Mr. Hale in charge of accounts for Roe & Co., Mr. Wagstaff could concentrate on the task in hand, resulting in 20 tons 16 cwts. of copper ore weighed in total for August and September and a final amount of 27 tons 18 cwts. on 21st October before winter set in. Charles seemed determined to make ore available as soon as possible, because his miners took out the floor of Cobbler's Level using gunpowder, eventually raising ore from two shafts, Bonsor East and Bonsor West.

* * * * * * *

Gunpowder was expensive, requiring great care and attention at all times, and its use in British mining was still at a comparatively early stage. It was a mixture of saltpetre, charcoal and sulphur in the ratio 75:15:10; the first known written formula appeared in a Chinese treatise completed in 1044 with the title *Wu Ching Tsung Yao'* In exactly the same way as silk had entered Europe, the use of saltpetre had been introduced also by the Arabs, in the first half of the13th century. Many attempts were made to produce artificially saltpetre in England but eventually the East India Co. had established a regular import trade from India during the 17th century. Sulphur was also imported from Italy.

Elizabeth I had granted royal letters patent to certain families who had thus monopolised production, especially close to the capital. In 1664 the Board of Ordnance was placed in control of the industry, giving rise to many centres of production. During the 1720s Woolley near Bath was supplying the mines of Wales and Cornwall and in the early 1760s a writer observed that along the banks of the River Mersey, between Liverpool and Warrington, were various kinds of mills "corn-mills, gun-powder mills, paper mills, oil-mills, slitting mills . . .".

The first recorded use of gunpowder in mining was at Ecton Copper mine in Stafforshire, 9 miles east of Matlock, close by the border with Derbyshire., though it is not necessarily the earliest mine where it was used. The mine had been re-opened by the 3rd Earl of Devonshire in 1660; a subsequent visit by Dr. Plot in 1680 provides much early information and indicates that although at the time of Dr. Plot's visit the mine had been closed for some time, it had been worked for several years by the Earl of Devonshire, Sir Richard Fleetwood and a Dutchman who "broke the rocks with gunpowder". The Ecton accounts reveal no use of gunpowder before 1665, in which year the mill and mine were let to a Dutchman with the unusual surname of Mumma. One can only assume a connection with a Jacob Mumma and Daniel Demetrius, two Dutchmen who had set up a brass wire mill at Esher in Surrey during 1649, close to the important gunpowder industry at Chilworth. Mr. Mumma worked Ecton mine until its closure in 1680, the workings traditionally taking place at the Dutchman mine. Ecton re-opened about 1693, but much draining was necessary, which revealed the early blast-holes and caused great interest amongst the miners. It was not until 1723 that the important period of mining began, with the Duke of Devonshire leasing the mine to a group of eight adventurers. On the surrender of their lease in 1739 the Duke allowed John Gilbert-Cooper, owner of the Denby smelter, a 21 year lease, from 12th December of that year.

This early use of gunpowder at Ecton must have called for the training of an elite group of miners to enable them to acquire the expertise necessary to carry out their duties of blasting ore from the mine. One such family of miners, who appear in the Low Peak or Wapentake of Wirksworth in the mid-17th century, were the Rooses. By coincidence Roose is a Dutch name, and although several members of the family lived in the Kingston-upon-Thames area in the 16th century, not too far from Esher, there was a John Roose recorded in Sheffield in the 1570s.

The first important member of note was a Richard Roose of Cromford who, at his death in

1697, left "all my part & part share & shares of all ground, moors or moors of ground and mineral possessions where ever" in equal shares to his wife Mary and son John. He seems to have been the patriarch of a branch of the Roose family of which several sons became skilled miners. By 1739, the will of his son, John, reveals that the family was working its own mine of Hard Hedg on Cromford Moor. His grandson, another John, having gained the reputation of a skilful miner, was called upon to serve as part of a twelve man jury of Low Peak miners regarding an important dispute in 1745 between the proprietors of two mines in the High Peak. He eventually gained a senior position in a Welsh mine which he would retain until his death in 1761.

The year 1702 was the year in which Jonathan Roose of Birchover married Mary Dakin at Youlgreave. In due course his son, Thomas, a miner, baptised his eldest son, Jonathan, at Youlgreave on 10th February 1732. The family connection between the two branches has not yet been established, but Jonathan of Youlgreave was later to play an important part in the life of Charles Roe. As Charles required experienced miners for blasting ore from the Bonsor vein at Coniston, he must have recruited men from Derbyshire, and one of the likely candidates was Jonathan Roose, then 25 years of age. (Not only was Jonathan to prove himself worthy of taking responsibility in the mines but he was also to prove himself quite a charmer with the ladies). It must be admitted Jonathan never referred to an early mining period in the Lake District, only that "he had been brought up to the Business of Mining" and had "practised it from his Infancy as well in the Lead mines in Derbyshire as in other mine works in Wales". Local men from Coniston would also be recruited but, as in the Welsh mines, the more experienced Derbyshire miners were needed at the onset to train and supervise the more inexperienced local labour. This was a role which Cornish miners had also filled at various periods in history, and would do so again by the end of the century.

At this point a mention must be made of another family which, like the Rooses, established itself in the vicinity of Ecton during the mid-17th century. Surprisingly the surname was Roe, but once again insufficient information in available records leaves an hiatus with regard to the family tree.

In 1671 Richard Roe died in the picturesque village of Parwich, and by the end of the century other family members were residing in Brassington and Bradbourne. During the 18th century two became vicars, Thomas of Bradbourne and his cousin George of Parwich. Where this branch originated from is not known, although the close relationship between these different family groups is easily discernible within the area. One fact which could be significant is that Alathea, Countess of Arundel, patron of the living of St. Peter and St. Paul in Wem in the early 17th century, was at the same time patron of Bradbourne Church and the daughter church of Brassington. (Today the reverse applies i.e. Bradbourne is subordinate to Brassington). Is it possible that two members of the Roe family were originally favoured with livings by the Countess, one in Wem and the other in Bradbourne? Perhaps in time answers will be found.

One member of this Roe contingent is of interest historically. Thomas of Ballidon near Bradbourne left a will in 1717 which is accompanied by a remarkably informative inventory. Thomas, an ironmonger by trade, left all his goods in his Winster shop (just north of Wirksworth) and elsewhere to his brother, Samuel and sister, Elizabeth. Out of the 146 items listed, apart from everyday articles such as pans, laces, tobacco, sugar, seeds, herbs, thread, buttons, silk, mohair and knitting needles (the latter valued at one shilling), unusual items such as "Long & short Hair 6s.", the remainder fall into three categories:

a) Items normally associated with ironmongery e.g. locks, padlocks, nails, tacks etc.
b) Items relating to the local textile industry e.g. a cask of copperas, ten pairs of wool cards.
c) Supplies for the mines including large ropes, several bundles of hemp, and last but by no means least, "A Hundred pound of Gunpowder £3 6s 6d".

It can be seen, therefore, that from this small Winster shop miners from the surrounding area were able to obtain their provisions.

* * * * * * *

Gunpowder was traditionally packed in oak barrels and kegs of various sizes, the 100 lb. barrel being used as the standard unit of weight when sold. Gunpowder was always stored well away from other buildings and areas of activity until needed, but was regularly inspected. Its usage involved a good deal of straw, not only to hold the charges, and to make mats for kneeling on whilst the holes were drilled, but also for fuses. At threshing time it was one man's duty to go round farms in the vicinity of the mine and select suitable straws from which fuses could be made.

At Coniston, before the ore could be blasted out, a certain portion of the floor would have to be removed by the laborious hand method of picks and hammers, until a sufficiently large vertical or sloping surface had been created in which to place the charges. The Derbyshire miners employed by Charles Roe excelled at this and they literally left their mark wherever they worked with their closely spaced pickmarks and small cross-section. They were experts and took a pride in their mining abilities.

It was also important to obtain maximum effect from the gunpowder used, in the interests of economy, and it was, therefore, essential to understand the direction of the fault lines in the rocks , so that the optimum degree of fragmentation was engendered when the explosion occurred. Hole spacing also affected fragmentation, and a better result was obtained using two rows instead of one. It must have been necessary for two miners to light the fuses at the same time, but lighting one row with longer fuses first and then the other.

The holes were made by a tool called an auger which was usually 2 ft long and steeled at the end in a wedge-shape. The miner grasped this with his left hand, turning it round continuously whilst forcing it into the rock with blows from a six-pound hammer. The resulting hole was usually 14 to 18 ins deep. Sometimes water was poured in if it had been made at a downward angle, and then dried out with a rag. Next a brown paper bag, containing 5 ozs. of gunpowder, was pushed to the extremity of the hole and a pricker (a thin iron rod) left in place touching the bag whilst the hole was packed as tightly as possible with small stones and clay. One of the specially selected straws, known as a staff straw, was then filled with gunpowder, and after careful removal of the pricker, inserted in its place to act as the fuse. This was primed with a match which the miner ignited with an old tarred rag. Needless to say great agility would be required by miners lighting fuses, in order to extricate themselves before the impending force of the blast.

Once the dust had settled and it was considered safe, work resumed to clear away the rocks which had broken off in a variety of shapes and sizes. The larger ones would have to be broken further by hand, and any pieces containing ore roughly cleaned and stacked ready for the women. Waste would be removed using wheel barrows with solid wooden wheels and deposited on a part of the site, which hopefully would be considered of no use for future mining prospects. At other mines, as work advanced, waste was often conveniently tipped into abandoned workings, but at Coniston the topography was such that this was not necessary.

It is interesting to note that in a survey of mines carried out in 1959, it was considered feasible to retrieve copper ore from waste abandoned by the old miners of previous generations. The extensive dumps at Coniston in parts averaged 1.5% copper, with a general average of 0.9%. The original ore as obtained by Roe & Co. was calculated to average only 3% in the poorer part of the vein but 8-9% in the richer part. As previously stated, as mining is becoming more uneconomical today, recovery from the old abandoned dumps is practised at a content of only 0.5% to 0.7%.

The Coniston ore was mostly copper and iron pyrites containing a considerable quantity of sulphur, making it difficult to smelt. The iron pyrites could possibly be represented by the hogsheads of "Copperas Ore" which began to make their way up the River Weaver in small but consistent consignments from March 1758. By July, each was referred to as a "Cask of Coppar", the weight given as 2cwts. per cask; this suggests that the ore was now being converted into copperas before transportation, implying a possible link with the Atkinson ironworks. Although copperas would be sent coastwise direct to Liverpool and Chester from Whitehaven, the copper ore (chalcopyrite) followed a different route.

When the Backbarrow Co. had leased the iron forge in 1735 for 21 years, included as part of the equipment was a "Three Ton Coal Boat" used to carry charcoal, iron and wood. Whether or not this was available for the use of the copper mine when the forge houses were leased by Tissington & Co. is not known. However, William Rigg, who lived at Greenodd and was lessee of the stone quarries on the Le Fleming estate, had a good sturdy boat with which to ply up and down Lake Coniston carrying, not only stones from his quarries, but a variety of goods and equipment for other people. He also acted as postman and messenger, in which capacity he was often engaged by the Le Flemings. It seems probable that after the ore had been packed in either casks or sacks and taken down to the lake-side, he would arrange for its onward journey down the lake to Nibthwaite, from where it was carted to either Penny Bridge or Greenodd. The latter was a small but busy port from which the ore would have been taken across Morecambe Bay.

At this period the nearby town of Ulverston was a town of growing prosperity, due largely to its export of oats, barley and beans, the latter sent in large quantities coastwise to Liverpool as food for the negroes in the Guinea Trade. The town being situated inland, and Morecambe Bay notorious for its quick sands, it must have been necessary for smaller vessels to take cargoes to the sea-going ships anchored in the Bay which were "employed" by the town, or else boat them to Glasson Dock or Fleetwood, so that larger vessels plying between Liverpool and Lancaster could take them on board. This would also pertain to the copper ore.

The first consignment of copper ore to pay toll of 1s. 3d. per ton on the River Weaver, was on 3rd October 1759. It weighed 18 tons 18 cwts. and was quickly followed by two further cargoes, 25 tons 10 cwts. and 19 tons 10 cwts. on 13th and 17th respectively. Unfortunately the consignee's name is absent from the records, but whereas one would presume the destination of the Coniston ore to be the Patten copper works at Bank Quay, Warrington on the River Mersey, the fact that it came up the River Weaver instead, indicates that it must have been en route for the improbable destination of Macclesfield.

11
THE BATTLES BEGIN

the smoke of the country went up
as the smoke of a furnace.

The year 1756 had not only been significant for Charles Roe, but also for his brother, James. James, although appearing to be on good terms with his patron of Disley, Peter Legh the younger, did not enjoy the same intimacy as he had previously held with Peter Legh's uncle. Matters had been brought to a head in August 1752, five months before his marriage to Elizabeth, when the question of who should benefit from the seat rents of Disley church had become a debatable issue. This was always a provocative subject, not only from the point of view of rents received, but more importantly of ownership and distribution.

Pews could be bought by individuals for their own use, for family or friends, or whosoever they wished. The individual paid an annual rent for the privilege to the church which, in effect, was comparable to a ground rent for a property. Seats or pews were willed on death, or sold by placing advertisements in newspapers or places of public notice e.g. pinned up on the inside of the door of the local barber's shop. They were included on property deeds and if, for example, someone bought a house close by the Parochial Chapel in Macclesfield, it was highly probable that the owner/occupiers also owned their own pew in the Chapel, and the new purchasers would be delighted to discover that their prospective residence was endowed with such an item of convenience and aggrandisement. If the vendor was moving within the area, then he might wish to retain his pew, or if moving out of town he could sublease to someone else, ensuring that on the occasion of his return visits, the pew was available for his and the family's use. Upper gallery pews or seats were always the most desirable, and much preferred to those down below. When one became vacated great 'battles' ensued for possession, usually by those beneath. In one particular instance in Liverpool, feelings ran so high on the subject that when the church had to be rebuilt, it was actually demolished leaving the pews intact, and reconstructed around its cherished interior.

Pews could also be leased direct from the Church for an annual rental, and any profits received were often given to the parson as an addition to his stipend, or used by the patron as he so desired. The pews which were privately owned usually had a door at the end which bore the initial of the original owner, either by carving or plaque, (many from earlier periods were dated) and could also be fastened, this not only had the desired effect of keeping trespassers at bay, but during winter months, the exclusion of icy draughts was also commendable. The luxury of central heating, however inadequate, was far away and only a few could claim to be comparable to the King, George II, who had the facility and enjoyment of his own fireplace besides the royal pew at St. Martins.

The problem concerning the Disley rents seems to have arisen inadvertently from James Roe's own action, or more accurately inaction, at an earlier time, when he had been offered the curacy by Peter Legh the elder. The solicitor, Samuel Harriman, who delivered the proposal, specifically mentioned that Rev. James would be entitled to the profits from the seats. Accordingly the Steward of the Lyme estate let it be known amongst the congregation that if anyone wished to have their own pews they could do so. The response was so small that James "declin'd to collect" the rents, allowing the persons in question the benefit of their own seats. But in the meantime circumstances had changed and James Roe in no uncertain terms, obviously exacerbated by this faction in his congregation, pointed out to his patron that:

"These very People had so ungratefully insulted both yo'r Uncle & Me I thought there was no Reason to excuse them paying for their Seats as usual . . . but not with(ou)t first acquainting you w'th it".

Peter Legh the younger had apparently rejected Rev. James's claim and denounced his action, but James Roe was not to be put off, continuing:

"it must be very hard to be debarr'd from receiving what the People have voluntarily contracted for & are both able & willing to pay . . . what little Fortune I had was sunk in my Education & y(e)t This is All I have to subsist on, You canot wonder if I am unwilling to give it up."

The outcome is unknown, but the letter would do nothing towards relaxing the tension which had crept into their relationship.

By 1756 James's wife, Elizabeth, had given birth to two sons, Charles and William, (who, sadly, had died within a few months) and a daughter, Hester Ann, born on the 31st January of that year. The close relationship between the Roe family and the Leghs of Adlington, all Royalists and Tories, was further cemented by Hester Legh becoming the baby's godmother and the child in consequence baptised Hester.

On 13th March James Roe wrote to Peter Legh at Lyme Hall advising him that "On Monday last we buried poor Mr. Robinson . . . & Mr. Downes (our present Mayer) has been so kind to give me a Nomination to succeed him". James, anxious to make his position clear, explained that he wished to keep the living at Disley by "putting in a Curate". This was usual, the parson would pay for his own curate out of his salary and they would both share the duties. If the curate was young, it was an excellent 'apprenticeship' and, in due course, if he performed well, he could hope to be recommended to a position of vicar and be provided with a living of his own, if and when an appropriate vacancy arose. James supplied details of his estimated income i.e. £70 per annum from St. Michael's, which included the parsonage house valued at £7 (presumably still leased to a tenant), which together with Disley "means my annual income (including the house as above) will not exceed £100".

He must be forgiven for not mentioning his income from the Derbyshire lead mines because, although he signed for his share of the profit from the Mineral Account relating to Consolidated Titles etc. for the year ending 29th June 1754, Charles and Rowland Atkinson were recorded as joint owners of the shares on 3rd September 1755 when the proprietors met to appoint a new overseer, George Owtram, in place of William Hill (who had, of course, been discharged for neglecting his duties). The 1754 profit was negligible; in total James received £17 8 $9^3/4$d. but he had to pay one of the working partners, Jonathan Oxley, £10 10 3d. for attending to the weighing, selling and reckoning of the ore on his behalf, so he was left with £6 18 $6^3/4$d.

His letter of 13th March was followed by another four days later (17th) adding weight to a recommendation already made on behalf of Mr. Booth, Curate of Taxall, for the curacy of Disley. James considered him to be "a very promising, sensible man" who was also willing "to undertake the School", as the death of the headmaster had left the position vacant.

Before the arrival of the second letter at Lyme Hall, Peter Legh the younger had already put pen to paper on the 16th, first congratulating James Roe on his impending appointment at St. Michael's, but continuing in a slightly disparaging tone:

". . . it has long been my resolution to have a Resident Minister at Disley first, for ye convenience of the people, and secondly for my own convenience of ye family at Lyme to be certain of having a respectable person to read prayer Each day (when) ye family are at Lyme".

His curt letter was concluded "I hope you'll give up ys (this) one as you've accepted ye other".

James refused to be outmanoeuvred, appreciating that his second letter would have arrived at Lyme after Peter Legh's initial reply. He again wrote on 20th March, "I heartily wish the Curacy of Macclesf'd was likely to be so beneficial as to afford me an Opportunity of obliging you by giving up Disley, with't injuring my own Family". His skilfully worded letter, no doubt endorsed by a few appropriate remarks succinctly delivered on his behalf by John Stafford and Charles Legh, had the desired effect. After resolving one or two complications which had arisen in the meantime, Mr. Booth was accepted as schoolmaster and curate of Disley, with James reducing his own share of the stipend to little more than one third instead of a half. For the moment all was amicably settled and resolved, but Peter Legh was never one to be happily persuaded from his entrenched position; taciturn by nature, he would await his opportunity to seek retribution.

James took up his duties as prime curate of St. Michael's from 1st May 1756, and eventually settled into a house on Back Street directly opposite to the school house in which his sister, Mary, her husband and, by then, two young daughters lived. The street, today known as King Edward Street, runs parallel to Chestergate for some distance before the two converge and, therefore, the two residences were only a very short walk away from the house of brother Charles and his family; in fact, from the front upper windows of Charles Roe's property, a good view of his brother's and sister's homes would have been possible.

* * * * * * *

On the opposite side of Chestergate from the Roe mansion was an inn, the keeper of which, Robert Harrop, was a tenant of General Cholmondeley's. Together with the land on which the inn stood, Mr. Harrop also leased from the Cholmondeley Estate a plot of land and a meadow. His holding was adjacent to a farm situated between Chestergate and Back Street, which in turn lay opposite to the northern boundary of Charles Roe's land.

The lower end of Chestergate, beyond the area of farmland, was beginning to develop with the construction of rows of cottages to accommodate still further the increasing population. Purpose built workshops (referred to as workhouses) were already in evidence, taking the place of the old twisting crofts, as Charles Roe's mills had made the majority of them obsolete. Only a few Dissenters would preserve their independence by retaining them, but even they would soon succumb to the modernisation process, as industry took its first faltering steps towards automation on a grand scale.

In all there were seventeen workhouses out of which only five were of any significance, and these five had more than likely only absorbed a small proportion of the workforce, possibly 200 people between them.

Although many of the additional members of the population had leased plots of land with their cottages, yet they would have to purchase bread or bake their own loaves at the bakehouse. In the larger burgages, now sub-divided, more families would be using the same garden plot and therefore a salient fact emerges, people were unable to be as self-sufficient as previously. Now they were relying more and more on purchasing food from the market and the bakehouse, but as they had a dependable source of income in the form of a wage each week, this was no detriment initially. However, one can imagine that the baker had to take on more employees in an effort to cope efficiently with the increased demand; people would be encouraged to buy grain from the market, produce their own bread, but still have it baked at the bakehouse. The system would obviously start to break down. The baker would expect more money and the suppliers of grain likewise. Macclesfield was becoming an affluent town and therefore why should they not have a share in it? Some of the workers, faced with the reality that their wages were limited, thus making no allowance for this sort of situation, felt obliged to act; they were beginning to enjoy the smaller luxuries of life and were not willing to give them up without a struggle. Things were finally brought to a head in December 1757 when the Mayor, Aldermen and Burgesses agreed to suspend tollage for a year to encourage farmers to bring their corn to the market and sell at lower prices. As though to ensure effective legislation, a crowd had forced one of the suppliers of meal, Richard Pimlott, to bring four horse loads to the market, at an agreed price of 20s. a load, just before and again just after the Corporation meeting of the 15th December. Although the Georgians had no word for it, they were experiencing the throes of inflation.

* * * * * * *

Whilst apparent domestic tranquillity and prosperity were working their way through the streets of Macclesfield, together with all their associated problems, and echoing the trend in the rest of the country, the northern population, either consciously or sub-consciously, was making a firm bid for its independence from London, by developing road and sea communications in a more positive way. The 18th century was progressing towards an important period for the advancement of the professions, and the laying down of strong foundations upon which the British Civil Service could thrive, placing it in a class of its own, to be admired, respected and envied throughout the rest of the world. And as the northern ports took on a new importance, the watchful eye of H.M. Customs was ever vigilant; but it was the members of military who were about to prove their worth.

> "Many of those who have studied the military and political history of the eighteenth century will have encountered criticisms of the officers and men who composed the British Army of the period. The former are often stated to have been ignorant of their job, and the latter represented as the dregs of the nation's manhood, who could only be held to their duty by a harsh and inhuman discipline. To me it seemed that if this assessment were correct, then the achievements of the British Army are incomprehensible. No army can be successful in war against well-trained and well-armed opponents, unless its regimental officers have a sound knowledge of their profession and its rank and file are animated by a high morale, together with confidence in themselves, their leaders and their weapons".

So wrote Colonel H.C.B. Rogers O.B.E. in the introduction to his book *The British Army of the Eighteenth Century* published in 1977.

During the next few years of the mid-eighteenth century the army would gain great victories making it difficult for anyone to refute Colonel Rogers's claim that "having regard to its size . . . never in military history has any other army over a similar period surpassed it in fighting ability".

In time of war, short periods of enlistment were introduced. Apart from one such period during 1745, impressment had not been enforced since Queen Anne's reign until the years 1756 and 1757. Men under 17 and over 45 years of age were exempt, together with "known Papists" and those under 5 ft 4 ins in height. It was difficult in some instances, however, to prove a person's birthday, and whether by accident or design, many young boys and one or two older men found themselves enlisted.

From its very nature the British navy had suffered a much more chequered history than the army. Until the Civil War naval conditions were appalling, but after the Restoration, it was the work of Samuel Pepys as Secretary of the Admiralty, together with James, Duke of York, who had improved conditions. With the downfall of James II in 1688 Pepys lost his position, allowing one or two naval captains to take advantage of the situation by swindling prize money distributions.

During Queen Anne's reign the sailor's lot had improved considerably. Several trials of this period by court martial exhibit a sense of justice and fairness with all evidence being admitted; in fact, in many cases the seamen were found not guilty and the officers who had brought charges were admonished.

Peter Kemp, a former naval officer and distinguished naval historian, wrote in his book *The British Sailor,* published in 1970:

> "That service on the lower deck was not so unpopular as many writers make out is proved by the large number of men who regularly re-engaged when their commission was legally ended. It was the rule rather than the exception for them to do so."

The Navy was now standing on the threshold of its golden age, with Admiral Anson as First Lord of the Admiralty, and it was only a question of time before pamphlets would be circulated encouraging recruitment and stressing the prizes to be gained. Next came the Royal Proclamation offering rewards for deserters when they were reported, and finally when there was no other alternative the Navy had to apply to Parliament for permission to press. This was a legal procedure and legally controlled. Certain groups were exempt including crews of mayoral barges, a number of merchant ships, Thames watermen and their apprentices and employees of Trinity House, and no press was allowed in the City of London unless the Lord Mayor gave his consent.

In the colonies permission had to be obtained from the Governor and council, but this only applied to seamen and mariners (the latter from merchant vessels), never to landsmen. Each ship carried a few negroes who were not indentured slaves and many captains liked them because they were willing and efficient seamen. Even Francis Barber, who had taken up duties as Dr. Samuel Johnson's faithful negro servant in 1752, at one point in his career decided to go to sea. The good Doctor did not dissuade him but was happy to receive him back into his employ when Francis's ambition had been satisfied.

The situation in which Britain found herself at the beginning of 1756 had inevitably been brought about by a series of complexities which had gradually intensified over the previous seven years. After the Treaty of Aix-la-Chapelle had concluded the War of the Austrian Succession in 1748, there had been an uneasy peace engendering many rivalries which were to culminate ultimately in the outbreak of the Seven Years War. Although Britain and France had been the main signatories on the 1748 peace agreement, yet the fight continued overseas. The French had defiantly pushed further into North America, establishing Fort Duquesne in the Ohio valley the year after the treaty had been signed. Efforts by George Washington in 1754 and General Braddock in 1755 to drive them out of the region had failed, producing a retaliatory action from the government by sending Admiral Boscawen to attack a French convoy off the coast of Newfoundland, bound for Canada. Sea fog saved the French and during the following months, the British navy seized more than 300 French merchant ships, although Louis XV, King of France, put off the inevitable declaration of war until May 1756, after the French navy had proved its strength by taking Minorca from Britain in the preceding month of April. Admiral Byng's failure to save the island, although it has long been argued that his orders to sail into the Mediterranean were sent much too late, paid the highest possible price – a court martial, then execution by shooting on his own quarter-deck at Portsmouth.

The shock to the British public and the repercussions were enormous. Minorca had been Britain's largest overseas base the loss of which brought about the replacement of the Duke of Newcastle as Prime Minister by William Pitt the Elder. Pitt increased the size of both the army and navy dramatically, for which Parliament voted £10 million in 1758, together with

£1 million pounds paid to the American colonies. During the preceding year most of the European powers except Spain, Holland and Piedmont had become involved, although most of the fighting was to take place east of the Rhine with the struggle between Austria and Prussia (the latter in the form of Frederick the Great), both insisting on dominating German affairs.

With all the preparations for war, and alarm amongst the British merchants intent on preserving their valuable trading routes, ships and possessions, the inevitable demand for armaments, gunpowder, and other related items, increased, initiating the structure of a highly skilled metallurgic industry as envisaged by Prince Rupert in the 17th century. In addition, the demand for domestic and industrial items was steadily increasing both at home and abroad. Exports of wrought copper and brassware had gradually risen from the beginning of the century. Between 1700-09, 92 tons had been sent overseas, which more or less doubled each decade, reaching a total of 1243 tons for the years 1750-59. Details of British copper mined support these figures, averaging approximately 400 tons per annum circa 1725 and reaching almost 2000 tons per annum in 1758; these estimated figures relate to metal (ie. copper retrieved from ore and not the ore itself). It is interesting to see that at least three-quarters of English copper being produced at this period was from Cornish mines.

Charles, with his incomparable flair for business, could not resist the challenge, particularly as fate had once again contrived to place an unusual set of circumstances at his disposal.

* * * * * * *

With the commencement of war in 1756, the silk business, which was already proving to be a lucrative source of income, had been given an extra boost with the decline of French imports. Charles saw this as an opportunity to put his money to practical use. He was not one for building country mansions or 'resting on his laurels'; his house and land were adequate for his needs, despite the fact that in addition to William, Catherine and Samuel (the surviving children from his first marriage), he and Mary had produced Martha, Robert, Mary and Frances during the first five years of theirs. His mind as ever dictated economy and, as in the case of the silk industry, he must have questioned the purpose of supplying everyone else with raw materials when he could be manufacturing products himself. This time, however, it was a vastly different proposition from that of building a silk mill; only he knew how much time, perseverance and energy that particular project had taken to achieve. Lesser mortals would not even have considered the idea, but Charles described as "enterprising, emulous and indefatigable" was known to consider that "what were Difficulties to others, were Incitements to Action in him", and began to look around for an ideal site on which to build a copper smelter.

There is little doubt he would have acknowledged already the prospect of mining within the vicinity of Macclesfield, and in doing so found the site for the location of his intended premises. The old copper mine on Macclesfield Common had, of course, been leased for 21 years from 21st May 1736. Although very little mining had taken place, the legality of the lease, the dubious legislation surrounding copper mining, and the fact that William Stanhope, Baron Harrington (advanced to Earl on 9th February 1742) had been involved, had ensured that the Mayor, Aldermen and Burgesses had maintained a diplomatic and discreet non-involvement of the area concerned. Charles would have learnt the details of the lease transferred to Marriot and Marsden, the associates in the linen thread trade of Manchester, and would have known that whatever arguments had gone before, the lease had well and truly expired in 1757. Another reassuring circumstance, so far as the Corporation was concerned, would have been the death of the 1st. Earl of Harrington in 1756. His successor, son William, survivor of twins, was a somewhat eccentric individual who had acquired the nickname "Peter Shambles" because of his peculiar gait. As Viscount Petersham he had represented Bury St. Edmunds in Parliament from 1747 to 1756, and had led a distinguished army career. He was an agreeable character who seemed totally unconcerned about his rights on Macclesfield Common and, therefore, it was only a question of time before Charles had persuaded other members of the Corporation to allow him to present his proposals at a public assembly.

Company Articles state:

"by virtue of two several Grants or Licences bearing date respectively the first and Nineteenth days of August One thousand seven hundred and fifty eight and made at the Public Meetings or Assemblies of the then Mayor Aldermen and Burgesses . . . of Macclesfield and the freeholders thereof and other Persons having or claiming Rights of Common of Pastures in and upon the Waste Lands . . . belonging to the said Borough of Macclesfield . . ."

Charles Roe in partnership with Rowland Atkinson had been granted his enclosure. The proceedings were duly noted in the Corporation Minute Book on 19th August 1758 as follows:

"That Mr. Charles Roe and Mr. Rowland Atkinson two of the Burgesses of this Borough (as far as in the said Mayor Aldermen & Burgesses lies or they have the power to grant) may have liberty to inclose forty yards square out of the waste lands in Macclesfield aforesaid at or near a place in the Common there called Highledge and may erect thereupon a Smelting Mill paying to the Overseers of the Poor of Macclesfield aforesaid for the time being the sum of five shillings yearly for the use of the Poor of Macclesfield aforesaid from the time the said Building shall be inclosed and so long as the same shall remain standing and continue to be used as a Smelting Mill or for any other purpose by them the said Charles Roe and Rowland Atkinson or any other persons claiming under them or either of them".

Understandably there was still a shadow of doubt in the minds of one or two members present, so the recorded Minutes were apropos to their sentiments. Nevertheless Charles had achieved his aim and claimed an area of 1600 square yards (about one third of a statute acre) which included the site of the original buddles for the copper mine, incorporating a good supply of water from the Black Brook on the Common. The buddles, already having been dug out, would make excellent bases upon which to lay the grates for the furnace fires.

A good deal of assistance would be needed in the construction of the original furnaces, which no doubt were completed with help from the Atkinson family, particularly as Cookson Atkinson, 19 years of age, was shortly afterwards allowed into the partnership, presumably with financial assistance from his father, Dr. John, either by gift or inheritance. He would attain the age of 21 years on 2nd October 1760, which seems the most likely date for his admission.

Although iron smelting is vastly different in principle from that of copper, requiring higher temperatures but yet a straight forward enough operation, the actual physical building and lining of the copper furnaces would be more readily understood and more quickly executed by employees with experience of an iron foundry. Another source of co-operation could have been Thomas Patten of Warrington: certainly there was to be no animosity shown between the two establishments, in fact quite the reverse, and there is no evidence to suggest that they ever considered each other as rivals.

The melting temperature of iron is 1536°C. achieved by use of a blast furnace, which in the 18th century was operated with large bellows made mostly from hides and motivated by water; these forced a cold blast of air into the iron furnace during smelting.

On the other hand lead, which melts at a relatively low temperature of 327°C. and copper,

ENCLOSURE 1804

Compiled from the Macclesfield Corporation terrier and the Macclesfield Enclosure Map 1804 (held by CCALS). The plan demonstrates the position of Charles Roe's smeltworks on Macclesfield Common in relation to the present layout of the area.

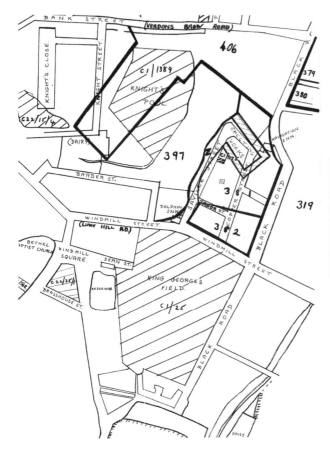

381 Roe & Co	–	2 acres, 2 roods, 11 perches
383, 397 & 319	–	H. M. King
379-380	–	Roe & Co
Z	–	Access to site

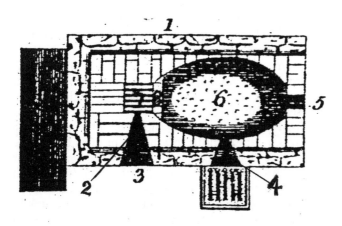

Upper plan of copper smelter:
1 Outer wall.
2 Draught hole connecting with ash hole.
3. Door where coal is shovelled in.
4. Place where an outlet is made allowing melted metal to flow from furnace.
5 Opening through which impurities (scoria) are skimmed off.
6. Basin of sand in which metal melts. A hole in the domed roof allows ore to be tipped in.
7 Fireplace with iron grate.
8 The bridge - a small one brick thick partition over which heat and flames pass into the furnace area.

requiring a temperature of 1083°C. are readily smelted in a reverberatory furnace, also known as a wind or English furnace, especially by the Germans of the 18th century.

A reverbatory furnace, commonly known in England as a copula, is an open flame fuel-fired furnace in which the charge (i.e. the ore or alloys of the metal required) is melted by radiation from the hot walls and roof, and by convection from the movement of hot gases. Heat is transferred directly to the melt instead of through containing walls, thus creating a furnace with a high thermal efficiency, capable of rapid melting.

Today in a foundry of eight reverberatory furnaces only six are in operation at one time, whilst two are being relined or on standby. Because of the high thermal conductivity of the refraction, insulation must be used between the lining and the furnace shell, and this is usually brick. A properly installed furnace lining gives long service and is a negligible factor in the cost of melting copper. It is undesirable to permit slag to build up in the furnace as it attacks the lining, necessitating patching, repairing or relining.

Good copper smelting requires speed, not only to reduce cost but also to minimise contamination from the atmosphere and from the vapour of volatile alloying elements, particularly zinc. In a neutral atmosphere, a protective cover, usually charcoal, may be used to minimise further contamination from oxygen and hydrogen. If hydrogen is present it will be rejected by the metal during solidification and cause unsound castings. Oxygen contaminates by forming metallic oxides when entering the molten copper. In the 18th century broken glass or sand was used as a flux and added to the smelt for cleaning, and this is still continued with the addition of common bottle glass.

It is essential that furnace temperatures are controlled, which creates no problem today, but in the 18th century this would be difficult to achieve, relying only on the judgement and experience of the man in charge of the fire.

Another critical operation requiring the greatest expertise is pouring. The temperature at which pouring can take place is extremely important, particularly at the final melting, and the molten copper must remain between 1260°C and 1315°C during the whole of the pouring process. If the temperature is above optimum there is a decrease in the tensile strength. This also occurs if the temperature falls rapidly below optimum because of the inability of the metal to feed properly, therefore working at such high temperatures in the 18th century required the greatest skill and judgement in deciding when pouring was viable, because of the limited temperature range in which it could take place, and was dangerous for the workers. Once pouring had commenced it would have been executed with great rapidity, otherwise the copper, when in a solid and cold state, not having the required tensile strength, would crack and break with usage or when it was being worked into articles or rolled.

Rakes, stirring rods and other tools for melting operations have always been made from iron, since iron is almost insoluble in molten copper alloys and any slight contamination can be tolerated. As in earlier periods, today many copper workers prefer tools of wrought iron which is stronger than pig (or cast) iron, the former being worked as in the making of horse shoes, whilst the latter is poured into moulds, which on solidification takes on a relatively more brittle property. Today only copper refining takes place in the U.K.

Although at present no detailed descriptions appear to exist of the original copper works on Macclesfield Common, it is possible to achieve an adequate idea of the development taking place from comparison with other sites, and from a brief understanding of the operations relating to copper smelting as set out above.

Two important sources of information for this period are accounts given by two Swedish visitors. The first, Emanuel Swedenborg, was a genius. Born in Stockholm during 1688 he became a scientist, engineer, anatomist and statesman, but he is now better remembered for his secular work and practical psychology. Brass and copper were important to Swedish economy, so the King of Sweden, Charles XII, commissioned Swedenborg to travel extensively throughout Europe and submit a detailed report on the metallurgic industries of each country.

He visitied Britain in 1710-12, but much of his work on technology, published in *De Ferro* and *De Cupro,* was based on reports from travellers such as Cletscher and Kalmeter submitted to him as an officer of the Board of Mines. His journey as "Assessor Extraordinary of the Board of Mines" began in 1721. The comprehensive account of his findings, written in Latin and beautifully executed with diagrams and illustrations, was eventually published in 1734.

Some 20 years later, appreciating that the English were beginning to acquire skills and knowledge of mining and smelting from which they were becoming formidable competitors, Reinhold R. Angerstein toured this country and wrote *A Journal of a Journey through England in the years 1753, 1754 and 1755.* Unfortunately this was just prior to the period of Charles Roe's involvement in the industry and consequently no details pertaining to the Macclesfield operations are included. However, the two reports, combined with an excellent Cornish publication written later in the century, have contributed considerably towards providing the following information.

The first requisite building of importance would be the calciner. In this most of the copper ores would receive an initial roasting to rid them of large quantities of impurities such as sulphur and arsenic and also reduced the bulk. As noted already there is a great variety of copper ores, numbering more than 160, with most of them based mainly on sulphides i.e. containing varying amounts of sulphur. To work economically the calciner would have been a brick building of approximately 24 ft in length and 18 ft in width. Inside a hearth or bed would have been laid out flat, measuring 18 ft long by 13 ft wide, with a height of almost 3 ft. The back of the calciner would have been constructed in a concave shape to reflect back the heat which passed over the ore from a fireplace at the front of the hearth. The fireplace would only have measured about $3^{1}/_{2}$ ft by 2 ft to a depth of 2 ft, but once the fire had been kindled and the heat built up, the ore itself burned with a "sulphureous flame". It was not necessary to add further fuel, because once the flame on the ore had burnt itself out, the ore was considered to be sufficiently calcined.

Next, a group of smelthouses would be constructed. These appear to have been built at least in pairs, but on occasion four or more were erected together, resembling a row of cottages. Each smelthouse, often referred to as a smelter or furnace, was built of brick or stone approximately 18 ft long, 12 ft wide and $9^{1}/_{2}$ ft high.

Ordinary bricks were already being produced at the brickworks on Macclesfield Common, on the site adjacent to the copper mine, and as such were readily available. They would be shaped with wooden moulds and stacked carefully, allowing them to be either sun dried or slowly dried in a low temperature kiln, otherwise they were liable to explode when finally baked in a kiln which produced temperatures as high as those at which copper melts.

The bricks between the furnace shell and the lining, and also the bricks used to build the hearths, would have to be fire bricks which could withstand very high temperatures, and consequently "Brickmakers rooms" were built for making and drying fire bricks. Ordinary bricks could be made with a variety of clays but fire bricks were different. In Cornwall "talcy" clays were used which came from soft "grouan" (growan - this is china clay or kaolin): Stourbridge clay was also considered excellent for the purpose. Not only was the clay used for fire bricks but it was mixed with sand to join the fire bricks together, in exactly the same way as mortar used by builders. It is of interest to note that by 1775 Josiah Wedgwood was experimenting with a white china clay which Dr. Gell of Hopton had obtained from Brassington; and the following year, William Duesbury of the Derby pot works, also anxious to have a local supply of suitable clay, had claimed ground near to the village under the old lead mining laws of Derbyshire. What had inspired their interest in the area? In all probability they had discovered that Charles Roe had been using clays from the Brassington estate for many years in the construction of his furnaces.

* * * * * * *

There is no doubt that mining and smelting in this country, and in particular copper smelting, was the catalyst which brought about the production of porcelain in imitation of the superb Chinese porcelains imported in vast quantities by the East India Company, which after years of experimentation resulted in the compilation of recipes for English bone china, primarily by the Spode manufactory, which earned it the accolade of being the finest in the world.

The three main ingredients of bone china are:

1) Calcined bones . . . "the best that can be used are the leg bones of oxen and cows but on no account horses bones as they are open and spongey".
2) China clay or kaolin.
3) China stone or petuntse.

A Quaker brass producer of Bristol, by the name of Benjamin Lund, had been carrying out experiments to simplify the production of brass from copper, calamine (a form of zinc used at that period in brass production), and charcoal. To this end he had registered Patent No. 495 on 3rd February 1728, and again three months later in partnership with a Francis Hauksbee on the 9th May. The significant part of the patent was that moulds were cast, turned and fitted together leaving a space between them to the desired thickness of the vessel required, and holes made in various parts of the moulds to allow air to escape. These holes were filled with a porous material to prevent the metal running out. What this material was is not stated, but several years later, on 7th March 1749, Lund was granted a licence to obtain soaprock from near the Lizard in Cornwall. Kaolin is porous but soaprock is not.

An ordinary porcelain body requires temperatures of 900°C to 1000°C; bone china, however, has to be fired between 1200°C to 1250°C, almost those at which copper melts, and it seems reasonable to deduce that Mr. Lund had been experimenting with various types of clays from Cornwall for his brass and copper receptacles, which in his smelters had produced some surprising results, resembling the body of the Chinese porcelains. So inspired was he that he began the manufacture of porcelain in Bristol during 1749, and on 4th June 1751 'The Worcester Porcelain Company' was formed to acquire the Bristol undertaking.

It can be no coincidence that Richard Champion, a member of the great Quaker family of copper and brass manufacturers of Bristol, entered into partnership with a Quaker chemist, Dr. Cookworthy of Plymouth, in order to produce "true porcelain". The Champions, connected with the Cornish mines since 1719 through the syndicate headed by John Coster, were involved with many patents concerning metallurgy and clays. It was found that if a perforated ladle was protected with Stourbridge clay, it could withstand the heat of molten copper being poured through it. (This process was concerned with the granulation of copper in order to produce brass).

Dr. Cookworthy claimed to have found kaolin in an old mine near Helston in Cornwall about 1755, and after further searching also found china stone or petuntse near St. Austell. He later wrote:

"Caulin (Kaolin). This material in the Chinese way of speaking constitutes the bones as the Petunse does the flesh of Chinaware . . . There are inexhaustible stones of this Caulin in the two Western counties (Devon and Cornwall). The use, it's commonly put to, is in mending the tin furnaces and the fire places of the fire-engines; for which t'is very proper".

The Champions were well adept in their acquisition of patents as part of their efforts to sustain as much industrial monopolisation as possible. The very nature of some manufacturing processes made it impossible to be specific, and they used this to great advantage, so that if anyone came remotely near to effecting a similar process they could claim infringement.

There seems no doubt that Champion had encouraged Dr. Cookworthy in his search, knowing the nature of Benjamin Lund's experiments. What must have surprised Champion was that Lund had not effected a patent, so Champion, presumably short of money or wishing to remain anonymous, must have encouraged Dr. Cookworthy to obtain a patent during that year of 1758 for the manufacture of true porcelain. As Lund had not included kaolin in his recipe, his was a hard paste porcelain. The patent taken out by Dr. Cookworthy in 1758 covered for the inclusion of kaolin which made his a soft paste porcelain.

Production commenced in Plymouth but was shortly moved to Bristol under the supervision of Richard Champion, and it was only a matter of time before he would purchase the whole enterprise including the patent. It was on its expiration in 1775 that a legal battle would ensue when Champion applied for renewal, causing such a fierce remonstration by a group of potters under the leadership of Josiah Wedgwood, that Champion stood no chance of success, thus assuring the availability of kaolin to all those concerned with porcelain experimentation, which would be used to great advantage by the potters in Staffordshire.

* * * * * * *

Charles Roe was fortunate that all his remaining building materials were available locally, particularly siliceous sandstones which, when mixed with clay, make ideal fire bricks for furnaces, especially when – as in the 18th century – pink gritstone (now known as Chatsworth Grit) from the quarry on the Common would have been crushed and added to the mix. Ordinary bricks were smaller than today, and would remain so until 1784 when, to compensate partially for a reduction on tea duty, Pitt was to introduce a brick tax which inevitably resulted in larger bricks being produced, some measuring as today, $2^1/_4$"x $3^3/_4$"x 8", many larger. Fire bricks were considerably larger than ordinary building bricks, measuring a good 16" long by 8"x 8"; several years later, after the dismantling of the smelters, many were utilised in the construction of walls. At present some remain in the wall surrounding the yard at the rear of the *Navigation Inn* on Black Road in Macclesfield and appropriately more or less indicate the eastern extremity of the original smeltworks.

Once the fire bricks had been put in place within each furnace, creating a curved ceiling to reflect back the heat, a hearth was built up 3 ft above the level of the ground to contain the melting area, the latter ideally measuring about 8 ft long, 4 ft 8 ins wide and 2 ft in height.

As in the case of the boles set high on the Derbyshire hills, where primitive lead smelting had taken place for centuries, it was important that the draught holes, through which air was drawn in by the fire, should face the prevailing winds. Each fireplace would be built almost 3 ft by 2 ft in size at one end of the melting area, with a small partition one brick thick dividing the two. The bottom of the fireplace was a grid made of cast iron set partly over a large pit into which the ashes could fall and through which air could enter. After passing over the fire and smelt, the resultant smoke and hot air containing impurities, rose to the apex of the roof and were carried to a height of about 30 ft through a chimney, before being expelled into the atmosphere.

Great care and attention were given to lining each furnace, which was achieved with a paste of burnt bone ash. The reason behind this is best explained in a conversation between James Boswell and his great friend and companion, Dr. Johnson:

Boswell: "I observe in London that the poor go about and gather bones, which I understand are manufactured."
Johnson: "Yes, Sir, they boil them, and extract a grease from them for greasing wheels and other purposes. Of the best pieces they make a mock ivory, which is used for hafts of knives and various other things; the coarser pieces they burn and pound and sell the ashes."

Boswell: "For what purpose, Sir?"

Johnson: "Why, Sir, for making a furnace for the chemists for melting iron. A paste made of burnt bones will stand a stronger heat than anything else. Consider, Sir! if you are to melt iron, you cannot line your pot with brass, because it is softer than iron, and would melt sooner; nor with iron, for though malleable iron is harder than cast iron, yet it would not do; but a paste of burnt bones will not melt."

Although Dr. Johnson specifically mentions iron smelting, evidence exists to indicate that bone ash linings were also being used for copper smelting and the refining of silver from both copper and lead.

One can now appreciate the inclusion of bone ashes in the early soft paste porcelains such as Bow (1749-1763) and Chelsea (1750-1765). Their use in smelt linings was to withstand high temperatures and reflect back heat, which would make them an ideal constituent for inclusion in porcellaneous bodies, particularly tea bowls, teapots and dishes. The Bow and Chelsea manufactories used neither kaolin nor petuntse in their recipes, and it is surprising that it took almost half a century before Josiah Spode II experimented by combining the three ingredients of kaolin, petuntse and bone ashes, together with one or two minor additions, to produce bone china.

After the paste of calcined bones had been applied to the walls and ceiling of the copper furnace, the inner part of the floor was lined with sand.

The district around Macclesfield forms one of the most important sources of foundry sand in the country, with the main quarries at Congleton to the south and Chelford to the west. This would be the sand used to cover the furnace bottoms and also to create a basin at the side of each furnace in which "oblong traces" were made to receive the molten matt or black copper.

The refiner was identical to the smelters except the sand inside the furnace was formed into a basin shape instead of being flat, because at the final melting the copper, now virtually rid of all impurities, was not tapped but "laded out by an Iron ladle".

There was a hole in the roof or crown of each smelter through which the ore or charge was dropped in. Three further accesses were necessary to each furnace, all at ground level and all covered by doors. There was one through which coke was shovelled onto the fire; one by which the metal could be tapped, and a third, slightly larger, through which slag, floating on the surface of the molten metal, could be skimmed off.

A later description of the Roe smeltworks indicates that further additional buildings included stables, a blacksmith's shop, and what were said to be "rooms in which to store charcoal, coke and iron". An assay office was essential and a small house in which the overseer lived; copper smelting continued 24 hours per day as it was uneconomical to allow those smelters in operation to lose heat, and therefore some responsible person would have to be close by at all times. Needless to say the building of the house would be on the south-westerly side of the site in the hope that the strong prevailing winds would carry away and rapidly disperse the 'obnoxious' fumes in the opposite direction. No complaints are recorded by anyone on the Common objecting to the smoke and fumes, nor do any of the earlier visitors passing through the town mention the smelter, which one would expect to have been conspicuous by its billowing sulphurous clouds, therefore one must conclude that Charles had made a wise decision when placing his furnaces at a safe distance from the town, with any detrimental effects felt in an area which was of minimal interest to a vast majority of people. It also proves that the maintenance of the works must have been given priority, because each time furnaces were put out for repairing purposes, the chimneys would also have to be thoroughly cleaned to remove particles of sulphur and other impurities which had built up inside, thus reducing contamination escaping into the atmosphere.

* * * * * * *

William Roe was 12 years old when his father and Uncle Rowland were given permission for the encroachment on the Common. Already he would be conversant with his father's silk interests, yet despite the fact his grandfather, Samuel Lankford, was also very much involved in the trade, William showed no inclination or desire to be likewise engaged. His interest was in copper smelting, and just as his father had acquired a vast knowledge of mining in his youth, which he would endeavour to pass on to the boy, William's perception of the smelter constructed on Macclesfield Common during the spring and summer of 1759, was sufficient to ensure a dedication to the trade of which his father would be proud.

The boy had possibly already visited Mr. Patten's works at Warrington, and one can imagine the excitement he felt as he saw the buildings taking shape during his frequent visits on horseback to the Common with his father. After many hundreds of bricks had been dried and baked, one of the first buildings to be erected on site would be the blacksmith's forge, necessary for providing tools, grates for fireplaces, hinges, locks and a whole multitude of other items including horse shoes and parts for wagons. The blacksmiths would always remain busy as everything needed to be kept in constant repair after the initial construction work had been completed. Coopers were also an integral part of the industry for keeping in good condition the vast stock of barrels and hogsheads, often referred to as casks, which were about to undertake a lifetime of phenomenal journeys, putting their counterparts in the beer trade to shame.

The buildings were constructed around a courtyard, a similar arrangement to that of the large silk mill, excepting the entrance to the smeltworks was from the west. Judging from the size of the original plot of land and subsequent alterations, apart from the calciner, refiner and other requisite buildings, it seems feasible to assume that one row of five smelters was initially provided.

The easiest part of the operation had now been completed, but the most difficult was about to begin – ensuring a steady supply of raw materials, training workmen in the 'art and mystery of copper smelting' and producing a very high quality copper.

At the commencement of the first smelting it was necessary to build up a considerable amount of heat in the furnaces. In his book *A Collection of Letters For the Improvement of Husbandry and Trade,* c. 1681, Houghton described the smelting of copper using the "choyfest" (choicest) coals, but not very small pieces. The bricks had to be wider than those for lead smelting so they could hold more coals (this presumably refers to the size of the melt area). The ore, broken into pieces the size of hazel nuts, was alternated with layers of charcoal, each layer one inch thick, forming four in all. To sustain the high temperatures required, it was necessary for two men, using two pairs of "hand-Bellowes", to blow very strongly. This proved to be an unsatisfactory process causing much trial and error, but on 28th August 1684 a Richard Brett and Henry Howard had been granted a patent for "Melting or smelting copper and tin ores in furnaces with sea coal or pit coal" (which may indicate a difference between the two types of coal at that period.) Unfortunately no specification is given. Years later, on 21st April 1722, George Moore, a merchant of Lambeth in Surrey, obtained a patent for "Refining copper by air and blast with furnaces and sea coal", but it was left to Abraham Darby, through his experiments with cast iron at Coalbrookdale, to discover that coal was ideal for smelting when converted to coke.

Coal contains varying amounts of sulphur which, when burnt in the presence of iron, forms compounds rendering the iron brittle and unfit for use. During the 18th century, to rid coal of its sulphur content, it was burnt in covered heaps in exactly the same way as wood for the production of charcoal; in fact, by this method, coal became a form of charcoal, hard, strong and full of little holes to which was given the name coke. Coke, being almost pure carbon, not only burnt more easily but was capable of producing very high temperatures.

Although bellows remained a necessity for iron furnaces, the use of coke in copper smelting virtually eliminated their employ.

Charles had obviously negotiated a coal lease for Macclesfield Common on behalf of Roe & Co. with the Earl of Harrington. This mine was to become known as Greenaway colliery, with the lease expiring on 29th May 1779. One must assume that it was for 21 years and therefore obtained during 1758, just prior to the negotiations for the proposed smelter site. Unfortunately the coal was not of a particularly good quality, graded by modern Coal Industry methods as 900 in some parts and 600 in others. It would have been possible, however, to produce reasonable coke from the 600 grade, although at that period both were probably mixed together.

Within the coal district of Macclesfield, encompassing the villages of Hurdsfield, Rainow, Bollington, Adlington, Pott-Shrigley, Lyme, Worth, Poynton and Norbury, coals were not sold by weight but by quality and quantity, making it difficult to compare one colliery with another. The system seemed to be closely related to that operating in Derbyshire where, except for a few instances, coal pits were worked by lessees who paid rent of approximately £50 to £100 per acre, with measurement of the mines and works taken each year. Charles Roe's agent at the copper works calculated that there were "10 Hoops of Coal in a square Yard". A hoop presumably related to a wooden version of a laundry basket complete with handles, which was used in mines. It resembled the sawn off part of a cask and was of adequate depth to accommodate one hoop or circular band of metal, sufficient to hold the staves together. As the calculation was used with reference to Cheshire acres, the agent reckoned 102,400 hoops per acre, but with the "gettable coals" as three quarters i.e. 76,800. A "Quarter of Coals" was 16 Hoops, which allowed for 4,800 Quarters to be raised from each Cheshire acre, and as the charge was 10d. per Quarter, the charge to lease each acre was £200. This compared favourably with rents in the Derbyshire coalfields, remembering that a Cheshire acre was a little more than double that of a statute acre.

Wood required for charcoal was bought locally and known as cord-wood. The name derived from the method of measuring with a piece of cord; a pile of wood 8 ft long, 4 ft wide by 4 ft high was known in quantity as a cord; thus wood piled up for fuel was also sold by the cord. Charcoal combined with turf had been used in smelting for centuries but, as the forests were rapidly receding, it had obviated the quest for an alternative fuel supply. The charcoal used by Roe & Co. was not for fuel but part of the actual smelting process.

Last, and by no means least, was the problem of a dependable supply of copper ores.

* * * * * * *

The first consignments of Coniston ore would be transported to Macclesfield either by packhorses or waggon, after their arrival at the quayside in Northwich during October, 1759. The most likely mode of transport would be by waggon pulled by one horse (with a horse at the rear in case of difficulties) or oxen. A waggon drawn by two horses could transport a ton of materials. Although packhorses were by this time a much sturdier breed than those of Elizabethan days, with Welsh ponies and steady Galloways preferred, and the occasional farm horses employed part-time, yet they were only capable of carrying 2cwts. each, one to each pannier. With an adequate load, therefore, unless inclement weather conditions prevailed, it was preferable to engage three horses with a waggon than ten packhorses if the route was suitable.

Whilst it was proving feasible to transport Coniston ores to Macclesfield, yet this one source was insufficient for the intended production of copper. As chemical composition and reactions were still not properly understood, the advice followed in relation to copper smelting was that of the 16th century Augsburg miners who stressed that "melting many sorts of ewres [ores] to gither is the most proffet and will melt a greattayll souner" [a great deal sooner]. Poorer ores, were mixed with richer ones. It aided the smelting of the former which acted as a flux saving money on fluorspar. Consequently Charles Roe would probably need to have at least one other source of copper ore to make his smelting a viable proposition. Although documentary evidence is non-existent, circumstantial evidence strongly points to Alderley Edge as the additional supplier; in fact Alderley could have been the original, making Coniston the supplementary one.

At this time The Edge was still Waste or Common land but eventually would be allocated under the *Nether Alderley Enclosure of Commons Act, 1775* "amongst parties proportionally to yearly value according to present Land Tax charged" with the following stipulation included:

> "Sir John Thomas Stanley his heirs and Assigns Lords of the Manor shall . . . take hold and enjoy All Mines and Minerals whatsoever and all Quarries of Stone . . . in through or under All that part of the said Common or Waste Grounds within the said Manor called Alderley Edge . . . (with) powers of getting working loading taking and carrying away all such Mines Minerals and Quarries" etc.

Early 19th century reminiscences of an old labourer, William Faringdon, employed on the Stanley Estate in Alderley Park, were to shed some light on the speculators known to have worked The Edge during the previous century, and he refers to Mr. Roe, who had undertaken to work the mines either "in Sir Edward Stanley's time or soon after . . ." Sir Edward had died in 1755, having suffered a fit whilst returning in his coach from a visit to Adlington Hall.

Sir Edward's will prepared in 1750, five years before his death, although containing considerable instructions in relation to the administration of his various estates in London, Somerset and Cheshire is, however, lacking in detail relating to specific lands, tenants and leases; nowhere, however, is there a mention of mines in his capacity as Lord of the Soil of Alderley Edge, and there is no codicil, so the commencement of mining in Alderley by Roe & Co. appears to more or less coincide with that of Coniston in 1756.

The will is revealing in that it mentions Charles Legh, Esq. of Adlington Hall as one of the Trustees in the event of the death of Sir Edward's wife, 'Dame Mary', and also gives authority to, amongst others, John Baskervyle of Withington for the execution of leases in order to provide income from the various estates. John Baskervyle was, of course, a lawyer and associate of John Stafford, both of the Inner Temple, and one of the parties concerned with the purchase of Charles Roe's house on Chestergate, Macclesfield in July 1752. There seems little doubt that some collaboration took place between the two lawyers, John Stafford and John Baskervyle, together with Charles Roe and Charles Legh; the latter being the probable communicator of the possibility of mining on The Edge (see chapter 2).

Fragmentary documentation has helped towards a clearer understanding of events that had taken place in and around the Alderley area from the late 17th century onwards, particularly as there is later evidence of significant lead deposits in the form of galena (lead sulphide) having been found there. It now seems certain that during the 1696 dispute Thomas Legh of The Ridge had endeavoured to claim his mining rights under the pretence of lead mining, but with the hope of finding copper ore.

Thomas Crosse, merchant of Liverpool and Chorley near Preston (although described as of Manchester), lessee of the copper mines from Sir Thomas Stanley, Lord of the Soil, at the time of the dispute, was in fact, a kinsman of the Leghs of Adlington Hall, and it was to be his descendants who would inherit the Adlington Estate in the early 19th century. He was the son of John, who had married Ann Yate, a member of a very important Dissenting family from near Whitchurch in Shropshire. Thomas, himself, married into the eminent Clayton family, originally from Clayton-le-Moors near Blackburn, but by this period merchants of Liverpool, Manchester and London.

Beneath Alderley Edge, and a little to the north-east, was the small hamlet of Mottram Andrew (today Mottram St. Andrew) in which was situated Mottram Hall. An impressive advertisement had appeared in *The Manchester Magazine* on Tuesday, 12th July 1743 referring to the sale of "The Capital Messuage or Mannor Houfe called Mottram Hall" together with about 137 Cheshire acres, 20 of which contained a wood of 3000 oak trees. It stated:

> "The house is pleasantly situated and there are stables, Coach-houfes and other Conveniences for a Gentleman's Family and it stands about fix miles from Stockport and three Miles from Macclesfield".

Out of the four names quoted for enquiries, two are significant: Dr. Clayton of Little Harwood, Blackburn and Mr. Yate of Whitchurch, Shropshire, both related by marriage to the Crosse family. It must also be remembered that Mr. Abbadine (or Hibberdine, as previously discussed) was said to have been working the mines at Alderley on behalf of a Shropshire gentleman, and that a member of the Clayton family, William, had sold his half share in the Macclesfield Copperas House works on the 31st January 1734. Both copper and iron pyrites are present in the Alderley mines and it seems reasonable to assume that the copperas works had been started with the intention of processing the iron pyrites from those mines. Because of subsequent developments, it is also possible that mining trials were carried out on that part of the land belonging to Mottram Hall which lay in a direct line north to north-east of the mineral vein being exploited on The Edge.

After this second burst of activity the mines appear to have been unworked for at least 20 years until Charles Roe took an interest in them. His observations on site would be as described by the old labourer of the Alderley Estate, William Faringdon. He remembered the mines "having been once taken on some kind of agreement" by Mr. Abbadine of Shropshire who then drove a tunnel from Dickens Wood to the Engine-Shaft near the Great Quarry. This tunnel was cut through sandstone to a height of 5 ft and one yard wide, and at the same time a smelting house was built near the Edge House. Mr. Faringdon also recalled that Abbadine had been ruined by his speculations. This is entirely possible because, although the malachite ore of Alderley gave every appearance of being rich, it proved extremely difficult to smelt. Ores from The Edge have been found to contain varying amounts of arsenic, and it seems feasible to assume that the miners were totally unaware of the advice given by those from Augsberg in the Elizabethan Period that it was a much easier process to smelt ores from different mines together, rather than one mine only.

There seems little doubt that Charles Roe would have made himself fully conversant with all the anomalies of copper smelting before attempting the complex operation for himself. Having obtained his lease from the Executors of the estate, his miners presumably reworked and extended the Engine Vein, and although no production figures are available, it was later reported that for a time they got a considerable quantity of ore "so much . . . as to give them a clear profit of £50 per week". It is almost impossible to calculate the tonnage represented by this figure, as it is not known what price per ton Charles would have charged to his smelting accounts, but in the broadest possible terms it seems likely that at least 100 tons per week would have been necessary to support the statement. Initially very little ore would have been raised until the levels had been cleared and drained but, after 18 months or so, one can assume that sufficient quantities of ore were being won for Charles to feel confident in securing a site on which to build his smelter.

Once the smelter had been successfully completed, and as far as possible all necessary steps taken to ensure a constant supply of raw materials, then the final and decisive stage would have been reached. Young William must have shared the excitement felt by his father and others as the furnace fires were lit, and slowly but surely the operation got underway.

* * * * * * *

After the initial supply of wood and coal had been kindled within each furnace hearth, William would observe the use of coal (available close by on the Common) shovelled into each smelter through the appropriate aperture, after which the cover or iron door would be carefully secured in order to build up a high temperature within the melt area. Air drawn in through the firehole at the end of the furnace would soon create a good blaze. It would be pointed out to William that two of the furnaces were temporarily not in use, as these would be kept on standby ready for the time when two of the operative smelters would need attention involving repairing and patching. At the same time as the smelters were lit the preparation of the copper ores would be taking place.

Apart from the better quality ore, already segregated by the women, some of whom, a later observer discovered, had been brought from Derbyshire to work at Alderley, all other ores were presumably stored separately, making it easier to assess how much Coniston ore would be required to add to that of Alderley in order to facilitate economic smelting. At this early stage, the bulk of ore was probably obtained from The Edge and transported by waggon along the highway favoured by the contingent of Bonnie Prince Charlie's forces on that fateful day of 1745. The route continued down into the town, passing Charles Roe's house on Chestergate. One suspects that each driver would have to report his arrival by visiting the Company office next to the house, before proceeding down Barn Street and across Parsonage Green for the unenviable drag up Lunt Hill road to the smelter site on the Common. There large heaps of ore would have materially altered the contours of land in the immediate vicinity of the works, and careful weighing and discharging of loads would have been insisted upon, in an attempt to keep some semblance of order in an otherwise random situation.

After various trials and errors, a desired admix of ores would be established in a fixed quantity, and this, referred to as the charge and weighing (which was anything from 10 to 40 cwts.), was then spread across the floor of the calciner and set alight. This mass was frequently stirred for about 12 hours so that it would not melt; however, a rich ore would require only 6 to 8 hours. The purpose of the operation was to rid the ore of a portion of its sulphur and arsenic content, after which it was then melted in a second furnace with an addition of approximately the same weight of raw ore. This time the fire was intense, which had the effect of melting the copper after about 4 hours. The slag floating on the surface, principally formed from iron impurities, was skimmed off by an iron rake called a rabble. At this stage further quantities of ore could be added, with skimming taking place three times within a further period of 12 hours. The coarse molten metal, now known as regulus, was "let out by a tap-hole in the side of the furnace". In Cornwall it was immediately run into a bed of sand to form pigs, but before these had cooled they were transported in iron wheel barrows to a trough or cistern where they were plunged into cold water. As Charles had a constant supply of cold running water through the site, from the Black Brook on Macclesfield Common, he could have used a method similar to that reported by Garner in his *Natural History of the County of Staffordshire*, published in 1844 i.e. to run the regulus immediately into cold water, by which it formed dark coarse shot with a metal content of possibly a third of the whole.

Next it was necessary to crush the regulus almost into granules. Women, sometimes with the aid of children, could be used to buck it, but the most efficient method was to use a horse-mill, where the horse pulled round a grinding stone or, alternatively, the stone could be pushed with human hands by means of a large wooden handle attached to a central post. A much preferred method at Bristol was to granulate the regulus by passing it through a sieve in the form of a ladle protected by a layer of potter's clay and perforated with holes. This was carried out over cold water so that the regulus instantly poured into it, and the drops thus formed became granules; again a method well suited to the Macclesfield operation.

The resultant recalcined granules were recalcined, and then a repeat of the melting process took place producing a matte or regulous known as blue metal, with a copper content of about 66%. According to the quality of the copper content this procedure was repeated over and over again. With a rich ore, three or four times was adequate, but with poorer ores it was known to take up to twenty recalcinings and remeltings to achieve satisfactory results. The removal of impurities was aided by the addition of broken bottle glass, but it was appreciated that sand containing a high silica content could be used instead, and as the siliceous sandstones of the Macclesfield area were of exceptional quality this would seem to have been a more practical alternative for the local works.

Because of the complexity of obtaining pure copper, only workers experienced in the art of refining could competently judge when the matte had reached the desired state known as white metal, copper content 75%, so that it could be calcined for the last time and then transported to the coarse refiner. After melting, the molten copper was laded out with iron ladles, one ladle full at a time, into large oblong iron pots or moulds. On solidification this was known as blister copper, a name derived from the blistered surface of the metal due to the expulsion of the gas sulphur dioxide.

For the final refining and toughening process, the brittle, crystalline, purplish-red metal was taken to the refiner where it was melted down, covered with charcoal and then poled. The poling process was carried out by means of a wooden pole of green wood, the most effectual being that of a pine or silver birch tree. The pole was used to stir the molten metal, which put back oxygen taken out during smelting, otherwise the desired malleability of the copper was not achieved on solidification. Great care was needed, however, because an excess of poling resulted in a reverse action taking place with oxygen once again expelled, in which case the only course to pursue was to open up the refiner, allowing air to be freely admitted.

Today furnaces have their own circulators, but in the 18th century it would have been necessary to stir continually in order to have a uniform smelt, so that when a sample was taken it was representative of the whole. Pure copper begins to run at 1083°C; depending on impurities, however, it can be taken up to 1700°C but no higher.

Copper smelting is based on the principle described by Agricola in the 16th century, practised in the 18th century, and still pertaining today: copper has a greater affinity for sulphur than iron, and iron has a greater affinity for oxygen than copper.

After refining the molten copper was 'laded out' into whatever shapes of moulds were considered desirable. The usual form was that of pigs or ingots, but on occasion cakes were made.

Once the Macclesfield smelters were fully operational they would burn night and day for months. It would be stressed by the experienced furnace men training others that on no account must slag be allowed to build up within the smelters, otherwise damage to the furnace linings would occur causing considerable expense in repairs.

During the first two or three weeks of smelting one wonders how many times Charles visited the works, and how many sleepless nights he suffered, until the first true copper ingots were produced. His outlay must have been considerable, and his sense of achievement on seeing those first ingots, well deserved; what other industries are more diametrically opposite than textiles and heavy metals, and in particular silk and copper? Yet both of these, requiring the greatest expertise within their own spheres, demonstrate the remarkable versatility of the man, especially at that mid-18th century period of English history.

12
THE GREAT PARTNERSHIP

Men at some time are masters of their fates.

On 25th October 1760 "His majesty George II died at Kensington in the 77 year of his Age & 34 of his reign". This entry appeared in the diary of a young lady visitor to London by the name of Caroline Powys. She continued "It was astonishing to see the amazing consternation, bustle & confusion, an event like this quite unexpected made in a Metropolis such as London, I happened to be out that morn before it was known, it was published about 12 when instantly the streets were in a buzz the black cloth carrying about and in a $^1/_2$ an hour every Shop was hung with Appendages of Mourning which was not put off till the Sunday sennight following. (i.e. the black drapes were not taken down until Sunday week). The Bowels were brought privately from Kensington and Buried in Henry VII Chaple and the night after the body was brought and deposited in State for interment on the next day".

This remarkable scene was the finale to a remarkable period. Great ministers had emerged in government, amongst whom were Sir Robert Walpole and William Pitt the Elder, and although the Seven Years War continued, great successes had already been achieved. Robert Clive, who at the age of 19 years had been a clerk in the employ of the East India Company, but who had subsequently joined the army, accomplished a great victory in India over the Nabob Surat-ud Dowlah at the Battle of Plassey in 1757, and established British power in Calcutta. General Wolfe had also accomplished a brilliant victory at Quebec in 1759 against the French, establishing British power in Canada, added to which, in the same year, a French defeat at the Battle of Minden by Ferdinand of Brunswick had been made possible by a British Infantry contingent.

The year 1759 had also proved a notable one for British sea-power with the capture of the valuable sugar island Guadeloupe in the West Indies and the French slave trading posts of Senegal and Gorée in West Africa. Admiral Boscawen had once more proved his worth by destroying the French Mediterranean fleet off Lagos Bay along the coast of Portugal, and towards the end of the year, in November, Admiral Hawke had inflicted another demoralising blow to the French navy when, despite appalling conditions, he had defeated the fleet from Brest in the shallow waters of Quiberon Bay.

British morale had never been better and George III, whose father, Frederick, Prince of Wales, had predeceased him, took over the throne from his grandfather with a devotion to England that was far beyond that demonstrated by either of his two predecessors.

It was crucial that British military and naval domination in certain regions was maintained in order to support a vast communications network, vital to our merchantmen plying to and fro across the oceans of the world. This fact was now becoming a reality as the demand for British goods, and those obtained through our trading posts overseas, was reaching a critical level, especially in the North American continent where development was rapidly taking place. Significant family and social links as ever played their part, and the old established Virginian families, and those from the West Indies, having the necessary resources and connections, used these to weave their way into the fabric of society in the expanding colonies such as Maryland, the Carolinas and most particularly, Pennsylvania. Factors were busily employed establishing important trading routes which, as far as possible, would be trustworthy and reliable, eliminating unpredictability and risk. British lives and goods were valuable. The colonists were not only demanding the necessities of life, such as linen, frying pans and millstones, but an astounding array of luxury goods, which were about to find their way across the Atlantic, both for personal use and trading purposes, particularly with the Indians.

* * * * * * *

Charles Roe had chosen the perfect time to extend his commercial interests, and although his involvement in the silk mill continued, more and more his occupation and attention were taken up by the demands of the prospective copper trade.

An almost immediate problem needing to be resolved was that of adequate quantities of good quality coal suitable for conversion into coke. Although local supplies temporarily sufficed, Charles appreciated that it was only a question of time before a secondary source would be essential, and once again the 'helping hand' seems to have been that of John Stafford.

The Stafford family connections in and around the High Peak of Derbyshire made it inevitable that many people in that area were conversant with John Stafford's reputation as a lawyer. He was also well-known in his capacity as Clerk of the Halmote Court (i.e. the Court of the Manor and Forest of Macclesfield) a position held since his promotion from Deputy in 1740. As the condition of the Court house, shared by the Macclesfield Corporation, left much to be desired, John Stafford carried out many of his legal duties in his offices within his dwelling-house on Jordangate, and it had been there, on 8th August 1757, that a significant action had taken place.

An Indenture dated 4th February 1752 relates to lands in Disley; it had been executed on behalf of two members of the Clayton family and others, amongst whom was a member of the Brocklehurst family and a Stafford. The eventual redeemer of their loans, in the amount of £1311 13s., was Thomas Tatton, related to John Stafford's wife, with a sum of £279 5s. still outstanding to Edward Brereton Clayton. Seizure at Court was inevitable, and "by virtue of Common Recovery and Surrender according to the Custom of the Manor and Forest of Macclesfield" which had taken place on 11th May 1757, the action was completed on 8th August following. The gentleman who redeemed the whole of these loans, for all intents and purposes, was a stranger to the Macclesfield area. The fact that he could command such a sum must have set many tongues wagging, but this impressive man, with a confidence second to none, had the ability to make the right decisions at the right times. His name was Brian Hodgson.

The properties granted to him comprised seven dwelling-houses with lands, part of a wood bounded by a watercourse with permission to obtain timber, and all appurtenances including mines and quarries. In due course one of the tenements in particular, known as Hogg Bank (today Hagg Bank farm), would be found to contain important coal seams.

Brian Hodgson, described on the Indenture as "of Buxton", was at some point introduced to Charles Roe. Theirs was to be a working partnership which would never founder, carried out with complete trust and mutual respect for the remainder of their lives.

Perhaps Charles, like everyone else, never really discovered the source of Brian Hodgson's wealth, but the facts, which are irrefutable, were known at that time. Brian was a younger son of Robert Hodgson and his wife, Margaret, of the county town of Stafford. His father was a tobacconist and 'Undertaker of Church Briefs'. The latter, an unusual but lucrative occupation, stemmed from the fact that a group in Stafford (in effect a legal firm) had acquired the monopoly of handling national appeals on behalf of any church in the country which had suffered a disaster e.g. the collapse of a spire or the flooding of premises. This monopoly was mainly due to Robert Hodgson's efforts, as he had been responsible for reducing charges for the briefs, which had forced another potential 'Undertaker' from Stafford to give up the business.

Son Brian during his late twenties had met and married Elizabeth Alcock, one of the three daughters of Thomas, landlord of a very famous inn, *The George* at Stamford in Northamptonshire (today Lincolnshire). This suggests that Brian was involved in his father's business interests, because Stafford and Stamford had been linked by trade from at least the medieval period. There are indications that the Alcock family also originated in Staffordshire, but from the area around Uttoxeter, where a group of them remained on the Staffordshire/Derbyshire border throughout the 18th century. On 10th July 1740 an advertisement appeared in the *Stamford Mercury*:

> "Whereas, Thomas Alcock, who kept the *George* in St. Martin's, Stamford Baron, is lately dead this is therefore to inform the public that the said Inn will continue to be kept by Brian Hodgson, his son-in-law; where all persons will be sure of meeting with an agreeable entertainment. N.B. – All persons indebted to the said Thomas Alcock are desired to pay their respective debts to Brian Hodgson aforesaid, who is empowered to receive the same".

Brian's first child, a son baptised Robert as recently as 28th June 1740 at St. Martin's Without, Stamford, was the possible reason why his wife, Elizabeth, obtained "Admin. of the Goods Chattels and Credits of Thomas Alcock, late of Stamford Baron in the County of Northants widower deceased" . . . on the 29th July, because she was the mother of the eldest (and only) male heir. It seems apparent that Thomas Alcock had almost certainly died suddenly, allowing no time for a will to be prepared. He must have accrued a small fortune because *The George* had a reputation for famous clientele, which included the Duke of Cumberland. Situated on the Great North Road it had begun life a few centuries earlier as a hospital administered by monks. In the Elizabethan period it was already a hostelry which had, with subsequent additions, become an inn of some consequence by the 18th century. Brian and Elizabeth remained as hosts for 10 years, during which time they produced a further eight children; then an unexpected move took place. At some time during the year 1750-51 the family took over the hostelry of Buxton Hall together with its famous spa water baths.

What had prompted this move is difficult to ascertain, but the lure of lead seems a not too unreasonable assumption because of the rapidity with which Brian Hodgson became involved in the local lead mining industry.

The accounts of William Roberts, kept on behalf of the Duke of Devonshire for the Liberties of Taddington, Monyash etc. including "the Manner of Hartington" and relating to the quarter 29th September 1751 to 25th March 1752, contain an item of 10 guineas paid by Mr. Hodgson and partners for the purchase of "the Lord's Mear . . . at Chance Myne in Hartington". Roberts also claimed ^{15}/₆d. "Expenses Disbursed concerning the Lords Mear at Chance Myne in Hartington Lyberty". Flooding must have occurred because in 1754 a Lords Meer was valued "in a vein that Mr. Hodgson and partners are driving in for a sough to relieve Chance Mine in Hartington". These are the only references remaining of this venture, which more than likely took place on ground situated on the shale and gritstone facing the eastern slopes of Axe Edge. It has proved impossible to trace this mine with certainty, or to establish who the partners were, but little ore could have been retrieved during the two years or so of the undertaking.

A mystery also remains concerning the terms by which Brian Hodgson took over the lease of Buxton Hall, as it was already leased by the Duke of Devonshire to Alexander Taylor for 21 years from Lady Day 1746 at a substantial rent of £145 per annum. However, Alexander Taylor had died, so one can only assume that the lease to Brian Hodgson was on similar terms. By the mid 1740s, Mary, one of the sisters of Brian Hodgson's wife, was married to Job Gibbons who, in some capacity, was connected with the Duke of Devonshire's estate; and it must have been through their associations with Buxton that Brian Hodgson had learnt of the availability of the Buxton Hall lease, with the additional inducement of investing in lead mining as the head of a partnership which presumably included his brother-in-law, or at least some acquaintances of his.

Buxton Hall was a posting station; obviously a valuable source of income. It was ideally situated on the important coach route from Manchester via Stockport to London, with postal customers covering a wide area, including the Lyme Hall Estate of the Legh family. The patronage thus created would provide important connections as people came and went, collecting and delivering mail and packages, keeping up to date with news and gossip from a variety of sources, and making additional demands for beer, wine and victuals together with feed and stabling for their horses, enhancing still further the profits of the hostelry.

The scene was set, and Brian Hodgson, obviously with a surfeit of money, was looking for investments which, although speculative, would give him a good chance of making a real fortune so that he could indulge himself further in his passion for horses, especially breeding and racing. Whilst landlord of *The George* he had taken a prominent part in the local race meetings at Stamford, and an advertisement in the Chester newspaper, Adams *Weekly Courant* dated 16th April 1754, signified his intention of continuing accordingly:

> "Mr. HODGSON for the better Convenience of Gent Breeders proposes to have his STALLION (which has cover'd Mares these last 3 seasons at Warrington) to be there Tues to Fri & from Fri to Tues at Manchester during Season & to Cover Mares $\frac{1}{2}$gn. each Mare & 1/- the Servant. Money to be paid at Stable door".

From his frequent visits to Warrington Brian Hodgson would have had the opportunity to observe the importance of Thomas Patten's copper works at Bank Quay, and also to intermingle at the race meetings with a growing number of merchants, town dignitaries, members of the professions, the military and not forgetting the aristocracy who, like himself, totally ignored any attempts to confine horse breeding to anything except useful purposes. Even in Carlisle on 18th July 1754, John Pearson, Town Clerk, began his letter to Sir William Fleming at Rydal Hall near Coniston with the sentence "I deferr'd writing to you as Mr. Atkinson gave me hope of seeing you at the Races here". As in church on Sundays this was another excellent means of making contacts, business propositions and finding out who was who, but this time it was on a much grander scale.

In addition to leasing Buxton Hall Brian Hodgson had also entered into a lease for farm land, imperative for his horses, visitors' horses, and to supplement the needs of his growing family together with the tables of the many guests who crowded in from dawn till dusk, whatever the season. The lease, effected with the Duke of Devonshire, was for 14 years from 25th March 1753 at an annual rental of £30. The land comprised Fearn House and Needham farms in Buxton, but was afterwards simply referred to as Mr. Hodgson's farm.

Brian Hodgson's presence at Buxton Hall seems to have had an almost immediate effect. His boundless energy, coupled with his experiences as landlord of *The George* brought a verve to the whole proceedings which guaranteed a perpetual clientele from all levels of society. During his occupancy the patronage of the baths is known to have included the Bishop of St. Asaph, the Lord Chief Justice Wills, the Duchess of Portland and by no means least amongst others, Josiah Wedgwood, who on 15th May 1762 would write to his great friend and associate, Thomas Bentley, in Liverpool, "Be so kind to tell Mr. Turner I hope to be at Buxton in about three weeks & should be very glad to see any of my Liverpool friends there"; and yet again two years later, "Do you go into Derbyshire this year?" By February 1765 Josiah's involvement in Buxton would be such that he would attend a meeting at Monyash to settle a petition for a turnpike system linking Buxton to Bakewell, which, after passing through the important village of Longnor, where several packhorse trails met, would go thence to Leek and Newcastle-under-Lyme.

* * * * * * *

Buxton always created a great scramble for accommodation, and those residing, albeit temporarily, at The Hall or the Eagle and Child (another property belonging to the Duke of Devonshire) had the privilege of bathing at an earlier hour than those who came "from any other lodging house". This was probably met with a sigh of relief on occasion, because it was said that "some persons have been obliged to seek lodgings in neighbouring villages".

The baths, formed in the shape of an oblong, measured 30 ft from east to west and 15 ft wide. They were fed by a spring at the western end, with a flood gate "by means of which the water was let out" at the eastern end. The wall was built with limestone and appeared to be of 'rude' workmanship. On the outside it was covered with a strong cement which, according to one observer, was most probably designed to prevent the cold water mixing with the hot. The floor was formed with "plaister and appeared not to have fuffered any material injury from time". Strong oak beams were laid on top of the walls which were firmly connected together at the four corners. The whole had been converted into three baths. The first, for gentlemen, had been there from "time immemorial", but the ladies' was more modern. The third, appropriated later to the use of the poor, was probably created under Brian Hodgson's supervision. All three adjoined, but in "distinct apartments".

In the original gentlemen's bath the water rose on the south-east side out of a strata of limestone, however, in the other two it issued "through several seams in the floor". An estimated calculation suggested that all the springs together supplied water at a rate of 60 gallons each minute, sufficient to fill the original bath to a height of 5 ft in 50 minutes, but requiring 2 hours 50 minutes to fill all three. The bath water, considered to be transparent, sparkling and "highly grateful to the palate", had an almost constant temperature of 82 F.

The aforementioned observer also reported:

> "There is an inconvenience attending the gentleman's bath which it is more eafy to point out than to remedy. Thofe who make ufe of it, are obliged to drefs and undrefs in the bath room itself and all the time are expofed to the warm and moist air with which it is filled.
>
> Tho' the ladies bath is not subject to the inconvenience I have now mentioned, yet it will admit of improvement. If the dressing room opened directly into the bath room such an alteration would render it more fafe and commodious".

Despite these criticisms, conditions had vastly improved since the time of Celia Fiennes's visit in the late 17th century, as witnessed by her chronicles:

> " . . . there is no peace nor quiet with one Company coming and another going into the Bath or coming out; that makes so many strive to be in this house because the Bath is in it . . . there is 10 or 12 Springs that bubble up that are a little warme . . . and not a quick spring so that its not capable of being cleansed after every body has been in, its warme enough just to open the pores of ones body but not to cause sweat; I was in it and it made me shake, its farre from the heate that is in the Somersetshire Baths; its cover'd over the top, but not ceiled and there is an open place in the middle like a tunnell, which pours the cold down on your head; it would in my thoughts be better if it were exposed all to the aire and sunn; there is a pavement of stone on one side at the brim to walke on with benches of stone to sitt on; you must have a Guide that swims with you, you may stand in some place and hold by a chaine and the water is not above your neck, but in other parts very deep and strong, it will turn you down; about 10 or 12 yards distant is a spring called St. Anns Well which is for drinking, they have arch'd it up that its much hotter, it heates

the cup you take it up in . . . the taste is not unpleasant but rather like milk . . ."

Miss Fiennes's illuminating descriptions of accommodation difficulties, for example:

"if you have not Company enough of your own to fill a room they will be ready to put others into the same chamber, and sometymes they are so crowded that three must lye in a bed"

suggest a callous state of affairs. However, those of the 18th century, whilst appearing similarly horrendous, do seem to promote a greater semblance of decency apart from one small innuendo: Buxton was described as "a place for pleasure as well as health", a possible precursor to a remark included in a letter by one female writer who felt obliged to comment "by all accounts Buxton is a shocking place". Unfortunately she did not elucidate in what context the remark was made, but one has to give benefit of doubt and suggest that the statement was directed at conditions found to exist in some of the smaller houses.

A visitor, during the Hodgson tenure, described The Hall as:

" . . . a large, Modern, Freestone building one part as a parapet wall and lead cover, on which Noblemen and Gentlemen in fair weather kill time, when it hangs heavy upon their hands – Thro' a spacious Lobby leads to a Fleet of steps devided in the middle, which opens to the Bath . . . The Water is of a blood warm quantity, remarkably transparent, that a pin may be discovered at six Yds. distance. Several half pence lye at the bottom which are changed by the quality of the Water to the Colour of Silver . . . Near the Bath and the Well are fine Gravel walks through delightful avenues, by a neat Canal and fish pond."

* * * * * * *

Despite all the veracities or otherwise, Brian Hodgson's clientele must have provided him with a substantial income during the first four years of his tenancy because, on 26th November 1754 he was one of a trio who invested a considerable sum of money in the purchase of a large estate in Derbyshire. The estate, held under mortgage of £5,500 was part of the lands and manors of an important Leicestershire family called Boothby, and as Sir Thomas had died, it was incumbent upon the trustees to pay the interest due on the mortgage payments together with an annual annuity of £250 to the widow, Sarah. To assist the trustees, the trio of Brian Hodgson, Nicholas Twigg and George Goodwin paid an amount of £13,344 for "the absolute purchase" of the manor, lands, tenements, watercourses etc. including woods, mines and quarries. It is of interest to note that although 18th century Indentures appear pedantic in the recitation of numerous types of appurtenances which could be part of a property, yet it was essential to cover for every eventuality should a legal dispute subsequently arise; however, the inclusion of woods, quarries, mines and such like, in a general sense and not specifically named, were not usually included on deeds unless there was some evidence of their existence already, or a likelihood of the land being used accordingly. As both Nicholas Twigg and George Goodwin were members of prominent lead mining families in the Peak of Derbyshire, part of the estate must have been purchased for the intention of mineral exploitation. Much of the estate was tenanted, so an income of rents was already assured from the several properties inclusive of farms and dwelling-houses, but one property in Ashbourne itself was specifically mentioned as untenanted; this was a house and malt mill previously in the tenancy of John Taylor, father of Dr. Taylor, intimate friend of Samuel Johnson. This third share purchase of almost £4,500 by Brian Hodgson was certainly a considerable sum, and made at the time of his apparent loss of interest in the Chance Mine near Hartington village.

The next Hodgson business venture appears to have been the purchase of the land in Disley during 1757, with a view to developing coal pits; so at the time of his introduction to Charles Roe his business interests were consequential. On the other hand Charles's credentials, relative to a partnership in the copper trade, were equally imposing. He had a share in the large Macclesfield silk mill, his own mercantile business under the name of Chas. Roe & Co., mining interests at both Coniston and Alderley Edge, and his own smeltworks on Macclesfield Common. The great difference between the two was that Brian Hodgson had reserves and easily disposable assets, whereas any money Charles had accrued was well and truly tied up in all his business investments, to the extent that it was not possible for him to redeem the mortgage on his Chestergate property; but who was to know?

The most likely time for Brian Hodgson's entry into the partnership with Charles and Rowland Atkinson was during the year 1760, probably about the same time as the admittance of Cookson Atkinson during the month of October. The coal pits at Disley were never part of Chas. Roe & Co. but always owned by the Hodgson family; consequently purchases would be made by the one company from the other.

Charles continued to use the name Chas. Roe & Co., often abbreviated to Roe & Co.; it would have been foolish to adopt a new one, he had important contacts and was widely known, but as his own mercantile business diminished, the name came to represent the copper company. The original shares c. 1760 appear to have been in fourths, one each to Rowland Atkinson (38 years of age), Cookson Atkinson (21 years), Brian Hodgson (51 years) and Charles Roe (46 years).

Rowland Atkinson took no part in the running of the business and was an inactive, or to use a more modern expression, sleeping partner. He was already fully engaged in his endeavours to extend the curriculum of the Macclesfield Free Grammar School, which was so well managed by its Governors that it was the wealthiest in Cheshire. His desire was to appoint:

" . . . other persons to be under the directions of the Master to instruct the Scholars in Writing Accounts Mathematicks and Foreign Languages . . . and to allow such persons reasonable salaries out of the Revenues of the said School".

However an application to the Court of Chancery two years later (1st September 1762) was to produce an adverse judgement, as it was considered that the description of the Foundation by the Donor "comprehends no more than reading the Mother Tongue [English] and teaching the learned Languages [Latin and Greek]". The only way in which this arrangement could be altered was by means of a Private Bill through Parliament, which was not forthcoming until after Rowland Atkinson's death. His salary was increased to £100 per annum which suggests he took on additional duties. Unfortunately no record of the names of the Governors exists at this period, but without doubt Charles Roe was amongst them, upholding the Roe family tradition of encouraging education. He, more than anyone, knew the importance of "Writing Accounts and Mathematicks", imperative for success in the modern business world which was rapidly advancing; his name is included on the next available list of Governors some years later.

* * * * * * *

Amongst other family affairs were the deaths of two important personalities, almost within a year of each other. The first, in 1759, was that of the former headmaster of Stockport Grammar School, Rev. Joseph Dale, at the good age of 80 years. It is said that "Dale's ability and constant service were eloquently recorded" by the patrons of the school, the Goldsmiths Guild of London, in their Court Book on 25th April 1754. Dale had retired on 20th December 1750, but the property belonging to the Grammar School was in his tenure until 1752. His will, though complicated, reveals considerable wealth in the form of properties in Stockport and elsewhere, a bond of £8,000 placed out at interest with his son, Edward, and several household items. Most of this was probably due to inheritance and the remainder from very good business investments with his son; it was certainly not due to the remuneration received from any of his many duties within the church or school. He made several provisions for his widow and grandchildren, including Harry Lankford and his brother, Samuel Jnr. sons of Samuel Snr., who were to receive £200 each, one year after his wife's death. The bulk of the estate, of course, would be eventually settled on his eldest son, Edward. The proposed bequests could only take place if not "occasioned by the Misbehaviour and Misconduct of all and every one of them", a decision which he left dependent upon the judgement of two of his friends.

The second death was that of Samuel Lankford Snr. in the month of April 1760. His will, prepared in 1758, also contained several bequests, one or two of which directly affected Charles Roe's affairs. The most significant was that the Lankford share of the silk mill partnership "entered into with Mr. Charles Roe and Mr. John Robinson of Macclesfield" was to be given to his eldest son, Harry; there is no mention of any copper mining shares.

As Robinson had died early in 1756 (his position at St. Michael's taken by Charles's brother, James), in all probability his interest in the silk mill had been taken by his son, John, married in 1754 to Mary Burgess at Prestbury and later designated 'Button Merchant'.

Charles must have been far from happy with the Lankford arrangement, but he had to accept it. A father with a strong and powerful personality often spawns offspring who are weak and indecisive, as appears to be the case with Harry Lankford. Harry had attained the age of 21 years in 1756, and yet in spite of this, his father had not bought nor allowed him a share in any business enterprise, which suggests a lack of confidence in his son's ability to succeed. Nevertheless, he does seem to have given some encouragement towards Harry's independence because, having come of age, the young man took up residence in the hamlet of Mottram Andrew; a surprising choice.

During the war, the silk trade had, of course, been experiencing boom years; it was estimated that from 1752 to 1760, 140,000 bales of silk per annum had been imported through the Port of London from China, by the East India Company, and the partnership engaged in "the Trade or Business of Silk Throwsters, Merchants Dealers & partners by buying Raw and unmanufactured Silks and throwing and twisting the same and afterwards selling such Silks when thrown and also by buying Silks and selling the same again" would have obtained considerable benefit from this importation. Charles, able to rely upon the judgement and experience of Samuel Snr. and his capability of undertaking many responsibilities for the silk business, could direct his own concentration and energies in the promotion of his copper interests, an absolute necessity at this time; but now, this sudden change of personalities left much to be desired, placing extra pressures and anxieties on his already overburdened shoulders; however, his discernment of priorities never faltered, and whilst the silk trade was in the ascendant, he must have thought that Samuel Glover and partners could play an inconspicuous role in monitoring the day to day business of the silk mills.

Also under the terms of Samuel Lankford's will, his younger son, Samuel, was to receive property in the parish of Sheen, Staffordshire, (which was actually from the marriage settlement of his father's first wife, upon her first marriage to the Vicar of Sheen's son) together with the sum of £3,000. The remainder of the estate was left to Harry, and in the event of his death, further provisions were stipulated.

The estate at Brassington is not specifically mentioned and must have been accounted for in the marriage settlement between Lankford's daughter, Elizabeth and Charles Roe, (which is included in the will) so in effect Charles would hold this estate in trust for his three surviving children from that marriage, Catherine, William and Samuel, and still retain the use of it.

Samuel Lankford nominated both his sons, Harry and Samuel, as Executors, but Harry, feeling unshackled at last, burst forth with a vengeance, determined to demonstrate his independence to the world. His first action was solely to prove his father's will, and then he "possessed himself of the said estate" executing a bond with interest in favour of his brother, Samuel. Poor Samuel, caught totally unawares, was to wait for some considerable time before being able to recoup his inheritance. Harry now had the means to marry well, and on 20th June 1761 he married Sarah, the eldest daughter of John Stafford, in the Parish Church of Prestbury. Sarah was just a few months younger than her husband.

In order to accommodate them, John Stafford took an unusual step; not long after the marriage, on 12th October 1761, the orphan, Elizabeth Blagg, then 21 years of age, signed a deed confirming that from 1st December of that year the Fence Estate would be surrendered to John Stafford "that he might be perfect tenant of the premises". He, in turn, allowed Harry and Sarah to live there, but under what terms is not known; Elizabeth should have been recompensed in some way.

Because of John Stafford's work for the Earl of Derby, he had built up many important contacts over the years in Liverpool, and it does seem as though Elizabeth was treated as a member of the family and taken to the town on several occasions. There she met a prominent Liverpool merchant, Thomas Smyth, whose grandfather had been Lord Bishop of Limerick, and whose father, also Thomas, third son of the Bishop, had been a member of the Middle Temple at the same time as Elizabeth's uncle, Edward Blagg of Hurdsfield. The Smyth residence and business premises were on Paradise Street in Liverpool, and after their marriage on 19th December 1762, also at Prestbury Parish Church, Elizabeth moved to that town. They became an important part of Liverpool society, yet were to make many visits to Macclesfield over the next few years and, due to a strange quirk of fate, would find themselves residing in Fence House in their old age; but much was to happen in the meantime.

A letter exists dated 20th March 1760, just prior to Samuel Lankford Snr.'s death, and at the time when Harry was living in Mottram Andrew. The writer, John Rotton of Duffield, had entered into partnership with John Gilbert-Cooper in his smeltworks at Denby and was also connected with the copper rolling mills in Derby, using ores from the Duke of Devonshire's mine at Ecton Hill on the Staffordshire border. The addressee was a Robert Shore of Snitterton near Matlock, a person of some repute in the lead mining community of the Low Peak of Derbyshire:

"Sir,
 I wrote to Mr. Lankford & aquainted him with what you mention'd to me, & yesterday I received a letter from his Son who informs me that his Father is very Ill, but as soon as he is better he will come over, and we will then waite on you in order to Settle the Affaire you talk't to me about . . .".

The three individuals were probably known to each other because of the connection with the Duke of Devonshire's mine at Ecton Hill. But what the 'affair' was, which involved them, remains a mystery. It is more than likely that Robert Shore was the baby baptised in the principal church of Derby, All Saints (today Derby Cathedral) on 30th October 1735, and named after his father; this suggests they lived close to the silk mill. As he grew up Robert became a book-keeper. He would have been familiar with the lead brought from the smelt mills in the Matlock area and carted through the town on its way to Wilne Ferry, for transportation by river to Hull, which must have inspired him to seek a position within the mining community in the Wapentake of Wirksworth.

The story returns to Mottram Andrew where, not far from the parish boundary, on Alderley Edge Charles Roe's men were busy reworking the mines. Until recently it has always been assumed that the mineral veins of Alderley continued somewhat abatedly into the parish of

Mottram St. Andrew, but it is now known that a geological fault runs between the two. In the 18th century the three parishes of Mottram Andrew, Over Alderley and Nether Alderley contained several halls; many still exist today as farmhouses. A significant number, including Mottram Hall already mentioned, were occupied by Dissenting families; not really surprising when one considers that the Cromwellian General, William Brereton, had lived close by at Handforth near Wilmslow. These families, such as the Mottersheads, in addition to their farms had become deeply involved in the mohair, linen and silk trade, particularly in the production of buttons. From the late 17th century onwards, due to the general increase in affluence, the old Elizabethan buildings were being replaced or modernised with the use of bricks, stones or slates, and it was often the result of quarrying which revealed mineral veins, causing speculative bursts of activity from small groups within the area.

Such was the situation around Alderley where several deeds mention in a general way mines and quarries. One in particular for Lowerhouse (farm), belonging to Thomas Mottershead, with land adjacent to the Mottram Hall Estate, is dated as early as 1675. Another for a messuage in Mere near Knutsford, by the name of Hough Hall, dated 1717, actually mentions "Lead, Copper, Coal, Ironstone & Limestone . . ." One of the persons concerned in leasing the Hall was Nathaniel Hough of the City of London, Clerk, and one of the lives used was John Hough of St. Andrews, Devonshire Street, London, apothecary. It is very tempting to believe that at this early date they were connected with the Hough Level in the Alderley Edge mine, later to be reworked by Charles Roe's men, especially as a John Hough was managing an estate somewhere in Over Alderley and overseeing the mines on behalf of Thomas Crosse and the London merchants at the time of the 1696 dispute. Perhaps Nathaniel, clerk, and John, apothecary, were in some way related to the overseer.

It has not been possible to locate the Hall in which Harry Lankford lived, but the choice in Mottram at that period is somewhat limited, and one wonders if it was Mottram Old Hall itself which was under lease. The present mines of Mottram, near the Kirkleyditch quarry, lie contiguous with what were boundary lines of 18th century estates, and one of them is definitely on land originally part of the Mottram Hall estate. This, of course, could have been worked later by Yate and Clayton. Evidence strongly suggests that Samuel Lankford Snr., seeing his former son-in-law's success in the Alderley mines, began speculating in Mottram and found some lead and copper, leaving son Harry resident on site.

Just a short distance away, over the hill and on the other side of the Stanley estate was Heaward Hall, owned by William Fallows until his death. It can be no coincidence that his son, William, lived in Derby and attended Derby All Saints church and must have been known to the Shore family. Robert Shore at this time was possibly attending to some business on behalf of the Denby partnership in connection with the ores received from Ecton Hill, but the expiration of the lease was imminent in October, 1760 and the Duke of Devonshire had made it clear that he had every intention of working the mines on his own behalf. Having heard that lead and copper had been found in Mottram, could Robert Shore possibly have been intent on managing the prospective business on behalf of the Lankfords? A recommendation from John Rotton would certainly not have gone amiss, or some arrangement by which he could work for both establishments at the same time. In the event Samuel Lankford Snr. died the following month and Harry's first priority was his marriage; the reason for his removal to Fence House is difficult to deduce, unless someone else, anxious to carry out trials, had offered him generous compensation for the lease in Mottram.

On the expiration of the Ecton lease, the 4th Duke of Devonshire took over the mines and appointed a new agent to supervise the whole proceedings; this was none other than Robert Shore of Snitterton near Matlock.

* * * * * * *

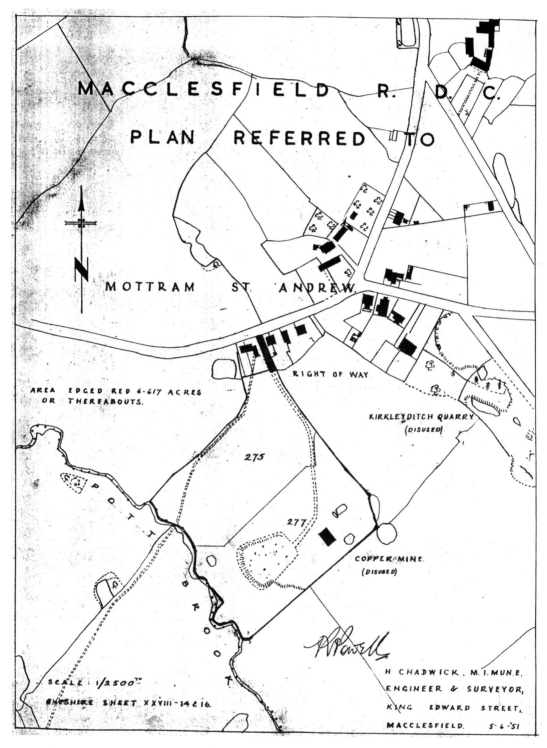

Plan showing position of copper mine in Mottram St. Andrew courtesy of Macclesfield Borough Council.

Robert Shore must have been very proud of his new appointment; William, 4th Duke of Devonshire, was a prominent Whig politician, Lord Lieutenant of Ireland (as his father had been when promoting Handel's Irish tour), and in the early months of the war, from November 1756 to May 1757, although only nominally, had been Prime Minister of England.

Chatsworth House, home of the Devonshire family for several generations and originally built by Bess of Hardwick, had been subjected to extensive alterations, particularly by the 1st Duke, a direct descendant of the famous lady. The 4th Duke, more interested in the expansive park and garden and the view from his windows than the house itself, commissioned the architect, James Paine, to build new stables together with a bridge across the newly altered river course. He also desired the famous landscape gardener, Lancelot (Capability) Brown, to rid the park of the 1st Duke's formal garden, replacing it with a more natural and romantic look. The profits from Ecton copper mine would contribute considerably towards the expenditure of such a scheme.

The 4th Duke began to take a more critical look at his business affairs, and on discovering some anomalies, became embroiled in two important disputes.

The first was in connection with a productive lead mine called Portaway in the Liberty of Winster, for which an ancestor of the Duke's had obtained a lease of mineral rights from the Crown. The Duke together with several others, amongst whom was Nicholas Twigg (third share owner of the Boothby estate with Brian Hodgson and George Goodwin), Anthony Tissington (associate of Charles Roe and original shareholder in Coniston mine) and Philip Gell (chemist and associate of Josiah Wedgwood), were partners and proprietors of the Portaway mine. The Crown, or in this instance, the 4th Duke as lessee, was entitled to receive a duty called Lott and Cope which, in the Liberty of Winster, was every 13th dish of Bing and Peazy only, considered as Lott; and 4d.(old pence) for each load of all ore, known as Cope. The grading of ore was as follows:

Bing: the richest part of the ore, separated out by the women and made merchantable and fit for smelting by using a chipping hammer only.

Peazy: the remaining ore buddled to remove earth, clay etc. then bucked into small pieces and placed in a sieve for further washing in a "Vatt or Vessel filled with Water". A riddle was next used, having holes of a certain size, and the pieces remaining in the riddle were termed Peazy but those which passed through the sieve were known as Smytham.

The last and fourth grade was Belland which, until the 1730s, had not been worth retrieving from the waste and rubbish, but a new method of washing, buddling and cleansing had been discovered which had made recovery of part of this ore worthwhile.

The 4th Duke challenged his partners, insisting that he was being denied his full payment of Lott, because the Peazy was being beaten so fine by the buckers that most of it was passing through the riddle. A litigation transpired and, although the miners argued that it was not worth the time and energy to pulverise the ore more than was necessary, the Duke won his case early in 1760. Thus prompted, he now turned his attention to Ecton Hill, where his auditor discovered that the Cope had never been collected during the lifetime of the Duke's father. His legal advisers were divided on this issue, and whether or not the Duke succeeded in recovering the duty is not known. It is strange that it had taken him so long to put 'his own house in order', because little more than two years earlier, through his parliamentary connections, he had offered assistance to the Earl of Powis, who had bid for a lead mine, Esgair-mwyn, situated to the south-east of the coastal town of Aberystwyth, near the shores of Llyn Teifi. It was a similar situation to that of the Portaway mine, except the Crown did not lease out the mineral rights and therefore was entitled to the duty and not Lord Powis. Competition for the mine had been strong and the Earl had to guarantee half the ore as duty to obtain the lease.

It could have been concern within the Treasury over the high percentage of ore payable as duty, and the apparent paucity of it, that alerted someone to have a discreet 'invigilation' carried out. The Duke, active in government, was an excellent adjunct in such a situation. He sent John Roose of Cromford to Central Wales, the skillful and superior miner upon whose judgement and abilities the Duke had often relied in the superintending of his own mining interests. This was a man who could be trusted, and the Duke's faith was soon rewarded.

* * * * * * *

On 1st December 1757 a letter was written to the Earl of Powis at Powis Castle near Welshpool from the nearby town of Montgomery. The writer, John Paynter, by an agreement between the Duke of Devonshire and Lord Powis, was allowed to work at the mine "to Instruct . . . Agents and Miners in the Business". Heavy rain could not be prevented from flooding the works and a temporary stoppage was inevitable so, having put pen to paper, Paynter proposed to visit the Earl, and had already begun his journey. He was obviously in a panic; his letter continued with information obtained from a working associate and friend of John Roose at the mine, "Mr. Roose is gone to London . . . to complain that Yr. Lordship does not get so much ore as you might do and that the King's Interest has been neglected . . . The Duke of Devonshire has sent to London for a copy of the Grant & has taken Counsel's opinion upon it" . . . Paynter referred to drunken miners and villians that had been dismissed for thieving, but it is difficult to decide whether he was alluding to the miners who were already employed at the mine or those sent from Derbyshire to help. He continued somewhat ambiguously, "I have, of late, been the more surprised at this sort of Behaviour, because I take all opportunities of shewing a Civility to Mr. Roose as being an Agent to some of My Lord Duke's Family".

Whatever the period one learns that as a general rule it is inadvisable to accept letters, or indeed any form of literature, at face value, without first obtaining some knowledge of the author, if at all possible. In this case, information gleaned from other sources, reveals John Paynter as an unreliable and devious character.

His career had begun in North Wales on the estate of Penrhyn close to "the little city of" Bangor. The estate had been in possession of the Williams family at the end of the seventeenth century when, probably due to marriage settlements, it had been divided between Gwen and Anne by their father Sir Robert; both these ladies made very interesting marriages.

Gwen became espoused to Sir Walter Yonge, 3rd. bart. M.P. for Honiton in Devon and one of the Commissioners of Customs, but he had died on 17th July 1731, so the half share of the estate passed eventually to their grandson, George, upon the death of his father, Sir William, in 1755. George, also M.P. for Honiton from 1754 was destined to become one of the Lords of the Admiralty (1766-1770) and Master of the Mint (July 1794-February 1799); the latter reflecting his mining interests in both the south-west of England and North Wales.

Anne married Thomas Warburton of Winnington, Cheshire who was a younger half brother to Sir Peter Warburton of Arley Hall; and again there is no escaping the important mining connections within the family. Sir Peter's mother was a daughter of Sir Thomas Myddleton of Chirk Castle just to the north of Oswestry, a family whose name was synonymous primarily with lead mining but also with silver. In the early seventeenth century the Myddletons could boast of their Lord Mayor of London, Sir Thomas, who held the lease of The Mines Royal and made very important contributions to mining. Sir Peter himself, had married Martha, heiress of Thomas Dockwra of Hertfordshire, a member of a famous copper smelting family. The Dockwra Copper Company had been established in 1692 along the banks of the River Mousley near Esher in Surrey. Brass was also produced using Swedish copper, and a wire factory set up for the important pin making trade. Finally Sir Peter's granddaughter, Diana, married Sir Richard Grosvenor whose ancestor and namesake had received a grant from King Charles I in 1634, as a consequence of which he had become possessor of the most valuable tract of lead mining property in Wales, extending from Holywell through Halkin Mountain to Minera.

In 1736 John Paynter completed the first of his account books for Penrhyn as agent to the Warburton family. Twelve more were to follow up to and including the year 1744, correctly kept to all appearances. But on 12th October 1742 John Paynter had started complaints against the last three agents of Vaenol, an estate situated immediately south of Bangor which had connections with Penrhyn. It comprised Vaenol House and grounds adjacent to the small port of Dinorwic, and lands stretching inland up the magnificent Llanberis Pass to the waters of Llyn Padarn and the village of Llanberis, an area described some years later by the traveller, Henry Shrine, as "extremely pleasant, being interspersed with various gentle acclivities (gaps) which formed the entrance to as many wooded vallies, and penetrated in sight into the hollows of those high impending mountains which hid Snowdon from our view".

The estate was shortly to pass into the hands of Thomas Assheton. The Assheton family, a very old Lancashire family from Middleton, a little to the north-east of Manchester, were comparable to the Clayton family of Little Harwood near Blackburn. By the18th century they were established in many areas and Thomas (Snr.), resident at Bowden in Cheshire, not too far distant from Macclesfield, had married Harriet the daughter of the Rt. Hon. John Smith, Speaker of the House of Commons, whose estate was at South Tedworth in Hampshire. Harriet's brother, Captain William Smith, inherited his father's Hampshire estate and lands in Caernarvonshire including Vaenol, but on his death, having no heir, these passed to Thomas (Jnr.) son of his sister Harriet who, because of legalities, took the surname Smith together with the estates and henceforth was known as Thomas Assheton Smith. Before this occurred, however, John Paynter had made an abrupt exit from the Penrhyn estate as witnessed by a letter from the new agent, Robert Bridge, to Mrs. Warburton in Chester on 7th November 1745.

At the commencement of his duties, Bridge discovered that Paynter had bequeathed him a bundle of iron hoops, an oak table, lumber not worth 20/- and money missing from the accounts of £880. He had made an effort to meet Paynter but the latter "had left towards Cheshire". Nothing further is known of Paynter's actual activities until his presence at Esgairmwyn in the employ of Lord Powis during the late 1750s.

About the same time as the 4th Duke of Devonshire was showing concern regarding the lead mine in 1757, another local employee, Lewis Morris, had written to Lord Powis concerning bad management at the mine by the duo John Paynter and John Ball, which he claimed was to the detriment of both the Crown and Lord Powis, thus supporting the findings of John Roose. At some time after this episode Paynter appears to have been offering his services to the Myddleton family of Chirk Castle, and his delightful self-recommendation is beyond comment. He wrote that he had once received income of £1,400 per annum and had been offered by Sir Robert Walpole the position of his secretary as Chancellor of the Exchequer but due to Sir Robert's downfall had decided to seek a future abroad. He was then appointed Governor of the Cape Coast or Fort St. James, but Mr. Corbett had asked for his assistance on his Cheshire estate for a few days, after which he had become involved in a lead mine and was "swindled".

It is surprising that John Paynter, styled "principal director of His Majesty's mine at Esgairmwyn" managed to retain this post until his death in 1772, the same year as the death of Lord Powis; but the Earl, like many of his fellow peers, was caught up in the web of government and spent a considerable length of time away from his Welsh estate, especially in London. He had inherited the estate from a distant cousin, so his dedication and knowledge were possibly somewhat limited, particularly on the question of whose judgement and information could be trusted. Whilst the 'machinery' of the large estate purported to be of adequate ability for its survival, it seemed a better option to leave well alone rather than interfere and disturb what relative efficiency remained. The Duke of Devonshire, on the other hand, had no such qualms, his family had been involved in their estates for several generations, passing down information from father to son, and their retainers likewise, so he never hesitated to make adjustments when necessary.

The year 1761 was significant in many respects, beginning with the death of John Roose, whose position at Esgair-mwyn was eagerly sought by John Ball. His letter to Lord Powis on 28th May also included the information "Paynter's leg is in a bad way", no doubt a situation which was used to good effect by Paynter in an attempt to hold onto his position. The death of John Roose meant that the Duke of Devonshire had lost an excellent retainer; the work of supervising the weighing of ore at Esgair-mwyn had only been subsidiary to his main employment with the 4th Duke, and as his home had always remained at Bonsall in Derbyshire, he must have undertaken many arduous journeys to and from the lead mine in Central Wales. As recently as 1760, when the Ecton mine lease was reaching termination, John Roose had carried out a survey, drawn a plan of the workings and on 21st April set down calculations of the number of dishes of ore for the Duke. Four months later, on 26th August, John Rotton, writing from his home in Duffield to the Duke, advised him that Mr. Twigg "thinks Mr. Roose will not be able to go down into the Mine at Ecton to Value the things there therefore (if he is not) beg you will send someboddy Else to meet Mr. Twigg to settle things next week". Perhaps John Roose was already feeling unwell, although he does not seem to have made a will, however, his time spent in Central Wales is significant because he would communicate the state of mining in that area to his associates and family in Derbyshire.

The Duke of Devonshire was not the only one to be experiencing mining problems, as Charles Roe was soon to discover.

* * * * * * *

After the death of Sir William Fleming of Rydal Hall in the Lake District during 1757, the estate had passed to his young son, Sir Michael, 4th Bart. who was only eight years of age; this had complicated matters because of the involvement of guardians, one of whom was the powerful character Sir James Lowther, Earl of Lonsdale, who, because of a by-election in April of that year, had been returned as a Whig M.P. for Cumberland.

At the Coniston mine a routine had been established with ore weighed at fairly regular intervals, usually four times a year and, presumably to accommodate the smooth running of the estate, payments made on account. Dr. Atkinson paid £50 on 10th May 1760 relating to the year 1759, and made two further payments of £25 and £50 on the 13th and 27th 1762 respectively, for the year 1760, and again in April of that year for 1760/61 of £55. It remained difficult physically to move money around the country, so the most logical arrangement would be for Dr. Atkinson to pay sufficient expenses on site to cover for his son's share of the partnership.

During 1760 ore had been quickly dispatched for Macclesfield in consignments of approximately 20 to 30 tons each month. It was inevitable that due to obstacles en route, such as inclement weather, the passage of ore up the River Weaver was not as consistent as at the beginning of the journey, nevertheless, by 12th December 1760 in total 360 tons of copper ore had been recorded in the River Weaver toll books from the commencement of mining at Coniston. This poses an important question, altogether only 312 tons had actually been weighed at the mine up to December 1760, and although the weighing of ore at one location might not have been as accurate as at another, yet the slight discrepancies which might have occurred during 1759/60 are not likely to account for the whole of the additional 48 tons of ore which came up the river, particularly as the difference becomes even more pronounced as time passes. It seems most unlikely that this ore was on account of Thomas Patten, because it would have been illogical for him to have allowed unsmelted ore to travel all the way to Cheadle in Staffordshire, as it was more economical to smelt it at Bank Quay, Warrington and then transfer it as pigs. Only one conclusion can be drawn: there was another source of copper ore for the Macclesfield smelter.

Although the additional copper ore would not have been destined for Cheadle, the consignments of calamine on the River Weaver must have been. There had been insufficient time for Charles Roe to have established a brass works, (although he soon began to realise that to make any progress at all in the copper industry, this was essential) and in any event the calamine consignments abruptly ceased on 1st July 1760; presumably due to the availability of further supplies for the Cheadle works from the Bonsall area of Derbyshire.

Meanwhile, on site at Coniston, with Sir William gone and Sir James Lowther otherwise engaged, one or two retainers were taking matters into their own hands. Dr. Atkinson endeavoured as much as possible to keep control of things and to work in a responsible way with the estate employees, but it was not always possible. In the first instance it was difficult to find adequate accommodation for some of the miners, and as the lease of the old Quaker partnership for the iron forge had ceased in 1757, Dr. Atkinson sent workmen to view the forge in order to estimate the amount of "putting it into proper condition for lodgings for ye Work people". The forge houses had already been leased by Tissington & Co. from 1757 for some of their workmen, but on 12th September 1759 the company, busily employed elsewhere in the area, acquired mining rights at Tilberthwaite from Sir John Pennington and withdrew from mining at Coniston, leaving the forge houses to be taken over by Roe & Co. They abandoned tools on site worth £40, which Charles Roe's men were able to use, and Anthony Tissington sold his $^{13}/_{24}$th share of the mine to Roe & Co. for which Mr. Hale made out a receipt and took over the accounts. Dr. Atkinson appreciated that if the lease of the forge houses had been available from 1757, then the forge itself was also available for leasing. On receipt of the workmen's report he wrote from his house in Kendal on 2nd June 1760 to the Chief Steward of the estate, John Moore, who was in charge of keeping all the account books, and pointed out that £50 expenses would cover for the conversion, thus providing the estate with workmen's rents of £6 to £7 per annum.

John Moore in turn wrote to his assistant steward, Michael Knott, enquiring about the termination of the 1735 lease of which he knew nothing. Michael Knott also had no knowledge of it "I cannot remember that ever I heard Old Sr. Wm. Fleming name it, or that I have seen any writings relative thereto. . ." but he did enquire of Lady Fleming, who confirmed that she held the lease and schedule for the forge. By this time it was the end of October and with winter approaching all were anxious to settle the matter, so John Moore sent his son to see Lady Fleming and retrieve the necessary documents. Immediately upon their receipt, he wrote to the agent of the Quaker partnership ". . . I find the lessees were to keep the forge in sufficient repair and deliver it up as such at the end of the term. Now I take it for granted, the gentlemen are very sensible that part of the lease has not been performed . . ." He suggested meeting on site on the 2nd November to settle the matter. It would seem that the matter was never properly settled because the forge was eventually dismantled in 1766, but repair bills exist for which there is good reason to suppose that they relate to the houses (originally a hammermen's house and two coal houses) and that they were kept in reasonable condition.

After John Moore's efforts to resolve the problem of the forge in 1760, what can only been seen as retaliation by James Dixon, the man appointed "to the Office of my Bailiff untill I shall Appoint another" by Sir William Fleming "to make Distrefs as often as there shall be Occasion . . ." took place. Dixon, amongst others, began a campaign of harassment on the unsuspecting miners until finally they 'downed tools' and started on their journey home. Fortunately they were stopped at Kendal by Dr. Atkinson who listened to their tales of woe and persuaded them to return to the mine. When Charles Roe heard the news he was furious.

Sir William's death had caused concern regarding the Coniston lease, but Mr. Atkinson (possibly Cookson) had been assured by Sir James Lowther that the lease, effected between Sir William, Charles Roe and Rowland Atkinson, would be honoured. Charles now took the opportunity to advise John Moore by letter on 10th October 1761 of this guarantee and at the same time give vent to his feelings regarding the intolerable situation. His awkward and abrupt style was an obvious embarrassment to him, but he forced himself to say what needed to be said, after all his future, that of his family and many others depended on it. By nature Charles was not a gambling man, but at this time he had reached deep into his resources and financially there was no room for manoeuvre. He would not wish to upset his relationship with Brian Hodgson at the very outset of the partnership by showing any indications of failure or an inability to handle the situation, so despite awareness of his somewhat incoherent style, his pride and determination took over, resulting in the apparent boldness of the letter:

" Sir, I rece'd yors & Acknowledge the favour to all the partners not only for that, but in any Instances you have shewn of yr Good Wishes to our Undrtaking. I can't say but [that] We are much more Satisfied of our Safety as to the lease, as Mr. Atkinson inform'd Us of Sr James's firm promise to Him, that We shd Enjoy it as it now stands, [and] for my part I think Us as safe undr Sr James's promise, as if a fresh Instrumt [lease] had been made, which is the Reason [why] you see Us after having laid out a very large Sume [of money] to have Enter'd on that Expensive Sough & probably may of [start] Another without wch the Mine never can Answer, undr the best Managemt upon Earth, We find the Upper Works won't do, all our hopes are in the Undr Ones; but We shd go on wth cheerfullness to make a perfect Tryal, if We cou'd keep our Workmen Quietly [contented], in this. We have been interrupted greatly, & part[icular]ly of late, by Dixon. Now a stop must be put to this, Cost what it will, & Were We certain [that] the Mine wou'd Answer [contain copper ore] when the Sough is up [finished], upon wch all depends, We shd not mind Spendg a Hundred or two on him [presumably payment on account for ore to be weighed], but being Oblig'd to do it now, when that and all is at hazard, bears hard upon Us, & your & Sr James's Influence on the neighbourhd, Dixon in particulr, wd be kind to Us, but [also] Absolutely necessary to Sr Michal's Interest, let Us succeed or not at the Mine, yet I hope On our own Acct, Our Conduct & Expenses considered, Sr. James will look on Us as having done for the Interest of ye Minor [young Sir Michael], what the Tisingtons (or I believe any other) wou'd not Venture to do, but Sold to us first [the $^{13}/_{24}$th share] rather than do it. The reason is plain that Dixon must be Trounced by Us, or some One, Or the Mine given Up, & I firmly believe if Doctor Atkinson had not stop'd the Men at Kendall, All had been Over wth the Mine – for had these Men told such dismall Stories Amongst their neighbrs [? in Derbyshire] – (e.g.) that they were continually threatned wth being sent for Soldiers, transportd, took up as Vagrants, & that they had been Servd wth Warrants & forcd on that Acct from yir Work before the justices, etc. etc. & [had to] go to Lancaster [Assizes], in this Case the Mine might have Stood Unwrought, & Our Money have been Sunk, for it would have been impossible to perswade any more hands to come there, & who then wou'd have Enter'd on it Again in such Circumsts. Being in haste I am Oblig'd to Conclude – with thanks for yr Letter & all favours, in desiring Yr Assistance on Occasn
I am Sir Yr very h(umb)le Servt."

Ironically, what the miners did not know was that whilst they were employed they would not be conscripted into the army, only unemployed ones were, and therefore they stood in grave danger of being enlisted by the very fact that they had run away from the mine. It would also seem that some of their Quaker pacifist neighbours were likewise unaware of the facts. Miners were a necessity in any army; the Board of Ordnance had the responsibility of providing a train composed of artillery equipment, spare gun carriages, ammunition carts and wagons, pontoons and their carriages, wagons for artillery and engineer stores and finally specialist vehicles. One of the latter was a tumbril i.e. a two-wheeled cart drawn by two horses and used to carry the tools of the pioneers and miners. The pioneers were there to mend roads, whilst the company of miners used their skills and abilities as appropriate and were the fore-runners of today's Royal Engineers.

With the Coniston miners safely back at work Charles Roe's attention was once more anxiously focused on the Macclesfield copper works. With successful smelting underway the time was approaching for expansion, and he must have been contemplating the setting up of brass works, without which his copper production was for a limited market only. This was again a comparable situation to that of the silk mill, only this time any enlargement of premises would be on common ground not private, and therefore seen as an encroachment. Charles, desirous as always to have the law on his side, must have been the imperceptible party to "Proposals for Inclosing Macclesfield Comons" instigated in 1761. A note thereon stated:

> "The Earl of Harrington as Lefsee of the King is Lord of the Manor and as such is intitiled to the Soil and all Mines and Minerals therein – And Note the Herbage has time out of mind been claimed and enjoyed by the Freemen of the Borough or Corporation of Macclesfield and the Freeholders in Comon without Suit or limitation."

It was proposed that $1/7$th of the land be allocated to Lord Harrington together with his retention of mines and minerals (except stone). The other important item was "That the Cottages & Incroachments be confirmed to the present pofsefsors".

Amongst the remaining proposals was one for ensuring that all profits made out of the residue of the waste or common lands were to be held by Trustees, and an annuity of £50 paid to the prime curate "whose present certain provision is but about £40 per annum". The prime curate was, of course, Rev. James Roe, and in view of all these initial proposals, it would be impossible for Charles not to have been involved, or indeed not to have been the main instigator of the scheme. He, for once, kept a low profile whilst John Stafford was, as usual, 'at the helm', with the Earl of Harrington happily complying with the requirements of his designated role as mediator.

The Earl, whose home was the beautiful Elvaston estate of over 200 acres of woods and parkland on the outskirts of Derby, now ranked Lt. General in the army, wrote to his fellow officer, General Cholmondeley, to advise him of the suggested enclosure. They were distantly related and had both served at the Battle of Fontenoy in the Austrian Netherlands during the spring of 1745 where, despite the fact that the Earl of Harrington had distinguished himself, the Duke of Cumberland's army had been defeated. The troops had then received an urgent recall to England to intercept Bonnie Prince Charlie and his forces on their advance towards Derby.

John Stafford, Charles Roe and other interested parties must have judged that both William Stanhope and James Cholmondeley were dedicated to their military careers and as such had outgrown their interest in small town politics. The Earl, true to his eccentric nature, was quite oblivious of his rights or otherwise on Macclesfield Common and was only too happy to help in whatever way he could for the good of all – as it was presented to him, of course. General Cholmondeley had no imperial desires in Macclesfield; the vast Cholmondeley estates in Cheshire, Ireland and elsewhere were under the control of his brother, George 3rd. Earl. James was a widower with no children, so his substantial land holdings in the town would pass to his brother's family upon his death, and a few more acres on Macclesfield Common would not make much difference either way.

But despite General Cholmondeley's acquiesence, his Chester solicitor held a different view and, being confined with a cold, the solicitor immediately sent his son to Macclesfield to make enquiries. The son reported that the Cholmondeley tenants were ignorant of the proposals so he "applied to Mr. Stafford to know on what Plan the Scheme was laid". John Stafford informed him "that Mr Grey Lord Harrington's agent had had a Meeting or two with him and some others in the Town . . ." to which the solicitor retorted that General Cholmondeley "ought to have been acquainted with the Intention of this Inclosure" and the principal tenants given notice to attend a meeting "in order to put the Inclosing the Comons on a fair footing". His main argument was that Lord Harrington had no estate in Macclesfield and as "upwards of 300 Cheshire acres of Land" was involved together with mineral rights, he would gain more benefit than General Cholmondeley who owned "near a fourth part of the whole Land in Macclesfield". Furthermore the agents of both the Earls of Derby and Courtown had no knowledge of the scheme, neither had it been possible to visit Mr. Pickford who "lives at New Castle under Lime", an obvious error which should have read Ashton-under-Lyne. The Cholmondeley tenants were found to be against the proposition and after talking with Lord Harrington's agent, the young man concluded that the Earl had wished to sound out the reactions of General Cholmondeley before making the scheme public.

The warning bells had sounded and by July 1762 nothing was resolved; the General having asked his solicitor "to meet the agents of the other Gentlemen who may be affected by Lord Harrington inclosing the Common", and let him know "what others who have any property intend to do" and if there was to be no disadvantage to either himself or his tenants he "would be glad to oblige his Lordship", left the matter in his attorney's hands. His reasonable and accommodating attitude seems to have bewildered and perplexed the solicitor who took great pains to reiterate all the legal implications, but as the attorney "had not heard a syllable . . . if any meeting intended to be held or by whom" and no bill was ever presented to Parliament, the whole plan seems to have died a natural death. From the onset the obstacles seemed unsurmountable but Charles was becoming a worried man and at this stage in his life, his eagerness to succeed seems to have clouded his judgement to some extent, appearing to give rise to the philosophy "the end justifies the means". He had no option but to continue seeking alternatives in the hope that, having kept the courage of his convictions, his aspirations in some way would finally be realised.

The situation regarding ore supplies had, to a great extent, already been alleviated by the fact that as soon as Ecton copper mine was out of lease in 1760 a system of ticketing had been established, similar to that of Cornwall, and Roe & Co. were able to bid for ore alongside "Thomas Patten Esq." and "Messrs. Cooper & Co." (of Denby). Over the next few years this would prove to be the most important source of copper ore for the Macclesfield smelter as hundreds of tons would be carried, either by long trains of packhorses (known as jags) or later possibly waggons, over moors set in a landscape thick with peat, until they reached Macclesfield Common. It is not known which route they would have taken. An Act of 1759 had included the widening and improving of the 12 mile stretch of road (A 537) between Buxton and Macclesfield, which would be turnpiked from 1762. However, to avoid paying charges the jags may have taken an old trail via Flash Bottom and Sutton Common, but this would have been dangerous during winter months when deep snow was often experienced.

Whichever route was taken, the prospect of Black Road and the smelter coming into view on Macclesfield Common, must have been most welcome as the beasts of burden made their final approach. Their arrival would be greeted with a bustle of activity as pannier after pannier was emptied of its ore.

The heaps of ore, from which ever source, must have been protected in some way, because long exposure to weathering, particularly heavy rain, could rob them of a percentage of the precious metal; especially vulnerable were those which might contain a small proportion of silver. This was particularly emphasized by Emanuel Swedenborg in his *Regnum Minerale* published in 1734, when he wrote:

". . . in some places the heap is covered by dampened mineral dust . . . if not reinforced by a cover; for if rain had seeped down into the heap, it was discovered that the stone was, as it were, corroded by the rain water and that the metal itself was suffering loss . . . also in these circumstances the metal becomes molten with extreme difficulty".

The copper ores from Ecton Mine proved to be reasonably rich (although they did not contain silver) having an average copper content of 15% in the 18th century, almost double that of Coniston. Some early19th century findings reported at least 40% in some parts but this has been disputed. A fascinating blend of minerals lay deep within the hill. As at Coniston the dominant one was the brassy chalcopyrite, but in the lower levels vivid streaks of blue azurite and green malachite were found interspersed with deposits of galena (lead) and the white or colourless crystalline rock, calcite. This variety of minerals created many beautiful formations including crystal-lined cavities, and several superb specimens were retrieved from the Ecton mines.

The first two lots of ore purchased by Roe & Co. were on 12th February 1761. Altogether eight lots were purchased that year totally 213 tons 13 cwts. the last being on the 1st October. Out of these only two lots were annotated as from the Starr shaft, a level of slightly inferior ore, for which £6 and £7 18 81/2d. per ton were paid; whenever possible the superior botham (bottom) ore was purchased with prices ranging from £9 to £14 5 3d. per ton.

The method of payment was interesting. The amounts paid do not agree the price of lots purchased, and suggests that a deposit was made, with the balance due on delivery of the ore. The first payment "by a bill of Mr. Hodgson" was £100 on the 9th April. Charles paid the next £364 12s. by bills on the 13th July, but the remainder were paid by Brian Hodgson. In all, that year Brian Hodgson contributed £2,361 8s., a considerable sum, again a more than probable arrangement for the purchase of his shares in the company.

The last two payments of the year totalling £632 16s. were made in cash. Brian Hodgson was able to do this because on the 14th October he had sold his "undivided 3rd part . . . which then remained unsold at the price or sum of £5,250" of the Boothby estate to John Twigg, son of Nicholas deceased, one of the original 3rd share owners, and therefore had sufficient cash on hand to make the payments of 3rd and 26th November. The significant phrase is "which then remained unsold", because later evidence indicates that Brian Hodgson had already purchased certain properties for himself out of the estate, which he would retain for the rest of his life.

* * * * * * *

Payment by bills was by far the most accepted method, and these were often transferred from one individual to another until, when appropriate, they were redeemed for cash. Early in 1762 an anonymous author wrote an *Essay on Paper Circulation* and stated "We know well enough now that bank notes and bankers bills are really a species of money". Until this time very little business at the Bank of England had been provided by provincial traders, including those from Scotland and Wales. The largest customer was the Government followed by The East India Co. Private trade was small by comparison and mostly came from London companies, merchants and shopkeepers of many origins e.g. London Jews, and Dutchmen who had settled in the capital together with a few Huguenots. All this was about to change as over the next 20 years development of country banking systems would rapidly increase. Very few country banks existed as such up to 1750, but note issues suggest the existence of banks in Nottingham, Norwich, Bristol, Gloucester and Stafford, cities which were at the crossroads of trade. Elsewhere, during the next two decades, many little shops and warehouses labelled themselves "The Bank" and discounted notes; unfortunately many were to fail.

Cash was difficult to come by. Gold was coined regularly and kept in stock, but the stocks of silver were declining, with coins of bad condition in circulation. Small silver change was extremely difficult to get hold of, and the Bank of England had nothing whatever to do with copper coinage.

How the system worked in general is neatly illustrated by Charles Roe's arrangements, and conveniently introduces the fifth partner of Roe & Co. from this early period. Charles Roe's bills for the Ecton ore would have been discounted by the person whose name was stipulated on them, which in this instance was Edward Pitts an important London merchant.

Edward Pitts, partner of Roe & Co., was a middle-aged man and near neighbour of Cousin Christopher in the City. At this time Christopher Roe lived on Watling Street, which still runs in an east to west direction, parallel to the western side of Cannon Street and facing the Mansion House at its eastern extremity. On the other side of the Mansion House, Cannon Street continues to The Monument, from where Gracechurch Street runs north, linking Cannon Street to Cornhill. Situated in "Grace Church Street" were the business premises of Edward Pitts, pin maker, who was described in the copper works deeds as "possessed of (under alia) certain Mills & other buildings, matters & things then mentioned"; an intriguing statement which time has yet to unravel. The suggestion is one of a considerable business, which for some reason was carried on under an assumed name, and the "Mills" referred to could relate to any one of several industries including silk. Alternatively, Edward Pitts could have been acting for someone else who wished to remain incognito; but the former seems the more logical alternative taking into consideration the fortune he would eventually put in trust for his nephews and nieces. He owned an appreciable estate in Oxfordshire and married Mary Battiscomb in 1743 when she was only 18 years of age. His wife appears to have died young for there were no children from the marriage, but his partner was his wife's brother, John. His kindness and generosity were considerable, and he was on excellent terms with his sister, Prudence, wife of Richard, a member of the Good family who had lived in the Southwark area of London since the days of Henry VIII. His friends included an engraver of Moorfields and a "gunner" (gunsmith) of Cannon Street.

The entry of Edward Pitts into the partnership could have been at the same time as Messrs. Cookson and Hodgson, but was possibly slightly later, during the spring of 1761. His inclusion, apparently kept secret from all his relatives, was yet again a useful and necessary expedient; for a period he would be able to discount bills equal to the value of his shares in Roe & Co. and would also provide a prudent business outlet for the sale of copper and (when established) brass.

Edward Pitts's own requirement was brass wire, to be drawn incredibly fine by his wire-drawers. The wire was cut into lengths, which seemed a rather haphazard affair, because at least nine different sizes of pins have been discovered on one archeological site, demonstrating that sometimes the thickness of the pins was the same, but the lengths varied. The next stage was to make the heads by cutting into slices a thicker piece of wire. These early types of pins seem to have been made by a more primitive method than later, with the shank dipped in molten tin (melting point only 232o C) which acted as a solder, and when pressed onto the head formed a blob (similar in appearance to pins used today for keeping new shirts in place when wrapped in cellophane). The final process was that of pointing with the use of a file. As expected the pins were fairly expensive to buy, a lading bound for Philadelphia from London in 1764 includes:

6 doz.	fine Pinns	6/-	£1 16 0d.
6 doz.	-	10/-	£3 0 0d.

Part of the pin maker's trade was also to make needles, predominantly sewing needles, for which steel wire was used. A relatively small demand for pins to set in wool-cards would still exist, but would contribute very little to the industry as a whole; in 1747 it had been described as "but an indifferent business". Remarkably the pin making industry was to grow considerably during the next few years, much of it due to exports.

Another matter of importance, destined also to promote the copper trade, was an experiment taking place in the West Indies during 1761. As early as 13th Aug. 1687 a Thomas Agar had obtained patent No. 254 "for the manufacture of milled lead for the sheathing and preservation of ships and other things" . . . which must have proved unsuccessful. Extra layers of wood for sheathing ships had also been tested in the intervening years, but now the experiment involved copper, and the naval vessel *Alarm* was sheathed on her hull with thin copper sheets, held in place with copper nails. Some form of sheathing was necessary because in tropical waters Toredo worms bored through the hulls of wooden ships below the water line, and in a very short time the hulls had almost rotted away, causing many tragedies. Timber was becoming scarce in England for ship building; many Liverpool merchants found it cheaper to have their vessels built in the area of the River Elizabeth in Virginia, sailed across the Atlantic to Liverpool and then re-registered. The naval experiment appeared to be a great success even improving the performance of the ship, because not only did the copper sheathing discourage attacks by toredo worms but also the attachment of barnacles and weeds, and this allowed for a speed of 13 to 15 knots instead of the usual 11.

* * * * * * *

Two events took place in September 1761 which excited great national interest. The first was the marriage of George III to the princess Sophia Charlotte of Mecklenburg-Strelitz: she was 17 years of age. This marriage on the 8th of the month was destined to last for 50 years and produce fifteen children during the first 22 years, eleven of whom survived. The second, exactly two weeks later, was their coronation in Westminster Abbey at which the Earl of Harrington's wife, Caroline, one of the renowned beauties of the period, was "cov'd with all the diamonds she could borrow, hire or seize" and was "the finest figure at a distance". The carved and gilded coronation chairs used by King George III and Queen Charlotte were afterwards acquired by William, 4th Duke of Devonshire, Lord Chamberlain, as a perquisite of office. Complete with footstools they remain as a permanent feature, to be admired by many visitors, in the State Music Room of Chatsworth House.

13
INTO WALES

Let not ambition mock their useful toil,
Their homely joys and destiny obscure.

Samuel Wright from Nether Knutsford, Cheshire, kinsman and close associate of John Stafford, was a solicitor of some regard, with diverse business connections in and around the Manchester area. Amongst his clients were the Asshetons of Ashley Hall, Bowden, whom he had represented since the 1750s.

On 13th October 1756, during the period of William Smith's ownership of the Vaenol Estate near Bangor and Caernarvon, a mining lease had been effected with his nephew, Thomas Assheton, and several others amongst whom were a merchant and a goldsmith from Chester, and also from the city Thomas Slaughter, Esq., husband of Anne (née Warburton, whose grandfather was Sir George of Arley Hall), Anne's cousin, General Hugh Warburton, who was by that time in possession of half the Penrhyn Estate, and Sir George Yonge, owner of the other half; yet again vital family links, which on this occasion, associated East Cheshire with North Wales, and Samuel Wright likewise.

The mining lease related to copper, lead, tin, caulke, calamine and silver etc. under three farms: 'Talmignedd, parish Llanllyfni, Frieth and Drwsycoad, parishes of Llandurog and Beddgelert'. The copy lease does not record the term of years, only that $\frac{1}{6}$ part of ores was payable. Nothing more is known of this mining, but it seems possible that a small quantity of ore was found because these areas were later worked to some advantage, particularly in the 19th century when the Tal-y-sarn mine at Llanllyfni produced chalcopyrite richer than that of the adjoining lode in the Drws-y-coed mine, the latter producing assays of 10% to 12% metallic copper. In addition to the copper pyrites Drws-y-coed produced some Peacock copper and the green carbonate, malachite.

Not too far distant, on the Penrhyn Estate, General Warburton was encouraging the quarrying of slates and hones. The hone stone from the Nant-y-benglog quarry near Ogwen Lake was a valuable commodity in the 18th century, not only used for sharpening domestic and commercial tools, but also surgeons' scalpels. Perhaps stimulated by the findings on the neighbouring Vaenol Estate, a partnership was formed in 1759 between General Warburton, Sir George Yonge, Francis Lloyd, a doctor from Anglesey and also High Sheriff of the Isle, and John Ellis, Vicar of Bangor and Archdeacon of Merioneth. The latter was father to Hugh Ellis, destined to become the husband of Ann, Samuel Wright's daughter and an attorney of Porth-yr-Aur near Bangor. The partnership, known as the Llanberis Mine Co., also decided to carry out mineral trials in three areas where quarrying was taking place, presumably because there was evidence on site of the presence of minerals.

Mr. Ellis acted as Trustee and took "a great deal of Trouble in paying and receiving of Money keeping Accts settling with Miners & others employed in & conducting Trials" . . . Three of the ventures were on the Penrhyn Estate, one at Capel Curig to the south-east of Lake Ogwen, another at Dinas to the north of the lake, referred to as Coed-y-dinas on the northern edge of the small town of Bethesda, and the third at a place called Do'lawen just below Llyn Meirig, neither of which exist today because of the huge expansion of the Penrhyn slate quarries. In order to carry out further trials, which took place on the Vaenol Estate, and suggests that Thomas Assheton and partners had ceased their venture, the Penrhyn steward, Richard Hughes, obtained a lease for which he charged £14 12 6d. expenses to the partnership. On 14th May 1761 the two partners "J. Ellis" and "Fran: Lloyd" signed a statement which began "Whereas the Agent employed by the Rest of the Company cannot agree in the Manner how the works at Do'lawen shod be carried on . . . We cannot approve the Method proposed by Mr. Climo (Clymo - a Cornishman sent to the area at the request of Sir George) as it has and will be a very expensive and very ineffectual Tryal". They had no objection to the trial being carried out by Climo and were willing to waive any claims for ore found if Sir George and party agreed to pay all expenses, otherwise "Whereas without Unanimity and Harmony among the partners no work can be carried on in a proper Manner or to profit We propose to purchase the Shares of such persons as will not agree to carry on the Works in a proper Manner". This statement was delivered to Mr. Climo for the attention of Sir George.

The outcome seems to have been that the partners separated into two groups and worked their own particular mines, but Mr. Closs, previously appointed company agent, remained over all. Mr. Climo, apparently aided by the Penrhyn steward, Richard Hughes, and others, monopolised the tools and equipment of the company at Do'lawen and carried out his own trials. In that area, just to the south of Bethesda around Nant Ffrancon, a Welsh writer in 1866 would relate that Cornish miners had worked for about seven years circa 1760-70 "and the candles were not extinguished day or night". One of the many subsequent travellers to the area, William Williams, in 1802, would describe several workings in which copper had been and was still being retrieved, but few were successful. The levels, some denominated Ceunant Copper Mine, Llandegai produced iron pyrites together with chalcopyrite.

Part of the ore, retrieved by the Llanberis Mine Co. before the dispute, was bought by "the Macclesf'd Co. according to Mr. Ellis's Orders by (i.e. from) Mr. Closs the Company's Agent". One suspects the involvement of Samuel Wright; without doubt the Vicar of Bangor much preferred to sell his ore to the brother of the Prime Curate of Macclesfield, otherwise John Champion, busily employed in both the Flintshire and Llanberis areas, would most certainly have purchased it for his Quaker family in Bristol. Mr. Ellis employed William Edwards to ship the ore for Macclesfield, but "Wm. Edwards by some Means or other procured the Remittances" and refused to give them to Mr. Ellis. It would take a further five years before Mr. Ellis's grievances were set out in a memorandum directed for Mr. Wright's attention on 15th September 1768. In addition to his legal work for the Vaenol Estate, Samuel Wright was by then also engaged in a professional capacity with Penrhyn.

There can be no doubt that the ore travelling up the River Weaver, additional to that of Coniston, was purchased from the Penrhyn proprietors under the guise of the Llanberis Mine Co., until at least 1764. An unusually large consignment of 41 tons is recorded on 17th May 1760, which almost accounts for the additional 48 tons to the month of December in that year. Often small discrepancies are the results of clerical error, and in later years, when it is possible to compare the River Weaver books completed at the beginning of the river journey, with the Northwich Tonnage of Up-Goods completed at the end of the trip by a more meticulous clerk, (by this time the Weaver was navigable to Winsford and some goods did travel further but not for Roe & Co.) small differences do occur from time to time e.g.:

24th June 1769	River Weaver	Copper Blocks 7 tons 9 cwts.
	Northwich	Copper Blocks 5 tons 1 cwt. Bar Iron 2 tons.

In reality it was unnecessary to record individual items within a particular consignment because the charge for everything was 1s. 3d. a ton. However, it might have been a form of safeguard to

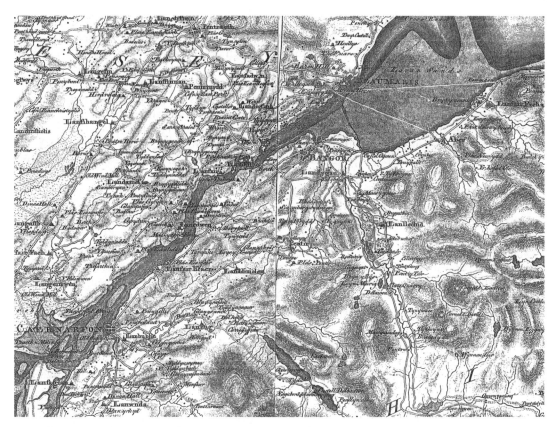

Map of the Menai Strait. Details from a John Evans map of c. 1795. Marked are the ferry crossings and also Do'lawen, situated on the route south from Bangor to Capel Cerrig close by Llyn Meirig.

have a more concise record kept at Northwich both as a cross check for weight charged and also, in the case of absent cargo, as a means of identifying on which particular section of the journey the goods had gone missing.

During the 18 months to June 1762, consignments totalling 385 tons 14 cwts. of copper ore are recorded in the River Weaver books as travelling up river, of which slightly more than 200 tons were from the Coniston mine, leaving an approximate amount of 185 tons from Llanberis. The next 18 months to December 1763 show a decline in Coniston ore received, only 127 tons 2 cwts. whereas the River Weaver total is 421 tons 18 cwts. suggesting just over $294^1/_2$ tons from North Wales.

As if to emphasise the origin of some of the ore destined for Macclesfield, John Paynter incredibly appeared on the scene, which later caused disparity. Although 18 years since his abrupt departure from Penrhyn, the man's audacity knew no bounds for he would still be remembered within the area. The mine at Esgair-mwyn near Aberystwyth was beginning to show signs of, what would prove to be, a temporary decline, and with only part of his attention required at this time he looked for additional employment elsewhere. Having already contacted the Myddletons of Chirk Castle, Paynter next approached Sir Roger Mostyn of Mostyn on the Welsh bank of the River Dee Estuary, just north of Holywell, and suggested that he should be allowed to carry out assays in the area of Snowdonia, an area which he knew very well. Sir Roger, member of another family with long standing lead mining interests, instructed him to take samples, but out of necessity the assays had to be carried out in the town of Denbigh. Whilst on his mission for Sir Roger, ever vigilant to seize an opportunity of enlarging his finances, he became acquainted with John Champion and his partner, Paul Panton, of Holywell and, more importantly, Mr. Closs, manager of the Llanberis Mine Co. He struck a bargain with John Closs, commencing 13th November 1762, whereby he would work all the slime or waste ore on site "& was to have for his Trouble ⁴/₇ths of the ore". The task was completed in nine months, during which time he assayed for the company "for which he was obliged to go to Denbigh", and also instructed John Closs in the procedure of assaying.

Some years later (1768) when an effort was being made to untangle the complexities of this early mining period, John Paynter said that he had been taking samples for the company "perhaps 2 years or upwards" before he took the washing bargain in November 1762. He had apparently forgotten that his leg was in a bad way during May 1761, which must have considerably hindered his journeys by horseback for an appreciable period through what was often rough and bleak terrain. He insisted on referring to himself as assaymaster for the company, but enquiries revealed otherwise.

It transpired that before John Paynter's arrival, the workmen in general had been paid "by the yard for raising Ore until the Washing Bargain", after which they were paid by the ton, so there had been "little Occasion for a afsaymaster" previously. After Mr. Closs had been trained in the 'art' of assaying, "J.P. made no afsays for that Company except once on a Difference between the Macclesfield Company's afsaymaster's & J. Closs when J.P. went to Denbigh and fixed the afsay". This is positive evidence that Roe & Co. were still purchasing ore from the Llanberis Mine Co. in the latter part of the year 1763, and judging from the large quantities en route to Macclesfield, must have included ore from Sir George Yonge's contingent.

John Paynter's eventual account from 13th November 1762 until 7th February 1765 sought to justify his retention of cash received to cover expenditure as assaymaster, when in fact this was not the case. The apparent total of £252 3 1¹/₂d. (over £25,000 today) for the two and a quarter year period was a useful part-time remuneration, particularly as in addition to this, he seemed to be charging each of his three employers for travelling to and from Denbigh, when actually he could assay for all of them at the same time, making only one return journey. His cessation on 5th February 1765 would conveniently coincide with renewed activity at Esgair-mwyn when a new level proved good.

A small piece of paper dated October 1764, has fortunately survived the ravages of time. It relates to "A Bargain proposed to be sett/ if approved of by the Company" between Mr. Smith (of Vaenol) and Morris Williams "in the Valley by the Castle". It purports to be for one year only to allow a trial to be made on condition that Mr. Smith received ¹/₇th of every ton of copper or lead ore raised or dressed and Mr. Williams was "to pay to the Llanberis Mine Company the sum of 40/- clear Profit out of every ton" . . . An indication that the Llanberis Mine Co. still held a lease for mining on the Vaenol Estate and was still in existence.

Purchases from Ecton continued, but unfortunately the tonnage is not known for the two years 1762 and 1763, however, it suffices to say that total bills of £3095 1 11d. and £2920 19 6d. respectively, are recorded representing slightly more in quantity than 1761 (213 tons 13 cwts.). It must be remembered that the Ecton ore was at least double or even treble the richness of that from the Llanberis area.

Whilst the spasmodic mining was taking place in and around Snowdonia, the concurrent events taking place in and around Macclesfield were to alter considerably the pattern of Charles Roe's life.

To begin with, by the end of 1760 five more silk mills of appreciable size, together with at least a dozen inferior ones, had mushroomed in the town, the proprietors eager to take advantage of the unexpected demand for English silk due to restrictions of war imports. In an industrial sense, nothing like this had ever happened before on such a grand scale, so it is hardly surprising that no-one had considered the possibility of the prosperity coming to an end, but end it did with great rapidity, due mostly to the inability of obtaining raw silk from China.

The problems had hardly begun in 1761 when an effort was made to restrict the importation of ribbands, laces and girdles made from silk or a mixture of 'other Stuff" with silk. A law, passed in the time of Henry VII, was referred to, but "great Quantities are now coming in in spite of other Laws in being" and so further legislation (Cap. XXI) was passed authorising the seizure of such merchandise together with a fine of £50.

Charles, now inexorably committed to the copper business with the expansion of the partnership, saw that his only course of action was the withdrawal of his money from the silk enterprise, otherwise the financing of brass production would be prohibitive. On 1st January 1762 William Harper, a mercer and probable kinsman of Rev. James Roe's wife, Elizabeth, was considered sufficiently experienced to carry out a valuation of all assets relating to the silk business in which Charles had shares. William Harper had lived in London for some time and possibly intended obtaining a loan for Charles or buying a share for himself, but in the event it was John Stafford's son, William, solicitor, and brother-in-law to Harry Lankford, who purchased a $^1/_5$th share from Charles Roe. The valuation produced the following details:

After deduction of bad and other debts,

Roe	£ 6,113 17 10d.	($^2/_5$ths share).
Lankford	£ 7,848 17 2d.	($^2/_5$ths share).
Robinson	£ 2,649 3 2d.	($^1/_5$th share).
TOTAL	£16,611 18 2d.	(today more than £1$^1/_2$ million).

It is not known how much was paid by William Stafford for his $^1/_5$th share, but it must have been in the region of £2,500 to £3,000. The buildings, premises, machinery and utensils, valued at £2,800, only accounted for approximately $^1/_6$th of the whole and indicates the extremely high value of silk and the large stock on hand.

As the year 1762 progressed, four of the larger silk establishments saw a small deterioration in business, but the large silk mill of the Glover and Roe partnerships maintained production; it would be months before anyone realised the severity of the situation. Without the assistance of modern financing the old established company, instead of having reserves of money in a bank, held reserves of stock in their warehouses. Whilst demand continued they would be able to supply for some considerable time and most likely assumed they could overcome any crisis; so it was business as usual.

The complicated water supply to the large silk mill functioned well, but for some reason, possibly due to the death of the Countess of Fauconberg (1760) , the lease for the water rights of the Sutton corn mills, dated 25th March 1750, had to be renewed in 1762, although it should have continued until 1771. The opportunity was taken to increase substantially the rental payable each year from £2 2s. to £85; the family no doubt appreciating the importance of the water supply to the mill. It could not have come at a more inappropriate time and presumably because of the large increase in rental, Charles brought in the Glover partnership resulting in a renewal of lease to Charles Roe, Harry Lankford, John Robinson, Samuel Glover, William Greaves and Samuel Huxley, but not William Stafford. It was to run for an unusual period of 19 years from 5th April 1762, and by strange coincidence would almost be the length of lease for the remainder of Charles Roe's own life.

One suspects that it was Charles's intention to withdraw fully from the silk partnership as of 1st January 1762, but in order to allow the remaining partners adequate time in which to obtain sufficient capital to purchase his interests, he agreed to retain a $^1/_5$th share temporarily.

On 29th November 1762, quietly and unobtrusively, William, Earl of Harrington acquired a Crown lease which, from an outsider's point of view, would hardly have warranted further attention. It related to Macclesfield Common, for which the Harringtons had, of course, held mining rights under lease for many years. When the eventual details came to light, the true purpose of the lease was still not obvious because it had been contained within a mass of inconsequential detail, and suggests some very clever legal work on the part of John Stafford in co-operation with both the Earl of Harrington and his agent:

"Whereas His Majesty did demise unto the Earl of Harrington All that cottage erection parcel of land containing 3 acres then lately inclosed from & out of the waste called Whalley Waste lying on the West part of a house late belonging to one Sarfson Widow & then in occupation of Edward Barlow Francis Barlow & Ralph Barlow and all that Mine or pits of coal already found & opened together with full power to sink pits . . .
Also all that parcel of land demised to William Earl of Harrington on which lately erected two small Outilsts & a small Gable End adjacent the house of Jonathon Pickford called the Malthouse also permission to erect Mills, Smelthouses" . . .

The "cottage erection" referred to must have represented the copper works, and the 3 acres of land together with "all that parcel of land" demised to the Earl was, in total, the additional 4 acres upon which all new buildings would be accommodated for the eventual expansion of the copper works and development of the brass complex.

In fairness to all concerned, apart from the fact that Charles would face the possibility of losing a small fortune should he be limited to copper production only, the industry was vital to British economy, particularly with experimentation of machinery taking place, and would benefit many people, not only in the immediate vicinity of the works, but over a considerable area. The Earl of Harrington with his military and government connections would very much appreciate the necessity for this metallurgic industry and the obligation to encourage its growth. The arguments for the increased demand of brass and copper, not only from the commercial point of view but also domestic, were convincing. An inventory contained within a property deed for a large house near Warrington in 1761 lists many brass locks and keys, and in the cellar two brass cocks and a funnel (usually copper). Although several of the listed items were made of iron e.g. implements for cooking and carving such as scewers, and pewter plates remained popular, yet the predominant items in the kitchen were made from either brass or copper, as the following extracts indicate:

'A Brass plate Warmer
7 Copper Saucepans & 3 covers
Copper boiling pot and cover fixed in the Chimney
three copper boiling pots and covers
2 Copper fish Kettles plates and covers
A copper Fish Kettle
A large copper stew pan and cover
three lesser copper stew pans and covers
A copper frying pan
A large copper dripping pan
A Brass Skimmer Ladle and Slice
A pair of brass scales & 4 brass weights (also 4 lead weights)
A Copper Chocolate pott and Mill
A Brass Mortar & Iron Pestle
A Copper preserving pan
A Copper warming pan
A large copper Drinking pot
A pint copper Drinking pot
Copper Coal Scuttle
2 Copper Tea Kettles
A pair of Copper Scales
A Brass Tinder Box
7 Brass flat candlesticks.'

The copper utensils would of course be lined with tin, but the brass were not, even though as early as 12th November 1673 a William Chamberlayne had been granted patent no. 171 for plating and tinning iron, copper, steel, brass and items comprising all other metals.

Also there is evidence, although slender, to support the notion that Charles Roe had in mind the production of brass buttons.

Buttons were always in great demand, having been an important part of fashion for centuries as evidenced by 14th century church effigies. The wide-skirted long coats for gentlemen, popular since the days of James II, and each often sporting at least 60 buttons, had begun to lose their fullness; in fact the ascension to the throne of George III in 1760 had heralded the beginning of a 30 year period of constant changes in fashion. Side pleats were moved to the back of coats, with fronts sloping away at the sides. Sleeves became longer and more fitted, but the number of buttons, although often complemented by false button holes woven in strips, remained as desirable as ever. They were an integral part of coats, gorgeously embroidered sleeveless waistcoats and buttoned up breeches. Ladies' coats were likewise endowed, worn over full bodied dresses. There was also a demand for military buttons which were made of metal never fabric; gilt or silver for officers, pewter for lower ranks.

Metal buttons had been in production for many years. Black latten, made in Bristol, was used by Birmingham braziers in fashioning their buttons, but English brass for a considerable period had been "so hard, flowy & scurvy" that its use had been restricted.

Growing affluence was creating a society desirous and appreciative of beautiful objects which were also works of art. Elaborately designed snuff boxes, delightful pieces of exquisite jewellery, pretentious shoe buckles, fobs, seals and watchkeys dangling from a variety of metal chains, all were highly prized and highly paid for. Many of these wonderful pieces, purchased in London shops, were made by Birmingham craftsmen amongst whom was one rapidly gaining fame, Matthew Boulton. He is better remembered for his connections with James Watt and steam engines, but this was still in the future when he took over his father's manufactory in 1759.

Matthew Snr. had served his time as a toymaker and subsequently made a good living producing buckles and buttons, so in due course his son set up his own business as a buckle maker. Matthew Jnr.'s ambitions as a silversmith soon made obsolete his father's old premises on Snow Hill, Birmingham and in 1759 he had begun the building of his famous Soho manufactory on Handsworth Heath, which was actually just over the border in Staffordshire. He, like so many other individuals, soon discovered that further resources were necessary, so during the year 1762/63 took into partnership John Fothergill (born in Russia but son of a probable English merchant) and began producing superb buttons, many with mother of pearl inlay embellished with multi-coloured stones. Some had faceted steel centres, whilst others had mounts of gilt ormolu, objects which Fothergill would have no difficulty in presenting to London society, but at attractively lower prices than others on the market.

Matthew hated London and sent all his silver work to be assayed in Chester. His fanaticism on the subject would eventually culminate in the establishment of the Birmingham Assay Office in 1773. His "magnificent pile of buildings", half completed by 1762, were situated on open heath land in full view of all travellers journeying north from Birmingham along Great Hampton Street.

Charles Roe would be perfectly well aware of the impending challenge to the traditional Macclesfield buttons embroidered with mohair and silk. Mr. Boulton with his newly acquired partner, Mr. Fothergill, was intent on capturing the attention of London's famous clientele.

In many ways Matthew Boulton was a strange character, with streaks of eccentricity in his nature. The mysterious death of his first wife, Mary, dragged from a pond in 1759, and his marriage to her sister, Anne, during the following year, provided a platform for gossip. His second marriage took place at St. Mary's, Rotherhithe, and strictly speaking under Church law was illegal. Whether or not the parson was aware of the facts is a matter for conjecture, but from Matthew's point of view, judging from his commitments at this time, it was an absolute necessity to retain the status quo as regards the marriage settlement, which would irrevocably be tied up with all his business obligations. Although he grew to dominate the toy manufacturing industry of Birmingham, he was not the only one producing metal buttons, as witnessed by reference to Birmingham directories of the period. In fact, by 1767 there would be 100 button makers in the city.

A very important group of merchants occupied premises at 32 Snow Hill, and were near neighbours of the old Boulton establishment. These merchants, Messrs. Welch, Wilkinson & Startin, not only handled the small wares of the enlarging city, but were a vital link in the export market for other areas, Macclesfield included. As groups of these specialist factors began to multiply throughout the country, more and more manufacturers were making use of their services, and Charles Roe, himself conversant with all the problems of conveying goods over great distances, and arranging sales, also began to appreciate the expediency of using such services as and when appropriate.

Macclesfield buttons still held popularity, especially in America, though one suspects that what was becoming unfashionable in England was conveniently sent to the Colonies where often styles and designs appeared to lag behind those of their English counterparts by at least a decade. A particular type of button, which seems to have been produced only in the Macclesfield area, remained a good export item to North America. It was described as a "Death head" button, which presumably depicted a skull or skull and crossbones, and was made either as a coat or breast (waistcoat) button. The only colour recorded is scarlet, made with "2 cord" or "3 cord", which must have referred to the plies. The stock in hand of one Macclesfield shop/warehouse of the period shows supplies on hand of just over 6 lbs. of 3 Cord Button Work and 2½ lbs. of 2 Cord Button Work, but unfortunately does not indicate the material. Although pounds of silk, mohair graded coarse, fine, "Superffine" and thrown, threaded horse hair and silk hair were present in large quantities, yet only occasionally are items qualified by colour, as in the instance of "Scarlet silk" and "Scarlet mohair". The premises also contained the following:

							£	s	d
"275	Bags	2	Cord Death head Buttons	12x12	3/9d.		51	11	3
28	Bags	2	Cord Death head Breast		2/10d.		3	19	4
102	Bags	3	Cord Death head	12x12	4/10d.		24	13	0
1	Bag	3	Cord Breast				0	4	0"

Local manufacture is indicated because the stock included "Death heads Molds"; as is, surprisingly, the production of horn buttons (usually attributed to Sheffield and Birmingham).

Messrs. Welch, Wilkinson & Startin, by today's standards, were responsible for a muti-million pound business. Goods assembled by them from a variety of sources were consigned to one of their shipping agents in London "with instructions to Ship & fully insure on board first Vefsell for Philadelphia for the Account & Risque of Mefsrs. Baynton Wharton & Morgan Merchts of that City". B.W.M. & Co. was the trademark of a highly successful partnership at the centre of a distribution network, not only covering the hinterland of the strategically placed port along the banks of the River Delaware, but across Pennsylvania, reaching Fort Pitt by way of river. Formerly built by the French and named Fort Duquesne, but captured by General Forbes in 1758, Fort Pitt was "the key to the great unbounded west", and a critical link in communications encompassing the Great Lakes and our newly acquired conquests in Canada.

Completed on the 30th August 1763 a bill of lading bound for B.W.M. & Co. from London lists Item No. 37 as a trunk containing:

					£	s	d
"133	Bags	Scarfe	Deathhead Coat & Crest Buttons	$^5/_6$	37	2	6
5	Bags	do	Scarlet & Crimson Ingrain	$^6/_6$	1	12	6
6	Bags	do	do all waistcoat	5/-	1	10	0
14	Bags	do	Black Blue Green & Buff do	4/-	2	16	0
30	Bags	rich 3 Cord scarlet silk twist Coat & breast		6/6	9	15	0
8	Bags		do all breast	5/-	2	0	0
2	Bags	do	Ingrain	6/-		12	0
30 lbs	fine silk & hair twist			18/-	32	8	0
2 lbs	do		Scarlet & Crimson	22/-	2	4	0
10 lbs	Rich Scarfe Silk Twist			28/-	14	0	0
1/2 lb	do		Scarlet & Crimfon	32/-		16	0"

(N.B. do = ditto. Scarfe is presumably derived from the verb to scarf meaning to cover etc.).

The total value for this one trunk alone was £104 16s., which one might be inclined to regard dismissively as a few bags of buttons and a few pounds of silk twist, yet if any comparison can be made, the value today would be in excess of £10,500. The ships often had upwards of 80 chests listed containing a variety of goods i.e. blue and white cups amd saucers, tea pots, butter boats and basons, dozens of silk handkerchiefs and knee garters, materials including printed linens, considerable quantities of brass wire and scores of barrels, many containing gun powder.

Although the contents of the trunk listed as item 37 provide copious information, they still do not reveal the materials of the death head buttons; never-the-less, these, together with several other silk items such as the handkerchiefs, knee garters and sewing silks, without a doubt were from merchants within the Macclesfield area, particularly as it is known from a later source that Charles Roe was dealing through Welch, Wilkinson and Startin of Birmingham.

The origin of the death head is intriguing. The emblem, representing mortality, was popular in the medieval period, often displayed on rings, and probably connected with plagues. Extensive searches have failed to produce a logical explanation for its unique appearance on Macclesfield buttons at this time, but one piece of information is worthy of note, two of the brasses relating to the Yate family of Dearnford Hall, one mile from Whitchurch, display the skull and crossbones. This was the family who were related to the Claytons (one of whom was a button merchant in Macclesfield) and the Crosse family of Chorley and Liverpool, and were also involved with the sale of Mottram Hall in 1742. Three further brasses, originally in the Dissenting Chapel of Whitchurch, also display the emblem of the death head and represent the deaths of members of other families related by marriage to the Yates. The existence of the death head on the Whitchurch brasses does prove that it was still in vogue at that period, for whatever reason. However, why they should have been popular in the Philadelphia area remains a mystery.

Some of these buttons could have made the long journey to Fort Pitt, but the recording of such items in the Fort Pitt Day Books is less accurate, and only small consignments of buttons, usually a gross or a dozen each time are listed, often with very little description at this early period.

With regard to population, the world was still a very small place in the 1760s. Many powerful bonds existed between the different branches of important mercantile families in both the vicinities of Manchester and Philadelphia. The Finneys of Fulshaw Hall, having provided a Provincial Councillor and Judge (Samuel) and a Provincial Councillor and High Sheriff (brother, Captain John) of Philadelphia County at the turn of the century, had become a prolific family owning much land. Nor were the Asshetons to be ignored when Robert, son of William (closely related to Thomas of Bowden) became Town Clerk of Philadelphia, taking office alongside Samuel Finney I and his brother. Robert Assheton was first cousin to William Penn.

(Although William Penn had pronounced himself Quaker, yet there had been many squabbles between him and his Quaker compatriots to whom he had sold land. His sons returned to the Church of England and two of them, Richard and Thomas, gave land for the building of the beautiful church of St. Peter on Pine Street, Philadelphia, in which the first service was held on the 4th September 1761.)

Another suggestion for the manufacture of the scarlet death head buttons has been made by an American archivist, and in light of the above family connections cannot be disregarded, that there were symbols of Free Masonry,

Alongside the mohair and silk buttons bound for Philadelphia in the early 1760s were considerable quantities of gilt buttons, with some described as "Dollar Buttons". Slightly later American examples of military buttons are extant, amongst which can be found specimens bearing an eagle and inscribed E PLURIBUS UNUM (translated – one of many), similar to those appearing on the American silver dollar; one can only conjecture that some of the gilt buttons thus described were of similar style. It is interesting to consider the fact that after the American Revolution, when coinage was in a deplorable state and all sorts of tokens made use of, one school of thought considers the employment of buttons as coinage a more than probable occurrence. Perhaps the flattened dollar button was the precursor of a coin destined to become one of the world's most famous monetary units. This consideration apart, metal buttons were in great demand, and as Matthew Boulton seemed intent on supplying the more elaborate specimens for wealthy customers, there was a considerable void to be filled amongst the masses of the Middle Class, and already there were many Birmingham button makers who were rising to the challenge.

Metal buttons were made by Roe & Co. at their works on Macclesfield Common, but it is difficult to say from what date. Charles, having been a button merchant for a considerable part of his life, seems unlikely to have discarded this integral part of his business. His monument states that he "carried on the Button and Twist manufacture in this Town" and "first established here . . . the Silk and Copper Manufactories", but it does not qualify the button and twist manufacture as silk, supporting the fact that much of the early production included mohair and horsehair etc. Could it be that the later production of buttons was brass or even pewter? Such an assumption seems further substantiated by a letter from Matthew Boulton some years later (1775 - but still during Charles Roe's lifetime) to Samuel Roe, who was by then acting as secretary to the copper company. Samuel had enquired on behalf of a friend regarding a "steam wheel for the purpose of turning a silk mill" and the reply was supplemented by the remark "It's probable I may come soon to Macclesfield, as I want a few female button workers". Matthew Boulton never made fabric buttons; the inference is that females were assembling the various parts of metal buttons, and that such were to be found in Macclesfield.

Early metal buttons, particularly the military ones which are extant, appear not to have been solid cast in one piece, but had wooden or bone cores. The desired metal was embossed with a design in an almost identical method to that of coinage i.e. a shaped block containing the pattern in reverse, known as a die, which in effect acted as a mould, held tight in a drop forge or press. The pieces of metal of appropriate size, destined to be the fronts of buttons, were each in turn inserted beneath the die and, with the use of a lever or crank operated by an individual, struck down upon so that the die, acting as a hammer head, left the impression of the design upon the metal. It was usual for the back of each button to have a loop attached to the middle of the disc by a short shank, all made from the same metal as the front. The final stage was to enclose a wooden core with a front and back, which were joined together by crimping the edges around the perimeter. The early shanks were made by hand, but, as demand increased a method of casting was developed, eventually superceded by the use of machinery.

Metal buttons on jackets and coats were not directly stitched on as today, but a row of eyelets was made, with each eyelet corresponding to a button hole or false button hole as desired. Each button in turn was pushed through the fabric so that its loop projected through its own individual eyelet on the reverse side, and a thong, usually of leather, was threaded through each loop from one end to the other, then secured at both ends. Another method, particularly popular with the more elaborate buttons, was to supply them beautifully boxed with their own individual rings similar to miniature key rings, so that as each loop was pushed through the eyelet a ring was secured through the loop, making it impossible for the button to fall off. The advantage of these systems was that buttons could easily be changed as and when required.

These were the challenge to the Macclesfield button industry which would hardly be affected by the depletion of raw silk imports from China. The remainder of the silk industry was affected, however, and the year 1763 saw a considerable fall in production of all silk establishments with the Roe and Glover complex reduced by a quarter, making it imperative for Charles to retrieve as much money as he could from his silk investments before it was too late, but this was still not possible and must have caused him grave anxiety.

The apparent departure from Macclesfield of John Guardivaglio, son of one of the Italians instrumental in the construction of the first silk mill in Derby, appears to coincide with this period. His subsequent movements are not known until he and his wife, Mary, are recorded as the parents of a son, John, baptised at St. Mary's Stockport on 8th April 1769. The family were to remain in that area for a considerable period, with the children eventually marrying into families of some consequence (not, as erroneously deduced by one historian, living out their days in abject poverty).

After the acquisition of the Crown lease relating to Macclesfield Common in November 1762 by William, Earl of Harrington, one can assume that Charles Roe, as sub-lessee, wasted no time in obtaining permission from the Earl to extend the smelthouses and begin experimentation of the complicated production of brass. At the same time he was also seeking a site suitable for the construction of a brass rolling mill, wire mill, annealing house with oven and several other buildings pertinent to the operations. There would have to be a sufficient supply of water which, when harnessed, would eventually have power to rotate five water wheels ranging from 18 to 22 feet in diameter, in turn capable of operating the machinery in the mills. Charles must have scoured the area around Macclesfield until he found the ideal location, then once again his enthusiasm and powers of persuasion came into play.

The land, situated in the parish of Astbury, was almost on the boundary of the town of – Congleton at a place called Eaton, and only six miles to the south-west of the parent works on Macclesfield Common. The Indenture dated 27th April 1763 between George Lee of Eaton and Charles Roe suggests that Lee held manorial rights under lease and possibly also the land, but the phraseology in parts is quite amusing, reflecting Charles Roe's persistence in achieving his aims. The 99 year lease, operative from 12th May 1763 at, what was at the time of signing, a fairly substantial annual rental of £30 10s, states that Charles:

"hath apply'd to requested and desir'd the said George Lee to grant him a Lease of the Mefsuage and Lands with the appurtenances . . . (and) to grant him the Liberty and Privilege of erecting one or more Water Mill or Mills and to make such Wares (weirs) Mill Damms or reservoirs for Water and likewise such subterraneous Passages for water as the said Charles Roe shall think fitt or be advised to. And the said George Lee apprehending it may be doubtfull if he can legally grant the aforesaid Liberties and Priviliges . . . but nevertheless he is willing and consenting thereto so farr as he may lawfully consent to the same especially in regard to the Covenants and Agreements of the said Charles Roe hereinafter contain'd with respect to the damage to be occasioned by . . . the Exercise."

The land and buildings referred to were tenanted and sub-tenanted but an agreement was reached by all concerned to include land called the Nursery, planted with trees, and part of the Tann house tenement "intended to be covered with water", excluding, however, the Round Meadow containing an acre and 14 perches, and reserving the royalties of hunting, hawking and fishing to George Lee and his heirs. In total the area covered by the works and appurtenances when completed was just over 17 acres, as shown by a plan of the site eventually drawn in 1777. Liberty was given to "Cut down and carry away the Timber or sink Mines get prepare carry away Stone plaster"(etc.) in any part of the close called the Field behind Daven (River Dane) where the mills and buildings were intended to be built within 40 yards of the weir. The rental, to begin on the following 12th May, was payable in two equal instalments. The usual clause of maintaining and keeping in good repair was included, with inspections by George Lee, his heirs, agents or surveyors permitted at least twice a year. At the termination of the lease, again the usual conditions of vacating the premises "quietly" and giving up all buildings both newly erected or already on site when the lease came into effect, were stipulated. An important final clause specified that Charles had also to cover any legal charges by George Lee and his neighbours in case they had to sue him for damages such as overflowing of the weir. Such damages were to be assessed within six months by two reputable independent "Farmers".

The choice of name for the site is a little difficult to understand. It became known as the Havannah Works or Havannah (a name retained to this day) presumably because in 1762, during the final months of the Seven Years War, after many successes in the West Indies, the British Navy finally captured Havana, capital of the Spanish Island of Cuba, together with twelve ships and £3 million in gold and silver. However, during February 1763 by the Treaty of Paris between Britain, Spain and France, Havana was exchanged for Florida by the Spaniards, and France regained most of her West Indian islands by surrendering Canada and the right to fortify her factories in India. The Treaty of Paris was signed prior to Charles Roe's acquisition of the site at Eaton, and possibly he was not aware of the situation.

One person very upset by the surprising outcome of the treaty was Pitt, who struggled to Parliament from his sick-bed to denounce the terms as ruinous, particularly as France had recovered all her valuable West Indian islands of St. Lucia, Martinique and Guadeloupe leaving Britain with the inconsequential ones of Tobago, St. Vincent and Dominica. There had been debate upon the preference of retaining Guadeloupe (captured in 1759) instead of Canada, but concern for consolidation in North America made Canada the obvious choice.

Charles Roe's father-in-law, Joseph Stockdale, had financed the journey of his second eldest son, Joseph, to Guadeloupe and continued to send several sums of money presumably for business transactions. The reversal of policy due to loss of the island forced young Joseph to take up residence on the nearest British possession, which was the island of Dominica. The group of islands comprising Guadeloupe were valued for their sugar production but Dominica, lying between Guadeloupe to the north and Martinique to the south, contained mountains of volcanic origin clad in high forest, resulting in the mining of pumice. It was also important for fruit production, in particular bananas, grapefruits, limes and oranges; another valuable asset was coconuts from which oils and fats were obtained for the manufacture of soap. Taking into account the sugar production of Guadeloupe and the fats and oils of Dominica, it seems evident that Joseph was there to sell coppers and other related goods, and in return to buy whatever would make a profit. No doubt he was responsible for the occasional boxes of lemons (weighing 1 cwt. each) and chest of oranges which made their way up the River Weaver on account of Chas. Roe & Co.

The main initial purpose of the Havannah site was the rolling of copper sheets and production of brass wire. The former to satisfy the demand of the West Indian markets for coppers and similar items, and the latter for pin makers such as Edward Pitts, who in turn were being called upon by the factors to supply markets overseas, especially those of the North American continent. Havannah, a name adopted in haste, must have represented to Charles Roe the opportunity for a vast commercial enterprise in the West Indies in co-operation with his wife's family, and was perhaps also symbolic of the copper company's hope of emulating the fortune gained in gold and silver by the British Navy during their capture of the Spanish city.

At this moment in time when the future was beginning to look more secure, Mary, Charles Roe's second wife, was expecting her eighth and final child.

During the previous year of 1762, on 4th August, John Wesley had preached in Macclesfield. Prior to this his journal only records three previous visits in the years 1747, 1759 and 1761, but the latter must have convinced him of his growing popularity in the town, and for the next few years his visits were to become an annual event. Wesley's sincerity and commitment to his convictions appear to be beyond reproach, but sadly none of his sermons or profound words of wisdom have been recorded with much alacrity. His journal adequately sets forth his day by day business engagements and prejudices, but even his diary, written in shorthand, and in the process of being transcribed in America, has yet to produce any deep philosophical awakenings. It has revealed that when it suited his purpose he was capable of using situations within the Church of England to justify his own actions as part of his campaign against the 'unrighteous', whilst at the same time objecting to such formalities. His zeal on occasion could make him seem unkind and his words at times cruel. His total abhorrence for prosperity or wealth is vividly described and woe betide anyone who made a fortune, he never forgave them.

There had been an instance in America, during his visit of 1737, when he had refused Holy Communion to one particular lady. It must be admitted that there was a personal involvement, but he took revenge by humiliating her unnecessarily. He quoted "So many as intend to be partakers of the Holy Communion shall signify their names to the Curate at least some time the day before . . . and if any . . . have done any wrong to his neighbours by word or deed, so that the congregation be thereby offended, the Curate . . . shall advertise him that in any wise he presume not to come to the Lord's Table until be hath openly declared himself to have truly repented". This was a legacy from the Roman Catholic Church's requirement for Confession on a day prior to that on which Holy Communion was offered, part of the ritual to which Wesley strongly objected and yet which he had no compunction in using to satisfy his his own vindictiveness. She had not done so, and thus was his response.

His notes regarding his visit to Macclesfield on 4th August 1762 tell of the "Case of Ann Hooley" who was talking in the street with two young women. As John Wesley passed by he spoke to the two young ladies but apparently ignored Miss Hooley, who was, of course, a member of an important Macclesfield family. The child, for she was only 13 years of age, immediately burst into tears and said "What am I so great a sinner that he won't speak to me?" By his own words she was inconsolable, and about midnight so great was her distress that Wesley was sent for to comfort her. She died a few months later.

On 20th June 1763 Wesley was again briefly in Macclesfield; he later wrote a short account of Mrs. R(oe) "who was in the society at London from a child but after she was married to a rich man durst not own a poor despised people". He recounted that she had broken through the crowd to talk with him, and continued "A few words which I then spoke never left her, not even in the trying hour during the illness which came . . . feeling her strength was quite exhausted, she said with a smile "Death, thou art welcome!" and resigned her spirit". Baby Jane, born on 5th July 1763, was exactly one month old when her mother was buried at St. Michael's on the 5th August.

At the time of Mary's death, Catherine, Charles Roe's eldest child, was 18 years of age and William little more than 16 years. Their younger brother, Samuel, now 13 years old, was still at grammar school, but the remaining seven half brothers and sisters were all under the age of 10 years, a formidable responsibility for anyone to take on. Although Catherine would bear a greater part of that responsibility, yet she was cushioned to a degree by the fact that her father could afford servants and nursemaids, unlike the Castleton household of the previous generation. This sudden promotion to head of the household, although temporarily, gave her a dominance which would assert itself after her marriage, causing many problems with servants in her own household. She was devoted to brother, William, her only constant in a rapidly changing world, but even his presence in the home would be limited as father and son put duty to business first. So many people were now becoming dependent upon the copper company for their livelihoods that the thought of failure was inconceivable.

During this same year problems arose at the Alderley Edge mines, one of the four important sources of copper ore for the Macclesfield smelter at this time. It was mainly due to flooding in the Engine Vein, hence the increased purchase of ore from North Wales, which would certainly not please Charles with his 'built-in' code of self-sufficiency. Almost immediately steps were taken to remedy the situation as Brian Hodgson, together with his eldest son, Robert, who by this time had gained useful experience of mining in his charge of the coal business at Disley, elected to go into North Wales on behalf of Roe & Co. to view the prospects. At this juncture they obviously appreciated the difficulties faced by Charles, whose presence would be needed nearer home.

In the late summer of 1763 the Hodgsons travelled extensively with their agent, who must have been either Samuel Howson or Jonathan Roose. It seems certain that the Derbyshire and East Cheshire connections in that region had brought the possibility of mining to their attention. John Twigg, one of Brian Hodgson Snr.'s former third share partners in the Boothby Estate, had been a partner in several mining ventures in Merionethshire from 1760 to 1762.

Whether or not the younger Jonathan Roose had assisted at Coniston may never be known, but he would definitely be associated with the partnership by this time, because from 1st January 1763 Charles and Brian Hodgson, Rev. Seward of Lichfield and a handful of minor investors had formed a partnership to work the Gorsey Dale mine at Bonsall near Winster, in the immediate vicinity of Jonathan Roose's home in the village of Youlgreave.

Published in 1789 "A view of the present state of Derbyshire" by James Pilkington reveals "Copper ore has yet been found only in small quantities in Derbyshire. Pieces about twelve inches in circumference and detached from any vein are frequently met with at Matlock. Others of a much larger size have also been found at Bonfal and converted into Copper. They were discovered, some lying on the furface of the ground, and the rest in a neighbouring walled fence." Although the Gorsey Dale venture was in lead mining country, the hope of discovering a vein of copper ore must have been paramount; in this they did not succeed, but just as important was the discovery of calamine which was to supply at least half the quantity required for the Macclesfield brass production until the beginning of the 19th century. Remarkably this is the only mine in Derbyshire in which Charles and Brian Hodgson invested together. It was not worked as Roe & Co. but as a separate venture with calamine sold to the company.

Charles still retained his several interests in the lead mines of the Eyam area, originally inherited from his father, and from January 1763 he and Rowland Atkinson took up a joint $1/_{24}$th share in Froggart Grove near Eyam. Surprisingly they only held the share for two years although the mine produced a total profit of £1,043 in 1763 and £704 in 1764, well worth the investment.

Brian Hodgson also made investments in lead mines from 1st January 1763. He held a $1/_{24}$th share in Eyam Dale Sough near the village of Foolow, a $1/_{24}$th share in Oxclose Sough near Winster, and in the same area a $2/_{24}$th share in Placket Mine. Although he was to hold these shares for many years, the fortunes of the mines varied considerably; some years a substantial profit would be made but other years considerable losses. However, it was within the shareholders of these mines that future investors would be found to support the mining activities of Roe & Co.

On 10th June 1763 John Paynter had written to the Earl of Powis, who at that date was making one of his customary visits to London and staying on Albermarle Street just off

Piccadilly. Paynter complained about the scarcity of miners in Mid-Wales, pointing out that the Halkin Mountains were full of ore and also full of miners. He commented that he had been visited by Mr. Cartwright with whom he had discussed the possibility of bargain takers (persons eager to take leases of land in order to carry out trials – but the trials were proving costly).

Mr. Cartwright, Christian name John, was to become a key figure in events concerning Roe & Co., not only during the following months, but also for many years. He, like John Paynter, was an opportunist, but lacked much of the latter's daring and flair. By trade he was a bricklayer from Staffordshire and yet had managed to acquire a more desirable position as retainer within Sir Nicholas Bayly's household at Plas Newydd on the Isle of Anglesey, and was rapidly gaining advancement to positions of greater authority which were more than commensurate with his abilities.

John Cartwright's arrival at Plas Newydd is not really surprising when one considers the series of events which had taken place.

On 23rd and 24th March 1736 an Indenture had been executed in consideration of a marriage settlement between Nicholas Bayly, eldest son and heir of Sir Edward (grandson of the Right Rev. Lewis Bayly Bishop of Bangor) and Caroline Paget, daughter of the Hon. Colonel Thomas Paget (cousin to Henry, 7th Lord Paget and 1st Earl of Uxbridge, at one time M.P. for Staffordshire).

Lord Paget had carried out considerable repairs and refurbishment of his house on his Staffordshire estate of Beaudesert during the years 1740-43, and it was more than probable that John Cartwright was involved. He is not specifically mentioned in the accounts but was presumably employed as a workman. There were also coal mines in the vicinity which provided the Paget family with additional income, the knowledge of which seems to have been used later by Cartwright to good effect. The death of Lord Paget took place in 1743, when he was succeeded by his grandson Henry, 8th Baron Paget and 2nd Earl of Uxbridge. It was this Earl of Uxbridge who never married but who continued the close family relationship between himself and the Baylys of Plas Newydd. After all, Caroline was his second cousin and, although the Uxbridge title would become extinct on his death, the barony in fee of Paget would pass to Caroline's eldest son, Henry, as next male heir. Due to the death of Sir Edward Bayly, Caroline's husband was now Sir Nicholas, 2nd Baronet of Plas Newydd.

Caroline and Sir Nicholas produced seven children, the first three of whom were sons. She was a devoted and loyal wife, her letters and portrait suggest a person of quiet charm who was contented with the simplest things in life. Not so Sir Nicholas, who lavishly overspent and indulged in his passion for females at every opportunity. His actions and reasoning on occasion were often unpredictable and quite idiotic. His attentions were given to as little as possible, except for the ladies, and he was quite contented to allow anyone who so desired to take responsibility for his estate. Whenever his military career permitted his sole concern was to enjoy the social life of London, financed by his estate income which he expected to be provided by his steward, whatever the circumstances. Here was the ideal opportunity for John Cartwright, who must have learnt of Sir Nicholas's intention of emulating Lord Paget by carrying out alterations to his family seat at Plas Newydd. The first phase of work took place between the years 1745-53, when Sir Nicholas decided to make Gothic additions to the east front of the old house. With the 7th Lord Paget dead one can imagine that Cartwright presented himself as an accomplished builder, for detailed correspondence is extant between Sir Nicholas and John Cartwright who acted as his agent, and which, from an architectural point of view, provides an excellent picture of the proceedings.

As expected Sir Nicholas took on the role of architect, the result being that the "Battlements of the East front" have been described as "almost literally of the pasteboard variety". During this escapade Cartwright also took over the development of coal mines on Sir Nicholas's estate, and eventually found himself in the position of steward.

As the years had passed, Caroline had spent much time in London, eventually almost taking up permanent residence there. During one of Sir Nicholas's visits to Plas Newydd she had written him a delightful letter. Addressed to "My Dear Life" and dated Saturday night, 18th August 1750, she proceeded to give an account of a dinner which she had arranged that day for Lord Uxbridge and friends, his Lordship being "just come to town". She had been lucky the previous day because "Mr. Revel sent me a side of venison & Mrs. Standlock some Partridge Sir Wm. brough fish . . . now I will tell yo my Dinner I had a Soop at Top (of the table) at the Bottom a Sadle of Mutton Sweet Breads & Pudings & Fish to remove the 2d corse I had 4 Partridge at top Pidgeons at Bottom an apricot tart & white fricace (sauce) at the first corse the venison Pastey was on the side table with the salade".

During the year 1760 Sir Nicholas found himself enmeshed in an intimate affair with a Miss Sarah Griffith, daughter of William Griffith, Linen Draper of Norris Street, Parish of St. James in the City of Westminster. He legally admitted his paternity in respect of their son, William Chevalier, alias Bayly, and set about devising a way of providing maintenance firstly, by Deed Poll on 28th November 1760. He promised that if the child survived his mother, Sarah, then he or his administrators would pay to the child a sum of £50 per annum for the remainder of the child's life. One assumes that Sir Nicholas promptly forgot his resolution and the affair, but was eventually pushed into a more acceptable arrangement, because finally on 2nd March 1762, when the child was almost 16 months old, he sent an eviction order to a Mr. Morris Thomas which read:

> "I hereby give Notice that you are to quit the ffarm you hold of Lord Powis' and me Called Penrhyndee in the Parish of Lan-ingan in the County of Carnarvon with all and Singular the Appurtenances at all saints next ensuing Dated this 10th day of April 1762."

This was followed, less than two weeks later, by the signing of a lease on 15th March, between Sir Nicholas and "Miss Sarah Griffith and Wm. Chevalier alias Bayly my Natural Son" in respect of the property. Very little information was included, only the details of the Deed Poll.

It seems strange that Sir Nicholas had sole power to evict a tenant whose tenancy was held jointly from himself and Lord Powis, and, indeed, to execute the lease. In all probability the copy of the eviction letter pinned to the lease was feigned by him; no mention of it arises on any subsequent deeds, nor does the matter of £50 per annum for the child, William Chevalier. There is the possibility, of course, that the child had died, and if so it was very convenient for it allowed Sir Nicholas, together with Lord Powis, to lease to John Cartwright "Land now in possession of Morris Thomas in the Parish of Llanigen" from 29th September 1762. The details on the lease suggest that Cartwright was already in possession of the site; he was given full power to set up engines for emptying and draining water from the mines, and also allowed the use of quarry stones for erecting and repairing buildings, and clay, from which bricks could be made for the same purpose. The yearly rental was £10.

This mine of Penrhyn Du had been described by a writer, T. Fuller, in 1662 (when it was considered the best in Wales) as situated "so near the sea that they may cast the oure into the ship". A letter written on 28th April 1668 stated, "since October last our best worke were drowned out and wee have gotten butt small stone of oare ever since". By 1734 it was reported that much money had been spent in clearing the mine of water and waste material, but once again, in 1748, it had proved impossible to keep the water at bay.

John Cartwright, amateur as he was in such matters, must have calculated that he could inspire interest in the mine amongst his contacts from the mining fraternity on the Staffordshire/Derbyshire border. He still made visits home from time to time, in fact his solicitor, Mr. George Greatbach, lived in Newcastle-under-Lyme. An important associate was Adam Simpson, Barmaster of Bonsall, whose business partner, Thomas Walker, was rapidly becoming a merchant of considerable standing in Manchester, having (together with his two sons) occupancy of business premises by St. Mary's Churchyard and connections with the merchants Marsden and Marriott.

A further stipulation of the Penrhyn Du lease related to mineral extraction and was to run from 25th March 1763 for a term of 20 years and 6 months, paying every 7th dish of ore i.e. lead, tin, copper or other metals except the waste ore. John Cartwright was obliged to expend £200 within two years for opening up the old pits and draining the mine by "putting in a pair of Stampers at the mouth of the Old Level", and keeping at all times four able and experienced workmen on site who were to endeavour to mine using their best skills.

The expenditure must have seemed a formidable sum to John Cartwright and within a few weeks had panicked him into giving up the idea of lead mining, but necessity forced him to find someone as soon as possible who could take over the lease and therefore relieve him of his difficulties. There seems little doubt that the information was relayed to Roe & Co. from contacts in Bonsall, but Brian Hodgson, not wishing to appear too eager, made it part of a grander scheme.

On 19th October 1763 John Paynter wrote to Lord Powis informing him that "Messrs. Hudson (Hodgson) and son with their agent & Mr. Cartwright came to the cottage in their way from his lordship's manors that they have been surveying in order to commence trials". Roe & Co. seemed just as eager to mine lead as copper for Brian Hodgson enquired about the mine at Esgair-mwyn, the information of which must have come from the Roose family, however, Paynter told them that he thought it was the intention of Lord Powis to work the mine for himself.

Once again there appears to have been a strange pattern to the sequence of events which had taken place. On 10th October, John Cartwright had claimed "One Night's Charges" of 6/- for meeting "Mr. Hodson" (Hodgson) at Bangor. The following evening he was visiting Llanerchymedd, a village on Anglesey close by an area called Parys Mountain where Sir Nicholas had interests. On 12th October he returned to Bangor to meet "Mr. Roe". At this time both senior partners of Roe & Co. must have agreed to lease Penrhyn Du, but whether or not they appreciated that the lease would have to be countersigned and agreed to by both Sir Nicholas and Lord Powis, is a matter for conjecture, because no mention of this is made in Paynter's letter to Lord Powis written exactly one week after Charles Roe's visit to Bangor. When the lease for Penrhyn Du was eventually drawn up, it was retrospectively dated from Charles Roe's visit of the 12th October, which suggests that Cartwright in his anxiety to re-lease offered it to Charles from that day. Charles and Brian Hodgson being men of their word and used to dealing with Derbyshire business men whose codes and ethics were religiously adhered to, assumed that the lease would be quickly executed, and on the strength of Cartwright's word, took possession of the mine placing Jonathan Roose in charge of operations.

About the same time Brian Hodgson also surveyed a disused mine referred to as near "Keightly (Caethle) Old Mine works" on the waste of the Bryndinnas Hills, near Tywyn, Merionethshire, which was on land belonging to Lord Powis. The mine, though apparently unworked since 1755, had shown prospects and was ideally situated. The carriage of ore down to Aberdovy, a busy little outport of Chester, was comparatively easy, as the distance from the entrance of the narrow valley in which the mine was situated, to the port, was only a couple of miles. The boat, after taking ore on board, would be able to sail directly across the northern part of Cardigan Bay, passing the Islands of St. Tudwal and Mercross, to reach the steep rugged headland overlooking Abersoch (a port which at this time had considerable trade with Ireland) on which the Penrhyn Du mine was situated. Further ore would be conveniently taken on board and the whole boated through the Menai Strait en route for the port of Liverpool and its inevitable journey up the River Weaver.

With greater involvement in North Wales taking place, not surprisingly the idea of a canal scheme for Macclesfield was beginning to gain favour to facilitate the carriage of raw materials to the area, stimulated by an already successful venture operated by His Grace, the Duke of Bridgewater.

Francis Egerton, 3rd Duke of Bridgewater, had been a sickly child and was subsequently sent on a Grand Tour of Europe in the hope of recovering his health. At the age of 16 years he had seen and become enraptured with the Languedoc canal in France, and when he had eventually inherited the family estates, after finally suffering the humiliation of rejection by his fiancée, Elizabeth, widow of the Duke of Hamilton, he had diverted his passion into making his dreams become a reality. James Brindley, by then a prominent and experienced engineer, was commissioned to construct a canal into the Duke's coal mine at Worsley near Manchester.

Brindley carried out a survey in 1759, and an Act of Parliament the following year allowed him to begin, what would prove to be in modern terms, another great tourist attraction, comparable to the Derby Silk Mill. When completed barges of coal crossed over an aqueduct from the collieries at Worsley to Manchester. At Castlefield the river Medlock had been skillfully taken under the canal by a tunnel, which increased the force of water, allowing Brindley to use it to good advantage. This great force of water power was able to turn a waterwheel of sufficient capability to hoist coal from the barges to street level. The Duke, in his anxiety to succeed, mortgaged estates and sold land, and it was calculated that the canal eventually cost £1,000 per mile to complete.

The Duke, of course, was not the first person to have successfully built a canal in England, already there were many networks in East Anglia as a result of Dutch influence. But this time Brindley's genius had ensured that an impossibility had become a reality and many lessons had been learnt from the proceedings.

It has been argued that Brindley was illiterate, in the sense that he could neither read nor write, but kept everything in his head. This is not true, to the initiated his diaries are decipherable, and one wonders if he intentionally chose not to commit some of his ideas to paper. After all, once completed, what better than a full scale working model which could prove its worth. Every circumstance was different, and one feels that Brindley's logical mind and common sense saw everything as simple facts for which there was no need to effect complicated diagrams. If a problem arose he solved it. Even on his eventual death bed (1772), having caught cold whilst surveying an intended branch of the Trent and Mersey canal for a syndicate headed by the potter, Josiah Wedgwood, a difficulty arose and the builders came to him with the news that a section of canal was leaking. His advice was to puddle it i.e. to make sure that there was a sufficient layer of clay, stones etc. to act as a barrier against water seepage. The workmen departed but later returned claiming failure, Brindley however persisted and reportedly told them to puddle it and puddle it, again and again until the leak was stopped; this time they were successful.

The Duke of Bridgewater, savouring his triumph, pressed on with plans to build a canal which would link Manchester to the River Mersey and thus to Liverpool. It is not surprising, therefore, to read the report "In 1763 Macclesfield business men applied to the Duke of Bridgewater, requesting that he should cut a branch to Macclesfield from his proposed canal". He declined due to insurmountable difficulties, one of which must have been the fact that Sir George Warren, lord of the manors of Stockport amd Poynton and owner of considerable coal seams, had been the successful suitor of a rich young heiress, Miss Jane Revell, with whom he had eloped and married in Edinburgh during 1758; the unsuccessful suitor was Francis, 3rd Duke of Bridgewater. The young Duke, with his affectations of grandeur, was so bitterly and emotionally upset by the episode, that the mere suggestion of a scheme in which Sir George was in the slightest way involved, must have ensured total opposition from His Grace at all costs.

Meanwhile, Charles Roe, having negotiated the Penrhyn Du lease on 12th October 1763, would have swiftly returned home, because four days later, on the 16th his brother, Rev. James delivered an important sermon entitled "True Religion", in the Parochial Chapel of Congleton. Its impact was such that it was later published together with a sermon preached in St. Michael's, Macclesfield, before one of the Societies of Artificers. The latter, presented as "The Way to Enjoy Life and Fee Good Days", was another great success. He praised the members of the Friendly Society, gathered there to hear his words, for their charity work and great endeavours in giving assistance to all and every member "rendered incapable of Bufineff". In his conclusion he pointed out that "foolish Talking and Jefting . . . is now become fo much the Cuftom, that it usually takes up the greatest Part of the Converfation, whatever Company you fall into . . . Not that the Gospel is an Enemy to all Mirth", and asked them to remember I Corinthians, Chapter 15, verse 33:

"Be not deceived: evil communications corrupt good manners".

A 1918 Survey of Penrhyn Du reproduced by kind permission of the owner.

Footnote: The English translation of the name Penrhyn Du is the Black Cape (or headland). The survey recorded the locations of the old mine shafts relating to the disused lead mine.

14
BRASS

his father was . . . a worker in brass: and he was
filled with wisdom, and understanding, and cunning
to work all things in brass.

The year 1764 was to be one of great struggle and strife for Charles Roe, during which he would finally sever his connections with the silk trade after an involvement of almost 35 years.

On the 9th April a considerable crowd of journeymen silk weavers (described as several thousand) marched in procession from Spitalfields. Distributing handbills en route, they carried a petition to King George III at the Queen's palace in St. James's Park. The petition set forth their grievances, highlighting the miserable conditions of themselves and their families which they blamed on the "clandestine importation of French silks".

In verification of this state of affairs an article, published by the *Chronicle* newspaper in April, related that a London customs' officer had confiscated a large book of French wrought silk patterns. Agents had been visiting mercers and other silk dealers with the book to enable them to obtain orders; the French silks were reportedly offered at 5/- to £5 per yard. The newspaper item concluded in an amusingly practical and sensible manner:

> "It is hoped, that these patterns will be preserved, by those who have the power, for the benefit of our own silk manufacture, and that no application will be available to have them restored to French emissaries or their abettors."

The Macclesfield silk mills were now showing an appreciable decline in the production of thrown silk, the lesser ones each having reduced their employees from 200 or 300 to a mere skeleton force of around 20 to 30. The large silk mill, which had successfully managed to stave off competition for almost three years, suddenly and drastically felt the impact of economic crisis, and the partnership of Messrs. Lankford, Robinson and Stafford ceased production entirely. Amazingly, in spite of this, on the 24th July Charles managed to exact a promise for the sum of £3,808 15 3d. (original value £3,435 9 2½d.) less the amount of monies drawn out by him since 1st January 1764, from the three partners in exchange for his remaining ⅕th share. (In modern terms this would represent more than £⅓ million). The transaction was finally completed by the 26th November when a new agreement was signed and the business valued at £19,023 12 11½d., representing today a business of approximately £2 million. This gave Harry Lankford a half share in the business with quarter shares to each of the other two partners Robinson and Stafford. The money was desperately needed by Charles Roe as commitments in the copper business increased day by day.

In the first instance, whilst Havannah was obviously being developed at this time, priority had to be given to the copper mining, and as the situation at Alderley Edge rapidly deteriorated indicators suggest that Josiah Wagstaffe was brought from Coniston to remedy matters, for it is his initials I.W. (the Roman letter I frequently used at this period to represent I or J) which are chiselled into the wall of Brinlow Sough accompanied by the date 1764. This sough, urgently required to unwater the Engine Vein and recently rediscovered by the Derbyshire Caving Club, shows the remarkable skill of Charles Roe's 18th century miners, for their hand-picked walls, together with the economical coffin shape of the passages, demonstrate the care and artistry employed in such undertakings by the Derbyshire miners. Unfortunately the sough did not quite reach its destination, failing by only 20 yards, the miners no doubt presuming that they had missed their target (as in the case of the Brookhead Sough near Eyam developed to drain the Hucklow Edge Vein, but driven at too high a contour).

At the same time, or within a very short period, hand-picked levels were also worked in the Engine Vein itself, and further evidence on site shows 18th century activity just over the parish border in Over Alderley, now known as the Stormy Point mines, though whether or not the latter is attributable to Roe & Co. is difficult to deduce because of subsequent workings.

The Coniston mine delivered 132 tons of copper ore that year, mostly during the summer and autumn months, which were supplemented by just over 77 tons, presumably from the Llanberis area of North Wales, although a small amount could have been retrieved from Bryndinnas near Tywyn, if trials had already begun in anticipation of the lease. Purchases of Ecton ore, made during May, June and September, totalled £1,814 2 0d. (today almost £200,000) and represent a tonnage of approximately one third less than the previous year's purchases at the mine.

Evidence exists to support only one other source of copper for the Macclesfield smelter during the year; not surprisingly it was Middleton Tyas where Tissington & Co. were already busily engaged, and where Josiah Wagstaffe would be given his next position. During 1764 the following purchases were made:

4 tons	10 cwts.	2 qtrs.	0 lbs.	@ £44		per ton	=	£198 0	0d.
3 tons	8 cwts.	2 qtrs.	9 lbs.	@ £13	6 10d.	per ton	=	£ 43 9	6d.
1 ton	9 cwts.	2 qrts.	0 lbs.	@ £22 13	1d.	per ton	=	£ 32 18	0d.

This ore, was (remarkably), 66% metal and only needed to be roasted once prior to refining. This copper would travel either as pigs, blocks or cakes, but the route taken is open to conjecture. Items of "casks of copper", which could of course relate to copperas, still appear in the River Weaver books at this time. One in particular on 27th October 1764, consigned to "Rowe & Co.", shows 18 casks containing in total 3 tons 1 cwt. of copper.

A cask could be of any size, and where complete information is given in the River Weaver books, a cask of copperas usually weighed 2 cwts. with an occasional one of 3 cwts.

Although there were slight variations in weight between individual blocks and likewise pigs (which is to be expected as the filling of moulds was done manually), yet as near as possible one block weighed slightly more than 3 cwts. (i.e. 336 lbs.) and a pig almost 66 lbs. As each of the aforementioned 18 casks contained an average weight of 3½ cwts. (approximately 392 lbs), a reasonably assumption is that 6 pigs were packed into each cask.

It is not impossible for these to have travelled from Middleton Tyas along Brampton High Lane via the villages of Richmond, Askrigg and Ingleton to the port of Lancaster, as an Act of Parliament in 1751 (Anno 24 Geo III Cap.XVII) provided for the turnpiking and repairing of this route. Once at Lancaster Quay they would follow the same course as the Coniston ore; in fact the 18 casks of copper were accompanied up the River Weaver by a consignment of 25 tons of copper ore.

As the turnpiking of roads gathered momentum, apart from the obvious main routes between towns, it is interesting to discover that what are now regarded as minor roads, or indeed ones traversing regions considered to be 'off the beaten track', were some of the earliest to gain attention because of their primary concern with mining activities.

The purchase of ore from Middleton Tyas must have been made to compensate for the lack of production at Alderley Edge. It is difficult to make a comparison between the copper ores of both areas because at Alderley the richness varied considerably. In the sandstone it barely averaged 2% (1.97% copper oxide) but rich patches of copper carbonate did occur in rock which was otherwise barren, giving a yield of $7^{1}/_{2}$% copper. If overall an average content of 4-5% is presumed to have been achieved by Roe & Co. then approximately 18 tons of Alderley ore would be replaced by 1 ton of smelted ore from Middleton Tyas. As the 1764 total purchases from Middleton Tyas were almost $9^{1}/_{2}$ tons, Charles must have been hoping for a yield of somewhere in the region of 160-170 tons of copper ores from the Edge.

Even when mines were making losses and working at a minimum, it must be remembered that often some ore was being won, but in this instance the retrievable ore must have been negligible for quite some time. Unfortunately the cause for concern was not only confined to the sources of copper ore, even the Gorsey Dale mine near Bonsall, after an excellent start in the first year 1763 with a profit of £48 5 1d., produced a loss of £139 1 7d. during 1764. This, however, proved to be only temporary as the following three years were to show substantial profits, but meanwhile it did necessitate a search for an additional source of calamine, imperative for the experimentation of brass production which was already taking place on Macclesfield Common.

An interesting by-product from the minerals mined in Gorsey Dale was jewellery. It was in this mine that toadstone was found. Derbyshire toadstone is a speckled basalt which is sometimes toad-like in appearance, although it has been said that the name came from miners seeking richer minerals,who, on digging out a piece of barren rock, would remark "It's t'od stone agin" (It's that old stone again).

Whatever the derivation of the name, basalt is solidified lava, dark green or brown in colour, which when originally formed became full of holes from escaping gases as the cooling process took place. The Derbyshire toadstone was the result of later impregnation by other minerals such as calcite, which filled up the holes thus creating an attractive speckled effect. Small quantities of agate have been found in the area, and it is more than likely that small pieces of this mineral were used for setting in jewellery and not the speckled toadstone, if the specimens today are anything to judge by.

However, the interest and fascination created by some of the minor minerals could not outweigh the importance of the need to find those such as zinc, required in large quantities by British industry.

Today the zinc ore of commercial importance is blende, which is zinc sulphide (one form of which is cadmium, although not recognised as a separate mineral until 1817 by Strohmeyer). It frequently occurs with lead, and the resemblance between the two originally gave rise to the Continental miners calling it deceiving ore "because while often resembling galena it yielded no lead". In the mid-18th century the preferred alternative was of course zinc carbonate, commonly known as calamine.

Swedenborg during his travels in England in the early 1720s reported that large amounts of the calamine stone were being mined, particularly in lead mines. It was pale red in colour but heavier than the rest of the earth. Mining operations for the stone were called 'Calamine Pits' and varied in depth from 9 to 45 ulnae (ulna - one of the bones in the forearm). The ore was crushed so that the lead could be picked out of it, otherwise the melting and mixing with yellow copper ore could be difficult, having a detrimental effect. The pale red deposits were considered to be the best kind of ore and also the ones containing white veins. Once the ore had been segregated it was ground into dust with the help of a millstone 'set up perpendicular' and then the dust put into a furnace to be burnt or calcined.

Swedenborg's description of the process is translated as follows:

"The calamine stone furnace is similar to the ordinary reverberative furnace; a flame is prepared from twigs and leaves and, having been introduced into the furnace through an intermediate aperture it is caused to rebound and move rapidly to and fro onto the top surface of the aforementioned stone; the dust in there lies layered to a thickness of 4 or 5 fingers (digitus); there is some as it were, drawing off the flame by a little chimney or oven constructed at the side of the furnace; the quantity of dust burnt is 1 TONN (or $7^{1}/_{2}$ nautical pounds) the burning operation goes on for the space of 6 hours, the heat will be moderate and always constant, and so that the calcination may also be consistent, the dust is turned around (? turned over). When this calcinating fire is finished, the substance appears melted in small pieces and it is then ground down again into dust under the millstone. There are here two types of calamine stone, one which is white in colour and the other red and both are mixed together without discrimination."

Once the calamine had been processed it became known as spelter and then, consisting of about 98% zinc, was shovelled into bags ready for transportation to the centres of brass making.

According to Swedenborg the principal place for English brass manufacture was Baptist Mills, the impressive works of Nehemiah Champion at Bristol. By the time of Angerstein's visit several more centres were in production and his travels of 1754 allowed him to view the most important ones. Bristol was still at the forefront of the brass industry now represented by The Great Brass Company and the Warmley Company, both of which had roots in the old company of Baptist Mills but were formidable rivals.

Nehemiah Champion's patent of 1723 had almost expired as his son, William, was busily engaged in carrying out experiments to obtain zinc from calamine. Within a short period he had accomplished his task, allowing him to acquire patent No. 564 on 1st July 1738. This should have marked the beginning of his success, but in the event the reverse applied. William claimed later that he could sell his zinc for as little as £48 per ton whereas the Bristol merchants, who were importing the spelter, were charging as high as £260-£280 per ton; they drastically reduced prices, and although William argued that they must have been selling at a loss, yet, unable to compete, he was forced out of the spelter trade. Despite this he later fought unsuccessfully for the renewal of his patent, with the possible intention of selling the process to the highest bidder.

After Nehemiah's demise in 1747 William Champion continued to work for some time with his uncle, Richard, in the old company, but certain of his actions were to cause dissension, so he was finally dismissed. His immediate response was to move five miles east of Bristol and construct his own impressive Warmley copper and brass works, which he endeavoured to operate with workmen enticed from the old company. Such was the extent of ill feeling towards him that one individual wrote "As to Mr. Champion, I think there are few mortals queerer."

William's eldest brother, John, although inheriting some shares in the company, moved to Holywell in North Wales and, as already mentioned, became involved in his own projects. He appears to have remained on amicable terms with William, whom he supplied with calamine and Black Jack, the latter a form of zinc sulphide or blende. John Champion, like other members of his family, was adept at carrying out experiments and proficient in obtaining patents. Whilst others struggled with the sulphide ores he effected the following:

Patent No. 569, 10th September 1739 "Making tough brittle metals from sulphurous minerals; mixing same with other metals."

Patent No. 726, 28th July 1758 "Preparing spelter & brass made from a mineral not before used for the purpose".

Angerstein was very impressed with what he saw of the Warmley works and, after receiving the greatest co-operation from William Champion and his book-keeper, was able to give an extensive account of the establishment in his report.

The furnaces he numbered as 15 for copper, 12 brass, 4 spelter or zinc; also on site were small mills for kettles, rolling mills for kettle plates, a battery mill and mills for rolling, slitting and drawing brass wire both thick and fine. The machinery was worked by a Newcomen engine located down stream which pumped water back into the upper pond for recycling. However, despite external appearances, by 1764 William Champion was in financial difficulties, which during the following year were to force him into borrowing large sums of money (subject to high interest rates) for sustaining the Warmley works.

The old company at Baptist Mills, whilst continuing to make brass there, had taken over the lease of Sir Abraham Elton's Conham Works two miles from Bristol at Crew's Hole, after his grandson's bankruptcy of 1745. Sir Abraham, a devout Unitarian, had originally built up an important business, but the old company rebuilt the copper smelters which, according to Angerstein, numbered "no less than 49" with an additional 17 other furnaces half a mile away; the latter possibly representing brass works. Angerstein also visited many of the company's premises between Bath and Bristol on the river Avon and its tributaries, the whole referred to as The Great Brass Company.

There was also a brass warehouse in the centre of Bristol belonging to the company known variously as The Brass Warehouse Co., The Brass Wire Co. (from 1768), or simply B.W.Co.

The London Copper Co. had an extensive copper smelting works four miles from Redbrook, west of the Forest of Dean. The copper, for the most part, was refined at Vauxhall near London and kept in "the store-house" for use by London brass founders who seem to have been concentrated in the Snow Hill area of Holborn (unfortunately, at present very few details of the London brass industry are known).

Angerstein's progress enabled him to inspect the Patten copper works at Warrington where he discovered that only 6 out of the 12 smelters were in operation, but this would shortly be rectified with the start of the Seven Years War in 1756. The copper ore, purchased in Cornwall at £8 to £10 per ton, was processed in a like manner to that of the Bristol and Welsh smelters and then sold to the Company's brass works on the Spout Farm site near Cheadle in Staffordshire. There, with the addition of charcoal and Derbyshire calamine, brass was made partly for supplying the nearby wire mill in anticipation of the African trade, and partly for the provision of ingot brass demanded by the rapidly developing Midland hardware market.

Birmingham had an estimated population of just over 5,000 in the middle of the 17th century, which was said to have trebled by 1700, although this seems likely to have been somewhat exaggerated. Nevertheless the lack of guild restrictions encouraged a further influx of craftsmen and their families, (conveniently assumed to be a 50% increase) during the first 30 years of the 18th century. The streets teemed with metal workers, presenting Thomas Patten with a convenient market for his copper and brass.

Birmingham did have its own brass works, but the demand from the toymakers was increasing at such a rate, with exports reaching France, Italy, what is now Germany, and as far away as St. Petersburg in Russia (where a large contingent of British factors were domiciled and attended the Russia Chapel, which for convenience was considered part of the London Diocese) that the market seemed insatiable.

In 1754 the proprietor of the Birmingham brass works was cited as Mr. Turner: by the time Roe & Co. were in full production John and William Turner, Brassfounders, of the same address had business dealings with Matthew Boulton. Situated on Coleshill Street, the works provided Angerstein with the opportunity of obtaining an excellent description of the brass making process still in vogue at that period.

* * * * * * *

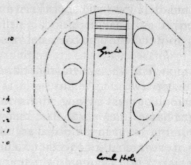

A spelter furnace described in a letter of 1794, together with the process of producing brass. By permission of Llyfrgell Genedlaethol Cymru/The National Library of Wales. (ref. 12513E f6).

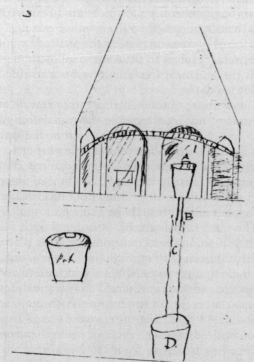

On the Coleshill site were nine furnaces, three under each roof and all fired with coal. Each melting took 10 hours using 3 cwts. of coal together with calamine from Derbyshire and copper from Wales. Into each furnace were placed nine pots, measuring 14 ins in height and almost twice the width at the top as the bottom, presumably made from clay. In all 41 lbs of copper, 50 lbs of brass-ore (calamine) and a quantity of coal were sufficient to fill the ninepots of one furnace. Each pot was initially covered at the bottom with a "mingled mass" of coals and calamine "which was hard packed" to protect the base of the pot. The next layer was described as "small copper" i.e. pellets or granules, known in Bristol as shot, which in turn was again covered with coals and brass-ore. The coals referred to must have been charcoal, because ordinary coal with its sulphur content was impracticable, causing fractures on solidification. The whole melt from nine pots produced 75 lbs. of brass which could be sold for £4 10s. per cwt.

The method of brass making, known as cementation, was a somewhat erratic and arduous process involving much waste. The idea was to encourage the copper to absorb as much zinc as possible, but so much depended on the purity of the ingredients and the responsible way in which they were mixed together, that only the most skilful workmen could be entrusted with the task. Wood charcoal, which always contains a little potassium carbonate, has the power of absorbing gases to a remarkable degree, and would encourage the removal of carbon dioxide or carbon monoxide from the mix. Later it became possible to melt the copper and zinc and stir together, giving a much more uniform mass and brass of superior quality, but at this earlier date, any excess heat applied to melt the copper resulted in vaporisation of the zinc before absorption could take place. Technically, it should have been possible for the copper to absorb sufficient zinc for a 30% zinc content in the resulting brass. Earlier brass founders had rarely succeeded in this, but the importance and experimentation of obtaining spelter of the highest quality had at last been appreciated during the early years of the 18th century.

Zinc is a metal which is easily boiled, allowing William Champion to effect a method of distillation by allowing the zinc vapour to pass through an iron pipe which ran downwards through the furnace floor into a vessel of water. Eventually this method was to prove extremely successful with the later recognition of various forms of zinc increasing the availability of the metal, particularly the more abundant zinc sulphide. However, the traditional method of preparing spelter, as observed by Swedenborg, is the one most likely to have been retained whilst good deposits of calamine were still readily available.

The brass making methods used by Roe & Co. were more than likely those in operation at the Cheadle works of Thomas Patten & Co. Although not mentioned in the translation of Angerstein's Journals, the cementation process at Cheadle varied slightly from the one attributed to the Turner foundry in Birmingham. In the Staffordshire foundry the proportion of copper to calamine was 1:2 by weight, which together with charcoal were placed in crucibles or clay pots of about 12 ins in height. Each container was then sealed and eight of them positioned in each furnace so as to describe a circle around a large "king pot" or crucible. Every 12 hours the pots were unsealed, the slag skimmed off and the remaining molten matter poured into the large central crucible. This routine presumably continued until the large pot was full, which would then receive a final skimming before the pouring took place. If made from best copper, granite moulds were filled; if from "common copper", iron moulds.

The granite moulds (Roe & Co. used Cornish Moor stones) produced 'slips' which measured $4\frac{1}{2}$ ft. long, $4\frac{1}{2}$ ins wide and $\frac{1}{4}$ in thick, these would then be transported to Havannah for rolling into thin sheets only $\frac{1}{16}$ in thick. The next stage involved slitting the sheets into strings ready for drawing through dies to produce round wire. The slitters were sets of iron discs with extremely sharp edges, and Patten's comprised two sets, each 12 ins in diameter and width. They were powered by water and reduced each 'slip' of $4\frac{1}{2}$ ins to 26 square rods. The rods were drawn seven times through a die which made them round, and then through seven dies to draw them fine. Because the method hardened the brass, the wire had to be heated red hot at each stage. The iron moulds produced slabs of ingot brass which were easily remelted by the Midland brassfounders.

Roe & Co. had four brass battery mills and a rolling mill at Bosley, and although brass battery is not mentioned at Cheadle, the methods in use at other works must have been similar to those adopted at the Bosley mills. For battery the granite moulds used were larger, producing 'slips', or slabs as they were known elsewhere, of about 6ft x 3ft, which were in a tilted cradle for pouring and lowered horizontally for removal. The rectangular slabs were then cut into rounds by heavy shears ready for battery.

The hammers used for battery were lightweight compared with those in heavy iron working. They operated between 200-225 blows per minute, and as the brass hardened with each blow, the sound of the hammer changed pitch enabling the hammerman to know when he needed to move the hammer to a softer part.

Each of the annealing ovens at Bosley would be a kind of large muffle furnace to stop gases from the fuel contaminating the metal. It would then be allowed to cool in situ before removal and dispatch.

The only other brass works which attracted Angerstein's attention, and that only briefly, were situated at Wednesbury to the north of Birmingham. The works had been recently built by a "Mr. Voad . . . consisting in 2 furnaces . . . which gets its copper from Bristol and the brass-ore from Darbyshire". (Wednesbury was the site of a vast coalfield where a dreadful accident had occurred on 20th June 1731 when a collier had been "most dismally scorched & roasted to death by ye Hellish Wildfire").

A tribute must be paid to the Continental brass workers without whose help the British industry would not have made such rapid progress. It was Abraham Darby who was said to have gone initially "to Holland" and hired Dutch workmen to assist in setting up the brass works at Baptist Mills.

William Champion, in turn, whilst still quite young, had travelled extensively on the Continent to acquaint himself with the best methods of brass production, and one of Thomas Patten's agents, in 1735, had been paid a fee of 2 guineas for encouraging the German, John Essor, to emigrate and act as chief melter at Cheadle. The family name was Anglicised to Keys, and his descendants would retain their posts as chief melters with the company until the mid-19th century, when the opportunity would arise for them to purchase the Cheadle site and the nearby Whiston Copper Works.

Certainly Roe & Co. needed the assistance of an experienced brass worker to train apprentices, but who fulfilled this role is not known, however, circumstantial evidence suggests that Thomas Patten's establishment provided the expertise.

Only one Macclesfield brass worker, by the name of James Swindells, has been traced from this early period. He must have been out of apprenticeship when he married Mary Warren at St. Michael's during the following year (26th October 1765), for his occupation is given as brass caster in the Parish register. As Roe & Co. did not make brass before 1763-64 it seems likely that James Swindells had started his apprenticeship as a metal worker with the company at the commencement of the copper smelting operations in 1758.

Three other employees on the brass making site, which was situated on the adjoining parish boundary of Sutton, lived in that parish. All were calamine dressers and listed as Roman Catholics on the 1767 Parish Returns to the House of Lords. Two of them, Daniel Melampy and Patrick Cassidy had Irish names and had just completed 18 months and 2½ years respectively with the company; the third, William Bassall was also a recent arrival to the area. In addition three more newcomers to Sutton were listed as 'Servants to Copper Comp.' i.e. James Bassall and wife, probable relatives of the calamine dresser, William, and a Thomas Bottom. The latter, with yet another Irish name, had arrived at the same time as Daniel Melampy and William Bassall to join Patrick Cassidy (a David Melampy is listed as a copper dresser at Ecton on 29th November 1760). This advent of apparently Irish workers is not surprising when considering that Thomas Patten was buying ores from Wicklow in Ireland at this time. It is more than likely some of the employees had followed the ore across the Irish Sea to take up employment at the Cheadle works, later transferring to the Macclesfield company.

* * * * * * *

From the details of the cementation process it can be seen that the proportion of calamine in the mix was far greater than that of copper, so it is not surprising to discover large quantities of calamine transported once more on the River Weaver from April 1764. The sources of this calamine have not as yet been established with certainty, but from later information there were only two areas from which deposits realistically could have been extracted and transported in this manner, Somerset and the region of North Wales closest to the Dee estuary.

Fortunately one volume of the 'River Dee Register of Vessels' 1740-1769 is extant, together with the Chester City Port Books for the period. When coupled with the River Weaver information, an interesting pattern of calamine movement emerges.

In the River Dee Register, apart from three entries, all consignments of calamine were from the port of Baghalt (Bagillt) on the North Wales coast of the Dee estuary. The other three were from the nearby ports of Greenfield (April 1762), Holywell (July 1763) and Mostyn (March 1764). The quantities shipped were not excessive but nevertheless significant.

Before 1760 only one calamine entry appears i.e. 4th June 1755 to Bristol 30 tons in the *Sea Horse*, which was obviously a sea-going vessel.

(The characteristic English coaster of the period was the brig or brigantine, two distinct types of vessel at this time, only later becoming one and the same. The tonnage was usually between 100 to 200, but to be able to negotiate certain parts of river estuaries smaller boats were required of about 40 to 80 tons. In the Severn estuary these were known as trows, whereas in the Dee and Mersey, ponts and sloops were in use. These smaller vessels carried only one mast but the coasters had at least two.)

There seems little doubt that the one large consignment of calamine in 1755 related to the brass industry of the Champions, but after that a pattern became established whereby all consignments of lead, calamine and such like from the Dee estuary, and in particular thousands of tons of coal from the remarkable workings of the Quaker colliery under the sea at Point of Ayr, were all taken to Chester. The city acted as a large administrative and distribution centre, collecting port dues and overseeing the dispersal of goods into its hinterland and far beyond. A decade later a visitor would observe "there is a custom-house with a collector, comptroller, searcher & 21 inferior officers to prevent smuggling & to take care of coasting vessels."

A large market existed in the rapidly expanding port of Liverpool, and during the 1720s Acts of Parliament had ensured improvements to the rivers Mersey and Irwell, contemporaneously with those of the Weaver. At that time, along the Wirral shore between Poole Hall and Ince, a narrow track, built in part as a causeway, ran to the tiny Poole's wharf. From there vessels plied to and fro across the Mersey estuary whilst goods were carried in waggons to and from the quay, mostly loaded or unloaded in the city.

The Mersey, notorious for its tides, had seen the gradual erosion of trade to the important medieval port of Runcorn, with its subsequent diminution. No such consideration was given to Poole's wharf, which was swiftly and completely swept away by surging tides about the year 1750-1751. Prompt action was necessary and on 25th March 1752, Lord Cholmondeley (brother of the General) concluded an important 'Agreement' with a group of merchants whereby he leased his "Wharfe or Key Near the River Weaver called Frodsham Key" to John Blackburne Esq. of Orford, Lancs. and several others. The most significant group of merchants were eight from Northwich, amongst whom was Thomas Marshall, salt proprietor and one of the most important carriers of goods on the river. In particular he transported salt and coal, but was also engaged by Josiah Wedgwood to transport clay for his potteries. Of the 12 remaining merchants, two were from Liverpool, one from Manchester and the others from elsewhere in the region.

The Agreement, which was for 21 years, allowed the:

> "Proprietors or owners of Severall Boats Barges Lighters Flats and other vessels employed and used on the said River in carrying Salt, Salt Rock and other Merchandizes to pass the said Key to and from the Port of Liverpool and elsewhere . . ."

paying the sum of five shillings for each boat. Each of the party of 20 who had signed and set their seal to the document were also allowed access for their "Boatmen Bargemen Workmen or Crew" belonging to their vessels.

With this vital link once more established, heavy materials could once again be more conveniently conveyed than by road, at least for a good part of the journey, although there were many who disagreed with this as attempts to consolidate a canal scheme got underway.

On the other side of the Wirral Peninsula, as early as 1674, a survey carried out by Mr. Andrew Yarranton, a river surveyor of the same calibre as Sorocold, had inspired considerable investment in a canal scheme as part of the improvements contained in several Acts of Parliament relating to the Dee estuary. Unfortunately the expenses proved enormous, forcing many to sell shares, but eventually Thomas Pennant, the famous author, reported that a "plan was brought to a considerable degree of utility; and a fine canal formed, guarded by vast banks, in which the river is confined for the space of ten miles; along which ships of three hundred and fifty tons burthen may safely be brought up to the quays."

Although much attention had be given to the rivers and estuaries, yet the roads had not been entirely neglected. During the 1750s much activity on Halkyn Mountain and elsewhere in the region had caused considerable repairs and turnpiking of roads from Mold to Conwy; this was further extended by a road widening programme, suggesting that many waggons and carriages were using these routes.

With the various transportation options in mind, it is easier to understand the entries, or lack of entries, relating to calamine in the available registers, and also to deduce its destination. The following yearly totals are given to the nearest ton:

River Weaver Tonnage Account Books. Commencing 1st January 1757.	Calamine.	
	1757	101 tons
	1758	63 tons
	1759	52 tons
Last entry 1st July 1760.	1760	45 tons
River Dee Register of Vessels 1740-69. Commencing 26th August 1760.	Calamine to Chester.	
	1760	18 tons.
	1761	54 tons.
	1762	59 tons.
(Calamine to Chester continued)	1763	54 tons.
Last entry 2nd October 1764.	1764	26 tons.

Until evidence is found to the contrary one is entitled to presume that all the above consignments were destined for Thomas Patten & Co. as theirs was the only brass works with connections in the North West until at least 1763-64. From August 1760, as the calamine did not continue up the River Weaver, it now seems possible that Patten & Co. had started brass production at Warrington in addition to Cheadle, or else were transporting the calamine overland to Cheadle in waggons with the copper blocks from the Warrington smelters. The calamine arriving in Chester would, of course, have been loaded in waggons and taken to Frodsham Quay for their journey by boat up the Mersey, past Runcorn to Warrington. The last entry of 2nd October 1764 adds weight to the argument, because during the year Thomas Patten acquired several leases in and around the Greenfield Valley with the intention of building a brass battery mill. This would be in full production, including the making of brass, by 20th August 1766. In the meantime, however, after a lapse of almost 4 years, from the 4th April 1764, regular consignments of calamine once again began to make their way up the River Weaver.

These consignments were to continue for several years with a total annual tonnage often three times, and in some years, at least four times that of the above entries. It is not until 1769 that the consignee's name is given in the Up-tonnage books and in every instance the calamine is destined for Roe & Co. Therefore it seems reasonable to assume that the calamine travelling on the Weaver in 1764, in total 173 tons, was to supplement the dearth of production from Derbyshire, and was the result of Charles Roe's search for further deposits in other areas.

Calamine was definitely being bought from Somerset by the Macclesfield company within the decade, and there is no evidence to suggest purchases were not being made from 1764.

Sir John Thomas Stanley of Alderley was in possession of family estates at Burnham-on-Sea and neighbouring Berrow and Brent within a few miles of the Mendip Hills, from where calamine for the Bristol brass industry had been mined for many years. But the connection in the area was more than likely forged by Thomas Brock, who had been Town Clerk of Chester from 7th April 1757.

There was a large contingent of Brocks in and around the city of Bath, and Thomas Brock's adherence to the area suggests a close relationship. In fact his daughter, Elizabeth, was shortly to marry the famous architect John Wood the Younger, who in 1764 was completing the construction of the Crescent in Bath, originally designed by his father before his early death of 1754. As a token of the marriage settlement John Wood was to finish the building of, and name Brock Street during the following year. He was a member of the Establishment, baptised at Bath Abbey on 25th February 1728, making him senior to Elizabeth by 16 years. The marriage must have given great satisfaction to Thomas Brock, whose second son, William, was now a Church of England minister.

In the extreme north-western corner of the Mendips lies the parish of Rowberrow within the Diocese of Bath and Wells; but as part of an endowment from Henry VIII in June 1542, the manor of Rowberrow had become integrated into the episcopal estate of the Bishop of Bristol, and in the 1760s was occupied by a family called Swymmer. They were kinsmen of the Fane family i.e. Earls of Westmorland, and also distantly related to the then Bishop of Bristol, Thomas Newton. A close friend, associate and, one suspects, relative was Christopher Battiscombe, which suggests a possible relationship with the deceased wife of Edward Pitts.

The Georgian desire for health and happiness, as already portrayed by the Buxton gatherings, was on a far grander scale in the city of Bath, encouraging vast building projects in the Classical style, compatible with the original salubrious Roman baths. These in turn promoted the city's appeal still further, not only to the attentive London society, but also to celebrities from elsewhere.

A Road Act of 1753 had kept pace with developments, allowing turnpiking and repairing of roads between Glastonbury and Wells, along the Great West Road to Bath, and from Wells to Bristol. Further Acts of 1760 had endeavoured to make more efficient the roads to Bath and Bristol, the latter including a bridge improvement.

As might be expected, Thomas Brock had London business connections, dealing through the famous Grecian Coffee-House. It stood in Deveraux (Devereux) Court behind the premises and tea shop of Messrs. Twinings, No. 216 Essex Street in the Strand. This coffee-house had a reputation for its literary clientele such as Goldsmith, Addison and Pope, and was often frequented by members of the Royal Society.

This was the fraternity in which Thomas Brock moved, one which took great pleasure in the seasonal gatherings of Bath for the enjoyment of the spa waters, much preferred to those of Buxton by Celia Fiennes more than half a century earlier, when she considered the Somerset baths and springs considerably hotter; a sentiment echoed also some 30 years later by Daniel Defoe when he could "hardly be persuaded to come out of the bath".

Apart from his position as Town Clerk of Chester, which was of course only part-time, Thomas Brock, like many others including John Stafford, had his own private legal practice. This provided him with the opportunity to acquire a considerable knowledge of business propositions, particularly in North Wales, and also to invest heavily in property.

At some point in time Charles Roe made an agreement with the Swymmer family to purchase calamine from the pits belonging to the Rowberrow Manor. It was stored in buildings constructed for the purpose at Winterhead, about a mile or so from the village of Shipham along an indifferent cart track, which in times of bad weather disintegrated into a quagmire.

Apparently the Bishop of Bristol, although having jurisdiction in the manor including the responsibility of holding court to maintain laws and customs, was not entitled to a proportion of the calamine sales; this was the right of the Swymmers as Lords of the Manor. They engaged Robert Phippen to oversee operations and he lived with his large family in a hill farm close to the pits, in a very bleak and exposed area. The entitlement of the Lord of the Manor was "1/4 of the calamy that is dug i.e. 5 cwts out of every ton."

Lead mining was prolific in the surrounding hills, having existed from at least Roman times, and was responsible for a considerable export trade through Bristol in the 14th century. The Mendips, as in other mining areas, had its own code of laws, together with a community of lead miners by all accounts similar to those of the Castleton area of Derbyshire who lived in Peak Hole i.e. "a stage or two beyond Christendom".

An interesting custom pertained whereby miners left their tools and ore, often in the open air but sometimes in a hut, "without much apprehension of having them taken away". If a workman was convicted of theft, he forfeited his right to work the mines and was condemned to a particularly poignant form of punishment called 'Burning of the Hill'. The culprit "with his hands and feet at liberty", was shut up in one of the little tool huts, with ferns and dry scrub placed around the outside; these were then simultaneously set alight on all sides. The encased man was left to make his escape as best he could "by breaking open his prison, and rushing through the fire."

It must be remembered that the dangers of lead poisoning were grossly underestimated, and just handling the lead over a long period could cause brain damage by its absorption into the blood stream. One can understand the sentiments expressed by a Bristol schoolmaster's genteel daughter who, having visited the area, later wrote, "Among the most depraved and wretched were Shipham and Rowberrow, two mining villages at the top of Mendip; the people savage and depraved almost even beyond Cheddar, brutal in their natures and ferocious in their manners."

* * * * * * *

The mining of calamine had, of course, begun late in the reign of Elizabeth I, and an excellent contemporary description of Mendips mining practices in the mid-1760s (published 1769) includes a detailed account of calamine treatment.

The mines of 'Lapis Calaminaris' were found on the western slopes of the hills, with the veins of white, red, grey or black running between the rocks. The veins in the limestone were generally wider than those of lead, but in the harder rocks much narrower, although a considerable quantity of lead was found with the calamine.

When a sufficient amount of calamine had been collected it was washed, cleansed and buddled. The washing took place within a small enclosure; there a clear stream ran through where boards or"'turfs" had been laid. The calamine was shovelled and turned, allowing the stream to carry away many impure and earthy parts, whilst the lead, calamine and "other stony substances" were left behind. When the calamine was considered clean, a quantity of the mix was placed in a sieve of strong wire and dipped in a large tub of water several times, being shaken up and down in-between whiles. This had the effect of encouraging the spar particles to float on top, which were then skimmed off and thrown away, with the calamine forming a layer in the middle and the lead beneath. The calamine was scooped off and spread onto the floor so that any remaining stones etc. could be picked out by hand. On many occasions such was the quality of the calamine that it could be brought straight from the pits and taken to the calciners. The correspondent continued:

> "The calamine being thus prepared, they carry it to the calcining oven, which is built in the fame form as that ufed by bakers, but much larger: on one side of it is a hearth, divided from the oven itfelf by a partition open at the top, by which means the flame paffes over the calamine, and calcines it. The fire is common pit-coal, which is thrown upon the hearth, and there lighted with charcoal. In about four or five hours, during which the calamine is turned feveral times with long iron rakes, it is, in general, fufficiently calcined: but this is not always the cafe; for fome being much harder than others, requires a longer time. When it is fufficiently calcined, they beat it to powder, by long iron hammers, on a thick plank, picking out what stones they find among it; by which means the calamine is at last reduced to duft, and then fit for fale. Its principal ufe is to turn copper into brafs."

The calamine could have been taken overland to Bristol and shipped via Liverpool for passage up the River Weaver, but no such evidence exists in the Bristol Port records. Only one item entered 12th July 1764: one basket of yellow earth, can be traced, bound for Liverpool.

The most convenient way would have been to cart it to the village of Rackley, only three miles from Winterhead, for transportation down the navigable part of the River Axe. This way the calamine would reach the coast just south of Weston-super-Mare at the village of Uphill (the route by which the calamine would be taken to the smelters of South Wales), from where it could have completed the journey to the Mersey estuary by transference to a sea-going vessel.

Another route, along the tedious meandering River Severn to Shrewsbury, seems the most likely; this had been established for centuries and was particularly used in the 16th and 17th centuries by merchants from as far away as Manchester and Sheffield, anxious to use the port facilities of Bristol. From Shrewsbury a packhorse route led northwards through Whitchurch, Northwich, Middlewich and Knutsford, then to Stockport and Manchester. Hence the connection between the Yate family of Whitchurch and the Claytons of Manchester, all vital links in a long mercantile trail. A second important way led directly from Whitchurch in a north-westerly direction, passing Bickerton copper mine en route for Chester.

Another two years would elapse before an Act of Parliament was passed to make a "Cut or Canal" linking the River Severn with the River Trent which, after many objections, would finally be completed in the year 1772 creating a prosperous new township called Stourport. Before this, it is difficult to find evidence as to which way the Somerset calamine travelled to Macclesfield.

Buttons, silks, Indian cottons, haberdashery and similar items were ideal merchandise for long packhorse journeys, but heavy goods such as minerals were transported as much as possible by water, often in bulk. Of course, the calamine would be calcined and therefore lighter in weight than lead or copper ores.

As can be seen from the information available, what had begun in 1736 as an ill-advised mining speculation on Macclesfield Common, but turned to advantage by Charles Roe, was now becoming a business of enormous proportions. Ironically it was to be through his lesser investments in the lead trade that prosperity for Charles and his family would indirectly be brought about, and also his third successful and final marriage.

* * * * * * *

During the early months of 1764 Charles had waited in vain for the execution of the lease in respect of the lead mine Penrhyn Du. Jonathan Roose and his men were hard at work draining water out of the mine, which was no easy task as the workings had reached a considerable depth. The costs of the operation were mounting rapidly, so finally, when the first year was almost at an end, after making many endeavours through his own agents and those of Sir Nicholas's, Charles took to his horse to make the long arduous journey to Plas Newydd.

The first part of the journey to Chester should have presented no problems although it was early autumn. Upon his arrival in the city Charles would have called to pay his respects to his good friend Thomas Brock, and more than likely stayed with the family, giving the two men an opportunity to discuss business matters. There is the possibility that Charles had already broached the subject of calamine purchases late in 1763, during his hasty visit to Anglesey in response to the Hodgsons' surveys in North Wales. If so, then as already discussed, the result could have been help from Thomas Brock in acquiring supplies from Somerset, which were possibly proving an expensive option.

The desirable alternative was to obtain supplies from the county of Flintshire, stretching along the southern shore of the Dee Estuary. Here also the Swymmer family of Somerset had interests in a joint concern known as "The Lords of Mold", but only later does evidence exist of Roe & Co.'s involvement in that area. With much of the production already committed to certain markets, the problem was availability of leases. Within the region already strong ties existed with Derbyshire cultivated over a long period. Even within the Roe family the connections, though somewhat distant by this time, nevertheless existed.

Flintshire is a county in two parts, with the smaller detached portion (Maelor) intruding, as it were, into the north-west corner of Shropshire. It was in this satellite area that Charles Roe's cousin, Rev. Samuel, son of Uncle William, vicar of Frodesley and Pitchford, had held the position of curate-in-charge for the parish of Overton from 1739 to 1745. Because of the close bonds between the two branches of the family, there is little doubt that as a young button merchant Charles would have visited his cousin on his journeys to and from Chester, and therefore knew the area well.

Even at the time of cousin Samuel's arrival, the Roes were already known due to the fact that a great uncle, having died young and without issue, had left a widow, Mrs. Magdalene Roe, in possession of property at Abenbury Fechan, just over the border in Denbighshire and close to Wrexham. The property included a forge which, towards the end of the 18th century, would be developed into an important site by the famous ironmaster, John Wilkinson. Mrs. Magdalene Roe subsequently married Rev. Parry of Oswestry, whose family were involved in the mines of North Wales, particularly Flintshire. At her death a legal wrangle took place amongst the next of kin, culminating in a court case (1753). This included the Roe family who should have been compensated in some way for the original marriage settlement. The forge was charged in the Abenbury Fechan Rate Books to "Mrs. Magdalene Roe or tenant" from 1715 to 1725, obviously providing the widow with income from rents.

The Brock family also owned lands in Denbighshire close to Wrexham, in the parish of Gresford. This property, in their possession from at least the late 17th century, had been bequeathed from one heir to the next (all Brock family pewterers of Chester) until 1759 when, without children, Thomas's uncle Richard had left the property to his wife. However, the Brock interests in the area had provided legal work for Thomas, and his first property investment. On 30th July 1752 he had lent money to David Ledsham, a Chester baker, to include in the marriage settlement of his joiner son. The security was property in Minera, parish of Wrexham and the inevitable took place; possession was legally obtained in the court at Ruthin with Thomas Brock becoming owner of two messuages, two gardens, two orchards, four acres of land, four acres of meadow and four acres of pasture.

An interesting account concerning the brass candelabra of Gresford Parish Church (All Saints) has emerged. Having reviewed all available information the anecdote is as follows: during 1739, Thomas Brock Snr. brazier of Chester had been approached to supply a brass candelabrum for the church. This was made, duly accepted and hung, with the following entry written in the Churchwarden's accounts:

> "April ye 9th, 1739.
>
>   £   s   d
>
> Pd. Mr. Brock towards the Sconc ..   20 0 0 "

The candelabrum must have been greatly admired, because in 1747 Thomas Snr. was asked to supply a matching partner for his original. This was also made, dated 1747 and inscribed with the Churchwarden's names but within a few months, for some reason, the undated one from 1739 was in need of repair, and once again the workshop of Thomas Brock was used. On this occasion it appears that this candelabrum was inscribed also with the Churchwardens' names and given the date of repair 1748. With the work completed a clash of personalities took place, indicated by the following entry in the vestry book:

> "Ordered, that, whereas the Inhabitants of this Parish are dissatisfyed with Mr. Brock the Brazier's Bill for the Repair of the Church sconch, Charles Leadward, one of the Churchwardens do and shall give notice to the said Mr. Brock that he is required to name an Indifferent workman on his part, and the Parishioners to name another, to value the sd. work, and that the sd. Charles Leadward be impowered, if He can, to agree and make up the matter in dispute with the sd. Mr. Brock – as witness our Hands December 27, 1748".

The outcome is unknown, but by 1903 only the "fine brass candelabrum" of 1747 would remain, hanging from the roof in the centre of the nave "by very handsome wrought iron work" which still retained a considerable amount of gilding. The observer noted that the names of the churchwardens were engraved on the upper half of the globe upside down, whilst they were "repeated again, in proper manner on the lower (half)". It was presumed that Mr. Brock had apparently mistaken the upper for the lower half, whereas the probable truth is that his apprentice had given the wrong half to the engraver.

Without doubt the missing candelabrum of 1739, repaired, inscribed and dated 1748, was the one located at the address 71-2 Buckingham Gate London in 1956, for it bears all the names of the Gresford churchwardens together with the date of 1748.

Several candelabra within the region have tentatively been attributed to the Brock workshop, such as in St. John Baptist's, Chester, the churches of Erbistock in Denbighshire, Hanmer and Overton in Flintshire, the latter dated 1746, where on 30th October Rev. Samuel Roe married Ellen, a daughter of Thomas Roberts.

* * * * * * *

The greater part of Flintshire, along the southern shore of the Dee Estuary, had seen the discovery of calamine in 1720 by John Barrow, a Somerset miner, conversant with the ore in his home county because of the demand from the Bristol brass industry. By 1727 plentiful supplies had been uncovered in the nearby mines of Lord Plymouth near Whitford, but the most remarkable discovery occurred in 1756 on Sir George Wynne's old Halkyn property, which had just been sold by his widow to Lord Grosvenor (worked as Saith-aelwyd Shaft). This had been followed by a further find in the Crown property of Dyserth.

As in Somerset, lead mining was the precursor and had long stimulated a Derbyshire interest in the region. Evidence exists to support the fact that skilled miners from Derbyshire had been 'encouraged' (sometimes by force) to work in the mines of Flintshire from at least the Middle Ages. Even the lead mining laws of the two regions were so much akin, that one wonders if Edward I, after confirming the Derbyshire rights and privileges under the Great Seal at Ashbourne in 1288, had been instrumental in suggesting the same for North Wales during his extensive programme of castle building.

The resurgence of lead mining in North Wales had begun, as in England, after the Restoration. In the 1690s Thomas Cheney was engaged as chief mineral agent for Lord Grosvenor on Halkyn Mountain, when one of the richest rakes was discovered and named after him. It was his son, Edward, Lord of the Manor of Monyash, who had married Elizabeth Sleigh, half sister of Charles Roe's first wife, resulting in the Brassington Estate being held in trust and enjoyed by the Roe family because of Elizabeth's mother's marriage to Samuel Lankford Snr. Another son, Thomas Cheney, had succeeded his father as the Grosvenor mineral agent, whilst a daughter, Elizabeth, married John Twigg of Holme, who purchased the greater part of Brian Hodgson's share of the Boothby Estate at Ashbourne.

In 1694 Quaker interests were served by the London Lead Co. which was to operate in the area around Holywell for virtually 100 years, smelting its ores at Gadlis. Derbyshire workmen were engaged from time to time and the Quakers, as already mentioned, extended their operations in Derbyshire when they leased premises for smelting at Ashover in 1734.

Because of the Cheney presence, a group of Derbyshire gentry, including Henry Thornhill and Brian Hodgson's later business associate, Nicholas Twigg, had formed a partnership called 'Pentre', whose results were so impressive that the Quakers, working close by, resolved to continue operations in their unprofitable Maeslygan mine.

At the same time "Mr. Thornhill & Partners" held shares on Mold Mountain from 1718 to 1738 and continued mining in the area with help from further investments by, amongst others, Richard Richardson, goldsmith and Thomas Slaughter, both of Chester (the latter High Sheriff of Cheshire 1755, associate and kinsman of Thomas Assheton).

Nicholas Twigg in partnership with another Derbyshire mining associate, leased land from the Pennant family and built an important smelter at Bagillt, which from 1752 was leased to members of the Smedley family, who would remain in possession until their bankruptcy of 1779. Two of the family, Thomas and Francis, also joined the Mold mining 'conglomerate' together with the London lawyer, Paul Panton of Lincoln's Inn, business associate of John Champion and his son of the same name. This group built themselves a smelter at Nantymoch near Holywell, which was the probable reason for Nicholas Twigg's withdrawal from the Bagillt smelter. (Because of the weight involved it was always easier to smelt lead, like iron, as near to the mines as possible).

The partnership of Thornhill, Twigg & Sons was well-known to Charles Roe, for it had a group shareholding in the Eyam mines known as Bradshaw & Butler's Old New Engines Sough. By the 1760s, instead of receiving money for his shares in the mines of Eyam, Charles was claiming his entitlement of the ore, proving his commitment to the lead trade in addition to copper and brass.

* * * * * * *

On leaving Chester in 1764, bound for Plas Newydd. Charles could have taken the more direct road through Flint and Holywell, but more than likely made a small detour to Mold, enabling him to enquire of the calamine prospects amongst the Derbyshire agents. From

Mold the way would lead him to the "fair, populous " and busy town of Denbigh, important for its assaying facilities because of its convenient position in relation to the lead mines of the surrounding region.

The next part of the journey led past falls and over rivers, descending to the ancient castellated town of Aberconwy and renowned for its abundance of fish and "pearls out of its Black Shells". Anyone travelling by coach, even from the direction of Shrewsbury, had to go via Chester and St. Asaph, which necessitated a perilous ferry crossing to the town.

From Conwy the coastal route via Penmaenmawr to Bangor was the most difficult and dangerous. Overhanging cliffs and crumbling track along the very edge of Conwy Bay resulted in many accidents, particularly during spells of inclement weather. Even the crossing to the Isle of Anglesey was not without its perils; the desirability of a bridge becoming a reality only after several more decades. In all there were five ferries from different points on the mainland. The most northerly was across Lavan Sands to Beaumaris, but only seasoned travellers dared to choose this route because, without a perfect knowledge of tides in the area, a late arrival of just half-an-hour meant that they were swept away.

The next ferry south, convenient for Bangor, operated slightly north of where the Menai Bridge (built 1825) now spans the Strait. *The George Inn*, aptly sited on the mainland to accommodate passengers, was one of the reasons why several important personages preferred this ferry route, such as Jonathan Swift in 1727.

A third ferry crossed from the tiny fishing quay of Dinorwig at the southern end of the Vaynol Estate, providing the shortest journey to Plas Newydd on the island. This might have proved more convenient for Charles, otherwise he would certainly have chosen the one located outside *"The George Inn"*, for the two remaining ferries served the southern end of the Menai Strait, one at the entrance to the waterway from Belan Fort (now a dock) to Abermenai Point, and the other between Caernarfon and Tan-y-foel.

Plas Newydd was inconveniently situated on the banks of a river and "protected on each side by a small growth of trees". A traveller remarked "although great sums have been expended . . . it is . . . by no means either elegant or remarkable."

Charles Roe's arrival at the house must have been perceived by Sir Nicholas Bayly, who no doubt took much pleasure in complimenting himself on his own perspicacity in the matter, for it appears that Sir Nicholas had further plans in mind, hence the deliberate postponement of the legalities confirming the Penrhyn Du lease to Roe & Co.

Under the terms of the marriage settlement of March 1736, in consideration of the enormous sum of £4,000 given by the Hon. Colonel Thomas Pagett for his daughter Caroline's marriage portion, Sir Edward's contribution on behalf of his son had included manors, lands etc. in the Welsh counties of "Anglesey, Denbigh and Carnarvon" together with those in Down and Lowth and "divers other places in Ireland". Much of this property had obviously descended through the family from great grandfather the Right Rev. Lewis Bayly, Bishop of Bangor. Situated in the north-eastern region of Anglesey was Trysclwyn mountain consisting of two estates; the eastern part called Cerrig y Bleiddia was part of the Bayly estates, but the western part, presumably because of a legacy or marriage settlement between two daughters (as in the instance of the Penrhyn estate), was held jointly but in equal undivided moieties; an unusual arrangement no doubt conceived to prevent the very thing that it would ultimately create – a legal wrangle. Sir Nicholas being one of the half share owners had leased the other half in 1753 from his coheir, William Lewis, for a term of 14 years, rental £25 per annum, and then sub-leased the whole of this estate called "Paris" (often spelt as now Parys) to Thomas Price, who at once became 'Tenant-in-Common' with Sir Nicholas.

When visiting the area a decade later, Thomas Pennant wrote a brief history of the location and set the scene for what was to become yet another obligatory sojourn on the 'Grand Tour' of Wales. He suggested that Parys Mountain was so called after Robert Parys, chamberlain of North Wales in the reign of Henry IV. In appearance the mountain, in reality a hill, was composed of "enormous rocks of coarse white quartz". Pennant was in no doubt that ancient workings had existed, if not in prehistoric times, most certainly during the Roman occupation, as several Roman coins, cakes of copper and traces of charcoal had been found in various parts of the island. The discovery of Roman foundry remains at Caer-rhun (originally Canovium) four miles above Conwy, in particular a mass of copper impressed "SOCIO ROME" adds weight to the argument that Roman mining took place within the vicinity. Two ancient grooved hammer stones, found at the top of a low peat covered mound near the old windmill on Parys in 1936 and now in the British Museum, confirm early interest in the site.

After the Restoration, during the revival of mining, some attention was paid to Anglesey, but although one or two learned visitors suspected the presence of iron, copper and lead yet no concerted effort was made to carry out trials, the only mining development being that of coal.

Apart from Sir Nicholas's endeavours to increase coal production by placing John Cartwright in charge of operations, another important area for coal was on the Penrhos estate near Holyhead. The death of a barrister, Hugh Owen, in 1742 left the estate as inheritance to a baby girl, Margaret Owen. She grew into a beautiful young woman who was painted by Reynolds, and in 1763 had married Sir John Thomas Stanley of Alderley. Under the terms of their marriage settlement Alderley Hall, Park and demesne lands were to be excluded, and also, presumably, Lord Stanley's rights as Lord of the Soil of Alderley Edge, for no mention is made of the copper mining lease in the settlement. Included was property in Chester, land in Nether and Over Alderley, an estate in Somerset and with Margaret's portion, the Welsh estate of Penrhos with income from coal mining leases.

During the year prior to Lord Stanley's marriage a character called Alexander Frazier had arrived on Angelsey with the intention of searching for ore, and according to Pennant "called on Sir Nichols Bayly and gave him so flattering an account of the prospect, as induced him to make a trial, and sink shafts. Ore was discovered, but before any quantity could be gotten, the mines were overpowered with water".

Before the flooding took over, Sir Nicholas had informed his family of the find; they, apart from himself, were staying at the London residence in Bond Street, and it was from there that the eldest son, Henry, addressed a letter to his father on 27th September 1762. Together with various snippets of news he wrote "I congratulate you upon finding a Copper Mine & heartily wish it may turn out according to your expectations."

Caroline wrote to her husband on the 2nd October, setting down further items of interest and concluding:

"I had a very agreeable dream last night of Placenewith The gardens and grounds about it were quite beautifull and extremely fine. if your Copper mine turns out as great as they have flatterd you it will I shall be tempted to pay a visit once more to Anglesea." Whether or not Caroline managed a further visit to Anglesey is unknown, but in a little more than three years' time she would be dead and Sir Nicholas's involvements with his lady friends were to become so entangled that he would almost sacrifice the Welsh estate to cover his 'commitments' and completely ignore the necessity of making any provisions for his six younger children in the event of his own death.

It must be remembered that Sir Nicholas's main career was a military one, a tradition strongly upheld within the family resulting in his grandson, Henry, becoming second in command to Wellington at Waterloo. Perhaps, therefore, to a certain degree Sir Nicholas could be forgiven his somewhat idiosyncratic life style. Certainly Caroline thought so, concluding her letter with one of her usual terms of endearment, "I am, Dear Sir Nicholas, your affectionate Wife."

Once flooding of the Parys mine had occurred, the inexperience of the miners rendered it impossible for them to proceed further, and Sir Nicholas must have felt bitterly disappointed. It can be no coincidence that after meeting Brian Hodgson at Bangor on 10th October,

1763, the following day John Cartwright visited Llanerchymedd, a village near Parys Mountain, before returning to Bangor for his rendezvous with Charles Roe. One is forced to conclude that Brian Hodgson was taken to survey the Parys mine but rejected its viability and so dissuaded Charles from attempting the project, concentrating instead on the more promising venture at Penrhyn Du.

Perhaps Lord Stanley, knowing the efforts which Charles Roe's miners were putting into their work at Alderley, and being aware of the Macclesfield company's need to supply its own ore rather than pay dearly for supplies as from Ecton and Middleton Tyas, had let it be known that Sir Nicholas's mines might prove successful to an experienced team. He could also have been endeavouring to show an amicable and neighbourly attitude towards the Baylys having recently married the Penrhos heiress. (Even today the present Lord Stanley shows great consideration for others, and though the family home and sheep farm is a little removed from the original, yet it is tucked beneath Parys Mountain with voluminous heaps of waste material providing a back drop to the cobbled courtyard and outbuildings.)

Sir Nicholas's determination to have further trials for copper ore carried out on his estate had evidently borne fruit; a brief note in John Cartwright's account book reads "1764 Mr. Roe came to Plas Newydd and agreed for Paris Mountain." The bait had been successful so far as Sir Nicholas was concerned, but still he tarried, and if a judgement can be made from later events, must have been hoping that a lucky strike in either of the mines would give him the opportunity to manipulate the verbal bargain agreed to, before it was committed to paper. However, Charles was no fool and would not have agreed to any conditions which were beyond his power to control. On this occasion he would have viewed the Parys site personally and appreciated that the situation had altered considerably since Brian Hodgson's visit. Men and equipment were now within easy reach at Penrhyn Du and Jonathan Roose was on hand to oversee operations. Charles, realising that it was imperative for an immediate decision to be made, took full responsibility for the bargain, thus agreeing to a lease on a one to one basis i.e. between Sir Nicholas and himself only.

Some time after returning to Macclesfield he was visited by John Cartwright, who must have brought drafts of the leases for approval and also delivered the message that Lord Powis "chose Sir Nich's sh'd sign first" in respect of the Penrhyn Du lease. Instead, however, Mr. Nicklin, Cartwright's deputy, had been sent to London to obtain the signature of Lord Powis prior to that of Sir Nicholas, an action which he communicated to Charles Roe upon his arrival in the capital. Charles somewhat surprised by the news, pondered what further procrastinations Sir Nicholas had in mind and quickly wrote to the Earl in Albermarle Street, London, on the 18th December to persuade him to sign first, otherwise Mr. Nicklin "must have Another journey without it. I hope Yr. Lordship will sign as it needs not be delivered without Sir Nich's & Cartwright signing . . . I can scarce keep the Partners (so very Tidious & expensive has the endeavouring to get this Lease been) from Throwing up & Resolving (to) proceed no farther . . ." In this instance an abrupt style was inappropriate, so Charles tempered his letter accordingly, pointing out that "Mr. Nicklin knows every Transaction from first to last, & can inform Yr. Ldship We have in no Case veared from the first Agreement." Mr. Nicklin was in a position to verify that Sir Nicholas had raised no objections to signing the lease when Charles was at Plas Newydd, and Lord Powis was also informed "We have bought the Stock upon the ffarm etc . . . & several Shafts etc: that were Open'd, We are to pay, on the Leases being Sign'd & brot hither."

This letter must have produced the desired effect for both leases were safely delivered.

The Penrhyn Du lease read as commencing 12th October 1763, between "the Right Hon'ble Earl Powis and Sir Nicholas Bayly of the first part, John Cartwright of the second part and Bryan Hodgson of Buxton in the County of Derby Gent. and Charles Roe of Macclesfield in the County of Chester, Gent".

The old mines had already been worked 30 yards deeper than the old level, but Brian

Hodgson and Charles agreed that they would carry on the mining 10 yards deeper so as to make 'an effectual trial', and for this purpose were given three years. Having created new workings or openings these were not to be filled in but left for further use.

John Cartwright was paid £142 10s. in consideration of the transfer and allowed to keep his buildings, but take the ore he already had on bank by a certain date. He was also allowed the right "to direct & turn the Watercourse of the Spring lying above the ffarm house . . . through and over any part of the said Lands and premises where the said John Cartwright his Exors. (etc) may from time to time think it expedient for the more effectual buddling washing and cleaning the said Ore and Minerals." This could have caused problems initially but Charles was relying on the experience and personality of Jonathan Roose to handle the situation appropriately.

Messrs. Hodgson & Roe were allowed full mining rights to dig soughs etc. erect buildings and have right of way across land for horses, carts, carriages and so forth. Any trespass or damage had to be referred to two impartial persons, one chosen by the lessees and one by the tenants or occupiers at the time. The term of the lease was 21 years paying $1/10$th of the 'Produce' (i.e. the ore made merchantable) for the first two years, and $1/8$th for the remainder of the lease.

The Indenture for Parys Mountain was dated 10th October 1764 by which Sir Nicholas leased all mines and minerals of lead and copper and all other minerals, in or under land belonging to a certain farm called 'Cerrig y Bledio' in the Parish of Amlwch to Charles Roe or his assigns. All rights of digging were allowed and water rights for buddling etc. and the usual rights of access for workmen and conveyances. The quarrying of stone was of course included for the erection of buildings as required, and permission to use engines, the latter necessary if water had to be pumped from the workings. The clause concerning trespass and damage was the same as for Penrhyn Du, as was the term of the lease i.e. 21 years. The duty payable was set as "one full eighth part" of merchantable ore for the whole of the 21 years, but Sir Nicholas did have an option included whereby if he preferred to receive the value in money instead of in kind, then he could do so. He was determined to cover for every eventuality and had every conceivable circumstance pedantically set down, stressing that everything had to be carried out "in a skillful and workmanlike manner".

It seems obvious that Sir Nicholas did not personally dictate all the terms of the lease, which was more than likely prepared by his solicitor in London, but that someone with a knowledge of mining and the site had assisted.

There was a specific stipulation which is difficult to believe Charles would normally have agreed to beforehand: within the space of two years "now next ensuing" (note: not from the date of the lease but from the date it was prepared, which is unknown) a sough or tunnel was to be driven "from the Turbary on the South East side of a certain hill or mountain called by the name of Paris Mountain . . . unto that part of the said mountain where there are now two pits or shafts sunk . . . called by the names of Fair Chance and Golden Venture being by computation 400 yards." In carrying out this stipulation, should the company use any of the old workings already opened at Sir Nicholas's expense, then he was to be compensated by a like figure within two months. Obviously it was a sly endeavour to recoup his money, because if the miners did not use the old workings then they would more than likely have to take a more circuitous route, adding further expense to the venture in any event. During the first year six able miners had to be constantly employed on site, and for the remaining years, ten.

Sir Nicholas, determined to keep tight control on matters, insisted on inspectors having access at all times and being kept informed of any proposed soughs or tunnels which could be determined either by the company or himself. The company had to keep books from which copies could be made, and carry out stringent checks on the storage of ore with a view to paying duty. In any event the Derbyshire miners would have carried out these conditions as part of their duties; ironically Sir Nicholas's behaviour, indicative of mistrust or treating them as novices, would have been better directed against his own retainers.

Because of the difficulty of operations at Penrhyn Du, the partners had expended almost £800 during 1764 and what must have been a similar figure at Alderley Edge. Finding supplementary supplies of ore, and the difficulties and costs of transportation over great distances must have created many worries for Charles Roe, not least until the 26th November 1764, when he was finally freed from his financial anxieties with regard to the silk trade.

Shortly before this, and just after the Roe visit to Anglesey, Brian Hodgson decided that the time was right for his eldest son, Robert, then 23 years of age, to be admitted to the Roe & Co. partnership. Although no details exist of the original number of shares, it is known that Brian Hodgson's was divided into four equal parts, one of which he gave to Robert. From a later statement of shareholders it has been possible to assess the early composition of the company and the subsequent movement of shares. In 1764 the position was as follows:

Charles Roe	$4/14$	
Rowland Atkinson)	$2/14$	Rowland $1^1/2 = {}^1/14 + {}^1/28$
Cookson Atkinson)		Cookson $^1/2 = {}^1/28$
Brian Hodgson	$4/14$	gift of $^1/14$ to son Robert on 5/11/64.
Edward Pitts	$4/14$	

* * * * * * *

The partners of the copper company were not the only ones to have been busily engaged during the year. The newspapers of 1764 provide various reports of John Wesley's peregrinations; from the Hull Estuary in April, through the Yorkshire Dales to Scotland in May, Liverpool in mid-July and Bath in September, all visits were noted and commented upon. His remarks concerning Liverpool were very edifying. "Many of the rich and fashionable were there, and behaved with decency. Indeed I have always observed more courtesy and humanity at Liverpool than at most sea-ports in England."

The Public Advertiser in June had proudly announced a performance by "the celebrated & astonishing Master MOZART, lately arrived, a child of 7 years of Age" and considered him to be the "most amazing Genius that has appeared in any Age." He was actually $8^1/2$ years old at that time.

On 4th September the Duke of Devonshire, seeking relief from the effects of his epileptic fits, had gone to Aix-la-Chapelle, then part of France and famed for its mineral waters. (He had obviously gained little benefit from his own baths at Buxton). By the 3rd October, when visiting the Spa in Ostend, he died. Naturally it was necessary to transport his body back across the Channel for burial, and on the 31st October the gossips were busy spreading the news that Customs officials had inspected the corpse for contraband, an action later denied.

The death of the 4th Duke left his three young sons as minors and his affairs in the hands of Trustees and Guardians. It left the town of Macclesfield without a powerful supporter in the House of Lords during the crucial stages of a bill, in respect of a canal scheme, to be prepared and presented to Parliament during the next few months.

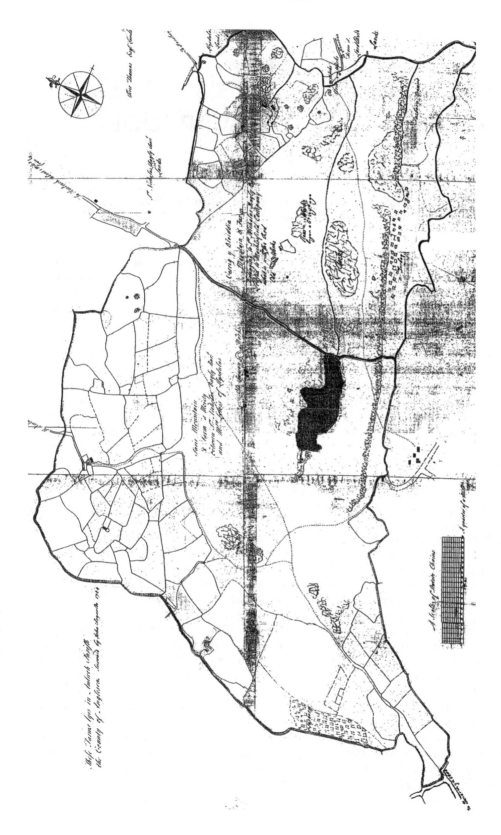

The Original Survey of Parys Mountain 1764 showing the Cerrigy y Bleiddia portion on the east, leased to Roe & Co., as one third of the whole area. Reproduced by kind permission of the Flintshire Record Office. Ref. D/kk/534.

15
WHICH WAY TO LIVERPOOL?

Where wealth and freedom reign contentment fails,
And honour sinks where commerce long prevails.

In the late summer of 1764, on the 28th August, 10 cwts. of copper items contained in two casks, had been transported from Northwich down the River Weaver to Liverpool, consigned to John Rogerson, a well-known merchant and carrier of the city. During the following spring, on the 8th March, a further consignment, weighing 2 tons 7 cwts. was meticulously entered in his book by the River Weaver clerk as "Copper in Boxes", and also taken down river on behalf of the same consignee.

This was the beginning of a steadily growing stream of goods which would make their way down river to Liverpool over the next few years.

Prior to this only two items are noted, both for 1762. That was the year in which Charles had requested withdrawal from the silk mill on the 1st January, and four days later, on the 5th, a small consignment of 15 cwts. of copper went down to Liverpool. On the 2nd June, John Rogerson also conveyed 5 tons of copper plates down river. These were more than likely from the Macclesfield smelter as copper production must have been tentatively underway by this time.

No further items of copper moving down river appear until 1764, the year in which Charles finally managed the withdrawal of his money from the silk trade. It is no coincidence that on 21st June 1765 the following advertisement was placed in *Williamson's Liverpool Advertiser*:

> "John Walker, of Hanover Street, Liverpool, begs to inform the publick that he has now got an assortment of rowl'd copper from Charles Rowe, Esq. and Co. Works near Congleton, and will always have a regular and constant supply of all sorts; where braziers may depend upon being served on the lowest terms and copper of the best quality; plates for sheathing are roll'd to any thickness required."

At last Charles Roe had been forced to turn his attention to Liverpool, but nothing was ever easy. Despite John Stafford's professional commitments in and around the city, it was to be a hard and bitter contest to gain a permanent foothold within the jealously guarded commercial circles already set in place during the three preceding decades. And if John Rogerson had been engaged initially as a carrier, the contract had certainly not continued.

The merchant who extended the helping hand, as observed from the advertisement, was John Walker, member of a family long established in Liverpool and, one suspects, related to the important mercantile family of the same name in Manchester. There is no doubt that the Claytons from both towns were the same kith and kin, and during the 17th century both these Lancashire families had provided mayors, civic dignitaries and eminent citizens in the then small but busy port of Liverpool on the Mersey estuary.

* * * * * * *

From its earliest beginnings the town of Liverpool has attracted controversy. Considering that the history of the borough left much to be desired, attempts by later historians, hoping to prove its existence before the 12th century, resulted in fabrication of charters by certain individuals, but after disregarding these forgeries, evidence strongly points to its foundation by King John.

A deed dated 28th August 1207 proves that he exchanged one piece of land for another, taking possession of the portion called Liverpul (the first occurrence of the name in the records). King John's Charter granted freedom of liberties and customs for those "who shall take burgages", suggesting very little occupation of the area at that time. His interest in the site was purely strategical, engendered by his desire for the establishment of a garrison town complete with castle, from where stores and troops could be shipped to Ireland and Wales.

The development of Liverpool as a port was to be a long and tedious progress. During the 15th century two titled families emerged to dominate the politics of the area, both holding estates of similar value; the Molyneuxs of Sefton, who were frequent custodians of the castle, and the Stanleys of Lathom (later Earls of Derby) who held the borough of Liverpool. It is interesting to note that Richard III, in order to maintain the support of these families, allowed certain privileges, one of which was the "rangeship of Macclesfield Forest" to the Stanleys. Although of the same political persuasion and united by marriage, rivalries between the two families soon brought about such violence within the borough that the King intervened to restore peace.

In 1623, by provision of the Charter, Robert Dobson was appointed first common or town clerk of the small corporation. Unfortunately his example left much to be desired for, having levied fines which he left unrecorded, he was prosecuted, convicted and expected to resign. He remained defiant, challenging the authority of the mayor and burgesses from which a legal wrangle ensued culminating in his dismissal, but still he would not accept defeat, refusing to give up his books and the corporation seal. After further litigation and a judgement in favour of the corporation at the assizes, he was finally 'got rid of'.

It was not long before history repeated itself, another town clerk, Mr. T. Sandford, was dismissed from office in 1707 "for a number of high omissions and irregular transactions". On this occasion, however, his successor was required to pay Mr.Sandford a pension of £40 for life, and upon his death 100 guineas to his executors.

The emblem of the Liver Bird, accepted by many as originally representing the eagle of King John, was destined to undergo several artistic variations from its probable inception as the crest of the first tiny citadel, until the present day. (Recent moves within the council for its 'extermination' have brought about such a wave of protestations from the people of Liverpool, that at least for the present its survival has been guaranteed). By the late 17th century the Liver Bird was a fledgling determined to spread its wings. Increased trade and stability after the Restoration had doubled the population to an estimated 6,000, which included many Dissenters, and already the strong determination to fashion its own destiny had begun to take root.

Celia Fiennes recorded "the first original was a few fishermens houses and now is grown to a large fine town and (still) but a parish and one Church tho' there be 24 streets in it". She considered the streets very handsome, with houses built high of brick and stone, complemented by a fine Exchange and Town Hall in classical style, the whole resembling London in miniature.

There is no doubt that Liverpool's development over the centuries had been stinted because of the limited harbour facilities. The estuary, often stormy and exposed to strong winds and currents, produced tides of at least 30 ft with little available shelter for shipping except in the tiny creek, effectively a small lake or pool.

At various times a breakwater, then a bridge and sluices, were built to exert some sort of control over the water entering into the pool. The pool itself was later enlarged and deepened,

A View of Liverpool 1728 - St. Nicholas's church is on the extreme left; the King's Dock and the glassworks are on the right of the engraving.

but it was not until 1708 that positive steps were taken to plan a dock. A letter dated 29th February 1709, written by John Ward M.P., lawyer of Capesthorne Hall, from the House of Commons, reported "Our Leverpool Members are like to obtain a Bill for a Dock for ye advantage of their town which will be very injurous to our County of Chester being a tax upon our Cheese".

This was an important issue as Cheshire cheese was considered the best in England, except for the Cheddar of Somerset, and by the middle of the century some 14,000 tons would be shipped annually to London cheesemongers, with almost the same quantity distributed between Scotland, Ireland and the regions supplied by the rivers Trent and Mersey. These figures could be somewhat inflated to add weight to the arguments. Nevertheless, the Dock Act was passed that year enabling work to begin, but construction took several years. In 1715, although a few small vessels were allowed access, a further Act was necessary to allow completion of the work, but Liverpool, whilst gaining her independence from the head port of Chester, was unique by the fact that she was allowed no member ports.

Daniel Defoe, who had witnessed considerable changes in the prosperous and thriving town between his two visits of 1680 and 1690, was astonished to discover a two fold increase in its augmentation during his tour of 1725-26. He felt inspired to write "Liverpoole is one of the wonders of Britain, and that more, in my opinion, than any of the wonders of the Peak". His enquiries and observations ascertained confirmation that Liverpool not only rivalled Bristol in the trade with Virginia and the West Indies, but her merchants had "almost become like the Londoners, universal merchants", sending ships to Norway, Hamburg, the Baltic, Holland and Flanders. Whilst Bristol virtually monopolised the Irish trade from Dublin in the east to Galloway in the west, Liverpool was now able to command the east and northern shores from Dublin to Londonderry. Likewise Bristol held trading reciprocities with South Wales, and Liverpool with North Wales, and whilst Bristol trade dominated in the south-western counties, Liverpool was now able to dominate in the north-west, creating an influx of mercantile offspring from many areas including, as particularly mentioned, those from Chester and Lancaster.

The first map of the town was produced by J.Chadwick in 1725 and depicts a Liver Bird of dove-like tranquillity bearing an olive branch in its beak, offering a simile with the story of Noah. Ships returning from long voyages fraught with danger, were always grateful to see the small castellated fortress of their home port coming into view across the deep, dark waters. By ancient established custom a ship's captain could arrange in advance for a peal of bells to be rung by the "Old Church Ringers", when his ship was sighted off shore. It was the seamen's way of offering thanks to the Almighty for their safe return. Payment was made in advance to the sexton, who in turn paid the bellringers; but eventually it came to light that "persons unknown" had obtained money from sea captains by pretending to be the sexton.

The Old Church was the Liverpool Parish Church of Our Lady and St. Nicholas, affectionately known as 'St. Nicks'. Originally a small private chapel probably existed within the castle walls, but within a short period of time a chapel would have been built for the small community, and was certainly in existence by the year 1257. Given the name of St. Mary del Quay and subject to the mother church of Walton, it stood on the very edge of the water.

In 1356 the king authorised the mayor of Liverpool to acquire land for a new chapel from the Duke of Lancaster, (for which he paid £10) expressly "to perform divine service every day in the Chapel of the Blessed Virgin Mary and St. Nicholas at Liverpool". This chapel was erected on land just to the east of St. Mary del Quay and in 1361, because of the ravages of the plague, a temporary licence was issued by the Bishop of Lichfield and Coventry commissioning the dedication of the chapel and cemetery of St. Nicholas, thus allowing burials to take place locally instead of at Walton. Five months later the new church received its official dedication to St. Nicholas, patron saint of mariners, and attracted benefactors who endowed it with altars and gifts, eventually including a priest to "teach and keep a grammar school".

The Reformation reduced its fabric almost to obsolescence, so that during the reign Elizabeth I , "A byll for erectyage of a parish church at Lyverpole" was read on 14th May 1571. By the following year, on 31st May 1572, during the First Session of a New Parliament, the Bill had been altered to "A byll for the chappell of Lerpoole that the same may be a parish churche by the name of St. Paule", but objections were raised.

On the 10th June this Bill received its second reading and again objections were raised, this time by Mr. Selinger who "Liketh not yt (that it) should beare the name of St. Paule." The Bill was sent for alteration and no further reference to the subject is at present available. The outcome seems apparent, however, suggesting that the chapel dedicated in 1361 was enlarged and allowed to retain the name of St. Nicholas.

Both Celia Fiennes and Daniel Defoe would have seen a small, unexceptional church with a steeple comprising a tower surmounted by a spire. This original nondescript spire was replaced in 1747 by one of more grandiose proportions, and someone who lived 'within its shadow' and would have witnessed the construction was John Walker, Snr.

* * * * * * *

After his marriage in the church on 20th August 1699, it was not until 12th April 1720 that John Walker and his wife, Elizabeth, took up residence in a house "north of old Church Steeple" leased from Liverpool Corporation. All Liverpool Corporation leases in the 18th century were for three lives and 21 years, accordingly the lives of their three sons were entered on the lease. This property remained with the family until the lease was surrendered on 4th August 1764, at which date it was described as of "Old Church yard".

John Walker, merchant's clerk of Rainford Square, baptised his second son, John at St. Nicholas's on 3rd January 1752. There is little doubt that the Walker family had accumulated a considerable fortune, making it possible for one of their progeny, another John, to lease a dwelling house and warehouse on Hanover Street from the Corporation, just before the relinquishment of the Old Churchyard lease. These were situated on the south-west side of Hanover Street, and on the "garden ground" of the premises the younger John Walker, now a merchant, quickly built two more warehouses, at least one part of which he subleased. The area covered was impressive; the original house and warehouse had a frontage of almost 61 ft and the remaining ground covered a triangular area measuring approximately '56ft. x 165ft. x 201ft.' In a little more than a year the small family of John, his wife, Elizabeth and their son, John, again had their lives added to a Corporation lease in respect of two houses adjacent to one of the warehouses. This further lease of the 3rd March consolidated their business premises, which were to become the first tangible outlet for Charles Roe's copper goods in the rapidly expanding territory of Liverpool Corporation.

The metamorphosis of the Liver Bird was soon to take place, transforming it into an elongated character resembling a greedy and rapacious Cormorant, with foliage still concomitantly held in its beak, uncannily symbolic of the struggle for power which was taking place within the Corporation.

* * * * * * *

After the early 18th century influx of merchants into the town, inspired by Virginia tobacco and Lancashire cottons, the freemen of Liverpool seemed of one accord in adopting a policy whereby the Corporation acquired as much land as possible and leased it only to its own freemen. That way a tight control was kept on commerce, ensuring that interlopers were debarred as far as possible within the limits of the borough. Important merchants from outside the borough whose trading practices had long been integrated with those of Liverpool, were allowed to trade free with other freemen, provided they paid a substantial sum for the privilege, but a very strict watch was kept to discourage defaulting.

Whereas in London the framework of guilds had endeavoured to monopolise trade for centuries, with outsiders working through guild members (a system which was beginning to lose authority by the mid-18th century), the only possible way to evade the restrictions imposed by the stranglehold of Liverpool Corporation, was to liaise with a freeman. This had the effect of placing that freeman (albeit unofficial) in the unenviable position of being accountable for his 'confederate's' actions. The impression gained is that the older Liverpool families did not quite sympathise with the restrictive necessities desired by their newer townsmen, after all they had already experienced an incursion into their territory, but new interests have a habit of forceful consolidation in the hope of keeping the old subdued and the potential discouraged.

Amongst the older families, and somewhat aligned with the Walkers and Claytons were the names of Shaw, Blundell and Johnson, merchants whose integrity was sufficiently strong to withstand the constraining tactics of others, and amongst whom Roe & Co. would find their champions.

Two bills of lading still exist in Pennsylvania verifying that on 20th March 1764, a ship called *Friendship* was riding at anchor in the River Thames, London, bound for Philadelphia. The casks, boxes and cases of merchandise taken on board were destined for Messrs. Baynton Wharton & Morgan by order of R. Neave & Son. The signature of the Master was John Walker and tallies with that placed against an entry in the Liverpool Plantation Books (an early form of ship registration), sworn on 8th July 1765 as a third share owner of "the Ship Peggy of Liverpool whereof Robert Allanby is at present Master being a square sterned Vefsell burthen about One hundred and forty tons was built at Liverpool in the present year" John Walker had obviously delivered goods from Liverpool to London, and was then able to refill the space with whatever cargo he could obtain, for the long journey across the Atlantic.

Further entries in the Plantation Books confirm John Walker's involvement with other ships and suggest his actual participation in their construction. Whether or not he was the same John Walker as the merchant of Hanover Street, is unclear, but, if not, there is definitely a close relationship, and one or the same person, subleased a wharf on the South Shore from a prosperous ship builder, Richard Golightly.

The Golightly family appear in Liverpool about 1730, which conveniently seems to coincide with Richard's marriage. He and his wife, Sarah, did not attend the Old Church but the comparatively modern one of St. Peter's, built in 1704. Liverpool had achieved parochial status in 1699. However, as the town expanded northwards from the Old Dock, and the area to the east of Frog Lane (later renamed Hanover Street) became urbanised, although remaining a single parish, the building of St. Peter's church resulted in Liverpool having two joint Rectors. Corporation land meant Corporation power, and not only had the appointment of ministers to the churches to be sanctioned by the Corporation, but also all other positions including church organists.

Richard and Sarah Golightly produced eight children in 18 years, all baptised at St. Peter's and all daughters except one, son Thomas. Born in 1732 and next to the eldest, young Thomas eventually obtained his freedom and became a wine merchant on reaching his majority. With his father's wealth and an abundance of female attention, not surprisingly Thomas grew into a dandified young man. His affectations and misplaced sense of humour inspired him to found an exclusive dining club called "The Unanimous Society" within one week of his 21st birthday. The members met primarily in Liverpool, but on occasion also in Prescot, Ormskirk and Warrington. The meetings took place every Saturday evening from the first Saturday in September to the last in April. There was a fine for "disclosing the secrets of the Society to anyone except a Brother Member" and several other fines included one for getting married. He charged 14s. 0d. (today almost £15) for "One dozen claret" and 6s. 0d. for a gallon of rum.

Thomas, unlike his father, became associated with St. Nicholas's, eventually renting his own pew and obtaining the contract for supplying the church with Communion wine.

The family lived in property on the east side of Mersey Street, close by the Old Dock. This property, leased from the Corporation in 1737, was added to in 1750 by another Corporation lease for a large adjoining estate which included a warehouse and yard. In addition to this, from December 1744 two houses on Duke Street were acquired by Corporation lease and subleased within six months. Richard Golightly was a part share owner of a Greenland whaler, and purchased a half share of a captured French vessel in 1749, but this ship was lost coming out of the ice.

The move to Mersey Street in 1737 was probably the result of an Act of Parliament in that year to enlarge the port facilities, first by the construction of a dry dock and secondly by the addition of a second wet dock to the south of the entrance to the Old Dock. When the opportunity arose on 30th May 1745, Richard Golightly took a lease from the Corporation of "A piece of Ground situated South Side Wall Dock containing to the front along the south Warfs of said Dock 17 feet 10 inches and in depth 108 feet 6 inches."

The shore line shortly gained the attention of the Corporation, and on 8th October 1762 four important leases were granted in respect of:

"A Piece of Ground formerly Part of the South Shore or Sea Strand within the Limits of the Corporation of Liverpoole and lately Inclosed from the Sea or River Mersey by a large Stone Wall built to the westward for Inclosing the same and preserving it from the Inundation of the Said River."

The piece of ground was divided into four parts from north to south, with the estuary running along the western side of each. The most northerly one was not given a reference, but the others were marked A B and C on the plan. By the time Eyes produced his map of

1765 two small basins or harbours had been made, one between the first and A plots, and the second between B and C plots. The annotations show plot B leased by Richard Golightly, timber merchant, and measuring 80 yards along the Mersey shore, with a northern boundary of 138 yards, a southern one of 170 yards, but the boundary along a proposed road to run virtually parallel with the shore, was just over 80 yards, making the plot of uniform width.

About this time, because of John Walker's commitment to the merchant shipping business, he leased from Richard Golightly the whole or part of plot B. Thomas had more than likely intervened on his behalf, anxious to strengthen a bond with an old established family and desirous of gaining a favourable position within the congregation of St. Nicholas's.

How Charles Roe first contacted John Walker is not known. The most logical approach would have been through John Stafford's social connections in the town, particularly his close relationship with the merchant Thomas Smyth and his wife, Elizabeth, formerly Miss Blagge of Macclesfield. Their visits to John Stafford's Macclesfield home, and the growing popularity of balls and assemblies in the East Cheshire town at which a great and varied company assembled, would present Charles with the opportunity of discussing business matters. Young William Roe, now almost 20 years of age, was to become a great friend of the Smyths and, true to his nature, would display a deep sense of loyalty to the couple in later years, indicative of a very close relationship between the two families.

* * * * * * *

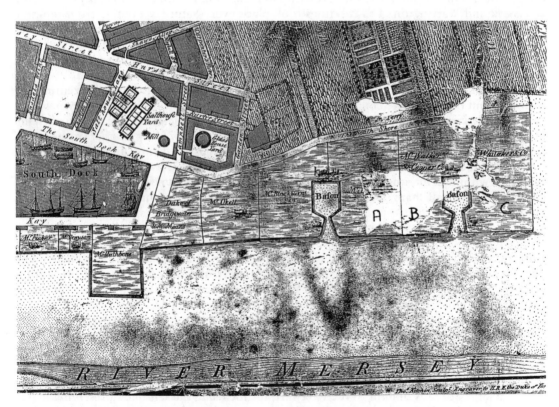

Details from Thomas Kitchin's map of 1770 – the site of the original Roe & Co. copper smelter on Liverpool's South Shore is shown as plot 'B'.

The rapid interest of Liverpool Corporation in improving dock facilities, accompanied by an equally active spate of warehouse building on the part of merchants such as the Walkers and Golightlys, was due in no small part to an "Act for extending and improving the Trade to Africa" passed in 1750 (Anno 23 Geo II Cap.31). Trading was "to be free and open to all His Majesty's Subjects" upon payment by each person of forty shillings, to either the Chamberlain of London, the Clerk of the Merchants Hall in Bristol or the Town Clerk of Liverpool.

Each of the three places was to appoint individual committees of freemen to meet within their respective boroughs, but each was to choose annually, by election, three of their members for the purpose of representation on the Management Committee of the new company, whose meetings were to be held in London.

The new company established by the Act, and named "The Company of Merchants trading to Africa", was entitled to claim possession of the "Charter, Forts, Castles and Military Stores, Canoe Men, Castle Slaves and all their Property on the Coast of Africa, their goods and merchandizes only excepted" relating to the old Royal African Company of England. Various other rules and regulations were laid down, amongst which each freeman was to be given a certificate upon payment of his fee.

The forts had to be maintained and improved, and an important clause stipulated:

> "That no Commander or Mafter of any Ship trading to Africa, fhall by Fraud, Force or Violence, or by any other indirect Practice whatfoever, take on board or carry away from the Coaft of Africa, any Negro or Native of the faid Country, or commit or fuffer to be committed, any Violence on the Natives to the Prejudice of the faid Trade."

Any person committing such a crime was to be fined £100. As an extension of this and other clauses, Commissioned Officers of His Majesty's Navy stationed on board warships, and under orders to cruise within the limits of the territorial waters, had authority to inspect and examine the state of conditions of forts, settlements, slaves and so forth, and to submit reports to Parliament. This also included inspection of any vessels entering or leaving the designated areas.

Liverpool, having been granted an equal share in the trading partnership which had previously been dominated by London and Bristol, responded by beginning a programme of sea shore development which, of course, was to have far reaching effects.

* * * * * * *

After the leasing of Frodsham Quay in 1752 from Earl Cholmondeley, the activities linking the various merchants and carriers, not only of Liverpool and its hinterland, but deep into the counties of Lancashire and Cheshire, intensified, as the scramble for trade reached a new level. It soon became apparent that Liverpool was pledged to dominance in the north-west and obviously intent on enlargement of its port, particularly as the number of ships involved in the African trade is said to have reached 88 by 1751.

Rivalries between the two counties would have to be quelled if constructive methods of improving transportation facilities were to be achieved, especially those dictated by water. The Sankey canal had been completed from the St. Helens coalfield to the River Mersey, between 1755-57; fuel being a priority for any expanding population. The Duke of Bridgewater had followed with the construction of his Worsley canal, completed in 1761, but saw this as part of a larger scheme to link Manchester to the Mersey Estuary and thus to Liverpool. Almost immediately he began the extension of the east to west branch into Cheshire, intending to follow a route south of the course of the Mersey and terminating into the estuary near Runcorn; this was still under construction in 1765.

The River Weaver Trustees, having devoted a good deal of time, money and energy on river improvements particularly during the 1720s, also found it necessary to keep pace with developments. Merchants and carriers such as Thomas Marshall of Northwich, had increased their activities after the acquisition of Frodsham Quay, and by 1760 interested parties had let it be known that a new commission was intended for the river. In order to gain support from all sides, it was to be constituted from members in Cheshire, but also to include two members from Lancashire and the Mayor and Aldermen of Liverpool Corporation.

There was a suggestion "of having 5ft. water to Northwich", against which objections were raised, and also "constructing our Locks bigger especially at Northwich". John Stafford was engaged both for advice and also for preparation of the bill, about which he reported on 11th March 1760, "This day the bill was brought into the House by Lord Strange."

Despite improvements, Josiah Wedgwood wrote in April 1765: "the Locks or Floods on the Weaver interrupt its Navigation which sometimes happens for months together," and was easily persuaded to consider a canal scheme which would eventually link the quay of Wilden (Wilne) Ferry, just south of Derby, to the Potteries before travelling northwards to the Mersey estuary. Cornish clay could then more easily be moved from Liverpool to Stoke, with the pottery destined for America taking the opposite direction, whilst that bound for London could be loaded at the quayside in Stoke and boated all the way to Hull. There, together with a multitude of other goods including Derbyshire lead, it would make the coastwise journey as usual in sea-going vessels bound for the Thames Estuary.

The Duke of Bridgewater, subsequently considered by some to be megalomanic, had become obsessed with the idea of monopolising canal building in England. He had a confidant in Lord Gower, later to become Marquis of Stafford, and there is little doubt that Josiah Wedgwood was cajoled into supporting a scheme which was already well and truly planned. Josiah in many ways showed a great naivety, never considering that a Duke, just like any other human being, was capable of deceit. He felt flattered when the Duke of Bridgewater, through his agent, had reserved for him his chosen piece of land by which the canal would pass; land necessary to fulfil the Wedgwood dream, for it was Josiah's intention of building a modern manufactory or pottery which would be the envy of all.

On 2nd March 1765 Josiah Wedgwood wrote to Sir William Meredith, Tory M.P. for Liverpool, who resided at Henbury Hall near Macclesfield. The purport of his letter was concern regarding a new pottery established in South Carolina, and the poaching of some of his men, including master potters, by an agent of the concern. He argued that whilst the home consumption of his products was "very trifling" by comparison with "an amazing quantity of white stone ware & some of the finer kinds" sent to the Continent, the North American market was also very important. Technically, he did have a valid point, because although copper was being mined in the Newark area of New Jersey in North America, no smelting was allowed anywhere in British colonies at this time, and ore had to be exported to Britain for processing. The same argument could be applied to clay, and in the past consignments had been sent from America and experimented with in England, but had been considered inferior to English clays.

Another letter to his brother, John, in London dated during the following week (11th March) confirmed that "on Friday last I dined with Mr. Brindley the Duke of Bridgewater's engineer", during which they discussed the plan of a survey for a navigation from Hull or Wilden Ferry to Burslem just north of Stoke.

In the meantime an independent project was taking shape within Cheshire to provide the county with a more efficient waterway, but which, at the same time, would endeavour to accommodate the desires of those on the fringes of the scheme.

The social gatherings in and around Macclesfield, often taking place in the public house called *The Angel,* (which now had a number of guest rooms and a large assembly room overlooking the Market Place) or lavishly provided by the Legh family at Adlington Hall, presented the perfect setting in which the gentlemen could espouse still further their ideas for a canal scheme, first mooted in 1763.

Charles Roe set himself the task of recruiting prospective shareholders, amongst whom were the lords of the manor whose land was likely to be affected by the cutting of the channel. Because of the weight and influence of the local Cheshire gentry and business men, John Stafford, to a certain extent, was coerced into joining the movement, for he found himself in a somewhat impalpable situation having prepared the River Weaver bill. He was also an extremely busy man, with responsibilities weighing heavily upon his shoulders. By now, well past his mid-50s, he must have been gravely concerned about his son, William's, involvement in the silk mill. Once again his professional services were required on presentation to Parliament in 1765 of a petition drawn from every branch and area of the English silk industry, and it could be no comfort to have to support the fact that owing to the "Difficulties in getting proper Silk for the Ufe of the Throwfter the Trade is almost totally ruined."

So far as a canal scheme was concerned he, like Charles Roe, was unable to invest financially, having regard for his marriage settlement in which the Tatton family was involved. Because of this relationship he was kinsman to the Duke of Bridgewater, which could have created some disparity with the Tattons, but it must be said that it certainly never restrained him from making fierce criticisms of the Duke at a later date.

In better times the silk trade had managed quite well without a canal, however Charles, in trying to allay the gloom and despondency of the depression in the town, was hoping that a canal would bring new incentives and prosperity to the area, a sentiment to which John Stafford seemed a little indifferent. Charles Roe, with his usual enthusiasm left no stone unturned in his efforts to achieve success; even Edward Pitts of Gracechurch Street, London promised financial support, but unfortunately it could never have been envisaged that Sir George Warren's inclusion would be the cause of such embitterment to the Duke of Bridgewater, as to jeopardise the whole scheme. This is the only conclusion which can be drawn for what was shortly to take place, because no logical explanation can be justified.

* * * * * * *

There were several reasons from Charles Roe's point of view, why it was imperative to have a more efficient means of transport to and from Liverpool. Apart from the fact that he had now gained a foothold in the town's commerce, which meant the beginnings of a flow of copper and brass goods to the port, two other important steps had been taken to ensure the continuity of supplies of raw materials to the Macclesfield smelters. By 1765 the sources of copper ore in North Wales were depleted: the Llanberis mines had petered out, little or no copper had surfaced at Bryn Dinas near Tywyn, so the venture proved short-lived, whilst Penrhyn Du remained non-efficacious. The completion of the Bryn Dinas lease had, in fact, been delayed, but on this occasion the fault lay with the mineral agent who wrote to Lord Powis on 9th February 1765:

> "In regard to the lease Your Lordship intended for Messrs. Hodgson & Roe in Merionethshire . . . The Macclesfield Company have agreed for the Work . . . at Bryndinnas Hills near Towyn Merioneth at $1/8$th – for Penryndu in Carnarvonshire upon the Terms settled by Sr. Nicholas Baylie, in Montgomeryshire the Royalty is fix'd generally at $1/8$th.
>
> I was unwilling My Lord to give any Instructions for a lease (to Mr. Davies, solicitor of Elsemeer) until I knew the certain Terms agreed upon between Your Lordship & Mr. Hodgson. And I humbly hope Your Lordship will not impute any thing to my neglect . . ."

By the 1st March the mineral agent, Mr. Hennings, had confirmed to Lord Powis that he had instructed Mr. Davies to draw up a lease "for Mr. Hodgson & Co. of the two different places on the Waste in Merionethshire (vizt) Bryndinnas, and that near Keightly Old Mineworks." Because of the difficulties of obtaining copper ore from the company mines, Charles Roe had no alternative but to consider the purchase of ores from Cornwall, and as a consequence he engaged his old friend and associate Legh Dickenson, formerly of Manchester, to bid for copper ores by ticketing on behalf of Roe & Co.

Legh Dickenson and Patience now had a son of six years, named William Churchill after his grandfather, and at this time Patience was expecting a daughter, to be christened Elizabeth in March 1766. There was to be no clash of loyalties because William Churchill Snr., after managing the Dolcoath mine so successfully for over 30 years, had recently died and Patience proved his will in London on 6th May 1765. After making provision for his widow, Elizabeth, the estate was to pass eventually to his grandson, William Churchill Dickenson. Dolcoath passed to another concern and Legh Dickenson, who had never held interests in the mine, was to prove himself a loyal and reliable addition to the firm of Roe & Co.

During 1765 he purchased a total of 216 tons of copper ore which travelled up the River Weaver in what appears to be fairly large consignments of around 40 tons, from the 20th June onwards. A further 112 tons 15 cwts. came from Coniston, but this leaves approximately 63 tons unaccounted for on the Weaver, suggesting an additional unidentified source. A final purchase of copper from Middleton Tyas, charged as 8 tons @ £31 1 6d. per ton in the mine accounts, was despatched to "Messrs. Roe & Co. of Macclesfield" during December.

The other positive step taken by Charles Roe was with regard to calamine supplies. In Bakewell lived an important family called Denman, kinsmen to the prolific Buxton family of Brassington with whom Charles was conversant because of his visits to the Brassington estate.

* * * * * * *

The patriarch of the Denman 'clan' was John a doctor. who, until his death in 1752, had been called upon from time to time to treat employees of the Devonshire estate. Son, Joseph, followed in his father's footsteps and was a doctor in Buxton, later to become a J.P. and Deputy Lieutenant of Derbyshire. He must have been an associate of Brian Hodgson and was possibly the family doctor, although sometimes in his association with the lead mines he is referred to as Dr. Joseph of Bakewell.

Another son, Thomas, became an eminent physician in London. His son of the same name was destined to become 1st Baron Denman of Dovedale in recognition of his distinguished career as an advocate.

As the family was known both to Charles Roe and Brian Hodgson, it seems a matter of course that they should engage a John Denman as mineral agent to oversee supplies of calamine from the Halkyn Mountain region of North Wales. This John of Bakewell, who appears to have been the nephew of Dr. John because he is not referred to as 'Junior', seems to have trained more as an apothecary than doctor, becoming involved in mineralogy. Hardly surprising when the medical profession was busily experimenting with new concoctions from a variety of minerals e.g. zinc oxide reduced to powder and made into an ointment.

John Denman's first appearance in North Wales is indicated by two entries in the Chester City Port Records. The first on 12th February 1765 shows that he consigned just over 17 tons of calamine to Liverpool. The transaction was handled by Edward Litherland, a merchant of the city, who obtained carriage aboard a vessel called *The Squirrel*. Whereas calcined calamine was always in bags, unusually this ore was in bulk suggesting that it had not been treated. A further load of almost 10 tons was shipped to Liverpool on the 16th May aboard the *Hopewell*, master David Jones. But at this time John Denman was able to lease an important piece of land, which placed him in the position of creating his own smaller business within the larger concern of Roe & Co.

From the previous year of 1764, Thomas Patten's company, intent on producing brass in the Greenfield Valley, had been working through an agent, Thomas Meredith, to obtain land leases in the Holywell area, effectively consolidating and expanding their mining activities and copper and battery works. The company held a lease of land near Mold (which when compared with Holywell is only half the distance from Chester) and finding it no longer desirable, gave John Denman the opportunity to sublease with rights to make dams and set up engines etc. This lease for Bryn-celyn near the village of Gwernafield and two miles west of Mold, suggests that Patten & Co. were seeking calamine, but Bryn-celyn became predominantly a lead mine, although early 20th century mining did produce a small proportion of zinc blende (sulphide) from adjacent shafts. It is hardly surprising that Patten & Co. would not be interested in the sulphide when calamine was more readily available in the area around Holywell, nor the lead, which required smelting. Also, the permission given to John Denman for making dams and setting up engines, strongly implies that there were drainage problems in the shafts. Roe & Co. already having interests in lead and knowing the market well would find it convenient to have the mine worked, especially as there was always the possibility of finding calamine in that area.

At about the same time John Denman joined the Derbyshire partnership of Messrs. Thornhill and Twigg in a lease of other neighbouring mines in the parishes of Kilken and Mold. The lease, dated 20th February 1758, was originally in the holding of John Griffiths and Thomas Jones, but upon the death of the latter Mrs. Mary Jones replaced him and was presumably his widow. The minerals referred to were lead, copper, caulk and calamine, and the mine, Puddyn Susan; because of its relationship to Bryn-celyn, must have been the same workings as the Erw-felin Vein on the northern bank of the River Alyn, west of Rhydymwyn village, which was supposed to have been known originally as Vein Susan.

John Denman was now able to supervise the purchase of local calamine. Having tested its quality and sent samples for approval, he would be responsible for overseeing the dressing and calcining of the ore, after which it would be placed in bags ready for transit. He would also be responsible for any lead retrieved.

A visitor to the area later in the century was to describe smelting houses in the immediate vicinity of the river "for fusing the ore, and casting it into pigs", and half a mile away further down the valley, a mill worked by a water wheel for rolling the lead into sheets; a complex undoubtedly constructed by John Denman as mineral agent on behalf of the Macclesfield company.

Because of the nearness of Chester it would be more logical to cart the minerals overland and thus avoid port dues. The roads were kept in good repair to the city and the route to Frodsham Quay was well organised, enabling the lead to be boated to Liverpool or the calamine to take the onward journey up the Weaver. The coastal port of Flint would otherwise have been the nearest port of embarkation, yet in the time it took to reach Flint the goods could be most of the way to Chester, and not only would the Chester City port dues be avoided, but in the case of the calamine, those also of Liverpool.

The lines of communication were now in place for large quantities of materials to arrive at Frodsham Quay in preparation for their final laborious journey across Cheshire. A canal scheme in conjunction with the River Weaver would certainly speed up deliveries, and was also the most economic option. An ideal route would be eastwards from Northwich, passing close by Alderley Edge and Mottram Andrew, at which point a branch was envisaged south to Macclesfield, whilst the main route continued northwards through the coal mining region of Worth, Poynton and Norbury to Stockport and Manchester. Seven years of coal supplies from Macclesfield Common had seen a depletion of coal reserves, and the difficulties of the Hodgson coal-getters at Disley, to supply sufficient quantities of coal to the Macclesfield smelters, would be greatly eased by such a scheme.

Consideration was given to the desires of the Staffordshire potteries by suggesting that the canal from the River Trent to Burslem could proceed in a northerly direction across the western part of the county, by-passing Sandbach and falling in to the other waterways near Northwich. This way there would then be two options for carriers, the first to continue as usual on the Weaver, or the second to link into the Duke of Bridgewater's canal when completed, and reach the estuary near Runcorn. This seemed an excellent idea, because it would stop any monopoly, particularly by the Duke of Bridgewater, and would help to keep transportation costs to a minimum. Also the time, efforts and expenses of everyone thus far involved would not have been wasted as everyone would benefit. A final consideration was given to the idea that a branch could be cut westwards from Stockport to link directly with the Duke's canal, and that way the Duke was assured of all business from the Mersey Estuary to Stockport and Manchester. No better scheme could have been planned.

* * * * * * *

In the midst of the deliberations and negotiations, Charles Roe suffered another personal loss; his brother, James, died on the 12th April and was buried in St. Michael's churchyard, leaving his widow, Elizabeth, to bring up their two surviving children, Hester Ann, nine years of age and her younger brother, James, of six years. No one could have understood their situation better than Charles, so out of respect for his brother he discreetly took responsibility for the small family. Elizabeth very much appreciated her brother-in-law's concern, however, she endeavoured to be as financially independent as she could, not wishing to take advantage of his generosity. The two sermons, published whilst James was living, were shortly republished in book form together with a further 18, and a second edition was to follow in 1767. The proceeds were for the benefit of the widow and children, and Hester Legh of Adlington Hall magnanimously ensured that the Legh family bought no less than 14 copies.

Whilst Charles was able to provide some stability for the family, neither he nor Elizabeth appreciated the extent to which the death of her father had affected young Hester, and whilst she grappled with the trauma, her mind became very much obsessed with the fear of her own death. Already, when only five years of age, Hester had experienced the death of one of her younger brothers from smallpox, an event which had deeply affected her.

Rev. James had been "A Man of strict Morals", teaching his children the fear of sin, with the most severe admonitions given on the subject of telling lies. "The Sabbath was kept Strictly sacred", and not only was praying encouraged by attendances at church, but additionally by family prayer at home, a principle which Charles and his family also upheld.

A year earlier James Roe had suffered a serious illness from which death seemed inevitable, but he had made a miraculous recovery. During the illness hallucinations had caused him to have a remarkable dream, after which he had felt such a sense of joy and happiness that during his final months he was at peace with the world, never again being angered by anything or anyone. Hester's recollections infer a somewhat different state of affairs earlier, hardly surprising when her father's relationship with Peter Legh the younger of Lyme Hall had been so precarious. The upset regarding the curacy of Disley had extended into a long drawn out affair, culminating on 11th February 1760, when James had written to his patron, "your sister inform'd me yt (that) Mr.Booth had incurr'd your Displeasure, & yt it w'd be agreable to you to have him remov'd from the Cure of Disley" . . . James had already persuaded Mr. Booth to accept the curacy of Marple, available from Midsummer, but required him to remain master of Disley school. He asked permission of Peter Legh to find a replacement for the curacy of Disley only: the outcome is unknown.

Hester grieved long and hard over her father's death, during which time she sat, read or wept with her mother. Concern for her condition soon encouraged relatives and friends to invite her to their homes, but their well-intentioned jocularity as part of their endeavours to draw her out of her serious state of mind, were considered by Hester to be a form of derision.

Elizabeth quietly encouraged her daughter to learn to dance. Her father had considered her too young for such frivolities, at the same time warning her against reading novels and romances. His over-protectiveness had never really been understood; it was not that he objected to balls, assemblies, plays or novels in general, but that unless proper supervision was given to young people, the newly extolled code of moral freedom was likely to encourage dissipation.

Hester's conscience was soon persuaded to overcome her inhibitions. She became proficient at dancing and began to enjoy parties, which in turn created a love and desire for fashionable dress and a passion for reading as many novels and romances as she could find. She attended plays, and at last seemed normal and well again, but her great extremes of character and deeply intense nature should have been a warning. The philosophical undercurrent remained, and as part of a religious campaign in later years she would write, "In short, I fell into all the vain customs & pleasures of a delusive world as far as my situation in life would admit; and even beyond the proper limits of that station God had placed me in".

Uncle Charles was a straightforward, down-to-earth man. His Christianity never aspired to ethereal levels, but to an everyday common sense practicality which had at its heart the strong Roe doctrine of public service. Mark Anthony's eulogy at the death of Brutus could not have been more appropriate in describing Charles Roe's nature "with his general honest thought and common good to all". Charles's greatest weakness was his inability to comprehend that he could not satisfy "all of the people all of the time". If he had taken the trouble to try to understand his niece a little better, it is still doubtful whether or not the storms ahead could have been avoided. His primary concern was with the business upon which so many people depended, and whilst keeping her welfare in mind, Charles left the state of Hester's mind to her mother's charge.

Charles himself had a deeply intensive nature, and was not without passion, attributes which he failed to recognise as inherent in his niece. Unfortunately in Hester they developed into a form of stubbornness tinged with a religious fanaticism which often clouded her judgement, whereas Charles was able to channel his into a potent source of energy, enabling him to overcome what to others would have been insurmountable obstacles and defeat; a characteristic best illustrated by his determination to succeed in Liverpool.

* * * * * * *

On 2nd May 1765 Josiah and Richard Wedgwood attended a meeting called by "the Committee of the River Weaver Navigation at the Crown in Northwich", and took along the proposals for their scheme from Wilden near Derby to Frodsham Bridge, by which they had no intention of linking in with the Weaver navigation. In order to persuade them to join their system to the Weaver, Mr. Pownall of Liverpool promised to assist the surveyor, Mr. Henshall "in surveying and taking proper Levells of the Country from Winsford Bridge (head of the Weaver navigation) to Lawton (Church Lawton near Kidsgrove just north of Stoke-on-Trent) and where else it might be necessary". The Trustees also promised lower tariffs on their waterway for the Trent and Mersey users.

On Monday 6th May the surveying began, and for the first two days Josiah Wedgwood was present. The survey to Lawton was completed, but then the "Promoters of the Wilden Scheme" (Trent and Mersey scheme) had their own survey carried out from Lawton, by Middlewich, to the river Weaver at Northwich.

A public meeting was organised on the 13th May at Newcastle-under-Lyme by the Weaver Trustees, but few attended, so it was postponed until the 27th June. At this meeting Mr. Brayne of the Weaver Committee put forward proposals to induce the Staffordshire contingent to consider joining their system, and asked for any offers or suggestions of any kind which could be considered, but none were forthcoming. The matter was to be left until the General Meeting of the 5th December allowing adequate time for private discussions amongst the various parties, and on the appointed date Mr. Brayne and Mr. Pownall were asked to contact Josiah Wedgwood and any other key promoters of the Wilden scheme, to see what decisions had been arrived at.

Josiah Wedgwood, however, requested that they meet at an inn in Newcastle on the following Sunday. The meeting took place with Josiah supported by four or five other persons. Messrs. Brayne and Pownall disclosed that it was the intention to make the river navigable for vessels of 120 tons and, as Josiah subsequently commented, Northwich would become to Liverpool what Gainsborough was to Hull.

At this juncture Josiah Wedgwood foolishly began a game of deceit, unbecoming of his position as a respected member of the Potteries community. He was, by religion, a Dissenter, as were most of his business associates, and years of defiance against the Establishment had left their mark. Josiah, whilst appearing to be co-operative, was actually hoping to gain time for 'his' scheme, so he told Messrs. Brayne and Pownall that as so few gentlemen were present "he must consult and then send an answer . . . but no answer ever came".

Unknown to the Weaver Committee the Duke of Bridgewater's 'cronies' had been at work, encouraging the belief that a 'Grand Scheme' was afoot whereby Manchester would be linked directly with the town of Liverpool by canal, thus cutting out the necessity of using the Mersey estuary.

At first Josiah was cautious and sceptical, but during December a meeting with James Brindley satisfied all his queries about the scheme, so he encouraged his friend Thomas Bentley, then resident in Liverpool, to stir up enthusiasm amongst the city merchants for the building of the canal and begin a collection of subscriptions.

A week or so later, on a Wednesday evening, the Duke of Bridgewater stayed at Trentham overnight en route for London, and sent for Josiah to breakfast with him together with one or two more, amongst whom was John Gilbert "his steward of the works". Josiah's impression was that the Duke and Mr. Gilbert had "some secret design of their own", for they requested that the plan in which Thomas Bentley had become involved "might not be mentioned at present" as "great things might be done at a proper time".

At the same time an anonymous letter was published in a newspaper by someone accusing "some Cheshire gentlemen" of contemplating a scheme whereby the Duke's navigation would be surrounded, depriving the country "of any possibility of ever having it extended either into Staffordshire or any other part". This was, of course, a complete fabrication to try to hinder the preparation of a draft Bill for the Cheshire scheme which had been discussed by more than 40 gentlemen and traders at the *George Inn*, Knutsford on both the 3rd and 12th December, where Charles Roe was appointed as one of the six persons designated to receive subscriptions. Immediately after the first meeting of the 3rd Charles wrote from Northwich to Josiah Wedgwood (letter dated the 4th December):

> "We had a meeting yesterday at Knutsford, when we had most of the Gentn. of this County, the Landowners & others & also several from Manchester – & the plan of our intended navigation as well as the conditions so far agreed to, that we have no doubt of succeding especially as the money to prosecute it is ready, & a very powerfull set of Gentn. to espouse it, of which I shall only name Sr. Wm. Meredith Sir Chas. Saunders & Sir Geoe Warren – so that it (is) morally impossible we shoud fail of success – I desire you'll come over hither (you may guess why & I assure you I mean it for your interest) to morrow, as soon as convenient, that I may have some conversation with you
>
> & I am Sir etc.
>
> Chas. Roe.
>
> P.S. Sir Geoe Warren will be here & there will be many more Gentn. on another occasion."

Charles as usual, eager to finalise matters, wanted everyone to move as quickly as he did. It is interesting to note the importance he attached to Sir George Warren's inclusion in the proceedings. Sir George also considered his position an important one, for he sent a representative to Manchester in order to gather together members of the old Mersey and Irwell Navigation "to make head against his Grace".

Meanwhile Wedgwood would not or could not make the meeting at Northwich, but chose instead to accept an invitation to visit Sir William Meredith at Henbury Hall and Charles Roe in Macclesfield, intending that Thomas Bentley should travel from Liverpool to accompany him. In the event he visited alone, but wrote an account of what took place, to his friend the following weekend.

He arrived at Henbury just ahead of Sir William on the Sunday evening (a week or so prior to his meeting with Bridgewater at Trentham) and, as an overnight guest, was able to discuss the idea of a canal navigation which could continue all the way to Liverpool. Sir William assured Wedgwood that the Cheshire Gentlemen would take on the burden and expense of cutting a canal from Lawton to Northwich, and with the capability of the river improved to accommodate vessels of 120 tons, ships would be able to take goods from there to any part of the world. (A scheme which obviously would not meet with approval in certain quarters of Liverpool Corporation, but for those gentlemen already holding interests in the Weaver, it would make no difference.)

The Wedgwood conscience was beginning to weigh heavy as he later admitted to Bentley, "After these offers & Afsurances what reasons could I give why we wo'd not terminate at N[orth] W[ich]."

It was obvious that Sir William supported the Cheshire plan, which included the Weaver navigation, much to Wedgwood's dismay. However, the master potter wrote to his friend in Liverpool hoping that Thomas Bentley in some way would be able to gain Sir William's support for their intended plan instead. Such was the Duke's scheming that Josiah concluded "I am ord'd, when our battle waxeth hot, which it soon will do, to keep 4 or 5 running footmen at my elbow & trust nothing of consequence to the post".

On the following Wednesday he dined with Charles Roe in his Chestergate home and spent the afternoon there, after which he "lay at Henbury" before hurrying to Knutsford the next morning in the hope of seeing or hearing something of Thomas Bentley. The remainder of his time was busily taken up with asking the consent of land owners to carry the waterway across their estates "and have been so succefsull as scarcely to meet with a denial". But still he desperately wanted a meeting with Bentley, whose opinion he valued considerably, and was moved to write one of his occasional juvenescent outbursts, "cannot you pofsibly come to Burslem once in your life?"

The subversive activities of the Grand Scheme supporters were about to be revealed as John Stafford, on behalf of the Weaver Trustees, made his way down to Wolsley Bridge, just north-east of the town of Stafford, to attend a meeting of the Trent and Mersey promoters on the 30th December.

At Stone he met by chance Mr. Tarlton and Mr. Scrope Colquith representing Liverpool Corporation, from whom he learnt "that a scheme had been formed a considerable time ago, by the people of Burslem in Conjunctin with the Duke of Bridgewater, to make a Navigable Canal from Whieldon Ferry to the Town of Liverpool, to which they had given Encourgement, and had suscribed £200 out of their publick fund, towards obtaining an Act for the purpose, being of Opinion Canal Navigations are much preferrable to River Navigations. However, it had recently transpired that the promoters of the scheme did not intend "to carry the Canal over the Mersey", hardly surprising as the Duke of Bridgewater was desperately short of money having heavily mortgaged his estates. This had placed the Liverpool merchants in a dilemma because, if the canal was to terminate at the Hempstones near Runcorn, "it wo'd be lyable to the same Objections with respect to Stoppages by the Neap Tides, as the Weaver Navigation".

The next morning they arrived at Wolsley Bridge by 11 o'clock and found few present, but within the hour "many of the Neighbouring Gentlemen attended" including Lord Gower who had spent the previous evening with Mr. Gilbert at Lichfield, where a meeting with the 'Burslemites' had "Settled the Plan of Operation for the next day".

The meeting commenced with Lord Gower proposing an application to Parliament for an Act to construct a canal from Wilden Ferry to the River Mersey. Mr. Pownall then presented his plan for an extension of the canal to Winsford Bridge, which John Stafford considered to be "a very honest way of thinking", but Lord Gower insisted that his proposals "were Enough for the present, and other improvements might be Grafted upon it hereafter".

The wording of the Act was then discussed and Mr. Colquit, on behalf of Liverpool Corporation, queried the words "to the Mersey", and asked where the canal would be brought to, pointing out that the suggestion was the canal would go into and not over the river, but Mr. Gilbert "artfully parryed them off". Further discussions covered subscriptions and expenses adjudged necessary by James Brindley, bringing the total estimated costs to £101,000, (which seems a very reasonable sum for such an undertaking).

John Stafford's remarks to his kinsman, Samuel Wright, solicitor of Knutsford, when reporting details of the meeting, reveal his utter contempt for what was taking place, appreciating that the Duke would be in a position to "draw all the Carriage between the two Great Ports of Liverpool & Hull & a great deal from the interior parts of the country into his canal."

Whilst at the meeting Mr. Stafford had been approached by an acquaintance who had asked him "whether the Cheshire Gentlemen were come to oppose the Scheme", to which he answered "by no means", but they had hoped for an enlargement of it. He found it extraordinary that the details were not to be expounded, nor had he heard of any surveys carried out by Brindley in Cheshire. He was immediately informed that Mr. Brindley had been interrupted in his work, but as only one land owner had been involved in Brindley's expulsion from his land, John Stafford guessed that the incident had been made good use of to obtain passage of an Act which was so vague that, in effect, Bridgewater would be given carte blanche to do whatever he so desired, and:

> "By that means I presume he will become the largest dealer as a Carrier in Europe, with this peculiar Circumstance, that he'l, in great Measure, be unaccountable for any Miscarriages – as it will be much more prudent for a Party Injured to sit down with the Loss [i.e. to accept the loss], than to seek any other recompence, than what he will graciously Condescend to Give – A Monopoly in the hands of a peer of the Realm, refusing to Waive his Priviledge, Seems such a Monster, as I hope this Land of Liberty will never suffer to live."

Strong words from John Stafford, now a much older and wiser man than in the days of Bonnie Prince Charlie's visit.

One can imagine Charles Roe's reaction upon hearing the details from John Stafford, as expressed to Samuel Wright:

> "And as to the Macclesfield Scheme, it was not even so much as Once mentioned, so Contemptible are we in the Eyes of the Great Schemers of Staffordshire, for my Own part, I was not Sorry for it, but my Neighbour Roe wishes he had been there, and thinks he cou'd have made it very evident, that our Scheme, will Shew the Burslemites the Way into the Weaver . . ."

In writing his letter to Samuel Wright on 3rd January 1766, John Stafford inspired himself to throw his full support behind the scheme, commenting "I am now Convinced more than ever, That our Scheme will not Only be very beneficial to the interior parts of the County, but also be a very Great advantage to the Weaver Navigation – And I hope nothing will obstruct it." The Duke's agents were well prepared, and James Brindley, unwilling to jeopardise Bridgewater's patronage, supported their theory that the Macclesfield scheme would drain all the water from the area, thus obstructing the 'Grand Design'. An objection which had already been proved false as part of the survey.

It also came to light that the course of the Trent and Mersey was to be altered and carried through Middlewich, running alongside the Weaver for a considerable distance, the object being "to steal the Trade" from the river. Small wonder great consternation was felt; this very lucrative trade, substantially of salt and cheese, would be subsidising the merchants from the counties of Lancashire and Staffordshire. For the magnitude of this situation to be appreciated and put into perspective, a comparable outcome today would be for the Cheshire residents to pay a large proportion of their Cheshire County rates, to the County Councils of Lancashire and Staffordshire, and hope that in return, some contribution might be made to Cheshire.

It was evident that both groups would persist in their desires to push a Bill through Parliament for their own particular plan.

So angry was Charles Roe, with the lack of honesty and principle on the part of the Trent and Mersey schemers, that he must have taken some action in order to communicate to Josiah Wedgwood exactly what he thought about the matter, as did Sir William Meredith. The outcome was that Wedgwood received a letter (from whom is not obvious, but almost certainly from Sir William), the contents of which compelled him to send it to his solicitor, Mr. Hodson. Perhaps he was hoping for encouragement to sue, but this he did not receive, only the return of the letter with the solicitor's comments. Wedgwood, still anxious to satisfy his displeasure, sent the letter to Thomas Bentley on 14th January 1766, terminating his screed with the following two paragraphs:

"I am greatly pleased with Mr. Hodson's Letter – which fully convinces me that if any of us Navigators are slip'd beside ourselves, it is our quondom Friend of Macclesfield – Poor Man! how he raves! – I hope one Month's Confinement to the Debates in Westminster hall will perfectly cure him (this suggests Sir William) – Have I liberty to make what use I please of this Letter? – I have not undergone so severe a piece of Self denial a long time as I shall do today, by not daring without your leave, to inclose this letter to the Duke by this post & I send this upward of seven miles that you may have it time enough to return an answer by Saturday.
It cannot hurt either you or Mr. Hodson with His Grace & Mr. Roe cannot be more obnoxious than he had already made himself, nor do I want it at all to answer that purpose, but of a much more important one of letting His G- know what that Country in general thinks of his design, in a way that he cannot suspect, was at first intended for that purpose – You will easily know, by recollecting some serious questions you asked me in a former Letter, the Effect I mean it to have:
  Time obliges me to conclude Myself
  Your affectionate Friend   J.W. for yr, perusal only."

It seems apparent that Thomas Bentley was suspicious of the Bridgewater plan, and Wedgwood thought that he had found a way to ensure the Duke's commitment to it, but he had completely underestimated the unscrupulousness of His Grace. One wonders what Josiah's thoughts were when, in the aftermath of the Duke's scheme being approved by Parliament, he was almost deprived of his plot of land, because Bridgewater's intention was to sell it to one of his 'accomplices'. It was Wedgwood's turn to be angry; however he was placated and the Duke finally allowed him to purchase the land in July 1766, blaming the misunderstanding on someone else. This site was destined to become Etruria, for which Josiah paid the substantial sum of £3,000.

As for the Macclesfield scheme, a petition was presented to Parliament on15th January 1766 and referred to a committee on the 7th February, with the Duke's friends giving "all the Trouble they co'd". Charles Roe appeared personally to deal with many of the questions, and apart from a little confusion by the surveyor, support from Golburn and Pownall of Liverpool Corporation satisfied the committee members. As this committee included Sir George Warren and Sir William Meredith it would have been surprising if the Commons had not given leave to bring in the Bill, which received its third reading on the 27th March, before passing to the House of Lords.

From that moment, the Duke of Bridgewater was present at all the debates, petitioning vigorously against the Macclesfield Bill with evidence given by James Brindley. Charles once again attended, stressing all the advantages, particularly those relating to the collieries (Norbury and Poynton being worked by Sir George Warren and Peter Legh of Lyme). The Bill was adjourned until the 21st April, when a further adjournment of three months was given.

It must have seemed to Charles Roe that everything possible had been done. Even the fact that canals are more readily frozen up in winter than the running water of rivers, had been highlighted, as witnessed by the severity of the weather in January of that year. The Sankey Navigation "was stop't within four or five days after the Frost began", and the Duke of Bridgewater had been put to considerable expense to keep the Worsley canal navigable, which could only be achieved with James Brindley's help. The engineer had invented a machine drawn by mules to break up the ice, and then kept a vessel plying to and fro "to keep the Pafsage open". It was evident that there would be little reward in pursuing the quest further, and although Charles had given up on the canal scheme, the possibility of a more advantageous plan occurred to him, so whilst the Bill was left to gather dust, he was already actively considering another important alternative.

One thing was certain, Charles Roe would never use the Bridgewater canal, and although the Duke had apparently succeeded in his intentions, William Roe would never forget the upset caused to his father: it would be many years before the Duke was taught a lesson, and without Charles's presence only William would have the satisfaction of having the last word.

The House of Commons before its destruction by enemy bombing during World War II.

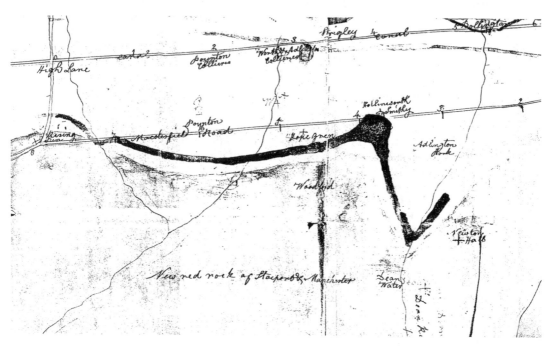

An early 19th century plan of the collieries near Poynton. These would have benefited from the construction of a canal under the scheme proposed by George Warren, Charles Roe and 'other Cheshire Gentlemen'. Courtesy of The John Ryland's Library, from the Bromley Davenport collection.

16
SUPPLIES AND DEMAND

These little things are great to little man.

With the cessation of hostilities at the end of the Seven Years War in 1763, Europe had quickly and eagerly settled down to enjoy a period of domesticity, though it must be appreciated that even during periods of war in the 18th century, fighting was localised with little prohibitive effect on travel and commerce; people simply avoided battlefields and cities under siege. War, however, still created an air of despondency and unease, projecting an overriding mantle of restraint, but with the resumption of peace, once more attention could be lavished on literature and the arts with particular consideration given to fashion.

An exciting period of experimentation was beginning, with a diffusion of ideas between Italy, France and England. The Georgian Court continued to dictate fashion, and sumptuously embroidered dresses and jackets remained in favour for formal wear, made from velvet, satin or silk, with men's waistcoats mostly sleeveless. The dress coat for men began to appear with a narrow standing collar, destined to become increasingly higher as George III's reign progressed. The full-skirted gowns of fashionable ladies were supported initially by three metallic hoops sewn to the material of the skirt. The overgown remained open at the front displaying a richly embroidered or quilted petticoat, whilst dresses in the home were more practical, remaining narrower and plainer.

Perukes were still very much in demand, but the long curling periwigs of French origin, fashionable since the beginning of Charles II's reign, were losing favour amongst the younger generation of gentlemen who preferred a shorter, simpler style. On the other hand ladies' hair styles, which had started the century with the simple elegance of drawn back hair and soft curls falling over the shoulders, were about to take on new dimensions; the mid-1760s were the start of a decade when fashion would run riot.

The hooped skirt, first round in shape as introduced by the actresses of the Comédie Italienne to a very mixed reception, soon became oval. Its sideways dimensions supported by whale bones, were to be stretched to the point of absurdity whereby ladies, unable to pass through doorways in the normal manner, were forced to turn sideways to accomplish the feat. They were unable to use sedan chairs or narrow carriages, unable to reach the hand of an escort, and were to find dancing a matter of utmost dexterity.

Whilst hip lines mushroomed to irrational proportions women's hair styles mushroomed to farcical heights, arranged with the aid of high frames or pads to which false curls and ringlets were attached. A profusion of flowers, feathers, jewellery, ribbons and whatsoever could be used, (such as model sailing ships) bedecked elaborate coiffures, with new styles invented to suit every possible occasion, particularly by the famous hairdresser, Leonard. When the wife of the English ambassador to Turkey, Lady Montagu, returned to England from Constantinople with the news that inoculation against smallpox was rapidly spreading through many countries, Leonard promptly designed a style called 'Inoculation' – unfortunately no description of this splendiferous creation is available.

Shoes were beautifully made of leather with rounded toes and small heels for both men and women, but fashion soon dictated that the sensible clog-like footwear, so adept for walking along rough road and pathways, was abandoned for all social gatherings. More elegantly styled footwear with pointed toes was preferred, with fastenings of oval or square buckles. Ladies sported embroidered silk or velvet shoes, often made from material to match their outfits. Silk stockings for the wealthy and best occasions were an absolute necessity, with cotton or wool for those of humbler means. White was the most popular colour, although ladies often wore blue or green, with dark colours preferred to accompany dark leather riding boots.

Females everywhere adored accessories; lace caps (mostly worn at home), large hats with wide brims perched at the front of headdresses, gloves, parasols copied from the Chinese and jewellery made of paste, all held pride of place. Assemblies provided the opportunity for wearing masks, a delightful idea from Venice, or for carrying exquisite little purses and gorgeously decorated fans. Shawls and hooded capes protected the ladies, whilst the men still wore three cornered hats, although sporting gentlemen usually wore beavers.

The most outlandish fashions would, of course, be more prevalent in London; there a gentlemen's club called Macaroni set the fashion in foppish attire, inspiring many young men such as Thomas Golightly of Liverpool to take their ideas to the provinces.

By the 1760s young men and women, whose fathers and uncles had worked long and hard during the preceding two decades, were coming-of-age. Many were the second generation of an expanding merchant and manufacturing middle class responsible for bringing great wealth and opportunities to these islands, merchants and others who had travelled great distances, often overseas, and endured all sorts of problems both physical and financial in their anxiety to provide their offspring with a better and more secure future. This younger generation had to be trained and schooled in all aspects of manufacturing and production to enable them to sustain the vital branches of commerce already set in place. Even young women, some left as widows, would soon prove themselves just as competent as men in running businesses when occasion demanded.

But this younger generation, whilst accepting that hard work and responsibilities were inevitable, were less inclined to sacrifice and more desirous to indulge themselves in the pleasures and privileges that money can buy. They copied the fashions and manners of the aristocracy and, although individually on a much smaller scale, yet cumulatively creating a considerable demand for exquisite and beautiful objects. Craftsmen were paid well for their work, so not only did the silversmiths, jewellers, tailors, dressmakers, toymakers, porcelain manufacturers, cabinet makers and other producers of luxury goods benefit, but also the butcher, the baker and the candlestick maker who were all regarded as important and well-to-do members of society.

London streets, walks and pleasure gardens, in particular Vauxhall and Ranelagh, were more conducive to the displays of fashionable attire than the steep narrow winding thoroughfare of Mill Street in Macclesfield or the cramped accommodation facilities of the inns and houses of Buxton. The cities of Bath, Gloucester and Bristol would more readily follow the lead of the capital, with Chester, Liverpool, Manchester and York not far behind. But even in these cities one suspects a pronounced note of sobriety. Although European Court dress still dictated fashion, with its surprising desire to copy and adapt peasant styles at this period, the strong forces of religion remained very much in evidence. Such frivolous dress would not be tolerated by many Dissenters, particularly Quakers, and fashion within the Colonies of North America was to remain more practical and subdued.

Whereas the aristocratic Roman Catholic families of the Continent were attired in the most sumptuous garments and jewels, in England the flair for fashion lay very much in the hands of the Church of England families, and even parsons' wives were not beyond the allure of fine jewellery and clothes.

The most expensive and fashionable dress of the British aristocracy would be retained in their residences in London and the Home Counties. The Earl of Harrington's wife, who was a great leader of fashion, or the wives of Lord Powis and the Duke of Bedford (the latter owning extensive areas of land in London, particularly around Bloomsbury) would dress in the most elaborate fashion for attendance at Court or for assemblies elsewhere in the capital. The list was endless: both Lord Lucan and the Duke of Richmond held estates in Ireland to which they retired from time to time, but when duty called they hastened to London, where their families could take advantage of enjoying the social scene. The Duke of Richmond was fortunate in having a splendid house by the Thames with an excellent view of the river, recorded for future generations by the famous Italian painter, Canaletto.

Visits to provincial estates provided an opportunity for displaying the latest Continental (via London) styles in the form of a new gown or jacket, a daring new colour of wig or a more unusual shaped riding boot with the back cut out. The local gentry, many of whom frequently visited London and reported back to wives and daughters, would have the satisfaction of having their narratives verified. It was one thing to hear what people were wearing and daring to emulate it oneself, but quite a different matter to copy what one could see being worn. In larger towns and villages the subsequent demands on the local dressmaker, tailor and hairdresser to acquire similar patterns and materials, or the local seamstress and barber in more remote localities, would be considerable.

The wealthy families of North Wales and Cheshire, amongst whom were the Grosvenors and Brocks, apart from having London arrangements, also held town houses in Chester, the nearest county town to their country estates; this was mirrored in other counties and regions throughout the British Isles by many other families in similar situations.

In the first instance, of course, it was a necessity to acquire a burgage in town if a person wished to benefit from the advantages of becoming a burgess. It was also essential to maintain town houses because of the difficulties of travel and often a convenient way of investing money. The fact that they were symbols of affluence or wealth was initially of secondary consideration, but one which was beginning to gain favour and priority amongst the nouveau riche.

Chester, "a very large and opulent town, beautified with many good buildings", was a centre for commerce, large fairs, horse racing and Corporation meetings, making a town house a more practical option than staying at an inn. All family members and servants could commute as convenient, with wives and children preferring to stay in town during the season of plays, balls and assemblies which fell between the beginning of November and the end of March. Dancing was held fortnightly at *The Hotel* on Monday evenings, with a Card Assembly every Thursday. Tea was served for a charge of sixpence or one shilling, and the universal passion for bowls could be satisfied on the immaculately maintained bowling green adjoining. Perhaps the restrictive fashions made it more a game for men, whilst the audience, predominantly female, watched, gossiped and sipped tea; however, not to be outdone, an enthusiasm for archery was soon to be cultivated amongst the women folk.

The bowling green of the 18th century, together with all its appendages and facilities, would find its comparison today in the modern leisure centre.

An occasional V.I.P. passing through the town, usually en route for Ireland, gave members of the Corporation and their wives an opportunity to entertain the celebrity in the Pentice (town hall). Funds were limited but did allow for a present, in one instance of sweetmeats, to be made to the spouse of the voyager. The opportunity would be taken to display the Corporation plate, whilst members and their ladies were able to air their fineries.

Naturally London Society operated on a much grander scale, allowing for a greater range of activities. London was also a beautiful city, with many aspects and views captured on canvas by Canaletto. He had arrived in this country during 1746 at the age of 49 years, and apart from one brief visit to Venice in 1750, remained for a further five years before finally returning to his Venetian home where he would die in 1768. He painted Westminster Bridge, opened in 1750, which gave London its second thoroughfare across the Thames.

In the City, Cornhill, having recovered from a devastating fire in 1748 during which 100 houses, including many famous coffee houses, had been destroyed and several lives lost, suffered a similar fate during 1765. The fire reached Threadneedle Street but was fortunately contained. One can imagine the horror and consternation felt by Cousin Christopher, Edward Pitts and their families, living in such close proximity to the disaster. The shock experienced by the linen draper, Robert Mandeville, must have been immense, and although only a young man he was to die within a couple of years.

Another character who witnessed the inferno was John Harriott, a young man who, according to his later writings, must have been 20 years old at the time. He compared the incident with a fire experienced whilst on duty in India, which on that occasion had been started deliberately to clear a path through thick grasses and foliage, allowing access to the summit of a hill.

"It spread in a complete circle, and the loud snapping and crackling of the flames was similar to that which I had known from a fire at Cornhill, in London, when the four corners were all on fire at the same time".

The Bank of England, which had originally commenced operations in a hired room in the Mercers' Hall in 1694, was moved into the house of the then Governor, Sir John Houblon, on Threadneedle Street in 1734. The addition of adjacent land acquisitions allowed for modest extensions and enlargement within 20 years; however, having survived the threat of fire in 1765 it was to remain virtually unaltered, hidden from view by surrounding houses, until almost the end of Charles Roe's life.

The population of the capital was steadily increasing, aided by an influx of skilled workers from the Continent. Since William and Mary's reign Dutch workmen had arrived, often referred to as Germans because of their accents, and with the advent of the Hanoverian Monarchy many German families, particularly from the region around Hamburg, had also made their way across the Channel. Ironically they were often referred to as Hollanders, but some were from the disputed territories of Schleswig and Holstein on the borders of Mecklenburg (home of George III's wife, Queen Charlotte) and considered themselves Danish by character and tradition. Whereas the French Protestants had tended to continue their trades in silver work, textiles and porcelain, the Hanseatic families were proficient in sugar baking, the production of small metal wares and heavy pottery such as storage jars and bottles.

The City of London traditionally contained within one square mile, saw her ever increasing population and commerce pushing outwards the boundaries of the Metropolis. Slowly but surely encroachment and absorption of the surrounding manors and villages was taking place, a situation which would rapidly accelerate within a generation; but unfortunately the facilities provided by the Port of London were unable to follow suit. This unbelievable situation, brought about by lack of Customs facilities, had presented Liverpool in particular with the opportunity for expansion.

* * * * * * *

During the late Middle Ages many of the northern ports, such as Hull and York, had rivalled London, but began to decline because of what they saw as a deliberate policy of domination on the part of London merchants. The northern cloth trade was poached to the extent that wealthy chapmen and excellent clothiers had moved to the Capital, creating deteriorations in port facilities elsewhere. Soon London and the Belgian port of Antwerp controlled much of the European cloth trade, as cloth made in London was shipped to Antwerp for finishing before distribution took place throughout north-eastern Europe. However, Antwerp's precarious position during the wars of the period, encouraged English merchants to move their centre of operations to Emden on the Ems Estuary, (today just over the north-eastern border of Holland in Germany) and later to Hamburg. During the Elizabethan era the trade with Hamburg was considerable.

In respect of Royal Customs, it was the Elizabethan Parliament which had laid down legislation to clarify the situation. The definition of a head port was not a place convenient for loading or unloading ships, but a port where such activities were permitted in the presence of the Collector of Royal Customs. Other havens were placed under the jurisdiction of the appropriate head port, with resident deputy officers to officiate. In the case of creeks or minor inlets, exporting and importing was illegal without a special licence or "sufferance". Under the Act (I Eliz.I cII) apart from definition, the exact location of all Legal Quays was set down, but surprisingly it was to be this very legislation which in due course would restrict the growth of the Port of London, causing great difficulties in the 18th century and allowing Liverpool to seize her opportunity.

The Pool of London, being such an immense area of water, could well accommodate all shipping which rode at anchor in mid-stream until lightermen were able to load and unload cargoes. The problem was lack of available land to extend the area of the Legal Quay, and without increased Customs facilities the volume of river traffic was subjected to longer and more expensive waits. Merchants petitioned in vain during 1762 and again in 1765 for an extension of the Legal Quay, but private land owners had already leased wharfs to wharfingers and merchants for inland trade on the Thames, so the quality of service for sea-going vessels was already under threat. The situation was only slightly alleviated by Sufferance Wharfes where certain goods could be handled; these stretched for almost 3,000 feet on the south bank below Old London Bridge and about 800 feet below the Tower on the north bank, but were of little effect.

The development down river had already well and truly encroached into the manor of Stepney, east of the City. Recorded in the Domesday Book as belonging to the Bishops of London, Stepney stretched from the City to the River Lea and from the Thames to Hackney. The old Saxon church, dedicated to St. Dunstan (formerly Dunstan, Bishop of London 959-961) had witnessed the building of the White Chapel of St. Mary Matfellon in the west of the parish during the early 14th closely followed, in 1311, by the chapel of Stratford Bow near Bow bridge for the parishioners in the east.

London merchants had eagerly sought sites for the building of country residences, and during the reign of Henry VII two important developments took place. The first was a strong wave of Protestantism with total rejection of the Roman Catholic faith, and the second was the growth of three naval establishments at Ratcliffe, Blackwall and Deptford.

Another intrusion into stepney was inspired by English privateers, already active from Bristol. London merchants gave encouragement in promoting the building of houses and shipyards along the Thames, first at Ratcliffe, then Limehouse and finally Blackwall. Intrinsically linked with this progression was the establishment of Trinity House, the Company of Merchant Adventurers and the Muscovy Company.

One famous name, whose family was to become synonymous with the parish, particularly the hamlet of Whitechapel, was that of the famous Elizabethan admiral, Sir John Hawkyns. Stepney was also to become home to many more great naval characters because of the proximity of the naval yards.

On 12th April 1551 the manor of Stepney had been given to Edward VI, ending the 500 year old connection with the Bishops of London. Almost immediately it was granted to Sir Thomas Wentworth, member of an old Yorkshire family, thus suggesting a reason for the settlement in the parish of other Yorkshire families, as the link between the estates took place.

A business which was to grow in importance throughout the area, with the development of the West Indian trade, was that of sugar baking. As early as 1597 the firm of Gardiner & Co. is recorded as sugar refiners in Ratcliffe.

From time to time the parish experienced considerable upsurges in population, although usually only of a temporary nature, as people left the City at the outbreak of plagues. One overwhelming occasion was at the time of the Great Fire when merchants arrived with carts full of possessions and goods seeking help from friends and relatives. The large houses were soon full to overflowing and, after the extent of the conflagration was known, temporary offices were set up until the return to the City could be organised, much to the chagrin of many Stepney residents.

With the steady increase in population and commerce, not only did the naval establishments contribute to the prosperity of Stepney manor, but also the East India Company. Under the terms of the monopoly of the Eastern trade, all ships of the company were restricted to the Port of London, which for convenience had always been the Blackwall Reach of the river. Such was the concern for security, as river traffic rapidly increased causing delays, losses and damage due to lighters endeavouring to weave their way through the Pool to and from the East Indiamen, that the company had all its goods landed at Blackwall. This created extra activity as processions of goods, under armed escort, frequently made their way from the wharfs to the East India warehouse in the City. The manor of Stepney was, therefore, the vital link between the City and its overseas trade.

* * * * * * *

Whereas the City was the centre of commerce, Westminster was the centre of political and religious life. Originally the two were linked by a bridle path and cart track, which had developed into an avenue of stately houses with beautiful gardens by the Elizabethan period. Those on the southern side sloped gently to the edge of the river, where convenient landing stages were constructed to enable their occupiers, mostly noblemen and their families, to be boated down to London Bridge or up to Whitehall Stairs.

18th century hackney carriages found the narrowness of this thoroughfare, known as The Strand, totally inadequate. There was much complaint about noise and congestion, although in reality it was quite wide, especially when compared with the vast majority of streets and avenues in the capital. Crowds milled to and fro, anxious to frequent the coffee houses, taverns and tearooms which now lined the street, mostly on the southern side.

Occasionally there were complaints about gutters blocked by ashes, fish bones and scraps of meat etc., but the Georgians had become so inculcated with the idea of aesthetic awareness, which in turn had stimulated a responsibility for landscape and townscape, that their complaints must be kept in perspective. What they considered as dirty and polluted today would hardly be noticed, so unconcerned are we about the volume of litter and rubbish which blows about our town and city streets. Georgians made use of everything they could, so there was little waste left to throw away. With no packaging, wrappers or carrier bags, most of the waste consisted of offals and left-over food which could be fed to animals or easily burnt on the abundance of open kitchen fires. Scavengers were vigilant in retrieving bones either for the local glue factory, or as noted by Dr. Johnson, the local foundry; until recent times the rag and bone man with his horse and cart was still a regular visitor to many towns and villages.

It is easy to criticise the location of 18th century manufactories such as glassworks, sugar houses, potteries, smelters and dyeworks, which often appeared in the middle of a picturesque village or near residential areas of a city. No one wanted to invite complaints about the production of obnoxious fumes so, as far as possible, the direction of prevailing winds was taken into account. The availability of the labour force had to be considered, with cottages and houses provided for some employees. Often properties were adapted or new ones built, but the result was the same, manufactories with the greater part of their employees living adjacent to or within easy walking distance of their gates. The Georgian mind saw these mini-complexes as part of the scenery, whether rural, urban or metropolitan and, as such, endeavoured to keep them unobtrusive. Mills were surrounded by gardens and trees, smelters accompanied by farms, glassworks and sugar houses lay alongside fields, walks and avenues, with their classical facades mirrored by ornamental ponds. It seemed as though everywhere efforts were made to present a pretty picture, portraying the Georgian obsession for attention to detail. Georgians were working hard and playing hard, though in what proportion depended very much on the individual.

Amidst all the hustle, bustle and excitement of London life Brian Hodgson's brother-in-law, maintained a family residence on Parliament Street in the City of Westminster. This was part of a new development completed between the years 1741-50 to provide approach improvements for the ambitious Westminster Bridge scheme. The street, taken across the courts and alleys which had initially replaced the Palace bowling green, was first rated in 1750 and belonged to Westminster Abbey. There were many large residences rated between £2 and £3 some of which appear to have been shared by two parties. The Webster family leased their property from 1760, with a modest rating for the area of 15s. 7^1/$_2$d. which suggests occupation of part of a smaller residence at the southern end of the street. Close by on Whitehall were the important buildings of The Treasury, Plantation Office, Judge Advocate's Office and War Office.

The Hodgsons appear to have used this residence when visiting London, for on the 13th May of the same year, 1765, Brian and Elizabeth's eldest daughter, Margaret, 24 years of age, was married from this address to a remarkable man, Rev. Beilby Porteus.

* * * * * * *

The Porteus family was originally from Virginia where Beilby's parents had maintained family estates for many years. His mother, distantly related to the Duchess of Marlborough, was the daughter of Colonel Jennings, superintendent of Indian affairs for the colony and, for a period, Deputy Governor. His father's ill health together with a desire to provide the children with a good education, forced the family to return to England. They settled in York where Beilby was born on the 8th and baptised on 21st May 1731, the eighteenth child out of what was to be a family of nineteen children. Beilby received his good education, first at York and then at the impressive school of Ripon. On 1st June 1748 he was admitted as a sizar at Christ's College, Cambridge where he proved himself to be an excellent scholar winning a medal for classics.

Distinctive by his threadbare coat, Beilby never considered himself to be anything but ordinary. He loved writing poetry and consequently took a literary course; however, his main concern was education, a subject to which he eagerly dedicated himself for much of the remainder of his life. Sadly he and Margaret were to have no children, so he embraced everyone else's as though they were his own. A great argument of the period was the use of the Bible in schools to teach children to read, for many considered that children regarded the stories as "a kind of Aesop's Fables". Beilby argued the contrary, it was good to sow good seed, and though it might lie on the surface or slip into some crevice apparently lost, yet when the opportunity arose, it would "burst into birth" and totally regenerate all around it.

In 1752 he was made a fellow of his college and eventually, after resigning all interests and devoting himself to private study for two years, was ordained deacon and priest in 1757.

At this time Cambridge University "had taken to itself a kind of pride as being the support of whig principles and accused its sister-university rather unjustly of toryism originated in the royal parliament held at Oxford in the civil wars". Beilby, in a life of "public turmoil and contest", made it a rule never to interfere in politics, a principle which the hierarchy of the Church of England might do well to observe today.

By a remarkable coincidence, Thomas Secker, whose letters to his family in Chesterfield had been so interesting, was now to be instrumental in shaping Beilby's future. Bishop Secker, previously of Bristol and then of Oxford, had preached a sermon at the time of Queen Caroline's death which had so impressed George II that he had asked the Bishop to try to effect a reconciliation between himself and his eldest son, Frederick, Prince of Wales. Although unsuccessful with this mission, Thomas Secker did baptise many of the Prince's children including the future George III.

As Bishop of Oxford he attended Blenheim Palace and ministered to Sarah, Duchess of Marlborough, which suggests that he must have become acquainted with the distantly related Porteus family.

In 1750 he succeeded his friend as Dean of St, Paul's and then became Archbishop of Canterbury in 1758. Having already baptised and confirmed the heir to the throne, in 1761 he was able to crown George III and conduct his marriage ceremony. The King presented a miniature portrait of himself to the Archbishop, as a token of the esteem in which Thomas Secker was held.

Meanwhile Beilby was hard at work correcting parts of the Bible which had been incorrectly translated from the Greek text, and acquiring considerable knowledge and understanding of the Jews and Jewish Law. In 1760 he had published *The Character of David. King of Israel impartially stated* from which Archbishop Secker recognised the excellence and potentiality of this impressive young man. Early in 1762 Thomas Secker appointed Rev. Porteus as one of his domestic chaplains, and upon Beilby's marriage to Margaret Hodgson gave him two small livings in Kent which he shortly resigned when he took up the living of Hunton in the same county. This was unusual as he was entitled to retain these livings, but having already acquired Peterborough the previous year he felt that two were sufficient for his position, thus allowing another clergyman to benefit from his gesture.

Brian Hodgson must have experienced a great deal of satisfaction from this marriage, and whilst Charles Roe was struggling through one of the most difficult periods of his life, the Hodgson good fortune continued with the marriage of the second eldest son, Brian Jnr. This marriage to Ellen Hodson took place in The Collegiate Church (Christ's Church) now Manchester Cathedral on 26th May 1766. As can be judged from her portrait, she was considered "very plain but of higher birth" than her husband.

About the time of his second son's marriage Brian Snr. retired from Buxton Hall, allowing the newly married couple to take over the business. His choice of residence was in Ashbourne, Derbyshire where he appears to have converted the house, malt mill and appurtenances, formerly in the tenure of Dr. Taylor's father and sub-tenanted, into a substantial residence known thereafter as The Grey House.

* * * * * * *

It is known that Robert Adam, the famous Georgian architect, was engaged by Sir Nathaniel Curzon (shortly to become Lord Scarsdale), an investor in Derbyshire lead mines, to enlarge and rebuild his family home at Kedleston. At the same time Dr. Taylor had several additions made to his father's Jacobean house in Church Street, Ashbourne, transforming it into a very fine residence of "exceptional splendour". It has been argued that the designs used were those of Robert Adam, as they display many features similar to those seen at Kedleston Hall. It has also been suggested that the architect James Paine was involved, who could have adapted the Adam designs for his own purposes. As a consequence of this he is additionally attributed with the extensive rebuilding of The Grey House for Brian Hodgson on stylistic grounds; the Venetian window is surmounted by a Spalato, characteristic of James Paine's villa designs.

Recent suggestions, however, include the name of the architect, Joseph Pickford of Derby (precursor of Adam at Kedleston) who took responsibility for the refurbishment of Dr. Taylor's house; from this he is also tentatively given credit for the facade of No.61.

The Grey House still stands at 61 Church Street, next door to the Elizabethan Grammar School and opposite The Mansion, former residence of Dr. Taylor and retreat of Samuel Johnson. Brian Hodgson, well pleased with his house, was to remain there for the rest of his life. He was close to Uttoxeter for the horse races, and could superintend the purchases by the Roe & Co. employees of copper ores from Ecton Hill just seven miles north-west of Ashbourne, which remained considerable.

After the completion of the Havannah works in 1763 and the acquisition of the Liverpool outlet through John Walker, purchases of Ecton ore in 1765 reached a record level of £6,214 18 6d. (according to the Ecton accounts) against which payment of £5,097 18 1d. was made by bills (cash payment of four shillings only, which must have been a tip to someone). With this vast amount of business taking place it was necessary for one of the senior partners to be close at hand, to be able to take decisions should any unexpected emergencies arise.

* * * * * * *

The work at both Alderley Edge and Coniston remained slow and arduous, and out of the total tonnage of copper ores transported on the River Weaver, for the period January 1765 to March 1766, 112 tons 15cwts. came from Coniston, leaving 265 tons attributable to Cornwall and elsewhere. The Cornish Ore Sales figures record purchases by "Rowe & Co." Macclesfield as 216 tons for 1765 and 208 tons for 1766, which suggests that the greater part of the 265 tons was from Cornwall. The account for the "Llanberris Mining Co". ends on 7th February 1765, but with John Paynter's figures presenting a somewhat obscure picture it is possible that a few tons of ore also came from this source.

The stocks of ore at the Macclesfield smelter were further supplemented by purchases from Middleton Tyas as follows:

Delivered December 1765	8 tons	@ £31 1 6d.	£248 12 0d.
To 1st August 1766 almost	6¼ tons	@ £35 3 9d.	£218 4 0d.
Plus	3 tons	@ £20 2 0d.	£ 60 6 0d.

These relatively small purchases in weight represent today a total value well in excess of £50,000.

At this period Josiah Wagstaff took up duties at Middleton from where he wrote on16th March 1766 to Robert Barker, now engaged by Tissington & Co. at Leadhills near Dumfries. There had been a misunderstanding with regard to the rent of the forge houses at Coniston which the Macclesfield company had taken over from Tissington & Co. in 1760 for accommodation of their miners. Cash payments appear in the Coniston accounts for Roe & Co. in respect of rent for forge houses from 1760 onwards, but it emerged that Mr. Wagstaff had received money from Tissington & Co. for the 1760 rent which he had passed to Mr. Hale on his arrival from Derbyshire. Mr. Hale had credited Tissington & Co. with the appropriate amount from the Roe & Co. takeover but either, must have forgotten to pass on the remainder due for 1760 together with the Roe & Co. rent, or the Le Fleming Chief Steward, John Moore, had not realised that the Roe & Co. rent also included the proportion from Tissington & Co. Either way the whole matter was amicably settled and the reputations of Messrs. Wagstaff and Hale were never in dispute.

Josiah Wagstaff, in writing his letter, took the opportunity to advise his friend, Robert Barker, "We still keep raising some ore, but yet are not to call rich, but are still in hopes of doing better this Summer", which suggests that Roe & Co., apart from purchasing ore at the site, were also carrying out trials and mining on their own account, possibly subleasing from Tissington & Co. Josiah was obviously labouring under great difficulties at this time due to personal problems. "My Wife has been extreem(ly) ill, & I expected no other than Death.

She is Some little better, at prefent, but yet not out of danger".

In spite of all the difficulties, hazards and distances involved, the choice of employees made by Roe & Co., and the policies adopted, were bearing fruit. Rewards and help were given to those who worked well, but negligence or slovenly work was immediately admonished, and in extreme cases a hearing called, after which a fine or dismissal might be the outcome. The business was steadily improving as reflected, not only by the supplies in the River Weaver books to the Macclesfield smelter, but also the demands made upon the company for finished goods.

After the third and final consignment to John Rogerson of Liverpool in March 1765, and the subsequent advertisement of June in Williamson's *Liverpool Advertiser*, small but significant items of copper and brass began to appear in the Weaver books under the name of John Walker; evidence that he personally was handling the transportation arrangements for the company goods to Liverpool, thus saving commission payable to an independent carrier.

* * * * * * *

The important foothold gained in Liverpool, together with what must have been an expanding market elsewhere, particularly in Birmingham and London, as the demand for objets d'art, kitchen utensils and commercial coppers increased, inspired Charles Roe to search for a further site to complement the already successful undertaking at Havannah near Congleton. Once again the choice of location could not have been better. Like Havannah it was sited on the River Daven (Dane) and at the same distance from Macclesfield, but whereas Havannah is slightly south-west, Bosley is slightly south-east of the town. This time the land belonged to William, Earl of Harrington, and with the arrangements for Macclesfield Common working well, the Harrington steward no doubt gave assistance in making available this further piece of land which would be of great benefit to the company.

The closes, part of Bosley Manor known as Daven Meadows, and the Stable Croft contained 11 acres. Included also was part of Kennersbank Wood and land bounded by a road linking Key Green to Linford (Lymford) Bridge, providing an additional 5 acres. Sufficient time was allowed for the partners to fence in these 5 acres after which "such fences" were to be kept in repair. Permission was given for buildings to be erected, and for stones to be taken from the Dane for the purpose, together with the making of a weir on the river or any other brook or stream. In addition the road could be redirected to provide more space for buildings, with cuts made to carry water from the river.

Trees could be planted as necessary and cut down, and old stocks used, but the only important exception was a group of oak trees reserved for the Earl and his heirs. For the purpose of identification a schedule of these oaks was drawn up on the back of the lease. Each had been given a number and carefully listed with its length in feet and its thickness in square inches e.g.:

	length feet	square inches.
No. 1.	15	10
No. 2.	12	3
No. 3.	14	6

The yearly rental of £25 was payable in two equal instalments still using the Ecclesiastical calendar dates of Lady Day and Michaelmas Day.

It is interesting to see the 'admixture' of personalities and partners appearing on the lease at this time, as funding must have been minimal with all the commitments thus far enacted. Five of the company partners, Charles Roe, Rowland Atkinson, Robert Hodgson (the latter now also of Macclesfield), Brian Hodgson Snr. of Ashbourne and Cookson Atkinson of

Westmorland, were joined in this particular venture by the Liverpool merchant, John Walker, and Charles Roe's father-in-law, Joseph Stockdale of St. Martin's-in-the-Fields. Messrs. Walker and Stockdale were obviously in possession of important retail outlets in two of England's premier ports.

The development of Bosley appears to have been very much the same as Havannah, with cottages and gardens provided for employees together with the necessary warehouses, "Blacksmiths, Millwrights, Carpenters and Coopers Shops" erected close by. However, whereas Bosley would eventually have copper rolling mills like Havannah, initially the site contained brass mills and facilities for hammering copper sheets. This latter process was essential for toughening the metal when producing large coppers for the rum and sugar industries, (in particular those of the West Indies) and vessels such as tun dishes (i.e. large funnels used in the brewing and dyeing industries). This suggests that for a time the greater part of copper rolling was carried out at Havannah and then sent to Bosley for hammering as desired.

The reason for the delay in building another copper rolling mill at Bosley may have been financial, unless the demand at that stage was insufficient to warrant one, the priority being given to a brass rolling mill and brass battery mills instead.

In order to work the rollers through which the brass passed a substantial source of energy was required. This was supplied by water driving a large water wheel which ultimately was accompanied by four more, one to work each of the battery mills, thus bringing the total to five as at Havannah. Although the size of the Bosley wheels is unknown they must have been of similar proportions to those of Havannah which ranged from 18 ft to 22 ft in diameter.

In the first instance one weir was built upstream from the brass mills, with a head and fall of water described as "25 feet 3 inches", which together with the natural downhill flow of the river provided a fall of 40 ft within one mile. The weir was constructed in large steps, but the immense volume of water hammering upon the sills for an appreciable length of time wore away this interesting feature, until today the fall appears obliquely straight.

A cut or leat was then constructed from just above this original (today the upper) weir, which led into a specifically constructed mill pool. At the opposite end a sluice gate directed and controlled a stream into a further channel for supplying the water wheels capable of producing 300 h.p. Today on site there remains hidden below ground an elaborate network of tunnels indicative of the distribution of water to each of the five wheels.

The building (or mills) was constructed on the eastern bank of the river, with the race passing along the eastern side, into which the water wheels must have been set: but whether they were undershot or overshot is now difficult to ascertain. The main channel has survived without the mill pond, and the force of water rushing through the large pipe bursts forth to effect a drop of several feet before re-entering the Dane below the mills; an impressive sight.

The rolling mills contained rollers of 2 ft or 4 ft in width, however it is known that the mills at Bosley were initially equipped with 4 ft rollers and the work subcontracted to a firm called Malpas & Co., with articles of employment correctly entered into. This was yet again an instance of a smaller company operating within a larger concern, so typical of the Georgian industrial scene.

The copper or brass ingots/cakes were first heated and then either poured into moulds to form thin plate, usually a half to three quarters of an inch thick, with the width presumably appropriate for the width of the rollers used, or flattened by a hammer and then rolled, forming a round or oval shape convenient for working into different sorts of vessels. Before each rolling the plate had to be heated and, depending on the thinness required, the rollers adjusted to make a narrower space through which to pass the hot sheets.

Brass production on Macclesfield Common had evidently reached a good standard and was easily delivered to the two sites. The important manufacture of wire for supplying pin makers such as Edward Pitts, would remain at Havannah, with brass battery produced only at Bosley. This indicates the practicality of harnessing the considerable force of water at

Bosley in such a way, as to direct its concentrated energy to the machinery within the battery mills for working large hammers, which were, of course, imperative for pounding the brass slabs.

Each water wheel turned a shaft which extended into the building: within each battery mill the shaft rotated several smaller wheels or cogs set with large protruding and appropriately spaced wooden teeth called cams. As each cam in turn struck one end of a pivoted wooden bar, this had the effect of raising its opposite end, to which was fixed the iron hammer head. The cam moved on, driven by the motion of the wheels, and drove the end of the hammer shaft onto a metal striking-plate fixed to the stand frame, the rebound from which gave greater force to the blow of the hammer on the metal object held below on an anvil.

These large hammers, called tilt hammers, had heads of various weights and shapes in order to produce a variety of articles; some of them weighed as much as 500lbs, although as previously stated they were considered light when compared with those used in an iron foundry. The work was highly skilled and could be dangerous if the wrong hammer head was used for that particular plate (i.e. piece) of brass or copper, sometimes resulting in damage both to the metal and workman from whose hands the object had been unceremoniously knocked. A deep pan or vessel could only be formed by a series of several hammerings, and between these the object was returned to one of the annealing ovens on site to heat it to "a full red heat". This process was necessary to restore the malleability and ductability of the metal, otherwise when cold 'metal fatigue' was likely to occur causing cracking of the fabric due to its brittle nature. The actual hammered sheet brass was known as latten, whilst today we refer to the copper sheets hammered in this way as 'beaten copper'.

At the same time as brass battery and beaten copper were being produced at Bosley, brass at Havannah was being prepared for conversion into wire. For this purpose a wire mill had been constructed together with a long chamber over the annealing house and oven.The Havannah wire, after the final annealing, was coiled and fastened into bundles ready for transportation; it appears to have travelled in this form without protection from the elements.

Brass objects which were cast in sand moulds, known as 'brazen wares', could easily be produced on Macclesfield Common, and also copper objects such as large kettles. But the rolling of sheets had to be carried out at Havannah and Bosley because of insufficient power in the water supply from the Common for the working of rolling mills.

Of the eight cottages and gardens provided at Bosley for the workmen, two were integrated into the main part of the works close to the northern end, whilst the other six were built on the opposite side of the roadway which traversed the site from Key Green to Linford Bridge. These cottages still remain on site, although the two within the main building have been adapted for office use.

* * * * * * *

During the development of Havannah William Roe was in his late teens, and with the development of Bosley he came of age. The considerable experience gained by him was shortly to be put to the test, as his father, indefatigable as ever, was pressing ahead with more important plans.

Charles was relentless, driven by a desire to overcome the disagreeable episode of the Macclesfield Canal Scheme, and determined not to be out-manoeuvred. If he did stop to draw breath it was only momentarily whilst he married for a third and final time. Having agreed and signed the lease for Bosley as from 1st August 1766, his marriage took place at Prestbury Parish Church on the 23rd October. He was fortunate, yet again, to have met someone who would prove to be good, reliable and dedicated, not only as a wife but also as a mother, no easy task with a 'ready-made' family of nine surviving children.

Rachel obviously chose to disregard the imposition, particularly as she was a mature 33 years of age and had not previously been married. Charles was her senior by 18 years, a circumstance not unusual in Georgian Society. Nor was the reverse, as more and more wealthy elderly widows found themselves desirous of the flirtatious attentions bestowed by handsome, underprivileged young men. Marriage contracts began to take on new meanings with one party more than happy to 'accommodate' the other, often at considerable expense, and although these were the exceptions rather than the rule, they provided copious gossip and speculation around the dinner tables of the wealthy, with the possibility of runaway marriages at Gretna Green or, in extreme cases, abduction. Fortunately this was not a situation with which the Roe family had to contend, at least, not for the present.

Whatever Charles Roe's daughter, Catherine, thought about the marriage is difficult to assess, but there was no hint of disapproval on William's part, in fact his relationship with his step-mother would prove to be one of mutual respect and understanding as the years progressed.

Daughters, Mary and Frances, aged 9 and 10 years respectively, were sure to prove their worth. Inseparable, known to the world at large as Polly and Fanny, and somewhat in awe of their father, these benevolent young souls were to become symbols of piety and 'doers' of good deeds, in their efforts to act out their Christian beliefs amongst the less fortunate families of Macclesfield. It is inconceivable that they would cause their step-mother any distress, unlike other members of the family, however well-intentioned the thoughts and actions of those other members were at the time.

Charles, more than occupied with business matters, left Rachel to impose her striking personality on all who met her. She was considered "a fine lady", revealing a brief glimpse of her otherwise elusive upbringing, and encouraging a desire to discover the reason for her somewhat sudden and mysterious appearance within the Roe family circle.

The Harriotts were not a very prodigious family, but can be traced in Northamptonshire at the end of the 17th century, where the main branch had lived for several generations. There, at Weston-by-Welland, three brothers were baptised William, Thomas and John, names which would predominate within the family throughout the 18th century. The Harriotts were responsible members of society, some following the trade of tanners, but as the mercantile wealth of the country increased one or two members moved into Essex. Although their offspring were primarily involved in farming as the demand for food within the metropolis increased, yet the lure of the London trade soon attracted their attention. Through marriage the family connections were consolidated; they developed a "liquor-business", became tobacco traders and had associates in banking and Lloyds. One of them married at the Mercers' Hall Chapel, Cheapside in 1738, suggesting a possible commitment to the textile trade. It is not surprising, therefore, to discover Harriott links with the West Indies, and in particular Jamaica, by the mid-century, where the potential for further business success lay.

It was in the Jamaican county of St. Elizabeth that William and John, kinsmen and probable brothers, eventually owned estates. This was an area where even today large sugar plantations flourish. In close proximity was the prosperous estate of John Pennant who resided in the parish of St. George, Hanover Square, London, and whose son, Richard, married one of the heiresses of the Penrhyn estate in North Wales on 13th November 1765, exactly three weeks after Charles Roe's third marriage. Richard Pennant was soon to become an important figure in Liverpool.

Of the two Harriotts residing in Jamaica little is known except that William held an influential position, reflected in his marriage to Anne, the daughter of Le Baron Penevayre. This title appears to relate to the Netherlands rather than France, and could either be purchased or given in recognition of diplomatic service. William's daughter, Anne, married on 1st January 1752 a mature young man of 32 years, Samuel Jebb. Samuel, born in Chesterfield, Derbyshire and educated at Trinity College, Cambridge, is described as "sometime of Kingston in Jamaica", hence his introduction to Anne Harriott.

The patriarch of the important Chesterfield family of Jebb was Joshua, a hosier and alderman. Although the Jebbs were Non-jurors (a small sect arising from the fact that six Church of England bishops had refused to swear allegiance to King William III, although they had taken the oath for James II) they were to become a very well educated and distinguished group. Originally from Nottingham, and certainly known to Charles Roe as a more than casual acquaintance, one is tempted to deduce that Joshua Jebb had business dealings with Samuel Lankford, and that Charles had continued to supply the hosier with silk after Samuel's demise. In addition, because of increased activity in the lead mines of Derbyshire during the years 1765 and 1766, it would have been necessary for Charles to undertake many journeys to Chesterfield in the course of business, to superintend the smelting and shipment of the lead ore from the Bonsall mine.

After his withdrawal from the Macclesfield silk mill at the end of 1764 there seems little doubt that Charles would have attended the Jebb residence to pay his respects, explain his position, and possibly make an offer to ensure a continuous supply of silk for the Chesterfield business. Whatever the reason for his visits, Charles must have been introduced to Rachel, daughter of John Harriott of St. Elizabeth County, Jamaica, at Tapton Grove, the large residence of Joshua, or at the home of his son, Samuel. Rachel's father had evidently sent his daughter to England either for education, a visit, or the most likely alternative, to remain permanently with relatives. Life in the colonies was extremely difficult at times; the ravages of disease terminated many young lives and, particularly in the West Indies, there was a frequent fear of hurricanes which not only cost people their estates and hard won fortunes, but often their lives.

A Miss Harriott of Macclesfield is listed as a subscriber to James Roe's *Sermons* which, although not published till 15th November 1766, would have been subscribed to earlier, before her marriage to Charles on the 23rd October. (This is on the assumption that the Miss Harriott referred to was Rachel). She would have to be resident in the parish to enable the marriage to take place at Prestbury, and the other strong possibility is that she was already engaged as a governess to the Roe children, a situation ideally suited to her age and maturity.

Another vital link in the chain was the fact that Samuel Jebb's uncle, Avery and his wife, Alice lived in Manchester and attended St. Anne's church. A great stalwart of St. Anne's was Thomas Walker, now become one of the most affluent Manchester merchants and friend and business partner of Adam Simpson, Barmaster of Bonsall in Derbyshire.

Rachel Harriott's allegiance to the Church of England was never in doubt, so Charles must have felt contented by the fact that the children would not be influenced by any Dissenting tendencies from his wife. But fate has a habit of playing tricks and ironically when the challenge came it was to be fostered from a very unexpected quarter. For the present the children obediently followed their step-mother's example as she settled into her maternal role in the Chestergate home.

The two youngest daughters would warrant considerable attention, for the family had been without a mother almost three years and Margaret was only five years old, with Jane little more than three. Like their elder sisters each had a soubriquet, Margaret became Peggy and Jane assumed Jenny.

The boys, Charles and Joseph, seven years and six years respectively, formed a special bond with elder brother, Robert, who was $11^1/_2$ years at the time of his father's third marriage. Robert, although only eight years of age at his own mother's death, was said to have been her favourite. He was a particularly kind and thoughtful boy, and in him Charles Roe saw his opportunity to continue the family tradition of providing a minister for the Church of England. Circumstances had deprived Charles of his opportunity of entering the Church, and likewise his eldest son, William, but he was determined that his ambitions for Robert would be fulfilled.

There seems little doubt that Charles had met Rachel through his business connections and association with the Jebbs, and having hopefully solved his family problems he could once more concentrate on business matters.

* * * * * * *

Although the combined Hodgson and Roe investments in Gorsey Dale near Winster had suffered a substantial loss in 1764, the following two years produced their greatest profits in that mine i.e.1765 £737 0 8½d.,1766 £871 14 2d. – a remarkable achievement and one which would provide a substantial supply of calamine for the company.

During 1766 the first accounts for the Penrhyn Du lead mine, on behalf of Sir Nicholas Bayly and Lord Powis, were completed by John Cartwright as at 6th May. His ore account, together with his share of the rent, totalled £95 18 1d. Roe & Co. were credited with a cash payment of £95 12 10d. but no breakdown is given. Out of the total of £191 10 11d. Cartwright claimed back £115 10 0d. as "Expences by Several Journeys to promote ye busfnefs of sd. mine" . The balance provided Sir Nicholas and Lord Powis with only £38 0 5½d. each.

When the final account was subsequently submitted it clearly showed no copper raised: however, Roe & Co. were able to produce "Potter's Ore" priced at £10 10s. per ton in addition to lead ore priced at £9 5s. or £9 2s. per ton.

In a mine where silver predominated, potter's ore was considered waste. It was lead ore in which only the smallest traces of silver could be found and being uneconomical to separate was considered "fit only for glazing pottery". From the potter's point of view this ore was much desired for glazing purposes, and documentation exists to show that by the 1740s potters of Burslem were paying £9 per ton for this finer type of lead ore, as opposed to £8 per ton for the ordinary. A small market for potter's ore existed in Hamburg and the Netherlands, but continental wars often disrupted trade until, finally, the ore from North Wales found its way to Bideford and Liverpool. It was to the latter destination that Roe & Co. sent their ores and forged important links with families who had connections in the pottery trade.

It must be remembered that early tortoise-shell and agate wares, together with the vibrant decoration on tin glaze and delft wares, were coloured in various ways by using oxides of manganese, cobalt, copper and iron. Manganese was not officially recognised as a separate metallic chemical element until 1774, when discovered by Gahn, nevertheless, under the name of 'wad' or 'blacking' the black oxide was in demand by potters. Periodically it has been found (sometimes in yellow clay) in the region of the North Hendre mine near Mold, together with zinc blende (Black Jack), lead, silver and needles of copper pyrites. It would have been conveniently available both for the potters of Liverpool and Staffordshire in the 18th century. As John Denman on behalf of Roe & Co. was established in the Mold area by 1765, it is not beyond the bounds of possibility that the company were supplying additional materials to some of the Liverpool potters.

With regard to cobalt, long used by the Chinese in the decoration of blue and white wares and obtained through their early trading links with Persia, such was the expense of importation that in 1756 the Society for the Encouragement of the Arts (The Royal Society from the mid-19th century) had offered a prize to encourage its discovery in the United Kingdom. From time to time small quantities had been found in Cornish mines, but it would not be until 1775 that Francis Beauchamp, in driving an adit through part of his estate at Pengreep in Gwennap, Cornwall would accidentally discover a lode of cobalt 3 ft in breadth, for which he was awarded the 30 guineas prize. By 1778 it would be reported that "it did not last long due to water in the workings".

Although the cobalt mine at Alderley Edge would not be discovered until the early 19th century, geologically it is not impossible for small deposits to have been found earlier. Whereas the Cornish ore was described as 'grey cobalt', Alderley was black cobalt ochre "in form of grains of blueish black colours", and considered of inferior quality to that produced from the German mines of Saxony. Nevertheless, despite its later rejection by Josiah Wedgwood's nephew, it would be 'packed in tubs' and sent to Pontefract in Yorkshire where treatment would render it smalt or zaffre, in which form it was readily acceptable to the pottery industry. Technically, therefore, it would have been possible for Roe & Co. to have been supplying small quantities of the ore to Liverpool at this earlier period. None is recorded in the River Weaver books, but, as previously mentioned, often the clerk was not specific when recording the contents of a cask, he was more concerned with the weight and charge of 1s. 3d. per ton.

Not only potters but artists and painters were reliant on the produce of mines e.g. zinc white, cobalt blue, bright yellow (later called cadmium) and red lead, the latter produced from a form of lead called litharge. Litharge was very rare, found mostly in an area just north of Rhydymwyn which eventually became the North Hendre mine.

In the early 1760s entries appear in the Chester City Port books for white lead, red lead and litharge to Liverpool, mostly consigned from Thomas Smedley of the important lead smelter at Bagillt in North Wales, but his name must have been used as a matter of convenience, because many mining individuals and partnerships were shareholders in the smelter, including John Denman. From 1765 onwards Denman was, of course, primarily concerned with the lead of Roe & Co. and the works near Rhydymwyn.

With the increased activity in North Wales and the decision to make substantial purchases of Cornish copper ores, Charles Roe determined to establish a copper smelter in Liverpool. This would reduce the bulky ore to unrefined copper: a greater convenience for the journey to Macclesfield.

17
THE LIVERPOOL SMELTER

Wealth gotten by vanity shall be diminished
but he that gathereth by labour shall increase.

John Walker, confident of his position amongst the old established families of Liverpool, must never have considered that any reasonable business proposition in which he might engage, would be called into question.

Whatever had been the outcome of the Macclesfield canal scheme it would seem that discussions were already taking place for enabling Roe & Co. to locate a smelter in Liverpool. The whole plan was dependent on a good coal supply and a suitable site being found, problems to which John Walker in some measure provided an answer. It is certainly no coincidence that little more than three months after the Canal Bill's adjournment on 21st April 1766, he was included in the partnership for the development of the Bosley site. This seems to have been part of a reciprocal arrangement whereby Roe & Co. entered into partnership with John Walker in Liverpool, thus sharing plot "B" on the South Shore or Sea Strand, subleased by Walker from Richard Golightly.

The quayside was ideally situated for the construction of a smelter. Its location, at the virtual extremity of the South Shore, was well away from any buildings in town which spread outwards in a north to north-westerly direction from the shore, ensuring that the prevailing winds could quickly disperse any smoke or fumes in the opposite direction away from the inhabitants. The nearby salt and glassworks and the sugar house were actually built several blocks further inland, closer to the Old Dock, and as no apparent complaints had been forthcoming with regard to their smoke emissions, all seemed well. In fact, from 5th November 1766 Thomas Golightly had become a partner in the 'Old Glasshouse', joining a distinguished group of Liverpool merchants, amongst whom was the Crosby family.

Agreement to the plan would have been sought from Richard Golightly and also his fellow members of the Corporation from whom the original lease was held; with no hint of discouragement the scheme went ahead.

As a new smelter would take months to construct, equip and bring into production, no time was lost. William Roe, 21 years of age on 10th April 1767, had been schooled and trained for the important opportunity which now presented itself. Evidently he removed to Liverpool at this time to take charge of the works and must have been accompanied by experienced workmen from Macclesfield. He shortly leased a residence at 19 Cable Street, a few blocks north of the Old Dock, but not too far distant from the South Shore.

The work would have progressed rapidly during the summertime because the winter of 1767 was one of particular severity. The mayor of Liverpool at this time, Thomas Johnson, anxious to relieve the distress of many townsmen, persuaded other Corporation members to allow an ambitious project to be undertaken. To the east of the town was Quarry Hill from where building stone had been excavated for some considerable time, but which presented an unpleasant blot on the landscape. Johnson's plan, to which the Corporation agreed, was to create an artificial hill in order to hide the obtrusion, in front of which a terrace or promenade was intended. The scheme was a great success, employing a large number of men. The completed terrace was named Mount Zion, and with the arrival of better weather gardens were set, appropriately known as Mount Gardens, which provided an excellent panoramic view of the town and river Mersey.

The smeltworks were fully operational from 1st January 1768. Under normal conditions it would have taken a couple of years to complete the task, but the time scale was somewhat reduced because refining was to continue in Macclesfield. Even so, taking into consideration the amount of work involved and any delays due to adverse weather conditions, it seems likely that the project had commenced in the autumn of 1766.

Unfortunately, whilst building was taking place, yet another obstacle appeared on the horizon. This time it was the "Rt. Hnble Norborne, Lord Bottetourt and others concerned in a Manufacture of Brass and Copper commonly called the Warmley Company in the Parish of Siston and County of Gloster" petitioning for a Royal Charter. Behind the scenes William Champion was at work: Lord Bottetourt, an important coal proprietor, and others had invested large sums of money with Champion, consequently the public at large was presented with a very favourable impression of the works. However, by 1765, large loans and crippling interest rates saw them on the verge of bankruptcy. Champion and the others gambled that if they received a Royal Charter of Incorporation, the money would flow in and all would be well. They had reckoned without the combined might of all the other copper and brass concerns, which would certainly not stand idly by to see one company monopolise the whole industry.

As soon as the warrant was issued in April 1767, giving authority for the preparation of the Charter of Incorporation, the petitions against it were immediate. Even so, after lengthy legal proceedings, the Attorney General could find no point of law which forbad the granting of letters patent and accordingly a second warrant was issued allowing preparation of the Charter. The time had now arrived for appeals against it to be made to the Lords' Committee of the Privy Seal.

In the list of petitioners Charles Roe and Copper Company of Macclesfield was tenth and last. It argued that several of the brass and copper companies:

"have great reason to think themselves equally entitled to Royal Favor. The Warmley Company being of a later standing than five companies in the ten who carry on the Brass and Copper Manufactory in this Kingdom at great Expense".

A plausible point was that if the Warmley Company was given power to raise capital of £400,000, whilst the ores "raised in the Kingdom annually amount to no more that £300,000" this must surely be considered a monopoly.

The Macclesfield company had already expended £15,500 and "have still a considerable sum to add before the Works be compleated". By March 1768, three months after operations had begun at the Liverpool smelter, the Warmley Company was defeated. William Champion, desperate to save himself from ruin (bankruptcy being considered a sin in the eyes of the Quaker community) secretly tried to withdraw some of his money from the concern; the following month discovery meant dismissal, with bankruptcy in March 1769; he subsequently emigrated to America.

* * * * * * *

The construction of the Liverpool smeltworks would have employed local men as labourers, together with blacksmiths, coopers, bricklayers and others, but the development of the furnaces could never have been contemplated without the help of experienced men from Macclesfield, and the certain knowledge that a good supply of top quality coal was available.

At this period in South Lancashire the four most important coal mining families and suppliers were those of Gerard, Mackay, Legh and Clayton who, by working in a series of cartels, dominated the Sankey trade.

In 1762 Messrs. Legh (Peter Legh of Lyme Hall) and Mackay had opened the St. Helen's colliery, and Mackay extended his interests into Sutton and Eccleston. By 1767 Peter Legh's colliery at Haydock Park, the nearest one to Liverpool, was exhausted and closed but was rapidly replaced by opening a new mine nearby called Florida. None of the Legh colliery ledgers reveal any coal purchases by Roe & Co. from the South Lancashire sites. On 24th November 1761 John Walker had purchased 32 tons, but a later order by him was deleted. Thomas Marshall, salt proprietor and carrier, had an account with Peter Legh, although not excessive; however the Legh collieries were committed to providing Thomas Patten, copper smelter of Warrington, with 24 tons each day, for which the average daily payment was £5, this account had been honoured since 1759.

From a later reference Roe & Co. made a contract to purchase coal from the Parr Colliery Company whose ownership must have been in the hands of either Mackay or Clayton. John Mackay had moved into the area in the 1760s, after the Clayton family, but as he was not approached by the Macclesfield Company for several years, it seems logical to conclude that the supplier was the Parr colliery on the Parr Hall Estate belonging to the Clayton family. It also appears that this was the only probable supplier for the Liverpool smelter during 1767, as extensive searches through National Coal Board archives relating to old mines, and the Molyneux collection relating to Liverpool and the surrounding areas, including Croxteth, contain no recorded purchases of coal by the company.

In any event, apart from the fact that rich coal seams existed on the Parr Hall Estate, so that quality and supply were adequately achieved, the important Georgain social connections were already in place.

Alderman William Clayton, mayor of Liverpool in 1689, was descended from the Clayton family of Clayton Hall, Manchester, and kinsman to the Claytons of Macclesfield and the surrounding area. His marriage to Elizabeth, daughter of George Leigh of Oughtrington on the outskirts of Lymm in Cheshire, had provided the family with many social connections in that vicinity. Lymm, almost equidistant between Knutsford and Warrington, was a vital link in the chain of communications from Macclesfield to Liverpool.

In 1709 Alderman Clayton had died, leaving his widow to bring up five surviving daughters out of nine children, the youngest of whom, Sarah, was three years old. A widow relied heavily on relatives who usually had been designated guardians and trustees for her children, managers of family estates, businesses and affairs, which included payments of her widow's dues as stipulated by her marriage settlement. This obviously inspired an unceasing round of social visits between relatives, whereby younger family members grew to know cousins almost as well as brothers and sisters. There is little doubt that, with the Clayton and Yates family involvement at Mottram Hall and both having kinsmen in Liverpool, the young daughters of William Clayton would have known something of the principal families in the Macclesfield area.

There were also the seasonal visits to Bath, almost suggesting a simile for Jane Austen's novel *Northanger Abbey* (although not written and published until the early 19th century). From these threads of Georgian intercourse, particularly accentuated by the sparse population of the period, Sarah Clayton knew of John Ward, eminent lawyer and grand old man of Capesthorne Hall near Macclesfield.

Before his death in 1748 John Ward was held in high esteem amongst his neighbours and associates in the vicinity of Macclesfield Forest and was evidently well-known amongst his fraternal business and social associates in London, Bath and elsewhere. His home, relatively close to Alderley Edge and Mottram Andrew, must have provided a venue for social gatherings, especially after its rebuilding.

One of Sarah Clayton's letters states that John Wood (Snr.) of Bath planned Mr. Ward's house at Capesthorne: she also wrote that she had enquired of "Mrs. Shaw and several others" who knew Capesthorne. (There was an important Shaw family having members in both Warrington and Liverpool at that time.) This commission of 1731, together with others, would eventually recommend John Wood Snr. to Liverpool Corporation for the building of a magnificent Exchange to incorporate a new town hall. The Exchange agreement was entered into on 11th July 1749 with both father and son working in conjunction, but John Wood Snr. died in 1754, just before its completion.

The 'Great Conveyancer' seems to have spent an appreciable amount of time in Bath, for between 1733-34 John Wood Snr. together with 11 other subscribers, had built St. Mary's Chapel for the use of residents in the vicinity of Queen Square, Bath, the documentation for which was "settled by Mr. Ward, the great Conveyancer". John Ward also contributed 20 guineas to the Bath Hospital building fund in 1737 and two years later became a Trustee and Governor, a project for which John Wood was an enthusiastic promoter.

John Ward, legal adviser to the Leghs of Lyme, and also a close personal friend of Peter Legh the elder, became M.P. for Newton, Lancashire in 1705 (a borough in which the Legh family had great influence). His encouragement of the Legh coal mining business, as already witnessed by his letter in 1704 regarding Lord Barnard, would eventually have brought him into contact with other prospectors or landowners in Lancashire, amongst whom would have been Alderman Clayton of Liverpool.

In due course Sarah Clayton inherited an interest in the Parr Hall Estate near St. Helen's from her father. Having discovered the existence of rich coal measures, she worked her collieries from 1754. Sarah, who never married, was dedicated to her four sisters, and having laid out "her new intended square" viz. Clayton Square in Liverpool during the preceding 18 months, had named the adjacent streets after her brothers-in-law, Houghton, Parker, Tyrer and Case. The son of the last mentioned, her nephew, Thomas Case, became her partner in a coal business on Water Street, Liverpool which operated under the name Clayton, Case & Co. On 17th April 1758 an advertisement was placed in Williamson's *Liverpool Advertiser* declaring two delphs of coal had been opened at Sarah Clayton's Parr collieries, and coal was being offered at 4s. 2d. per ton at the pit head, 7s. 0d. alongside ships in Liverpool and 7s. 6d. in the town of Liverpool (approximately $^1/_5$ the price of high grade coal today).

It has been suggested that Thomas Case was of the same family as Abraham Case, the inventor and populariser of clothwork or high top buttons at Shaftesbury. Known as 'Dorset Thread Buttons', the majority were white, some worked with linen thread on a circle of wire. Abraham's grandson, Peter, had succeeded to the business in 1758 at Bere Regis: it is of interest to note that the family name could be a corruption of Kaas, the Dutch word for cheese, a possible indication that at some time the family had moved across the Channel to England, and a reminder that the Dutch had been suppliers of large quantities of buttons at an earlier period. This business also suggests the original link between the Case and Clayton families, as William Clayton of Macclesfield was, of course, occasionally referred to as a button merchant.

The Clayton family, like the Walkers, had been amongst the small group of merchants who had settled in the tiny port at the mouth of the Mersey Estuary in the 17th century. The diminutive integrated congregation of St. Nicholas's, bonded together by trust and determination, formed the backbone of the Corporation. If a newcomer was found acceptable by one, then others would follow, a situation guaranteed only to last whilst numbers were small and before breakaway groups began to emerge. The Roe links were now established and with John Walker's influence the coal supply for the Liverpool smelter was contracted for.

* * * * * * *

Apart from coal, it was difficult at this time to locate sources for the copper ore supply. One must assume, of course, that whatever ore was still being won at Alderley Edge or bought at Ecton Mine was taken directly to the Macclesfield smelter and therefore would not appear in the River Weaver books.

During 1767, whilst the construction of the Liverpool smelter was under way, supplies of copper ore travelling up the Weaver reached almost 600 tons, a hundred less than the previous year. It is reasonable to suppose that a greater part, if not all of this ore, was destined for Roe & Co. in Macclesfield. Surprisingly Legh Dickenson purchased only 159 tons on behalf of the company in Cornwall and Coniston's rapidly decreasing output produced 25 tons 4 cwts., which leaves a little more than 400 tons unaccounted for (almost the same situation as the previous year).

It is doubtful whether Roe & Co. would have purchased ore from New York or the Wicklow mines in Ireland at this time, and it is unlikely that such large quantities were available from Llanberis, although mining there appears to have continued in some form or other, as odd references indicate the existence of the company until 1804, but unfortunately at present no further relevant mining details can be traced. However, it is obvious that another important source of copper ore existed, and one area more than any other could provide the answer.

The area in question is Blackcraig hill, five miles north-west of Wigtown in Kirkcudbrightshire and just across the Solway Firth from Workington and Whitehaven. One brief reference relating to the working of the old mines reveals that in 1763, whilst building a military road, a soldier discovered ore. Soon afterwards prospecting began "and the ore produced was shipped to Chester for smelting". Mining would certainly not have been fully under way until 1764, and a group of miners en route from the Leadhills district did soon discover a copper mine which yielded ore in the form of chalcopyrite; later the mines produced predominantly lead ore. The output for the early years is stated as 400 tons per annum, but by 1793 it had fallen to 30 tons.

This source of copper ore does conveniently coincide with the unaccountable ore coming up the Weaver viz. 1765 63 tons; 1766 406 tons; 1767 414 tons. Admittedly the 63 tons in respect of 1765 could have included some ore from Llanberis, but would not account for the whole of the differential in the years 1766 and 1767. From 1768 the ores, of course, went direct to the Liverpool smelter, and as the port books are no longer extant due to war damage, no details exist to indicate the tonnage of imported ore received by William Roe, it is therefore impossible to say whether or not the supply of this additional ore continued. Tissington & Co. were active in that part of Scotland, especially around Leadhills, and Charles Roe's close association with the partnership could account for his knowledge of this source. One could argue that the Blackcraig ore was destined for the Patten smelters at Warrington, but it would have been more practical to take it via Liverpool up the Mersey Estuary to Bank Quay. The only other smelters in the region capable of handling an extra 400 tons per annum were those of Roe & Co.

Another, though diminutive contributor at this time, was Parys Mountain on Anglesey, for Thomas Pennant later wrote "ore was discovered, but the expences overbalanced the profits. They continued working to great loss: and at length determined to give the affair up".

John Cartwright's correspondence indicates that only 31 tons 14 cwts. were despatched in 1766 (value £669 1 10d.) this included the $1/_8$th Duty ore of Sir Nicholas Bayly which the company had smelted on his behalf and then purchased from him. A note in true Charles Roe style was added to the bill in favour of Sir Nicholas, "The above is a Free Value of the Ore upon carriage and More than anybody else will give for it for which you have overdraft".

This is certainly true, for the following year, 1767, Roe & Co. paid Sir Nicholas £21 12 5d. a ton after processing, after which they terminated the agreement, whereas for 1768 Cartwright received £17 15s. a ton for the Duty ore from Mr. Dumbell partner to Thomas Patten of Warrington. From then on the Warrington company must have considered the arrangement a gross imposition and only bought the Duty ore raw, so that they received the profit from the smelting and selling on.

* * * * * * *

An interesting memorandum in Cartwright's letter book states that the 1766 and 1767 ore "was raised in the Tenement called perircarrag and no part of the above ore raised upon Cerrig y Bleiddia or Paris Mtn. Neither is the said Tenemt under lease To Chas Roe & Coy".

This seems strange; whilst this tenement can no longer be traced, it must have been situated close to the boundary of the Cerrig y Bleiddia site, possibly on land held jointly by Sir Nicholas and the Lewis family, but more than likely on other land held solely by Sir Nicholas. Jonathan Roose would certainly have had enough sense not to flaunt any mining activities in direct contradiction of the lease. The site could have been one worked at an earlier period and with encouragement from Cartwright, who himself was keen to find and work a copper mine, had been re-opened. At this point Cartwright appears to have turned a blind eye and there were no murmurings from Sir Nicholas.

Jonathan was obviously under orders to co-operate amicably with the workmen of Sir Nicholas but, in handling John Cartwright, he appears to have had no easy task, for Cartwright was beginning to show his lack of ability as his responsibilities increased.

The first indication of any disparity between the two agents is a letter written by Jonathan Roose from the farm at Penrhyn Du on 30th November 1766 to Cartwright. This was the second letter Jonathan had written, fearing the first might have gone astray. He was sorry to learn that Cartwright's leg was still in a bad way as he had hoped for a visit from Cartwright before the latter left on an intended journey. (It is difficult once again, not to compare Cartwright with John Paynter) Jonathan had been on Anglesey, presumably overseeing work at Parys Mountain, but on returning home had been disappointed to discover that their vessel had been thrown onto a sand bank during a storm, obliging him to wait until the next spring tide for a replacement. The intention then was to load the newly acquired vessel with ore and settle the account.

Once more flooding was causing problems in the Penrhyn Du mine, for Jonathan reminded Cartwright of his promise to obtain an "Injun at Minarah", which would be a steam engine to pump water out of the workings. There is a brief reference to lead mine workings at Minera near Wrexham at this time, which states that these mines were finally flooded in 1776 and closed for a short period, so Cartwright must have claimed a contact with the mining fraternity in that area. Jonathan, taking Cartwright at his word, had written a long letter to Charles Roe explaining the situation and enclosing correspondence from Lord Powis. Having informed Cartwright of his action he continued, "Now if you could come here at the time I've mentioned, I probably might have Mr. Roe's answer."

Evidently Cartwright had complained also about the condition of the horses at the mine, from which a surprised Jonathan Roose assured him that they had not got "the Scab", for if they had then all the horses would have been affected. He tactfully suggested that Cartwright could send them to Parys Mountain "twill Save me the trouble of sending others there – If we have any other that youd like better, your wellcome to them".

Anxious that Cartwright should have a copy of the accounts as soon as possible, Jonathan suggested an alternative meeting place of better convenience in 'Carnarvon', the date to be during the following week.

By 30th December Sir Nicholas, writing from London, was complaining to Cartwright, "I wish you w(oul)d be less sparing of yr. paper and lett me hear where you are and what progress you have made." He queried the settling of the accounts with Mr. Roe, which suggests that Cartwright still had not attended to them.

One possible reason was that, as building on the Liverpool smelter site progressed,

Cartwright himself had become intent on finding copper ore in North Wales, despite his trials and tribulations at the Penrhyn Du lead mine. He commissioned a report "Observations relating to the Mines in Carnarvonshire as to the discovery of Copper Mines" together with "Observations relating to the Working & raising Ore out of Copper Mines" dated 2nd January 1767. (The author of these observations was Moses Orme, responsible for assaying ore at Warrington and a member of a family who had lived near Liverpool for centuries.)

However Cartwright's letter book does contain an entry for 27th February 1767 "Set out To Macclesfield to Settle Paris Mtn acct. paid on road £1 3 6d." By 5th March he was in Macclesfield but returned home shortly afterwards.

On 2nd July he was again travelling to Macclesfield "to settle for the Duty ore from Paris Mtn". He claimed expenses for staying in town on the nights of 7th, 9th and 10th of July, but apparently stayed somewhere else on the 8th. He was possibly attending to some personal business or visiting Warrington, because on the 18th the Duty ore was sent there for smelting. This suggests that at that time Roe & Co. had declined handling this ore.

By the time the 1768 Duty ore was ready for despatch Cartwright was in a quandary having appreciated his foolishness in receiving a lesser price from the Warrington company, so he craftily wrote a letter to Charles Roe informing him that the Warrington company intended to bid for the ore. Judging from his mild, yet extremely polite answer, Charles must have been extremely amused. He informed Cartwright that the company had a 'just' price in mind which Jonathan (Roose) already knew of and rightly pointed out that the fairest way was by ticketing as at Ecton or in Cornwall: "Each put their Ticket into the Hatt and you open and read them and the Highest Bidder takes the ore."

The saga of the Duty ore is complete, as Roe & Co. seemed quite happy for the Patten group of Warrington to out bid them in every subsequent year.

* * * * * * *

Meanwhile much had taken place and Jonathan Roose had not been idle. In his first few months at Penrhyn Du he had met, courted and was about to marry a local girl, when Elizabeth Thompson arrived from Derbyshire. Nineteen years old and pregnant, it hardly seems likely that all alone she would have made the long, arduous journey from her home in Wirksworth to the bleak Lleyn Peninsula. One wonders what took place regarding broken promises and marriage settlements, but Elizabeth won the day. She and Jonathan were finally married by Licence on 11th June 1764 in the Llanengan church where their son, Thomas, was baptised almost two months later on 9th August. He was to be the first of eight sons and two daughters born to the couple.

Initially Jonathan seems to have taken up residence at the farmhouse of Penrhyn Du whilst concentrating his efforts at the lead mine.

Another Derbyshire man, Samuel Howson, had been sent by Roe & Co. to be agent at Parys Mountain from 25th April 1765 and an Edward Steel was engaged by Cartwright to oversee operations there on behalf of Sir Nicholas. Henceforth the main focus of Cartwright's attentions seems to be his own personal aspirations, causing untold problems for everyone else concerned.

After Cartwright's visit to Macclesfield in early July 1767 regarding Duty ore, he was again on Anglesey supervising the weighing of ore at Parys Mountain by the 19th. What passed between him and Jonathan Roose may never be known, but it was significant enough for him to accompany Jonathan all the way back to Macclesfield on the 22nd. From the outcome of the visit the problem seems to have been Pebrhyn Du, partly confirmed by a brief note against Cartwright's expenses, "about penrhyn du and paris Mtn."

On 25th July, Jonathan Roose was present in Charles Roe's house on Chestergate, Macclesfield, when Charles wrote a letter to Lord Powis, presumably for Jonathan to deliver on his return journey to North Wales. This was obviously the most expedient way of dealing with matters relating to Penrhyn Du, as between Cartwright and Sir Nicholas communications seemed somewhat lacking. Charles set out the company's resolution to sell the tools, engines and equipment at the mine "at Michaelmas next" (29th September 1767).

By the terms of the lease the lessors were allowed first refusal for buying any of the equipment on site, after a fair valuation. Charles gave notice that should they not wish to do so then "we may dispose of them . . . as we dont Intend to continue to work the mine". By this statement Charles Roe was emphasising the fact that the Macclesfield company then had the right and intended to dispose of the equipment, the word "may" being used in its sense of "being permitted to". In his usual straight forward manner he added, "I think it but Just to Inform you, that you may Lease it to Others for it is very wrong to keep possession when we dont Intend to work."

Following this Cartwright personally delivered a letter to Charles Roe from Lord Powis and Sir Nicholas saying neither wanted to be purchasers of the equipment nor did they wish to undertake any further mining operations. The date of this is unknown.

On 9th December 1767 a letter, signed by John Cartwright, but neatly written by someone else on his behalf, was sent from Plasnewydd, Sir Nicholas's estate, to Lord Powis. His confirmation "I went with Mr. Roe's Agent to penrhyndu the 19th of the Last month, & took pofsesion in the works in your name & Sir Nicholas's. . ." leaves no doubt that Roe & Co. had given up their operations at the lead mine.

The final accounts from Jonathan Roose, for the period 12th December 1766 to 19th Noember 1767, meticulously list the weights of ore from individual companies (bargain takers) working the site and the $\frac{1}{8}$th duty payable on each, giving a grand total of £16 5 1$\frac{1}{2}$d.

One of the shareholders of the mine, Messrs. Barkers & Wilkinson, lead smelters of East Moor near Chesterfield, reckoned a total loss for Penrhyn Du of £1740 4 9d. This related to the period from the commencement of the partnership on 2nd April 1764, until the cessation of mining on 6th March 1767; small wonder Roe & Co. were anxious to rid themselves of the mine.

In spite of this, seven weeks later, on 20th January 1768, Cartwright submitted his own proposals for working the mine once more, convinced that there was plenty of ore in the bottoms and that the water could be pumped out. His proposals included erecting a water engine, with a lease effective from 25th March 1768. However, a dramatic event was about to take place, one which would alter considerably the lives of all concerned, and force Cartwright to postpone his leasing of Penrhyn Du until 29th June 1768.

Much confusion has previously arisen from the way in which copies of correspondence and accounts have been written up in John Cartwright's letter books; it is now obvious that on at least two occasions incorrect dates were entered by the clerk.

In August 1768 the clerk wrote up copies of letters and notes relating to the Duty ore from the previous year i.e. 25th July 1767, and one, on page 42 dated "Aug 16th 1768", should also read 1767. This latter note from Cartwright reads:

> "Waited on Mr. Roe and Mr. Hudson [Hodgson] at Macclesfield by Sir Nicho s Bayly's Orders for them to give up Penrhyn Du lease and Mr. Hudson answered for Mr. Roe and Mr. Adheson [Atkinson] and declared that Penrhyn Du lease should not be given up".

This note seems absurd. Charles Roe had already put in writing the company's intention of withdrawing at Michaelmas and Cartwright, presumably on this visit, must have brought the answer that Bayly and Lord Powis had declined the offer of either purchasing equipment or mining it themselves. Perhaps Sir Nicholas was under the impression that Roe & Co. should actually hand over their copy of the lease, or was it Cartwright's idea to cover up the fact that he desperately needed all the equipment leaving on site? Certainly from the wranglings which ensued the latter seems a possibility.

Cartwright accused Jonathan Roose of destroying pumps which had been installed by the previous company of Mr. Griffiths, costing "upwards of Six Hundred pounds". These pumps had been underwater for some time and as Cartwright had insisted all along that he would set up a steam engine, Jonathan must have considered their removal an essential part of leaving the mine in a safe and workable condition. Jonathan also took some of the materials to Parys Mountain where his efforts were now to be concentrated.

In the event the solicitor, Samuel Wright of Knutsford, together with Samuel Howson and others decided to join Cartwright in working the Penrhyn Du mine using local labour. The workings would be extended on 24th June 1769 when Cartwright leased land from the adjoining landowner William Smith of South Tedworth, Southampton, who was related to the Assheton family.

A report prepared some years later was to reveal Cartwright's irresponsible work:

"At TYDDYN TALGOCH in LLANENGAN the lands have suffered very much by the Mine Company of Penrhyn Du who sunk several shafts in it and left 'em open, and the heaps of rubble delved therefrom not trimmed or levelled".

As the Liverpool smelter was operational from 1st January 1768, orders must have been sent to Legh Dickenson to increase the company ticketing in Cornwall, for during that year 608 tons of Cornish ore were bought. This was a large purchase for Roe & Co., Thomas Patten of Warrington only acquired 347 tons but, compared to the other seven concerns bidding at this time (excluding William Champion who was on the verge of bankruptcy), this tonnage was small. Theirs averaged between 3 to 4,000 tons each, with two slightly less. The two North West companies, however, were actively surveying for ore deposits and supplementing by purchases as necessary, mostly from Ecton Mine, whereas most of the other brass and copper concerns were heavily reliant on purchases of Cornish ore for their smelters.

The 1767 ore bought by Roe & Co. from Ecton Mine in Staffordshire totalled £2,073 6 6d. and during that year, in an effort to clear some of the outstanding arrears from previous years, the company remitted an amazing £4,205 6 0d. according to Robert Shore's accounts as mine manager. This implies that the Macclesfield smelter was working to full capacity and about this time became the responsibility of Cookson Atkinson from Kendal, Westmorland, nephew of Rowland. His role at the Coniston mine was now at an end.

The decision to cease operations at Coniston must have been taken about the same time as that of Penrhyn Du, because accounts reveal a final payment of rent for "Coniston Forge & house £2 5 0d." up till 28th February 1767. Ore would continue to be cleared, weighed and despatched from the site until 3rd January 1769.

The company was now 'streamlining' operations and intent on cutting costs where appropriate. Not only had the lead mine at Penrhyn Du made a considerable loss, but operations on Parys Mountain had also produced an almost identical drain on resources. New shareholders had apparently been admitted to help with financing; as from 1st August 1765 Barkers & Wilkinson had taken a 2/24th share for £500. This partnership, established in 1729 by William Barker, steward to the Duke of Devonshire, to smelt Derbyshire lead ore, had continued in the capable hands of two more family members, Alexander and Thomas (steward to the Duke of Rutland). Thomas's uncle was none other than Robert Charlesworth of Castleton, great friend, associate and subsequent trustee of Charles Roe's deceased father, so the business relationship between the families had existed for some considerable time. The Chesterfield company must also have known Brian Hodgson Snr. in connection with his lead mining activities in Derbyshire. However, after two years' investments Barkers & Wilkinson's reckonings produced a total loss of £1,498 7 11d. for the Parys mine venture and it was time to withdraw. Luckily for him, Brian Hodgson Jnr. now landlord of The Old Hall Inn, Buxton decided to purchase their share, possibly having more faith in Jonathan Roose's undivided attention on the site now that Penrhyn Du had been disposed of.

* * * * * * *

The activities on Parys Mountain, during the winter and early spring of 1767/68, must have been very disappointing and Thomas Pennant records that Roe & Co. gave their agent orders to cease operations:

> "but he, as a final attempt, divided his men into ten separate companies of three or four in a partnership, and let them sink shafts in various places, about eight hundred yards eastward of a place called the Golden Venture, on a presumption that a spring which issued from near the spot, must have come from a body of mineral. His conjecture was right, for in less than two days they met with, at the depth of seven feet from the surface, the solid mineral, which proved to be the vast body which has since been worked to such advantage. The day this discovery was made was 2nd March 1768 (St. Chad's Day) which has ever since been observed as a festival by the miners".

The agent concerned was Jonathan Roose, as witnessed by his epitaph in the graveyard of Amlwch Parish Church:

> "He first yon Mountain's wondous riches found,
> First drew its minerals blushing from the ground,
> He heard the Miners first exulting shout."

Unfortunately, apart from the above, neither Jonathan Roose nor Roe & Co. have ever been given the full credit they deserve for the copper ore discovery on Parys Mountain, nor the professional way in which they would develop the site and conduct business.

It has recently been suggested that Roe & Co. concealed their find on the Mountain for some time, but this is totally illogical, there was no possible reason for doing so. This erroneous deduction has been made because the clerk entering up Cartwright's expenses for 1768 at the end of the year, incorrectly wrote "15th feb ry Sett out to Macclesfd by Sir Nic's Order to purchase share of Paris Mountn Mine." when the date should have been 15th March. This is easily confirmed by reference to the copy letters and notes.

On 16th March Jonathan Roose, who now had much to discuss with his employers, wrote urgently to Cartwright "I purpose going to Macclesfield with you if you can stay till next Monday" . . . but Cartwright had already left the previous day, in fact a memorandum clearly dated "March ye 15th 1768" begins "Set out to Macclesfield by Sir Nichs Bayly's Order To Mr. Roe with an unlimited power to purchase shares of the copper mine at Paris Mountain."

According to Cartwright Charles Roe said there was to be a meeting of the company at Macclesfield when he would put forward the proposal that Sir Nicholas should have a share with them in the mine. This company, to all intents and purposes a subsidiary of Roe & Co., had been specifically formed to work the Cerrig Y Bleiddia estate on Parys Mountain and was appropriately called 'The Paris Mountain Company'.

Cartwright to a certain degree had 'jumped the gun', because Jonathan's letter of 16th March pointed out that a greater part of the samples, which Cartwright intended to take for assaying, were insufficient and more were needed. He continued that if Cartwright had already left for Macclesfield then he would remain to level the ground, make a new trial and draw a plan. It seems obvious that the discovery, of what was to become the "vast body", of ore had only occurred within a few days and not weeks before, otherwise confirmation of the assays would have been received and a plan completed.

At the beginning of May, John Denman, the Roe & Co. agent at Holywell was sent to inspect the Parys Mountain site and Cartwright instructed to meet him. A consultation took place during which Cartwright, knowing his master well, used his persuasion to encourage John Denman and Jonathan Roose to intercede with Charles Roe on Sir Nicholas's behalf for a $\frac{1}{8}$th share in the mine. All agreed that this was probably the best, by which the inference seems to be the most amicable solution.

Early in June Charles Roe, accompanied by John Denman, was on Parys Mountain where he informed Cartwright that it had been agreed to allow Sir Nicholas a $\frac{1}{8}$th share of the mine "he paying $\frac{1}{8}$ share of the Expences". Cartwright accepted this on behalf of his master but, when he returned home and reported to Sir Nicholas, the latter greedily insisted on having a $\frac{1}{4}$ share. Cartwright told him that "it was Not in Mr. Roe's power to let him have Any More than $\frac{1}{8}$ as the Coy had settled it". Sir Nicholas's reply, that if he could not have a $\frac{1}{4}$ share then he would accept $\frac{1}{8}$th, seemed to satisfy Cartwright.

Within two or three days Charles and Mr. Denman arrived at Plas Newydd to speak with Sir Nicholas. Charles informed the baronet of the company resolution to offer him a $\frac{1}{8}$th share and immediately Sir Nicholas pressed for more. After the procrastinations concerning Penrhyn Du and the incessant complaints from Cartwright, this proved too much for Charles Roe, whose imperious temper got the better of him. A dispute took place and Cartwright, anxious to placate the visitor, accompanied him to the stables where Charles took to his horse. John Denman must have been in close pursuit for Cartwright told both of them that he would endeavour "to have everything Reconciled" and proposed making a journey to Newcastle-under-Lyme and Macclesfield in three weeks time to settle matters.

Charles must have been anxious to return home, for on 12th July Rachel gave birth to their one and only child, a son, named John Harriott after her father. In the years to come this son would find more affinity with brother William and his family than any other. Rachel was 33 years of age, not young by any means to be giving birth to a first child, particularly in the 18th century, and Charles must have found it impossible to forget that his second wife, Mary, had died only one month after giving birth to daughter Jane, at the age of 34 years. His relief and gratitude for the safe delivery would have put him in a better frame of mind for reconsidering the situation on Parys Mountain, which he obviously discussed with the other partners.

In the event Sir Nicholas's share was not claimed, for Cartwright now allowed his personal affairs to take precedence and "being disappointed by Businefs" did not undertake the journey. He subsequently received a letter from Charles Roe confirming the company resolution to continue with their shares, presumably without Sir Nicholas as word had not been sent. Immediately upon receiving this news Sir Nicholas ordered Cartwright to Macclesfield in order to claim the $\frac{1}{8}$th share which Cartwright had originally accepted on his behalf. Cartwright met with "Mr. Roe and Mr. Adheson" (Atkinson), but if Charles was having any pangs of conscience and about to relent, he was overshadowed by Brian Hodgson, whose seniority and firmness took command. Who better than a former innkeeper to understand human nature, and who better to handle it? Without hesitation he answered for all concerned that "Sir Nicholas Bayly had no right to $\frac{1}{8}$th share of the mine, neither should he have any share", and that should have been the end of the matter.

Sir Nicholas must have been very aggrieved and yet he only had himself to blame, but his agitations continued, with Cartwright, no doubt, bearing the brunt of them. Poor Jonathan Roose could not escape the machinations and at some point had been forced to call upon Sir Nicholas and make a subsequent journey to Macclesfield; Sir Nicholas was still insisting on having his $\frac{1}{8}$th share. Cartwright, meanwhile, was concentrating his efforts on the situation at the Penrhyn Du lead mine.

Charles must have appreciated the difficulties under which Jonathan Roose was working and generously sought a solution. He put pen to paper on 7th January 1769 briefly setting out all that had passed between the company, Sir Nicholas and Cartwright, adding "Our Inclination to live in Harmony & Friendship (& no other motive, for we will defend our Rights) . . ." had persuaded him to reconsider the situation. He set out a list of proposals intended to remove some of the absurd stipulations from the original lease and suggested tearing up the old one and having a new one prepared. Also Cartwright was refusing to give up some of the equipment at the lead mine, which included two steam engines known as whimsies, and this Charles now demanded. Additionally he asked that the vein of ore worked by Jonathan Roose be included in the lease for Cerrig y Bleddia.

Charles had definitely made up his mind that this was the baronet's final chance, "Excuse my saying you'll have no more offers . . ." He signed the letter "Yours To Commd" and emphatically stated that there were to be no negotiations with Cartwright. Charles waited for the command or instructions from Sir Nicholas regarding the purchase of the share, but no answer came, only indications that Cartwright and Jonathan Roose had once more been discussing the matter, much to the disapproval of Charles Roe. On 6th March he sent a final letter to Sir Nicholas by Jonathan Roose, which clarified the position viz: that the agents had no right to negotiate, and requested an answer by the 20th, otherwise the company would feel free from any obligations to allow Sir Nicholas his purchase of "$\frac{1}{8}$ of the mine".

The main problem on both sides was probably financial. Charles had pointed out that £800 had been expended up to the previous Christmas and £300 since, to which, of course, Sir Nicholas was expected to contribute $\frac{1}{8}$th in taking up his share. It is evident that neither Sir Nicholas nor his steward were able to find the money to cover these expenses.

The Paris Mountain Company needed extra cash; houses had now to be built for workmen and consideration given for a road from the site down to the port of Amlwch, amongst other things. In the event Barkers and Wilkinson once more joined the partnership, together with other investors from the Derbyshire lead mines including Thomas Southern and his associate Mr. Wall. Sir Nicholas had missed an excellent opportunity.

Life was going to be made extremely difficult for Jonathan Roose who, by July 1768, had moved with his family to Amlwch. Not only would he have difficult weather conditions to contend with, sea mists and fog could descend suddenly even on a bright summer's day, but the constant irritant of Cartwright being as awkward as possible.

During the latter half of the previous year Cartwright had been scheming once more. He had engaged William Elliott from Derbyshire as overseer at Penrhyn Du. The Elliotts were neighbours of Adam Simpson who was about to retire as Barmaster in Bonsall after 20 years.

Simpson held various investments in Derbyshire lead mines and was also involved in other areas such as Flintshire. Evidently the Elliots kept him informed of developments in North Wales and William Elliot's reports in particular had roused his interest in the Lleyn Peninsula to which he journeyed, somewhat incognito, and met Cartwright.

Perhaps Cartwright knew more about Simpson than he pretended, as he evidently went to great lengths to entertain the Barmaster. Having returned home to Bonsall Simpson wrote to Cartwright on 1st December 1768 briefly referring to his mining interests and purporting to be a "Very Considerable dealer". His comments are interesting and reveal the obvious regard in which he held the mining abilities of Roe & Co. He showed concern when learning of their relinquishment of the Penrhyn Du lease, which suggested that the mining was not worth their efforts, but for some reason did not discourage Cartwright – however, his main interest was Parys Mountain.

By strange coincidence Simpson's travelling companion on his outward journey to North Wales had been Brian Hodgson, so perhaps some of the intelligence information to him about the site had come from that quarter. He had certainly visited Parys Mountain before returning home, but not at Brian Hodgson's invitation because he did not see Brian Hodgson again during his visit. His observations led him to believe that there was "a great deal of both lead and copper" to be had, for which he was more than happy to enter into partnership with Cartwright and hoped for a large share, commenting "Somebody must have a Chance on the other side of the road". This unknowingly sowed the seed from which an incredible legal dispute would grow and, although not directly involving Roe & Co. in the first instance, would encroach upon their well-doing from time to time and ultimately have a profound effect.

Simpson had learnt that the remaining land on the Mountain, not under lease to Roe & Co. was held jointly by Sir Nicholas and the trustees of William Lewis deceased whose widow, sister and niece would in turn receive benefit from the estate. He could not have appreciated the complexities with which the land had been left under the terms of a very intricate will.

Adam Simpson in his role of Barmaster was, of course, well versed in the laws of mining and would often be called upon to settle disputes such as land ownership, encroachments and other legalities, so his professional advice was that there should be no problems. He suggested the submission of a Bill in Equity, after which the area or field concerned would be bought by the Lord Chancellor, divided in two and the half belonging to the Lewis family given to the person in that family who was entitled to benefit from it at that time. The inference appears to be that if Sir Nicholas had already started trials on one half, then that would be the half he would be allocated. Obviously the parties concerned would be able to repossess by payment of legal dues.

As the situation was fraught with ambiguities, Sir Nicholas, who must have appreciated that the minerals could be anywhere on any part of the land, decided to seek approval from the heirs of William Lewis with a view to a joint mining venture. Young Mary, the niece, had just married Rev. Edward Hughes who immediately took control of the situation on behalf of his wife, and at this time Sir Nicholas's offer was refused.

Mary's father, Rev. Robert Lewis, Chancellor of Bangor Diocese was possibly also rector of Mold in 1763 when he leased the tithes to Henry Swymmer, Esq. of Bristol, one of the Lords of Mold. This could explain why a survey of Parys Mountain, carried out in 1764 by John Reynolds and clearly prepared to show the site leased to Roe & Co. was deposited with a firm of Mold solicitors. Perhaps Lewis anticipating problems with Sir Nicholas at a later date was ensuring that his family had a copy plan showing the area under lease to the Macclesfield company. Another explanation could be that it came from John Denman or another of the Roe employees in Flintshire; but whatever the reason for its solitary existence amongst a large and varied solicitors' collection, it is an incredible find and helps answer many questions.

The survey clearly shows that from the original Parys Mountain site (including Cerrig y Bleiddia) the "Macclesfield" company had been granted lease for little more than $1/3$rd of the land area, which lay in the eastern portion. It did not include what was later to become the Mona Mine; Roe & Co. never mined nor had any connection with this mine, they were quite definitely restricted to the area contained within their original lease. Only after the expiration of their lease in 1785 would their particular area come under the jurisdiction of the Mona Mine Company. (Survey reproduced on page 272).

A 1926 O.S. map shows a large group of buildings occupying approximately half of the original Roe & Co. site and by then, such had been the extent of mining over the preceding 160 years, that the entire original site only represented about $1/10$th of the whole.

The results of ore samples sent for assaying by Jonathan Roose are not known, but modern geological analysis reveals a yield of between only 3-5% metallic copper in the original area mined by the Paris Mountain Company. The area is one of shales with lodes which are not true fissure-veins, hence the difficulty in initially locating copper ore, which is predominantly chalcopyrite. Iron pyrites (Fool's Gold) is much in evidence and apart from the chalcopyrite the other important ore of the mine is bluestone. This bluish-grey material, whilst containing the aforementioned minerals, also contains galena (lead), blende (zinc) and chalcocite, a copper ore with a grey-black sooty appearance but extremely rich in content. This ore, however, is a complex sulphide and as previously mentioned any sulphurous ore at that period was more difficult to smelt.

To assist miners a concise little book had been published entitled *The Miners Guide or Compleat Miner* by William Hardy. A second edition of 1762 and dedicated "To the Most Noble Prince William his Grace The Duke of Devonshire" sets out all the rules, regulations and methods of mining with lots of 'helpful' advice, such as:

"The Methods of discovering Veins are various, fometimes one Way and fometimes another, according as it happens; . . . they are many a Time found by mere Accident, as by a Plow running over it, or a Horfe treading upon loose Earth and laying the Vein bare to Sight or a Mole cafting up fome pieces in the Mould, which commonly proceed from a Vein."

All sorts of suggestions were put forward for discovering the veins e.g. "chiefly on Hills that confift in Lime-ftone" etc. As can be seen it was literally very much a hit or miss affair and the hill, generously called Parys Mountain, had long teased all those adventurers who had dreamed of making their fortunes from it.

* * * * * * *

At last the fortunes of Roe & Co. were beginning to look brighter as the Weaver books reveal a steadily increasing procession of items both up and down river, particularly during 1769. From May onwards, virtually without exception, the Northwich Tonnage of Up-Goods gives the name of the consignee as Charles Roe & Co.

Almost weekly copper pigs or blocks, with a total weight of between 1-2 tons, made their way from the Liverpool smelter to Macclesfield Common for refining. Also, possibly because of the lack of storage space in Liverpool or the necessity to mix ores for easier smelting, occasional consignments of copper ore, averaging 30 tons, still continued up river.

Finished items travelling in the opposite direction were mostly referred to as brass and copper, but from time to time were more detailed:

Aug. 18th	(Ship) *Hopewell*	10 tubs Brass	1 ton 15 cwts.
Oct. 31st	*Dolphin*	Brass wire	1 ton 10 cwts.
Nov. 3rd	*Marlborough*	120 Rings of wire	1 ton 10 cwts.
Nov. 14th	*Hopewell*	Guana kettles	2 tons 2 cwts.

All these above entries were consigned to William Roe who is recorded as a merchant on Cable Street in Gore's *Liverpool Directory* of 1769. John Walker's name was still entered for goods to Liverpool until the advent of William Roe on 18th August. Only one further consignment of "4 Neptunes" on 5th September is noted for "Mr. Walker" and thereafter it is always William Roe.

John Walker's death must have been sudden and unexpected because, in spite of all his mercantile involvements, he had no time to prepare a will and his widow, Elizabeth, obtained Administration of the estate. This death would have been a considerable blow to Charles Roe, particularly as John Walker had had a strong voice within Liverpool Corporation, as evidenced by the outcome of a Council Meeting on 7th December 1768.

The smelter had been operational for almost one year when the following had been recorded in the Liverpool Town Book:

"This Council having obtained a Counsel's Opinion that the Smelting of Copper Ore in the new erected smelting houses on the South Side of the Town is a public

Nuisance to the Neighbourhood and great and daily Complaints being made to this Council by many of their Tenants of or against such Work & Mr, Alderman Goore having reported to this Council that Mr. Walker had told him that the said Company were going to remove the Smelting of this Ore to some part of Wales – It is ordered that the Town Clerk so wait on Mr. Walker in the Name of the Council to know when they will remove this Nuisance and to have their positive Answer hereto to prevent any adverse Measures being taken to remove the said Works."

This promotes some interesting conjectures, particularly as it is the only entry in the Liverpool Town Books which refers to the adverse effects of the smelter. Whatever legal actions subsequently took place during the aftermath of this meeting, they certainly went unrecorded so far as the Corporation was concerned.

The problem had actually begun two months earlier when the *Liverpool Chronicle*, issued on Thursday 15th September, carried an article which at first glance appeared to be the work of an eccentric. It began by quoting "And as to his benevolence, he exerted fo much that he had thereby difobliged all his neighbours". It continued "Reader, whoever thou art, thou wilt be aftonished at the above sentence", which even for that period had an antiquated yet poetic ring to it. The anonymous author wished "to point at the malignity of one of the moft impudent and pernicious nuifances ever obtruded on a neighbourhood". The object of his displeasure was, of course, the copper works, but apparently he had little support, for he compared those who were surprised at his remonstrations to "village curs at his heels".

His irony in condemning the copper works is shown by the way in which he compares it with the other similar manufactories in the area. The steam from the sugar house was considered "balsamic", that of the salt house, "antiseptic"; the smoke of the glass works was "nothing obnoxious" and that of the foundry had "virtues of challybeate water". Needless to say the smoke of the copper works was "poifon of a moft acrumonious nature".

One is left with a picture of a large group of Liverpool residents who, before the establishment of the smelter, left behind the white sandy beaches, as they considerably extended their nightly perambulations to encompass the industrial South Shore, thus allowing themselves the pleasure of inhaling the profusion of health giving aromatic concoctions, before gracefully retiring to bed.

Someone was obviously at work behind the scenes intent on the downfall of Roe & Co. It can be no coincidence that just a few hundred yards further along the South Shore, immediately adjacent to the South Dock, glass and salt houses, was a plot leased jointly by the "Duke of Bridgewater & Mr. Mears". Nor can it be a coincidence that the Dissenting groups in Liverpool, which included associates of Wedgwood and Bentley, had a very strong voice through their monopoly of the publishing industry. Evidently the upset regarding the Macclesfield Canal Scheme had not been forgotten.

After the great discovery on Parys Mountain, Charles must have considered building a smelter on Anglesey, but inadequate supplies of good quality coal on the island and the restrictive carriage and duty costs from the mainland were prohibitive. His efforts to find another suitable smelter site continued; the business was expanding and any further moves would have to take into consideration the necessity of finding an appropriate coal supply.

As often happens in life, the efforts initiated in overcoming adverse events can suddenly find reward in quite unexpected ways, but for the present Charles would have to struggle on, as one cirsis after another presented itself. Not only had John Walker's death disrupted events in Liverpool, but Charles Roe's private affairs had received a jolt when in April 1768 another unexpected death, that of Robert Mandeville, linen draper of Cornhill, had upset the arrangements regarding the loan on his Chestergate house.

* * * * * * *

Robert Mandeville's will (proved 17th August 1768) had left his affairs in the hands of trustees. The original loan of £1,000 @ 4% was possibly called in by them, for on 12th April Charles had hurriedly borrowed money from the mercer William Harpur and an Elizabeth Roberts, a widow of Chester, to cover.

At the same time Samuel Holland, druggist of London, decided to call in his loan of £1,000 and Charles was again compelled to borrow from Elizabeth Roberts; this time the amount was £1,200. Elizabeth Roberts could have been a kinswoman of Charles Roe because of his cousin Samuel's marriage to Ellen Roberts at Overton, Flinthsire. Widow Roberts appears to have been a client of Thomas Brock, Town Clerk of Chester, so it could be through him that Charles Roe obtained the money. Thomas Brock, always with an eye for a good investment, would soon learn of the confirmation of the Paris Mountain Company's assays, for about that time he personally advanced the remainder of the money and released William Harpur from the loan.

Through his various investments in North Wales Thomas Brock's affinity with the Wrexham area had remained, and it is no surprise that on 31st May 1766 his name had been added with others to a deed of assignment for a considerable estate at Broughton. The mortgage was for £12,000 (at least £1¼ million today) in respect of a mansion house called Plas Hallcock Issa, lands in both Broughton and Brymbo, a house called Bellan and one in Gwersyllt which included "all mines and minerals thereunder".

There is no doubt that because of the Brock clientele amongst the mining fraternity in North Wales, Charles had approached the Town Clerk in his efforts to obtain additional coal supplies, and now with the possible intention of re-locating the Liverpool smelter in Flintshire. After all it was just as easy to transport copper ore to Greenfield or Bagillt, in fact the lead ore from Penrhyn Du had already taken this route. The first cargo, before October 1765, had actually been sold to Mr. Roberts of Neath in Glamorgan, but then John Denman, who by this time was already dealing with calamine in Flintshire, established himself in the lead market. He accepted delivery at Holywell of the three other lead cargoes from Penrhyn Du and sold them on to an important dealer, Mrs. Richardson of Chester.

Thomas Brock needed little persuading to assist Charles Roe; on 5th July 1769 Brock offered £2,300 for part of the vast estate in Broughton and acquired the house, Plas Hallcock Issa, lands, two cottages and a blacksmith's shop, but most important of all "coal mines in all or any of the premises, with whimseys and other machines".

This considerable property he divided and on part of the land built a large house called Bryn Mally. According to one authority the spelling should be "Bryn Mali", meaning Mary's Hill, leaving little doubt that Thomas Brock had named it after his wife Mary. He also added eight cottages to the two already in Broughton. It would be strange if John Wood the Younger had not helped his father-in-law with the plans for building Bryn Mally.

All these properties, together with the blacksmith's shop, coal mines, whimseys and machines Thomas Brock leased to Charles Roe. It seems apparent that Charles already had miners on site before the completion of the buildings; a lease dated 10th October 1769 between himself and Thomas Brock, for the extension of a sough into adjoining lands, states that Brock had lately leased the estate to Charles Roe. As Brock had purchased Plas Hallcock Issa on the 5th July, Charles must have taken possession of the land shortly afterwards and continued work on the sough until October, when it reached the boundary. The estate lease was for 31 years "rendering ¹/₇ of the coal raised to Brock".

The sough, begun to drain the mines, which presumably became known as the famous "Ffrwd Level", had to be continued into land already leased to Martha Morgan, widow of Stanstye Hall and subleased by her to a miner, John Price of Gwersyllt. Thomas Brock negotiated the release to Charles, from which compensation of £10 per annum was paid to the widow with a ¹/₇ of coal production to himself, as before. As Roe & Co. always treated their own employees fairly it would not be surprising to discover that John Price was hired by the company.

The Bryn Mally colliery rapidly developed and, although subsequently passing through several hands, would remain in production until 1935. The operations by Roe & Co. were similar to those at Penrhyn Du, for coal was wound up to the surface using "whimseys" operated by the power of horses plodding round in pairs, with each pair changed every two hours. Some whimseys at other pits were operated by men or steam engines; all consisted of a wooden frame which was easily movable, with a pulley and ropes which lifted the buckets of coal up to the surface by means of a large rotating iron wheel. The ones using horses were often called 'Cog and Run'.

The roads in the area left much to be desired, so during the worst of the winter months loads of coal were heaped up in adjoining fields. With the arrival of better weather it was carried away in panniers on the backs of horses or donkeys and presumably loaded onto boats at Farndon, from where the River Dee was navigable down to Chester. But even this part of the journey could not have been without its hazards, particularly with springtime flooding due to melting snow on the Welsh Mountains. On arrival in Chester the coal would be despatched to Liverpool as soon as possible.

* * * * * * *

During 1769 Joseph Wright of Derby set up a temporary studio in Liverpool. The small boy, who had briefly encountered Bonnie Prince Charlie's soldiers whilst staying with his family at Repton in 1745, had grown into an exceptional artist. He had twice studied in London with the portrait painter Hudson and his attention to detail had earned him the reputation of being a very accurate painter.

One story relates how Mrs. Morewood of Alfreton Hall Derbyshire had accompanied a friend to view Wright's paintings and was quite taken with the portraits of three young children who had just released a dove. So intent was she on obtaining a better view of the painting, she asked her friend to remove the birdcage which was obstructing part of her view. Wright thanked the lady for her unintentional compliment – the birdcage was part of the painting.

Liverpool was acquiring a reputation for its encouragement of the Arts. Already a theatre existed on the east side of, what was appropriately called, Drury Lane. The London theatres were closed during summer months, so it became customary for their most famous actors and actresses to travel north and spend the summer season in Liverpool.

During the 1769 season John Stafford, who was fond of plays, had taken his entire family to Liverpool. He seemed very much aware of Joseph Wright's reputation, in fact Wright had been well and truly occupied cleaning and restoring several oil paintings for the Earl of Harrington at Elvaston near Derby. Possibly because of his legal work concerning the Harrington leases in Macclesfield, John Stafford had somehow learnt of Wright's talents, and Wright, short of work at that time, had accepted two commissions from him. There is also a suggestion that Joseph Wright was distantly related to the Staffords, through their relationship to Samuel Wright the solicitor of Nether Knutsford. The painter evidently undertook the work in John Stafford's Jordangate house, for "Mr.Stafford" and "Miss Stafford" are recorded as sitters in Macclesfield, total fee for both £10 10s. The fee was extremely reasonable, only half of the usual £10 10s. for one sitter. One authority has suggested a link through Free Masonry, which was beginning to gain strength. Certainly this link existed between Wright, Josiah Wedgwood and other members of the Lunar Society, but no evidence has come to light suggesting that either Charles Roe, Brian Hodgson or their immediate associates were ever drawn into such societies, in fact quite the reverse.

Unfortunately no date is recorded for Wright's work in Macclesfield, but it does seem to precede his commissions in Liverpool, for there John Stafford had the entire family portraits painted at £10 10s. each. They are recorded as "Two Miss Staffords", "Mr. Stafford", "Mr.

Wm. Stafford", "Mrs. Lankford", and "Mr. Sam. Lankford". Also amongst the sitters was "Mr. Rowe" fee £10 10s., no doubt encouraged by the Stafford enthusiasm.

Charles Roe must have taken the opportunity to make use of John Stafford's presence in his capacity as legal adviser and valued associate of certain members of Liverpool Society. He was made aware of Viscount Molyneux's intended leasing of part of the Toxteth Park Estate, which lay a little farther along the estuary and adjoined property belonging to Liverpool Corporation.

Charles, by recommendation, met a Mr. Chapman who promised to negotiate for a lease with James Chadwick of Mount Pleasant, Liverpool, agent to the Viscount. This gave Roe & Co. some bargaining power when the case of *The Liverpool Corporation versus the Macclesfield Copper Company* was heard at the Lent Lancaster Assizes in 1770.

Without John Walker's presence certain members of Liverpool Corporation were obviously intent on disbelieving the assurances of Roe & Co. that the copper works would be removed. The Corporation legal fees eventually totalled well in excess of £500 as they managed to rally 35 witnesses "who proved beyond a doubt" that the smelter was "a nuisance to the neighbourhood". The company promised to discontinue the calcining of ore immediately and were allowed two years in which to remove the works to a more "remote situation".

With fumes considered a danger to health and "injurous to herbage", it was not a good recommendation in support of the bid to move to Toxteth Park. It must have seemed to Charles that every time he managed to solve one considerable problem, fate was eagerly waiting to throw yet another in his path. Having no alternative, a notice appeared in the *Liverpool Advertiser* of 14th September 1770 announcing the sale by auction of:

> "All the Yard and Dock belonging to the Proprietors of the Copper Works; as well as four very good and convenient Houses; and all other buildings, out-buildings, and other appurtenances belonging to the same . . ."

The premises were offered for inspection at any time, with enquiries to be directed to William Roe or in his absence the foreman at the South Shore works.

18
THE MACCLESFIELD
COPPER COMPANY

These glancing sideways in a straight career,
Yet each confin'd to their respective sphere.

Although business negotiations had taken up a good deal of time since the building of the Liverpool smelter, Charles Roe also had to consider a marriage settlement for his eldest child, daughter Catherine. This did need careful consideration, particularly as Catherine's intended was Rev. Ralph, son of Francis Nicholson deceased, former apothecary of Macclesfield. Having matriculated and become a Fellow of Brazenose College, Oxford on 2nd November 1756, Ralph had been ordained the following February by none other than Thomas Secker, at that time Bishop of Oxford; he then took the living of Didcot, Berkshire and was 35 years of age when he proposed marriage to 25 year old Catherine.

The availability of funds or property was a crucial issue, so Charles took an unusual step. So far as he was able he set aside sums of money (in the form of bonds) to be loaned out. He managed five in all viz: £400, £480, £200, £50 and £100 making a grand total of £1,230, but, instead of transferring them to Ralph Nicholson, he put them in trust. This meant that his Son-in-law could never get his hands on the capital but was to receive all interest from the investments twice yearly on 7th February and 7th August.

It was a very clever plan, for Rev. Ralph, benefiting from the investments, was not penalised in any way but Charles, in effect, was retaining control, for he selected as trustees son William and Harry Lankford. One reason for this arrangement could have been the unpredictability of the Nicholson family; after all they did seem to experience more than their fair share of family disputes, especially regarding legacies. Another could have been that, in extreme circumstances, Charles would not be tempted to use the capital but make other arrangements; he was retaining his company shares for his sons.

The marriage took place by Licence at Prestbury on 4th February 1769. Just before the ceremony an Indenture was signed in respect of the bonds and securities purchased by Charles but now the responsibility of the trustees. Rev. Ralph's future accounts would meticulously show the amounts of interest received, affectionately recording them from "Father Roe" in respect of his "dear Wife's Fortune".

From July 1768 Ralph had been carrying out an extensive refurbishment of what was to be Catherine's new home. Amongst other things the large bedroom had been papered and new fireplace mouldings made, together with shelves for shoes. By the time Catherine moved in, masons had already begun work on the gardens, which was to take until 1776 to complete. In total the refurbishment would eventually cost in excess of £456 but the source of this sum is not known. Also Rev. Ralph cherished a considerable library, which he would continue to enlarge throughout his life until it eventually comprised almost 1,000 books.

Apart from the wedding, the only other notable episode of 1769 was that concerning a lead mine near Mold in Flintshire.

* * * * * * *

The first intimation of this mine is in the *Derby Mercury*, issue 15th July 1768. The advertisement is for a sale by auction of mining shares at the "House of Mr. William Hilton, being the Sign of the Angel in Macclesfield", held on Tuesday 9th August 1768. Charles must have seen the notice which included, "One Ounce in a Lead Mine called Loggerheads two Miles from Mould in Flintshire, in Lease from Mrs. Jones".

The English mine shares were usually offered in multiples of 6, 8, or 24, but the Welsh were in Ounce. The word is derived from the Latin word 'uncia' meaning $^1/_{12}$th part. This small and inconsequential notice represents a very interesting story, particularly as once again Thomas Brock, Town Clerk of Chester, was involved.

During the Civil War lands in possession of James, Earl of Derby, had been sequestrated at the time of his execution. This involved a promise of the payment of an enormous fine by his son, Charles, in order to repossess. Even after the Restoration the younger Earl of Derby was unable, through loans, to achieve his ambition, so he had to sell some of the properties to the people with whom he had effected the loans.

One such property was the Manor of Mold, Flintshire, which was conveyed to Captain Andrew Ellis. This was presumably an army officer although, of course, it could have referred to the captain of a mine. Other lands in the area were conveyed to two other families, but the mineral rights of the whole area were to be divided equally between the three parties. Thus the name "Lords of Mold" came into being.

Captain Ellis's share eventually "passed by will in 1710 of Andrew Langley to his nephew Anthony Swymmer". Anthony Swymmer lived in Jamaica where son Anthony was born in 1725. In 1729 the father died and the Manor of Mold passed to his son and because of his minority his two uncles became unofficial trustees.

There were good prospects of getting coal and lead in the waste lands of the Manor but no one would take up the leases, so the uncles, Henry and William Swymmer finally obtained an Act of Parliament by which the King appointed them 'Guardians and Trustees' of young Anthony from 26th March 1737 until he reached his majority at 21 years. The uncles were also cousins of William Swymmer, who by his marriage became involved with the calamine deposits in the parish of Rowberrow, Somerset, where, at a much later date, Roe & Co. would become involved.

By 1757 Anthony Langley Swymmer had returned to England, married and taken up residence at Longwood House near Southampton. Uncle Henry of Bristol appears to have borrowed money to keep the estate in order, and was presumably entitled to fees for the administration of it. In the event Anthony transferred the royalties of the mines to his uncle and others. He never visited Wales but, from evidence in a litigation case, the estate was well looked after by his employees who even took on the might of the Grosvenor family when their miners intruded over the boundary to work a very rich vein of lead ore.

The steward of the estate was William Brock, a possible kinsman of Thomas. The lease for one of the nearby farms called Gwernafield was, as previously mentioned, held by Thomas Jones who had become involved in mining the neighbouring vein called Puddyn Susan for the remainder of the lease, dated 20th February 1758, the transfer of which had been dealt with by Thomas Brock. Thomas Jones had, of course, died and been replaced by his wife, Mary, in partnership with John Griffiths. She is presumably the "Mrs. Jones" referred to in the *Derby Mercury* advertisement of 15th July 1768 in connection with the lead mine of Loggerheads near Mold.

Roe & Co. were already working the Bryn-celyn mine, in close proximity to the above, where several whim-shafts in the eastern section were being sunk in the Lower Coal Measures. Evidence today suggests that substantive quantities of ore were obtained from within these coal seams, a most unusual occurrence, in fact it is said to be the only case known. The coal was therefore conveniently on site for smelting the lead ore.

The lease for the Loggerheads Mine was taken up by the Roe syndicate, (amongst the shareholders was Charles Roe, Lankford & Co., Thomas Walker, merchant of Manchester and Adam Simpson, former Barmaster of Bonsall) and from 29th September 1769 John Parry and partners were paid for driving shafts and draining water out, with William Kirkland as overseer. The Kirklands were a Lake District family so it is possible that, with the cessation of mining at Coniston, not only had Cookson Atkinson moved south, but also William Kirkland.

As work progressed, by 1770 the Jones family had joined the Parrys in the actual mining activities alongside two members of the Cheney family and one or two more individuals. The work proceeded well but there remains little evidence of much ore extraction, however during the winter of 1772-73 Charles Roe and Thomas Walker found it necessary to visit Lord Grosvenor. At this point the work appears to have reached the River Alyn which was the boundary of Lord Grosvenor's land. The pair were successful in their endeavour to continue the workings into Grosvenor territory, for on 23rd February 1773, as was customary when celebrations took place, ale and bread were purchased for the miners "when Making the Ware {weir} cross the River".

A considerable amount of work was done that year, including the construction of a cabin and whimsey shaft, with reckonings henceforth entered as "Loggerheads and Pengearrach Mines". Evidence today suggests that these two mines later became the Llynypandu mine which would be taken over, in due course, by "John Wilkinson Esq., the great Ironmaster" and considered "the most considerable lead mining speculation in England"; it adjoined the Bryn-celyn mine (later to become the Pen-y-fron).

Galena (lead) and blende (Black Jack or zinc sulphide) were mostly mined in Bryn-celyn. John Champion, of course, had been sending Black Jack to his brother William in Bristol before the latter's bankruptcy, so with correct roasting the sulphur could be driven out of the zinc ore and when crushed, used in exactly the same way as calamine for brass making.

Although the Loggerheads mine section, west of the river, proved of little value, the eastern part, driven through Lord Grosvenor's land, would prove extremely rich until excessive flooding took place. Site evidence reveals the use of pumps, themselves operated by water power.

Further Roe & Co. activities are suggested in the area. A vein known as Erw-felin was said to be the same as Vein Susan (? Puddyn Susan), but underlies south. Adjacent Erw and Parry veins are almost in line, the latter crossing the high road 600 yds. west of Halkyn Hall. Waste from Parry's mine reveals crystals of transparent spar with needles of copper pyrites embedded in them, which suggests that Charles Roe was hoping to find copper ore in the area. Also, in a group of mines on Halkyn Mountain, there is a Wagstaff Lode. This could be coincidence, but it is possible that Josiah, having completed duty at Middleton Tyas was now mining near Mold. Josiah could have been working alongside Anthony Tissington & Co. but was almost certainly sub-contracting for Charles Roe.

As John Denman was responsible for the purchase and calcining of calamine, it would be logical for coal from the Bryn Mally colliery to be delivered to him for conversion into coke. A geological survey suggests that the coal from that area had a high sulphur content and would need to be roasted in exactly the same way as the zinc ores. Obviously the same calcining house could not be used because of contamination, but the conversion of coal to coke before its journey to Liverpool does seem a practical one. The coal would be reduced to 75% carbon, ideal for the high temperatures required to smelt copper and also less bulky, thus cheaper to transport.

An interesting note in a survey states that near Holywell, where calamine had been worked since 1740, it was referred to locally as 'coke'. The derivation of this is unknown but does suggest a relationship in the processing of calamine with that of coal.

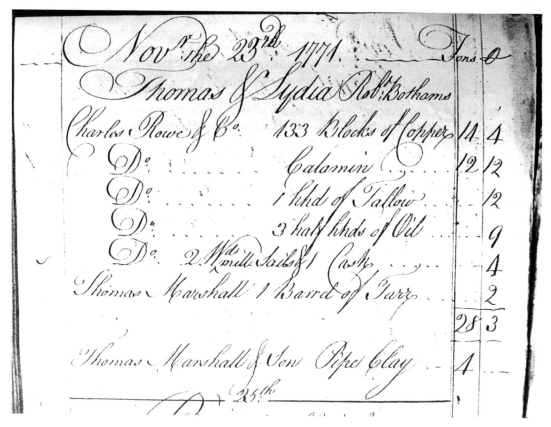

Entry from the Northwich Tonnage of Up-goods. Reproduced courtesy of CCALS ref. LNW 11/2

About this time the Alderley Edge mines were abandoned due to flooding and the Derbyshire miners and equipment on site were transferred to Parys Mountain on Anglesey. It is also conceivable that some of the miners would have joined the teams near Mold, particularly if they had worked with Josiah Wagstaff previously.

Activity was now increasing across the Dee and Mersey Estuaries and correspondingly along the River Weaver. On 13th December 1769 the first batch of six "Neptunes" was conveyed down river to William Roe & Co. Between 21st February and 11th July 1770, 31 more Neptunes, each weighing almost half a ton, took the same route. These large copper receptacles were doubtless on their way to the West Indies at the request of Charles Roe's brother-in-law, for use in the sugar and rum industries. (Later neptunes were saucer shaped plates, but judging from the weight of these earlier ones they must have been of considerable size).

Every two or three days between $1\frac{1}{2}$ and $3\frac{1}{2}$ tons of brass and copper items were despatched from the Macclesfield area, creating an almost continuous stream of traffic conveying goods to the port of Liverpool on behalf of the company.

Occasional bars of iron came up river, retrieved from the slag skimmed off the contents of the Liverpool smelthouses, in all probability due mostly to the iron pyrites content in the Parys Mountain ores. An intriguing item comprising 21 tons of French burr stones, renowned for their use as millstones, was recorded during March 1770. Although seeming to be an isolated item, the significance of this particular cargo would not reveal itself for a further twelve months.

By 1771 other odd items of interest began to appear: tallow, oil, a cask of tongues, pipes of wine, kelp (important as manure, especially from Red Wharf Bay, Anglesey) boxes of lemons, casks of biscuits and a small firkin of herrings, all consigned to Charles Roe. But an entry for 4th March 1771, confirming a removal from Liverpool to Macclesfield of "Mr. Roe's workman Household goods 4 cwts", is the start to unravelling the mystery of the millstones. It marks the beginning of a flow up river of an unusual group of items comprising screws, nails, blocks, crucibles, lead, a cask of mill cogs, 356 feet of "deal balk" and 18 cwts. of pott metal (the latter accompanied by a cask of wine). Pott metal was a form of cast iron but different from common pig iron; as the name implies it was used for making pots. The mystery is finally solved on 23rd November 1771 when tallow, oil and calamine were accompanied by two windmill sails; Charles Roe's plans to build a windmill in Macclesfield were underway.

The necessity of bringing a builder from Liverpool was obvious; there were no large windmills in the Macclesfield area and therefore no expertise for such a scheme, but the Liverpool skyline was accentuated by windmill sails, making the source of both materials and constructor a palpable one.

The site for the mill, intended for grinding calamine, hence the purchase of French burr stones, had been carefully chosen on Macclesfield Common. Unlike the Mersey Estuary, where strong south-westerlies provided a valuable source of power on many days of the year, the atmospherics on the Common were far less predictable, as time and experience would show. However, a windmill in Liverpool would not have been worth while, for the calamine would have had to be redirected from Flintshire, and only a small proportion, if any, at this time was passing through the port from Somerset en route for Macclesfield. The most important source of calamine remained at Bonsall in Derbyshire, and therefore it was more sensible to roast the ore on site and send it to Macclesfield for crushing.

The windmill was constructed on the southern side of the smelthouses, but lower down the hill, on a site which today roughly corresponds with the eastern end of St. Peter's Church, yet on the opposite side of Windmill Street. This was the beginning of a large development through which water from the Black Brook, having traversed the copper smelting site, was diverted in a southerly direction until it passed through a small unadopted area before entering a large sough to fall several feet into the River Bollin.

The area, adjacent to the windmill, was designated for the construction of a considerable brass works and during 1772 hearth stones, riddles, sieve bottoms, a dozen iron shovels and a hammer (of large size) also made their way along the Weaver to Macclesfield. And because of future development on site the Derbyshire calamine could be sent raw for dressing (washing) and calcining (roasting) in addition to crushing. The confidence with which the company now operated was due mainly to the progress on Parys Mountain and the successful relocation of smelting operations in Liverpool.

* * * * * * *

After Charles Roe's initial contacts with Lord Molyneux, through his agent, Charles had put pen to paper on 30th December 1769, addressing the letter to James Chadwick. At that time he was confident that the Liverpool furnaces would not have to be removed from their original site, even suggesting that if Lord Molyneux was anxious on this point, then a clause could be added to the lease forbidding their removal to Toxteth Park. Should a move become necessary, Charles had in mind a more southerly site along the shore, at Knots Hole. However, this was as far from the available Toxteth site, in one direction, as the original Liverpool smelters were in the other, suggesting that Roe & Co. were seeking as many options as possible and had in mind the development of better harbour facilities.

The area on offer, in Toxteth Park, was a 500 yards stretch of waterfront next to the Liverpool Corporation boundary.

One week later Charles addressed a second letter to Thomas, not James, Chadwick in order to clarify the actual depth of land he desired, "as far into the Sea or River as We chuse to take in – And 30 or 40 Yards of Land in the Fields above high Water Mark." This would enable the company to complete walls and yards and at the same time provide quay facilities for the growing fleet of vessels plying to and fro from North Wales, carrying bulky cargoes on behalf of the company. It would also avoid the heavy port dues of Liverpool, for with John Walker gone, there was no Freeman to deal through in the port.

Amongst other terms, Charles offered a rent of £50 per annum and a lease for 3 lives + 21 years, with a fine payable on the death of a life. He added his usual P.S. "Excuse my being in a hurry" and left Mr. Chapman to discuss the finer details with Mr. Chadwick.

At that time there was a great scramble by Liverpool merchants anxious to take up leases in Toxteth Park. A group of them, requiring "a Spot of Ground for a Timber Yard", had already made offers, together with a Mr. Whittaker, who specifically asked for "500 yards of shore under Toxteth Park".

The idea was to develop the land and then sublease, or sell the developments, to others. Although there is no documentary evidence to support what went on behind the scenes, someone must have been working very hard on Charles Roe's behalf. By 15th June 1770 he wrote "I Agree to My Lord Mollineux's Terms for both Places – Along the Shore," but expressed a hope for an amendment to the usual Liverpool terms of 3 lives + 21 yrs. and a fine payable on death. He suggested a definite fixed fine every 20 yrs. i.e. £75 after 20 yrs., £150 after 40 yrs., and so forth.

Liverpool Corporation's decision was to allow Roe & Co. two years in which to remove the smelters elsewhere, and Charles, never one to tarry, instantly took action. Remarkably, during 1771, the smelters were dismantled and rebuilt in Toxteth Park, just beyond the Liverpool Corporation boundary, but at what price?

The Right Honourable Sir Charles William Molyneux Baronet, first Earl of Sefton from that year and Irish Peer, must have reconsidered the situation. Although his family was strong in the Roman Catholic faith and recusants from the time of the Reformation, yet he had been brought up a Protestant by Protestant guardians.

Toxteth Park had great potential for development, but Lord Molyneux must have found himself in an extremely awkward position. Liverpool Corporation was powerful enough to make life very difficult for the nobility in the area, and had done so on several occasions. If Lord Molyneux could find someone who had the ability and apparent financial backing to begin a comprehensive development of Toxteth Park, then this would create an ideal situation, thus avoiding piecemeal growth. It would also act as a buffer against further expansion by the Corporation along the South Shore, and from this point of view Charles Roe was the most suitable 'applicant', having himself born the brunt of a particularly vicious campaign of exclusion within Corporation territory.

In fairness it must be said that Liverpool Corporation had been the 'instrument' by which legal action had been brought about, rather than the instigator. From Lord Molyneux's view point, however, Charles was hardly likely to succumb to any future demands for subleasing from Liverpool Corporation.

One can only assume that in exchange for allowing the relocation of the smelters on the Toxteth Shore, Lord Molyneux had some sort of reciprocal arrangement in mind, for his plans concerned an "intended Town of Harrington". He was, in effect, taking a gamble, which relied heavily on Charles Roe's conscience and respect for fair dealings, but the Earl must have been reassured by someone of the Macclesfield merchant's character.

In the first instance a lease for 80 years was granted on 1st May 1772, but with effect from 29th September 1770. In order to allow Roe & Co. time to convert the proposed area for usage, rent of £7 10s was waived for each of the first 3 years, until 29th September 1773.

The parcels of leased land were known as the Lower Croft, the Roughs and the Great Sea

Hay and measured 30 yards deep by 150 yards in length, with a further area down to the water line, in front of the above. This left an odd adjoining piece of land, only 10 yards square, which was also leased for use as "a reservoir for water to scour and cleane such Dock or Docks or other sluices as may be made within the said premises".

The lease ensured repairs to buildings "or other works for melting or refining of copper" and allowed for clay, marl, earth gravel and other similar materials to be obtained for building purposes from a close called Barn Bay, and stone from the Roughs close. Permission was also given for bore holes to be made in the adjacent Claughton's meadows and, most importantly, the laying of pipes to carry the water to appropriate sites.

In order to be financially secure a new syndicate was formed consisting of Charles Roe; son William, merchant of Liverpool; brother-in-law, Rowland Atkinson, headmaster; Rowland's nephew, Cookson Atkinson, now a merchant of Macclesfield; Brian Hodgson Snr. of Ashbourne and son, Robert, (now residing at Daisybank near Congleton, having been put in charge of the Havannah site); Edward Pitts, merchant of London; Legh Dickenson of Redruth, Cornwall and last, but by no means least, Thomas Weaver and John Jeffreys, merchants of Gloucester.

Evidently, about this time, the company was still contemplating building smelters elsewhere, despite the move to Toxteth Park. The latter appears to have been considered only as a necessary expedient, for the focus of operations, hopefully, was to be near Parys Mountain, as evidenced by efforts to obtain importation of coal free of Duties to Anglesey.

The coal on Anglesey was not of a sufficiently high quality to produce the intense heat required for copper smelting. It could, of course, be used for calcining the ore and working fire (atmospheric steam) engines for pumping water from the mines, but it was most unlikely that the main coal proprietor, Sir Nicholas Bayly, would offer Roe & Co. any favourable terms, in fact quite the reverse. Most of the Anglesey coal was destined for Dublin as household coal; Dublin was growing into the fourth largest city in Europe at this time and the Bayly connections were well established, for Sir Nicholas had inherited estates there.

All goods entering United Kingdom ports had to pay Customs Duties which, together with the carriage costs, made the importation of high quality coal from South Lancashire to the island prohibitive. It was necessary, therefore, to try to obtain a reduction of Duties through an Act of Parliament. Having suffered the failure of one defeat (the Macclesfield Canal scheme), the company decided on an entirely different approach.

No Public Meetings were advertised, in fact the proceedings took place as quickly and quietly as possible, which did attract later accusations:

> "no Notice of applying for their Bill was ever given to ye proprietors of Estates in Anglesea or ye Parties to be affected by ye Act but on ye Contrary that it was attempted to be made part of ye Sinking Fund Bill & by that means to be pafsed without striking ye Attention of ye Persons interested in the Consequences of it."

Needless to say it failed, due mainly to objections from Cornwall, but in its defence on this occasion a pamphlet was published: *REPLY On the Part of the Proprietors of the Anglesea Copper and Lead-Mines to a Paper called an Answer to their Case*.

The unknown writer pointed out support given by Birmingham manufacturers, who now received their metals at prices some 15% less than those when Cornwall held a virtual monopoly. Cornish mines had been exempted from paying Duty on coal importations for working fire engines and other necessities, and the Anglesey mines were only asking to be placed "upon an equal Footing". They were already at a great disadvantage because the majority of Anglesey ores were of very poor quality, thus many tons had to be raised to equal the copper content of one ton of Cornish ore.

Cornish miners argued that many of their mines were "one hundred and fifty Fathoms deep" (a fathom = 6 feet) and difficult to work, employing 21 fire engines (to pump out water), whereas the Anglesey mines were not more than 30 or 40 yards deep. The Anglesey case concentrated on the fact that in the not too distant future fire engines would be required for pumping purposes; it would be foolish to wait until that time and delay workings, with yet another Bill required, creating a complete waste of public expenditure and proceedings in the House of Commons.

By this pamphlet Roe & Co. were obviously intent on repairing public relations, although they had been very discreet in the use of their name, referred to only as "proprietors of the Anglesey mines". However, with yet another failure in Parliament, Charles now had no alternative but to come to a permanent agreement with Lord Molyneux, whose time for recompense had arrived.

* * * * * * *

It is now apparent that between the signing of the lease on 1st May 1772 and the date of the first payment of rent on 29th September 1773, Charles Roe had been forced to consider a lease of much greater complexity than he had originally intended, especially as the surprising result of the Lent Assizes judgement in Lancaster had forced the removal of the smelters. Lord Molyneux's persistence in his creation of a new township, Charles Roe's inability to obtain a more economic smelting site in North Wales and, no doubt, pressure from the agents concerned, saw a substantial addition to the original lease.

At this time Charles was not feeling well. Apart from the considerable business responsibilities which he was shouldering he had endeavoured to keep up with commitments in Macclesfield. On 2nd March 1770 he had taken the opportunity to extend his lease of the Dams area close to his land near the centre of town. He now leased several closes in Macclesfield Park called the Chamber Thorns, the Higher Dams, the Rough Dams, totalling 10 acres together with the 3 acres of the Lower Dams and compensated Joseph Pickford for the remainder of the lease with a payment of £755. Part of the land was already under lease to two individuals and Charles was allowed to claim the annual rents from them.

Until the year 1765 Charles had regularly attended the Macclesfield Assemblies of Mayor, Aldermen & Burgesses, always taking his civic duties seriously, but from then on company business could not be postponed. His attendances became more infrequent and evidently he was developing stomach problems; hardly surprising when considering the distances travelled on horse back at all times of year and in all conditions, irregular eating habits and the necessity of drinking large quantities of wines and port for fear of contaminated water.

The family made frequent visits to Adlington Hall and during 1770 Charles gave Charles Legh a recipe "For ye Gout ye Stomnick or any Cholicky Complaint", which the latter assiduously copied into his Common Day Book. Although the stomach complaint presents no surprise, the remedy certainly does – "Infuse one Ounce of Ginger sliced in a Quart of Madeira Wine. Take Three Spoonfulles once a day". It hardly suggests a soothing cure for an upset stomach, but evidently it worked. (Charles Legh's notebook contains an interesting collection of verse, remedies and advice, and one wonders if his note on page 72 was ever attempted, "To prevent being troubled with Gnats in Bed Lay Horse Dung on ye Floor".)

Despite all the concerns with Toxteth, Charles Roe managed a Corporation meeting in Macclesfield on 9th October 1772 (he had been elected a capital burgess from the previous week), but his very shaky signature suggests that he was suffering from a severe illness.

* * * * * * *

By 29th September 1773 Charles had agreed with the Earl of Sefton for an area of Toxteth Park comprising 50 acres 3 roods and 21 perches, which in due course would be developed "into a Town or Village to be called Harrington and good substantial and Convenient Dwelling Houses to be Erected & Built thereon with Streets", according to a plan annexed to the agreement.

The lots of land now leased were numbered 25, 26, 27 and 28 on the plan. The copper smelting site and subsequent quay and basin excavations were all contained within lots 25 and 26. Lot 27 was virtually all water, which actually extended one third of the way across lot 26. The subsequent infilling of lot 26 and the dock construction between lots 25 and 26 would cost Roe & Co. £2,000 (not too far short of £¼ million today). Lot 28 was converted into a mill dam and sold to a Mr. Jackson for £600, the rent, of course, still payable by the company as a form of ground rent.

In total length the four lots were 704 yards and in depth 235 yards for which the annual rent was £65, but the fines every 20 years had substantially increased, i.e. £130 on 29th September 1793 and £260 on 29th September 1813, and so forth. No time scale was stipulated for the considerable undertaking – it was envisaged that eventually 117 houses would be built by Roe & Co. at a cost of £300 each – but nevertheless at that particular juncture the prospect must have seemed awesome.

Hardly had the lease come into effect and the first payment made in September, 1773, than other proprietors, leasing land within the proposed development area, began to make overtures to Lord Molyneux's agents requesting rates be fixed for any quays which they could have use of. Charles Roe was completely taken by surprise at this request and pointed out to the agent that his agreement "was made, not only unconnected with them or any other persons, but was before the Town of Harrington was thought of . . . The Docks and Quays will and only can, find their own value when compleated, and all I can say, is that we shall be glad to give a preference to his Lordship's Tenants upon every occasion in our power."

The getting of stone and clay for building purposes had been restricted to the first 20 years of the lease, but Charles used the opportunity to request that this be allowed for the whole term of leasing.

Lord Molyneux's agent in Warrington was in complete agreement with the Roe comments and advised his Lordship accordingly, which seems to have settled the matter.

* * * * * * *

Within a few months the Toxteth smelters were visited by someone who fortunately recorded his observations. Sir John Morris, a lawyer from South Wales, was an ardent traveller and kept Common Place books. His Continental meanderings from 1772 to 1774 make interesting reading, particularly his visit to Amsterdam where he observed:

> "The girls are forward & impudent . . . others you may pick up to go to their own houses . . . a Florin is enough for what we call a Flyer . . . I think they have most of them a better appearance than most of the Covent Garden Street walkers: many of these girls are German, some French".

Arriving back in London during May 1774, he took the Liverpool Coach via Highgate, St. Alban's, Coventry and arrived in Lichfield at 8 o'clock in the evening. The coach left before 2 a.m. travelling via Newcastle (under Lyme) to arrive in Warrington at 5 o'clock in the afternoon, with Sir John complaining bitterly about the "common types" in his coach, the worst one being a "cheesemongering Scotchman of Liverpool".

About a mile and a half from Liverpool the coach crossed the Bridgewater Canal from where John Morris took a boat to Manchester. The trackskuyt (pleasure boat), pulled by one horse, was "not so large or well shaped as those in Holland". The journey of 20 miles took 5 hours to complete, with two stops of ten minutes each for the horse to rest and passengers to enjoy refreshments.

Morris stayed overnight in Manchester, meeting some people from Ireland, including two Dublin students. Late the following evening he managed to find a chaise for Runcorn, where he met some sailors from Aberystwyth who knew his family in Swansea.

The next evening he continued his journey on the *London Machine*. From 1750 some London routes used a conveyance called a "Caravan", similar to the Gipsy vans but fitted inside with benches for 8, 12 or even 18 persons and pulled by "6 able horses". The year 1764 saw the introduction of the "Machine", with fares reduced in the summer time because the journey was quicker; winter fares had to take into account an extra overnight stay. At the time of Sir John's journey a new Flying Machine had been built, taking advantage of new turnpiked roads. It was reckoned to halve the time of travelling and had a further considerable advantage – steel springs.

Unfortunately only when the coach was passing the Patten Copper Works at Warrington did Sir John learn of it, with much regret, for it was then too late to arrange a visit. His father had been proprietor of a copper smelting establishment in Swansea from 1717 to 1730, hence his interest.

On arrival in Liverpool, during Saturday 21st May, he lodged in a good inn called *The Talbot*, but it was not until the following Tuesday, after three days of exploration, that he learnt "Messrs. Rowe & Co. have a Copper works in ye skirts of this Town: I thought indeed to have heard so before". The next day he set forth on a visit and discovered the smelters about a mile from town on the river side, no longer in the 'skirts' of Liverpool because "being considered a nuisance was compelled to be removed".

Sir John was impressed with what he saw, but forgot to make a note of the number of furnaces, although he considered them "not even so large as those at Middlebank at Swansea". He found them cool and well contrived, but of particular interest was the roof, for instead of finding cross beams he seemed to recall an arch of bricks and, from memory, added two small diagrams to his notes.

He was unable to speak to the foreman who was ill; however, one of the workmen who had taken his place supplied Morris with some very interesting information. He learnt that most of the ore came from Cornwall, some of which was red in colour and did not need calcining before it arrived. Presumably this red ore was bornite, an ore with a copper content of 63.5%, thus making the payment of high carriage costs worthwhile. It would also explain the quantities of iron retrieved, for apart from copper, bornite contains iron (and sulphur) which would be additional to the iron obtained from the pyrites of the Anglesey ores.

Morris learnt also that ores arriving from Anglesey and Flintshire were likewise red in colour because they had already been calcined. This confirms that Roe & Co. had ceased roasting the Parys Mountain ores in Liverpool, as promised at Lancaster Assizes, and were now roasting them on site. But the calcined ore from Flintshire is intriguing, the inference being that it was copper ore not calamine, especially as the colour was red, not white or yellow. Calamine would not have been used at Toxteth, for there is no mention of brass manufacture on the site, in fact at this time it would not have been possible; the refining expertise remained on Macclesfield Common and brass could only be made from the finest refined copper, hence the building of the adjoining brass houses. One can only assume, therefore, that some copper ore was being mined in Flintshire and calcined by John Denman alongside calamine and possibly Bryn Mally coal. It must be admitted that John Morris does not mention any coal from North Wales, commenting only "They have their coal from ye works up ye River near Warrington".

The workmen claimed that they produced more copper than the Patten works, yet this left Morris in some doubt. Their wages were 15 pence for a 12 hour working day, 7 days per week for the first year. The second year saw a rise to 16 pence with the foreman earning 20 shillings for his 7 day week. Morris, of course, was talking to the day shift, but there must have been a night shift also, whose wages are unknown. He also noted that the Liverpool

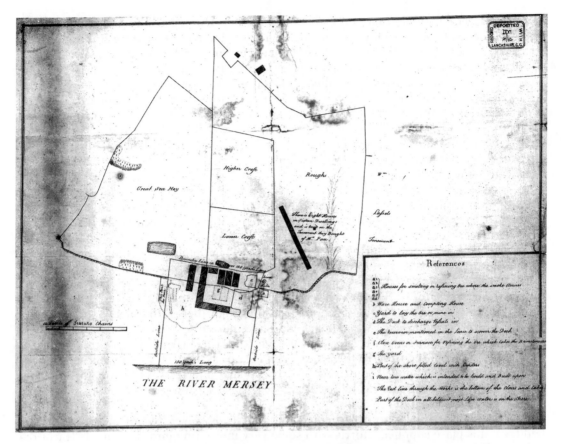

A plan of the Roe & Co. Toxteth copper works reproduced from the Molyneux collection (DDM H/62) courtesy of Lancashire R.O.

Corporation quarry men earned 18 pence a day, but comparison is difficult, the quarry was an enormous undertaking reckoned by Morris to be "as grand as any Quarry in Europe".

With his Liverpool visit drawing to a close, unfortunately John Morris was delayed by bad weather in his attempt to sail to Scotland. The journey to Liverpool appears in his third notebook; his first contains extracts from his father's smelting records, one of which is of particular interest:

> "The Furnaces are pulled down generally after a year's use. In making up the value of stock, the Furnace Bottoms are always calculated. And the value set upon them in proportion to their lives of working & from former experience because we are obliged to value these furnace bottoms whilst standing".

Presumably this practice would be the norm in most 18th century smelting works. As previously noted the furnace bottoms were made of iron because it has a much higher melting point (1533°C) than copper (1083°C).

* * * * * * *

Mining activities on Parys Mountain had increased dramatically within the last five years, as witnessed by the application to Parliament for exemption from Customs Duties on coal, the opposition suggesting "Have not their Gains for these last five Years been immense, not to say exorbitant?" The answer "Very far from it". Whatever the financial truth, bearing in mind the considerable sums invested, the level of activity was such that it had created an impression of great prosperity.

A meeting of the Paris Mountain Company took place on 14th February 1772. Unfortunately Jonathan Roose had taken advantage of his position and started his own importation business, which included "Cloth, Flower [flour], Meal, Butter and other things", apparently compelling the miners to buy their commodities from him.

It had also come to the attention of the company that in order to obtain mining contracts or shipments of ore, the "Bargain-takers and other workmen" had been paying gratuities to Jonathan Roose or other Agents; this was strictly against company rules.

An order was issued that the sale of commodities was to end by 1st May and workmen had to be paid in cash only. This is definite proof that Roe & Co. would not tolerate the truck system i.e. payments in kind to employees, which often had a devastating effect.

Samuel Howson was instructed to attend when any company business was transacted by Jonathan Roose, including overseeing the book-keeping and accounts. Jonathan, together with any other agents who did not abide by company regulations, faced instant dismissal.

Charles Roe must have been very disappointed with Jonathan's behaviour, and Jonathan must have regretted the error of his ways; he was to remain in the employment of the company for many years to come and from all accounts remain a loyal and dependable servant.

The local parson, Rev. Mr. Owen, had asked permission to preach in English to the workmen on Parys Mountain who were not Welsh. Mr. Owen had extracted a promise from Sir Nicholas for half his annual fee of £20, so Roe & Co. agreed that it was reasonable for them to pay the other £10. (An amusing comment, rather than a proviso, appears in the Minutes, "If Sir Nicholas Bailey Bart condescends to pay"). Here again is an instance of an Industrial chaplain at work in the 18th century as at the collieries on Macclesfield Common.

A decision was taken to stop the new mining of low grade ores, which would be near the surface, and to put as many men as possible to work on driving a level in a specific area. This could only mean that the intention was to reach the richer ore in the lower stratum.

The final order directed Samuel Howson to "attend upon Sir Nicholas Bailey's Agents" so that a good road could be made from the mine to Port Amlwch, each concern making half the road.

The next General Meeting was to be held Midsummer at Buxton, no doubt in the Old Hall Hotel under the auspices of Brian Hodgson Jnr. As most of the shareholders were from Derbyshire, this would seem to be a greater convenience.

It is surprising that Sir Nicholas should be concerned with either Rev. Owen's proposal or the suggestion of a decent road from the Mountain to Amlwch. However, having had his appeal for a joint mining venture with the Lewis-Hughes family quashed by the Court of Great Sessions, for which he had to bear the costs, he had taken matters into his own hands. In March 1770 his miners had entered the Parys Farm on the joint estate and dug pits. Operations ceased for a short period but four months later, in July, the Bayly agents set miners to work once again and soon engaged 200 men on site. In the event Rev. Hughes now approached Sir Nicholas with a view to accepting a joint mining venture, but this time Sir Nicholas stubbornly refused.

For some time the Bayly actions went unchallenged, then, taking the attitude that he was succeeding in regarding the jurisdiction of the Parys Farm as his own, Sir Nicholas forced the tenant, Thomas Price, to pay the whole of the rent to him and disregard the arrangements by which half went to the Lewis landlord. By remitting the appropriate payment himself to the landlord, Sir Nicholas was obviously hoping to establish a precedent. This was the catalyst for an extraordinary turn of events which brought to prominence a certain Thomas Williams.

* * * * * * *

In his late thirties and described only as an attorney, Williams had received legal training from Mr. Lloyd of Caerwys. He had soon become involved with legal matters pertaining to many of the landowning families in the region, particularly those of Anglesey. Ironically he had previously undertaken legal work for Sir Nicholas, but now wisely chose to support the injured parties. A Bill in Chancery was filed on behalf of Rev. Edward Hughes, his wife and their infant son, on 13th January 1772.

Sir Nicholas's eldest son, Henry, now Lord Paget (having assumed the title and arms on the death of his uncle and been summoned to Parliament 13th Jan 1770 as 9th Baron Paget) took legal opinion as to whether or not Thomas Williams should continue to act for him, as he had been informed of some misbehaviour towards his father; the opinion given was that the circumstances of the case should not debar Williams from doing so.

Roe & Co.'s agents, observing Sir Nicholas's miners on the land of Parys Farm, must never have doubted that his actions were anything but legal, hence the approach of Rev. Owen and the attempt to obtain a decent road from the mine to the port of Amlwch. They also offered to buy some of the ore which the Bayly contingent had accumulated on bank, but Sir Nicholas had to be consulted. As he was residing in London at that time several letters passed between him and Cartwright which indicate that he was considering the matter. From later submissions to the Court by Williams, it would appear that the ore was sold to a Crawford & Co. whose senior partner was a German. As this firm were "in bad credit" the German had "left this Kingdom" owing money to the Bayly concern, which was then irretrievable.

Meanwhile Thomas Williams saw an excellent opportunity presenting itself. He was a man of extreme cunning and persuasive talk. Miss Lewis, aunt of Rev. Hughes's wife, Mary, who was 'benefiting' from half the Parys Farm Estate during her lifetime, was now an elderly and infirm lady. The share of the estate could not have brought much income to her and, possibly because of mounting legal costs, she was persuaded by Thomas Williams to lease her life interest in the estate to him as part recompense. In the not too distant future this was an action she would regret, at which time Williams asked the solicitor, Mr. Lloyd, to assure her all was well. Lloyd appears to have stressed the point that Williams was in a better position than her to take whatever stance was necessary against the Bayly actions.

In effect Williams was now a partner with the Hughes family, which more or less gave him carte blanche to sue Sir Nicholas if he thought it necessary. There is no doubt that his 'line of thinking' took over, the main bone of contention becoming the incompetence of the Bayly employees and the wasted ores, which was hardly surprising with Cartwright in charge of operations.

Roe & Co. agents were approached for information regarding the working on the Parys Farm, as enquiries made of the Bayly employees had proved negative. They responded that it was not possible to give "any Particular Information having never seen any of the accounts" but they did manage to calculate that Sir Nicholas's men had "raised and carried off within 12 or 15 Months last past at least 3000 Tunn of Copper Ore" which was reckoned at delivery to be worth only £2 to £2 5s. per ton.

Without any treatment this was considered wasteful; the Paris Mountain Company had a very good routine for dealing with such low grade ores. Firstly the ore was roasted and then washed, keeping the water confined in pits until it had stagnated. The pits were filled with "considerable Quantities of Iron to Attract the Copper Particles" which sank to encrust the iron in the bottom of the pits. At midsummer of 1771, 60 tons of iron had been placed in the company pits and at the end of October, when the precipitated copper was scraped off, 8 tons of almost pure copper was retrieved valued at £60 per ton with hardly any corrosion to the iron.

The complaints against the Bayly methods were almost endless, including the fact that lead ores had been incorrectly washed and buddled so that "those most replete with Silver as well as the Lead were washed away".

All these matters were brought to the attention of the Court by Williams including the fact that the Bayly employees were conversant with the Roe methods but had made no effort to emulate them. So, not only was Williams intent on claiming half the mining profits to date on behalf of his clients, Lewis and Hughes, but also compensation for the irresponsible and negligent methods of working which resulted in loss of revenue. The effect was almost instantaneous, Sir Nicholas was forced to stop all mining activities on the Parys Farm Estate, meantime the wranglings in Court would continue for a further two years.

Early in the summer of 1774, Williams and Hughes, knowing Sir Nicholas's employees were still under a restraining court order, took possession of the mine, tools and equipment. Miners were quickly engaged and work advanced rapidly. The Court was in recess for the summer, so unable to take legal action himself, Sir Nicholas raged; his hands were tied until the Court resumed for the autumn term.

Without reiterating the claims and counterclaims it suffices to say that in January 1775 the Bayly employees were once more on site and working as a separate group, but in an apparently compatible manner. Behind the scenes preparations were taking place for a considerable legal battle.

Sir Nicholas, throughout the proceedings so far, had let it be known that Cartwright must take full responsibility for the accounts prepared and the state of the workings. Cartwright had over-reached himself far too long and died on 6th April 1775. This was at a crucial time, for Cartwright had been busy collecting affidavits and material in his own and, as a consequence, Sir Nicholas's defence. As expected, his untimely death appears to have had some effect on subsequent proceedings though not necessarily a retrograde one.

A decision was taken by the Court to seek a third agent, acceptable to all parties, who would be capable of acting as mediator. Whilst this process was taking place Sir Nicholas was debarred from further mining on the joint estate. Sir Nicholas, still residing in London, whether by choice or inadvertency, ignored the order. He had now formed a liaison with a Miss Anne Hunter whom he subsequently married, but there appears to have been some problem with regard to a marriage settlement, for during 1776 he pledged to her, by Deed Poll, a sum of £600 per annum. This was the same annual payment he had provided for his first wife, Caroline, until her death ten years previously. As a consequence of his non-compliance with the court order against mining, he was threatened with confinement in the Fleet Prison; this had the desired effect. Within a year the mining agent for each party i.e. Richard Bennet for the Hughes family and William Elliot for Sir Nicholas, had appointed a third independent agent, Henry Staples of Holywell, Flintshire. For a time the trio worked together in a effort to divide the ore raised between the proprietors.

During this period Roe & Co. had not been much affected by the dispute over the boundary on the land belonging to Parys Farm except for supplying the aforementioned information. Only Jonathan Roose had been particularly involved as he had been obliged to appear as a witness and swear an affidavit at the behest of Williams, on behalf of the Hughes family.

His name, together with that of John Denman of Holywell, appears in a memorandum drafted by Williams on 25th December 1775 when he put forward four names for consideration in regard to the post of third independent agent. It is difficult to believe that this was done with the consent of the Roe agents, who must have considered it could jeopardise their positions with the Macclesfield company. The paragraph in question appears to have been deleted from the draft and was probably never submitted, the consent of the two not having been gained in the meantime. However, it is interesting to see the high esteem in which both Jonathan Roose and John Denman were held by those outside the company.

Possibly in exchange for his co-operation with the affidavit, Jonathan was assisted in finding a plot of land in the Parish of Amlwch on which he could build an adequate residence. It is known that he was in possession of his house, named Mill Bank, by 1777.

* * * * * * *

Fortunately excellent descriptions have survived of the Roe & Co. mining operations on Parys Mountain in the mid-1770s. An unknown visitor, writing of his observations on Monday, 28th August 1775, began "This is a most surprising place where Copper Ore and Sulphur is raised in abundance, it's (sic) appearance is not like a Vein, but a whole Rock." The author describes how the ore was thrown into great heaps, intermixed with gorse and, by digging tunnels underneath in which fires were lit, set alight. The sulphur content easily ignited and became "Red soft stuff which serves for making Red paint for Gates and rough Doors." (This mode of painting is still used in Sweden).

Thomas Pennant's visits, which took place in the years 1773 and 1776 provide further details. The vast beds of ore were set on fire using a small quantity of coal. Some of the beds contained 400 tons of copper ore, others 2,000 tons, the former requiring four months "to be completely burnt", the latter "near ten".

Both visitors described the buddling and dressing places and appear fascinated by the precipitation pits, although Pennant remarked that this method "is not new; it has been practised long in the Wicklow mines in Ireland, and above a century in those of Hern-grundt in Hungary, where the precipitate is called Ziment copper". The unknown visitor relates that "any kind of Iron, Old, or new, wrought or Cast" was thrown into the pits and the resultant copper, when scraped off, was worth £45 to £50 per ton.

Thomas Pennant, being an eminent geologist, observed the proceedings through scientific eyes and reported accordingly. The pits were rectangular, measuring 36 ft in length, 12 ft to 15 ft in width but only 20 ins in depth. He noted that the best method was not only to collect in the pits water used from washing the raw ore, but also that which was lodged in the bottom of the mine workings and had a great concentration of minerals in it. The latter was drawn up "either by means of whimsies or windmills" and the water thus collected produced a weak solution of sulphuric acid in which the copper content was fairly rich. The pieces of submerged iron comprised old pans, hoops, anchors or anything that could be had, which must have made the scraping off of the copper difficult at times. This was in some way partly resolved as Pennant remarks . . . "of late for the convenience of management, the adventurers procure new plates, 4 feet long, 1½ feet broad, and ¾ inch [thick]."

These iron plates were immersed in the pits and almost immediately copper was precipitated onto them. In time the iron "gradually dissolved into a yellow ochre"; the plates were frequently taken out and the copper scraped off, which must have been a quicker, easier process than having to handle all sorts of odd shaped objects. However, it is recorded in later years, when groups of 'tourists' arrived to view the operation, submerged items such as horseshoes and other conveniently small objects attractively coated in copper, were sold as souvenirs.

The sludge or yellow ochre, which settled at the bottom of each pit, was also extremely valuable so, from time to time, the water was let out, the sludge dug out, dried and found to contain copper worth £50 per ton.

The unknown visitor also noticed on the mining site a "sort of Yellowish gritty Earth", which was stripped off to get to the rock of copper. At first this must have been considered waste, but then it was discovered to have a lead content, which after riddling (but not washing) produced 7-8% in each ton, worth 50 shillings "upon Bank" i.e. when ready for shipment.

* * * * * * *

It can be appreciated that by 1774 Roe & Co. had become an 'umbrella' beneath which many separate partnerships had collected, creating a situation of great complexity. Whilst the senior partners, Charles Roe and Brian Hodgson Snr., maintained their own separate investments in various lead mines and coal mines, the production of brass with the development of the Macclesfield brass works, and the deaths of two of the original five partners of 1764, appears to have forced their hand in seeking a remedy to the situation.

The outcome was a document dated 7th August 1774 entitled "Articles of Partnership Between Charles Roe Gentleman and other Partners in the Copper Company." The extant copy is of 25 pages and out of sheer necessity can be adequately simplified.

The "Indenture of Thirteen Parts" confusingly lists fifteen partners, each with his town or city of residence and, as appropriate, occupation. This is because in two instances two new partners jointly held one share or part. It continues by reciting "Grants or Licences" dated 1st and 19th August 1758 made at a Public Meeting in Macclesfield in relation to the smelter on the Common, referred to as on waste or common grounds "near a place there called High Ledge".

Next are briefly mentioned the lands near Eaton, Bosley and Congleton, with a further reference to land adjoining the "Town of Liverpool".

The purposes for the formation of the new partnership make interesting reading: "the Management . . . of Copper Works and the Art Mystery or Business of smelting refining and afsaying of Copper and other Ores and Minerals and in refining of Silver and making Cobalt and other matters and Things appertaining to the said Works". Here is a specific reference to cobalt used so prolifically by the pottery industry in its efforts to imitate the imported blue and white Chinese wares.

The engines, implements and utensils are categorised in the document for the sake of brevity, as are the ores in stock.

Although the partnership was now composed of fifteen individuals, the shares conveniently remained in fourteenths. Charles Roe retained two of his original four shares, one having been given to son William, now in sole charge of the Liverpool business, and the other purchased by Legh Dickenson of Cornwall, still responsible for buying and assaying Cornish ores on behalf of the company.

Out of the original two shares owned by Rowland Atkinson, Headmaster of Macclesfield Free Grammar School and married to Charles Roe's sister, Mary, a half share had been taken up by his nephew, Cookson Atkinson. This was presumably at the time when Cookson must have assisted with the setting up of the smelting operations on Macclesfield Common. He had, of course, subsequently taken up residence in the town, apparently during the winding down of mining activities at Coniston for, on the Bosley Deed of 1766, he is still shown as of Kendal, Westmorland.

Rowland Atkinson had died suddenly in August 1773 at the age of 51 years, and on the following 1st December his widow, Mary, had obtained Administration of his estate. From the date of the new partnership on 7th August 1774 Charles purchased the one and a half shares from sister, Mary, for a consideration of £5,066 0 2d. This was a considerable sum and, despite the fact Mary and the three surviving daughters would have to leave their home in the Grammar School and purchase other property, it gave Mary the necessary money with which to provide adequate marriage settlements for the girls in due course. Charles had taken care that young Mary, Ann and Frances now had the opportunity to marry well. Only Charles remained to look after his sister's family, his sister-in-law's family and his own.

The one and a half Atkinson shares were immediately purchased by Messrs. Smyth & Caldwell who appear for the first time in the 1774 *Liverpool Directory* as bankers trading as Charles Caldwell & Co. on Paradise St. William Roe was still resident at No. 19 Cable St. in 1774, a street which ran into Paradise St. at its eastern end.

The Smyth in this partnership was, of course, Thomas, married to Elizabeth Blagg of Macclesfield and good friend of John Stafford and the Roe family. By this time he had become a merchant of considerable importance, elected to the Chamber of Commerce. His partnership with Charles Caldwell appears to have arisen through an Irish connection.

As already mentioned Thomas Smyth's grandfather had been Bishop of Limerick and his father a member of the Middle Temple. The Caldwell family of Castle Caldwell were an important Irish family with several branches. Colonel Samuel Bagshawe, J.P. for Derbyshire and M.P. for Tallagh had married the daughter of the 3rd Baronet.

Charles Caldwell's grandfather, Andrew, was of Dublin and his father, Charles, also of the Middle Temple, but admitted 18 months earlier than Thomas Smyth's father. Charles Snr. became solicitor to the Customs of Dublin yet his three sons were born in Liverpool. The eldest was destined also for the legal profession, until he inherited a good estate in Ireland, then studies were promptly forgotten and he became a poet; the second entered the navy and would eventually gain the rank of admiral and be knighted, but Charles Jnr., attracted by commerce, remained in Liverpool to become a merchant.

By 1761 young Charles Caldwell was living in Lord St., which ran parallel to Cable St. and also entered Paradise St. at its eastern end. He appears to have become a partner in Oldham, Caldwell & Co., a firm dealing in sugar. Certainly by 1774 he had made sufficient money to have moved to a superior residence in the northern district of Bevington Bush and become principal partner in the banking concern. The banking house was adjacent to Thomas Smyth's business and private premises in Paradise St.

Charles Caldwell was very much a socialite, on occasion acting as steward for the races at Crosby. However, at times his behaviour could be somewhat unpredictable and he was never really to become an intimate part of the Roe organisation. From 30th July 1774 the banking firm were appointed receivers of light gold, in return for which they could issue "proper-weight coins". From their inclusion in the partnership it seems obvious that the Macclesfield company was using their banking facilities in Liverpool.

Out of the four original shares held by Brian Hodgson Snr. one, of course, had already been given to son, Robert, as a gift on 5th November 1764. Initially Robert's concern appears to have been with the family coal mines at Disley, where he could possibly have lived on site at Yeardsley Hall but, by 1766, he was living in Macclesfield. At some time he took responsibility for the Havannah works near Congleton, which logically should have been from when he acquired a share.

On 23rd May 1772 a Marriage Settlement was prepared between Robert and Mildred Porteus, sister of Beilby. Robert was to invest £4,000 in freehold lands, with the rents payable to Mildred during her lifetime, and a further £4,000 in Government Stocks etc. This was a considerable sum and in return Robert was to receive £1,200 with no stipulations. By this time he was already living at Daisy Bank near Congleton (a former Tatton family residence).

Under the partnership agreement of 7th August 1774 Robert now held an additional share from his father; in retrospect, this could have been held from the time of his marriage. Robert's trustee was Edward Leigh, solicitor of Greenhill, Staffordshire and married to sister, Elizabeth from 20th November 1767. And whilst Brian Hodgson Snr. retained only one share for himself, his fourth whole share was divided between Edward Leigh and son, Brian Hodgson Jnr. (i.e. $1/28$th share each).

Edward Pitts, pin maker of London, the remaining partner of 1764 who had also held four shares, had died in 1772. By his will, dated 13th February and proved three weeks later on 6th March 1772, he mysteriously makes no reference whatsoever to his connections with the Macclesfield company. It could be argued that he had already disposed of his shares, but this seems most unlikely. He had ceased to discount bills for Roe & Co. in connection with Ecton copper mine during 1768 but, incredibly, his name appears on the Toxteth Park lease dated 1st May 1772, although he had died two months earlier . The only explanation has to be that the lease was with effect from 29th September 1770, at which time he must still have been involved with the company. The signatures of all the participants in the leasing of the site are set out on the final page of the deed except, of course, that of Edward Pitts; nor is there one for a trustee or guarantor on behalf of his estate.

The original brass works deeds for Macclesfield Common are quite definite in the description of "one Edward Pitts possessed of (under alia) certain Mills & other buildings, matters and things". Mr. Pitts, having no children, left £500 and substantial property in Oxfordshire to his sister, Prudence, married to Richard Good. To Prudence's son, Edward, he left the lease of his dwellinghouse in Grace Church Street, London, all his "Stock in trade", £2,000 and the residue of his estate, except for several small bequests in Southwark and others to the family. The nephew must have maintained the business because the Macclesfield Copper Co. continued to supply him with wire.

There was a bequest to Edward's partner and brother-in-law, John Battiscombe and to his niece, Frances, married to John Fenton. The latter was possibly of a copper smelting firm, later selling copper to the East India Co. under the name of Messrs. Fenton & Chacewater Copper Co., and this could be the reason why Edward Pitts wished to be discreet regarding his business investments in Roe & Co.

As at 7th August 1774 the four former shares of Edward Pitts can be ascribed to five individuals.

One share had been taken up by John Atkinson Busfield. He was the eldest son of Rev, Christopher Atkinson, former headmaster of Macclesfield Free Grammar School and therefore nephew of Rowland. John had married an heiress in Yorkshire, Elizabeth Busfield, and on the death of her uncle had assumed the surname and arms of Busfield enabling his heirs to inherit the estate.

A second share had been taken up by Latham Arnold of London. He was a factor who, whilst not directly dealing with the East India Co., sold to the captains of its ships. As previously mentioned each crew member was entitled to carriage of a certain amount of goods for his own benefit, but stringent regulations ensured quotas were not exceeded. Obviously the captains were in the best position for making lucrative contracts and, as a consequence, Latham Arnold had important contacts, making him a valued member of the partnership.

Another share was held jointly by Thomas Weaver and John Jefferies (sometimes spelt Jefferis or Jeffreys), pin makers of Gloucester and important customers of Roe & Co.

Pin making, introduced into Gloucester during 1626 by a John Tilsley when the cloth trade was in decline, had grown into a considerable business by the 18th century, together with the wire trade. The chief market for Gloucester pins was London and by the 1770s the value of this trade was reckoned as £20,000 each year, with Messrs. Weaver and Jefferies considered as one of the most successful businesses.

The Jefferies family had long been established in the Gloucester area and John, a member of the Common Council elected Alderman in 1768, had been Mayor of Gloucester 1769-70. Thomas Weaver (with possible connections in mid-Wales) was a comparative newcomer to the city. He must have had strong ties with the Jefferies family for, so important was their friendship and such was their mutual respect and trust, that the partnership was carried on without any legal documents to control their business enterprise. This was a situation not to be tolerated by John Jefferies Jnr. in the not too distant future.

Money made by the partnership from their pin making activities had been used to purchase five dwellings (converted into seven) at the lower end of Oxbody Lane in the parish of St. Aldgate. The date of purchase was 24th November 1767 and the vendor John Cooke an apothecary of Gloucester. The buildings were rebuilt to provide several workshops, a compting house, warehouse and stables together with two residences, one for each partner. This contact provided the Macclesfield company with its final shareholder, John Cooke, apothecary, who bought the last of Edward Pitts's shares. This appears to have been purely an investment on the part of Mr. Cooke, as there are no indications that he was in anyway involved with the direct business of the company.

It can be argued that the year 1774 saw a turning point in the affairs of Roe & Co. Such was the magnitude of operations that it was no longer possible to confine investors, as much as it was desirous, to virtual family members. More and more the company was referred to as the Macclesfield Copper Company, however, Charles did obtain a proviso in the Articles that in all transactions relating to the "Copartnership" done in joint names, "the Name of Charles Roe shall on all such Occasions be first used or in the name or Designation of Charles Roe and Copper Company . . .".

Charles also appears to have retained the family name for his mining operations (the Paris Mountain Company excepted), but the world at large, having contracts with the copper and brass production side of the business, dealt mostly with the Macclesfield Copper Company.

19
BUSINESS, PLEASURE AND DUTY

When thou vowest a vow unto God, defer not to pay it.

The Minute Book of the Macclesfield Copper Company (1774-1833) commences with the first Annual General Meeting in Macclesfield on 19th August 1774. Eleven partners were present, the two absentees being Latham Arnold and John Jefferies.

Charles Roe, aged 59 years, was Chairman but seniority was held by Brian Hodgson Snr. at 65 years. Solicitor, Edward Leigh, who was to retain a copy of the Articles and be entrusted with the company's legal business, was a surprising 49 years old. He had married Elizabeth, almost twenty years his junior and daughter of Brian Hodgson Snr., when he was already 42 years of age. Of the remaining partners present most were in their thirties, with William Roe at 28 years very much the junior in age, though not in business acumen.

John Hale, the bookkeeper at Coniston, had been rewarded for his loyalty and hard work and was now, in effect, the company accountant. All books, accounts, deeds and other documentation were to be kept in an iron chest shortly to be fitted into the company office, which remained near the northern end of Barn Street (Churchill Way) adjacent to Charles Roe's house. Presumably the iron chest was that weighing 6 cwts. which had been transported along the River Weaver from Liverpool and recorded by the clerk on 18th Oct. 1773.

Cookson Atkinson, by this date in charge of the Bosley site, was required to submit weekly bills for expenses in order to receive cash reimbursements from Mr. Hale. Although he was a shareholder, Cookson was voted a salary of £50 per annum for his responsibilities at Bosley.

At this time a firm called Malpas & Co. were rolling brass at the Bosley Mills on a subcontract basis, but Cookson was asked to persuade them to give up the contract and put forward his plans for taking over the process. It was also decided that the 4 ft rollers on site should be replaced by 2 ft ones.

Attention was also given to the Macclesfield works. Firstly "the East end of the Old Smelting house" had to be prepared for storing charcoal. This, of course, was used as a cover on the surface of the molten metal to stop contamination by oxygen entering from the atmosphere. Two bings were also required for coal, in places convenient for the brass house. This suggests covered containers in which the coal could be heaped, but probably with some form of ventilation at the bottom to assist any wet coals in drying out.

Instructions were given to break up copper furnace bottoms and resmelt them either at Macclesfield or Liverpool; as previously mentioned these were of iron, and if John Morris's notebook is correct, as each smelter came out of commission for a period, to allow a complete overhaul to take place, the furnace bottom would be inspected and hopefully only need replacement at the most once each year. Any old iron at the Macclesfield works, which was not worth resmelting, was to be sold to Hugh Ford, an iron founder of Swan Bank, Congleton.

Presumably any old iron from the Liverpool works would be made use of for the precipitation pits on Parys Mountain.

William Roe had achieved great success with his smelters at Toxteth, which meant that the copper blocks travelling to Macclesfield only needed refining. Unfortunately Charles Roe, as manager of the Macclesfield works, was given the unenviable task of deciding which of the local work force could be dispensed with, as less smelting meant less workmen on the Common.

Robert Hodgson, living nearest, was asked to contact Mr. Moore, clerk to Henshall & Co. at Stoke, to encourage a better delivery of goods to Birmingham customers. Hugh Henshall, brother-in-law of James Brindley, had taken over the construction of the Trent and Mersey Canal from the time of Brindley's death in 1772. It would not be finished till 1777, but already goods were travelling on the completed section from Stoke to Birmingham and Henshall had set up a carrier business. Cookson Atkinson, or whoever made the journey first, was to give 2 guineas to the wharfinger in Birmingham "for his Extra Care" in delivering the Macclesfield goods to customers.

The weights from the Havannah site, used for weighing merchandise and other items, had to be brought to Macclesfield town and adjusted to the "Corporation Standard weights".

The new partnership was evidently starting as it intended to carry on, particularly with regard to debts. It was important for the old debts to be cleared and the bookkeeping corrected. William Sutton, a local brazier, was refused any further goods until his account was settled which, surprisingly, was quite large, £90 13 4d.

Two old debts related to mining; one to that part of the lead mine, Penrhyn Du, which had been leased from Assheton Smith (having succeeded to his uncle, William Smith's estate), for which an outstanding balance of £129 15 7d. was due from the attorney, Samuel Wright of Knutsford. The other, most certainly of some embarrassment, would have been outstanding for quite some time. It related to the Alderley Edge copper mine which had apparently been taken over by a London partnership, Messrs. Whitfield and Heaton. The amount was not particularly large, £40 7 10d. but it was due from John Stafford who had obviously finalised matters on behalf of the Macclesfield company. On this occasion Charles Roe and Robert Hodgson were asked to "go to Mr. Stafford & endeavour to settle with him the Debt . . .".

Poor John Stafford, after more than thirty years of arduous legal cases his health was beginning to suffer, but the truth of the matter probably lies in the fact that on 16th July 1773 Messrs. Lankford, Robinson and Stafford had been declared bankrupts. This was the silk partnership in which Charles Roe had previously been engaged and in which both the son and son-in-law of John Stafford had remained. How tragic and humiliating this must have been for the lawyer, particularly as his son-in-law, Harry Lankford, had contrived a considerable loan from John Stafford's wife's family, the Tattons.

* * * * * * *

Harry Lankford had married Sarah Stafford at Prestbury in 1761 yet, despite the petition to Parliament regarding the rapid deterioration of the silk trade, submitted in 1765, he had bought a substantial estate in Leek. At that time he and his wife were living in Fence House which was, of course, Elizabeth Blagg's old home. On 2nd April 1766 he had paid the considerable sum of £12,005 for a house and farm called Barnfield near Cheddleton in Staffordshire together with a large area of arable, pasture and meadow land which he leased out. Ten days later he borrowed £7,800 from William Tatton of "Withinshawe", which was advanced from the estate of Elizabeth Egerton, William Tatton's sister-in-law, who had died a spinster.

One suspects that the other part of the purchase price was John Stafford's dowry for his daughter, because other loans and property had been consolidated which, by 9th January 1770, had given rise to a very complicated situation. At that point it was agreed by all parties, John Stafford now included, to bar "all claims of Dower".

To add further to the confusion, on 20th July 1771, Harry was forced into effecting an

Indenture with his brother, Samuel, which says little for his character. When Charles Roe's first father-in-law, Samuel Lankford, had died, by his will dated 9th September 1758 he had left £3,000 to Samuel amongst other bequests, but Harry alone had proved the will and taken Samuel's £3,000 for his own use, giving Samuel a bond plus interest to cover. Now Samuel was in fear of never receiving his money, so Harry included him on the Leek property deeds.

On 12th August 1773 a meeting of creditors took place in the Angel Inn, Market Place, Macclesfield, under the auspices of the landlord William Hilton, according to a notice which had been entered in the *London Gazette*. By 6th April 1774 all the property and lands in Leek, including property at the upper end of Spout Street (now St. Edward Street), which had evidently been used by the silk partners for warehousing and other things, had been sold at Public Auction and realised £14,270; out of this Samuel received his £3,000 plus interest of £470.

Under the circumstances one suspects that previously Charles Roe had been willing to carry the Alderley mines debt for quite some time, but now the situation was more or less out of his hands; he had more partners to answer to, and those, on a less intimate basis, hence the approach to John Stafford for the outstanding debt.

* * * * * * *

Supplies for the new brass works were naturally of great concern, but the company policy was a sensible one, never to requisition unnecessary stocks for the Macclesfield works and, where it was essential to purchase from other concerns, only to purchase as and when the partnership agreed. At this time it was considered necessary to advise John Denman in Holywell not to exceed his purchase of 50 tons of calamine each quarter, and Legh Dickenson in Cornwall, to purchase no further supplies of copper ore "till further orders".

The calamine from Rowberrow in Somerset was causing problems, which suggests that by this time it was being purchased on a regular basis. Samuel, 25 years old and Charles Roe's third surviving child from his first marriage, was employed by the company, so to him fell the task of inspecting this particular ore and reporting when it was not clean. Meanwhile Brian Hodgson Snr. and Thomas Weaver were asked to "go into the West" and look for an alternative source.

Once again the problem seems to have arisen from the death of an owner of an appreciable estate. William Swymmer, Lord of the Manor of Rowberrow, had died in 1771. It had been his father, Henry, ship owner and Mayor of Bristol in 1713, who had been one of the guardians of young Anthony Langley Swymmer involved in the mining concern relating to the Lords of Mold in Flintshire. William Swymmer's son of the same name had also been left a minor, so three trustees were appointed, one of whom was Elizabeth, the widow. They were designated "Lords and Lady of the said manor in trust for William Swymmer".

Mrs. Swymmer had apparently continued the business interests in Rowberrow manor on behalf of her son, hence the references in the company's Minute Book to "Mrs. Swymmer's Calamine", but it now seemed that there had been an unfortunate deterioration of quality in supplies necessitating the search for an alternative source.

This first extant recorded A.G.M. of the Macclesfield Copper Company is important because it also reveals the extent to which the retail side of the business had progressed. The quality of its brass and copper production was such that some of the most important merchants in the country could now be approached for custom, whilst that of others had already been acquired.

One particular customer, John Darbyshire, was a brazier and merchant of Aston and Birmingham and owned the largest sugar cane estate in the West Indies at Tobago (later to be valued at £30,000). In 1774, however, Darbyshire must have been in financial difficulties because the estate was already heavily mortgaged and whichever of the company's representatives next visited Birmingham was instructed to attend "Mr. Darbyshire's affairs".

This does actually indicate just how well Roe & Co. had been conducting their own affairs because, commencing in 1772, there had been a financial crisis. The Bank of England had come under pressure from all sides during a European monetary crisis. The East India Company by then a considerable establishment with both military and political commitments, was deeply in debt and desperate for loans, but the Bank refused help. This was a perfectly responsible action to take because it was trying to support other concerns in difficulty. In 1772 the situation suddenly worsened as the Ayr Bank in Scotland collapsed.

Ayr Bank notes at the beginning of the year were said to represent two thirds of notes circulating in Scotland. To support this the bank had obtained short term credits with London banks but had over extended its business. The Ayr Bank was a private partnership without limited liability so, as the majority of its partners were substantial landowners, their properties flooded onto the market in order to meet their liabilities.

Panic ensued as people rushed to obtain cash, which had such disastrous repercussions throughout Britain and beyond, that on 22nd June 1772, the City of London was said to be in "uproar" and in "tears".

One prominent Edinburgh partnership, William Alexander & Sons, owned vast sugar estates in Grenada, which were already mortgaged to the Bank of England. The pressure proved too great and the Alexanders were declared bankrupts. John Darbyshire, at this period, was more fortunate and managed to survive for quite some time.

Measures were taken to stabilise the situation. In 1773 the Treasury was granted a substantial loan by the Bank of England for the relief of the East India Company, and the following year the Bank of Scotland was allowed to double its capital; both were by Act of Parliament.

The London banking house used by Roe & Co. was that of Messrs. Welch Rogers & Co. which happily survived the crisis and, as the economy began to recover, Roe & Co. were in an excellent position to take advantage. From the 17th century Wolverhampton had specialised in locks and buckles and the Macclesfield brass works undertook supplies to John Savage a brazier of High Green, whose premises were situated along the river towards Bilston. Another firm of considerable repute was Gibbins & Sons, locksmiths in Wolverhampton itself, which was also visited.

Just three days after this first A.G.M. the will of Charles Roe's second father-in-law was proved in London.

* * * * * * *

Joseph Stockdale had died a wealthy man in the Parish of St. Giles in the Fields, Middlesex. When he had removed from St. Martin's-in-the-Fields is difficult to deduce, but he could not have been resident there for long. It was an area where a large number of French Protestants had settled, having escaped the persecution in France after the Revocation of the Edict of Nantes in 1685. The area was not without its very wealthy families, having been amalgamated with Bloomsbury until 1724, but it did also have a very poor quarter known as 'The Rookery' where conditions were deplorable because of overcrowding by poor families.

Thomas Stockdale, the eldest son, who was within three days of his fortieth birthday on 26th August, was to receive £1,000 with the proviso that if no heirs of his reached 21 years then the money had to be returned to the estate. This considerable sum was apparently regarded as adequate by his father as "I have already given him a very handsome provision."

The second son, Joseph Jnr. who had lived in Guadeloupe but was then resident in Dominica, had likewise received substantial sums of money over a period of time amounting to at least £900, and was also to be given £1,000 if he returned to England within the year, otherwise it was to be sent to him.

Daughter Jane, a spinster still living at home, was left the house, goods, plate, china, linen, pictures and all other contents; an acknowledgement by her father "for the great care she hath taken of and for the duty and respect she hath always shown me."

The settlement of £500 in respect of Mary's marriage to Charles Roe was noted, with important provisions stipulated. Firstly, after payment of funeral expenses etc. the residue of the estate was to be divided equally between Jane and the children of Mary and Charles Roe, but the £500 already given was to be treated as part of the residue. Charles was expected to provide for his and Mary's children's education and maintenance during their minority, but if he should die or become insolvent "or be reduced to low circum-stances" then the children could be provided for, by the Executors, out of the money held in Trust. This must have been some consolation to Charles, although it would later cause much upset and strife within the family. However, Charles still held the responsibility for his first wife's marriage settlement with regard to Catherine, William and Samuel and the added complication of his third wife's welfare and their only son, John Harriott.

No mention is made of Joseph Stockdale's share of the lease for the Bosley works, which presumably represented the £500 investment from the marriage settlement; nor is there mention of it in the Minutes of the company.

* * * * * * *

The Minutes for the following month of September record an agent in Bristol with whom Robert Hodgson had dealings. Evidently the Bristol Wire Company was buying herring casks for transporting goods, so the agent, Mr. York, was asked to find a cooper in Bristol who would buy the same for the Macclesfield company, but making sure they were water tight.

(A great advantage by this time was the completion of the River Severn navigation and canal system in May 1772. This finally linked with the Trent and Mersey canal creating a much easier carriage of goods to Bewdley, Worcester, Tewkesbury, Gloucester and, of course, down the Severn Estuary to Bristol.)

Further business related to London i.e. Latham Arnold and other agents dealing with East India captains, and ingot brass by ship from Liverpool to a Mr. Fossick at Cotton's or Beale's wharf, for which he would supply warehousing.

Another concern was for a company vessel of about 30 tons, presumably for trips between North Wales and Liverpool, as William Roe was advised to obtain information from the Warrington Company (Patten's), including what 'burthen' such a vessel would provide.

It was also decided that the following six partners were to be considered inactive (i.e. sleeping partners):

John Cooke	Charles Caldwell
Brian Hodgson Jnr.	Latham Arnold
Edward Leigh	John Atkinson Busfield

At the following month's meeting each of the six was voted £50 per annum from the commencement of the partnership. It is interesting to note that Edward Leigh must have made a decision not to take up any legal work on behalf of the company. In only three years time James Boswell, whilst visiting Dr. Johnson at Dr. Taylor's house in Ashbourne (The Mansion in Church Street), would write "A Counsellor Leigh, no longer in practice, but who acquired an estate in the neighbourhood, dined with us". His further comment, that Leigh was "More Squire than Counsellor", hints at a somewhat slothful character who did not quite endear himself to his father-in-law, Brian Hodgson Snr. He never acted on behalf of Brian Snr., whose attorney was Francis Beresford of Ashbourne.

After the meeting of 29th October the following meeting was postponed until 31st January 1775 at which six of the active partners were present. The agenda, although short, is of significance because it does reveal that until that day coal had been supplied to the Toxteth smelters by the Parr Colliery Company, but that future supplies would come from 'Mr. Mackay', with whom the partners now signed an agreement. He was to be paid £50 per annum in addition to the price of the coals from either the "Raven Head or Thatto Heath" collieries if he agreed to the same price as those previously supplied from the Parr Colliery Company.

This change of supplier must have been the result of the predicament in which the unfortunate Sarah Clayton found herself. During 1773 and 1774 she had sued Alexander Tarbuck, her colliery manager of Parr, for irregularities in bookkeeping, misappropriation of money and neglect of workings, from which she had suffered a great loss. (On 19th June 1778 she would be declared bankrupt, as reported in Williamson's *Liverpool Advertiser*).

The only other business discussed at the company meeting was the admittance of another partner from the following A.G.M. in August 1775, at which time he would pay "the Sum which (the) said share comes to in ppn. (proportion) to Capital as shall appear at that time". This particular gentleman, Edward Hawkins, was to play a significant role, not only in the future of the Macclesfield Copper Company, but in Macclesfield itself.

The February, April and May meetings of 1775 indicate an increased demand for wire and a request for a ring of Bristol wire to be used as a pattern by the workmen of Havannah.

The brass production was evidently increased as John Denman was instructed to purchase an additional 200 tons of calamine, but then to revert back to 200 tons per annum (i.e. 50 tons each quarter). The stipulation for this ore is always that it must be "Groove" or "Grove" calamine, but what this particular specification means is difficult to deduce for grove or groove meant a mine or pit. The suggestion seems to be that it should not be calcined but raw, or from a large deposit rather than a small vein.

Some upset had occurred at Bosley and "Mr. Hodgson", most likely Robert, was instructed to "call on" Cookson Atkinson. He was to be informed that the company had lost confidence in the way in which he handled business and that from the next A.G.M. someone else would take his place, including the occupation of the house he held from the company. This was certainly a drastic step and one wonders what Charles Roe's thoughts must have been on the matter. Evidently the person chosen to take Cookson's place was Edward Hawkins. Cookson agreed to offer his share to the company in August following.

Edward Hawkins was instructed to travel to Wolverhampton where he would meet Charles Roe and presumably be informed of his future position. "Mr. Hodgson" (? Robert), after a visit to Birmingham, was to join Charles and Thomas Weaver on a journey to Rowberrow in Somerset.

Although the supply of well dressed calamine for brass making was now causing problems, at last the supplies of copper ore were on a more permanent and regular basis. The smaller uneconomic mines had been abandoned so that at this period the Toxteth smelters were reliant, primarily on Parys Mountain ore, but also on best quality Cornish ore (which facilitated smelting) and any copper ore retrieved in the course of mining operations near Mold in Flintshire.

Since the great find on Parys Mountain, the supplies of Cornish ore had varied a good deal. In 1769 the purchase was 411 tons followed by 842 tons in 1770, 540 tons in 1771 but only 3701/2 tons in 1772, however the latter figure represents a particularly rich copper content. In 1773 a considerable quantity was bought, 913 tons, the highest yearly Cornish purchase to date. (Unfortunately the book containing records of purchases 1774 to 1777 is missing).

The available figures for the Paris Mountain Co. production are extremely impressive:

January to December 1769	2,856 tons.
January to December 1770	4,319 tons.

Out of the 1770 figure 43 tons 4 cwts. are noted as "Calcined" or "Burnt" ore, the remainder were raw ore after the sorting and dressing processes. Obviously the calcined copper ore, although having had the sulphur expelled still retained some impurities such as lead or iron and does represent a much greater initial tonnage of raw ore.

The first batch of calcined ore is recorded on 11th August 1770, which must have been as a direct result of Charles Roe's promise at the Lancaster Assizes to terminate the calcining of ore in the original Liverpool smelters. Although some of the ore had already been transported to Liverpool and roasted there for two and a half years, yet there must have remained on bank at the mine something in the region of 5,000 tons which would need to be calcined before delivery to the new smelters at Toxteth.

From April 1771 there are two distinct sets of figures, the first showing raw ore weighed together with its 1/8th duty ore; the second showing burnt ore weighed also with the appropriate 1/8th duty ore. This is confusing because surely Sir Nicholas was not receiving duty twice, once on the raw ore before calcining and then after it had been calcined. In no way does the first set of figures bear any relationship to the second.

The 1771 total of raw ore is 740 tons 1 cwt. and calcined 520 tons 15 cwts. However, by October 1771 the calcined ore in quantity had actually overtaken the unburnt. This double set of figures ceases on 14th July 1772, at which point it would appear that as much raw ore as was possible, had been calcined; from then on a new set of accounts must have been prepared for calcined ore only, which regrettably appears to be no longer extant.

* * * * * * *

Although the commencement of the Liverpool smelter on 1st January 1768 had seen an appreciable decline of copper ore consignments to Macclesfield along the River Weaver, yet it was not until the Toxteth smelters were fully operational that these cargoes finally came to an end. After the occasional freights of 1772 a final 20 tons is recorded on 13th December 1773. This ore was obviously needed to complete the smelting of the remaining stocks of copper ore on the Macclesfield Common site, the greater part of which would have been purchased from Ecton Mine until the year 1771.

Had it been economical and convenient to continue full smelting operations at Macclesfield then there is little doubt that the company would have done so. The chain of circumstances, however, appears to have reduced operations to refining only, which conveniently coincides with the formation of the new partnership in August 1774.

In the first place local coal supplies had become a problem. The sparsity of coal deposits on Macclesfield Common had been referred to in the original petition for the Macclesfield canal scheme, when great emphasis had been made of the ability to supply Macclesfield with coal from the collieries of Norbury, Poynton and Worth. By 1771 the situation was critical and on 27th February Charles Roe had written to Richard Orford, Steward to the Leghs of Lyme, stating that an agreement had been made with Mr. Venables to take one half of coals from the Sponds Colliery, which was apparently leased from Peter Legh. The agreement was for 11 years for which Charles had requested an extension.

Secondly, Robert Shore, the Devonshire agent at Ecton copper mine, was faced with a very complicated situation. After the death of the 4th Duke in 1764 two sets of accounts had to be legally prepared, one for the Guardians of the Duke's son and heir (who was still a minor), the other for the Trustees of the younger sons, who were entitled to payments from their father's estate.

The profit from mining was divided up as the year progressed and Robert Shore pointed out on one occasion to the auditor, the profits for the first six months of 1766 were easily wiped out by a particularly high expenditure at the Ecton Mine. However, with further sales of ore still to be made he hoped for a substantial profit by the end of the year. The auditor was Godfrey Heathcote, a Chesterfield solicitor, who had the considerable responsibility for all legal and many other administrative matters relating to the estate.

In 1764, shortly after the 4th Duke's death Shore had charged a sum of £1.090 16s 9d. expenses to both the Guardians' and Trustees' accounts, which went unnoticed for some considerable time. Whether or not this was initially a deliberate attempt of fraud on the part of Robert Shore may never be known, but his accounts are very difficult to reconcile. He must have pleaded that it was an error, which was apparently accepted. But the Trustees were in a position to argue that the sum could have been invested and accruing interest, and where was the money?

Whatever his shortcomings Shore literally paid for them. Together with an initial cash payment of £90 16 9d. he was forced to obtain a loan of £1,000 @ 3% interest with guaranteed annual repayments. In the event he was allowed to continue in what he would consider to be a prestigious position, and was extremely lucky not to have been sued by the estate.

On 30th May 1768 Samuel Roe, 18 years of age and acting as Company Secretary, wrote in a delightful flourishing hand to Robert Shore. Obviously mindful of his newly acquired post he began "Mr. Shore!" "Sir!". The request, which has the hallmark of Charles Roe's dictate, was for the copper ore at Ecton to be weighed in parcels of 30 or 40 tons each, keeping the lots for the different companies separate and then sampled. "This is done in Cornwall & wou'd be the most pleas'y Method to us in respt to Ecton Ore".

Shore sent this letter to Mr. Heathcote in Chesterfield with his own recommendation that the request be refused on economic grounds, pointing out the necessity of requiring more time, effort, space and buildings, should it be accepted by the Guardians. Without doubt this request was refused, for the young Duke would attain his majority the following year and had already formed his own plans for organising his affairs. During the previous year, in June 1767, one of the Duke's uncles and guardians, George Cavendish, had been approached by no less a person than the Governor of the Company of Copper Mines in England, who was considering sending an agent to one of the Ecton ore sales. He had hinted at a deal to their "mutual advantage", which George Cavendish felt merited further enquiry.

On 25th January 1769 an anxious letter was addressed to Mr. Heathcote by Robert Hurst, one of Thomas Patten's partners from their Cheadle works in Staffordshire. It had come to his notice that a new smelter was soon to be established in the area, and it had been suggested, much to his surprise, that the Duke and his agents were the proposers. He pointed out that the Cheadle Company had been located for the 'sole' purpose of purchasing Ecton ores, which they had faithfully done, to the considerable benefit of the Duke. Mr. Hurst had endeavoured to find out the truth from other sources, as the Cheadle Company stood to lose a great deal of money, but had been unable to do so. He was anxious for clarification of the rumours, which he refused to believe until he had received Mr. Heathcote's answer.

A smelting furnace had actually been constructed at Ecton in 1767, to accompany a calciner of 1764. From 1770 William, 5th Duke of Devonshire, did smelt all his own ores and by 1772 there were 12 men employed as smelters at Whiston near to Cheadle in Staffordshire.

Considering the close affinity between the Macclesfield and Cheadle works, the pending 'sword of Damocles' must have been discussed between them. This would, of course, have put further pressure on Charles Roe, who at that time was having problems with the location of the Liverpool smelters.

Mr. Heathcote's reaction is not known but he was carrying out an audit of the Ecton accounts and had apparently written to Roe & Co. asking for details of ore purchases and prices paid. Having received no answer he asked Robert Shore to obtain a reply, which to modern eyes would seem an odd action to take, as apparently suspicions of further fraud were now coming to light.

On 5th February 1769 Shore wrote to Heathcote from his house at Snitterton stating that he had sent a "special Mefsinger" to Macclesfield and the reply received was enclosed. This time Samuel was acting alone, reflected in the less formal style of his letter. He wrote that his father and Mr. Hodgson had left for Liverpool that morning but were expected back "on Saturday - when you may expect a Lr.[letter] from them". Feeling obliged to offer some sort of rationale for their inattentiveness he continued in a somewhat amusingly adolescent vein "I carn't think that Mr. Heathcote was refus'd . . . I dare say they had forgotten it."

After the considerable ore purchases of previous years by the Macclesfield company, the 1968 total for Ecton ore was only £493 4 0d. but the arrears had been cleared by bills to be drawn on certain dates in London. Several of these bills were to be drawn on cousin Christopher Roe, who was still acting as a banker for the company at that time. But, at the beginning of 1769, a sum of £3,461 12 9d. appears in the accounts as arrears, which suggests that insufficient money was deposited with Christopher Roe when the bills were presented for payment. The situation was on occasion alleviated by bills drawn on Edward Pitts.

Roe & Co. were not the only partnership in arrears, Patten & Co. owed £2,475 14 6d. whilst Cooper & Co. had an outstanding £4,353 7 10d. Roe & Co. were bidding for the better grade ores and coarse copper whilst Patten & Co. were receiving mostly waste (the latter when processed would, of course, yield copper of equal quality). When the Roe & Co. figures were submitted (see appendix for details) they show the total tonnage purchased from 1762 to 1768 as 1,790, cost £27,235.

By 1770 the Roe partnership had made great efforts to settle the arrears; cousin Christopher was relieved of what must have been a considerable burden, as the banking affairs were put on a firm basis by the engagement of the bankers, Welch Rogers & Co. (abbreviated to Welch & Co.) in London. A letter addressed to Mr. Shore on 18th May 1771 hints at the financial difficulties of that period by being obliged for "a litle indulgence at this time & if we exceed the time we have no objections to allowing you Interest".

The final regular purchase of Ecton ore was 94 tons on 30th August 1771, value £1,598. As Roe & Co. had agreed to interest payments if necessary with Robert Shore, these appear to have been included in the final settlement made by Welch & Co. in two instalments, £537 drawn 14th October and £1250 drawn 3rd November.

Taking into consideration the rumours regarding the availability of Ecton ore purchases and the not too happy relationship regarding methods used, the successful relocation of the smelters from Liverpool to Toxteth by 1772 and the progress on Parys Mountain, the time had conveniently arrived, as mentioned previously, to wind down smelting operations on Macclesfield Common to refining only and look to the expansion of the brass works.

* * * * * * *

There is one further letter from the office of Godfrey Heathcote which deserves notice, if only for its illuminating glimpse of the period and confirmation of the larger-than-life character of Brian Hodgson Snr.

Initially the letter was addressed to "His Grace the Duke of Devonshire" from Trallee in Ireland on 30th November 1768. The young Duke William, at 20 years of age was still a minor therefore, whatever his thoughts on the matter, the letter was redirected to the Chesterfield solicitor presumably for the ultimate attention of the Guardians. It was written by young Job Gibbons whose mother, Mary, was sister to Brian Hodgson's wife.

Job reveals, by a brief résumé of his life, that he had attended "Sheffield free school" where he gained an excellent knowledge of mathematics. During his subsequent apprenticeship his name appeared in the *Gentleman's diary for the year 1763*, having been able to solve several mathematical problems. After serving his apprenticeship, his desire for travel encouraged him to enlist in "Collonel Haylers regiment of light Horse" in which he had served four years. In January 1768 the troops were in Tallow, County Waterford where he met and married the daughter of a tanner, a clever girl "of good character a protestant".

Shortly before writing, his wife had given birth, but on his small amount of army pay Job found it difficult to maintain them. His father-in-law had promised assistance, enabling Job to purchase his discharge by paying £10 into the stockpurse.

Job, obviously anxious for better things, was petitioning for work in the Revenue as a gauger. (Gaugers were excisemen who had the responsibility of determining by measurement the capacity of vessels or containers, and the amounts they contained, a position for which Job was suitably qualified.) The well written letter to the Duke is punctuated by sentences of heart-rending appeal:

> "I have not a friend in the world That I would get to petition Your Grace but Mr Hodgson or his son Brian Who keeps the bath now, & as I have disoblig'd them by Inlisting & being Wild as it is term'd in England if a young man inlists, although I have wrote to them, they have not sent me an answer . . ."

What happened to Job is unknown, but his mother, a widow, was later living in Windsor where there was a large military establishment, which does suggest that he attained promotion in the army. One can only imagine Brian Hodgson's anger had he learnt of the letter, as indicated by Job's penultimate plea, "I beg Your Grace wont let Mr. Hodgson know that I was so bold to write To You, as I am fearful of his displeasure . . ."

* * * * * * *

Despite all the financial and business aggravations of the early 1770s Charles Roe still found time for social, religious and family matters.

On 22nd January 1770 son, Robert, had entered Manchester Grammar School, followed by nephew, James, on 4th October 1771, son of his deceased brother. This was in preparation for their eventual matriculation at Brasenose College, Oxford in anticipation of their future careers as clergymen of the Church of England.

Manchester seemed to encourage a love of social activities, for whenever Robert returned home to Macclesfield he attended "nightly dancings with the young people of the town". James too led a very full social life, much to the detriment of his mother's finances as acknowledged by sister, Hester, when she later wrote . . . "I reflected how much had been expended on my poor extravagant Bro'[ther]."

Hester and her mother spent most of the summer months at Adlington Hall where she was a particular favourite of her godmother, the wife of Charles Legh. There she was encouraged to mix in 'high society' and dress "in A manner suitable to such Company". There seems little doubt that other members of the Roe family attended the gatherings, which included musical evenings, playing cards, assemblies and balls.

Although travelling and company business must have taken up a considerable proportion of Charles Roe's everyday life, yet he and wife, Rachel, made time for social visits to the Jebb family in Chesterfield. During 1771, when involved in negotiating with Peter Legh the younger of Lyme regarding coal leases, which required assurances that the Legh "pleasure Roads" would not be spoilt, the implied apology for the delay was that "Mrs. Roe and I were detained longer yn [than] intended" in Chesterfield.

It seems probable that this particular visit to Chesterfield also included business dealings with the solicitor, Godfrey Heathcote, regarding the termination of Ecton ore purchases and the final settlement from Welch & Co. There is also a suggestion that the Jebb family connections were significant in the discussion of religious matters, and especially Charles Roe's turn of thinking.

There is no doubt that Charles was a religious man. His father's orthodoxy, even to the extent of entering the Latin names for each of his children in the Castleton registers, is very evident, yet his mother's family had within its ranks those who appear to have had some sympathy with the Puritan cause of the previous century. Charles had obviously absorbed the effects of all the different points of view during his early impressionable years, and drawn his own conclusions. The undeniable influences of his elder brothers, William and James, had encouraged a "right of centre" attitude in his approach to religious matters. Charles could never deny the Sovereign's position as Head of the Church of England, nor the principles and rituals to which he had been accustomed, but he did see the influence that personalities such as John Wesley were exerting, and recognised the need for some reform and easier understanding of the Scriptures amongst the rapidly increasing population.

His passion for music also entered the equation and he must have taken into consideration the charge of Methodism made against any Evangelical clergyman who was successful in "crowding his Church", encouraging hymn singing and speaking with "Communicants at the Sacrament".

After the death of his brother James, Charles appears to have been quite happy with his replacement, John Burscoe, licensed as Prime Curate of St. Michael's on 19th June 1765. The nomination was always at the behest of the Mayor (who in that year happened to be Harry Lankford) and the concurrence of the Bishop of Chester.

Rev. Burscoe was a 'local ' man, from Wybunbury in Cheshire and graduate of Brasenose College, Oxford. There is no record or intimation of any discords during his ministry, and when the position of Assistant Curate became vacant, due to Peter Mayer's acceptance as Vicar of Prestbury, Charles decided to use his influence in the question of a replacement. One can only assume that he discussed the matter with the Jebbs, from which an important recommendation was made.

Samuel Jebb's cousin, related to Charles Roe's wife, Rachel, through marriage, was an extremely well educated man. Born in London 1736 and named after his father, Dr. John Jebb, he completed his grammar school education at Chesterfield and then attended the University of Dublin in 1753 before admittance to St. Peter's College, Cambridge on 9th November 1754. Two years later a severe illness took him to Bath for recovery, after which he returned to university and successfully gained a Master of Arts and then Fellowship (1st. July 1761).

The following year John Jebb was ordained deacon at Buckden and admitted into priest's orders on 25th September 1763. During the winter of 1770 he published his *Short account of theological lectures w*hich was well received, but a certain faction had already stirred up trouble by deliberately misunderstanding them at their original presentation, and took offence, labelling him a "protestant christian".

Five years earlier his philosophical publication *Excerpta Quaedam E Newton I* had amongst the list of its subscribers the Rt. Hon. Lord Grey of Dunham Massey, members of the Denman family of Derbyshire and other Jebb family members, the Rt. Hon. Countess of Stamford, members of mining families such as Morewood and Parry, his dear friend the late Rev. William Unwin M.A. and significantly Rev. Mr. Porteus M.A. late Fellow of Christ College, Cambridge. Evidently Beilby Porteus was empathetically inclined to support John Jebb's theological premiss, and Charles Roe must have been aware of this.

During the early 1770s John Jebb was busy at Cambridge, helping to lay the foundations for university reform. Many debates took place, but despite his liberal views he was the one who, from 1773, fought hard to establish annual examinations within the university. It was through one of Jebb's associates, Rev. Lindsay, that an impressionable young man was introduced to him.

* * * * * * *

David Simpson, from the village of Ingleby Arncliffe near Northallerton in Yorkshire, close to the copper mines of Middleton Tyas, had at last found his vocation. His father, Ralph, held the important position of farm bailiff which enabled him to provide adequately for his family of seven children, comprising five daughters and two sons.

Young David had begun his education with Mr. Dawson, a clergyman of Northallerton, but after 12 months was admitted to Scorton Grammar School just three miles south of Middleton Tyas where he was one of eighty pupils under the headship of Rev. John Noble. He was a good mathematician yet from this early age became interested in religious teachings. From October 1765 he attended St. John's College, Cambridge until he gained his degree in 1769.

Whilst at Cambridge he was drawn into many controversies and almost became a Calvinist. This evidently stemmed from his conviction that he had been called to do God's service, supported by the Calvinistic belief that a person's destiny is preordained and nothing can alter it. However, a mathematical brain can often be at a disadvantage, particularly when dealing with human nature and in that respect David Simpson would show a profound naivety at times.

After his ordination by the Bishop of London, Rev. Simpson became curate of Ramsden Bellhouse in Essex, assisting his very good friend, William Unwin, rector of Grimston near King's Lynn and great ally of Dr. John Jebb. The area was described as "bleak, flat and unhealthy" with much river and canal traffic, as the roads were in great need of repair.

In spite of the fact David Simpson made quite an impression on the local farming community, yet he remained for only one year. His departure in 1771 was inexplicable, even to himself, and initially proved detrimental. His move to Buckingham, a more prosperous parish of lace manufacturers, was to assist an old and infirmed man, Rev. Thomas Price. Perhaps he saw an opportunity for reinspiring the local populace with his fire and determination but if so he had greatly miscalculated. Whilst the Simpson sermons had 'washed over' the agricultural community of Ramsden Bellhouse, the same sermons promoted outrage in the new parish, resulting in a request that the Bishop withdraw his licence.

Bishop Green, a well-known outspoken opponent of the practice of Methodism, at this time was somewhat constrained, obviously bearing in mind the comment of Thomas Secker, then Archbishop of Canterbury, that Methodists were a "well meaning sort of people". His brusque audience with Simpson resulted in the admonition, "If, Sir, you are determined to do your duty, as a clergyman aught to do, you must everywhere expect to meet with opposition."

Meanwhile, judging from later events, Charles Roe seemed determined to find a suitable candidate to assist John Burscoe at St. Michael's and was obviously making enquiries; that David Simpson's name was suggested initially by the Jebbs, is very evident. It also seems possible Charles would have made further enquiries regarding Simpson through his cousin, Rev. Samuel Roe, vicar of Stotfold in Bedfordshire (from 1754) and only 30 miles from Buckingham. Certainly the controversy was widespread and Samuel would have been well aware of the gossip within neighbouring parishes.

Charles could not directly nominate David Simpson for the position of Assistant Curate at St. Michael's, only encourage the choice. Even so he did appreciate that a personal approach was necessary and so invited the young man to visit Macclesfield.

Simpson's friends were already busy on his behalf; one had suggested his name to the eccentric Lady Huntingdon as someone sympathetic to the Calvinist cause; her offer he declined, accepting instead Charles Roe's invitation to be a guest of the Roe family, and accordingly arrived at the Chestergate home in June 1772.

Having satisfied himself as to the suitability of Rev. Simpson, Charles in his inimitable way made certain that there would be no ambiguity as regards the legalities and outcome of this particular man becoming Assistant Curate at St. Michael's. Obviously John Burscoe was also involved in the decision making, and if the entry in the Bishop's Act Books is to be believed, so were many more residents.

On 2nd October 1772 Charles had, of course, been elected a capital burgess and at the same time James Rowson was chosen for mayor. One week later David Simpson was admitted as a burgess 'ex gratia' (i.e. without having to pay a fee) as also was John Dickenson Esq. of Taxall (related to Legh Dickenson, the Roe agent in Cornwall).

Within two weeks David Simpson was granted his licence. The entry recorded by the Bishop's clerk at Chester on 15th October reads "at the Nomination of John Burscoe Cl. the Prime Minister the Wardens and principal Inhabitants of the Town".

This was the period of Charles Roe's illness and strange to relate soon afterwards David Simpson also fell seriously ill. He was betrothed to Miss Ann Waldy of Yarm in Yorkshire, but as a consequence of his infirmity had to postpone the marriage until Charles Roe's wife, Rachel, had nursed him back to health.

The mysterious illness continued to work its way through town, as though determined to change the course of Macclesfield history, for in at least two other instances it would prove fatal. By February 1773 John Burscoe was dead and buried, leaving David Simpson temporarily in charge of the Parochial Chapel.

Young Robert Roe, returning home from Manchester for the Whitsuntide holidays, discovered a very different scene from when he left and later expressed himself as being full of "grief and amazement" to find that David Simpson "had turned all things upside down". Whilst admitting Mr. Simpson seemed a candid pious man, yet his influence in the Roe household was such that assemblies and the like were now considered "trifling amusements" and the children forbidden to attend, which brought forth the observation from Robert that his sisters "were as grave as old women". He rebelled; his own mother, who had been an exemplary Christian and Methodist at heart, had adored him and led him to believe that he was a devout son, so the present persecution seemed unjustified.

Hester too, whilst spending the summer at Adlington Hall with her mother, heard the gossip relating to the 'Methodist' minister her uncle had brought to the town, and of his preachings directed against all her "favourite diversions". Her own father's aversion to Methodism had cultivated a similar prejudice within her, and she vowed never to be 'converted'. On returning home, like Robert before her, she would find Macclesfield "in an alarm" and determined not to hear David Simpson preach. But, with assurances from Uncle Roe and some of her cousins that he was an excellent man, Hester would shortly relent.

Robert was not the only one to find David Simpson's moralizations too oppressive; soon complaints began in many quarters. Yet in spite of this, every Sunday David Simpson addressed a congregation which filled St. Michael's Chapel, giving him much encouragement and support.

The Simpson marriage took place on 27th May, after which the couple accepted accommodation offered in the Roe household until their own house was ready for occupation during the following September. It must have been built on Charles Roe's land for it "stood almost next, in the street fronting the fields, an attraction to the bride who had a love for the open country". And although Rachel Roe had appeared to approve of David Simpson's choice of bride, yet Ann Simpson expressed her unease in a letter to relatives when she wrote that Mrs. Roe seemed slightly prejudiced against Methodists. Ann was the niece of Edward Waldy who happened to be a great friend of Rev. John Wesley. Even so Rachel never faltered in showing kindness or giving generous assistance to the young couple.

It seems strange that Charles Roe should have abruptly and suddenly become extremely and obsessively concerned with the morality of others. The aftermath of his illness must have been partly to blame, as he and David Simpson would have considered themselves very lucky to have survived. The Wesleyan principles of penitence and self denial seem to have come into play, whilst Charles, guided by David Simpson, struggled with his conscience. It must have occurred to him that the wealth and prosperity which he was helping to create, were not only being used to improve some people's lives but at the same time encouraging greed and deception in others.

With John Burscoe's death it seemed an almost foregone conclusion that David Simpson would take his place as Prime Curate of St. Michael's, which is obviously what Charles Roe intended. Even if there was opposition to his sermons, Simpson was so confident of his ability to succeed to the post that he had already approached a friend to consider becoming Assistant Curate in his place.

Now begins an extraordinary and abtruse sequence of events, not helped by the fact that there is an uncanny dearth of information both in the Corporation records and those of St. Michael's.

Once again recorded at Chester, but on 17th June 1773, an entry in the Bishop's Act Books confirms the granting of a licence to Thomas Hewson Clerk "to the Chapel of Macclesfield Co. Chester", however the name of the nominator is left blank.

There was an arrangement whereby both the Bishop of Chester and Mayor of Macclesfield had to approve the appointment. In the past it would appear that the candidate chosen by the Mayor and Corporation of Macclesfield had met with the Bishop's concurrence. This time, however, it is apparent that the higher authority had taken the matter in hand without consultation.

Thomas Hewson does not appear as an entrant to either Oxford or Cambridge university, which is very unusual, the records being fairly comprehensive at that period. However, the Hewson or Hughson family were established in Frodsham and Chester, and Thomas was possibly the child baptised at Chester Cathedral on 10th March 1740. Two earlier family members had attended Brasenose College, Oxford, so the Macclesfield connection was there. It has been suggested that Thomas could have been a chorister of Chester Cathedral and as a consequence obtained his Ordination.

Considering all the known facts, it does seem that the Bishop of Chester was conferring a favour on someone he knew well, rather than deliberately excluding David Simpson. In the event there was nothing Charles Roe, James Rowson or anyone else could do, except that James Rowson appears to have withheld his name as nominator.

David Simpson, therefore, remained as Assistant Curate at St. Michael's, unaware of the difficulties ahead. During the summer of 1773 Charles, of course, was very much involved with affairs in Liverpool, and as the Simpsons moved into their new home he was busy with the developments on the Toxteth Park site.

Another question now begs an answer: unusual though it may seem, in order to encourage the acceptance of David Simpson as Prime Curate, had Charles Roe made some sort of offer to the Corporation regarding a burial ground?

20
TRAGEDY AND TRIUMPH

The stone which the builders refused
is become the head stone of the corner.

Before the founding of the Parochial Chapel in 1278 the inhabitants of Macclesfield had been buried in the graveyard of the Church of Prestbury. The construction of the Macclesfield chapel allowed for burials to take place within the building until 1686. The most influential residents could choose their special site before a particular altar, paying a mortuary fee to the priest and, in some instances, establishing a chantry. Bones of other residents were retrieved from graves and housed in an adjoining charnel house when space was required for further burials.

By 1686 the crowded vaults and facilities of the chapel could no longer accommodate further bodies and a petition was organised. As the Bishopric of Chester was vacant from mid-July to mid-October 1686, the request became the responsibility of the Archbishop of York. But the Archbishopric of York was also vacant and so Dr. Tobias Wickham, Dean of York, was the one who granted a licence permitting burials to take place outside the chapel, in an area "conveniently contiguous" (sic) and already fenced out. Translated from the Latin it was referred to as the old school or church garden.

By the mid-18th century this plot of land had almost reached 'saturation point' and the powers that be were experiencing considerable difficulty in deciding what to do next. Whatever happened it would involve considerable expense and would have to be paid for by some means of raising revenue. There was also the problem of finding a suitable plot of land and its availability.

Perhaps John Burscoe's burial in February 1773 finally brought matters to a head and presented Charles Roe with an ideal opportunity to exert his influence. In one particular part of his lower field, close by the Dams Brook, was an area called 'The Marled Bank', aptly named because of its clay content and the ideal constituent for burial grounds. From the very outset of his plans Charles intended building a chapel on site, if only for the convenience of burials.

A survey was an absolute necessity, and after completion the documentation was vested with Macclesfield Corporation, a copy of which was later kept by Peter Wright, Town Clerk (a possible son or relative of Samuel Wright of Nether Knutsford). This solicitor's copy is unfortunately without its drawings and the Corporation manuscripts cannot be traced, so the name of the individual who carried out the survey is unknown.

The identity of the surveyor, who would also be author of the architectural drawings, is intriguing. One school of thought favours Joseph Pickford as he was closely associated with the painter Joseph Wright of Derby, but the reason given, that Freemasonry was the binding element, certainly does not apply to Charles Roe, in fact quite the reverse. Thorough research has failed to reveal any membership of any Lodges by any of the copper company partners.

Freemasonry was still in its infancy at the beginning of the 18th century and seemed to attract those who, although having a strong sense of fellowship and justice in one way or another, were, to a certain degree, outcasts of the Establishment and frowned upon for their outlandish activities e.g. compounding scientific theories or becoming members of illicit clubs such as 'The Hell Fire Club' of West Wycombe. Even the great Benjamin Franklyn was later to be found amongst such company.

Military lodges were of prime importance, where officers and men met on equal terms and the camaraderie was at its most prolific. However, when recalling the antics of Sir Peter Davenport, or the clandestine activities of Josiah Wedgwood and his associates with regard to the canal scheme, Charles Roe, Brian Hodgson and company would hardly have welcomed an association with these societies. In any event their religious principles would have been a barrier against such immature rituals.

It was a well-known fact that most 18th century architects were members of the Society, because it was almost impossible for them to succeed otherwise, but obviously it did not follow that their clientele were all Freemasons. From 1768 onwards many of Charles Roe's ideas and materials came from Liverpool, and it is worth considering his associations in that city as an indicator for what transpired.

Following John Walker's death it must have been a difficult task for William Roe to extend business affiliations in the port, although greatly aided by Thomas Smyth and his own staunch and very mature personality. There was a group of Liverpool merchants with family roots in and around Warrington, and these are the ones who appear to have extended a helping hand, no doubt supported by Thomas Patten who was never a rival but a partner on the national 'stage'.

John Stafford's support is also evident, as it does seem that after he and family members had been sitters for Wright of Derby in 1769, during a visit to Liverpool, it was his persuasion which had encouraged Charles Roe to stay still long enough for his portrait to be captured on canvas. Certainly the Stafford cravat, coat and waistcoat appear in both portraits, so the introduction of Charles Roe by John Stafford to Joseph Wright is a fair conclusion.

Although the founding of the Royal Academy of Arts had taken place towards the end of 1768 Wright, supported by friends including artists such as Stubbs and Romney, continued to exhibit at the Incorporated Society of Artists in London for some time. Included in the group was another close friend and possibly kinsman from Derby, Peter Perez Burdett.

Burdett was a true genius and circumstantial evidence also suggests kinship with Sir Robert Burdett of Foremark Hall, Derbyshire. He was primarily a mathematician, with an intense interest in science and technology, yet he was endowed with considerable artistic talent and part of a musical group formed in Derby, in which Joseph Wright sang and played the flute, whilst he was master of the cello. He had a keen eye and his perspective was particularly brilliant. It is known that he provided Wright with drawings of technical subjects to include in paintings, as seen in 'The Alchemist'.

It seemed as though Burdett's talents were limitless, for he also achieved acknowledgement as a remarkable surveyor and engineer. He took on the colossal task of surveying and producing a map of Derbyshire, after considering a prize of "not exceeding one hundred Pounds", offered by the 'Society for the Encouragement of Arts, Manufactures and Commerce' in 1762, to promote publication of more detailed and accurate county maps.

The onerous task, with assistance, took from 1762 to 1767, but Burdett could never have calculated the enormity of the expenditure in spite of receiving the full prize of £100, for he was repeatedly in and out of debt. Together with his wife, and about the same time as Joseph Wright, he moved to Liverpool in 1769 and was almost immediately elected first President of the Liverpool Society of Artists. There he lectured on perspective and the art of design, sharing the course with, amongst others, the well-known architect, William Everard. Other members of the Society included John and Charles Eyes, architects, the former responsible for the 1768 map of Liverpool, and John Wyke watchmaker.

Perhaps feeling encouraged by a greater support in Liverpool than Derby, Burdett set about organising a survey of Lancashire with the intention of producing another county map, but lack of sponsorship and a tour of France in 1771 saw the project abandoned. On returning from France he spent the next two or three years producing some of the finest aquatints seen in England which were exhibited at the Society of Artists in London.

As a consequence Burdett also undertook drawings to be reproduced as decoration on Josiah Wedgwood's pottery and experimented by engraving the copper plates himself. Partly by rejection and partly by complaints of exorbitant fees, Josiah Wedgwood dispensed with Burdett's services, which infuriated the latter and led to much bitter correspondence between the two.

Meanwhile Burdett had surveyed a route for the Liverpool promoters of the Leeds and Liverpool canal (1769), surveyed and published a Chart of the Harbour of Liverpool (1771) and in association with Thomas Boydell, compiled details and a plan of the land and premises belonging to the River Dee Company between the City of Chester and the towns of Flint and Parkgate (1772).

Taking into consideration the Cheshire influence in the port of Liverpool, it is not surprising that Burdett was persuaded to undertake a survey of the county as a natural progression from the River Dee plan. His Derbyshire map had been engraved in the London workshop of Thomas Kitchen, and would have cost him dearly, but now he seemed intent on engraving the Cheshire map himself.

In 1774 Burdett was living at 39 Old Hall St. Liverpool, situated only two blocks away from St. Paul's Church. The church was relatively new, having been built in the years 1765 to 1769 of yellow sandstone which was considered by some to mar its appearance. Its lofty dome and columns seemed to ape its magnificent namesake in the City of London yet, set in its own fashionable square, for some reason it was never very popular. Initially, however, it was patronised by several members of the Liverpool Society of Artists.

It is significant that amongst the congregation was Samuel Shaw, purchaser of a lease from the Corporation for three pews in the North Gallery, commencing on 31st July 1769 for 2,000 years. He was William Roe's future father-in-law.

Another pew owner, John Wyke, together with a partner, had a large warehouse in Wyke's Court, Dale Street. There they not only produced a great variety of clocks and watches, but supplied other clock and watch makers with parts and also jewellers, braziers and mechanics; this included files, tools and a variety of other items. There seems little doubt that William Roe, still resident in Cable Street, and presumably maintaining the warehousing facilities in Hanover Street, as John Walker's widow had taken over the lease, must have been a supplier of their brass and copper.

Another contributor to St. Paul's, John Okill, a very wealthy timber merchant and closely related to Samuel Shaw, chose as an Executor for his will, Thomas Boydell, associate of Peter Perez Burdett for the River Dee survey. By the early 1770s, therefore, Burdett was intimately involved with this group of merchants.

About this time Burdett, with assistants, began surveying in earnest for his map of Cheshire and one suspects that he personally undertook work in and around the area of Macclesfield. His fascination with 'modern technology' must surely have guaranteed his presence on site at the important Roe copper and brass works. He accurately sited the Old King's Mill on Mill Green and the Roe windmill on the Common and correctly drew attention to the 'FORGE' at Bosley. Modern criticism suggests that the latter is incorrect, inferring an iron forge, but Burdett was correct, for a forge was a workshop containing a fire or hearth for melting any form of metal.

The inclusion of the symbol for the Macclesfield windmill indicates that the survey was carried out after its construction during the early months of 1772. If Burdett was in the area at that time then surely this would have been seen by Charles Roe as a perfect opportunity to make use of his talents. Also Burdett had fallen out with Wedgwood, no doubt a redeeming factor so far as Charles Roe was concerned, and would be in need of copper plates, which were expensive items, on which to engrave his map, Charles Roe was not averse to considering payments in kind, as an expedient, if all parties were in agreement. At a later date Vivian, the great copper master of Cornwall and subsequently South Wales, owed money for copper to Roe & Co., so he was asked to send a consignment of tin to the value of the copper – a metal needed for lining copper vessels in order to prevent poisoning.

The survey of the Roe land appears to have been completed during the spring of 1773. By 17th June, of course, Thomas Hewson was installed as Prime Curate of St. Michael's and Charles, by that date deeply committed, went ahead with the legalities for the graveyard.

By Indentures of 20th and 21st July 1773, between firstly, Charles Roe, secondly Samuel Glover of Macclesfield and John Birtles of Sutton, wardens of St. Michael's Parochial Chapel and thirdly the Mayor, Aldermen & Burgesses of Macclesfield, Charles "granted bargained sold" a piece of land "lately inclosed out of a certain Field in Macclesfield called The Marled Bank", measuring from east to west 80 yards and in breadth north to south 70 yards. Free access was guaranteed by way of a cart road through another of his adjoining fields called Fair Steads.

The deed of 21st July makes clear the necessity for the additional burial ground "by reason of the great Increase of the Inhabitants" and affirms that Charles Roe "at the instance" of the Chapel Wardens and other inhabitants "hath agreed to vest in and convey to the said Mayor, Aldermen & Burgesses" that part of the Marled Bank measuring 70 yards x 80 yards which had already been staked out. (This measurement was taken from what is today the corner of Bridge Street with Great King Street).

To facilitate payment by the Corporation the agreement was that Charles gave a quarter of the whole area i.e. the northern quarter, for the burials of poor people free of charge. Out of the remaining area he was to be allowed a site on which to build an "Oratory or Chapel for the hearing of Divine Service according to the Rite and Ceremonies of the Church of England." The remaining area was divided into plots 8 ft by 5 ft which Charles or his heirs were allowed to sell at "not exceeding " two guineas each. In this way Charles was given monetary recompense for providing the Corporation with the burial ground. In the event he allowed sale of the plots for £1 11 6d. a considerable saving to the purchaser of at least £55 by today's values, and it was not until January 1780 that the price was raised to £2 2s.

Obviously access would have to be provided for horses, carriages and hearse and it is possible from information on site to speculate as to the original intended layout, including the carriageways.

From east to west 23 rows of 28 graves per row were excavated, lined with bricks and whitewashed; a professional job, no doubt completed by a team of miners. The rows were lettered A to Z as in the Roman alphabet, so I and J were the same, as were U and V. Having run out of letters the final row was added as ZZ. None of the plots L and M were ever sold, allowing for a carriageway of 16 ft in width running from north to south (which remains in situ, but narrower by some 3 ft). This arrangement indicates an original plan of ten rows on the eastern part of the graveyard and thirteen on the west. No carriage way was laid on the western side, only a path of one grave in width i.e. 8 ft, so taking into consideration the width of 80 yards or 240 ft overall, the remaining 32 ft must have been intended for a broad carriageway along the eastern side. From the boundary of the paupers' plot at the northern end, the 28 rows of graves were laid towards the southern end, leaving a carriageway of 17½ ft along the south side.

The deed stipulates that within 12 months Charles Roe must build a brick wall and gate to enclose the cemetery, which seems to indicate only one entrance/exit. Carriages and horses were difficult to manoeuvre, but if the entrance was from the north and along the 16 ft wide carriageway, it would be possible to turn left at the southern end and then left again into the 32 ft wide carriage way. The extra width on this eastern side would then have been sufficient to turn a procession of horses and carriages headed by a horse-drawn hearse, enabling them to exit along the same route by which they had entered.

Consideration can now be given to the intended site and size of the oratory or chapel. An oratory was a very small building usually containing one large room only. Presumably its size would conveniently cover multiples of graves, which would suggest dimensions in the ratio of 8:5, referred to in the world of Greek classical architecture as the 'Golden Section' and beautifully illustrated by the Parthenon on the Acropolis in Athens.

Initially Charles Roe claimed six plots for his family vault viz. 10, 11 and 12 of rows N and O, which presumably were intended to be next to or near the chapel. If the chapel was to cover an area of seven rows each way viz. 13 to 17 (incl.) of rows N to T (incl.) then together with the Roe vault it would have been in the middle of the western side of the 16 ft wide carriageway, excluding the pauper ground. This would also mean that in length the chapel would have been exactly half of the width of the western section, thus measuring 56 ft in length and 35 ft in width. These dimensions are important in determining what happened later. For someone with a good sound basic knowledge of architecture the plan for such a chapel would have been comparatively easy, and Peter Perez Burdett was such a person.

Dr. William Enfield, at one time a Dissenting minister in Liverpool until he moved to the Warrington Academy in 1770, had inherited a collection of notes and information intended for a history of the city. He completed the work (publication date 1774) with assistance from several contributors including Burdett. Burdett produced eight illustrations of Liverpool churches, including those of St. Paul, St. Thomas, St. Peter and the old Parish Church of St. Nicholas. His accompanying comments drew a significant acknowledgement from Dr. Enfield, "For the preceding remarks on Architecture of the Public Structures, the Editor is indebted to the ingenious Mr. Burdett".

Assuming that Burdett had carried out the survey for Charles Roe, it is possible, of course, that an architect such as William Everard or John and Charles Eyes could have drawn the plan for the chapel, but further consequential facts do seem to favour Burdett as both surveyor and architect.

During 1774 Burdett appears to have become thoroughly disillusioned with the lack of support from members of the British brotherhood, some of whom were evidently using his talents for their benefit without due credit. Heavily in debt he accepted an invitation to the Court of the Margrave of Baden (Germany) and by January 1775 was part of an official military topographical survey team in the post of geographical engineer. He was soon to attain the rank of Major and receive just reward for his work, becoming a master in an important architectural drawing school. The year 1784 would see a new market place planned for Karlsruhe comprising a church, vicarage, town hall, prince's school and other public buildings. Although several prominent architects were to be involved in the scheme, Burdett was consulted about the overall planning, and gave advice as to the height and length of various structures. Not until 1797 was the chosen architect, Weinbrenner, given authority to proceed, but did complain that Burdett's plans were "too monotonous". Burdett, however, was no longer present to hear the criticism, he had been taken ill and died during 1793; his final resting place, the cemetery of Karlsruhe.

Meanwhile, returning to the Macclesfield cemetery, hardly had excavations begun for the new burial ground when, as previously mentioned, Rowland Atkinson, headmaster of the Grammar School and Charles Roe's brother-in-law, died suddenly. The epidemic sweeping through the town had claimed yet another life, and ironically, by this strange quirk of fate, he became the first person to be buried in the new ground. The Atkinson plot was 8 ft x 20 ft, comprising H 1-4, for which six guineas were paid but, unfortunately, the gravestone is no longer extant and re-arrangement of other stones gives a false attribution to the plot. His burial was entered in St. Michael's register on 14th August 1773, in compliance with the stipulation contained in the deed of conveyance that the new burial ground was the same as a "Coemetery or Burial Ground to the Parochial Chapel of Macclesfield", with burial fees belonging to the Minister of St. Michael's "for the time being".

Charles Roe must have considered that his generosity to the town had been more than adequate in ensuring good relations amongst the different facets of the local community, yet it was not to be, Thomas Hewson had a mind and will of his own.

* * * * * * *

On 9th December 1773 Rev. Hewson married Hannah Lockett at Prestbury, a widow with two children, and by early 1774 Hannah was again pregnant. The stipend of the Prime Curate of St. Michael's was barely sufficient to support its incumbent and family and there seems to have been no opportunity for Thomas Hewson to supplement his income. Although Charles Roe had lent a helping hand to both his own brother and John Robinson, Hewson appears to have alienated himself in that particular quarter.

In the first instance Hewson refused to acknowledge the shared preaching arrangements with David Simpson, an agreement which had stood between the Prime Curate and Assistant Curate since the time when Charles Roe's father, Thomas, had arrived in town. Hewson claimed the right to preach "as often as he liked" and the antagonism went deeper as anonymous pamphlets were apparently printed on the subject and circulated. Finally a parochial meeting was called at which a truce was declared.

Secondly, Rev. Hewson, feeling himself in a somewhat isolated position was said to be envious of David Simpson's popularity. This time the crisis occurred because Simpson had been asked to preach a "Charity Sermon" which Hewson forbad him to do. Several members of the congregation followed Hewson to his house and complained about his attitude.

The Mayor for that year was John Ryle, a great supporter of the Evangelical movement within the Church of England, and Easter Day of 1774 saw John Wesley, on his annual visit, walk in procession to St. Michael's together with John Ryle and the two ministers, Hewson and Simpson. What Thomas Hewson thought about this is not recorded, but one suspects that he was none too happy. David Simpson, on the other hand, already very much aware of the Wesleyan principles through his wife's family, embraced the opportunity wholeheartedly for he had not previously met John Wesley. This was the beginning of a very strong personal relationship between the two men, although as always Wesley seems to have kept his discreet cool distance, quite happy to allow David Simpson to 'carry his banner' and make all the advances.

Whilst John Wesley's personal impact had a profound effect on David Simpson, so in turn did David Simpson's influence surprisingly affect Robert, now returned to Manchester University. Robert reconsidered the Simpson criticism and persuasive arguments and, having undergone a change of heart, was judged by his friends to have become Methodist in attitude. He soon left Manchester behind and matriculated at Brasenose College, Oxford on 18th May 1774, aged 20 years.

Charles Roe must have felt extremely satisfied and proud of his son, for the opportunity denied, not only to himself but also to his eldest sons William and Samuel, had at last been given to one of his offspring. Here was the chance for Robert to fulfil one of his father's greatest ambitions, the continuation of the Church of England ministry in his branch of the family. Despite the considerable business pressures at that time, there seems little doubt that Charles must have felt something was going according to plan yet, paradoxically, in the midst of turmoil and great stress it is often the very thing which appears to present no problems that finally causes grief, whilst everything else resolves itself.

David Simpson continued on his 'collision course' by preaching a sermon "Marriage honorable, Whoredom damnable" with such emphasis that it gave great offence to a particular "local magnate". This sermon, which also appeared in print with several others, entitled *Useful and Important Subjects*, published by T. Bayley of Macclesfield during 1774, was based upon the seventh Commandment "Thou shalt not commit Adultery". Simpson's outspokenness knew no bounds, "Scores of the young Women in this Town, have, at different Times fallen a Prey to the deceitful Arts of lewd, wicked and defigning Men". His opinion, that it was common "even amongst those who affect to call themselves Gentlemen", had obviously struck a chord with someone, for amongst the complaints to the Bishop was one requesting the withdrawal of David Simpson's licence. It has always been considered that the 'gentleman' in question was Sir William Meredith of Henbury Hall, but on closer examination the assumption is not such an obvious one.

* * * * * * *

After the ascent to the throne of George III on 25th October 1760, a new parliament was convened in March 1761. Sir William, having addressed a public meeting at the Golden Lion in Liverpool during the previous January had been unanimously adopted as M.P., having become a very popular candidate. As ever election fever took hold and Sir William was accused of being a Jacobite, having insisted on drinking a toast of "Down with the Rump" in the presence of some of his Dissenting tenants. However, after an election of six days, he was voted in and subsequently occupied "a position of considerable eminence in the House of Commons". In July 1765 he was appointed Lord of the Admiralty and re-elected in December of that year without opposition. As already seen he was a great supporter of the Macclesfield Canal Scheme, even entertaining Josiah Wedgwood at Henbury Hall.

One of the great debates of the period was whether or not young men entering university with the intention of becoming priests, should be compelled to sign their concurrence to the Thirty-nine Articles of the Church of England before commencing their studies. It was a subject which "much occupied" the attention of Dr. John Jebb M.D. F.R.S., who had published a letter on the subject in August 1773. He argued that where a lord of a manor built a church for his tenants and endowed it with glebe and tithes, he should have a right of choice to nominate a person to officiate in that church or chapel as long as the candidate had been "canonically ordained", not be enforced. For whatever reason it was a cause which Sir William Meredith took up by entering a debate in the Commons. He commenced with a synopsis of several religions, including those of Calvin, Luther and the Armenians, then cited instances of hardship by those who could not agree with the Articles and, as a consequence of which, had been forced to give up their livings.

Edmund Burke responded for over an hour, concluding "this motion would, if agreed to, turn the House of Commons into a cock-pit of religious controversy" . . .

Lord George Cavendish wanted "One grand national church" with free toleration enabling everyone "to think as he pleased". In the event the motion was not carried.

It would be naive to suggest that the respect in which Sir William was held, particularly in his office as Comptroller of the Household, precluded him from any involvement with members of the female sex. But what seems surprising is that Sir William was able to attend services at St. Michael's chapel with such regularity that David Simpson was guaranteed his presence on the day on which Simpson was allowed to preach, especially on that particular day with that particular sermon. Perhaps someone had requested Sir William's presence in order to see for himself the 'over-righteous' minister's approach and the subject matter of the sermon was pure coincidence, the reaction to which was later misconstrued. The Bishop of Chester was certainly not pressurised into taking any drastic steps and acquiesced with the status quo for a period.

Business as usual continued for Roe & Co. with, of course, the first A.G.M. of the Macclesfield Copper Company taking place on 19th August in the company offices adjacent to Charles Roe's house. By the time of the following month's meeting on 22nd September, David Simpson's life had altered considerably.

* * * * * * *

On the 31st August Ann Simpson had given birth to a daughter, Ann Waldy, but little more than two weeks later had died on the 16th September. The next day David Simpson purchased plots K 1 and 2 in the new burial ground and Ann was buried in the former, next but one to Rowland Atkinson. At this time Rachel Harriott was a great help in the Atkinson household, ably assisted by Charles Roe's daughters, Mary and Frances.

This tragic event appears to have been the catalyst for Charles Roe's decision not to build his oratory or chapel in the graveyard. Desperation on the part of Rev. Hewson, making him awkward and obstructive, must also have been an underlying factor, for undoubtedly his attitude would have contributed, in no small way, to the diminution of David Simpson's stipend, a situation which Charles Roe would certainly not tolerate.

Charles was never one to enter rashly upon any scheme, but having made up his mind he was never one for half measures. The formation of the Macclesfield Copper Company must have eased his worries and financial burdens to some degree, and matters were proceeding on a firm, secure basis so that he was in a better position to afford another of his life's ambitions. Despite the fact his estate on Chestergate was still subject to a large loan, he decided to use his business profits for the building of a chapel or church on a much grander scale than he had originally envisaged. As patron he would have choice of presentation and, apart from David Simpson, there was also Robert's future to consider. Charles was far from well; with a rising mortality rate in the town, perhaps he felt there was no time to lose.

The plot chosen for the intended chapel (later to be named Christ Church) was still part of the Marled Bank, but directly adjacent to the south carriageway of the graveyard, on Charles Roe's private land; this is the reason for today's somewhat incongruous feel to the overall plan when viewed from a southerly direction looking north. The church appears wedged on the last available strip of suitable land, bounded by Waterloo Street West, but it was originally perched at the top of the short but rapid decline to the Dam's Brook. The view from the other three directions is very impressive with the full vista of what is now the garden and adjoining car park extending on the northern side of Christ Church. The Roe family had their own private pathway leading from their garden behind the Chestergate house, down through the fields and orchard until it joined the carriageway giving right of access through Fair Steads to the cemetery gates. The position of Christ Church, therefore, presented the finest view from their (and everyone else's) approach.

Charles would have been completely undaunted by the idea of a grander scheme; after all he was no novice when it came to building projects. He had seen the construction of two silk mills in Macclesfield, three copper smelting works (one on Macclesfield Common and two in Liverpool, the latter completed with harbour facilities), brass and copper rolling mills and workers cottages at Bosley and Havannah, and finally a windmill and brass works at Snow Hill on Macclesfield Common; no mean achievements.

The structure of Christ Church suggests that Charles used the original plans for the oratory and simply doubled the dimensions for the main body of the church. Additions included a small extension on the eastern end for the accommodation of the altar, and what now appears to be a disproportionately tall square tower at the western end (probably never included in the original plans). It would have been a comparatively easy task to alter other features to fit the larger size of the building. The plain yet elegant style would certainly be in keeping with Burdett's creativity, with a few additional embellishments traceable to Liverpool churches of the period, in particular St. Anne's and St. Thomas's.

St. Anne's had been built by three private individuals as recently as 1770 (architect unknown) and consecrated two years later. It was a very fashionable, elegant church with a square tower, but no steeple, bedecked with Chinese pinnacles and other finials which continued at regular intervals around the edges of its roof. The Christ Church tower, with its four large

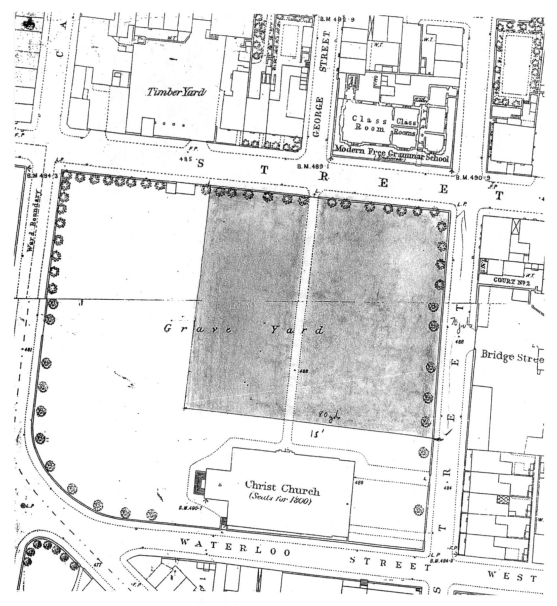

A survey of Christ Church 1871 adapted to show the size of the original graveyard which is the shaded area on the plan. Taken from the O.S. 1871.

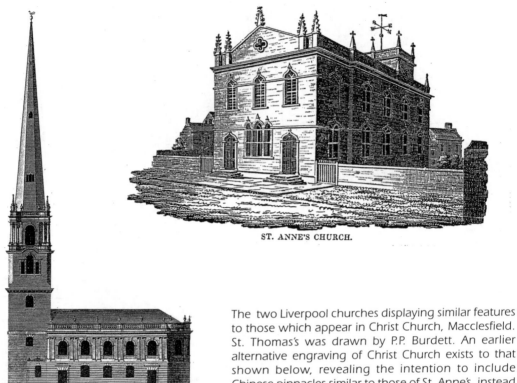

ST. ANNE'S CHURCH.

St. Thomas's Church.

The two Liverpool churches displaying similar features to those which appear in Christ Church, Macclesfield. St. Thomas's was drawn by P.P. Burdett. An earlier alternative engraving of Christ Church exists to that shown below, revealing the intention to include Chinese pinnacles similar to those of St. Anne's, instead of the urn-like finials.

engraving of Christ Church.
Courtesy of T. Brinton.

belfry windows, one on each side of the upper part, are identical to the windows of St. Anne's, whilst the remaining windows in the tower and main body of the church copy the upper windows of St. Thomas's. The large Venetian window over the altar of Christ Church is also reminiscent of the one depicted in the tower of St. Thomas's.

A lady visitor to Liverpool during February 1775 wrote of St. Thomas's that the church was very light and elegantly simple, with an organ in its gallery and clock below. The interior of St. Anne's was noted as having "a neat range of pews, which are divided into aisles" with a gallery supported by slender iron columns. Both descriptions could equally serve for Christ Church when completed. St. Thomas's was the church which John Wesley attended when in Liverpool and St. Anne's would shortly witness the marriage of William Roe to Hannah Shaw.

Charles Roe, well prepared, saw the actual building work commence with the main body of the church in the spring of 1775, for during the winter months building materials had travelled up the Weaver from Liverpool. The first consignment, on 9th December 1774, was for "60 firr balk". A balk was a roughly squared heavy timber beam, and this consignment, weighing 41 tons 2 cwts. represented 2,080 ft of fir timber, without doubt from Virginia. On the 19th December it was rapidly followed by 13 bags of lead weighing one ton, and during the next few months further lead arrived, initially in casks but then as pigs, for its employment as gutterings, pipes and roofing etc. This would have been obtained by Roe & Co. during mining operations in North Wales.

The consignments of fir timber were considerable; between 18th February and 24th June 1775 31 fir balk were transported, each measuring approximately 48 ft in length and just under a ton in weight i.e. a little more than 19 cwts. These were followed by 10 shorter beams of 30-35 feet each and three longer ones of 50-55 feet each. (Total length 505 ft, total weight 10 tons 2 cwts.) When added to the original consignment of 9th December, altogether the length of timbers transported overland from Northwich to Macclesfield were in the region of 4,083 ft. The most obvious method of transportation would have been to use a sledge-like contraption pulled by a team of oxen.

Iron for the ironwork, including the twelve slender columns to support the gallery, was also carried by boats along the River Weaver from the Liverpool smelters. Sometimes described as bars, sometimes as blocks, with weights that varied from piece to piece, the first 50 "barrs iron" were charged for on 1st March 1775 weighing 1 ton, followed by 45 blocks 27th May, (5 tons 9 cwts.) with a further 40 blocks on 29th June and 36 bars on 7th August. Two final consignments of 12 and 51 iron bars were not received until January and February 1776, respectively, but by this date the main body of the church had been completed, leaving the tower for construction during the spring and summer of 1776.

Fortunately the summer of 1775 had been hot and dry, allowing the first phase of construction to be carried out in the short time of five months to October. Bricks would have been made in their thousands on the Common, but it is not known where the huge oak trees, from which the roof timbers were formed to cover the internal span of 65 ft, came from. For centuries the Leghs of Lyme had supplied oak locally for important buildings, and it could have been possible for Peter Legh to have supplied timber from his estates in south Lancashire. However, taking into consideration the depletion of the local forests, the size of beams required and the fact that no oaks are recorded as travelling up the Weaver at this time, negating Ireland as a possible source, the most likely supplier was the Forest of Dean from where the Royal Navy obtained timbers for its ships.

* * * * * * *

With considerable building work taking place and the local interest which must have been engendered, it seems strange that both Robert and his cousin, Hester, made no mention of the proceedings in their well-kept diaries. Hester's was compiled at different periods; one later version was intended for publication and edited accordingly, which has given rise to incorrect dating on occasion. Nevertheless, it is obvious that for some reason she deliberately ignored the building of the church, an omission which resulted from her having become a fervent Methodist, surprisingly the very thing which Charles Roe wanted to avoid but which he had inadvertently encouraged, for Hester had heeded the advice given and had listened to Rev. Simpson's words. As a result, by Easter 1774, although only 18 years old, she had become so distressed and dissatisfied with her lifestyle that she 'ripped up' her fine clothes and cut short her hair. Encouraged by a neighbour to hear a Methodist minister preach she set out early one morning. Her mother's fury was such that Hester was ordered to leave the house, but Uncle Roe intervened; instead she was confined to the house and visitied by several relatives and friends intent on changing her mind. The summer visit to Adlington Hall was endured, though Hester stubbornly refusing to socialize. As a consequence she was told by her godmother, Hester Legh, that if she continued to act accordingly then she must expect nothing in return. Hester's thoughts ran deep; she felt the need to serve others, and if her mother would not allow her to work as a servant in their own household then she would go elsewhere.

Having returned home in October 1774 Hester argued for her independence. Her mother, having sought the advice of friends, agreed; for all thought that if Hester was given the opportunity to work as a servant she would soon "weary of hard labour ". Within a month the strain began to tell and Hester's mother admonished her, as she would have done any domestic servant who had not carried out her duties properly. Hester, overburdened both in mind and body, went to hear John Wesley preach during his visit early in the spring of 1775. With further encouragement from her cousin, young Charles Roe, Hester's devotion to John Wesley was established and, having found support from Charles Jnr., she turned her attention to his brother, Robert, who had, of course, matriculated at Brasenose College, Oxford the previous year.

Robert had a great many things on his mind and as he repeatedly turned to Hester for advice, so more and more she took control of his thoughts with her reasonings and persuasive manner.

Of all Charles Roe's sons Robert was her favourite and there is a slight suggestion that she might have been tempted to marry him, had he asked. Robert, however, appears to have had no such thoughts, his mind was too intent on theological matters, apparently regarding Hester more as a sister than a partner. In the not too distant future the same could not be said of his brothers, Joseph and Charles Jnr., for in Hester's eyes she was to be relentlessly pursued, especially by the latter, but somehow manage to retain a cool, aloof attitude whilst at the same time encouraging them also to Methodism.

Charles Roe was completely oblivious to what was taking place. During the summer of 1775 Hester was a constant visitor in her uncle's house, as Robert, home from Oxford for his long vacation, sought her companionship.

Towards the end of the summer a great tragedy occurred which Hester later incorrectly recorded as on Tuesday 19th September, when it apparently related to Tuesday 28th August. The bearer of the news that morning was Robert, who was so deeply affected by what he had learnt, that he naively vowed to "forsake All vain Amusements" in his endeavour to become more devout.

The surprising news must have been a great shock to many as the story was recounted, and to no one more so than Charles Roe. Hester's version, as heard from Robert, was that John Stafford "Attorney in this Town Grown of late years very sick by his employments" had been to the playhouse on the previous evening to see a performance of Oliver Goldsmith's play, *The Good-Natur'd Man*. In the middle of the play, which Hester described as "A Witty Burlesque upon ye tricks practised by lawyers", John Stafford became uneasy and let it be known that he felt very ill. At once a chaise was called and he hurried home where he was put to bed. That very morning at 7 o'clock was "found A Corps – it is confidently reported his throat is cut by his own hands".

What could possibly have taken place to create such remorse, depression or guilt causing someone as venerable as John Stafford to act in such a way? Suicide was seen as a sin in the eyes of the Church, assuming it was suicide; his will dated 10th February 1775 goes some way towards confirming this assumption.

By any standard, John Stafford should have been a wealthy man. His land holdings, as part of his Jordangate House estate, were considerable, but nothing when compared to his Derbyshire estates. In the area around Chapel-en-le-Frith, Bowden Middlecale and the hamlet of Kinder he owned over 1,000 acres. The clue to his demise seems to be the instructions that if there was not sufficient money to pay off debts and legacies then the lands had to be sold as soon as possible by the Executors, from which they were to give a yearly sum to his son, William, sufficient for his support and maintenance until all claims were satisfied. John Stafford was, therefore, heavily in debt, hence the difficulty experienced by Roe & Co. in obtaining settlement for the Alderley Edge copper mine.

The family extravagances could have been a contributory factor, but the most obvious explanation must be John Stafford's support for both his son, William, and son-in-law, Harry Lankford, at the time of their declared bankruptcy, as witnessed by a notice in the *London Gazette* of 20th July 1773. As already mentioned, a subsequent meeting of creditors at the *Angel Inn*, Macclesfield on the 12th August, forced a sale of estates and effects by Public Auction; a considerable humiliation for the former Town Clerk. Yet even this burden would have been small in comparison to the knowledge that his London associates would also have gained notice of this undesirable state of affairs.

It is possible that John Stafford 'played for time' by borrowing money from clients' estates for which he held the responsibility of administration, as in the case of the former Elizabeth Blagge. Son-in-law, Harry Lankford, was in possession of the Fence House estate in Hurdsfield between the years 1766 and 1773, and possibly longer (i.e. from the time of his marriage to Sarah Stafford in 1761, until John Stafford's death), but there is no evidence of the Smyths taking legal action for recovery of the property.

The only certainty is that John Stafford's failing health pushed him into taking that final awful, desperate and drastic step, and perhaps in some way the Goldsmith play does hold the key to the mystery, as so many similarities occur between the on stage and off stage dramas.

* * * * * * *

In brief, the play revolves around a young lawyer called Honeywood whose generosity to deserving, but mostly undeserving individuals, has plunged him deeply into debt. He finally learns the error of his ways by the surreptitious help of a young heiress who has fallen in love with him.

The first Act begins with Sir William, Honeywood's uncle, a lawyer of repute who has practised in Italy for many years, returning to London intent on teaching his nephew a lesson. The young heiress, Miss Richland, has an unscrupulous guardian, another lawyer called Croaker, whose designs have ensured that either she marries his son or loses half her fortune in refusing.

Sir William has recently covered a debt on behalf of his nephew whose foolishness, in giving surety for an unreliable acquaintance, has seen the latter abscond with great rapidity. Sir William, now in the guise of an unknown individual, takes Court action in order to recover the debt from his nephew. By Act 3, which occurs almost half way through the play, the bailiffs (albeit quite amiable and understanding characters, particularly when compensated for any inconvenience caused) arrive at Honeywood's house. Could this have been the point at which John Stafford became uneasy and chose to leave?

John Stafford's frame of mind could not have been helped by certain lines within the play, such as those from Act I:

> "It's a melancholy consideration indeed, that our chief comforts often produce our greatest anxieties" (Honeywood).
>
> "Ah, my dear friend, these were the very words of poor Dick Doleful to me not a week before he made away with himself" (Croker).

When under considerable pressure people are often forced into taking actions totally alien to their nature, and all the years of trust and admiration are swept away in an instant. John Stafford was buried in an unmarked grave, presumably at St. Michael's, for the entry there on 1st September 1775 simply reads "John Stafford Gent. Alderman of Macclesfield". (No grave was bought at Christ Church). With that he slipped quietly out of mind, leaving behind an uncomfortable situation for his family from which a good deal of resentment, towards those supposedly responsible, would grow.

* * * * * * *

Hardly had John Stafford's burial taken place than notices appeared in *The Manchester Mercury*, the content of which must have been a welcomed distraction for many. Charles Roe had organised a magnificent concert to celebrate 'the Opening of the Organ' at the New Church in Macclesfield. Performances were arranged for three days, Wednesday the 11th October to Friday the 13th October 1775. The doors were to be opened at 9.30 a.m. with the concert from 11 a.m. Tickets for the gallery were priced 4 shillings, with those for the main body of the church 3 shillings.

"The Sacred Oratorio of the Messiah" was scheduled for the daytime performance on the Wednesday, "The Oratorio of Judas Maccabaeus" for Thursday with a "Miscellaneous Concert" in the evening, followed by a ball. As a Macclesfield Copper Company meeting was arranged for Friday the 13th, the principal partners would conveniently be in Macclesfield for the Thursday and Friday performances and are recorded as Brian Hodgson, Snr., Robert Hodgson, Edward Leigh, Thomas Smyth, William Roe and Edward Hawkins. (The latter had been admitted as a partner for a $^1/_{15}$th share from 17th August 1775 valued at the astonishing sum of £6,167 7 9½d. for which he had paid £3,647 7 9½d., leaving £2,500 payable within 12 months at a rate of 5% interest).

The town of Macclesfield could never before have witnessed a celebration of such magnitude; the performers were some of the country's finest. The most famous was Johann Christian Fischer (born Freiburg 1733), a German oboist (the instrument known as a hautboy) whose first public appearance in London, June 1768, had coincided with that of J.C.Bach on the piano. The pair, together with C.F.Abel, were responsible for many concerts, with Fischer performing frequently at Vauxhall Gardens, various provincial festivals and at court.

Fischer not only played solos during the Christ Church festivities, but was accompanied by the also famous Thomas Pinto, first violin, in presenting concertos between Acts on each of the three days.

Pinto, son of a Neapolitan civil servant, was one of the most prominent violinists in Britain. He played in many provincial and London theatres including, for a time, the King's Theatre (known as 'The Opera House') where he had been principal violinist before taking up residence in Edinburgh during 1770. His daughter, Julia, accompanied him to Christ Church and sang in the Oratorios together with Mrs. Hudson and Mr. Norris.

Mrs. Hudson, an actress and singer, who often sang at Vauxhall Gardens, had performed Oratorios in York during the 1769/70 season. She is probably the artist referred to by the famous Kitty Clive on 23rd November 1773, "Mrs. Hudson is an agreeable woman but I am afraid she will Break in two, I never so (sic) anything human so thin".

Thomas Norris, although well-known as an organist and composer, was even better known for his outstanding tenor voice. He held several posts at Oxford University and gave weekly concerts in the Music Room there.

Little is known of the two remaining vocalists, Miss Radcliffe and Mr. Nield, engaged for minor parts, but both were possibly related to two more famous singers who had connections with Westminster Abbey.

Apart from Fischer and Pinto the other instrumentalists comprised Mrs. Hudson's husband as second violin and Mr. Jobson on harpsichord.

The choruses were sung by "the best Singers from Hey, Oldham, Manchester, Liverpool & other parts of Lancashire etc." with "The Whole conducted by Dr. Wainwright" whose brother, Richard, former organist of St. Ann's but then of the Collegiate Church in Manchester (now the Cathedral), was engaged to play the Christ Church organ for the Opening.

Dr. John Wainwright, son of a Stockport organist and composer, had succeeded to the post of organist in the Collegiate Church of Manchester upon his father's death in 1768. After taking music degrees at Oxford during April 1774, he had become organist of St. Peter's, Liverpool from 1st March 1775, and had been replaced by his brother, Richard, at the Collegiate Church.

Hester's diary entry for Saturday, 14th October 1775 reads:

"Though I have been much tried by Charles Roe (Jnr.) repeating his former offers - But ye Lord I know will keep me. I was very happy at ye Oratorio on ye Opening of ye New Church ye Messiah was perform'd & ye Chorus Trumpets & Kettledrum etc. raised my views to that long'd for day When "ye trumpet shall sound & ye Dead shall be raised".

Charles Roe Snr.'s choice of Handel's music and its performers was no coincidence; the appropriation for the introduction of a very special organ into the New Church auditorium was complete. The organ had been purchased from the London Opera House (not the Royal Opera House, Covent Garden) which was known at various times as the Queen's Theatre, the King's Theatre, the Italian Opera House or simply 'The Opera House'; today the occupier on site is Her Majesty's Theatre in the Haymarket. The general alternative appellation at all times appears to be the Haymarket Theatre. This was the theatre adjacent to Joseph Stockdale's former house in the parish of St. Martin's-in-the-Fields and very much connected with Handel.

After a brief visit Handel had settled in London late in 1710 when he was invited to write an opera for the director of the Queen's Theatre. He did return to Hanover at different periods for several months but, unfortunately, fell out with the court, having overstayed his visits to England. The problem was eventually resolved and Handel restored to favour when the Elector of Hanover became George I; Handel had successfully written the 'Water Music'. Later that year the Haymarket Theatre, patronised by George I, was the only theatre to have the opening of its season delayed because of the Jacobite incursion.

John James Heidegger, son of a Swiss clergyman, had become manager of the Haymarket Theatre in 1713 and introduced masquerades, said to be 'the rage of the town'. Although George II had appointed Heidegger master of the revels yet, due to public pressure, a royal proclamation had to be issued against them, at which time Heidegger and Handel began an operatic partnership. They remained together at the Haymarket until June 1734 when, due to a dispute between Senesino, the famous Italian opera singer, and Handel the theatre was closed. Not until 1737 did the theatre once again open its doors when Handel returned and Heidegger was restored as manager. About this time an organ must have been installed, for it is first mentioned on 28th March 1738 when a Benefit Concert was held for Handel in the presence of the Prince and Princess of Wales. The programme comprised an Oratorio and a concert by Handel on the organ, which proved a resounding success.

Much to Handel's chagrin very little money was spent on theatre organs because theatres were in the habit of burning down; nor were they very large instruments. Handel's compositions for the harpsichord could also be played on the English organ and he referred to his own harpsichord as his 'little organ'. Handel was delighted by the fact that although pedals had been in use for centuries in Europe, yet the English organ was without (and would remain so until well into the 19th century). The organ in the Haymarket Theatre, therefore, would be a small pedal-less English organ.

Handel died in 1759, but his old pupil John Christopher Smith continued his master's Oratorio performances until he retired to Bath in 1774. Meanwhile in May 1773 the King's Theatre had been purchased and refurbished by Yates and Brookes, hoping to obtain permission to alternate plays with operas, however, the Lord Chamberlain refused the application. The theatre reopened in November 1773 at a time when theatre organs were falling from favour and "By Command of their Majesties" a final organ concert was arranged for 8th March 1775. The organist on that occasion was the lesser known Bach (Johann Sebastian had died in 1750) who played a new concerto written by Handel before his death.

There seems little doubt that this was the organ which received its grand Opening in the New Church, Macclesfield in October 1775. A tentative Victorian note records that Samuel Green was responsible for the removal of the instrument from the London Opera House to Christ Church. Samuel Green was a partner with John Byfield Jnr. in the firm started by Bridge, Byfield Snr. and Jordan. At that period there were very few reputable organ builders and whilst Handel had favoured organs built by Richard Bridge, which would seem to suggest that this organ had been of his creation, yet an interesting story is told by composer, Charles Jennens, who had visited Handel on 18th September 1738:

> "Mr. Handel's head is full of Maggots than ever . . .His second Maggot is an Organ of 500£ price, which (because he is overstock'd with Money) he as bespoke of one Moss of Barnet: this Organ, he says, is so contriv'd, that as he sits at it, he has a better command of his Performers than he us'd to have; & he is highly delighted to think with what exactness his Oratorio will be perform'd by the help of this Organ: so that for the future, instead of beating time at his Oratorio's. he is to sit at the Organ all the time with his back to the Audience. . .".

All the other organs owned personally by Handel have been traced except this particular one, which therefore is a good candidate for that purchased by Charles Roe. Thomas Pinto would certainly have been familiar with the organ, having held the position of principal violinist at the King's Theatre for a period, and although he would be dead by 1784, of the other performers in the New Church concerts, Thomas Norris, Robert Hudson and Johann C. Fischer would all take part in the Handel Musical Commemorations commencing in that year of 1784 at Westminster Abbey: in particular Fischer's performances would receive exceptional praise from George III.

The first resident organist of the New Church, who must have felt privileged to play such an instrument, was John Francis Stanton; little is known of him except for the inscription on his gravestone confirming his brief status, for he died on 24th April 1777. He was replaced by Anaeus Maclardie from London, who would shortly marry the daughter of John Hale (Roe & Co.'s faithful bookkeeper). And it was Maclardie who would later inform his choirboys of the provenance of the organ; yet the name of the builder goes unrecorded.

* * * * * * *

After the Simpson sermons of 1774 relations between Thomas Hewson and David Simpson had deteriorated rapidly, until finally Bishop Markham wrote a letter of restraint to Rev. Simpson, having received complaints at the time of his Visitation. The Bishop had underestimated David Simpson's popularity, for the latter had still been asked to baptise children and church women, which he continued to do in his own home. From February 1775 Rev. Simpson recorded the baptisms in what was to become the first Christ Church register, although the church itself was unable to accommodate baptisms for quite some time.

No baptisms are recorded between 31st July and 17th September 1775, presumably as a result of the Bishop's letter, but then a small number appear once more in the register for the months of October and November. Thomas Hewson, having in mind his small stipend, was upset and wrote to the Bishop on 19th November 1775 pointing out that Simpson's actions were causing "a great Lofs with respect to the Surplice Fees". Worse still, since the Bishop's letter to David Simpson, Charles Roe was refusing to allow burials in the new burial ground. Technically the only way he could have done this is by not allowing access across his field called 'Fair Steads' and by arguing that although he had granted the land to the Corporation for burials, he had still not received full recompense as most of the graves had to be sold - an unusual situation. Thomas Hewson's letter continued by painting an illuminating picture of the difficulties in finding burial space in St. Michael's graveyard:

> "I have known it very lately, that the Coffins have been oblig'd to be taken up, & carried into the Chapel & remain there while another has been buried, & the People Dispers'd, & then the others brot back into the same Grave, so that there has not, when cover'd, been a foot depth of Soil upon them – I, as well as other Gentlemen in Macclesfield, have seen a Scull wch has been taken up, but could not be avoided, & thrown into a place where the Bones usually taken up in making graves are put, wth flesh upon it in a corrupted State; which is certainly disagreeable to any person induced with the last Spark of Humanity & may, in all Probability, be the Cause of some Pestilential Disorder amongst us . . .".

The last sentence is an obvious reminder of the illness working its way through town which, in all probability, was a severe form of influenza.

Bishop Markham, son of an army Major, was wise enough not to become needlessly involved. He did not withdraw David Simpson's licence, in fact he did nothing. There is a strong likelihood that Charles Legh, patron of Prestbury Parish Church would have spoken to the Bishop in defence of the Roe and Simpson situation, as intimated by a letter from Charles Roe to Bishop Markham dated 19th March 1776:

> "It is nearly five months since I wrote concerning the Chapel I have erected, encouraged thereto by what your Ldship said, that one or two more Churches were wanted in the Town.
> As I offer'd a Salary adequate to all reasonable demands, I must own I did expect a kind Ear from your Ldship. I am not ashamed to say my motive was Love and Gratitude to GOD. I entreat your Ldship's favor and good Opinion. I hope when your Ldship comes to be informed of my real Character and conduct every Vile Aspersion and Misrepresentation will be dispersed. . . I have given the privilege of Burial Ground to him (Thomas Hewson), paying the common Fee to the Old Church . . . But as I never granted, or was asked to grant, an exclusive Right to the Minister of the Old Church, I must beg leave to assure your Lordship I never shall submit to it".

This letter refers to Charles Roe's desire for the Consecration of the New Church and is indicative of the fact that he must never have considered the possibility of any obstacle standing in the way of it. Meanwhile the church was, by status, a private chapel built by a private individual.

* * * * * * *

At the time of the 'Opening of the Organ' the pews were fitted but the interior remained as an auditorium. The seating capacity was approximately 450 in the gallery and 850 down in the main body of the chapel. It seems more than likely that by Christmas 1775 the chapel would have been appropriately furnished i.e. an altar table placed beneath the Venetian window in the eastern extension or sanctuary, with five large marble tablets inscribed and mounted on the three surrounding walls. Two displayed the 'Ten Commandments' and the remaining three, 'The Lord's Prayer', 'The Creed', and words from 'The Eucharist'.

The elegant font, on its round platform of greyish white marble mottled with dark grey to bluish black veins, suggests best quality Derbyshire marble from the mines near Monyash. Charles Roe's sister-in-law, Elizabeth Cheney of Monyash, widow of Edward, an important mining manager in the area, had died in June 1772 and, although Charles has sold several of his Derbyshire lead mining shares on 3rd December 1773, still his connections in the area remained.

The question of lighting partially presents a problem. There were apparently three large candelabra suspended from the ceiling over the central aisle, with a fourth hanging from the middle of the dome above the altar table. The gallery was illuminated by three smaller versions on each of the north and south sides, whilst sconces, appropriately fixed on walls, pews and organ, made up the deficiency in luminosity. The whole must have presented a superb scene, as dozens of candles glowed alongside their gleaming brass fittings, branches and orbs, with light reflected inwards from the bright white interior, accentuating the slender iron columns and other features, the details of which were highlighted in gold.

The maker and the present whereabouts of these candlesticks is unknown, yet they would have been superb pieces, a grand advertisement for the brass of Roe & Co. The most obvious place of manufacture would have been the Brock workshop in Chester, however, commencing on 12th May 1772 advertisements had been placed in *Adams Weekly Courant,* the first of which read:

> "Alderman Brock of this City is selling up his shop goods which consist of all sorts of copper wares and pewter goods of the best kind and as he is leaving of the business everybody indebted to him are desired to come and pay the same to him . . .".

During the time of the sale customers could still have copper and brass items made, and tinning and mending work continued. The notices appeared for quite some time, until finally on 12th April 1774 it was printed that goods not sold would be returned to Alderman Brock's house in Fleshmonger's Lane. It was about this time that Thomas Brock came into possession of Bostock Hall, Davenham.

Even the renowned former Brock apprentice, John Thomas, who was the possible maker of a candelabrum in Congleton Parish Church, had also ceased business in 1774. The North West expertise was almost at an end, so perhaps Charles attempted the manufacture himself with purchased moulds, otherwise London seems the most likely place of origin.

Within the chapel it was most important to keep draughts at bay, therefore windows were made solid (i.e. without the facility of opening) and all pews had doors. At each inner corner of the western end a small porch gave protection against draughts admitted by a large outer door. Between these two entrances, at the end of the central aisle, the font was placed. It stood directly in front of the choir vestry door and was accompanied, on its southern side, by a stove - ideally placed for winter baptisms. The flue from this stove passed through the vestry wall and joined that of the chimney from the vestry fireplace for an unusual exit through the eastern wall of the tower. On completion of the tower, during the early months of 1776, the vestry became part of the ground floor. This conveniently facilitated the ascent of choir members to the gallery by means of a stairway, which led directly to a doorway behind the organ, allowing them to take up their positions on either side of the instrument. On their way through the door they would have passed the organ blower, for at this early date air was pumped manually to the instrument. Victorian accounts credit quarterly payments to this particular individual, which possibly pertained earlier.

The free pews for the poor were along the back of the gallery, and all those sitting upstairs were able to use two enclosed staircases at each inner corner of the eastern end of the building.

The magnificent three-tier pulpit, 12 ft in height and placed in the centre aisle, ensured that the preacher was in line with the first row of pews nearest the altar, and was also on a level with the gallery. Times were changing, the old rituals were now being enhanced by a more emphatic preaching of the Gospel. Whereas for many years it had been the practice of certain Church of England clergy to pay scholars and others to write their sermons for them (even Dr. Johnson had assisted his good friend Dr. Taylor on occasion), the theatrical exercise was becoming abhorrent, thus paving the way for a more sincere, devout and meaningful presentation by a believable cleric, as in the instance of David Simpson.

On 24th April 1776 one of the Buxton family arrived in Macclesfield to pay his respects to Charles Roe. Thomas Buxton, formerly in the army, lived in Bradbourne close by the Brassington Estate and was on tour, visiting old friends and relatives. There is little doubt that his curiosity to see the New Church had encouraged his visit. After spending time in Derby and the enjoyment of a fishing trip in Bakewell, within a day or so he had arrived in Macclesfield via Leek at 5.45p.m., conveniently in time to dine with "Mr. Rooe". He was taken to see the New Church which he recalled as having internal dimensions of 35 yards by 20 yards, divided into different sized seats which Charles Roe intended to sell. He considered the structure as regular and elegant with a good organ and squared tower to hold eight bells, "tho I think it will be soon enough to ring ye bells when it is Consecrated wh. Mr. Rooe cannot get done at present, nor is he likely to".

Thomas Buxton also called to see "Mr. Euson, Clergiman of ye Old Church" who informed him that Charles Roe's chapel could not be consecrated without his consent and this he would never give whilst David Simpson remained as "officiating Clergiman", whom he accused of being a Methodist. Once again Charles Roe's triumph was incomplete and David Simpson, "hindered from preaching" at St. Michael's, read the chapel services and gave after dinner sermons (presumably on Sundays) in the Roe household. This effectively gave him the temporary status of chaplain to the family, although he was still officially assistant curate of St. Michael's.

* * * * * * *

Robert Roe had been present on one of the 'after dinner' occasions before returning to Oxford and as a result, with great encouragement from Hester, had joined local class meetings formed to inspire Methodism. On leaving Macclesfield he was accompanied by his brother, Joseph, as far as Leek. Joseph had also attended the classes, thus providing further encouragement for Robert's weakening resolve. Samuel, who must have been engaged on company business, also joined his brother; he attended Robert from Leek to Birmingham about which Robert later wrote that Samuel "behaved very kind; there is something very noble and generous in his spirit".

Suffering from complete exhaustion Robert arrived at Oxford University after travelling all night; feeling that he had left all his friends behind, an inevitable depression set in. He found himself in conflict with his tutors, who evidently saw no justification in the disclosure of his Methodist views, one of whom chastised him for spending his father's money to no purpose. By January 1776, having obtained his father's permission, Robert had taken leave and was staying in London with Aunt Stockdale, sister of his deceased mother. New Year's Day saw him join a meeting to hear John Wesley preach and, together with Aunt Stockdale, he attended the Covenant at Spitalfields, having been given a ticket by the incomparable preacher.

Robert's disturbed state of mind was leading to ill health; tuberculosis, together with smallpox, were the two most feared infectious diseases of the period, and most prolific. The former, referred to as consumption was, and still remains, a debilitating disease, causing the victim to appear ashen in colour with a semblance of wasting away. Until recent years there was very little hope of a cure, so inevitably with the illness's progression a disturbed psychological effect often emerged. Robert's university friends had cause for concern as they considered he was "going into a consumption". Nevertheless Robert continued his affiliations with the Methodists, which brought about a crisis with his college. By April 1776 he had returned to Macclesfield but all was not well.

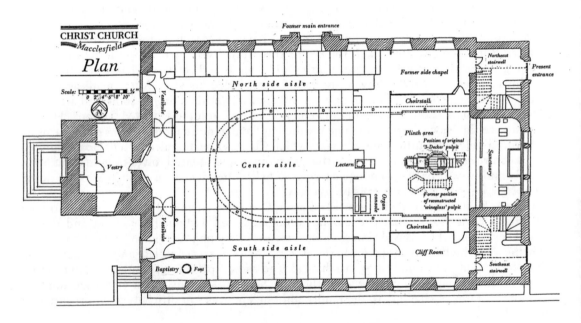

Plan of Christ Church. Courtesy of T. Brinton.

21

FAMILIES

Their inward thought is that their houses shall continue
forever, and their dwelling places to all generations.

On 9th April 1776, the day prior to William Roe's 30th birthday, he married Hannah Shaw who was 22 years of age. Details of the marriage settlement are not known, but there were no provisions made in relation to the copper company. Because of the stranglehold of Liverpool Corporation with regard to land deals, investment in property was at a premium and therefore out of the question, so one can only assume that an investment was made in one of the Shaw enterprises; William Roe, however, does not appear in any of the lists of merchants trading to Africa.

The marriage having taken place in the fashionable church of St. Anne's, Richmond in Liverpool, William and Hannah took up residence in the elegant thoroughfare of Duke Street, a little to the east of Cable Street, from where they attended St. George's Church. (Presumably this was the church previously attended by William as it was just across the square from his former residence in Cable Street.). The two witnesses to the marriage were the merchants Thomas Crowder and John Brock; the latter appears to have been one of the sons of Thomas, Town Clerk of Chester. Also, two months earlier, on 2nd February 1776, the Liverpool Town Books record that Rev. William Brock had altered the lives on his Corporation lease for a tenanted house in Paradise Street together with a warehouse at the rear on Manesty's Lane. Manesty's Lane was almost a continuation of Duke Street across Hanover Street, and about this time Roe & Co. moved their warehousing arrangements to Manesty's Lane.

The family into which William married had a history almost paralleling that of the Roe family. The Shaws probably originated in Shaw, close by Oldham, just to the northeast of Manchester, from where they eventually spread out across Lancashire, from the Lancaster area in the north to Warrington and then Liverpool in the south. Several were Church of England clergymen and headmasters, and so strong was the tradition of teaching in the family that it is more than likely Edmund Shaa from Dukinfield (a goldsmith and subsequent Lord Mayor of London in 1483), who by his will founded Stockport Grammar School, was an ancestor.

By the mid-18th century a Thomas Shaw was Principal of St. Edward's College, Oxford and another Rev. Thomas, headmaster of the Free Grammar School in Bolton, whilst yet another Thomas had become an important member of Liverpool Corporation (Bailiff in 1738 and Mayor, 1747) and owner of a pot works in the city.

Members of Hannah's branch of the family had settled in and around Warrington before establishing themselves in Liverpool. The patriarch, Samuel, (Hannah's great grandfather) matriculated at Queen's College, Cambridge 5th May 1670, was ordained priest 20th September 1674 and obtained his M.A. in Oxford 1677. His first appointment was as headmaster in Wigan, where he remained until 1686 when he became headmaster of the Warrington Grammar School. He married the Rector's daughter, Ann, and himself became Rector of Warrington at St. Elfin's in 1690.

Rev. Samuel acquired a reputation for his verses, which included writing a Latin ode to the newly appointed Bishop Cartwright of Chester, for which he duly received his Warrington living. He was an energetic man and soon gained a position of some esteem when he became one of the four King's preachers in Lancashire. He took charge of the demolition and rebuilding of St. Elfin's steeple and, together with friends, also rebuilt the school house. He even found time to promote the Warrington Clergy Society, established by the Bishop and his Archdeacon for assisting widows and families of clergymen.

Rev. Samuel died in September 1718; his will, proved on 31st October contained several bequests to the poor of Warrington and also Sutton near Frodsham, where another group of the Shaw family appears to have lived. Many family members received bequests, which included cousins such as the 'Okell' (Okill) family.

St. George's Church in Liverpool had been built in 1726 by James Shaw, a builder from Newton-le-Willows, aided by his brothers, one of whom was a Thomas. They were certainly related to Rev. Samuel and possibly his nephews, for Thomas was taken to Warrington to be baptised by Samuel. It was this Thomas who would become Mayor of Liverpool and, amongst other things, acquired a pot works, no doubt with assistance from his close relative, John Okill.

Okill, as previously mentioned, was a timber merchant of some standing, such that by 1739 he had obtained the first Liverpool contract from the Commissioners of the Navy. He initially built the *Hastings*, a ship of 44 guns, and completed a further eight naval vessels between 1740 and 1758. Although he was a member of the Merchants trading to Africa, he was not actively involved in the slave trade.

Okill was first recorded in Liverpool on 12th December 1719 at about the age of 30 years, when the Corporation clerk registered him as leasing "A Pott house now made into a Glass house, Wind Mill and small piece of ground". However, the interest in pottery must have continued elsewhere, for by his will of 1769 he left his "pott house Mill Outbuildings Utensills" in Toxteth Park to his nephew, John. John was responsible for the sale notice placed in the *Liverpool Advertiser* of 29th October 1773, suggesting his lack of interest in the concern. The stock included materials for manufacturing purposes and a large assortment of cream colour or Queen's earthenware made on site, with the "workmen and customers fixed".

In true Georgian style the family is once again seen to be self supportive i.e. Okill no doubt supplying timber to the Shaws for building purposes, and they perhaps helping with ship building in between-whiles and supplying clay, dug from the local pits initially for brick making, but some of which must have proved a suitable constituent for pottery making.

It is interesting to note that amongst the Okill bequests was a gift of £10 to Cuthbert Ridley, organist of Macclesfield, together with an annuity of £10 per annum each to Cuthbert's wife and youngest daughter, Ann.

John Okill died four years after the preparation of his will, whereas Rev. Samuel Shaw of Warrington, having prepared his will in 1713, had died five years later. Samuel left quite specific instructions for his wife's administration of his estate, particularly with regard to the distribution of property and money amongst members of his family, yet incredibly, one hundred years later, in 1813, because of his wife's failure to make a will, a problem would arise with a property in Appleton near Warrington. Meanwhile son, John, replaced his father as Rector of Warrington, but Hannah Roe's grandfather, the eldest son Samuel, was already established as a Liverpool merchant.

Having served his apprenticeship, Hannah's grandfather had become a woollen-draper in High Street. He received from his father, Rev. Samuel, an estate in Statham which he would be able to include in his marriage settlement, for he married Hannah Blundell on 28th Febrary 1717.

The Blundells were another important mercantile family and when, tragically, Samuel the woollen-draper died before the birth of his first child, (a son, Samuel, baptised 11th May 1718) the widow, Hannah, appears to have returned to her family so that the child was brought up amongst merchants trading to Africa. She was given administration of her husband's estate together with Bryan Blundell (? brother).

Rev. Samuel, of course, died later the same year, yet made no further provision for his little grandson, a negligence which seems totally out of character; perhaps he considered that the child was already well provided for.

Bryan Blundell was a very good friend of the Dissenting Minister of the Key St. Chapel in Liverpool, Rev. Christopher Bassnett, so much so that Bassnett preached and published a sermon for him. Bassnett, son of a Chester apothecary, came from a family of divided loyalties at the time of the Restoration; his branch of the family had remained Dissenters. Bryan Blundell took a particular interest in merchant sailors and their families and was Captain of the *Cleveland*, so Bassnett preached part of the published sermon before the ship's company on Thursday, 13th December 1711 and the remainder in the Meeting House the following day. It was Rev. Bassnett's daughter, Ann, who married the woollen-draper's son, Samuel, at St. Peter's, Liverpool on 28th April 1745. From this marriage came three surviving sons and at least two younger sisters, one of whom, Hannah, was destined to marry William Roe. So just as in the Roe family, where the Dissenting influence came from Charles Roe's maternal relatives, it was likewise in Hannah's.

Throughout the early years of his marriage Hannah's father, Samuel, is recorded as a merchant of Dale Street and is not to be confused with a relative and potter of the same name in Lord Street. Hannah's three brothers, Samuel, Christopher and John, aged 25 years, 22 years and 21 years respectively, were admitted Freemen 'by Birthright' of Liverpool Corporation on 3rd March 1773, each paying 3s. 4d. And whilst brother, Samuel, appears to have worked independently, Christopher and John were very much a partnership; but it was Christopher Shaw in particular who seems to have regarded William Roe as an elder brother.

There were many ships registered to members of the Shaw family which, at times, makes attribution difficult, but there seems little doubt that the "Headboat Sterned Ship" called *Hannah* of 200 tons, built at Norfolk, Virginia and registered 30th September 1769 belonged to Hannah's father.

* * * * * * *

The Shaws were fortunate that their election to the Freemanship of Liverpool Corporation was a comparatively easy procedure with minimal cost. Others out of apprenticeship often paid 6/8d. whereas outsiders, referred to as "Foreigners" could be forced into paying considerable sums in order to avoid Town Dues. One example is John Sparling, a merchant from the Lancaster area, who paid 50 guineas in 1764. By the early 1770s, however, his ruthless incorrigible character gained him a dominant position in Liverpool affairs and a fortune from his dealings.

Elected bailiff in 1768 Sparling was quick to appreciate the fanaticism of the Corporation for land purchases. The sea shore was obviously the most important area for development, particularly as the sea-going trade was rapidly increasing, thus creating a desirability for additional dock facilities. Sparling, therefore, enclosed a piece of land along the shore line and initially offered it to two individuals on lease, but in October 1774 Liverpool Corporation agreed to purchase at, what was then, the current value with the addition of expenses incurred in enclosing it.

During the following month of November the Corporation sent a deputation to Lord Sefton, in order to purchase "all the interests that his Ancestors have held around Lord St.", and also agreed to pay Sparling £1,450 for his piece of land.

Sparling, meanwhile, became one of seven Common Councilmen on a newly formed "Committee of Trade of the Town of Liverpool" which agreed to hold annual meetings each April. The minutes of the first meeting record that "the remainder of Ald. Sparling's Ground inclosed along the Sea Shore be now purchased from him by the Corporation for the sum of 5,000 guineas". Within the space of six months Sparling, in effect, was more than half way to becoming the equivalent of a modern millionaire.

The intriguing part of the story lies in the fact that in the first instance Sparling had gained a foothold in the port of Liverpool because of trading connections between Virginia and the port of Lancaster. He had lived in Virginia for 13 years, during which time he and his partner took shares in vessels with the Blundell family, an extension of which was the apparent influence with Hannah's father, Samuel Shaw, to gain entry into Liverpool Society. Relations between the two deteriorated rapidly during the early 1760s, when their business dealings ceased, and whenever Sparling was present at a Liverpool Corporation meeting, Samuel Shaw was absent. It seemed inevitable that Sparling would extend his considerable influence in certain quarters for an appreciable time yet to come. Someone who unwittingly became his ally was the inimitable Thomas Golightly, mayor in 1772, although Sparling does not seem to have been a member of Golightly's exclusive dining club – the Unanimous Society.

Unfortunately another 'foreigner' had quite a different tale to tell regarding his freedom of Liverpool.

* * * * * * *

Thomas Marshall was as important to Northwich as was Thomas Patten to Warrington or Charles Roe to Macclesfield. The Marshalls had built up a fortune in the local salt industry and Thomas, in expanding his father's business interests, had become an important carrier of goods along the River Weaver. Whilst he was busy carrying his company's salt and coals (the latter from his leasing of Lancashire collieries) to Liverpool, the return journeys were made profitable by contracts for bringing a variety of goods up-river on behalf of others. One such customer was Josiah Wedgwood, who wrote in July 1766:

> "Messrs Marshals of Northwich are the Gentm. my former Cargoes of Clay were consign'd to there . . . I believe they perform'd their parts very regularly & well, & when that is the case I never like to alter."

This refers to Cornish clay transported by sea-going vessels to the port of Liverpool, and from there conveyed to Staffordshire by the Marshalls.

Surprisingly at a Liverpool Council meeting held on 4th February 1767 Thomas Marshall Snr. had been accused of defrauding the Mayor, Bailiffs and Burgesses of Liverpool and was summoned to appear before them. The case centred around a merchant, Joseph Pieters of Antwerp in the Austrian Netherlands, "a foreigner" who was not free and to whom Thomas Marshall had sold several hundred bushels of white and rock salt. It was stated that Marshall had "covenously & deceitfully under Colour" and using his own status as a freeman, permitted salt to be loaded aboard a Liverpool vessel for shipment to Ostend. However, "by the ancient and immemorial usage & customs of the said Town of Liverpool", immediately the vessel set sail Pieters was liable for port dues which had not been paid.

Several other instances were quoted, demonstrating the vigilance with which trade was carried on within the port, and Thomas Marshall was ineluctably "disfranchized & expulsed" from his freedom. It does not necessarily indicate personal involvement by Thomas Marshall, it could have been due to a fraudulent employee. In the long term it probably had little effect; the Marshalls were certainly far from being bankrupted and had a steadily increasing clientele who, within a couple of decades, would be joined by 'Messrs. Roe & Co. of Macclesfield'.

The last item appearing in the River Weaver Account Books consigned to 'Chas. Roe Esq & Co.' is for 166 copper blocks weighing 20 tons 17 cwts. and windmill sails 2 cwts. on 4th March

The Navigation Inn built partly over the area previously occupied by the eastern end of the Roe smelthouses; the earlier inn adjoining the site was probably part of the premises for the benefit of the workmen.

The base of a furnace discovered when excavating a garage floor opposite the Navigation Inn. Courtesy of the owner.

The old engine house on Ecton Hill, built in 1788. The roof has been lowered.

Ecton Sough or Deep Adit driven in 1774, reopened in 1984.

Penrhyn Du; the view from the site of the lead mine looking across Cardigan Bay.

The farm leased by Roe & Co.

Penrhyn Du; site of the old lead mine.

Keightly near Tywyn, site of an unsuccessful mining venture by Roe & Co.

Pot used for brass making, height 14 inches. From the Brookhouse site, Cheadle. Courtesy of Matlock Museum.

Havannah at Eaton near Congleton. The site was built for the rolling of copper sheets and the making of brass wire. The weir, which was constructed 10 feet high, worked 5 wheels.

The stone cottages built at Bosley by Roe & Co, for their workmen.

Details of the original ceiling inside one of the cottages.

The remains of 18th century industrial buildings opposite the above cottages on the site of the Lower Mills Bosley.

River Weaver at Northwich.

Locks on the River Weaver at Northwich.

The Toxteth Smelters as represented on the Roe monument in Christ Church. On the right hand side can be seen a ship sailing to the quay.

Christ Church, built 1775-1776 courtesy of A. Rowbotham.

Plas Newydd, Anglesey; home of Sir Nicholas Bayly. The nearest ferry crossing across the Menai Strait was on the right of the photograph. Courtesy of L. Porter.

The Roe Windmill on Macclesfield Common early in the 19th century. In the centre of the picture can be seen Christ Church tower with the tower of St. Michael's on the extreme right.

Windmills of Liverpool from an engraving 'Liverpool from Lime Street 1797' by W. Herdman c. 1840 courtesy of T. Thomas.

The Roe family coat of arms. The Roe family descended from King Cadwaller who died in Rome in 688. His son Edwal Wyrch or 'the Roe' became the first King of Wales.

The Roe Monument Christ Church in Macclesfield.

Entrance to St. John's College, Cambridge. The bell tower, where James Roe rang the bell is seen at the rear on the left hand side.

Dr. Porteus, artist unknown, courtesy of the Bishop of London.

Left: Inside view of the King's Theatre in the Haymarket, c. 18th century.

Right: Rev. David Simpson, Macclesfield Museums Trust.

Below: John Wesley's Death Bed scene by Marshall Claxton R.A. courtesy of The Methodist Church Overseas Division. Hester Ann Rogers is standing second right of Wesley and Rev. Rogers third right, the child is their son, James.

Below: Rare bust of John Wesley c. 1791.

Duke Street, Liverpool, where William and Hannah Roe had their first home at no.5. The house, with its two neighbours, is long gone, having been demolished in the early 19th century to make way for a corn mill.

Roe Alley, Liverpool. A reminder of the original way leading to the rear of no. 5 Duke Street. The name Roe Street still exists incorporated into the new development of St. John's Market.

Looking towards Lime Street, Liverpool. The area developed in the late 18th century by William Roe and John Shaw. The photo is taken from what would have been the rear of William Roe's house in Queen Square.

The River Bank Works built for Roe & Co. by William Roe and Edward Hawkins c. 1785, on the banks of the brook called Nant-hil in Flintshire. The engraving was used by Thomas Pennant in his *History of the Parishes of Whitford and Holywell* 1796.

The Great Orme, Llandudno, scene of much mining activity in the late 18th century which included Roe & Co. in their attempt to replace the ores of Parys Mountain after the termination of their lease in 1785.

Hawkins & Mills Bank (1787 c.1799). Entry was by the door on the left, and the bank occupied part of the first floor above what is now the appropriately named 'Silver Coin' premises. In the Market Place, Macclesfield.

Edward Hawkins, painted by Thomas Lawrence, early 19th century.

Neath Abbey near Swansea. Right: A modern reminder on houses built on the nearby site of the original cottages of Roe & Co. close by the copper smelters, and subsequently used by the Cheadle Co. for their employees.'

Plaque on the cottage named Cheadle Works.

Above: Macclesfield Tokens courtesy of The British Museum.

Right: An Irish Cronebane Token. Courtesy of Dr R. Doty.

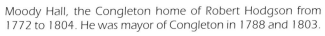

Moody Hall, the Congleton home of Robert Hodgson from 1772 to 1804. He was mayor of Congleton in 1788 and 1803.

Miniature of Brian Hodgson Jnr. courtesy of D. Bates.

The farm of Persabus leased by Roe & Co. in the middle of their designated mining area on Islay.

The Crinan Canal.

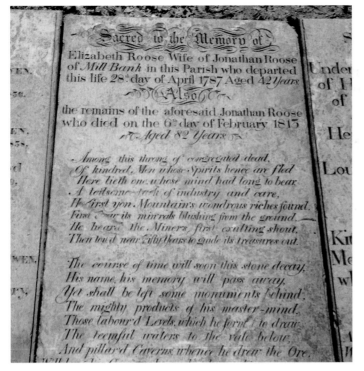

Sacred to the Memory of

Elizabeth Roose Wife of Jonathan Roose
of *Mill Bank* in this Parish who departed
this life 28 day of April 1787 Aged 42 Years

Also

the remains of the aforesaid Jonathan Roose
who died on the 6 day of February 1813
Aged 82 Years

Among this throng of congregated dead,
Of kindred Men whose Spirits hence are fled
Here lieth one whose mind had long to bear
A toilsome task of industry and care.
He first yon Mountain's wondrous riches found,
First saw its minerals blushing from the ground,
He heard the Miners first exulting shout,
Then toil'd near fifty Years to guide its treasures out.

The course of time will soon this stone decay,
His name, his memory will pass away,
Yet shall be left some monuments behind,
The mighty products of his master-mind,
Those labour'd Levels which he form'd to draw
The teemful waters to the vale below,
And pillar'd Caverns whence he drew the Ore,

Left: The gravestone of Jonathan Roose, Amlwch Parish Church. Anglesey.

Below: Cronebane Mine at The Meeting of the Waters, County Wicklow, Republic of Ireland.

Above: Cerrig y Bleddia farm now in ruins, leased by Roe & Co. on Parys Mountain.

Left: The Port of Amlwch developed for the transit of copper ore to the mainland.

Below: Precipitation pits on Parys Mountain c. 1920 filled with 'any old iron'. They had been created originally by Roe & Co. some 150 years earlier. Courtesy of Anglesey County Archives Service.

1776. (This neatly confirms that it was necessary to replace windmill sails approximately every two years – the originals having arrived in November 1771 were replaced in November 1773 and again in March 1776).

Apart from a few consignments to William "Rowe" during the following 18 months, Thomas Marshall Jnr. would successfully transport all further items including copper, copper blocks, calamine, a rare batch of hearthstones and an odd quantity of iron, on behalf of the Macclesfield Company for the foreseeable future. One reason for this change in policy could have been William's marriage, from which he would automatically gain more personal responsibilities, and also the fact that extra duties, placed on him by an expanding and successful business, took up more and more of his valuable time.

* * * * * * *

The Company Minutes for the first half-year of 1776 imply a considerable increase in both copper and brass production, proportionate to the increased activities of the partners.

Legh Dickenson was ordered to purchase and ship immediately 100 tons of Cornish copper, and Jonathan Roose was likewise instructed to purchase from W. Hughes (representing the consortium of Sir N. Bayly, the Hughes family and Thomas Williams) a further 100 tons of copper ore. "Mr. Hodgson" was to approach Robert Shore at Ecton for 8 to 10 tons of copper, which indicates smelted copper in the form of ingots, not ore. This came mostly from chalcopyrite (copper ore containing 34.6% copper) with a small proportion of the very rich ores chalcocite (copper content 79.9%) and bornite (62.5%), representing approximately 25 tons of raw ore. Although this amount seems somewhat insignificant, yet a comparison with Parys Mountain ore would mean that 200 tons of the latter would need to be processed in order to procure an equivalent amount of copper ready for refining.

More "Scull iron" (rough or waste) was sought from Reynolds Gesley & Co. and if they could not supply then other Houses in the same trade were to be approached. This indicates greater production from the precipitation pits on Parys Mountain, suggesting that more scrap iron was needed than Roe & Co. were able to retrieve from their smelters.

Apart from Ecton, all other instructions directly affected William Roe in Liverpool, including one to examine the stocks in the Liverpool warehouse "on [the] last Friday in every Month" accompanied by Mr. James's clerk (presumably Mr. James was chief tenant of the warehouse). On 1st July 1776 orders were given for William Roe to erect two more furnaces for smelting and refining copper, yet a further indication of increased production and demand. This is also confirmed by a letter to Messrs. French & Hobson of London, advising that because of large orders their requirement for 20 tons of copper could not be met before September.

Unfortunately the calamine supplies were once more giving cause for concern. After losses for the years 1768-1772 the Gorsey Dale Mine at Bonsall in Derbyshire recorded a small profit of £24 1 10d. for 1773, followed by a good year's profit of £207 7 3d. for 1774. However, despite an optimistic outlook it would be a further nine years before a small profit could again be recorded; meanwhile, although losses were not substantial, they must have resulted in a depletion of calamine stocks, and an annotation of "no ore" can be found against the years 1778-79.

The A.G.M. of 17th August 1775 reveals that Brian Hodgson Snr. was asked to reduce the price of raw calamine to 5/- per ton for purchase by the company. Apparently the calcining of the Bonsall calamine was on a sub-contract basis and instructions were given to send no more than 3 tons each week, presumably because of storage difficulties, although new buildings had just been completed for the storage of calamine on Macclesfield Common.

One can only assume that at this time the greater proportion of calamine was coming from the "Pennygarrick" (Pen-y-Gareg) Mine near Mold in Flintshire, together with purchases from other mines in the area. The Roe & Co. mine was, of course, the extension of the

Loggerheads Mine originally leased from Mrs. Jones, and brought into existence when Charles Roe and Thomas Walker of Manchester had made an agreement with Lord Grosvenor to extend workings into his land from 3rd January 1774.

A considerable amount of work had taken place in the two years between June 1774 and June 1776, with total expenditure of £1,206 11 3d. The agent in charge was Adam Woodward with William Kirkland remaining as mining manager and overseer. Any lead retrieved was sold to the Smedley smelters near Bagillt; no production details are extant, but the calamine entries in the River Weaver Account Books are a useful substitute.

The total tonnage of calcined calamine transported up the Weaver for Roe & Co. in 1773 was 282 tons and 17 cwts., slightly more than the previous year's total of 220 tons 18 cwts; this increased dramatically to 374 tons 6 cwts. in 1774, reducing to 236 tons the following year with only 112 tons 6 cwts. for 1776. The figure for 1774 must reflect the opening of the Pennygarrick Mine. Occasionally the number of bags is recorded together with the tonnage, which initially points to a fairly consistent size of bag e.g.:

19th November 1773	400 bags	20 tons.
11th March 1774	1236 bags	61 tons 18 cwts.
19th April 1775	518 bags	25 tons 10 cwts.

This infers that each bag and its contents weighed close to 1 cwt., yet other entries contradict this. For example, an entry for 2nd October 1775 records only 298 bags weighing 20 tons and on 8th February 1776, 506 bags weighing 27 tons 6 cwts. It probably depended on where the ore had been calcined and bagged,

During the Swymmer problems of 1774, regarding calamine from Somerset, Brian Hodgson Snr. and Thomas Weaver had been asked to "go into ye West" to negotiate with Lord Paulett (whose family estates were near Bridgwater) for the purchase of calamine. Whether or not anything transpired is not clear, yet on 4th November 1775 letters were sent to agents and 'Swymmer' to look for a place to store 150 tons of the ore.

By the 5th December a decision had been made to send letters to both Messrs. Swymmer and Michael Blackwall regarding the dressing process. Michael Blackwall, a Roe & Co. employee from Derbyshire, was possibly the son of William, baptised at Wirksworth on 27th February 1740. (It is interesting to note that in the early boundary dispute between the Lords of Mold and the Grosvenors, a Bryan Blackwall of Chester and a Thomas Blackwall appeared as witnesses in Court, which suggests that members of the Derbyshire family were already employed in Flintshire).

Evidently matters did not improve, for in March 1776 another employee, Thomas Botham, was asked to dress 5 tons of Mendip calamine and keep account of how much waste there was in each ton, an indication that the washing and dressing process was still not being carried out to the satisfaction of the company. The outcome was a letter from Charles Roe cancelling the agreement with Mrs. Swymmer, and recorded at the company meeting of the 6th May. She was also advised that a company representative would shortly call to ensure cancellation, and as a consequence "Mr. Hawkins and Mr. Weaver" were asked to settle the affair with her.

The only other concern of any magnitude at this time was the extension of the Grand Trunk navigation, for which a Bill was to be introduced into Parliament early in 1776. A letter was speedily written to Nathaniel Pattison, partner of the Congleton Silk Mill, to be vigilant in ensuring that a clause was inserted restricting the volume of water to be taken from the River Dane. The scheme had been attempted two years earlier bringing protestations from the owners of mills along the river; Roe & Co.'s concern would be to guard against the creation of any impediment likely to affect the water supply powering the mills of Bosley and Havannah.

* * * * * * *

Apart from company business, the completion of the New Church had remained an issue for Charles Roe during the first three months of the year. The tower was finished by 24th April, as evidenced by Thomas Buxton's interesting comments, from which he infers that 8 bells were intended to be hung, whereas 10 bells weighing 24 cwts. were actually cast. The bellfounder was Thomas Rudhall of the City of Gloucester, whose great-grandfather had established the family business by producing his first peal of bells in 1684.

Unfortunately no original records remain, only a Victorian list of bells cast. However, it has been possible on occasion to compare individual church records with the list, which, in these particular instances happily verifies that the number of bells cast is correct, and also does allow for rough dating. The list is definitely in chronological order from 1684 to 1830; immediately following the entry of 10 bells cast for the New Church, Macclesfield, is one which reads "8 bells weighing 19 cwts. for the Old Church, Macclesfield".

The Parochial Chapel could only boast of six bells from 1701, when two new ones had been added to the original four. The eight new bells were hung in 1777 and must have followed the Roe bells up the River Severn, therefore it is reasonable to assume that within a few months of the completion of the tower, Charles would have had his bells installed, shortly before those of St. Michael's in 1777.

It has been argued by some and repeated by many that Charles Roe deliberately chose to have the Christ Church (New Church) tower constructed to a greater height than that of St. Michael's out of spite, because of his problems with Rev. Thomas Hewson but, by nature, Charles Roe was not a petty man. From the events of his life so far it can be seen that he was meticulous, thorough, fastidious, sentimental, very fond of music but above all, a very practical man. The height of the tower ensures that all four clock faces can be seen at a considerable distance, even from the site of the former brass and copper works on the Common; the clock of St. Michael's is barely visible. This was important in an 18th century town where many mill and other workers had early starts to their day.

The second consideration must have been the effectiveness of the bells. With eight, instead of six, as at St. Michael's, so many more changes could be rung, and the fact that his brother James had entered St. John's College, Cambridge on the 'Bell scholarship', must have evoked a desire in Charles Roe's mind to be able to produce the finest peal of bells for many miles around. Thomas Hewson's embittered and troubled mind could only have interpreted the whole grandiose scheme as a deliberate personal attack, to which he had responded by ordering an equal number of bells for St. Michael's. Of course, he would not have been alone in making this decision and must have been supported by, amongst others, someone who was rapidly becoming one of the chief Roe antagonists, Peter Wright, Town Clerk. In the event Charles was not to be outdone.

There seems little doubt that the Wright family in some way regarded Charles as partially responsible for John Stafford's demise. There is no denying that John Stafford, although often in the background, had supported the Roe ventures and worked to encourage favours for the company. Yet, on the other hand, Charles was a fair minded man; perhaps the Wrights felt that he could have been more supportive towards John Stafford during his family's crisis, by not pressing for the redemption of his equity in the silk mill, or even later, when demanding what was a comparatively small sum due from the Alderley Edge mine. More than most Charles knew what it was like to fight for survival, but obviously felt the need to put the welfare of his considerably extended family first, and it must be said that John Stafford's son-in-law, Harry Lankford, had acted in a very irresponsible manner by purchasing the Cheddleton Estate at enormous cost, forcing himself to obtain a considerable loan from the Tatton family.

Whatever the pros and cons there was now a divided camp, the Old Church versus the

New; without doubt, on this occasion, Charles, good as any man at keeping score and angry at Hewson's meddlings, secured the casting of ten bells instead of eight, thus winning that particular competition. The bells were hung high up in the tower which would later cause considerable problems because of the level of oscillation. Today six of the original ten bells remain and bear the following inscriptions:

3rd: *THOS. RUDHALL GLOUCESTER, 1777.*

4th: *WE WERE CAST AT THE EXPENSE OF CHARLES ROE, ESQ., 1777.*

5th: *SUCCESS TO TRADE, 1777.*

6th: *PROSPERITY TO THIS TOWN, 1777.*

7th: *PEACE AND GOOD NEIGHBOURHOOD, 1777.*

8th: *T.R. 1777.*

(The 1st and 2nd bells have been replaced and the 9th and 10th recast).

The fortunate though depleted details regarding the bells are a definite plus in an otherwise deficient record of original furnishings for the church. No information is available regarding the original large clock in the tower, though it was more than likely of Liverpool origin.

The clock within the main body of the building, which hung on the wall beneath where the organ sat in the upper gallery, has survived. The maker, John Kaye (or Caye) of Liverpool is recorded in Dale Street circa 1760-71, the street in which Samuel Shaw resided. From the 1780s he would become involved with large church clocks, as recorded at St. Peter's and St. Nicholas's, but whether or not he would have had the expertise to build the large tower clock for the New Church at this early date, is unknown. However, another conceivable candidate was John Wyke.

From 1772 John Kaye's address became No. 2 Wyke's Court, Dale Street (though he had probably occupied the premises from 1760). This suggests a close working relationship with Wyke for, as previously mentioned, Messrs. Wyke and Green had a considerable workshop or manufactory in Wyke's Court which supplied a variety of clocks, watches, spare parts, tools and other items, whilst at the same time producing some extremely beautiful and excellent mechanical instruments. So considerable was the Wyke business that it even operated as a bank, discounting notes for customers. The additional fact of Wyke's association with St. Paul's Church together with Peter Perez Burdett and Samuel Shaw, seems a somewhat positive, though not conclusive, indicator of his involvement in the production of the New Church tower clock.

In the building of his church, Charles Roe, as much as possible, would have used his own men and resources, and where outside workmanship was necessary, would have supplied, as far as possible, the desired materials. There is no doubt that the copper used in the making of bronze for the church bells would have been in the form of Roe & Co ingots, and purchased from the company by Charles Roe personally.

(Bronze is principally composed of copper and tin, usually in the proportion of 90% copper to 10% tin . As copper is a relatively soft metal and somewhat difficult to pour when molten, the addition of tin gives it increased strength and fluidity. Other alloys such as zinc and lead can be used in differing proportions according to each founder's 'secret formula' but, by ancient custom, only bell-founders are restricted to an almost constant recipe of 78% copper to 22% tin.)

The transportation of the bells from the Gloucester foundry to Macclesfield would have been no mean achievement considering their awkward bulk. However, facilities were in place for the transportation of Roe & Co. stocks to and from Gloucester, so arrangements should have been comparatively easy to make. One particular person who must have been of assistance was Edward Hawkins, and his entry into the company at this time does help further the suggestion that the huge oak timbers for the New Church roof had come from the Forest of Dean, the area of his birth. Edward, born 20th June 1749 and baptised in Newnham three weeks later on the 11th July, was the youngest surviving child of Thomas and Elizabeth Hawkins. Thomas's progeny always claimed descent from the famous Elizabethan Admiral, Sir John Hawkins and circumstantial evidence does go some way towards supporting this claim, evoking a desire to know more about this intriguing family.

* * * * * * *

John Hawkins from Devon, had married Katherine Godstone at St. Dunstan-in-the-East near London, on 20th January 1566 and six months later his son was born. The child was baptised Richard after Katherine's father, and not John, which is a little surprising given his father's fame and fortune. Richard was Sir John's only legitimate child, but there is a reference to "a base son" said to be captain of a ship in 1587. This has been dismissed by historians, who construed it to be a slight on Richard by a man "full of rancour" towards his father. However, the register of St. Dunstan-in-the-East records a John Hawkins baptised 24th January 1563, with the name of the parent left blank. Admiral Hawkins resided in that parish for at least 30 years before his death in 1595, inspiring a monument to be erected in the church to his memory. There seems a strong possibility that the child John was his illegitimate son.

The legitimate main branch of the family can be identified as remaining in the parish of St. Dunstan in Stepney, with frequent occurrences of the Christian names Richard and John. Their later movements are readily traceable by use of the family coat of arms. Other family members, of what appears to be the illegitimate line, begin to appear in the parish of St. Mary, Whitechapel by the 17th century, and apart from one couple taking up residence in St. Martin's-in-the-Fields (1641) it is not until the last quarter of that century that many more family members appear in this parish.

It is illuminating to trace the movements of this important mercantile family along the main trading routes e.g. Faringdon on the River Thames, Huntley and Newnham in Gloucestershire, Chester and even Macclesfield.

In the early18th century three brothers, John, Thomas and Samuel Hawkins spent time between Huntley and St. Martin's-in-the-Fields. At this time a John Hawkins is recorded in Macclesfield (1719); his nephew, William became Town Clerk, remaining till his death in 1748, when he was replaced by John Stafford.

Charles Roe's second marriage at St. Martin's-in-the-Fields, and the fact that in 1750 a member of a Macclesfield family was a weaver in the parish, does seem to confirm strong mercantile links between the two communities, at least in relation to the silk trade. Also, for some inexplicable reason, there was a sense of 'belonging' on the part of Edward Hawkins as soon as he arrived in Macclesfield. When admitted as a Roe & Co. partner in August 1775 he was described as "now of Newnham", but only two months later, on 13th October, was admitted as a burgess of Macclesfield Borough.

The Hawkins were a prolific family and Samuel of Huntley had, amongst his offspring, two sons, Samuel (baptised 1696) and Edward's father Thomas (baptised 1702). Young Samuel returned to London, married and settled in Whitechapel where he became an important builder and property owner. He eventually developed the area of Goodman's Fields, became a churchwarden of St. Mary Matfellon and, close by the church, owned a sugar house which was tenanted. His son, Samuel (baptised 1728) became treasurer of St. Mary's church and charity school, and a magistrate of the parish. Together with his elder brother, Edward, Samuel was a partner in their father's building firm and, because of the rapidly expanding East India trade encouraging affluent merchants and naval personnel into the parish, the brothers became extremely wealthy from property development. Apparently business was also booming in some of the more insalubrious parts of the parish, for on 29th January 1754 Edward, together with another parish constable, claimed £350 expenses in prosecuting "Bawdy Houses".

Their father died in 1771 and left his considerable estate to be divided between his two sons. Edward inherited houses, workshops and sawmills in Lemon (Lehman) Street. Samuel became the owner of property in Stepney Manor comprising the sugar house, dwelling houses and appurtenances in Church Lane near "White Chapel Church"; in St. George's parish, Middlesex, he also inherited the public house called *The George* together with its garden, eight small cottages and gardens, and in Whitechapel a house and workshop. Finally he received houses, a workshop, warehouses and storehouses on the west side of Lemon Street and Ayliff Street etc. most of which was tenanted property, one in particular occupied by a brewer and pipemaker.

Amongst their father's other bequests his brother Thomas of Newnham and his wife were given £50 each "for Mourning", and his nephew, Edward, received £200.

In order to accommodate nephew Edward's subsequent entry into Roe & Co. on 17th August 1775, the shares, previously in fourteenths, were increased to fifteenths and the person nominated by Edward to inherit his share, should anything untoward happen to him, was his cousin Edward Hawkins of "Lemon Street Goodman Fields". One suspects that a greater part of the initial considerable payment of £3,667 7 9½d. was borrowed from Cousin Edward of Whitechapel.

Edward's father, Thomas, is first recorded in Newnham on the estuary of the River Severn, when he signed the Church Wardens' minutes on 9th September 1750 at the age of 48 years. The inference is that he had only recently moved to Newnham, because from that date onwards he is very much involved in Newnham affairs, yet Thomas and Elizabeth earlier baptised several children at Newnham. There was another Thomas living in Newnham at that time, making it is difficult to judge, even with bequests in wills, which of the older children belonged to which family, or even if Edward's father was married twice.

Speculation apart Thomas was an important merchant participating in the sea-going trade. By the mid-18th century the Newnham trade was mostly with Drogheda (where another important branch of the Hawkins family lived), Dublin and other Irish ports to where the locally produced cider and bark were conveyed. However, in the early 1750s occasional voyages to London began, and by 1762 Thomas Hawkins had a ship called *Newnham* which at that time was the only vessel sailing between the port and London because of the danger of privateers in the Channel due to the Seven Years War.

At the end of the war Thomas Hawkins entered into partnership with a young local lawyer, Robert Pyrke, and on 5th March 1764, with the launch of their new brig the *Severn*, Hawkins, Pyrke & Co. began a regular service to the capital. Over the next few years a significant fleet of vessels was built and goods, brought down the River Severn by trows, were transferred to the sea-going vessels at Newnham Quay. From 1767 the London warehousing arrangements were dealt with by the wharfinger at Hilditch's Wharf, Southwark.

Unfortunately the Gloucester Port Books, covering the Severn outports including Newnham, are only extant to the end of 1765, but it seems evident from the inclusion of Edward Hawkins of Newnham as a Roe & Co. partner in 1775 that Macclesfield goods were, by then, being conveyed to London via Newnham.

(In August 1774 a London agent Fossick (of Millis & Fossick) had been given the franchise for selling ingot brass on behalf of Roe & Co. September 1774 saw 12 tons sent, six by one ship and six by another, from Liverpool to Cotten's or Beale's Wharf in London. From 1769 to 1772 Daniel Fossick had periodically sold copper to the East India Company but on whose behalf is not known. By the spring of 1775 Millis & Fossick were also selling wire on behalf of Roe & Co.)

In August 1775 Edward Hawkins was, of course, residing in Newnham, but one suspects that he had previously been schooled in the family timber business in Whitechapel. At this time Charles Roe was intent on travelling to London to "procure a Sale of Copper to the East India Company", but he was still recovering from his serious illness, so the task fell to Robert Hodgson accompanied by William Roe. Gaining a foothold in the extremely lucrative trade with the East India Company was a very difficult business and only attainable through bidding at their sales, which for many years had been dominated by the copper companies of Bristol, Swansea and London. At last Roe & Co. were successful and are included for the first time in transactions for the period August 1776 to April 1777.

In all, eleven companies supplied copper during this term, and apart from four, each averaged circa 1,200-1,300 tons, resulting in an average total price to each of about £5,500. The largest sale was from another newcomer, John Dawes of London, a banker, whose 1,581 tons sold for £6,087 1 0d. Apart from two comparatively small sales by Isaac Elton & Copper Co. and a John Furly, Roe & Co. managed a sale of 1,080 tons 21 cwts., price £4212 14s. (today not far short of £½ million). This was the beginning of a valuable annual source of income for Roe & Co. which would continue for almost a decade.

On 8th April 1776 Thomas Hawkins, far from well, had prepared his will, leaving all his estate to his wife Elizabeth for life, and after her decease to Edward, apart from £200 for daughter Sarah. Thomas died on 12th November 1776 at which time Edward appears to have taken his father's place temporarily in the day-to-day running of the business at Newnham. Just over a year later, a note in the Macclesfield Copper Company minutes of 18th November 1777 reveals a Mr. Wilkinson delivering copper to Chester and Hilditch's Wharf, Southwark, by which date Edward had returned once more to Macclesfield.

One can only assume a close working relationship between Edward and Robert Hodgson for, at Ashbourne on 25th October 1777, "Edward Hawkins of the parish of Prestbury in the County of Chester . . . made Oath that he was of the Age of twenty three years & upwards, & a Bachelor that he intended to marry Ellen Hodgson of the parish of Ashbourne in the County of Derby . . . Spinster aged twenty one years & upwards".

The wording of this marriage licence is unusual, for Edward was actually 28 years of age, and Ellen, Brian Hodgson's next to youngest daughter and Robert's sister, was 25 years of age.

On 6th January 1778, possibly as an investment resulting from Edward's marriage settlement, a lease was effected between Robert Pyrke and Messrs, Hawkins & Co. The term was 21 years with an annual rental of £30 in respect of the Newnham wharf or quay "adjoining the River Severn", complete with new crane "lately erected" upon the wharf, and the storehouse or shed. Apart from Edward Hawkins, who appears on the lease as a merchant of Macclesfield, the partnership of Hawkins & Co. included John Wood, a glover and merchant of Hereford and former partner of Thomas Hawkins, Richard Hilditch of Newnham, merchant and Charles Yoxall of Southwark, wharfinger.

Edward and Ellen Hawkins were now possibly residing in a property close by Charles Roe's house in Macclesfield, but on the opposite side of Chestergate; a property which they were certainly in possession of by the turn of the century. The first born child, a son Edward Thomas, who appears to have died early, was baptised at St. Michael's in September 1778. This seems an odd decision to have made, taking into consideration the antagonism between Charles Roe and Rev. Hewson, however, matters had moved on apace and Thomas Hewson had succumbed to the "Pestilential Disorder" and been buried during the previous month of August. Room must have been found in the Parochial Chapel burial ground for his interment, for there his gravestone has survived.

Who christened the Hawkin's baby is difficult to deduce, for David Simpson had already resigned his post as Assistant Curate of St. Michael's prior to Hewson's death, when licence had been given to Rev. William Greene to replace Simpson on 11th June 1778.

* * * * * * *

On 9th October 1778 two important licences were granted for Macclesfield by the Bishop of Chester. The first was sanctioning the appointment of Rev. John Lingard as Prime Curate of St. Michael's, at the nomination of the mayor, Rowland Gould. The second was in respect of David Simpson's appointment "to the new Chapel in Macclesfield till it is Consecrated at the Nomination or appointment conditionally of Peter Mayer Cl(erk) – Vicar of Prestbury and Charles Roe Esq."

Charles was on the point of overcoming one of the greatest obstacles he had ever encountered, the reluctance of the Bishop of Chester to proceed with the consecration of the New Church. He must have felt that a miracle had taken place because, on 20th December 1776, a few months after the completion of building work in the spring of 1776, Rev. Beilby Porteus had:

> "kissed the King's hand on his promotion to the see of Chester: a preferment on his own part perfectly unsolicited, and so entirely unlooked for, that, till a short time before it happened, he had not the smallest expectation of it".

Bishop Beilby immediately resigned the living of Lambeth, which he was entitled to retain, in order to concentrate on the affairs of the large diocese now in his care, and moved to Chester on 4th July 1777.

Yet even this fortuitous turn of events had not automatically guaranteed Charles Roe's desideratum and it took a considerable amount of diplomacy on the part of the Bishop to reach a satisfactory outcome. Immediately upon the death of Rev. Hewson the Mayor, Rowland Gould had chosen David Simpson for the vacancy of Prime Curate, no doubt with great encouragement from Charles Roe, but Peter Wright wasted no time in sending a petition against this proposal to the Bishop. On 17th August 1778, only four days after Hewson's burial, Rowland Gould and David Simpson hurried to Chester for an audience with the Bishop, and the following day the Bishop's clerk wrote a letter to Peter Wright.

Bishop Beilby was a man of integrity and his first priority was that any action taken should be on a legal basis. He questioned "in whom the Right of Nomination of the Prime Curate is vested", and had requested the Mayor to search for the original Grant, as the one held by Peter Wright as Town Clerk appeared to be only a copy. The whole issue had been clouded by the fact that the previous Bishop of Chester had taken the nomination upon himself, suggesting that the Mayor's entitlement was only arbitrary.

Secondly, objection had been made against Simpson being granted any licence at all, which would also have debarred him from taking up a ministry elsewhere in the diocese, but as Beilby pointed out the petition was "not sufficient for withholding a Licence from Mr. Simpson". The Bishop then cleverly drew everyone's attention to the fact that as the £50 stipend for the Prime Curacy came from the Crown, he would have to certify to both Crown and Treasury that the appointment was with his full approval, but this he found impossible to do as he could not ignore the petition from the Town Clerk. Under the circumstances "he supposed that the £50 payable by the Crown would be withheld". This would certainly cause panic amongst the burgesses of Macclesfield; however, the Bishop skilfully gave them an alternative, as set down by his clerk:

"Mr. Simpson has been nominated by Mr. Roe to his Church and I believe he has not been licenced thereto; Indeed I think the Church is not consecrated, But the Bishop seems to think it wou'd be unreasonable that Mr. Simpson should lose both . . . supposing him to be properly and legally nominated to either Church".

The result was a compromise, as evidenced by the licences of 9th October 1778, but one which Charles and David Simpson must have greatly welcomed, particularly as Simpson had remarried in the October of the previous year. In some respects David Simpson's naivety was partly to blame for the situation. During the troubles with Hewson and the conveyancing of the burial ground, Charles Roe, in thinking out loud, had discussed the idea of building his own church in which Simpson could minister, with David Simpson himself. One great difficulty was, of course, how to overcome the problem of "Consecration and Patronage". Had David Simpson known Charles Roe better he would have left matters in Charles Roe's capable hands, but instead he sought advice from amongst the Methodist fraternity, and the eccentric Countess of Huntingdon came to hear of it. "Her Ladyship . . . said if Mr. Roe would build a Church she would patronise it". This offer was the last thing Charles needed, for the Countess, whilst Methodist at heart, had formed her own small religious body known as the "Connexion" which would later become closely allied with the Congregationalists. Charles Roe had no intention of building a church which was anything other than Church of England, yet rumours set tongues wagging and from the very outset the label 'Methodist' became attached to the whole project, quite erroneously.

Charles, very much aware of the problems this supposed association was creating, particularly with regard to the question of consecration, began a battle against any suggestion of Methodism, either with regard to the New Church or his own family.

* * * * * * *

The first to feel the real impact of Charles Roe's bitterness and wrath was Robert who, having returned home in April 1776, was spending the summer in Macclesfield. On 3rd August one of Robert's sisters asked to accompany him to a Methodist meeting but Robert, knowing full well his father's wishes, set out alone. His sister then called for Cousin Rachel, and as Robert later wrote "which I was sorry for, as I knew it would prejudice my father against her".

Neither Charles nor Robert was in good health, which is always a recipe for misunderstandings, particularly as Robert had failed to appreciate the considerable difficulties under which his father was labouring. Robert had grown up in a comparatively easy atmosphere, it was William who had born the brunt of those early years of worry and strife, and it was William who had shouldered immense responsibilities at the age of 21 years, when he had successfully taken on the task of superintending the Liverpool branch of the business.

Had William lived nearer, or Robert visited Liverpool on occasion, one suspects Robert's stubbornness would have been less acute, certainly this was the case with Charles Jnr., however the paths of the two half-brothers rarely crossed, as each was totally committed to his own "sphere of operations", so William's role as Robert's mentor had been usurped by Cousin Hester with her dogged persuasiveness.

Following Robert's Methodist meeting of 3rd August, he wrote "When I came home my Father declared I should not come anymore into his house. He said my Cousin had been the ruin of all his children".

Hester's account of the incident, supposedly written the following day (although written in retrospect for publication at a later date) varies slightly. "I hear my Uncle Roe . . . has ord'd them [Robert etc.] to forbid me ever entering his Doors & tells them he will punish them severely if they come where I am". Hester's simplistic outlook created an incapability of understanding, what she considered to be, her uncle's irrational attitude. She reflected that her friend Polly, also a Methodist, had been "turned out by her Mother" in the spring of 1776, but when Hester had spoken of this to her uncle, he had immediately offered Polly a place in his home until her mother was willing "to take her back".

(Shortly after this incident John Wesley visited Macclesfield and Hester spent an hour with him "at old Mr. Ryles", after which he departed for Manchester).

Young Charles Roe had once again been soliciting Hester's affections on the pretext of converting to Methodism; Hester, whilst not wishing to discourage the latter had assiduously resisted the former. Suddenly, in May 1776, Charles Jnr. was taken seriously ill and begged for her presence. Mrs. Roe sent a message for her to attend: Hester wrote "I dealt very plainly with him & did not stay long – being determined not to be left with him alone – While at prayer, My Aunt seem'd Deeply Affected".

Evidently Mrs. Roe had spoken well of Hester for Uncle Charles assisted her with pocket money when her mother refused, and told his children that Hester was the one "he wish'd them to take after". Hester's contempt was obvious as she wrote "& Now - Because I do not need his fr'dship this very Person forsakes me for doing everything which at first engaged him in my favour".

Charles Roe, busy with so many weighty matters, had failed to appreciate the effect of Hester's actions and preachings, not only upon his family but also amongst his servants. It was as though, with the completion of his church, Charles had not expected Hester's Methodist crusade to continue, because he was now able to provide a more evangelical form of service in the town. In contemplating the situation the reality must have suddenly impacted on his mind. There is little doubt that Hester's rides out with young Charles and also with Joseph were then seen as part of her campaign.

Charles Roe's fury was understandable. He was probably angry with himself for underestimating what, from his point of view, was the gravity of the situation, and for allowing Hester to "pull the wool over his eyes". He was never one to admit defeat; with other disputes, such as the Anglesey mining problems and Sir Nicholas Bayly, and even the formidable question of relocating the Liverpool smelters, he had eventually won the day, but here was a young girl, his deceased brother's daughter, whom he had supported and cared for, who was stubbornly refusing to see beyond her own emotional needs. This time he could find no answer and his patience was at an end.

Rachel Harriott, whom the children regarded as "Mother", being very well thought of and respected by them, and obviously concerned for both her husband's and Robert's health, intervened to try to alleviate the situation. She pleaded with the children only to make concessions, but Robert wrote "which we durst not do for conscience sake".

On 27th August Robert and Charles Jnr., having attended chapel, returned home to be told by Joseph that they had been "turned out". Robert must have intended to return to Oxford, but Mrs. Roe begged his father to allow him to spend a long vacation in London with Aunt Stockdale. Here, once more, is a discrepancy between Robert's version and that recorded by Hester, both of which were edited many years later for inclusion in a Methodist magazine. Robert infers an abrupt decision on his father's part to turn them out of the house, but Hester reveals that Charles Roe gave them time to think things over. He demanded a promise that they would forsake Methodism, which they tenaciously refused to do, until finally he threatened them with disinheritance.

The threat was not as drastic as first appears for, by the terms of their grandfather's will, Joseph Stockdale had left the residue of his estate to be divided between his daughter, Aunt Jane Stockdale, and themselves as children of his daughter Mary; the residue must have been a fairly substantial sum. There was one important stipulation, each share could not be received by each individual grandchild until the age of 21 years. Robert, born 26th February 1754, was already 21 years of age and had therefore received his inheritance, but Charles Jnr. and Joseph would not receive theirs until 25th March 1780 and 5th May 1781 respectively. Charles Snr. was obviously counting on the fact that whilst Robert was able to support himself, the other two would find it difficult and would therefore choose to remain at home and obey his commands. Young Charles relented and asked his father's pardon, much to Hester's chagrin, but she happily wrote on Saturday 7th September, "Coz Robert & Joe are immoveable & he has turn'd them both out".

Once again Hester's dating is called into question, for on 8th September Robert reveals that he had not seen his father for five days and continues with a very moving account of that day's events. "I ventured this morning into my Father's kitchen, the backway & unexpectedly met him . . . we both stood motionless for sometime".

One wonders how many parents and children have experienced a like situation; each feeling unable to speak for fear the words uttered will cause offence, yet each desperately anxious for reassurance that their former mutual affections, though somewhat sullied, are substantially the same. The parent, still eager to command respect tries hard not to demand it, and the child, somewhat bewildered and hurt that the threat of rejection has finally been carried out, whilst anxious for forgiveness, does not want to jeopardize the newly acquired independence. Each remains guarded until the one with least pride finally gives ground.

Robert broke the silence by asking how his father was. Charles said sternly "What have you to say for yourself?" Robert repeated his question, to which Charles replied, "Pretty well". Robert in order to palliate his situation asked for his father's blessing, but Charles, perhaps guessing his thoughts, turned away and said, "I have nothing to do with you". By "noon" the Roe conscience had been hard at work and Charles Snr. sent Charles Jnr. to ask his brothers if they would dine with them that evening.

. . . "accordingly we went. Restraint by degrees wore off and all seemed well; but at half past ten at night he began to upbraid us in severe language indeed. He said we were bringing his grey hairs with sorrow to the grave: that we had nothing more to expect from him: and that perhaps we should never see him more. He said I [Robert] was to live on my own money in London henceforth and take my chance etc. I saw he expected me to ask pardon: but this I durst not do as it would be acknowledging That to be wrong which I had done from a sense of duty".

As his parents left for Liverpool the next day, Robert took his leave but was very upset. He set out for London two days later, having said his farewells to other members of the family including Hester. With much on his mind Robert rode all night and arrived at Aunt Jane's about 8 o'clock on the evening of the 12th September.

Charles Roe's visit to Liverpool must have been of short duration, for the Company Minute Book contains the signatures of himself and William, verifying their presence in Macclesfield on 17th September. Other members present were Brian Hodgson and son, Robert, Edward Leigh and Edward Hawkins, the latter once more instructed to "go into the West" and cancel Mrs. Swymmer's contract; also, an important decision was made to add six more furnaces "to the two lately erected at Liverpool".

Whilst his father's mind was again drawn towards business matters, Robert Roe remained in London until 5th May 1777 when he returned to Brasenose College, Oxford in very low spirits, "I . . . came to my lonely room, without fire, without friend." On 10th June he despairingly wrote, "My father never writes O how this grieves me!"

An unexpected letter arrived from his father on the 2nd October, which at first Robert was afraid to open, but to his surprise "it was the most kind of any received of late". Charles Snr., perhaps appreciating Robert's decision to remain in Oxford in order to attempt, for the fourth time, a pass in his aural examination before the Principal and Fellows of his college, was hoping to provide, no doubt, some moral support by writing thus. But Robert was once again to be faced with disappointment, as others, including his tutor, had objected to him being granted "the Grace", by which he would be given licence to move on and take his degree. He was subjected to a very strict examination during which he learnt that his morals and conduct were not called into question; he did agree with the stance that laymen praying in a private house or in public should not assume "the character of a Minister in administering the Sacraments", but the accusation against him, of frequently attending "the Meetings of the People called Methodists", was one which he could not deny. For this reason he was taken to task, the interpretation being an unwillingness to discuss his "scruples of conscience" with either his tutor or the others present. Under the circumstances, as further progress was impossible, his wish to enter Worcester College was denied.

On 2nd January 1778 Robert wrote to advise his father of the refusal, but in return received news of his father's ill health. By the first week in February a message was sent for Robert to visit a family acquaintance in Shropshire "to consult with him". Robert dutifully obeyed, and after several nights en route finally reached his destination, where he was unexpectedly joined, on the 24th February, by both Mrs. Roe and Rev. Simpson. Together with friends, Rachel Harriott and David Simpson did their utmost to dissuade Robert from attending further Methodist meetings, but to no avail. Robert learnt that his father intended to "ask the Bishop to force the College to give me a Testimonial".

The Bishop was John Green, Bishop of Lincoln, but his involvement by Charles Roe is not, at first, perspicuous. The Bishop, who held a residuary canonry of St. Paul's Cathedral and mostly resided in Amen Court, had been vice-chancellor of Cambridge. Charles, however, was evidently appealing to John Green in his capacity as Bishop of Lincoln, for it was one of his predecessors, William Smyth who, together with Richard Sutton of Sutton near Macclesfield, had founded Brasenose College.

The situation was a delicate one as Green had anonymously attacked the Methodists by publishing the *Principles and Practises of the Methodists* shortly before his appointment as Bishop of Lincoln in 1761. A further intended publication was discouraged by Archbishop Secker because of its ferocity, a circumstance of which Charles Roe was probably unaware. Even so he would have had little choice in the selection of someone who was in an appropriate position to intercede on Robert's behalf. It did not take long before the reality of the situation was well and truly put into perspective, for Robert and the family friend, having "received shameful treatment" from the Principal of the College in Oxford, set out for London intent on finding the Bishop of Lincoln. At the second attempt of calling the Bishop agreed to meet with them; he was "civil" but insisted that "none but the College" could determine Robert's case.

Whilst Robert returned to Shropshire, the friend hurried to Macclesfield to report to the Roe family and subsequently returned with an affectionate letter for Robert from his father. The letter also brought some surprising revelations regarding Hester and young Charles Roe, which Robert found incredible to believe, "Surely she is falsely accused".

Poor Hester deserved some sympathy, for her mother had been very ill for several months. Mrs.Legh of Adlington Hall had hurried to their home when first she received news of Elizabeth Roe's illness and, bringing with her a servant, organised as much help as possible. After arduously nursing her mother for long periods, Hester herself became ill, but, refusing all medical help, turned instead to a Methodist preacher and gradually recovered.

During the spring of 1778 John Wesley made his annual visit to the town. Two years earlier Hester, of course, had spent time with him at "old Mr, Ryles", but his visit of the previous year (9th April 1777) had been a very different affair, for he had preached in the New Church, presumably at the invitation of David Simpson. He praised the building as being "the most elegant that I have seen in the kingdom". Although Wesley had preached in Macclesfield on the following evening, it is unclear whether or not this also took place in Charles Roe's church (his usual habit was to address a gathering at Mr. Ryle's house, or if the numbers were excessive, to make use of the adjacent grassy expanse of Parsonage Green). It is evident that at this time Charles Roe intervened, for Wesley never set foot inside the church again until after Charles Roe's death. There appears to have been no argument with David Simpson, who surprisingly acquiesced, and must have taken into consideration the problems and sacrifices which Charles was making in order to achieve his objectives.

John Wesley's visit of Saturday 21st March 1778 was very brief indeed, he did not preach nor even stay overnight. His later excuse was his hurry to reach Ireland yet, despite this, he spent the evening in Manchester and then time in Liverpool, admittedly whilst waiting for a particular vessel recommended by a friend. Prior to his Macclesfield visit he had preached in Newcastle-under-Lyme, and had his haste been of such necessity, then surely he would have travelled the old pilgrims' route from there to Parkgate, for the sailing to Ireland? Wesley's Saturday visit to Macclesfield suggests that he was hoping to assist David Simpson with the Sunday service in the New Church; however, an awkward situation and respect for David Simpson's predicament had possibly inspired his unobtrusive exit from town – a very uncharacteristic action for Wesley to take.

An unprecedented event took place on 16th September 1778 and one which had been foreshadowed by an incident witnessed by Robert when visiting Whitchurch the preceding 8th May. "We were all much alarmed at the apprehension of an earthquake, hearing a loud, rumbling noise, and as we thought feeling a shaking of the ground."

The "awful earthquake" of September, as Hester's account recalls, occurred in the middle of a service which she was attending at the New Church, when the whole building "rocked like a cradle". The noise resembled thunder and many kneeling were thrown forward. Suddenly panic ensued, as people, fearing that the tower was about to collapse, rushed through the doors at the eastern end of the church "shrieking and crying for mercy". Many were bruised and suffered severely from shock, whilst those who fainted were lucky not to be trampled to death. Hester concealed her own reactions but Beilby Porteus, feeling it incumbent upon himself as Bishop of Chester to quell any hysteria, published a pamphlet entitled *A letter to the Inhabitants of Manchester, Macclesfield & the adjacent part on the occasion of the Late Earthquake in these places.*

Superstition was still very much a part of everyday concepts, and those, swathed in religious fanaticism, saw the earthquake as a punishment from God. Bishop Porteus, making full use of his adroitness, pointed out that those living in the affected area should not consider themselves "more wicked" than the rest of their "Countrymen", but to regard the event as a monitor, effectual in inducing people's minds to reflect upon their bad deeds, and by so doing make an effort to right their wrongs. Part of his address is a useful gauge in acting as a barometer for the period:

> "By the flourishing State of your Trade and Manufactures, you have for many Years been advancing rapidly in Wealth and Population. Your Towns are every Day growing in Size and Splendour; many of the higher Ranks amongst you live in no fmall Degree of Opulence; their Inferiors, in Eafe and Plenty. What the ufual Fruits of Fuch Affluence as this are, is but too well known. Intemperance and Licentioufnefs of Manners; a wanton and foolifh Extravagance in Drefs; in Equipage, in Houses, in Furniture, in Entertainments; a Paffion for luxurious Indulgencies and frivolous Amufements; a gay thoughtlefs Indifference about a future Life, and every Thing connected with it; a Neglect of Divine Worship, a Profanation of the Day peculiarly fet a-part for it, and perhaps, to crown all, a Difbelief and Contempt of the Gospel."

.

About this time Robert returned home, but finding his father away dubiously awaited his return, fearing an unhappy reunion. His alarm was unfounded for Charles Roe greeted his son with great affection; but the next few months were to witness a considerable strain put upon their relationship. Robert's presence in the house was short-lived as he again took up his former associations with his Methodist friends and conversed with John Wesley during a visit to John Ryle's house. Within a few days Mrs. Roe arrived with the message that his father desired him to leave town, but Robert strongly objected and wrote, "I think my father is very unkind; for seeing he has cast me off, it is reasonable I should live where I most conveniently can".

What to Robert seemed like his father's total irrational behaviour at this time stemmed from the spirit of a weary, troubled 63-year-old man with bad health, who was desperate for the consecration of his church. The building, as David Simpson later broadcast, had cost Charles Roe "upwards of £6,000". He could have used the money to purchase a grand estate or build himself a fine house; his Chestergate home was still mortgaged, and even that he did not redeem because of his conviction that Macclesfield needed a new church. To make matters worse the American Declaration of Independence on 4th July, 1776 was beginning to have effect, and the company was experiencing some financial difficulties.

Before long an unexpected letter to Robert gave hope that the Bishop of Lincoln was considering his ordination, and as a consequence he set out for London on 24th November, where he had been directed to meet his father. A discussion took place between the two during which Robert confessed that he had no objection to signing the 39 Articles of the Church of England, and with this in mind, Charles Roe made strenuous efforts to gain an audience with the Bishop. The second attempt was successful, but Charles, over-anxious and determined to gain his Lordship's consent, forced Robert to discuss John Wesley and the Methodists, giving the Bishop (who was not considered a particularly intelligent man) the opportunity of asking several questions which he might otherwise have considered unnecessary. As Bishop Green absented himself to look for a book, Robert upbraided his father:

> "Sir, I have to oblige you, gone to the utmost stretch, so that I am scarcely satisfied with myself. I therefore insist upon it, you press me no further, lest I make such answers as you and the Bishop did not approve of. I am determined not to forsake Mr. Wesley or his people."

That evening Robert spoke plainly, in an effort to finally force his father to understand his position. He was happy to sign 'the Articles' but if the Bishop or anyone else took this as an indication of his rejection of the Methodists then he would not subscribe to them. The irony of the situation was that the same doggedly determined spirit, as inherited by his son, which had always been such an asset to Charles Roe, was now the very trait which was working against him and thwarting his every move. Putting pen to paper Robert wrote: "My father was greatly agitated; sometimes he stormed, sometimes entreated, at others reasoned and then wept."

Three times Charles Roe kept an appointment with the Bishop of Lincoln, but on each occasion he was left waiting, so finally Charles sent one of his 'severe' letters, with surprising results. The Bishop promised ordination if two Fellows and the Principal would sign Robert's testimonial, for he considered it "a shame" that Robert should be expected to complete a further three years. Leaving Robert in London, Charles returned home a contented man.

The months passed, during which Robert, whilst staying with Aunt Stockdale, was offered two curacies but which, under the circumstances, he had to refuse. When the Bishop of Lincoln's letter finally arrived in Macclesfield Charles Roe must have been devastated, for Robert's tutor and Principal at Oxford had advised that he considered Robert had meant "to mislead his Lordship". Charles wrote a letter to Robert in March 1779 demanding his return to Oxford, which Robert refused to do. A letter from sister Peggy informed Robert of his father's displeasure at his defiance, and Robert, now apparently on the verge of a nervous breakdown, was left to wander and seek solace amongst his various Methodist acquaintances and friends in various parts of the country.

22
BUSINESS AS USUAL

Except the Lord build the house, they labour
in vain that build it.

Despite all the personal setbacks during the period from mid-1776 until the spring of 1779, it was otherwise very much business as usual for Charles Roe and the copper company. The initial trading boom, which had obviously inspired an extension of the Liverpool smeltworks, in turn produced more work for the Assay Master in Cornwall, on whose behalf Legh Dickenson had written during the spring of 1776 requesting an increase in expenses to cover for the engagement of an assistant. The reply was brusque; the copper company would not allow £40 per annum for such a purpose, as the payment of £60 per annum to the Assay Master was considered sufficient for the amount of business involved.

The £60 per annum presumably related to Roe & Co.'s portion of the Assay Master's salary, the remainder would be shared between all the other copper concerns purchasing ore in that area of Cornwall. (An extant schedule of "Copper Ores sampled the 26th June 1777, and Sold the 10th July 1777, at Redruth" lists twelve other "Buyers Names" apart from "Dicksfon"). By the following meeting of the 6th May the company, for some unknown reason, had agreed to allow Legh Dickenson £80 per annum for a clerk. At the A.G.M. of August 1776 he was requested to ship all casting stones on hand and to buy no more. These Cornish stones would be used as moulds, particularly for brass objects, and therefore utilised at the brass works on Macclesfield Common.

Problems concerning the work of employees local to Macclesfield had arisen, but the matter was dealt with promptly and appears to have come about from the misdemeanours of only three or four workmen. Work had to be redone, and in June 1776 a Mr. Krinks was allowed six guineas for losses he had incurred in soldering, hammering and turning a batch of naps (bowls), which had taken him five weeks to complete.

A new employee, Edward Harvey, was engaged from 7th August 1776, at a salary of £40 per annum, to produce a machine for cutting brass plates into slips (long narrow strips) at the Havannah works. This salary was revised to £50 per annum the following year, an indication of Edward Harvey's good work. He was also sent to visit the principal manufacturers of Sheffield so that he could observe the different processes involved in making various articles; from these observations it was envisaged that he would then be able to make judgements and improve the rolling methods of the mills at Havannah and Bosley, thus supplying a better quality of rolled brass and copper to the manufacturers.

About this time Robert Hodgson appears to have moved from Daisy Bank into Congleton itself, and taken a lease of Moody Hall. Circumstances also suggest, that with the departure of Cookson Atkinson from the company and the arrival of Edward Hawkins, Robert was now in charge of the day to day running of Havannah and Bosley.

During the spring of 1777 it was decided to increase the power of the copper battery mills at Bosley by building a weir across the river. Mat Henshall of Congleton was approached for an estimate, and was told that the weir must hold for 20 years at a height of 6 ft. The weir was subsequently completed by him; however, in May 1778 there is a suggestion that it was giving cause for concern, because a sheeting was ordered to be laid as soon as possible. This would refer to a layer of stones built in a series of mini-terraces over which the water flowed in the form of a small waterfall. The stones were necessary to give extra protection and act as a buffer against the possibility of a partial collapse or disintegration of the weir.

Edward Hawkins seems to have been engaged for the supervision of the brass works on Macclesfield Common, with jurisdiction also at Bosley in so far as it affected brass production on site i.e. the brass battery mill. Whilst Robert Hodgson involved himself in the making of a cast iron cylinder and other equipment for annealing wire, Edward Hawkins, between journeys as a Roe & Co., salesman (which entailed trips to Dublin on occasion) became so proficient in his management of brass production, that the company advised him to take out a patent in his own name. Accordingly "Hawkins Specification for Shaven or Bright Brass, A.D. 1778 No. 1189" came into being, in which he is described as a merchant of Congleton. Dated 13th March and enrolled 16th April 1778, the specification gives very little detail as to the exact processes involved, only that the "Method of Making Shaven or Bright Latten" was "By rolling, battering or hammering (and shaving for scraping) sheet brass".

The period was also one of great activity as regards acquisition of contracts with various merchants and companies, e.g. W. & T. Turner or Birch & Villiers, both brassfounders of Birmingham and the latter also pewterers; Brown & Luxford, pinmakers of Houndsditch (close by Bishopsgate); French & Hobson or Yates, Dunn & Parker, merchants of Liverpool; Cowcher & Son and John Adey, both pinmakers of Gloucester. The latter two companies ranked with Weaver and Jefferies as the three most prodigious pin producers, if not in the country, then certainly in Gloucester. William Cowcher, like John Jefferies, was an alderman of the city, but apparent rivalry between himself and John Adey had resulted in a dispute over the purchase of Roe & Co. brass, which Edward Hawkins was sent to resolve.

* * * * * * *

In 1774, the year of the Macclesfield Copper Company's formation, John Jefferies had begun his second term as mayor of Gloucester, whilst his son, John Jr. was chosen 'Bailiff of the City and Sheriff of the County'. On 10th August 1778 the father prepared his will and died almost immediately afterwards. This will relates that John Snr. had transferred "a considerable Stock-in-Trade" in several of his partnerships to his son, prior to the young man's marriage. The trustees, his "good friend" Thomas Weaver and John Baylis, woolstapler of Gloucester, were given administration of the remainder of his estate in respect of the grandchildren from his daughters' marriages.

John Jefferies Jnr. had married Charles Roe's niece, Ann Atkinson, second daughter of Rowland Atkinson deceased, former headmaster of Macclesfield Free Grammar School, at Prestbury on 25th May 1775. Three months later, on 17th August, John Snr. had relinquished his one half share in the copper company in favour of his son, who thus became a partner. Ann was fortunate to have married into one of the most consequential families of Gloucester, without doubt helped by the considerable sum received by her mother from her late father's share of the Macclesfield business – and all thanks to Uncle Roe.

Barely had his father drawn his last breath than John Jefferies Jnr. acted swiftly in obtaining execution of an Indenture dated 14th August 1778. It recites that with money received from their pinmaking partnership, Thomas Weaver and John Jefferies Snr. had bought several properties and rebuilt a compting house, workshops, warehouses, stables and other buildings "for convenience of respective habitations". John Jefferies Snr. had then purchased from Thomas Weaver two of the messuages (actually cottages) which he had subsequently demolished in order to build a 'Mansion House' on the site. This had been done on trust, so the conveyance had not been completed legally. Son, John Jnr., having replaced his deceased father in the pin-making partnership, went to court to claim ownership, not only of that particular property, but also of a large house with brewhouse and certain other workshops and buildings, which he considered appropriate to his share of the company business.

Thomas Weaver did agree to sign all the necessary legal documents, and as a consequence was fined for not having previously legally conveyed the first mentioned properties to John Jefferies Snr. Young Alderman Jefferies and his wife, Ann, immediately sold this property (i.e. the then Mansion House) to John Baylis.

Whether or not by coincidence or as a consequence of Alderman Jefferies's actions, the apothecary John Cooke withdrew from the copper company. The resignation of his share was accepted at the A.G.M. of 20th August 1778, for which he was to receive £6,347 15 4d. Efforts were made to find a replacement and Mr. Forbes, agent to the Admiralty, was approached but declined the offer. Cooke was therefore offered repayment by instalments, with the addition of interest as appropriate, and for the time being the share was held in abeyance.

Some readjustment of shares had already taken place, as instanced by the admittance of Edward Hawkins to the partnership when the shares had been increased to 15 instead of 14. This was because Cookson Atkinson had chosen not to withdraw his capital at that time, however, one year later (17th August 1776) he had withdrawn, and with no offers received for his half share, the company decided to redistribute it between the remaining partners and so create 14 and a half shares instead of 15, but it was easier to regard a whole share as $^2/_{29}$ths.

Until the upset between Thomas Weaver and young Alderman Jefferies their share had been held jointly, but from August 1778 it was divided equally, and accordingly a $^1/_{29}$th share was "placed to each credit" by request. This also resulted in the $^3/_{29}$th share of Thomas Smyth and Charles Caldwell being divided equally between them, instead of jointly as before.

At the time of the redistribution of Cookson Atkinson's share Charles Roe, who held two whole shares, was then allocated $^4/_{29}$ths. However, from 7th August 1777 he had transferred a half share, or $^1/_{29}$th, to his son, Samuel, from which date the latter was considered a partner. Samuel's career was advancing nicely; from October 1775, partnered by Samuel Glover, he had taken over part of the Waterside tenement at Disley from Brian Hodgson Snr. The property included a dwellinghouse; but the interest, apart from investment, was possibly the production of coal. From August 1776 Samuel's work with the company had been recognised when he was voted a salary of £50 per annum but, at the age of almost 28 years, this had ceased on his admittance as a partner with a half share well in excess of £3,000. Should the question of matrimony arise, Samuel was now in an eligible position.

At this time (1777) an important decision was taken to delegate command, probably as a result of Charles Roe's continuing ill health. Charles was appointed "Director to superintend [the] Works at Macclesfield", which was possibly done to minimise his necessity to travel; Robert Hodgson was likewise appointed for Havannah, Edward Hawkins for Bosley and William Roe confirmed for Liverpool, for which each was to receive £120 per annum.

William Roe's responsibilities also extended to the old works on the South Shore, which had been converted to a timber yard since the move to Toxteth Park. The property was proving difficult to sell, but William agreed to lease it for seven years to Smallshaw and Rogers from April 1777, on the understanding that if a sale was successful then they would withdraw upon 12 months notice; the rent was a useful £100 per annum. The next important task was the deepening of the dock at the Toxteth works by 4 ft, to facilitate the vessels carrying coal. It was also intended to erect a crane in order to speed up the unloading process and, taking into account the increased trade for the coal merchant John Mackay, William Roe was asked to propose to him that he should share the expenses with the copper company.

Apart from the larger issues, many minor problems arose for William. In December 1776 he found himself involved in the recovery of damages from the owner and captain of a vessel lost during the previous winter, which had been laden with copper ore. In the spring of 1779 he was advised not to send wire on vessels bound for Dublin which carried salt on board, an obvious indication that contamination had taken place.

The wire was transported as rings and would not conveniently fit into containers, which did cause problems on occasion. Wire travelling to Hull by river had been intermixed with wire from other manufacturers by the agent at Gainsborough, so it was decided to fix a 'small Brass Ticket marked C.R. & Co.' to every ring of wire for the benefit of the agent, Caleb Maulin. He was also asked to take extra care when handling these consignments, for the company valued its customers. Finally at the A.G.M. of August 1778 a decision was taken to have cases made for all wire conveyed to London, of a size to hold a 'convenient' number of rings. There were at least three sizes of wire viz. 'Standard, Midling' and 'Short'; sometimes the Midling wire was referred to as 'Old Midling' which, when re-sorted into either Short or Midling, was reckoned as 60 strings for a ring of Midling. Despite all efforts the problems continued, for in February 1779 a letter was sent to Caleb Maulin informing him that several customers had complained of the mishandling of their wire consignments, for which the company insisted on redress; not even this had the desired effect and the saga was to continue for some time.

Apart from problems with the rings of wire, difficulties continued in respect of calamine supplies. August 1776 saw an order issued to John Denman to take stock of the calamine on hand and send no more supplies for the present. He was required to send a statement of expenses for the Holywell Sough and asked to discharge an employee. Something serious had happened, for not only was Thomas Bottom discharged but also his father, and Denman was specifically instructed that they were to be forbidden entry to any Roe & Co. premises. A sample of 'calamy' (the colloquial name for calamine) was subsequently received from the agent, but considered unsatisfactory.

During December 1776 Edward Hawkins was asked to visit Shipham near Rowberrow, Somerset and examine the storage buildings close by at Winterhead, to assess the stock of calamine there. The latter place is aptly named; it was not the best time of year for such a visit, but it was necessary to make enquiries of Mr. Phippen regarding Michael Blackwall's conduct.

The situation had apparently inspired a rethink as to calamine supplies, for by September 1777 a consignment of zinc ores was en route to the port of Lancaster, destined for Liverpool. The most likely source of this ore was the Grassington mines of North Yorkshire, from where it would have been carried by pack horses, via the village of Ingleton, down to the Lancaster quayside.

At this time further problems arose in North Wales, stimulating Charles Roe into writing one of his arraigning letters. The subject of his displeasure was William Kirkland, who was refusing to co-operate with the agent, Adam Woodward, at the 'Pennygarrack Quinn' mine near Mold. The latter was instructed to take Kirkland to the mine in order to set the necessary bargains (i.e. to agree which miner should work which section), and also to advise Kirkland that Charles Roe was insisting on being paid his last quarter's share of the profit. In the event of Kirkland's lack of co-operation an explanation in writing was demanded from him immediately.

The mine had actually been working at a loss for some time. Expenses for the year ending 24th June 1777 resulted in an overall loss of £298 8 2d. From 24th June 1777 the expenses of a new sough "Waggon Gate" totalled £561 19 2d., offset by ore sales of £496 9 8d., resulting in a loss of £65 9 6d. No further details are available for this mine but, because of the difficulties which had arisen, it would appear that this new sough had proved disappointing and that mining had been abandoned about this time. The notebook containing the aforementioned details was utilised much later for household accounts and other items in Liverpool but, unfortunately, two or three pages following the details of the loss to 31st December 1777 have been torn out, making it impossible to judge whether or not further information was originally extant. Brief leasing details, relating to the years 1774-77 only, appear on subsequent pages, suggesting a cessation of mining at the close of 1777.

Until this period the old accounting procedures had been followed i.e. any expenses incurred were divided equally between the partners or shareholders, who paid in money to cover, as and when required. Any profits from ore or merchandise sales were divided between them at the end of each quarter. Those, of course, who had regular duties with the company and were not sleeping or inactive partners, in addition benefited by receipt of an appropriate salary, reviewed yearly each August at the A.G.M.

As regards the Macclesfield Copper Company, the only one of the Roe & Co. concerns for which complete minutes are extant, the A.G.M. of 17th Aug. 1776, Item 38 records "That for the future the Books . . . be kept in the true Mercantile Stile of the Book keeping that is by double Entry and the Italian Method." The company was modernising. At the same time pressure was put on Charles Roe to lease to the company the land "whereon the Compting House stands" for 99 years. Occupation of the house by John Hale, the faithful bookkeeper, was to continue at an annual rental of £12 8 6d. fixed by the Committee. Charles, however, must have considered the rent unreasonable, for he did not comply with the request for a further twelve months, at which time the rent was then agreed at £8 8s. a year.

From an auditing point of view an important part of company business, much of which was carried out on trust, was the purchase of ore, exemplified by the situation in Cornwall with its unique ticketing procedures. In order to avoid embezzlement by employees, who had an ideal opportunity to subsequently alter tickets or collude with one another, Roe & Co. and Thomas Patten's company of Warrington made an agreement. From time to time William Roe and William Dumbell (chemist and partner of Thomas Patten) met to compare Cornish ticketing. It is to the credit of Legh Dickenson that he was never found wanting, although on occasion he was asked to submit the ticketing information on a more regular basis.

It was, of course, absolutely vital for brass production that the calamine used was of the best quality and also had been dressed and cleaned properly before calcining took place. During February 1778 it was found necessary to review the situation with regard to the Derbyshire calamine, and to this end 'Mr. Hodgson' (presumably Brian Snr.) was asked to purchase a piece of ground at Bonsall on which buildings were to be constructed for cleaning and calcining the zinc ore. One year later Mr. Phippen was instructed to buy 100 tons of Mendip calamine and to order Michael Blackwall to return home. In the event Michael Blackwall must have pleaded for more time; it was not until September 1779 that William Phippen received a company letter, directing him to inform the employee that as of that date his wages ceased, and to pay him £5 expenses "in case he chooses to return to Derbyshire".

Other mining concerns of the period were the disposal of company property at Middleton Tyas (which was presumably storage facilities and equipment on site) and the outstanding settlement of the Penrhyn Du account. In June 1778 it became expedient to offer 2,000 tons of Parys Mountain ore (already calcined) to Freeman & Co. of Bristol, Lockwood & Co. of Swansea, Pengrees & Co. of Snow Hill, London, three of the companies engaged in selling copper to the East India Company, and a fourth, Tyndale & Co. of Bristol. The latter was possibly associated with Isaac Elton & Co. who were also providers of copper to the East India Company.

General business involved the collection of overdue accounts, with William Roe left to chase those owed by Liverpool merchants. Because of the unpredictability of canal navigation, especially during winter months when ice presented a particular hazard, a consideration was given to the idea of establishing a warehouse in Birmingham for those in the brass trade; but opinions had first to be sought. Meanwhile all goods from the Liverpool warehouse had been relocated by William to that of Thomas Smyth, per instructions received. As a consequence Mr. Hale found himself travelling to Liverpool in the autumn of 1778 "with Books to settle Mr. James's a/cs.".

Freight charges had come under scrutiny in November and December of 1777, as efforts were made to establish costs between certain wharves, especially on the Trent and Mersey navigation and at the ports of Liverpool and London. This became a periodic exercise, yet, as later minutes reveal, the company had no intention of altering its shipping arrangements, but was merely placing itself in a better bargaining position for obtaining comparable or reduced rates from its regular wharfingers.

Closer to home Edward Hawkins and Harvey were engaged in a project with the Hughes family, the latter being responsible for rolling copper at Bosley. The intention was to build another furnace for heating copper ready for pickling, the method used for cleaning copper wire with acid. Unfortunately, on the last day of 1778, William and Thomas Hughes were given notice that unless their behaviour improved within six months, their employment would be terminated.

Another employee, who had been summoned to appear before the Committee to answer charges made against him, was Thomas Johnson. He was responsible for the company's wood at Buglawton, where he met Robert Hodgson and Edward Hawkins in July 1777 for an inspection of timber stocks. His vindication seems apparent, for three months later a contract was made with the partnership of Johnson and Rowley for all their cord-wood; by this date however they appear to have been leasing a wood at Odd Rode in the parish of Astbury from Robert Hodgson. One can only conclude that the timbers available for felling at Buglawton had been exhausted. This cord-wood, which was usually stacks of timbers of about 4 ft in length and ideal for fuel, was probably required by the company for making charcoal.

Another important consideration of 1777 was the manufacture of fire bricks for the smelters on Macclesfield Common, a task subcontracted to John Swindells. A costing of the work was called for from Samuel Roe, in order to assess the viability of continuing with the arrangement.

* * * * * * *

Thus far one would be forgiven for assuming that the company was proceeding very well and that any cost cutting exercises, such as the transfer of Liverpool stock to the Smyth warehouse or concern over freight charges, were part and parcel of a prudent company policy. Indeed they were, but they had also become an absolute necessity, for all was not well.

The first intimation of an impending crisis occurs in the company minutes of 5th March 1778, which note that arrangements had been made for the partners to borrow "Six or eight thousand pounds to replace sums of money that have been called in by Co." By the end of August Legh Dickenson was told that the financial situation would not allow for his withdrawal of £1,000 in less than nine or twelve months, from the company bankers. In addition each shareholder was to advance £250 for each $1/_{29}$th share held to the bankers, Welch Rogers & Co., before the following 1st January, for which interest of 5% would be paid. This was despite record sales to the East India Company during the previous year of 1777, which for May and June had totalled just over 2,941 tons of copper, value £11,483 2 0d.

A meeting was arranged at Warrington during December whereby all Macclesfield Company members, including William Roe and Thomas Smyth from Liverpool, met with the Warrington Company partners to agree an agenda for a further combined meeting with the Bristol Company. This was an important amalgamation of ideas to preserve their business interests during a difficult period, and the start of a combination which would benefit all. It was based on trust and respect, although from time to time if the gentleman's agreement was found to be lapsing e.g. competition through price cutting, it was quickly brought to the attention of those concerned.

The final decisive indicator of the severe decline in business was the consideration given to reducing the number of Liverpool smelters early in 1779. Dramatic events had called for drastic actions and yet there is no hint as to the nature of the former in the company minutes, Hester's or Robert's diaries or, in fact, in many other day books or diaries of the period. Yet, at that time, one of the most important episodes in modern history was taking place.

Initially even the Government was inclined to ignore what was ill-judged as a 'riot' in the Thirteen Colonies of North America. The population there, during the first 60 years of the 18th century, had increased six fold and continued apace. The colonists expected protection and policing, which were provided by the British Army.

At the end of the Seven Years War in 1763 there had been hopes of substantially reducing the cost of maintaining both the army and navy, by placing them in reserve. However, the cost of maintaining the forces in the American Colonies, which included that of the navy's significant role in transporting both troops and supplies, was a considerable burden on the Government. Modern American estimates suggest a figure five times that of the income received by the Government from the colonies, although this was never highlighted at the time. Consequently taxes were enforced by Acts of Parliament, but bitterly disliked e.g. *The Sugar Act (1764)*, *The American Stamp Act* (1765, but later repealed) and the notorious *Tea Act (1767)*. All were opposed by William Pitt the Elder (Earl of Chatham) who, on 30th May 1777, made his memorable speech in Parliament which included the phrase "You cannot conquer the Americans". He died less than one year later. The poignancy of this remark appears to have forced the reality of the situation on an otherwise disbelieving public, particularly as things were not going well with what had grown into all out warfare. Even the Declaration of Independence, on 4th July 1776 in Philadelphia, had not been given due credence, and was obviously considered by many to be a histrionic gesture which would soon be relegated to obsoletism. But the defiance and ability of the American forces had been grossly underestimated and every battle won by the British, as in the instance of Bunker Hill near Boston in 1775, was unfortunately pyrrhic.

The realisation that the colonies were not teeming with loyalists, and the considerable loss of heart on the part of the British soldiers to kill those whom they considered countrymen, caused a rethink. It has even been suggested that the officers on both sides, being Freemasons, were reluctant to engage in combat against each other. The solution became painfully obvious as the war began to spread worldwide; Britain had to withdraw in order to limit damage.

* * * * * * *

The key to the decline of trade lies with the British Navy. In times of war only half of its service is in the movement of squadrons and engagement in battles, the other half is to protect trade. The outbreak of hostilities with the colonists brought to light the great naval predicament; although vast sums of money had been voted by Parliament for improvement of the fleet, which had seen rapid deterioration since the Seven Years War, yet due to the unreliability of contractors etc. funds had been squandered. One glaring example was the *Dragon*, built in a hurry with green timbers and launched in 1760, it had rotted by 1771.

In 1773 the Admiralty had endeavoured to take stock of its vessels, which proved an extremely difficult operation. The list of ships in full sea pay included those in the dockyards awaiting repairs. Others were awaiting appointments of captains, which could take months; meanwhile the ships lay unmanned. By the summer of 1778, when France declared her intention of supporting the American Colonies, but with the hope that relations with Britain would not be strained, the Admiralty was unable to find 50 line-of-battle ships fit for sea.

The previous year of 1777 had seen the preparation of a French fleet at Toulon, with its subsequent commission of patrolling the seas between New England and the West Indies. Inevitably, whatever the rhetoric, the initial French operations inflicted heavy damage on the West Indian trade but, by December 1778, as a retaliatory measure the Western Squadron of 43 battleships had been formed under Viscount Augustus Keppel. Meanwhile for several months the British and French fleets had played 'cat and mouse' manoeuvres around the West Indian islands.

The Americans were proving successful in taking prizes, so much so that by 1778 it was reckoned there were at least 173 American privateers. Hostilities at sea continued along the eastern seaboard of North America and south to the West Indies, with storms and hurricanes playing their part in denying a British success. In fact Admiral John Byron (grandfather of the poet), already nicknamed "Foul Weather Jack" by his men for his unfortunate ability to encounter storms, continued to warrant his soubriquet. Even Admiral Keppel, with his newly formed Western Squadron, had dashed Admiralty hopes of a resounding victory over the French fleet at Brest, by not engaging in battle. It was an important opportunity lost and the "much debated battle of Ushant", in July 1778, was considered "little more than a feeble parade". It evoked a quarrel of national proportions with Admiral Kepple eventually facing court-martial.

The American privateers continued to have an appreciable effect on trade, encouraged by the French, who openly repaired and fitted out the American ships in French ports. This supports the fact that the American presence was felt as close to home as the Channel, and also extended along the coastline of the Iberian Peninsula and North Africa, and even into the waters of the Mediterranean Sea.

The naval response was to increase vessels employed on "Convoy and Cruising". Twenty four cruisers were employed in British waters, eight of which were merchant vessels hired or bought by the navy and each equipped with 20 small guns. Between them they cruised all round the coasts, and were individually stationed in ports such as North Shields, Liverpool, Leith, Bristol, Greenock, and Plymouth. Four guarded routes to the Channel Islands, one cruised from Belfast Lough to the Mull of Kintyre and another, the Irish Channel.

Eighteen ships were on convoy duty of which the *Belleisle,* equipped with 44 guns, had the important task of escorting the East India trade home from St. Helena. Others included the *Warwick,* used to convoy trade between Cork in Ireland and Canada, and the *Ranger,* which "attended the Yarmouth Herring Fishery" and then returned to the outer part of the Thames Estaury known as the Nore. (For centuries British vessels had gathered at the Nore for the hazardous journey through the Channel, before separating to continue their voyages to distant parts). A further four ships were employed to protect the important Hudson's Bay trade and two, each carrying 50 guns, cruised along the Portuguese coast.

Despite the considerable periphery of operations, the incipient effect on trade must have been devastating, as indicated by the only extant list of ships clearing the port of Liverpool to a specific region. The early 1760s had produced a yearly average of 65 ships carrying goods to the coast of Africa; this had steadily increased to 90 by 1769 and at least 100 by the early 1770s, followed by:

1774	92 vessels		1777	30	vessels
1775	81	"	1778	26	"
1776	57	"	1779	11	"

The above figures dramatically demonstrate the impact of the war on the commerce of Liverpool and the consequent recession experienced by merchants such as Roe & Co. The outlook remained bleak, for in the summer of 1779 Spain joined forces with France against the common enemy, with the Dutch conveniently 'waiting in the wings'.

The court martial of Admiral Keppel, after his dismal failure to defeat the French fleet at the battle of Ushant in July 1778, though vigorously impugned by his friends, had taken place from 7th January to 11th February 1779 and ended in his acquittal. Because of his ill health, Keppel's advocates had supported a private bill though Parliament during the first week of January, by which he was allowed to stand trial on shore and not, as naval law dictated, on his flagship in Portsmouth. By coincidence the bill, ANNO 19 George III CAP VI, was followed by (CAP VII) "An Act for making the Church or Chapel erected by Charles

Roe Efquire, in the Town of Macclesfield, in the County Palatine of Chefter, a perpetual Cure and Benefice, and for endowing the fame, and vefting the Right of Nomination or Prefentation thereof in the faid Charles Roe, his Heirs and Affigns, and for other Purpofes."

* * * * * * *

At last Charles Roe had obtained legal status for his chapel, but at a price, for he had agreed with Rev. Peter Mayer, Vicar of the mother church of Prestbury, that he would provide the latter with £200 for "augmenting the Maintainence of the Ministers of the Chapels of Rainow and Saltersford within the said Parish of Prestbury" and also lying within the area of Macclesfield Forest. This substantial sum had to be paid by 29th September otherwise the Act would be declared "null and void". One vital provision, the agreement to which had been obtained in advance by Charles with both Peter Mayer and Charles Legh of Adlington, Patron of Prestbury Parish Church, was that he (and also his heirs) would have right of nomination and presentation of the Minister to the new chapel, now to be called Christ Church, to which Beilby Porteus as Lord Bishop of Chester had given his consent.

Other details included the appointment of Wardens, Organists, Sextons and any other officers by Charles Roe as patron (and subsequently his heirs), with the Wardens appointed annually. The Wardens' obligations involved letting a certain number of pews, sufficient to provide an annual income of £180, which was necessary to cover the payment of salaries or stipends to the Minister, Clerk, Organist, Sexton etc. Two pews were specifically reserved; one "numbered with the Figures 61" for the Curate and the other "numbered with the Figures 74" for the Church Wardens. All other pews or seats could be sold or let at the discretion of Charles Roe and his heirs. Rents were due half-yearly at Christmas (Feast Day of the Nativity of our Saviour Christ i.e. 25th December) and Midsummer (Feast Day of Saint John the Baptist i.e. 24th June), and had to be recorded in an account book. If any rent remained unpaid "by the Space of Thirty Days" then the pew could be relet and action taken for recovery of the debt.

The stipend of the Curate was set down as £100, payable by the Wardens half-yearly on the same due dates as the rents, with the first payment to be made on Christmas Day following the consecration of the chapel. The Wardens were also responsible for making payment of all other salaries and for providing bread and wine for Communion, books and surplices, and for keeping in repair the walls, gates, chapel and yard together with the clock, bells and any other appurtenances.

Two important specifications were embodied in the Christ Church Act to preserve the rights and privileges of both Prestbury Parish Church and the Parochial Chapel of Macclesfield; firstly the prohibition of the creation of a new parish; and secondly the preservation of revenues. The latter created complications; no marriages or burials within Christ Church itself were to be allowed, and any burials in the graveyard, or christenings were to be "registered as usual in the Register of the old Chapel" with payment of double fees. One half of such fees was to be paid weekly (or as received) to the Minister, Clerk and Sexton of the Parochial Chapel.

The only specific reference to the burial ground is interesting in light of what had gone before, and reads:

"Whereas Charles Roe . . . hath also allotted, set out, and enclosed, a Piece of Ground (which hath been already consecrated) as and for a Cemetery or Burying-ground belonging to the said Church or Chapel, containing Eighty Yards in Length, and Seventy Yards in Breadth, Part of a certain Field commonly called The Marly Bank, the Property of the said Charles Roe."

There is no reference to the conveyance of this plot to the Mayor, Aldermen and Burgesses, yet Charles Roe had "allotted, set out, and enclosed" it, albeit at their request. One is forced to consider the notion that the carefully chosen wording of the Act was a deliberate ploy to encourage the idea that the plot of land or graveyard was a legal appurtenance of Christ Church and not a Public Cemetery used as an extension of St. Michael's graveyard. Rev, Hewson was no longer present to air his objections, and after all that had taken place Charles was more than likely regretting his apparent inducement to the Corporation. However, the Indentures of lease and release, dated 20th and 21st July 1773 had been copied, and the copies verified as true on 6th June 1775 by no less a person than the Town Clerk, Peter Wright and witnessed by a David Mears, then kept by the former. The originals have disappeared together with the relevant Vestry Minutes for the period 1760 to 1794, relating to St. Michael's Church, the only hiatus in what appears to be an otherwise complete collection of parochial records preserved from the Elizabethan period.

With the payment of £200 to Rev. Peter Mayer by the 29th September Charles Roe was officially able to offer the New Church "to be severed from all common and profane Uses and to dedicate and consecrate the same for the Worship and Service of Almighty God." There was nothing further to delay the Consecration Service which took place on Tuesday 16th November. This time there was no copper company meeting to coincide with the event, for the November Meeting had been arranged for the 30th. The choice of name is interesting and possibly taken from Christ Church in Spitalfields with its close association with the silk trade and cousin Christopher.

The Consecration Service commenced with Beilby Porteus reciting the Act of Parliament before a crowded congregation which included, not only the Vicar of Prestbury and Prime Curate of St. Michael's, but also clergy from the neighbouring villages of Astbury, Alderley, Baddiley and Siddington. He confirmed that Charles Roe had completed the chapel and furnished it with a Communion table, font, pulpit, reading desk and all other necessities as contained in the Act, which amplified the gesture as, "for the Performance of Divine Service, according to the Rites and Ceremonies of the Church of England." Charles Roe signed to acknowledge the forfeiture of any rights he had previously held in the church or yard, and to ratify his promise that Christ Church would be regarded as a holy place and used accordingly.

The very next day i.e. 17th November, a licence was granted to Rev. David Simpson making his temporary curacy at the "new Chapel" a permanent one at "the Church or Chapel of Christ in Macclesfield, on the Nomination of Charles Roe of Macclesfield aforesaid Patron."

Ironically Robert Roe was not present to see one of his father's dearest wishes fulfilled and one can only imagine the inner grief of his father, when facing the probability that Robert would never become minister there. Robert's thoughts on the subject are unrecorded for, due to ill health, his journal had been neglected for several months.

Even Hester Ann Roe's journal is obstinately silent regarding the consecration of her uncle's church, yet on personal matters she was surprisingly forthcoming.

* * * * * * *

After the dreadful experience of the September earthquake in 1778, Hester had spent several weeks at Adlington Hall, during which time she was plagued once more by her recurring ill health. The summer of 1779 saw her recover sufficiently to begin a round of visits to Methodist friends in other parts of Cheshire. She rode off with cousin Joseph Roe to Nantwich where her good friend, Miss Salmon, joined them for a visit to Chester. They dined and stayed overnight at Mr. Platt's on Friday, 11th June, "being nearer ye Boat then it is at Nantwich", for their intention was to travel to the city by canal.

The next day the trio rode the seven or eight miles to the waterway through very heavy rain where, once on board the boat, Hester fell asleep, later to awake feeling "refreshed". At this time the canal terminated just outside the city, which entailed a walk of about one mile. The rain continued heavy as the small group made its way towards Mr. Bennett's shop. Hester later wrote "<u>He</u> was <u>there</u> I tho[ugh]t D[ea]r Miss Salmon to have fainted – Coz Joseph was struck pale w'th astonishment" . . . She was referring to young Charles Roe. Hester, apparently unperturbed by the encounter, behaved in a cool, rational manner, for it had crossed her mind, whilst sailing along the canal, that Charles Jnr. might be in Chester.

Young Charles, having been encouraged, quite erroneously, by many of Hester's "religious" friends, believed her to be in love with him to the extent that her "health and life" depended upon him marrying her. Hester vehemently refused to converse with him, yet he followed her everywhere, professing his love. Whenever Hester was out in company, even when she was deep in conversation with others, young Charles disrupted the proceedings by attempting to force his attentions on her; but to everyone"s "astonishment" Hester held firm, tenaciously refusing to acknowledge his presence. Charles Jnr., barely 20 years of age, was an emotional young man whose protestations, according to Hester's notes, included threats of shooting her, shooting himself, shooting his brother (presumably Joseph) and also many of her friends. However, after only two days of "resistances" on Hester's part, he left Chester and returned to Liverpool.

The following day, Tuesday 15th June, Hester and Joseph set out for Malpas, where they remained for two weeks before returning to the Salmon household in Nantwich. Mr. and Mrs. Salmon had already left for Shrewsbury but had given instructions that Hester was to remain as long as possible which, in the event, was only two days. Hester returned home where she remained for several months. During August a letter arrived from Miss Salmon, who was visiting friends in Halifax, containing the unhappy news that Robert was ill in Leeds. By December Hester's mother and their maid were also very ill.

* * * * * * *

Charles Roe Snr.'s health continued to give cause for concern, although he was present at every company meeting throughout the year of 1779 which, as near as possible, took place on a monthly basis; he was obviously intent on asserting his considerable influence for as long as possible. Together with Edward Hawkins he attended the East India Company sales in London during August, but both returned for the important A.G.M. on the 25th, when eleven partners were present.

From this time onwards Joseph Cooke, solicitor of Jordangate in Macclesfield, was engaged to act in all legal matters on behalf of the company within the town and its environs, and was instructed to enforce payment of the principal and interest due from the Commissioners of the Bosley Turnpike.

Evidently a site at Bonsall had been found for the processing of calamine, as a rent of £5 per annum was agreed in respect of a dwelling rented there by a William Brace.

John Denman, who had been asked for some considerable time to forward "the reckonings" and a copy of the lease for the Holway Sough, was once again prompted to despatch the documentation.

As previously noted the first half of the 1770s had seen well over 200 tons of calamine each year brought up the River Weaver for Roe & Co. The total of just over 112 tons in 1776 was a drastic reduction, and the figure of only 91 tons for 1777 does support the winding down of calamine supplies from the Holway Sough. However, the year 1778 provides a more back-to-normal figure of $247^1/_2$ tons, with a slight reduction to at least 185 tons during 1779. Circumstantial evidence suggests that this new source of calamine was from North Yorkshire, for only two months after the A.G.M. William Roe was instructed to purchase Captain Overend's share of the "Calamy works in Yorkshire" which, from subsequent meetings, is referred to as a "Calamine mine in Wensley dale". A later deed reveals Peter Wilson Overend mining on his own account at Bewerley, 10 miles east of Grassington.

With the calamine problems hopefully in the process of being resolved Roe & Co. were also compelled to consider coal supplies. John Mackay had sent a "great Quantity of small Coal" to the Liverpool works, although he knew it to be "totally unfit for the Furnaces", (a complaint later echoed by Thomas Williams of Anglesey after having acquired a smeltworks in South Lancashire). Mackay was to be sent a letter of complaint, giving details of the losses incurred for the last quarter. The lease for the colliery on Macclesfield Common (Greenaway) expired on 29th May 1779 and a reckoning was taken of the stock of coals 'on the Bank'. Possibly because of this an agreement was drawn up, for one year only, with four local dealers for coals from the Sponds Colliery near Pott Shrigley, to be delivered to the works on Macclesfield Common. It is possible that the Greenaway lease was renewed at this time, however, the coal seams, of no great depth to begin with, were thinning considerably and although the quality was good it was only of use as house coal.

Edward Hawkins was kept busy in his capacity as salesman; during the year of 1779 he visited Derby and London, and his trips to Ireland must have been a success, for the company now recorded a warehouse in Dublin in addition to those of London and Liverpool.

A further warehouse was planned at the Red Bull Wharf, Lawton on the Trent and Mersey canal, the nearest point to Havannah and Bosley. With Robert Hodgson appointed to act on behalf of the company in negotiating a lease for an appropriate piece of land on which to build, he attended a navigation meeting at Stone in Staffordshire.

A final item of 1778 had been to note a renewal of lease, early in 1779, with William Armett Esq. for Dean's meadow and road. This land lay virtually contiguous to the Havannah works and would appear to have been leased shortly after the initial development of the site by the Macclesfield company.

The efforts of Edward Hawkins, with his invaluable connections in East London, accompanied by William Roe, were beginning to pay dividends. In July 1778 they had succeeded in securing further sales with the East India Company which brought the year's total to 1,842 tons, value £7,840 6s. This part of the business had obviously been given priority as the Atlantic trade continued in depression and "Charles Roe & Copper Co." proved to be the largest supplier of copper to the East India Company in that year. By June 1779 William Roe was insuring every ton of copper shipped from Liverpool to the East India Company for 60 guineas, a considerable valuation.

Edward Hawkins and William Roe had also approached William Forbes, in an effort to sell 'Tile Copper' to the Admiralty. This was impure copper, described as iron copper, for it was the scruff skimmed off the surface of the molten metals in the furnaces and allowed to solidify into flat cakes, ideal as ballast for ships. An extension of this visit was to persuade the agent to order copper sheets from the company, for at last the Admiralty, taking heed of its naval commanders, had begun in earnest to sheathe its ships.

Meanwhile William Roe had become involved with experiments concerning the calcining of Parys Mountain ores. His patent no.1216 enrolled 1st July 1779 (the specification of which he had acknowledged on 14th June) refers to a new process for extracting sulphur from poor copper and lead ores and "rendering such poor ores as were before Unsaleable as Valuable and Saleable as any Ores". The idea must have been conceived partially from a wish to control the obnoxious fumes emitted by the huge smouldering heaps of sulphurous ores on the mountainside, and also from an inherent desire to waste as little as possible.

The plan was to construct stone or brick kilns in whatever shape or size was necessary i.e. circular, oblong etc. with a capacity from (say) 5 tons to 2,000 tons. Fireplaces with open roofs were to be built at convenient distances within the outer walls and each covered by an iron grille to allow the heated draught to rise through, yet at the same time prevent the ore from falling down onto the fire.

First the ore had to be sorted and the larger pieces placed in the kilns as the initial layer. This was followed by a layer of smaller pieces which in turn received a covering of brick, stone, slate, sods of earth or soil, the latter having apertures left in various parts for the smoke and sulphur to pass through.

The practical application of the patent required the construction of a horizontal brick chimney or flue along the ridge of the heap of ore within each kiln. The smoke was drawn through a vent along this main chimney and into two or three other flues, all of which led off the main flue at intervals but in the same direction, until they entered a large arched chamber. There the smoke "condenses and falls to the ground in real Sulphur of Fire yellow powder where it lies perhaps a foot or more deep." After collection it was boiled and cooled, becoming "hard as a Rock" on solidification, in which form it was sold to gunpowder manufacturers etc. as "Stone Brimstone". Although the profits realised from this part of the business were comparatively small, yet the product was extremely important, for otherwise the sulphur, needed urgently by the munitions makers, had to be imported from Italy. Another lucrative by-product was silver, now easily extracted from the calcined ores by the washing and buddling processes, as it was no longer contaminated by the presence of sulphur particles.

The patent would appear to be a straightforward natural progression from the work overseen by William Roe on behalf of Roe & Co., as in the instance of Edward Hawkins's patent, but behind the scenes an incredibly devious scheme was being hatched by certain individuals, of which the company was obviously unaware.

* * * * * * *

The episode had begun the previous year when John Champion Jnr. had written a letter dated 12th March, to Sir Nicholas. "I am the acting Partner . . . of a Company who have long ago had a Patent in course (which we can seal any day) for . . . making Brimstone." He continued by stating that the amount of sulphur in the Anglesey ore would make the workings worthwhile, and proposed that his partnership would build and pay for the necessary kilns, whilst Sir Nicholas could provide men to wheel the ore in and out of them.

His second proposal was far more significant; he had recently visited Parys Mountain and from his observations had concluded that improvements could be made for mining it, therefore he had approached "some Men of Businefs of my acquaintance, men of very large property, that we should make application to you for the whole or part of the said Mine;" and inferred an offer of a beneficial lease.

Sir Nicholas, taking the bait, had quickly replied, for a further letter was sent by John Champion Jnr. on 11th April acknowledging one from Sir Nicholas. Evidently the leasing of the mine was the important issue but John Champion Jnr., presumably taken a little by surprise at the speed with which Sir Nicholas replied, began to procrastinate by declaring that further enquiries and consultations were necessary. He did, however, provide answers to some of Sir Nicholas's queries regarding the calcining process, by giving assurances that the copper ore was not injured in any way, and that, although it would lose weight, he could not say by how much. The kilns were to be situated on the mountain near the sea. He wrote again on the 27th April stating that the intention was to offer "so much per ton", but after consultations Sir Nicholas's suggestion, "that of paying a yearly income" was approved of so he asked Sir Nicholas to make a "demand upon us".

This time Sir Nicholas was having second thoughts and delayed his reply. John Champion Jnr. anxious to pursue the matter, wrote again on 24th May . . . "if you are not dispos'd to treat with us for the Mine, . . . consider . . . the Brimstone making", and surprisingly continue:

"As acting Partner of the Brimstone Company I have taken Mr. William Roe of Liverpool into Partnership & under Right of the Brimstone Concern Patent he is authorised to carry on this concern at Liverpool & on Paris Mountain."

This is so blatantly fallacious one wonders how he expected to get away with it. Under the Articles of Agreement for the Macclesfield Copper Company William Roe was debarred from entering a partnership with any outsider and William certainly would not have contravened the Articles. Also the patent did not exist in John Champion's nor anyone else's name until William Roe acknowledged his own patent on 14th June, which does appear to refer to the same process. If John Champion Jnr. had been responsible for the experimentations and then found himself without financial support in taking out the patent, it does seem possible that he had approached William Roe with a view to selling him the process. There is no denying that for long enough the Quaker family of Champions had been experimenting with sulphur extraction from various ores, and there is little doubt that John Champion Jnr. would have learnt the importance of acquiring patents, with all their lucrative advantages, from his elders.

Subsequent correspondence suggests that Champion was working on his own behalf to procure a monopoly of sulphur extraction by the new process, for he was trying to inveigle, not only William Roe and Sir Nicholas into his scheme but also, Rev. Edward Hughes. To each he offered the same terms i.e. for his payment of £50 per annum and construction of the kilns he would calcine all their ores and retain the profits from the brimstone. They, of course, were expected to provide workmen for breaking down the ore and then for loading and emptying the kilns. His enticement to each was that he had already received agreement from one of the others. He even instructed Sir Nicholas to write "on condition that Mr, Hughes gives his consent" on his document, having already told him that Hughes had agreed to the terms. The footnote to the Champion letter of 24th May is intriguing:

> "Please to observe that Mr. Roe has no concern nor any knowledge of my application to you about the Mine, tho' he is my Partner in making Brimstone from Anglesey copper ore."

At this juncture Sir Nicholas Bayly approached Roe & Co. with a proposal for them to lease his share of the moiety held with Hughes. Circumstantial evidence suggests that he was determined to receive $1/3$rd duty ore, but this time Roe & Co. were in no hurry to reply. Their reluctance is hardly surprising, and maybe sensing that no other mining company would be willing to agree to such a high duty charge when taking into account the difficulties of extraction, they decided to bide their time. Perhaps they would later rue their misjudgement, for although they were correct in deducing that another mining company would not be involved, they had reckoned without a London broker and an Anglesey attorney.

On 31st August 1778, whilst still contriving to procure both patent and customers for his calcining schemes, John Champion Jnr. wrote once more to Sir Nicholas and added a further footnote regarding the mining lease. As Roe & Co. had failed to contact Sir Nicholas, Champion suggested their "disapprobation" of the offer, which had been promised to him in the event of their refusal. His final known words on the matter were that if he received the offer in writing, then he would "set out for the Mine immediately", make the "final calculations" and meet Sir Nicholas "in Town" (presumably London).

Only three months later, in November , Sir Nicholas "Demised all his Moiety" of the Parys Mountain mines held equally with Rev, Hughes, to Mr. John Dawes for 21 years "at Certain Rents and Duties". One suspects that Dawes was one of the "Men of Businefs and "very large profit" referred to by Champion, but further indicators suggest that in the first instance they had both been solicited by none other than Thomas Williams.

* * * * * * *

John Dawes of Highbury House, Middlesex, was a broker who first appears in the East India accounts for 1777 together with Roe & Co. His sale of 3,721 tons of copper was the largest in that year, with Roe & Co. superseding him during 1778. In 1775 a John Dawes of Cannonbury House, Middlesex had been engaged by the Duke of Devonshire to sell Ecton ore. The 1777 tonnage sold to the East India Co. by Dawes under this contract was only 199 tons, therefore Dawes must have had other contracts at this period for more than one concern.

Circumstantial evidence suggests that Dawes was possibly selling copper on behalf of Williams, who from that year had surreptitiously taken an interest in a smeltworks called Upper Bank or Plas Uchaf near Swansea, South Wales.

The works were originally set up for smelting lead in the late 1750s and had been in the ownership of a London Alderman, Chauncy Townsend and his son-in-law John Smith, who happened to be solicitor for the East India Company. In 1777 the works changed hands and began smelting copper; the new owners, of whom little is known, traded as Joseph Rotton & Co. and yet this must have been the business where Williams was principal partner for he complained to Lloyd (see below) early in 1780 of being "considerably cheated by our first agent there", but fortunately had made a large profit for 1779. Williams evidently realised, unlike Sir Nicholas and Hughes, that a significant amount of money was to be made from smelting and that he could purchase all the ores on Parys Mountain, except those of Roe & Co. comparatively easily. However, knowing the antagonism which existed between himself and Sir Nicholas, resulting from the part he had played in the earlier litigations, he worked in utmost secrecy, later admitting to a friend "I don't tell anybody even my own", and added with admonition "much less you".

Sir Nicholas, totally unaware of the deception which was taking place, had accepted the offer from Dawes, which included payment of 1/3rd. duty ore, but Dawes was acting as Trustee for Thomas Williams. A later dispute reveals that Williams offered Dawes, in return for his trouble, either a share in the concern or "a certain sum of money"; Dawes chose the former. The leases granted by Sir Nicholas and dated 14th and 17th November 1778, were effective from 12th November. Dawes later confirmed in court that whilst he owned a 1/3rd. share, he held the remaining 2/3rds on behalf of Thomas Williams of Llanidan. It was such a closely kept secret that even in four years time i.e. 1782, when a report of the workings would be commissioned, it would state "A New Company seems to have been formed and it is not clear who is involved except a Mr. Dawes".

A complication arose when Williams admitted his "Friend and acquaintance" Hugh Lloyd into the partnerhsip for a quarter of an ounce or 1/64th share. This was either a relative of, or Dr. Hugh Francis Lloyd from Fynachdy, Anglesey, a former High Sheriff and partner in the Llanberis Company at the time of the dispute in the early 1760s. When Lloyd later arraigned Williams regarding an extension of his share, Williams declared that Lloyd had "repeatedly requested" a share in the concern, and yet a letter addressed to Hugh Lloyd from Williams on 8th September 1779 suggests a different story:

> "From your silence I might suppose the Mine concern is beneath your attention, but perhaps your Patriotick Spirit wo'd not of late admit of any such private considerations. However we are going on Swimmingly at Paris Mountain but confoundedly in Debt . . ."

Apparently the company had bought up all the old Bayly stocks including the duty ore from Roe & Co. until Sir Nicholas had "not a single lump left". Williams's letter was written with the intention of persuading Hugh Lloyd to invest further in a smeltworks in Lancashire which Williams had just inspected. The suggested deposit was £360 with a possible £50 later, and the comment that "our friend Dawes can sell the Copper as fast as it is smelted" does imply a business association already established between Williams and Dawes before their venture into mining. Williams's cupidity got the better of him as he wrote "we can now avail ourselves of the smelting profits and put them in our pockets". Inevitably he proudly boasted that the "Lancashire scheme" had "vexed the Liverpool and Warington Smelting company", an obvious reference to Roe & Co. and Thomas Patten, but being "out of their power" there was nothing they could do about it. From whom Williams purchased the Ravenhead Smelting Works is difficult to deduce, for there is a mention of the deposit not yet paid to a Mrs. Carreg.

* * * * * * *

For some time to come there were to be no obvious clashes between the various groups on Parys Mountain, and however thwarted John Champion Jnr. must have felt with regard to the sulphur extraction process, his frustrations could not have lasted long for he died in August 1779.

By November unfortunately Latham Arnold, partner and London agent for the East India captains, had also died and his close associate Robert Pyrke of Newnham requested that the Macclesfield company take his share. It was pointed out that under the Articles there was no obligation to do so, but a promise was made to "look out for a purchaser" and failing that consideration would be given to taking back the share on the same terms as those of Messrs. Cooke and Pitt.

In retrospect perhaps Roe & Co. had panicked unnecessarily, having over-estimated the extent of the trading crisis. Shipments of ore from Parys Mountain to the Liverpool smelters had been withheld between 1st. November 1778 and 1st. March 1779, resulting in the partial shut down of the works. The East India sales had certainly saved the day but no one could have predicted the speed with which the Admiralty would move, in an endeavour to sheathe as many ships as possible in as short a time as possible.

The inspiration behind this sudden change of naval policy could have been the alarm caused by the French Admiral D'Orvilliers who, having been joined by the Spanish fleet in June 1779, almost reached Plymouth on the 14th August and in the process captured the *Ardent*. The attack was countered successfully by William Bastard in charge of the Plymouth garrison yet, despite the fact that the French and Spanish fleets commanded the Channel for four days, for some inexplicable reason they never capitalised on their success.

23

THE END OF AN ERA

... two vessels of fine copper, precious as gold.

Early in the spring of 1780 a powerful French fleet, having sailed from Brest, arrived in the West Indies. The British fleet, with Admiral Rodney in command, after carrying stores and soldiers to Mediterranean fortresses, was now ready to reinforce the Caribbean and the copper sheathing of ships became imperative for gaining advantage over the enemy.

As previously mentioned a frigate in full sail could reach 13 to 15 knots but barnacles and weed growth on the hull, particularly in tropical waters, reduced speeds to 11 knots and also reduced manoeuvrability. The experiments of 1761 with the frigate, *Alarm,* had shown that copper sheathing prevented such contamination and also, of course, guarded against rot from the actions of the teredo worms.

It was estimated that to sheathe a First Rate ship 17 tons of copper would be required in the form of 4,000 sheets (which allows for an approximate weight of 10 lbs per sheet), with 30 cwts. of copper nails to fasten them. This is a somewhat arbitrary estimate as initially thicker sheets were used, referred to as "of 22 ozs." but this was shortly reduced to "thin Copper of 16 to 18 ozs." This possibly indicates weight per square foot, which does give a remarkably thin layer of copper, seemingly compensated by the application of an extra coat of white lead paint, making three coats in all.

Already by 13th January 1780 a Roe & Co. invoice confirms that at least three cases of copper sheathing, containing respectively 65, 75 and 75 sheets, had been consigned to London. Addressed to "Mr. William Forbes, Primrose street, Bishopsgate Street London". It also contained a letter pointing out that the usual disruptions due to frost had occurred on the canal (from Staffordshire through the Midlands) but that the sheathing would arrive in due course via Gainsborough. Edward Hawkins also advised "we continue to make considerable quantites of sheathing at all our Mills which shall be delivered at Liverpool to the Ametys desire". The Naval Minute Book for Tuesday 2nd May 1780 records that the Master of the *Amitys Desire* at Liverpool was to take on board as much copper as Mr. Forbes's agent had to hand, and not to delay in "proceeding with the first Convoy".

At this time also the Admiralty was receiving copper sheathing for the Portsmouth Yard from Sir Herbert Mackworth's company (Gnoll) in South Wales and held a further contract with the Mines Royal Company. William Forbes was under contract to copper bottom the *Nemesis,* and the Roe consignments via Gainsborough appear to have been part of this. Having completed the task Forbes was asked by the Admiralty to state the lowest price he would accept for coppering the 'Dodalus' [*Daedalus*], which had to include three coats of white lead on each copper plate. The *Daedalus* was to be fitted out at Liverpool for Channel service, and the comment, that if the price for the white lead could not be agreed with Mr. Fisher then to suggest an alternative sub-contractor, once again indicates involvement by Roe & Co. Edward Hawkins's letter of the13th January concludes ". . . our Mr. Wm Roe will send You Mr. Fisher's receit for sheath(in)g deliv'd to him . . ."

The second week of May 1780 saw the Admiralty clerk extremely busy issuing orders to the stores at Sheerness and Deptford in respect of copper sheets, nails and fastenings to be delivered to the naval dockyards of Plymouth and Chatham. Portsmouth also received orders to refit and copper the *Diligente* and *Monarco* after the *Prince William* and *Minerva* were taken into the dock.On Thursday 11th May 1780 a note was made to inform Roe & Co.:

> "it is not in our power to order Bills to be made out till the Copper is rec'd at the Yard, which we hope will be soon, as we are in daily expectation of hearing of the Transport with it sailing for Plymouth. And that we are not in want of any further quantity at present."

An interesting note is recorded on the 16th May to advise Messrs. Smallshaw & Rogers of the agreement made with Mr. Hillhouse to copper the *Cleopatra*. Messrs. Smallshaw & Rogers were the Roe & Co. lessees of the old smeltworks site, now a timber yard, on the Liverpool South Shore, and had obviously been recruited in the drive to expedite the sheathing programme.

Whilst the company made great efforts to maintain a share of this lucrative market, Charles Roe's health continued to give cause for concern, so much so that a trip to Bath had been considered necessary. Although he was present at the February company meeting, all meetings were then postponed till 7th June 1780 "on a/c of absences". It appears, however, that his indomitable spirit was still very much in evidence, for a Roe & Co. deputation met with those from the Bristol and Warrington companies in Shrewsbury during March, and suggests that his outward journey was planned to enable him to take part, after which he completed the journey to the spa town.

* * * * * * *

Amongst the clientele who regularly frequented Bath were many familiar names; Sir George Warren, K.B. who owned collieries at Poynton near Macclesfield; Viscount Molyneux, landlord of the Toxteth Park Estate; the Earl of Harrington from whom Roe & Co. leased the Bosley estate; Earl and the Hon. Paulett, who owned calamine lands in Somerset; Sir James Lowther, owner of mines in the Lake District. Others, included on the list of Nobility and Gentry, were the Duke of Marlborough, the Marquis of Carnarvon and the Earl of Radnor.

Amongst the 'lesser mortals' there was Thomas Brock of Chester together with Sir Herbert Mackworth, owner of the Gnoll Company South Wales, John Stafford's son, William of Macclesfield and John Jefferies of Gloucester. Jefferies was in the enviable position of having apartments in the Royal Crescent close by Thomas Brock's residence, whilst Sir Herbert and William Stafford were also near neighbours, having bought new residences on River(s) St. adjacent to The Crescent.

Where the Roe family stayed on this occasion is not recorded, but the visit was of short duration, possibly eight weeks, for Hester recounted that Uncle Roe returned to Macclesfield on 12th May, two weeks earlier than expected. Charles Jnr. had once again been causing problems for Hester, but as a consequence of her Uncle's return his "designs" had been "frustrated" and, much to Hester's surprise, young Charles was ordered to return to Liverpool by his father.

The summer of 1780 progressed quietly enough with its tinges of domesticity and no undue alarms. Hester and her brother, James, visited Adlington Hall on 16th June where their mother was spending her usual sojourn. One week later a Friday evening Charity Sermon was delivered at Christ Church, followed by a concert with music from the *Messiah;* the proceeds were used to fund education for the poorer children of the town. Hester, busy as ever amongst her Methodist friends, was annoyed to learn that Aunt Atkinson had accused her of neglecting her mother, who was suffering badly with rheumatism. Within a short time Hester was once again complaining of headaches and feeling exhausted.

The house of Thomas Brock on the corner of Upper Church Street, Bath. It is now an extension of the Crescent, but was unattached when originally built.

* * * * * * *

The company A.G.M. appears to have taken place in Macclesfield as usual during August when nine members were present, including Thomas Weaver from Gloucester. A decision was taken to melt down all stocks of short wire and discontinue its production. Samuel Roe was instructed to meet with Mr. Orford, steward of the Lyme Estate, to discuss terms for a lease of Sponds Colliery; meantime Mr. Cooke, the company solicitor, was to draft an appropriate lease.

An intriguing note refers to a payment of £3,000, due to the Executors of Lord Strange (son of the Earl of Derby) which was to be "paid off", this possibly relates to mortgaged premises in Liverpool which, with the consent of Lord Derby, were to be re-assigned. Little is known of this property but, it could relate to that later appearing in Brian Hodgson Snr.'s will.

Another directive to William Roe suggests that the company held a lease of "Mrs. Parr's Estate at the Copper Works in Croxteth Park", for he was asked to procure an additional life in it whilst applying to Lord Sefton for a reversionary lease. This is the first intimation of this lease and although somewhat ambiguous, appears to relate to a farm, certainly in possession of Roe & Co. at a later date, lying adjacent to the Toxteth smelters.

Edward Harvey remained busily engaged at Havannah; having altered an oven for annealing bright latten, he was made responsible for purchasing and transporting cordwood to the works and was accordingly voted an extra payment of five guineas per year for this contract. In addition he gained extra duties as and when they arose e.g. together with a workman he was sent to London on 8th September to inspect the stock of wire held by Mr. Bevington (which had become contaminated over a period) and to make saleable as much as possible. Another important decision was to find him "a young promising boy" for an apprenticeship and another for William Krinks, both employees evidently proving to be conscientious, hardworking and producing work of a high quality.

Edward Leigh, married to Brian Hodgson's daughter, Elizabeth, finally severed his connections with the copper company by transferring his share to his brother-in-law , Francis Ferneyhough. (Ferneyhough, a druggist of Hatton St., Holborn in London, had married Catherine Hodgson in 1774 and was obviously in possession of a considerable fortune.) The enmity which evidently existed, at least on Brian Hodgson's side of their relationship, must have had something to do with Leigh's decision and before long he was investing in the Cheadle Copper Company.

Only four members were present on 28th September when the company meeting was held in Congleton. Brian Hodgson Snr., son Robert, Edward Hawkins and Thomas Smyth made up the complement, but little business was dealt with. However, it is apparent that Roe & Co. were by then aware of the association between Thomas Williams and John Dawes, for a directive to William Roe requested him "to make some agree[men]t with Messrs. Williams Dawes & Co." regarding the matter of calcining their ores in covered kilns, the implication being that the fumes from the other side of Parys Mountain were creating a nuisance.

About this time the Clerk to the Navy Board in London appears to have been working in some confusion, which is hardly surprising given the enormity of his task with regard to the purchasing and supplying of copper sheets and nails to the various yards, sub-contractors and ships. Following the rejection of the Roe & Co. offer of the 11th May, William Roe was surprised to receive a letter from the Clerk complaining that he was expecting a delivery of 60 tons of copper which had not arrived. In reply William, writing almost immediately on 7th June, pointed out that their proposals had not been accepted and there, for the time being, the matter rested whilst the Clerk concentrated on other urgent issues. (The month of July would witness the start of the hurricane season in the West Indies and it was imperative to arrange an escort for the merchantmen returning home. Ten naval ships were sent to Jamaica allowing Admiral Rodney to sail for North America with a like number.)

On 7th August the Admiralty clerk advised the acceptance of the Roe & Co. offer which was 11 shillings per pound weight for any copper sent to Liverpool. The same price was agreed for 60 tons to be delivered to Plymouth in five months or less, with an additional £4 per ton for carriage and a request that "they will send as much of it as they can each month". Two days later he informed the officers at Plymouth not to send any copper to Liverpool for the *Alligator* as arrangements were already made, and at the same time he again wrote to Roe & Co. directing them to deliver 850 sheets to Mr. Marshall (presumably Thomas Marshall for transportation along the River Weaver). On receipt of the copper by the overseers it was to be painted three times.

Nothing further is noted on the subject until 23rd October when Roe & Co. were informed not to depend on naval ships for transporting the sheathing destined for Plymouth from Liverpool. Two days later the company took the decision to send the copper plates relating to this contract, via the canal and River Severn to Bristol, then overland to Plymouth. This route was as a result of an Act of Parliament (20 Geo III cap 59) which forbad the conveying of copper sheets or bars coastwise to prevent capture by the enemy. An infringement carried a fine of £100 per cwt. which emphatically underlines the importance of the operation. Whether or not the company resolution was a coincidence or as a result of the naval communication (which is entirely possible given the excellent postal arrangments of the period) is difficult to say. What is not in doubt is the promptness with which Roe & Co. acted realizing that they had been working under a misapprehension i.e. the navy was prepared to transport its own urgently needed copper from Liverpool to Plymouth.

A somewhat disgruntled comment appears in the Navy Board Minutes of 28th November:

"Messrs Roe & Co. – Acquaint them they must deliver the whole of the Copper at Plymouth and that if they do not fulfill their Contract with more dispatch we must declare against having any further transactions with them."

But Roe & Co. had been given five months from 7th August in which to complete the order, and not from 11th May, when their offer had been rejected not confirmed. This unfortunate gaffe by the clerk has led to one historian charging Roe & Co. with "seriously mismanaging" this contract, when in fact Roe & Co. should be congratulated for completing it in less than four months.

One of the Shaw family was also admonished by the Admiralty for not complying with his contract for tallow, but the tallow arrived the following day of 30th November and was accepted. Circumstantial evidence suggests that the Roe & Co. copper sheets arrived at the same time, for a new contract was made with the company on the 8th December. This time they were allowed until March 1781 to provide Plymouth with a further 60 tons, the remainder (amount not stated) to be sent in 14 ton consignments each month.

The initial rush by the Admiralty to sheathe its ships with copper was almost at an end. The hostilities in the West Indies would last a further eighteen months until the spring of 1782 when, on 12th April, a great naval battle would take place. Admiral Rodney, aided by Sir Samuel Hood, would inflict the most decisive defeat on the French off Dominica, heralding the way for peace with the American States in 1783. (Incidentally, this battle produced a new style of strategy which would become so important during the Napoleonic Wars.)

September 1782 would establish the impregnability of Gibraltar by its ability to withstand the final attack of the Spaniards supported by a French force; and the fighting in the East, particularly around Madras and the Bay of Bengal, would flare only when the West Indian hostilities drew to a close. Yet even there the French Admiral Suffren would finally disengage on 29th June 1783 on receiving news of the peace preliminaries signed in Europe on the preceding 20th January.

It would be some time before an unfortunate and totally unpredictable problem arose with copper sheathing. Whereas it had been appreciated that the sheets had to be fitted with either copper or brass nails, the former presenting problems because of the comparative softness of the metal, the effect on the original iron fastenings of the ships' timbers had been totally overlooked. The heads of iron bolts etc. in the inevitable prevailing damp conditions, reacted with the copper causing pitting and eventual rupture of the area, creating a dangerous situation when the sheets became dislodged. But these problems, together with many others, were for the future, as the Admiralty purveyors secured orders for their copper during the final months of 1780.

Although the naval contracts must have both delighted and relieved the partners of the Macclesfield Copper Company, Charles Roe was in no position to appreciate the pervading atmosphere within the company, for he was lying "dangerously ill & given up by ye Physicians" in Chesterfield.

It seems possible that he might have contracted an infection which had considerably weakened his already debilitated constitution. Hester's diary reveals another wave of illness in the Macclesfield area during early September. Her brother James, arriving with a friend from Manchester on the 5th, dined at a local inn then, hurriedly taking a coach, disappeared for several days leaving his mother to pay the bill. He returned on 17th September complaining that he had been ill, although in this instance Hester's suspicions were soon proved correct; he had escorted a young lady and a group of friends to Manchester and "treated them to a Concert & Ball . . ." Hester herself was suffering for quite some time with a swollen face and sore eyes.

On Saturday afternoon, 30th September, a servant arrived from the Jebb residence in Chesterfield with news of her uncle's illness. Hester immediately wrote to Robert in London, sending him the additional sad news that his brother, Samuel, was also on the point of death. Robert's conscience weighed heavy; he had been visited by a family friend, Mr. Pugh, on the 6th of the month, who had asked him to return home, but Robert could see no purpose in the visit, unaware of the distressing circumstances which were developing. After a brief respite for prayers and contemplation he set out on his long journey, completing the 89 miles to Birmingham the following day.

The next day's ride took him to Derby where, exhausted, he stayed overnight and began to worry as to whether or not Samuel was still alive. He pressed on to Matlock, then only a "straggling village, built in a very romantic manner". The cottages between the baths and the bridge were built mostly along the rocky ledges of the small ravine with the floor of one almost touching the roof of the one beneath. Robert had little time to waste and finding no one with any immediate news, despite his acute tiredness, rode the final lap to Chesterfield.

His unannounced arrival placed the Jebbs in a somewhat difficult position, but evidently they promised to tell his father of his presence when convenient, so the young man decided to stay at a local inn. The night passed with no message from his father and he later learned that "they were a long time before they durst tell him of my arrival". Charles Roe's refusal to see his son, and his agitated reaction when questioning the motives behind Robert's sudden appearance, forced the Jebbs to change the conversation in order to pacify him. Mrs. Jebb bided her time and then, returning to the subject, said that nothing but love could have motivated Robert into attempting such a journey in such a bad state of health. "Love" said Charles "I cannot believe it, but if I must see him, let it be now. I will give him an hour."

Robert hastened upstairs, threw himself at his father's feet and asked for his blessing. Charles, trembling, reiterated his past grievances concerning the young man's behaviour, but this time Robert 'held his tongue', respecting the severity of his father's illness and also the wishes of his mother (Rachel Harriott) not to upset him.

Shortly afterwards everyone was called to dinner and as Robert's offer to remain was rejected, he began to make his way downstairs but then was recalled by his father. Charles, in an effort to make light his concerns, jokingly broached the subject of Robert and marriage, suggesting a particularly wealthy young lady for a wife. Robert said that a fortune was nothing to him and proceeded to describe the character he would wish for in a wife. Charles commented "you are honest, but too nice Robert". One suspects that Charles Roe's concern was in the event of a marriage between Robert and cousin Hester, for when Robert indicated his intention to return to Macclesfield, his father refused to sanction the idea. Robert's stubbornness got the better of him and he declared that if permission was denied (presumably to stay at the family home) then he would depart without it.

This sudden show of defiance on Robert's part had an immediate therapeutic effect on his father, or so it would seem, but was probably coupled with the abatement of the infection, for Charles Roe's physician, Dr. Coxen, who had been called from Macclesfield, returned to town on the 9th October expressing hopes of a recovery. David Simpson too, having played his part, returned on the evening of Thursday the 12th, but with a more subdued report. On Friday the 13th Hester received news of Robert's reconciliation with his father "My Uncle rec'd him kindly Clasping him with much Affection in his Arms", which gives a slightly different nuance to the situation than that presented by Robert's version.

A week later Rev. Collins called at the family home on Chestergate and took part in a religious discussion whilst walking in the garden with Frances Roe and her visiting cousin, Hester. The following day Charles, still very poorly, arrived, having already extracted a promise from Robert that as soon as possible he would take Samuel, who was by now "in a deep consumption", to Bristol and remain to look after him. Robert himself was not well, evidently suffering from the early stages of tuberculosis, as revealed by the recurring symptoms of his self-pitying syndrome. His accusations of his father's unkind behaviour, after his visits to Collins, David Simpson and his aunt, are made without any consideration for his father's point of view; Charles, aware that Robert was regularly out visiting, was obviously imagining the worst and ordered an early departure for Bristol the next morning.

To add to the drama, young Charles arrived from Liverpool to break the news of his marriage to the family. First he confided in Robert, but his planned confession to his father was thwarted by the latter's refusal to see him. Rachel Harriott, acting in her usual role as mediator, endeavoured "as if by accident" to gain young Charles an entry to his father's room, but a rebuff, in the form of instant dismissal, quickly followed.

Robert's poignant entry in his journal on 1st November, as later accredited and published in the *Arminian Magazine,* does much to stir the emotions:

"I set off with my brother for Bristol Strange behaviour to desire <u>me</u> to go such a journey; myself an invalid and distressed in my circumstances, without giving me a farthing to defray my expences! Yea and at a time when it will effectually hinder my ordination."

Charles Snr. was obviously fully aware of the practicalities of the situation and must have taken into account the fact that the visit to the warm baths of Hotwell near Bristol would be beneficial, not only to Samuel, but also to Robert. These Bristol 'waters' were judged fourth in prominence after Bath, Buxton and Matlock and much cleaner and cooler, being considered greatly beneficial to those suffering with ulcers, internal haemorrhages and inflammations and therefore particularly efficacious "in confumptions".

Meanwhile, Hester, learning with astonishment of young Charles Roe's marriage to a very young lady, Mary Rylands, on 17th June 1780 at St. Nicholas's, Liverpool, thanked the Lord for preserving her "from ye snares this poor Young Man laid for my feet". A visit from Aunt Rachel and Cousin Polly confirmed their intention of setting off for Bath the next morning with her uncle. As Hester wrote her diary entry for Thursday, 2nd November 1780, her grief seemed genuine, "I was much Affected when my Uncles Coach went past this Morning - As very few expect he will return Alive."

During the week following the departure many Macclesfield families fell ill with "a Raging Fever" and several died; others, who escaped the infection, were afraid to come into contact with those who were ill, dreading the effects of the disease.

By 27th November word arrived that Samuel Roe was beyond help and Robert accordingly moved him to Bath to be with members of the family. Evidently the Roes had taken rooms just to the north of the Abbey and close by the river, for an entry appears in the Walcot Poor Rates Book (November 1780) for "Mrs. Row & C[ompany]" on Northgate St. Charles Snr. in his endeavours to rally Samuel, reminded him of the winter season of balls and assemblies just beginning in Macclesfield, but could not resist a cautionary sentiment as one from an older generation to the next, "They will see the folly of these things by and by." Samuel's mind, however, was concerned with his own spiritual well-being, and a sudden and strong desire to talk to Rev. Simpson in Macclesfield compelled his father to make arrangements for his return.

Despite William Roe's considerable responsibilities, not only with company but family matters (by now William and Hannah had four daughters, the youngest born 30th June 1780, and Hannah was again pregnant), he arrived in Bath to take on the onerous task of accompanying both Samuel and Robert home.

Robert's Methodist sympathies surfaced as he considered the fact that Samuel might never reach Macclesfield alive and decided to take on the role of confessor for his brother. There was no other way but to tell Samuel of his predicament. Samuel, having already prepared himself for the worst, did not need telling and admitted to Robert that the reason for his return to Cheshire was to speak with David Simpson and make his confession. Before the little group departed the family gathered together for a private Communion and Samuel, as a final gesture yet hardly able to breathe, knelt before his father for his blessing. Even Polly was present although she too was very ill.

A strange looking carriage called a "Bed-machine" was ordered and when it arrived Samuel, in a feeble and pathetic condition, was carried out through a crowd of people and lifted onto it. He was able to lie full length on the bed part whilst his brothers sat at his feet. If necessary the carriage, drawn by six horses, could have accommodated four sitting passengers apart from the invalid. The journey was soon underway and the nearer to home they came, the happier Samuel grew, but the final evening of Wednesday the 27th December necessitated an overnight stay in Leek, where they were received with great "kindness and affection" by Mr. and Mrs. Daintry. Robert retired to bed having bid goodnight to Samuel, never expecting to be wakened next morning with the news of Samuel's death.

A further day was spent at Leek whilst preparations were made and a message sent ahead to Macclesfield; on Friday the 29th December Samuel's corpse was brought home. The new family vault, close by the eastern end of his father's church, witnessed his interment the following Sunday before morning service, but Charles Snr., too ill to travel any great distance, was to remain in Somerset until the spring of 1781.

Samuel's half-sister, Peggy, 19 years of age, had travelled from the Roe household in Liverpool to join the small family group, an action much appreciated by Hester. David Simpson had also travelled far, having been called into Yorkshire to attend his dying father on Thursday the 7th December, but was able to return in time for Christmas and, of course, Samuel's funeral.

* * * * * * *

With time precious and journeys difficult it is not surprising that the company meeting scheduled for 11th January 1781, was brought forward to the 2nd, no doubt in order to accommodate William Roe. Brian Hodgson Snr. and his two sons, Robert and Brian, attended together with Edward Hawkins. The business under discussion mostly related to quantity and prices of copper in dealing with the various agents, but two important items concerned a replacement for Edward Hughes, who had been asked to leave, and the setting-up of a meeting with Capt. Overend to discuss the leasing of a calamine mine in Wensleydale, Yorkshire.

By the February meeting William's great organising ability began to come into play, as he shouldered more and more company and family burdens. At each future meeting every Company Director was asked to exchange the minutes for that part of the business under his control, with those of the other Directors, to ensure that all had a "clear & competent knowledge" of the whole structure of the concern.

A surprising directive instructed Edward Hawkins to join Charles Roe Snr. in Bath and accompany him, together with a deputation from the Warrington Company, to see the Committee of the Bristol Brass Wire Company, in order to advise of the misconduct of their agent in Birmingham. Charles Roe's unquenchable thirst for business and his relentless desire to right wrongs would not permit his physical weaknesses to inhibit his ability to function. Even as late as the 6th April his presence was required at Stourport to attend an important General Meeting of the 'Makers of Brass Wyre', but this was to be his final engagement before the small family group returned home to Macclesfield.

* * * * * * *

Robert had remained in his father's house whilst he awaited the return of the family. At the end of March he had been visited by two Methodist friends from Leeds, one of whom, Mr. Rogers, was a preacher. Robert held Rogers in high esteem and brought Hester to meet him; she too was very impressed but could never have considered that this man would be the key to her future happiness. John Wesley made his annual appearance in town, although on this occasion only briefly, yet still forcing Hester's mother to ensure that her daughter's visit to John Ryle's house, in order to speak with the ageing preacher, was of limited duration.

Charles Roe's return placed great restrictions on Robert as his father, grown "very peevish" with ill health, made more and more demands upon him. The constant requests for Robert to sit and read aloud became wearisome and the young man's health suffered further. Finally, on Sunday the 29th April, Charles Roe's condition became so grave and his spirit so restless that Robert in despair sent for David Simpson to pray with them. Having made no will Charles called the family together the following morning and with Simpson present told them all of his wishes concerning his "temporal" affairs. He then prayed that God would bless Rachel Harriott and all the children and made his farewells calling each by name, but young Charles and Joseph were not present.

(It is easy to understand Charles Roe's reluctance to prepare a will; company assets were far too complicated to set down in detail and he must have known that William's integrity was beyond reproach when dealing with such matters and sorting out the complications of the various marriage settlements; also, it is one thing to threaten a child with disinheritance in order to gain some obedience, but quite a different matter to set it down in black and white. Circumstances can change quite rapidly, as Charles knew well from his own business experiences, and his judgement evidently dictated that it was far better to let matters take their course under the watchful eye of David Simpson and William's guiding hand.)

About midnight the indefatigable man of former years was almost gone, yet when daylight came he rallied a little, calling for Rev. Simpson and his absent children, Charles and Joseph, and was heard to say "poor Charles I forgive him!". Hester joined her cousins for the day's long vigil, which lasted throughout Wednesday, but was fortunately broken for a short spell with the arrival of young Charles at noon. His father embraced him affectionately and kissed him three times. Robert, evidently moved by this event, later wrote "we begged my Cousin R [oe = Hester] to inform my brother Joseph . . . by an express".

Charles Snr. lay quiet and peaceful all night, then suddenly, about 10 a.m., he opened his eyes, smiled and drew his last breath. Hester heard the news from a tearful servant as she entered her uncle's home later that morning. Joseph, having received her urgent message, rode hard the 200 miles from London in 26 hours and arrived completely exhausted at 9 o'clock in the evening of Friday, the 4th May, only to learn with great anguish that his father had died the previous day.

The funeral was arranged for the following Tuesday evening of the 8th May. Evening funerals were customary, a practice possibly carried over from the days of the plagues when bodies were left outside doors after dark and carried away in carts for mass burial, although an alternative reason could have been the premium at which daylight hours were set, particularly when working the land or taking into consideration commercial interests. The latter suggestion is, to some degree, supported by extracts from a letter recommending a certain person for a curacy in Dorking and also indicates that by the late18th century the custom was on the point of falling into obsolescence ". . . he has given offence to some of the tradesmen in this town by objecting to attend funerals after sunset, which, after my enquiries, I find to be a circumstance objected to in general by all clergymen."

If David Simpson held any strong views on the subject they were certainly not set down, and in any event he would have put aside all objections for his Patron and sponsor who had risked so much on his behalf. As dusk fell and the funeral procession began, the solemnity of the occasion was recorded by Hester and is best conveyed in her own words:

". . . my Dr. Uncles Corps was Carried in great Pomp by his own Horses & to ye New Church & attended wth Torches & A great concourse of People – but ye Horses being unaccustomed to be ornamented with B[lack] Cloth & escutcheions etc. wd hardly proceed – he was interrd by Mr.Simpson in ye Vault he had so lately prepared – & this much feared & much loved Man is now Committed to Corruption & ye Grave!"

PART 3

24
THE AFTERMATH

As their shape varies various is the name,
Different their parts, nor is their strength the same.

In the year following Charles Roe's death there came to England a 25 year old teacher of philosophy, Carl Philip Moritz; his letters to a German friend convey an infinitely more eclectic view of society than that recorded by his English predecessors viz: Fiennes and Defoe, for he is observing with the eyes of a foreigner. In presenting his impressions it becomes apparent just how much Charles Roe's generation had achieved, and espouses the theme of the Bishop Porteus's treatise as to the growth in both size and splendour of towns, and the increasing passion for luxuries and frivolous amusements.

Moritz's first impressions, when sailing up the Thames, were of a considerable maritime commerce complemented by "neat villages and pretty little towns". The approach from Greenwich to London, thronged with people walking, riding or driving, was seen to be much busier than the busiest streets in Berlin and Moritz noticed that many of those on horseback were bespectacled, even the younger riders. His eulogies on the state of buildings and streets, particularly the "delightful side-streets" leading from the Strand to the Thames, leave one in no doubt of the depth of his admiration.

Moritz's considerable regard for the English landscape and townscape however did fall short of that he held for his esteemed homeland, but when it came to personal appearance, he was forced to admit that the English were more handsome and better dressed. From the highest to the lowest they were neat and clean for even beggars wore clean shirts under their rags. From his later peregrinations outside London he observed that the poorest women, distinguished by their short red cloaks, wore hats comparable to those of their wealthier sisters.

Having watched a funeral procession Moritz confirmed that an influenza epidemic was claiming many lives, as in Berlin. His delightful description of a coffin ironically seems to epitomise the English way of life:

"English coffins are economically designed to fit the shape of the corpse – flat and broad on top, the middle bowed and tapering from there almost to a point at the foot, for all the world like an oversize violin case."

Because of his pecuniary situation, gastronomic delights eluded him, however his meals were wholesome, consisting of pickled salmon, wheaten bread, butter and Cheshire cheese, the latter apparently still a great favourite in the capital. Dinner comprised a piece of "half-boiled or roast meat" and a few green cabbages served in a white sauce. At teatime he thoroughly enjoyed the buttered bread toasted on a fork in front of the fire until the butter soaked through. But his description of coffee as "an atrocious mess of brown water" is all too familiar, despite his protestations and suggestions as to how many cupfuls should be made from half an ounce.

Moritz was greatly impressed with the general public's understanding of English literature and its knowledge of authors, adequately illustrated by the many editions of their works. He approved of the cheaper pocket sized publications, especially the poetic ones, which encouraged the "common people" to buy, giving them a good basis for discussions with anyone and everyone; an excellent class leveller.

His descriptions of the pleasure gardens, Vauxhall and Ranelagh, support the sublime to the ridiculous state of English manners and etiquette by this period, and his visit to the House of Commons produced a shocked revelation on hearing the extent of personal abuse bandied about, translated into persecution by the press; he understood there was corruption but also that there were genuine moves to expose it.

As German lodges had contributed funds towards the considerable costs incurred in the building of the Freemasons' Salon in the Freemasons' Tavern, Moritz paid an obligatory visit. The Salon received his admiration, however he was highly critical of the general proceedings of freemasonry in England. German lodges provided masons with a unanimity of high ideals but most of their English counterparts had "degenerated into drinking-clubs". Before long he was travelling out of London intent on heading north.

Moritz decided to proceed on foot intending to walk at least to Oxford. One evening, as it was growing late, he had reconciled himself to spending a night in the open air, when he was suddenly aware of an approaching fellow pedestrian who turned out to be the vicar of Dorchester returning to college after conducting his Sunday preaching in his parish church. This pleasant young man swept the otherwise tired Moritz along with him to Oxford where, although it was almost the middle of the night, the vicar introduced him to "a whole roomful of clergymen in their gowns and cravats sitting round a great table with their beer-mugs in front of them". Moritz was soon in high spirits and appreciating the wit and good humour joined in the lively debates about the Bible and German universities. This was obviously a very different life style from the prosaic existence which young Robert Roe had carved out for himself.

After two days in Oxford the German decided to visit Derbyshire but was advised to go by coach. This time he was told that anyone on foot was regarded as 'disreputable'; even the poorest individuals saved up their money for the half price facility of travelling on top of the coach, which could prove to be a death-defying ordeal at times.

Soon Moritz was heading north and asked a fellow passenger why he thought the English were reluctant to walk any distance and received the reply "They are too rich and too lazy". He endured the somewhat erratic journey to Birmingham where he hoped to make use of an introduction to Fothergill (Matthew Boulton's partner) only to discover that the talented Russian born artist had died the previous week. With the visit cut short Moritz once again continued on foot, this time in the direction of Derby, and although booed and hissed at en route he was pleasantly surprised to discover a few welcoming inns.

The busy town of Derby made little impression on the perambulating teacher so he quickly departed for Matlock Bath along the route so fervently ridden by Robert Roe in the autumn of 1780. In this part of Derbyshire Moritz perceived that whilst English inns usually displayed pictures and prints of the Royal Family as a group and occasionally Hogarth scenes, the portrait of the King of Prussia was also in vogue (a probable sign of the presence of German miners within the local community). An inconsequential Matlock was reached via a bridge spanning the river at the northern end of the impressive ravine, but the traffic was considerable because of the popularity of the baths.

Having decided to visit the Devil's Cavern in Castleton Moritz traversed the countryside via the villages of Bakewell, Ashford, Wardlow and Tideswell; finding a convivial small inn at the latter place he again enjoyed a lunch of Cheshire cheese, this time toasted in front of the fire. The next morning, although it was Sunday, he visited a local barber with the landlord of the inn and was surprised at the stir created by his newly purchased London hat which, because of its quality, was admired with some awe.

The next part of the journey was to take him to Charles Roe's birthplace where little seems to have changed, except perhaps the expansion of the village constructed within the cavern and the increased activity of rope making as evidenced by a group of large wheels. Moritz's escorted journey by candlelight, firstly through a small door sited beyond the smoky cottages in the far wall of the cavern, then partly by boat along a subterranean river where the dipping roof allowed very little room for the passage across, filled him with wonder and amazement. The petrified plants and animals were too numerous to examine in the time available, but leaves little doubt that there Charles Roe would have spent many hours of his early childhood, overcoming any fears of darkness and confinement and cultivating a passion for mineralogy which had remained with him for the rest of his life.

It was almost time for Moritz to return south yet not before he had visited Mam Tor, thrown his pebble into the proverbial Eldon Hole and been told many of the fascinating fairy tales and myths which had abounded in the area for generations.

Moritz returned via Nottingham, not Derby, and thought the town to be the "loveliest and neatest" he had seen outside London. On arriving in Leicester, as time was of the essence in taking up an offer of a sea passage from London to Hamburg, he opted for a coach ride to the capital. Unfortunately all the inside seats were taken and his one and only experience of riding on the outside, albeit just to Northampton but squatting on the roof with nothing to hold on to, would never be forgotten. Yet even the final part of the trip, with accommodation inside, left much to be desired because of incompatible travelling companions. However he reached his ship in time, having collected enough information for his fascinating narrative on England and the English.

* * * * * * *

Some years earlier Brian Hodgson had found himself travelling alongside Dr. Johnson in North Wales and although unrecorded, conversationally that journey had probably passed quite congenially, since Dr. Johnson and Brian Hodgson were acquainted, having met as dinner guests at Dr. Taylor's house in Ashbourne. The coach journey to Bangor via Penmaenmawr had taken them along what had been a very precarious and dangerous route until two years previous when, in 1772, a wall had been built on the seaward side. This shielded travellers from the precipices which lurked beside an otherwise excellent road, constructed along a shelf in the huge rock face. Evidently Johnson had regretted his brief glimpse of Chester en route, for in 1779 Boswell, who was on his way to Carlisle, stopped off to meet Beilby Porteus, the newly appointed Bishop of Chester, and reported back to Johnson:

> "The Bishop treated me with a kindness which was very flattering. I told him that you regretted you had seen so little of Chester. His Lordship bade me tell you that he should be glad to show you more of it. I am proud to find the friendship with which you honour me is known in so many places."

This meeting took place shortly before the Bishop's consecration of Christ Church in Macclesfield and in the not too distant future once again his ecclesiastical duties would involve him directly in Roe affairs, when William accepted the formidable task of administrator of his late father's estate. On 20th June 1781 each family member, who was not a minor, signed an affidavit declaring their refusal to act and granting "William Roe of Liverpool" the responsibility.

Rachel Harriott, only 46 years of age, signed first as widow of the deceased. Next in succession were Rev. Ralph Nicholson and wife Catherine, still residents of Didcot, Berkshire followed by the children of Charles Roe's second marriage. Sons Robert, Charles and Joseph signed in order of seniority with daughters Mary and Frances signing last. Margaret was little more than 20 years of age and Jane almost 18 years and therefore as minors prohibited frm signing. The same proviso applied to Charles Roe's only child from his third marriage, John Harriott, who would attain 13 years of age on 12th July 1781; on that very day William Roe "took the usual oath as Administrator in common form" in the Consistory Court of Chester, and was allowed until the end of July 1782 to deliver an account of the estate. Meanwhile a bond for an estimated value of £30,000 was lodged with Bishop Beilby as Lord Bishop of Chester, head of the Consistory Court. Two guarantors were necessary to support the bond, in this instance an onerous commitment because of the considerable sum involved, but the Shaw family was willing to oblige; Samuel Shaw Esq. and John Shaw Merchant, both of Liverpool signed the covenant.

John Shaw was, of course, William's youngest brother-in-law and Samuel his father-in-law, however the latter's somewhat shaky signature is indicative of some health problem, for St. Nicholas's register in Liverpool records that on 15th September 1781 Samuel Shaw (Snr.) "of this Town Merchant" died at Knutsford in Cheshire from where he was "brought to his house in Pitt St. on the 17th instant & from thence buried on the 19th September".

Perhaps appreciating the difficulties created for William by his father's noncommittal to paper of his last wishes, Samuel Shaw had prepared his will on 26th August 1781 and, as property was held in different counties, had registered it in the Prerogative Court of Canterbury. The eldest son, Samuel, received the paternal estate in Warrington and Lymm together with £500 to be paid two years after death and a further £500 one year after that. The remainder of the considerable estate i.e. that part which Hannah's father had worked for and purchased or leased with his own money, he divided between his two younger sons Christopher and John and his son-in-law William Roe. Amongst the property in Liverpool this latter estate included the three pews in the North Gallery of St. Paul's Church; a warehouse on the east side of Bromfield St; ground and premises on the south side of Whitechapel called Potters' Gardens and a field or close of ground measuring one acre, one rood and one perch on part of which two buildings had been erected.

It is interesting to note that son, John, having given up ownership of a ship called *Bella* (built in Bristol 1763) on 21st, August 1781, just three months later and obviously after the death of his father, purchased a "prize from the French built in Marseilles". The ship was valued by Customs and John, having paid the appropriate price, renamed her *Sam* of Liverpool; a reminder of Georgian sentimentality.

The summer of 1781 had also claimed another indomitable spirit when Charles Legh of Adlington Hall died in July; Hester records the news on Thursday morning the 26th of the month, and her inevitable "awful reflections on What he has been . . ." would no doubt have amused the old man beyond measure. He had led a hearty life to the age of 83 years and still prided himself on his prowess as a poet. In a *Farewell to Buxton* on 29th July 1779 his verses reveal a happy congeniality amongst the company with whom he drank, ate "Old England's Roast Beef", played cards and danced to the tunes of the fiddlers, often joining the latter with fiddle in hand to assist in their musical escapades. He continued to write a verse on his birthday till the end of his life, but perhaps the most poignant was that written "On my Birth-day 1770":

> "The Birth-day (never let it be forgot)
> Knits on ye Line of Life another Knot:
> Extend This Gracious Lord! though weak at best
> To join through Death ye Temple of thy Rest."

His most outrageous was that on his 83rd birthday in 1780:

"He's not Bard born but loses Time,
Straining to Tag a Verse with Rhyme,
Far better let Him Strain to Sh-t.
A Stool may stop a Rhyming Fit,
If Costive let him daily Doze
Over John Westly's Purging Prose."

* * * * * * *

The conglomeration of William Roe's duties and responsibilities since the beginning of his father's last fatal illness, had kept him so preoccupied, that delayed christenings for two of his daughters meant three were christened at the same time. Taking into account the high rate of infant mortality this was extremely unusual for the period, yet St. George's register in Liverpool records the baptisms of Hannah, born 11th June 1779, Rachel Harriot (*sic.*), born 30th June 1780 and Catherine, born 4th July 1781 all on 3rd October 1781.

A glimpse at the Company Minute Book confirms William's absence from both the meeting of the 17th September held in Warrington and that of the 18th October in Congleton; rarely had he missed one meeting but never two in succession. These meetings also indicate a change in policy; until Charles Roe's death all meetings had taken place in Macclesfield, presumably within the company premises adjacent to Charles Roe's house, but now the power base was divided as never before, so conformity gave way to convenience. Yet despite the fact that occasional meetings would be held elsewhere, such as Warrington or Congleton, still the A.G.M.s remained in Macclesfield.

Meetings were also held periodically by the Mining Company, sometimes referred to in the Copper Company Minutes, but unfortunately the book for the former has never come to light, however scraps of evidence imply that the venue had varied from time to time to allow a greater degree of convenience, thus operating a less rigid routine than that set by the Copper Company.

No specific reference appears in the Copper Company Minutes regarding Charles Roe's death, only that William as nominee of his late father was entitled to succeed to his father's shares. What happened to Samuel's share is something of a mystery, but as the shares in total were now reduced to thirteen, one has to assume that as Samuel's nominee would have been his father, his entitlement would also have passed to William. Taking into account later information the division now appears to be as follows:

William Roe	$^1/_{13}$ own + $^2/_{13}$ inherited.
Legh Dickenson	$^1/_{13}$
Thomas Smyth	$^3/_4$ of $^1/_{13}$
Charles Caldwell	$^3/_4$ of $^1/_{13}$
John Atkinson Busfield	$^1/_{13}$
Brian Hodgson Snr.	$^1/_{13}$
Robert Hodgson	$^2/_{13}$
Brian Hodgson Jnr.	$^1/_2$ of $^1/_{13}$
Francis Ferneyhough	$^1/_2$ of $^1/_{13}$
Edward Hawkins	$^1/_{13}$
Thomas Weaver	$^1/_2$ of $^1/_{13}$
John Jefferies	$^1/_{13}$

This synopsis includes a half share which is difficult to account for, but the options are limited. John Jefferies appears to have increased his share from half to a whole one by purchasing part of that held by the company in lieu of John Cooke. He paid £2,369 16 6d on 25th August 1779, but it would seem that he had lent the company money as an indemnification against Cooke's claim and the transaction was therefore a straightforward assignment to cover the company bond to Cooke.

Each partner was allowed to nominate a son or sons (this included in-laws) to succeed to his share upon death, although there had been one exception, Latham Arnold who, having no son, had taken the advice to nominate his daughter in his last Will and Testament, but in the event the trustees were anxious to sell. The company was able to release £3,133 7 8d. to the four London trustees on 20th August 1782 which appears to represent only half a share. A deed of the same date, between Arnold's Executors and the remaining copper company partners, confirms the sum paid together with a "General Mutual release" between the partners which can only relate to the redistribution of the other half share between them. Now it was William's turn to become the exception, with three daughters, no son and no other close family members left as shareholders of the company, he chose to elect Thomas Smyth as trustee for his children's shares should the question of inheritance arise. However, the birth of Charles Samuel on 25th September 1782 allowed William to name his son as his successor at the A.G.M. of August 1783 in lieu of Thomas Smyth's nomination.

* * * * * * *

Business was brisk at this period thanks, of course, to the Navy which meant all active partners were busily engaged in keeping operations running smoothly. As the sheathing took utmost priority more copper ore was required for the smelters and orders of August 1781 included requests for the purchase of 400 tons from Williams at Amwlch, an unspecified amount from the Duke of Devonshire via his London agent and the preparation of an application to import ore, duty free, from Ireland. There was even a suggestion of acquiring shares in the Mixon copper mine located four miles east of Leek in Staffordshire, close by the Derbyshire border. The outcome of these enquiries is not known except by April 1782 a letter had been sent to Mr. Kyan, partner of Colonel Camac who traded as the Hibernian Mine Co. in County Wicklow, Ireland, making an offer for his ores and precipitated copper. Within a decade Roe & Co. were certainly receiving Irish ore in Liverpool, but not duty free; as yet the date from which this importation commenced is uncertain.

In compliance with the naval request for an extra coat of white paint, the agent must have agreed with the Macclesfield Copper Company to have the sheathing coated white on one side before leaving the mills. A further request for the sheets to be encased for their journey to Plymouth was also agreed with Mr. Forbes, and the price fixed, for which the Navy Board was duly invoiced.

It was also important to encourage the domestic and overseas trade whenever possible, which included sheathing for merchant vessels. By November 1781 Mr. Satterthwaite, the Lancaster agent, was asked to sell copper sheathing and also African battery if possible, offering him the same commission as Mr. James the Liverpool agent. His response must have been unenthusiastic, for a planned Lancaster warehouse was disregarded and the request modified to obtaining orders for copper sheathing which would be dealt with in Liverpool.

The brass trade was evidently in decline, for although various sorts of copper were sent to Hamburg and Ostend at the request of Messrs. W & T Raikes during January 1782, yet the company decided not to purchase brass chippings for remelting from Mr. Pengree's company because of the state of the ingot trade. However, wire was still very much in demand, with one of the Birmingham factors, William Welch, still handling orders together with those for black latten. In December 1779 William Roe had endeavoured to engage a workman, dismissed by Tyndale & Elton of Bristol, for the production of black latten i.e. copper treated with a varnish which created a black glossy lacquered surface; the process was often referred to as japanning resulting in the commercial name of 'Japan Copper'. Due to the increased naval demand for sheathing by February 1782, the employee then engaged in producing black latten was switched to making nails.

The demand for nails must have been considerable because of the number required to hold each copper sheet in place, but even the Navy seemed unsure as to how many were needed. On examining the accounts of the Plymouth yard in May 1780 it was found that different quantities were used on ships of the same rating, so an enquiry was launched. An interesting note in the Navy Minutes for the same month records an order to the storekeeper at Sheerness, advising him to instruct the agent Mr. Forbes to send copper nails in future in small casks and also "to hasten the Copper Nails due" to the Portsmouth yard. Because of Forbes's involvement it seems entirely possible that the nails referred to were the product of the Macclesfield Copper Company.

The period was not without its difficulties; flooding at Havannah had caused problems with an adjacent land owner Mr. Armett, whose meadow of just over three statute acres was up stream and enclosed on two sides by a bend in the river. The dam at the Havannah works had evidently built up too high a head of water, causing an overflow into Amett's land, despite the fact that a sluice-way controlled by gates ran alongside the weir. One can only assume that bad weather or misjudgement by the employee in charge of operating the sluice, or both, had contributed to the situation. Compensation was sought by Armett, and, with Joseph Cooke acting on behalf of the copper company, an opinion was obtained from a barrister, Mr. Foster Bower. Armett was sent an offer based on the arbitration but failed to reply in the time allowed, so officially the action had lapsed, however the company decided to pay the undisclosed sum as discretionary compensation.

Throughout the summer and autumn of 1781 complaints had regularly been made to the 'Commissioners of the Navigation Company' at Stone in an effort to obtain the promised lease for a wharf on the canal side of the Red Bull Inn at Lawton. In addition there had been delays in forwarding the Roe & Co. copper from the existing wharf, but after several months of persistent badgering Robert Hodgson seems to have been successful. By August 1783 he was directing the wharfinger at Lawton to place the goods, as soon as received, in the warehouse and obtain from each boatman an acknowledgement in writing of their good condition immediately they were taken on board. The lease, however, was a different proposition, taking until 1789 to acquire and then only from a local landowner of an adjoining estate.

Certain company employees were also causing problems. William and Thomas Hughes, copper rollers at Havannah, were again in trouble, together with another workman called Malpas. By October 1782 several complaints were received insisting that the copper sheathing was not sufficiently pickled, so it was decided to fine the three culprits 5 shillings for every substandard sheet produced. Another employee by the name of Sylvester had been given notice on 29th August 1782 with salary paid up to 7th September, and each partner was asked to make enquiries regarding a suitable replacement. This case is an intriguing one because in August 1778 Sylvester's salary had been reduced by £10 per annum, which implies that for some reason his output had lessened. Sylvester must have pleaded his case and the outcome suggests that he was more than likely disabled and had been transferred from elsewhere, possibly Liverpool, for on 13th December 1782 the company agreed that his salary should be calculated at £40 per annum for the period he had spent in Macclesfield. If the reduction of £10 in August 1778 had limited his salary to £30 per annum, then by giving him the extra £10 for the previous four years, in effect he would receive at least an extra year and a quarter's salary "not for services rendered but from motive of compassion". A further dismissal took place at Bosley in July 1783 when Ralph Maydew was replaced by another workman at the site.

Even the Cornish operatives, superintended so successfully by Legh Dickenson for almost

25 years, were giving cause for concern. One can only assume that Dickenson had made a decision to become an inactive partner, an action possibly precipitated by Charles Roe's death. Surprisingly, for the first time ever, he had made the long journey north to attend the A.G.M. in Macclesfield on 24th August 1781, as though wishing to pay his last respects to someone who had given him support in the aftermath of the Bonnie Prince Charlie episode. He was no longer a young man and the loyal company servant most probably wished to discuss his future intentions during this visit, culminating in a second and final appearance at a company meeting one year later. Circumstantial evidence suggests that this second visit was to advise what arrangements had been put in place regarding new agents; unfortunately the agents proved incompetent and by May 1783, after "repeated blunderings" were given notice to leave at Midsummer. As regards assaying, the outcome of an idea to approach Thomas Williams of Anglesey with an offer for contributing towards the expenses of his Cornish assaymaster, appears to have materialised and an agreement made.

* * * * * * *

At this time relations between Roe & Co. and the Williams partnership were quite amicable and there was no reason to suspect that they would continue otherwise. Cartwright was long gone and Sir Nicholas had abandoned Plas Newydd and family for a life of pleasure in London. He had married one of his mistresses, Miss Ann Hunter of Epsom, Surrey and when things did not work out, had taken to living with a Miss Mary Gordon. His death on 8th December 1782 left matters in some confusion. The £600 per annum which Sir Nicholas had provided for his first wife, Caroline, under the terms of their marriage settlement, were also agreed for his second wife, Ann, but true to form Sir Nicholas was in arrears with the payments and Dame Ann held bonds totalling £1,800, a considerable sum. Henry, Rt. Hon. Earl of Uxbridge, as eldest son, now inherited his father's estates in Wales and Ireland; however, Sir Nicholas had failed to provide for his six younger children in his will. Matters were finally resolved when Ann, who received the house on Bond Street including all the furnishings and coaches etc. relinquished the arrears and any future payments, allowing Henry to inherit the estate without any obligatory payments to her. Henry, acknowledging his father's oversight, agreed to pay £5,000 + interest for the benefit of his brother and four surviving younger sisters, allowing each to inherit at least £1,000; sadly his sister, Caroline, had died. Miss Mary Gordon was certainly not overlooked, for amongst Sir Nicholas's bequests was one in her favour for the sum of £1,500. Because of his inheritance Henry would shortly be drawn into the affairs of Parys Mountain, a situation which would be used to great advantage by Thomas Williams.

Meanwhile, returning to the affairs of the Macclesfield Copper Company, all was not doom and gloom; many employees were proving their worth and were rewarded accordingly, some with contracts and others pecuniarily.

* * * * * * *

In July 1781 a legal agreement was made with Thomas Gidson to supply the brass house on Macclesfield Common with pots. In May 1783, William Krinks the solderer had his contract extended by 21 years, with the understanding that Elisha Rigley would be apprenticed to him for seven years. A guinea reward was given to I. Salt and H. Houseland for the "good Quality of their Brass" and at the same meeting, in August 1783, it was decided that each workman who could not produce a certificate guaranteeing the quality of his brass, in future would be fined not less than 2 guineas per annum. Joseph Wilshaw was offered an incentive to bring "to perfection casting of Plates for metal Wyre" with the promise of a bonus.

The company had again shown consideration upon the death of one of the Harvey family.

The widow of William Harvey would continue to receive her late husband's salary from October 1781 whilst her eldest son was being trained by Edward and Robert Harvey (together with the shortly to be admonished Malpas). The Harveys were asked to continue their duties at Havannah whilst preparing William Harvey's son to take his father's place. Edward Harvey was obviously still held in high esteem as £10 per annum was voted to him to cover the board of his apprentice, Thomas Harrison. An additional bonus of £50 would be paid during the seven years of Harrison's apprenticeship for instructing the young man "in the several branches of the concern at Bosley", an obvious indication of Harrison's intended future placement.

As always the supplies and quality of the two great essentials, calamine and coal, could not be ignored. Because of the temporary abatement of the ingot trade during 1781, purchases of calamine from Derbyshire, Flintshire and Somerset were halted until further notice. This conveniently provided an opportunity to re-establish contact with Captain Overend regarding his calamine works in Yorkshire, a matter unattended to by William Roe since the autumn of 1779. Details of proposals for a "fair trial" (essential to confirm the quality of the zinc ore) were set out in a letter, including an explanation for the delay.

By the autumn of 1781 William Brace, who was in charge of the calamine works at Bonsall in Derbyshire, was sent, together with his son, to the Overend works in order to select 30 tons for trial. This ore was then sent to Lancaster from where the Captain was requested to despatch it to Macclesfield at the end of February, 1782. On the following 5th April Captain Overend requested payment, but Roe & Co. replied that the consignee, Mr. Barrow, had demanded sufficient remittance to cover the full value of the merchandise, a demand not readily acceded to by the company, as it understood that Captain Overend would be expecting settlement of the account. A reply from the Captain was not forthcoming, which seems to have stimulated further enquiries, after which Mr. Barrow received an agreement from Roe & Co. on 29th August that payment would be made to him on condition that he indemnified them against Overend's claim.

This once again highlights the financial difficulties of the period, particularly with regard to the lack of branch banking, and suggests that Overend was in debt to Barrow who resorted to recouping at least some of the money owed through a third party. The method was effective, saving legal action and costs, but it was dependent on co-operation from the third party which would need to establish the validity of the debt before agreeing to payment. It also suggests that Roe & Co. were allowed some discount as recompense for their trouble.

As regards calamine perhaps the difficult situation created a dilemma with a subsequent policy re-think, for immediately a decision was taken to use Mendip ore in the production of "arco" brass (presumably brass used in making curved containers such as dishes, pans and kettles etc. but not wire) which had proved as good as Derbyshire in trial. By December it was agreed to mix the Mendip calamine with that of Flintshire in the brass recipe required for making wire, and an order for a further 100 tons was sent to John Denman in Flintshire two months later. Alongside the calamine policy re-adjustments went others for coal leases.

At the time of John Stafford's death his daughter and son-in-law (Harry Lankford) had been resident in Fence House, the former Blagge estate, but the death of William Stafford in 1777 appears to have encouraged the couple's return to Cumberland House on Jordangate, allowing Thomas Smyth to take possession of the estate on behalf of his wife, the former Elizabeth Blagge. Thomas Smyth could now exploit the coal reserves to the advantage of all concerned. In May 1781 the company proposed a survey resulting in the preparation of a lease by Mr. Cooke and in the meantime work was suspended at the Greenaway mine on Macclesfield Common allowing a reduction of the stock piles at the works.

Next came a review of coals delivered from the Spond's colliery near Pott Shrigley on the Legh of Lyme estate. Charles Roe's original plea of 27th Febru, 1771, to have his half of the lease extended beyond the 11 years agreed with Mr. Venables, holder of the other half of the lease, had apparently fallen on deaf ears, for it had become necessary to obtain a new lease. With Samuel Roe no longer present to negotiate, the task fell to Edward Hawkins. He appears to have been more than successful, managing to gain an advantageous rate of carriage, so much so that Brian Hodgson was advised to inform his tenants the transportation cost was six pence a ton cheaper than they could provide. Despite the close relationship between himself and the Hodgson clan, Edward Hawkins always appears to act impartially, as in this instance, putting the interests of the copper company first.

In the spring of 1783 Holland, who was Robert Hodgson's overseer at the Odd Rode colliery, was asked to accompany a Richard Gaskell around the site with a view to employing him as a banksman. If Gaskell was considered suitable then Robert Hodgson would agree terms and conditions with him. At the same time a contract was drawn up with Ford (possibly Hugh Ford the ironfounder of Congleton) for working his nearby colliery at Odd Rode.

Even the Liverpool works came under scrutiny in December 1782 when additional bings (i.e. containers) for storing coal and iron were approved, but they had to be installed as cheaply as possible.

Behind the scenes debts were being chased, in particular those relating to tenants of the Liverpool South Shore on the original smelter site. Mr. Chadwick, responsible for collecting the rents due, was on the point of being sued by Joseph Cooke on behalf of the copper company, as payment had been outstanding for some time. Efforts also continued in the bid to sell the property but as the financial situation generally remained grave, there were no takers.

As Cornish ticketing was of great concern, not only were tickets (for audit purposes) exchanged with the Bristol and Warrington companies, but the net was widened to include Williams of Anglesey, Mark Harford & Co. of Bristol and even the Mines Royal and Cornish Copper Company. Co-operation between the companies within the syndicate continued strong as ever with Mr. Dumbell of Warrington suggesting to Macclesfield and Bristol that, in order to cut costs, allowances to the larger wire customers should be reduced and a general warehouse for African battery established in Liverpool.

In August 1782 Charles Roe Jnr. had been engaged by the company in Liverpool to assist the senior agent Mr. Watkinson. His task was to acquire orders for sheathing, nails and battery for which he would receive $2^1/_2$% commission, but it was on condition that he or Mr. Watkinson was in constant attendance at the 'Counting House' in Liverpool. The arrangement did not last long, barely one year, as Charles was replaced by John Johnson in August 1783 and appears to have returned to Macclesfield.

Strenuous efforts were made to regain orders at the East India Company sales, for whilst Roe & Co had acquired important naval contracts, during 1781 they had been excluded from the East India purchases together with virtually every other company. The war with the American Colonies was at last having an effect in the East and orders were greatly reduced; in desperation Thomas Williams, who must have had a considerable stock of ore on bank, had apparently taken matters into his own hands and, presumably using his connection with the East India Company solicitor John Smith, had managed to dominate the sales. In that year the name of John Dawes no longer appears in the East India accounts but is replaced by The Paris Mine Company, and signals the start of a protracted campaign by the unscrupulous Williams to rid himself of Dawes. Out of total purchases of 11,215 tons of copper ore Williams is credited with 8,833 tons, selling at approximately £4 10s. per ton. Another newcomer, John Heaton, the Duke of Devonshire's audition and land agent, supplied 2,364 tons, leaving just over 18 tons from the agent William Forbes, who had also never previously appeared in the accounts.

Matters had more or less returned to normal during 1782 with Roe & Co. selling £7,098 13s. of copper to the East India Company out of a total of £85,940 (representing 19,348 tons). The sales for 1783 would prove phenomenal as East India Company purchases almost doubled from those of the previous year, totalling in value £150,476 out of which Roe & Co. received £17,647. (i.e. approximately the same proportion as the previous year). Thomas Williams's short meteoric dominance of this particular market was at an end, at least for the time being; from 1783 until 1789 the names of John Dawes and the Paris Mine Company are absent from the East India records, and when the company eventually reappears it is under the name of Thomas Williams.

* * * * * * *

Leaving business matters aside for a while, it is of interest to return to the various members of the Roe family and observe their reactions in the wake of Charles Roe's death. The person most affected was, of course, William Roe who, despite having to allow a certain priority to company matters, had also to give serious consideration to the administration of his father's estate. The fact that his presence was required almost continually in Liverpool complicated affairs in Macclesfield, not so much from the business point of view (although supervision of the works on Macclesfield Common would have to be resolved) but more particularly with the family.

William's principal duty was to Rachel Harriott, by which he was committed to providing a roof over her head for the rest of her life, and an adequate income to support both herself and son, John, in the event of the company's non-survival. The Chestergate house was still mortgaged and the loan, obtained through Thomas Brock of Chester on behalf of a client, Mrs. Elizabeth Roberts, would have to be redeemed. Mrs. Roberts had died leaving two daughters, Susannah Roberts and Elizabeth Tonman, both of whom were in receipt of the interest due on the loan. William, with the help of his friend and banker, Thomas Smyth of Liverpool, paid Susannah Roberts (executrix of her mother's estate) £2,200 on 8th July 1783, thus entering into possession of his father's estate in Macclesfield. Rachel Harriott was therefore guaranteed rent free possession of the house for the remainder of her life and able to provide a home for her son, John and the daughters of Charles Roe's second marriage, although alternative arrangements concerning the youngest, 18 year old Jenny, would soon be made.

Fortunately Hester continued the entries in her journal providing much poignant information during this pivotal chapter of Roe family history. She had attended Christ Church on the Sunday of the week following her uncle's burial to hear David Simpson preach the funeral sermon, during which reference was made to Charles Roe's monument (although the latter was unrecorded by Hester). There seems little doubt that it could not have been completed in the ten days between Charles Roe's death and the narration; the most likely synopsis is that William Roe had commissioned the memorial and, in so doing, had devised the inscription with David Simpson's approval, who would therefore be familiar with its content in advance. The eventual obituary could not have been better executed and must indicate William's authorship, for it seems apparent that no other person could have been in such an authoritative position for providing the remarkably concise and accurate résumé of Charles Roe's life.

Simpson pointed out that at the start of the Christ Church building work Charles Roe's finances must have been "inconfiderable"; there was also a wife and eleven children "unprovided for", yet the inevitability of building costs in excess of "fix thoufand pounds" had not been a deterrent. The incentive was recorded "on the foundation of the ftructure – In gratitude to God for a variety of favours through life received." Once building work began "the principal part of the genteel fortune, which his family and children at prefent enjoy, was poured into his lap . . ."

No one can argue with these words; before 1775 the whole of Charles Roe's income had been tied up in his numerous business projects and, having relocated the Liverpool Works at

Toxteth Park with the subsequent formation of the Macclesfield Copper Company in 1774, he had taken a gamble. The war with the American Colonies had mushroomed beyond everyone's imagination, creating the sharp decline in trade together with considerable anxieties, yet with fortitude the company had survived to allow Charles his fortune. Many other entrepreneurs in similar circumstances had acquired country estates and mansion-houses, but Charles Roe had chosen to provide a much needed church for Macclesfield, even to the extent of allowing the mortgage on his Chestergate home to remain unredeemed, by which his family were effectively "unprovided for".

When completed, the Roe memorial, 12 ft in height and just under 5 ft at its widest part, was mounted high up on the southern wall of the small chancel where it remains today. The sculptor John Bacon R.A. had built up a considerable reputation for public monuments after completing a bust of the King for the hall of Christ Church, Oxford, encouraged by the Archbishop of York. Charles Roe's superbly executed memorial comprises a full length female figure of the Genius of the Arts holding a large cog-wheel in her left hand, whilst her right supports a medallion portraying his head. She is sitting on a tableau representing the three most important projects of Charles Roe's life, the large silk mill, Christ Church and the Liverpool smelter in Toxteth Park. The inscription covers the base whilst the Roe coat of arms, surmounted by a funerary urn, is set at the apex of the configuration, adding a dash of Georgian decorum to the overall work. Hester's silence on the subject is to be expected, her main concern was promoting the Methodist cause and influencing cousin Robert's affairs.

On Monday 21st May, almost two weeks after the funeral, Miss Stockdale arrived from London and told Robert she would see "Justice done to all her Sisters Children . . .". The following week she called to see Hester and was apparently "very kind and affectionate" before returning south again.

During the next few months Hester found herself frustrated by the behaviour of both Robert and Joseph; the latter becoming more and more domineering, creating a fractious relationship between Robert and herself. Finally, in August, Hester left for a visit to Yorkshire with a Methodist friend where, one month later, she was joined by Robert. The pair returned to Macclesfield via Manchester arriving home on the 7th September both, as yet, totally unaware that in the not too distant future a drama would begin to unfold.

Towards the end of the month Robert, in his naivety, took an absurd step by inviting a group of Methodist friends along to Hester's house after a meeting; the outcome was an "enraged" Elizabeth Roe who threatened to show the supposed 'ringleader' Billy Sharpley the door. The next morning James Roe, who was visiting Adlington Hall, sent word that Hester had been invited to join him for the day and, at Mrs. Legh's command, the chaise duly arrived. Perhaps in order to placate her mother, Hester accepted, but in doing so missed an urgent visit by Joseph Roe who, having received letters from Bristol informing him that his sister Peggy was dangerously ill, had hurried over to convey the news.

Nothing further on the matter was reported for months. The New Year came and went with Joseph accusing Hester of unfairly interfering in Robert's affairs, for Robert had received word that there was a chance of Ordination but had been persuaded by Hester that his destiny lay in Methodism. Joseph's behaviour was erratic, one minute acting as accuser, the next wishing to endear himself until he finally confessed his love for her. Hester, aggrieved at his audacity in suggesting that unless she ignored Robert in deference to him then their friendship would cease, defiant and angry chastised him.

Good Friday heralded the appearance of John Wesley preaching in Christ Church, a remit of policy which must have taken much soul searching on the part of David Simpson now that his benefactor was no longer present to oppose. But the encouragement must have come from Bryan Bury Collins, the newly licensed assistant curate of Christ Church. He was yet another graduate of St. John's College, Cambridge, who, having been nominated by David Simpson, commenced duties on 21st October 1781 with a stipend of £40 per annum.

Collins was a disciple of the Wesleys which had caused problems because of the reluctance of several Bishops to grant him priest's orders. He became involved in field preaching, particularly in Yorkshire and London, which brought from John Wesley his usual disclaimer, "Mr. Collins is not under my direction – nor am I at all accountable for any steps he takes." Collins married on 21st September 1780, a possible indicator of a desire to lead a more settled life, and was subsequently accepted for Christ Church. Whether or not his Wesleyan 'soul' was as sincere as his Methodist tendencies portrayed, is another matter, for eventually he would adopt the surname and arms of his maternal uncle in order to inherit a large estate, an action of which John Wesley would certainly not have approved had he still been alive.

The Good Friday service of 1782, during which Wesley assisted David Simpson in administering "the sacrament to about 1,300", was remembered for the exceptional performance of the organist, Aneas Maclardie. Although nothing is known of Maclardie's early life, the fact that Charles Roe engaged him in London for his Macclesfield church suggests an organist of excellent repute. Wesley was so moved by the occasion that he commented to the organist at the end of the service " . . . if I could ensure a similar performance to yours this afternoon I would have an organ introduced into everyone of our chapels."

At this period organs were losing their popularity in theatres and playhouses so it remained the domain of churches and chapels to provide a fitting environment in which the repertoires of many first-rate organists could be performed. It is easy, therefore, to appreciate Maclardie's enthusiasm in accepting the position of choir master and organist in what many would consider to be a provincial chapel, yet one where music was allowed its rightful appreciation and place. Having settled in Macclesfield, he married Sarah, the daughter of John Hale, on 16th January 1782 at the fashionable parish church of Prestbury.

In the meantime Robert Roe, who initially had taken lodgings with a friend, John Barber, but because of family illness had been forced to leave, found himself lodging at Aunt Roe's, much to Hester's delight. Early in February 1782 Jane Stockdale wrote from Bristol to advise that Peggy, suffering from a dangerous relapse, was not expected to live. On 7th March Mary, widow of Rowland Atkinson and the last surviving child of Rev. Thomas of Castleton, died, and Hester was asked by her cousin Mary to assist in the preparations for her aunt's funeral, with which she willingly complied. Opposite was the house where her father had died some years earlier; an observation made with much emotion.

At this time Robert was engaged in building his own house at the western end of Chestergate close by his father's church but not on Roe land. The plot, which abutted the south side of the street was part of the North Orchard belonging to Worth Hall; apart from the northern boundary the whole parcel of land belonging to the hall was surrounded on three sides by Roe meadows. Robert's close friendship with Peter Goostree 'of the Waters' (Waters Green) was causing Hester some concern, for the young man appeared to be steering Robert away from Methodism. Joseph, as though still anxious to direct Hester's affections away from Robert, criticised his brother's preaching, presumably in the hope of encouraging Robert's disenchantment with the Methodist cause culminating in abandonment by Hester. Joseph's action could not have had a more perverse effect on his intended aspirations, as usual he had totally underestimated Hester's stubborn, wilful and persistent nature (a family trait used to such good effect in his lifetime by her uncle Charles); Robert's conversion would not be given up so easily.

On 21st March Hester received word from Miss Stockdale that Peggy was steadily improving, however the drama was about to begin.

Three weeks later Joseph received a letter with the disturbing news that Peggy had had a dangerous relapse, which greatly upset Robert and the very next day, although Sunday, he too received a letter entreating him to accompany Joseph to Bristol at once for Peggy was not expected to live beyond a fortnight. As the Bristol coach left early everyone was up at 3 o'clock, but Joseph had mishandled the arrangements and the coach left without the brothers.

Robert decided to take a chaise yet Joseph refused to share and having ordered the saddling of his own horse, galloped off much to Robert's dismay, for Joseph was aware that because of his ill health Robert was unable to ride on horseback.

At last, towards the end of April (1782) Robert reached Bristol where he was preaching, and finding Peggy almost fully recovered, wrote home immediately to convey the glad tidings then returned shortly afterwards with a half guinea for Hester from Aunt Stockdale.

By early May Robert's house was finished and with furnishings under consideration Hester's advice was sought, yet within six weeks Robert declared that if in the near future he did not feel better, he would sell the house and leave Macclesfield.

Joseph's return to the town was delayed until after the June Fair; in fact he arrived on Tuesday 2nd July with news of Peggy's amazing recovery and the imminent arrival of Aunt Stockdale and the trustees of her father's will. Doubtless with this visit in mind Robert asked Hester to accompany him to the Atkinson household for the purpose of buying a bed.

Jane Stockdale was expected that Saturday by midday in time for dinner at Robert's new house, to which both Hester and Joseph had been invited. In the event the party from London did not arrive at the Angel Inn till afternoon and shortly afterwards one of the trustees, Daniel Golden, the linen draper of St. Clement Danes Parish, called to escort them to the inn where Miss Stockdale was waiting. It was decided that the trustees could stay overnight at Robert's house and accordingly all were invited to have supper there. Jane Stockdale's intimate and friendly conversation with Hester revealed her concurrence to the proposed arrangements for young Jenny to move into Robert's house under Hester's care. It was also intended that Hester and her mother should live in the new house and receive payment from Joseph Stockdale's estate for looking after both Robert and Jenny, a subject yet to be discussed with the trustees and therefore one of confidentiality for the present.

The weekend passed with Robert "much tried by the Trustees" and forced to beg Hester's help in assisting his aunt before Jane Stockdale and the trustees departed for Liverpool on the following Wednesday. Miss Stockdale rewarded Hester for her kindness with a present of a black silk cloak trimmed "with a good Edging". (Just one week earlier Hester had received a gift of a chintz gown, muslin apron and handkerchief case from her godmother, Mrs. Legh, who was visiting Chester.)

The Liverpool visit lasted about four days with the London trio arriving back in Macclesfield at almost midnight on Sunday 21st July. The next day Hester, "having gone into the Market for them", helped Miss Stockdale prepare dinner, but it was not until the following day of Tuesday that Hester learnt many more details. William Roe had resolved the complications of his father's estate and Miss Stockdale confirmed that her nephews' and nieces' affairs were "better than expected", in fact they would receive "very handsome Fortunes". Jenny's move to the new house was also discussed with William and all agreed it was the best course of action for the present.

Robert's aggravation with the trustees was renewed when they expressed criticisms of his house, but during a walk with Hester he confided that they were very displeased with Joseph who had made great endeavours to take control of his sister Peggy's fortune. Whilst at the bank and with the trustees present, realising that he had been thwarted by them, Joseph had flown into a rage. However, unknown to Hester, difficulties had arisen in Bristol and for the second time Mr. Golden journeyed to Liverpool, presumably to consult further with William.

Hester did not visit Robert's house until the weekend when she discovered a scene of great despondency, with Jane Stockdale the worst affected. Robert, feeling under some duress, could say very little, only that it involved Peggy and as a consequence Joseph had gone to Bristol, but Miss Stockdale's hints inferred disapproval of Peggy's conduct. Whilst further news was awaited Jane Stockdale and the trustees spent one afternoon drinking tea with Rachel Harriott and, according to Hester, "told her Miss Jenny must leave her". This somewhat abrupt resolution could not have been very gratifying for Rachel Harriott, as both Robert and Hester had always recorded her attentions to her stepchildren's welfare as of the best. The main consideration behind Jenny's intended removal from the Roe household must have been the desire for Jenny to remain true to Methodism, as dictated by the Stockdale family. One can imagine Rachel Harriott's surprise and, no doubt, protestations at the intended removal of her stepdaughter from her care, especially taking into account the seeds of gossip which would be sown quite unnecessarily.

Jane Stockdale, this time accompanied by trustee John Davis, the ironmonger and brazier of St. Andrews Parish, Holborn, wasted no time in calling on Hester's mother to make the final arrangements. It was proposed to pay Hester £20 per annum and to pay her mother £60 per annum for the keep of both Robert and Jenny with an additional £10 "for the House"; mother and daughter would presumably live in Robert's new house rent free. Hester spent virtually the whole of Friday with Miss Stockdale and Messrs. Golden and Davis during which she was warned (although one suspects with very little foundation) that she must expect "envy and ill will from Mrs. Roe".

The weekend passed without incident but Monday revealed all, for as Hester made her way to the Barber household she met Mr. Golden. His news was distressing; Peggy had formed a relationship with Mr. Bulgin's brother "A Carnal Young Man at Bristol" (the inference being that Mr. Bulgin was already known to the Roe family). Peggy had moved into the young man's house and was refusing to leave Bristol, hence Joseph's hurry to force her return, but without success. Under the circumstances the trustees and Miss Stockdale were leaving for Bristol the next day.

The affair appears to have had a demoralising effect on Jane Stockdale creating an irrationality of action, for she again visited Rachel Harriott and "ord'd Coz. Jenny" to be brought to her the next morning so that she could leave her with Hester. It was as though, being unable to influence Peggy's situation for the present, all her anger and frustration had been directed at the Roe household. Hester was pleaded with to stay at Robert's house, taking care of Jenny and sleeping there until her mother could move in, which Jane Stockdale hoped would be as soon as possible. The reckoning had been made without taking into consideration Elizabeth Roe's ability to think and act for herself; the entry in Hester's diary for Thursday, 8th August 1782 records her mother's fury together with the following:

"She told me She wd keep her goods & stay at her own house & I might Live with
my Gentleman as a Mistress & keep his house if I pleased".

Her wrath having been expended Elizabeth Roe packed up her daughter's belongings and sent them to Robert's house where Hester, with her usual imperviousness, unpacked and arranged them. The situation was never going to be an easy one and Miss Stockdale, in trying to salvage what remained from one adversity, had created another.

25
ALL GOOD THINGS

Take ye heed, watch and pray:
for ye know not when the time is.

Robert Roe died during the early hours of Sunday, 15th September 1782. The events of the last few weeks of his life were meticulously recorded by Hester, though at what time is difficult to deduce, for her diaries were supplemented by notebooks which had obviously been completed at a later date for publication purposes.

One month before his death Robert had received a further offer of Ordination and in contrary mood declared that if he accepted he would have to leave 'Maxfield' but as it had always been his desire "to live and die here", so he chose to stay. A brief note by Hester records "P.G. (Peter Goosetree) now sleeps with him" and could account for the change of heart. His sisters, Polly and Fanny, called to relay family news and young Jenny had developed such an affection for Hester that at the merest suggestion of her returning to live at Mrs. Roe's she wept uncontrollably on Hester's shoulder.

Robert's condition grew rapidly worse yet he struggled on, still holding his young men's religious meetings although with great difficulty; he was plagued with symptoms of what appeared to be a very heavy cold. "P.G." spent the whole of Friday, 20th August papering an upstairs room for Robert, who foolishly remained to assist his good friend. That afternoon workmen arrived to put up a spout and in doing so took out the sashes which left the windows wide open. It was a cold day but Robert, wanting to complete the decorating, worked on in the room for a further two hours until finally, cold and exhausted almost to the point of collapse, he retired downstairs. Hester was quick to provide him with rum and then a cup of cocoa, after which he felt much better but went to bed early.

By the weekend Robert was so ill that Hester felt compelled to stay with him all day and subsequently decided it was time for Dr. Coxon to be called in, although persuading Robert to agree was difficult and initially he refused. William Roe, in Macclesfield for the A.G.M. of Thursday, 29th August accompanied his half-brother Charles to Robert's house on the day preceding the meeting and, according to Hester "made a Joke of his illness". After walking about with them for some time Robert again felt weak and collapsed when they had gone. Hester insisted that Dr. Coxon must be called in, otherwise Miss Stockdale would blame her for his worsening condition, so Robert promised to reconsider the matter but not until the following day, when at last he relented.

Visitors came and went, including Rachel Harriott who was at first forbidden to enter his room; Charles visited each day and grew graver with each visit, until finally the weekend brought David Simpson to administer the Sacrament.

After a change of medication and several visits by Dr. Coxon, on Friday 6th September Robert decided to consider the preparation of his will. At first he thought of leaving "P.G." £300 but then decided £100 would be sufficient (still a considerable sum for a friend). The house could be sold to clear debts and Hester provided with £20 per annum as Robert deduced "I do not expect your Mother would leave you much". Joseph was a problem for, although he had been very unkind on occasion, he appeared to have undergone a recent change of heart which earned him equal consideration with his sisters. Although able to request singing at his funeral Robert could only hope that Jenny would be allowed to remain with Hester, for whatever his wishes were on that score, he was unable to intervene.

The time had arrived for Dr. Coxon to seek a second opinion and Dr. Hall was sent for. Both considered that Robert had endured many years of stress and Dr. Hall approved the awful treatment of creating a blister on his breast already begun by Dr. Coxon.

David Simpson found himself in a difficult position; he had been approached by many relatives and friends showing concern with regard to the preparation of Robert's will, and after careful consideration felt that Hester's well-being must be safeguarded, he therefore judged the time right to broach the subject. At first Hester was afraid to bring any pressure to bear on Robert, but, finding him more rested after a comfortable night, obtained his agreement for David Simpson to set down the details, as Robert's opposition to the involvement of the solicitor, Mr. Cooke, was total.

Initially Robert, before discussing his bequests with her, asked Hester if she knew how much his share of his father's estate would be. Hester reckoned about £1,500 so Robert determined "Well then you shall have £600". Hester protested but Robert had reconsidered his original plan of leaving her mother £200 and herself £400; so resolute was he to secure her independence that the capital was to be paid and not held in trust. Peter Goosetree would receive his £100 and some silver buckles; the "Young Men" in his religious group a half guinea each; a mourning suit for his boy (servant); certain books for David Simpson and others for Hester together with his pocket handkerchiefs and John Wesley's picture. Brother Joe was to inherit his best clothes and Matty Ridgway his shirts. Brother Charles was to have £10 per annum "for if I leave him the capital he shall spend it".

Robert's final decision took into account Peggy's failing health and convinced she would die, would leave no bequest: "she will only leave it to Mr. Croxton". Hester thought Peggy should have her share and David Simpson wanted the £10 per annum to Charles Jnr. withheld and kept for his wife and children should he die. Simpson also named Jane Stockdale as Executrix but Robert insisted that the clergyman himself should be Executor so that, instead of receiving payment for the task, he would receive part of the book collection. Simpson feared that Joseph, who was hoping for possession of the books, would be displeased with this arrangement but Robert was adamant, "his share of my Grandfather's was 4 or 5 Hundred pds. more than mine & I think none of them will have reason to complain." This latter comment is intriguing for nowhere in Joseph Stockdale's will does it specify as to how much each child of his daughter Mary should receive, only that the residue should be divided equally, therefore it must have been the result of actions by Jane Stockdale and the Trustees that this anomaly had arisen.

Robert's will, dated 9th September 1782 and proved the following 9th December, was as he had intimated, despite the objections from David Simpson and his cousin, but he omitted to commit to paper the disposal of most of his personal effects, trusting in Hester's probity to carry out his last verbal wishes. His greatest concern had been the guardianship of his private papers which he had begged Hester to undertake. He also asked her to promise not to reveal his bequest to her in case it should spoil any provisions her godmother, Hester Legh, should make.

In the event only one of Robert's predictions would appear to have come true, Hester Legh would leave just £10 each to Hester and her mother, Elizabeth Roe, but his judgement of Hester's mother was ill-conceived. She was to die on 10th April 1790, yet in her will of 1787 she would appoint Hester sole Executrix and meticulously divide her estate between Hester and James after payment of debts and rewards to her servants. At that time Hester would be in Ireland, having married the Methodist Minister and widower James Rogers at Prestbury on 19th August 1784. She had met him for the first time on 27th March 1781 in Macclesfield and had then written "I never saw him before but he seems A Dear Man & simple as A little Child."

Charles Roe Jnr. would die in 1790 shortly followed by his wife, Mary, leaving their only surviving child, a daughter Jane, to be taken care of by William Roe and his family in Liverpool; and Joseph did cause problems which began even before Robert's death.

* * * * * * *

On Friday 13th September (1782) Joseph called to question Robert about his will but Robert was too ill to respond. The next day, whilst wrapped in a blanket and supported by two friends (to allow his bed to be made) Robert's troubled mind would not be appeased until he had given a brief account of the resistance he had met with at College; at the home of the Nicholsons' in Didcot; from his father and the Bishop of Lincoln etc. in their vain attempts to dissuade him from Methodism. Exhausted and in the final stages of what appears to have been tuberculosis, he died a few hours later.

During the day David Simpson called and Hester was at last able to cry before beginning the mourning ritual. A message was sent to "Mrs. Roe" in the hope of borrowing linen for the bedroom hangings "but she refused any except some which did us little good" so David Simpson supplied a sufficient quantity. Rachel Harriott's response could have been the result of superstitions which surrounded any suggestion of 'consumption' (tuberculosis). Even in recent times houses were fumigated after an occupant's suspected diagnosis was confirmed, and it seems more than likely that the Georgian deathbed drapes from such a case would have been burnt. Bearing in mind that the drapes which Rachel had were probably those from her husband's deathbed, she might be forgiven for not wanting to part with them under such circumstances, however uncharitable that might appear to Hester.

Joseph arrived early to pay his respects but unsuccessfully returned later to enquire of Hester's share of the estate. The Atkinson girls called and expressed the hope that Robert had left her "a Handsome Legacy" as Dr. Coxon had informed them of the extent of her nursing care.

Another day passed during which Joseph stayed most of the time with Hester and Cousin Jenny and an evening visit by David Simpson allowed for a discussion of the funeral, scheduled for the following afternoon.

Tuesday morning the 17th September dawned and Hester went into the room where Robert's corpse lay to wipe his face with brandy. She grieved, especially when the lead coffin arrived and Robert was 'made up' and prepared for his final journey. She was supported by her aunt, Rachel Harriott and William Roe, both acting in a polite and decent manner, and by her cousins of whom Polly and Fanny in particular showed their affections. All was well with Charles and Joseph until the will was read, at which point they did not conceal their displeasure, Charles with his £10 per annum and Joseph at the appointment of Rev. Simpson as Executor, the consequent gift of books and Peter Goosetree's legacy of £100.

The funeral was attended by a huge concourse of people who had to be held back by ushers, which Hester recorded as larger than that of her Uncle Roe's funeral. The four mourners in the coach were her cousins William, Charles, Joseph and young John Harriott (then only 14 years of age); eight more men including the organist and clerk walked in procession, but the vicar (presumably of Prestbury) although invited did not attend. Robert's wish for singing could not have been better fulfilled, for sixty singers took their places and were joined by others as they sang inside the church and also at the grave side.

With the funeral over Hester's first task was to sort through Robert's papers and burn those which she felt he would have wanted destroyed. In the process of doing so Joseph arrived, questioned her actions and gave vent to his anger regarding the will by asking who was present when it was prepared. His interrogation continued with a demand to know whose responsibility it had been to set down the details and who had suggested the bequests, David Simpson or herself. The badgering persisted the next day as Hester walked in the garden with Fanny, who became upset at her brother's insinuation that he did not believe it to be Robert's will. After lunch Joseph returned to make a catalogue of Robert's books, but said nothing further.

Joseph's bad behaviour continued until the weekend, then he gained access to Robert's study where he was alone for some time. After his departure Hester's mother asked why Joseph had been looking through the drawers in the study when she thought they had been locked. On entering the room Hester discovered that one of the drawers had been prised open and would no longer lock; her assumption was that Joseph must have thought his brother had left her "something secret", when in reality he was probably searching for another will.

One of the servants, Martha Ridgway, also mentioned she had seen Joseph take a pocket handkerchief (a gift from Hester) out of the pocket of one of Robert's suits. Joseph, delighted with his discovery, declared "I wish I had more & I will never part with this". Hester, not realising the handkerchief had been left in the pocket and obviously annoyed, wrote in parentheses "wh he left me". Although Robert's will makes no specific mention of such items, Martha Ridgway was a witness to it together with husband Peter and another servant, all of whom presumably would have heard Robert's verbal wishes on such matters.

* * * * * * *

The Ridgway family were loyal servants to the Roes, and as a consequence of Martha's husband Peter having worked for Charles Roe Snr., and her subsequent widowhood, she would be left seven guineas in Frances Roe's will of 10th May 1783.

Peggy Roe did not die early as Robert expected and was also included in Frances's will, part of her bequest being Robert's watch which he had left to Frances. Nor would Peggy be forgotten in her sister Mary's will, prepared on 11th July 1787, by which she would receive Mary's gold watch, several gowns of silk and finest linen (two of which were her late mother's) together with a share of the residue of the estate. Someone obviously spoke out against one or two omissions, for on the same day Mary added a Codicil, part of which read:

> "To my Sister Margaret Racster I give and bequeath the sum of Four hundred Pounds as a Compensation for what she would have received if my late Brother Robert had lived to alter his Will in her Favour as he had proposed . . ."

Evidently Peggy had extricated herself from the affair with Bulgin's brother and made an approved marriage, for Mary also added the purchase of a mourning ring for "my Brother-in-Law Racster".

Although other members of the Roe family viz: William, Catherine, Rachel Harriott, John and Elizabeth had been excluded from Robert's will, they were quite definitely included in the wills of both Frances and Mary and from their bequests were all regarded with much affection and loyalty. Even the wives of Charles Jnr. and William were not forgotten, suggesting that with Robert's death came a greater cohesion and tranquillity within the family.

Joseph was 22 years of age when Robert died and of all Charles Roe's children he is the one who still remains something of a mystery. Nothing is known of his education, but having become a fervent Methodist seems to have gone his own way, often complaining to Hester about the hypocrisy of some of the new members who joined their group. He had obviously received the inheritance from Grandfather Stockdale's will the previous year, when he was 21 years old and appears to have spent time in London with Aunt Jane. One can only assume that whatever business concerns he had were through his London connections, for he was never involved with the Macclesfield Copper Company. At a later date he would certainly have interests in the Congleton silk industry, which suggests they could have been held earlier, but initially he was to become very much involved in the civic life of Macclesfield, as his father before him, holding the office of Mayor for the year 1791-92. What thoughts he had on Hester's marriage in August 1784 are not known, though two months later, on the 7th

October, he would marry a Martha Whittaker at Prestbury and is recorded as a resident of Chestergate, Macclesfield.

The whole episode vividly portrays the characters of those involved and their interrelationships, whilst at the same time proving that often Robert's judgement could be somewhat lacking.

* * * * * * *

Whilst the Macclesfield Roes settled back into their lives of domesticity and local politics William Roe, having satisfactorily appeased the Stockdale faction and discharged his duties to the family with regard to his father's will, now had many more serious matters to occupy his mind. His concerns were framed against the background of the rapidly developing city of Liverpool which provided contemplation for actions, not only on a local but on a national scale.

However, the first priority was a replacement for Charles Roe Snr. in his capacity as supervisor of the Macclesfield works. This was achieved at the A.G.M. of 29th August 1783 when the shares were increased from 13 to 14 allowing "Abraham Mills Esq. late of Gerston Co. Devon" to be admitted as a partner. For this share Mills paid the considerable sum of £7,301 8 11d. and was then appointed a Director "taking upon him chief inspection of Copper & Brass Works on the Common at Macclesfield". Taking into consideration the economic situation, this sudden appearance of a seemingly wealthy man, unconnected with the copper industry, is intriguing; time would provide evidence of his apparent great charm and personality and would also confirm his ability to be extremely adept at public relations.

According to his gravestone Mills should have been born circa 1749, but his date and place of baptism at present remain elusive, leaving one to suspect that he was probably born a little earlier. The nomination of his brother Henry of Surrey, a wealthy timber merchant, to be his successor in the event of death, suggests that, like Edward Hawkins before him, he had borrowed money from a family member in order to purchase his share. From other available information it would seem that the initial contact with the copper company was in fact through the acquaintance of Edward Hawkins.

A brief note by a Derbyshire antiquarian infers that at an early age Mills had served in the 116th Regiment of Foot. Army Lists record an Abraham Mills appointed Ensign of the company of Invalids in the Scilly Isles in July 1757 but no longer in the unit by 1761. By 1763 the Invalids had become the 116th Regiment of Foot having been raised by Major Robert Ackland on 14th February 1762, from which date Abraham Mills is recorded as an Ensign. By the year 1763 Abraham Mills of Roe & Co. would have been at least 12 years of age, making it possible that this is the same person, but suggesting that the earlier Mills in the Scilly Isles was more than likely a relative. He remained with the unit until 1767, despite a renumbering in 1765 when the 116th became "Seventy-third Regiment of Foot, Invalids" which was finally disbanded in 1771.

On 20th September 1779 Mills leased a "Mansion House" in Higher Gerston parish between Torquay and Plymouth from William Bastard of Kitley, Devon. From the details given this was a substantial property comprising a "Great Parlour" and "Little Parlour", two brewhouses, four cellars and a "Great Cellar with the Binns . . . with the Pump therein", kitchen, housekeeper's room, scullery, mealhouse, pantry, goosehouse and "Necefsary", several chambers of various sizes, two or three courtyards one leading to the Hall and one to the stables. There was also a pigeon house, laundry (over the stables), carpenter's shop, coach house and a further stable for six horses. The closes of land included an orchard, and there were rights for shooting and fowling.

The timing of the granting of this lease could be coincidental but, if considered with other factors, it does suggest that Mills may have had a hand in assisting William Bastard (Colonel in the East Devonshire Militia) in repelling the French attack on the Plymouth arsenal in

August 1779. The Naval Abstract of Contracts Minutes record "Henry Mills & Son having certified 25th July 1778 to have received in Forest of Dean Timber to be delivered to H M Stores at Plymouth". A further note of 5th May 1780 confirms that "Mr. Mills" had supplied iron ballast to the Woolwich officers. Abraham Mills was evidently overseeing part of the family business i.e. the delivery of oak from the Forest of Dean and shipped via Newnham Quay (hence the Hawkins connection) for delivery to the naval yard at Plymouth. This also means that Mills must have been aware of the lucrative contract held by Roe & Co. for providing copper sheathing to the Plymouth yard; one can only assume he had become conversant with the important iron smelting industry in the Forest of Dean, which gave him sufficient expertise (or the panache to imply that he had) to take on supervision of the Macclesfield works, although producing copper not iron. By this period it would have been no difficult task as William Roe, of course, had perfected smelting in Liverpool confining the Macclesfield works to refining only.

The Gerston lease records Mills as formerly of Exeter and the Mills family were certainly prevalent in that area with the Christian names of Henry and Abraham proving popular. Unfortunately war time destruction of records creates difficulty with relationships, but one important factor cannot be overlooked, John Russell, fourth Duke of Bedford, owned extensive estates in the West Country and had been created Lord-Lieutenant of Devonshire in 1751. He had a reputation for being warm hearted and thoroughly honest but had an unfortunate knack of being taken in by unscrupulous, politically motivated greedy individuals. He was very successful in his post at the Admiralty where he actively engaged in promoting officers, reforming dockyards and fitting out ships for service, although he personally had led a distinguished army career. His mother was the daughter and heir of John Howland of Streatham and through her marriage to his father, the Bedfords had acquired a large estate at Rotherhithe on which the Howland Great Wet Dock had been constructed between 1697 and 1700 to which two dry docks were soon added. Although the first half of the 18th century saw no great expansion, for the East Indiamen were adequately built, repaired and catered for at the Blackwall Dock, the second half saw business increasing.

On 17th March 1768 Henry Mills, timber merchant, insured a considerable new development in Lavender St. Rotherhithe with the Sun Insurance Co. This was within half a mile of the Howland Dock and comprised a new dwelling house with adjoining warehouses occupied by himself, several houses, one with warehouses, another with stables and two workshops used by lighter builders, all leased to tenants, with the total value of the complex for insurance purposes assessed at £1,900. One cannot help but speculate that the Mills family, through their various connections, had succeeded in gaining favour with the Duke of Bedford and as a consequence acquired a very lucrative naval contract and the facility for constructing this important Rotherhithe development.

Be that as it may, a not inconsequential gentleman arrived in Macclesfield and from later evidence would prove Jonathan Roose to be a novice when it came to charming the ladies. It is not known whether or not he was a widower at the time of his arrival, but he only had one legitimate surviving child, Mary Ann, described in his will years later as his "legitimate daughter of late wife, Mary". Surprisingly he never remarried, which does suggest that his wife lived for quite some time, but he did lease Fence House from Thomas Smyth of Liverpool, which provided yet another outlet for his unbounding versatility – coal mining. Logically he was in the right position to superintend the coal getting from the Smyth estate and probably as a result of this Edward Hawkins and the solicitor, Joseph Cooke, decided to form a partnership for operating a new colliery close by on Macclesfield Common. This in no way contravened the company Articles of Partnership which related specifically to the smelting and refining business and associate processes; mining was quite separate allowing each partner to invest as and when he chose.

Edward Hawkins, unlike William Roe and Robert Hodgson, certainly had no practical mining experience but no doubt relied on the latter for advice. The area in question was under lease from the Crown to the Earl of Harrington from 10th May 1766 for 26½ years (i.e. till November 1793) and for a payment of £400 Hawkins and Cooke purchased the leasehold for what appears to have been the remainder of the lease (i.e. from 10th November 1783 which would be for 10 years). Some coal getting was already in progress by the Barlow family, though only on a small scale, so Hawkins and Cooke obtained permission to take over the existing pits (which must have been agreed beforehand with the Barlows), open up new ones and sink shafts etc. in a concerted effort to increase coal supplies.

* * * * * * *

It had now become time for William Roe to reconsider his position within the company's scheme of things. According to the Articles it was sufficient for only three members of the elected committee to hold a meeting and conduct business. William, however, must have been acutely aware of his onerous position now that his father and brother, Samuel, had died. Brian Hodgson Snr. was still very much in the picture together with his sons, Robert and Brian Jnr. and although Edward Hawkins tended to take an independent stance, yet he was related to them and an associate of Abraham Mills. Whilst there had never been any obvious dissension between the parties, the balance of power was now tilted in favour of the Hodgsons and this William must have felt obliged to remedy.

From the minutes of the company meetings it soon becomes obvious that although John Atkinson Busfield was still an inactive partner, yet his attendances increased, as did his interest in company business. He was the sole remaining representative of the Atkinson family and there seems little doubt that William must have spelt out the problems concerning the situation and gained his extra support.

Busfield had enjoyed considerable success in the intervening years from when he first acquired a share following the death of Edward Pitts, until 1783 when he was 44 years of age. The adopted surname and estate from his wife's uncle had gained him a position as a senior magistrate in the West Riding of Yorkshire. He was described contemporaneously as a "kind-hearted gentlemanly man", a sympathiser with the poor and tolerator of Methodist prayer meetings. In fact he had apparently heard Wesley preach in 1776 and having admired his stance, during a subsequent visit to Bingley on Saturday, 1st August 1778 had invited the preacher to view his considerable estate which he had greatly improved.

Busfield had originally bought a large farmhouse called Spring Head near Bingley which he then converted into a fashionable mansion renamed Myrtle Grove. The house stood at the top of a wooded hill adjacent to another covered with tall oak trees. A river, flowing between the two, allowed him to create walkways which provided excellent views of the valley, and the description by Wesley at least suggests that in the first instance the minister appeared to appreciate the place.

In April of the following year (1779), having preached in Bingley church, Wesley was once more invited to dine with Busfield "in his little paradise"; on this occasion one cannot help but detect a note of sarcasm in Wesley's comment as he wrote that new improvements continued apace and privately questioned Busfield's justification for such things ". . .it can give no happiness unless God is there". Wesley went quickly on his way to Otley and seems to have closed his mind to both Busfield and his estate. Whether Busfield was aware of his 'rejection' or not, it certainly did not deter him from taking a more responsible role with regard to the copper company and its commercial advantages.

From subsequent proceedings Busfield was able to shoulder some of the responsibilities regarding mining facilities in Yorkshire, particularly in respect of calamine and Captain Overend, thus providing William Roe with a reliable associate.

William also knew that he could rely implicitly on Thomas Smyth's support, but Charles

Caldwell was a different matter, for the latter had never attended a company meeting.

The Liverpool end of the business was a considerable responsibility and with the company now tightening its rules whereby each committee member must forfeit a half guinea for non-attendance, unless ill or otherwise engaged on company business, the question difficult to answer must have been who to leave in overall charge during absences, especially with regard to the Toxteth works. As it was, both William Roe and Thomas Smyth rarely missed a meeting, which must have taken up at least three to five days of their time on each occasion, when allowing for the journeys to and from the different venues. Also Thomas Smyth had been elected Mayor's Bailiff of Liverpool on 18th October 1782, a position demanding his attendance at corporation meetings on a more regular basis. The problem was quickly and somewhat mysteriously resolved with the emergence of someone who, like Smyth, would prove to be an extremely dependable and dedicated member of the team, John Johnson.

There seems little doubt that Johnson was in some way related to the famous mayor of Liverpool, Thomas Johnson and also to John Johnson renowned for his brewery in Dale Street, but his own branch of the family, although merchants, seem to have been involved with canvas and sail making. Like the Shaws they originated in Warrington where members of the family remained and had become pin manufacturers. On 30th October 1778 there is a record of a naval contract with a John Johnson for canvas to be delivered to Deptford in "12 weeks time". Although deductions can only be based on circumstantial evidence, yet the fact that at the same time the Navy was receiving tallow from Samuel Shaw, copper sheathing and bolts from Roe & Co. and timber from Henry Mills & Son does beg forgiveness if one is incorrect in confidently assuming that this John Johnson was the one admitted into the copper company. The question is "how?" for no mention is made in the minutes.

Under the Articles of Partnership should a committee member die then a majority of members could elect another "interested" person and the logical conclusion is that William Roe had given the trusteeship of his late brother, Samuel's share to Johnson, who was then elected to the committee but with the unusual proviso that either he or Thomas Smyth would attend future meetings. William's original intention must have been to admit his half-brother, Charles Jnr. in place of Samuel, as evidenced by the employment of young Charles as a salesman with Watkinson in Liverpool. But Charles Jnr. evidently wasted the opportunity and was, of course, replaced the following year by Johnson, proving that Hester's comments and David Simpson's apprehension as to his character, were justified.

A further fact cannot be overlooked; as the development of Toxteth Park rapidly advanced, particularly after the establishment of the Roe & Co. works with its influx of workers, it was soon apparent that the foundation of a Church of England church was imperative. The Earl of Sefton gave a plot of land for the purpose and by Articles of Agreement dated 20th April 1773 the proposal to build St. James's on part of a close called the New Field in Toxteth Park was confirmed.

Several people formed a committee and contributed £100 each, totalling £2,700 towards building costs; two committee members were John Johnson and John Pemberton "Sailmakers" (a Liverpool Corporation lease of 4th June 1777 records their interest in a property on the eastside of Paradise Street). This John Johnson was in an ideal position to oversee, when necessary, the smeltworks in Toxteth Park and, because of his affiliation with St. James's, would know well many Roe & Co. employees from their attendances at the church, which when completed had opened for Divine Service on 4th June 1775. Early registers record the names of several copper smelters with an occasional wire drawer or nailmaker; labourers and coopers also appear, some of whom must have worked for the company. Many of these families were to remain in the company's employ for a very long time; of particular note are the surnames of Jones, Roberts and Ovens with the latter family especially prominent (in fact a company note of 2nd September 1784 suggests that William Ovens should visit Cornwall "for his improvement in the art of assaying").

St. James's, Toxteth.

Entered on the inside cover of the earliest register is a memorandum which reads:

"that George son of Charles & Ann Caldwell was Born June 12 1773 and was Baptized some time in the said month; and William son of the said Parents was Born May 5 1774 and was baptized sometime within the said month also Ann daughter of the said Charles & Ann Caldwell was born Dec 8 1779 and baptized sometime within the said month of December – Which Baptisms were neglected to be inserted in any Register. This Memorandum was made by particular Desire of the said Mr. Charles Caldwell May 25 1784."

(Charles Caldwell was certainly an enigma, in his eventual will prepared in 1813 his above-named children, together with a younger daughter, Harriet, are qualified also as the children of "Ann Ashton late of Liverpool deceased"; this appears to imply illegitimacy.)

There is no evidence that the Roe family initially contributed in any way to St. James's, which is understandable when considering the expenditure involved in transferring the works from the Liverpool South Shore to Toxteth and Charles Roe Snr.'s additional commitment to the building of his own chapel in Macclesfield at that period.

* * * * * * *

The members of the Roe & Co. committee, having resolved the managerial problems, once again turned their attention to production, with emphasis on quality. The policy of fining for bad work continued with some vigour, but on the other hand employees such as Salt and Houselander received a guinea reward for the excellence of their brass.

In November 1783 Brian Hodgson Jnr. was excused attending a meeting as he had taken one of his sons to Glasgow for what appears to have been the start of an apprenticeship. This link with the Scottish port would be of some significance to the company in the not too distant future. William Roe was also excused, as the letter advising him of the meeting had been misdirected. After a further brief meeting held in Macclesfield during January 1784 the subsequent one of the 1st April, this time in Warrington, again saw William absent; on this rare occasion he was very ill and although he recovered, tragically two of his children died.

The first was young Charles Samuel on 27th April, just 17 months old; the second was daughter Catherine on 18th June, nearly 3 years of age. Their deaths were recorded on the memorial which stood over the family tomb in the graveyard of their grandfather's church, Christ Church, in Macclesfield, from which one may assume that their little bodies were brought there for burial. Fortunately daughters, Ann (7 years), Hannah (6 years), Elizabeth (almost 5 years) and Rachel Harriot (almost 4 years) survived; miraculously so did baby William born 4th January 1784 who would now replace brother Charles Samuel as his father's heir.

William Snr.'s susceptibility to illness at this time, although of sufficient severity to have caused the deaths of two of his children, perhaps indicates the extreme pressures he was under. Not only had he dealt with the difficulties arising from his father's estate successfully, organised the retention of the balance of Roe power within the company for the sake of his family but, following in the footsteps of Thomas Smyth, had been elected one of the two Liverpool Bailiffs in 1783, despite the fact he was not a freeman of the port.

* * * * * * *

Liverpool Corporation had its own peculiarities much contested for centuries. The original charter from King John allowed certain privileges for anyone who leased a burgage tenement from the Crown, but gave no provision for any form of local government. Henry III extended the charter by allowing power to the burgesses for the election of officers who were called Bailiffs and the creation of a court to deal with offenders and dispense punishment. A quite separate guild was formed from the burgesses for trading rights, which over a period of time admitted 'foreigners' on payment of a fee or fine. But it would seem that the 'elite' band of burgesses from the established council continued to meet from time to time, causing dissension until the reign of Elizabeth I, when the Mayor took matters into his own hands. He decided that together with the Aldermen and twenty four free burgesses and inhabitants, a council should legally be formed to govern the town. The burgesses of the Common Council, however, took matters into their own hands, continued as usual, and if a vacancy occurred voted amongst themselves for a person most suitable to fill the position. Apparently this is how William Roe became a member of the Common Council and Bailiff of Liverpool because, although the Restoration brought further legislation sanctioning the Common Council, it did little to alter the established procedure.

This sudden desire on William's part to become a more active participant in Liverpool affairs, was possibly the result of both his father's and father-in-law's deaths, after all he was the one who, at that time, had fathered the heir for both families and it was now imperative to maintain the vital links within the Establishment. It could also have been the determining factor in his decision to build a grand family residence within the confines of Toxteth Park, for which he was granted a piece of land on 17th October 1783 (leased by Thomas Gildart from Lord Molyneux) measuring 28 yards x 150 yards on the "South side of new Street intended to be called High Park St." Subsequent Liverpool directories although recording William Roe, Esq. at "High-park" also record "Roe Wm, & Co. Copper Warehouse Manesty's Lane". Yet within three years or so he would have leased this mansion called "Fair View" to his good friend, Thomas Smyth, and returned to town residing at 3 Shaw Place close by the Haymarket. One can only assume that part of the Fair View premises, situated high up the hill from the Mersey estuary and copper works, was set aside for company business.

The year 1784 saw William Roe becoming more closely associated with his brothers-in-law, John and Christopher Shaw, partly because of the trusteeship of Samuel Shaw Snr.'s will. Their

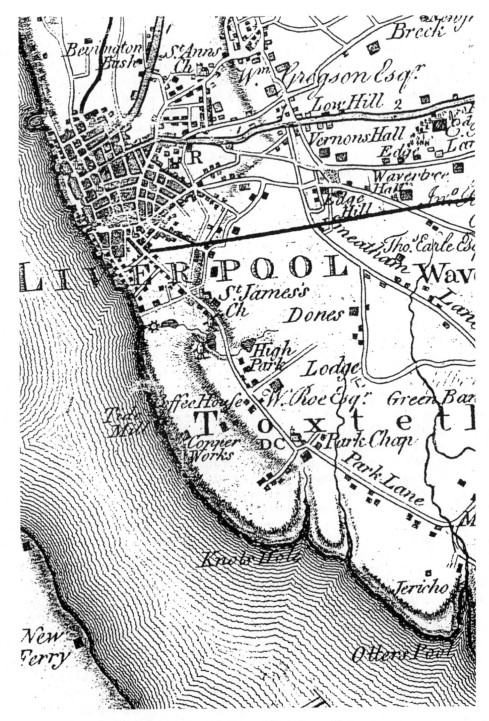

Details taken from a 'Survey of the County of Lancaster' by William Yates 1786. The Roe influence in Toxteth is clearly visible with the siting of the 'Copper Works', the residence of 'W. Roe Esqr' and 'St. James's Ch[urch]

names appear on Corporation leases for a large warehouse on the east side of Bromfield St., overall size a little more than 68 ft square and also a piece of ground and premises on the south side of White-chapel called Potters Gardens. On 9th January 1784 they were registered as co-owners of a ship *Asia* captured from the French and legally condemned in the High Admiralty 29th January 1781 then bought and made seaworthy by the trio. They were already in possession of another French prize of 1782, the sister ship *Europe*, similarly condemned and restored to use, only to be burnt "on the coast of Africa" 22nd September 1788.

It is interesting to note the large number of baptisms for black servants in St. James's earliest register e.g. "Jemmy Africa negro native of Gold Coast". One of the most noteworthy would be made in 1796 "Samuel Baron son of the African King, Oaramby, alias Johnson, was bapt. Jan 21st". During the 1780s about 80 black children, sons and daughters of African merchants, were sent to Liverpool as temporary residents by their fathers for primary education.

* * * * * * *

By this period steps had already been taken towards the abolition of slave trading, a movement supposedly begun with a meeting of a committee founded by the Society of Friends in April 1783. The next five years would see an escalation in support of a bill to outlaw the trade and one of its chief protagonists was Bishop Beilby Porteus.

On 11th February 1783 the Bishop had preached before the Society for the Propagation of the Gospel on the subject of "the Negroes in the British West-India Islands". It was the culmination of months of correspondence with several West Indian landowners both abroad and in Britain. From the result of his enquiries he deduced that the Africans were in a deplorable situation and was determined to act. The Society, which had a trust estate in Barbadoes, was itself responsible for 300 slaves and therefore in an excellent position to set an example. The Bishop's keenness to educate children with the use of the Bible once again came to the fore, as he preached in favour of "a regular system of religious instruction" for the workers of the plantations. He suggested that the Society set aside funds for the purpose, which met with general approval.

Encouraged by the support he received Beilby set out his scheme to the Society, but much to his disbelief after only four hours of debating, the members, having thanked him for "the great pains and trouble he had taken" concluded that "at that time (it was) unadvisable to adopt the plan". The Bishop's comments, echoing those of Edmund Gibson, Bishop of London (1723-48) who had once found himself in a similar position, reflect his utter dismay and consternation at the rebuff, "Nothing less than an absolute demonstrable impossibility should have discouraged us from the attempt". The Bishop however was not easily deflected from his chosen path of duty and, though thwarted for the present, his resolve was undiminished, meantime he worked tirelessly within the Diocese of Chester. Having the care and welfare of his clergy at heart besides that of his laymen and women, he was successful in establishing a relief fund for those clergymen whose stipends barely reached subsistence level.

At this juncture it must be pointed out that William Roe was never a member of the 'African Company of Merchants Trading from Liverpool'. The Shaws, through the Blundell family connection, had been, but with the admittance of John Sparling as a freeman of the company in 1771, the sheer ferocity of his dominance saw the gradual withdawal of the Shaws who had served on the committee at various times; the last occasion was that of Samuel Shaw Jnr. in 1779. Sparling's purchase of St. Domingo House in Everton for £3,470 ensured his total commitment to the slave trade and any suggestion of Abolition was fiercely contested by him.

At future Liverpool Corporation meetings where petitions were signed to Parliament for non-Abolition, William Roe was markedly absent. Thomas Smyth's indefatigability ensured his presence but like Bishop Beilby, with overwhelming opposition there was little he could do for the present. His son William (tutor to the Sheridan family) did join an Anglican

Society but again was constrained in his support for Abolition. It was early days and people had to be won over quietly. Even the Roscoe Circle, with its aims firmly fixed on Abolition, would have to work discreetly behind the scenes.

Surprisingly one national voice who pressed the need for caution in the desire for Abolition was Dr. Johnson. Whilst admitting that "men in their original state were equal" and that any slave must have been "brought into the merchant's power" by either fraud or violence, yet he firmly believed "it would be extreme cruelty to the African Savages, a portion of whom it saves from massacre or intolerable bondage in their own country, and introduces into a much happier state of life; especially now when their passage to the West Indies, and their treatment there, is humanely regulated. To abolish this trade would be to ". . . shut the gates of mercy on mankind". Whilst Boswell adamantly recorded his disapproval of Johnson's stance, there is no evidence to suggest that the faithful black servant, Francis Barber, made his objections known, in fact, who better than he to have made known these matters to Dr. Johnson in the first place.

Others must have been gravely concerned about developments in New York. After the attainment of peace early in 1783 between the American States and Great Britain most of the Rhode Island inhabitants had agreed to free all their slaves. A visitor at that time was John Harriott who, in his memoirs "Struggles Through Life", later wrote the following:

> ". . .the fact is, that, instead of becoming industrious and living comfortably, they became a pest to society. Not knowing how to enjoy a sudden burst of liberty, they gave themselves up to all manner of rioting and excess of debauchery. To themselves, the consequence is that they do not propogate their own species as much as when they were well clothed, fed and kept to regular hours, by their former masters. They are now idle and lazy to a proverb, nor can they be induced to do a little work but at extravagant wages. What money they earn, they chiefly buy spirits with for their night-frolics, when the few, that have been prevaild on to go to service, and tempted to join them and are soon persuaded to rob their masters or mistresses in order to support these nocturnal riots, where all kinds of debauchery are practised.
>
> There are some few exceptions, but I understand they chiefly were to be found among those negroes whose emancipation from the yoke of slavery was gradual."

Societies for emancipation had been set up in various parts, principally by the Quakers but John Harriott complained that their methods were neither just nor honest.

Whilst passions ran high on the subject, particularly in the ports of Bristol and Liverpool, in the quiet respectable little town of Ashbourne in Derbyshire on 12th December 1784 Brian Hodgson Snr. quietly passed away. This marked the end of an era as far as the copper company was concerned; the event was reported as follows in Drewry's *Derby Mercury*:

> "On Sunday last died at Ashbourne, much advanced in Years, Brian Hodgson, Gent – He formerly kept the Hall at Buxton where he acquired a large Fortune."

Until the present day this insert has perpetuated the myth that Brian Hodgson's fortune was made as a Buxton innkeeper. Whilst accepting it certainly played a part in his financial situation it was negligible compared with his returns from Roe & Co. It seems strange that the partnership with Charles Roe has hardly warranted attention and suggests that Hodgson was not one to boast of his investments. One suspects also that Ashbourne's genteel society was not adept at hard-headed bargaining or desirous of discussing business matters during its after dinner soirées. In its pleasant rural setting the delightful market town appeared to rely on its academics and members of the professions to provide more favoured intellectual conversation.

* * * * * * *

Brian Hodgson's will, prepared on 1st June 1784, reveals that he must have been aware of his impending demise having "lately made a vault in the west end of Ashbourne Parish Church". His wife, Elizabeth, inherited the "Dwelling House'"(Grey House) in Ashbourne with the coach house, stables and other buildings; in addition other holdings included land in Offcote and Underwood (Parish of Ashbourne) and lands and buildings in "Chappell in the Frith" known as Spire Hollin Farm. Elizabeth was also entitled to the household furniture, wines and liquors, husbandry implements, live and dead stock, and her husband's horses. (A Horse Tax Return for 1784 shows Brian Hodgson in possession of two drays). The only charge on this bequest was an annuity of £30 per annum payable out of the rents received from Spire Hollin Farm to a nephew, John Grace.

After Elizabeth's death the two administrators (one of whom was the Ashbourne solicitor, Francis Beresford) were instructed to sell everything except a picture of Brian Hodgson's father and a sofa in the parlour, both reserved for son Robert. Also exempted was a set of chairs with "worked seats" together with a screen "the work of my dear Daughter Elizabeth Leigh", which she was to be given.

A somewhat strange bequest of one acre of land in Cheadle, Staffordshire was also made to daughter Elizabeth and possibly intended to accommodate her horse; it adjoined an estate included as part of her marriage settlement. After her death the acre was to be regarded as part of the adjoining estate which, at the time of her father's death, was more than likely mortgaged to pay off her husband's debts.

Lands were still held in Disley, Cheshire, including a copyhold farm from which widow Elizabeth was to receive an annuity of £20 per annum for life from the rents. This property was left to Robert for his own use whilst the nephew, John Grace, was given use of the lands at Fairfield (now occupied by the Pavilion Gardens in Buxton) for his lifetime only, with the proviso they would then pass to Brian Hodgson Jnr. and his heirs.

Sons Brian and Robert were to inherit in equal moieties their father's share of a piece of land called 'the new Inclosure' near Liverpool; this obviously relates to land leased because of the activities of the copper company.

All the mining shares, which included Brian Hodgson's "one sixth" or "four twenty fourth shares in copper and lead mines at Paris (*sic.*) Mountain, Anglesey" and several shares in Derbyshire (not specified) were to be adminstered by his trustees; out of the clear profits his widow was to receive a one seventh part, the remainder to be treated as residue of the estate.

Hodgson's holdings in "a joint Trade now carried on under the Name and Designation of Roe and Company" which he referred to as "frequently fluctuating" were also entrusted to his administrators. They, in turn, were instructed to sell to son Brian Jnr. and son-in-law, Edward Hawkins at the price fixed by the Articles of Partnership, but if either refused the offer then the unsold shares were to be offered to Brian Hodgson Snr.'s other children or his grandchildren. In the event of further refusals the shares were to pass to the company for disposal and the money realised taken as part of the residual estate.

Confirmation of a "Deed of Gift" in writing by which son Robert had received a quarter of his father's shares in Roe & Co. on 5th November 1764 was also included.

Hodgson charged his two sons Robert and Brian Jnr. together with Edward Hawkins to invest the considerable sum of £6,000 in Government or other Securities and pay the dividends or interest to his widow; after her death this investment was to be considered as part of the estate. He also confirmed that this provision was in lieu of any third claim of Dower. In addition Elizabeth was to received an immediate payment of £100, with the same sum paid to each of her two widowed sisters, Mrs. Catherine Webster, still resident in Parliament St., Westminster and Mrs. Mary Gibbons (whose son Job had written the appealing letter from Tralee in Ireland to the young Duke of Devonshire on 30th November 1768) now resident in Windsor.

An interesting bequest was to a family in Stamford, Lincolnshire where Brian Hodgson Snr.'s early days had been spent helping to run his father-in-law's famous inn. The Stevensons, father and son, had borrowed a not inconsequential sum of £200 on which interest was regularly paid. Hodgson instructed that the interest must be paid by the husband to his wife, Sarah, for her own use and after her death the capital should be shared amongst all the children (if more than one). It was an interesting way in which to clear the debt for succeeding generations. Nor were the Hodgson family servants forgotten, each duly received £5.

Hodgson's contributions to his four daughters' marriage settlements had been £2,400 each, now, in addition to these vast sums, he bequeathed a further £2,600 each to be paid one year after his death. As Catherine Ferneyhough was already a widow she was to receive her portion personally. "Beilby – Lord Bishop of Chester" and Edward Hawkins would receive the bequests on behalf of their wives but a special proviso was made for Elizabeth (wife of Edward Leigh). Her extra £2,600 was to be invested by three of the trustees i.e. Robert and Brian Hodgson Jnr. and Edward Hawkins, in Government or other Securities and the interest paid to whoever Elizabeth Leigh should direct to receive it in writing, an arrangement to be adhered to whilst her husband was still living.

There seems little doubt that Edward Leigh had got himself into financial difficulties probably as a result of his affluent lifestyle, bad investments or both and Brian Hodgson Snr. was evidently determined that Leigh would spend no more of his daughter's inheritance. His will specifically states that the extra money "shall not be subject to the Control, Debts or Engagements of the said Edward Leigh". If daughter Elizabeth predeceased her husband then the money was to be willed by Elizabeth to a responsible person as trustee for her children. In addition to the three aforementioned trustees, Brian Hodgson also appointed his widow and Bishop Beilby.

It was extremely difficult at that period to value estates in advance of sales and many trustees struggled with encumbrances brought about by bequests in wills. Brian Hodgson Snr. appreciating that this sort of predicament could occur, allowed for any shortfall by specifying that if the extra bequests to his daughters could not be fully met, then they must be deferred until after his wife's death when the assets of the estate would be fully realized.

In due course the residue was to be divided into six equal parts and distributed between his two sons and four daughters as under the terms already stipulated i.e. Edward Hawkins and Beilby Porteus receiving the shares appropriate to their wives.

This is an impressive will and if seen in context with Charles Roe's circumstances at the time of his death, one can appreciate the enormity of Wiliam Roe's task in administering his father's estate, which was of far greater complexity.

* * * * * * *

The Derbyshire lead mine shares are difficult to assess. At various times, particularly in the 1760s Brian Hodgson Snr. had held investments in:

Placket Mine	$^2/_{24}$th.)	
Eyam Dale Sough	$^1/_{24}$th.)	All from January 1763
Oxclose Sough	$^1/_{24}$th.)	– problems with water in this mine 1772 continued till 1780.
Mawry Mine Sough	$^1/_{24}$th.	(19/9/64) still held 1773 but mine abandoned 1775.
Calver Mill Sough	$^1/_{48}$th.	(January 1765) still held 1770 but mine then under water and was abandoned 1774.
Noon Nick	$^1/_{24}$th.	(1/1/66) Executors still investing in 1795.
Watergrove	?	(January 1774) in Middleton Dale. Executors still investing 1802.
Haredale	$^1/_{24}$th	(1776) No further details.

It is doubtful whether or not much profit was gained by these investments, where records do survive the losses far outweigh the profits. Some were new mining ventures which by their nature incurred large losses because of expenditure in the early years (i.e. 1760s) but had one or two profitable years in the early 1770s.

Ironically, the Gorsey Dale mine near Winster, the only one recorded with investments from both Charles Roe and Brian Hodgson Snr., after making losses of varying amounts (from as high as £534 10 1d. in 1769 to only £18 11 10d. in 1777) in 1783 began to make a small profit. Whilst Charles Roe's share had been $^1/_{48}$th and Brian Hodgson's $^1/_{12}$th yet the Executors for both would continue the investments long after calamine was required by Roe & Co. The records are extant to 1802 and though profits each year barely reached double figures, yet from 1783 onwards no losses are recorded.

The investments were all managed by John Barker of Barkers and Wilkinson and his copy letters to investors reveal much interesting information. One, concerning Robert Shore, by then the former Duke of Devonshire's agent at Ecton, and dated 20th March 1780 confirms that he had once more fallen foul of fraud, but this time of an even graver nature:

"We have made but little workmanship either at Winster Pitts or Oxclose lately as you will perceive by the a/c this is partly owing to the veins affording but little Ore & partly to the loss we have met with in parting with our Overseer (Mr. Shore) whose affairs were & are so embarrassed that he has been obliged to seek out employment at a distance and is now (I believe) erecting Copper Works near you.

Whether he means to do business in this County anymore or not is at present uncertain, this is unfortunate for the Oxclose partnership as we know not any person equal in ability & practical knowledge of the Veins whom we can with propriety put into his place."

A further letter of the 2nd June was sent to Shore exhorting him to return and deal with a problem relating to an investor in the Mixon mine just over the Staffordshire border. Barker was obviously unaware of the magnitude of Shore's indebtedness. The original debt of £1,000 to the Devonshire estate had not been cleared and over £3,000 was now missing at Ecton. Unfortunately the lack of adequate branch banks and the mechanism by which loans were obtained against property left much to be desired. Time after time merchants and others were borrowing to pay off debts until the whole situation spiralled out of control.

In 1779 a meeting had taken place in Buxton to put forward the Duke's scheme for building "The Crescent". When completed this considerable building with a span of 275 ft would accommodate seven boarding houses, each with eleven rooms, a hotel of twenty rooms and at the eastern end an Assembly Room 75$^1/_2$ ft in length with both a height and width of 30 ft. The meeting was a heated affair during which Brian Hodgson Jnr. (keeper of the Old Hall from the time of his father's retirement to Ashbourne) walked out with his supporters. He had evidently calculated that the development would ruin his business, whilst at the same time his rent, payable to the Duke, would substantially increase. By 1781, when the foundations for The Crescent were dug revealing the old Roman bath, Brian Jnr. had retired to Wootton Lodge in Staffordshire not too far distant from Ashbourne, but would still retain his shares in the copper company.

The death of Brian Hodgson Snr. could not have occurred at a more significant time; the Parys Mountain mining lease was due to expire on 10th October 1785 and with considerable activity taking place behind the scenes William Roe was about to discover what a ruthless adversary Thomas Williams could be.

26
CONSIDERABLE CHANGES

Think not to-morrow can repay
The pleasures that we lose today.

Shortly after Thomas Williams's successful coup of 1778, when Sir Nicholas Bayly had unwittingly leased his moiety of Parys Mountain to John Dawes not realising that Dawes was acting as trustee for two thirds of the lease on behalf of Williams, an agreement was reached with Rev. Hughes to "Occupy the Lands and work the Mines jointly" as from 1st January 1779. The shares of the whole venture were accordingly divided $^3/_6$ths to Hughes: $^2/_6$ths to Thomas Williams and $^1/_6$th to John Dawes.

By 1780 Williams was embroiled in a dispute in which legal opinion was very much against him. The case was brought by a Henry Prichard who had been approached by Williams in an attempt to bludgeon him into agreeing to the construction of a new private road across his lands. Prichard and fellow residents soon realised that the new road was "merely for the convenience of carrying the copper ore to the port of Amlwch". The old road, which linked the market towns of Llanerchymedd and Amlwch, passed within 600 yards from where the new one was proposed and could easily be repaired and widened for a tenth of the cost of the new one. Williams, described as "lately a practising attorney but now acts as a justice of the peace", persuaded one of the Quarter Session J.Ps. Mr. Sparrow to act supposedly on behalf of the residents of the township of Llanryllan who were responsible for the maintenance of the roads in the parish. Sparrow appeared in person to confirm the residents' desire for a new road. Mr. Goodman, an attorney involved in business with Williams, stated that he would accept a fine of £200 on behalf of Prichard and others towards the cost of the new road; but none of them had engaged either Sparrow or Goodman to speak for them.

Williams also ensured that a sworn jury was made up of his own servants or agents in order to assess the amount of compensation payable to Prichard for the intrusion. A judgement was made which was considered by Williams to be far in excess of what should be paid and the jury were told from the Bench to say nothing but must consider the valuation as set down by witnesses. Accordingly a piece of paper was passed to them with the sum under consideration written on it, they retired only to return inevitably with a verdict agreeing the sum as dictated by the witnesses.

Henry Prichard took action and obtained some important legal opinions from the Inns of Court all condemning the "improper conduct" of the magistrates and confirming that the Act of Parliament 13 Geo. 3, used so effectively by Williams, was for repairing old roads and not for creating new ones. One Middle Temple barrister went so far as to say "the justices have abused the public trust" and recommended that Goodman be sued and an appeal made to the King's Bench at the next Quarter Sessions. It was obvious that Williams would stop at nothing in his quest for wealth and power.

During 1782 a survey of the progess of mining on Parys Mountain appears to have been commissioned; by whom and from whom is at first not at all obvious, however, the eventual report, made up from information collated at various times, has been attributed to Thomas

Harrison steward of Beaudesert, Staffordshire and chief agent of Lord Paget. It is possible that the initial inspiration for the report was the fact that Sir Nicholas Bayly had already fallen seriously ill and was not expected to live, therefore his eldest son and heir, Lord Paget, would be anxious to discover the apparent state of his future inheritance from his father. This is in part supported by a comment written in the notes, "Will Lord Paget on the demise of Sir Nicholas Bayly have it in his power to make void the Leases or not?".

The account, a copy of which was entered in a large notebook purchased from a bookseller and stationer of The Strand, London, commences with the words "Extracts and heads of Sir Nicholas Bayley's Case and Suit with Edward Hughes Clk and others and the proceedings thereon" and had obviously been prepared by someone unfamiliar with the area or the people concerned. It began with a grand resumé of the situation regarding legal ownership of the land and the difficulties under which Roe & Co. had first worked the mine. After mentioning the lucky strike, a quick calculation deduced that as Sir Nicholas was by then (1782) receiving almost £3,000 per annum for his $\frac{1}{8}$th duty ore, the gross annual value of the mine would be somewhere in the region of £24,000. Enquiries must have been made to ascertain that the net profits were approximately £15,000 leaving a simple calculation for expenses as £6,000.

The author was completely baffled by the dearth of information regarding the 'New Co.' and could only report the involvement of a Mr. Dawes. However, he does appear to have gathered snippets of gossip inferring a connection between Sir Nicholas, Dawes, Rev. Hughes and Thomas Williams, which one suspects had been volunteered by employees of Roe & Co., but lacking anything positive chose to compare the workings of the Old Company with those of the New and report what was taking place on site.

The method used by Roe & Co. was to dig pits "said to be 30yds deep" until they reached the extremely hard yellow bed of ore with its high copper content. The shafts were then worked as a coal pit i.e. 6 or 7 ft in one direction and 4 or 5 ft in the other, from which the author deduced that working in this way must be expensive.

The New Company, whilst emulating this method, were still mining close to the surface but had begun blasting the bed or rock with gunpowder. This innovation had created a huge chasm signified by loud explosions every four to five minutes which were clearly heard amongst the rocks in the surrounding area of the approach to the mine.

At this stage of the report the writer allowed himself the comment that had both mines been out of lease when the grant to Dawes was made then he was convinced that a third duty could have been obtained for the whole enterprise and probably even a half. He confirmed that Sir Nicholas had offered Roe & Co. the additional lease at one third duty but had been refused. Various calculations followed as to the future potential of the mines and a conclusion drawn that as Roe & Co. had only three years left in which to extract ore before the lease was renewable, there was nothing in their lease to stop them "plundering with a vengeance" by using the easiest methods to extract the ore with total disregard to the state of the mine.

This disparaging comment might have been more aptly applied to Jonathan Cartwright and his employees, for the professionalism with which Roe & Co. had always carried out their mining was hardly likely to be jeopardised at this time. In any event irresponsible mining methods would ultimately bring about the opposite effect, a probable collapse of shafts spelling danger for the workmen with possible loss of life and creating even greater difficulty in retrieving ore and getting it to the surface. A further view, that Roe & Co. were under no obligation to clear ore from the site as it was brought to the surface, seems rather ridiculous under the circumstances, given the topography of the area and the treatment necessary to make the copper smeltable, or, as appropriate, saleable. Here was someone totally unfamiliar with the working of copper mines and the Anglesey mines in particular, where the processes adopted had been specifically devised to suit local conditions. Roe & Co. would be as anxious as anyone to remove the calcined or precipitated ore from site otherwise weathering might rob it of some of its copper content. It would appear, therefore, that grounds for a future legal dispute were already being sought.

Sir Nicholas's steward, Hugh Price, no doubt anticipating that he would 'come under fire' for any shortcomings which might surface should Sir Nicholas die, was eager to exonerate himself from an apparent lack of vigilance in the acquittal of his duties. He emphatically declared that he had "repeatedly requested" a copy of the lease (i.e.between Sir Nicholas and Charles Roe) but the Baronet had kept all negotiations secret and even received the payments direct from Roe & Co. Hugh Price conjectured that Sir Nicholas was embarrassed by the whole affair having agreed "to inadequate terms". With nothing further to work from but Price's interpolations the writer deduced that the lease to Dawes had "been more cautiously made than that to the Old Company".

The scene which greeted anyone visiting Parys Mountain for the first time must have been awesome, and the writer could not resist including a description of the unedifiying environment:

> ". . . not a blade of any sort can live where the Smoke reaches as is evident from the burning of Ore which destroys and has destroyed every thing of the Vegetable kind within its reach, and such is the stench of it, as well as its tendency to suffocation, that no mortal being can think of living near such works, but those who are employed in them."

There follows a detailed account of the processes taking place on site and the observation that both companies were using the same sorting and calcining methods; however, the writer noted the additional process carried out by the Old Company of "making Sulphur or Brimstone". Roe & Co.'s request for their neighbours to use flues in order to reduce contamination by sulphurous fumes must have been acceded to in part, for the report includes a note that the New Company had arches in their works, some of which housed considerable quantities of yellow dust, but because the patent was held by the Old Company "they don't seem to pay much regard to it".

The precipitation pits also received a full and efficient survey, after which the question of constructing smeltworks on site was analysed then rejected as too expensive an option.

About 800 people were judged to be employed by the New Company at their mine named Mona, compared with 400 by Roe & Co. Taking into consideration that the area of land under lease in respect of the Cerrig y Bleiddia mine was half that of the Mona Mine, then the number of employees was in correct proportion. However, if one also takes into consideration the enormous profits being made by Roe & Co. and the indebtedness of the Mona Mine (according to Williams in 1779) this must stand as testimony to the professional and responsible way in which Roe & Co. were working their smaller area of Parys Mountain.

The writer next proceeded with an inspection of the Port of Amlwch, recording that the New Company had gone to considerable expense in purchasing "Estates adjacent to the Port". Sir Nicholas's quay of 60 yards, which was on a long term lease from the owner, was in great need of repair doubling the cost of loading vessels when compared with that of others. Hugh Price again insisted that he had made representations to Sir Nicholas about the problem but had been ignored.

Meanwhile Sir Nicholas died and was succeeded by his son, Lord Paget as 3rd Baronet, who was subsequently elevated to Earl of Uxbridge on 19th April 1784.

Now in a more commanding position, the compiler of the report was able to state that the Mona Mine Co.'s ores were shipped from Amlwch under the direction of John Price to Michael Hughes at the Stanley Smelting Works (in Lancashire) or to Mr. Richard Jenkinson at the Middle Bank Smelting Works, Swansea. This is not strictly chronological, for although Williams was in the process of adding these two smelting works to his small but rapidly growing empire, the ores were still being smelted at the new Ravenhead Works in Lancashire, where production had begun in October 1780 (Stanley would be purchased from Thomas Patten's Warrington company in 1785 and in operation once more by 1786) and the Upper Bank Works near Swansea (the Middle Bank works were apparently bought in 1787 although they could have been acquired surreptitiously a little earlier). The writer also verified the competent way in which the duty ores from the Parys Mine (Roe & Co.) for the Earl of Uxbridge were accounted for and assayed.

The ores were weighed daily and at each pair of scales a man was on duty to record the figures and take a sample from each barrow. Roe & Co. also had a 'Tallyman' who checked the figures with the agent employed by the Earl of Uxbridge and with the 'Bargain takers' (those in charge of each group of miners). This would ensure that at all stages the figures were correct and the risk of embezzlement kept to a minimum.

At the end of each day's weighings the two Tallymen went together to apportion the samples in a securely locked building. Each had a key to a different lock so that one could not enter without the other. The samples were kept till the end of each quarter when John Price superintended the division of each sample into four. Two were taken by Roe & Co. and the other two by John Price. Each company then sent one of their samples to their respective assayer, retaining one should a check become necessary. Price usually received his analysis from an Edward Steel within the week; this was then compared with that obtained by Roe & Co. and if the two more or less agreed then the account was dealt with and settled.

On the assumption that Thomas Harrison was the author of the report, then his style of presentation was certainly more official and straightforward than that contained in his letters to Lord Paget. The latter reveal passages which are quite melodramatic at times, as in the instance of his letter dated 19th January 1784 when, having worked on the cash accounts, Harrison declared "to my great Mortification, I have already proceeded enough to put me in a cold Sweat". Despite the considerable sum of £14,000 received for copper ore and rents during the months of December and January, he discovered that Lord Paget's "wants" far exceeded the incomings and could find no way of solving the problem. A brief comment towards the end of the letter indicates that Roe & Co. had been in communication at some stage, for he had not heard from 'Mr. Hawkins' since Lord Paget had left Beaudesert.

By the 9th February Thomas Smyth had evidently become involved, having written to say he would take a lease of the Cerrig y Bleiddia mine upon any terms Lord Paget was willing to offer; this Harrison viewed with suspicion. Still preoccupied with sorting out his accounts and anxious to impress upon Lord Paget the amount of time now taken up by the extra bookkeeping, he wrote that his son had "not spent a day in any other Business since the 25th December" and that he personally had also spent three quarters of his time working towards their completion, which was still some way off. The mention of Lord Paget's "dejection" over some other matter becomes plainer in Harrison's follow up-letter of the next week.

Having been paid a visit by Smyth, during which the future of the Cerrig y Bleiddia mine was discussed at length, Harrison wrote reassuringly. Smyth had read out a report of a survey from which the prospects of the mine were very much uncertain, the contents of which had obviously already been conveyed to Lord Paget. Harrison, wishing to dispel the latter's gloom, pointed out that "Mines were uncertain Things" and he was not unduly concerned as the lease had almost two years to run and circumstances could change quite rapidly. He related that he had advised Smyth to make the best possible offer, who at length "proposed giving the Duty of a third", the same as that paid by Dawes. Smyth then held firm making it clear that under the circumstances he could not increase the bid.

* * * * * * *

At this juncture Roe & Co. were perfecting bolts for the Admiralty sheathing so that by April 1784 a letter was sent to Williams advising him that if the new bolts were accepted then the company would be unable to supply him with block copper (obviously this would be needed for Roe & Co.'s own contract). A letter in the same vein was sent to Welch in Birmingham, but his referred to ingots. Here Roe & Co. were acting in a responsible manner and giving these customers a chance to find an alternative supplier. The Regency Period with its concern for etiquette and good manners was still a little way off, but even so gentlemen were expected to act as gentlemen and no one could have imagined the deceit and sheer vindictiveness with which Williams was about to act.

The interesting question is why Williams would be buying block copper from Roe & Co. when, if he was actually short of supplies, he could have bought calcined ore much cheaper and smelted it himself at his modern and extensive Ravenhead works. The only logical explanation appears to be that the copper "brought to perfection" by William Roe in Liverpool was of the finest quality, and this Williams needed, for he too had entered the race, not only to supply the British navy with copper bolts but also Continental dockyards, and in particular those of the former enemy, France.

The whole project had arisen because of difficulties now being faced by the Navy as a result of the reaction between the iron bolts and fastenings securing the wooden hulls and the copper plates. By the end of 1782 the Admiralty and Navy Board were having second thoughts about the initial advantages of copper sheathing, having received reports of the loss of H.M. *Centaur* and other vessels which suggested that disaster had struck due to the detachment of plates and the subsequent foundering of the ships.

The French navy, eager to catch up with the advantages gained by their former enemy, had also suffered the loss of two of their most famous vessels, *Ville de Paris* and *Glorieux* after having them copper-bottomed. It must be noted, however, that this information came from a report presented to Parliament by Thomas Williams. Whatever the French claimed British naval records maintain that at the Battle of the Saintes on 12th April 1782 Admiral Rodney's flagship *Formidable* cut through the French line, withheld fire until the precise moment and struck the *Ville de Paris* so decisively with her broadsides that every gun shot told and only one musket was able to return fire. Nevertheless the outlook was not good unless someone could produce bolts of adequate length and hardness to hold wooden planks in place. The copper sheathing was secured by short copper nails, sufficient in themselves but not when other factors came into play.

* * * * * * *

In an effort to cut costs Williams used Dawes to present a petition for an Act of Parliament, to be effective from 24th June 1782, for reducing the duty on coal imports to Anglesey. This had, of course, been tried before in 1773 by Roe & Co. and again in 1779 by Dawes following the commencement of his copper lease on 14th November 1778. The 1782 proposals, attributed to Dawes but no doubt under Williams's dictate, set down the intention of acquiring "Rowe's bargain if he declines it" and building smeltworks on the island, as it was considered a nuisance to smelt at Swansea, Liverpool and other places. Appreciating that diplomacy was needed when handling Sir Nicholas Bayly, Dawes offered to buy coals from the Baronet if the price was as cheap as elsewhere and also promised that if Sir Nicholas was disadvantaged in anyway by the plans then he would "desist".

The bill, passed by the House of Commons, met instant opposition in the Lords. It was pointed out that Sir Nicholas and Lord Paget had "considerable Collieries or Coal Works in ye Isle of Anglesea which have been worked at a great Expence" and would be reduced in value if the duty was abolished, thus encouraging coal importations. Emphasis was also placed on the fact that the two previous bills had been quashed and if this one succeeded would "be prejudicial to every other Smelter of Ores in ye Kingdom" enabling Dawes & Co. to "undersell other Miners". The bill was rejected and Williams thwarted for the present.

In a letter dated 24th September 1782 Thomas Williams informed Matthew Boulton that he had "a year's stock of ore" on site and must have been desperate for a large contract, for on 1st June 1782 he, together with Dawes, had leased the mines of Maes Cariadog and Dinas in the parish of Llandegai (close by Bangor) from Richard Pennant Esq. The duty payable was $1/8$th ore and this new venture must have represented a heavy potentially financial commitment. Williams had little knowledge of mining, in fact the piecemeal way in which the Mona Mine had been worked for years could not have boded well for any great profit making in the immediate future, hence his remark of 1779 that it was "confoundedly in debt". His exuberance on receiving the two years' accounts for smelting to 31st March 1781, which included profits from the large sales to the East India Company must have been his salvation, but only momentarily. Without sales the company would be doomed; apart from the finances involved in the new mining project, the money invested in the Ravenhead works must have been substantial, for Williams wrote to Hugh Lloyd of Denmark St., London on 23rd October 1784 telling him not to expect a remittance as "The Concern will not yet bear a dividend". Whether or not this was strictly true is difficult to determine, Williams could have been playing for time, however his sly comment "unless you sho'd chose that of double the Sum you paid – to Relinquish your claim" had a surprising effect.

Lloyd, apparently angry at the offer and jibe, tried to turn the tables on Williams by insisting that he was entitled to a share of the combined Bayley and Hughes estate of the Mona Mine and so claimed two 64th shares out of Williams's $2/6$th share. Williams, of course, had offered a one 64th share limited to the Bayly moiety only, so various legal opinions were sought. All agreed that whilst the case was not a clear one yet overall Williams had not increased his holdings and consequently the consensus was that Lloyd was still only entitled to a one 64th of the whole. The new arrangement with Rev. Hughes was simply to cut costs.

Thomas Williams's contempt for his former friend is adequately demonstrated by a final letter of 2nd April 1785 in which 'Dear Hugo' has become 'Mr. Lloyd' who was advised that in the instance of further claims, the grounds on which they were based must be fully supported by receipts etc. and recommends "Mr. Lld to postpone his journey into Wales untill these matters are fixd".

Behind the scenes Williams had turned to the Birmingham market for his survival by engaging a more than competent metallurgist to work on the production of copper bolts, and William Collins was granted a patent on 22nd October 1783. A London coppersmith, William Forbes, had already patented a process in July 1783, but subsequent trials had proved his bolts to be unsuitable. Collins soon teamed up with John Westwood, also of Birmingham, to produce "Patent Copper Ship Bolts" and both insisted that the copper should be as pure as possible.

By now Williams's situation must have worsened considerably. He had no naval contract for copper sheathing and his meteoric success with the East India sales was at an end. However, his display of sheer confidence, ebullience and court room patter, coupled with his ability to know exactly whom to target in order to carry through his schemes, won the day. Unknown to Matthew Boulton, whose loyalty was very much with the Cornish mines, the manager of his "plated manufactory" was persuaded to buy from the Parys Mine Company. On discovering that between "£5 and 6,000 worth of copper" had been purchased during 1784, Boulton admonished the person concerned, although having to admit that the quality of copper "is the finest I have ever used". He learnt from his manager, who had also considered it of the best quality, that he had purchased it more cheaply than was possible from anywhere else. Even so, from Williams's point of view, this was only a small fraction of what would be needed to keep the company afloat. But he was a survivor and so resorted to ruthless selling methods by engaging as his combatant Pascoe Grenfell, a merchant already operating in Charlotte Row near Mansion-house Street, London in 1783; Grenfell now needed the ammunition with which to do battle.

Despite the fact that Williams's smelters were producing fine copper and that Williams had evidently enrolled the assistance of Robert Shore, the former Duke's agent from Ecton Mine, he would have wanted to be absolutely certain of success. As it took years of hard work and experience to produce copper of the finest quality, it does not seem too far-fetched to suggest that Williams was using the Roe & Co. copper blocks (which only needed refining) in the production of those bolts to be used in the naval trials. If he was successful in gaining the contract then he could resort to using his own copper again and who would know?

An important part of the strategy was to court the French and this is where Grenfell played his part well. He organised teams to visit the Continent targeting the French dockyards where he demonstrated the superiority of British bolts, nails and even rudder fittings.

On 10th February 1784 a group of French munition experts visited England and, whether by coincidence or not, a considerable proportion of their report was taken up by their visits to the Ravenhead smeltworks and a manufactory near Holywell in which Williams was also a partner.

Thomas Patten & Co. had been established in the Greenfield Valley near Holywell since 1743, but at the same time as Williams was developing the Ravenhead Works on the doorstep of the Warrington company's Stanley Works, he was also constructing a large manufactory for producing brass wire and copper nails close by the Warrington company's Greenfield battery mill. The wire mill accompanied a pond or reservoir fed by the Holywell stream and just below this, where another pond was situated, were located the copper rolling mills visited by the French team.

There is little doubt that Williams was well prepared for the visit and put on the best show possible, evidently feigning full production despite his depleting contracts. His exaggerations knew no bounds, unless one can blame errors in translation, for the Frenchmen were informed that the company was supplying the bolts and nails "used in all dockyards" and selling sheathing to "all the naval powers in Europe". The team was also well-informed regarding the cost of materials and the price of copper etc. from which they concluded that before taking into account employees' wages or any interest paid, the business must be worth £29,000 a year.

As potential customers, generalities should have been sufficient, but Williams was obviously anxious to present a very successful business.

If anything like these considerable profits was being made at this time, why was it that within a few months Williams, anxious to obtain a small engine for the Ravenhead stamp mill from no less a person than Matthew Boulton, was disputing the rent for such an item? Boulton, aware of the poor quality of the local Lancashire coals, calculated a feasible rental of £30 per annum, but was willing to reduce it to £20 in order to encourage further business; Williams, still not satisfied, argued that it would probably be used for only half the time and therefore offered £10 a year or £100 to purchase.

The outcome was one of fraud and deceit. Williams approached the ironmaster John Wilkinson, who illegally provided the engine based on the Boulton and Watt patent. This was not the only occasion on which Wilkinson would violate the conditions of the patent and, where he was caught out, Boulton and Watt charged him premiums for the use of their invention.

If, as the Williams's contingent were claiming, the bolts produced from the Collins and Westwood patents had been accepted by the Navy Board for all the dockyards, it seems strange that Abraham Mills should be sent to attend the trial of the Roe & Co. bolts in April 1784, two months after the visit of the French munitions team. By June Edward Hawkins accompanied the second delivery of copper bolts to enable him to tender for a copper nails contract. At the same time a letter was sent to Williams querying the prices his company paid for manufacturing copper bolts; presumably this referred to the premiums paid for the use of the various patents. Roe & Co. had evidently relied on the skill of their employees Harvey and Malpas to produce theirs and the trial appears to have been a success, for the two were rewarded with "30/-" in July "for making Copper Bolts". On 25th November a request for payment from the Navy Board for copper bolts "sent on Trial to Deptford yard" was ordered. (Unfortunately the Navy Board Minutes are not specific on the bolt issue. A reference in December 1786 relates to a pattern for copper screws being sent to Deptford and Woolwich Officers with instructions to make two moulds. One was to be returned with the pattern for forwarding to the contractor (name not given) and the other mould was to be kept in the dockyards' store.)

Early in 1785 the Gnoll Copper Company, being part of the cartel, had become concerned about price cutting by the Parys Mine Company and wrote to advise Roe & Co. of the situation. It is interesting to note that someone was sent to see "Mr. Hughes", not Williams, who denied that a Roe & Co. customer had been offered cut-price copper. At the Macclesfield company meeting in Warrington on 19th March it was decided to send a reassuring letter to the Gnoll Company based on information available and their own local knowledge. By this date the Parys Mine Company had been given a Government contract encouraging Roe & Co. to believe that as a consequence Williams had no quantity of manufactured copper to sell, supported by the fact that he had been forced to buy copper from others to fulfill the contract. In retrospect, if this was the case then Williams had miscalculated by making the cheap sales to the Boulton manufactory in his panic to sell, thereby depleting his own stock of copper and forcing him to pay higher prices for its replacement. On the other hand it could have been his excuse for purchasing William Roe's copper blocks from Toxteth, needed for the manufacture of bolts to satisfy the naval trials. Roe & Co., assuredly convinced of their reasoning, were evidently prompted into making the enquiry regarding the cost to Williams of making the bolts, for they would have calculated that their price to the Navy Board was a fair one, and with expenses less than those incurred by Williams their tender should have won them the contract; they deduced, therefore, that Williams's transaction must be unprofitable. They also pointed out to the Gnoll Company that without help from other companies Williams could not possibly complete his commitment.

* * * * * * *

Until this period the copper industry as a whole had steadily increased as the 18th century progressed. From figures now available, whether from mining, smelting or producing brass and copper goods, the profits had been fairly well distributed. It had not been without its ups and downs, nor had individual concerns, but in general the system worked well. The so-called cartel of Associated Smelters has been accused by some modern historians of keeping prices artificially high, when in reality it was endeavouring to maintain fair prices so everyone had a chance to survive; but all that was about to change.

Unfortunately Williams appears to have had a peculiar streak in his nature; he was perfectly capable of living well off his legal fees, after all he had, in the past, procured many clients in North Wales, yet, whilst he liked to think it was his patriotic fervour which dictated his ambitions making the survival of his copper concern paramount, it becomes increasingly obvious that personal greed was his motivation. Should anyone dare to cross his bows he regarded it as a personal affront and laid schemes to humiliate and even ruin those whom he came to regard as competitors. Matthew Boulton, when writing to Watt on 26th July 1785 would comment "He is not a man to be trifled with. . ."

By 1787 an associate writing to Boulton would reveal that Williams was selling copper privately under the market price, remarking "It is hard to know how to manage a man of his revengeful & artful disposition."

To have any chance of success Williams had to gain more power and control, which necessitated the acquisition of the Cerrig y Bleiddia mining lease, and to this end he concentrated all his efforts during the latter half of 1784.

Thomas Harrison was having problems with the copper ore accounts which needed "settling and adjusting", claiming it was due to some irregularity concerning matters which had been discussed in advance with Williams and therefore should not have occurred. Williams, for his part, preferred not to correspond on the subject but invited Harrison to London for discussions. On 21st August 1784 Harrison reported to Lord Paget (now Earl of Uxbridge) that on the day of his arrival in the capital he and Williams had worked on the calculations till midnight and through the whole of the next day, until the matter was settled. The letter continues by urging the Earl to make a decision on whether or not he intends to work the Cerrig y Bleddia mine for himself or lease it to a tenant on the expiration of the Roe & Co. lease. From this one suspects that Williams had broached the subject and begun preparing the ground for his approach to the problem of acquiring the lease by feeding Harrison some convincing ideas.

Two weeks later the Earl advised Harrison that he intended working the mine for himself. Harrison again put pen to paper on 5th September, but from his exhuberant response, promising to "make it productive in the fullest manner " by "great Care & great Attention" and the "best portion of Skill & Judgement" with the "greatest Activity & Exertion we are capable of." There is more than a slight suggestion of apprehension at the prospect. The decision foretold far greater responsibility for Harrison with no extra reward, and therefore left him ripe for alternative suggestions.

Within the week the Earl of Uxbridge had chided Harrison for not visiting Anglesey, which in turn produced a befuddled reply in relation to Harrison's intentions, but the man was obviously playing for time due to the considerably increased burden of his duties. Williams had exerted pressure, anxious to know whether or not he was to have "a Finger in the Pye", but was informed that "Patience is a cardinel Virtue". Harrison intended to visit Anglesey at the end of the month when he would let it be known that the Earl intended working the mine for himself and therefore any further enquiries would be unnecessary. But Williams refused to accept the situation and became relentless in his efforts to secure the lease. He took both Thomas Harrison and the Earl of Uxbridge on a grand tour of his business establishment, visiting Ravenhead, Greenfield and finally Anglesey. His 'rehearsal' with the French team no doubt stood him in good stead, for by November he was endeavouring to negotiate terms.

As already related, the following month saw the death of Brian Hodgson Snr. and with none of the original partners at the helm, the Macclesfield Copper Company was left in the hands of the second generation.

* * * * * * *

There seems little doubt that William Roe's illness during that early summer had put pressure on the other partners and somewhat disrupted the flow of company business, particularly with regard to mining in North Wales, but even so it is doubtful whether Roe & Co. were really enthusiastic about renewing their Parys Mountain lease. By then the rich vein of copper would have been extensively worked out leaving the poorer ores and precipitation pits for the future, and the lease did restrict their mining to an area of the mountain which in proportion to the whole was very small. Also the proposed duty of one third was extremely high, therefore if a half had to be offered in order to compete with Williams, Dawes & Co. the risk was not worth taking.

William Roe had not been idle and already alternative sources were being sought. Under the direction of the Penrhyn Estate steward and 'Mr. Barker' of Barkers & Wilkinson, Derbyshire explorations had been undertaken once more in the Conwy Valley and some 'sulphur ore' recovered. Between May and September 1783 the ore was purchased by William

Roe for the Liverpool smeltworks and William Bridge, formerly of Conway Furness but now of Amlwch. Although the copper content seemed high, later analysis disclosed arsenic mixed in with the ore which would have created difficulties in smelting and, whether by choice or not, the venture appears to have ceased shortly afterwards. At the A.G.M. of August 1785 it was proposed to purchase William Bridge's share in the Llandudno Mine to add to the three shares already held; this is the first intimation of Roe & Co.'s involvement with this mine.

The Great Orme's Head at Llandudno is a promontory of carboniferous limestone making it a unique location for copper mines and, as at Ecton Hill in Staffordshire, these were found to be predominantly of copper (chalcopyrite to a depth of 600 ft with some malachite and a little azurite) with only minor lodes of lead. Apart from prehistoric and Roman mining the revival had begun in earnest, as elsewhere, in the late 17th century with the formation of the Welsh Copper Company (1694). The land on the rocky mountainous headland was mainly divided between the Bishop of Bangor and the Mostyn family. The Bishop, as Lord of the Manor of Gogarth, was entitled to rights on the open common, but the Mostyns, over a long period, had enclosed their parcels of adjoining land in a somewhat piecemeal fashion; however, each respective landlord had augmented his income by granting mining leases.

In February 1783 Sir Roger Mostyn had granted just such a lease to John Lloyd a lawyer of Wigfair, Denbighshire in trust for several others including Rev. John Ellis (of the Llanberis Mining Company) and William Bridge. The latter was already complaining that unless a "proper agent" was employed then "we [Messrs Lloyd, Bridge and Ellis] shall forthwith apply to the Court of Chancery for leave to make such an appointment."

At this time another company was apparently working an adjoining mine on the Bishop of Bangor's land and Bridge accused Lloyd of conspiring with Sir Roger Mostyn in allowing this group of miners the use of a level already worked through the Mostyn lands, which gave the group an advantage. The situation was reminiscent of 1747 when the great dispute arose concerning the lead mining soughs along Eyam Edge in Derbyshire and the outcome, as then, appears to have been the same i.e. combination. A meeting for all those who intended to become partners with Sir Roger Mostyn to work the venture was proposed for the 10th March when £800 in shares would be advanced.

One can only assume that Roe & Co. were either part of the original group working the Bishop of Bangor's mine or more than likely bought three shares on the 10th March, at which time it would have been appropriate for the Llandudno Mine Company to come into being. By purchasing Bridge's share the four gave Roe & Co. a quarter holding in the new concern.

On 5th April 1785 Lord Penrhyn together with William Roe and Thomas Smyth leased the minerals under Ty'n yr-hwylfa farm, Llandudno for a period of 21 years from Lord Bulkeley (son-in-law of Sir George Warren of Poynton near Macclesfield). A duty ore of $1/8$th was payable and the usual stipulations made regarding the ore being rendered merchantable, damage limitations, buildings to be kept in good repair etc. Weighing would take place every six months, notified in advance to Lord Bulkeley so that his Steward or agents could attend, and during the first three years £300 had to be expended and a report made. At any one time six workmen were to be engaged on site with at least one pit operational, and if the site was vacated for a period of more than two months then the lease was void. The prospects must have looked good, for Roe & Co. were now concentrating their efforts in the area as an apparent insurance against the loss of the Cerrig y Bleiddia mine.

* * * * * * *

It was also becoming imperative to find further calamine supplies as the demand for brass was dramatically increasing, reflected in an order of April 1785 to add four fires to the four in "Peacock's (brass) House" on Macclesfield Common and "that they be large enough to contain 9 pots each."

Throughout 1784, although calamine was still being bought in the Mendips and Flintshire, efforts had been made to purchase the Duke of Bolton's calamine works in Yorkshire through an agent called Maud. However, these efforts do not appear to have been successful, for in April 1785 it was suggested that Robert and Brian Hodgson should approach Thomas Southern of Derbyshire (an associate of the Barker family and also a partner in the Paris Mountain Co.) with a view to purchasing the whole or part of his share in the Yorkshire calamine works which were leased to him and others by the Duke of Bolton. The Hodgsons were also asked to attend a sale of land at Bonsall, owned by a Mr. Simpson, and "endeavour to purchase such part as they may judge eligible for a further supply of Derbyshire Calamine. . ."

The Bonsall bid seems to have been successful but it is doubtful if the Yorkshire one was concluded. Circumstantial evidence suggests that Thomas Southern was of Wensley near Wirksworth in Derbyshire and father of John who, at the age of 24 years in 1782, had been introduced by Matthew Boulton to James Watt as a potential employee. The dour Scot expressed reservations, but the young engineer was employed and would prove himself such an asset that, for the last five years of his life (1810-1815), he would be a partner in their concern. Because of this association and other possible factors such as Roe & Co.'s impending termination of their Parys Mountain operations and Boulton's increasing involvement with Willliams, perhaps Southern was not so easily persuaded to give up his calamine interests to the Macclesfield company. Instead, what appears to be an alternative, is recorded; as from 18th October 1785 it was agreed with an agent called Carter that Roe & Co. would employ 20 men in mining lead and calamine on Crickheath Hill and Moylydd at Llanymynech near Oswestry, Shropshire. The Roe & Co. agent was to be Joseph Simpson's son from Bonsall with a salary of £40 per annum from the date he took up residence there, which suggests that this was perhaps part of the deal in acquiring the extra land at Bonsall.

Almost one month earlier, on the 22nd September, William Roe and Edward Hawkins had signed a lease with Thomas Pennant Esq. for a piece of land on the banks of the Nant-hil-brwc, (a small stream in the Greenfield Valley) which was held in trust by Edward Hawkins on behalf of the company until the intended development plans could be finalised. Roe & Co. proposed building a large calamine house and calciners, not only for their own benefit but for a combination of brass producers which included Pengree's and the Cheadle and Bristol companies. An annual rental of 8% of the value of the buildings was proposed which all the concerns would share, but first agreement had to be reached.

* * * * * * *

The company of Thomas Patten Jnr. had, of course, been operating in the valley since 1743. By the early 1750s the site contained a copper mill making 'Guinea rods' for the African market and copper rolling mills. A later addition was the brass wire mill. In 1767 a separate partnership was formed to control both the Greenfield site and the brass ingot house at Cheadle in Staffordshire under the name of the Warrington Copper & Brass Co. At this time the copper smelting part of the business was actually moved from Warrington to Cheadle and the former works leased out. When Sir Nicholas Bayly decided to use the Warrington company for smelting his Parys Mountain ores from the Mona Mine and the duty ores from Roe & Co., Patten, in order to accommodate the arrangement, for convenience built the Stanley copper smelter in the township of Ashton-in-Makerfield near St. Helens in 1771.

Thomas Patten Jnr. died in 1772 leaving the next generation to build on his success. Perhaps if Charles Roe, Brian Hodgson Snr. or Thomas Patten Jnr. had still been alive they, with their knowledge of business practice and people, would have seen through Williams's scheming and not allowed his disruptive plans to take their course. Instead the Warrington company, realising that Williams and his partners would be smelting all Anglesey ores, allowed him the purchase of the Stanley and Greenfield works and consolidated their very successful business at Cheadle. Two important factors dictated the decision viz; the Duke of Devonshire's compliance in allowing purchases of the rich Ecton ores and the Birmingham market's demands for more and more brass. Thus Roe & Co.'s confidence in reaching an agreement for supplying calamine to Cheadle was justified; relations between the two companies had always been propitious and the new arrangement was to last for quite some time.

George Pengree & Co. smelters and brass producers of Snow Hill, London, had been supplying the East India Company amongst others for many years. In 1769 they had taken a site at the Middle Bank Works (or Plas Canol) near Swansea in South Wales and in that year began purchasing Cornish copper ore which averaged at least 2,000 tons each year. They also appear to have been treating calamine there, possibly through a subsidiary, but all operations ceased in 1785 and the works would be under the control of Thomas Williams by 1787; the result was that no further transactions appear to have taken place between Pengree's and Roe & Co.

In December 1785 the Bristol Wire Company partners were approached by Roe & Co. for an agreement to pay part of the expenses incurred in the building of the River Bank calamine house, followed one month later by the proposed rent. The rental was to be shared in proportion to the quantity of calamine (either calcined or raw) shipped annually to each company. But the Bristol Wire Company's response was inevitably hesitant because they too, like George Pengree & Co. were under pressure due to their heavy reliance on Cornish ore. From the late 1760s the company had bought an average 4,000 tons of Cornish copper ore each year, with an incredible 7,101 tons in 1779 out of a total 30,337 tons. It has been estimated that by 1780 Birmingham manufacturers were consuming an average of at least 1,000 tons of brass per annum and were therefore an important market for Bristol. In that year the syndicate of brass producers had been forced to raise prices by £12 to £84 per ton and immediately the protests began.

* * * * * * *

It was inevitable that the Cornish mines, worked so successfully for centuries, would eventually experience difficulties. As the mines went deeper, flooding got worse and by the mid-18th century the old Newcomen steam engine, with its limited capacity, was unable to cope with the situation. The challenge was taken up by several Cornish engineers; another engineer, Smeaton, by 1775 was working on a modification of the Newcomen engine which provided additional pressure and allowed pumping from a depth of 60 fathoms at the Chacewater mine. His success doubled the efficiency of the original machine but exacerbated the coal problem. The bigger the steam engine, the greater its appetite for coal, yet there were no coal mines in Cornwall and coal was expensive to bring any distance, so that at this time more than half the pumping engines in the county (i.e. at least twenty) were in any event out of action. It was also soon realised that the ultimate pumping capacity of the improved engine was 80 fathoms; there was no alternative but to turn to James Watt in Birmingham for help, as his new engine, with its separate condenser, had considerable potential.

Ironically Matthew Boulton was automatically involved, being a member of the partnership, but he was also involved as a purchaser of silver, copper and brass for his manufactory – two conflicting interests so far as finances were concerned.

In 1777 the first Boulton and Watt engine was working in Cornwall and within six years the duo had supplied half the county's requirement. Not only did the new engines have greater power but fuel consumption was actually reduced. Watt obtained an extension of his patent for a further 25 years during which time the mining companies could either lease an engine for an annual fee based on a third of the fuel saved (which inevitably led to a fixed rate), or could purchase outright for payment of 10 years rental. The fees were soon to become a source of grievance to the Cornishmen who regarded the firm as outsiders. Those working Poldice mine, for example, had agreed to a payment of £1,500 per annum for two engines. Soon Boulton and Watt found themselves accepting mining shares in lieu of payment. At least Boulton accepted readily but there were to be great arguments with Watt.

The situation reached crisis point in 1780. Until that date total Cornish ore production (almost 28,000 tons in 1771 with an estimated average copper content of 12% i.e. 3347 tons sold for £189,609; just over £56 per ton) had remained on a fairly even basis for the last decade. Half the period averaged £55 per ton and the other half £45.

In 1779 total production reached a virtual all time high of 31,000 tons (price £46 6s. per ton) and although the 1780 production figure was back to that of 1778 (around 24,500 tons) yet the price had soared to its highest level of £58 3s. per ton. Actually this was only £2 more per ton than in the early 1770s but the rapid and excessive outcry was presumably based on the assumption that if resistance was not immediate then prices would continue to rise. In particular pressure was exerted by the Birmingham manufacturers on the brass producers in the hope of restraining prices. This was a formidable task taking into account the mounting expenses in the Cornish mines, although surprisingly production totalled almost 29,000 tons in 1781, at a price of £51 16s. per ton, despite Thomas Williams's monopoly of the East India sales. Even 1782 produced little less in total tonnage although the price had dropped to £45 3s. per ton; yet the fact that Williams had sold ore on such a large scale in 1781 and undercut the market, sent shock waves through the industry which reverberated in Cornwall.

The Cornishmen's resentment was acute; they contemplated a petition for repealing the extension to the Watt patent, but nothing transpired. Boulton and Watt, with their increased business commitments in the county, had seriously considered moving to Cornwall but in this particular instance the Cornishmens' rancour won the day and the pair remained in the Midlands.

By 1785 a dissatisfied group had formed a syndicate to establish the Cornish Metal Company with the idea of stabilising Cornish copper prices by smelting their own ores and finally abolishing the system of ticketing. Chief amongst them was Boulton who unfortunately was incapable of managing his own business affairs let alone those of a company with subscriptions targeted at £500,000. (He had originally resisted the idea of Cornwall expanding its smelting facilities because he was associated with the Fenton Copper Company). The other 'heavyweights' included the ironmaster John Wilkinson; potter, Josiah Wedgwood and a powerful Quaker group led by the Fox family of Cornwall. Amongst the rest were James Watt and John Dawes.

The Cornish copper mining interests were by this time in the hands of John Vivian, who appears to have been a man of great integrity and fairness, but already Williams had sown the seeds of discontent whilst blatantly offering what appeared to be a helping hand. His persuasive tongue initially did much to convince the Cornish contingent that the Associated Smelters (which of course included Roe & Co., the Cheadle, Bristol and Gnoll companies) "had done their best to create emnity between Cornwall and Anglesey". Williams boasted of his sales to foreign markets and produced evidence of a successful cut-price strategy, then he and Wilkinson succeeded in executing one of the greatest confidence tricks the industry had ever been subjected to. Williams feigned agreement with the idea of considerably expanding the Cornish smelting facilities in order to be self-sufficient but then, in April 1785, came up with the idea of a corporate venture whereby three smeltworks, in close proximity to Swansea and under the control of one agent, would work for the combined mining industry of Cornwall and Anglesey.

Months of meetings, dealings and strategies ensued and inevitably, slowly but surely, Williams gained the upper hand. At this juncture Lord Paget was finally persuaded to allow Thomas Williams a quarter share of the Cerrig y Bleiddia mine, but as always the legalities would take some time to complete. About the same period a pamphlet was published on the state of the copper works in Cornwall and Anglesey. The anonymous author let it be known that whereas Cornwall (and Devon) had received substantial benefit from the importation of coals duty free for smelting ores since the year 1710, it was intended to obtain the same benefit for Angelsey.

Reference was made to the two previous failed attempts due to opposition in the Lords, but objections previously made by Lord Paget "have since been removed". A petition in respect of a bill had been submitted to the House of Commons on the 3rd February last but opposition in the Committee made it necessary for "the attendance and support of every candid Friend . . .". There seems little doubt of the authorship of the circular and of the fear it must have engendered in the hearts of Cornish miners at the thought of still cheaper copper flooding the market from Anglesey. If any had previously doubted the wisdom of a combined scheme this portent must have been the final inducement for them to join in the proposed arrangements.

Confidence in the scheme was of utmost priority so Wilkinson gambled, without doubt at Williams's behest, by pledging £25,000 as his subscription. The response was immediate encouraging many to buy into the scheme and Boulton, initially in control, placed his Cornish agent, Thomas Wilson, in his stead. The subscription list closed on 1st September 1785 but the treaty was not due to be consolidated until May 1786. Williams and Dawes reneged their commitments and Wilkinson, who was to ensure total advantage to Williams during all subsequent negotiations, would later demand half his subscription from the Welshman. The whole scheme was to operate for seven years but apparently Williams was soon up to his old tricks again, surreptitiously selling cheaper copper, in part evidenced by Roe & Co.'s approach to Hughes regarding the offer made to one of their customers; meanwhile he was about to gain his prize in respect of Parys Mountain.

* * * * * * *

On the same day as the subscription list was closed Thomas Harrison found himself writing a hasty letter in reply to one received from Lord Paget, who had enclosed correspondence from Roe & Co. Harrison deduced it was "the Composition of Mr. Smyth" and that the company may possibly have been begging a favoured response from the Earl which could be used to their advantage should difficulties arise regarding their former conduct. He suggested that Lord Paget should write a letter to them stating that he acknowledged the letter which had been forwarded to his agent for attention, or words to that effect. Harrison declared that he would see Williams first before answering the letter 'more fully' but then launched into one of his conjectural tirades which seemed to make no sense whatsoever, and concluded with an apparent contradiction of his original views on the subject. He defended Williams, who had evidently been dealing with Roe & Co., and wrote "He has not said that they would be permitted to carry away all the Ore they should raise, but if he had exprefsly said so, there could not have been any Harm in it, Because it would only have been telling them That they had permission to do what they know, Your Lordship has not the power to prevent . . ". He continued by suggesting that he felt his presence at the mine "at the Time of the Expiration of their Term" was not a necessity as John Price would be competent to set the men to work etc. a sentiment which he was convinced Williams agreed with. Valuation of the tools and engines would be decided by referees and could be settled with Roe & Co. at some point en route via Liverpool. However, in concluding Harrison had no alternative but to state that should his presence be considered necessary "I will most afsuredly be there."

Evidently Thomas Harrison's presence was necessary, for he was assuredly there and wrote to Lord Paget from Amlwch on 11th October 1785 confirming that possession of the Cerrig y Bleiddia mine had taken place the previous day. Agreement had been reached for the purchase of Roe & Co.'s engines, tools, equipment and iron etc. for which they had been paid £2,013 6s. and had gone. But this was not to be the end of the matter, as indicated by Harrison, "with respect to non-performance of covenants nothing is or will be settled but by a suit and a Jury". At this point Williams appears to have kept quiet, presumably because he had no legal grounds on which to interfere, a situation which would shortly be reversed.

By Christmas, Harrison was planning to visit Anglesey for the New Year's Day festivities, but Williams assured him that it was not at all necessary for him to be there. Williams had, in fact, planned a 'snug Party' in his parlour on the Sunday and arranged for 150 or 200 neighbours to dine in the Hall "take a Drink and all go home in goodtime that night." His advice to Harrison was that it "would not look well" if he appeared and suggested that he should defer the journey; for what reason is not at all clear but sufficient to conclude that evidently some plot was afoot. Harrison then decided to meet Williams at Ravenhead to settle the business of having a ship (i.e. a packet-boat) built for the works. In conclusion he assured Lord Paget that Williams had reported all was well on Parys Mountain and should money be needed then it would not be their fault for he had already advanced £6,000 as Lord Paget's share.

On 1st March 1786 a deed was finally drawn up and signed by which Lord Paget leased a quarter share of the Cerrig y Bleiddia mine (which comprised all minerals recovered) to Williams for a nominal fee of £16 per annum. The Earl retained for himself the three quarter shares, but it would not be long before Harrison would appreciate the magnitude of the arrangement as more and more money was demanded on the pretext of investment and repairing the supposed damage done by Roe & Co.

The convolutions of the Cornish scheme were now evolving, which would eventually spell disaster for the community and no one seemed aware of the fact that Thomas Williams was plotting to acquire his own private enterprise. Within three years he would personally purchase a copper works at Marlow on the Thames from George Pengree & Co. and a second works close by at Wraysbury from the Mackworth family. These would go some way towards satisfying his lust for power and prestige, as shortly afterwards he would be elected M.P. for Marlow.

Despite Roe & Co.'s logical deduction that unless others supplied Williams he would not be able to fulfill his contracts, some of those others had obviously panicked and played into his hands. Certainly Boulton, after a series of meetings with Williams in London, came away full of admiration for the man and dispelled all Watt's gloom and despondency, so much so that Watt had let it be known if companies did not join in the treaty then they stood little chance of purchasing Cornish ore. Those dependent on that ore, yet having doubts about Williams's trustworthiness, (for he was a comparative newcomer in the business) must have felt they had little choice and five of them, including the Gnoll Company, had acceded. The outcome was that Williams had not only triumphed in strengthening his control in Anglesey but had succeeded in his efforts to split the Associated Smelters. The Mines Royal was excluded and in June 1786 offered a lease to Roe & Co. for a mine on the Isle of Man, however the Macclesfield partnership declined the offer.

The Duke of Devonshire together with the Cheadle and Macclesfield concerns was somewhat on the periphery of the grand alliance. All three were very much self-sufficient, mining virtually all their own ores and their prices, therefore, would normally be competitive and fair. However both Roe & Co. and Cheadle had remained loyal to the cartel for the sake of stability, particularly with regard to the companies of South Wales and Bristol who would otherwise be disadvantaged because of their greater dependency on Cornish ores. It could be argued that the Cheadle and Macclesfield companies were therefore gaining a larger profit, but on the other hand they could easily have cut prices and gained a greater share of the market. They chose to help the industry as a whole and work in unison with the rest. Now under Williams's influence it was rapidly deteriorating into a 'free for all' and as over-production would soon become a problem, Cornwall was bound to lose out.

* * * * * * *

At this time Roe & Co. had been experiencing problems close to home. There had been some form of dispute at the Bosley brass works in the winter of 1784 resulting in the dismissal of the son of an experienced worker and fines for eight others (including the young man's father) for leaving the site.

The next quandary was at Havannah in the following spring of 1785 when employees were unable to complete orders due to an insufficient water supply. A directive was issued on the March to erect a fire engine at the works immediately. This brought them into contact with Boulton and Watt, to whom a letter was sent on 20th April stressing the urgent need for a fire engine which would recycle all the waste water "running with moderate velocity" through a space of 9 square feet. However, more specific information was required, so that on the 11th May a letter detailing the problems was sent to the Birmingham partnership, together with comprehensive measurements of the water system and small diagrams in the margin of the first page. The idea was to recyle the waste water which had passed over the 10 ft high wear and through a shuttle (i.e. a flood-gate allowing regulation of the water flow) providing an opening of little more than 18 ins but which was capable of supplying sufficient water power to work the wheels. It was estimated, therefore, that the waste water would need to be pumped to a height of 15 ft to complete the cycle. The letter concluded with a request for an estimate of the cost and size of an appropriate engine.

On 16th August 1785 Watt, writing a very interesting letter from Birmingham to Boulton at the Chacewater mine in Truro, Cornwall, included the following details:

"I was at Mefsrs Roe & Cos. Brafs works, their causway of water is amazing they have 5 wheels, the one belonging to the wire mill requires constant water & may be replaced by a 20 horse rotative Engine. Mr. Hawkins, one of the partners, was exceedingly kind. After we had seen the mills he took me to dine at Congleton at Mr. Hodsons his Brother-in-law, who is also a partner, and is just returned from Scotland, where the Company have taken a lease of the Lead & Copper mines of I[s]lay he says the latter are very promising & I have heard so formerly. After dinner Mr. Hawkins went to church and I was left alone with Mr. Hodson he said that they had 12 years stocks of Ores on hand & besides the fair prospects of the I[s]lay mine had other resources which were not publickly known, that they would be willing to enter into a treaty of amity with the Cornish M. Compy and that they would be proved always to act honourably, they seem to feel the disgrace of being left out of which however they acquit you but seem to give Wms the credit, though they did not say so. For my part I think it would be right to make some bargain with them as to prices, especially as they seem to give up the idea of buying ores. I have no high opinion of some of the companies you have got & think it would be right to keep on neighbourly terms with those who can subsist without you. I promised to write to you and after sounding your colleagues if you find anything can be done I think you should write to them. It is certainly the interest of the C. compy to avoid competition."

(A somewhat ominous note, apparently a postscript, is written in the left hand margin of the first page by Watt: "It is thought there will be a war soon, French money has been bestowed plentifully in Ireland.")

This appears to be one of the rare occasions on which Boulton concurred with Watt's request, for a letter was sent to Vivian from the Macclesfield company meeting in Liverpool on the 18th October accepting "the reserved $\frac{1}{8}$ of the Ore of Cornwall" and agreeing to buy "on same terms as Bristol B.W.Co." This resulted in the cancellation of Roe & Co.'s agreement with Thomas Williams to pay part of his Cornish agent's salary, as purchase by ticketing was no longer necessary; the agent John Martyn was advised of the decision within three months of the Vivian agreement.

October was proving to be a busy month. John Hurd, a Birmingham associate of Boulton and Watt, had been working on an idea to resolve the anomalies of the city's brass trade. Two meetings had been held by the Birmingham Metal Company, the first to explain "the great revolution that has taken place in the Copper Trade" and the second (which included a vote of thanks to Boulton for his work regarding "the interest of the town") to discuss regulations for the brass trade. During the latter Hurd presented his proposals, which were favourably received and subsequently submitted by him to Boulton in Truro for approval.

The plan was to provide a general warehouse for Birmingham and district which would be supplied by the various brass manufacturers according to certain quotas. Obviously the Birmingham Metal Company would be allowed the largest quota of 200 tons of brass out of 1,000 and the remainder were set out as follows:

"The Bristol B.W. Co.	150 tons	
Freeman & Co.	100	"
Macclesfield Co.	100	"
Smethwick Co.	100	"
Lockwood Morris & Co.	50	"
Cheadle Co.	50	"
Pengree & Co.	50	"
Emerson & Co.	50	"

The proof, that Thomas Williams at this time was not producing brass, is found in the final item – " and in case they should go into the Trade I would add The Paris Mine Co. 150 tons." This list confirms that Roe & Co. were considered joint third in the top brass suppliers to Birmingham at that time.

John Hurd's letter to Boulton, dated the 22nd October, also included information relating to Roe & Co. On a visit to London he had been 'solicited' by both the Macclesfield and Cheadle concerns to sign an agreement for the purchase price of brass. He could not agree their terms because although the subject appeared to be 'Common Brass' yet it left room for the price of 'Yellow brass' to fluctuate from which he concluded that they would try to undersell each other as formerly. They asked Hurd to make a proposal, from which he suggested a difference between 'Common' and 'Yellow or Ashmetal' of 10s. 0d. i.e. 75s. 0d. and 65s. 0d. respectively. The Cheadle Company represented by Lee agreed; Edward Hawkins "I fancy would have agreed to it but the B.W.Co. (Bristol Wire Company represented by Harford) . . . objected to it."

Hurd later spoke to Hawkins and told him of the plan regarding the Birmingham warehouse hoping he would communicate the details to Harford. This he did, but whilst Harford thought well of the scheme he considered the timing wrong because of "the revolution in the Copper Trade". Hawkins returned to Birmingham a week later and supported what Harford had said considering that "the consumers of Brafs wou'd be too much alarm'd." But Hurd was not to be put off and wrote enthusiastically to Boulton that the Birmingham Metal Company should forge ahead, as it represented a considerable number of consumers. The scheme, however, never materialised.

* * * * * * *

By March 1786 Roe & Co. had decided not to undertake "any expensive plan of improvement" at Havannah because of the state of the copper trade and instead asked a local engineer to judge which repairs were necessary. Now concerned to enhance their stocks of copper ore with an eye to brass production, a letter was sent 'demanding' their fourth share of ores unsold at Llandudno and also that of any future ores raised there. Legal opinion had already been taken regarding the Llandudno lease, for one of the partners considered that the lease allowed for the sale of the ores in general; the Macclesfield partners were certain they had a right to claim their proportion as ore raised, and were evidently proved correct.

Two further areas in North Wales warranted their attention at this period, but very little information remains. One speculation was in the Conwy Valley under a farm and lands called Bodiddabach in the parish of Gyffin comprising lead and copper mines previously leased to an Owen Owens, who appears to have had a connection with the mining at Llandudno. The lease was signed by William Roe and Thomas Smyth with Sir Roger Mostyn on 29th September 1786 and was to run for 21 years. The other venture, for which no documentary evidence remains, only tantalising references in various sources, was in the Llanberis area. Yet whilst the greatest priority was to find a reliable source of ore to replace the eventual dwindling stocks from Parys Mountain, William Roe, who was foremost in experience in such matters, found his time increasingly taken up with litigations initiated by Lord Uxbridge.

It is doubtful if the Earl had any knowledge of mining and was therefore totally reliant on Harrison and his observations of the situation on Parys Mountain. He would also have no confidence to embroil himself in a series of long, drawn out and expensive litigations, unlike his father before him, unless encouraged to do so by someone with an authoritative genre. Once again circumstantial evidence indicates that Thomas Williams, through Harrison, was that person. One need not look far to discover Harrison and Williams working together behind the scenes, in part evidenced by Harrison's inclusion in one of the manufacturing partnerships.

A letter dated 11th May 1786 written by Harrison suggests some upset between Williams and Lord Uxbridge, which seems to have occurred because Harrison had concealed something from the Earl and begged His Lordship to hear his version. Once again his obsequious and rambling style does little to elucidate matters but the gist of it appears to relate to the formation of the two companies relevant to the Mona Mine, now incorporating the Cerrig y Bleiddia area.

Firstly there was the Stanley Smelting Company in which Lord Uxbridge had been granted half a share; Williams held a quarter, whilst the remaining quarter was held by the quartet of John Wilkinson, the ironmaster, Michael Hughes, manager of the works, John Dawes and Thomas Harrison. This company had two smeltworks, one at St. Helens and the other at Swansea.

Secondly there was the manufactory in Flintshire carried on under the name of the Greenfield Copper & Brass Co. but in which Lord Uxbridge held no share. However, together with Williams there were six other partners, one of whom was again Thomas Harrison. In inferring mitigating circumstances Harrison wrote "The adjudgement of Matters on which depend all the future plans & Prospects of a Man's Life must to that Man necefsarily be of the utmost Importence". Was this his excuse for acquiring a share in the Holywell concern? Whatever the answer he had certainly found sufficient capital to invest in both companies, unless the latter was a reward for services rendered.

In the same letter Harrison confessed "I am sorry to tell your Lordship there is another Subject . . . distrefsing & embarrafsing" which he had been unable to resolve. He quoted several payments, either already expended or shortly demanded, in respect of the Mona Mine and summarised that "the immense Sum of £20,000 or more" had been "swallowed up in a narrow Space of Time." This is an incredible amount, given that Lord Uxbridge already owned the mine and that more than £2,000 had been paid to Roe & Co. for all the equipment etc.

Thomas Williams knew that the mining part of the business was the most expensive to operate and also the most unpredictable. There is no doubt that he took full advantage of Lord Uxbridge's ignorance of the subject to finance his own way out of trouble. It was Lord Uxbridge who would have to bear the cost of the Court Case as sole owner of the Cerrig y Bleiddia mine at the time of Roe & Co.'s lease. It is interesting to note that Harrison and Williams would soon "boast" of expecting an award for damages against Roe & Co. of not less than £20,000, which must have been the incentive for Lord Uxbridge to press for damages: This was his only hope of recompense for Harrison's actions in undertaking such vast expenditure on his behalf.

Four months later Harrison was busy on Parys Mountain collecting evidence for the suit, at which time he had already filled "Near 150 Pages of Folio", however he had to report that he had heard nothing from William Roe (who had now taken charge of matters on behalf of Roe & Co.) but was expecting an attorney, another Mr. Harrison from Daventry, who would select the most appropriate documentation in support of the claim.

Evidently William Roe, appreciating the identity of the real adversary, had taken steps to ensure that the circumstances would be judged by those well outside Williams's sphere of influence on Anglesey. Consequently seven Shropshire gentlemen and a Sheriff arrived at Parys Mountain to act as a jury when viewing the supposed damage at the mine. Thomas Williams, confident of a successful outcome, could never have imagined that he was about to be outwitted by William Roe.

The group had been on site only a short time when a message arrived from Roe & Co. requesting that the dispute be settled in some other way rather than "going to the Afsizes". Harrison and the others agreed to hear what Roe & Co. had to say and "Mefsrs Roe & Smyth with their attorney Mr. Leigh of Liverpool soon appeared at our office at the Mountain, anxiety was visible in their Countenances." The Uxbridge group were anxious to accept arbitration (it was less expensive and they would have felt certain of receiving some payment for damages) but for a while pretended otherwise, then agreed that the jury could select three or five of their number to act as arbitrators, hear the evidence and settle the dispute. The Sheriff was advised of the decision and accordingly reported to the jury; they conceived many difficulties until finally the two attorneys representing the respective parties met in private. It was then agreed that the whole of the jury would undertake the task, but first expected an agreement to be signed immediately and arbitrator bonds executed by both parties in the sum of £20,000 each, demonstrating an acceptance of the arbitrators' decision.

Harrison and his group expected the arbitrators to stay and "complete the Business", but the tables were turned. Through delaying matters not only had William Roe ensured that Harrison and other employees had spent a great deal of time and expense collecting information unnecessarily, but now they would be forced to journey to Oswestry where the arbitrators expected them to attend a meeting on 16th August. Undaunted Harrison, acting as Lord Uxbridge's representative, then took the arbitrators "over the whole work" commentating with appropriate malevolence, whilst Bridge, present on behalf of Roe & Co., in no way interrupted the performance. Harrison's report to Lord Uxbridge concluded in his usual didactic manner proclaiming anxiety, distress and embarrassment at the outcome whilst being "so agitated with this distrefsing appointment that I hardly closed my Eyes all night."

There is now a significant dearth of information in the correspondence of both the Beaudesert and Plas Newydd estates, nor is any reference made to the outcome of the law suit in the Macclesfield Copper Company Minute book, but fortunately a transcript of a letter written by Edward Hawkins to John Atkinson Busfield reveals the outcome. Written in Macclesfield on 19th February 1787. Hawkins, whilst appreciating that Busfield had already been informed of "the Awards of the Seven Arbitrators in favour of Mr. Roe" doubts if he is aware that "Affidavits had been exhibited in the Court of Kings bench to prevent that Award being made a Rule of Court and . . . to set it aside". However, the Award was confirmed by two judges who severely admonished Williams and Harrison for their conduct in the affair, to the great satisfaction of Roe & Co. who had considered the pair as "antagonists".

Hawkins's letter also confirms that Williams "and his new Allies the Cornish Metal Compy" were equally unsuccessful in obtaining a Navy contract for sheathing and sales with the East India Company during the 1786 season. The Macclesfield partnership had secured the supplies for all the Navy dockyards but had allowed Mr. Raby, who together with Thoyt & Co. had supplied all the East India copper for 1786, the contracts for Portsmouth and Plymouth. From later evidence Roe & Co. were supplying manufactured copper to Thoyt & Co. which was then converted into copper sheathing enabling them to fulfil their part of the naval contract. Raby had sold copper to the East India Company on behalf of Roe & Co., suggesting reciprocity amongst those concerned.

Hawkins was also keen to point out to Busfield that the Roe & Co. prices were fair and conformed to the regulations set out by the treaty of May 1786 between Cornwall and Anglesey; in fact "the purchasers of Copper give us universally the preferences".

On the state of trade in general he was optimistic. Because the African Trade continued well there was a corresponding increase in the demand for wire, which was a great aid to Roe & Co. as this was the "least profitable" part of their manufacturing processes. Also exports to France attracted only 10% duty which increased the demand for Birmingham goods and in turn created a larger market for ingot brass and tile copper.

Information regarding the mines was set out concisely and is important, for it reveals that from the two in Wales, one had already produced "a considerable quantity of rich Ore" which seemed likely to continue and the other, which was in the early stages of development, had produced some good ore. These comments appear to refer to Llandudno and Llanberis respectively, however there is a dearth of information regarding the Bodiddabach lease. A report of an unnamed mine in June 1786 refers to a "great abundance" of surface water, although where the land was high the workings were less than two yards deep, suggesting problems at Llandudno. Another mine was eventually abandoned in January 1788, having proved a "Blank"; this could account for the subsequent total lack of reference to the Bodiddabach site. What Hawkins's letter does provide is definite evidence of further mining at Coniston in the Lake District.

The original Coniston lease had expired in 1777 after 21 years, but very little mining had taken place during the last decade. However on 21st January 1778 Charles Roe had renewed the lease for a further term of 26 years paying the same duty as previously i.e. $1/12$th ore but none for the first six months, proving that the mine had been dormant for some time. (This is also confirmed by a letter of April 1775 from a speculator who was enquiring if the mines were out of lease, as he had received an enquiry from two of the old miners.) It was not until three years later that an agent from Kendal writing to a friend was able to report "I hope there begins to be a pretty good Prospect for Copper at Conistone, the steward, Jno, (Jonathan) Ball, told me at the Court yesterday that he has a Ton ready drefs'd and amongst it two Lumps of Ore 8lb. each".

By 1783 Sir Michael le Fleming was advised by his steward that there were 17 or 18 men constantly at work and producing "a good quantity of ore" with 15 tons ready for weighing. It had become necessary to erect an engine for stamping or crushing a large quantity of small ore, mined at the beginning of the new venture, but which could not be weighed until it had also been washed; a further problem had then arisen because of the need to find some sycamore wood for the water wheel. The steward sold the men four trees from the estate and with Sir Michael's approval felled an oak tree with which to build the engine. The former were poor quality costing 1s. to 1s. 6d. a foot but 16 feet of the oak was bought at 2s. per foot.

Unfortunately no accounts have survived for this period of mining at Coniston yet the mines were obviously once again in full production as evidenced by Hawkins's comment in his letter to Busfield, "we obtain a good deal of Ore . . ." A further letter the following year reveals, "we have better prospects we have found the Vein in Calbeck fells and are pursuing it . . ." He also confirmed a contract with John Heaton, the Duke of Devonshire's auditor and land agent who would supply the copper battery mill.

There is an interesting reference to the mines of Cronebawn and Ballymurtagh in Ireland which for certain reasons the company had not generally disclosed and are probably the ones referred to in Watt's letter of 16th August 1785 as "other resources not publickly known". Hawkins predicted that there were considerable quantites of poor ores to be had, as good as those from Parys Mountain and, perhaps with a twinge of nostalgia, added "tho' we ne'er shall, take her for all in all, look on her like again."

27
THE BEGINNING OF THE END

Those mighty periods of years
Which seem to us so vast,
Appear no more before thy sight
Than yesterday that's past.

The years immediately following the termination of the Parys Mountain lease mark a period of intense activity on the part of the five principal Macclesfield Copper Company partners, not only in their co-operative ventures but also in their other distinct and personal careers, which were now beginning to take shape.

Thomas Smyth was, of course, already a successful Liverpool merchant and banker when he and Caldwell purchased their company shares in 1774, but now his commitment to local government affairs intensified. On 28th March 1784 the banker's clerk of Caldwell & Co., having completed his "Servitude", paid his fine of 6s. 8d. and was admitted a freeman of Liverpool; this appears to have allowed Smyth the opportunity to delegate more duties to the young James Carmichael, enabling Smyth to spend more and more time on Corporation matters.

Liverpool Corporation was entering a new phase of development, in order to accommodate the rapidly increasing populace, which correspondingly created ambitious new plans. Apart from the domestic schemes of employing a surgeon for the "Recovery of Drowned Persons" and setting up a patrol of twenty men to combat burglaries and street robberies, the most important project, sanctified by Act of Parliament in April 1785, was the construction of two new docks. The Old Dry Dock, allowing access to the Old King's Dock, had already been flanked by the Salthouse Dock constructed on the south in 1753 and the George Dock on the north by 1767, but the volume of trade had continued to increase with such speed that it was imperative to undertake a major development of further docking facilities.

The success of the Act never seemed in doubt for already, on 24th December 1784, the Corporation had bought four plots of land on the South Shore which virtually encompassed two private docks, one of which was the site of Roe & Co.'s old copper works. This was a very fortuitous outcome for the company after years of struggling to sell the site. A note in the Liverpool Corporation Minutes of 2nd February 1785 confirms:

> "That the several purchases made by the Corp[oratio]n from Thomas Whitaker, William Roe & Co. Richard Kent & John Blackburn amounting to £29,000 be carried into execution & that the said purch[ase]. moneys shall be respectively secured to the several Sellers by Bonds etc. at the rate of £4 10s being the usual interest paid by the Corpn."

Just how much Roe & Co. received for their plot is not known but the Blackburn parcel, which appears to have been slightly smaller than a quarter of the whole estate, sold for £6,000; therefore it can be safely assumed that Roe & Co. would have received something in

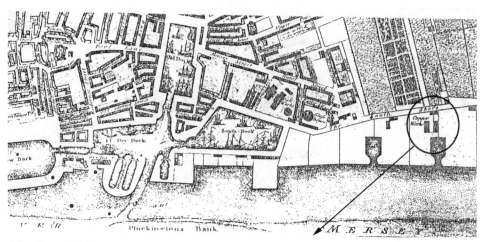

John Eyes 1768.

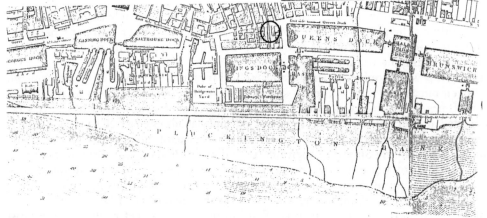

Jonathan Bennison 1835.

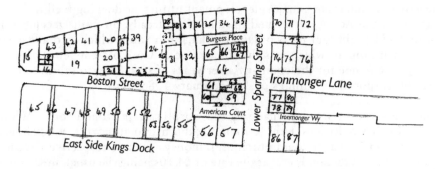

By 1845 most of the above plots had been acquired by Liverpool Corporation. Nos. 70-72 were in the area occupied by the original Roe & Co. smelter. The whole site became Wapping Dock which opened to shipping 9th May 1855. Plan deposited in the Office of the Clerk of the Peace for the County Palatine of Lancaster., 29 November 1845. Reproduced by kind permission of the Lancashire Record Office Ref: P DH27.

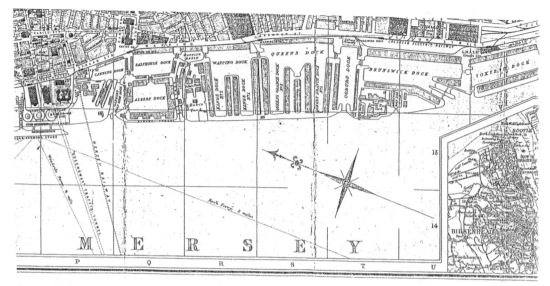

J. Bartholomew & Son Ltd. c. 1930s.

the region of £8,000, for theirs was the largest holding (which at some point had evidently been bought by the company from the Golightly family).

Amongst the special committee members appointed to advise on the new docks were Thomas Smyth, William Roe and Thomas Golightly. Many regulations were introduced to ensure the greater efficiency of the harbour, especially in the handling of cargoes and their security. The fear of fire was ever present, particularly as the Old King's Dock reached into the city and therefore any ship at anchor which caught alight was a danger to the whole community. Already heavy fines were in place to combat any lading of gunpowder within the docks, lighted candles (except those in lanterns), smokers of uncapped or uncovered pipes of tobacco and hot irons where tar or pitch was stored.

One year later William Roe was again a member of another committee, this time to improve communications to the area of the proposed new docks, for the city streets were narrow and in need of great improvement. It was a considerable task including compulsory purchases of property to enable the widening of thoroughfares and an additional plan for building almshouses.

Despite their heavy Corporation commitments, William Roe (elected Bailiff for 1786-87) and Thomas Smyth continued to superintend the Llandudno mining area on behalf of the company and had, of course, also agreed a mining lease for Bodiddabach in the then county of Caernarfon, signed on 29th September 1786 with Sir Roger Mostyn. It is logical, therefore, to assume that they also superintended the initial workings of the new venture, situated just south of the town of Conwy and appropriately close to Llandudno, that is until the apparent abandonment of the site some 18 months later.

By the autumn of 1786 the new Liverpool dock estate, covering just over 14 acres in the area of Wapping, was under construction. The new King's Dock was completed first and opened on 3rd October 1788, whilst the Queen's Dock, somewhat delayed, would eventually receive its first ship on 17th April 1796, by which time Roe & Co. would no longer have a Liverpool smelter.

However, much was to happen in the meantime, beginning with the Corporation's refusal on 4th June 1788 to allow the Duke of Bridgewater a renewal of his lease in Wapping. The Duke had been in possession of a valuable plot of land at the southern end of the Salthouse Dock where, by 1773, he had constructed a dock and outer channel to facilitate easier connections between his canal and the harbour, supported by extensive warehousing. At first glance this seemed to be a straightforward matter, the culmination of plans on the part of the Docks Committee to incorporate the area into the new Dock Estate. William Roe and Thomas Smyth were both present when the refusal was made and William was again in attendance on 3rd September when the Duke sent in his second petition. Not until March 1789 did a committee meet to consider the Duke's request and William Roe, whilst attending other meetings regarding the new development, was markedly absent. The matter dragged on.

On 14th July 1789 a serious step was taken, when the Corporation Treasurer was suspended, whilst a committee examined all the cash books, papers and documents, resulting also in the suspension of the Clerk to the Treasurer. Almost immediately Thomas Golightly was appointed Treasurer with confirmation of his position on 5th August; for the first time in Liverpool Corporation's history this was to be a full time salaried permanent position in exchange for which Golightly gave up his private business "so as not to interfere with the Public interest". Despite the fact that he was something of a dilettante in private life, history would prove him to be a thoroughly honest, competent and honourable member of Liverpool Corporation.

During the meeting it was decided that the Corporation funds would "be lodged equally" in the banks of Smyth & Caldwell and their agency bank in London, Messrs. Gregson & Co. At this juncture Thomas Smyth obtained permission from the Macclesfield Copper Company to transfer his share to his brother-in-law, John Pendred Scott of Ballygammon, Ireland who was then admitted as his successor, but with the proviso that Smyth should continue in trust as a partner for him. There are two possible reasons for this action, one politically motivated, taking into account the animosity which existed within Liverpool Corporation at this time, for two months later Thomas Smyth was elected Mayor (and his daughter married John Johnson of London a possible relative of his close associate of the same name); the other is dealt with in the next chapter.

On 2nd June 1790 it was noted in the Corporation Minutes that "a most eloquent letter" had been sent by Thomas Smyth to the Duke of Bridgewater on behalf of the Corporation, expressing their earnest desire that he should not think they were unappreciative of everything he had done for public benefit. From his following reply, which was read out aloud, the matter was evidently not so straightforward as first appears and one is left wondering whether or not certain sentiments expressed by the Macclesfield company duo had influenced the resulting procrastinations:

> "Since the appl[icatio]n. I made to the Corp[oratio]n. in 1776 for the Extension of my premises which was refused me as not consistent with the safety of the port of Liverpool & which at that time was also refused Mr. Rathbone for the like reasons but afterwards it being granted him, I applied a second time to Mr . Birch, the then Mayer and from that appl[icatio]n. I rec'd no answer".

The Duke was therefore determined to sue and had taken out a lawsuit against the Trustees of the late William Rathbone. The Trustees begged the Corporation to pay the legal expenses for their defence; payment was agreed and allowed for in the Treasurer's accounts.

Although positive proof is lacking to support the notion that William Roe had a hand in the matter, yet he must have felt extremely satisfied that his father's old antagonist had been balked in his designs and put to a great deal of trouble for the past 14 years; some small recompense for the Duke's treatment of those dedicated to the provision of a canal for Macclesfield.

As Thomas Smyth's year as Mayor drew to a close he was appointed a J.P. and automatically became Coroner for the succeeding year but just when Liverpool Corporation's stability seemed assured, Sparling was elected Mayor. Within four months an intriguing power struggle began to develop, the catalyst of which was the election of Charles Caldwell and three others by the burgesses to become council-men. It seems strange that William Roe and Thomas Smyth had not previously endeavoured to obtain the election of Caldwell on the Common Council when a vacancy occurred. It is interesting to note, however, that Caldwell's first attendance at a Roe & Co. meeting had not been until 18th September 1786 when held in Liverpool, and his second attendance on 9th May 1789; again the venue was Liverpool. This suggests his unreliablilty and that, for whatever reason, he was now being courted by Sparling. The obvious justification for his inclusion in the company must have been the banking facilities provided for Corporation funds.

The protestations from the Common Council members against the election of Caldwell and company were immediate and strong, reiterating their predecessors' claims that it was not in accordance with the ancient customs of the Borough and Corporation and therefore the election procedure was null and void. Thomas Smyth moved that it be put to the vote and having received an affirmative had it recorded in the Minutes Book that the Mayor, John Sparling and the two bailiffs, Moss and Tarleton, had acted in an illegal manner. It transpired that the three had held a meeting in an attempt to make a by-law which would allow their choice of council-men and also insist that the Treasurer present his accounts to the Mayor, who in turn would ask four of the Common Council to audit them. This seems too much of a coincidence considering that Sparling and his bailiffs had four new council members in mind, for with the accounts under their control and Caldwell involved, suspicions were bound to be aroused.

The leader of the Common Council at once convened a committee to prevent "illegal attacks" upon the Corporation and asked Sparling and his cohorts to leave. A vote confirmed agreement with the action taken but Sparling, upon leaving the room, instantly returned and "discharged" the meeting. Totally undeterred, the Common Council continued with its business, thanked Thomas Smyth "for his great service" as Chief Magistrate and voted him the usual 500 guineas.

It was not long before Thomas Golightly refused a request by Sparling, now Mayor, to have the books audited by Sparling's chosen few and the latter, comparable to Thomas Williams of Anglesey by nature, began to work behind the scenes. Soon a petition was organised to legalise Sparling's actions until finally Thomas Golightly was summoned to appear at Lancaster Assizes (on Sparling's original home territory) where judgement went against him. The Common Council refused to accept the verdict and a retrial was proposed.

By July 1791 Thomas Golightly, having borrowed £12,000 on behalf of the Corporation from the banks of Gregson & Co. and Caldwell & Co. suggested that, in order to raise revenue, bonds at 4.5%, affixed with the Common Seal, should be issued. The second judgement was by jury and yet again resulted in defeat, but once more a retrial was accepted. The burgesses, appreciating that Corporation funds were almost exhausted by their actions, abandoned further litigation. How the outcome affected Sparling is difficult to judge, but he virtually abandoned Corporation business for the remainder of his year as Mayor, leaving his deputy to attend meetings etc., though needless to say he was voted the customary 500 guineas in due course.

* * * * * * *

At the same time as Liverpool Corporation was utilising William Roe's expertise in its ambitious development programme, he and his brother-in-law, John Shaw, began their own development of the area which today lies immediately to the west and south of St. George's Hall. On 1st December 1787 they leased from the Corporation sixteen substantial plots of land with houses and buildings in Great Charlotte St., the Haymarket, St. John's Lane and Lime St. which, given time, would take on a new character.

The following year of 1788 saw William at his indefatigable best. Firstly on 23rd February he was appointed one of only nine Commissioners of English Customs. This was an extremely important and prestigious position attracting a considerable salary of £1,000 per annum.

Until the Commonwealth period the business of customs had been farmed out, then the Long Parliament not only appointed Commissioners for the English Customs, but created a separate Excise service with its own Commissioners. Further alterations took place and Charles II once more placed the Revenues in farm. During the 18th century the build up of trade, commensurate with a wealthy and increasing population, had placed extra pressures on the Customs Service so that at the time of William Roe's entry it was decided to appoint by a sign manual two joint chairmen.

One can only speculate on how William Roe achieved his appointment. It so happened that at this time Liverpool Corporation was under pressure from the Board of Customs for the provision of a new Custom House. The old one built in 1721-22 and situated at the eastern end of the Old Dock, was a very impressive building. Drawn by Peter Perez Burdett in the early 1770s it had a spacious yard at the rear and several warehouses. The first initial problems, however, arose from the East India Company's monopoly, whereby all its goods were imported through London and attracted high duties. Liverpool, Bristol and other outports, needing these goods for part of the African trade, had to receive them delivered under seal by land carriage; they were then placed under the King's Locks until released for exportation.

Liverpool's warehousing facilities were soon to become "grievously deficient" and the port's Collector of Customs proposed a plan to build a warehouse specifically for the company. It was a complicated process as the intended site was on Corporation land which involved obtaining a lease on behalf of His Majesty from either the landlord (Moorcroft) or the Corporation. All was finally settled and the building completed in 1744 but inevitably by the 1780s the booming trade had once again placed pressure on the beleaguered Collector, even before the construction of the new Docks Estate had begun. A report by the Inspector General in 1782 recorded that "difficulties arise from not having a fit place to examine Irish Linens and that great Injury is liable to be rec'd from their being wetted by sudden showers of Rain".

As ground landlord the Corporation had a right to specify the type of building and materials it wanted on the site; this, in effect, was a form of planning, although at this period still very much on a private basis. The Commisioners requested that plans be submitted for approval, but this was the start of a very long drawn out wrangle which would take years to resolve and, from either point of view, William Roe must have found himself caught up in the conflict.

Amongst his other commitments were William's interests in shipping. On 18th September 1787, together with his partners Christopher and John Shaw, William sold a sloop named *William* registered in County Fife, Scotland during 1775. They were still in possession of the brigantine *Charles*, which would not be sold until 17th July 1794 but, as trustees of Samuel Shaw deceased, did, of course, lose the ship *Europe* in September 1788. On 5th April 1788 William bought a share in another brigantine *Lucy*, registered Chepstow 1779, which was comparable in size to the *William*. This time his partners were Thomas Smyth and John Johnson; in due course the ship was sold to Christopher and John Shaw on 6th January 1790.

John Johnson held interests in several vessels at various times with other merchants yet the one which related directly to Roe & Co. was the brig *Brothers* registered at Northwich 1786; bought 16th March 1789. Apart from Johnson the other owners were William "Row". Thomas Smyth and Charles Caldwell. It would remain in their possession until 18th July 1795 when sold to and registered by the residents of Weymouth.

In addition to William Roe's local government and Civil Service careers and his commitments to Roe & Co. he was still very much aware of his family responsibilities. Having completed the administration of his father's estate he was now drawn into the affairs of the Nicholson family. As he and sister Catherine were the only surviving children from Charles Roe's first marriage it seems natural that their family ties were particularly strong. Catherine and husband Rev. Ralph had resided in Didcot, Berkshire until 1785 where, judging from their meticulously recorded accounts, they kept an extremely fashionable vicarage. Twelve pages, containing approximately thirty items per page, reveal purchases of high quality furniture, furnishings and household goods in every conceivable shape and size from a large bird cage, oyster knives, a grindstone and water tub, an ice tray, cuckoo clock, great ladder, several sets of superb cutlery, mahogany tables, chairs, a harpsichord and carpets (two of which were purchased in London; one Chinese) to beds, bed linen and so forth, including a remarkably comprehensive and valuable library.

Apart from Catherine's desire to be near her brother William and his prodigious family, Liverpool society evidently beckoned, for by 1785, the Nicholsons also had a residence on Merseyside which, over the next six years was completely furnished in the same extravagant manner as that of Didcot. Of their three sons only William survived to be heir and was 11 years old on their arrival in Lancashire. All three daughters, Catherine, Helen and Elizabeth, would grow up attending the scintillating assemblies of the Liverpool fraternity and there, in the busy vibrant port, their mother Catherine would remain after her widowhood of 1792.

A Directory of 1790 lists Rev. Nicholson as residing "back of St. James' Harrington". An incorrect record of his burial in the 1792 Register was later altered to "He died December 26th & was buried December 30th" aged 57 years. Young William Nicholson was by then only 18 years of age.

Whilst still at Didcot, in 1783, Ralph had prepared his will leaving Catherine the Chadkirk Estate near Stockport; property in Sutton adjacent to Macclesfield; all the household goods and his valuable collection of books and manuscripts. After Catherine's death her inheritance was to pass to their son William. In order to make provision for the three daughters, a charge of £1,000 was to be made on the above estate which, together with the Macclesfield properties, money out on loan and rents from holdings in Marple and Bramhall, was to be shared equally between the three. Catherine was nominated Executrix by her husband and, together with William Roe and Harry Lankford (now of Stockport) the two Executors, was to be guardian for the children.

What inspired Catherine suddenly to prepare her will on 1st January 1792 is difficult to deduce, unless her husband was already ill, although he is included in the bequests. The contents are a fascinating reflection of her life style; her jewellery included a watch, a diamond and garnet ring, bracelets and a locket set with pearls, a pearl necklace, several other rings and a silver snuff box with a lapis lazuli stone. Further items were inevitably intimate and personal, an exposition of the depth of Georgian sentimentality. One such piece was a ring inherited from her half sister Mary Roe containing a lock of her late father's hair. Her husband, for his life time, was to have possession of a locket decorated with an angel and child and containing hair from their deceased son, Ralph; after his death it was to pass to son, William. Rev. Ralph was also bequeathed a silver snuffbox decorated with a design made from Samuel Roe's hair, Catherine's deceased brother.

The portion of Catherine's marriage settlement, totalling £1,230 and given in the form of bonds by Charles Roe, was still invested in loans; by a series of provisions this sum was to be held in trust for the benefit of her children. With the death of her husband, Catherine's financial situation was set to become a very complicated affair, creating problems into which several family members would ultimately be drawn.

It is interesting to note that William Roe's busy life style had once again disrupted the normal pattern relating to his childrens' baptisms, with surprising results. Son and heir, William Jnr., born on 4th January 1784 was not baptised until 31st August 1785 at St. Peter's Church yet, on the same day, the sixth daughter, Frances, born 20th March 1785 was baptised at St. James's, Toxteth Park. The latter suggests a possible baptism by uncle Ralph, newly arrived in Liverpool and living next to St. James's. The intriguing question is why young William was not baptised at the same time as his sister; one can only deduce that as son and heir he had to have an appropriate christening perhaps with the wishes of the Shaw family in mind. St. Peter's, at this period, held the status of senior Church of England church in Liverpool whilst the others, including St. Nicholas's, were in effect chapelry status. One could equally well ponder why Frances was not baptised with her brother; the choice of St. James's was obviously a gesture of goodwill, not only to cement family relationships but also as a possible acknowledgement of the fact that the church was attended by the Roe & Co. workmen and their families living in the Toxteth area.

For some reason during 1788 William Roe (apart from having the satisfaction of his five week old son, Christopher Shaw's baptism at St. Peter's on 25th August) had decided to sell his father's two properties relating to the first Lankford marriage. Without doubt these would have formed part of his father's first marriage settlement and one suspects that it was done to assist Catherine financially. The first sale was that of the premises at Brassington in Derbyshire on 28th June, (though few details are known) followed by the property in Jordangate, Macclesfield on 20th October. In the intervening years the latter had been converted into three dwellings and the twisting croft at the rear into gardens for the residences.

* * * * * * *

Whilst William Roe and Thomas Smyth indubitably combined operations around the Liverpool area, in Macclesfield Edward Hawkins found himself working closely with Abraham Mills; the two inevitably teamed up with Robert Hodgson (still resident at Moody Hall, Congleton) whilst conducting company business, but when it came to personal careers Hawkins made a very brave decision to become a banker. It was not the best of times to have made such a choice but, although his experience was somewhat limited, he had seemingly gained some knowledge in the company's counting-house; also there was always Thomas Smyth to offer advice.

The first intimation of the Hawkins's bank is a note in the company Minute Book at the A.G.M. of 25th August 1785 "The Counting House be moved to Mr. Hawkins as soon as he has made a convenient building for that purpose." That this refers to the banking part of the business in addition to the accounts is verified on the following 8th March when an instruction was given to take all bills of £20 or less from the bank and also a week's supply of cash, allowing the bank a $^1/_4$ per cent on the account. Unable to find a suitable building Hawkins was allowed to rent the company counting-house for ten guineas per annum from 7th August 1786, which also included the occasional use of the Committee Room.

Within a few months suitable premises were found; according to a local chronicler, Corry, writing in 1817, the first Macclesfield bank was opened by Hawkins and Mills on Jordangate in 1787. Apart from a couple of items of correspondence signed Hawkins Mills & Co., one of which is addressed to Dr. Busfield on 18th October 1789 enclosing a draught for £135 as requested, this is the only evidence for Abraham Mills's initial involvement in the business.

Apparently there was at least one other partner, the son of Brian Hodgson, Jnr. (former landlord of the Old Hall, Buxton and shortly to move from Wootton Lodge in Staffordshire to Crakemarsh Hall, north of Uttoxeter). The young man, yet another Brian, had attended Manchester Grammar School and was 21 years of age in 1787, but whether or not he was engaged by his uncle Edward at the start of the business is not known; however he was employed by the copper company at that time. At the A.G.M. of 1786 he had been voted 20 guineas as an "acknowledgement of his services" and was allowed a salary of £50 per annum from the 7th August of that year. His employment continued for two years, then he was promoted to permanent membership of the committee joining the five senior members.

(Years later Edward Hawkins, when writing to Dr. Busfield on 5th May 1796, would apologise for the young man's inattention to his duties. The reason expounded aptly reflects the considerable changes in attitudes taking place during this period, as the Nation's wealth continued its course of corruption, creating a more lax and permissive society:

" . . . my nephew's best excuse is that a Lady occupied so much of his mind he forgot you. he will be married in a very short time and after a while will be as steady to his business as heretofore".

That such a business letter could be written would certainly have been beyond the belief of either the late Charles Roe or Brian Hodgson Snr., though in mitigation the young man was married only eleven days later on 16th May at the Collegiate Church of Manchester (now Manchester Cathedral).

The premises on Jordangate (today part of the Market Place) appear to have been utilised by Joseph Cooke, the company solicitor, as an office (he was also Deputy Clerk of the Manor and Forest Court of Macclesfield). Together with his wife, Ann and son, Charles, the solicitor lived in a substantial property next to the inn called *The Bull's Head,* but in order to accommodate his business a wall had been built to create the office, with its own separate doorway between the two premises, complete with courtyard at the rear. The doorway allowed access to a steep flight of stairs (still in existence) which led to a first floor room at the front of the dwelling-house but quite separate from the residential part.

Joseph Cooke died on 8th April 1788 and his son took over the office; Hawkins evidently rented his share of it for the bank, and the partnership with Cooke in the colliery enterprise on Macclesfield Common seems to have continued with the son, for Land Tax returns contain an item on Jordangate "Coalmines Roe & Co." proprietor the Earl of Harrington.

An interesting outcome of the establishment of the bank was the decision by Roe & Co. to produce their own copper coinage in the form of halfpence tokens.

* * * * * * *

The national coinage had been in a deplorable state for years because there was no provision for periodic renewal. After issuing 200 tons of 'Tower' halfpence and farthings during 1771-75, the Government took the decision to concern itself only with gold and silver coinage, so it was left to others to produce copper tokens, an unsatisfactory situation as it led to the creation of many forgeries. Encouraged by the Master of the Mint several anxious individuals from the Exchequer and Mint united to embark upon a reform of the British coinage. It was an expensive business, however, and not until 1787 was there an issue of silver money when £55,459 of shillings and sixpences were struck at the Mint situated in the Tower of London. (The recoining of gold money had taken place between 1774-78 but this was of little help for those companies with employees to pay).

A sightseer has left a valuable description of the Royal Mint; published in 1769, it underlines the intricacy of coining and leaves no doubt as to the magnitude of the labour intensive stamping operation still in use at that period before Matthew Boulton began construction of his mint at the Soho manufactory in 1788.

The visitor entering the Tower saw the Mint Office on the left hand side not far from the gate. The initial processes were kept from public view until the stamping stage was reached, and this was executed with an engine worked by three sometimes four, men. The engine was capable of impressing the coin on both sides at the same time. It comprised a worm screw "terminating in a spindle, just in the same manner as the letter press for printing books." The die (on which a die-sinker would have engraved the desired pattern) was then screwed to the lower end of the spindle directly above a recess into which was fixed the die for the reverse design. Each round blank or planchet was placed in turn on the lower die, but if a gold one it had been carefully weighed first, then the spindle was pulled hard down "with a jerk" resulting in one embossed coin. The visitor was full of admiration for the coiner, "The whole process is performed with amazing dexterity; for as fast as the men who work the engine can turn the spindle, so fast does another twitch out with his middle finger that which was stamped, while with his finger and thumb he places another that is unstamped. The silver & gold thus stamped, are delivered to be milled round the edges, the manner of performing which is a secret never shown to any body."

Therefore in handling gold and silver coinage the Mint was milling the edges last, this was the most difficult part of coining for it produced the regular ribbed markings around the narrow outer edge. But when it came to producing copper tokens by those outside the employ of the Mint, it was found more expedient to prepare the blanks by milling and cleaning first before striking, and with this in mind Roe & Co. contemplated the problem of acquiring sufficient copper coinage with which to pay their employees.

The A.G.M. of 1787 reveals the first intimation of Macclesfield tokens when it was decided to obtain a pattern for blanks and an estimate of the cost of coining halfpence for Ireland in addition to that for Great Britain. (It is interesting to note that the Bank of Ireland had been established by Charter on 15th May 1783).

By December the Treasury, aware of the need for coinage of smaller denominations, but also aware of the Mint's antiquated machinery, which if adapted for copper coinage would run at a loss, decided to resolve the problem by offering a contract for the undertaking; Roe & Co. immediately sent in their application. Nothing appears to have transpired, for one year later the company, now desperate for copper coinage and following the example set by Thomas Williams for his Parys Mine Company, decided to produce their own copper tokens. (The first Parys Mine Company tokens are dated 1787 and on the obverse sport a Druid's head encircled by oak branches, a design later used for Cornish tokens. On the reverse is *P M Co.* and *We promise to pay the bearer on demand one penny*. These tokens are often erroneously attributed to the Macclesfield Copper Company because of the previous connections with Anglesey.)

The designs for the Roe &Co. coinage "for the use of the respective works" were approved at a meeting held in Warrington on Monday, 19th January 1789 when Edward Hawkins was asked to find "some able artist in Birmingham to execute the Die for a Copper Coin".

Matthew Boulton, appreciating that there was very little difference between embossing buttons and coins (except brute force!) was evidently working behind the scenes to obtain the Government contract for himself. A copy letter, undated but obviously written early in 1789, reveals his anxiety on the matter. It is addressed to none other than Lord Hawesbury (otherwise Charles Jenkinson, Master of the Mint from 1775) expressing his dismay at the increasing 'evil' of receiving halfpence at tollgates, two thirds of which were counterfeit. He revealed that officials and residents of Stockport in Cheshire had published a resolution only to accept the copper coinage of the Anglesey company, and in addition he had just learnt that the Macclesfield Copper Company was following Anglesey's example and had begun production of 40 tons of coins, to be called Macclesfield halfpence. Not only were the latter being produced but others for Ireland with St. Patrick's head on one side; these were intended for "their own private trade" and not for the Irish Government. Boulton was convinced others would follow suit and with firmness concluded "unless the growing mischief is put a Stop to by the hand of power"; he achieved his aim and in due course was granted the Government contract but the execution of it would take some considerable time, with delays and deferrals on both sides. One unlooked-for complication was the illness of King George III which raised the question of the sovereign's head appearing on the coinage, and not until 1797 would Boulton be granted his first regal copper coinage, meantime he was to provide copper tokens.

As already mentioned the most difficult part of coining was the preparation of the blanks by milling the outer edges. Whilst on a visit to France in the latter part of 1786 Boulton had met a character called Jean-Pierre Droz who had impressed him with an invention which not only produced the milled edge, but allowed for the inclusion of lettering in relief; this was an almost foolproof way of combating counterfeiting. However, Thomas Williams was also fighting for Droz's attentions, having initially joined the race for the Government contract, and although Droz chose to court Boulton, after many vicissitudes Boulton's workmen succeeded in perfecting the operation without Droz's supposed indispensability.

It is known that the Parys Mine Company had actually produced copper tokens at the Holywell site and then moved operations to Birmingham, and Thomas Williams, now having to hand over production to Boulton, was trying to sell him the stamping machine. It does seem possible therefore that Roe & Co. had coined for themselves the first few batches of the 1789 halfpence series with 'R & Co.' under a beehive and six bees, arced by 'MACCLESFIELD' on the obverse, with the female figure of Genuis (looking like an industrialised Britannia) copied from the Roe monument in Christ Church on the reverse. If so these would have been made in the works on Macclesfield Common where security was tightest and access to the bank almost immediate.

Some of these early tokens have not been milled with the same expertise as the later series begun in 1790, when the beehive and 'R & Co.' was superseded by a very fine reproduction of Charles Roe's head, again copied from the Christ Church monument. The fact that Roe & Co. tendered for the copper coinage contract surely proves that they had the capability to produce some form of coinage.

Examples of a Macclesfield halfpence have survived with the obverse sporting an owl over the 'R. & Co.' and the reverse, three castles. Other examples have *Chester* instead of *Macclesfield* on the obverse, but none bear a date. Some regard these as counterfeit, yet circumstantial evidence does suggest that they are genuine, made by Peter Kempson a Birmingham coiner , and possibly some of the earliest in use by the company. At the start of the 19th century Charles Pye, a famous Birmingham engraver, would compile details of *Provincial Coins and Tokens* for the years 1787 to 1801 to be printed in Birmingham by London publishers. He accredits Kempson with producing 5 cwts of the three castles version for Macclesfield. Perhaps not satisfied with the results the Macclesfield partners quickly decided to produce their own with blanks supplied from elsewhere, and approached John Westwood, a button manufacturer of Birmingham to make and mill the blanks. Westwood, for whatever reason, passed on the information to Boulton, and one can only speculate that he had learnt of Boulton's pending contract and had no intention of being sued over the affair.

Certainly the exchange of letters between Boulton and Roe & Co. from March to November 1789 suggests this. Boulton pointed out that Westwood had asked him to execute the dies and strike the pieces, which he was willing to do provided the mode of payment was agreed. The company had already negotiated a price with Westwood for "completing the manufacture" and to cover the cost of packing; the account was to be paid quarterly. They pointed out, therefore, that it was up to Matthew Boulton to agree a price with Westwood (in effect as a subcontractor) which would be covered by reimbursement in the quarterly account, this was, of course, normal business practice at that period. Boulton, however, was in a better position to appreciate Westwood's declining financial situation and informed Roe & Co. accordingly, so it was agreed that Edward Hawkins would pay Boulton direct when visiting Birmingham.

By the end of May 1789 Westwood had sent Boulton 10 tons of blanks with the edges milled and ready for annealing and cleaning etc., with a further 4 tons awaiting despatch, but Boulton wanted payment to cover the packing, which had already been allowed Westwood. The 1789 account was finally agreed and the details entered into the Soho accounts viz:

"Charge by Boulton for coining to 11th January 1790   £756   8   3d.
 (20 tons 14 cwts. 1 qu. 25 lbs 2ozs @ £36 10s. per ton)
Paid by Roe & Co. December 1789   £383   7   9d.
                                    Outstanding   £373   0   6d.
Collected personally by M. Boulton   £ 26   5   0d.
                                                            £346 15   6d.
Less shruff metal sold to J. Westwood   £ 82 17   6d.
                                    Then Due   £263 18   0d."

Unfortunately the bookkeeping is somewhat confused by the fact that Boulton was charging Westwood with expenses for rolling copper etc. (but on whose behalf is not clear) and there are no records available for what Roe & Co. were charged by Westwood, or indeed paid him.

Also on 21st August 1789 "Chas. Roe & Co." were charged by Boulton for three silver medals at 6s. 2d. each i.e. 18s. 6d., but why these were made is not known; it was forty years since the smelters on Macclesfield Common had begun production so they could have been given to long serving employees.

When the Macclesfield Copper Company met in Warrington on 5th January 1790 Edward Hawkins was asked to attend a meeting of Westwood's assigns to prove the company's debt, (which suggests Westwood was on the verge of bankruptcy) and also to settle the account in dispute with Boulton, but inevitably the matter dragged on. Westwood appears to have survived with the aid of a large loan from one of Boulton's associates for, on 19th March 1790, 5 tons of plate copper were sent to him from Macclesfield to be coined "according to speciman handed us by Westwood". As a consequence Boulton, when writing to his friend and business associate Samuel Garbett on 11th September, confirmed that the Macclesfield Company had ordered a further 25 tons of coins from Westwood in addition to the recent issue of 21 tons and that the new order was to have "the Head of old Roe upon them . . ." this suggests that the previous 21 tons were still sporting the beehive design and possibly St. Patrick's bust for Ireland. Judging from surviving examples each of these coins weighed just under half an ounce which would give 36 to the pound, this sounds a reasonable assumption given that 12 pence equalled one shilling and would allow for easy reckoning, and for four weeks commencing 10th January 1791 one ton of plate copper was sent each week to Westwood.

By 26th December 1792 the Soho accounts show a total debt for Roe & Co. of £2,053 6 8d. simply referred to as "for 20 tons of copper". This considerable figure suggests that, in addition to the charges for coining, the company had accepted Boulton's offer of 16th March 1789 to provide 20 tons of copper @ £77 per ton (£1,540) possibly as part of the agreement made by Roe & Co. to continue purchasing a proportion of Cornish ore each year. The difference of £513 6 8d. presumably relates to a charge for coining during 1791, unless the £263 18s. was still outstanding. For reasons best known to himself Boulton's book-keeper, at this stage in the proceedings, was far from efficient so further charges could have been paid by Roe & Co. From Boulton's records there is no disputing that 21 tons had already been coined and that he had provided a further 20 tons. From the Macclesfield Copper Company records a further 4 tons are recorded as despatched to Westwood in January 1791, but not all consignments are necessarily mentioned in the company minutes. This is obviously the minimum tonnage sent for coining, however it still provides a far greater quantity of tokens issued by the Macclesfield Copper Company than has hitherto been appreciated.

It is extremely difficult to judge the total number of tokens produced taking into account all the various issues, including those for Ireland. From the new issue bearing Charles Roe's head a hundredweight would have produced 4,032 tokens, suggesting 80,640 per ton. As this issue initially was to be 25 tons it implies that at least two million (viz. 2,016,000) were issued for 1790-91, and the previous 21 tons relating to the beehive and possibly St. Patrick designs is more than one and a half million (viz. 1,693,440). Even these estimates seem conservative when allowing a possible 25,000 for the three castles series; issues of the Roe head halfpence for 1792; and last but by no means least 30 variations of the Cronebane series for which the Macclesfield Copper Company paid freight and insurance, with the Irish Mine Company paying the importation duty, although some of the latter's tokens must have been produced from the 21 tons.

Extant examples of the Macclesfield tokens include 7 variations of the beehive design, and for the "Roe head" 12 variations for 1790, 28 for 1791 and only 4 for 1792 (although only the slightest difference in design is discernible) but of course there could have been several more issues. In 1801 the company would begin a rigorous campaign to remove all tokens from circulation with the intention of melting them down; finally hand bills were to be distributed informing the public that after 28th February 1802 none would be redeemable. Considering this was a time of depression during the Napoleonic Wars it is surprising how many have survived.

A penny piece was produced in 1790 said to have been made by Westwood for collectors, but this has been disputed; it is of the 'Roe head' series and could have been made for circulation but then discontinued as the halfpence pieces would have proved more convenient. Some counterfeits have survived suggesting more originally, and one or two hybrid coins called 'Mules' i.e. one side stamped for the Macclesfield Copper Company whilst the other side has no connection whatsoever. The greatest counterfeiting took place in Ireland, to date 24 examples are known with 20 mules, a far greater number than was usual.

These copper tokens were a remarkable success and greatly admired, even by the acrimonious John Byng who, whilst en route for Macclesfield in 1790, happened to pass through the village of Fairfield in Derbyshire: " . . .at the Turnpike I was surprised to receive in Change the Anglesea, and Macclesfield Half Pence, a better Coinage and of more beauty than that of the Mint and not so likely to be counterfeited." The vast majority of the Roe & Co. halfpence read *Payable at Macclesfield Liverpool or Congleton* and in addition thousands bore the mark X with a dot on either side which indicated that John Gregory Hancock was the die-sinker (i.e. engraver). Hancock was employed by Boulton on a sub-contract basis and produced many superb designs including the Druid's head for the Anglesey (Thomas Williams) tokens, which was presumably what John Byng had received as part of his change together with the Macclesfield halfpence.

* * * * * * *

Remarkably Byng's congeniality remained for some time and his brief perambulation around Macclesfield produced a glowing report, having discovered that the copper works had brought prosperity to the town which was "enriching" and "increasing" because of it. He once more commented on the coinage which was circulated far and wide "of much better make and Value than Government can afford, of these, new ones, I sent for Sixpenny-worth." He astutely observed that the sight of a place surrounded by brick kilns was a sure sign of success and noted the newly paved streets; the new church (Christ Church) although without reference to Charles Roe, and the silk mills of "good Account". His abode for the evening was none other than the *Old Angel Inn* under the proprietorship of Samuel Goodwin where he happily attacked "a boild Buttock of A Bull" commenting, with slight acrimony, "(such a thing as I have seen in Porridge Island) but Hunger is not refined."

However some two years later, during a return tour of 1792, there was no containing Byng's disgruntled self and his words flowed forceful as ever, "I put up at the best tho' a bad inn (where I have been before), The Angel, where the house was so crouded by a grand dinner, – that I betook myself into a small room behind the bar, desiring to be serv'd from the remains of the grand dinner". He asked, . . . "of whom is the Club formed?". The reply was that elderly women of the town had formed a Sick & Burial Society and had met to "settle their accounts and enjoy themselves over a good dinner", from which Byng benefited considerably by being served one of their "good" hams.

The next day it was time for sightseeing and he began, more or less, with a reiteration of his comments from two years earlier adding a further observation that the good health of the residents must have been due to the number of 'water-carters', but his composure was soon to be disturbed. Byng had decided on a visit to the copper works on Macclesfield Common which, like many other manufactories of the period, were open for public viewing. It was not an easy journey, even by horse, and having descended the steep decline of Mill Street he decided to visit a silk mill in the lower part of town, which could possibly have been one originally part of the Roe complex. Evidently he was accompanied by someone, who was more than likely a fellow traveller also staying at *The Angel*, as he wrote, "but when I came to Mr. Roe's great copper works, we were refused admittance, from the want of a ticket which we should have applied for: now was this not very provoking? And to have to trudge a mile back to Mr. R's banking house. So I was properly peevish at the inn; where they knew my intentions: but the weird women had bewitch'd them." Small wonder Byng was annoyed, for the bank was only one minute's walk from *The Angel Inn*, just along the next block.

"Horses in hand, we return'd to the copper works; where I took an accurate, and gratifying survey, of their mixing, melting and flat'ning the copper; a most unwholesome employ, for which the workmen, I think, are meanly pay'd, as the best earn but 14s. per week."

Another contemporary description of the works provides a far more comprehensive account of the procedures. The 'Smelting House', where the copper ore was first melted, was a large building with an open "counter-yard" in the middle about 30 yards square. Great quantities of shot or pellets were made; these would be for the production of brass, as the copper would more easily absorb the calamine if it was in small pieces. Workmen also made large white bricks for constructing the ovens (the most likely use would be for the linings as these, of course, were constantly in need of repair) and also big deep pots to melt the ore in, likened to "garden pots, but much larger".

The large windmill was said to be between the smelting house and the brass houses and used for grinding the ore. This is somewhat misleading; the smelting house was higher up on the Common, nearer the collieries, whereas the windmill and adjacent brass works were on a lower level and a little to the south-west of the smelting house. The mill ground the roasted or calcined zinc ore, calamine, not copper ore. An early 19th century engraving of the stone built windmill shows it to be "a tower mill . . . containing four floors, with a dome shaped cap and four common (cloth-set) anti-clockwise rotating sails, which were operated from ground level."

Close by the windmill, mention is made of a long one storey building comprising the calamine houses. Here calamine was washed and filtered several times suggesting that it was received in a raw state, in all probability brought from Bonsall in Derbyshire. After this process it would have needed to be dried and roasted in the calcining ovens before crushing between the French burr stones of the windmill; however no mention is made of the roasting process, but a later sale notice confirms that there was another long range of buildings for drying and storing the calamine.

The brass houses were seen as "lofty buildings where brass wire, pan bottoms and large quantities of brass nails were made and also copper sheets for ships." This description is surprising, suggesting that the inquirer had asked what articles were produced from the brass and copper without actually seeing the manufacture, and had assumed that they were made on Macclesfield Common, whereas the brass houses were where the brass was made and then poured into moulds forming ingots or plates for convenient transportation. The moulds for the brass plates were made from casting stones shipped from Redruth in Cornwall, otherwise known as 'Cornish Moor Stones', so it would have been convenient to cast the pan bottoms in the immediate vicinity of the brass houses, but production of the other items on this site has to be speculative.

There was a nail makers' workshop close by the smelting house; however the brass wire was primarily produced at the Havannah site where brass bolts were also made. There too were the copper rolling mills for the production of the sheets intended for sheathing vessels, and all using the brass and copper from Macclesfield Common, hence the company's investment in "Turnpike Securities" with regard to the road leading south from Macclesfield (A523) in the direction of Bosley and Havannah.

It is the Bosley site which has always held the reputation for nail making. The brass nails were a considerable size, at least a foot in length with enormous heads the size of a small plate, and were being used to secure the timbers of wooden ships instead of iron ones, thus eliminating contamination on contact with the copper sheathing. The copper sheets were secured with copper nails, some of which were possibly being produced on Macclesfield Common in addition to Bosley when orders warranted it, otherwise one would have expected the nailers on the Common to have been producing ordinary nails both for the domestic market and the company's own use.

The description ends with a reference to three large reservoirs of water "for the supply of the works" which were located in front of the brass houses, together with a row of dwelling-houses for workmen. There were actually 29 houses, each with a garden, and situated at the southern end of the site, presumably in the hope of encouraging prevailing winds to carry away any obnoxious fumes and smoke, though one can well imagine that the stench must have been quite overwhelming at times, but not in the same league as that experienced by those living close to the smelting house, particularly in the early days before copper refining only was taking place.

Neither John Byng nor the anonymous visitor mention the workshops of the blacksmiths, carpenters, coopers etc. nor the Assay Office, perhaps this is because from a visitor's point of view the brass works were considered more interesting and less fumy than the smelting house site. The Roe & Co. employees were, of course, comparatively well paid in relation to other similar industries and could earn bonuses for good work. Byng's comment on the subject of pay was obviously a general one, appreciating the magnitude of skill and stamina required to perfect the different processes essential in the production of high quality copper and brass. He soon departed south for Staffordshire, but sadly left no record of his dealings at Messrs. Hawkins & Mills bank.

* * * * * * *

In addition to Edward Hawkins's banking enterprise and civic commitments to Macclesfield, including his mayoralty of 1782-83, he was elected a governor of Macclesfield Grammar School on 8th November 1785 as a replacement for Rev. Peter Mayer who had died. The Grammar School was experiencing a period of modernisation and needed someone with good business acumen to control its investments and help realise its full potential.

On 10th November 1788 Hawkins reported to a committee, formed to survey all the school properties, that William Roe was willing to purchase a plot of land in Chestergate owned by the school, containing two houses, a garden and smithy for £400; this was accepted and the conveyance made in 1789. Also the school profits of £368 1 7d. for the year ending in 1788 were to be paid into the "Macclesfield Bank", which would be that of Hawkins, Mills & Co. At the same time Hawkins was one of a three man committee instructed to find an additional master for teaching reading, writing and arithmetic, and an appropriate house for the new master to live in. On 7th June 1790 Hawkins was able to report that a suitable house and schoolroom had been found and a lease prepared. It was at this meeting that Abraham Mills joined his fellow copper company and banking partner on the Board of School Governors.

By nature Mills was not a parochial man and therefore only involved himself in Macclesfield affairs just so far as it was necessary. He was never really part of any great decision making within the company, although his name appears in several different contexts, but this is the clue to his most valuable asset – public relations. He was the one used to solicit business with the Navy Board; a feasible commission bearing in mind the Plymouth connections. And his choice as 'envoy', sent to explore the possibilities for proposed new ventures, seems to have satisfied his somewhat nomadic disposition. This newly acquired diplomatic role, coupled with his rapidly increasing knowledge of the mining industry, provided him with yet another diversification, a desire for academic recognition.

In 1789, at the age of 50 years, Mills presented himself as a not inconsequential geological expert when he wrote to Richard Kirwin, Fellow of the Royal Society and Member of the Royal Irish Academy. Kirwin had produced a paper on "coal-mines in the neighbourhood of Newcaftle and Whitehaven" and had inadvertently extended his observations to apply to English collieries in general. Mills wrote to correct the supposition and included a very detailed account and diagram of the Blakelow colliery on Macclesfield Common, one mile south-east of the town. Kirwin accepted the correction and, by way of apology, graciously put forward Mills's paper which was read to the Royal Irish Academy on 5th December 1789.

The method used at Blakelow was to drive an adit or sough from the lower ground so that it cut into the coal seam as deeply as possible. This allowed the water to drain off and then the level could be worked as far as possible until "interrupted by a fault". The decision would then be taken to sink a shaft (called a pit) from the surface above, down to the level, to follow the new line of the seam. The collier, using his pick, cut out the coal from the floor first, but only about 4 ins in thickness, and then, with wedges, broke it from the roof. The coal was cut out to about 3 yards and a pillar, about ³/₄ of a yard wide, left to support the roof. The collier lay on his side wearing a piece of leather on his knee called a 'cap', one on his thigh called a 'pilch' and another on his arm called an 'elbow patch' and wore only a pair of 'flannel drawers' (i.e. pants similar to pyjama trousers but made from a thick kind of woollen fabric).The coal was put in a basket and dragged by the collier on a little sledge to the foot of the shaft; not an easy task as he slid along on his side, feet first, dragging the sledge behind him. The basket was then lifted to the surface by a horse gin or whimsey.

Often the roof required extra support and a lot of timber was used underground, particularly as the coal pillars were hewn away periodically to allow a better flow of fresh air to circulate. Also expensive machinery was used to draw off the water which continued to seep into the workings. The seams were less than 2 ft in places, but the main seam proved to be of good quality coal and therefore extraction was considered well worthwhile.

Mills, seemingly inspired by his success, particularly as Kirwin referred to him as "an eminent miner in Cheshire", began to involve himself in more geological explorations. Strange as it may seem the extant Roe & Co. records give no indication that his newly acquired expertise was initially put to use by them, all suggestions are that William Roe and Robert Hodgson remained the two principal partners with sufficient competency to keep control of any mining surveys; subsequent mining leases always bear the name of either one or the other of them but not so Abraham Mills. Proof of the Mills paradox is perhaps best demonstrated by the extraordinary situation with regard to the mining on Islay.

* * * * * * *

The initial Roe & Co. interest in the Scottish island's mineral potential had possibly been aroused by Brian Hodgson Jnr. when accompanying his son to Glasgow in November 1783. Knowing that the Cerrig-y-Bleiddia lease on Parys Mountain was drawing to a close, he must have been keen to hear of any prospects in the region, particularly as Tissington & Co. had been involved in the Leadhills area.

Lead mines on Islay had been known for centuries; local myths and legends had attributed their existence to the Norsemen, but the first recorded mention of 1549 appears in *The Book of Islay* compiled in the late Victorian Period.

By 1680 Sir John Campbell was the lessor, but the complicated agreements under which sublessees were subsequently to operate was to play havoc with finances and any future long term plans for investors. From 1720 to 1760 various groups from Glasgow succumbed to the difficulties of the situation, until finally in 1763 Charles Freebairn took over the mines on behalf of himself and two Campbells. He predicted that it would take five years to bring the mines to a profitable state and by 1769 was maintaining his theory having recently made two important discoveries.

The first was at the farm of Mulreesh, inspiring him to write "at present there is not a more promising work in Brittain, not one carried on at so moderate an expence". The second was a vein of copper at the farm of Kilslevan, referred to by Freebairn as "the most promising sort I ever saw in Isla". This he had begun to work and after three days had retrieved a hundredweight of ore and traced the vein for a quarter of a mile further. But despite all optimism progress was slow and in fact had reached such a critical stage by 1770 that the laird demanded a report, which was not satisfactory. Shortly afterwards Freebairn disappeared for some time, which leaves one to deduce that the cost of extraction needed to be addressed and he had gone in search of financial backing; at one stage he had considered offering shares in the operation.

Meanwhile the laird commissioned a second survey from Alexander Shirriff, manager for Lord Hopetoun at the Leadhills mines on the mainland. Shirriff reported on seven lead mines and one copper mine with calculations showing that the Islay lead expenses were less than half those of Leadhills; he corroborated Freebairn's expectations, considering the prospects good, so when the latter returned work continued. From February 1769 to October 1774, 260 tons of bar lead (pigs), 72 tons of lead ore and 90 tons of lead slag were produced.

Towards the end of this period the next visitor to arrive on the island was Thomas Pennant engaged in collating information for his proposed book *A Tour of Scotland and Voyage to the Hebrides*. He arrived in Islay on the 1st July 1772 to be "hospitably received" by Charles Freebairn who lived in Freeport near Port Askaig, close by the air furnace where the ore was smelted. (Today this latter site is said to be occupied by the Caol Ila distillery). When visiting the mines next day Pennant discovered that the copper was "mixed" with the lead ore "which occasions expense and trouble in the separation". (The copper deposits were in the form of chalcopyrite). He described the lead ore as good, existing in veins of various thicknesses which, after smelting, sold as pigs. He was told that the copper content was 33 pounds per hundred (whether or not this indicates 33% or 33 pounds per hundredweight is difficult to determine, but the implication is one of a rich ore) with 40 ounces of silver from every ton of metal. Freebairn, no doubt anxious to present a lucrative enterprise, let it be known that under his management he had "brought in six thousand pounds".

Richard Crawford, a Glasgow merchant, was certainly impressed and in 1776 began financing the Islay mining expenses by way of loans, whilst at the same time taking rough and dressed ore for sale, that is until 1781 when a legal battle ensued. Crawford had obviously been kept in ignorance of the fact that Freebairn had borrowed "considerable sums" from an Edinburgh banker. A statement by Isaac Grant, Writer to the Signet, declared that from the mining accounts he had inspected, the gross profit had never covered the cost of operations. Crawford had evidently been deluded, and sorting out the debts took time, but the outcome seems to have resulted in one of the Campbells, Walter of Shawfield, becoming owner and lessor of the land, for it is from the latter that Roe & Co. obtained their leases.

From all accounts the prospects were good and any previous failings the results of bad management, therefore it is easy to understand why Roe & Co., with their vast knowledge of mining and adequate finances, took on the challenge with confidence. In all, three leases were executed, dated the 18th May and 14th and 20th June 1786 and the three Roe & Co. representatives were Robert Hodgson of Congleton, Thomas Smyth of Liverpool and Edward Hawkins of Macclesfield. (Unfortunately there is no trace of the original leases but it is possible to gain much information from a copy of the "Renounciation" document drawn up in 1799 but not recorded in the Books of Council and Session until 1803.)

The overall leasing was, in fact, taken from 12th November 1785, the date said to have been the time of entry on site. The stipulations are unusual; firstly, on or before 1st July 1786, the company had to ascertain a position for a fixed pillar to be taken as the centre of a circle six miles in diameter; when put in place the pillar had to be given an inscription "declaring it the center". Mining was limited to the area within the circle but only on Walter Campbell's land.

There is no written indication of the position of the stone yet a large standing stone close by Finlaggan Farm, is exactly three miles south-east of Port Askaig and a half mile to the east of Mulreesh and would qualify well for the marker, given its exact distance of 3 miles from the nearest point on the coast. Under the terms of the lease the company had guaranteed to drive two levels at Mulreesh and Gartness, subject to the normal leasing arrangements. This lease was for the usual local term of 36 years but no other details are specified, however as subsequent extant leases were also for 36 years (extending to 42 years if necessary) it is not unreasonable to assume that the Roe & Co. "tack" payment was the same as for those i.e.

First twelve years	$1/12$ share or dish.
Second twelve years	$1/10$ share or dish.
Third twelve years	$1/8$ share or dish.

In addition to the mining a lease was granted for the farm called 'Persaboles' (today Persabus), situated one mile south-east of Port Askaig, but it did not include "a small Cottage lately built upon the Sound, with a small park around it."

As evidenced by James Watt's letter to Matthew Boulton on 16th August 1785, negotiations had already taken place some time earlier, for Robert Hodgson had by then just returned from Scotland after finalising matters on behalf of the company.

Mulreeshhad been worked by Freebairn from 1760, sometimes with vigour, but only spasmodically as allowed by the geological complexities. Islay is overlaid by a massive bed of limestone about 50 ft in depth in which the mineral veins occur, in particular stretching from Port Askaig south-westwardly to Bridgend. The region, once subjected to volcanic action, has outcrops of igneous rocks, and earth movements have created folds in the strata. Modern surveying techniques have revealed very little depth to the striated mineral lodes, but where the folding has created intersections, richer pockets of ore occur which, when discovered by the 18th century prospectors, led them to believe that a rich substantial vein of ore was about to be revealed, especially around the village of Ballygrant where the ribboned veins are most numerous.

Ballygrant is on the main road between Bridgend and Port Askaig. To reach Mulreesh, about 2 miles south-west of the port, one has to travel along the main road, and about half way between Port Askaig and Ballygrant branch off in a northerly direction, either at the tiny village of Kiells or a nearby track. Mulreesh is only half a mile from the road and there the remains of a dam and sluice, once used to work the mill and dressing plant, are still evident. The 1770 survey reported workings to a depth of 22 fathoms (132 ft) along the main vein for a distance of 14 fathoms (84 ft). Subsequent workings have reached a depth of 240 ft by using four levels each 60 ft apart, but how much of this relates to Roe & Co. is not known.

The Gartness mine, now difficult to position, has been taken as that situated about half a mile south-east of Ballygrant, on what was said to be Gartness Farm but now absent from modern maps. There is a line of old workings indicated by flooded shafts and subsidence extending about a quarter of a mile along a vein, reported as only 2 ft wide, containing galena (lead) and native silver. Just 150 yards to the west another vein shows signs of open-cast workings and small trials.

It is difficult to believe that Roe & Co. did not work the mine at Kilslevan, or at least carry out trials there, for it is little more than a mile north-east of Gartness and the only one where copper ore had been discovered. Just one company comment on the Islay mining is to be found in a letter addressed to Dr. Busfield on 30th April 1788, "In Islay there is some Ore raised and more got in the bottoms ready for raising as soon as proper Machinery and good weather (both rare in that Climate) will enable the Agent to set about it." The agent was apparently a Mr. Hutton who, by November, was asked to select from the Maxwell & Co. stock copper which would sell in Glasgow, despatching the remainder to Liverpool. But whatever ore was retrieved by the company it seems most likely to have been predominently lead with a little silver, for in the month of July 1790 they relinquished their occupation of the mines. At first Walter Campbell took out a Summons, but afterwards agreed to accept the surrender of the lease and dropped the claims after the "Renounciation" document had been prepared and signed by all the three representative partners.

Given that Abraham Mills is in no way mentioned in connection with the mining activities on Islay and that his name was not included on the lease as representing the company, it is surprising to discover his article 'Observations on the Whyn Dykes of Ilay' addressed to John Lloyd Esq. F.R.S. appearing in *The New Annual Register of History, Politics and Literature For the Year 1790*. It is evident from the content that mining had ceased on the island prior to his visit, which must have taken place, therefore, after the month of July.

* * * * * * *

On the previous 28th May Mills had been instructed to apply to the Bishop of Bangor for a 'fresh' lease of the Llandudno Mine (suggesting that trials had been unsuccessful and needed to be carried out elsewhere on the Bishop's moeity), and in June, as previously mentioned, he had attended Macclesfield Grammar School when confirmed a Governor. After his appearance at the A.G. M. of the 10th August, the next scheduled meeting was not until 11th November, which would have provided ample time for his own private wanderings. From November 1790 to March 1791 the copper company held a regular monthly meeting with Mills always in attendance, not only in Macclesfield but twice in Warrington and once in Liverpool. As his 'Observations' patently took place in favourable weather conditions, this suggests a mid-August to September or possibly October tour, but nowhere does he reveal his association with the mining concern.

The subject matter is contained in two letters, the second of which is the most significant because of its background mining information. Taking into account the fact that geology was in its early infancy, the descriptions, by modern standards, would be well suited for inclusion in a sophisticated rambler's guide, but Mills, however, was assuredly purporting to be something of a geological expert. The "whyn dykes" of Islay are the black volcanic outcrops of basalt which litter the landscape, often forming ridges; and after ploughing through a somewhat tedious commentary on the terrain in general, Mills eventually took a boat from Freeport "intending to vifit the cave Eamawr on the weftern fide of the ifland". Arriving on a white shingly beach he walked three miles over moors and pastures across the north-western area of the island, but returned to the beach for his boat trip back to Freeport. He next began his tour of the mining areas.

This time Mills set out for Shinegart, a lead mine about a mile and a half west of Ballygrant and close by the southern end of Loch Finlaggan. His route took him close by Persabus Farm where he commented on a very large 'Whyn Dyke' and other features, but soon reached the mine. It had been included in Shirriff's 1770 survey as having a vein of ore 8 ins in width yet had been abandoned because of problems with flooding. The information provided by Mills suggests that Roe & Co. had reworked the site but to no avail:

> "This vein had been formerly worked; but, when the old workings were cleared out, was found not worth purfuing."

Today evidence remains of the old shaft together with a dam and sluice.

For his next perambulation Mills again passed Persabus, but on this occasion was heading for the Gartness lead mine in the centre of the limestone. Once more his remarks suggest mining by Roe & Co., for having described the largest dyke he had ever seen, he mentions two shafts which had been cut through it, Abel's and Hodgson's, the latter at least must have been worked on behalf of the Macclesfield company. And his further comment "much work has been done here, but at present there are no great profpects of fussefs", had obviously been learnt from personal knowledge gained within the company.

Mills next proceeded to the lead mines at Ardachie, just to the south of Gartness, but his only mention of a vein "which has formerly been much wrought" and had in fact been included in Shirriff's 1770 report, seems to indicate no involvement by Roe & Co.

* * * * * * *

Although the company lost interest in the area and concentrated all efforts in North Wales, Robert Hodgson did not, for by 1793 his name is included as a subscriber to the Crinan Canal scheme authorised by Act of Parliament in that year. Of all the partners Robert Hodgson is perhaps the one who appears to have had the most dispassionate nature, yet like the others took on civic responsibilities and was elected mayor of Congleton in 1789. By this time he had four young sons and two surviving daughters and apart from company business concentrated his efforts on his collieries. As in the Roe family, where William and Catherine had a special bonding, Robert and his wife Mildred had close ties with Bishop Beilby Porteus and his wife Margaret, particularly as the latter were childless.

Robert's eldest son, Robert Jnr., a pupil of Macclesfield Grammar School, would soon enter Peterhouse College, Cambridge at the early age of 15 years. Because of the complicated family tree young Robert was both the great nephew and nephew of the Bishop. He was to be especially influenced by his uncle, becoming first priest then a deacon of London (1796), Dean of Chester (1816-20) and finally Chaplain to the King and rector of St. George's, Hanover Square.

On leaving Chester in 1787 Beilby had become Bishop of London and continued his considerable work for the underprivileged, in particular giving assistance to the poorer London parishes. With persuasion, his opposition to Sunday entertainments (the latter generally promoted by the wealthy) had a successful outcome, and he would eventually find himself with the onerous task of preparing Princess Charlotte (born 7th January 1796) for her role as the future Queen of England. The respect and admiration which he commanded would eventually translate itself into a substantial book by his nephew after the Bishop's death.

Meanwhile, possibly because of Robert Hodgson's personal connections with Chester and the increasing company activities and speculations in North Wales, Roe & Co. had been contemplating moving operations from Liverpool to Chester.

28
ON THE MOVE

. . . in this moment there is life and food
For future years.

By the late 18th century the trade of Chester had long been eclipsed by that of Liverpool, but nevertheless remained of sufficient volume to warrant retention of its "custom-house with a collector, comptroller, searcher and twenty inferior officers to prevent smuggling". The largest part of the trade was with Ireland, as Pennant pointed out, after perusing the Customs records of vessels entering and leaving the port.

A contemporary description of the city paints a glowing account of its attributes. The wall, 20 ft high and 7 ft wide, had become the 'Grand Promenade' of the 'Beaus and Belles' on fine evenings and a healthy walk for 'Valetudinarians' each morning. The shops and galleries were extolled upon, some adopted by 'Loungers' on rainy afternoons. Evening entertainments included balls and the theatre, with the latter attracting 'Good Performers' from the London stage.

Race days were more popular than ever, still combining with the great fairs and drawing crowds of visitors over their five day duration. Tradesmen and merchants of all descriptions, particularly those from Bristol and Dublin, flooded into the city from considerable distances to attend the events.

Chester had also grown into an important centre for sales of ore, as indicated by general correspondence in 1783. Nor did Roe & Co. miss the opportunities provided; on 5th January 1790 William Roe was asked to attend the sale of Mr. Vaughan's ore at Chester, after Thomas, one of the Ovens family from Toxteth, had travelled to the mine at 'Dolgelly' in North Wales to take samples.

John Byng, whilst travelling through North Wales during 1781 had mentioned Dolgellau where he stayed at an inn:

> "Our company of today was a young clerk of Liverpool; to which town there being much trade carried on from this neighbourhood, many young men come here, to learn the language and arrange the business."

Incidentally, three years later, whilst on a similar trek, he happened to visit Plas Newydd and wrote.

> "I shou'd mention that in Ld. Uxbridge's chapel are kept wheels, carriages and all kind of timber: and that it stinks, most abundantly of drying sea-fish. How devout an age do we live in !!"

On that occasion he subsequently passed St. Asaph where, on high ground he visited a smelter close to lead mines and observed the process. He ascertained that the smelter belonged to a Mrs. Vicars (actually Mary Vigars) at which 30 tons of lead, value £17 per ton. were smelted each week. He also visited neighbouring collieries, assuming them to be "likewise

Historic houses in Chester.

her property" where he saw coal "craned up from the pitts", commenting on its cheapness at 5/- per cart load.

(Mrs. Vigars had inherited the Bagillt smelter and equipment from her deceased husband, Henry, a former mayor of Chester and steward to the Grosvenor family; he had bought the enterprise when the Smedleys were declared bankrupt in 1779. A letter of January 1783 confirms annuity payments, totally £15, paid by Mrs. Vigars's agent to Charles Roe's widow in respect of a lead account for 1781).

An interesting feature of Chester at this period was that the weekly markets, held Wednesdays and Saturdays on Northgate Street, were largely supplied from Wales. Some 300 or 400 Welsh women, dressed in blue felt hats, striped woollen gowns and cloaks, each with a basket full of home produce covered with a napkin, lined Bridge Street. On Fridays the women supplied the coal market; each loaded and drove a one horse cart into the street until, arranged in rows, they sold their coals at 6d. per cwt. This coal was obviously for domestic consumption, but Roe & Co., whilst considering the relocation of the Toxteth smelters to the vicinity of Chester, must have taken into account the accessibility of sufficiently high quality supplies from the Wrexham area, as the leases acquired by Charles Roe from Thomas Brock were the inheritance of William Roe from the time of his father's death.

In the intervening period William had allowed a certain Richard Kirk the lease and contract for working part of the Bryn Mally colliery known as Hallcock Isa, but Kirk had unfortunately run into difficulties, accumulating arrears of both rent and coal duties. William, eager as always to overcome problems, thought out a complicated financial solution to assist all concerned, particularly as circumstantial evidence suggests that the Roes and Kirks had a long-standing acquaintance.

* * * * * * *

Richard Kirk was a member of the Kirk family of Chapel-en-le-Firth, only 12 miles north-east of Macclesfield, but just over the Derbyshire border; there, his uncle, Henry, owned the estate called Martinside. What inspired Richard to move to the village of Gwersyllt near Wrexham, is difficult to deduce; however, according to a local historian he is first mentioned there in 1775 being "of or near the Wheatsheaf", this neatly coincides with a lease he obtained from Richard, Earl of Grosvenor for a stone quarry called Pool Mouth in Broughton. About that period Thomas Brock divided his nearby estate and built Bryn Mally Hall together with several cottages and, whilst Brock's daughter was married to the famous architect John Wood the younger, in time, Frances, the second daughter of Richard Kirk, would marry an equally gifted architect, Thomas Penson. One cannot help but speculate that at Charles Roe's suggestion Richard Kirk had been offered the contract to supply quarry stones for the Brock building project, or that the Roes had used the Kirks to assist them with some of their own.

A decade later Kirk owned a dwelling house, buildings, a garden and two acres of land in Gwersyllt, four cottages and a smithy in Broughton and land in Brymbo, one acre of which had been separated from the rest and a house built on it. His financial difficulties seem to have arisen when he decided to speculate in the local lead mines, acquiring a $1/8$th share of St. Catharine's near Mold in 1786 and a $1/4$th share of Chye at Minera in 1787. (It is no longer possible to identify these mines). Coal was, of course, needed for the initial smelting and in 1787 Kirk had taken a half share in the Broughton colliery, but it seems likely that he was experiencing problems due to flooding and so invested in Bryn Mally two years later. Meanwhile he became indebted to William Roe for £320 2s. and the same sum to Richard Barker of Chester, one of the trustees of the lately deceased Thomas Brock. William's solution was for Kirk to pay off the debt to the Brock estate (for which Edward Hawkins was seconded as trustee for William, presumably to advance money from the bank to cover the payment) and then transfer to William property as collateral to cover the loan, with an additional interest charge of £52. The loan was then to be paid off in instalments of £50 each year on the 29th September.

An Indenture covering the whole complicated legalities was signed by William Roe and Richard Kirk on 17th April 1789. During that year Richard's uncle Henry died and he inherited the Martinside estate, but by 1792 had mortgaged part of the land to Richard Barker for £200; his difficulties were far from over: the advantage was with William Roe who now had control of additional coal and lead supplies from which the company would shortly profit.

* * * * * * *

A crisis was now looming in the copper industry as the 'Great Treaty' of March 1785, between Thomas Williams and the Cornish Metal Company, had stood little chance of success. The Cornishmen soon found themselves unable to sell an ever increasing stock pile of copper, whilst Williams's sales took priority. By 1787 relations between Boulton and Williams were strained and with resistance and rioting growing in Cornwall, Williams closed his Birmingham warehouse and offered his share of the market to Cornwall; Boulton and Watt, however, considered it but a token, for they were convinced he was still supplying his agent surreptitiously at a cut price. The year 1787 proved to be extremely difficult for Cornwall till on 11th October an agreement was reached with Williams to sell ores in a fairer ratio, but the Cornish miners refused. Finally in November Williams's ruthless tactics saw him triumph over all Vivian's efforts for independence, and Thomas Harrison, still agent to Lord Uxbridge, wrote "every ounce of copper produced by Cornwall is to be sold by Mr. Williams for five years and no other man upon earth is to sell an atom of it . . ."

The impact of this coup would not be felt for some time, but when it did begin in April 1789 Thomas Williams, on behalf of the syndicate, would utterly monopolise the East India purchases of copper for the following three years to April 1792. (In August 1790 Roe & Co. commented on the "disadvantageous state of the copper trade".) Williams's total ore sales for the period from April 1789 to April 1792 realised £77,377 17s. for 17,130 tons (i.e. just over £4 10s. per ton, a surprisingly high figure in the circumstances, suggesting that he was intent on raising copper prices). Ironically by the autumn of 1792 Abraham Mills would be tendering lead to the East India Company.

Under the circumstances Roe & Co., having anticipated the impending 'scourge', although at the time benefiting considerably from the copper contract with the Navy, began to concentrate on brass production; likewise the Cheadle Company.

On 29th November 1788, at a Macclesfield Copper Company meeting held in Buxton, John Denman and William Smedley were confirmed as joint agents for conducting the Flintshire calamine concern, and commission of 6s. 0d. per ton was to be divided equally between them. Although Smedley was to keep the accounts, all remittances were to be made to the partnership of Messrs. Denman and Smedley, and both had to be present when payments were made to avoid 'anomolies'.

Each month an account of all calamine bought, weighed, dressed and shipped, and all recorded payments had to be submitted to Macclesfield. Hugh Thomas was made responsible for inspecting "the picking at the Mines" and all the calamine bought, for which he was paid 15s. 0d. per week. He was also charged with ensuring that the dressing and calcining processes produced cleaner calamine than previously for delivery to the River Bank Works near Holywell. A further instruction related to the 'Crops & Weak' calamine (inferior) which had to be shipped in the proportion ²/₃rds to Macclesfield and ¹/₃rd to Cheadle, but care had to be taken to keep it separate from the rest and recorded as such on the invoice.

Joseph Simpson, still in charge of the Shropshire calamine supplies, also received orders to submit his accounts monthly to Macclesfield. Six months later a plan and estimate were immediately requested to enable a pair of rollers to be installed at the Holywell calamine works, presumably to improve the crushing of the calcined ore.

By August 1789 further development of the River Bank Works was underway when it was decided to construct a lead furnace, slag hearth and a hammer for buckering (i.e. to reduce to powder) the calamine. The lead furnace appears to be the outcome of William Roe's financial arrangements with Richard Kirk and resulted in both Denman and Smedley each receiving a salary of £50 per annum from 10th October 1790 for their additional duties in attending the lead smelting works. Unfortunately John Denman died during the summer of 1791 and the company recorded their sincere regrets for "the loss of our late valuable friend & Agent"; it was confirmed that his son William would be appointed joint agent in place of his father.

An interesting description of the River Bank complex would later appear in Thomas Pennant's *History of Holywell Parish* published 1796:

> "On the side of the rill (i.e. the small rivulet of Nant-hil-brwc) stand the works called the River Bank, established on my land, by leafe dated September 22, 1785, granted to Meffrs, William Roe and Edward Hawkins. Thefe buildings are employed for the double purposes of calcining calamine for the brafs-works at Cheadle and Macclesfield, and for the fmelting lead-ore. It has the advantage of a fmall ftream, which improves the operation of the latter.
>
> It turns two wheels, one of which is twenty-four feet in diameter, and from the size and breadth makes a noble appearance. At each end of thefe wheels is a balance wheel; one of them fets the great refining bellows in motion, and the other that of the flag-hearth.
>
> Here is alfo a curious contrivance for faving the calx of the lead-ore, which would otherwife have gone away in fmoke. It befides leffens the bad effects on the grounds above. For this purpofe two brick flues have been conftructed, one from each furnace; each of them is horizontal, and is fupported by three arches, and over each is a channel to contain a fmall current of water, for the purpofe of turning the wheels, and alfo to condenfe the fmoke in its paffage. Thefe flues converge, and meet a little beyond the third arch, and terminate in the condenfing room, to the walls of which the calx adheres. This room is opened three times a-year: the calx is taken out, and re-smelted with fome profit.
>
> The two flues, in iffuing out of the building, are united in one, and are continued, forming a right angle for a very confiderable way. Out of the end rifes a vertical flue, forty-three feet high, out of which the fmoke iffues. The length of the horizontal flues which pafs over the arches is fifty-feven feet; of the fingle one which paffes from the room which catches the calx, is two hundred and ten feet."

The advantage gained by Roe & Co. in expanding their Holywell site must be reflected in the mineral exportation figures of 1791 for the port of Chester:

	Foreign	Coastwise
Lead	540 tons	4,497 tons
Lead ore	150 tons	761 tons
Copper	Nil	933 tons
Brass	Nil	164 tons

The expansion of the River Bank works with its increased lead production was obviously not the only reason for the intended evacuation of the Toxteth site. The proposal to move must have been contemplated early in 1789 and was most likely prompted by what appears to have been a somewhat stifling situation arising within the port of Liverpool, created by politics and rivalries. The fact that Thomas Williams now had carte blanche to dictate copper prices in the town, could not have helped matters. But before any move could take place the first important obstacle to overcome was to obtain relinquishment of the Toxteth lease.

* * * * * * *

The election of Thomas Smyth as Mayor on 18th October 1789 provided the perfect opportunity for action; within five days he had written to Lord Molyneux expressing Liverpool Corporation's desire to purchase the Roe & Co. lease for Harrington. Smyth and the Earl seem to have been associates on as much a social as formal level, for Smyth conveyed his wife's compliments to Lady Sefton. Initially Smyth had personally approached the agent, Webster, but must have been asked by him to write formally to the Earl setting out all the details. Smyth's subsequent correspondence not only fulfills the request, but clearly indicates why he had transferred his $^1/_{12}$th share in the copper works to his brother-in-law John Pendred Scott on 20th August 1789 (for the considerable sum of £6,689 12 6d.).

The gist of the argument was that Liverpool Corporation wished to continue the vast dockland project to the south, and intended creating a large basin and dock at Harrington which, it was estimated, would greatly add value to Lord Molyneux's adjoining lands. However, it was vital that the lease be given to the Corporation "in perpetuity" otherwise it would be imprudent to spend public money on "commodious new docks and quays if at a later date they were to become private property."

On 21st December Thomas Smyth wrote a second letter, this time addressed to Webster; it included an invitation to breakfast at a quarter past nine on the following 26th January, after which they were to meet with the Docks Committee. The Committee had already decided to take a tough stance and Smyth accordingly passed on their sentiments, explaining that if the lease was not forthcoming the intended "Corporation Estate, called the Queen's Docks" would be rejected and improvements begun north of the town, although he thought the former better suited the community. He commented, "the trifling Share I hold in the Lease subjects (small as it is) my Advice to proceed from Motives of Interest, but I solemnly disavow them on this Occafion . . ." In conclusion he gave a firm promise never to broach the subject again as he felt certain that all his efforts would be rewarded.

As if in anticipation of success William Roe was authorised to reduce the number of employees at the Liverpool works. Another indicator of the proposed move was the appearance of the series of Roe & Co. halfpence pieces with *Chester* on the obverse, and the reverse identical to those for Macclesfield (produced by Kempson) i.e. embossed with three castles encircled by the four directions of the compass. It does seem possible that Hawkins Mills & Co. had in mind the idea of opening a branch bank in the city. Another important pointer to consider is the election of Robert Hodgson as a Common Councilman of Chester on 25th October 1792 (although it has been suggested that this refers to another Robert Hodgson of Doddlespool Hall on the Staffordshire and Cheshire border); this would have been an essential part of the strategy pending the removal of the centre of operations from Liverpool.

In the meantime the Earl of Sefton took legal advice on the proposed transfer of the lease, and was presented with a very comprehensive assessment of the situation, including a detailed plan of the area in question. The complicated legalities in respect of the lease originally granted to Charles Roe were reiterated, particularly the contemplated development of the town of Harrington. The advantages to Roe & Co. as lessees were judged against those as appropriate to the Earl.

The company had paid the rental for the first 16 years (i.e. to 29th September 1790) and spent £2,000 "in filling up and Inclosing" the sea shore and were asking £8,000 for the remaining three original lots. However, the proposal to build 177 houses at a cost of £50,000 was still an unfulfilled part of the covenant, but given the time scale involved was not as yet a breach of covenant.

The various observations included the important criterion that only "Mr. Roe" had the right to reclaim land below his lots out of the River Mersey (made possible by the shallow shelf extending to the south from Pluckington Bank) on which an important quay development was possible which, of course, would pass to Liverpool Corporation if the lease was transferred. Obviously this was the Corporation's intention in acquiring the lease, so that if the Corporation as lessee went to the expense of walling up and filling in the area adjoining its new docking facilities, in a few years time the flourishing trade would result in seeing that end of Liverpool next to Toxteth "covered with Buildings".

However, the final legal opinion, with its ominous tone, seems to have persuaded Lord Sefton to retain the status quo as regards the lease; it was considered that despite the Corporation's desire to enclose and create a new dock, "they want only to put old Ships in . . . and not their Loaded Ships as it does not seem likely they would send them into Toxteth Park to carry the Trade there to pay Duty, while they had any roome in their own Docks." It therefore seemed inevitable that the Corporation would build small houses in the area encouraging labourers to move in, which would be a burden on the poor rates and "create a bad Neighbourhood".

Roe & Co. must have been bitterly disappointed and surprised at the outcome, yet had no option but to continue as usual for the time being, despite a further setback of deteriorating coal supplies from Mackay, coupled with spiralling costs. At this time the Toxteth smelter contained 35 furnaces, employed 80 people and consumed between 10,000 and 12.000 tons of coal annually. Throughout the summer of 1791 adverts were placed in Gore's *Liverpool Advertiser* in the hope of securing coal supplies for at least one year, possibly longer, from 1st May 1792. This was the result of a decision made the previous February to insert notices in the Liverpool, Manchester and Chester newspapers from May onwards, inviting tenders for the Toxteth coal contract.

The expansion of the River Bank Works must have resulted in an increased coal consumption, inadvertently creating further problems for Toxteth. A letter dated 28th Jaury 1783 from the lead agent Thomas Smedley mentions the sloop *Venus,* owned by the Paris Mountain Company (i.e. Roe & Co.) on which he had managed to secure part of the lading for a lead customer, commenting that the vessel "plys fro' Greenfield to Liverpool frequently". This is the only mention of this particular small one masted craft which presumably was used for the transportation of the company's coal, calamine and lead etc. from North Wales, around the Wirral peninsula and across the Mersey estuary to Liverpool.

Quite suddenly, in May 1792, there was a re-assessment of policy and a Mr. Haddock, who had apparently come forward and offered coal supplies, was told that no agreement could be made with him until after the A.G.M. of 7th August as "we are to receive coals from Mr. Mackay's works until that date". However, it is obvious things were happening behind the scenes, for Abraham Mills was sent on a visit to a smeltworks in South Wales, after which he reported back to the committee.

* * * * * * *

There seems little doubt that the visit to South Wales by Abraham Mills had been suggested by the firm of Rupert Leigh & Co. who were manufacturers at Penclawdd on the Gower Peninsula near Swansea this was the name being used at that time by the Cheadle Company. They are first mentioned in the company minutes in November 1786 when it was decided to ask "Mr. Rupert Leigh & Purrell" their opinion on abolishing allowances given to large customers, of which "Mr. Weaver" was informed, obviously their contact in the area. One month later Leigh & Dagley(?) were present at a Roe & Co. meeting, "on behalf of the Cheadle Co.". Roe & Co. agreed to take the remaining stocks of manufactured neptunes, bolts and deep kettles off their hands; and at the same time discussed a partial advance on wire with regard to the Bristol Brass Wire Company and Purrell & Co.

By August 1787 it was noted that Rupert Leigh had to be sent the best block copper and in March 1789 Roe & Co. took out insurance in London to cover a consignment of copper to be shipped from Swansea to Liverpool. This suggests that Rupert Leigh had ceased the manufacture of articles and was instead refining copper. It is known that the Cheadle Brasswire Company set up operations at Penclawdd in 1792, which seems to indicate that Roe & Co. and the Cheadle concern were again working in unison to survive any competition from Thomas Williams and using the services of Rupert Leigh & Co. as a subcontractor. It is also apparent that Leigh & Co. had a reciprocal arrangement with the River Bank Works for lead smelting; the last item of the 1791 A.G.M. gives the sum of £6,000 as Roe & Co.'s proportion in the lead smelting concern and requires "Messrs R.S. Leigh & Co." to pay into the Macclesfield Bank £2,000 for their proportion up to the previous July.

Events now moved rapidly and the A.G.M. of August 1792 saw the commitment made to remove smelting operations from Toxteth to South Wales not Chester. Based on a report from Weaver and Mills, in the first instance it would be necessary to subcontract the smelting operations to allow time for Roe & Co. to erect their own smelters near to the River Neath. Contact had been made with Richard Parsons, an ironmaster of Cadoxton-juxta-Neath and he was asked to attend a Committee Meeting, bringing with him "such deeds as will enable them to judge of the eligibility of erecting Works on his premises."

Richard Parsons had negotiated a lease for the Ynissciuen colliery at the neighbouring village of Skewen, from Lord Dynevor of Dynevor Castle, Carmarthen and others; effective from 25th March 1791. Under the terms of the Indenture, signed on 29th January of that year, Parsons was not allowed to impound the water for the Abbey Copper Works (i.e. the Neath Abbey works owned by the Mines Royal Society) nor the grist mill near Neath Bridge. It was proposed to raise 2,000 "weys of coal" from a new colliery, payment set at 6s. 0d. per wey made a yearly rental of £600. And from the already established Abbey colliery 8s. 0d. a wey was reckoned which, for 2,000 weys, made a rental of £800 per year. Any additional coals raised at Ynissciuen would be charged at only 5s. 0d. per wey. The Indenture incorporated a contract to supply the Abbey Copper Works and the mill with all their required coals, and any brought from the Ynissciuen colliery would be transported along the River Neath at an agreed shipping price.

On 29th May 1792 Richard Parsons had obtained a further lease from the same lessors for a mill and foundry in the Vale of Cwmfelin in Cadoxton Parish and nine cottages near the foundry for his workmen and tenants. The premises had previously been used for the "battering of copper", but Parsons's lease provided for rolling iron plates and making cast iron goods. Also included was an area of land in the Vale measuring some 8 acres; it ran from below the grist mill and foundry (where the bridge crossed the Clydach Brook on the highway from Neath to Swansea) to the waterfall above the mill; the northern boundary was just short of the River Neath. Parsons subsequently subleased the mill and foundry on the 13th July to a partnership which included six members of the Fox family, who were iron founders, and also a Thomas Wilson, copper smelter of Truro. In the first instance he had possibly offered the lease to Roe & Co. but they may have declined, intent only on the possibility of developing the 8 acres of land.

Later in the year, encouraged by the feasibility of the proposed new plans, Abraham Mills, whilst travelling to Cornwall to "gain information" respecting the mining situation, was to see for himself how the arrangements for constructing the Roe & Co. smeltworks at Neath were proceeding. Possibly as a result of his visit a decision was taken to accept the offer made by the nearby smelter of Fenton & Co. (shortly to become the Rose Copper Co. in which Matthew Boulton had an interest) of a short term contract for smelting each month 200 tons of the Macclesfield company's copper ores. Mills also appears to have been busy and successful in acquiring much better facilities for the new site.

* * * * * * *

At this period Neath was a small town with a Corporation consisting of a portreeve, twelve aldermen and several burgesses. On the eastern side of the River Neath stood the Abbey ruins and also Gnoll Castle, the latter, built by Sir Herbert Mackworth, provided an excellent view of the whole town from its elevated position. On the western side of the river were located the copperworks of the Mines Royal established at Neath Abbey in 1584 by a Charter of Elizabeth I. The impressive smeltworks of the Mackworth family, subsequently incorporating several changes of management and name, including the English Copper Company were, at the time of Mills's visit, known as the Gnoll Works Company and stood, like the castle, on the eastern side of the river.

Having surveyed the locality, Mills must have decided that further property would have to be leased in order to accommodate the relocated smeltworks of the Macclesfield Copper Company with all its processes as it then operated in Toxteth. A considerable amount of negotiating appears to have taken place between the various parties from which Parsons was granted yet another lease by the same lessors, who had been made fully aware of Roe & Co.'s intentions. It is a testament to the trust which existed between all concerned that on 8th March 1793, before the signing of any further Indentures, the order was given to dismantle all the furnaces in the north range of buildings at the Harrington Works in Toxteth, together with the north calciners. This was a considerable undertaking as all the materials were to be shipped to Neath. At the same time the four Liverpool partners, Caldwell, Smyth, Roe and Johnson were made agents for the sale of the Toxteth copper works.

Almost three months later, on 30th May, Richard Parsons signed the additional lease with Lord Dynevor and the other five lessors, allowing him use of the Abbey yard and wharf which adjoined the old ruins and covered around 3 acres, and an additional 40 acres of the Salt Marsh. The latter, which lay opposite a timberyard, was bounded by the Clydach Brook on the north, the River Neath on the south and other marshes on the east. Out of this area Parsons retained 2 acres of the yard for his own use and the whole of the Salt Marsh. The remainder of the lease covered 6 acres of meadow land to the west of the Salt Marsh, with the Neath to Swansea turnpike road on the north, another road from the latter leading to the Abbey and timberyard on the east, the Greenway watercourse on the west and land occupied by the Mines Royal Copper Company on the south. A second meadow comprising a further 6 acres, adjacent to the last and near the Old Abbey, was also included. On the 22nd June Parsons subleased the 12 acres of meadow to Roe & Co. in addition to the wharf and remaining acre of yard. The lease also included the right to make a weir and floodgates from which water could be conveyed by pipes from the Clydach Brook to the premises, but the Abbey itself, with its gardens and nursery, were excluded.

Parsons's lease, which ran from 25th March 1793, was for 61 years for which he was to pay £60 yearly. He in turn subleased the requisite properties to Edward Hawkins and Abraham Mills "in Trust for Mefsrs. Roe & Copper Company" from the same date and for the same period; rental £40 yearly. Under the covenants in the lease Parsons was allowed to erect smelthouses and other necessary buildings on the site, and make a canal or iron rail road from the premises to either the Clydach Brook or the River Neath, whichever proved most convenient. "without interrupting the works intended to be occupied by Mefsrs, Roe & Co." He was also compelled to use only coal raised from the Abbey Estates. There were the usual stipulations regarding repairs, damages, notice to quit and so forth.

It is evident that he had obtained permission for the industrial development on behalf of Roe & Co. which was then included in their sublease. It covered the manufacture of all metals except iron, and they were to take responsibility for providing docks, quays, canals, railways and other constructions as appropriate, but without prejudicing the Brook or property belonging to the lessors who were the owners of Cadoxton Manor. An important condition was the coal supply. Roe & Co. were also compelled to use coal from the Abbey and Court Rydhyr Estates so long as there was a sufficient quantity, thus protecting Richard Parsons's coal leases.

On 8th July Parsons was advised by the Macclesfield partners that they had received the copy lease for the land on which the smeltworks were to be built; it also incorporated the coal contract. At the same time arrangements were made to send all copper ores from Coniston, Llanberis and Ireland to Fenton & Co. until their contract was fulfilled. But at the A.G.M. of the following month this decision was rescinded and the ores redirected to Rupert Leigh & Co. at Penclawdd. Apparently Fenton & Co. had produced some poor quality copper necessitating a further refining process for which Roe & Co. were seeking compensation. Accepting their incompetency, Fenton & Co. offered relinquishment of their contract, which was accepted. How they entered into the scheme of things in the first place is difficult to comprehend, perhaps they were part of a strategy to keep on good terms with the Birmingham manufacturers.

* * * * * * *

Those present at the 1793 A.G.M. in Macclesfield also witnessed the penultimate chapter in the life of the Harrington Works. All the wrought iron from the furnaces was consigned to Macclesfield, whilst the cast iron plates, having been cut to a "proper size", were to accompany the scrap iron to Wicklow (for which the Irish mining company would be charged £5 per ton).

How long it took to reassemble the smelters in Neath and bring them once more into full production is not known, but smelting on a limited scale did begin on 1st January 1794 under the direction of a 'Mr. Place'. He was instructed to use only one calciner and the 'required furnaces to work with'. Members of the Place family had been employed as managers by the Mines Royal Copper Co. for a long period and at this time the manager was John Place; but whether or not he was also acting on a subcontract basis for Roe & Co. or whether it was another family member who was involved, is difficult to deduce.

On 15th February 1794 Roe & Co. sent a petition to the Board of Customs:

> "Our House is Roe & Company . . . extensively concerned in smelting & manufacturing Copper ore & are likewise concerned in Copper Mines in various parts of this Kingdom & also in the Kingdom of Ireland, our smelting works were situated within a short distance of the Town of Liverpool, & by . . . indulgence we were permitted to land our ores . . . but the high price of labour and coals at that Port, has obliged us to remove our Works to the Port of Neath . . . and in the month of January of the present year, we imported from Wicklow in Ireland to the Port of Neath, per our Brig, the Irish Miner, a Cargo of Copper ore which is subject to an heavy duty on importation . . ."

This petition, of course, could in no way affect the importation duty, that would have to be done by inclusion in an Act of Parliament (the company had applied to the First Lord of the Treasury for free importation of Irish ore in May 1792, but without success). Obviously it was being used as a lever to persuade the Comptroller that it was worthwhile for officers to undertake the occasional stint of duty at Roe & Co.'s private quay because of the large amount of duty involved. Having been allowed the concession of unloading ore directly onto the company's quay at Harrington, which came under the jurisdiction of the Liverpool Custom House, it had seemed reasonable to conclude that a similar arrangement could be made with the Swansea Custom House with regard to the company's quay at Neath Abbey, but not so. The Swansea customs officers complained bitterly of their 8 mile journey to oversee the unloading; demanded that the master of the *Irish Miner* travel to the Swansea Custom House to make entry of his ship, and that their considerable fee of six guineas be paid by the company. With the reimbursement went a request to facilitate further importations at the Neath Abbey quay and the ability to make entry there instead of the Swansea Custom House, for which Roe & Co. were willing to pay expenses at a fixed rate.

Further correspondence is difficult to trace except a letter of February 1794 from the Collector & Comptroller of Customs at Swansea to the Board of Customs indicating that "the trade of Neath is so trifling as to render the establishing the officers there wholly unnecessary." However it would seem that, given time, an adequate fee and the realisation that the business was larger than expected, the mission was eventually accomplished, for a drawing of Neath Abbey ruins published in 1811 includes seagoing vessels anchored at the quayside.

From the extant correspondence it is interesting to note that despite William Roe's position as a Commissioner of Customs, in no way did he try to influence the outcome, nor in fact did he declare his interests; he was a man who strenuously lived his professional life very much 'according to the book'.

Although there are several references to the company vessel *Irish Miner* it has not been possible to discover when it was first owned, suggesting that it may have been registered in Dublin having belonged originally to the Irish mining concern and then acquired by Roe & Co. but transferred to their Irish subsidiary. On 5th January 1790 the Macclesfield Copper Company authorised a sum of 20 guineas to be paid to Nathaniel Litherland "late Master of *Irish Miner*" for his services on board the vessel. Despite the fact that the brig is recorded as arriving in Liverpool from Wicklow in the shipping supplement of the *Manchester Mercury* of 15th February 1791, laden with copper ore for W. Roe & Co. comprising 8 hogsheads, 1 barrel and 56 bags (packed) and 83 and a half tons (loose) yet it does not appear as an asset in the balance sheet to 5th July of that year; in fact John Johnson (Jnr.) of Liverpool would be instructed to "dispose" of the vessel in May 1792.

On 1st March 1791 the arrival of the *Mary Ann* from Wicklow, reported as carrying 33½ tons of ore for the same consignee, suggests that for some reason the *Irish Miner* had become unoperational. But the Customs records support the fact that a vessel of the same name was still operating from Wicklow in 1794 as evidenced by its arrival at the Neath Abbey quay. The brig had in fact left Wicklow in December 1793 and returned in March 1794, however, the final mention is in October of 1794 when the Master Jonathan Parkes was ordered to be discharged as soon as possible and a replacement found.

There are three vessels only appearing in that first recorded balance sheet to 5th July 1791 viz; *Brothers*, *Union* and *St. Patrick*. The brigantine *Brothers*, then valued at £525, was the one purchased in March 1789. The *Union* appears to be the brigantine newly built and registered at Northwich in June 1788; it was just over 62 ft in length and by 1791 valued at £630, suggesting it was superior to the *Brothers*. In May 1790 Thomas Smyth had been asked to "apply for protection" for these latter two vessels which were to be engaged later that summer for transporting ore from Cornwall, but by December other vessels from the ports of either Liverpool or Chester were to be used for the Cornish run on a subcontract basis. In due course, similar arrangements appear to have been made between Wicklow and Neath, for the names of several vessels are noted in the expenditure accounts of the Irish subsidiary.

The *St. Patrick* was the result of a company decision taken on 8th September 1789 to have a lighter built at Northwich able to carry 40 tons at "the smallest possible draft of water", for conveying Irish ore from the port of Wicklow to seagoing vessels; its value in July 1791 was £158 13 7d. One month later it was decided to "fit up" this flat for carrying goods between Northwich and Liverpool and at the same time build a warehouse in Northwich with a suitable person to take charge. After just one year it was considered necessary to purchase a replacement for the *St. Patrick*, but instead the *Union* appears to have been converted into a flat and eventually sold in 1804 to a consortium including the Roose family of Amlwch.

A flat or lighter was quite a small vessel with a flat bottom and more manoeuvrable than a large ship in and out of ports, so was an ideal vessel to use as a go-between from harbour to seagoing vessel. The *St. Patrick*, however, on its longer duty sailing from east to west along the mouth of the Mersey Estuary would have had a tricky journey because of strong tides and prevailing winds, not to mention inclement weather conditions and therefore a larger, more seaworthy vessel would be appropriate.

* * * * * * *

It is now appropriate to unravel the mystery of the Irish mining operations, impossible to glean from the nebulous information produced by Roe & Co. in their desperate search for another reliable source of copper ore to replace that of Parys Mountain.

Mining had been underway in County Wicklow since 1734. The first extant reference is a partnership lease at Tigroney to the east of Meeting of the Waters and close by Castle Howard. By 1752 it was estimated that 500 people were employed at Cronebane, adjacent to Tigroney on the east side of the Avoca River, where deposits of valuable silver had been discovered. To the west of the river there had been a further mining speculation at Ballymurtagh which had

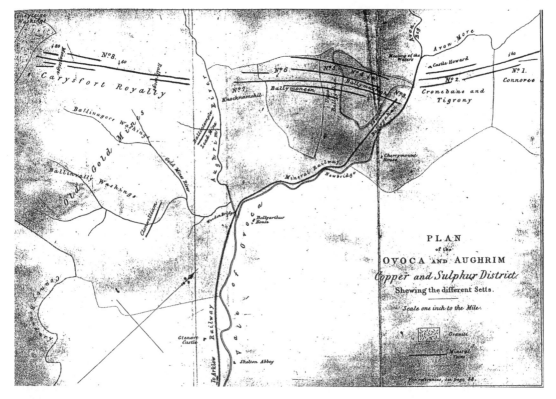

Map c.1850 showing the position of the Cronebane and Tigrony mining areas in County Wicklow in relation to Meeting of the Waters.

subsequently petered out. Geologically the area is in the copper and sulphur district of the Wicklow Mountains and, being on a par with Parys Mountain, the most successful method of collecting the low grade copper deposits was by using the same precipitation process; consequently scrap iron was submerged in the waters running from the mine with proceeds estimated to be £1,000 per annum. Unfortunately the effect on the environment was devastating with the ruin of rich salmon fisheries and the extermination of all fish life down to the town of Arklow on the coast.

By 1780 John Howard Kyan was mining at both Ballymurtagh and Cronebane and, with the prospects considered good, had managed to acquire parliamentary grants in the years 1783 and 1785 for the construction of smeltworks; but the operation had proved too difficult for him.

There is little doubt that Roe & Co. would be well-known in the region, taking into account Thomas Smyth's family connections and a warehouse in Dublin; thus their offer of April 1782, to purchase both ore and precipitated copper from Kyan, was the start of a more permanent business relationship. As matters progressed Kyan was obviously looking for capital to relieve his beleaguered financial situation therefore an alliance with Roe & Co. could not have come at a more appropriate time for all concerned.

Initially a leasing arrangement was agreed some time during 1786, which presumably would be for a year, allowing time for the Macclesfield partnership to carry out trials. One must conclude some were successful, for Roe & Co. then purchased the mineral rights of Tigroney and Cronebane from Kyan. Work began in May 1787, with the first expenditure account prepared the following month; by July there were 100 employees on site and the outcome was the establishment of a separate company with the name of Associated Irish Mines Company, more conveniently known as the A.I.M. Co. which held its first meeting in August 1787.

The name had obviously been chosen with care and in the first instance the company would have operated as a partnership in exactly the same way as Roe & Co. with members of the committee entitled to take action on behalf of all concerned when sanctioned to do so. Here was the golden opportunity for Abraham Mills to make his presence felt and he, together with Thomas Weaver Snr. of Gloucester, became the Directors responsible for overseeing the Irish mining operations. It does appear, however, that Weaver was to be the one directly responsible for the mining side of the business, whilst Mills concerned himself with the less technical aspects. Weaver's commitment to the project was such that his young son, Thomas (born 1773) was encouraged to study geology and mineralogy and would soon be sent to continue his studies in Freiburg under the tutorship of the famous Abraham Werner from 1790 to 1794, and would prove to be a vital asset in the not too distant future.

From east to west the intended mining area incorporated the sets of Connoree (Connery), Cronebane and Tigroney, all to the east of the river, with Ballygahan and Ballymurtagh (adjacent to each other) to the west. The company must have agreed to carry out trials at Ballymurtagh with a view to extending their purchase of mineral rights, and there is a reference to "Mr. Kyan's north level" there in 1787, but by February of 1788 having discovered "Nothing of consequence" except some retrievable ore from Kyan's waste dump, it was decided to abandon the site unless "Mr. Kyan agrees upon more reasonable terms." This Kyan must have refused to do for he instantly formed a partnership with two brothers of the Camac family, establishing the Hibernian Mining Company, in order to work Ballymurtagh for themselves.

Relations between the two companies deteriorated rapidly, possibly because some of Kyan's personnel remained with the A.I.M.Co. An employee called Penrose wrote on 15th November 1791 "I was at Ballymurtagh when Lord Powerscourt was there fixing the boundary and as I had not been on the ground from the time we gave it up till now I was very desirous of seeing what they were about and made an attempt, but Mr. Kyan saw me & very soon met me "Sir, this is not your lode and your absence is at all times expected at Ballymurtagh." They are very great enemies to our men which we paid 10d. a day to, they pay 6d.".

Unfortunately for Kyan his headstrong action seems to have set him on the road to ruin as capital was squandered on useless enterprises over the next four years, whilst the A.I.M. Co. initially found success. Just one year after the start of mining at Cronebane a vein of rich ore, said to vary from 6 ft to 18 ft in width, was discovered, which fortunately would continue in production for several years.

Whilst the A.I.M. Co. circulated the Cronebane halfpence from 1789, procured on their behalf by Roe & Co. from Birmingham (die-sinker Hancock) the Hibernian Mining Company responded with several issues of their own. The Cronebane halfpence was beautifully made having the bust of St. Patrick on the obverse, complete with cowl, mitre and 'pastoral rod', whilst the reverse design was an unofficial arms and crest appropriately comprising a windlass, three pickaxes, two shovels and a bugle-horn.

From the outset Mills was very much involved in the company's Irish affairs and soon found for himself a niche in Dublin Society. Despite the fact that all indications would suggest he had become a member of one of Dublin's Masonic Lodges, yet no records can be traced to substantiate this idea. However, he seems to have courted not only the intellegentia of the city, as evidenced by his submissions to the Royal Irish Academy, but also a young widow, and this despite the fact that there is at least one known liaison in Macclesfield with an unmarried woman.

In mitigation Mills (in all probability a widower) presumably thought that the Royal Proclamation "for the encouragement of Piety and Virtue and for the preventing and punishing of Vice, Profanenefs, and Immoralty" of 1788, and seized upon by Rev. Simpson as the subject of a printed sermon addressed to the Justices of the Peace for Macclesfield in the form of a distributed pamphlet, had really nothing to do with what appears to have been his genuine affections for these female companions. Simpson used the Proclamation as a lever with which to withhold licences from "petty ale-houfes' considering many to be a "bane of good morals, horrible haunts and infernal abodes" where "wickednefs" was rife. The irony of King George III producing such a proclamation leaves one in no doubt of society's declining moralities at that time, and should question the way in which the modern world has pilloried such outstanding men as Lord Nelson and the Duke of Wellington for their affairs, as though they were exceptions to the rule, when in reality they were probably among the least promiscuous of the many.

Despite the attractions of Dublin, Mills did make visits to the mines, some details of which are recorded, as in November 1788 when an entry under Ballygahan reads "The alteration that Mr. Mills ordered to be made on the Horse Engine has made it work much better & we hope it will supply the wash & copper pitts with sufficient water". In January 1790 a site called 'Cronebane Coppice' is mentioned followed by "John Jeffreys & Co. as in our last – prospect much the same as when Mr. Mills saw it", indicating that Jefferies of Gloucester was still very much in evidence. By July 1791 a note proves Mills intervened at Cronebane Coppice when a plan was altered according to his orders and only miners were allowed to form partnerships.

By this time there had been trouble when the leaders of each mining team had been accused of "idleness" and their money withheld, they immediately 'downed tools' but after a short protest returned to work; swift action was then taken to dismiss the ringleaders. Mills subsequently inspected the Oak Vein at the Tigroney Canal Level and suspended operations. It must be remembered that at some time during the previous summer of 1790 Mills had visited and written his report on Islay, a tour more conveniently undertaken from Dublin via the north of Ireland than from elsewhere. But whichever route he took, the outcome seems to have inspired a thirst for mining above all else which would remain with him for the rest of his life.

Mills also took a keen interest in company personnel: Early in October 1787 he was enquiring what wages were being paid in Cornwall to skilled men attending the stamps. He was told 12s. 0d. per week although Mr. Price, who had a book on Cornish mines, said about 10s. 0d. per week. A month later William Roberts and Joseph Byrne, both formerly employed at Parys Mountain, were set to work on the construction of an oblong kiln, which suggests it was for calcining the sulphurous ore and collecting sulphur as previously done on Anglesey. A report written many years later appears to confirm this:

"In former days, a great part of the ores of the Ovoca mines were smelted on the spot. . . . The ore was broken into fragments the size of large walnuts, and, freed from the smaller particles, was placed in a low cylindrical kiln with flat bottom, capable of holding fifty or sixty tons of ore. On the opposite side of the kiln were four apertures, and these were connected across the bottom of the kiln by open flues of bricks. On the flues was placed a layer of heath and furze [gorse]; the kiln was then filled, and on the top of the ore was constructed a top-close flue, which led to an arched receiver sixty or seventy feet in length, four feet in breadth, and six feet high; the surface of the ore being covered close in all other parts. The kiln thus formed a retort on a large scale. Firing was now placed to the apertures, and continued until the ore in the vicinity acquired a red heat, when the openings were stopped, and the process of subli[mate], surrounded by red oxide of iron, might be found in each piece of burnt ore. In this state, the ore being steeped in water, a solution of sulphate of copper was obtained, and the copper precipitated by iron; and the kernels of the sulphuret, that remained without decomposition, were separated from the slimy oxide by washing."

The deposits of sulphur remaining in the kiln were refined and made into "cake and roll brimstone", a very useful by-product for the manufacture of gunpowder, which during the forthcoming war with France would sell at between £20 to £30 per ton.

Apart from Roberts and Byrne, several other employees also appear to have followed the company fortunes from Wales to Ireland, although for Joseph Byrne it was apparently a return home. Even Cornishmen were in evidence, but some not for long. In September 1793 five Cornish team leaders made a pact not to bid against each other when it was time for bargain taking, their dismissal was immediate and other mines in the area were warned of their behaviour.

The office of the A.I.M.Co. was 184 Great Britain St., Dublin (renamed Parnell St. in the mid-1920s) and was situated almost next door to Simpson's Hospital, a newly built facility opened in November 1781, but with North Great George St. separating the two. On this latter street at No. 3 lived an eminent physician, William Harvey, later to become President of the King's & Queen's College of Physicians and a governor of the Hospital for the Relief of Poor Lying-in Women. He, together with Brabazon Noble a merchant of Cronebane, appear to have been trustees for John Middleton Scott of Ballygammon, the heir of Thomas Smyth's deceased brother-in-

The new building on Parnell Street, Dublin, which has replaced the Georgian property 184 Great Britain Street, and has been appropriately named 'Avoca House'.

law and therefore entitled to his share. Negotiations took place and young Thomas Weaver, having returned from Freiburg and taken up residence in Cronebane, purchased one share in the Macclesfield Copper Co. for £4, 200 on 4th July 1794, and at some point 10 shares also in the A.I.M.Co., price unknown. Until that date and from at least 1791 Noble seems to have played an active role in the running of the business (possibly because young Scott was a minor). Noble's ship arrived from Liverpool in February 1794 bringing two pieces of copper wire, four sieves and four riddles for the mines and about the same time he supplied a large quantity of wines (including nine pipes of port) which obviously marked some special occasion.

Although at last there seemed much to celebrate in Ireland, on this side of the Irish Sea it was a different matter, the post-Parys Mountain period had witnessed some great losses in human terms, which the company acknowledged and from which they would never really recover.

* * * * * * *

Early in 1788 the sudden death of George Hurst, employed in the Macclesfield company office, was a considerable blow, and such was the regard for this "faithful Clerk" with the company lamenting "the Loss of so valuable a son" that it was decided to pay his mother an annuity for life, to compensate for the financial assistance he would otherwise have been able to give her. His clerical duties were shared by John Hale, young Brian Hodgson and another employee called Hopley with the salary subsequently divided between them.

In August 1790 John Hale was given the job of cashier at the same salary he had been paid as bookkeeper; his replacement would be expected to keep the mine account in addition to that of the copper company. Unfortunately Hale died on 13th October 1790 aged 61 years and his widow was initially allowed an annual pension of £10 from the date of his death, this was increased to £20 from August 1791 when his Executors paid the balance of a security payment. Four months later Hopley became cashier and was allowed rent free occupation of the house originally leased from Charles Roe for John Hale's benefit.

Apart from John Denman's demise at Holywell and other dedicated employees such as William Harvey (Havannah), George Hurst and John Hale, the company shareholders had also been affected. At only 55 years of age Legh Dickenson had died and been buried on 4th May 1787 in the village of Kenwyn just to the north-west of Truro. For his relatives, his death was the start of an administrative chain reaction of incredible complexity.

In brief, there were two local Cornish trustees responsible for selling his $1/14$th share in the Macclesfield Copper Company including an equal share of stock, buildings, furniture, tools, utensils and so forth, the proceeds from which were to be invested in 'Stock in the Public Funds'. The complications arose from the fact that his father, John, the Manchester merchant who had played host to Bonnie Prince Charlie, had left him an interest in the Birch Hall Estate, Rusholme, near Manchester and also £1,000 in trust for Elizabeth, Legh Dickenson's only daughter; Elizabeth's only brother, William Churchill Dickenson, was heir to their father's estate. Patience was still living and travelled to London where, as Executrix, she proved her husband's will on 2nd June 1787, from which she benefited by receiving all their household goods, furniture, horses and carriages, 'ready money', arrears of rents and debts. Young Elizabeth was to receive the handsome capital sum of £5,000 (which included the £1,000 from her grandfather) at either 21 years of age or upon marriage if sooner. Son William would inherit the considerable residue but, because his mother would shortly die intestate, he was plagued by unresolved legalities.

The problem arose because of the considerable properties in Lancashire, which fell within the jurisdiction of the Consistory Court in Chester as part of the Chester Diocese, demanding that Patience should have proved the will in that court. There was also the unresolved interest in the Birch Hall Estate, which was most likely in the form of rents received and therefore part of Patience's income, to which the young man would now have to prove his entitlement.

The copper company partners acted quickly and in August 1787 resolved to pay the residue of Legh Dickenson's share after deducting a proportion in respect of bad debts but, for some reason, payment was delayed inspiring the intervention of Elizabeth Dickenson and her attorney. One year later a list of bad debts was drawn up to the date of Dickenson's death with the recommendation that the appropriate proportion should be deducted and the matter left in Mills's capable hands "to make the best terms" with the two. Presumably this meant as little cash payable as possible and the remainder in the form of bonds with interest. Miss Dickenson wrote quickly, but the contents of her letter dated 25th August are not known, only that the company found them "inadmissible". She evidently contacted her brother who was sent a copy of the bad debts in March 1789, but again the outcome is unknown.

(By 1798 William Churchill Dickenson whilst a Lieutenant in the Royal Lancashire Volunteers stationed in Newport, Hampshire would be required to travel north in order to swear an oath in the Consistory Court at Chester however, unable to do so, he was given permission to appear before the Bishop of Winchester. Letters of Administration had to be granted in Chester which necessitated an abstract of Legh Dickenson's will accompanying the affidavit from the Bishop of Winchester confirming the young soldier's personal appearance and sworn oath; unfortunately there would be little time left in which to enjoy his inheritance as he would die unmarried in 1803.)

Also in March 1789 the company once more sought a reliable agent in Cornwall able to assay copper ore (no longer being sold there by ticketing since Thomas Williams's intervention), make purchases and send regular accounts. One year later a prospective agent, 'Mr. Magor', travelled to Macclesfield bringing with him security, which would be in the form of a bond to guard against embezzlement etc., and was engaged. Two months later he was instructed to send 500 tons of copper ore as soon as possible, and during the autumn attended and reported on an important meeting held in Truro, as none of the company partners were able to be present. The company proposed purchasing a small share in a Cornish mine which would allow them to be present at any meetings of the 'Cornish Copper Miners' but there is no evidence that this ever materialised. Magor continued sampling, weighing and shipping ores and in August 1791 was asked to ticket for some Somerset copper ore. Although Legh Dickenson had not actively worked for the company for some considerable time before his death, yet his knowledge and expertise would have been invaluable, particularly at so great a distance, so it was imperative that the company should have a conscientious, reliable agent in that area to compensate partially for Dickenson's demise, and Magor appears to have been that ideal replacement.

* * * * * * *

Two further, although rather minor, adjustments to the Roe & Co. shares had been made in January 1789; first, young Jane Roe's trustees accepted pay out of her portion as it was then valued; this was, of course, Jane's inheritance from her father's estate as determined by Wlliam Roe's administration. At the same time William Racster of Bristol accepted his share also at the book value; this had evidently been acquired as part of the marriage settlement when he married Margaret, the former Peggy Roe.

Three years later, in January 1792, John Jefferies representing Jefferies & Co. wrote, making a request to increase his shareholding in the company. This could have been inspired by the successful new development at Holywell, the Irish mining prospects and the fact that of late years his business interests had proved extremely lucrative. A business directory of Gloucester for 1784 still included an entry for 'Weaver & Jefferies pin-makers', but whether or not this partnership continued much longer is difficult to deduce. Although the older Thomas Weaver had become involved with the Wicklow project yet, at some time during 1788, he appears to have returned to Gloucester leaving Mills as 'caretaker in charge' and therefore responsible for all the aspects of the mining venture until the advent of his son.

During 1788 King George III, his wife, Queen Charlotte and four of the princesses made an official visit to the city of Gloucester. They met the ecclesiastical contingent which comprised the Bishop, Dean, Chapter and clergy of the district, then the Mayor and Corporation with the Town Clerk presenting an address on behalf of his fellow members. Thomas Weaver and John Jefferies were, of course, both aldermen and presumably present on what for them would have been an extremely important occasion, in which event they would have made a somewhat rapid exit from the proceedings, because immediately afterwards the royal party visited "the pin manufactory of Messrs. Weaver & Co.", (N.B. not Weaver & Jefferies). The Weavers would remain in the King St. premises for many years to come, and although the younger Thomas made his career in Ireland, at some point in time his brothers Charles and Edward became involved with the pin manufactory.

The fact that John Jefferies Jnr., anxious to increase his Roe & Co. share in January 1792, was acting alone and not on behalf of himself and Weaver as partners and joint shareholders, seems to suggest a split in the partnership at some juncture. Some years later both the older Thomas Weaver and John Jefferies are referred to as merchants of Gloucester.

* * * * * * *

As regards the mining at this period, it is evident from the company minutes that, apart from the Avoca Valley in Ireland, the main sites for the copper ore supplies were Coniston and Llanberis. Llandudno was proving problematical; in June 1791 the agent there had been asked to make up the account and not carry out further trials. This obviously referred to the mining venture under Ty'n-yr-hwylfa farm, leased from Lord Bulkeley, which must have proved unproductive. (The area would be reworked by others in the 19th century and become known as the New Mine).

The Llandudno Mine Company workings were also causing problems on the Bishop of Bangor's land, but this was mainly due to bad management; in August 1792 Roe & Co. demanded all outstanding payments, a deposit and a transfer of management to their control, otherwise they would "decline all further concern with it".

There had been occasional miscellaneous purchases of copper ores to supplement those of Cornwall and even two offers of shares in mines which, after the copper ore samples had been assayed, the company declined. One, in March 1786, had been from a member of the Champion family for which Roe & Co. had paid £50 to carry out trials. On the offer being declined, which included a new method of making brass, Champion immediately resorted to making legal threats which were entirely groundless.

A reference to the vein of copper at Calbeck fells is interesting. It was obviously being worked by April 1788, as mentioned in Hawkins's letter to Busfield, but apparently only on a small scale because of the "temporary disadvantage of want of hands". This mine appears to be the one referred to in a geological survey as Driggith Mine at the head of Driggith Beck just over three miles south of Calbeck. An historical note mentions that the mine "was opened in 1700, by a Mr. Row, who wrought it from shallow shafts and day-levels to a depth of 25 fms. and erected smelting-works near Carrock Beck."

From later 19th century information the smeltworks were for lead which yielded a small quantity of silver. Although lead ores predominated some copper pyrites and malachite were present. This information could be coincidental, but there is a strong suggestion that it relates to William Roe and that the Victorian originator of the information had inadvertently quoted the year 1700 instead of 1788. The mine, however, is not included by name in the balance sheet to 5th July 1791, but is more than likely part of the item referred to as "Coniston Mines"; by 1794 this appears in the singular as "Coniston Mine" and no further reference can be found for Calbeck.

A self-styled 'rambler', member of a guided party to the area in 1792, left a description of

Coniston mine. Whilst making an ascent he entered a tunnel and waded some 200 yards through deep water, expecting it to be a copper mine, but on meeting 'Cyclops' (a miner with a lantern strapped to his head) he learnt that the adit was for draining workings on the other side of the brook. The miner had a piece of copper ore which showed the copper content to be poor and not worth retrieving, confirming that at that time the mine was "rather barren", despite the fact that at 1st. February 1792 there were 283 tons 6 cwts. of copper ore on bank awaiting transportation to the smelters.

At the A.G.M. of August 1792 the partners were each handed a copy of the Coniston mining accounts with a request for payment of expenses, indicating a not inconsequential investment at that time.

The rambler soon discovered ". . .this mountain has been so productive, they do not doubt meeting success; they already get sufficient to keep some men at work. We went lower, where they pulverised it, and by different processes were preparing it for smelting, which is carried on in a country better supplied with coal, and more convenient for navigation".

Despite the advances in scientific knowledge, superstitions persisted as strong as in the days of Daniel Defoe, as witnessed by a tale related locally of an old man who had secretly gained a fortune. Some of his neighbours believed he had a copper mine somewhere in the mountains and often questioned him about his acquired wealth. One evening he finally told them that the devil had helped him get the copper; the next time he climbed the hill he never returned, but was found torn to pieces. Stories of ghosts abounded everywhere but the rambler reassured his readers that whilst half the population appeared to believe the tales, the spectres did no harm to anyone and therefore held an affectionate place in local folklore.

Another mystery relevant to the area, though this time a factual one, is the appearance of a Jonathan Roose who, together with a Christabella Sharp had several children baptised during the 1790s at Orton in Cumberland. It is not beyond the realms of possibility that this was the same Jonathan who had discovered the vein of copper ore on Parys Mountain, (the only other Jonathan in the family, a son born 1766, was well established as a Liverpool merchant). After bearing him ten children, Jonathan Snr.'s first wife Elizabeth had died in Amlwch during April of 1787, and although Jonathan had reached the age of 60 years by February 1791, totally undeterred he had begun an affair with an 18 year old daughter of a local farmer. Now a respected member of Amlwch society and a wealthy local businessman he found the history of thirty years previous repeating itself when he married Sarah Evans on 7th April 1792 in time to see their son, Benjamin, baptised on 12th May. Although Sarah would eventually bear him eleven children, five during the 1790s, yet there was still the opportunity for Jonathan to have travelled periodically to the Lakes whilst supervising further searches for copper, though not necessarily on behalf of Roe & Co. The company minutes do indicate that the agent at Coniston called "Rutter" had been accused of "breach of trust" in November 1788 and would therefore have been replaced.

At this period Jonathan's son, Stephen, was agent for the Parys Mountain operations, and is described by one visitor to Amlwch as having a "comfortable home"; evidently Jonathan had relinquished the post some time earlier.

Although operations on the Great Orme and in the Lake District were proving problematical at times yet the company's expectations were high. Llanberis continued to produce good ore but not in sufficient quantities to make a profit, so it was decided to alter the system of working, making it more convenient for both the miners and the smeltworkers. The copper content is recorded as 20% pure in parts, which obviously related to the 'good ore', but the poorer yet larger quantities were more difficult to retrieve, suggesting that the alternative Production method was the formation of precipitation pits attributed to Roe & Co. by a subsequent observer.

Another method was to calcine some of the poorer ores to rid them of the sulphur content. The alternative system must have been a success, for 18 months later Busfield was advised that "our Mineral prospects are considerably improved . . . we have no doubt of drawing an ample supply of Ores for the Liverpool works." Although this was a general comment one can assume that it included Llanberis otherwise Hawkins would have said so.

The Llyn Peris mine was situated near the "upper-end of the higher Lake" near Nant Peris. The ores were crushed in a stamping mill near to the lake which was described as having "fixed oaken beams shod with iron and placed perpendicularly side by side along a large trough; these beams are alternately raised by a waterwheel . . ." The same observer provided a description of the mine which consisted of "several galleries driven into Snowdon; the rock is hard whin and hornblende schiztus, the matrix quartz; the metal is a rich yellow ore, containing copper in unison with sulphur, the quantity procured is not very considerable".

After crushing, the ore was packed and transported across the lake in boats and then loaded into carts. Many visitors would later write about the area but Thomas Pennant is the one to mention a character called Margaret uch Evam of Penllyn, then about 90 years of age. She was renowned for her hunting, shooting and fishing and kept at least a dozen terriers, greyhounds and spaniels. Amongst her other attributes were those of being a good mechanic and joiner who, at the age of 70 years, was the best wrestler in the country having defeated several young men who had tried 'a fall' with her. "She shoed her own horses, made her own shoes, and built her own boats, while she was under contract to convey the copper ore down the lakes."

The ore, having been trundled from the lake side in carts down to the port of Caernarfon, was loaded on board vessels bound for the Mersey Estuary and the Toxeth works, that is until the order of 7th July 1793 when it was, of course, redirected to Fenton & Co. at Neath and then, almost immediately, shipped for Rupert Leigh & Co. , at Penclawdd near Swansea.

An interesting extension to this mining development is an apparent subleasing by Abraham Mills on behalf of Roe & Co. of a timber yard in the town of Caernarfon. At some time in the past this had been leased to the Llanberis Copper Mine Company by Thomas Assheton Smith, but on 1st October 1788 Thomas Wright, an attorney and son of the solicitor Samuel of Nether Knutsford, Cheshire, had acquired the lease for 21 years. It also included slate quarries and mining rights in the parishes of Llanberis, Llanddeiniolen and the manor of Dinorwig; rent £13 per annum. Evidently Mills subleased from Wright, but the details are illusive so it is possible that some of the mineral rights were also taken over. Wright did offer a lease of the Dryscoed (Drws-y-coed) mine to the company in the summer of 1792, but unfortunately this was declined; subsequent mining during the first half of the 19th century would produce 6,291 tons and the second half 8,566, with an average copper content of 9-14%. The mining at Llyn Peris does predate Wright's lease from Smith, suggesting that Roe & Co could have already been subleasing from the Llanberis Mine Company.

There is an intriguing mention of Alderley Edge in August 1791 where, as at Llandudno, instructions were given to make up the account, but this time the Committee would meet to decide whether or not to continue with trials. Alderley had, of course, been abandoned circa 1770, but the lease had subsequently been taken up by the Cheadle Company and worked until 1st February 1787. Meantime during 1775 an Enclosure of the Commons in Nether Alderley had taken place and by a deed dated 17th January of that year "all Mines and Minerals and all Quarries of Stone in or under a certain part of the Common or Waste Ground within the said Manor called Alderley-Edge" were to be reserved for Sir John Thomas Stanley and his heirs.

A somewhat confused recollection by an old labourer on the Stanley Estate in 1805, implies that Charles Roe and Abraham Mills were working together whilst mining The Edge, but this should obviously relate to the two separate periods in which Roe & Co. had an interest in the area. It does seem evident that Mills was left to supervise the trials during the renewed interest in the Alderley mines, which had probably begun in 1788 when Edward Hawkins leased a farm in Over Alderley very close to the mine workings. A letter of 1791 addressed to Sir John Stanley from a Mr. Radcliffe suggests that Roe & Co. had indeed ceased trials and that Radcliffe was the new lessee ". . . The mine goes on well but the lead is not in one place. The copper continues good. Eight women are employed in dressing the copper and a woman came out of Derbyshire to wash the lead."

The second period of Roe & Co. mining at Alderley must have been brief, for the company accounts to 5th July 1791 only include shares in the copper mines of Llandudno, Coniston and Ireland, and also in the Holway level (predominantly lead with some calamine). Nor is Llanymynech included, and coupled with the comment written by a traveller in that part of Shropshire some six years later that very little mining had taken place "of late years", one can confidently assume this source of calamine had ceased by 1791. The Bonsall estate was still intact, and occasional references imply that purchases of the zinc ore were still taking place in Yorkshire. In August 1792 a letter was sent to the King of Prussia's Mines in Silesia requesting a few tons of calamine for sampling, though no further reference is made to this source.

Other assets appearing in the balance sheet to 5th July 1791 include, of course, the collieries. Whilst coal supplies continued to be delivered from mines owned by individual partners, yet the company had extended their holdings as Roe & Co. The valuations provide a good indication of comparative sizes: by far the largest colliery on Macclesfield Common was Greenaway at the northern end, with the Blakelow workings on the southern side only half the size. Ford's colliery at Odd Rode near Congleton was comparable to Blakelow, but the largest investment was in the Hall Colliery at Bollington, the village on the north-eastern side of Macclesfield, where the shares held were of slightly greater value (£1,020 12 6d.) than the Greenaway Mine, shortly to become known as the Great Mine.

By November 1792 the workings at Bollington were beginning to flood and Robert Hodgson, on behalf of the company, was asked to propose to the other shareholders that a fire engine should be installed at joint expense. This appears to be the colliery in which a "Mr. Vardon" had an interest. Mills and Hawkins had been asked to negotiate with him for a quarter share in the concern early in 1785. Later information records Messrs. Vardon and Upton as holding a joint share, whilst a further share was held by a Joshua Wood.

Amongst the items relating to stocks and buildings appearing in the balance sheet were the warehousing facilities close by the Red Bull Inn at Lawton. Taken on a 21 year lease of 2s. 6d. per annum in 1789 from John Lawton they were insured for £500 in August 1791, although their book value stood at only £246 8 7d.

Another interesting item was Whetton Mill, (not to be confused with Wetton Mill in the Manifold Valley and near to the Ecton Mine). It appears to have been acquired because of a dispute with a James Meredith who is listed in a Manchester Directory of 1788 as a pinmaker of Hanging Ditch. Meredith had accrued a large debt with the Macclesfield Copper Company and as early as 1784 was asked to execute a bond in the company's favour for the considerable sum of £2,000, together with an assignment of the mill lease. The matter inevitably dragged on until, in August 1790, Hawkins and Mills were asked to attend a meeting of arbitrators in Manchester. The verdict evidently favoured Roe & Co., for they had a stock of copper on the mill premises valued at £313 17s. in July 1791; they then decided to advertise the lease for sale in October 1792, but without success. About one year later Edward Hawkins was asked to take Edward Harvey from the Havannah Works to Whetton Mill with the intention of converting part of the premises into a copper rolling mill if at all possible. The lease was still held in 1794 when the premises were referred to as a building, suggesting that the copper rolling idea had not been feasible.

The company assets in the 1791 balance sheet total little less than £200.000 which today would provide a valuation of at least £20 million.

Unfortunately a chain of events was already underway which would not only see the eventual demise of Roe & Co., but would completely alter the economic and therefore the social and political structures of this country, for on 14th July 1789 the French Revolution had begun in earnest with the storming of the Bastille prison in Paris.

29
THE TWILIGHT YEARS

The bird of Time has but a little way
To flutter – and the Bird is on the Wing.

It is usually the economic rather than the moral desires of a nation which create revolution, and despite the cries of "Liberty; equality; fraternity", it was the serious financial state of France in 1787 which was the initial culprit for what followed. Years of war had depleted her treasury, and although the American War of Independence had been successful, France had invested a fortune in providing troops and naval assistance to a cause from which she would make no financial gain, whilst ironically, Britain, having lost her American colonies would see her trade across the Atlantic increase appreciably; family ties were strong.

France had also seen a fortune spent on royal palaces, particularly during the reign of Louis XV, and there was a sharp contrast between the affluent upper class of the nobility and the vast peasant class with its predominance of agricultural labourers, between which two there was very little respect. King Louis XVI's solution was to summon members of the nobility to a council in the hope that they would agree to pay a larger share of taxes; but all in vain. The nobility recommended a meeting of the states-general representing the commons or middle classes. The procrastinations saw the Bastille in ruins and the commons united as one under the guise of the National Assembly.

Inevitably factions set to work behind the scenes, and what had been welcomed initially by certain members of the British public who were in a position to know and care about what was happening across the Channel, began to turn into a nightmare of horrors and destruction, culminating in the execution of Louis XVI.

The king met his death by guillotine on 21st January 1793 in a city virtually blanketed by an eerie silence; and the rest of Europe woke up to the fact that this was far more serious than had been anticipated.

The revolutionaries had already declared war on Austria and invaded her Netherlands in 1792. As a consequence Austria received Prussian support and an invasion of France followed, but in retaliation the French revolutionary army marched from the Netherlands across the Rhine and captured Brussels. The next step was the declaration that the river Scheldt was open to all international commerce; Britain, however, in concluding a trade agreement with the Dutch, had respected their rights on the river. Realising that Britain and Holland were about to declare war, France declared first on 1st February 1793.

Confidence was shattered and it was the Stock Market which bore the brunt of it as many old established businesses began to fail. In little more than six weeks the firm of Forbes & Gregory of Aldermanbury, London was declared bankrupt. This was the London banking agency for Smyth and Caldwell, and the *London Gazette* notice of 19th March was shortly followed by that for Charles Caldwell & Co. of Liverpool on 30th March. Of the four established banks in Liverpool unfortunately Caldwell & Co. was the only one which could not withstand the pressure due to a large investment in the cotton trade.

On the outbreak of war with France the price of cotton had fallen rapidly and British

Government stocks followed; the mercantile business of Smyth & Caldwell, in which Forbes and Gregory were partners, was therefore ruined, for they had a large stock of cotton in their Liverpool warehouses on Paradise St. and Manesty's Lane, as did many of their clients. When the mercantile business failed so did the bank with what must have been disastrous results, for Thomas Golightly, as Treasurer of Liverpool Corporation, had, of course, been given permission in August 1789 to bank part of the Corporation's funds with Smyth and Caldwell.

What happened to the account for Roe & Co., opened in August 1791, in respect of the Liverpool branch of their business, is uncertain, for no mention is made in any correspondence. Bankruptcies are never 'convenient' but this one could not have occurred at a more significant time, for the order had barely been given to dismantle the furnaces in the north range at Toxteth for their removal to Neath.

The assignees for the Smyth and Caldwell bankruptcy ordered a public sale of their stock comprising West Indian cotton, Pernambuco (Brazilian) cotton, Jamaica sugar and London refined sugar. Finally the humiliating sight of their household goods being removed from their respective residences, took place.

First it was the turn of Thomas Smyth who said goodbye to prints, a large collection of plate and "the finest wines, brandy, and rum perhaps in the country" together with many other items including furniture, and all removed from Fairview in Toxteth, the house he was presumably renting from William Roe. The sale took place quickly on 11th June and also included the contents of the business premises on Paradise Street.

Next it was Caldwell's turn as the sale of contents from his house in St. James's Street followed on the 24th of the month. At the A.G.M. on 7th August the company agreed to accept his share and make the appropriate payment to the assignees. From the previous A.G.M. of August 1792 the shares had been divided into 64ths. Smyth's share, however, was under dispute, but Roe & Co., having taken legal advice, assured the assignees that the "Assignment" dated 20th August 1789 was binding and therefore that share had transferred to John Pendredd Scott whose representatives would deal with any queries. By February 1794 Roe & Co. had heard nothing further regarding the Caldwell share, nor could they calculate the value of any residuary interests of Smyth's until a statement of bad debts had been received.

The only other investments by the duo appear to have been in the Llanberis Mine for which William Roe was 'empowered' to purchase the two $\frac{1}{8}$th shares at £200 each.

For some time afterwards Caldwell lived in St. Anne's Street, Liverpool but circumstantial evidence suggests that William Roe gave considerable support to Thomas Smyth and that Smyth was given the facility of using Fairview as his residence for as long as he should require it. His name continues to appear as a Common Councilman for Liverpool until 1814, although the last meeting attended by him would be in July 1806.

At this period the law governing the administration of bankrupt estates left much to be desired and would not be amended until 1826 As a consequence the renewal commission of the Smyth and Caldwell bankruptcy would not take place until 1st December 1832, long after the deaths of the two partners.

Smyth's estate in Macclesfield, which included the colliery under lease to Roe & Co., remained intact, presumably because it was part of the marriage settlement. In time he did take up permanent residence there but, in the interim, whilst arguably domiciled in Macclesfield, he does appear to have divided his time between his Hurdsfield estate and Liverpool, allowing for the fact, of course, that the enigmatic Abraham Mills had once again moved residence.

For a time the Macclesfield bank was able to hold firm, but it too had not been without its difficulties. Shortly after becoming operative (probably in 1785) the bank had arranged a loan for an Edward Maddock enabling him to build a cotton mill in Macclesfield, but in

1791 circumstances forced Hawkins & Co. to require full redemption of the loan. Whether or not it was a political move is difficult to deduce, but cotton prices were already beginning to fall and this was the period when company capital was very much tied up with the production of the Macclesfield tokens. Maddock, in order to finance his way out of difficulty, did what was common practice at that period; whilst repaying one loan he negotiated another. He sold the newly built cotton mill and lease of land to a partnership, but obtained another loan privately for the purchase of further property, having made a small profit between the two deals.

The new purchase comprised part of the original glebe land and old parsonage house of Macclesfield (today site of the Paradise Mill – a working silk mill) on Park Green. Maddock then used the buildings as collateral for an additional loan of £1,000, and when unable to repay, approached yet another individual called Hilditch for £1,500 in order to clear the £1,000 debt.

Evidently seisin took place and the property, which in the interim seems to have been developed and extended, became a pawn in the financial complexities of the period; within a year, whilst remaining unoccupied, it passed from Hilditch to Clayton then to Legh.

The latter was Thomas Legh who married Abraham Mills's daughter, Mary Anne, at Prestbury on 20th August 1792. Thomas was descended from an important local family, Legh of Ridge, entitled to bear a coat of arms and boast of a monumental brass in St. Michael's church representing a medieval ancestor, Roger Legh of Ridge and his wife Elizabeth. It does seem possible that the purchase of the Park Green property was an investment as part of the marriage settlement, for adjacent to what was by then the main house, there was also a cotton shop or factory with a second house (the former parsonage) adjoining the north-west gable of the factory.

In 1794 the Bishop of Chester (successor to Beilby Porteus who was by then Bishop of London) declared that the covenant dated 18th September 1781 by which Rev. Jennings had sold the parsonage to a former mayor of Macclesfield, Rowland Gould, was invalid and instructed the vicar to reclaim the house as church property. The subsequent progressive conveyances meant that Thomas Legh was the one who had to defend his right to the property, and as a consequence challenged the judgement of the Diocese of Chester in court. Evidently he won, for shortly afterwards Abraham Mills purchased the whole of the small estate from him for £1,600; however, at some point Edward Hawkins became owner of part of the site, suggesting that initially a loan had been obtained from the bank by Mills, enabling him to make the purchase.

Mills, whilst apparently taking up residence in the grander and larger house on the site in 1794, let the factory and what had been the old parsonage house, to which was soon added a row of cottages. Thus Thomas Smyth was able to gain occupancy of his wife's former family residence, Fence House.

* * * * * * *

During this period John Johnson began to play a more active role in company affairs, presumably in compensation for Thomas Smyth's somewhat compromising situation, and together with William Roe was given charge of disposing of the company's Liverpool assets. In an effort to sell the residue of the Toxteth copper works Roe and Johnson offered the complex to Lord Sefton in April 1794 for £2,500, with the slag heap as an additional asset for £1,000, a possible initiative inspired by Lord Sefton's offer to take over the lease of the adjoining farm and land rented to the company by Mrs. Parr at £120 per annum. Although Roe & Co. happily accepted the latter, Lord Sefton's reluctance to reciprocate must have once again dashed hopes of an early end to the Toxteth crisis.

By August 1795 the agent remaining on site at the Liverpool works was instructed to supervise the sale of slag and stop cattle and people encroaching on the premises and farm land, emphasising that if necessary any trespass would be dealt with "as Law allows". Offers for the stock of cast iron had been made by two individuals, Fawcett and Watson, but it had not been collected; they were given seven days in which to remove it otherwise the sale was "considered void". All the remaining copper and brass rods were returned to the Havannah works where they were made into wire for button shanks.

As John Johnson was by this time very much involved with operations in Liverpool, allowing William Roe to attend to matters in Neath, it was decided to pay him a salary of £120 per annum instead of commission only. Finally, on 14th March 1796 the pair were able to sign a lease with a Liverpool merchant, Samuel Worthington. The document quoted details of the original lease between the Earl of Sefton and Roe & Co. and the subsequent development of the site comprising buildings for copper smelting, a quay and expansion into the River Mersey itself. As previously, the agreed price was £2,500 and £1,000 for the copper slag. Roe & Co. were allowed three months in which to remove all items not included in the sale e.g. lead, lead ore, lead slag, cast and uncast iron and firebricks.

Worthington obviously intended to continue copper smelting on the site, for on 1st August 1796 he was given permission by Lord Penrhyn to search for minerals, including copper, on the Penrhyn estate in the parishes of Llandegai, Llanllechid and Bangor. But although the lease was signed, the release (usually signed the following day to complete the transaction) was not. Perhaps Worthington was playing for time and had underestimated the difficulties involved in copper smelting or was unsuccessful in finding copper ore, but in any event Lord Sefton had no desire to see copper smelting continue on the site. For whichever reason it was not until three years later, on 8th August 1799, that the sale lease was finally signed by all the Macclesfield company partners and Samuel Worthington, by which time Worthington had set himself up as an earthenware manufacturer in addition to his trade as a merchant. Inflation was taking its toll, the sale price had increased to £5,000 and Worthington, evidently experiencing financial difficulties, agreed to the execution of a £7,000 bond (presumably to avoid paying interest on a cumulative basis) "for peaceable enjoyment" of the premises in Toxteth Park.

In the interim, in order to assist the agent with the sales of slag, the weighing machine from the Macclesfield brass-works had been sent to Liverpool, from where, one year later, it appeared "fixed upon (the) railway leading to coal bins near Neath Abbey works". The old weighing machine from the brass-works found its way to Bosley. With the demise of the Toxteth works Johnson dismissed the wharfinger at Northwich and terminated the lease for the warehouse.

It is interesting to note that seven months after signing the sale lease, Worthington, in partnership with three other Liverpool merchants (Holland, Hurry and Humble) leased a mill for grinding flints, water grist mills, a farm and 24 acres, an ochre works and mill dams from Lord Penrhyn for 21 years at a rental of £720. One of the partners, Samuel Holland, had been very involved in the development of the Ffestiniog slate quarries and therefore would be a useful addition to the partnership. One year later (25th March 1801) the lease was extended to include quarrying for stones, but by then Hurry had withdrawn from the business. On 1st August 1801 the three remaining partners obtained a contract for a supply of slates from the Penrhyn quarries with the details precisely defined, for contracts were already in place to supply John Furey of Warrington and Wyatts, the famous London architects. Finally on 12th November 1806, with an investment of £25,000 made up of 50 shares each of £500, the Herculaneum Pottery Company was established to produce porcelain, and would find an important market in the United States despite all the adversities of the Napoleonic Wars.

With all the trials and tribulations of the period the Hodgsons too had not escaped the repercussions; during the two years 1793 and 1794 the brothers Robert and Brian Jnr. had begun to borrow large sums of money, with the property at Disley comprising Yeardsley

Hall, the adjoining land and colliery initially used as collateral. The brothers were, of course, each entitled to a $\frac{1}{6}$th share of the residue of their father's estate upon the death of their mother, and as at least £6,000 was invested on her behalf, it followed that each (or their heirs) was guaranteed at least £1,000 in due course. During 1793 in total Brian Jnr. borrowed £2,500. The following year Robert sold a house and land in Wagg Street, Congleton and, together with other property, two pew seats in "Congleton Chapel" and two seats in Astbury Church. Still needing a further £2,000 he used his interests in the Disley colliery and estate in order to secure a loan of comparable value.

* * * * * * *

Apart from the considerable financial demands created by the move from Toxteth to Neath, there was a never ending drain on company resources, as the search for copper continued on the mainland in the hope of reducing the quantities of ore imported from Ireland with their restrictive import duties. In April 1793 each partner had been required to pay Hawkins Mills & Co. £100 for every $\frac{1}{64}$th share held in order to facilitate the purchase of Cornish ore, and by 1795 Mr. Magor was shipping Cornish ores to Neath from the mines of Wheal Jewel and North Downs.

At the August meeting of 1793 it was decided to accept a lease offered by Sir Roger Mostyn for a mine "under a messuage, tenement & lands in the parish of Bethgelert co. Caernavon called Havodyllan". The mine, situated to the south-east of the village of Beddgelert, had originally been under lease to others for 21 years from 1762, but with little success. The indenture was finally signed on 29th September 1794 between Sir Roger and Robert Hodgson, Edward Hawkins and Abraham Mills, the latter still " of Hurdsfield" at that date. The lease, again for 21 years, had a rent of $\frac{1}{9}$th part of ores raised for the first 11 years and $\frac{1}{8}$th thereafter. The mine is listed as an asset, value £4 17 6d. only, on 15th August 1794, just six weeks prior to the signing of the lease proving that trials had already begun.

During the August meeting of 1794 a reappraisal and valuation of the whole business took place culminating in a decision (taken two months later) to draw up new Articles of Partnership. Events had moved rapidly, and with the unfortunate exclusion of Smyth and Caldwell from the partnership and the need to incorporate new partners into the scheme of things, the local attorney Peter Wright was, surprisingly, given the commission.

One new partner was John Harriott Roe, admitted with a $\frac{1}{64}$th share in August 1793 which had been held in trust for him by William Roe from his late father's estate. And, as already mentioned, there was also the admittance of Thomas Weaver Jnr. in July 1794. Another, yet not so new, partner was James Clegg, a Liverpool solicitor who, up to this time, had only been given one brief mention in the company minutes when Charles Caldwell had transferred a half share to him on 29th August 1786. The reason for this is not at all obvious, but one suspects it could have been a convenient way for Caldwell to settle a debt for services rendered. Clegg's first attendance at a company meeting was not until 1st October 1794 in Macclesfield when, after Peter Wright's apparent reluctance to act for the company, Clegg began his role as another useful company asset. But even Clegg showed signs of inertia when faced with the preparation of the Articles and was still being asked to "expedite" their completion in August 1796.

Meanwhile the Cheadle Company partners were also under considerable financial pressure and took steps to alleviate the situation by attempting to dispose of some of their assets, creating further difficulties for the Macclesfield partnership. In the spring of 1794 Cheadle decided to sell a quarter share of the Cromford calamine lease, but Roe & Co., on resolving not to follow suit, requested an increased responsibility for the management of the mine.

Cheadle also advised Roe & Co. of their intention to withdraw from the lead trade which would dramatically affect the stability of production at the River Bank Works near Holywell.

Roe & Co. immediately offered a lease of the works to Lord Grosvenor and advised Cheadle that if the offer was accepted they would expect to have "use of the works free of all and whatever, except a proportion of the ground rent payable to Mr. Pennant." If successful, Cheadle would be paid their share of the capital invested as soon as possible.

Problems had arisen during the previous summer of 1793 when the Macclesfield partners had learnt of some misconduct relating to the two Holywell agents, and a meeting with Cheadle quickly followed. No doubt warnings were given to the suspected pair and matters improved for a while. Two years later, after Lord Grosvenor's apparent rejection of the lease offer, Roe & Co. recommended to Cheadle that the two be dismissed and replaced by one new agent only, having already told Cheadle that they had no desire to purchase the latter's share of the works but instead were willing to join them in disposing of the whole site. Yet still no resolution presented itself and matters dragged on, even after a suggestion to Cheadle in April 1797 that the works should be advertised for sale by auction; Flintshire calamine was once more shipped to Macclesfield in its raw state.

In a desperate attempt to resolve the situation, during 1797 Roe & Co. agreed to purchase the Cheadle share of the works if John Wilkinson, the ironmaster, concluded a smelting contract with them by the autumn. Wilkinson, wily as ever, offered Cheadle £350 for their share, and Cheadle did the honourable thing by offering it to Roe & Co. for the same price; it was accepted together with a proposal from a Mr. Clay to rent the premises if he was prepared to pay an annual rental of £160. Mr. Hodgson (presumably Robert) was sent immediately to take stock and make a valuation of the tools and furnaces which he then submitted to Clay.

Times, however, were becoming progressively more difficult, as acknowledged by Rev. Warner of Bath during his tour of the area in 1799. He wrote, "War, which never fails to produce individual distress, as well as public misery, has so reduced the price of lead, that mines can scarcely continue to exist."

As late as October of that year the buildings at Holywell were valued at £984 2 1½d. in the balance sheet when the Macclesfield Committee was empowered to "dispose of them". Further offers came from a Benjamin Hughes of Birmingham and a Mr. Myers Marshall. Finally, in May 1800, Mr. Marshall's offer of £2,060 for the purchase of the site was accepted and presumably completed, for no item relating to the River Bank or Holywell Works appears in the accounts to 18th November 1800, only the Holway Mine.

* * * * * * *

The lead mine, known variously as 'Old Holloway", 'Holway' or the 'Holywell Level' had ironically proved itself consistently productive despite the growing economic crisis of the period. Thomas Pennant's initial visit to and account of the mine, some four years prior to that of Rev. Warner's, gives a more general geological and touristic view. Whilst the latter, preferring more substance, concentrated specifically on mineralogy, industry and the lives of the people.

Pennant, accompanied by his two sons, arrived at the entrance to the mine on 21st September 1795, from where they were piloted by the "honest" agent, Thomas Edwards, along the subterranean waterways whilst passing through several caverns. Edwards was the agent sanctioned by Roe & Co. in July 1793 to sell sufficient lead to cover the expense of working the mine and, judging from Pennant's epithet, was presumably the replacement for the two previous employees. Pennant's journey was quite eventful, lighted by candles placed along the sides of the barge. After negotiating several tunnels the thunderous noise of an underground waterfall was heard, causing great alarm, but passing close by the spot and experiencing only a rise in the water level and a strong tidal effect, they soon reached the end of their tour, judging that the 'cascade' was probably one of the sources feeding the nearby St. Winifred's holy well, a place of pilgrimage for centuries.

Rev. Warner's account of the subterranean adventure is even more detailed than the former because of his obvious interest in people. Having described the caverns and gothic arch hewn out of quartz, he and his associates were startled by the sudden appearance of two "extraordinary figures" each holding a flaming torch and marching their way down the archway. The first was a giant of a man, wearing miner's clothes and a fur cap, closely followed by a slightly smaller companion dressed likewise who turned out to be Mr. Edwards "the able and diligent agent of the mine".

Warner's narrative also lists the products of the mine as limestone (burnt for manure and buildings), chert or felsite (a hard stone used in the potteries), calamine, Zinc blende or black jack and the most important, lead ore. The lead was the most valuable, being mined and brought to the mouth of the level by workmen at an agreed price per ton. Before the war rates were high, as much as £13 to £15 per ton, but by then (1799) had been drastically reduced to no more than £7 to £8 per ton.

Sixty five men were employed, yet all in poor health because of the necessity to work alternatively in the wet and cold conditions underground and then return to the heat of the surface. They were "pale, wan and weak", many affected by a debilitating condition called 'ballan' i.e. constipation of the bowels from inhaling particles of lead, although Rev. Warner did also suggest that their unhealthy pallor could be due in part to the large quantities of liquor "to which they are fatally attached", or their favourite pastime of "smoaking". He observed young boys of 10 or 12 years of age with 2 inch pipes in their mouths "breathing smoke and flame from morning to night." Yet, despite these observations, he concluded that although mining was a dangerous occupation there were very few serious accidents because of the expert way in which the miners worked.

Tales were told of many narrow escapes, but the one affectionately related by Warner was of a workman in a mine near Holywell who fell almost a hundred and fifty feet. His workmates above guessed instant death, but the miner, totally unperturbed, called back up the shaft "Ecod, I've broke my clogs."

On 7th October 1799 Roe & Co. reckoned they had lead ore to the value of £400 on bank at the Holway Mine, but this was obviously somewhat superficial, given that lead prices were plummeting, which must have been a constant source of agitation. In August 1798 the value had been £750, but with the need to discharge debts Mills attended a winter meeting of the Holywell Lead Mine Company to recommend a sale of both lead and calamine, which could account for some of the reduction in the valuation figure.

Meanwhile the mining near Beddgelert continued with trials of copper and appears to have been a speculative undertaking to replace the sudden failure of Llanberis, for no mention is made of the latter from August 1793 till April 1798 when samples of Llanberis ore were sent to William Roe via Chester. Roe & Co. were certainly reworking the Llanberis mine at the turn of the century as noted by various visitors to the area, and during November 1800 further ore samples would be sent to Dublin, presumably for assaying and Abraham Mills's attention.

The Llandudno mining lease from the Bishop of Bangor had met with some success. However, Roe & Co. in an effort to retain as much capital as possible for as long as possible, had accrued a large deficit. Abraham Mills, in charge of the operation, had claimed expenses for the Macclesfield company's working of the mine together with carriage and shipping charges, duty payable to the Bishop and other miscellaneous expenses. As the most convenient way was for the company to be paid in kind (i.e. copper ore) this had been done, but the Bishop had received his duty in cash, after which any excess profits and a proportion of the expenses were payable to the Llandudno Mine Company to be distributed as shares. For the years 1793 to 5th July 1801 a total of £1,079 13 1½d. was due to be transferred from Roe & Co. to the Llandudno Mine Company.

The copper mining problems in North Wales would have arisen, of course, with or without a war, but events on the Continent had certainly affected the most profitable parts of the business and nowhere more so than in Ireland.

* * * * * * *

At first glance the Irish problem is an intriguing one, but many interesting forces were at work and explanations are not too difficult to find when remembering the postscript in Watt's letter of 16th August 1785 to Boulton that "French money has been bestowed plentifully in Ireland".

The links between France and Ireland were considerable, especially amongst the Roman Catholic mercantile families, strengthened by their support of the exiled English court of James II in the late 17th century. Also long held grievances, not only amongst the Roman Catholic community but within Dissenting groups, had been passed down from one generation to the next. Just as in Britain, where no one could hold public office unless they could produce a 'Sacrament Certificate' confirming they were communicants of the Church of England, so the Irish Parliament ensured a similar commitment to the Protestant Episcopalian Church of Ireland. By an Act of 1720 the British Government declared its right to legislate for Ireland, and Irish law cases requiring the powers of a supreme court were transferred to the House of Lords. The American Declaration of Independence, therefore, greatly affected the vast majority of those in Ireland excluded from the Establishment and, being further inspired by the French Revolution, some Dissenters and Roman Catholics combined to form an association known as the United Irishmen in 1791, intent on agitation.

The Hibernian Mining Company was known to have engaged a number of rebels expelled from County Louth in 1792, and as John Howard Kyan was a close relative of a local Wexford leader of the United Irishmen, and the Camac brothers were thought to be republican sympathisers, tensions were rapidly increasing within the mining communities of the Wicklow area.

When France declared war, the British Government, hoping to gain support from the large group of Irish Roman Catholics, gave them the right to take up most public offices, but a few months later there was an extraordinary turn of events; gold was discovered on the north-east side of the Croaghin Mountain, the summit of which was the boundary between the counties of Wicklow and Wexford.

On 3rd November 1795 Abraham Mills visited the site and sent a full report to the Royal Society of London, where it was read to members on 17th December. Grains of gold had been discovered in the sand and gravel of a stream flowing through a great ravine to join the River Aughrim. (Attracting further tributaries en route, the river then takes the name of Avoca and enters the sea near Arklow). The greatest interest was in an area of about half a mile in length just before the confluence, where the Arklow road led to a ford adjoined. The land was in the barony of Arklow and county of Wicklow but, whilst belonging to the Earl of Carysfort, was claimed by the Earl of Ormond in respect of mineral rights.

Once the discovery was publicised, people from the surrounding areas quickly moved in, and from early September 1795 worked feverishly to earn their fortunes. Their enterprise was short-lived, for the Kildare militia arrived on 15th October to take possession on behalf of the government until the legalities were fully investigated. Everyone left quietly, and although Mills considered their haphazard methods of periodically turning the course of the stream, digging holes and washing the silt in bowls and sieves as "flovenly & hafty", yet the value of the gold retrieved was reckoned as "three thousand pounds Irish fterling" having been sold to various people at £3 15s. per ounce. The profitable gold stream works were continued on an official basis until 1798, but no effort was made to trace the true source of the gold at that time.

There is no doubt that the French Republican government learnt very quickly of the discovery of gold in Ireland, and it can be no coincidence that General Lazare Hoche, commander of the Republican Army, was persuasive in gaining permission to invade Ireland not England in 1796. France was full of Irish exiles, and whilst some actually spied for the British government others supported the French. Roman Catholic families such as the Byrnes had risen to prominence both in Dublin, where Edward Byrne was judged to be the wealthiest merchant, and on the Continent where a John Byrne had been established in Bordeaux from 1757. Significantly a younger member of the family, Miles Byrne, had spent much of his childhood on the banks of the Avoca, where his mother's family lived, and such was French interest in the Irish mines that a French periodical entitled *Journal des Mines* contained a remarkably accurate report of the Avoca mines, including a description of the copper tokens in circulation. (When taking into consideration that the A.I.M. Co. managed 64 variations between 1789 and 1795, 42 of which relate to 1789, but the Hibernian company are known to have produced at least 185 variants in 1792 alone, there seems to be a strong hint of French assistance with the latter).

Gold was difficult to find in Europe; the main sources were Mexico, Russia and Hungary with only minor production from Sweden and the Italian States. The French mint at Toulouse had formerly been supplied from the region of Southern France bordering the Pyrenees, but now an incredible opportunity had presented itself, not only did the French government have the chance to acquire some valuable copper mines but also a relatively accessible and promising gold mine.

From the spring of 1795 the British navy had been left to fight single-handed at sea, and whilst the French army was being reorganised by Napoleon after his triumphant success in defence of the Tuileries against a rebellion in October 1795 and had begun a brilliant military campaign across the Continent to defeat the Austrians and Italians, yet the French navy was greatly underfunded. Thomas Williams had been supplying French naval yards with copper sheathing surreptitiously; when later confronted with this he commented that if they had not bought it from him they would have bought it elsewhere. Terrible winter storms had caused great damage, more to the French navy than English, and France was desperately short of food, having first suffered a failed harvest in 1793 and become dependent on American grain. The sooner France could acquire gold for her coinage and copper for her naval sheathing, the more food could be imported and the more popular the government would be, no doubt inspiring plans for an Irish invasion to be set in motion during 1796. Rumours abounded and the British government, unable to learn any specific details, ensured the fleet was on full alert.

On 16th December Hoche, in command of 14,750 soldiers, set sail with supplies in a French fleet of 37 vessels, but a strong south-westerly wind soon dispersed the ships and scattered them into an area of rain, mists and fog. By 19th December the wind had changed direction and only a handful of French ships found themselves off the southern coast of Ireland and could easily have taken Cork where there was a large store of military and naval supplies. But Hoche was elsewhere so the immediate command hesitated; by the 25th December an easterly wind blew fiercely down the bay and the French Admiral Bouvet was forced to sea and returned to Brest.

Two or three other ships reached the mouth of the Shannon and also returned to France but not before one of them had succeeded in capturing the *Cumberland* a trading ship with 30 English soldiers on board returning from the West Indies. All passengers and crew were taken on board the Frenchman and the *Cumberland* was sent to France as a prize. A spell of atrocious weather followed during which the French captain was seen and attacked by two English naval vessels in an engagement which lasted all night. When daylight came one English ship escaped; the other had been driven onto the French shore, but the French vessel lay on her side and was pounded by breakers for two days without any hope of assistance. Conditions were terrible, with an attempt to lower boats filled with women and children ending in disaster; they were dashed to pieces. The English soldiers and crew did their best to help all concerned, and when a rescue was effected the French government released the surviving English because of their "supreme, humane conduct" and gave rewards in cash to many.

It was now becoming obvious to everyone that the French were intent on invasion, and perhaps many Irishmen had been forewarned, especially those like the Camac brothers who had each taken charge of a corps of yeomanry in 1796 recruited from within the Hibernian Mining Company, many of whom were United Irishmen. One of their number, described as an "agent provocateur", had already been active in the area stirring up trouble, but his denunciation in due course resulted in the disbandonment of the Camac yeomanry in March 1798. Nevertheless the seeds of rebellion were sown.

The expense accounts for the A.I.M. Co. verify that Abraham Mills was frequently in Ireland during 1795. He twice visited Dublin in February and March; was present at Cronebane in November and travelled from England to Cronebane in December. At this time Cronebane was the major site with lesser workings at Tigroney, and although Connery had ceased production by February 1793 and Ballygahan by March 1795, yet one year later Ballygahan was again operative but providing precipitated copper only.

Roe & Co. could not afford to take chances and during 1796 Abraham Mills, by then in his mid-forties, must have been flattered to find himself in uniform once more, designated Captain of the Cronebane Corps who were volunteers of the A.I.M. Co. His second in command was 'First Lieutenant Weaver' supported by Second Lieutenant Blood. The A.I.M. Co. had every intention of guarding its investments, for almost £49,000 had been spent on developing the mines, including the payroll, since 1787. The company provided uniforms for the 'Volunteers' at a cost of £150 2 2d. , a drum price £2 10 11d. and was shortly importing arms through Wicklow.

The following year witnessed an extraordinary turn of events, if the French government's motives are to be believed. There were those in France who had openly challenged the revolutionary regime, many were royalists and Roman Catholics, but the government was determined to crush all opposition, so they were driven 'underground'. Known as emigrés many fled the country to fight the cause from a distance whilst others congregated along the coast, mostly in Brittany, and created as much havoc as possible. They burned, pillaged, murdered and obstructed proceedings to the best of their abilities. Many were caught and imprisoned but the French government, tiring of overcrowded cells full of rabble-rousers, came up with an incredible idea. The scheme was to transport as many of the troublemakers as possible across the Channel and 'dump' them on the English coast where, it was assumed, they would continue their outrageous activities and cause great damage. At the very least they would be out of the way and one less headache for the revolutionaries. Consequently in February 1797 four vessels were dispatched with prisoners on board, eventually landing 1,500 men at Fishguard on the Pembrokeshire coast.

The French ships were hardly out of sight before the interlopers surrendered peacefully to Lord Cawdor leading a much smaller force of Welsh militia. Led by an American adventurer called Tate, the French men had no intention of risking their lives unnecessarily, but the sudden appearance of so large a number on British soil caused great panic, and one only has to look at a map of Wales to appreciate just how close they were to the Swansea area and how easily a greater force could have severely disrupted the manufacturing industries of South Wales. Roe & Co. must have been extremely concerned, but John Place, manager of the Mines Royal Co. was able to write in one of his company books "6 March. – Tis not true that the French had landed at Swansea".

The British government wasted no time in demanding an exchange of prisoners, but the French declined on the pretext that they did not want the rabble returning to France. Only after being threatened with a reverse operation, did the thought of several hundred marauders let loose somewhere along the French coast bring the French government to its senses.

About this time Liverpool became a centre for the detention of French prisoners and the gaol, built in Great Howard Street in 1786 but still unoccupied, was put to good use. By the end of 1798 there were 4,000 prisoners in the city, many of whom performed plays for the general public, made trinkets, toys and such like, which were sold for the purpose of purchasing extra comforts for themselves. In 1802, with the unexpected signing of the Peace of Amiens, many would be released to return home, but others would choose to stay.

The Fishguard episode is difficult to comprehend and would appear more logical if the real object of the exercise was to land the prisoners on the Irish coast somewhere between Wexford and Wicklow (i.e. on the opposite side of St. George's Channel). Sailing ships were at the mercy of winds and tides and needed a good deal of luck to complete successful ventures, so the possibility of Ireland, and in particular Wexford or Wicklow as the intended destination cannot be ruled out; the French government was hardly likely to reveal its true intent at this stage. Subsequent information has revealed a plan to take Chester and Liverpool, but even that does not detract from the idea that the acquisition of copper and gold was the ultimate target. Yet although the fiasco was over before it had barely begun, the ensuing widespread panic created serious undertones.

During the next few months the management of the A.I.M. Co. was extremely vigilant and a decision was taken to ask each of the Volunteers to make a solemn oath swearing that he would not join the United Irishmen and would remain loyal to King George III. Unable to do so 44 men had to be dismissed and replaced by those willing to declare allegiance; this would obviously cause dissent, but the year 1797 was proving to be one of alarms and high tensions. Spain, having joined the French by declaring war in October 1796, was preparing for combined naval operations, which would also include the Dutch fleet, in the invasion of England. Fortunately Admiral Jervis sighted the Spaniards en route for Brest and the English fleet managed a decisive victory in the Battle of Cape St. Vincent on 14th February 1797. Nelson was beginning to make his presence felt by capturing two prizes. Another great victory was won by Admiral Duncan at Camperdown (off the north coast of Holland) on the 11th October when the Dutch fleet was defeated in just two and a half hours. Yet despite the uplifting of morale everyone knew that the danger was far from over.

By now the disturbances generally in Ireland were taking on a more serious nature as rumours and counter rumours abounded, and in the New Year of 1798 one of Roe & Co. Volunteers acted as a guard when escorting prisoners to Wicklow. Perhaps as a security measure, a new set of uniforms was provided for the corps during April 1798.

* * * * * * *

Across the Channel, Napoleon, having conquered the Austrians and Italians, deprived the city state of Venice of her 1,100 years of independence, and subjected the Pope to some humiliating conditions, had returned in triumph to Paris in November 1797. After the abortive attempts to invade the British Isles, at last the French felt they had a personality who could accomplish the task, so in the New Year of 1798 Napoleon was commissioned to prepare for a full-scale operation. Hopes must have been high amongst the Irish Republicans but, after surveying the Channel coast, Napoleon decided that it was premature to attempt such a considerable undertaking and instead set about raising his "army of England" for action at a future date. His next strategy was ingenious, to capture the British wealth and destroy the British army in India.

Since the second half of the 17th century permanent British troops had been recruited by the East India Company to serve in regiments abroad in defence of the company's forts, trading posts and settlements, and nowhere more so than in India. Napoleon, growing up on the island of Corsica, had viewed the world with a different perspective from those born and raised in France. His way to India, like Alexander before him, was overland from Egypt.

On the 2nd May Nelson was dispatched to the Mediterranean and subsequently given ships and a command with which to patrol the sea off the French port of Toulon, but during a refitting operation Napoleon, and ships crowded with troops and supplies, sailed out of the port on 20th May bound for Egypt. Nelson, on returning to patrol duty, found the French fleet gone and could not discover its destination.

It is difficult to appreciate the depth of fear and terror felt by the British public at this time. Napoleon had gained an awesome reputation and might even then be sailing for the Irish Sea, having given Jervis the slip off Cadiz. The circumstances strongly suggest that five days later it was the expected arrival of the French fleet off Ireland which started the Irish rebellion in a dramatic way.

The British government had passed an Act of Parliament in 1794 to set up a voluntary cavalry force of yeomen, and the Irish yeomanry had been particularly active in suppressing subversion and taking prisoners. The situation was already volatile when, for some inexplicable reason during an altercation, yeomen guarding a building full of detainees at Carnew only seven miles to the south-west of the gold mining area of Wicklow, set fire to the place killing all those within; as though a bomb had exploded, suddenly bigotry was let loose. The rebellion quickly spread and houses and businesses of both Protestants and Roman Catholics were systematically burnt throughout north Wexford and Wicklow, the two most Protestant counties outside Ulster.

The Cronebane Volunteers were evidently very active, for work at the mines was suspended between 31st May and 30th September "in consequence of the unhappy disturbances which broke out into open acts of violence in this country." The first priority would be protection of the company premises together with the lives of the work force and their families. There was already a heavy Irish yeomanry presence in the area because of the gold mining operations, so the damage to domestic property was far less locally than elsewhere in County Wicklow, although the Volunteers did support the local community by sending ninety of their members to Rathdrum. An interesting tuition fee for "Cronebane Drummers and Fifers" appears in the company expenses for August, suggesting they were 'on the march'. During their three months in service each Volunteer was paid a sum comparable to what he would have earned in wages, but the cost to the company, not only from accrued expenses but actual loss of profits, must have been considerable.

The Hibernian Mining Company was already in an untenable situation before the rebellion began, due mainly to its irresponsible mining methods, which could have been one of the reasons why Kyan became embroiled in the troubles, in the hope of being able to reclaim the management of the profitable Cronebane mine. But when Colonel Camac filed a suit in the High Court of Chancery against him during 1798, mining ground to a halt and Kyan was destined for ruin. There was no easy way out, the French were elsewhere and the fact that Kyan's father-in-law, Thomas Sutton, had been an important financier in Paris before the French Revolution, was now of no use to him.

Surprisingly the main French force commanded by Napoleon was 'researching' its way through Egypt in an effort to satisfy his insatiable curiosity with Egyptology. And Nelson, having correctly calculated that the French had sailed eastwards, finally destroyed Napoleon's fleet in Aboukir Bay during the night of 1st August. Just six days later, with the English fleet occupied in the Mediterranean, the French Government began yet another attempt to invade Ireland. One squadron reached Killala Bay on the north-east coast between Mayo and Sligo but shortly after landing, the officer and troops involved surrendered at Ballina.

An alarm was raised in the autumn when a French squadron was sighted off the west coast of Ireland on 11th October, however, during a series of fights English ships were able to capture six French frigates. Other stray ships appeared, but hurriedly returned to France when discovering the fate of their squadron. A further squadron, sailing from Rochefort on the 12th October, again managed to reach Killala Bay but, finding it impossible to land, was sighted then chased back to France having thrown guns overboard in order to lighten the ships.

With the realisation that there was much to lose in Ireland, the Macclesfield partnership made an important decision to form a private limited company, which was Incorporated by an Act of the Irish Parliament on 7th November 1798. This meant that, should any financial difficulties arise requiring the wind up of the company, the creditors could not claim any personal property from individual company members. Also only two original members were necessary to form the company and only one director required, although there was a restriction on the right to transfer shares.

The two original members were "Abraham Mills of Macclesfield & Cronebane' Chairman and "Thomas Weaver of Cronebane" Director. Mills was also proxy for William Roe (Liverpool); Edward Hawkins and Roe & Co. (Macclesfield); Robert Hodgson (Congleton) and Brian Hodgson (Crakemarsh, Staffs.) Thomas Weaver was proxy for both his father and John "Jeffries" of Gloucester. In addition to these nine partners, who were also shareholders. There were three more units of shares relating to the assignees of Thomas Smyth, Charles Caldwell and Brabazon Noble. Each unit was of 50 shares and apart from William Roe and John Jefferies of Gloucester who held half a unit each (i.e. 25 shares each) and Thomas Weaver Snr. and his son, Thomas, who divided a unit 40 shares and 10 shares respectively, all other eight holdings were of 50 shares each. The total was therefore 500 shares, value £100 each (£50,000).

It was at this time that French public opinion began to turn against the Revolutionary government and Napoleon, having spent a year in Egypt and Syria losing men to disease, hunger, plague and fatalities as they battled against the Turks, was recalled to France. A successful coup saw a new constitution proclaimed on 29th December 1799 with Napoleon as First Consul, but exactly what effect this would have on the situation was anybody's guess.

Meanwhile Roe & Co., "the present purchasers of the Cronebane ores", who had been trying for years to obtain a reduction of import duties on Irish ore decided to petition once more, but were advised to refer their grievances to a committee already set up to inquire into the copper trade in general. There is little doubt that this was the product of agitations on the part of Thomas Williams, who had learnt of the government's intention to restrict the exportation of copper by the East India Company. He was now fighting for his existence.

* * * * * * *

About the spring of 1793, as the effects of the French Revolution intervened, even Williams had finally accepted that it was becoming increasingly necessary for companies to put aside antagonism and rivalry for the sake of survival, also the Mona Mine was beginning to fail. When negotiating a large contract, which he knew he could not fulfil, he allowed Roe & Co. a share, as in the instance of the naval bolt contracts. Williams was by then in the advantageous position of concentrating the copper sheathing and bolts production in his own works at Temple Mills, Marlow, a site ideally located because of its proximity to the south-eastern naval yards and the merchant vessels of London.

In July 1793 Robert Hodgson had been sent to tender copper for the naval dockyards of Chatham and Sheerness, unless he could agree a share of a general contract with Williams which would allow the Macclesfield partners to provide a proportion of copper equal to the supply required for the two yards. By October 1794 Roe & Co., obviously intent on streamlining the business, offered the remainder of their East India contract to Williams followed by their Liverpool stock of African goods in May 1795.

Williams, already appreciating the potentials of a self-owned banking system, had founded, together with other partners, the Chester and North Wales Bank in 1792; branches at Bangor and Caernarfon were also opened in that year and in Chester during 1793. When the panic of 1797 arose and people rushed to withdraw their savings, Williams simply closed the Chester branch until the storm abated. He would find it to be a very useful provider of a £30,000 loan at the beginning of 1801 until, by some miraculous book-keeping and the creation of yet another subsidiary company, it allowed him to recover a greater part of the capital. But debts were mounting due to his inability to find cheaper sources of copper.

The last great strike on Parys Mountain had produced 2,931 tons of reasonably rich ore in a period of just three months during 1787, at which Williams must have been rubbing his hands with glee; however, the reservations set out by Abraham Mills on behalf of Roe & Co. in their negotiations for a renewed lease, suddenly became a reality. The rich vein was worked out leaving only the poorer ores with their higher retrievable costs, so that by the mid-1790s production had fallen to barely 2,000 tons each year. Yet, although Williams was so desperate for ore, his sheer ruthless and vindictive nature would not allow him to support Roe & Co. in their bid to import Irish ores duty free.

The parliamentary inquiry began on 5th April 1799 when George Simcox, representing the manufacturers of Birmingham, came before the committee. He was asked what reductions had occurred during the previous seven years, and answered that consumption of copper in 1792 had been 1,500 to 2,000 tons but by then was "may be" 1,000 tons. He argued that no manufacturer of heavy goods could make a profit without raising prices, and whilst prices of goods had increased initially after 1792 they did gradually reduce again, but certain articles, in particular brass foundry, had risen sharply during 1797 and since then the manufacturers had absorbed the increases themselves.

Next it was the turn of Abraham Mills who was questioned about the Irish ore situation. His answers were clear and concise; about 1,000 tons average had been raised for each of three years from the Cronebane Mine Company, Wicklow, and of similar quality to Cornish ores. There was a mine on the other side of the river called Ballymurtagh, but he had no knowledge of its production. He agreed that it was possible to contract for 120 tons of ore for the next three years, but when asked if he would contract for 500 tons at any price he emphatically answered "No".

The following day Simcox was recalled and asked if he had ever imported foreign copper, to which he replied "Not immediately" (presumably meaning not directly, but obviously purchases from Roe & Co. would include Irish copper) and that he had no knowledge of the price of foreign copper.

Simcox was immediately followed by John Vivian on behalf of the Cornish mines who, when asked to provide the profits and expenses for the last seven years, had only the figures for the last six months to hand. He did, however, volunteer to send immediately to Cornwall for the information and meantime requested to be allowed to present those he had brought with him. He explained that the Cornish mines had been divided into three groups; the old deep mines which were producing more than half the copper raised in Cornwall and about $^2/_5$ths of the copper in Great Britain; the mines where costs just exceeded ore sales and therefore accrued a proportionately small loss and those which were a 'dead loss'.

The inquiry dragged on for several days until on 20th April Thomas Williams "a Member of the Houfe" and therefore secure in the knowledge that his position as M.P. for Marlow had already given him a platform from which to pontificate, began his convoluted deliberations. In compliance with a request to give an account of the copper trade he gave a resumé of the copper industry from the late 17th century, and although not entirely correct, it was sufficient for his purpose and no doubt satisfied his streak of egoism. On arriving at the year 1773 he pointed out that new copper mines had been discovered in Derbyshire and Wales resulting in falling prices until 1781, then a great competition had taken place at East India House between Cornwall and Anglesey, with the result that Cornwall sacrificed £25,000 to keep Anglesey copper out of the market.

When later reading the published report Roe & Co. must have been appalled at the way Williams had manipulated the facts, for he had completely concealed his involvement with the Anglesey mining until much later, and therefore as the report stood it could easily have been construed that Roe & Co. were the instigators of the destruction of the Cornish mines which, of course, could not have been further from the truth.

Williams continued that "a warm Conteft" had ensued between all the copper companies from then on, and Cornwall had lowered prices in order to compete but then "proposed to me to come to terms with them". In 1787 "some Difagreements arofe between the Cornish Metal Company and myself refpecting the Proportion of Sales at Market . . . I was enabled to conduct the Businefs so as to despose of the great Stock of the Cornish Metal Company" (possibly by buying some of this ore cheaply for his own works near London).

He argued that the East India Company had greatly benefited from the competition and also other copper purchasers, and then went on to dispute the figures produced by Simcox for Birmingham. He spoke of his experience of keeping a warehouse there from 1781 to 1791 when he supplied ²/₃rds or more of the city's requirements which amounted to 1,100 tons per annum. (This is proof that Boulton and Watt were correct in deducing Williams had been selling copper from his Birmingham warehouse after he had supposedly closed it down due to the dispute of 1787). He derided Simcox & Co. for recommencing the ticketing system in Cornwall during 1792, complaining that they had opened up old Cornish mines, purchased smeltworks and raised copper prices, which he considered "odious", and that Simcox at the same time had proposed the importation of foreign ore duty free and the prohibition of English copper exports. Small wonder Williams was eager to reap revenge, for Simcox could not have proposed any better ways of putting him out of business. Williams, as always, knew how to turn an argument to his benefit, and knowing Boulton was panicking about his shares in the Cornish mines, had written to him to prove Simcox had exaggerated the figures by asking Boulton to supply a catalogue proving that many of the Birmingham goods did not contain copper e.g. steel buckles, and other items made of glass and mother of pearl etc.

At this point Williams mentioned the difficulties experienced with copper sheathing but emphasised his great patriotism by his experiments to help the British Navy with the problems of bolts. He stressed that all these parts of the trade depended on the mines of "our Country, and the Spirit and Enterprize of our People in carrying them on . . ." He gave details of the losses and waste in foreign mines, yet all were supported by their respective governments, and with a final burst pronounced that if the government had supported Cornwall in 1783 "England might this Day have been the greatest and moft flourishing Mineral Country in all Europe . . ." Instead of support he insisted that the govenment had created nothing but restrictions, prohibition and taxes. He was obviously furious that the exportation of copper sheathing, around 1780, had been prohibited "under the mistaken and ruinous Notion of depriving our Enemies, the French, of Copper Sheathing for their Ships during the American War", resulting in the French erecting their own copper works followed by Spain and Italy. When asked where the French had bought their supplies of copper Williams denied any knowledge of it but stated that 14 or 15 years ago their copper came principally from Smyrna and Constantinople, with considerable quantities from South America and a little from Sweden.

With regard to his copper warehouse in Birmingham, Williams said he had withdrawn because his agent of seven or eight years had died leaving considerable debts on the books, some of which he had been unable to recover. He found it difficult to satisfy customers there and decided to have no further dealings with them.

His response to the next question revealed that merchant ships had more copper fastenings in them than naval vessels, because more copper nails were used throughout the hulls especially below water, and also more deck nails.

The next query was with regard to how the East India Company contracted for their supplies of copper. With a somewhat tongue-in-cheek reply Williams verified that the company advertised for tenders to be placed on a certain day and all those interested sent in tenders sealed on that day, but that it meant little "of late years". A few days beforehand the copper companies met to discuss how much each wished to tender for and "to what Amount". In general it was agreed that they would contract according to the amount of stocks held within the last twelve months and also estimate a fair price according to the standard of those ores. The East India Company, knowing this price, then contracted for a certain amount e.g. 1,500 tons, and according to quality, purchased at various prices but always bearing in mind the average price.

At last the vital questions were asked; what would be the consequence of a temporary halt to trade with India and secondly the effect of stopping the exportation of copper and allowing the importation of duty free ore?

To the first Williams answered that it was not immediately obvious what would happen but the Armenian mines had already sent some copper to India, though not in the form required; however, it was possible to satisfy India's wants from Armenia. The Indians had bought various copper and brass articles from England, but if this was impeded then they would build their own manufactories and use Persian copper, so the trade with England would be lost. To the second he commented tersely that he remembered a time when the mines "in this Country" would have prospered with the usual duty on imported ore, but whilst the expense of working mines increased, the ore prices would follow suit.

The Inspector General's Office of the London Custom House then presented a report of foreign wrought and unwrought copper and copper ore imported in a series of decades from 1710 to 1790, and then yearly from 1791 to 1799, with the concluding comment "The Copper Ore was almost wholly imported from Ireland". Therefore any suggestion that the importation of foreign copper ore would in any way be detrimental to mining within the British Isles was a myth.

With the enquiry at an end Williams increased his purchases of copper ores, and during the two years of 1799 and 1800 appears to have been supplementing the heavy decline in production on Anglesey; he had, however, won a reprieve.

Mills, as chairman of the A.I.M.Co., would make a further attempt to obtain abolition of the duty on imported ores late in 1801, but before that time, in fact one year before on 18th November 1800, quite suddenly and abruptly a decision was taken to dissolve the Macclesfield Copper Company partnership as soon as possible. Whilst bad debts were to be written off, an effort had to be made to collect those considered retrievable, but all the Macclesfield works, stock and materials had to be disposed of, including one of the mills (either Bosley or Havannah), and all outstanding bonds settled; the gamble to concentrate on brass production had evidently not paid off.

* * * * * * *

Hopes must have been high five years earlier when in August 1793 Hawkins and Mills had been empowered to purchase land and houses adjoining the brass-works on Macclesfield Common (apparently from a member of the Wagstaff family). An almost immediate decline in the wire trade saw an order issued in the following December to use six brass hearths only for casting wire plates, eleven for battery plates and four for ingots. By April 1796 it had become necessary to reduce the labourers at each brass hearth in order to save money paid out in wages, and the A.G.M. of August 1798 ordered the fires for making ingot brass to be put out and the six redundant workmen offered work in Neath at the "present rate paid there."

Hawkins, in explaining the financial situation when writing to Busfield on 5th May 1796, advised him of a resolution by which each partner was asked to advance the considerable sum of £500 for each whole share, but several had not complied with the order. A substantial loan of £6,000 in respect of the Irish Mine Company had been discharged during the course of the previous year, partly by drafts from the Macclesfield Bank and partly by Roe & Co., which would account for most of the demand, but extra capital was no doubt required for two important reasons.

Firstly the Macclesfield Canal was at last seriously considered possible, and a decision to bring it from the Grand Trunk Canal near the Red Bull wharf at Buglawton, via Bosley to Macclesfield was of enormous advantage to the copper company, therefore ten shares were purchased. Such was the boost to confidence that Brian Hodgson transferred to his son, Brian (recently married on 16th May and still an employee of the bank) two and a half $^{1}/_{64}$th shares allowing the young man to be admitted as a partner from 5th July 1796. The August meeting sanctioned Hawkins to double the canal subscription should further funds be needed.

Secondly, by an Act of Parliament 36 Geo 3 1796, proposals were set out for the Enclosure of Macclesfield Common which would radically affect the company's position, as the copper and brass-works were spread out over a large area. Not only would capital be required to purchase the leasehold of the allotted portions of land but, appreciating that the canal would pass across the Common close to the higher copper works, and that building a wharf in the vicinity was an absolute necessity, it was imperative for the company, or one of the partners, to acquire the appropriate allotments adjoining the proposed route. This could prove to be an expensive business depending on how those allotments were allocated.

As far as possible enclosure had to be seen to be fair and therefore certain guidelines had to be followed. The proposals relating to Macclesfield Common (and also to the two smaller commons of Long Moss and Whirley to the west of the town) were set out in the Act.

Because the King was Lord of the Manor of Macclesfield he had to receive one tenth of the common or waste ground within the Borough. The Mayor, Aldermen and Burgesses, with their exclusive rights over certain springs and watercourses granted by Charles II, were to be awarded allotments which would include such springs and watercourses, whilst at the same time incorporating a certain width of land on either side. This would allow the town's water supply to continue unimpeded; however, the total area of land allotted to the Corporation was restricted to between 60-66 acres only. There were also further grants to the Corporation for water pipes to the town, areas reserved for fairs and markets and compensation for the withdrawal of rights of common pasture.

An important clause affecting Roe & Co. was the one relating to coal. His Majesty and the lessees were allowed to mine under the new allotments and use the 'pits, shafts, levels, soughs or tunnels' already opened, and also permitted right of way for carts and waggons to transport the coal, whilst an additional proviso empowered the Corporation to examine the condition of the collieries from time to time. Further permission was given for extending the colliery enterprise to include the conversion of coal to 'charcoal' (coke) and to dig clay for brick making.

At this time Macclesfield Common contained about 750 unenclosed acres to be apportioned between slightly fewer than 300 proprietors, so enclosure was bound to become a long drawn out and difficult process because of the numerous complexities involved. Many private negotiations took place, particularly amongst those where fragmented awards were proposed, so that people were able to exchange allotments in order to consolidate their future holdings.

Initially the land was divided and staked out, with each enclosure given a number. For sale purposes the numbered enclosures became lots and so temporarily acquired an additional number. The whole process was carried out by three commissioners, Josiah Potts, Samuel Sleigh and Thomas Rowley; the latter from Leek was an associate of the copper company. Apart from the grants of ownership where encroachment had taken place, offers could now begin for the remaining available lots, but one suspects it was very much organised on the East India company sales principle i.e. a general meeting first before the official gathering.

Where disputes arose two referees could be called upon, one by each party, and a further arbitrator if necessary. In the event of a particular award not being taken up, the commissioners could dispose of the lot by auction.

In the midst of these domestic affairs the reverberations of war finally reached Macclesfield Common and, like their Irish counterparts, some of the employees were enlisted for militia training. In April 1798 the order was made for ten of the workmen to be "cloathed and trained to Arms in conjunction with any Association formed for the protection of the town and neighbourhood of Macclesfield". This was extended to include the satellite works where the directors were given similar instructions, encouraging a proportion of the employees to join "any Association in their respective districts".

On 22nd August 1798 the copper company partners agreed to the purchase of eight lots on the common numbered 10-15, 27 and 31, by Edward Hawkins and the younger Brian Hodgson as representatives of the company. At the same time the two, accompanied by Thomas Weaver, were asked to negotiate with an adjoining proprietor, Mr. Saywell regarding the pools and watercourses on that part of the Common (this was presumably James Saywell described in 1818 as a warehouseman and a subsequent owner of property in the area – the newly constructed street would be named Saywell, corrupted later to the present day Saville Street). Evidently the pools, necessary for the supply of water to the copper works, had fallen into an adjoining lot, and there was also the problem of the water conveyed from the copper works down to the brass-works on the other side of Lunt Hill (now Windmill Street) for which rights would need to be established.

Apart from the land enclosure there was the 'Cottage' enclosure which established the right of ownership of every individual to the buildings which they had either built or bought. Roe & Co. were, therefore, legally confirmed as owners of their industrial buildings. The brass-works (lots 10-15 corresponding to enclosures 166, 168-170, 177 and 177A) covered 4 acres and 36 perches, although 166 was on the northern side of Lunt Hill Road and nearer the copper-works and seems to have been used as a brick yard.

The copper-works (lot 27, enclosure 381) occupied 2 acres 2 roods and 11 perches, and there was also a small piece of land (lot 31, enclosure 383) only 2 perches on the south-west corner of what it today Black Road and Blakelow Road, presumably for the convenience of the colliery, the entrance to which was just across the way. On 7th October 1799 the company confirmed the purchase of these plots totalling 7 acres 1 rood and 16 perches for £600, calculated on a rental of £30 per annum for 25 years.

The Macclesfield Commons and Cottage Enclosures were finally completed and published in 1804 from which the full extent of acquisitions can clearly be seen.

In addition to the above original allotments, the company also purchased a further four enclosures (377-380) which ran north to south and allowed for prime position along the proposed canal route across that part of the common. The most northerly one (377) of exactly one acre was sold to defray costs, leaving the other three comprising a parcel of land 4 acres 2 roods and 9 perches which today runs along the eastern side of Black Road with its eastern boundary contiguous with the canal.

William Roe, the only partner with anything like a private fortune still intact, acquired the reversion of 23 allotments with tenants high up on the common, close by Blakelow Road (enclosures 93-103, 144, 146-150, 184-189). Number 187 was tenanted by the copper company and from its situation again appears to have been related to the nearby coal seams, as do a further four gains, giving William an additional $23\frac{1}{2}$ acres stretching across the upper part of the common (enclosures 56, 145, 182, 183), presumably bearing in mind any future need for opening up new pits.

The Bollington colliery, valued at just over £6,270 in August 1794 had been running at a loss for some time, and the company had been pressing the other investors, Verdon, Upton and Wood for payment of their proportion of the losses since August 1795. In contrast, however, matters had materially improved on Macclesfield Common, for in August 1797 John Jones was voted a five guineas reward for producing a profit at Greenaway "which under his predecessor had worked at a loss for many years."

There remained the problem of water rights without which the company could not operate. Initially all seemed well; the commissioners stipulated that the streams and watercourses leading through and under several of the allotments granted to the King had to remain unaltered and (no doubt under Thomas Rowley's influence) that the soughs or tunnels "through which the same flow shall at all times hereafter be kept in repair by Messrs. Roe & Co. and the Owners for the time being of the Buildings called the Copper-works." However, although at present no evidence can be found to support the theory, it does seem likely that there were problems with Saywell who subsequently appears to have developed his site and would be keen to avoid any interference from not the most desirable of industrial neighbours.

The severe decline in the brass trade and the results of the House of Commons report were certainly the greatest contributors to the order given to close down the brass-works on or before 5th July 1800. Agents and workmen were given "proper" notice by the directors, who were also responsible for disposing of the stock as soon as possible. On 5th February 1801 it was decided to offer the brass-works, houses and adjoining land to the partnership of "Daintry & Royle", silk manufacturers of Park Green, Macclesfield who had already taken over the bank of Hawkins Mills & Co. by October 1799. Meanwhile the workmen at the brass-works had put forward a proposition to continue producing brass but to be paid by the ton; this was accepted. The proposal to close down the button shank concern might also have been rescinded, as by tradition buttons continued to be produced in that area for many decades. At the same time several more steps were taken towards selling off other parts of the business.

A surveyor was engaged to value the works and buildings at Macclesfield, Bosley and Havannah, and Mr. Magor was instructed to cease sampling, assaying and ticketing in Cornwall and give his "servants" notice to leave at the end of the quarter. His salary would continue to be paid until 5th July 1801 when the assay office would close, but he was asked if he would be willing to carry on employment on a hire basis. His agreement is evident by his offer to invest his own money in the Truro assay office.

Following an inspection of Bollington colliery (proposed in July 1798 but only to be undertaken by someone trustworthy who would submit an accurate report) it was decided to sink an existing shaft by a further 5 yards and work a "drift of 20 yds. in the back level" towards the twitch (i.e. a compressed and narrow vein). This would provide a better assessment in considering the validity of selling the colliery. A shaft at Blakelow was likewise to be sunk, but in this instance the lease was offered for sale.

By October the bonds relating to the £6,270 loan had been cleared, and after recording a valuation of £1,020 for Bollington colliery to the end of the previous financial year, Vardon, Upton and Wood were told that the company intended to quit the workings and sell the materials. This was obviously due to an accruing bad debt which appears in the accounts to 5th July 1802 as £1,313 6 2d. Evidently no offers were forthcoming; in fact Vardon and Upton appear to have discreetly withdrawn, for in August 1803 Wood was the only person advised that the engine and materials were to be sold by auction at Bollington; this was the end of Roe & Co.'s interest in the business.

Blakelow, on the other hand, must have looked promising because Abraham Mills decided to take up the offer of the lease, and was charged £10 in February 1802 for materials and equipment.

Nationally matters were improving. By this time the English fleet was establishing its superiority in the Baltic and had won a great sea battle off Copenhagen in the spring of 1801, just nine days after the murder of Czar Paul of Russia (24th March). The Czar had been one of the key figures in the French coalition, but it was not to be so for his son,

Alexander I, who refused to follow his father's lead because of pressure from within Russia itself. Napoleon's fury at this turn of events, which severely disrupted his policy of excluding all British ships from continental ports, produced a sudden determination to invade and conquer England. Troops were marshalled along the northern coast of France and an enormous flotilla prepared for transportation purposes. But, despite the insistence of the British navy that the scheme "simply would not work", fear amongst the British public was at such a level that the government signed an armistice, ratified at Amiens on 27th March 1802. The celebrations, however, were short-lived for it turned out to be an uneasy peace as Napoleon continued the build-up of his invasion force across the Channel.

30
PEACE AT LAST

With the Peace of Amiens came a breathing space of only fourteen months before hostilities between France and England were resumed. Initially, from the point of view of the Macclesfield Copper Company partners, it allowed time in which to persuade would-be purchasers that the business still had potential; but to no avail. Whilst the older partners might have felt equipped to deal with anything that fate had in store for them, the younger ones must have been very uneasy, especially Thomas Weaver and the young Brian Hodgson. The latter had seen his career in the Macclesfield Bank come to an abrupt end with its transfer to Daintry and Ryle, and with his son only two years old and his wife, Catherine, expecting their third child, he was particularly vulnerable. Unable to purchase his own residence he was leasing Lower Beech House and farm; it was, however, an impressive estate on the outskirts of Macclesfield and previously rented by William Roe's brother Joseph.

Lower Beech. Sketch by V. B. Morgan from an original engraving.

Edward Hawkins and Abraham Mills had both reached their early fifties, and whilst their own immediate circumstances were suspect, yet they had the security of knowing that family wealth existed as a contingency should matters go dramatically wrong. Unfortunately the Hodgsons were without such luxury; their family fortune, like the Roes, had been won over two generations in the North of England, without the security of substantial property investments in the Capital, and to see it slipping away through no fault of their own must have been devastating.

William Roe, on the other hand, through a fortunate marriage, success in the Civil Service and a prudent life style had created financial stability for his family. Like his father before him he did not take lightly his position as head of the Roe family; but there were limits to what he could do, or would wish to do, for, apart from everything else, he was committed to the Liverpool property development which he and his brother-in-law, Alderman John Shaw, had begun on 1st December 1787.

The original intention had been to create a crescent on the east side of Great Charlotte Street but the plans were altered and Queen Square laid out instead. The square was defined on the east and north by the building of "good houses", but the roperies restricted development on the western side, for they were an extremely important facet of Liverpool business. Not only did they provide ropes for maritime needs but also supplied the mining communities as far afield as the Castleton area of Derbyshire and Ecton Mine. For example, in 1773 the Liverpool merchant William Earle had sent four engine ropes to the Oxclough Sough by waggon via Manchester; three of the ropes were 70 fathoms long (420 ft), the fourth was 74 fathoms long (444 ft) with two measuring 5 ins in circumference and the other two, a half inch thicker. It can be appreciated, therefore, that the production of such ropes required an extremely long site and one which could not be relocated in a hurry, so the roperies remained.

On a plot adjacent to property owned by John Shaw, William Roe built his grand residence which occupied the north side of Queen Square as No. 9. It originally comprised four storeys with a frontage to the square of 75 ft 6 ins. The three upper storeys each had seven windows; the ground floor sported a fine stone portico entrance complete with columns, and was accompanied by three windows on either side. (It was later altered and extended by subsequent owners, spoiling the original classical design and Georgian symmetry). In depth the whole plot averaged just over 100 ft with the house probably taking up the first 40 ft or so, leaving room for a reasonably sized garden. William took the opportunity to provide an interesting feature for this rear garden, which became a local attraction. The street leading out of the southern side of the

Queen Square, Liverpool 1920. The Stork Hotel was originally built by
William Roe in 1812 as his residence.

square was named Roe Street and near to where it joined St. John's Lane was an ancient well known as 'Old Fall Well', which had supplied fresh water for centuries on the edge of the Great Heath. In the early 1790s modern development in the area had rendered it obsolete, so William was able to conduct the water through a series of pipes to his garden, where it performed as an attractive fountain for several years.

This was certainly the time for building property as the population was witnessing a phenomenal increase, so much so that the first official census took place in 1801. Macclesfield had doubled since the mid-century to 8,743, and mostly within a generation if property deeds are to be considered as an additional indicator. This was nothing compared with Liverpool, which saw a 1773 population of almost 34,500 reach a recorded figure of 83,708 by 1801. Even this latter figure was disputed by an historian who had discovered that the published 1801 figures were on the low side, because families were inclined to miss off many of their younger sons in the fear that they would be taken for military service. Also, since the start of the war the standard of record keeping was abysmal, as many of the qualified clerks were already serving in the Forces. One only has to look at the River Weaver tonnage books and the Land Tax Returns for Macclesfield to appreciate that the previously meticulously kept records were no longer. Therefore one would expect a less than accurate gathering of information, particularly as it was such a massive undertaking and being attempted for the first time.

The reasons put forward for this population 'explosion' are equally divided between advances in medicine, particularly in the care of pregnant women; a better understanding of hygiene, diet and surgery, much of this attributed to naval doctors serving with the fleet, and inoculation, especially against smallpox. If votes were cast, they would have to come out heavily in favour of the latter as being the greatest contributor. Rev. David Simpson published a 'Discourse on Inoculation for the Small-pox', addressed to the doctors and surgeons of Macclesfield on 30th January 1789 by which he cited cases of total success and took the lead in promoting a programme of inoculation for the town. With the previously high infant mortality rate and many who remained unmarried, especially those females who really were afraid of childbirth because of what they had witnessed or heard personally, it would only require two or three children in a family to survive and reproduce, and within a generation the population would have doubled. Smallpox was the greatest killer, followed by influenza and tuberculosis, for which there was no cure.

With the purge on smallpox during the 1790s a dramatic change took place. Bigger families meant more mouths to feed and more houses needed for accommodation and whereas earlier a large townhouse had a substantial garden at the rear, suddenly the owner was allowing another house to be built, often quite literally 'at the bottom of the garden'. By 1825 plots which had once contained one house, would not only have two on site but quite often four. It is interesting to note that in a city such as Chester, which still possessed the grand Elizabethan mansions known as The Rows, a parallel process was taking place. In the 1790s each one was subdivided so that it accommodated two families instead of one, and by 1825 would be subdivided again to allow space for four families. The time was right therefore for speculating in property, but whilst William Roe was able to take the opportunity, the Hodgsons could not; in fact, quite the reverse, for Robert, of course, had been forced to sell his in an effort to pay off debts.

Meanwhile, William's widowed sister, Catherine, also finding herself in debt, during 1795 had asked the company to purchase her share proportion held by William Roe as nominee of his late father's estate. She was to be disappointed, for not only did the partners refuse, but asked her to repay "the money which at her urgent request was advanced to her", and continued – "we conjecture that her son's Coming of Age will enable her to make repayment without inconvenience." The conjecture, of course, could not have been more wrong for, as previously noted, Rev. Ralph had left all his properties to Catherine's use during the remainder of her life after which son, William, was to inherit the Chadkirk Estate near Stockport. But even then William Nicholson had to ensure that the charge of £1,000, placed on both that and the Sutton Estate (adjacent to Macclesfield), by his father, had to be met for the marriage settlements of his three sisters.

Having graduated from Brasenose College, Oxford, William had joined the army and in 1798 was a captain in the 2nd Royal Lancashire Militia. Someone must have paid for the purchase of his commission, and as Uncle William continued nominee for his mother, one suspects that William Roe did support his nephew. In the meantime, however, William Roe appears to have taken a firm stand in not assisting Catherine further with her financial difficulties, as evidenced by a letter from Michael Daintry dated 18th October 1797.

Michael Daintry, of the partnership Daintry and Ryle, was married to the daughter of Catherine and William's aunt and her second husband, the apothecary Francis Nicholson, which meant that Margaret Daintry was half-sister to Catherine's deceased husband, Ralph. Catherine, desperate for help, had approached them with her problems and Michael Daintry, acting on her behalf, had discussed matters with her son, William Nicholson. The outcome was Daintry's letter to Catherine on 18th October in which he wrote:

> "William in a very respectfull manner agreed to every proposal in your favour. To raise £300 for ye discharge of all your debts – and to make out your Income £300 per annum. We advised him to pay all you ord'd immediately – Should he not have done this, but left you money for that purpose, be carefull to take regular discharges for each payment that he may, if he pleases, see and examine them – In future have no Bills."

In return William Nicholson requested some security which was yet to be agreed, but his specific wish was to inherit his father's superb library after his mother's death, a demand which Michael Daintry considered "very reasonable". Daintry advised Catherine to consult with her brother (William Roe) when the proposals had been 'drawn up', and then added a word of advice, "Always keep on the best terms with your son – because he is generous, Affectionate and Virtuous."

In recognition of her son's financial support Catherine agreed to allow his claim for the furniture and any other part of her estate after her death, which occurred in the spring of 1801. William Nicholson was satisfied but had reckoned without the proposed marriage of his sister, Catherine, and on 10th July 1801 found himself writing from his army camp in reply to a letter received from Uncle William now resident in Queen Square, Liverpool. The general naivety of his letter and his exuberant finale reveal a young man with a mind very much on other matters; in fact he had fallen in love with one of William Roe's daughters, his cousin Hannah, and so intent was he on completing his own marriage arrangements that his sister's situation took a distant second place.

His sister's fiancé, Robinson, was a very influential man and had objected to Captain Nicholson's claim of entitlement to his mother's chattels after her death, and also demanded the promised monetary portion towards the marriage settlement which his mother had insisted was tied up in the copper company assets. This had prompted Robinson to write to William Roe as nominee of Catherine's company share, presumably in the hope that William would possibly purchase his late sister's entitlement and bring to an end the financial deadlock. But William Roe had no room for manoeuvre, his commitments were considerable. He had already been pressurised by the other partners to collect an outstanding debt of £137 9s. from his brother Joseph, and there was a further problem, the date for the realisation of Rachel Harriott's assets had passed. With some diplomacy William Roe had evidently been able to persuade Rachel to leave the money invested in the company for the time being, on the understanding that it would be equal to a 5% dividend, for which she would receive an annual payment.

In addition, William Roe had already accepted Catherine's company bond of £273 17 3d. on his own account and, one suspects, obtained employment for his nephew with the company, for the company minutes do confirm that 'Mr. Nicholson' was employed by the company from at least 1799. In October of that year it was agreed to increase his salary to £100 per annum from the following 5th July; this employ would be in addition to his army career. By April 1802 there is a clear indication that William Nicholson was keeping the company books, and must have been attending to other company concerns such as the collection of bad debts.

Apart from family matters, William Roe had also been very much involved with the removal of the Liverpool smelters to Neath. Having accepted responsibility for the assaying and been appointed joint Director of the South Wales works in August 1796, he received a salary of £60 per annum and a vote of thanks for his efforts. He felt no compunction, therefore, in leaving his nephew to deal with Robinson's letter.

Young Captain Nicholson was quick to point out to his uncle that he had met Robinson and his sister in London and thought he had adequately explained the situation. He had shown his sister all the sums advanced to his "much lamented Mother" at various times, and could see no other way to claim recompense but by reserving her furniture and other parts of her estate for himself in lieu of the money advanced. He argued that his mother should have been given a bond from the Macclesfield Copper Company as proof for Robinson, and that he would approach his attorney, Mr. Walker, who was present when his mother had verbally made her commitment to him. He also hoped that Mr. Walker would advise him how best to pay the money left by his father's will, commenting "I know of no other mode than by raining it on the Estates", which would, of course, leave him in great difficulties.

However, seeming to have disposed of the problem by putting pen to paper, William Nicholson returned to his immediate concern, that of receiving his uncle's blessing and the hand of his cousin in marriage. As the young officer declared, his uncle was well aware of his financial situation, and the thought of any pecuniary arrangements on his uncle's part was far from his mind. A cynic might say that he was fortunate to have found such an ideal match, otherwise his chances of a good marriage were slim indeed. But in any event times were changing, and from the spontaneity of his acknowledged sentiments, William Nicholson's affections for Hannah do portray a genuine sincerity. They were married on 4th May 1802 at St. Anne's Church, Liverpool, and the young Captain was promoted to Major the following year.

There seems little doubt that William Roe was very generous with the couple; in his will, subsequently prepared in 1821, William refers to all the marriage settlements of his then married daughters, in an effort to equalise the distribution of his wealth; all, that is, except for the one relating to daughter Hannah, which is carefully concealed.

* * * * * * *

Apart from the problems of establishing the Neath Abbey Works, William Roe had not been idle in chasing up further sources of copper ore. The Coniston mine had finally been abandoned in 1795, for on 27th July of that year, Abraham Mills sent a letter to the agent in Kendal, Thomas Harrison, informing him that the mine had been unproductive for some time and the decision taken to "discontinue the working". Unfortunately there was still plenty of ore to be found, but having proved illusive to Roe & Co. it would be others, some years later, who would reap the rewards. Yet William Roe had still not lost interest in the Lake District.

Just two miles north of Coniston was the manor of Tilberthwaite owned by Sir John Pennington of Muncaster House. In 1759 Anthony Tissington, together with the Barkers of Derbyshire, had been working the area for copper but, judging from present day observations, not to any great extent. On 19th July 1799 William Roe agreed a one year lease with Lord Muncaster, paying $1/15$th part of all ores found, which does suggest a recognition of the difficulties involved. William was to keep at least four workmen on site "with liberty to drive Drifts & carry up Levels" and to provide copies of the accounts. The next proviso is interesting, inferring that the agreement was just between Lord Muncaster and William Roe, not Roe & Co. ; if, within that year, William decided the mining propects looked worthwhile, then he personally "by writing under his own hand" had to agree a further lease for at least 21 years. Evidently he never took up this option.

The main or North Lode was worked to 120 fathoms but the other older workings amounted to little, in places revealing veins with only minute traces of copper. A deep adit was driven near the slate quarries in Yewdale Valley, but which of these workings are attributable to William Roe's men and not Tissington & Co. or others, cannot be confirmed. In 1850 the mine would be re-opened yet not until the end of the 19th century did any worthwhile operations take place.

At the same time as Tilberthwaite was under consideration, William Roe also took an interest in a mine called 'Texel' near Fremington, Swaledale, just a little to the east of Richmond in North Yorkshire. The only evidence supporting this is recorded in a small notebook belonging to William, but subsequently re-used for other purposes. Written on the inside cover is the information that on 3rd September 1799 he undertook a journey from "Liverpool to Fremington & back to consult with Mr. Clayton & Brear about carrying on the Mine". He was absent for eleven days and charged £9 12 6d. expenses. On 15th December William sent a John Davies on the same journey to ask Mr. Clayton's advice about "working the same mine". This time the ten day visit cost £3 19 0d. Unfortunately the first page of the notebook has been torn out in order to make use of the remaining pages for household accounts and details relating to the administration of his sister Catherine's estate, due to her subsequent death.

One poignant entry of 8th April (1801) suggests that Catherine was possibly living with the Roes at the time of her death, for it shows a cash payment of £20 to a Dr. Branebreth "for his attendance on Mrs. Nicholson before and during her last illness".

The brief but significant reference to Texel does suggest that trials were already in progress by September 1799 yet, like Tilberthwaite, never really amounted to anything. It also implies that William Roe had personally financed both operations, and in the event made the right decision not to expend any further sums from his hard earned fortune.

Edward Hawkins, on the other hand, had gambled on the fact that in the not too distant future he would inherit part of the family's substantial holdings in East London from his uncle, Samuel. When offered the opportunity to purchase the Neath Abbey Works on 6th July 1801, he had accepted, and must have felt vindicated in taking such a decision with the restoration of peace by the treaty of Amiens some months later.

* * * * * * *

At the time of the A.G.M. of August 1794 the Neath smelting works had been valued at £2,961 5 9d. but were far from being completed. Five years later the value was reckoned as £8,087 5 3d., almost £1,000 more than the works on Macclesfield Common. The build up had started in 1795 when the Liverpool rollers and engine together with the Coniston ore and firebricks had all been shipped to Neath. William Roe and Thomas Weaver Snr. had taken stock, and a decision was made to build a house for the agent; with further houses to be built as and when required.

By February 1796 Parsons was supplying coals to the works but had not yet completed the supply of water, and was still being pressed to do so six months later. He proposed new coal supplies viz; ⁶/₇ths from a new level, unpicked and ¹/₇th of the 'Skewan' binding coal and one wey of the Cwm Valyn coals each week for the refineries, charge 36s. 0d. per wey instead of 32s. 6d. (In this instance a wey seems to be a little less than 5 tons). With this contract in mind the weighing machine from Toxteth (originally, of course, from Macclesfield brass-works) was fixed on the railway leading to the coal bins near the Abbey works. However there were complaints about coal supplies; John Place, the Mines Royal Company manager, wrote in his account book on 8th May 1797 that Parsons "should send better coal and further measure", a grievance echoed by Thomas Weaver who happened to be visiting Place at the time.

During August 1797 the new coal rates were agreed with Parsons, and an attempt made to persuade him to export coals to the Irish Mines at the same price. Also Weaver had been successful in leasing a plot of land on behalf of the company from the Lords of Neath Abbey. It was close to the works and an ideal site for the agent's house, which was to have sufficient rooms to accommodate any of the visiting partners.

Meanwhile Place could not rid himself of his problems. In the past the Mines Royal employees had argued that the quality of the coal had been so bad they were unable to work, and on one occasion had left the site for two days. Parsons had counter-attacked by saying that the men were stealing coal for their own use, and as though suggesting this accusation had some validity, the workmen waited till mid-winter before leaving the site on 11th January 1798, arguing that they were working for less money than those employed by Roe & Co. But one week later, after Price had promised them an extra sixpence per day, bringing their wages up to 16 shillings per week, they returned. Price must have been extremely concerned about their action for there were 38 furnaces under his control, whilst on the nearby site the Macclesfield company works still remained uncompleted. It must be said that Price was paying 42 shillings per wey for his company's coal, a higher price than Roe & Co., so perhaps the whole episode was, in some respects, contrived by Parsons in order to gain better regulation for his coal contracts and more profit.

At this particular juncture Roe & Co. agreed to pay Hawkins £300 per annum as "Principal Director" of the copper company, which included the superintending of the Bosley works. Young Brian Hodgson was also voted £120 per annum and both to be retrospectively paid from 5th July 1796. Edward Hawkins continued in his role as school governor of the Macclesfield grammar school and played an active part on a committee controlling the school's investments; he also remained a burgess of Macclesfield Corporation.

Meanwhile the agent's house in Neath was built, and in August 1798 Richard Morgan was sanctioned to have the building "roofed and secured" and to send an estimate for "finishing and furnishing" the property to the company. He was awarded a pay rise to £140 each year with a further sum of £10 until the house was completed. Credit was also arranged with a local bank to enable him to purchase supplies for the Neath Abbey works.

A possible relative, Edward Morgan, who had been accepted as an apprentice in August 1796, was to learn "the Art of Assay" under instruction from Benjamin Magor, the company's Cornish agent, during 1798.

October 1799 saw preparations underway for making firebricks out of local clay deposits near Neath, but it was at this time, of course, that the move to import duty free ores from Ireland failed, and with a deepening depression the order was given to advance no further sums to any of the copper company partners.

The decision to cease brass production from 5th July 1800 still allowed Edward Hawkins to remain Principal Director of the copper company, but with a reduction in salary to £250 per annum. On the other hand young Brian Hodgson gained the £50, having been appointed second director, allowing him £200 per annum. But Thomas Weaver Snr. continued his overseeing of the Neath works at his then current salary of £60 per annum, and there was no wage rise for Richard Morgan, who was told that as he now occupied the agent's house, this was considered as a "sufficient increase in salary".

With brass production at an end the order had been given to purchase no further ores from Cornwall, and to halt the transportation of copper from Neath to Macclesfield from 25th December 1801. The second, somewhat abrupt decision to dissolve the partnership totally, saw the purchase of ores abandoned and a message sent to the Associated Irish Mine Company to that effect, with the Roe & Co. contract terminated on 24th June 1801. However, as Hawkins had agreed the date of transfer to him of the Neath works as 25th December 1801, Mills was asked to make a contract with him to continue supplying Irish ore from that date. In the event Hawkins agreed to take all the A.I.M. Co.'s ore from 1st January 1802 for three years, but limited to 5,000 tons or less each year, with provision made for terminating the contract by either party upon six months' notice.

Hawkins was certainly accepting a considerable financial burden, for apart from the valuation of the actual works, which stood at £8,367 in November 1800 and was to be the agreed purchase price, there were the tools, equipment and stock of ores to take into account. Another important item was the furnace bottoms, to be priced as agreed by two separate people, together with any other relevant articles. And if any disagreement over valuations should occur, then an 'umpire' was to be called in; but as expected the latter option was unnecessary, as Hawkins agreed the price arrived at by Mr. Dagley (of the Cheadle company) who carried out a survey and valuation.

Dagley also made an offer to purchase the stock of calamine at the Bonsall works, which was accepted. His assessment of the Neath Abbey works was produced in January 1803 and shows that Edward Hawkins had taken over 7 ore furnaces, 3 metal calciners, 8 roasters and 2 refining furnaces; a total of 20 ovens. This proves that the works had fallen far short of reaching the Toxteth capacity of 35 furnaces and, when considering John Price's note, that on 18th March 1796 he had 35 furnaces working (out of a known total of 38), were consequently dwarfed by their near neighbour the Mines Royal Company.

Edward Morgan's allowance of £35 3 4d. per annum, to cover board and washing whilst at Truro, continued to be paid by Roe & Co. whilst he remained in the company's employ.

Richard Morgan was allowed to continue weighing and sampling the ores on hand until the transfer to Hawkins on 25th December, at which date he would send the final sealed sample to Cronebane for assaying. He was also charged rent for the area of land known as 'The Marshes', adjacent to the Abbey, onto which he had driven his cattle.

It is evident that Roe & Co. had been smelting ores for others as, apart from a contract renewed yearly with Fox & Co., suggesting the latter were rolling copper in addition to iron plates, there is a mention of an order for a Mr. Daniel which was to be completed by Hawkins.

Finally, all the leases and contracts undertaken by Roe & Co. in connection with the Neath Abbey works were ordered to be assigned to Hawkins. He agreed to pay £7,000 by December (1801) and the remainder within nine months of "taking possession"; but in order to legalise the agreement he made out a bond which was held by the Macclesfield solicitor, Cooke, and a Mr. Hogg (the probable owner of Charles Roe's original silk mill establishment in Macclesfield, and perhaps connected with the Edinburgh banker of the same name).

With the decision taken to advertise company lands and buildings for sale at the *Old Angel Inn,* Macclesfield on Wednesday 14th October 1801, but by private sale should the option

To be Sold by Auction,

At the Old Angel, in Macclesfield,

On THURSDAY the 29th of this inftant OCTOBER,

AT TEN O'CLOCK IN THE FORENOON;

In fuch Lots, and according to fuch Conditions, as fhall be fpecified in Particulars, to be had at the time and place of Sale.

ALL that Pile of Buildings, fituate on the Common, and near to the Town of Macclesfield, heretofore ufed for fmelting and refining Copper, containing at prefent, only five Furnaces, (others having been taken down) Blackfmiths, Carpenters, Nailmakers, Brafs-founders, and Coopers Shops; Brickmakers Rooms, for making and drying Fire Brick, Charcoal, Coak and Iron Rooms; Affay Office, formerly a fmall Dwelling-houfe, two Stables, and other conveniences, with good Water near the Premifes.

About 11 Acres of Land, ftatute meafure, freehold, and the Leafe of 13 Acres, held under the Corporation of Macclesfield, for a Term; 30 Years of which are unexpired, at the Yearly Rent of 35l. all lately inclofed and improved.

ALL that Range of Buildings, fituate on the faid Common, but nearer to the Town, now ufed for making Brafs; containing 40 Furnaces, two Warehoufes, with Rooms over for making Cafting Pots, a fmall Shop for Brafs-foundry, inclofed Coal Yards; two long ranges of Building, ufed for dreffing, drying, and keeping Calamine: Twenty-nine Houfes, with Gardens to each: a Field adjoining the Brafs Houfes, abounding with excellent Clay, for making Brick; a Wind-mill, lately fitted up for grinding Corn, with drying Kiln and Warehoufe, clofe to the Road, and moft conveniently fituated.

About 300 Tons of Fire Stone, and 120 Tons of Fire Clay, of fuperior quality, for making Cafting Pots and Fire Bricks.—About 28,000 Fire Brick of various fizes.—About 240,000 common Bricks, for Building—About 2000 Cafting Pots, of an excellent quality, and well feafoned. —78 Gornifh Moor Stones, 36 of which are new, and 42 in ufe for cafting Brafs Plates.—About 300 Tons of Calamine, of various forts, prepared for making Brafs.

ALL that Range of Buildings, fituate at Bofley, in the County of Chefter, fix Miles from Macclesfield, and fix from Leek; where a Branch of the Grand Trunk Canal is now completed to: with the Pools, Dams, five large Water Wheels, Annealing Ovens, and every other convenience, for making Brafs Battery: containing a Rolling, and four Battery Mills, the head and fall 25 feet 3 inches, and the fupply of Water conftant: together with eight Cottages, and Gardens, Blackfmiths, Millwrights, Carpenters, and Coopers Shops.

ALL that other Mill, fituate at Bofley aforefaid, now ufed for Rolling and Hammering Copper; with Warehoufes, for Raw and Manufactured Copper adjoining thereto; two Dwelling-houfes with Gardens, for the Workmen; the head and fall is 14 feet 9 Inches, and the fupply the fame, as to the upper Mills before mentioned.

A handfome Brick Dwelling-houfe, fafhed, and very well finifhed, fuitable for a fmall Family, with a good Garden, Stable, and fixteen Acres of Land.

The whole of the Premifes at Bofley, are held under Leafe, from the Earl of Harrington, for 99 Years, from 29th of September 1766, at the fmall Yearly Rent of 25l.

The Turnpike Road, from the Staffordfhire Collieries, runs through the Premifes, and that from Macclesfield to Leek, very near to them.

ALL that Pile of Building, fituate at a place called the Havannah; within two Miles of Congleton, in the faid County, and adjoining to the Turnpike Road, leading from thence to Macclesfield, and now ufed for making Brafs Wire, and Rolling Copper Sheets and Bolts: having five Water Wheels, from 18 to 22 feet diameter, with head and fall, of 13 feet 3 inches, and the whole River Dane for fupply. The Premifes confift of a Brafs Rolling Mill, a Wire Mill, and long Chamber over, Annealing Houfe and Oven, Copper Mill, Blackfmiths, Millwrights, and Carpenters Shops: two Warehoufes, feven Cottages with Gardens, Sheds for Wood, Charcoal, &c. together with eight Acres of Land, the whole under Leafe, from Richard Ayton Lee, Efq. for 99 Years, from the 12th of May 1763; at the very low Rent of 30l. 10s. per Annum.

ALSO a very valuable freehold piece of meadow Land, adjoining to the Premifes, containing fix Acres.

ALL that Warehoufe, with the Crane and other conveniences, fituate on the Staffordfhire Canal, near to the Red Bull, in Lawton, and held by Leafe from John Lawton, Efq., from the 2nd of February 1789, for 21 Years, at the Yearly acknowledgement of 2s. 6d. and renewable at the fame rate.

Thomas Maydew, at the Macclesfield Brafs Works, will fhew all the Premifes there; and John Edwards, at the Bofley Works, will fhew thofe and the Havannah Premifes: and further particulars may be had at the Office of Mr. Cooke, Attorney, or the Counting Houfe of Meffrs. Roe and Co. in Macclesfield.

Bayley, Printer, Macclesfield.

The sale notice which appeared in the Manchester Mercury 20th Oct. 1801. It was also distributed in the form of handbills.

present itself sooner, Hawkins, after placing adverts in the London, Birmingham, Sheffield, Manchester and other appropriate papers (with the date of sale now fixed as Thursday 29th October), hurried off to Neath. Unfortunately he neglected to present his accounts as "Receiver and Treasurer' of the grammar school to the committee on 11th August 1802, and six months later a letter was sent requesting him to present the statement to the governors at their next meeting. Hawkins complied and submitted his accounts on 10th December 1803 which showed that up to his relinquishment of the post on 19th April 1802 he had in hand the sum of £162 19 8d. This was a substantial figure, so the clerk was directed to advise Hawkins to pay the sum plus interest into Daintry & Ryle's bank, the governors also elected Michael Daintry,' of the estate called Byrons, in Sutton', to take the place of Edward Hawkins who had "lately gone to reside at Neath in the county of Glamorgan".

Things were not so simple from the point of view of Macclesfield Corporation; Hawkins still owned property within the borough and his business activities continued, therefore it was not until 11th May 1810 that a note could be entered in the Corporation Minutes stating "Mr. Hawkins, Capital Burgess" no longer lived in Macclesfield; at the same time a letter was sent requesting his resignation of office, to which he evidently agreed.

* * * * * * *

Whether or not the advertised sale went ahead on 29th October 1801, is debatable, for none of the company properties was sold, despite the fact that the windmill had been converted to a corn grinding mill and many of the furnaces dismantled, leaving only five copper smelters on the upper common. In November further steps were taken to limit the damage to the business due to the continuing economic depression; all copper tokens were to be melted down when presented for payment, and notice given to the two supervisors of the rolling mills, John Edwards and James Malpas, to leave on the following 25th March.

During 1802 strenuous efforts were made to sell or lease the remaining properties by reducing them into smaller viable units. The Havannah works were initially offered to a Mr. Vernon in February for one year only at £300. At the same time the Lower Mills at Bosley were offered for sale at £2,500, but six months later the works were dismantled and all surplus materials sold, with the company cottages offered to the tenants at £3 per annum from the 29th September 1802. Having decided that the most logical action was to divide all the company properties between some of the partners, who would act as trustees for the sales, a trust deed was drawn up naming William Roe, Edward Hawkins and Abraham Mills as those nominated for the task from August 1802.

In April 1803 it was judged appropriate to convert both the Havannah and Bosley mills into cotton works suitable for letting, but before any further steps could be taken hostilities with the French resumed with a vengeance. Ironically it was at this period that the silk industry in Macclesfield witnessed a revival. Weaving had been introduced about 1790 and with the dearth of French silks, English production increased, accelerated by the demands of war and the British Navy for squares and handkerchiefs; many of the latter were in the form of kerchiefs of a considerable size worn by sailors and subsequently replaced by the sailor collar, whilst others were black silk neckcloths "commonly used round the head by a gun's crew".

However, with war once more casting its gloomy shadow on companies such as Roe & Co. the partnership carried out an appraisal of debts which did indicate solvency and therefore confidence to weather the gathering storm. The good debts were reckoned as £26,390 11 3d. with stock, securities and property valued at £29,760 7 5d. and bad debts £825 13s. They were able to discharge their own debts on bonds of £31,475 by March 1804 with only £6,158 still outstanding; this latter sum was left to be paid by those partners who were "debtors to (the) concern".

By August 1803 it had been agreed to lease the Upper Mill (i.e. brass mills) at Bosley for six years to John Edwards who had formed a partnership. But after further negotiations the brass mills were altered "at the least expence" according to a plan put forward by Edwards & Co., and with the work completed in March 1804 a lease for 20 years was signed; rental £402 3 8d. per annum less ground rent £35 = £377 3 8d. (sic) this should, of course, be £367 3 8d. The Lower Mill remained unconverted because of a possible interest by Beresford & Co. silk manufacturers, but evidently nothing came of this enquiry, for on 14th December 1805 Robert Hodgson noted that it was to be offered to a William Pointon for £2,500.

Havannah was let at £350 per annum (tenant unknown) together with the farm at £22 10s. less the ground rent of £55 10s. making a net rent of £317 per annum. The Havannah meadow was let separately at £12 per annum. By May 1805 the tenant of the farm, Thomas Clowes, was sent notice to quit on the following 25th September, with the intention of letting it for pasture at a more realistic rental of £52 10s. per annum, whilst in December the tools and machinery from the mills were offered to "Messrs. Key & Co." at a reasonable price. Presumably this relates to the Keys family; originally German with the name of Essor they had later adopted the English name. Thomas Patten Snr. had brought John Essor to England in 1735 to supervise the smelting process at his Cheadle brass-works, and the subsequent Keys descendants would retain the position of chief smelters until finally purchasing the business in the mid-19th century.

On Macclesfield Common the various houses were let to tenants for a total of £200 per annum, but a small group of dwellings was allocated to the windmill, which the company hoped to lease en bloc although the rent was not specified. However, the primary concern was still the sale of assets, but meanwhile, after all the carts and horses had been sold, the land was let for pasture. The only other property of specific mention is the house at Fairsteads, transferred by Charles Roe to the company for use by the company secretary, and the original home of John Hale. This was offered for sale at £300, indicating a fairly substantial residence.

Other assets still attributable to the company in 1805 were the Irish Mine shares, the Holway Mine shares, the lease of Lawton Wharf (adjacent to the Red Bull Inn, Buglawton) and securities on the Bosley Road and Congleton Road turnpikes. No mention is made of the Macclesfield canal shares nor the mines of Llandudno, Havod-y-llan or Llanberis; nor the warehouse at Northwich which had been finally relinquished at the end of 1801.

* * * * * * *

In 1800 William Cleaver had become Bishop of Bangor and must have decided to offer Roe & Co. a lease for the Llandudno Mine, possibly having knowledge of the former difficulties and Roe & Co.'s desire to take charge. A copy of the proposed lease was drawn up and dated 30th June 1801, but times had changed and the partners declined the offer, deciding instead to continue raising ore by the ton until their current lease expired on 16th October 1803. By August 1802 the Llandudno Mine shares were considered to be of no value and an observer of the period wrote that the mines were being worked "with very little spirit and with profits not at all commensurate with the production . . ." Evidently the mining company was wound up at the end of the lease, for in October 1804 Mills was indemnified against any claims "that may be made against him by the late Llandudno Mine Co. or any persons." Also he had in hand a profit of £364 19 1d. from the sale of Llandudno ores, and after a final adjustment a small dividend was paid to each partner.

The Havod-y-llan Mine is last mentioned in July 1802 when little more than £35 worth of stock and materials are recorded. But the Llanberis Mine Company was a considerable investment valued in excess of £4,000 which had had a recorded workforce of between 80 to 100 men in 1798 whilst "their womenfolk tended the small grazing farms which still formed the chief household support." William Williams visited the area when writing his *Observations on the Snowdon Mountains* published in 1802; his comment on the 'Copper-Mine', though brief, is nevertheless significant:

> "Near the upper-end of the higher Lake a mineral enterprize was undertaken, about A.D. 1763 or 1764; and though a vaft quantity of copper ore was found, yet it fell infinitely fhort of rewarding the adventurers. This work was difcontinued fome years after; but now is worked again under Mr. Roe and Co. and much ore has been obtained from it. I cannot learn what profit it yields; but I fuppofe little or nothing."

So once again Llanberis was proving unprofitable to work, and in October 1804 it was decided to transfer any payments received by Roe & Co. to individual partners' accounts, but this was rescinded in December 1805. By then the Llanberis debts were mounting, so an alternative was found; those partners holding shares in both the Irish and Welsh mines were to use future dividends from the former to cover the losses of the latter.

Fortunately, after the struggles of the 1790s, the Irish situation had greatly improved, and by 1800, with the rebellion past, the Irish mines had once more begun to produce a considerable profit. Whereas the past decade had only once seen production of over 1,000 tons raised in 1797, reduced to just over 498 tons in 1799, the figures for the following three years 1800-02 averaged little less than 2,000 tons each year, with the total value of ore sold almost £29,100, a very large sum.

On 21st January 1802 a meeting of the English partners took place in Macclesfield with only John Jefferies absent; he had written to excuse himself because of "lameness". At this meeting a significant gesture was made when the company resolved to present 'Captain' Mills with silver plate worth 50 guineas for his "spirited and judicious conduct . . . during the momentous period of the rebellion in Ireland." First Lieutenant Weaver was likewise honoured with plate to the value of 30 guineas and Second Lieutenant Blood similarly received plate worth 20 guineas. The Irish mining prospects appeared good, but the spring of 1803 brought an epidemic of influenza which almost closed the workings and reduced production for the year by a third; it was to return three years later. It did not deter the Cronebane Volunteers, however, who were supplied with 102 new uniforms in 1804 and the guardhouses at Rathdrum and the gold mines were still maintained.

Abraham Mills, following his previous articles on collieries (1789), the whyn dykes of Islay (1790) and the discovery of gold in Wicklow (1795) had been asked to complete a report of the latter for the Lord Lieutenant of Ireland, which he submitted in August 1801. From this a second report and government survey were commissioned, and, aided by Thomas Weaver Jnr. and a Thomas King, Mills submitted his findings on 8th March 1802 from "No. 3 Spring-Gardens" London. The area concerned was the Croaghan Mountain, and having recited the previous locations at which traces of gold were found along the sides of the river beds, and the sites of the old mines, Mills suggested that a level should be driven in the north-west area of the region, to cross "all the veins, which are feen in the Ballinvally Stream". He concluded with a flourishing report on similar undertakings in "his Majesty's Hanoverian dominions", South America, Mexico (with a reference to R. Kirwan), Russia, Hungary, scattered deposits in Spain, Italy and Norway, and gold carried down by the river Rhine from Switzerland; then included a table of individual mines and their annual productions together with the types of minerals found. He had certainly built up a strong reputation for himself, though how much was his own work and how much was attributable to others is difficult to deduce. At least in his opening gambit to the 'Second Report' Mills does allow for a combined operation, having written "we have now the honor to fend the plan and fection of the principal auriferous stream, and the map of Croaghan".

The fortunate productivity of the A.I.M. Co. was salvation for the Hodgsons who, during April 1802, were asked to deposit their Irish mining shares as security against debts. (On 5th July 1804 one of the Hodgsons, probably the elder Brian of Uttoxeter, would transfer 25 shares to John Jefferies for £2,500).

By October 1804 it is apparent that William Nicholson could no longer sustain his employ with Roe & Co. due to the necessity of committing himself totally to his army career. John Johnson was assigned the Nicholson duties and allowed 2½% commission on all monies collected. Unfortunately the most significant debt was that relating to Edward Hawkins, and the partners felt that they had no alternative but to seek legal advice in finding a way of forcing him to pay the balance due, so a resolution to that effect was made on 23rd May 1805.

As the year progressed William Roe became more and more committed to his Civil Service career and was appointed Joint Chairman of the Commissioners of Customs on the 11th August, with an additional salary of £500; this brought his total annual salary to £1,500 (not far short of £200,000 today). The extent of his jurisdiction was considerable, often requiring his presence in the London Custom House on Thomas Street situated between the docks of Billingsgate and the Tower, from where he was often in contact with the Chancellor of the Exchequer. In April 1806 he was there writing on behalf of an officer in the seaport of Newhaven, Sussex, who was being considered for retirement on the grounds of ill health; and later advising against the purchase of premises in Drury Lane for use of the Commissioners. Meanwhile one of the most important events in English history had taken place when Lord Nelson, supported by Collingwood, defeated the combined fleets of France and Spain off Cape Trafalgar on 21st October 1805. At last the fear of invasion was virtually at an end, yet Napoleon's conquests on the Continent continued, and the years of war dragged on.

* * * * * * *

In 1804 the election for Recorder of Macclesfield took place. The position of Recorder was an extremely important and prestigious one held by a magistrate or judge, who was given criminal and civil jurisdiction in a particular city or borough. The Macclesfield contest was between the Whig candidate, the Hon. James Abercrombie and John Harriott Roe for the Tories. Several new burgesses were sworn in (including William Roe, who had relinquished his place on the Common Council of Liverpool as early as 1797), swelling their number to 271, of whom 112 voted for Abercrombie and 128 for Roe; 31 abstained.

William Roe came from Liverpool and walked at the head of a jubilant Roe parade through the town and was greeted warmly and kissed by the aldermen. A superb new flag was carried along, with the 'New Church' (Christ Church) painted on one side and "Roe and the Town and Trade of Macclesfield for Ever" on the other. As the crowd passed into Chestergate, accompanied by a group of militia, they stopped outside Rachel Harriott's house for some time, chanting "Roe for Ever'." Half the town was dressed in blue and in the evening Joseph Roe, who had "exerted himself greatly", gave a ball at the young ladies' school where all the females, including the governess and teachers, wore blue ribands.

During April 1804 John Roe arrived unexpectedly one evening in Queen Square, Liverpool, much to the chagrin of William Roe's wife, Hannah, who had to move some of the children from their bed because of "the one he should have slept in being taken over to be washed". Hannah received no apology and commented that he never wrote letters but always appeared at his convenience whether or not it suited them.

The reason for this unheralded visit is not mentioned, but later he did write to inform them of his marriage to Hannah Ramsden on 29th May at Ardwick-le-Street near Doncaster in Yorkshire. John Roe had decided to divide his time between his mother-in-law's house, his mother's house and those of his friends, to save expense. Hannah's harsh comment "he is very much reprobated at Macclesfield for his covetiousnefs", intimates that she knew nothing of the accumulating business difficulties nor, in fact, finances in general, and even less of the ambiguous situation in which John Harriott found himself, otherwise she might have been more understanding and sympathetic. Hannah had known nothing but financial stability all her life, and had been surrounded by family who were able to support her and offer the best of everything; John Harriott's situation had been very different; he was only 12 years old when his father died intestate, leaving his mother in a heavily mortgaged property.

Nothing is known of John Harriott's career until admitted to the company with the 1/64th share from his father's estate in August 1793. By that time he was a surprising 25 years of age, which suggests that he had probably insisted on the transfer of the share. William Roe, who was in a better position than anyone to understand the financial difficulties, had possibly held onto the share appreciating the adverse situation; after all John Roe's admittance could not have come at a worse time, for it meant that he was yet another partner with whom to share the losses, as and when they arose.

The unknown factor is what, if anything, had Rachel Harriott inherited from her father, or Charles Roe received as her dowry. Many bankruptcies had taken place in the West Indies due to war, appalling weather conditions, especially hurricanes, and disease, so it is likely that Rachel received little or nothing from her late father's estate, and this could be the reason why William Roe had redeemed the mortgage on the Chestergate house, ensuring that Rachel had a roof over her head. The deeds remained in his name and therefore allowed him to take his place amongst the freemen of the borough, but Rachel Harriott was certainly entitled to some benefit from her marriage, and that was now due from the copper company. Her only recourse was to press for this legitimate inheritance from her late husband's estate at every available opportunity. In all probability she had turned to her Jebb relations in Chesterfield when it came to requesting help with her son's career. They were an extremely influential family one of whom, Sir Richard, had become physician not only to the Westminster hospital but also George III and the Prince of Wales. Joshua Jebb of Walton Lodge, Chesterfield, a J.P. of Derbyshire, was in an ideal position to recommend and obtain a legal post for John Roe, which in part is supported by the fact that the young man had met and married someone from the Doncaster area.

Yet John Harriott must have felt very aggrieved, as circumstances appeared to dictate that he was being deprived of his inheritance, which could account for the fact that his age was 35 at the time of his marriage, as he had not been able to provide an adequate marriage settlement sooner. And his "covetousness", far from being a ploy with which to force William's hand, was most likely the result of absolute necessity. His hurried visit to Queen Square in April 1804, between his successful bid for Recorder and his marriage, suggests that he had gone to seek financial assistance from his eldest brother. It is difficult to believe that William would have refused such a request under the circumstances It also allows for, though does not excuse, John Roe's arrogant attitude to the world in general, an attitude developed from the necessity to conceal his position as the 'poor relative' who had to go begging 'cap in hand' to receive what he considered rightfully his and his mother's. The impression created by William's wealth and influence must have caused him great frustration, and with his mind aggravated by money matters and his intolerable situation, good manners and regard for others were unfortunately the least of his concerns.

* * * * * * *

Another victim of the period was Edward Hawkins, who was beginning to feel the strain of his ambitious schemes. His cousin, Edward of Whitechapel, had died on 12th February 1780 leaving a considerable fortune, but most of it was held in trust for certain relatives, as Edward of Whitechapel and his wife, Ann (formerly Schumaker) had no children. Out of the several bequests Edward (of Macclesfield) was to receive the rents and profits of the Huntley estate in Gloucestershire for life, after which they would pass to his children. Cousin Edward of Whitechapel also stated "I forgive my said Cousin all such Sum and Sums of Money as he may owe me at the time of my decease." The sum outstanding must have been considerable, for there was a proviso that within three months Edward of Macclesfield must make out a bond for £3,000 payable to his children after his own death. This does seem to confirm that most, if not all, of the original sum paid by him for the purchase of a Roe & Co. share, had been borrowed from his cousin in East London.

In simple terms the will set up extremely complicated trust funds, and it is obvious that the intention of Edward of Whitechapel was to secure the futures of his cousins' children and perpetuate the family name of Hawkins. Edward of Macclesfield's eldest son had died, but his second child, Edward Jnr. arrived four month's after his cousin's death with the assurance that he, and any other children yet to be born, would in time inherit a fortune; although of course Edward Snr. was obliged to contribute the additional sum of £3,000. When, on 6th July 1801 Edward Snr. was offered the purchase of the Neath Works he took a calculated risk in accepting. By then his eldest son, Edward, was just 21 years of age and would therefore benefit from entering a partnership with his father, and Edward Snr. must have had in mind that he had inherited a share of the Newnham business from his own father.

Thomas Hawkins had worked hard with partners to build up the shipping company, but even in his own lifetime there had been stiff competition (e.g. in 1768 customers had been lured into using vessels at Hay's Wharf, Southwark "under colour and pretence of being Newnham vessels"). When Robert Pyrke died insolvent in May 1780 the Newnham company had to be wound up, despite the fact that only two years earlier the investment in new equipment had been made at the Newnham Quay. It took several years to sort out Pyrke's affairs, and another partner, Richard Hilditch, was declared bankrupt resulting in the sale of assets including the three remaining brigs. Edward Hawkins Snr. could have gained little financially from the enterprise, especially if, as suspected, his marrige settlement had been invested in the business; yet, by 1801, once more he was willing to put his business abilities to the test.

At the time of the transfer of the Neath Abbey works in December 1801, cousin Samuel of Whitechapel was celebrating his 73rd birthday and had apparently remained a bachelor all his life. Edward Snr. therefore must have judged (and possibly it had been discussed) that apart from the inheritance due to his family from the 1780 will, the substantial holdings left to Samuel by his brother, and Samuel's own estate, would in time considerably benefit either himself or his children. In the meantime the problem was how to raise the purchase money for the Neath Abbey works. Edward obviously had no intention of prejudicing whatever cousin Samuel might bequeath him, by asking for money in advance. Also, having been forgiven repayment of the large sum loaned by Edward of Whitechapel, the pressure was on to prove himself capable of managing his own finances; and this is very much reflected in the manner in which Edward of Whitechapel had prepared his will.

To all intents and purposes Edward Hawkins Snr. had become the owner of the Neath Abbey works from 25th December 1801, but little is known of how he operated the business.

He apparently took as a partner his eldest son, Edward, and was possibly assisted by his second son, Samuel. On 5th July 1802 a schedule records his enormous debt to the Macclesfield company as £11,286 18 3d. plus an additional figure of £121 12 3d. for stock at the Neath Abbey works (a total well in excess of a million pounds at today's values), but whether or not he had paid the initial £7,000 is not recorded, nor are any further payments he did or did not make during the succeeding period. From the large sum outstanding at 5th July 1802 it can be confidently assumed that the initial payment of £7,000 was by bond.

Surprisingly the Cheadle Company minute book establishes that on 19th August 1803 the partners decided to approach Edward Hawkins in the hope that he would "dispose of a part of Neath Copperworks & part of his lease of a Colliery which supplies same". Yet despite his financial problems Edward appears to have stubbornly held onto the assets as if expecting some miraculous turn of fortune. However, on 5th March 1805 he wrote to Roe & Co. seemingly setting out mitigating circumstances for his inability to meet his financial commitments; but, having considered the letter, Roe & Co. decided on 23rd May (as previously mentioned) that they had no alternative but to take legal action to recover the sum due.

The December meeting of 1805 began on the 10th of the month and stretched to five days; there was much to discuss. Letters had passed between Johnson and Hawkins regarding the outstanding debt, not only for the Neath Abbey works and stock, but also for the balance due from the Macclesfield bank; but to no avail. The partners present therefore regretted the "powerful necessity" to take action immediately, feeling it was their duty, not only to themselves but also their families, to collect what was due.

Ironically Edward's cousin Samuel of Whitechapel had prepared his will on 8th November 1804, evidently in a poor state of health, and died on 29th December 1805. Edward was executor together with a Richard Radford of Chiswick, Middlesex. Once again the will was complex and the executors had much to do in administering the various bequests of the estate. So apart from all the worries and frustrations of running the Neath Abbey works and sorting out his financial problems, Edward Snr. now had increased responsibilities as joint administrator of this considerable estate in East London, which in many ways was not to his benefit but to that of his children and in particular his eldest son, Edward Jnr.

A trust fund was set up for Edward's children and as his brother before him, Samuel gave several comparatively 'minor' bequests to friends and relatives, yet many more to charitable organisations Another £100 was to be spent on repairing the Hawkins family tomb in St. Mary's and for a monument there in memory of his father and brother.

Samuel's will reveals the considerable fortune inherited and enlarged upon by the two Hawkins brothers of East London, especially when taking into consideration that the parish of Whitechapel was one of the wealthiest in England at that time. Yet, despite this fact, to a great extent Edward Snr.'s hands were tied; the fortune was there but most of it not at his disposal. However Edward was shrewd enough to realise that it could work to his advantage, and circumstantial evidence indicates that he was able to raise loans against his implied wealth. He even had his portrait painted at this period by the famous portrait painter, Thomas Lawrence; but it reveals a man of gaunt features suggesting a person of little humour or personality, not an obvious recipe for promoting success.

Edward's own will, eventually prepared on 18th December 1813, records that he had subsequently borrowed money from his two sons, Edward and Samuel, for which he provided securities. However, he did have unspecified loans which his sons were left to redeem out of the sale of assets, although the latter did not include his interests in the East London estate which were charged with £600 per annum for his widow's benefit. Initially Edward Snr. must have felt confident that the loans were only on a temporary basis, no doubt assuming that his business ventures would soon produce profits capable of reducing all his outstanding debts; an illusion under which he was still labouring at the time of preparing his will. In the meantime he took some surprising decisions.

* * * * * * *

After the copper company meeting of December 1805 it was almost two years before the partners reconvened to discuss further the dissolution of their partnership, but first a more immediate matter was dealt with. By September 1807 Charles Cooke, son of the late Macclesfield attorney with an interest in the collieries on the Common, had diverted the water from the pool at the brass-works site and had been helping himself to clay from the company ditch at the eastern end of the yard; he was threatened with court action. For some reason Roe & Co. decided to build a brick kiln in the vicinity on the company field in Sutton, during the following winter, possibly as a deterrent to Cooke's enterprise.

The question of the continuation of the partnership in some ways remained unresolved yet, after further consultations, the legality of the situation dictated that whilst some company commitments were bound to continue, especially in the sphere of mining, so must the partnership; however, the following month steps were taken to simplify matters. The buildings and land in the "neighbourhood of Macclesfield" were to be improved, some by conversion into dwellings, and then divided between the individual partners as part of their personal share of the remaining company assets.

At this time Edward Hawkins Snr. asked for Robert Hodgson's bond of £6,000 to be transferred to him and, together with his own debt to the company (including that from

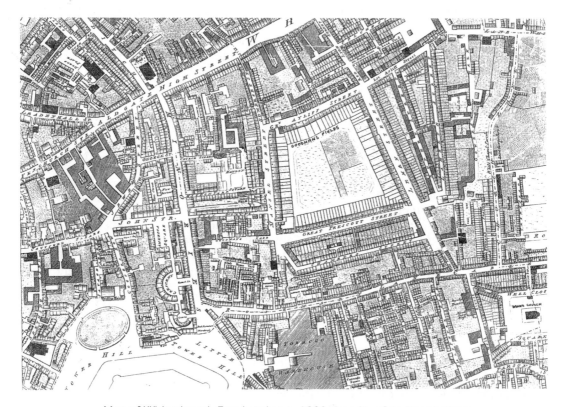

Map of Whitechapel, East London c. 1800 showing Goodman's Fields
and Leman Street in the centre, where many properties were owned by the Hawkins Family.

the bank), he contracted to make half-yearly payments until the whole of the debt was cleared. The partners, appreciating his change of circumstances, accepted this, though it does seem possible they had only been given half the picture. The surprise was Edward Hawkins's acceptance of Robert Hodgson's debt, although they were, of course, brothers-in-law and had always worked closely together. Robert, having completed his second term as mayor of Congleton in 1803 at the age of 63 years, moved shortly afterwards to St. Alban's. By the autumn of 1807 he must have been feeling very unwell and, perhaps realising that he did not have long to live, was anxious to put his affairs in order. One can only assume that a discussion took place between himself and Edward Hawkins Snr. from which an agreement was reached for Edward to accept Robert's debt of £6,000 in return for Robert's share of the company assets. Having received the concurrence of the other partners at the October meeting, Robert prepared his will on 6th November 1807 and died during the winter of the following year on 10th December 1808.

By his will Robert left his properties in and around Congleton for the benefit of his widow, Mildred, together with the remainder of the lease on his house in St. Alban's and the household contents. The three trustees (one of whom was his nephew Brian Hodgson the Younger, who had been forced to leave the Lower Beech estate and first take up temporary residence in Macclesfield Town and then Congleton) were to manage his share in the Llandudno copper mine and premises close by, under lease from Thomas Mostyn. This does indicate renewal of mining on the Great Orme after 1805 and was probably undertaken by the partnership including Edward Hawkins Jnr., who, having married in September 1806, had then moved to North Wales.

Robert's other assets were his shares in the "Irish Mine Company", the Crinan Canal Company and the heavily mortgaged estate at Disley with its collieries. Once again trustees were left with a difficult and unenviable task, for they had to realise £3,000 from the sale of assets to invest in government stocks, and pay £1,270 to Robert's son Beilby for an advance he had made to his father. The money invested was primarily for the widow's benefit and then for the children, although Robert included a kindly plea to his son Beilby to "consider" those of his brothers and sisters who might need his assistance. Unfortunately Beilby, a judge in India, had little time to consider anything, for he died there on 2nd July 1809 at the age of only 33 years, barely six weeks after his Uncle Beilby's death.

* * * * * * *

One of the last duties performed by Bishop Beilby was to request and be granted an audience with the Prince of Wales. Within a few days the exhausted Bishop, feeling that his life was drawing to a close, asked to be moved from his summer residence at Sundridge back to his London residence, Fulham Palace, where he died three days later.

Beliby's achievements were endless. He distributed his wealth amongst many causes including the poorer clergymen, and was one of the "earliest promoters and most strenuous advocates" for the Abolition of the Slave Trade. A bill finally receive Royal Assent on 25th March 1807 stating that no vessels were to clear out for slaves after the 1st May. Beilby declared "The Act which has just passed . . . will reflect immortal honour on the British Parliament and the British Nation." He urged for programmes of integration to take place, the most important being the education of the black children and also their religious education, and amongst his many bequests he left £1,000 to be invested for this purpose. The Bishop's lifetime investments included one as a shareholder in the Swansea canal, perhaps on the advice of his brother-in-law, Edward Hawkins Snr.

By this juncture Edward Hawkins Snr. had become an established member of Swansea society. He appears in the list of subscribers to the Theatre Royal which opened on Bank St.

in 1807, by which he nominated two of his daughters as shareholders. Amongst the other important local family names listed is that of John Stroud, also of Neath, who had become a partner in a Swansea bank during 1804. Together with Edward Hawkins and his son, Edward; Rees Williams, a local landowner with mining interests who had allowed Fox & Co. a lease of his iron stone mines on his Aberpergwn estate; William Gronow a surgeon and Griffith Llewellyn, Stroud established the Neath Bank on Wind St. Swansea during 1809, but withdrew one year later. The Hawkins remained in the concern until 1813, although, by then, had relinquished their interests in the Neath Abbey works, from which a very complex situation would evolve.

* * * * * * *

Whilst Napoleon's schemes of invading England had gone considerably awry (as predicted by the British Navy), leaving his flotilla of over 2,000 small craft rotting along the northern coast of France, having been torn apart by storms particularly those of June 1804, and his fleet smashed by Lord Nelson at Trafalgar, yet Napoleon was far from giving up in his determination to bring Britain to her knees. His next plan of action was to exclude all British goods from continental ports; a policy which met with some resistance from other European rulers, especially the Russian Czar.

On 2nd December 1805 Napoleon inflicted a resounding defeat on the combined forces of Russia and Austria at Austerlitz. During February 1806 the French seized Naples, thus cutting off an important British trading link. The Prussians were next to feel Napoleon's wrath with yet another glorious victory for the French at the battle of Jena on 14th October 1806. Not surprisingly Napoleon began to hear rumours of Russian resistance and marched for Poland via Berlin where he learnt that Alexander I had taken possession of some of the Polish states.

Russian defiance proved stronger than anticipated and for a short while French pride was badly shaken, then began a considerable struggle along the Vistula in appalling weather conditions, with the French Emperor engaged in outwitting an army he had greatly underestimated. Battles continued until well beyond the New Year.

In the early summer of 1807, on 14th June, the Russian army suffered its final great defeat at Friedland forcing the emperor Alexander I to seek an armistice. The result was the famous meeting between the two emperors in a specially constructed pavilion on a raft floating on the river Niemen near Tilsit. Peace was concluded on 9th July and England yet again found one of her greatest trading links severed. Temporarily the impact on the Baltic trade was devastating, and as Napoleon increased his grip on the continental ports, the warehouses of England were bulging with goods destined for export, until saturation point was reached. As the demand for goods slumped almost overnight, likewise the markets for raw materials.

There is no way in which Edward Hawkins could have averted a disaster, and although he was not the only purchaser of A.I.M. Co. ores, he must have been top of the list. The result was, that from 1808 the A.I.M. Co. had no option but to wind down operations, yet at the same time retain a team of miners to drive a deep level in an effort to keep the mines clear of water should hopes for later reworking become a reality.

By 1810 Abraham Mills was writing "everything is going steadily to ruin." The irony of the situation could not have been lost on anyone connected with Roe & Co; after several years of searchings, trials and considerable investment they had at last found a replacement for Parys Mountain, but to little avail. Incidentally their old adversary Thomas Williams had died in 1802, weaving his web of financial intrigues till the very end and leaving the subsequent partnership of Pascoe Grenfell and his eldest son Owen Williams with loans of a few thousand pounds; now everyone was feeling the strain, including the Cheadle Company.

By 1809 Edward Hawkins had, of course, become a partner in the Neath Bank, and whether or not it was his cajoling that brought about the desired effect backed by a promise of a bank loan, may never be known, but his offer "to dispose of his Copper Works" to the Cheadle Company was debated by them on 11th December 1810 and finally accepted. Although further details of the transactions are lacking (possibly with good intent) by March 1812 Cheadle was instructing Mr. Plumbe "to use every exertion to forward a Case of such best Copper from Neath Abbey Works by way of mixture to work off the present Stock of Copper on hand", and a one penny copper token was also produced that year with the obverse inscribed "the Cheadle Copper Co," and the reverse "London, Cheadle and Neath"; this seems evidence enough that they were in possession of the works. Under the circumstances the move was a foolish one, but when things become desperate people clutch at straws and not surprisingly the Cheadle partners were soon no better placed than Edward Hawkins had been.

Meanwhile Edward Hawkins, having rid himself of one burden unexpectedly appears to have acquired another, with the considerable estate in Whitechapel and Stepney, East London. It affected that part of the Goodman's Fields estate purchased by both Edward Hawkins of Whitechapel and his brother Samuel from a John Newnham. The whole complicated business ended in Chancery during 1814 when large chunks of the estate were sold at auction. This must have caused problems for the Hawkins trustees, although later deeds support the fact that young Edward and Samuel were in possession of at least part, if not all of their inheritance by renegotiation (i.e. leases relating to ground rents).Obviously all these different traumas affected Edward Snr.'s ability to honour his agreement with Roe & Co., and in the spring of 1811 to try to resolve the situation a meeting was arranged. One of Edward's daughters had married Thomas Pickford, a wealthy carrier and haulier whose estate was at Deanwater near Poynton just to the north of Macclesfield, and whilst on a visit Edward met there William Roe, Abraham Mills and John Johnson. A copy of the company minutes recorded at Liverpool on 19th April was taken along and duly read and signed by Hawkins on 12th May.

Several matters had arisen, in particular the money owed to Rachel Harriott and to the executors of Mary Roe, a matter which William Roe had put forward and for which he tried to obtain payment. John Johnson, however, had offered £200 only on account of a £1,000 bond to Mary's executors, claiming "I believe J.H. Roe to be the instigator & from his former conduct I am reluctant to put my hand into the a/c which may enable other persons to claim." This was a reference to an action brought against John Johnson by Rachel Harriott and recorded in May 1810. She had claimed £4,830 12 6d. but Johnson had insisted that without the consent of the majority he could only pay out interest, not capital. The outcome had been that William Roe, Abraham Mills, John Johnson and Thomas Weaver (the latter acting for his brothers Charles and Edward), as the majority had "resolved to indemnify" Johnson against damages. This minute is annotated "I hereby enter my protest against the resolution, J.H. Roe." Johnson was also given additional powers to enable him to sell or dispose of any company assets on the best terms possible.

Another interesting yet somewhat surprising initiative is also revealed by the minutes of 19th April 1811; Brian Hodgson the Younger had become involved in the business at Havannah. William Harvey had remained on site and from 10th May 1810 was charged a rent of £5 per annum for his house and an increased rent of £10 per annum for part of the wire room. Hodgson gave the company a bond for £866 15 3½d. to cover the period from 5th July 1804 for rolling copper at the works, and on 11th April 1811 accepted a further lease for 7 years "subject to agreements". There is no indication that he was in anyway connected with the Hawkins business, but was probably using up the large stocks of copper from the redundant smelters on Macclesfield Common.

Edward Hawkins Snr., having agreed the minutes of the April meeting, must then have been forced into some serious discussions about the Neath Abbey works; discussions which were certainly kept "off the record", but after which the status quo was allowed to continue for some time.

* * * * * * *

At this period the lower mills at Bosley were converted into cotton mills and William Roe agreed to accept them, together with adjacent houses and land (total value £5,000), as his personal share of the company assets. The Roe & Co. bond in his favour was therefore cancelled and he took possession on 1st January 1813. These years had been far from easy for him, having suffered a great loss when his eldest son and namesake died unexpectedly on 20th March 1809 whilst visiting Rachel Harriott in her Chestergate home. A surviving letter, written by John Harriott Roe in reply to one received from William Nicholson, encapsulates the effect of the tragedy on the whole family. "Alas! how sudden! and how destressing . . . Who indeed can supply the void". John Roe concluded his letter with the "necessity of bringing an action against Mr. Johnson on my Mother's hand." He deduced that his brother, William, was offended by his action as he had not heard from him for quite some time, "I can only lament, that he does not see things in their proper light." Although his message was at an end, the tragedies continued.

First, Jane Roe, the only surviving member of Charles Roe Jnr.'s family, died in Liverpool during February 1811. She was presumably under the guardianship of William and close to his family, for he announced the news in the *Liverpool Advertiser*. She too was placed in the family vault at Christ Church, Macclesfield. Then John Roe's wife, Hannah, died on 8th April 1812 at Tyers Hall leaving him with three young sons. Within two years (i.e. 30th March 1814) he married Dorothy Berridge, the widow of a vicar from Lincolnshire.

William Nicholson was now well established in Liverpool, having transferred from the Lancashire Militia to become deputy lieutenant in the Liverpool Militia. He had served as Bailiff for the city in 1810, was elected Mayor in 1813 and, as was customary, served as Coroner and J.P. for 1814. The Roe & Co. influence, evident so long in the Corporation by the presence of Thomas Smyth and William Roe (although the latter had slowly relinquished his position in deference to his Civil Service career) was now taken over by the younger man, and was one which he would retain until his death in 1832 at the age of 58 years. As one modern historian has pointed out, in the years prior to 1780 the burgesses of Liverpool were predominantly Whig "but then surprisingly the town became more Tory".

Another old adversary, Sparling, had died in 1800, having built a "palatial-looking" residence which became known as St. Domingo, a reminder of his slave trading activities. Sparling had also prepared for himself a tomb of appropriate grandeur in Walton churchyard directly opposite, so that each day he had the satisfaction of viewing his monument through his windows. His will stipulated that his heirs were to retain the property and his son did live there for some time until scandal forced him abroad during 1804. Relatives eventually obtained an Act of Parliament in order to sell the property, which in the meantime was let as an army barracks.

Whilst the military presence in Liverpool remained high it was a good excuse for balls and celebrations whenever possible. In September 1806, whilst guests of the Earl of Derby at Knowsley Park, the Prince of Wales and the Duke of Clarence (the future William IV) were invited to a magnificent banquet at Liverpool's town hall where several military personnel were amongst the guests. By 1810 George III's health had deteriorated to such an extent that he had become incapable of ruling and the Prince of Wales was accepted as Regent.

The following year saw the Russian Emperor Alexander allowing British goods to pass through his domains for various destinations on the Continent. Napoleon at first tried diplomacy, but Alexander was already negotiating with England, Sweden, Austria and Prussia. Conflict loomed as the French Emperor assembled the largest army ever seen in Europe, more than half a million men, and declared war on Russia 20th June 1812. He swept all before him forcing a Russian retreat after a ferocious battle at Borodino on the 7th September.

In Liverpool a fund was set up for "the Relief of the Russian Peasantry", but the French were unstoppable and soon took Moscow. Napoleon, considering he had left nothing to chance, had reckoned without a Russian will determined even to sacrifice the great city of Moscow in its efforts to defeat his army; within two days a fire was started. The Russian Emperor had already taken the precaution of sending all his diamonds, other valuables and ships to England. But even if the treasures had been there they could not buy food for the French troops, nor replenish other supplies which were destroyed with great rapidity, so Napoleon ordered a full retreat, but then delayed in order to retrieve his heavy artillery.

Fate delivered a brutal blow, the bitter cold arrived suddenly three weeks early, and almost all the horses, 30,000 of them, perished overnight. The retreat continued in appalling conditions and thousands perished. Napoleon made good his escape, arriving in Warsaw on 10th December. News of what was now considered to be his defeat was rapidly relayed to England, and by 14th December Gore's *Liverpool Advertiser* was reporting on the celebrations in the city.

The previous year of 1812 had provided Britain with near starvation due to a bad harvest, further exacerbated in ports such as Liverpool where very few ships could gain entry to bring in supplies, but now an atmosphere of victory prevailed. Everyone vied with each other to produce the best and most colourful illuminations, and there was a brilliant firework display on Everton Brow creating a glow in the evening sky visible as far as Chester. William Roe's house in Queen Square was singled out for special note as it was "beautifully lighted" with wax and small transparancies depicting emblems of the allies viz: Great Britain, Prussia, Sweden, Russia, Spain and Germany. The celebrations were, of course, premature and the incomparable Napoleon, having reached Paris on 18th December, declared his intention of completing his continental system the following year.

Whilst Napoleon's Russian campaign had been underway, the swansong of Roe & Co. was taking place as the partners agreed to a valuation and division of all assets, allocated according to their respective interests in the company. This included the mining shares of both the Holway and Irish mines, with the latter transferred "according to the act of parliament." The deeds for the various transfers, particularly the properties and plots of land on Macclesfield Common, were finally drawn up in time for the A.G.M. of 24th August 1813, and the firm of Roe & Co. ceased to exist. It did continue however as the late Roe & Co. to allow time for the collection of debts, payment of dividends and any business relating to the mining interests including the Macclesfield colliery, which from 1792 had been worked across the boundary of Macclesfield Common and into the neighbouring parish of Sutton.

On 19th April 1814 surprisingly a meeting took place in Burnley, a Lancashire town close to the boundary with Yorkshire. The significance of this is that only two members were present, John Atkinson Busfield (now a senior magistrate), and his son William Busfield J.P., both still resident in the West Riding of Yorkshire. Burnley, renowned for its cotton industry and coal mines must have held some interest for the father and son, which was possibly an investment in the collieries because of their involvement with other mining concerns. Their company meeting put forward a resolution for the agent at Holywell to sell all the mining shares for not less than £5000. This was confirmed by William Roe in Liverpool on 28th April on behalf of the others, however Jefferies and Brian Hodgson the younger recorded their disapproval in Gloucester on 28th May declaring that they would "not sell or dispose of our shares at any price." The only other item to receive attention at this time was the difficulty in obtaining payment from Captain Smith, owner of the Llanberis mine, and the suggested recommendation of threatening litigation for the recovery of his share of the losses in the concern.

Across the English Channel Napoleon Bonaparte was also forcing the pace, and incredibly soon had another French army in the field despite the phenomenal losses suffered during his winter campaign, only this time it was a much younger, inexperienced one. The allies, having already gained several footholds on the Continent, succeeded in invading France and on 31st March 1814 entered Paris. Louis XVIII returned to the city from England as the senate announced Napoleon's abdication, and the former French Emperor was taken from Fontainebleau to his exile on the island of Elba.

Although the winter of 1813-14 had been a particularly severe one in many ways, the following spring brought peace with France and the beginnings of a negotiated peace with America. Further rejoicings during the summer months were still denied their full maturity when, having learnt that his exile was shortly to be lived out on the isolated island of St. Helena not Elba, Napoleon boldly sailed for France on 26th February 1815. As on so many previous occasions his dynamic personality won the day, and those sent to intercept him instead fell in behind, swelling his support The battle of Waterloo on 18th June 1815, when Wellington assisted by the Prussian General Blucher delivered Napoleon's final crushing defeat, is well documented, but Napoleon's letter to the Prince Regent requesting exile in England is not so well-known. His audacity had failed and soon he was on his way to St. Helena and life could return to some sort of normality. There was peace at last.

FINALE

31
THE FINAL CHAPTER

On the evening of 7th March 1816 Edward Hawkins Snr. died quite suddenly in his home at Court Herbert within a mile or so of the Neath Abbey works. He had "retired to rest apparently in perfect health" as reported in the *Gentleman's Magazine* for April 1816. The remaining Macclesfield company partners acted swiftly; they had done their best to accommodate his aberrations but the code of loyalty could no longer be sustained, they had their own futures to consider.

Despite the fact Napoleon had been defeated, and the harvests of 1814 and 1815 had provided plenty, still the warehouses were full of goods, many deteriorating, which could not be sold due to the poor economic state of the Continent.

Surprisingly the situation was initially exacerbated by thousands of British subjects rushing overseas, having been forced to curtail their life styles during the years of war. It was, in fact, a real problem, debated by Parliament when it was discovered that from 1814 to February 1816 the figure for those sailing from Dover alone reached 90,230, of which 13,000 remained permanently abroad. Many headed for Boulogne hoping to "dodge their creditors", yet all spent lavishly. This was the period when whole retinues departed, including amongst them the famous poets Byron, Keats and Shelley, which caused a considerable drain on capital. The result was a year of "high taxation, high prices and enforced austerity" during 1817.

The sons of Edward Hawkins Snr., who were in a much better position financially than their father had been, now had to bear the brunt of his chaotic financial legacy. The company minutes record that on 28th October 1812, at the same time as William Roe had accepted the cotton mills at Bosley, John Jefferies agreed to take the Havannah works. The latter was valued by a surveyor from Liverpool and another recommended by Peter Marsland, owner of the Stockport silk mill (which suggests that a silk mill had by then been erected on the site); the third, Thomas Rowley (one of the commissioners of the Macclesfield Common Enclosure) gave a valuation for the adjoining meadow. One month later a Liverpool company, Horne & Stackhouse were interested in purchasing the works, but, when the sale failed, the property, described as "the land, buildings & appurtenances" was allotted to Edward Hawkins Snr. instead of Jefferies. This was an incredible turn of events which at first suggests that Hawkins was willing to trade his position in the Neath Bank for what he considered to be a better proposition; however, it was another financial ploy to assist Jefferies.

On 12th May 1813 the legalities were completed and the site, referred to as "improved and developed", included several cottages and their tenants, but Brian Hodgson the younger was not amongst them, having apparently given up his lease. The value was taken as an average of the three received and comprised £3,850 for the buildings + appurtenances, and £450 for the adjacent Dean Meadow, formerly part of Armett's. Almost immediately Edward Hawkins Snr. sold the whole property except Dean Meadow (which he retained) to John Jefferies (still of Gloucester) for a loan of £4,300 + interest. The transfer took place on 24th August, but whether or not Jefferies realised that the included meadow land known as Armett's had been subdivided and a new one called Dean created, is difficult to judge. However, after their father's death the Hawkins's children sold Dean Meadow to a Thomas Davis as trustee

Survey of Neath Abbey Estate 1770-71

Map of Court-Herbert Demesne page 25

Above: Neath Abbey 1811 including the 'Shipping Place' and the copper works.

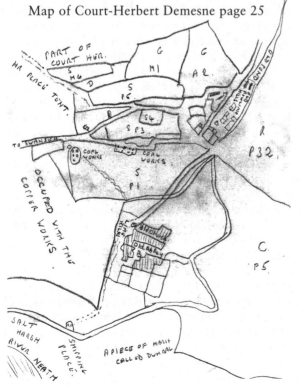

by kind permission of City Records Office Swansea Ref: D/D DE/157

Left: is an extract from a survey of the Court Herbert Estate (City R.O. Swansea) relevant to the above view. The 'Old Abbey' is marked 'B' in the centre of the plan; the 'Shipping Place' is to the south and the area 'Occupied with the Copper Works' indicates the position of the Roe & Co. site in-between.

for John Jefferies in November 1816.

John Jefferies died during 1818 and his seven children inherited the property, one of whom was Rowland Jefferies, a captain in the East India Company's service in Madras, and another son Charles Jefferies, described as "of Havannah Mills", a lieutenant in the Royal Navy.

Not so easy to resolve was the situation regarding the Neath Abbey works. Although Edward Hawkins Snr. had technically been the owner from 25th December 1801, yet he had never been able to redeem his mortgage plus interest with Roe & Co., so the Macclesfield partners could legally have claimed the property by seizure. However, it was now also mortgaged by the Cheadle Company but again payments were overdue, this time to Hawkins, giving rise to a complicated situation. The case placed in the hands of a Liverpool solicitor. It does seem possible that Hawkins, in accepting the Havannah works had agreed to transfer those of Neath Abbey back to the company. This would still have left him in debt because of the amount of interest which had accrued from the initial loan, but does seem to justify (at least from his point of view but not from Jefferies's) the sale of Havannah, because the interest received from the loan made to Jefferies could be offset against that outstanding to Roe & Co.

The manager of the Cheadle works, Dr. Plumbe, had begun his own personal enterprise as a manufacturer of sulphuric acid at the nearby Melin Gryddan chemical works in 1813; his co-partner Joseph Gibbins is shown as a banker, but in reality the latter was probably only the lender of capital. This does suggest that the doctor felt financially confident in attempting such an undertaking, perhaps with the somewhat misguided notion that should the Cheadle company's investments fail, the Roe & Co. finances would be able to support his scheme. Presumably the truth had finally begun to dawn three years later when Dr. Plumbe "retired" from the works, this was shortly before a local solicitor, William Gwyn. attorning for the Liverpool solicitor acting on behalf of the late firm of Roe & Co., escorted him from his home at Longford Court to the Neath Abbey premises where notice was served on him demanding possession. The date was 17th January 1817 and Gwyn had just returned from serving notice on Edward Hawkins Jnr. demanding his quittance of the Salt Marshes adjacent to the works. Young Hawkins, who was by then living in Dylais two miles from Neath, happened to be away in London, so the notice was left with his housekeeper.

Gwyn was having a busy day, for he next delivered his final notice to a Mr. Allen at the agent's house demanding possession of the house and premises, then completed the legalities by visiting the premises at the Salt Marsh. On the 25th April Hawkins Jnr. was at Court Herbert where Gwyn and his clerk caught up with him, but Hawkins refused to allow them to take possession of the marshland. On 2nd May Gwyn was again obliged to serve Hawkins with a copy of the original writ, for which he once more travelled to Dylais.

It is apparent from subsequent information that compromises were reached and court action averted, although the usual hiatus as to what actually took place is all too apparent. The Cheadle company minutes, however, do record years of difficulties, yet payment must have been made to the Macclesfield Copper Company to allow Cheadle to retain the works. The minutes of the Macclesfield company reveal nothing. A meeting took place at the *Angel Inn*, Macclesfield on 24th April 1816 after which the next recorded meeting of the "Proprietors of the late firm Roe & Co." was at the Exchange Buildings in Liverpool on 13th June 1831, yet much had taken place in those intervening years.

The only conceivable action to fit the circumstantial evidence is that Roe & Co. were again legally considered owners of the works in 1813, but that the Cheadle Company renegotiated the loan for possession of the works with the Macclesfield partnership from early in 1817 to avoid court action. Because Roe & Co. are referred to as once more being connected with Neath Abbey from 1813, it does add weight to the idea that Edward Hawkins Snr. in May of that year, gave up Neath Abbey when taking Havannah, for by the A.G.M. of August 1813 the firm of Roe & Co. had ceased to exist.

There is also a suggestion that, as the Cheadle Company partners struggled on, they came to some arrangement with the neighbouring Crown Copper Company, but in 1821 John Keates, manager of the Cheadle works in Staffordshire, was sent to close down the Neath Abbey works. The furnace bottoms were knocked out, and other items, which could not be removed to the Staffordshire site, were sold to Vivian & Sons.

The meeting at the Exchange Buildings, Liverpool in 1831 records that "All claims & suit against the Cheadle & Crown Company on acct (account) of premises at Neath Abbey be entirely abandoned."

* * * * * * *

After the controversy of 1813 young Edward Hawkins had apparently acquiesced, but he did not remain long in South Wales for he was living in Surrey by 1819. Earlier in his career during his stay in North Wales he had become an expert botanist and was made a fellow of the Linnean Society in 1806. This was probably the reason for the defense of his occupation of the Salt Marsh near Neath Abbey; but apart from a naturalist's point of view, the stigma of such an eviction would be difficult to bear within the close knit community of the Neath area. He was able to take with him to Surrey a superb service of Swansea china, specially hand-painted for him with illustrations taken from Sowerby's book called *Botany*. He had also amassed a considerable collection of prints and books relating to the city of Chester.

In Surrey Edward was free to pursue a surprising career; by 1821 he was a fellow of the Royal Society (later vice-president) but in 1826 was appointed Keeper of Antiquities at the British Museum, a post he would retain until his 80th year in 1860. His contributions to the various collections at the museum, which included many publications, and in particular the setting-up of what would become its remarkable coinage and medals collections, is outstanding, but his greatest achievements were his own collection of British medals (purchased by the Trustees in 1860) and his book *The Silver Coins of England* (1841). The latter is still regarded as the standard work although revised since the first edition because of the many hoards of coins which subsequently have come to light with "soil disturbances" and building work. For this reason the second edition of 1876 was revised by one of his grandsons and prefixed "as a grandson of the author, he was unwilling that his grandfather's work should either be edited by a stranger or superceded by any new publication. He has therefore undertaken the duty; and in doing so he has been compelled, very unwillingly, to make considerable alterations in the original text." Hawkins the Younger had obviously been inspired by his father's, and later his own connections with the world of banking, stimulating his fascination with coinage.

Brian Hodgson Jnr. had left Crakemarsh for Uttoxeter in 1800 where he spent his final years, firstly in the vicarage and then in the 'old house opposite the church' until his death on 3rd November 1827 aged 85 years. He was interred in Ashbourne Church near his parents and was subsequently followed by his wife, Ellen, who died on 11th April 1830 aged 91 years. His son Brian the Younger was living in Bologne, France by 1825.

Another Hodgson family member who has a significant role in British history is Rev. Robert Hodgson, Dean of Carlisle, and eldest son of Robert and Mildred Hodgson; educated at Macclesfield Grammar School and Peterhouse, Cambridge, he had served as chaplain to Bishop Porteus and become rector of St. George's, Hanover Square in 1803. He accepted the parish of Hillingdon with Uxbridge in 1810, the Archdeaconry of St. Alban's (1814-1816) and later the Deanery of Chester. He resigned the latter in favour of Carlisle during 1820, but died at his house in Lower Grosvenor Street, Westminster on 10th October 1844. His granddaughter, Frances Dora Smith, married Charles Lyon-Bowes (later Bowes-Lyon) and by that became the grandmother of the late Queen Elizabeth, the Queen Mother.

Of the remaining copper company partners, Thomas Smyth died at his residence 'The Fence' in Hurdsfield, adjoining Macclesfield, on 12th July 1824 aged 87 years. Thomas Smyth's partner of many years, Charles Caldwell, lived out his days in Liverpool, dying at 7 Bold

Street on 10th January 1814 aged 75 years. Despite the bankruptcy he was able to leave an interesting will. First appears the apparent confirmation that his four children, William, George, Ann and Harriet, were all illegitimate but had the same mother, Ann Ashton, who had died earlier. He left two estates in Ireland, one called Harold's Cross near Dublin and the other, Adams Town land in Co. Kilkenny amongst other bequests. To assist his son, George, with the trusteeship he appointed his relative and good friend, Mr. Haywood adding (no doubt with a modicum of Irish charm) "I trust my worthy friend Mr. Haywood will forgive my requesting him to take a share of trouble in this business & add this last obligation to many others I am indebted to him for." So concluded the life of yet another intriguing Georgian character.

The younger Weavers, although latecomers to the enterprise, but nevertheless part of the story, failed in their efforts to keep their father's pin business afloat, despite innovative patents for pin production worked on by Charles Weaver in partnerhsip with a John Leigh Bradbury. On 15th December 1817, together with several others, the *Gloucester Journal* announced that "a Commission of Bankrupt is awarded and issued forth against Edward Weaver and Charles Weaver, both of the city of Gloucester, Pin-Manufacturers, Dealers, Chapmen, and Copartners . . ." Finally the sale by auction appeared in the issue for 23rd March 1818.

Their brother, Thomas, having been well educated, fared much better. Initially he was committed to the Irish concern; in March 1811 he produced a table of the production figures from the commencement of operations in 1787 until that date, to give a "retrospective view of the annual proceedings" based on the fact that "so little work has been done in the mine within the last 3 years." A decision was taken to sell, and the auction took place on 27th June 1811 when it was recorded that Lieutenant Colonel Robert Haward bought the Cronebane mine for £2,500. In the September account Mills was credited with the expenses of the Cronebane sale, a John Davies received commission for the same and a fee of 5s. 5d. was paid for entry of the sale at the Customs House. The expenditure account was concluded in March 1812 showing that during the final six months expenses of only £111 2 3d were necessary for Cronebane, £65 4 5d. for Tigroney, £425 5 1d. for "General" items and on "Land and Royalty" £42 5 10d. The mystery is what happened next, for in August 1814 Mills was attempting to find a lessee for the mine.

Individual details remain unclear, but Cronebane and Tigroney had always been worked as two separate mines. Cronebane was the oldest, and the adit had been driven "in a considerable distance up the hill" but entirely within the townland of Cronebane. The lower Tigroney mine, which was extended by Thomas Weaver, had begun with a deep adit worked from the river Avoca and was continued through the townland of Tigroney into the Lower Cronebane workings. But it was never extended to reach the upper mine. Either Haward had only bought the upper Cronebane mine or he had died or been killed before payment was made and the workings had been neglected; without money to sue, the A.I.M. Co. would have been forced to retake the mine. The only certainty is that the years to 1817 proved to be extremely difficult ones with losses mounting to almost £4,000, and the partners had no option but to cover the deficit out of their own pockets. Unfortunately Thomas Weaver had nothing left to give and, because of his arrears, was not entitled to vote at the meeting which took place on 22nd April 1817 at the Royal Exchange, Dublin. On this occasion the only other person present, apart from Abraham Mills and Thomas Weaver, was John Johnson who, in addition to representing himself, was proxy for all the other members. (The previous year's A.I.M. Co. meeting had taken place in Macclesfield and had been well attended).

At this juncture it was decided to advertise the Irish mine for sale at £6,000, or otherwise by auction, and Thomas Weaver Jnr. took time out to write his *Memoirs on the Geological Relations of the East of Ireland* published in 1819. A report written on the mines of Wicklow in 1856 credits him with the extensive workings at Cronebane and Tigroney and mentions that the latter produced thousands of tons of black copper ore under his management. Weaver described Tigroney as having a bed of solid ore of one to three fathoms deep which yielded 5-7% copper, in parts made up of copper pyrites.

On 25th March 1823, by coincidence, the concern was leased to a Mr. Johnson for 21 years, but it is doubtful that this was in anyway connected with John Johnson of the Macclesfield company; however the average income from this source was £600 per annum. Within two years the lease for both mines was acquired by the Imperial Mining Company of Dublin which worked them until the early 1830s. During this period one final meeting took place at the Quadrant Hotel, Regent Street, London on 14th July 1828 for the remaining members whose connections had been through the original Macclesfield Copper Company; the now depleted group was reduced to representatives of only John Jefferies and Abraham Mills. By 1837 even they were gone.

With the leasing of the mine Thomas Weaver became an active member of the recently formed Geological Society and published further surveys of Gloucestershire, Somerset and Southern Ireland. He produced a paper concerning the fossil remains of the great Irish deer for the Royal Society in 1825 and was elected a fellow the following year. In all he wrote 20 geological papers for the society between 1820 and 1841, and at the same time travelled as a mining geologist in Mexico and the United States. The product of his latter endeavours was yet another series on the carboniferous rocks of America. He had been retired for some years when he died at this home in Pimlico, London on 2nd July 1850 aged 72 years.

Little more is known of John Johnson except that he had left Liverpool by 1813 to take up residence on the Arley Hall estate near Knutsford, Cheshire; a probable indicator of an earlier family connection. In April 1816 his profit and loss account, kept for the company, showed that he was holding credit of £1,388 10 1d., and he attended the mining company meeting in Macclesfield on 14th July 1818. He is also included in the final list of shareholders following the meeting at the Exchange Buildings in Liverpool during 1831, and had evidently been acting as company accountant in the intervening years, for he was asked to "co-operate" with Redish and Bird, a Liverpool accountancy firm engaged to take care of the winding up of the company.

* * * * * * *

For the remaining years of his life Abraham Mills appears to have divided most of his time between Southern Ireland and North Wales, yet obviously paying the occasional visit to Macclesfield where his daughter, Mary, and her family remained. His interest in the Parsonage Green property was not relinquished until 2nd July 1826 when he, together with others, sold it to a William Dickenson. His eldest grandson, James Legh, at some point in time had joined his grandfather in Ireland, for he died in Dublin on 19th February 1820.

Shortly afterwards Mills moved to Bodlondeb, a house and gardens which were part of an estate near Conwy in North Wales. Although the death of his grandson could have been a contributory factor in his decision to leave Ireland, yet there were certainly others. The leasing of the Irish mines by 1823 would have ensured that his attention was no longer necessary at Wicklow, and the end of his affair with the widow, Margaret Jane, in Dublin, which seems to have been brought about by her death, perhaps produced the realisation that it was once more time to move on.

North Wales must have been chosen as an appropriate place to settle because of the remaining mining interests in the vicinity, and the fact that Mills had forged many connections in the area over the years. An extant letter of 10th August 1792 from Mills to Thomas Wright of Knutsford (second son of the solicitor, Samuel Wright) indicates the designation of the area to Mills as agent for the copper company:

"In my way through Carnarvon I had the pleasure of seeing Mr. Ellis who mentioned that you was working at Drws y coed & expresfed a wish that our Company should join you in the adventure, in consequence of which I orderd Jones to go & view the Mine, which he did & rendered a report rather favourable to the undertaking – This report has been laid before the General meeting of our Company, who consider themselves obliged by the preference you give to them, but having come to a determination not to extend their Mineral concern, I am desired by them to decline your obliging offer."

This refusal, already mentioned earlier, was, of course, at the crucial period when the transfer of the Toxteth smelters was taking place. A further letter, annotated "What past between Harvey & me at the Hotel 14th Fby 1801", although unsigned, apparently relates to a Thomas Jones acting on behalf of Roe & Co. He had travelled down from Llanberis to a hotel in Carnarfon in order to settle some accounts with a Mr. Harvey. He was informed by the waiter that Harvey was "going to dinner", but, having asked for a message to be given of his arrival, was invited to join the dinner table.

Before dinner arrived the accounts relating to the purchase of barley for the miners' use and also the miners' other expenses were agreed, and after dinner the two retired to the "Other parlour." However, the Roe & Co. representative went to look for Hugh Hughes, who had arrived escorted by Euan Jones; the two were then able to witness the payment made by bill, value £70 15 6d. in respect of the miners' account, together with two guineas in gold. But when Thomas Jones insisted on receiving his commission, Harvey refused to accept the payment, arguing that Hughes had not paid the corn bill. Thomas Jones pointed out that the corn bill was not his responsibility and, as Harvey departed leaving the two guineas and remittance on the table, he picked them up and went to see an attorney, Williams, the next day. As he was in the attorney's office Harvey passed the window and Williams called him in; payment was made, receipts were signed, but Harvey, in no mood for being outmanoeuvred, still refused to pay the commission, insisting that he would make both Thomas Jones and Hughes responsible for the corn bill and asked Williams to proceed against Jones before he left town.

The outcome is unknown, as also is the one relating to a letter dated 29th July 1804 addressed directly to Abraham Mills from the same attorney. The subject was again Llanberis, this time relating to a Mr. Jones and his wife who were tenants of Thomas Assheton Smith. Jones worked a quarry on the Dinorwig Common and they lived in a tenanted house close by, which had a small piece of land adjoining. Evidently under the terms of the company lease with Smith, Abraham Mills had been instrumental in the issuing of a writ against the couple for the removal of an old gate and posts, for which the couple were to be ejected from the field. The attorney had been told that the gate and posts had not been "carried off the premises" but fixed in another part of the field. Mrs. Jones had made up her mind that she no longer wished to be a tenant, because without the field they could not keep a horse or cow. However, the couple intended suing, as they had discovered that although Smith had continued to pay a yearly rental for the Manor and premises of Dinorwig, the Treasury had discovered old grants which proved that the Crown was still 'Lord of the soil' and therefore held the right to sanction mining and quarrying leases. On occasion Smith had tried to "turn off" those quarrying for slates, and now his actions could be called into question.

These local disputes, of which there must have been more, no doubt added to Mills's decision for moving into the area. He was no longer a young man, although from all accounts appeared remarkably fit for his seventy or so years, nevertheless the arduous journeys, particularly during the winter periods, must have begun taking their toll, so once again his social connections seem to have paid off.

One of the trustees for the Conwy estate (which in 1821 was part of a marriage settlement when the heiress, Jane, married Sir David Erskine baronet) was Rev. Edward Owen, rector of Llaniestyn, Co. Carnarfon; his daughter, Catherine, married Edward Legh, the second grandson of Abraham Mills. Young Edward lived in Lewisham, Kent so perhaps a fortuitous visit to his grandfather at Bodlondeb had brought about his introduction to Catherine. Abraham Mills, however, could not have lived long in the rented property, for his burial took place in Conwy on 8th March 1828; he was recorded as aged 79 years. There is a certain poignancy about his final request, "And if I die at Bodlondeb or if I die elsewhere It is my desire to be buried in the plainest manner and without Funeral Pomp in the next adjacent usual plan of Burial." Mills had never purchased a burial plot in the Christ Church cemetery in Macclesfield, unlike Edward Hawkins who had actually purchased two, which ironically would always remain unoccupied.

Mills had prepared his will some six months earlier on 9th September 1827; it reveals a man of great sentiments, and one who acknowledged and accepted his responsibilities, for he did not neglect his illegitimate daughter. She was given his surname and placed in Miss Eliza's boarding school at No. 18 Dover Place, New Kent Road near London, within a mile or so from where his brother, Henry, lived.

Henry and two of Abraham's friends, Charles Bleasdale of Lancashire (previously of Threadneedle Street in the City of London) and Earles Cuthbert of Dublin, were entrusted with the sum of £500 as an investment for the maintenance and education of the child, described as "my Dear Child Mary Jane", the youngest daughter of Margaret Jane, widow, born in Dublin on 19th November 1819.

Mills also commended all his other family members to his brother's "paternal care", but, anxious to show some acknowledgement of his affection for his brother, yet at the same time appreciating his brother's considerable wealth, he left him a family heirloom. It was a two handled silver cup which had once belonged to their grandfather, Abraham, "said to have been presented to him by a person who he rescued from a House on Fire."

Nor did he forget his "Dear Friend Miss Anne Watson" of Macclesfield. He had put aside a diamond ring, to which he had attached her name, and asked that before it was given to her it should be engraved with his name and the date and time of his decease.

His legitimate daughter, Mary Legh, by then a widow, received the greater part of his estate. To granddaughter, Emma, the wife of Dr. Cannon, Mills left his late wife's miniature portrait; and to Emma's sister, Mary Anne Legh, a pair of pearl earrings and "all other pearl ornaments."

Various other comparatively minor sums were left to each of the grandchildren and friends, and in addition his grandson, Edward, also received his wearing apparel. All the residuary interests from the copper company i.e. property in Macclesfield and county Wicklow and shares in mines in the counties of Wicklow, Carnarfon and Flint, were to be disposed of by the trustees in order to meet his bequests.

* * * * * * *

Unfortunately very few details remain of the later period of mining; however by 1807 there is a reference to "the New Mine" on the Great Orme, Llandudno, which was worked mostly on the Mostyn land, with one level being shared by the 'Old' mining company in return for a payment of 2s. 6d. per annum: presumably the latter included the Roe & Co. partnership. In April 1812 Sir Thomas Mostyn leased mines in the parish of Llanasa, a little to the south-east of Prestatyn, to a group which included James Kyrke of Brymbo, but none of the extant Mostyn deeds for this period mention Roe & Co. or any of their individual partners by name. But it is evident that at some time circa 1806 Abraham Mills and others had agreed a lease with the new Bishop of Bangor John Randolph; an early 19th century writer, Edward Hyde Hall, in his *Description of Caernarvonshire* wrote an account of the crushing and washing of ore on the site, from where it was carted to the banks of the Conwy for shipment to Swansea (presumably destined for Edward Hawkins's smelters at Neath Abbey).

There was yet another bishop of Bangor appointed late in 1809; he was Henry William Majendie who had resided in Liverpool for some considerable time, and such was his influence in the city that in October 1809 the Corporation granted him the Freedom of the Borough. In eloquently flowing terms the Council recorded their regret at:

"his Lordship's Departure from this Diocese a regret which is more sincerely felt from a consciousness of the many Advantages which have been derived from his Lordship's constant Residence within this Diocese & from his unwearied endeavours to discharge with ardent zeal the High & Important Duties of his exalted Station."

It is not surprising, therefore, that from the quarter ending August 1812 the Bishop of Bangor drew up an agreement with Samuel Worthington of Llandegai (possibly the owner of the Herculaneum Pottery manufactory, or his father) to become agent for his $^1/_8$th duty payable by the partners of Roe & Co. on ore retrieved, for the two would have moved in some of the same Liverpool circles. Finally, in October 1824, the Bishop agreed a new lease with Worthington himself, duty payable $^1/_8$th, which covered the whole common, an area of some 700 statute acres. This marks the end of the Roe & Co. involvement on the Great Orme.

Remarkably the Busfields had still retained their company interests held jointly by the father, John Atkinson, and his eldest surviving son, William. In 1800 William married the sister of a baronet, and his father, by then a widower, married for the second time and became resident at Consonby Hall in Yorkshire. Wesley's influence had run its course and the Busfields had remained loyal to the Church of England. On 1st November 1812, when a division of the lots held by Roe & Co. on Macclesfield Common had taken place to the appropriate active partners, the Busfields received property equal in value to that allocated to William Roe, confirming that jointly they held the same number of shares as he did.

John Atkinson died on 26th March 1817 aged 78 years, and by his will, proved the following 22nd June, nominated son William heir to his estates. William Busfield was present at the final winding up of the company by the trustees on 11th May 1832; he subsequently became M.P. for Bradford from 1837 until his death in September 1851.

As his father came first in the order of Roe & Co. personnel, it is appropriate that William Roe should be last, although he did predecease Abraham Mills by almost a year, dying in Macclesfield on 27th March 1827, just two weeks before his 81st birthday.

William's large will, in respect of folios, disappointingly reveals comparatively little, except his considerable wealth. By this time it was no longer necessary to provide inventories, and whilst some continued to do so, William's trustees took the easier option; perhaps forgivable when considering his eighty years and the complicated state of his affairs. The will had been prepared as early as 22nd January, 1821, at which date, out of his original eleven daughters and three sons, ten daughters and one son had survived.

Under an agreement of 11th November 1783, following Samuel Shaw Snr.'s death, William Roe, as Hannah's husband and father of her children, had received one third of the Shaw estate for the use of those children. As acknowledged in his will, William possessed a considerable personal fortune quite separate from the third share of the Shaw estate. Between the two he contrived to leave to each of his daughters a total sum of £5,000 (over £1/2 million today), taking into consideration the sums already included in appropriate settlements for those already married. The residue was to be inherited by his only surviving son, Christopher Shaw Roe, together with his real estate which included the "advowson of Christ Church and all other rights and property in the same Church and its Cemetery" and a share in the Theatre Royal, Liverpool. Yet the full extent of his wealth will never accurately be known, only that William would have achieved the status of a mutimillionaire today. (For further details of his will and life see Biographical Notes in Appendix 1). William lived his final years with his son Christopher in Macclesfield until his death on 27th March 1827. He was buried in the family vault in Christ Church with the following inscription:

"he was an affectionalte Husband and Indulgent Parent a Man of benevolence and a sincere Friend and a firm upholder of the excellent principles of the Established Church."

Epilogue

Most historians will concede that the 18th century has remained a somewhat shadowy period. Far too often the Regency period, primarily because of its extant wealth of original correspondence and documentation, has been expanded to fill part of the gap between the Seven Years War and the Napoleonic Wars. However, with the aid of property deeds the lives of ordinary people, and the networks linking those lives can be better understood. The idea that predominantly there was a handful of wealthy aristocrats and thousands of downtrodden poor, disappears, also the deduction that local history was just that, with the vast majority of the people hardly moving outside their immediate area. Whilst journeying in comparative comfort along modern routes to destinations where Roe & Co. personnel were located, I began to appreciate what incredible people our 18th century ancestors were, and just how vibrant and mobile was the society in which they lived.

18th century property deeds contain a wealth of information often including copies of wills, marriage settlements, proofs of birth etc. and addresses. The greatest problem is pinpointing the present day property to which they relate if they have been separated from the modern deeds. Another problem is that one deed can rarely be used alone, it has to be seen as part of a group for a particular area, otherwise incorrect deductions can be made. For instance, any property which today is located on what was Charles Roe's estate in the middle of Macclesfield, will have the same Abstract of Title mentioning Charles Roe's name; this has led to at least three Georgian houses in the area being claimed as Charles Roe's residence. It is imperative, therefore, never to make a positive pronouncement unless at least one other source indicates the same fact.

Another important comprehension, revealed by property deeds, is that as the second half of the 18th century progressed, more and more property owners were living on credit, not only borrowing against the value of their properties, but far beyond. It was an incredible situation as a desperate individual would borrow from one creditor, then surreptitiously seek out another. By the time of the Napoleonic Wars the vast majority of property deeds examined reveal the extent of borrowing, which in some cases was three or four times the value of the collateral. Many were obviously hoping and gambling on an economic turn round, and staggered on from crisis to crisis. They were patently insolvent, but had the personality to persuade yet another associate to part with even more money than the last, and continued to bluff their way through their pretentious lifestyles leaving trustees and descendants bearing the brunt of their misguidances.

Only two generations earlier than the start of the Georgian Period, the Restoration of 1660 had taken place, which would cast its shadow over every aspect of English life for some considerable time to come. Like it or not, religion was continuing to be an important aspect of everyday life and simply could not be ignored. Little did I realise just how significant this comprehensivness would be; only when individuals began to group together under their various religious umbrellas did the truth dawn. The competition for industrial power and wealth had begun, stimulated by the founding of the Bank of England and religion, a far different concept than that previously offered of Boulton and Watt's steam engines.

And whilst mining has always been recognised as one of the prime factors in contributing towards the Industrial Revolution, yet the emphasis has been on coal and the production of coke, coupled with the iron industry. The mining of copper and casting of brass have never been given their proper places in the scheme of things. Ingenious projects incorporating water power and wind were already well established by 1717, as were Newcomen's early steam engines. Without the use of brass Watt would never have been able to build up sufficient pressure in his engines to create far more powerful machines than those built earlier by Newcomen, so the idea that the Industrial Revolution began with Boulton and Watt seems to be ignoring completely over half a century of hard working geniuses, such as the Pattens and Roes, who certainly warrant their place in history.

Charles Roe deserves credit for his building projects alone; a silk mill complex, three copper smelters (one with a harbour development), a brass works complete with windmill, two large industrial sites with rolling mills and other utilitarian buildings, and a large church. No mean achievement for a man who had died by the time the Boulton and Watt schemes were attracting serious attention.

Too much prominence has also been given to the wealthy merchant class of the 18th century. Whilst admitting it merits its place, yet the emphasis placed on its importance has overshadowed all other strata of society. The lawyers, civil servants, militia, naval personnel, doctors, chemists, professors and clergy were all there in great force, together with miners, engineers and surveyors, amongst others. It was a balanced society, just as today. And those of William Roe's stature were not only business men but deeply concerned with public duty and charitable works; they were the backbone of English society. Many held posts in government departments, intent on eradicating corruption and greed at the highest level. William and his colleagues in the Revenue were able to create a Customs Service which had a reputation for fairness, honesty and a commitment to duty which has remained to this day. Even figures on the periphery of this story had important roles to play, for whilst William and his Liverpool associates organised patrols to begin policing the streets of that great city, the adventurer John Harriott devised a plan to set up the first official river police force in London. It was established to combat plundering of naval ordnance and pilfering from the warehouses of the West Indian merchants along the Thames. Sugar was the prime target, but even the domestic trade of coal was severely hit. This was the forerunner of today's Pool of London police, and with Harriott an ardent Freemason it is not surprising that the tradition has remained within the force.

* * * * * * *

Charles Roe and Brian Hodgson could never be accused of living opulent life styles, in fact quite the reverse. Brian Hodgson lived out his days in the Grey House, Ashbourne with a small estate, and Charles Roe remained in his mortgaged property on Chestergate. It would have been easy for them to have built magnificent residences surrounded by large estates, Josiah Wedgwood and Thomas Williams felt no compunction in doing so. Charles Roe's surplus wealth was employed for the benefit of others, hopefully, as he judged, both spiritually and materially. That he battled to keep alive the principles of his Christian upbringing cannot be in doubt, and if this suggests "pride, greed or arrogance" in any small degree, then he must be forgiven. Only his enemies were capable of such calumny by promoting these deformations of character.

The story also brings to light the fact that the Church of England, far from losing its influence in society, was as strong as ever. When resistance to something grows, it is the strength of the constituent, not its weakness, that provokes such opposition. Bishops and clergy pervaded boardrooms, invested in industry; were headmasters of grammar schools, principals of colleges, writers of books and pamphlets, and great recorders of past history and contemporary events. They were the key figures within their own communities.

Another illuminating fact is that for centuries families could be traced along important trading routes as offspring intermarried; and conversely, trade routes can be traced by discovering the destination of family members, not only in Britain, but throughout the known world.

The family unit had remained throughout the 18th century, as the networking amongst families proved to be as strong as ever. Business after business was full of relatives, with the offspring of partners or associates regularly intermarrying. The marriage settlement has to be regarded as one of the most important aspects. It was consistently used to develop businesses and estates, not only amongst the aristocracy but amongst the vast majority of the middle classes, constituting yet another vital link in the commercial chain which has so often been overlooked.

The effects of the Napoleonic Wars cannot be underestimated in contributing to the ensuing economic disaster, and neither can the incredible increase in population, unfortunately accentuated by the fact that the two were concurrent. The 1780s and 90s were already witnessing the deterioration of the moral fabric of society, which reached a crescendo during the Regency period. When there is a dramatic upsurge in numbers, unless steps are taken in advance, authority loses control, as evidenced by the post war "bulge" in 1947. Teachers were overwhelmed by large class sizes and the resultant teenagers became the liberal rebels of the 1960s.

It is too simplistic to criticize from information which is easily available, or which appears to be the only extant data for a particular period. How we shall be judged in 200 years from the readily available information of today; newspapers full of disasters, drug abuse, plagues, scandals, fraud and hooliganism, coupled with the way we portray ourselves in films, poetry and literature? Is the picture we leave behind a true one for the vast majority of the population?

Interpretation of facts can also distort reality if taken out of context, and not related to the background from whence they came. In October 1773 Liverpool Corporation decreed that there was to be no tipping of rubbish near the North Dock or Pier, which some would construe as an indication of Liverpool's dirty streets. But further searching through records and prints should assure one that the reverse was true; in fact if anything did start to go wrong then the Corporation acted quickly to put things right. And how often have Acts of Parliament been quoted as a finite solution to a problem, when it was not what people were supposed to be doing that mattered, but what they were, in fact, actually doing?

Documentary evidence alone is generally not sufficient when making judgements. Society leaves records in the way it constructs towns, cities, ports and in the buildings themselves. Ruins can speak volumes, as we are constantly made aware of by archaeologists. Georgian buildings stand out for their elegance and charm; they are perfectly proportioned, embellished with classical designs both inside and out and are indicative of an attitude to life. This ensured that industrial complexes were laid out with beautifully designed forecourts and gardens, surrounded by trees and ponds, which attracted visitors by the thousand. But with the sudden population increases, whereas a large house once had a substantial garden to its credit, during the 1790s the owners, many of whom were experiencing the first throes of economic depression, seemed only too happy to allow another house to be built literally at the bottom of the garden. By 1825 two houses on a site had become four and, inevitably, insanitary conditions and overcrowding accelerated, creating a more widespread deterioration in health in addition to the periodic epidemics, the festering of which was ready to plague Victorian society.

The difference between living in the early 18th and early 19th centuries is aptly demonstrated by two poems. The first, written by Henry Carey (c. 1693-1745) and entitled "Sally in Our Alley" is light hearted, appealing and surprisingly Edwardian in style. His attitude to life is obviously carefree and happy, there is no mention of grief or worry, only a taken for granted attitude that all will be well and turn out as planned. Neither does he appear to consider finance a problem:

"When Christmas comes about again,
O, then I shall have money!
I'll hoard it up, and box it all,
And give it to my honey;" . . .

In stark contrast the poem written by Thomas Hood (1799-1825) entitled "The Song of the Shirt", reveals, in the first of its eleven verses, the depressing mood repeated throughout the entire poem:

"With fingers weary and worn,
With eyelids heavy and red,
A woman sat, in unwomanly rags,
Plying her needle and thread, –
Stitch! stitch! stitch!
In poverty, hunger, and dirt;
And still with a voice of dolorous pitch
She sang the "Song of the Shirt.

* * * * * * *

As societies move in one direction or another, it is the pull of individuals which matters most, and the extent of their influence on others for better or worse; they are the creators of history.

On several occasions I have been asked how much influence Charles Roe had in Macclesfield. Can anyone correctly quantify the influence of another on anything? It is, of course, dependent on personality and the ability to move others so that they react in a way desirable to what you want. But having done so, then the end result also becomes part of the equation. Just how much of the whole of the end result is attributable to the direct or indirect influence of one particular person, is obviously a subject for great debate. Additionally there is the question of whether or not the outcome is for the better, which generally means judging the effect of the repercussions on a larger section of the community.

Charles Roe's influence in the commercial world outside Macclesfield was certainly great, otherwise he would never have been able to achieve what he did i.e. the creation of a company which became one of the greatest brass and copper producers of the 18th century. There is no doubt that Charles Roe's ability to attract partners of a like calibre was crucial to the efficient working of the company. Surprisingly none of the Hodgsons intermarried with the Roes, but the Roe family members were much younger than the Hodgson clan. However, this in no way affected the loyalty shown, nor support given, to the various committee members in the early years.

Good and firm management affected the work force, who were treated well, and malpractice was certainly kept at bay, as in the instance of the rapid termination of the truck system which had been set up by Jonathan Roose on Anglesey. When comparisons are made with other local employees in the Liverpool and Swansea areas, Roe & Co. workmen received better wages, and were also provided with housing close by the various sites. Disputes were dealt with in a proper manner, with the people concerned appearing in person to put their case before the committee, or the committee members sometimes going on site to have a better grasp of the situation, as recorded at Bosley It is interesting to learn of the pension arrangements for employees and compensation for widows and orphans. Also the staff training, such as that for members of the Ovens family of Liverpool, who appear to have remained loyal to Roe & Co. for many years. *The Cambrian* newspaper of Swansea, on Saturday 28th April 1804, reported "Bankrupt awarded against John Ovens of the town of Cardiff. Tanner dealer & Chapman". One has to wonder if this was one of the faithful few who had transferred to the Neath Abbey works had been forced to 'go it alone'.

Roe & Co. were meticulous and efficient in their working methods. the company overseers were able to engage first class teams of workmen, especially in the mines. The remaining evidence on site, discovered during recent surveys, confirms this. Even the digging of tunnels was regarded an art form as the miners sculpted their way through the earth, transforming rocks into columns and passageways in the most economic and safest manner. It therefore seemed most unlikely that the Roe & Co. miners would have left the mine on Parys Mountain in an unworkable and dangerous condition for others to operate; Thomas Williams's propaganda proved ineffectual and his case was lost.

It is fortunate that the Macclesfield Copper Company minute book has survived, revealing the business acumen of the period. The frequent meetings between the numerous representatives of companies to solve major problems, despite the considerable distances covered and the inconveniences of travel, might surprise many senior executives today.

Not only is it surprising to discover the frequency with which long and often dangerous journeys were undertaken by company personnel, but the actual routes taken by goods is, at times, astonishing. One particular instance proves the point above all else, that of ore travelling by sea from Cornwall along the extemely difficult sea route around Wales (in stormy conditions captains sought refuge in Milford Haven or Dublin Bay). Having been unloaded in Liverpool or Toxteth it was smelted, cast into blocks or pigs, conveyed up the Weaver, brought overland from Northwich to be refined on Macclesfield Common, after which part of it began its journey south again. Carted to the sites of Bosley and Havannah it was either hammered or rolled into sheets ready for sheathing. Those copper sheets ordered by the Navy were either transported back to Liverpool for a further sea journey to the naval dockyards in the south, or taken south (eventually by canal) via the Bristol Channel. When the order came for no copper ladings around the coast because of fears of capture by the French, it was transported overland to the yards of Plymouth and Portsmouth, having almost completed an incredibly circuitous journey and still at a profit.

As for Charles Roe's influence within the town of Macclesfield, one would have had to sit in on many of the corporation meetings he attended, to hear how far his proposals were adopted. His influence in the outside world must have given him greater confidence when tackling local issues. Although silk twisting was already established in the town, primarily for the production of silk buttons, he was the one who had the ambition and drive to make it something greater. Without the establishment of the large silk mill in Macclesfield others might have been reluctant to follow suit, and the town would not have expanded as quickly as it did. His inability to force through a canal scheme, linking Macclesfield to the Midlands and Mersey, in no way diminished his plans: he determinedly found another way round the problem.

Although it became necessary to operate from sites such as Liverpool and North Wales, his business headquarters remained on Chestergate. Even after Charles Roe's death and the eventual transfer to Neath, still the hub of the Roe & Co. wheel never left Macclesfield, and William Roe, returning home on a permanent basis after almost 55 years, was well received. It was certainly William's influence and the memory of his father's achievements which gained his half-brother, John Harriott Roe, the requisite votes for the position of Recorder as evidenced by a family letter.

Perhaps Charles Roe's greatest challenge came in his private life as head of the family. He never shirked his responsibilities, taking care of both his sister and sister-in-law, and their families, when unexpected widowhood came; a characteristic inherited by eldest son, William, as demonstrated after his father's death. William was more resolute in preparing a will; yet had Charles really any choice in the matter of preparing his own? He loved all his children dearly; the tragedy was that his first wife had died early leaving him with a difficult choice. The children from the second marriage were certainly influenced by their relatives in London and their mother, yet, despite the fact his sentiments were vehemently opposed to Methodism, Charles's conscience would not allow him to commit to paper his total rejection of their blood ties. They were his children, and possibly for the first time in his life he chose to avoid an issue; a will was out of the question. This, in many ways, is a compliment to William's ability to deal with the outcome in a competent and just manner, a fact which his father never seemed to have doubted.

Another important area of influence for the Roe family was education. When considering that Charles Roe came from a family where five generations had produced Church of England clergy, many of whom were headmasters, it is not surprising that he very much involved himself in the town's academic life. He approved a petition to parliament which set out details for a new act, "to appoint additional Masters and Ushers with fuitable Salaries to instruct the youth educated at the said School in Writing Arithmetic Geography Navigation Mathematics modern Languages and such other useful Branches of Education". Even after Charles Roe's death the company continued to promote education. On 7th August 1787 a proposal was made to write to "some of our friends in Sheffield for (a) plan for establishing a Charity School". And later, after the renewal of mining in Llandudno during 1806, a school was established by the miners for poor children, with the master's salary set at £30 each year.

Charles Roe's daughter, Mary, who at the age of 30 years had prepared her will and died two years later as the tenant of Sutton Hall, had also made provision for the education of poor children. She chose David Simpson and the two chapel wardens of Christ Church to keep in trust £600. The sum was to be invested in Government stocks or other securities with the interest applied to "the Education of such poor Children in Reading and Writing and the four Rules in Arithmetic" as the trustees saw proper. In recognition of Mary's wishes "Miss Roe's Charity School" began at Christ Church on Lady Day, 25th March 1790 "for the education and religious instruction of children of the labouring poor residing within the township of Macclesfield and adjoining township of Sutton". This remained on the site until 1969 when it was renamed Bollinbrook School. At Easter 1972, as a C. of E. Aided school, it moved almost half a mile away to a new building on a new housing estate, where it remains to this day.

* * * * * * *

Athough Christ Church is now the focal point of a conservation area in which recent restoration work has taken place (thanks to the efforts of Macclesfield Borough Council), yet sadly the church itself is now under the jurisdiction of the Churches Conservation Trust. It is, however, still licensed for weddings and christenings, and regularly opens its doors to the public. The original Handel organ is long gone, having been replaced in time for the centenary celebrations of 1875 by one from the famous organ builders Gray and Davidson. Its subsequent disposal has remained a mystery.

Whilst the Havannah and Bosley sites still retain some features of their historic past, the brass works on Macclesfield Common have disappeared, remembered only by the street names of Calamine, Windmill and Snow Hill. The windmill had finally been bought by a miller of Bollington in 1813. The advertisement of the 17th April described it as:

"comprising a Wheat Mill, Oat Mill and Dressing Mill, three pair of stones, a Dressing machine and all proper sails, geer, tackle and appendages in good repair; and also the substantial Dwelling House, Drying Kiln, and Yard lying to the east of the said Windmill and near thereto" .

The area of land was said to be 1,645 square yards, and the final enticement read, "The Lunt Hill Road communicates immediately with the Great Thoroughfare through Macclesfield and its intended improvement will enhance the value of this property". By the 21st August the Bollington miller, William Boston, was advertising it for letting, and by November 1814 he included "Six newly erected houses east of windmill". The last reference to the mill on

Macclesfield Common is in the *Macclesfield Courier* of 29th May 1830 when Ryle Street is mentioned as being "near the Windmill in Lunt Hill".

During the early Victorian period (circa 1848) development of the area witnessed the construction of St. Peter's church on the northern side of Lunt Hill brow. About this time the windmill, situated across the road on the southern side, was dismantled and removed to Kerridge above the village of Bollington, where it remained until the last war. It had been redundant for many years, though a well-known landmark, but due to vandalism and courting couples, an offer to purchase the stones, by American forces stationed locally, was accepted by the owner. He told me that the stones were transported elsewhere and assumed that they had been used in the construction of a nearby military runway. Various communications with an American Association, some of whose members were stationed in wartime Cheshire, has yielded nothing. So, like the original Christ Church organ, another piece of Roe history has melted into obscurity, but at least a reminder of its former existence remains, Lunt Hill was renamed Windmill Street.

Further up the hill on Macclesfield Common, running in a northerly direction, is Copper Street adjacent to the site of the former copper works, but an overlooked fact begs recognition, the original name was Copper Mine Street, a poignant reminder of the early speculation by Peter Davenport, until someone, thinking it a mistake, had the name altered.

The Navigation Inn, adjoining Black Road and Copper Street, covers part of the site on which the eastern end of the Roe & Co. smelters were situated. When built, some of the large fire bricks from the smelthouses were utilised for the construction of its adjacent stone wall. To this day they remain *in situ*, as do others in the immediate vicinity used by locals in the building of their garden walls. The inn is probably that recorded earlier as *The Rose* on Copper Mine Street which, after completion of the Macclesfield Canal in 1831, became *The Navigation* on the adjoining Black Road. By 1834 the name of *The Rose* had been transferred to a new inn on Brasshouse Street near to the windmill site. The landlady, a character called Betty Bradbury, probably hoped that the transfer of name would encourage the former 'clientele' to walk the extra few hundred yards across the Common, leaving the *Navigation* to cope with the influx of bargees and other travellers along the new waterway.

Charles Roe's house on Chestergate remains, luckily rescued from the threat of demolition some years ago by the actions of a small group of devotees. It has since been sympathetically restored by its present owner.

The Grey House in Ashbourne, final residence of Brian Hodgson Snr. also remains, and is today the home and surgery of a dentist. Fortunately it has experienced a better fate than Charles Roe's house for, apart from a few interior touches of modernisation, the remainder and facade are virtually unaltered.

John Stafford's home in Jordangate, Macclesfield was drastically altered at the end of the 18th century after his suicide. The southern side remains with its superb Venetian window, but the garret or upper storey was removed together with a section at the northern end in the early 19th century. A complete new unit was then added on the northern side with its own entrance from the north. This addition became the premises of a solicitor, but was eventually incorporated into the original structure; today it is largely occupied by a doctor's surgery, with a couple of units on the upper floor let as business premises. Whilst other buildings, such as Fence House, are now long gone, Robert Roe's house on Chestergate has survived, although now converted into shop premises, and Moody Hall in Congleton is still standing.

Liverpool has witnessed many changes, and people still recall with affection the *Stork Hotel* (William Roe's former residence) and wonder why it was demolished not restored; yet there also, names remain as reminders of another era. A section of the modern development in the St. John's Market area has been designated Roe Street, and partially covers the original thoroughfare. And although William's former house on Duke Street, together with those of three of his neighbours, was replaced by a corn warehouse during the reign of William IV (1830-37), yet the remaining properties on the row leave a clear picture of exactly what the house would have looked like. Close by, leading towards the rear of the former premises is Roe Alley, obviously a one time access route to William's first family home.

St. James's church in Toxteth is now boarded up and sadly in a serious state of deterioration, despite having been included in Nikolaus Pevsner's *The Buildings of England - South Lancashire* together with a photograph of the Nicholson monument by Sir Francis Chantry.

In South Wales, whilst the indomitable ruins of Neath Abbey remain, all evidence of the smelters near the site have long since disappeared. The Neath Canal, which once divided the two areas, was redirected around the Abbey about a century ago, causing initial confusion as to the original location of the Roe & Co. copperworks. However, in the corner of an adjacent field are two or three houses, one of which bears the name "Cheadle Works", a probable indication that they stand on the site of those built originally by Roe & Co. for their site managers.

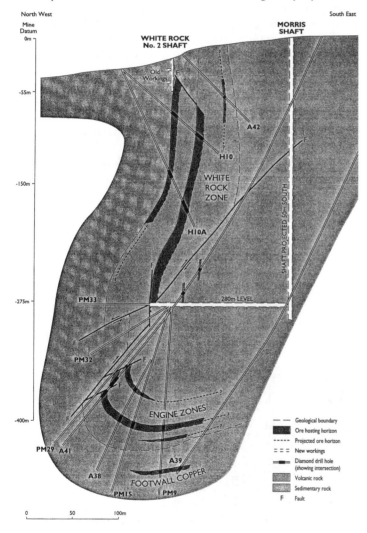

Section of Parys Mountain included in the Annual Report 1990 of Anglesey Mining plc. The 'Old Workings' shown left 'WHITE ROCK No. 2 SHAFT' are those of Roe & Co. indicating that they did reach a very rich vein. The workings of the Thomas William's group are just off the diagram to the right. An earlier section shows a basin-shaped chasm almost to the depth of the Roe workings, but there is no rich vein in that area. Reproduced by kind permission of Anglesey Mining plc.

The above illustration is reproduced by kind permission of Anglesey Mining plc. which, after four years of exploration and drilling, commenced mining at Pary Mountain in 1988. Unfortunately the 1990s saw a dramatic fall in the world price of copper and a further exploration of 1995 was therefore delayed. With prospects improving it is hoped that further progress can be made in the near future.

Many of the mining areas are well worth a visit, being located in some of the most beautiful regions of the British Isles. Parys Mountain on Anglesey and Coniston, in the Lake District, have been designated Heritage sites and are now organised for visitors. Islay still boasts its farmhouse at Persabus, as does Penrhyn Du in North Wales, and Jonathan Roose's house remains beside the road leading down to the port of Amlwch. His gravestone, fortunately preserved in the parish church yard, is unique, not only for its poem but for the reminder of his versatile fatherhood given by the various dates it contains, which at first glance seem incorrect but, of course, are not. Llanberis and Bethgelert, although somewhat remote, do inspire the imagination and help one to appreciate the difficulties faced by the miners and also those transporting ore down into the coastal areas, ready for loading aboard vessels. Thanks to their considerable endeavours new elements would be discovered, and the study of chemistry greatly advanced. Prince Rupert's ambitions were at long last bearing fruit, and he must be given some credit for his enthusiastic experiments which, although they did not immediately create a scientific revolution, certainly paved the way for one.

Of the London connections the church of St. Mary Matfelon in Whitechapel no longer exists. It was almost totally destroyed during a wartime bombing raid, and took with it all evidence of the Hawkins family monument, amongst others. The irony is easy to appreciate when considering how much they had provided for the parish and now much money they had spent on building and restoring the memorial in order to perpetuate their memory, especially as the brothers, Samuel and Edward, were connected by marriage to the old Germanic family of Schumaker. The whole area of their former holdings in Stepney and Whitechapel has been redeveloped, making it almost impossible to say with certainty where some of the buildings actually stood.

The area of East London where the church of St. Mary Matfelon stood until devastated by a bombing raid during World War II. All that remains is the one memorial, but not that provided by the Hawkins family.

As regards the Roe family, their direct influence in Macclesfield ceased on the death of Charles Roe's grandson, Christopher in 1854. Although Charles Roe's copper and brass works were long gone, his legacy of the silk industry would see Macclesfield foremost in the world for production during the 19th century and contributing greatly to the Second World War effort in the 20th, particularly with the prodution of parachutes.

APPENDIX I

THE ROE FAMILY PEDIGREE

1)   Rev. William and Robina
       *   William baptised 15th February 1618 Wem
           Richard baptised 29th September 1619 Wem
           Thomas baptised 25th May 1624 Wem (died young)
           Dorothy baptised 25th May 1624 Wem
           Sara baptised 24th September 1626 Wem
           Thomas baptised 3rd April 1628 Wem

2)   *   Rev. William and Elizabeth of Arlston
    ** Robert baptised c. 1646
        Richard baptised c. 1648
        Thomas baptised c. 1651
        Jane ?

3)   ** Rev. Robert and Elizabeth of Hadley.
    *** Thomas baptised 8th November 1670 Munslow
        William baptised 26th June 1672 Munslow (died young)
        Elizabeth baptised 7th July 1674 Munslow
        Robert baptised 2nd February 1677 Wem (died young)
        Jonathan baptised 31st May 1679 St. Mary's Shrewsbury
        Dorothy baptised 5th June 1681 Wem
        William baptised 16th November 1683 All Saints Wellington
        Jane baptised 1st June 1686 All Saints Wellington
        Alice baptised 7th June 1689 All Saints Wellington.

4) *** Rev. Thomas and Mary of Castleton.
        Thomas baptised 7th March 1700 Castleton
        Francis baptised 9th December 1701 Castleton
        William baptised 26th August 1703 Castleton
        Robert baptised 26th September 1705 Castleton (died young)
        John baptised 16th October 1707 Castleton (died young)
        James baptised 5th July 1711 Castleton
        Mary baptised 9th January 1713 Castleton
        CHARLES baptised 2nd June 1715 Castleton.

5)   **CHARLES** OF MACCLESFIELD and wives a) Elizabeth b) Mary C) Rachel.
         a) Catherine baptised 18th April 1745 Macclesfield
         William baptised 2nd May 1746 Macclesfield
         Charles baptised 24th July 1747 (died young)
         Samuel baptised 13th November 1749

         b) Martha baptised 4th February 1753 (died young)
         Robert baptised 8th March 1754
         Mary (known as Polly) baptised 30th October 1755
         Charles baptised 2nd April 1759
         Frances baptised 13th December 1756
         Joseph baptised 12th May 1760
         Margaret (known as Peggy) baptised 12th May 1761
         Jane born 5th July 1763 baptised ?

         c) John Harriott baptised 11th August 1768.

6)   **WILLIAM** and Hannah of Liverpool.
         Ann baptised 20th June 1777 St. George's Liverpool
         Elizabeth baptised 5th June 1778 St. George's Liverpool
         Hannah born 11th June 1779*
         Rachel Harriot born 30th June 1780*
         Catherine born 4th July 1781 (died young)*
         Charles Samuel baptised 26th November 1782 (died young)
         William baptised 31st August 1785 St. Peter's Liverpool
         Frances baptised 31 August 1785 (! the same day as William above) St. James's Toxteth.
         Christopher baptised 25th August 1788 St. Peter's Liverpool
         Lucy baptised 16th February 1790 St. Peter's Liverpool
         Helen (Ellen) baptised 1st August 1792 St. Peter's Liverpool
         Dorothea ?
         Mary ?
         Matilda ?

         * Baptised on 3rd October 1781 St. George's Liverpool

ADDITIONAL ROE FAMILY BIOGRAPHICAL NOTES

1) The family of Rev. James Roe

Hester Ann Rogers and her husband had, of course, departed for Dublin shortly after their marriage in the late summer of 1784 and worked hard, achieving a large increase in their congregation before moving to Cork. Apart from an occasional visit to a Manchester Conference they remained in Ireland until John Wesley called them to London in 1790. At the time of their marriage Rev. James Rogers had two surviving sons, Joseph almost 5 years old and Benjamin, 2 years and 8 months. His youngest son of only 13 months had died in June 1784 shortly before the marriage, and only five months after his first wife's death. Hester had immediately taken on the role of mother to the boys, but herself bore Rogers six children during the next ten years. The first three were born in Ireland, however the third barely survived and was buried six weeks later.

By 1790, John Wesley, who had suffered ill health for quite some time, must have appreciated that he had not long to live. The Conference of 1790 confirmed the appointment of Rev. Rogers to London, which meant that he and Hester were able to move into Wesley's house next to the New Chapel on City Road and between them take care of the elderly minister, whose increasing debility was causing concern. Hester took the position of housekeeper and Rev. James accompanied him on his daily missions. Unfortunately Hester was once more blighted by her periodic ill health, made worse by the fact that just before leaving Ireland two of the children, the maid and herself had all been seriously ill. There are slightly different versions of what then followed, but the fact remains that Hester was replaced in her role as carer for the preacher by a certain Elizabeth Ritchie.

Ritchie, having originally heard John Wesley preach in Yorkshire, became an ardent admirer and convert, and almost a daughter to the preacher. Her journal entries do reveal a slight hint of envy and jealousy after discovering that Hester was occupying, what she considered to be, her rightful place at his side.

Her own version claims that she visited their mutual friend, Mrs. James (the former Miss Salmon, now resident in London), during November 1790, where she learnt that Hester's ill health was prohibiting her from providing the care which Wesley needed, whereupon she "consented for a while to undertake her duties". Yet it is claimed that Wesley himself wrote personally to Elizabeth Ritchie and "insisted she should stay at the Chapel house". It is possible that Wesley was wearying of the large family living in the house. It was a very young family and the noise and clatterings up and down the narrow staircases, in what is a somewhat confining though charming house, must have been a little irritating at times.

Ritchie's account of those last few weeks of Wesley's life is full of her attentions to him, and the old man's devotion to her, quoting his own words "I should wish you to be with me in my dying moments; I would have you to close my eyes." It is strange to discover that nowhere does Wesley mention Hester in his journals; on his part there always seems to have been a desire to distance himself from her attentions, an attitude which no doubt stems from the fact that she was Charles Roe's niece and had caused considerable problems in Macclesfield, which had, quite unintentionally, greatly undermined his visits. On the other hand Hester was completely committed to Methodism and never ceased to work for his cause. She considered Elizabeth Ritchie to be a close friend, yet Ritchie implies acquaintance only, nevertheless the dismissive manner by which Hester was excluded from their considerations is cruel, to say the least.

Following Wesley's death on 2nd March 1791 there was certainly a partial vindictiveness shown by some towards the Rogers. In his will Wesley had confirmed his choice of James Rogers as one of the trustees sanctioned to preach in the chapel at City Road, and also to be a committee member for selecting preachers at Bath, yet there was dissension resulting in a move to Spitalfields chapel and then Birmingham. Hester, pregnant for the last time and weakened by her considerable exertions, died in childbirth on 10th October 1794. (The baby boy, John, lived only till 1st November). This time justice was done and a sermon preached in Hester's memory at St. Mary's Chapel in Birmingham followed by one in Spitalfields Chapel, after which her husband wrote a worthy obituary. Tragedy struck again some five months later when four year old Martha, debilitated by smallpox, died of tuberculosis. The housekeeping accounts include the funeral expenses which today would suggest a comparable sum:

Attending my Darlings)	
including Coffins Hat Bands)	£20 15 0d.
Dark Cotton for childrens' mourning	£ 1 0 7d.
Tomb stone, Ground etc for it	£ 8 0 1d.
Total funeral expense	£29 15 8d.

Rogers married for a third time in 1796 and, at the time of preparing his will on 21st October 1806, apart from his wife, he had two surviving children from each of his three marriages. On each was settled £800 with an additional £10 bequeathed to his servant, Isabella. This represents a figure in excess of £¹/₂ million today. In mitigation Rogers had asked Wesley before his death what part of his private income he should "save for my growing family" apart from his income from the church. Wesley characteristically replied that it was up to the individual concerned to judge what was best if he had children, but anyone who did not "aught to wind his bottom round the year" (a delightful expression using a nautical term, which meant that he should sum up his situation from time to time; in other words give as much as he could when he could). The magnitude of, what Rev. Rogers considered to be, his somewhat impoverished position, once again illustrates the considerable wealth which had accumulated in Britain by the end of the 18th century.

Hester's mother had predeceased her and, contrary to what Robert Roe had expected, she did not exclude Hester from her will prepared 5th August 1787, in fact far from it. As far as possible Elizabeth divided most of her possessions equally between Hester and her brother, James, with a meticulous account given of every item. Amongst the very personal items Hester received her mother's gold wedding ring and a mourning ring set with her father's hair.

James received two of his mother's gold rings, one set with his Uncle William's hair (i.e. Rev. William Roe who had been prime curate of the Macclesfield Parochial Chapel) and the other with a stone and his father's hair. He, like Hester was left several items of bed linen and towels, which included the "old linen" from Oxford (a probable souvenir from his university days), and an equal share of silverware including a small silver boat (presumably for sauces).

To her sister, Mary Braddock, Elizabeth left her settee complete with cushions and a mourning ring bought by her mother at the time of her father's death, but one which her mother had "lost the Stone out of." Conditional upon the servant, Ellen Woodward, remaining with Elizabeth until her death, she was to receive £10, an oak bureau, items of clothing comprising a pair of jumps (i.e. a form of underbodice), aprons both white and check, four neck handkerchiefs and day caps, six night caps and any other "Odd things" which Hester thought she should have. The remaining possessions, including a £50 security on the Leek Turnpike, were to be sold, and after deduction of funeral and other expenses, divided equally between her two siblings.

Hester's brother James, having graduated M.A. from Brasenose College, Oxford in June 1793 had previously accepted the curacy of Dorchester, just to the south of Oxford, in 1787 (the year of his mother's will). This he would hold for 50 years and in 1796 added to it the rectorship of Newbury in Berkshire. He died on 9th July 1838 at Newbury aged 80 years. A monument in the church not only records his own details but also those of his wife, Sophia (who had predeceased him in 1833 aged 74 years).

In all they had eight sons and two daughters, but the eldest, James, had died when only two. Of the others, Thomas, who entered military service with the East India Company in Bombay, had met and married his wife in Liverpool (West Derby), but she died in Bombay October 1827. Seven years later he married William Roe's youngest daughter, Lucy, at Newbury, proving once more the strong family ties which existed, and the fact that William Roe's family must have kept in close touch with his cousin James's family over the years.

James and Sophia's seventh son, born in May 1797 and appropriately named John Septimus Roe, is worthy of mention. With little money to spend on the education of their sons, John Septimus was sent to Christ's Hospital School in London, where, much against his own wishes but at his father's furious dictate, he entered the mathematical school two years later. The regime was strict, yet the boy was well prepared for a naval career by receiving a thorough education in navigation and maritime surveying. On 27th May 1813 his seven year apprenticeship, begun under the commander of H.M.S. *Rippon*, Sir Christopher Cole, saw his entry into the service as a midshipman. He made several eventful voyages in different ships, one as far as China, and his records, charts and sketches, both official and unofficial, portray his considerable talents at recording, writing and illustrating in a competent and extremely intelligent manner. His enormous output has resulted in a very valuable collection of papers which has fortunately survived to this day in Western Australia. After several promotions, his naval career ended on 5th December 1828 when he was appointed Surveyor General to the Swan River Colony in Western Australia. His arduous life, well documented in *Not An Idle Man* (J.L. Burton Jackson 1982), reveals his incredible fortitude and genius, particularly in laying out the cities of Perth and Fremantle. He died in 1878; until his retirement in 1871 he had completed 42 years of work filled "with determination and unswerving loyalty to do his job well."

2) The family of Charles Roe

Of Charles Roe's immediate family, whilst Catherine, William, John Harriott and some of their offspring had survived, out of the eight children from the second marriage there remained only Margaret (who had caused the problems in Bristol but finally married William Racster) and Joseph. Nothing further is known of Margaret, but Joseph, having vacated the Lower Beech Estate near Macclesfield in 1800 in favour of Brian Hodgson the younger, had taken over the occupancy of Moody Hall, Congleton, following the retirement of Robert Hodgson to St, Alban's. Married twice, only two of Joseph's five children survived to marry, in fact his eldest son, Joseph, and daughter, Jane, had predeceased him in 1817 and 1815 respectively, whilst Margaret followed shortly after his own death.

Joseph's will has left something of an enigma. It was prepared on 5th November 1816, and by it he gave his wife, Margaret, full authority to distribute all his "effects" amongst his children as she considered appropriate, "according to their good conduct". The important instructions are with regard to his business investments. He specified "I leave and bequeath Charles Roe all the Silk Machinery and Silk Geering in a certain Mill called Dane Mill in Congleton ", but on no account was this Charles Roe "of Congleton Silk Throwster" to be given the cotton machinery or cotton gearing, for these were to be inherited by his widow together with £600 owed by this particular Charles Roe to Joseph.

The identity of this Charles Roe is a mystery, but he does seem to qualify as a distant relative, and was most likely a grandson of Rev. Samuel of Stotfold, Bedfordshire (1754-80) and a great nephew of Cousin Christopher, the Spitalfield silk throwster. Christopher did have a nephew, Charles, who, according to his will, was a ribbon manufacturer of Coventry, and it is recorded that the manufacturers of ribbons for Coventry merchants had been established in Congleton from at least the mid-1750s. However, Charles died a bachelor on 29th November 1816 (some four months before Joseph prepared his will) and reveals no son, no connection with Congleton and no outstanding loan to Joseph. Because of Joseph's strong links with London, through his Stockdale relatives, it does suggest that this Congleton silk throwster was a Roe relative closely connected with one of his father's London cousins, albeit a possible illegitimate one.

Charles was also the name of one of John Harriott Roe's sons, but he was far too young to be involved in the Congleton business in 1817, and was, in fact, a scholar at Charterhouse (then in London) by 1823; both he and his elder brother, Samuel Ramsden Roe, became Church of England clergy in due course. Another son John, died young from fits, but was shortly replaced by a William, of whom little is known. All three were living and shared with their stepmother, Dorothy, their father's estate after John Harriott's death at his home, Grafton Manor in Worcestershire on 19th October, 1833.

John Harriott had been Recorder of Macclesfield for 30 years, and whilst brother William had, only so far as circumstances would allow, supported him, yet certain family members had remained in touch, as evidenced by John Roe's letter of 2nd April 1823. It was written to his great niece, Hannah, daughter of William and Hannah Nicholson, thanking her for advising him of Christopher Shaw Roe's marriage. His opening comment portrays something of a teasing nature by suggesting that, "as a descendant of a Roe and a Nicholson, of the present generation", it had "cost" her to write to him. He did, however, continue by expressing his delight and the hope that in the future their correspondence would carry on.

Between the Sessions held in Macclesfield he had been busy viewing houses in Berkshire and Wiltshire. He referred to William and Hannah Nicholson as "excellent correspondents" and mentioned that Mary Roe (the youngest daughter of his brother Joseph) had stayed with them on her return journey from visiting friends on the Isle of Wight. His curiousity and enquiries, with regard to a new bride in the Liverpool 'entourage', befits the Regency Period; "Pray say who she is, what she is, what family, what fortune, whether, amiable, accomplished, handsome, or otherwise: with what other little et ceterers you think desirable in a bride." After a résumé of the Cheltenham social scene, comprising balls and the like at which "all the world and his wife" appeared to be present, he signed himself "your affectionate Uncle J.H. Roe.' Ten years later he had died and, in keeping with family tradition, was buried in Christ Church, Macclesfield, where a marble plaque, in memory of both himself and his mother and bearing the Roe family coat of arms, was affixed high on the inner northern wall of Christ Church. It overlooks the altar and faces his father's superb memorial on the southern side.

* * * * * * *

An extraordinary period of history had taken place during William Roe's lifetime. Born during the aftermath of Bonnie Prince Charlie's campaign, William had witnessed the effects of the Seven Years War as a young teenager, the struggle for independence by the American colonies in his early thirties, troubles in Ireland and France in his fifties, and latterly the devastations of the Napoleonic Wars.

Deprived of a university education, as his father before him, yet sent to Liverpool at the age of 21 years to take control of a highly skilled and substantial business, William, as an outsider in the port, had succeeded against all the odds. He had married well and, despite his obvious advantageous connections through his in-laws, had contributed in no small way to the municipal affairs of the rapidly growing port. But his ultimate achievement was in his Revenue career, particularly when he was promoted Joint Chairman to the Commissioners of Customs. His responsibilities were considerable, varied and yet interesting, as evidenced by a series of letters relating to April and May 1813. They refer to packages sent aboard the Lord Lieutenant of Ireland's yacht from Dublin by the Duke of Richmond, which had been taken by lighter from the ship at Deptford to the Customs quay. Instructions were issued that these had to be delivered duty free to Richmond House, and William, having received assurances that no contraband was on board, issued orders accordingly. Letters passed to and fro each day from 18th to 20th May between the Inspectors of the River, the Warehouse Officer, William and the Board, until William could report that "none of the effects of the Duke of Richmond have been either seized or opened." Enclosed was a list of the 29 packages which included "a Picture of his Grace." All other articles on board had been placed in the Kings Warehouse awaiting instructions; the latter were quickly received from 'Mr. Peel', then Secretary for Ireland but later to become Sir Robert Peel.

Being contemporaneous with George III William would have been much better informed from an early age, than his father had been, of the political struggles at Westminster, due to the additional increase and expanding circulations of newspapers. His generation had witnessed the emergence of the brilliant statesman, William Pitt the Younger and the resurgence of art, literature and culture. There was the constant awareness of the great scandals of the period, amongst them the reported escapades of Lord Byron, ultimately overshadowed by those of the Prince Regent.

George III died on 29th January 1820 and the Prince Regent took the throne as George IV. The popularity of the sovereign had reached, what appeared to be, an all time low, by which the moral fabric of society seemed to have been tainted, and from which the likes of William Roe's family would not escape.

On 10th Sept. 1817, at the age of 71 years, William had faced, what must have been his greatest challenge, the death of his wife, Hannah. Her name is included with those other Roe family members buried in the Christ Church vault, but her touching and eulogistic obituary appeared in the *Liverpool Advertiser* on the 18th September. William continued in his role of Joint Chairman to the Commissioners of Customs until 17th February 1819 (he had been voted an additional increase in salary of £100 per annum from 15th February 1816), then Rachel Harriott, aged 84 years, died on 7th May of that year and, possibly as a result of this, he once more turned his attention to Macclesfield.

As early as 1787 William had leased a plot of land, close by the north-eastern corner of the Christ Church burial ground, to a William Croxton, with permission to build houses on the site. A year later began the sell off of the vast parkland in possession of Lord Cholmondeley, heir to the estate of his uncle, General Cholmondeley. At some point in time William Roe purchased the strip of land which ran contiguously along the southern side of Christ Church and beyond, and which contained a section of the Dams Brook. Here the brook flowed in an easterly direction, but then changed course to flow south into the area known as the Dams. This strip of meadow land was part of several plots for which Charles Roe had paid £750 in March 1770 to Joseph Pickford, to gain the unexpired terms of the leases from General Cholmondeley.

At the time of the Enclosure plan of 1804 there already existed a street leading from the main street (Mill Street), which traversed part of the strip of meadow land and then curved immediately northwards, to run alongside the eastern end of Christ Church and the burial ground. Although for the most part unadopted, except for a house now built on the Croxton plot (today No. 36 Bridge Street) this street was already named Roe Street. Before the corner turning north, part of the street (this section has retained the name of Roe) ran and still runs parallel to the Dams Brook, and it was on its southern side that William built three houses which were completed by 1810. These he let to tenants, except for a small unit which he retained for his own use. The largest one (now No. 67 Roe Street and occupied by a firm of solicitors) was taken by a surgeon, Samuel Stone, and possibly used as a surgery or even small infirmary, as his residence was on Jordangate. For some reason Samuel Stone became involved with the sale of the brass works on Macclesfield Common in 1813, as a trustee. The house is interesting because it contains fixtures and fittings (such as a copper fireplace) from a slightly earlier period, but, as nothing was wasted, it is highly probable that William used the fittings from the office at the brass works to furnish his newly built properties.

The westwardly continuation of Roe Street retains the name Shaw after Hannah's family name, and nearby Catherine Street remains in memory of William Roe's sister. There was once a Charles Street, but 'conveniently' demolished some time ago to make way for the present Duke Street car park; a situation similar to that of William's Liverpool residence which, having become the Stork Hotel in the mid-19th century, was demolished in the 1970s to make way for a car park adjacent to St. John's Market.

Apart from developing the area around his father's church, William also held the patronage of the living. He had had little time to consider the controversies which had been taking place, having left David Simpson to 'plot his own course', which had resulted in John Wesley's advent once more into the Christ Church pulpit. After his reappearance on Good Friday, 29th April 1782, Wesley visited Macclesfield on a further 11 occasions before his death in 1791; when referring to six of these he specifically mentions preaching in the church, yet surprisingly omits any mention of the Sunderland Street chapel built by his supporters in 1779.

William's resignation from H.M. Customs on 17th February 1819, at almost 73 years of age, seems to have been his first step towards anything like retirement. His presence in London would no longer be necessary, but he had still retained many of his considerable interests in Liverpool. The batch of Corporation leases granted in 1787 to himself and his brother-in-law, John Shaw, had in part been diminished in 1796 by regrants to others, but a substantial area around Queen Square was still retained by them. Their own personal leases in the area had been renewed on 31st October 1812, and apart from his own grand residence on the north side of the square, William, in the meantime, had built two more fine houses on the south side of the adjoining Shaw Place, and one on the east side of Great Charlotte Street.

John Shaw, however, having built his own mansion on Great Charlotte Street, just to the south of the square, preferred to retain his semi-rural position by not encouraging development immediately on his doorstep. On 11th September 1820 William did renew the leases of the then remaining seven plots of land in the area still held jointly with John Shaw; his son, Christopher, 32 years of age and still unmarried, was recorded as one of the lives on the leases. Despite this retention of Liverpool property, after his stepmother's death during the previous year, William continued to increase his interests in Macclesfield. Surprisingly, however, he does not appear to have taken up residence in his father's old Chestergate house but let it as a multiple tenancy, a policy continued by his son, Christopher, who inherited the property after William's death on 27th March 1827.

Unfortunately during the last decade of William's life the Macclesfield land tax returns leave much to be desired, so it is difficult to judge exactly where William lived on his return to the town. A small group of tenanted properties and land were charged to him and initially recorded as on Sunderland Street, but later returns prove this to have been a convenience, for they were sited on the nearby Macclesfield Common. The only property specifically shown as owned and occupied by him was the small maisonette created in 1819 out of the large house, 67 Roe Street, and let to Samuel Stone. Perhaps this was simply a temporary arrangement until William had time to sort out his affairs.

3) The family of William Roe

Although William's interests in the collieries near Wrexham had been relinquished during the early 1790s, at the time of the transfer to the Neath Abbey Works from Toxteth, yet it is evident that William's family had fostered strong links within the area. The Indenture of 1789, between Richard Kirk (then of Wrexham), William Roe and Edward Hawkins, had incorporated several properties in Broughton, Brymbo and Gwersilt; included in the tenants of Broughton was a John Jones of Wrexham who also held a half share in the Broughton colliery with his wife, Sarah. It is possibly their son or relative, John Jones who, on 6th May 1802 married William Roe's eldest daughter, Ann, aged 25 years. He was, by then, a much older man, widower and officer in the King's Own Regiment of Foot, living in Gresford near Wrexham. When William prepared his will, in January 1821, Jones had died and Ann had married a George Barratt. Originally she had exacted a promise from her father that, after her marriage to Jones, provision of £2,000 would be made for her in William's will, to which he had agreed. His reluctance in fulfilling this promise is evident from his bequest of £2,000 to the trustees for the benefit of Ann's two daughters, followed by the animadversion "although her conduct since then has given me just cause for not carrying such promise into execution." However, although William's chattels and the remainder of the estate were to be divided equally between all his children, Ann was excluded from this particular provision.

Richard Kirk and his wife, Ellen, (daughter of George Venables of Prestbury near Macclesfield) had produced five sons, but the two eldest would die unmarried. The fourth son, George, married William's daughter, Rachel Harriott, at St. Anne's Church, Gwersyllt Hill near Wrexham; she was 33 years old and George's senior by six months. William specified that Rachel Harriott's inheritance of £5,000 was for her own use and free from the debts of her husband, Each year she was to receive the interest from the investment, and her receipt was to be accepted as proof of William's proviso; following her death it had to be paid to her children as minors or until married, after which a share of the principal could be made.

Richard Kirk's fifth son. Richard Venables Kyrke (the sons preferred to use the old spelling of their surname) had eloped to Gretna Green with Harriet Anne, the eldest daughter of Ann and Captain Jones (and also Rachel Harriott's niece) where they were married on 5th October 1820. He was almost 33 years old but she was barely 17; in England the minimum age for marriage was 18, in Scotland only 16. Their son, Richard Venables was born on 11th June 1821. The marriage was declared legal by the Court of Chancery which was the probable justification for William including his granddaughter in his original will, however, after the death of her younger sister, Hannah, Harriet Anne was excluded from the inheritance by a codicil dated 29th March 1824, William having considered her "amply provided for".

Nor was this the end of the family intermarriages, one of William's younger daughters, Dorothea, married Henry Warbrick of Everton House, Liverpool on 22nd December 1812, and their daughter, Fanny, would eventually marry her cousin Richard Venables Jnr.

William added a second codicil to his will on 28th January 1825 reducing the legacy of £3,000 to Dorothea by £240 i.e. the sum he had loaned to her husband, with the stipulation that should further sums be advanced and remain unpaid, then the principal sum had to be reduced accordingly. As Rachel

Harriott had recently died, this same codicil allowed George Kyrke "a liberal sum of money" out of the yearly interest payable to his children, for their support and education, provided he too contributed towards their maintenance.

William's third and final codicil was added on 12th December 1825 when Helen, one of the youngest daughters (although by then 33 years old) was to marry a Macclesfield surgeon, James Cockson. William gave £2,000 towards the marriage settlement, and the provision for this in his original will was consequently revoked. Helen's marriage suggests that William Roe was certainly resident in Macclesfield by 1825, in fact he had most likely made a decision to return to the town shortly after his wife's burial at Christ Church in 1817, as and when circumstances permitted.

Christopher Shaw Roe finally married on 25th February 1823. His wife, Anne, was the daughter of Barker Bossley of Bakewell, and niece of Rev. George Bossley, vicar of Bakewell and rector of Clowne, Derbyshire. Again a further indication that William and his unmarried children had probably returned to Macclesfield sometime earlier. Christopher soon lived in a grand house and estate named Summer Hill on Chester Road, where he remained until his death on 28th February 1854. There seems little doubt that this is where William lived out his final days, for he is recorded as "of Summerhill, Macclesfield" in a history of *The Old Parish of Wrexham*, in 1821, although his will, prepared on 22nd January 1821 still described him as "of Liverpool". This does suggest that he was probably the original owner of the property Summer Hill which then passed to his son after his death.

The estate was a considerable size, the grounds of which were eventually occupied by the Parkside Mental Hospital for East Cheshire (now a housing estate) and the present West Park General Hopital on Victoria Road.

Like the Smyth estate of Fence House in Hurdsfield, Summer Hill not only provided its owners with a sophisticated water supply from a private reservoir, but also its tenants. The early 19th century saw Macclesfield Corporation desperate to supply its inhabitants with a decent water system, as the antiquated one of the17th century was proving totally inadequate for the rapidly expanding population, which had passed the 8,000 mark by 1800. In 1807 the Round Fountain was replaced by a filtering reservoir (final cost £1,800), but by 1822 an entirely new reservoir was required. By then, however, the Corporation was involved with a series of grandiose schemes concerning the town centre and a new magnificent town hall.

After further delays, procrastinations and bickerings, not until 1837 did it finally commit itself to the creation of Leadbeaters reservoir, and yet another saga was underway. Those areas of the town supplied with water from private systems were to be brought into the main Corporation scheme which, of course, included those of both the Smyth family and Charles Roe's grandson. On 4th May 1839 Mr. Broderick, of the newly formed Water Committee, recommended taking in 'Mr. Roe's' system immediately. A committee member, Mr. Gould, said the Roe tenants had virtually been supplied with the town's water already, as "It is impossible to drink Mr. Roe's Water". Mr. Broderick, a resident of that part of the town disclaimed the "imputation". After technical difficulties lasting well over three years, the system was finally completed at a considerably increased cost.

Perhaps this was the inspiration for Christopher Shaw Roe's interest in water schemes, as he generously contributed towards the baths at Buxton. In general, however, whilst devoting many years of his married life to public service and his grandfather's church, he seems to have lived very much the life of a country gentleman. His obituary in the local newspaper makes delightful reading, beginning "A painful gloom was cast over the inhabitants of this Borough generally on Tuesday morning last, by the sudden death of this lamented gentleman." It reminded everyone of his commitments, "It would be hardly possible to lay one's hand upon any plan, public or private, permanent or temporary, which had for its object the good of Macclesfield, with which Mr. Roe's name was not identified." His charitable causes were touched upon, extolling his virtues in florid Victorian rhetoric, "Many a cottage latch was lifted, and many a threshold crossed by him when the world saw nothing of the ministry of mercy". He died childless, and the family's close affiliations with Macclesfield, begun by Rev. Thomas Roe in the late17th, were almost at an end.

Christopher joined the others in the family vault and was simply added to the list on the gravestone as the "youngest and only surviving son of the above William Roe."

John Ralph (born 1811), the only surviving child of William Roe's daughter, Hannah and her husband

William Nicholson, married in 1837. During that year young Nicholson had taken the name of Shaw in order to inherit the vast estate and fortune of his great uncle, John Shaw. The Wirral estate of 1,000 acres, with its newly built hall, was Arrowe Park, and over the next century and a half both owner and estate would receive a considerable and enthusiastic press.

John Ralph, eventually High Sheriff of Cheshire, is known to have worked hard in administering the estate; together with his eldest son, William Otho, "trees by the thousand" were planted. The hall itself was extended several times; the final occasion providing accommodation for a considerable collection of 'trophies' i.e. nine tigers, black bears, elks, leopards, panthers, moose, yaks, bison etc. which William Otho had brought back from his hunting trips abroad. A private museum was also created comprising water colours, paintings, silver plate, a superb collection of glass wares, and pottery from the tombs of Cyprus said to be more than 2,000 years old. Nor was the furniture less impressive, as many of the rooms contained magnificent carved oak pieces.

The estate was eventually subdivided and sold, with the largest portion, almost half, bought by Birkenhead Corporation in 1928. Today it has gained notoriety and fame as the site of Arrowe Park Hospital.

* * * * * * *

APPENDIX 2

i) Sources of copper ore (in brief and listed chronologically).

Alderley Edge. Worked by Roe & Co. c. 1756-1770 and again c. 1788-91.

Coniston. Worked by Roe & Co. Lease 13th September 1756:

Ore weighings to nearest ton

1758	83	1764	109
1759	109	1765	112
1760	120	1766	79
1761	171	1767	25
1762	97	1768	7
1763	82	1769	15

No further ore weighings are recorded, however a further lease was signed 21st January 1778. Letter 23rd February 1781 referred to 'Pretty good prospect of oar' but yield seems to have been unimpressive. Company withdrew 27th July 1795, the mine had been unproductive for some time.

Ecton. Purchases by Roe & Co. from the Duke of Devonshire's mine as taken from Robert Shore's accounts:
Purchases commenced 12th February 1761, tonnage details are not shown for each individual company but as one large figure. The amounts paid were considerable:

	To nearest £.		To nearest £.
1761	2,726	1767	2,073
1762	3,095	1768	5,938
1763	2,921	1769	(no purchases but arrears
1764	1,814		of £3,000 paid.)
1765	6,215	1770	1,750
1766	4,574	1771	1,594

The 1771 arrears of £1,594 were paid 1772 and no further purchases made. Prior to 1761 only 25 tons of coarse ore are recorded to Roe & Co.

The figures submitted by Roe & Co are as follows:

	Tons.	Metal	To nearest £.
1761	?		
1762	231		3,728
1764	264		2,006
1765	381	7	6,606
1766	283	7	4,574
1767	240	5	3,925
1768	225	6	3,901
1769	none		

These figures are reconcilable for the years in which both sets of figures are available i.e. 1762-1769. The Ecton account total of money paid is £26,630 (which does not show any interest). The

Roe & Co. figures are 1,790 tons + 25 metal cost £26,835. In some years Roe & Co. did not pay the whole amount due and offered to pay interest on the amount carried over to the following year. The difference between what Roe & Co. paid and what the original cost was in the Ecton accounts if therefore £205.

The interest charged at that period was normally 4%. Although it is difficult to be absolutely accurate about what amounts of interest were calculated at which dates, the fact that £3,000 was carried over from 1768 to 1769 would attract interest of £120 for that year alone. Sometimes arrears occurred in other years, but then Roe & Co made extra payments during the following year, yet not clearing the whole of the debt until 1769.

Dolawen. 1761 ore sold to 'Macclesfield Co.'

Llanberis. 1762-65 some small purchases but no details known. Mining begun by Roe & Co. circa 1787, however it appears to have been unproductive from August 1793 to April 1798, then ore yields were considerable. There is no further mention after 1802 and company had ceased trading.

Blackcraig Hill, Kirkcudbrightshire ? Purchases a possibility c. 1763-66.

Bryndin(n)as Hills near Tywyn. Agreed for at the same time as Penrhyn du. Duty ore agreed as 1/8th for two places on 'Waste' : Keightly Old Mine Works and Bryndinnas Hills. Very little mining appears to have taken place. Mines shortly abandoned.

Parys Mountain. Leased from 10th October 1764. Great strike made on St. Chad's Day, 2nd March 1768. Lease terminated 1785.

Production began in July 1767 and to December 1768 2,304 tons were raised, mostly after the great strike.

For the period 21st January 1769 to 14th July 1772 9723 tons were raised (details from UW Bangor Mona Mine 3536)

Details are not available for the period 15th July 1772-September 1783 when the Dawes and Williams partnership were smelting the Duty ores, but it was reckoned in a report (UW Bangor Mss. 3544) that the profit to Roe & Co. was in the region of £15,000 per annum.

It has been possible to calculate ore production from details of the Duty ores for the period 8th September 1783 to 10th October 1785 when the lease of the Cerrig-y-Bleiddia mine ceased (UW Swansea Grenfell C1):

		Duty ore		Total ore to nearest ton
	1783	633 x 8	=	5,064
	1784	2218 x 8	=	17,744
to 10th October	1785	2024 x 8	=	16,192

This shows the considerable efforts made during the final two years to retrieve as much ore as possible, there was a considerable amount of ore on bank. Out of the above, a total of 21,295 tons of ore was finally shipped from Amlwch after the termination of the lease to 31st March 1788 (UW Bangor Mona Mine 3046).

Middleton Tyas. Purchases of rough smelted ore 1764-67, particularly rich. Prices varied between £31 to £43 per ton.

	Tonnage
1764	9 1/4
1765	8
1766	9 1/4
1767	13 1/2

Order made to dispose of company property on site 17th August 1775.

Cornwall. Purchases commenced 1765. (Except for Roe & Co. and Patten & Co. some other companies were purchasing averages of 2000-4,000 tons each year see NLW Ms 15103B to 15109B).

	Tonnage		Tonnage
1765	216	1770	842
1766	208	1771	540
1767	159	1772	370.5
1768	608	1773	913
1769	411	Book missing for years 1774-78.	

Apart from one purchase of 46 tons in 1781 no further purchases were made by Roe & Co. in the books available to 1785. The figures are not available for 1785-86 but it is known that purchases ceased in January 1786.

Conwy Valley. May-September 1783. Some sulphur ore was purchased and sent to William Roe in Liverpool.

Llandudno. Ty'n yr hwylfa. Leased from 5th April 1785 in the names of Lord Penrhyn, William Roe and Thomas Smyth from Lord Bulkeley.In August 1785 Roe & Co. proposed to purchase shares in the Llandudno Mine Co. working an adjoining set, and had done so by March 1786.

By 1788 Roe &Co. appear to have effected a further lease on adjoining ground with the Bishop of Bangor for A. Mills applied to the Bishop in May 1790 for a 'fresh' lease, but this was denied. Eventually in 1801 a new bishop offered a 'fresh' lease, but Roe & Co. declined. In 1802 the mine shares were considered to be of no value and operations ceased at the termination of their lease on 16th Oct.ober 1803.

It appears that in 1806 Robert Hodgson, Abraham Mills and Edward Hawkins Snr. reworked the mine in the hope of supplying the Neath Abbey Works then under the supposed ownership of Edward Hawkins, but no further details are known.

Islay, Scotland. First worked 12th November 1785 but leases drawn up from 18th May 1786 and 14th and 20th June 1786. Mining ceased 1790 resulting in the 'Renounciation' of 1799, registered 1803.

Bodiddabach. Gyffin co. Caernarfon. Leased from 29th September 1786 in the names of William Roe and Thomas Smyth from Sir Roger Mostyn. ? Abandoned January 1788.

Wicklow Ireland. Avoca Mines. Lease c. 1786; work began in earnest May 1787. Ballymurtagh was abandoned February 1788 having discovered "Nothing of consequence". Cronesbane proved to have a rich vein which produced copper ore for many years, and it was soon worked in conjunction with Tigroney.

The Associated Irish Mine Co. was incorporated by Act of Parliament 7th November 1798 and Edward Hawkins agreed to purchase all the ores for three years from 3rd November 1801. A crisis followed during the Napoleonic Wars and by 1811 it was decided to sell, but no takers resulted in the shares still being held in 1833.

Calbeck Fells. Lake District. This mine was being worked by April 1788 and some ore produced 1789 but had ceased by 1791.

Bethgelert. Hafod y Llan mine. Leased from 29th September 1794 in the names of R. Hodgson, E. Hawkins and A. Mills from Sir Roger Mostyn. Last mentioned 1802: details not known.

Tilberthwaite,Westmorland 1799. One letter only exists suggesting a lease between Lord Muncaster and William Roe, but nothing seems to have come from this.

Fremington, Yorkshire: Texel Mine from September to December 1799, trials but no further development.

* * * * * * *

ii) Sources of calamine and lead (in brief).

Gorsey-dale. Near Bonsall, Derbyshire. Calamine bought from 1763-1801. Both Charles Roe and Brian Hodgson Snr. were investors in the mine from 1st January 1763 and their executors continued to hold shares till after the Roe & Co. demise in 1801.

The mine was in profit to 1768 but then incurred heavy losses for 5 years. Productive for the years 1773 & 1774, but then small loses for the years to 1782 with no ore retrieved for 1779. From 1782 small profts were made each year.

Penrhryn Du. Leased from 12th October 1763, possession relinquished 19th November 1767. Lead only retrieved but yield poor. December 1766 produced only 1 ton 3cwts; and 1767, 81 tons 15cwts. (NLW Powis 3084).

Loggerheads. Near Mold. Predominantly lead but also calamine. It was worked from September 1769. From 3rd January 1774 work continued in conjunction with the **Pennygarrick Quin Mine** until December 1777.

Holway or Holywell Level. North Wales. Leased from Thomas Pennant 1774 it was predominantly a lead mine but rich in calamine in parts. Shares were still held in the mine at the final winding up of business in 1833 by former company shareholders or their heirs. No production figures are known.

Mendip Hills. Somerset. Calamine bought and treated on site from circa 1774 to 1781.

Wensleydale. North Yorkshire. Enquiries made in 1779 regarding the purchase of calamine works: few details known except that for a comparatively short period calamine was bought.

Llanymynech, Shropshire. Mostly a lead mine but calamine purchases made c. 1780s and early 1790s.

Appendix 3

Shares in Company

	1758	circa 1760	1764	1767	1772	1773	1774	1775
	thirds	fourteenths	fourteenths	fourteenths	fourteenths	fourteenths	fourteenths	fifteenths
Charles Roe	2	4	4	2	2	3.5	2	2
William Roe				1	1	1	1	1
Thomas Smyth &							1.5 (joint)	1.5 (joint)
Chas Caldwell (Joint)								
Legh Dickinson				1	1	1	1	1
Rowland Atkinson	1	1.5	1.5	1.5	1.5	died		
Cookson Atkinson		0.5	0.5	0.5	0.5	0.5	0.5	0.5
Brian Hodgson Snr		4	3	3	3	3	1	1
Robert Hodgson		1	1	1	1	1	2	2
Brian Hodgson Jnr							0.5	0.5
Edward Pitts		4	4	4	died			
J A Busfield					1	1	1	1
Lathom Arnold					1	1	1	1
Thomas Weaver &					1 (joint)	1 (joint)	1 (joint)	0.5 (TW)
John Jeffries Snr (Joint)								
John Jeffries Jnr								0.5
John Cooke					1	1	1	1
Edward Leigh							0.5	0.5
Edward Hawkins								1

	1776 twenty ninths	1777 twenty ninths	1778 twenty ninths	1779 thirteenths	1780 thirteenths	1781 thirteenths	1783 fourteenths
Charles Roe	4	3	3	1.5	1.5	died	
Samuel Roe		1	1	0.5	died		
William Roe	2	2	2	1	1 + 0.5 (trustee)	2.5	2.5
Thomas Smyth & Chas Caldwell (Joint)	3 (joint)	3 (joint)	3 (joint)	1.5 (joint)	1.5 (joint)	1.5 (joint)	1.5 (joint)
Legh Dickinson	2	2	2	1	1	1	1
Cookson Atkinson	withdrawn						
Brian Hodgson Snr	2	2	2	1	1	1	1
Robert Hodgson	4	4	4	2	2	2	2
Brian Hodgson Jnr	1	1	1	0.5	0.5	0.5	0.5
J A Busfield	2	2	2	1	1	1	1
Lathom Arnold	2	2	2	died			
Thomas Weaver	1	1	1	0.5	0.5	0.5	0.5
John Jeffries Jnr	1	1	1	1	1	1.5	1.5
John Cooke	2	2	(2) resigns				
Edward Leigh	1	1	1	0.5	transferred		
F Fernyhough					0.5	0.5	0.5
Edward Hawkins	2	2	2	1	1	1	1
Abraham Mills							1

	1784 (fourteenths)	1786 (fourteenths)	1787 (readjusted to twelfths details not known)	1793	1794 (twelfths)	1796 (twelfths)	1801 (Company begins to wind up)
William Roe	2	2					
John Harriet Roe				Aug 1793 admitted with part share from William Roe			
John Johnson	(?) 0.5	(?) 0.5					
Thomas Smyth & Chas Caldwell (Joint)	1.5 (joint)	0.75 bankrupt (TS)	0.75 Purchased from C.Caldwell (1786) died				
J Pendred Scott			Purchased T.Smyth's share (1789)		died, 3 trustees	0.75 3 trustees	no further details known until 1812
James Clegg	1	1					
Legh Dickenson	died						
Brian Hodgson Snr	2.5	2.5					
Robert Hodgson	0.5	0.5					
Brian Hodgson Jnr	0.5	0.5					
Elizabeth Leigh	1	1					
J A Busfield	0.5	0.5					
Thomas Weaver	1.5	1.5					
John Jefferies Jnr	0.5	0.5					
F Ferneyhough	0.5	0.5			0.5	died	
C. Ferneyhough (widow)						0.5 inherited	
Edward Hawkins	1	1					
Abraham Mills	1	1					

Although part of the Macclesfield Copper Company business ceased in 1801-1802 the Roe & Co. shareholders continued until August 1813, when they became shareholders of the late Roe & Co. However, only three mining projects appear to have been retained for investment:

a) The main colliery on Macclesfield Common appears to have been driven through the boundary into the adjoining parish of Sutton. From 1792 the Sutton Land Tax returns shows ' Mefs. Roe & Co.' paying 9/10d. but what this not excessive amount relates to, goes unrecorded. The property was previous let to a John Clowes by another owner. The Roe & Co. occupation continued to the death of William Roe in 1827 and then let. No further details are known.

b & c) In 1812 both the lead mine of Holway (Holywell) and the Irish mining concern show the same proportions of shares to the remaining shareholders:

	No. of shares
Robert Hodgson Exors.	8
Edward Hawkins	6
William Roe	4
J.A. Busfield & W. Busfield	4
Abraham Mills	4
Catherine Ferneyhough	4
John Jefferies (Jnr)	$^9/_{10}$ x 4
Brian Hodgson (Jnr)	2
J. Johnson	2
Thomas Weaver (Jnr)	2
Elizabeth Leigh	2
John Clegg	1½
William Roe nominee	$^8/_{10}$ x 1
John Harriott Roe	$^8/_{10}$ x 1
Unappropriated shares	1½

By 1831 the shares were as follows when the proprietors of the late firm of Roe & Co met:

	No. of shares
Brian Hodgson Exor. to late R. Hodgson	80
Ed. Hawkins Exor. to late E. Hawkins	60
Rev. E. Hodgson proxy for C. Ferneyhough	40
Edward Leigh proxy for late Adm. A. Mills	40
W. Busfield Exor. to late J.A. Busfield	40
Rev. E. Hodgson Exor. to late Brian Hodgson	20
Rev. Thomas Leigh proxy for Miss Margt. Leigh	20
Brian Hodgson (the Younger)	20
John Johnson	20
J.I Clegg	15
Christopher Shaw Roe	40
Christopher Shaw Roe proxy for W. Roe nominee	8

On 9th November 1833 the last meeting was recorded when the Macclesfield Partnership was finally terminated and a trust fund set up in its place. The final shares appear to be as those of 1831.

NOTES AND REFERENCES

Note: Apart from chapter 1 the references are listed under page and paragraph number. Where a paragraph continues onto the following page I have treated the continuation as number one of the following page. Many of the references are self-explanatory from the text, but where there is doubt I have specified in the notes and references, and have used op. cit. only where the information is set out fully within the same chapter.

Abbreviations:

Al. Oxon.	*Alumni Oxoniensis.*
Al. Cantab.	*Alumni Cantabrigiensis.*
Birk. PL	Birkenhead Public Library.
Birm. PL	Birmingham Public Library.
BL	British Library.
BLG	*Burke's Landed Gentry.*
CCALS	Cheshire and Chester Archives and Local Studies.
Ches. RO	Formerly the Cheshire Record Office now the CCALS.
Chester City RO	Now transferred to the Cheshire and Chester City Archives and Local Studies.
Chester PL	Chester Public Library.
Corn. CRO	Cornwall County Record Office, Truro.
CRO Swansea	City Record Office, County Hall, Swansea.
Cu. RO (K)	Cumbria Record Office, Keswick.
Cu. RO (C)	Cumbria Record Office, Carlisle.
Derby LS	Derby Local Studies Library.
Derby. RO	Derbyshire Record Office, Matlock.
Dev.C.	Duke of Devonshire colln. Chatsworth House, Derbyshire.
DNB	*Dictionary of National Biography.*
G. M/cr CRO	Greater Manchester County Record Office.
Gr. LRO	Greater London Record Office.
Guild.L	The Guildhall Library, City of London.
IGI	International Genealogical Index.
JHC	*Journals of the House of Commons.*
JRL	John Rylands Library, Manchester.
Lancs.	Lancashire.
Leeds Dist. Arch.	Leeds District Archives.
Leek PL	Leek Public Library.
Lich. JRO	Lichfield Joint Record Office.
Liv. PL	Liverpool Public Library.
Liv. Univ.	Liverpool University.
Macc.	Macclesfield.
Macc. BC	Macclesfield Borough Council, Town Hall, Macclesfield.
MCC	Minute Book of the Macclesfield Copper Co. 1774-1833 held in the John Rylands Library, Manchester.
M/cr. PL	Manchester Public Library, St, Peter's Square.(Archives).
M.G.S.	*Memoirs of the Geological Survey.*

MLS	Matlock Local Studies Library.
MM	Mona Mine colln. UW Bangor.
NA	National Archives (previously the Public Record Office).
NLI	National Library of Ireland, Dublin.
NLW	National Library of Wales, Aberystwyth.
NMGM	National Museums & Galleries on Merseyside, Liverpool.
NYCAD.	North Yorks. County Archives Department, Northallerton.
O.E.D.	*Oxford English Dictionary.*
Picton	Picton J.A. *Memorials of Liverpool* (2nd edn.1907).
SCA	Sheffield City Archives.
Shrop. RO	Shropshire Record Office.
Staffs. RO	Staffordshire Record Office.
Stock. L	Stockport Library.
THSL&C	*Transactions of the Historical Society of Lancashire & Cheshire*
T L&CAS	*Transactions of the Lancashire & Cheshire Antiquarian Society*
UW	*The University of Wales.*
VCH	*Victoria County History.*

Chapter 1

The information for this chapter has been gleaned from the following sources; content and dates will identify origin.
Quotation: Robert Burns.

Lich. JRO: Roe wills: William Roe the Elder of Arleston   1670
   William Roe of Arleston   1680
   Elizabeth Roe Admin. 1691
   Robert Roe of Hadley 1717

 Shropshire RO: a) Copy will Samuel Roe of Stotfold Beds. 1766.
   b) Map Hadley Township 1840 F/N Map.

Shrewsbury Public Lib. Deeds 18093, 136.

Lich. JRO: Bishops Visitations B/V/1/62, /77, /78, /80.

Hereford RO: Bishops Visitation (Munslow) 1670

Alumni Oxon & Cantab.

A Short History of the Parish Church of St. Peter & St. Paul, Wem. (1987).

VCH : Shropshire Vol X1 Telford.

DNB Prince Rupert - Arundel.

Arleston Mss. Brief architectural history of manor house kindly supplied by the owner in 1990.

Spufford, M. *The Great Reclothing of Rural England* (1984).

IGI and parish registers as appropriate.

Picton vol. 1 p.79 (James 1).

Woodward, I.*The Story of Wem* (1952) I am grateful to Mrs. Keeling-Roberts for providing a copy of this book and also for the extracts from Samuel Garbet's *History of Wem* (1818) relating to the Roe family.

Lockyer, R. *Tudor & Stuart Britain* 1471-1714, chap.XI James I.

Wheeler, H. (ed.)*The Wonderful Story of London* (Odham's Press 1930s) p.154.

JRL:*Travels of Pietro Della Valle* (1665, 1st pub. Rome 1650) includes: Sir Thos. Roe, *An Essay upon the Trade to Africa* (1711).

Fry, P. Somerset, *1000 Great Lives* (1975) ref. Oliver Cromwell.

Firth, C.B. *The Days of the Tudors & Stuarts* (1965) chap.XV1 re: Charles 1.

CCALS: Macc. Corpn. Minute Books 1619 -1744, LBM/1/2-3 2/6/1738.

CCALS: St. Michael's Churchwardens Accounts 1686-1751, 85/10/1.

Barker, T. *Memorials of a Dissenting Chapel* (1884) copy M/cr. PL.

Anstey, R. & Hair, P.E.H. 'Liverpool the African Slave Trade & Abolition' in the *Hist. Soc. of Lancs. & Ches.* occasional series 1776 vol 2.

* * * * * * *

Chapter 2

Quotation:	Psalm 121.
26:1-2	i) CCALS: LBM/1/2.
	ii) Parish registers as appropriate.
	iii) CCALS: LBM/1/2 Parsonage 17th May 1692.
	iv) *Al. Oxon.*: Rev. Thomas Roe.
27:2-3	Davies, C. Stella, *History of Macclesfield* (1961) Part 1.
27:4	Booth, P.H.W. *The financial administration of the lordship and county ofChester 1272-1377.* (pub. Chetham Soc. 1981) Chapter 4.
27:5	Lancs. RO: Earl of Derby Colln. 1551/20, 1709 survey.
27:6	Leeds Dist. Arch. Radcliffe Mss. Cheshire Deeds 103/2 (Jordangate). 27:7-28:1 Booth, *passim.*
28:3	i) Booth, op. cit. p.87.
	ii) 18th century property deeds Great King St. Macc. held by Robinson's Brewery, Stockport under the Red Lion, Catherine St.
28:4	Davies, op. cit. p.16.
28:5	i) For a description of a timber framed mill see Vince, John N.T. *Discovering Windmills* Shire pub. No. 13.
	ii) CCALS: LBM/1/2 Macc. malt mill 8th March 1691.
28:7	Quern: *Everyman's Encyclopaedia.*
29:2	i) Leeds Dist. Arch. Radcliffe Mss. Uncatalogued papers -
	ii) Exemplification Chas 5. 4th Dec. 1629/30.
	iii) Houghton, J. *A Collection of Letters for the Improvement of Husbandry & Trade* vol. 1 p. 63 No. 7 Thurs. 15th June 1682.
29:3	Radcliffe Mss. op. cit. uncatalogued papers 14th Jan. Chas 8.
29:4	Lancs.RO: Earl of Derby colln. bundle 1605 No. 5.
29:5	i) CCALS: will Richard Blachlach1635.
	ii) Leeds Dist. Arch. op. cit. Blachlach property deed 1632 14th Jan. Chas 8.
	iii) Leeds Dist. Arch. Radcliffe leases 103/109, 103/23.
29:6	Davies op. cit. pp.76-77.
29:7-30:1	Radclife Mss. op. cit. lease 103/62.
30:2	NA: E134, 14 Chas 2 Mich 26, 57743.
30:3	Ibid. uncatalogued John Pickford - Office of Clerkship 18th June 1661. 30:4
	i) CCALS: LBM/1/2.
	ii) Radcliffe Mss. op. cit. lease 103/37.
30:7-31:2	Ibid. misc. deeds 142 - 161.
31:3	i) Lancs. Parish Register Soc. vol. 65 (Ashton-under-Lyne) see also
	ii) Lancs. RO: Earl of Derby colln. lease 458/20.
31:4	Derby Local Studies 3226. Original Journal of George Fox.
31:6	Radclife Mss. op. cit. misc. deeds 263.
31:7	i) Ibid. copy will Jedediah 116/6.
	ii) Ibid. Subsidiary Deeds 1694-1741 103/129.
32:1-2	i) CCLAS: LBM/1/2: Streets, 13th Dec. 1677, 10th May 1679; Malt mill 14th Sept. 1694.
	ii) Leeds Dist. Arch. Radcliffe Mss. 103/101 (Tithe barn 12th Nov. 1711).
32:3-33:4	CCALS: LBM/1/2 or Leeds Dist. Arch. Radcliffe Mss. as appropriate.
33:5-6	i) Houghton, op. cit. vol. 1 no.12.16th Jan 1683, see also bread pp. 127-135.
	ii) Ibid. vol.2 recipes pp 108-139.
33:7-43:2	Chester City RO: Earwaker colln. CR 63/2/341.
34:3	CCALS: LBM/1/2, 3rd July 1676.
34:4-5	Chester City RO: Earwaker colln. CR 63/2/341.
34:6	Spufford M. *The Great Reclothing of England* (1984): chapmen.
34:7-35:1	CCALS: LBM/1/2.
35:2-4	Houghton op. cit. vol. 1 no.2.
35:5	i) *Barlow's Journal 1659-1703,* (Lubbock 1934).
	ii) Lancs RO: Earl of Derby colln. 1634 survey 1551/1- Philipp Holland.

35:6	CCALS: LBM/1/2 29th Aug. 1678.
35:7	Leeds Dist. Arch. Radcliffe Mss. 103/49.
36:1	*JHC:* 9th March 1737 (Linen).
36:2	i) Ches. County Council : Modern deed 3151 (Pack Horse Inn, Jordangate now the site of Macc. Public Library).
	ii) Young, A. *North of England Tour* (1771) 2nd. edn.
36:3	Houghton, op. cit. vol. 1 no. 5 27th April 1682.
36:4-6	i) Morse, H.B. *Trading to China* vol.1 (1926) - There was virtually no direct trade with China until Manchus settled in Amoy 1684. Many problems were encountered, then finally trading commenced, but there was no raw silk in the cargoes of 1695 and 1696, only wrought. First imports are recorded July 1697, ship *Nassau* from Amoy, 30 tons raw silk; November 1698, frigate *Fleet* from Amoy, 20 tons raw silk.
	ii) *Barlow's Journal* op. cit.
	iii) *JHC:* no. 849 -17th April 1702 (see also no. 863)
	iv)*The Silk Book* (The Silk & Rayon Users Association Inc. 1951). Morse, op. cit.
	v) *Barlow's Journal* op. cit.
36:7	CCALS: LBM/1/2 8th Oct. 1675.
37:1-3	i) Campsell, R. *The London Tradesman* 1747 (facsimile 1969 New York) - Turkey merchant. I am indebted to P. Latham for the loan of this book.
	ii) *JHC:* 9th March 1737 - Turkey merchants.
	iii) Dashwood, Sir Francis, *The Dashwoods of West Wycombe* (1987) p.13.
37:4	CCALS: LBM/1/2 11th Jan. 1686.
37:5	i) Laughton, J. *Origins of the Silk Industry* Source Book, Ches. Museums & Archives.
	ii) Johns, Rev. C.A. *The Forest Trees of Britain* (1919) pp 194-204.
37:6-38:1	i) Radcliffe Mss; op. cit. 103/118 6th March 1712.
	ii) Ibid: bundle 108 Indenture 5th March 1735 (Wortley).
	iii) JRL: Legh Mss. box K F, Surveys of Macc. School lands 1667 & 1731.
	iv) NA: E190 1433/4 1759, 1433/1 1760 et seq. Chester Port records.
	v) Houghton, op. cit. no.14, 14th March 1683.
38:3	i) CCALS: wills Dale and Allen 1696.
	ii) Woollen Acts: first legislation 1667, reinforced 1668, from then onwards there were several but evidently disregarded as the 18th century progressed. Reprinted 1814, copy M/cr. PL.
	iii) *Intreaty for Help* 1699 M/cr. PL.
38:4	Wilson, G.E. 'A History of Macclesfield Grammar School 1503-1890' unpublished M. Ed. thesis 1952 (University of Leeds).
38:5	Clapham, Sir John, *A History of the Bank of England* (1945).
39:6	CCALS: LBM/1/2 15th Sept. 1697.
39:7	CCALS: F2 D93 Abstract Quarter Sessions Nantwich 14th July 1696, see also D92, D90 & D88.
39:8-40:1	i) *DNB*: Prince Rupert.
	ii) Copper: Morse op. cit.
	Barlow op. cit.
	Roe, Thomas, 'A voyage to East India' in *Travels of Pietro della Valle* 1st pub. Rome 1650 reprint 1665 copy JRL.
40:4	i) BL: Harl. 2130 re: Thomas Legh, 46,464 - 10 April 1663; 46,472 - 24th Nov.1663; 46,488 - 1670/71; 46,525 - 7th March 1696.
	ii) Beaven, A.B. *Aldermen of the City of London* (1908).
41:1	i) Glover, S. *History & Gazetteer of the County of Derby* (1831) vol 1. part 1, Lead p.56 et seq.
	ii) SCA: Tibbit's colln. 366, printed pamphlet no.6 1721.
41:3	i) JRL: Box 5/17 Bromley Davenport colln. Nether Alderley - Enclosure of Commons 1775, deed 17th Jan 1775.
	ii) SCA: OD 260, Legh 21st April 1692.
41:4-42:2	CCALS: Quarter Sessions Nantwich op. cit.

42:3   i) Warrington, G. 'The Copper Mines of Alderley Edge' report from the *Journal of the Chester Archaeological Soc.* vol. 64 1981.

    ii) *Halsbury's Laws of England* Book 8, Manors: Nature and Origins, in particular Lord of the Manor nos. 48 & 49. N.B. these general rules apply to manorial lands but the land on Alderley Edge was waste or common, and as such the Stanley family should have held the manorial rights from the Crown allowing them to sublease, in the same way as the Duke of Devonshire operated in the Peak District of Derbyshire.

43:2-3   i) *Al. Oxon.*

    ii) CCALS: Nether Knutsford parish register.

43:5   i) Derby LS; Bagshawe family tree in *Bagshawe of Abney* Col. W.H.G. Bagshawe (London 1886).

    ii) Earl of Derby Archives Knowsley Park, Ches. 468/37 deed 17th Oct.1725.

43:6   i) CCALS: Ches. marriage licences.

    ii) JRL: Bagshawe muniments 14/2/14 Castleton 1st Jan.1696.

    iii) CCALS: will Mary Roe 1724, portrait.

44:4   Shawcross, Rev. W.H. *Some Notices of Castleton and its Old Inhabitants* (1903) quotes "Mr. Bagshawe's vicarage occupied the site of a garden near the Brook opposite Foxhill". (Rev. Edward Bagshawe, vicar of St. Edmund's, Castleton 1723-69 was successor to Thomas Roe). A barn is said to have been erected on the site of the former parsonage but was reported as demolished by 1845.

44:4-45:2   i) Morris, C. (ed.) *The Illustrated Journeys of Celia Fiennes 1685-c.1712* (1982) - chap. 4.

    ii) Lyson's *Derbyshire* (1817) p 72.

45:3   Glover, op. cit. part 1 p.56 - for plan of red-lead oven 18th & early 19th centuries see sheet in misc. correspondence Bag. 587(47) SCA.

Chapter 3

Quotation   'The Lord's Prayer'.

47:1   Derby RO: Castleton parish registers.

47:3   i) Macc. Town Hall, list of mayors.

    ii) CCALS: will Josiah Barbor 1704.

48:1   *Barlow's Journal* vol. 2 p 553. Many accounts of this storm are recorded e.g.Rev. Francis Blomefield in his account of the *City of Norwich* wrote '1703 Nov. 25th in the Night was a great Tempest and on the 26th a most prodigious Hurricane of Wind which did abundance of Damage both in Town and Country by blowing down Houses, Chimneys . . .'.

48:1-3   Derby. RO: Castleton parish register.

48:2-4   i) *BLG*: Bagshawe of Wormhill and Oakes-in-Norton.

    ii) JRl: Bagshawe muniments 24/2/14, 24/2/17, Richard Bagshawe mineral accounts 1709-1715.

    iii) SCA: OD 539, 264.

    iv) BL. Woolley manuscript also copy in Matlock Local Studies, M/f 6696 p.244 Castleton tithe paid to vicar, inquisition Henry VIII.

48:7-49:3   i) Derby. RO: 32a Glebe terriers, Castleton - three are extant relating to Rev. Thomas Roe for 1705, 1719, 1722.

    ii) Ford, T.D. and Rieuwerts, J.H. 'Odin Mine', *Bulletin of the Peak Dist. Mines Hist. Soc.* vol.6 no.4 Sept. 1976.

    iii) Bible: Deuteronomy chap.14, v. 22 et seq. "Thou shalt truly tithe all the increase of thy seed that the field bringeth forth year by year".

    iv) Glover, S. *History & Gazetteer of the County of Derby* (1831) vol.1 pt 1 p.62 Footnote: Tithes.

49:4   Derby RO: 32a Glebe terriers, Castleton.

49:5-50:1   i) SCA: OD 1495.

    ii) Weights: Dishes of Ore etc. are given in 'Life & History of Brassington Village Derbyshire', Supplement no.1 Derby RO and William Hardy's *Miner's Guide* (1762) Derby LS.

50:2   i) East India Co. lead account books were originally held in East India House but have been transferred to the British Library under the Oriental & India Office collection.

    ii) Bagshawe, Col. W.H.G. *The Bagshawes of Ford* (London 1886).

50:3	Ford, T. and Rieuwerts, J.H. op.cit.
50:4	i) SCA: TC 646 - School.
	ii) Derby. RO: Occasional Paper no.5 1983 (Richard Clark).
	iii) Lich. JRO: Papist Returns nos. 34 & 35.
51:1	Lich. JRO: B/V/1 93-95.
51:2	i) MLS: Derby School Register (1570-1901) 94.2-51D.
	ii) Derby LS: Retford Grammar School Register 1700-1730.
	iii) *Life of Dr. Beilby Porteus by a lay member of Merton College* (London 1810) copy held M/cr. PL.
51:4	Derby LS: *History of Derby* (1826 - "an account written by Mr. Woolley in 1712").
51:5	Beverley Church Records Office Archive, Beverley, Yorkshire.
51:6	NA: Navy Adm. 32/265, 36/2394 et seq.
52:1	Derby. RO: St. Edmund's parish register.
52:2	SCA: OD 298.
52:5-53:2	SCA: Bag. no.330 (Secker copy letters) & 319 (Whillock's notebook).
53:3	Garland Festival still performed each year on Oak Apple Day. Details from the Castleton Museum, Derbyshire.
53:5	SCA: Bag. no. 319.
53:6-54:1	i) Campbell, R. *The London Tradesman* 1747 (facsimile New York 1969) p.270 Tallow chandler.
	ii) Price, W. *Mineralogia Cornubiensis* 1778 (facsimile Truro 1972).
	Working of Mines: in particular see p.147 for the circulation of good air by pumps etc. and illustration plate 2d opposite.
	iii) Roberts, A. and Leach, J. *The Coal Mines of Buxton* (1985). The illustration on p.2 is of the air shaft chimney of Dane colliery visible from the Buxton to Congleton road (A54).
	iv) Rhodes, E. *Derbyshire Tourists' Guide & Travelling Companion* 1837). Chap. 2 description of Castleton and 'slickensides'.
	v) Ford, T. and Rieuwerts, J.H. *Lead Mining in the Peak District (*1968) p.16 'Ventilation'.
	vi) Daniel, C. *Derbyshire Traditions* p.69.
	vii)*Cotton's Angler* (1675).
54:3	Clergymen's sons e.g. Oliver Goldsmith, John and Charles Wesley, Horatio Nelson etc.
54:5-55:4	Derby LS: 6482 Houghton (1681) p.130 et seq.
55:5	Ches. RO: will Mary Roe Stockport 1724.
55:6-56:2	Derby LS: Derbyshire Miscellany pp. 350-351 copy letter.
56:3	i) Derby RO: St. Edmund's parish register: Francis.
	ii) Birk. PL: Macc. colln. B/V/7: Brasenose College.
56:4	Rhodes, op. cit.
57:2-3	i) SCA: Several lead mine reckoning books are held in the Oakes Deeds and Bagshawe collns. See also *Miner's Guide* by William Hardy (1762) and John Barker Letter Books no. 494 (1765-1811): letters to J. Stonehewer, 19th June 1769: Mr. Ryley, 23rd June 1774: William Earle, 26th Dec. 1776; Brian Hodgson, 24th Nov.1780.
	ii) Mining disputes: Little Pasture and Miners Engine lasted more than 50 years (1730s-1792), Magclough Sough and Great Brookhead was amicably settled 1746 (see chap. 8).
57:4-58:2	iii) Rieuwerts, J.H. *History and Gazetteer of the Lead Mine Soughs of Derbyshire* (1987).
	iv) SCA: Bag. 724 Foolow; Bag. 712 Have-at-All original list 1711; Bag 3509 Brookhead partners listed at the back of the book.
58:3	Derby.RO: 32A Glebe terrier 1705 final paragraph.
58:4	SCA: Bag. 319 and 330.
58:5-59:1	Clapham Sir John *A History of the Bank of England* (1945) - South Sea Bubble.
59:2	Lich. JRO: will: Dorothy Creswick 1720 (proved 1721) I am grateful to the wife of Rev. M.F. Collier for drawing my attention to this will.
59:3	i) Varley, B. *The History of Stockport Grammar School* (1957).
	ii) Ball, J. and W. *Stockport Grammar School 1487-1987* (1987).
	iii) CCALS: will: Joseph Dale Stockport 1759 (proved 1760).
59:5	SCA: Tibbitt's colln. school deed 646 1721/22.

60:2   Lich. JRO: will: Thomas Roe 1724.

60:3   Ches. RO: will: Mary Roe 1724.

60:4   Wadsworth, A.P. and de Lacy Mann, J. *The Cotton Trade and Industrial Lancashire 1600-1780* (1931) *passim*.

60:5-61:1   i) JRL: Legh of Lyme colln.

ii) G. M/cr CRO: colliery ledgers etc. catalogued under E17. Letter re: Bishop of Chester E17/89/1/30.

iii) Thomas Patten: details from a paper presented by Prof. J.R.Harris to Warrington Historical Soc. held in Warrington Public Library.

61:2   i) Robey, J.A. June 1971 *Bulletin of the Peak Dist. Mines Hist. Soc.* vol. 4, part 5, p. 350 - discussion of coal required.

ii) Stock. PL: Lyme Hall a/cs. Deed Box B/JJ/6/21A.

61:3   *Al. Oxon:* W. Roe

61:3-4 CCALS: will: Mary Roe Stockport 1724.

Chapter 4

Quotation: Bible, Proverbs ch.22 v.6.

62:2   CCALS: 85/10/1 St. Michael's Churchwarden's a/cs 1686-1751.

62:5-63:1   i) SCA; Bag. 587(14) partners at Eyam Groves.

ii) Rieuwerts, J.H. *History and Gazetteer of the Lead Mine Soughs of Derbyshire* (1987) see Brookhead, Magclough etc.

63:2   *Al. Cantab.* James Roe.

63:3   SCA: Bagshawe colln. general.

64:1   Defoe, Daniel, *The Tour* (1928 edition) intro. by G.D.H. Cole "It is here presented as he wrote it".

64:2   i) Education: for further details see 'Some Aspects of Education in

ii) Cheshire in the 18th century'. D. Robson *Cheetham Soc.* (M/cr.1966) vol XIII.

iii) *The Life of Dr. Beilby Porteous by a lay member of Merton College, Oxford* (1810).

iv) Examples of Charles Roe's letter endings:-

a)Collingwood, W.G. 'The Keswick and Coniston Mines', *Trans. Cumberland and Westmorland Antiqu. and Arch. Soc.*vol. XXVIII New series 1928 p.31.

b)Lancs.RO: DDM 50/20.

65:4-66:1   i) CCALS: St. Michael's register.

ii) Lancs.RO: Earl of Derby colln. 1551/20, 1709 Survey.

66:2   Calladine A. and Fricker J. *East Cheshire Textile Mills,* Royal Commission on the Historical Monuments of England (1993) pp.18-19.

66:3   i) General survey of extant wills as listed in Earwaker's *Cheshire Wills.*

ii) JRL: Bromley Davenport colln. letter (4 pages N.D.) to John Ward from J. Allen.

iii) Birk. PL: MA/5/1/4-5: Charter,

66:4   Warner, Sir Frank, *The Silk Industry of the United Kingdom* (1911) general references.

67:1   Birtles: Earl of Derby colln. Knowsley Park, bundle 468, deed 37, 17th Oct.1725.

67:5-6 i) Lankford: 1722 marriage at Ilam Church, Derby. registered 'of Leek'. 1736 Elected Warden of Leek and owned property on Spout St. (now S. Edward St. Leek).

I am grateful to Alan Bednall for this Lankford information.

ii) Derby LS: George Lankford the Younger, Notts. deeds 1695, 3rd Jan. 1715.

ii) Parish registers as appropriate.

iv) Derby LS: Ince pedigrees - microfilm.

v) Staffs. RO: D3272/1/4/3/42 - this deed includes a copy of Samuel Lankford's will and a note relating to the New Grange estate from Mr. Cruso, solicitor of Leek.

67:7   Porter, Lindsey, *Ecton Copper Mines* (2004). p.25.

67:8-68-2   Cox, J. *A Compleat History of Staffordshire* (1730).

68:4-69:1   i) Kerridge, E.*Textile Manufacturing in Early Modern England* (M/cr. Univ.Press 1985).

ii) Deeds for 60B, 62 & 62A Chestergate in possession of owner McMillan-Scott PLC.

69:2   Stock.L: deed B/LL/2/1/5 31st Jan. 1734.

69:4	i) Copperas or melanterite FeSO47H20 *Everyman's Encyclopedia*
	ii) Goodwin, J. *A Dyer's Manual* (1982).
69:6-70:2	i) M/cr PL: Nicholson colln. C17.
	ii) Birk.PL: B/V/5 Land Tax return 1743.
	iii) CCALS: LBM/1/2-3.
70:3-4	i) Stock. L. Lyme accounts deed box B/JJ/6/21A (earliest Bundle 1727-1738 kept by Peter Steel Jnr. Steward's overseer).
	ii) Copy will Joshua Mottershead with deeds 118 & 118A Mill St. in possession of the owner.
70:5	*Al. Cantab:* John Robinson.
71:4	Roe Monument, Christ Church, Macclesfield.
71:5	Den. E. Barbara, *Bramall Hall* (1977) Davenport pedigree.
72:1-73:1	i) Peter - possibly baptised at St. Martin's-in-the-Fields, Westminster 9th Nov. 1684.
	ii) BL: English Army Lists & Commission registers vol. VI 1661-1714 p.236,310, 378.
	iii) Rogers, Col. H.C.B. *The British Army of the Eighteenth Century* (1977).
	iv) Marriages: per Ormerod's *East Cheshire* Mary Thornycroft was a previous wife who died 8th Oct. 1721.
	v) Parish registers for Prestbury held locally by archivist record two more marriages, Martha Gollop 14th April 1713; Anne Sherwood 22nd April 1716.
	vi) Macc. B C: deeds C1/166.
	vii) BL: English Army lists op. cit. vol. VI p.896.
	viii) Stock. L: Lyme Hall accounts op. cit.
	ix) CCALS: St. Michael's register.
73:3	CCALS: Cholmondeley colln. includes plan of Macc. Park estate c.1778.
73:4-74:3	Chester City RO: Earwaker colln. CR63/2/341.
74:5-76:6	i) Craven, M. *A Derbyshire Armory* (Derbyshire Record Soc. vol. XVII 1991). Stafford family.
	ii) Derby LS: Stafford family pedigree see also:-
	a) Tilley, J. *Old Halls of Derbyshire* (1892) vol. 1 pp152-3.
	b) Bowles, C.E.B. *Stafford of Botham* (1915).
75:2	i) CCALS: will: John Stafford Feb. 1775- portrait. The family portraits passed down through the family until they were included in an auction at Eaton Hall, Retford, Notts. 30th & 31st May 1946, details from catalogue.
	ii) Stock.L: Lyme accounts op. cit.
75:4	i) JRL: Legh of Lyme colln. in particular letter 14th March 1733/34 from John Stafford addressed from Clifford's Inn.
	ii) Bowles op. cit. p.63.
75:5-76:1	Wheeler, Harold (ed.) *The Wonderful Story of London (c.1940)* chap. Ancient City of the Lawyers pp 375-388.
76:3	CCALS: LBM/I/I -3: items out of order.
76:4	i) Derby LS: 5977 deed Mellor.
	ii) CCALS: Taxal parish register.
	iii) JRL: Legh of Lyme colln. letter.
76:7-77:1	CCALS: LBM/I/I-3.
77:2	Ormerod, G. *The History of Cheshire.* (c.1825) vol. 3 p 819 Dukinfield Pedigree - Mary widow married Peter Davenport in 1736.

Chapter 5

Quotation:	Shakespeare.
78:1-2	I am grateful to the Borough Engineer's Department of Macc. Borough Council for supplying information and a report by E.R.Ford dated 28th March 1972 entitled "Leadbeaters Reservoir including catchments areas, inlets, draw-offs . . ." and also to North West Water Ltd., Great Sankey, Warrington for providing a detailed map of the area including reservoirs, streams and watercourses.
78:3	Pryce, W. *Mineralogia Cornubiensis* 1778 (facsimile Truro 1972). Section: Discovery of Mines.

79:1   CCALS: DFF/27/I Finney colln.

79:2   Staffs. RO: D(W) 1878/14 (D518) deed 21st May 1736 N.B. Copper St. Macclesfield, which today indicates the area of the original speculation, was initially called Copper Mine St. in the 19th century.

79:3-80:2   i) Yannopoulos, J.C. & Agarwal, J.C. *Extractive Metallurgy of Copper* vol. 1 (1976) pp. XV & XVI.

            ii) West, E.G. *Copper and its alloys* (1982).

            iii) *Source Book on Copper & Copper Alloys* (1979) A.S.M. Engineering Bookshelf, pub. The American Society for Metals.: Preface and Sect. 1.

            iv) Hamilton, Henry, *The English Brass & Copper Industries to 1800* (1926) Chap. 1 'The Beginnings'.

80:3-7   i) Collingwood, W.G. *Elizabethan Keswick* (1912 facsimile 1987) "Extracts from the Original Account Books 1564-1577 of the German Mines in the Archives of Augsburg" for additional information.

            ii) Hamilton op. cit. chap. 1.

81:1   i) Barbados: *Everyman's Encyclopedia*.

            ii) Grant, Alison, *Bristol and the Sugar Trade* (1981) : Jamaica.

81:4   Pryce op. cit. Copper smelting processes etc. chap. 2. p. 271 et seq.

86:6-82:3   Hornsby, Peter, *The Arthur Negus Guide to British Pewter, Copper and Brass* (1981) chap. 9.

82:6-83:5   i) Definition of a copper, Dr. Johnson's Dictionary (1755).

            ii) The use of coppers in the sugar industry: I am grateful to the archivist of the Tate & Lyle sugar refiners, London for this information.

            iii) Anstey,R. & Hair, P.E.H. (ed.) 'Liverpool the African Slave Trade & Abolition" in the *Hist. Soc. of Lancs & Ches.* occasional series 1776 vol 2, chap. 'The Atlantic Slave Trade & the economy of West Africa', by Marian Johnson.

            iv) Grant, op. cit. p.49.

83:7-8   Hamilton, op. cit. chap. IV.

84:1-4   i) Notes - N.J.Dibben Oct. 1988 prepared on behalf of the Derbyshire Caving Club for a Keele Univ. lecture.

            ii) For a discussion of the various theories relating to ore deposits at Alderley Edge see *M.G.S.* vol. XXX 'Copper Ores of the Midlands, Wales, The Lake District & the Isle of Man' pp.14-15.

84:6   Day Joan, *Bristol Brass* (1973) chap. 2: Darby.

84:7   Birk. PL: B/V/5.

84:8-85:2   i) I.G.I.: Hibberdine.

            ii) *THSL&C.* vol. lV p.189 letters relating to the button trade in the 17th century: Motterhead.

            iii) Chester City RO: Birch Collimore colln. D/BC deed 6th June Chas II 13th yr.

            iv) Leeds Dist. Arch: Radcliffe misc. deeds 121 (103/129) date 13th Oct. 1718 stipulates planning of land with "muck and manure" to be left on premises at the end of the lease.

            v) Deeds for the Grosvenor Centre (Macc. Indoor Market) seen at Solrs. Messrs. George Carters', Chancery Lane, London November 1988. Bundle 2, deed 5th Sept. 1715 re 17 & 19 Stanley St. etc.

85:3   i)Carlon, C.J. 'Bickerton Copper Mine' in *British Mining* no.16 Northern Mines Research Soc. Pub. (1981).

            ii) Kerry, Rev. Charles, 'Mackworth and its Castle and its Owners', in *Derby Arch. and Natural History Soc.* vol. XI (1889).

            iii) UW Swansea: G.F. D3 Minutes of the Fortunate Adventurers . . .1699-1707.

85:4   i) UW Swansea: Mackworth colln. notes and catalogue.

            ii) ibid. 1720 bundles 5&6 letter 208 from Sir Hubert to his father.

85:5-86:1   i) CCALS: DE 063 & 064, Bickerton.

            ii) Shrop. RO: 2284/1-49 Church family pprs., see also 4708 134-156 and family tree.

86:3-4   i) Day Joan, *Bristol Brass* (1973).

            ii) SCA: Bag. 330 Rev. Secker's quote taken from book copies of letters (1713-38).

86:5-87:4   i) CCALS: Finney colln. DFF extracts including mining records.

            ii) Wilmslow PL: article Lancs. & Ches. Hist. colln. article August 1853.

            iii) *Pennsylvania Hist. Soc.* colln: extensive article chap.7 'The Finney Family' in The Historical Soc. of Western PennsylvaniaLibrary, Pittsburg. Many Finney wills are held in the Philadelphia City Hall, Penn. U.S.A.

87:5   Pryce W. op. cit. 'Captain' see Management of Mines.

88:3	i) CCALS: DFF/27/1 End of partnership agreement 14th Feb. 1736.
	N.B. There was a Peter Davenport Finney I, grocer of Manchester and brother of Samuel Finney III, who died 1800, which suggests a family relationship.
88:4	Staffs. RO: D(W) 1878/14 (D518) deed 21st May 1736.
88:5	Robey, J.A. & Porter, L. *The Copper & Lead Mines of Ecton Hill, Staffordshire* (1972) p.68.
89:2	Pryce, W. op. cit.
89:3	Shaft - rear of property 160 Black Rd., Macc.
89:4-90:5	Chester City RO: CR63/2/341/133.
90:6	Wilmslow PL: Finney notes Lancs. & Ches. Hist. colln.
90:7	Shaw, William, *The Knights of England* London (1906) Peter Davenport knighted as a Crown Servant, Collector of Land Tax, Receiver General 8th June 1744.
90:8	Tilley, J. *Old Halls, Manors & Families of Derbyshire* (1892) : Chetham.
	Bowles, C.E.B. *Stafford of Botham* (1915)

Chapter 6

Quotation:	Oliver Goldsmith - The Traveller.
92:1	i) M/cr PL: pamphlet :Intreaty for Help on behalf of Eight silk weavers (1699).
	ii) Defoe, Daniel, *The Complete English Tradesman* (1727) chap. XXl N.B.*Barlow's Journal*, Third China Voyage 6th Jan 1701.
92:2	Morse, H.B. *East India Company Trading to China* (1926) vol.I.
92:3	Ibid. p.196 private trade.
92:4-93:1	Ibid. p.205 silk packaging.
93:2	Ibid. p. 158 tea beginning to displace silk.
93:3	Ibid. p.166 sago "as much as will fill all the hollow China Ware".
93:4	Ibid. chap. IX - 'The Conditions of Chinese Trade'.
93:5	Ibid. chap. X - 'The Council at Chusan'.
93:6	Act 1750: Geo.II 23 Cap. IX. Act for repealing duties on Chinese raw silk, from 24th June same as from Italy N.B. Geo.II Cap. XX. Act for encouraging the growth & culture of silk worms in H.M. colonies or American plantations.
93:7	Act 1736 Geo.II 9 Cap. V. Witchcraft.
93:8-94-3	*J.H.C.* Geo.II II Cap.II.
94:5-95:2	i) JRL: Legh of Lyme colln. Ward letter.
	ii) Lysons *Magna Britannia* (c. 1810) vol. 2 part 2 Rivers: see Weaver.
	iii) Route depicted on Bowen's map of Cheshire (1777) with annotation for Delamere Forest.
	iv) M/cr PL: *Journal of a Tour Through England* (1796) Ms. 942 J42.
95:3-96:1	i) Jackson, Gordon, *The History and Archaeology of Ports* (1983) : Chester: p. 15, 25, 33-34.
	ii) Pennant, Thomas, *Tours in Wales* (1773 & 1776) vol.1 pp. 245-7.
	iii) Hemingway's *History of Chester* (1831) vol. 1 p.266.
	iv)*England Described* (1776) Chapter: Cheshire - part of this description e.g. the floods, is based on Daniel Defoe's account in his *Tour through England and Wales* (1724-26).
	v) Spufford, Margaret, *The Great Reclothing of Rural England* (1984): Chester horse fairs.
	vi) CCALS: Q.D.N. I/5 River Dee Register of vessels.
	vii) Rhodes, J.N. 'Derbyshire Influences of Lead Mining in N. Wales' . . . (1968) in *Peak Dist. Mines Historical Soc.* vol. 3 part 6, pp. 339-351.
	viii) Chester PL: *Adams Weekly Courant* advert 1st Aug. 1744, "Several sorts of nets as Calling Cutter, Tramail & Partridge with Silk & Thread all fresh good & strong".
96:3	NA: E190: Port Books Chester.
96:7-97:2	i) CCALS: will: Philip Brock 1702, proved 1705.
	ii) Guild. L: Records of Huguenots.
	iii) CCALS: Chandeliers by Chester Brassfounders read by R. Sherlock to the Ches. Archaeological Soc. 8th March 1969: Brock the Elder p.40 et seq.
97:5	Leek PL: M/F St. Edmund's parish registers.

97:6	i) See in particular St. Mary the Virgin Church, Wirksworth.
	ii) *Boswell's Life of Johnson passim.*
98:2-99:1	i) Derby LS: 4467: *The Universal Magazine* for October 1748 pp. 147-8.
	ii) Derby LS: *History of Derby* (1826) contains an account written by 'Mr. Woolley in 1712' including St. Michael's parish.
	iii) Williamson F. *George Sorocold of Derby* (1926) pp. 59-64.
99:2-103:2	i) Derby LS: The several versions of the story and full details of the silk mill are catalogued in this library.
	ii) Mercers Hall, Irongmonger Lane, London. Records show Thomas Lombe as a freeman of company from 1707; Master 1727 and knighted same year 8th July; Alderman of Bassishaw Ward 1728 and Sheriff 1727-8. I am indebted to the achivist Anne F. Sutton for this information.
l03:4	Briggs, Asa, *A Social History of Engand* (1984): Coffee houses p. 207, illustration p. 242.
103:5-6	i) Wheeler Harold, (ed.) *The Wonderful Story of London* (1930s) pp. 451-4.
	ii) Mcr PL: notes in *The Holyhead Road* vol 2 and:-
	iii) 18th century county maps as appropriate.
103:7-104:5	i) William Salt Library, Staffs: Staffordshire Collns. Dr. Burney's Newspapers1710-27.
104:6	Moritz, C.P. *Journal of a Journey through England* (Germany 1783 reprint in English 1983) - Inn food.
105:1	Staffs. RO: D/603/K/5/2 quote from letter 11th May 1750 William Gibson to Lord Uxbridge.
105:2	i) Shrop. RO: D18093 - Roe pedigree devised by Henry Octavius Roe.
	ii) NA: Prob. 11/1301 - will Christopher Roe.
105:3	i) Wheeler op. cit. *passim* .
	ii) Ibid. p. 47-8.
106:1	Ibid. p.82 (Abbey) p.120 (Hall).
106:2	Ibid . p. 93.
106:3	i) Deeds 60B, 62 & 62A Chestergate (now known as Charles Roe House). I am indebted to the owner for sight of these.
	ii) CCALS: LBM 2039.
	iii) Chester PL: Adams *Weekly Courant* advert 25th Sept. 1752 and subsequent weeks.
l06:4	i) Feltwell, John, *The Story of Silk* (1990) p.22.
	ii) Wheeler, op. cit. p. 90-1.
	iii) Moritz, op. cit. Vauxhall & Ranelagh, see also *1764* ed. Jack Lindsay p.119.
106:6	i) Wheeler op. cit. p. 158 et seq. Guilds.
	ii) Guild. L: all extant Guild records checked i.e. Weavers, Pewterers, Founderers, Innholders, Silk throwsters and Haberdashers.
	I am grateful to the Secretary of the Drapers' Hall for assistance in checking its records and for the written information supplied by the archivist of the Mercers' Hall.
107:2	i) Guild. L: Rebuilding survey carried out on behalf of Chas. II after the Great Fire.
	ii) Dashwood, Sir Francis, *The Dashwoods of West Wycombe* (1987) p. 38
	iii) Wheeler, op. cit. p. 65 Barts Hosp. p. 63 Smithfield.
107:3	Ibid. p. 153.
107:4	Jordangate deeds in possession of author.
108:2	i) Stock. L: deed B/KK/5/30/6 Thomas Glover "of Prescott County Lancaster mercer', 4th Nov. 1701.
	ii) Guild. L: Sun Insurance records 15/465 year 1723 Thomas Glover M/cr.
	iii) See also 14/465 Thomas Dickenson, merchant M/cr. subleased his house to Thomas Glover and Henry Guest value £300 (1723).
108:3	Deeds for 18 Jordangate in possession of owners.
108:6	CCALS: LBM/1/2-3: the Macc. Corporation Minute books LBM/1/3 relates to 1734-1768, however LBM/1/2 also has some additional entries to 1744. At the back of LBM1/2/3, out of order, are some 'Admissions of Freemen' one of whom is Charles Roe "Admitted & sworn Gratis" on 8th Oct. 1742.

Chapter 7

Quotation:	Kipling (The Ballad of the King's Jest 1892).
110:1-2	*DNB*: Sir Thomas Lombe.
110:3	i) Maps: a) Stock. L: 1045 - 17th century Stockport.
	b) CCALS: DVE 3282 Stockport C. 1770.
	ii) Ches. RO: Acc. No. 1272 Deeds Stockport silk mill.
110:4	M/cr PL: M3/2/47.
110:5	IGI: Eyre - Elcocke Nantwich, Cheshire.
	ii) Lancs. RO: will T. Hadfield 28th Feb. 1752.
110:6-111:1	Ibid.
111:2	M/cr PL: C17.
111:3	*JHC*; Act II Geo II 9 MARTii 1737.
111:4	Earwaker, J.P. *East Cheshire* (1880) vol. II : Warren of Poynton.
111:5 -112:1	i) CCALS: Acc. no. 1272.
	ii) Goodway, Jill, A Dyer's Manual (1982).
	iii) Jenkins, J. Geraint, *The Welsh Woollen Industry* (Cardiff 1969): p.23.
112:1	CCALS: Acc.no.1272.
112:3 -112:6	i) Derby LS: notes on Bassano family.
	ii) Derby LS: M/F Parish registers.
113:3	JRL: Legh of Lyme colln. John Stafford letter.
113:4	G. M/cr CRO: C17 10/2 Thos. Eyre 1726.
114:3	Stock. L: plan of Park Mills 1842. For comparison of 1842 Stockport plan with the Derbysilk mill see chap.6.
114:4	i) Ball, J & W, *Stockport Grammar School* (1987): Joseph Dale.
	ii) CCALS: will Samuel Lankford 1760.
114:6-115:1	Porter, Lindsey, *Ecton Copper Mines* (2004) p.25.
115:2	Jordangate deed in possession of author (1788 William Roe).
115:4-116:1	i) Thomas Birtles: deeds 13th & 14th Feb. 1744 show Birtles paid £157 10s. for several dwellings including a shop, a barn, a building, several closes and "the other which when standing was known by the name of CLAPHAM HOUSE". It seems probable that Birtles had initially leased Clapham House, which was then partially demolished and 'modernised' by re- building the exterior. Although today Chatham St. exists close by, the deeds clearly refer to Clapham not Chatham House,which suggests someone misread the original name when selecting the one for the street.
	ii) JRL: Legh of Lyme colln. letter.
116:2	Ibid.
116:4	M/cr PL: C17.
116:5	Ches. RO: Macc. parish registers as appropriate.
116:7-117:2	i)Rieuwerts, J.H. *Mines of Derbyshire* (History & Gazeteer 1987) re: Brookhead Sough.
	ii) SCA: Bag C 587(70) re: Miners Engine and Moorwoods Engine.
117:3	JRL: Legh of Lyme colln. letter 8th Feb. 1743.
117:4	Ibid. Letter 17th Sept. 1743.
117:6	*Margate - A Recent History* (1736-1986), advert. p.4.
118:3	JRL: Legh of Lyme colln. Parson Parr, letter 17th Sept. 1743 and also letter 9th Aug. 1743.
118:4	Ibid. White, letter 17th Sept. 1743.
118:5	Ibid. Davenport, letter 9th Aug. 1743.
119:3	i) Shaw, William, *The Knights of England*, (London 1906).
	ii) JRL: Legh of Lyme colln. Letter 8th Oct. 1743.
119:4 -120:1	i) JRL: Bagshawe Muniments 13/3/180: will William Leese.
	ii) Ibid. 13/3/181: bond.
	iii) JRL: Bagshawe (Wormhill & Ford) letter 7th Oct. 1737.
120:2	Ibid.
120:3-4	i) Lich. JRO: Marriage licence 1743.
	ii) Ches. RO: will: William Hyde 1780.

120:6	i) Poorhouse: Mentioned in Abstract of Title (Arighi Bianchi & Co. deeds for Commercial Rd. in possession of owners) 12th & 13th Oct. 1780 as a building known as Methodists Old Chapel "which abutted on the south side to Macclesfield Poorhouse".
	ii) Ches. RO: 85/II/I St. Michael's Vestry Minutes 1685-1759 record on 10th Feb. 1757 "Present Poorhoufe shall with all convenient speed be enlarged for the use of the Poor of the Burrough of Macclesfield . .
121:4	i) Lancs. RO: 1551/20.
	ii) Leeds Dist. Arch: Radcliffe Mss. 121 (103/129) lease 5th May 1728.
121:5	Ches. RO: LBM 2039 c 1795 plan clearly shows watercourse between Parsonage Green and Waters Green.
122:4	i) Leeds Dist. Arch: Radcliffe Mss. Misc. Bundle 108 lease 4th Sept.1732.
	ii) Ches. RO: St. Michael's register, Macc. - Marriage 31st. Dec. 1732.
123:3	Jordangate deed 20th Oct. 1788 recites "the Ground . . . then lately divided into and used as three small Twisting Crofts but then and now converted into a Garden or Orchard" . . . In possession of author.
123:6 -124:3	For further reading re Lancashire textiles see:-
	i) Daniels G W. *The Early English Cotton Industry* (M/cr. Univ. Pr. 1920)
	ii) Wadsworth, A.P. & De Lacy, J. *The Cotton Trade & Industrial Lancashire 1600-1780.* (M/cr. Univ. Pr. 1931). N.B. this publication contains certain references which are of dubious origin e.g. p. 304 footnote 3, Warwickshire Journal , there was no such journal; p. 303 footnote 3, Crofton Ms. Clowes Deeds i 251 M/cr. Ref. Lib. this has also been impossible to trace.
	iii) Lankford: Information supplied by Alan Bednall.
	iv) JRL: Samuel Touchett & Co. correspondence 5th June 1761 et seq.
124:5 -133:3	The 'Bonnie Prince Charlie' episode has been taken from the following sources:-
	i) John Stafford's letters quoted by J.P.Earwaker in *East Cheshire* pp.34-9.
	ii) Creighton M. *Carlisle* (1889) copy Carlisle Ref. Library:-
	Johnston, Chevalier de, *Memoirs of the Rebellion in 1745/46* p.51 "John Hay who acted for a time as the Prince's Secretary states "there was a council of war held at Macclesfield . . . ".
	iii) Hannay, David, *A Short History of the Royal Navy 1689-1815* p. 122.
	iv) Dickenson family: Several references in M/cr. PL Local History & Archives, see in particular:-
	a) Swindells: M/cr. Street Series 2 pp. 208-11.
	b). M/cr. Directory 1788 Leary 942. 738. L4.
	v) Earl of Derby colln. Knowsley 470/31/16 Kettleshulme dispute.
	vi) John Stafford's letters op. cit.
	vii) Derby L S: Thompson Note Book no.4 Derby and the Scotch Rebellion of 1745 (Account taken from *History of England*, Knight & Co, 1841).
	viii) Wright family:' Wright of Derby' by W. Bemrose Jnr. in *The Reliquary* vol. IV.1863-64.
	ix) JRL: Legh of Lyme Mss. Ward letters.
	x) M/cr. PL: *Journey through England & Scotland* (pub. 1747) written by a soldier in the Duke of Cumberland's Army .(942. 075. VI.)

Chapter 8

Quotation:	Dr. S. Johnson, Prologue to *The Good-Natur'd Man* by O. Goldsmith.
134:1-2	i) Davies, C. Stella, (ed.) *History of Macclesfield* (1961).
	ii) Ibid, p.81.
134:3	CCALS: LBM/!/3.
134:4	i) CCALS: LBM/I/3, Stafford.
	ii) JRL: Legh of Lyme colln. Ward: letter 1744.
135:3	i) CCALS: Walter Smith notebooks uncatalogued N.B. No. 5 pp. 50-1 (extracts from Title deeds).
	ii) CCALS: St. Michael's register Macc.
135:4	JRL: Hester Ann Rogers Diaries, Blagg entry Thurs. 15th March 1781.
136:2	i) Walter Smith op. cit. p.29.
	ii) Ches. RO: will Hobson, Affidavit only 1743.

136:3   Macc. Library Local Hist. newspaper articles in Walter Smith file.

136:4   The Venetian window remains in Cumberland House, Jordangate, Macc.

136:6   i) I have attributed the alterations to Thomas Birtles because of details from the title deeds, held by the owner McMillan-Scott PLC. and circumstances pertaining at that time.
ii) JRL: 24/1/1 Misc. deeds and letter.

137:1   i) SCA: 1146 Oakes Deeds 1747.
ii) Walter Smith op. cit. No. 2, p.211 Rainow Hall.

137:3   i) Bingley Library; Atkinson Family History (dates verified with Troutbeck and Cumbria registers in Cu RO (K)).
ii) Cookson family of Newcastle-upon-Tyne, my thanks to P.W. King of Stourbridge for this information on their iron and lead interests in the Workington and Whitehaven area.

137:5   i) Ches. County Council: Modern Records, Jordangate Library deeds, Macc.
ii) Armstrong, J. *A History of Freemasonry in Cheshire* (1901) pp. 8-9.
iii) Ches. RO: SP3/15/6: Articles of Agreement, 28th May 1748.

137:6   i) Kendal Library; le Fleming family tree.
ii) Cu RO (K): D/12/108, D/13/111, Fleming's deeds and wills.

138:2-3   i) Cu RO (K): Atkinson family - several references in Index to Bound Manuscripts vols. I - XVI.
ii) Bingley Library, Yorks: Atkinson family indexed.
iii) Wilson, G.E. 'A History of the Macclesfield Grammar School', unpublished M. Ed. thesis 1952 (Leeds University), p.68 "One student . . . who attended St. John's College, Cambridge was a Thomas Swettenham, probably the son of a Governor who was admitted to the College as a pensioner in 1695".

138:4-5   Ibid. p.106.

139:1   i) Ibid. p.106.
ii) Cu RO (K): WD/Ry Box 85 Letter John Atkinson 17th Feb. 1752.
iii) Ibid. Letter, 6th April 1754 "The Sefsions here are on the 24th inst. . . . the Church of England".

139:2-5   i) SCA: Bag. colln. 587/58/17, see also 587/58/II which lists "Mr. Charles Roe" as receiving £25.
ii) SCA: Bag. colln. 587(47).

139:6 -140:1   Rieuwerts, J.H. *Mines of Derbyshire* (1987): Stoke Sough. See also:
SCA: Bag, colln. 587/58, dispute Stoke Sough A/c 5th Sept. 1748, "Due from Mr. Roe £1 10 0d."

140:2-3   i) Ibid. 587/I2. This clearly shows James Roe's signature on 12th Sept. 1754 "Rec'd the balance of these Accounts (Errors Excepted) by me".
ii) Ibid. 587/14 Old & New Bradshaw's.
iii) Ibid. 587/47/90.
iv) BL: Woolley Mss. and MLS: M/f 6696 p.10 et seq. Richard Bradshaw Esq. & Others V William Spence Esq. & Others.
v) Lich. JRO: wills: William Street 1733, Robt. Charlesworth 1735.

140:4-141:3   i) Chester City RO: CR63/2/341/72, letters of Tuition of Miss. Eliz. Davenport, 7th March 1747.
ii) CCALS: SP3/15/6 Old School House (1748-1871). SP3/19/4 Land, Back St. & Byron St. etc (1703-1870) see details of Agreement 28th May 1748.
iii) Ibid. SP3/I/2 - Petition to Parlt. 1744.

141:4   i) JRL: Legh of Lyme colln. letter 13th March 1756.
ii) UW Bangor; Plas Newydd Mss. VII.
iii) MM: 3025 27th Sept. 1762.
iv) Achify Llangefni, Anglesey; WDY/47.
v) M/cr PL: C17/3/20 Nicholson letter 1748.

141:5-6   i) Stock. L: M/f St. Mary's register.
ii) Mcr PL: C17/3/II3/I will Alice Nicholson.
iii) M/cr PL: C17/3/20

142:1-3   CCALS: will: Alex Elcock 1748.

142:5   Clapham, Sir John, *A History of the Bank of England* (1945).

143:1   Factory within a factory. A detailed example of this appears in Leonard Whiter's *Spode* (1978) p.38 & p.43.

143:2-3   i) Deductions regarding the buildings have been made by comparing the Stockport and Derby mills surveys.

ii) JRL: R67I67 Sermon: True Religion - Rev. J. Roe A.M.

143:4 -145:5 i) *JHC*; vol. XXX p.213 (1765).

ii) *The Silk Book* (The Silk & Rayon Users' Assn. London 1951):Reeling p.25.

iii) Ibid. chap.1.

iv) Ibid. chap.3.

147:3-6   i) Deeds 118 & 118A Mill St. Macc. seen at Natwest Bank by kind permission of the owner. These include a copy will of Joshua Mottershead, tallow chandler and soap maker.

ii) *The Silk Book* op. cit. Waste silk p.p.32-35.

147:7   Dyeing and trimming. I am grateful to Gene Burger M.A. Pittsburg, Penn. U.S.A. for this information.

148:2-4   i) *The Silk Book* op. cit. chap. 8.

ii) Silk Heritage Mills Survey:Turner's dyeworks.

iii) SL: B/LL/2/1/5

148:5   Leeds Dist. Arch.; Radcliffe Mss. Uncatalogued papers, Bundle 109, deed 1st May 1768.

148:6   Ibid. Huxley deeds 31st March 1752 & 1st June 1753.

149:2   Ibid. Bundle 108: Vardon deed 25th March 1743.

149:3   Ches. RO: LBM/1/3: Roe & Atkinson 30th Sept. 1748.

149:4   i) *Macc. Directory* 1825 p.46, "Having obtained a perfect model of the machinery employed in the silk mill in Derby he (Charles Roe) engaged a skilful mechanic, who erected a complete machine". Much of the information in the Directory is taken from *The History of Macclesfield*, J. Corry (1817) to which William Roe (son of Charles), Liverpool subscribed. Corry's information is not always accurate e.g. the date of commencement of Charles Roe's business on Parsonage Green was 1746 not 1756.

ii) Porter, Lindsey, *Ecton Copper Mines* (2004) p.26.

150:3-4   i) Leeds Dist. Arch: Radcliffe I, no.121 (103/129): Crooke, 29th Dec. 1736.

i) Queens Hotel, Waters Green, Abstract of Title - Tetley Walkers Brewery, Warrington.

ii) Leeds Dist. Arch.: Radcliffe 1, Misc. no. 259 Bundle 108 large deed 24th Oct. 1748.

ii) Ibid. George Grieves: No.I2I (I03/29) deed 13th Oct. 1718.

150:7-153:2 i) Op. cit. bundle 108 deed 24th Oct. 1748. Extract:

"that Brook Stream or Watercourse of him the said Joseph Pickford in Macclesfield in or near certain fields or parcels of land called the Eyes in possession of Thomas Vardon together with liberty to make erect upon or cross the said Brook Stream or Watercourse or otherwise any Ware (weir) or other devise whatsoever for the raising and impounding the Water ."

On all other property deeds within the area e.g. the Sunderland St. warehouse of Arighi Bianchi & Co. nowhere is the River Bollin mentioned by name, it is always referred to as" the Brook." Thomas Vardon, chapman of Macclesfield had leased a meadow close known as "the Eyes" from Pickford on 25th March 1743. This is described as situated at the eastern end of a messuage in possession of Urian Whilton, today the plot is occupied by the Sunderland St. surgery and other buildings overlooking the War Memorial Park on Park Green.

ii) CCALS: DDX 528/7/I/I. Plan of the Free Grammar School lands 1774: no. 4 refers to Halle Fields. Item Z clearly shows "Field next to Henry Verdon's House" and today this corresponds with the lower end of Brook St. on the opposite bank of the Bollin from George St.

iii) Wregelsworth, P. & Richardson, N. *The Pubs and Breweries of Macclesfield* (1990) no.2. p.9 quote "The Queen's Hotel was built on the site of a row of old cottages which in 1731 were sold to Edward Downes by Joseph Eccles". This deed is no longer with the current deeds held by Tetley Walker's Brewery, Warrington.

iv) CCALS: LBM 2039 Enclosure plan c. 1795/96.

v) Waters Green 1810 print held by Macclesfield Museum Trust, reproduced this chapter.

vi) Christ Church, Macclesfield: Charles Roe's monument.

vii) My thanks to H.J. Cookson, Managing Director of The Central Garage, Waters Green, for his help in allowing inspection of the property deeds and the site, and for other items of information.

153:3-154:1 i) Birk. PL: B/V/4, Land Tax 1756/57.

ii) Leeds Dist Arch: Pickford MSS. Uncatalogued papers, draft of marriage settlement c.1740.

iii) Duppa, R. (1816) *Life of Johnson* extracts from 'Tour in N. Wales'.

Chapter 9

Quotation: Robert Burns - First Epistle to Mr. Graham of Fintry.

156:1-3 Ches. County Council: Modern Deeds, HDT/7265. (See also deed CCALS: QDE 2/I7).

156:4 i) Earwaker, J.P. *East Cheshire* (1880) vol. II: p.442 Prestbury Parish.

Booklet: *Diocese of Shrewsbury 1851-1951* (Centenary Record):

"The faith in this part of Cheshire was kept alive by the owners of Suttton Hall until the eighteenth century when the 3rd. Earl of Fauconberg apostatized."

ii) Davies, C. Stella, *A History of Macclesfield* (1961) p.350.

157:1 SCA: Bag. colln. Book 500 Devonshire: 31st May 1766 'To Mr. Hadfield Sunday afternoon 10/6d'. also for 14th June 1766.

157:2 JRL: R 67I67 Sermon: True Religion.

157:3 i) CCALS: St. Michael's register.

ii) Eliz. Hooley married John Hulley, deed 23rd. Dec. 1737 for 27 Mill St. Macc. in possession of owners.

iii) CCALS: will Thomas Hooley 1745.

iv) JRL: Legh of Lyme colln. J. Roe letter 9th Aug. 1743. See also Chester City RO; Earwaker colln. CR63/2/34I - 'The Case of the Corporation of Macclesfield'.

157:5 *TL&CAS*; Chaloner, W.H. vol. LXII (1950/5I) part I p. 137.

159:2 The old reservoir site is reproduced on page 158 and taken from Ches. County Council Modern Deeds HDT/7265.

159:3 CCALS: St. Michael's register Macc.

159:4 i) Wilson, G.E. 'A History of the Macclesfield Grammar School 1503-1890', unpublished M. Ed. thesis 1952 (Leeds University).

ii) IGI Cheshire, Frances bapt. IIth Aug. 1749, 2nd. Frances bapt 9th Aug. 1757. John bapt. 23rd. July 1750 - no further mention.

159:5 i) Ches. RO: St. Michael's register.

ii) *Al Oxon.*; Rev. Ralph Nicholson.

159:6-160:1 i) Hancox, Joy, *Adlington Hall - A House and Its Family,* privately published. pp. 8-10 The Great Hall,

ii) 'Adlington Hall', *English Life Publication Ltd.* (1987).

160:4 *DNB*: Handel.

160:5 i) Hancox op.cit.

ii) Museum of Methodism, City Rd. London - Handel manuscripts.

160:6 i) *DNB*: Stanley (1714-1786).

ii) Hancox op. cit.

160:7-161:5 Adlington Hall (1987) op. cit.

161:6 Hall James, *A History of the Town & Parish of Nantwich* (1883), Davenport p. 303.

162:2 JRL: Legh of Lyme colln. Letter 9th Aug. 1743 from Rev. J. Roe to Peter Legh the Younger.

162:4-6 Derby LS: 4447 - *The Universal Magazine* October 1748. Also under this reference is 'A Short Tour in the Midland Counties of England - Summer 1772' which contains a mention of Matlock.

163:1 i) Hey, David, *Packmen Carriers and Packhorse Roads* (1980) p.I22.

ii) SCA: Bag. colln. John Barker Letter Books no. 494 II 1765-1811 - letter 24th Feb. 1774 to Rt. Hon. Lord George Cavendish, Berkley Squ. London.

163:2 i) Rhodes, J.N. 'Derbyshire Influences' . . . in *Peak Dist. Mines Hist. Soc.* vol.3 part 6 p.342 - Quaker Co.

ii) Rieuwerts, J.H. *Mines of Derbyshire* (1987) - Yatestoop.

163:6 i) MLS: Anthony Tissington mentioned in *A Walk Through Derbyshire* compiled by R. Simpson in 1827.

ii) MLS: Index. 6840 M/f 6696 Woolley: A. Tissington of Swanwick, Deputy Barmaster of Matlock.

iii) Ibid. Barmaster of Matlock 1738.

iv) Derby LS: Manuscript 253 - Rough terrier of Manor of Winster 1763.

164:1 Hornshaw, T.R. Copper Mining - Middleton Tyas (1975).

164:4   Glover, S. *History & Gazetteer of the County of Derby* (1831) vol.2 part I: Brassington pp. 169-173.

164:5   Robey, J.A. & Porter, L. *The Copper & Lead Mines of Ecton Hill, Staffordshire* (1972) p.19.

164:6   i) Map of Derby, Moneypenny 1791.

        ii) Liv. Univ: M.S. 7.I (22) Angerstein translation p.22.

        iii) Bradley, H.G. (ed.) *Ceramics of Derbyshire* 1750-1795.

165:1   *DNB*: John Gilbert-Cooper.

165:2   Hornshaw op. cit.

165:3   bid. Rev. Mawe.

165:5   i) Hornshaw op. cit. - Lady D'Arcy.

        ii) Sulphur - see later mining at Parys Mountain, Anglesey.

165:6-166:1   Hornshaw op. cit.

166:2   NYCAD: ZKU 2/10-44 - letter from Eaton.

166:4   i) My thanks to the Librarian of the Royal College of Organists for the information regarding theatre organs.

        ii) *DNB*: Handel.

166:5   i) NA: Prob 11/1000 - Will Joseph Stockdale 1774.

        ii) NA: Prob 11/1334 - Will John Roe 1800.

166:6-167:1   My thanks to the Archivist of the Bank of England for this information.

167:3   SCA: Bag. colln. 330 - letter 13th Sept. 1737.

167:5-6   The details of John Wesley's life can be found either at the City Road Museum, London or in the Wesley Collection at the John Rylands Library, Manchester.

167:7-168:2   Mc.Master, L. *A Short History of the Royal Parish of St. Martin's-in-the-Fields.* (1916).

168:4   My sincere thanks to Patrick Latham for discovering the discrepancy of the entry 'Bee' for 'Roe' in the parish register.

168:5   IGI.

168:6   Westminster City Archives; F2007 St. Martin's Vestry Minutes.

168:7   JRL: *Arminian Magazine* October 1783: Robert Roe p. 52I .

169:2   NA: Prob 11/1000 - Will Joseph Stockdale 1774.

169:4-5   i) Abstracts of Title in possession of each owner relating to the Red Lion Inn (now the Barnfield) Catharine St.; the former Albion Inn, Bridge St.; 60B, 62 and 62A Chestergate.

        ii) Chester PL: Adams *Weekly Courant.*

169:6   Ibid.

169:7   Abstracts of Title as above.

169:10   CCALS: St. Michael's register.

170:1   Abstracts of Title as above.

170:2   CCALS: LBM 2039 - plan of Macc. c.1804.

170:3   i) Leeds Dist. Arch: Radcliffe 121/103/129 deed 10th Sept. 1729.

        ii) CCALS: LBM 2039

        iii) CCALS: Acc 1128 Bd 5.

        iv) My thanks to Barclays Bank Ltd. for providing inspection of the I8th century deeds for the Park Green site and for permission to reproduce the relevant information; likewise to the Trustees of the United Reformed Church and their solicitor for the adjoining plot of land.

        v) Deeds 60B,62 and 62A Chestergate .

172:3-4   Lancs. RO: will T. Hadfield 1753.

        N.B. 1752 - in order to make the English calendar agree with that of most European countries, and with calculations made by astronomers, 11 days were removed from the year. The day after 2nd. September became 14th instead of the 3rd. New Year's Day had been taken as the Quarter Day 25th March, but now it became 1st. January. The Treasury, obviously wishing to avoid complicated calculations with regard to finances, chose to retain the 11 days, and so the Inland Revenue year end became the 5th April, which it has remained to this day.

172:5   CCALS. RO: will G. Nicholson 1756.

172:7   Town Hall Macc. List of Mayors.

173:2   i) Boswell's *Life of Samuel Johnson* (1926) pp.94-99.

ii) Several deeds relating to Macclesfield Park contain Abstracts of Title relating to the Earl Rivers inheritances and specifically except "the Chapel called Earl River's Chapel adjoining the Parochial Chapel of Macclesfield & the Sanctuary or Burial Ground under the same And all benefit and advantage of them."

173:3   Chester City RO: Earwaker CR63/2/341.
173:4   CCALS: DCHI - I84, Rental of Rock Savage Estate 1775.
174:2   CCALS: 85/I0/I St. Michael's Churchwarden Accounts 1686-1751.
174:3   Cu. RO (K): WD/Ry/Box 9I Coniston Copper Mine Lease 13th Sept.1765.

Chapter 10

Quotation: Mineralogia Cornubiensis, Dr. Garth's Dispensary p.112.
175:1   Cu. RO (K): WD/Ry/Box 20 - letter 9th Dec. 1754.
175:4   i) Ibid. Box 2I - lease 29th June 1748.
                ii) Cu. RO (C): D/PEN/Bundle 46.
175:5   i) Holland, E.G. *Coniston Copper* (1986) - Vipone p.6I. See also:-
                Cu.RO (K): WD/Ry/Box78 - letter 6th July 1754.
175:6-176:2   Ibid.
176:3   i) Holland op.cit. site details only.
                ii) Morton, John. *Thomas Bolton & Sons Ltd.* (1783-1983) p.15.
176:4   i) Indenture 12th March 1767 recites all previous deed including 12th July 1755. Documents held in a chest on premises of T. Bolton & Sons Ltd. Cheadle, Staffs, (owned by BICC Group of Companies since 1961).
                ii) N.L.W: RS I5I0IA et seq.- Cornish Ore Sales 1728 et seq.
176:5   Stock.L: B/LL/2/I/22 - deed 5th March 1754.
176:6   Truro RO: St. Euny Register.
177:2   Lewis W.J. *Lead Mining in Wales* (1967): Industry 1568-1690.
177:3-4   Information taken from the following sources:
                a) Barton, D.B. *A History of Copper Mining in Cornwall & Devon* (1967).
                b) Pryce, William, *Mineralogia Cornubienses* (1778): Introduction.
                c) Ibid chap 9 - The history of the copper, brass and bronze industry.
                d) Hornsby, Peter, *The Arthur Negus Guide to British Pewter, Copper and Brass*.
177:5   i) Donald, M.B. *Elizabethan Copper* (1955 repub.1989): Smythe pp.66-72.
                ii) Ibid. Frosse p.354.
177:6   Barton op. cit.: Coster (also mentioned in *Bristol Brass,* Joan Day 1973).
177:7   Morris, Chris. (ed.) *The Journeys of Celia Fiennes 1685-1712* (1982). pp. 205-206.
178:2   Mitchell, Frank, *Annals of an Ancient Town Redruth* : 1700 (1978).
178:5   Pryce op.cit. Introduction.
178:6   i) Corn CRO: DD EN/I69I - Copper accounts 1731-1775 North Downs Adventure (Dolcoath, Cambourne).
                ii) Mitchell op.cit.
                iii) Mines as recorded in notebook M.S.I5I0IA N.L.W.
179:2   Mitchell op. cit. 1740-47.
179:4   i) Corn. CRO: St. Euny registers.
                ii) Corn. CRO: will Francis Michell 24th April 1755, also copy will and documents relating to Admininstration 19th Sept. 1764.
179:5   IGI; Dickenson Family.
180:1-3   Pryce op.cit. Chapter: Discovery of Mines - Tin Mine.
180:4-7   i) Mitchell op.cit. 1726 - Ticketing.
                ii) Pryce op.cit. Table of Sales following Introduction.
                iii) Ibid. Chapter IV (p.287).
                iv) Mitchell op.cit.
                v) Pryce op.cit. Chapter IV.

	vi) Ibid. p.288.
181:2-182:1	i) Ibid. Sampling: Dressing copper & lead ores - Plate VI.
	ii) Ibid. p.288.
	iii) Ibid. Chapter: To Assay Copper Ore - Plate VI.
	iv) Mitchell op.cit. Crucibles 1760.
	v) Pryce op.cit. Chapter: Assaying - section Copper Ores.
	vi) Ibid. see Process XIV
182:2	Ibid. p.288 "Of the Sales of Copper Ores".
182:3-5	i) Ibid. pp 62-64 - description of Cornish Ores.
	ii) Whitten, D.G.A. & Brooks J.R.V. *The Penguin Dictionary of Geology* (1972): see Appendix: Table of Minerals. Comparison made with present day geological surveys of the area and descriptions.
183:1-2	Birk. PL: B/V/5.
183:3	Birk. PL: B/V/4.
183:4-8	Comparison between the previous two land tax returns for 1743 and 1756.
184:3	Marks & Spencer deeds with owners.
184:4	i) Jenkins, J. Geraint, *The Welsh Woollen Industry* (1969 Cardiff) p.II quote: "The custom of collecting urine from the homes of a district was well-known in many part of Wales until the end of the nineteenth century. In the Llanbryn-Mair district of Montgomeryshire urine was collected daily on behalf of a number of textile manufacturers. This was carried to the mill in a cask placed on a cart. In Cardiganshire too, It was customary for a man to gather urine from house to house and dispose of it to the fullers".
	ii) CCALS: LNW 9/7 - Copperas 1761: 29th July 8 hogsheads 8tons 1cwt. 5th Aug. 3 hogheads 1ton 10cwts. 19th Oct. 2 hogsheads 2tons 2cwts. All consigned to Thomas Ryle.
185:1	Marshall, J.D. & Davies-Shiel M. *Industrial Archeology of the Lake Counties* (1969) p.92 map.
185:4	Cu. RO (K): WD/Ry Box 80 - letter 1st. Aug. 1756 from J. Robinson to Sir William. Letter 30th July 1756 from Philip Harland to Sir William.
185:5	Durrant, David, *Bess of Hardwick* (reprint 1988) pp.80-8I.
	Morris op. cit. p108.
	Pilkington, J. *A View of the Present State of Derbyshire* (1789) pp.213-215.
185:7-186:2	Cu. RO (K): WD/Ry Box 91.
186:3	CCALS: LBM/I/3.
186:5	Cu. RO (K): WD/Ry Box 22 - letter 21st. Feb. 1766 R. Barber to John Moore. The locations are according to *Coniston Copper & History* by Eric G. Holland (1986) p. 63. As a geologist he has worked on the site. According to *Memoirs of the Geological Survey* vol XXX, Copper ores of the Midlands, Wales, The Lake District and the Isle of Man (Dewey & Eastwood p. 62) "the nomenclature of the veins is confused as workmen at different periods of the history of the mines have applied different names to the same vein and have given lode-names already in use to other lodes". This, however, does not confuse the observations on site where the earlier workings can be established because of the different mining techniques prevalent at different periods.
186:6-7	Tyson, Blake, 'Coniston Forge' in *Trans. of Cumberland & Westmorland Ant. & Arch. Soc.* vol. LXXXIX (1989).
187:1	Cu. RO (K): WD/Ry Box 85 - letter 15th Apr. 1750 from H.M. Hulme to Sir William.
187:2	Ibid. Box 22 - letter of authority.
187:4	Dr. Leigh - copy M/cr. PL.
187:5	SCA: Bag. C 383 - John Hale's "Stopadge Notes" Miners Engine 1741-47.
	SCA: Bag. C 587/58 - 17.
187:6	SCA: Bag. C 587 - 14.
187:7	Cu. RO (K): WD/Ry Box 113 - see summary at the end of accounts book and further details within accounts.
188:1	Holland op.cit. p. 6I - use of gunpowder.
188:2	Crocker, Gladys, *The Gunpowder Industry*, Shire pubs. (1986); see also *Mining History*- Bull. of the Peak Dist. Hist. Soc. vol.13 no.4 Winter 1997 pp. 24-43.
188:3	Croker op.cit.

188:4	Robey, J.A. & Porter, L. *The copper & Lead Mines of Ecton Hills, Staffordshire* (1972). pp.17-19.
188:5	IGI; Roose family.
189:1	i) Lich. JRO: will, Richard Roose 1697.
	ii) Lich. JRO: will, John Roose 1739.
	iii) BL: Woolley MSS. Folio 395 1745.
	iv) NLW Powis Colln. catalogue see in particular 3966 - letter from J. Paynter to Lord Powis 1st. Dec. 1757.
189:2	i)IGI & parish registers.
	ii)UW Bangor: Kinmel I808 - Deposition of J. Roose 18th Jan. 1775.
189:5	Lich. JRO: will Thomas Roe, Ballidon 1717. It is necessary to mention this Roe family because on occasion historians have erroneously concluded that a Thomas Roe of Parwich was the father of Charles Roe.
190:2	i) Crocker op.cit. p.21.
	ii) For the various methods used see W. Hooson, *Mines Dictionary* (Wrexham 1747) under Blasting etc.
	iii) Cockshutt, E. (1965) *Archaeologia Cambrensis* vol.CXIV p.99 et seq.
190:3	Brinlow Mine, Alderley Edge worked by Roe & Co. - per the DerbyshireCaving Club the 18th century workings are an excellent example of the company's mining techniques.
190:4	Misra, G.B. *Surface Mining* (1979) Section: Blasting.
190:5	Hooson op. cit.
190:7	*Future of Non Ferrous Mining in Great Britain and Ireland* (1959).
191:1	CCALS: LNW 9/7 - River Weaver Tonnage Accounts Book.
191:2	i) Tyson op. cit. p.202.
	ii) Cu. RO (K): WD/Ry Box 80 - letter William Rigg to Sir William 30th June 1749, "Yesterday I met with ye Master of a Ship bound for Dublin an According to Lady Fleming's request enquired ye price of feathers he says the best are Seven Shillings per stone the Duty threepence besides some Charge of Entry." There are also several entries in the Coniston 'Stone Quarries' accounts for William Rigg.
191:4	CCALS: LNW 9/7.

Chapter 11

Quotation:	Bible - Genesis 19 v.26.
192:1-4	JRL: Legh of Lyme colln. - letter 20th Aug. 1752 J. Roe to Peter Legh theYounger.
	a) For an example of a pew included in deeds see Ind. 1st. March 1804 Natwest Bank site Market Place, Macc. viz. "All that Dwelling house . . . and also the lowest seat but one in the second per from the front on the north side of the south alley going to the chancel in the Parochial Chapel of Macclesfield."
	b) St. Michael's register 8th Sept. 1771, " Harry Lankford Esq. bought from William Brookshead Esq. "3 Highermost seates in the I6 pews from the front on the right hand side of the middle aisle."
	c) *Macclesfield Courier & Herald* Sat. 30th July 1831, "Property to be sold by auction LOT V - A large and commodious Pew or Seat adjoining the South Aisle in the Parish Church of Nantwich . . . late in the occupation of the said William Sprout."
	d) St. Nicholas's, Liverpool - see notes on rebuilding begun 1775 in the Introduction to *Ancient Churches of the Liverpool Diocese* by Chas. Budden (1929).
	e) St. Edmund's church, Castleton in Derbyshire still contains pews with carvings on their doors; some on the north side of the nave bear the names of occupiers in the late 17th century.
	f) Mc. Master G.L (1916) *A Short History of the Royal Parish of St. Martin's -in-the-Fields.*
192:5-193:1	JRL: Legh of Lyme colln. - letter 20th Aug. 1752 J. Roe to Peter Legh the Younger.
193:4	CCALS: St. Michael's register: both sons were buried 2nd. Feb. 1755.
193:5	JRL: Legh of Lyme colln.
193:6	i) SCA: Bag.C587(12) 'Mr. Roe Mineral Acct Ending 29th June 1754".
	ii) Ibid. 584(14) 3rd Sept. 1755.
193:7-194:2	JRL: Legh of Lyme colln.
194:3	JRL: Hester Ann Rogers diary.
194:4	Deeds: Tetley Walker Brewery, Warrington.

194:5-6	Birk. PL: B/V/4 - Macc. Survey: Land Tax 1756/57.
194:7	CCALS: LBM/I/3 - tollage.
197:2	Hornsby, Peter, *The Arthur Negus Guide to Pewter, Copper and Brass* (1981) p.99.
197:4	Christ Church, Macc. Charles Roe monument inscription.
198:2	NMGM: 335 H2 Articles.
198:3	CCALS: LBM/I/3 .
198:6	Saville, J.P. *Iron & Steel* (World Resources 1976).
200:2-7	*Source Book on Copper & Copper Alloys.* ASM Engineering Bookshelf. (pub. 1979 by the American Society for Metals).
	Further information provided by BICC Cheadle, Staffs. (Goode) to whom I am indebted for a copy of *Thomas Bolton & Sons* 1783-1983 by J Morton.
200:9	i) Swedenborg (1734) copy in JRL.
	ii) Liv. Univ. Archives Ms.7-I (22). Rhys Jenkins collection, copies of the translation from the Angerstein Diary.
201:3-4	Pryce, William, *Mineralogia Cornubiensis* (1778 reprint 1972).
202:3-203:2	i) Science Library, London - Patents.
	ii) Ducret, Siegfried, *The Colour Treasury of 18th century Porcelain* (1976).
	iii) Price op.cit. p.31 - china clay.
203:4-5	i) Ibid. Chapter 2.
	ii) Ingpen, Roger (1907) Extracts from Boswell's *Life of Johnson* - year 1783.
203:6-204:1	Price op. cit. Chapter 2.
204:6-7	*Manchester Mercury* 20th Oct. 1801 - Sale by auction notice.
204:8	CCALS: QDE 2/10.
205:3	Saville op.cit. pp.14-15.
205:6-206:1	Derby. RO: D664/M/E3.
206:2	*Geological Survey of Great Britain* (H.M.S.O. 1968) pp. 263-264.
206:3	i) Glover, S. *Peak Guide*. (1830). Intro. vii.
	ii) Knowsley: Earl of Derby colln. 470/3/I5.
206:4	*O.E.D.* Cord-wood.
206:6	Hey, David, *Packmen, Carriers and Packhorse Roads*. (1980) chap.4.
207:1	Phillips, D. Rees, *History of the Vale of Neath* (1925) p. 267 - Frosse letter 7th March 1586.
207:2	JRL: Bromley Davenport colln. Box5/17.
207:3	Stanley, Hon. L.D. *Alderley Edge and its Neighbourhood*. (1843).
207:4	Ches. City RO: CR63/2/4I/3 - copy will E. Stanley 1750.
208:3	*TL&CAS*, 1901 vol. XIX pp. 106-109, 'Mining at Alderley Edge'- see references in footnotes.
209:3-210:3	i) Price op. cit. Chapter 2.
	ii) Day, Joan, *Bristol Brass* (1973) Chapter 3.
210:4-7	i) *Source Book on Copper & Copper Alloys* op. cit.
	ii) West, E.G. *Copper & its alloys.* (1982).
	iii) Information from BICC, Cheadle, Staffs.

Chapter 12

Quotation:	Shakespeare.
211:1	BL: Add. Mss. 42,160 Powys Diaries vol. 1.
212:1	Harrisburg Archives, Pennsylvania; M/f: ladings of Baynton, Wharton & Morgan. I am indebted to Gene Burger for bringing these to my attention.
212:5-7	JRL: Legh of Lyme colln. Box B box 1 Bundle of old deeds 1707-1799, Brian Hodgson's estate, Disley.
212:8	*VCH*; Staffs. pp. 215-216.
213:2	William Salt Library Staffs; Alcock family papers and genealogy.
213:3	NA: Admin T. Alcock 1741.
213:5	i) Derby. RO; 1288 M/L219.
	ii) Rieuwerts, J.H. *History & Gazetteer of the Leadmine Soughs of Derbyshire* (1987) p. 41.

213:6	Dev. C: Deeds.
214:2	JRL: Legh of Lyme colln.- letters B. Hodgson to R. Orford 1772 & 1777.
214:3	Chester PL - newspaper.
214:4	Cu. RO (K): WD/Ry/Box 85.
214:5	Dev. C: Alex. Barker accounts.
214:6	Buxton Library - Notes on Buxton Baths including:-

a) Axon, E. *Historical notes on Buxton, its Inhabitants and Visitors* (1948). - 1766 letter Mrs. Delaney to Duchess of Portland; 1750 letter from Mrs. Stapleton re: Bishop of St. Asaph etc.

b) For further references see *Buxton under the Duke of Devonshire*, G. Heape (1948) and Keele Univ. Library; Wedgwood Archives. - Devonshire footnote in letter from Burslem 28th May 1764.

215:1-216:2	i) Pilkington, J. A *View of the present State of Derbyshire* (1789) - Buxton Baths pp. 211-222.

ii) Morris, Chris. Ed. *The Illustrated Journeys of Celia Fiennes 1685-c.1712.* (1982) p. 108.

iii) Axon. op. cit.

iv) Pilkington op. cit. p.222.

v) Cu. RO (K): WD/TE/Box16/16 - A Buxtonian Expedition.

216:4	i) MLS: M/F 6696 fol.81-85 - Woolley.

ii) Dev. C: Barmaster's records, copy Indenture.

217:1	JRL: Legh of Lyme Box 1 - late B. Hodgson's Estate Disley, deed 6th Aug.1757.
217:4-5	i) CCALS: SP/3/I/2 - see also 'Some Aspects of Education in Cheshire in the 18th century' , D. Robson, in *Chetham Soc.* (M/cr.1966) vol. XIII.

ii) *Stockport Grammar School* (1487-1887), James & William Ball: Dale.

218:1	CCALS: will: Joseph Dale 1760.
218:2	CCALS: will: Samuel Lankford 1760.
218:3	CCALS: Register St. Peter's, Prestbury.
218:4	*TL&CAS*, vol. LXII (1950-51) Part 1 p. 137 H. Lankford cited as in the parish of Mottram Andrew by W.H. Chaloner.
218:5	i) *JHC*; vol. XXX 1765 p. 213 col.1.

ii) Staffs. RO: 1/4/3/47 - quote from property deed 13th Aug. 1773.

218:6-219:1	CCALS: will Samuel Lankford 1760.
219:2	CCALS: uncatalogued Walter Smith Notebook No.5 p.23.
219:3	i) Regr. of Admissions Middle Temple.

ii) Hughes, J. *Liverpool Banks and Bankers 1760-1837.* (1906) chap. VI.

iii) Picton vol. II p.148 no. 19 Paradise St.

iv) CCALS: Regr. St. Peter's, Prestbury.

219:4	Chesterfield PL: G. Heathcote colln.- Robert Shore letters.
219:5	Derby RO: Regr. All Saints, Derby.
220:2	JRL; Brooke of Mere colln. - Lowerhouse.
220:3-4	i) Macc B.C: C1/854 1951 plan.

ii) CCALS: D.S.A. 206 Nether Alderley.

220:5	Robey, J.A. & Porter L. *The Copper & Lead Mines of Ecton Hill, Staffordshire* (1972) p.21.
222:1-2	Chatsworth House Guide Book 1984.
222:4-223:1	i) MLS: Woolley Mss. M/f 6696 Portaway 1760. Mentioned by Robey & Porter op. cit. p. 21.

ii) NLW: Powis colln. 3966.

223:2	Ibid.
223:4	Shrine, H. *Two Tours Through Wales* 1798 pp. 203-204.
223:5	*BLG.*
223:6-224:1	Lewis, W.J. *Lead Mining in Wales* (1967) : Myddleton.
224:2	UW Bangor: Penrhyn Mss. 1643-56.
224:3	i) Shrine op. cit. p.211.

ii) Stock.L: B/KK/5/30/12 Deed 9th April 1773 including marriage settlement for T. A. Smith.

iii) UW Bangor: Penrhyn 1657.

224:4	Ibid.
224:5	NLW: Powis 3331 & 3907.

225:2	ibid 1290.
	Dev. C: H (3/2) 'Mr. John Roos's Plan'.
	Ibid. Rotton letter.
225:4	*DNB.*
225:5-226:1	Cu RO (K): WD/Ry/Box 113 Coniston A/c. Book.
	CCALS: LNW 9/6 & 9/7.
226:2	Ibid. Calamine 9/7.
226:3-227:1	Cu RO (K): WD/Ry/Box 22 - letter 2nd June 1760.
	Cu RO (C): D/PEN/46/90-99 - Tilberthwaite.
	Cu RO (K): WD/Ry/Box 22 - letter 21st Feb. 1766.
	Ibid. Letter 28th Oct. 1760.
	Ibid. Draft letter and repair bills.
	Ibid. Bailiff 1755.
	Collingwood, W.G. 'The Keswick and Coniston Mines' in *Trans. of Cumberland & Westmorland Ant. & Arch. Soc.* vol. XXVIII New Series 1928 pp.31-32.
227:2-228:1	Rogers, Col. H.C.B. (O.B.E.) *The British Army of the Eighteenth Century,* (1977) pp. 86-88.
228:2	CCALS: DCH/FF/13 - Enclosure.
228:5	D.N.B.
228:6-229:3	CCALS: DCH/FF/13 - letters 10th Nov. 1761 & 7th July 1762.
229:4	Robey & Porter op. cit. p. 67.
	Hey, D. *Packmen, Carriers and Packhorse Roads* (1980) p.155.
230:2	M.G.S. vol. XXX 'Copper Ores of the Midlands' . . . (1925) p.27.
230:3-5	Dev. C: Roe & Co. A/cs. for 'Copper ore taken up at Ecton Mine' 1761-67.
	Dev. C: Boothby Estates Indenture.
230:6-231:2	Clapham, Sir John, *The Bank of England* (1945).
231:3	Dev. C: op. cit Roe & Co. A/cs.
231:4	NA: Prob 11/976 - E. Pitts 1772.
231:6-232:1	i) Campbell, R. *The London Tradesman* (1747) p. 256 & 200.
	ii) Westmoreland County Hist. Soc. U.S.A.; Pins and information from the archaeological site of Hanna's Town, Pennsylvania.Harrisburg Archives; M/f Fort Pitt Day Book containing invoices from Barton, Wharton & Morgan (photocopies held by author). My thanks to Gene Burger for her hospitality and information during my visit.
232:2	i) Science Library, London: Patents.
	ii) Whitlock, P. & Pearce, W. *H.M.S. Victory & Admiral Lord Nelson* (booklet N.D. circa 1990) p.3: Copper.
	iii) NMGM: Plantation Books May 1765-December 1773.

Chapter 13

Quotation:	Elegy - Thomas Gray.
233:1	UW Bangor: The Bodvel Purchase part V - Early books in the hands of Samuel Wright of Nether Knutsford, associated with the Asshetons 1750-60s.
233:2	i) UW Bangor: Porth-yr-Aur 30679.
	ii) *MGS;* vol. XXX 'Copper Ores of the Midlands' . . . pp. 48-49.
233:2-4	Hubback, David, 'Time and the Valley' in *Caernarvonshire Hist. Soc. Trans.* vol. 35 1974 p.66: honestones. Also in same volume: Bassett, T.S. 'Diwysiant yn Nuffryn Ogwen' pp.73-77 - my sincere thanks to Mair Roberts of Merthyn, Henllan for her translation. (N.B. On p.75 Bassett states that in 1782 Roe & Co. carried out a test at Drws-y-Coed, this is incorrect, it was Thomas Williams of Anglesey.).
234:1-2	i) Ibid.
	ii) UW Bangor: Porth -y-Aur 30662.
	iii) Williams, William, *Observations on the Snowdon Mountains* (1802) p.64.
234:3	UW Bangor: Porth-y-Aur 30663.

234:4-235:2   CCALS: LNW 9/7 & 9/10.

235:3-236:1   i) NLW: Powis 3318, 3926, 3907.

           ii) UW Bangor: Porth-y-Aur 30665.

236:2   i) Ibid.

           ii) NLW: Powis 3318.

236:3-4   i) UW Bangor: Porth-y-Aur 30665.

           ii)NLW: Powis 30I6.

236:5   Caernarfon RO; Gwynedd Archives Service: Llanberis.

236:6   Dev. C: Ecton Mine A/cs.

236:8   *JHC*: vol.XXX appendix pp.215-219 (4th March 1765).

237:1   Ibid. pp.208-215.

237:2   *TL&CAS*; vol. LXII (Part I) p. I38 - Royal Depot Mills Mss.

237:4   *JHC*; vol. XXX pp.217-218 - figures.

237:5   *TL&CAS*; ibid. p.137 - W.H. Chaloner footnote.

237:7-238:1   Derby. RO: D664/M/E3.

238:3   JRL: Box XI/7 (1761) - House deed.

239:1   Staffs RO: D6I6/I - Brazier's A/c. Book (C.1768-9) and miscellaneous receipts for tinning etc. in the G. Heathcote uncatalogued colln. Chesterfield Public Library.

239:3-4   Bradfield, N. *Historical Costumes of England 1066-1968* (reprint 1977).

239:5-7&9   Delieb, Eric, *The Great Silver Manufactory* (1971).

240:1   Directories kindly supplied by Birmingham & Midlands Institute, Margaret St. Birmingham.

240:2   Ibid. 1770 p.72.

240:3-4   CCALS: deed D 174.

240:6-241:4   Harrisburg Archives - Fort Pitt Day Books - M/f & notes held by Westmoreland County Hist. Soc. U.S.A.

241:6-242:1   Library of the Hist. Soc. of Western Pennsylvania, Pittsburg U.S.A. - Finney notes and references held.

242:4   Birm. PL: Matthew Boulton Letter Book 1775-1778: 29th June 1775.

242:5-243:1   i) Notes from Gene Burger, Pittsburg U.S.A.

           ii) Hutton, W. *The History of Birmingham* (6th Edn. 1835) pp.17I-174: Buttons.

243:2   *JHC*; vol.XXX p.217.

243:3   Stock. L: M/f - parish registers of St. Mary's etc.

243:4   Birm. PL: Matthew Boulton pprs.- letter from J. Watt I6th Aug. 1785 p.2.

243:5-244:1   Staffs. RO: DW I909/A/8/I-I0.

244:2-3   Cowie, L.W. *Eighteenth Century Europe* (1963 reprint 1966) p.232.

244:4   i) NA: Prob 11/1000, will Joseph Stockdale 1774.

           ii) CCALS: 11/3 & 11/4 Northwich Tonnage of Up-Goods, see in particular I6th Dec. 1771 and 11th March 1774.

245:4-6   i)*The Journal of John Wesley* (Epworth Press 1960) - Sun. I0 th May 1747; Tues. 24th April 1759; Sun. 22nd March 1761.

           ii) Visits to America 16th August to 12th September 1737.

246:2   Alderley Edge: Brinlow Sough begun to unwater the Engine Vein has the inscription on the wall 'I. W.' Information from Derbyshire Caving Club.

246:3   Rhodes, J.N. 'Derbyshire Influences' . . . in *Bulletin of the Peak Dist. Mines Hist. Soc.* 1968 vol.3, part 6, p.348.

246:4   SCA: Bag. C 43IA. (1763-74).

246:5   Pilkington, J. *A View of the Present State of Derbyshire* (1789) vol. 1, chapter IV, section III p. I42.

246:6-7   SCA: Bag. C. 43IA (1763-74).

246:8-247:1   NLW: Powis 3318.

247:2   UW Bangor: Penrhyn Du leases 3554-3560.

247:4-5   i) JRL: Bromley-Davenport colln. no. 27- Estates of Earl of Uxbridge, 18th century.

           ii) *Burke's Peerage*: Anglesey - Marquis of.

247:6-7   Jackson-Stops Gervase, Plas Newydd 'A Property of the National Trust' in *Country Life* for 24th June, 1st July & 16th Sept. 1976: also 4th Aug. 1977.

248:1	UW Bangor: Plas Newydd Mss.- Caroline Bayly's letter 18th Aug. 1750.
248:2-4	UW Bangor: Penrhyn Du leases 3554-3560.
248:5	i) Fuller, T. *Histories of the Worthies of England* (1662) Nuttal Edition London 1840 as quoted in *Lead Mining in Wales* by W.J. Lewis (1969).
	ii) NLW: Powis 402 & 943.
248:6-249:1	i) M/cr. PL: Walker M9/40/2/22 (1770); M/CI28 (25th July 1760); M159/1/21/11; M159/1/46/8.
	ii) Derby LS: Derby Mercury 11th Feb. 1780; 29th Jan. 1760 (dissolution of partnership between Walker and Simpson).
249:2-3	UW Bangor: Penrhyn Du leases 3554-3560.
249:4	NLW : Powis 3I45.
249:5	UW Bangor: Mona Mine 3534 & Penrhyn Du leases 3554-3560.
249:6	NLW: Powis 3021.
250:2-4	Bode, Harold, *James Brindley* (1716-1772). Shire Pub.Ltd.1973.
250:5	Institution of Civil Engineers, London, no. 3461 J. Brindley notebook 1755-58. Birm. PL; J. Brindley notebook 1759-63. See also *Pitt's History of Staffordshire* (1817) pp.429-435.
250:6	Chaloner op. cit. p.145.
251	Roe's Sermons pub by A. Ward, Coney St., York, 1766, (copy with author).

Chapter 14

Quotation:	Bible - Kings 7 v.I4.
252:2-3	Lindsay, Jack, Ed. *1764*, (1959) p.104.
252:4	i) *JHC*: XXX pp.216-218.
	ii) Chaloner, W.C. 'Charles Roe of Macclesfield', in TL&CAS vol. LXII (part 1) p.138.
252:5-253:2	Inscription Brinlow Sough and other mining details per Derbyshire Caving Club.
253:3	i) Cu. RO (K): W/DRy Box113 - A/cs. of copper ore weighed at Coniston.
	ii) CCALS: LNW 9/8 - copper ore consignments on Weaver 1764.
	iii) Dev. C: Ecton a/cs.
253:4-5	NYCAD: ZAW 117-118 - Clifton Castle Archive.
254:2	SCA: Bag. C. 431A - Gorsey Dale.
254:3	Farey, John Snr. *Agriculture and Minerals of Derbyshire* (1811) vol. 1 p.259. Toadstone in O.E.D.
254:6	Street, A. & Alexander, W. *Metals in the Service of Man* (10th Edn. 1995) - Zinc pp. 178-182.
254:7-255:1	i) JRL: Swedenborg p. 343. I am grateful to Mrs. Margaret Birch for the English translation from the Latin of the process.
	ii) Liv. Univ. Library: M.S.7.I (22)28. - Angerstein.
255:4-5	Day, Joan, *Bristol Brass* (1973).
255:6	i) Ibid. Chapter 3.
	ii) NA: 1433/1, 1436/1, Chester City Port Books, Black Jack 11th Nov. 1759; 25th Jan. 1762 & 6th March 1762 etc.
255:7-256:6	i) Angerstein op. cit.
	ii) Delieb, E. & Roberts, M. *The Great Silver Manufactory* (1971) *passim*..
256:9	Angerstein op. cit. pp.1-2 of translation.
258:1	Ibid.
258:2	Hornsby, Peter, *The Arthur Negus Guide to British Pewter, Copper & Brass* (1981) p. 97, 100-101.
258:3	Day op. cit. p.76.
258:5-259:4	i) Morton, John, *Thomas Bolton & Sons Limited 1783-1983* (1983) p.14.
	ii) Some information kindly supplied by A.P.Woolrich.
259:5	i) Angerstein op. cit.
	ii) M/cr. PL:*The Holyhead Road vol.II* . Birmingham to Holyhead, Wednesbury registers.
259:6	Day op, cit. Chapter 2.
259:7	Morton op. cit.
259:9	CCALS: St. Michael's parish register.
259:10	Porter, Lindsey, *Ecton Copper Mines*, (2004) p.31 - David Malampy.

260:3-5	CCALS: QDN 1/5, LNW 9/8.
260:6	i) *Bristol & Gloucs. Arch. Soc. Transactions* vol. XCVii pp. 93-94.
	ii) Craig, R. & Jarvis, R. 'Liverpool Registry of Merchant Ships', in *Chetham Soc.* 3rd. series vol. 15 (1967).
260:7	i) CCALS: QDN 1/5.
	ii) *England Described* (1776): Chester - copy in M/cr. PL; 942.07 EI.
260:8	i) Picton, J.A. *Memorials of Liverpool* (1907) vol.1 p.165.
	ii) Porteous, J. Douglas, *Canal Ports* (1977) p. 108.
260:9-261:2	CCALS: D.C.H. FFl3 - deed 1752.
261:4	Pennant, T. *Tours in Wales* (reprint 1883) vol. 1 p.p. 246-248.
261:5	M/cr. PL: Statutes at Large (1751-67) 30 cap.LXIX, 1757.
261:6-262:2	i) CCALS:LNW 9/6, 9/7, QDN 1/5.
	ii) Davies, Kenneth,' Manufacturing Industries of the Greenfield Valley 1750-1900', unpublished Ph.D. thesis, 1985 (UW Bangor).
262:5	i) IGI: Somersetshire.
	ii) Bath City RO: Notes collated by author.
262:6	i) City of Bristol RO: EP/E/I7 - Manor of Rowberrow Diocesan Records 1407-1814.
	ii) Swymmer Pedigee and other information held by descendants still resident in Rowberrow and kindly forwarded for my information.
262:8	Act: Geo II 26 Cap. LXXVl.
262:9	CCALS: CR63/2/691/280.
263:4	MCC: earliest reference 19th Aug. 1774 Item 20; Winterhead, 17th Sept.1776 and visit to Winterhead by author.
263:5	i) City of Bristol RO: EP/E/l7/8 p.27.
	ii) Somerset RO: Phippen Pedigree.
262:6-264:2	i) Whitlock, Ralph, *Mining* (pub. Basford 1975) - Somerset P.64 et seq.
	ii) *England Displayed* (1769) vol.1 p.41.
264:5-6	i) County Map of Cheshire, Bowden 1777.
	ii) Porteous, J. Douglas, *Canal Ports* (1977) p.83 et seq.
265:4	i) Clwd RO: Lords of Mold papers held in Keene & Kelly colln. solicitors Mold.
	ii) Rhodes, J.N. 'Derbyshire Influences on lead mining in North Wales' . . . in 1968 *Bulletin of the Peak Dist. Mines Hist. Soc.* vol.3 part 6 pp.339-351.
265:5-6	i) Al. Cantab.
	ii) Palmer, A.N. *A History of the County Township of the Old Parish of Wrexham* (1903) p. 150.
	iii) Davies, Glyn, *Minera* (1964) p.13.
	iv) Depositions in the Court of Exchequer 27 Geo. 2 c.ll July ID 17 Sept. 1753, Oswestry Mich. 5.
265:7-266:1	i) CCALS: wills: Philip Brock 1705, Richard Brock 1730 & Richard Brock 1759.
	ii) Clwyd R.O: DD/HB 880-882. Deeds.
266:2-6	i) Sherlock, Robert, 'Chandeliers by Chester Brassfounders', in *Chester Arch. Soc. Journal* vol. 56 (1969) pp. 37-48.
	ii) Palmer op. cit. p.55.
266:7-267:1	Lewis, W.J. *Lead Mining in Wales* (1967): Calamine.
267:3	Rhodes, J.N. op. cit. pp. 347-348.
267:4-7	Ibid. pp.339-350 - various references.
267:8	SCA: Bag. C 587(12).
267:9-268:5	i) Journey extracted from following;-
	ii) JRL: R. 69086, *Dr. Johnson & Mrs. Thrale* (Duppa 1909) p. 239.
	iii) M/cr. PL: *The Holyhead Road* vol. II - Birmingham to Holyhead: Bangor.
	iv) Map featuring Menai Strait, John Evans 1795.
268:6	Report on the Manuscripts of the Earl of Verulam (H.M.S.O. 1906) p.265.
268:8	i) Staffs. RO: Case pprs. D603/L222.
	ii) JRL: Bromley-Davenport colln. Property deeds no.27.
	iii) Pennant op. cit. vol III, p.55 et seq.

	iv) UW Bangor: Mona Mine 1267 & 3544.
268:9-269:1	Pennant op. cit.
269:3	CCALS: DSA 205, 1-8.
269:5	UW Bangor: Mona Mine 3025.
269:6	Ibid. 3026.
269:8-270:1	Ibid. 3534, Cartwright's Acct. of Money etc. 1762- May 1769.
270:3	i) Ibid.
	ii) UW Bangor: Porth-yr-Aur 30618.
270:4	NWL: Powis colln. 3008.
270:5-271:3	UW Bangor: Misc. Deeds 3554-3560.
271:4-7	UW Bangor: Porth-yr-Aur 306l8.
272:4-7	Book *1764* op. cit. various references.

Chapter 15

Quotation:	Oliver Goldsmith, 'The Traveller'.
274:1-4	CCALS: LNW 9/8.
275:2-3	Picton vol. 1, p.9, 25, 31-37.
275:4	Ibid, p77.
275:5	bid. p.l57.
275:8	Ibid. p.2 & p.16.
275:9-276:1	i) Ibid. p. 114, 115, 139.
	ii) JRL: Legh of Lyme colln.
276:2	i) *England Described* (1776) copy M/cr. PL.
	ii) *The Natural History of Lancashire & Cheshire* p.242 - copy in M/cr. PL; 591. 94271 Mal.
276:3	Defoe, D. *Tours Through England & Wales* 1724-26. Letter X.
277:1	*The General Advertiser Liverpool*, Friday 14th Aug.1722 - Bellringers notice.
277:2-5	i) Jones, Thomas Lloyd, 'Liverpool Parish Church - A History and Guide' (1977).
	ii) *Proceedings in the Parliament of Elizabeth I* , vol.1 1558-81 (Leics. Univ. Press 1981). p. 252, 313, 384, 402.
277:7-278:1	Liv. PL: Liverpool Corpn. Leases, Register A, 12th April 1720.
278:6-279:1	i) Harrisburg Archives, Pennsylvania U.S.A; Bayton, Wharton & Morgan. (photocopies in possession of the author).
	ii) NMGM: Plantation Books.
279:2-5	i) Gerrard, G.A. J.P. - Article 'Thomas Golightly' in Liv. PL.
	ii) Jones op. cit.
	iii) Liv. PL: M/f Liverpool Town Books, examples 4th March 1767 & 5th July 1786.
	iv) Liv. PL: Liverpool Corpn. Leases, Register A.
279:6-280:1	i) Act II Geo. II. c.32 - 1737.
	ii) Liv. PL: Liverpool Corpn. Leases, Register A.
281:7	Picton vol. 1 p.182, for further details see also:-
	Troughton, T. *The History of Liverpool* (1810). p.265.
282:1-2	JRL: Arley Mss. - letter from George Heron to Peter Warburton dated 21st June 1760 refers to J. Stafford on 9th March 1760.
282:3-282:6	Keele Univ. Archives: Wedgwood letters, see also:-
	Porteous, J. Douglas, *Canal Ports* (1977) pp. 64-65.
283:2	*JHC*; vol. XXX p.215 Appendix l.
283:4	i)*TL&CAS*, vol.LXII p.151, pt.1 - W.C. Chaloner 'Charles Roe of Macclesfield'. List of shareholders.
	ii) Bick, David, *The Old Copper Mines of Snowdonia* (1982) p.86.
283:5-284:1	i) Williams, William, *Observations on the Snowdon Mountains* (1802) p.64.
	ii) NLW: Powis 3016 & 3021.
	No further mining at Bryn Dinas has come to light, and workings on site show little activity at this period. The trials appear to have been unsuccessful, suggesting a rescission of the agreements before the

	signing of the leases took place.
	iii) NLW: MS 15101A & 15102A - Cornish ore purchases 1727 et seq.
284:2	i) William Churchill Dickenson baptised 30th July 1758, Redruth.
	ii) Corn. CRO: DD EN/1691 - N. Downs Adventures (Dolcoath) Copper accounts 1731-1775.
	iii) Truro Museum Library: Portreath affairs, letter 27th April 1765 from Thomas Kevill to Francis Bassett.
284:3	i) CCALS: LNW 9/9. River Weaver.
	ii) Cu. RO (K): WD/RY Box 113. Coniston - John Moore's Estate Book.
	iii) NYCAD: ZAW 117-8 - Middleton Tyas.
284:4-5	i) *DNB:* Denman - see also Dubrett's Baron of Dovedale.
	ii) Chester City RO: TCP/5/136 - Town Clerk's Colln. Letter from Hugh Meredith mentions Denman in charge of mining.
285:2	i) Morton, John, *Thomas Bolton & Sons Limited* (1983) p.15.
	ii) Staffs. RO: M/f 58/1 (1765) Bryncelyn etc.
	iii) Smith, B, 'Lead and Zinc Ores . . . of North Wales' in MGS, vol. XIX p.81.
285:3	Chester City RO: TCP/8/92.
285:5	Smith, B. op. cit. p.83.
285:7	Chaloner op. cit. plate VII between p. 144 & 145.
286:2	'Twenty Sermons on Several Subjects & Occasions' printed by A. Ward, York (1766). Copy held by the late Charles Hadfield of Macclesfield who kindly brought it to my attention.
286:3-5	i) JRL: Methodist colln. 'A Short Account of ye Experience of Hester Ann Rogers Written by Herself' Cork. 30th August 1789.
	ii) JRL: Legh of Lyme colln. - letter 11th February 1760
286:6-287:3	'A Short Account of ye Experience of H.ester Ann Rogers. 'op. cit.
287:6-288:6	i) JRL: Arley Mss.
	ii) Keele Univ. Archives: Wedgwood.
288:7	i) *History of Inland Navigation* (1766) part 1 p.76.
	ii) Chaloner op. cit. pp. 147-148.
	iii) JRL: English Ms. 1101 p. 126.
	iv) Chaloner op. cit. p.148 footnote 47.
289:2-6	Keele Univ. Archives: Wedgwood 18106-25.
289:7-291:2	JRL: Warburton Muniments Box 1 - copy letter to Wright from J. Stafford 3rd. Jan. 1766.
291:4	Keele Univ. Archives: Wedgwood 18114-25.
291:5	Ibid. 18l23-25.
292:1	JRL: Arley Mss. letter from J. Stafford 8th Feb. 1766.
292:2	*JHC:* vol. XXX (1765-66) p. 453. For further details see Chaloner op. cit. pp. 151-156.

Chapter 16

Quotation:	Oliver Goldsmith,'The Traveller'.
294:1-295:3	Bradfield, N. *Historical Costumes of England 1066-1968* (1970). Contini, Mila, *FASHION* (1967).
296:5	*Georgian Chester* (Chester City RO Hist. pub. no.3 1987) Chapter VI.
296:7	Chester City RO; A/B/4 31st May 1745 - Assembly Books.
296:8	Wheeler, Harold, Ed. *The Wonderful Story of London* (1938) p.49.
297:2-3	Harriott, John, *Struggles Through Life* (London 1807) p.213.
297:4	i) Wheeler op. cit. p.220.
	ii) Chancellor, E. Beresford, *The XVIIIth Century in London* (1920) p.174.
297:7-298:3	i) Jackson, G. *The History & Archeology of Ports* (World's Works Ltd. 1983) pp. 16-19.
	ii) *Proceedings in the Parliaments of Elizabeth I* vol.1 1558-1581 (Leicester Univ. Press 1981) p. 390.
	iii) Jackson op. cit. p. 14, 54-55.
298:4-299:1	i) Hill, G.W. & Frere, W.H. Ed. *The Memorials of Stepney Parish* (1890/91).
	ii) *DNB:* Wentworth.
299:2	Jackson op. cit. p.55.

299:3-5	Wheeler op. cit. pp.189-191.
300:2	i) Information kindly supplied by Grosvenor Estate Holdings Ltd. London.
	ii) Westminster City Archives; M/f E412 et seq. - Rates Books.
300:3	i) Hodgson, R. *The Life* (1811) p.17.
	ii) Family notes compiled by Vere Hodgson 1975.
300:4-7	i) *The Life of Dr. Beilby Porteous by a lay-member of Merton College, Oxford* (London 1810).
	ii) Hodgson, R. op. cit.
301:1-3	*DNB*; Thomas Secker.
301:4	*The Life of Dr. Beilby Porteous . . .* op. cit.
301:5	Copy letter held by D.L. Bates (from Isabella Cunningham - grandmother Ellen).
301:6	These properties were retained from the sale of Brian Hodgson Snr.'s one third share of the Boothby Estate.
301:7-302:1	i) Derby LS: Extracts from *A Georgian Country House Ashbourne 1725-1825* part 1.
	ii) Derby LS:*Fashionable Society* , Ashbourne Local Hist. Group 1989 : 'The Grey House'.
302:2	Dev. C:. Ecton accounts.
302:3	i) CCALS: LNW 9/9.
	ii) Cum. RO (K): WD/Ry/Box 113 - Coniston A/cs.
	iii) NLW: 15107B - notebook.
	iv) UW Bangor: Porth-yr-Aur 30665.
302:4	NYCAD: ZAW Bundles 117-118 - Clifton Castle Archive.
302:5-303:1	Cum. RO (K): WD/Ry/Box 22 - letters 21st Feb. 1766 & 16th March 1766.
303:5-304:1	Derby. RO: D664/M/EI - Indenture 1st Aug. 1766.
304:2	i) Sale advert *Manchester Mercury* 20th Oct. 1801.
	ii) MCC: 25th Feb. 1777 & A.G.M. 19th Aug. 1774 no.24.
304:4-8	i) Birm. PL: Matthew Boulton colln. - Havannah -J. Watts letter 11th May 1785.
	ii) Information kindly supplied by Stuart Thompstone, Director of Bosley sawmills on 16th Aug. 1993.
	iii) MCC: 19th Aug. 1774 no. 24.
304:9-305:3	i) Hamilton, Henry, *The English Brass & Copper Industry to 1800* (1926), Chapter : Methods of Production.
	ii) Hornsby, Peter, *The Arthur Negus Guide to British Pewter, Copper & Brass* (1981), pp. 12-16.
	iii) Davies, Kenneth, 'Manufacturing Industries of the Greenfield Valley 1750-1900', unpublished Ph.D. thesis 1985 (UW Bangor).
	iv) Information kindly supplied by A.P. Woolrich.
	v) Morton, John, *Thomas Bolton & Sons Ltd.* (1983) pp.14-15.
305:4	i) MCC: 16th Sept. 1777.
	ii) Ibid 25th May 1779 no.7.
306:3	JRL: Diary - Hester Ann Rogers.
306:5	i) IGI: Harriott.
	ii) Harriott, John, *Struggles Through Life* vol.1 (1807).
	iii) *DNB*: John Harriott.
306:6	UW Bangor: Penrhyn Castle Mss. 1182 - The Jamaican Estates.
306:7	SCA: J.C. 1366 - Pedigree of Jebb of Chesterfield.
307:1	i) Chesterfield PL: Jebb family in *Old Halls , Manors & Families of Derbyshire.* (1892) pp. 88-89.
	ii) *Burke's Peerage & Baronetage.*
308:1	SCA: Bag. C. 431A.
308:2-3	NLW: Powis 3084.
308:4	i) *M.G.S.* vol. XIX *Zinc and Lead Ores . . . North Wales,* (1921) p.92.
	ii) NLW: Peniarth Ms. f89 and Powis 3756 & 4167.
308:5	*M.G.S.* vol.XIX ibid. p.11 & 77.
308:6	i) Pryce, W. *Mineralogia Cornubiensis* 1778 (facsimile Truro 1972): Cobalt.
	ii) Copeland, R. *Spode's Willow Pattern* (1980) p.18.
309:1	Notes supplied by N.J. Dibben of the Derbyshire Caving Club, October 1988. Keele University Day Course.
309:2	i) NA: El90 1433/1 et seq. - Chester City Ports Records.

ii) Rhodes, J.N. 'Derbyshire Influences' . . . in *Bulletin of the Peak Dist. Mines Soc.* 1968 vol.3 part 6 pp. 344-345.

Chapter 17

Quotation:	Bible - Proverbs 13 v.14.
310:2	i) Derby. RO: D664/M/El (Deed).
	ii) Eyes maps of Liverpool 1765 & 1768.
	iii) Liv. PL: Corporation Leases Book A 30th May 1745 & 8th Oct. 1762.
310:3	Cu. RO (K): WD/AG Box 111 - Old Glasshouse deed.
310:5	Gore's Liverpool Directories 1769 & 1774.
311:1	Picton vol. II p.262.
311:2	Liv. PL: Holt & Gregson XlX 75 no.77 - Johnsons' letter 30th Sept. 1792.
311:3-7	i) Day, Joan, *Bristol Brass* (1973) p.79 et seq.
	ii) NA: SP44/266A fol 31-33.
312:1-2	i) Langton, John, *Geographical Change & Industrial Revolution* (1979) pp.143-144.
	ii) G. M/cr CRO: E17/106/1
312:3	MCC: 31st. Jan. 1775.
312:5-313:2	i)*THSL&C*: vol.100 (1948) pp.55-72.
	ii) Ibid. vol. 121 (1969) pp.43 - 45. - Capesthorne Hall.
313:3	JRL: Legh of Lyme colln.
313:4	*THSL&C*: vols. 100 & 121 (ibid.)
313:5	i) Peacock, Primrose, *Buttons for the Collector*, (1972) p.10 - Dorset
	ii) Knowsley; Earl of Derby colln. Deed 468/37 - William Clayton.
313:6	Picton vol.1. p.143.
314:2	CCALS: LNW 9/9.
314:4	M.G.S. (1921) vol.XVII *The Lead, Zinc, . . . of Scotland.* p.48.
314:7	UW Bangor: Mona Mine a/cs. 3534 p.76.
314:8-315:1	Ibid. 35364 p.79, 3536.
315:2	Ibid. 3534 p.77.
315:5-8	UW Bangor: Plas Newydd Mss. VII no.8.
315:9	Ibid. no.9.
316:1	NLW: Powis 3848, 3846.
316:2-3	UW Bangor: Mona Mine 3534.
316:4-5	Ibid. p.40 Letter 9th July 1768 and 3536.
316:6	Much information generously made available by Mrs. R.F.Roose of Chester from Parish Registers and other original documentation in her possession.
316:8	UW Bangor: Kinmel 1807 & 1808.
316:9-317:3	i) UW Bangor: Mona Mine 3534
	ii) The letter is correctly dated 25th July 1767 pp.41-42.
317:4-5	NLW: Powis 3084-3085.
317:6	SCA: Bag. C. 431A p.3l 'Penrendew".
317:7	NLW: Powis 3531.
318:3	i) UW Bangor: Penrhyn Du leases 3554-3560.
	ii) UW Bangor: Porth-yr-Aur 30618
318:4	Roberts, R.O.' Farming in Caernarvonshire around 1800' p.19. Article in Caernarvonshire RO.
318:5	NLW: Notebook l5l07A.
318:6	Dev. C: Ecton Mine a/cs.
318:7	Cu. RO (K): WD/Ry Box 113 - Coniston a/cs.
318:8	SCA: Bag. C. 431A p.50 and notes accompanying collection.
319:2	Pennant, Thomas, *Tours in Wales* vol. III (reprint 1883).
319:5-320:1	UW Bangor: Mona Mine 3534 pp.35-38 & 80.
320:2	bid. pp.37-38.

320:5	CCALS: St. Michael's parish registers.
320:6	UW Bangor: Mona Mone 3534 pp.35-38 & 80.
320:7-321:2	Ibid. pp. 103-104.
321:2-3	Ibid. Letter dated 4th March.
321:4	SCA: Bag. C. 587(47) Signatories.
321:6	UW Bangor: Mona Mine 3534 pp.43-44.
321:7-322:3	Ibid. pp.45-46.
322:4	Harris, J.R. *The Copper King* (1964) pp.26-27.
322:5	Clwyd RO: D/KK/255 - Deed 16th June 1763.
322:6	Clwyd RO: D/KK/534.
322:8	M.G.S. (1921 & 1925) vol. XXX *Copper Ores of the Midlands* . . . pp.32-38.
323:4-7	CCALS: LNW 9/9.
323:8	Lancs. RO: will: John Walker, merchant Liverpool 1769.
325:1	NA: Prob 11 941 - Will Robert Mandeville.
325:2	Deeds 62/64 Chestergate in possession of owner.
325:3	Clwyd RO: D/W 49.
325:4	UW Bangor: Mona Mine 3534 pp.7-8.
325:5	Clwyd RO: DW/48 & 50.
325:6	Palmer, A.N. *A History of the County Townships of the Old Parish of Wrexham* (1903) p. 104.
325:7-8	i) Derby RO: Deed 513M/B8.
	ii) Palmer op. cit.
326:3-4	i) Bemrose, William, *The Life and Works of Joseph Wright A.R.A.* (1885).
	ii) Nicolson, Benedict, *Joseph Wright of Derby* (1968).
326:6-327:1	Ibid.
327:3	Lancs. RO: Molyneux colln. DDM 50/19.
327:4	NA: Annual Register XIII (1770) part 1 pp.96-97.

Chapter 18

Quotation:	Oliver Goldsmith, Vida's Game of Chess.
328:1-2	i) *Al. Oxon.*
	ii) M/cr. PL: C17/3/116/1 - copy will Catherine Nicholson.
329:3-5	i) Clwyd RO: Flintshire Hist. Soc. publication no.6 1916-17 - Lords of Mold.
	ii) Clwyd RO: D/KK/266 - Lords of Mold colln.
329:6	i) Clwyd RO: D/KK/274.
	ii) My thanks to David Rhys of Exeter for providing Swymmer family tree.
	iii) Clwyd RO: Kearne & Kelly colln. 294 bundle 1 - litigation.
329:8	i) Clwyd RO: D/KK/267 p.25 - Thomas Jones
	ii) Chester City RO: TCP/8/92.
329:9	M.G.S. vol.XIX p.80.
330:2-4	M/cr.PL C17/1/1 p1 & 23.
330:4-5	M.G.S. vol. XIX *Zinc and Lead Ores* . . . *North Wales* (1921) pp.82-83.
330:7	Ibid. p.79, 64 & 67.
330:9	Ibid. p.41.
331:1	Stanley, Hon. Miss L.D. *Alderley Edge and its Neighbourhood* (1843).
331:2-3	CCALS: LNW 9/10.
331:4-332:1	CCALS: Northwich Tonnage of Up-goods.
332:4	Macc. PL: L2(1) Macc. Express - Findings of wooden pipes and sough.
332:5	CCALS: Northwich Tonnage of Up-goods.
332:6	Lancs. RO: DDM 50/19 - Molyneux Colln.
333:1-2	Ibid. DDM 50/20.
333:3	Ibid. DDM 50/17 & 50/18.
333:4	Ibid. DDM 50/21.

333:9-334:3	Ibid. DDM 50/179.
334:4-335:2	Swansea PL: Two pamphlets c.1773 & 1785 under General References.
335:4	Leeds Dist. Arch: Radcliffe Mss. no.259 (108-110).
335:5-6	Liverpool Univ. L: M.S. 26.3.34 p.2.
335:7	CCALS: LBM/l/4.
335:8-336:3	Lancs. RO: DDM 50/30.
336:4-6	Ibid. DDM 50/22.
336:7-338:2	Swansea Univ: Morris Mss. - Robert Morris's notebooks l-6.
339:1	Swansea PL: Two pamphlets c. 1773 & 1785 in General References.
339:2-10	SCA: Bag. C.587 (47).
339:11-340:1	i) UW Bangor: Kinmel Mss. 1807-09 - The Parys Mountain Suite 1769-1776.
	ii) UW Bangor: Mona Mine 1269.
340:2	Ibid. 1270.
340:3	i) UW Bangor: Plas Newydd Mss. VII 38.
	ii) UW Bangor: Mona Mine 1269.
340:4	Harris, J.R. *The Copper King* (1964) pp.30-31.
340:6-341:2	UW Bangor: Kinmel 1807.
341:3-4	Harris op. cit. pp.32-33.
341:5	UW Bangor: Plas Newydd Mss. VII 56.
341:6	i) UW Bangor: Kinmel 1808.
	ii) JRL: Bromley Davenport colln. no.27 - deed 21st. March l807.
	iii) UW Bangor: Kinmel 1808 - Deposition sworn in Chester 26th Jan. 1776.
	iv) Harris op.cit. p.35.
341:7-8	UW Bangor: Kinmel 1808 - Deposition l8th June 1775.
341:9	Information from Mrs. R.F. Roose, Chester.
342:1-7	i) NLW: Powis 4131.
	ii) Pennant, Thomas, *Tours in Wales* vol.III (1773 & 1776) reprint 1883.
343:2-8	NMGM;: MDHB Deeds 335 H2 - Articles of Partnership.
343:9	Ibid. Deed 335 H3.
343:11	Hughes, John, *Liverpool Banks & Bankers 1760 - 1837* (1906) p.84.
344:1	JRL: Caldwell Family Mss.
344:2	i) Register of Admissions: Middle Temple.
	ii) *DNB*
344:3-4	Hughes op.cit. p.85.
344:5	List of subscribers to James Roe's sermons November 1766.
344:6	JRL: Legh of Lyme colln. Box 1 C22.
344:8	i) NA: Prob 11/976 - Will Edward Pitts 1772.
	ii) Dev. C: Ecton a/cs.
	iii) Lancs. RO: DDM 50/179.
345:1	i) Macc. BC: C22/25/1.
	ii) Op.cit. Will: Pitts.
345:2	Ibid.
345:4	Victorian Pedigree of Busfeild Family supplied by Bingley PL. N.B. the name is spelt Busfield on all company documents.
345:5	MCC: 22nd. Sept 1774.
345:7	i) *VCH* : vol. IV City of Gloucester.
	ii) Gloucs. RO: D3117/3953
	iii) *Bailey's Bristol Directory* 1784.
	iv) Gloucs. RO: Corporation Minute Book.
345:9	Gloucs. RO: Deed D3117/3953.
346:1	NMGM: MDHB Deed 335 H2.

Chapter 19

Quotation:	Bible - Ecclesiastes V v.4.
347:1-348:5	MCC.
348:6	Staffs. RO: D/3272/1/4/3/47.
328:7	bid. /4l-43.
348:8	Ibid. /44.
348:9-349-1	Ibid. /46.
349:2	Ibid. /47-49.
349:4-5	MCC.
349:6	i) My thanks to David Rhys of Exeter for a copy of the Swymmer/Fane (Earl of Westmorland) pedigree.
	ii) Clwyd RO: D/KK/274 - copy of Act.
349:7-8	MCC: For example see 19th Aug. 1774 no.20.
349:9	Birm. PL: Ms. 39/114 & 115 - Darbyshire A/c Books.
350:1	MCC.
350:2-6	i) Clapham, Sir John, *A History of the Bank of England* (1945).
	ii) Cameron, Alan, *Bank of Scotland 1695-1995* (1995) p.63.
350:7	MCC.
350:8	NA: Prob ll/l000 - Will Joseph Stockdale 1774.
350:9	Clinch, George, *Bloomsbury & St. Giles* (1890).
350:10-11	Ibid. will, Joseph Stockdale.
351:5	Porteous, J. Douglas, *Canal Ports* (1977) p.83 et seq.
351:7-9	i) MCC.
	ii) Riden, Philip, *The Butterley Company 1790-1830* (1990) - F. Beresford.
	iii) Derby. Record Soc. (2nd. Edn. 1990) vol. XVI pp.11-27.
351:10-352:1	MCC.
352:2	*THSL&C* vol.100 (1948) 'Sarah Clayton's letter and John Wood of Bath' by Stanley A. Harris, pp.55-72.
352:3	MCC.
352:9-10	NLW: 15103B-15109B.
353:1-4	UW Bangor: Mona Mine 3536.
353:7	JRL: Legh of Lyme colln.
353:8-354:7	Dev. C: Ecton.
354:8-355:1	Chesterfield PL: G. Heathcote colln. (uncatalogued).
355:2-5	Dev. C: Ecton a/cs.
355:7-356:3	Chesterfield PL: G. Heathcote colln. (uncatalogued).
356:6-7	*Arminian Magazine* 1783 pp.521-4.
	JRL: Methodist colln. - Hester Ann Rogers Journal.
356:8	JRL: Legh of Lyme colln.
357:2	Leedes Hunt, Rev. Alfred, *David Simpson* (1927) p.123.
357:4	*Al Oxon.*
357:5-6	SCA: J.C. 1366 - Jebb pedigree.
	Cambridge Univ. Peterhouse Library;*The Works of John Jebb with Memoirs . . .* John Disney D.D. FSA vol.1.
357:7	Cambridge Univ. Peterhouse Library: PET F537 Al.
357:8	Leedes Hunt op. cit. pp. 72-74, 88-89, 136-137, 143-144, 152.
358:1-6	Ibid. chap. V.
358:8-9	Ibid. chap. VI - especially pp.177-178.
358:10	CCALS: EDA 1/7 (1760-1776) fol. 138 - 15th Oct. 1772.
359:1	CCALS: LBM1/4.
359:2	CCALS: EDA 1/7 op. cit.
359:3	Leeds Hunt op. cit. chap. V.
359:5	*Arminian Magazine* 1783.
359:6	JRL: Methodist colln. Hester Ann Rogers Journal.

359:8 Leedes Hunt op. cit. chap. VI.
360:2 Ibid.
360:4 CCALS: EDA l/7 (1760-1776) fol. 141v 17th June 1773.
360:5 Birk. PL: C/IV/l7 - Macclesfield colln.

Chapter 20

Quotation: Bible - Psalm 118 v.22.
361:1-2 i) Article: *Macclesfield Courier & Herald* 1st. Jan. 1876.
ii) Information supplied by the librarians of York Minster Archives.
361:4-5 Birk. L: C/IV/16 - Macclesfield colln.
362:1-2 i) Dashwood, Sir. Francis, *The Dashwoods of West Wycombe* (1987) pp.47-48.
ii) Baigent, M. & Leigh, R. *The Temple and the Lodge* (1988) pp.293-294.
362:5 John Stafford portrait, Phillips Cat. Sale no. 23,852, 26th April 1982.
Charles Roe's portrait is exhibited West Park Museum, Macclesfield by kind permission of The Churches Conservation Trust.
362:6-8 i)*THSL&C:* vol. 115 pp. 117-119 - Peter Perez Burdett.
ii) Burdett's map of Derbyshire pub. by the Derbys. Arch. Soc. 1975 (edited by J.B. Harley, D.V. Fowkes & J.C. Harvey).
363:5 Picton vol. 1 pp.39-40.
363:6 Liv. PL: Corporation leases Regr.A. 31st July 1769.
363:7 Liv. PL: Hf 68l lWYK - Wyke & Green.
363:8 Lancs. RO: will, John Okill 1773.
364:2-5 Birk. L: C/IV/15 & C/IV/ 16 - Macclesfield colln.
365:4 Enfield, W. *An essay towards the history of Liverpool* (1773).
365:6 My thanks to Helen Warhurst Smith for her translations from the following publications:-
a) 'Beitråge zur geschichtlichen Landeskunde - Geographie, Geschichte Kartographie' (1968 Stuttgart) no.lll pp.l58-l65.
b) Hirsch Fritz, *Hundert Jahre Bauen und Schauen*, Bd 11 (Karlsruhe 1928) pp.451-455.
c) Weech Friedrich V. *Karlsruhe, Geschichte der Stadt und ihrer Verwaltung* Bd 1 (Karlsruhe 1895) p. 265.
365:7-366:1 i)Christ Church: Graveyard Transcripts Project - Family History Soc. March 1989, completed prior to extension of an area designated for conservation by Macc. Borough Council.
ii)Macc. L: M/f Christ Church burials included in St. Michael's registers.
366:3 St. Peter's register held by the Archivist at Prestbury.
366:4-6 Leedes Hunt, Rev. Alfred, *David Simpson* (1927) chap. 6.
366:7 *Arminian Magazine* October 1783, Robert Roe pp.521-524.
366:9-367:1 Leedes Hunt op. cit.
367:2 i) Picton vol 1 p.198, 201.
ii) Sermons: copies in Macc. L. Local Studies.
367:3 i) Leedes Hunt op. cit. pp. 88-89.
ii) Cambridge Univ. Peterhouse Library, *The Works of John Jebb with Memoirs* . . . John Disney D.D. FSA vol. III pp.143-148.
iii) *Parliamentary History* vol.17 11-14 Geo. 3 1771-1774. 'Debate on a Motion for Relief to the Clergy in the Matter of Subscriptions to the 39 articles', 5th May 1774. My thanks to Sir Nicholas Winterton M.P. for Macclesfield in helping to trace this debate.
367:4-5 Ibid.
368:1 CCALS: Christ Church registers.
368:4 CCALS: Plan LBM 2039. - the foundation stone was laid 5th Oct. 1774.
368:7 i) Liv. PL: St. Ann's Church in Wallace's *History of Liverpool* 1794.
ii) Enfield op. cit.- Illustrations.
371:2 Lady's Magazine February 1775 p.61 - description.
371:3-5 CCALS: Northwich Tonnage of Up-goods 11/4 & 11/5.
371:6 Simpson, David, 'Discussions on Several Subjects' (1788 et seq) p.422 - copy in Macc. L. Local Studies.

372:1-373:1   JRL: Methodist colln. Hester Ann Rogers' Journals.

373:3   CCALS: will, John Stafford 1775.

373:7-374:2   Goldsmith, O. *Poems and Plays* (reprint 1948) - 'The Good-Natur'd Man'.

374:4   *The Manchester Mercury, Harrop's General Advertiser* Tues. 19th Sept. 1775.

374:5   MCC.

374:6-375:6   i) Sadie, Stanley, Ed. *The New Grove Dictionary of Music and Musicians,* (reprint 1995)
ii) Highfill, PH., Burnim, K.A., & Langhaus, E.A., *A Biographical Dictionary of Actors, Actresses, Musicians, Dancers, Managers & Other Stage Personnel in London 1660-1800* (S. Illinois Univ, Press 1982).

375:7   Rogers op. cit.

375:8   i) *Macclesfield Courier and Herald* Sat. 13th Nov. 1875 'Correspondence' p.5
ii) Information supplied by The Theatre Museum, London.

375:9-376:1   Dean, W. & Knapp, J.H. *Handel's Operas 1704-1726* (1987).

376:2   i) Information obtained from the Royal College of Organist's Library.
ii) Wilson, Michael (Ed. by Sumner), *English Chamber Music* (1968) pp.8-9.

376:3   Westminster City Archives; H3 567, H2 107.

376:4   i) Information from David Wickens in conjunction with his book, *The Instruments oif Samuel Green.* Details held British Organ Archive Oxon.
ii) Burrows David, *Handel* (1994) p.202. - There is evidence in Christ Church today that, instead of the organist playing with his back to the congregation, as on the present Victorian replacement organ, the original allowed the organist to face the congregation and altar.
iii) Burrows, David, *Handel* (1994) p.202.

377:1-3   Birk. PL: C/IV/l9 - Macclesfield colln.

377:4   Leedes Hunt op. cit. p.219, 221 et seq.

378:2   As evidenced today with pews still in situ.

378:3   i) Advert: *Manchester Mercury* 16th Nov. 1773 p.3 & *Drewry's Derby Mercury* 26th Nov. 1773 p.1 and was repeated 12th & 19th Nov. & 3rd Dec. 1773. for lead mining shares.
ii) Cu. RO (K): WD/TE/Box 16/16. - 'A Buxtonian Expedition' contains a description of the marble works.

378:4   Recent analyses of paint samples by The Churches Conservation Trust have confirmed the original colour scheme as described.

378:5   Chester PL: Newspapers.

378:8-379:1   Evidence remaining in Christ Church today.

379:4-5   Derby LS: Derbyshire colln. 9233 - Diary of Thomas Buxton of Bradbourne.

379:6-380:2   *Arminian Magazine* October 1783 - Robert Roe pp.638-641, 19-22, 76-81.

Chapter 21

Quotation: Bible, Psalm 49 v.11

381:1   Liv. PL:352/MD1 - Committee Book of the African Company of Merchants Trading from Liverpool 1750-1820.

381:2   Liv. PL: Liverpool parish registers.
Liv. PL: Liverpool Town Books M/f 2/6.

381:3   I.G.I. Shaw Family.

381:4   M/cr. PL: M39/5/3/1 (1749), L 85/6/7/3 (1759) and Picton vol II p.297 - Thomas Shaw.

381:5-382:1   i) *Al. Cantab.*
ii) Warrington PL: Warrington Church Notes 1876 - 'St. Elfin's' by William Beaumont pp.84-93.

382:2   Lancs. RO will: Samuel Shaw 1718.

382:3   i) Picton vol. II p.297.
ii) James Shaw baptised son Thomas at St. Elfin's 31st May 1694.

382:4-7   i) Liv. PL: Okill: Stewart- Brown R. *Liverpool Shipping in the 18th Century* (1932) pp.117-118; Liverpool Corpn. Leases CLE/CON vol.3/2, 352.
ii) Lancs RO: will: John Okill 1773.

382:8	i) Lancs. RO: will: Samuel Shaw 1718 & oath of 1816.
	ii) CCALS: EDA 2/12 January 1813-July 1816 Bishop's Act Book - Oath llth March 1816.
382:9	i) Samuel baptised llth May 1718 St. Nicholas's, Liverpool.
	ii) Lancs. RO: will: Samuel Shaw of Warrington 1713 proved 1718.
382:10	Lancs. RO: Admin: Samuel Shaw 1718 (dated 12th March 1717).
383:2	Date of death 27th Sept. 1718.
383:3-4	i) Liv. PL: H9 252.7 pp. 32-45, Key St. Chapel, 'Ordination Sermon . . .' of Duke St.: children baptised St. Nicholas's e.g. Christopher 15th Feb.1751, Ann 22nd April 1756.
	ii) Liv. PL: Liverpool Town books M/f 2/6.
383:5	NMGM: Plantation Books May 1765 - December 1773.
383:6	Liv. PL: Liverpool Town books M/f 2/6.
383:7	Ibid. see 1st Oct. 1774.
383:8	Ibid. see 2nd Nov. 1774.
383:9-384:1	Liv. PL: H338 15PA - *The Firm of Sparling & Bolden of Liverpool 1788-99.*
384:4	i)*THSL&C* vol 117, 1965, p.59 - 'The Rise and Fall of the Marshalls of Northwich . . .' (1720-1917).
	ii) Keele Univ. archives: Wedgwood colln. E 18119-25.
384:6	Liv. PL: Liverpool Town books M/f 2/6.
384:7	Ibid. 16th Feb. 1767 & 4th March 1767.
384:8-385:1	CCALS: Northwich Tonnage of Up Goods 11/5.
385:3-6	MCC.
385:7	SCA: Bag. C. 431A.
385:8	MCC.
386:2	M/cr. PL: C17/1/1.
386:3	CCALS: Northwich Tonnage of Up Goods 11/3 & 11/4.
386:5-6	MCC.
386:6	Clwyd RO: Keane & Kelly colln. 294 Bundle 1 - Court Case.
386:7-8	MCC.
387:1-2	Ellacombe, Rev. H.T. *The Church Bells of Gloucestershire* (1881) and notes from Gloucs. RO.
387:3	Nichols, Ivor R. *A History of the Bells and the Ringers,* booklet - St. Michael's. Macclesfield (privately pub. 1992).
387:5	JRL: Legh of Lyme colln. Peter Wright to Peter Legh 15th August 1778.
388:3-4	i) Liv. PL: Hq 681 1FAI - copy Thesis 'Watch and Clockmaking 18th century Liverpool', Oliver Fairclough.
	ii) Liv. PL: V57 *Hist. Soc. Transactions.* 1905 pp.50-52 John Wyke (1720-1787).
	iii) Liv. PL: Hf 681 lWYK - Wyke & Green Watch & Clockmakers. (c1780).
388:6	Hauser Christian, *Art Foundry* (Paris 1972) pp. 17-20 : Bronze.
398:1	Ches. RO: parish registers.
389:2	IGI & *DNB.*
389:3-5	IGI.
389:6	i) Silk Heritage Museum, Macc: Deeds for Waters: Silk factory etc. with reference to William Sherwin, weaver.
	ii) MCC.
	iii) CCALS: LBM/l/4.
389:7-390:3	i) Greater London RO: P93/MRYl/90- St. Mary Matfellon, extracts from Vestry Books etc. N.B. 12th July 1731; 31st March 1746; 29th March 1752; 29th Jan. 1754; 4th April 1774.
	ii) NA: Prob ll/973 - Will: Samuel Shaw of Liverpool 1781.
390:4	MCC.
390:5	Gloucs. RO: P228 CW 2/1 - Bishop's Transcripts 1720-54, St. Peter's, Newnham.
390:6-7	*Bristol & Gloucestershire Arch. Soc. Transactions* XCVii, (1979) pp. 93-100 - 'The Newnham and London Traders' by N.M. Hibbert.
390:8	NA: Gloucester Port Records E190.
390:9-391:3	i) MCC.
	ii) BL: Oriental & India Office colln. L/AG/1/5/18-20.

	iii) NA: Prob 11/1026 - Will: Thomas Hawkins 1776.
	iv) MCC.
391:5-6	Lich. JRO: B/C/7 1777.
391:7	Gloucs. RO: 5D 2957/215 (19).
391:8	i) CCALS: LBM 2039, no.83 on Plan.
	ii) CCALS: parish registers.
392:1-2	CCALS: EDA 1/8.
392:3-4	Hodgson, Rev. R. *The Life* (1811) pp. 45-46 - Beilby Poteus.
392:5-7	Birk. PL: Macclesfield colln. C/IV/18.
393:2	Leedes Hunt, Rev. Alfred, *David Simpson* (1927) p.221.
393:4-7	i) *Arminian Magazine*, October 1783 pp. 76-81 - Robert Roe.
	ii) JRL: Methodist colln. *A Short Account of ye Experience of Hester Ann Rogers* (Cork 30th Aug. 1789). N.B. 7th May & 4th Aug. 1776.
394:7-8	*Arminian Magazine* op. cit. August 1776.
394:9-395:1	NA: Prob 11/1000 - Will: Joseph Sockdale 1774.
395:2	*Arminian Magazine* op. cit. pp. 76-81.
395:7	JRL: MCC.
395:8-396:1	*Arminian Magazine* op. cit. pp. 132-137.
396:2	Ibid. pp. 186-189.
396:3-4	Overton, Perry C. *Bishops of Lincoln 1761-1779*, pp.340-342 - John Green 54th Bishop. See also *DNB* entry.
396:4-5	*Arminian Magazine* op. cit. pp.186-l89.
396:6	Hester Ann Rogers op. cit. - after April 1777.
396:7	i) JRL: Methodist colln. *The Journal of John Wesley* (Epworth Press 1960), see 21st March 1778.
	ii) Ibid. 9th April 1777.
397:3	*Arminian Magazine* op. cit. pp.186-189.
397:4	i) Hester Ann Rogers op. cit.
	ii) M/cr. PL: Porteus pamphlet.
397:5	Ibid.
397:6-398:1	Hester Ann Rogers op. cit. pp. 303-307.
398:2	Macc. PL: 'Discourses on Several Subjects', Rev. D. Simpson - see p.423 'On Beneficence' also footnote p.213 of *Old Cheshire Churches* by Raymond Richards which gives cost 'near £8,000'.
398:3-6	Hester Ann Rogers op. cit. pp.358-362.

Chapter 22

Quotation:	Bible - Psalm 127 v1.
399:1-2	MCC.
399:2	Pryce, William, *Mineralogia Cornubiensis*, (1778 facsimile Truro 1972) - schedule opposite p.288.
399:3-400:2	MCC.
400:2	i) Ibid.
	ii) Science L: London - Patent.
400:3	MCC.
400:4	i) *VCH* vol. IV Gloucestershire pp. 130-131, City of Gloucester.
	ii) Gloucs. RO: D 3117/3955 - copy will.
400:5	i) St. Peter's register held by archivist at Prestbury.
	ii) MCC: A.G.M. item no.34.
400:6-401:2	Gloucs. RO: D3117/3953 - Deeds.
401:3-6	MCC.
401:6	JRL: Legh of Lyme colln. Box1 C22 deed 16th Oct. 1755 - Copy of Court Roll: Samuel Roe.
401:7-402:5	i) MCC.
	ii) Liverpool Univ. Archives: Letter 175.3.52 (187).
402:7	M/cr. PL: C17/1/1 - Nicholson colln.

403:3-405:1	MCC. (N.B. also 17th Sept. 1776).
405:2-3	i) Briggs, Asa, *A Social History of England* (1983) p.232.
	ii) *The Oxford Illustrated History of the British Army* ,(1994) pp. 121-2, 126, 132.
	iii) White, R.J. *The Age of George III* (1968) pp.91-93.
405:5-6	Hannay, David, *A Short History of the British Navy 1689-1815* (1909) pp.209 - 212.
405:7-406:1	Ibid. pp.221-228.
406:3-406:4	Ibid. p.213.
406:5-6	Troughton, T. *The History of Liverpool* (1810), p.265.
406:7	Hannay op. cit. p.228.
407:2-408:1	The Act: A.D. 1779 Anno 19 Geo. III Cap.VII.
408:2-3	CCALS: EDA 2/8 Fols. 17-29, (Act) 30 - Bishop's Transcripts.
408:4	CCALS: EDA 1/8 vol.29.
408:6-409:3	JRL: Methodist colln. - Journal of Hester Ann Rogers.
409:4-8	i) MCC.
	ii) CCALS: LNW 11/6, 11/7.
	iii) SCA: Bar. D805, Deed circa 1789 - Overend.
410:1-4	MCC.
410:5	BL: Oriental & India Office colln. L/AG/1/5/20.
410:6	MCC.
410:7-411:1	Science L: London - Patents.
411:2	UW Bangor: Mona Mine 3544 pp.13-14.
411:4-5	Ibid. 3028.
411:6	i) Ibid. 3029.
	ii) Ibid. 3030.
411:7	Ibid. 303l.
412:1	i) NMGM: 335 H2 - Articles of partnership.
	ii) UW Bangor: Mona Mine 3031.
412:3	Ibid. First paragraph.
412:4	bid. Footnote to 3032.
412:5	UW Bangor: Porth-yr-Aur 30636.
413:1-3	i) BL: Oriental & India Office colln. L/AG/1/5/20.
	ii) *Glamorgan County History*, vol.5 p. 58 & 88 (R.O. Roberts articles).
	iii) UW Bangor: Port-yr-Aur 30633 - copy letter 8th April 1800.
	iv) Ibid. Copy letter 8th Sept. 1779.
	v) Ibid. Copy letter 5th April 1800.
413:5	i) UW Bangor: Porth-yr-Aur 30636.
	ii) UW Bangor: Quote from Mona Mine Mss. 3544.
	iii) UW Bangor: Porth-yr-Aur 30636.
	iv) Ibid. 30633.
413:6-414:1	Ibid.
414:3-4	MCC.
414:5	Hannay op.cit. pp.241-242.

Chapter 23

Quotation:	Bible - Ezra 8 v.27.
415:1	Hannay, David, *A Short History of the British Navy 1689-1815* (1909).
415:3-416:2	i) Whitlock, P. & Pearce, W. *H.M.S. Victory and Admiral Lord Nelson*, (Booklet 1990s) p.3 - Copper.
	ii) AN: ADM 106/2063 - Naval Minutes, see 2nd, 4th & 29th May 1780.
	iii) Macc. Silk Heritage Archives: copy invoice and company letters.
416:3	MCC.
416:4-5	Bath City Archive: Rate books.
416:6-7	JRL: Methodist colln. Hester Ann Rogers' Journals.

417:1-418:2   MCC.
418:2-419:2   NA: ADM 106/2063, 2064 - Naval Minutes.
419:3   Hannay op. cit. p.279.
419:4   Ibid. p.280 & 286.
419:5   Whitlock & Pearce op. cit.
419:6-422:6   JRL: Methodist colln. Notes compiled from Hester's Journals and Robert Roe's extracts in the *Arminian Magazine* for October 1783.
422:4-6   MCC.
422:7-423:1   Hester Ann Rogers & *Arminian Magazine* op. cit.
422:3-4   Ibid.
423:5   Historical Monuments Commission - Earl of Verulam (H.M.S.O. 1906) p.155
423:6   Hester Ann Rogers op. cit.

Chapter 24

Quotation: Oliver Goldsmith - Vida's Game of Chess.
425:1-427:4   Details based on extracts from *Journeys of a German in England*, Carl Philip Moritz - first published in Germany 1783, translated by Reginald Nutter 1983 (London).
427:5   i) JRL; R73040 - Boswell's *Life of Johnson* vol.5 p.447.
    ii) Ingpen Roger, Ed. *Life of Samuel Johnson* (1907) - Carlisle 7th Nov.1779.
427:6-428:1   CCALS: Admin. Charles Roe 1781.
428:2   Liv. PL: St. Nicholas's Burials 178 no.284.
428:3   NA: Prob 11/1085 - Will Samuel Shaw 1781.
428:4   NMGM: Plantation Book 1779-1784.
428:5   i) JRL: Hester Ann Rogers' Journal.
    ii) Liv. Univ. Archives: Ms. 26.3.34. - Extracts from Charles Legh's Commonplace book.
429:2   Liv. PL: St. George's parish registers..
429:3   MCC.
431:2   NA: ADM 2603, 2604 - Naval Minutes.
431:3   MCC see 2nd July 1781 - settled 22nd May 1783.
431:4-432:1   MCC.
432:2   JRL: Bromley Davenport colln. no.27 Ireland & Wales: Estates of Earl of Uxbridge 18th century. Deeds 15th July 1784 & 21st March 1807 (including extracts from Sir Nicholas's will at P.C.C.).
432:4-433:3   MCC.
433:5-434:1   Ibid.
434:7-435:1   BL: Oriental & India Office colln. L/AG/1/5/21.
435:3   Deeds: 60B, 62 & 62A Chestergate in possession of the owner.
435:4-5   i) Hester Ann Rogers op. cit.
    ii) Macc. PL: *Discourses on Several Subjects,* by David Simpson - 'On Beneficence' p.422.
436:2   *DNB* Bacon.
436:3-7   i) Hester Ann Rogers op. cit.
    ii) *Al. Cantab*; Collins.
    iii) CCALS: EDA 1/8 nos. 66 & 68.
437:1   Ibid.
437:2   *The Journal of John Wesley* (Epworth Press 1960) p.346.
437:4   i) JRL: *Arminian Magazine* October 1783 - Robert Roe 24th June 1781.
    ii) Hester Ann Rogers op. cit. 7th Feb. 1782.
    iii) JRL: Methodist colln. Hester Ann Rogers diary 9th & 11th March 1782. There is overlapping at this period between the journals and diaries.
437:5   i) Ches. County Council Modern Deeds no. 2871.
    ii) Hester Ann Rogers op. cit. diaries March 1782 et seq.
437:6-439:5   Ibid.

Chapter 25

Quotation:	Bible- Mark 13 v.33.
440:1-441:5	JRL: Methodist colln. Hester Ann Rogers' diaries.
441:6	CCALS: will, Robert Roe 1782.
441:7	i) CCALS: will, Elizabeth Roe 1824 - Hester never proved this will and her brother, James, finally took up the Administration in 1824.
	ii) Hester Ann Rogers op. cit.
442:1	Gravestone Christ Church, Macclesfield and Parish registers.Jane's death was reported in the *Gore's General Advertiser* of Liverpool as 21st March 1811.
442:2-443:3	Hester Ann Rogers op. cit.
443:4-7	i) CCALS: will: Frances Roe 1783.
	ii) CCALS: will: Mary Roe 1787.
443:8	i) Hester Ann Rogers op. cit.
	ii) CCALS: will, Joseph Roe 1822 (this is a copy from P.C.C. proved 1821: Joseph had remarried on 20th June 1793 - Margaret Hopkins.)
	iii) CCALS: Macclesfield Land Tax Returns 1784 - M/f copy in Macc. PL.
444:4	MCC.
444:5	Gravestone - Bodlondeb Parish of Conway. Buried 8th March 1828.
444:6	Details kindly supplied by the Archivist of the National Army Museum, Chelsea.
444:7	i) Plymouth RO: Bastard Estates deed, property Higher Gerston.
	ii) National Army Museum - Bastard details.
	iii) NA: ADM 106 3613 (1778-1779).
	iv) NA: ADM 106 2603 (May - August 1780).
	v) Gloucs. RO: *A History of Dean's Woods as Producers of Timber* by Cyril E. Hart, Senior Verderer (1966) p. 141.
445:2	i) IGI.
	ii)*DNB*.
	iii) Jackson, Gordon, *The History and Archaeology of Ports* (World's Work Ltd. 1983) pp.43-45.
445:3	Guild. L: Sun Fire Insurance Book no. l8l, p.382, 17th March 1768.
445:4	i) NA: Prob. 11/1740 , will Abraham Mills 1828.
	ii)*Transactions of the Royal Academy* vol.3 (1790) p.54. Letter addressed by A. Mills from 'Fence-houfe, near Macclesfield, Cheshire Oct. 30 1789'. I am grateful to David Bates for bringing this letter to my attention.
446:1	Derby. RO; D 664/M/E3.
446:4-6	*The Journal of John Wesley* (Epworth Press 1960) p. 205 (also note), p.229.
446:7-447:2	MCC.
447:3	i) Warrington Library Family Index - Johnson.
	ii) NA: ADM 106 3613 - Naval Abstract of Contracts.
447:4	NMGM: MDHB Deeds 335/H2.
447:5	i) Act for St. James's - Geo III 14 (Decimo Quarto) cap.94.
	ii) Liv. PL: M/f 2/6 - Liverpool Town Books 4th Aug. 1777.
	iii) Liv. PL: St. James's register begins 1776. Bishop's transcripts are held in Lancs. RO.
448:1-2	Lancs. RO: will: Charles Caldwell 1813.
448:4-449:1	MCC.
449:4	Picton vol.1 p.67 & 69.
449:5	Lancs. RO: Molyneux pprs. DDM 50.
451:1	i) Liv. PL: Liverpool Corpn. Leases vol. 3/4 C Register 27th & 22nd July and 29th Dec. 1784.
	ii) NMGM: Plantation Books 1779-1784.
	Craig, R. & Jarvis, R. *Liverpool Registry of Merchant Ships* no.176 Chetham Society (M/cr.1967).
541:2	i) Liv. PL: St. James's register.
	ii) *THSL&C* Occasional series 1976 vol III. - Introduction to 'Liverpool the African Slave Trade and Abolition', edited by R. Anstey & P.E.H. Hair.

451:4-5	Hodgson, Robert, *The Life*, (1811) pp.85-91.
451:6	i) Liv. PL: 352/MDI - Committee Book of the Africa Co. of Merchants trading from Liverpool, 1750-1820.
	ii) Williams, Gomer, *The Liverpool Privateers*, (1897) pp.92-93.
451/7	i) Liver. PL: M/f 2/6 - for example see 14th Feb.1788.
	ii) Willams op. cit - Conclusion.
452:2	Ingpen, Roger, Ed. *Life of Samuel Johnson* (1907) pp. 734-735.
452:3-4	Harriott, John, *Struggles Through Life*, (1807) vol. II p.27.
453:1-454:6	CCALS: will: Brian Hodgson 1798 (Extracted from P.C.C.).
454:7-455:2	i) SCA: Bag. C 431A.
	ii) Ibid. book 482.
455:3-4	Ibid. book 494 - Barker letter book.
455:5	i) Details from Buxton L. and Archivist at Chatsworth House.
	ii) Derby LS: Register of Owners Horse Tax p.68 no. 11.

Chapter 26

Quotation:	Oliver Goldsmith, The Captivity - An Oratorio.
456:1	UW Bangor: Porth-yr-Aur 30636.
456:2-4	NLW: Esgair & Pantperthog 1025.
456:5-458:7	UW Bangor: Mona Mine 3544.
458:9-459:1	i) Ibid.
	ii) Harris, J.R. *The Copper King* (1964) p.53 & Appendix ll pp.168-18l.
459:2-3	UW Bangor: Mona Mine 3544 p.20.
459:4-6	Staffs. RO: Letter in ref. D603/K/9/12.
459:7-460:1	iMCC.
460:3	i) Whitlock, P. & Pearce, W. *H.M.S. Victory and Admiral Lord Nelson.* (Booklet 1990s) p.3.
	ii) *JHC :* Liv.470 no.54 pub. 22nd April 1799 - Report on the copper trade p.360, Report page 52.
460:4	i) Ibid.
	ii) Hannay, D. *A Short History of the British Navy 1689-1815,* (1909) p.279.
460:5-6	i) Staffs. RO: D603/L/2l9.
	ii) Swansea PL: Misc. copy white paper 'Account of the present State of the Copper Works in Cornwall & the Isle of Anglesey.' c.1785 p.2 para.6.
461:1	i) UW Bangor: Penrhyn Castle Mss. Uncatalogued lease 1st June 1782.
	ii) UW Bangor: Porth-yr-Aur 30433 no.3 (8th April 1781) & no.4; 30634.
461:2	Ibid. 30636.
461:3	Ibid. 30633.
461:4	Harris op. cit. pp.47-48.
461:5	i) Corn. CRO: DDX 318/1 - Wilson letters.
	ii) Harris op. cit. p.l54.
462:1	i) SCA: Bag. C. 494 11 1765-1811 - Devonshire Estate pprs. , letter 20th March 1780.
	ii) Robey, J.A. & Porter, L., *The Copper and Lead Mines of Ecton Hill, Staffordshire* (1972).
462:2	Harris op. cit.
462:3	i) Morton, J. *Thomas Bolton & Sons Ltd.* (1983) p.15.
	ii) Davies, Kenneth, 'Manufacturing Industries of the Greenfield Valley 1750-1900', unpublished PH.D. thesis, 1985 (UW Bangor). p.69.
462:4	i) Ibid. p.77.
	ii) Harris op. cit. p.49.
462:7-8	Harris op. cit. Appen. II. pp.173-174.
462:9-463:1	MCC (PRO ADM 106 2622).
463:2	MCC 19th March 1785.
463:4	Birm. PL: Matthew Boulton pprs.
463:5	Harrison p. cit. p.78.

464:2	Staffs. RO: D603/K/9/12.
464:3	Ibid. 5th Sept. 1784,
464:4	Ibid. 11th Sept. 1784; 27th Oct. & 16th Nov. 1784.
464:7-465:1	i)*Caernarvon Hist. Soc. Transactions* vol.35 (1974) 'Diwydiant yn Nyffryn Ogwen' by T.M. Bassett. pp. 75-76.
	ii) MCC.
465:2	*British Mining* No. 52, 'Great Orme Mines' by C.J. Williams (May 1995) p.6 & 14.
465:3	i) UW Bangor: Mostyn Mss. 7040.
	ii) UW Bangor: Port-yr-Aur 30661.
465:4	Ibid.
465:6	UW Bangor: Baron Hill 4334.
465:7	MCC.
466:1	Ibid. See in particular 21st July 1784 Ord. 7&8; 2nd Sept. 1784 Ord. 2; 27th April 1785 Ord. 2.
466:2	i) Dickinson, H.W. *James Watt Craftsman and Engineer* (1935) - Southern.
	ii) MCC.
466:3	i) Pennant, T. *History of the parishes of Whiteford and Holywell* (1796), p.273-274 - History of Holywell Parish.
	ii) MCC: 29th Dec. 1785; 27th Jan. 1786.
466:4	Morton. op. cit. pp.15-17.
467:2	i) BL: Oriental & India Office colln. in particular L/AG/l/5/l8-2l - Cash journals.
	ii) *Glamorgan County History* vol.5. p.88 - Chronological table by R.O.Roberts.
	iii) NLW: 15107B- 15109B.
467:3	i) MCC.
	ii) BL: Oriental & India Office colln. L/AG/1/5/18-20.
	iii) Day, Joan, *Bristol Brass* (1973) p.103.
467:4-468:1	Barton, D.B. *A History of Copper Mining in Cornwall and Devon* (1961) pp.26-31.
468:2-3	Author's calculations from Vivian's notebooks NLW 15l02B et. seq.; statistics as presented by Sir Charles Lemon in March 1838 are in *Cornish Mining* (1969) edited by Roger Burt pp.49-59. (Lemon's figures 1771-1784 vary only slightly from Vivian's totals).
468:4	Barton op. cit. p.34.
468:5-6	Harris op.cit. pp.55-60.
468:7-469:2	i) Ibid.
	ii) UW Bangor: Cerrig-y-bleddia misc. deeds 1st March 1786. (See also Baron Hill 3937 12th Nov. 1785.)
	iii) Swansea PL: Misc. c.1785 - Pamphlet "Account of the perfect State of the Copper-Works in Cornwall and the Isle of Anglesea, in which great National Advantages . . ."
469:3	Harris op. cit. p6l, 63 & 69.
469:4	Staffs RO: D 603/K/9/14 1st. Sept. 1785.
469:5-470:1	UW Bangor : this letter is quoted by W.H. Chaloner in *THSL&C* Pt.II vol.LXIII, footnote p.67 - unfortunately the reference is incorrect and the letter cannot be traced, however it does seem to fit the chronology, given that the lease to Williams & Co. (which has since been deposited at UW Bangor) runs from 10th Oct. 1785.
470:2	Staffs RO: D603/K/9/14 - 27th Dec. 1785.
470:3	UW Bangor: Cerrig-y-bleddia misc. deeds 1st. March 1786.
470:4	Harris op. cit. p.155.
470:5	i) Ibid. pp.58-60.
	ii) MCC 14th June 1786.
471:1	Ibid. 25th Nov. 1784.
471:2	i) Ibid.
	ii) Birm. PL: Matthew Boulton colln. Letter Box H.
471:3-4	Ibid.
471:5-472:1	MCC.
472:2-6	Birm. PL: Matthew Boulton colln. Letter Box H - letter 22nd Oct. 1785.
472:7-473:1	MCC: 8th & 30th March 1786.

473:2   i) UW Bangor: Mostyn Mss. 7042.

ii) Macc. Silk Heritage Archives: transcription of a letter 30th April 1788 originally held by Macc. L but now missing.

iii) MCC: 29th Aug. 1786 Ord. l9.

iv) Staffs. RO: D603/K/9/14.

473:3-474:1 Harris op. cit. p.52.

474:2   UW Bangor: Mona Mine 3033.

474:3-5   Ibid. 3034.

474:6-475:5 Macc. Silk Heritage Archives: transcript of letter.

475:6-7   i) Holland, E.G. *A History of Coniston Copper* (1986). - whilst the 1765 lease has been located in Box 9l of the Le Fleming colln. Cu. RO (K) at present the 1778 lease seen by Holland remains elusive.

ii) Cu. RO (K): WD/RY/84 - letter 23rd. Feb. 1781 from Harrison to a 'Friend'.

475:8-476:2 Macc. Silk Heritage Archives; transcripts of letters 19th Feb. 1787 & 30th April 1788.

Chapter 27

Quotation: Robert Burns, The First Six Verses of the Nineteenth Psalm (v.4).

477:2   Liv. PL: M/f 2/6 - Liverpool Town Books - minutes 4th Oct. 1783.

477:3   Ibid. November 1748 & 1st Dec. 1748.

477:4&479:1 i) Liv. PL: Corporation Leases Book vol. 3/2.

ii) Liv. PL: M/f 2/6 - minutes 2nd Feb. 1785.

479:2   Ibid. 21st April 1785 & 1st June 1785.

479:3   Ibid. 1st Feb. 1786.

479:5   Picton vol.1 pp.558-9.

479:6-480:1 i) Liv. PL: M/f 2/6.

ii) Picton op. cit.

480:2-3   i) Liv. PL: M/f 2/6.

ii) NMGM: 335 H 11 - Leases.

480:4-7   Liv. PL: M/f 2/6.

481:1   MCC.

481:2-5   i) Liv. PL: M/f 2/6.

ii) Picton vol. 1 pp.233-234.

481:6   Liv. PL: Corporation Leases Book 3/4 'C' Register.

481:1-2   Information supplied by the librarian of H.M. Customs, London.

482:3-5   Rideout, Eric H. *The Old Custom House*, (1928) pp. l-l3. copy Liv. PL.

482:6-7   Craig, R. & Jarvis, R. *Liverpool Registry of Merchant Ships*. Chetham Soc. (M/cr.1967) - Nos. 220, 76, 176, 129, & 39.

483:1-2   M/cr. PL: C/17/3/3 - Rev. R. Nicholson's Memorandum Book 1768 -1794.

483:4   M/cr. PL: C/17/3/115/1 - copy will.

483:5-6   M/cr. PL: C/17/3/116/1-3 copy will.

483:7-484:1 Liv. PL: Parish Registers.

484:2   i) Derby LS: Pedigrees etc. Thomas N. Ince. p.69.

ii) Jordangate deed in possession of the author.

484:4   MCC.

484:5-6   i) Corry, J. *The History of Macclesfield* (1817). p.74.

ii) Macc. Silk Heritage Archives; copy letter.

iii) *DNB* supplement vol.XXll p. 854 - Brian Hodgson (3).

iv) MCC.

484:7-485:1 Macc. Silk Heritage Archives: copy letter.

485:3-4   i) CCALS: DSA 210.

ii) Deeds for property 'Silver Coin', Market Place, Macc. with owners' solrs.

485:6   i) Clapham, Sir John, *A History of the Bank of England*, (1945).

ii) Hawkins, E. *Hawkin's Silver Coins of England* (3rd. edited edition 1887).

485:7-486:1   *England Displayed by a Society of Gentlemen,* vol.1.(1769) - Middlesex.

486:3-5   MCC.

486:6   Birm. PL: Matthew Boulton colln. Letter Box H2 doc.13.

487:2   Doty, R.G. *The Soho Mint and the Industrialization of Money* (1998) pp.27-36.

487:5   Birm. PL: Matthew Boulton colln. Letter Book W2.

487:6-488:3   Ibid. Coinage Day Book vol. 29, p.72 & 86.

488:4-5   i) MCC.

    ii) Birm. PL: Matthew Boulton coln. Letter Book O (1789 -1792) pp.53-54.

489:2-3   i) Dalton, R. & Hamer, S.H. *The Provincial Token Coinage of the 18th century,* (1910) pp.8-23.

    ii) Bell, R.C. *Commercial Coins 1787-1804* (1963). p.27, 232, 233.

489:4   i) M/cr. PL: *The Torrington Diaries* vol.1. 1790, p.28.

    ii) Information communicated personally by Dr. R. G. Doty of the Smithsonian Institute, Washington D.C.

489:5   i) *The Torrington Diaries* op. cit. p.33.

    ii) Deeds held by NatWest Bank Manchester - Samuel Goodwin.

489:6   *The Torrington Diaries* vol. III (abridged 1934) pp. 121-122.

490:4   *TL&CAS* vol. LXlll p.53 - pt.2 W.C. Chaloner 'Charles Roe of Macclesfield'.

490:5   For a description of the windmill see 'The Windmill Tower Warmley Brassworks South Gloucestershire', - a report submitted in October 1996 by Martin Watts to the Kingswood Heritage Museum Trust & S. Gloucs. Council, p.6.

490:6-491:4   Chaloner op. cit. and the Author's comments.

491:6   i) CCALS: LBM 1/4 11th Nov. 1782.

    ii) CCALS: SP3/15/6.

492:1-4   *Royal Irish Academy Trans.* vol. 2 (1787-88) pp. 157-170 - collieries: vol. 3 (1789-90) pp. 49-54 - collieries. I am indebted to David Bates for this valuable information.

492:2   N.B. see following meeting of 1st Nov. 1783.

493:2-7   Information gleaned from:-

    i) *The Book of Islay* (G. Gregory Smith 1895) pp.464-466.

    ii) *Memoirs of a Geological Survey* vol XVII - 'The Lead, Zinc, Copper and Nickel Ores of Scotland (H.M.S.O. 1921) pp. 65-72.

    iii) 'The Ancient Lead Mining Industry of Islay' No. 6, R.M. Callender (copy in The Museum of Islay Life).

    iv) *British Mining* No. 24, R.M. Callander & J. Macaulaw.

493:8-494:4   'Renounciation' and other documents are held in the Factor's Office of the Morrison Estate, Bridgend, Isle of Islay. I am grateful to the Factor, David B. Boyd for allowing sight of the documents, and also for providing other useful information, including a recent geological survey and maps of the area.

494:6-495:1   Ibid.

495:2   i) Silk Heritage Archives; copy letter.

    ii) MC: 26th Nov. 1788.

495:3   My thanks to David Bates for sending a copy of this article.

494:4   MCC.

495:5-496:3   Details from the article see 495:3

496:4   Crinan - Details kindly provided by the Local Studies Librarian of Argyll & Bute District Council.

496:5-7   Hodgson family - details colated from various self-explanatory sources, including the Earwaker colln. CR 63/2 now in the CCALS.

Chapter 28

Quotation: William Wordsworth, 'Tintern Abbey'.

497:1   Pennant, Thomas, *Tours in Wales* (1773 &1776) vol.1 (reprint 1883) pp. 246-253.

497:2-3   M/cr. PL: Ms.942.J42. - 'Journal of a Tour Through England in 1796'.

497:4   i) Chester City RO TCP/5/91, TCP/5/97.

    ii) MCC.

497:5-498:1   *The Torrington Diaries 1781-1794* , (Eyre & Spottiswoode 1934) p.152, 163-4, 173.

498:2   i) Rhodes, J.N. 'Derbyshire Influences of Lead Mining in N. Wales' . . . (1968) in *Peak Dist. Mines Historical Soc.* vol.3 part 6, p.345.

               ii) Chester City RO: TCP/5/42 & 46.

498:3   'Journal of a Tour Through England in 1796' op. cit.

498:4   Derby. RO: E 403A. - deed.

498:5   i) *The Reliquary* (Derbyshire) vol. VI (1865) pp.218-219.

               ii) Palmer, A.N. *History of the Thirteen County Townships of the Old Parish of Wrexham,* (1903) p.108.

               iii) Derby. RO: E 403A - stone quarry.

498:6-499:2   Ibid.

               iv)*The Reliquary* op. cit.

499:3   Harris, J.R. *The Copper King* (1964). pp.74-87.

499:4   i) BL: Oriental & India Office colln. L/AG/1/5/22 & 23.

               ii) MCC: A.G.M. 8th Aug. 1792, (12).

499:6-500:3   MCC.

500:4   Pennant op. cit. pp.273-274.

500:5   NLW: 2534B.

501:2-3   Lancs. RO: DDM 50/26.

501:4   Ibid. 50/27.

501:5   i) MCC: 5th Jan. 1790.

               ii) Chester coinage as illustrated by R. Dalton & S.H. Hamer in *The Provincial Token Coinage of the 18th Century* (1910), p.9.

               iii) Chester City RO: A/B/5/60 & 72. (See also letter of J. Johnson 20th Sept. 1792 in Holt & Gregson pprs. Liv. PL.).

501:6-502:3   Lancs. RO: DDM 50/30.

502:4   i) J. Johnson op. cit.

               ii) MCC: 15th Feb. 1791.

502:5   Chester City RO: TCP/5/48.

502:6-503:3   MCC.

503:4   CRO Swansea: D/D D1205.

503:5   i) Ibid. D 1198.

               ii) Phillips, D. Rhys, *History of the Vale of Neath* (1925) p.289.

503:6-504:1   MCC: 20th Nov. 1792; 8th March 1793.

504:2   i) Wood, John G. *The Principal Rivers of Wales* pt.1, (1813) p.82.

               ii) Phillips op cit. p.266.

504:3   MCC.

504:4-505:2   i) CRO Swansea: D/DD 1227/1.

               ii) Ibid. 1228/2.

505:3-4   MCC.

505:5   i) Ibid. 20th Dec. 1793.

               ii) Phillips op. cit. p.268.

505:6-506:2   i) Ibid. p.281.

               ii)*TL&CAS* vol. LXIII p.74 - pt. 2 W.C. Chaloner 'Charles Roe of Macclesfield'.

506:4-507:1   i) MCC.

               ii) Craig, R. & Jarvis, R. *Liverpool Registry of Merchant Ships* Chetham Soc. (M/cr.1967) nos. 39 & 150.

507:2   O.E.D.

507:3-508:2   *Wicklow History and Society* (1994) Chap. 19 pp.761 -762 : 'The Mining Community at Avoca 1780-1880' by D. Cowman.

508:4-5   i) NLI: M.s. 16304.

               ii) *DNB* Thomas Weaver (1733-1855).

508:6-509:1   i) NLI: M.s. 16304.

               ii) Ibid. 16309.

               iii) *Wicklow History and Society* op. cit. pp.762-763.

               iv) NLI: M.s. 16309 - Penrose.

509:2   *Mines of Wicklow* (1856) pp.56-57. (a fathom = 6 feet).

509:3   Bell, R.C. *Commercial Coins 1787-1804* (1963) pp.232-233.

509:4-5   i) NA: Prob 11/1740 - Will A. Mills 1828.

           ii) Macc. L: Simpson pamphlet.

509:6-7   i) NLI: M.s. 16304 - Proceedings.

           ii) Ibid. 16309.

510:1   i) Ibid. 16304.

           ii) *Mines of Wicklow* op. cit. pp.44-45. - Report.

510:3   NLI: M.s. 16305.

510:5-511:1 i) NLI: Dublin Directory 1810 and local map of period.

           ii) NMGM: Deed 335 H 12.

           iii) NLI: M.s. 16305.

511:3   MCC: 28th March 1788; A.G.M. 7th Aug. 1788.

511:4   Ibid. 10th Aug. 1790 (18); 11th Nov. 1790; 16th Aug. 1791 (14); 14th Dec. 1790.

511:5   Corn. CRO: Parish registers.

511:6-512:2 i) Lancs. RO: will: Legh Dickenson 1836. This copy will with legal proceedings is held because of the legalities regarding the Birch Hall Estate, Manchester.

           ii) MCC: 7th Aug. 1787 (26); 7th Aug. 1788 (17 & 18); 26th Nov. 1788; 13th March 1789.

512:3-4   MCC: 13th March 1789; 19th March 1790; 28th May 1790; 11th Nov. 1790; 16th Aug. 1791 (29); 19th Jan. 1789.

512:5   i) MCC: 10th Jan. 1792

           ii) Gloucs. RO: Bailey's British Directory 1784.

513:2   *Original History of the City of Gloucester* (1819) vol. II p.62.

513:3   NMGM: Deeds 335 H6 - partners 1782; 335 H15 - merchants 1799.

513:4   i) MCC.

           ii) *British Mining* No. 52 p.17 (Northern Mine Research Soc. May 1995).

513:5   MCC: 8th Aug. 1792 (14).

513:6   MCC: 8th March 1786; 7th May 1787; 29th Aug. 1786.

513:7-8   M.G.S. vol XXII 'The Lead and Zinc Ores of the Lake District' (1921) p.43.

513:9-514:4 i) *A Fortnight's Ramble to The Lakes"* by A Rambler in 1792 (Reprinted by Preston Publishing 1990) pp.43-45.

           ii) *Trans. of the Cumberland & West.morland Ant. & Arch. Soc.* vol. XXVIII New Series (1928) p.5.

           iii) MCC: 8th Aug. 1792.

514:5   i) I.G.I.

           ii) Information supplied from documentary evidence and parish registers by Mrs R.F. Roose, Chester.

           iii) MCC: 26th Nov. 1788.

           iv) Warner, Rev R. A*Walk Through Wales* (1798) p.283 - Amlwch.

514:7   i) Macc. Silk Heritage Archives: transcript of letter 30th April 1788 to Busfield, original now missing.

           ii) Dodd, A.H. *Industrial Revolution in North Wales* (UW Press 1971) p.165.

           iii) Bick, David, *The Old Copper Mines of Snowdonia* (1982) p.86.

           iv) Macc. Silk Heritage Archives: transcript of letter 16th Oct. 1789 to Busfield, original now missing. It appears that the transcripted phrase "as well as in Works". should read "as well as in Wales".

515:2-4   i) Williams, William, *Observations on the Snowdon Mountains* (1802) p.64.

           ii) Warner, Rev. R. op. cit. p.133.

           iii) Evans, Rev. J. *Tour Through Part of North Wales, in the year 1798 and other times.* p. 131.

           iv) Pennant,Thomas, *Tours in Wales* (originally undertaken in the years 1773 & 1776) vol. II p.320.

515:5   i) UW Bangor: Vaynol Deeds no. 506.

           ii) MCC: 8th Aug. 1792.

           iii) *Copper Mines in Great Britain* - 'The future of Non-Ferrous Mining in Great Britain and Ireland' (1959) - Snowdonia.

515:6-516:1 i) MCC: 16th Aug. 1791 (24).

           ii) *British Mining No.16* (1979) p.48 - 'Review of Mining in the Cheshire/Shropshire Basin' by Chris. J. Carlon.

iii) M/cr. PL: Bromley Davenport colln. Box5/17 - Nether Alderley Enclosure of Commons 1775.

iv) Stanley, Hon. Miss L.D. *Alderley Edge and its Neighbourhood* (1843).

v) CCALS: DSA 2l0 & 232 - deeds for farm confirmed by a visit to site.

vi)*TL&CAS* (1901) vol. XIX p.109.

516:2	i) MCC.
	ii) Warner, Rev. R. op. cit. p.192 (as quoted by W.H. Chaloner).
516:3-7	MCC.

Chapter 29

Quotation:	Edward Fitzgerald, The Rubaiyat of Omar Khayyam (v.II).
517:1-5	Firth, C.B. *From William lll to Waterloo* (10th edn. 1955) pp.251-259.
517:6-518:4	Hughes, John, *Liverpool Banks & Bankers 1760-1837* (1906) pp.84-87.
518:5	i) Ibid.
	ii) MCC.
518:6	Ibid. 8 July 1793 (27).
518:8	Firth op. cit. p.89.
519:1-5	i) CCALS: DDX 297.
	ii) Macc. Silk Heritage Archives: File M10 - Paradise Mill.
	iii) Ches. County Council: Modern Deeds 1431.
519:7	MCC: 14th April 1794.
519:8-520:2	i) MCC: A.G.M. August 1795.
	ii) NMGM: Deed 335 H13.
520:3	i) UW Bangor: Penrhyn 2033 - Agreement 1st. Aug. 1796 referred to in deed.
	ii) Lord Sefton correspondence 5th March 1800 quoted by J. Mayer in *History of the Art of Pottery in Liverpool* (1871) "Messrs. Worthington and others . . . threaten they will smelt Copper and other Ore unless Lord Sefton will grant them a lease of some premises adjoining . . .".
	iii) NMGM: Deed 335 H15.
520:4	MCC: 26th Sept. 1795; 29th Aug. 1796 (13, 10, 28).
520:5	i) UW Bangor: Penrhyn 2032 - Deed 24th March 1800. (There is a note in the catalogue of NLW under Samuel Holland.)
	ii) Ibid. 2035.
	iii) Ibid 2033.
520:6-521:1	JRL: Legh of Lyme colln. Box 1 C22 - Disley colliery deeds.
521:2	MCC: 30th April 1793; 3rd Feb. 1795.
521:3	i) MCC: 7th Aug. 1793 (15).
	ii) UW Bangor: Mostyn Mss. 7034, 7047.
521:4-5	MCC.
521:6-522:1	MCC: l4th April 1794; 1st Oct. 1794; 7th Aug. 1793 (25); A.G.M. August 1795 (6); 5th April 1797.
522:3	i) MCC l5th Aug. 1793 (30).
	ii) L&CAC vol.LXIII p.72 - pt.2 W.C. Chaloner 'Charles Roe of Macclesfield'.
	iii) MCC 22nd Aug. 1798 (9, 10, 11).
522:4	Warner Rev. R. *A Walk Through Wales* vol.II (1799) p.218.
522:5	MCC 7th Oct. 1799 (list & 26); 6th May 1800.
522:6-523:5	i) Pennant T. *History of Holywell Parish* (1796) pp.249-251.
	ii) Warner op. cit. pp.211-220.
523:6-7	MCC.
523:8	NLW: A/cs. 12513E ff7-9.
524:3-525:1	Brief details extracted from:-
	i) *The Emergence of Modern Ireland 1600-1900* (1981); chap. 10 - 'The '98 rebellion in Wexford and Wicklow' by L.M. Cullen, pp.210-232.
	ii) *Wicklow History and Society* (1994) Ken Hannigan & William Nolan Ed; chap.19 'The Mining Community at Avoca 1780-1880' by D. Cowman, pp.761-772.

iii) *Philosophical Trans. of the Royal Soc.* London (1796) pp.456-467.

iv) *Dublin Society Trans.* vol.III (1802) 'Second Report of the Wicklow Gold Mines", A. Mills, pp.91-97.

525:3-526:1   Hannay D. *A Short History of the Royal Navy 1689-1815* (1909); chap. Xl - 'The War Till the end of 1797' pp.323-384 passim.

526:2   Cowman op. cit.

526:3   NLI: Ms.16305.

526:4   NLI: Ms. 16306.

526:5-7   i) Hannay op.cit. 334-335.

ii) Phillips, D. Rees, *History of the Vale of Neath* (1925) p.269 - Place. 527:1 Picton vol.I p.247; vol.II p.44.

527:3   i) Cowman op. cit. p.770.

ii) Hannay op. cit. 346 et seq. , 352-4.

527:4   NLI: Ms. 16306 - Expenses account April 1798 for January.

527:5   Extracts from chaps. II-IV of *Life and Battles of Napoleon Bonaparte* (selected from the most authentic sources- W. Nicholson & Sons Ltd. London c 1870s.).

528:1   Hannay pp.388-390.

528:3   *The Oxford Illustrated History of the British Army* (1994) p.459.
Cullen op. cit. - extracts.

528:4   NLI: Ms.l6306 - Cowman op.cit. states that the report of October 1798 has been removed from the bound volume and, having been framed, now hangs in the bar of the Avoca Vale Hotel.

528:    i) Cowman op. cit. pp.763-764.

ii) Law, C.H. *Mines of Wicklow* (1856) p.47.

iii) Cullen op. cit. (see 8:5-9:3 i) p.225.

528:6-529:1   Hannay pp.39l-400.

529:2-3   NLI: Ms. l6309 - Company Minute Book.

529:4   *Life and Battles of Napoleon Bonaparte* op. cit. - extracts from chap. IV and pp.98-99.

529:5   *JHC* 54 pub. 22nd April 1799.

529:6   Harris, J.R. *The Copper King* (1964) pp.155-156.

529:7   MCC.

529:8-530:2   i) Harris op. cit. p.156.

ii) Pennant, T. *Tours in Wales* (omnibus ed. 1883) p.395 'Observations on the Present State' . . . quoted as vol.lll p.57.

530:3-532:4   *JHC* 54 op. cit.

532:5-6   i) Harris op. cit. p.155.

ii) NLI: Ms. 16309 - Minutes 16th Sept. 1801.

iii) MCC.

532:7   Ibid.

532:8-533:2   i) Macc. Silk Heritage Archives: transcripted letter.

ii) MCC: 7th May 1795; 21st April 1796; 29th Aug. 1796 (17); 15th Aug. 1797 (36).

533:3-6   The Act as stated.

533:7-534:1   i) CCALS: QDE 2/10 - map, LBM/3038 - enclosure.

ii) Macc. BC: C/22/25/1 - Thomas Rowley appears on these deeds for the brass works.

534:2   MCC: 24th April 1798.

534:3   i) Ibid.

ii) CCALS: Walter Smith notebooks no.7 p.17 & no.5 p.9.

534:4-8   CCALS: QDE 2/10 - map, LBM/3038 - enclosure.

534:9-535:1   MCC.

535:2   CCALS: LBM/3038.

535:3   MCC: 7th Oct. 1799 (16 & 24); 5th Feb. 1801 (4 & 9).

535:4   MCC: 5th Feb. 1801 (3, 2, 8); 6th July 1801 (1).

535:5   MCC: 5th Feb. 1801 (11 & 12).

536:6   MCC: 27th Oct. 1801 (1 & 7); 18th Nov. 1800 - copy of ledger opposite p.162. MCC: 21st Nov. 1801

(9); llth Feb. 1802 (7).

535:8-536:1 *Life and Battles of Napoleon Bonaparte* op. cit. pp. l06-l08.

Chapter 30

537:1   Lower Beech - my thanks to Molly Spinks for providing information from the Tytherinton Land Tax returns etc.

538:2   i) Picton vol.II p.173.

             ii) SCA: Bag.C. John Barker Letter Books no. 494 - letter 29th July 1773 to William Earle, Liverpool.

538:3-539:1 i) Liv. PL: Liverpool Corporation Leases Register C pp. 304-305.

             ii) Map of Liverpool 1807 - J. Britton.

             iii) Photographs: 'City of Liverpool Official Handbook' (1933-34) p.46 and *The Illustrated Liverpool News 1962.*

             iv) Picton vol.II p.174.

539:2   i) Troughton, T. *History of Liverpool* (1810) p.149 & 269.

             ii) Records held at Ches. RO.

539:3   Macc. L: copy of Simpson Discourse.

539:5-540:4 i) MCC: August 1795 (19).

             ii) M/cr. PL: C17 - Index for Nicholson family pprs.

             iii) Ibid. C/17/3/24.

540:5-541:1 i) Ibid. C/l7/3/35.

             ii) MCC: l5th Aug. 1797 (21); 24th April 1798 (5); 22nd Aug. 1798 (16).

541:2   MCC: 7th Oct. 1799 (9 & 22); 12th April l802 (3).

541:3   MCC: 29th Aug. 1796 (9) August 1795 (34).

541:4-5   M/cr. PL: C/17/3/35.

541:6   Lancs. RO: copy will: William Roe 28th June 1827.

541:7   *Trans. of Cumberland & Westmorland Ant. & Arch. Soc.* vol. XXVIII New Series (1928) p.5.

542:2   i) Cum. RO (K): WD/Ry Box 22- letter 21st Feb. 1766 R. Barker to J. Moore.

             ii) Holland, Eric G. *A History of Coniston Copper* (1986) p.60; Ind. 12th Sept. 1759.

             iii) Cumb. RO (C); D/PEN/Bundle 46 - letter 19th July 1799.

542:3   *M.G.S.* vol. XXX 'Copper Ores of the Midlands' . . . (1925) pp.66-68.

542:3-5   M/cr. PL: Cl7/3/6/9 - Texel details written in back of book upside down.

542:5-543:1 MCC: 6th July 1801 (8); 7th Oct. 1799; Aug. 1795 (4, 31, 23).

543:2   i) MCC: l2th Feb. 1796; 29th Aug. 1796 (12, 13).

             ii) Phillips, D. Rees, *History of the Vale of Neath* (1925) p.269.

543:3   MCC: l5th Aug. 1797 (20 & 6).

543:4   Phillips op. cit. pp.268-269.

543:5   i) MCC: 15th Aug. 1797 (37 & 36).

             ii) CCALS: SP3/15/6 - Minutes 26th Feb. 1803; LBM 1/4 -11th May1810.

543:6   MCC: 22nd Aug. 1798 (3, 22, 26).

543:7   MCC: 29th Aug. 1796 (14); 22nd Aug. 1798 (25).

543:8   MCC: 7th Oct. 1799 (6).

544:1   MCC: 7th Oct. 1799 (18, 19, 20); 18th Nov. l800 (6).

544:2   i) MCC: 5th Feb. 1801 (1, 2); 6th July 1801 (7, 6, 9); 2nd Nov.1801 (14, 15).

             ii) NLI: Ms. 16309 - A.I.M. Co. Minutes l6th Sept. 1801, 2lst Jan. 1802.

544:3   MCC: 18th Nov. 1800 (1); 6th July 1801 (8); 18th Nov. 1800 (l4); 15th Feb. 1801 (13); 2nd Aug. 1803 (3).

544:4   MCC: 2nd Nov. 1801 (11).

544:6   MCC: 2nd Nov. 1801 (13 & 12).

544:7   MCC: 2nd Nov. 1801 (15).

544:8   MCC: 2nd Nov. 1801 (14): 6th July 1801 (8).

544:9   MCC: 6th July 1801 (10).

546:1   i) Ibid

ii) CCALS: SP3/15/6 ; LBM 1/4.

546:3   i) Advert: *Manchester Mercury* 20th Oct. 1801.

ii) MCC: 2nd Nov. 1801 (10, 18).

546:4   MCC: 11th Feb. 1802 (l, 2); 4th Aug. 1802 (11, 17); 12th April 1802 (1); 4th Aug.1802 (6).

546:5   i) MCC: 28th April 1803 (3).

ii) Corry, J. *History of Macclesfield* (1817) p.75.

iii) Kemp, Peter, *The British Sailor* (1970) p.156.

546:6   MCC: 2nd Aug. 1803 (5); 2lst March 1804.

547:1   MCC: 2nd Aug. 1803 (4); 2lst March 1804; 10th to 14th Dec. 1805 (7).

547:2   i) MCC: 21st March 1804; 23rd May 1805 (2); 10th to 14th Dec. 1805 (see 13th).

ii) Morton, J. *Thomas Bolton & Sons Limited 1783-1983* (1983). p14.

547:3   MCC: 21st March 1804; 2nd Aug. 1803; llth Feb. 1802 (3).

547:6   i) N LW: B/DL/651.

ii) MCC: 27th Oct. 1801 (4). In July 1802 a statement on p.162 of the MCC shows Llandudno Mine Share 'wrote off' - bad debts £294 l0 7d.

iii) MCC: 4th Aug. 1802 (4) It seems probable that with Robert Hodgson and Abraham Mills as partners, Edward Hawkins accepted the lease from the Bishop of Bangor to supply his company works at Neath Abbey from 1803. The Bishop leased the mine to Samuel Worthington in October 1824; as leases were usually no longer than 21 years, 1803-1804 seems an appropriate time for the commencement of the Hawkins & Co, lease.

iv) MCC: l9th Oct. 1804 (1, 2).

547:7-548:1   i) MCC: Schedule p.l62. (July 1802).

ii) Dodd, A.H. *Industrial Revolution in North Wales* (UW 1971) p.165.

548:2   MCC: 19th Oct. 1804 (1).

548:3   MCC: Ms. 16309 - Weaver's production figures annexed to March quarter proceedings 1811.

548:4   NLI: Ms. 16307, 16309.

548:5-549:1   *Dublin Soc. Trans.* vol.III l9 pp. 1802.

549:2   MCC: l2th April 1802 (5).

549:3   MCC: l9th Oct. 1804 (3, 4); 23rd May 1805 (1).

549:4   i) Information kindly provided by H.M. Customs & Excise, London.

ii) BL: ADD M/s 33112 117V.

iii) BL: M/s 81373 115 R & V.

549:5   Corry op. cit. pp.84-92.

549:6   Mcr. PL: C17/3/56/2, C17/3/56/3.

549:7-550:2   Ibid. C17/3/32.

550:4-5   i) Chester City RO: CR63/2 - Earwaker colln. 1779 no.84 (Scholae Macc.)

ii) Robson, D. 'Some Aspects of Education in Cheshire' . . . in *Chetham Soc.* (M/cr. 1966) vol.XIII, Appen. V 1785.

iii) SCA: JC 1366 - Jebb pedigree and *DNB*.

iv) Marriage to Hannah Ramsden of Hampole 29th May 1804 Ardwick-le-Street or Doncaster.

551:1   i) NA: Prob 11/1062 - Will Edward Hawkins 26th Jan. 1780.

ii) John Rocque's map of London 1747.

551:2   i)Edward Thomas bapt. St. Michael's Macc. 12th Sept. 1778.

ii) Edward bapt. St. Michael's Macc. 6th June 1780.

551:3   *Bristol & Gloucs. Ant. Soc. Trans.* XCVII pp.93-98.

551:4   Samuel Hawkins bapt. St. Mary Matfelon, Whitechapel 12th Jan. 1723.

552:2   Staffs. RO: M/f 58/1 - (Company Minute Book remained with BICC at Cheadle).

552:3   i) MCC.

ii) Ibid.

552:4-5   NA: Prob 11/1436 - Will Samuel Hawkins proved 27th Jan. 1816.

552:6   A letter from Thomas Lawrence dated 7th June 1808, held by the British Library, apologizes to Edward Hawkins the Elder for the slowness in completing his portrait. Apart from the original portrait a copy exists, both painted by Lawrence. My thanks to David Bates for bringing this to my attention.

553:2   MCC: 2nd Sept. 1807.

553:3-554:1   MCC: 1st Oct. 1807.

554:2-3   NA: Prob 11/1497 - Will Robert Hodgson.

554:4-5   Hodgson, Rev. R. op. cit. p.249 et seq.

554:6-555:1   i) Swansea PL: Misc. list of subscribers to the Swansea Theatre.

               ii) Roberts, R.O. *Neath and District - a Symposium* pp.252-265 - Banking. See also Royal Institute of
               S. Wales Ms. J2 -' Early Neath Bank' by G.A. Taylor p.70; and 'A Description of Swansea and its
               Environs' (1813) p.18.

555:2-5   i) Hannay David, *A Short History of the Royal Navy* vol. 2 1689-1815 (1909) p.443, 456 et seq.

               ii) Guild. L: Russia Company Ms. 21377; Ms. 11,749; Ms. 11893/2; Ms.lll92B p.68.

555:6   i) Cowman, D. 'The Mining Community at Avoca' in *Wicklow History and Society* (1994) p.772.

               ii) Harris, J.R. The Copper King (2nd. Edition 2003) pp.154-157.

556:1   Staffs. RO: M/f 58/1 - 25th July 1800; 1806 et seq.

556:2   i) Gr. LRO: Leman Family of Northaw, Herts. female issue drawn up from Law Records etc. Copy of
               pedigree with notes for Stepney Manor. (Abstract of Title for Stepney Manor, C/93/1568).

               ii) Bethnal Green L: Indices have several references for Samuel & Edward Hawkins. e.g. 640, 561, 2163.
               Court case in deeds 849-860 Goodman's Fields (N.B. this part of estate not owned or leased by
               Hawkins family).

               iii) MCC: Liverpool 19th April 1811 p.181.

556:3   MCC: l0th May 1810.

556:4   MCC: dates as quoted.

557:2   M/cr. PL: C17/3/33/1.

557:3   i) *Gores General Advertiser*, Liverpool 21st March 1811. Jane died 22nd Feb. 1811 from inscription on
               Christ Church gravestone.

               ii) Details of John Harriott from *Cheshire Sheaf*, November 1935, 6736.

557:4   Liv. PL: M/f 2/6 - Liverpool Town Books.

557:5   Picton vol.II p.372.

557:6   Ibid. vol.I p.270.

558:1-3   *The Life and Battles of Napoleon Bonaparte* (c.1870s.) chap.XX.

558:4   Picton vol.I p.295.

558:5-559:1   i) MCC.

559:2-3   ii) Extracts from *The Life and Battles of Napoleon Bonaparte.*(1870s).

Chapter 31

561:3   Clapham, Sir John, *A History of the Bank of England* (1945).

561:4   MCC.

561:5&563:1   Ibid.

563:2   Staffs. RO: DW l909/A/8/1-10 - Deed 27th Oct. 1823.

563:2-564:2   i) Phillips, D. Rees, *History of the Vale of Neath* (1925) pp.282-283.

               ii) MCC: 13th June 1831.

564:3-4   i) *DNB* Edward Hawkins (1780-1867).

               ii) Hawkins, E. *The Silver Coins of England* (1841).

564:5   i) Macc. BC: C/22/25/1 - Title deeds brass works; these show Brian Hodgson the Younger as 'late of
               Harwich but now of Bologne in the Kingdom of France.' See also:

               ii) Hunter, Sir W.W. *Life of Brian Houghton Hodgson* (1896).

               iii) Lich. JRO: will: Brian Hodgson of Uttoxeter 1827.

564:7   i) Ches. County Council - Modern deeds former Macc. High School for Girls, Fence Ave. This property
               has since been sold.

               ii) CCALS: Walter Smith notebook no. 5 pp.30-31 - details of previous deeds from 1799.

               iii) Hughes, John, *Liverpool Banks and Bankers 1760-1837* (1906) p.87.

565:1   i) Ibid.

               ii) Lancs. RO: will:Charles Caldwell 1814.

565:2	i) Details supplied by Gloucester PL from contemporary newspapers etc.
	ii) Science L. London: Patent no.3555 A.D.1812.
565:3	NLI: Ms. 16308; 16309.
565:4	i) Law,C.H. *Mines of Wicklow* (1856) p.56.
	ii) NLI: Ms. 16309 25th April 1816; 29th April 1816, 22nd April 1817.
565:5	i) Ibid. l4th July 1818.
	ii) Law op. cit 57-58.
566:1	NLI: Ms. l6309 l4th July 1828 - Average receipts were £600 p.a.
566:2	*DNB* Thomas Weaver (1773-1855).
566:3	i) Macc. BC: C22/25/1 - lease llth May 1813.
	ii) The Arley Estate book of tenants includes a John Johnson of the village of Aston who had a son baptised in 1747.
	iii) NLI: Ms. 16309.
	iv) MCC.
566:4-5	i) UW Bangor: Deed 1431 - lease and release 1st & 2nd July 1826.
	ii) Earwaker, J.P. *East Cheshire* (1880) vol. 2 p.450 - Family tree Legh of Ridge.
	iii) UW Bangor: Bodlondeb Estate pprs.
566:6	UW Bangor: Porth-yr-Ayr 30685.
567:1-3	i) Ibid. 30668.
	ii) Ibid. 30667.
567:4	Ibid. 30670.
567:6-568:7	i) UW Bangor; Bodlondeb Estate pprs.
	ii) Caernarvon RO; Parish registers.
	iii) NA: Prob 11/1740 - Will Abraham Mills 1828.
	iv) Macc. L: M/f Christ Church burial records.
568:8	i) Williams, C.J. 'Great Orme Mines' in *British Mining No. 52* (May 1995) p.19.
	ii) UW Bangor: Mostyn leases 7042 et seq.
568:9-569:2	i) Liv. PL: M/f 2/6 Corporation Minutes October 1809.
	ii) NLW: B/DL/969.
	iii) Williams, C.J. op. cit. p.21 'Old Mine'.
569:4	i) Bradford PL: Pedigree Busfield family.
	ii) CCALS: QDE 2/10 Enclosure 1804 and MCC.
569:7	Lancs. RO: will, William Roe of Liverpool Esq. 28th June 1827 (Copy).

Additional Roe Biographical Notes

581:1-582:2	Information collated from various sources-
	i) 'The Experience and Spiritual letters of Mrs. Hester Ann Rogers* (Halifax 1845).
	ii) JRL: The Methodist colln which includes John Wesley journal; Rev. Rogers 'Housekeeping Accounts' etc., H.A. Rogers diaries and journals; Elizabeth Ritchie journal.
582:3-5	CCALS: will: Elizabeth Roe N.B. this was not proved until 1824.
582:6-7	*Cheshire Sheaf* October 1935 pp.83-84.
582:8-583:1	Burton Jackson, J.L. *Not An Idle Man* (Western Australia 1982) kindly sent by M.B. Roe, a descendant of John Septimus.
583:2	i) Macc. L: M/f Macclesfield Land Tax returns.
	ii) *Cheshire Sheaf* September 1935 (6689).
583:3	CCALS: will: Joseph Roe of Congleton 1822.
583:4	NA: Prob 11/1596 Charles Roe of Coventry 1817.
583:5	NA: Prob 11/1826 John Harriott Roe 1834.
583:6-584:2	i) M/cr. PL: C17/3/33/2.
	ii) M/cr. PL: C17/3/8l (letter 2nd April 1823).
	iii) Copy of a legal document with property deed relating to Rev. Charles Roe kindly received from Richard Longden of Macclesfield.

584:3	BL: Folios 81373 117v & 115v; 68398 257v; 37097 227v; 37098 57v, 49r, 51r, 94; 68402 167r.
585:1	Salary and dates supplied by the Librarian, Customs & Excise, London.
585:2	Deed 36 Bridge St. in owner's possession.
585:3	CCALS: LBM 2039.
585:5	JRL: Methodist colln. Wesley journals.
585:6-7	Liv. PL: Corporation leases vol. 3/4 'C' register pp.304-5. 345-6.
586:1-2	Macc. L: M/f Macclesfield Land Tax Returns.
586:3-5	i) Lancs. RO: will, William Roe op. cit.
	ii) Palmer, A.N. *History of the . . . Old Parish of Wrexham* (1903) p.108.
	Ibid.
587:3	*Cheshire Sheaf* December 1935 p.99.
587:5-6	i) CCALS: LBM 2703/l/4 see in particular l4th Oct. 1809, 6th Oct. 1837, 2nd May 1839.
	ii) Report of Water Committee in the issues of the *Macclesfield Courier & Herald* of 28th Oct. 1837; 8th March 1838; 9th Feb. 1839; 4th May 1839 et seq.
587:7	Obituary found amongst family papers and brought to my notice by Miss Helen T. Proctor, a descendant of William Roe of Macclesfield and Liverpool.
587:8	Gravestone, Christ Church.
587:9-588:3	i) Ellison Hale, Norman, *The Wirral Peninsula* (1955) pp.220-221.
	ii) Urnley Hale, Ken B. *The Illustrated Portrait of Wirral* (1987) pp.186-189.
	iii) Batsford, Alan B. *The Wirral* (1980) pp.184-185.
	I am grateful to Mrs. Pauline Schofield of The Wirral for supplying these references.

* * * * * * *

INDEX